Intermediate Accounting

Edition 2

Bart P. Hartman
St. Joseph's University

Robert M. Harper
California State University—Fresno

James A. Knoblett
University of Kentucky

Philip M. Reckers
Arizona State University

SOUTH-WESTERN College Publishing
An International Thomson Publishing Company

I(T)P®

International Thomson Publishing
South-Western College Publishing is an ITP Company.
The ITP trademark is used under license.

Accounting Team Director:	Richard K. Lindgren
Acquisitions Editor:	Alex von Rosenberg
Developmental Editor:	Mignon Worman
Production Editors:	Jason M. Fisher and Marci Dechter
Production House:	Litten Editing and Production
Composition and Art:	GGS Information Services
Team Assistants:	Rebecca Glaab and Katherine Meisenheimer
Internal Designer:	Ellen Pettengell Design
Cover Design:	Joseph Devine
Marketing Manager:	Matthew Filimonov
Photo Editor:	Jennifer Mayhall
Photo Credits:	© Jeff Greenberg
Cover Photograph:	Tony Ise/PhotoDisc, Copyright 1997

ISBN: 0–538–87890–8
2 3 4 5 6 7 8 9 VH 5 4 3 2 1 0 9 8 7
Printed in the United States of America

Library of Congress Cataloging-in-Publication Data

Intermediate accounting/Bart Hartman . . . [et al.]. — 2nd ed.
p. cm.
Includes indexes.
ISBN 0–538–87725–1 (alk. paper)
1. Accounting. I. Hartman, Bart P.
HF5635.I5295 1997 97–8393
657'.044—dc21 CIP

To our neglected families

Betsy and Trey

Deborah, Robin, and Kelly

Carole

Patricia, Brian, Colleen, and Ashley

BRIEF CONTENTS

Contents

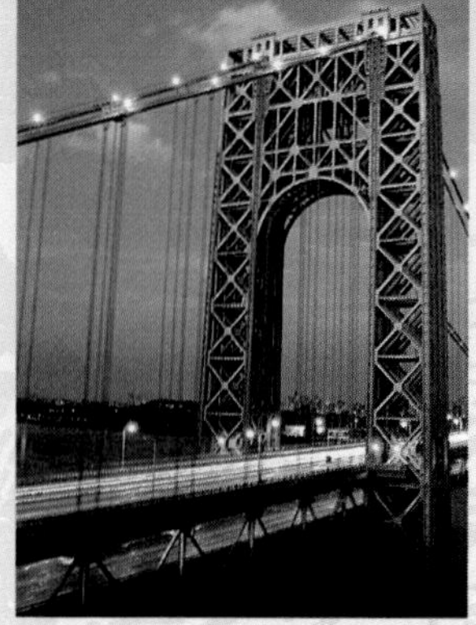

Preface

BRIDGE THE GAAP

From Point A to Points B & C

Are Intermediate Accounting students headed for jobs where their success will rely primarily on their technical skills? Or are they headed for careers in the global economy of the future where their success depends more on critical thinking and problem-solving skills? For most students the answer is both—therefore, teaching the Intermediate accounting course has become a balancing act.

This balance between the technical and practical demands of a modern accounting career was our primary concern as we designed and wrote *Intermediate Accounting*. We understood that students need to know and apply the principles of accounting, but that they also need to recognize and solve problems in the unpredictable, fast paced business world. Our **financial statement analysis framework** provides the perfect route to both of these important skill sets by bridging the gap between simply applying GAAP and making smart decisions on the job.

I intend to adopt the second edition. I felt that the student outcomes were what I had hoped for when I adopted the [first edition]; specifically, students were better able to see beyond debits and credits to broader issues of financial reporting.

– Jeannie Welsh
LaSalle University

Our financial statement analysis framework addresses two important sets of questions that students must be able to answer:

How? How are financial measures and ratios used to evaluate the health of a firm? How are they calculated? How are the components of ratios measured? How are accounting standards applied?

Why? Why are financial measures and ratios used by managers to understand the financial health of a firm? Why is more emphasis placed on certain measures than on others? Why are alternative valuation methods allowed in some cases but not in others?

The current approach to the intermediate accounting course, as reflected in most texts, is one of excessive detail and emphasis on learning all the standards. . . . These authors are to be congratulated for breaking the mold.

– Douglas Sharp
Wichita State University

When students understand *how*, they are well prepared for technical activities such as developing financial statements and completing the CPA exam. *Why*, on the other hand, builds the critical thinking skills described as essential by the AECC and prepares students for making informed and rational business decisions in the real world.

The strength of the financial analysis approach is that it perfectly frames for the student the financial health and activity of the firm for exploration in terms of both how and why. And because it addresses the preparation as well as the interpretation of financial data, financial statement analysis builds the set of skills that students need early in their careers—preparation and use of financial information—with bias toward neither.

BUILDING THE BRIDGE

The more conceptual approach is easier to follow because it provides a framework: the technical accounting is therefore more understandable.

– Anne Lee Bain
St. Cloud State University

THE BIG PICTURE Take a quick look at the Table of Contents; it tells an important story. The streamlined design of *Intermediate Accounting* allows students to absorb the details while keeping the big picture in focus. Following Part I, which provides accounting basics, we explore the financial position of the firm from the perspectives of profitability (Part II), liquidity (Part III), and solvency (Part IV). These three parts each examine one aspect of a firm's financial health, and as a group provide the complete picture. Part V addresses disclosure and reporting issues.

I wholeheartedly agree with your idea of a concise, brief book. I had been using [a competing text], which comes with a wheelbarrow to carry the book to class. I believe the coverage is complete, and twenty chapters with appropriate appendices is just about right.

– Al Oddo
Niagara University

STREAMLINED COVERAGE To preserve the big picture focus, we limited the text to a manageable 20 chapters without sacrificing the comprehensive coverage necessary to prepare for even the most demanding careers in accounting. We go beyond the numbers to teach problem solving. The moderate length sharply contrasts to many intermediate texts that have grown to encyclopedic proportions.

REAL WORLD EXAMPLES Real world examples abound to illustrate key issues; they open each chapter and are sprinkled throughout each chapter. Company names are highlighted when used in examples to illustrate chapter concepts. Stand-alone exhibits illustrate accounting methodology and calculations. We explore the advantages and disadvantages of alternate approaches to reporting and disclosure as well as the FASB's position on such issues.

ETHICS IN PRACTICE—"COOKING THE BOOKS"

"How Pressure to Raise Sales Led MiniScribe to Falsify Numbers"

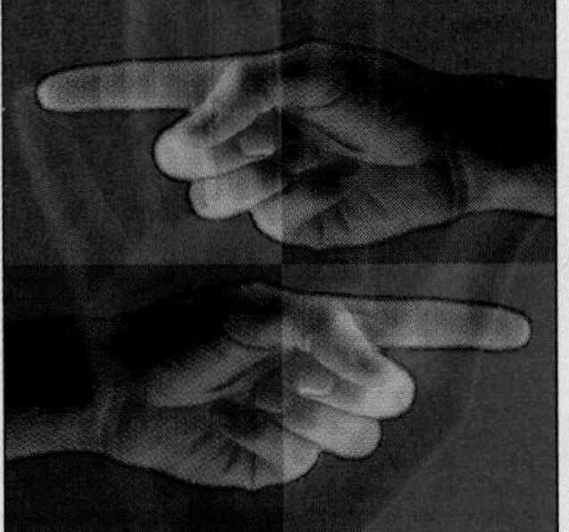

Last October, as other computer-disk drive companies were laying off hundreds of employees, ***MiniScribe Corporation*** announced its 13th consecutive record-breaking quarter. This time, however, the surge in sales sent a shiver of apprehension through MiniScribe's board.

"The balance sheet was scary," says William Hambrecht, one of the directors.

What worried Hambrecht was a sudden, three-month run-up in receivables to $173 million from $109 million, a 59% increase. Inventories were similarly bloated, swelling to $141 million from $93 million—a dangerous development because disk drives can become obsolete from one quarter to the next.

Seven months later, the portents that had worried Hambrecht generated grim headlines: MiniScribe's spectacular sales gain had been fabricated. In fact, the company acknowledged, it didn't know whether it could produce accurate financial statements for the prior three years.

Virtually all of MiniScribe's top management has been dismissed, and layoffs have shrunk worldwide employment to 5,700, from a peak of 8,350 a year ago. MiniScribe might have to write off as much as $200 million in bad inventory and uncollectible receivables.

Sales objectives became the company's driving force, . . . financial results became "the sole determinant" of whether bonuses were awarded. . . .

Hitting the number became a companywide obsession. Although many high-tech manufacturers accelerate shipments at the end of a quarter to boost sales,—a practice known as "stuffing the channel"—MiniScribe went several steps beyond that. On one occasion, an analyst relates, it shipped more than twice as many disk drives to a computer manufacturer as had been ordered; a former MiniScribe sales manager says the excess shipment was worth about $9 million. MiniScribe later said it had shipped the excess drives by mistake. The extras were returned—but by then MiniScribe had posted a sale at the higher number.

STRENGTHENING THE BRIDGE—CHANGES TO THE SECOND EDITION

The real [world] examples, . . . make [Hartman] more attractive than many intermediate texts.

– Karen Smith
Arizona State University

While the first edition was extremely well received and supported by students and instructors, we consulted with an impressive group of reviewers to update and further strengthen the text. This edition reflects their suggestions:

INCREASED END-OF-CHAPTER MATERIALS More than 50% of the EOC are new or revised. We have added more financial analysis exercises, problems, cases, and research activities, plus writing assignments that require students to identify and solve problems. These assignments have been developed in consultation with practicing accountants in order to foster those skills most important to the student's future career success.

The variety and mix of problem materials at the end of each chapter is the strongest feature of this text. These are excellent, and set this text apart from others in the field.

– Douglas Sharp
Wichita State University

END-OF-CHAPTER SAMPLE

P20–5 Economic Consequences of Disclosure
One of the chapter excerpts described the accounting technique for Goodwill by RJR Nabisco in its proposed spin-off of the food business from tobacco. After the details of the proposed offering were made public, and analysts had an opportunity to study it, the offering was canceled.

Required:

A. Briefly describe how the goodwill was to be accounted for in the offering.

B. Briefly describe the effect on projected earnings of the goodwill treatment.

PROBLEM SETS ON THE INTERNET Unique Feature! Unlike any other text on the market, we offer additional problems and solutions on the Internet. Instructors may download problems or direct students to the Hartman homepage at *http://www.swcollege.com/hartman.html.* Because we are committed to providing you current, accurate, first rate problem sets for instruction, we update the Internet problem sets every semester. For instructor access to protected material please contact us via e-mail at *accounting@swpco.com.*

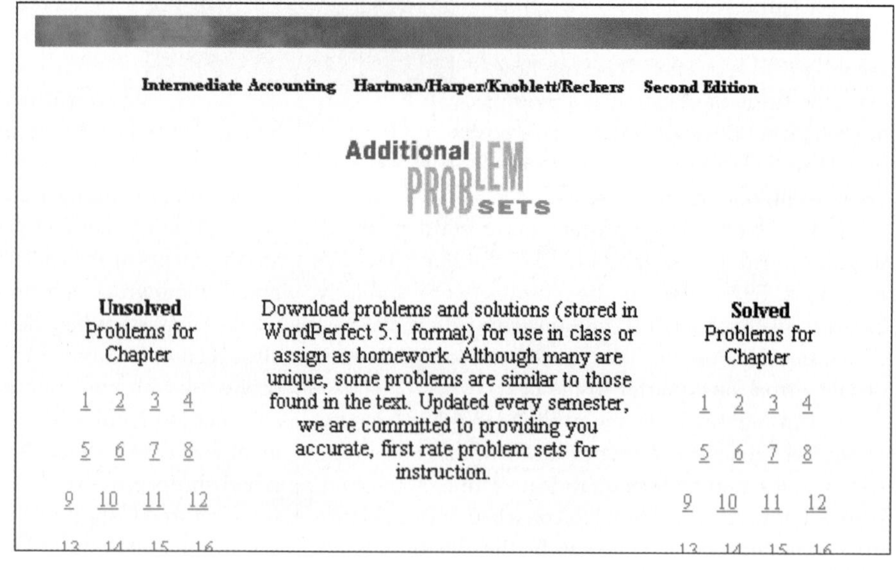

INTEGRATED INTERNET COVERAGE Click to the Hartman home page (*www.swcollege.com/hartman.html*) to access further information on companies mentioned in the text, to download instructor resources, and to read or submit great ideas for teaching intermediate accounting. This feature accentuates the power of the Internet in accounting education for both students and instructors. It also makes surfing the Net second nature to students, many of whom who will utilize its vast resources for decision-making in their future careers as accountants.

FINANCIAL STATEMENT DATABASE DISKETTE This database provides complete financial statements from 55 companies including many that are well-known to students. The database is keyed to exercises, problems, and research activities to build the student's financial statement analysis skills. Alternatively, many of the end-of-chapter problems may be solved using Internet resources such as EDGAR.

I am impressed with the software that is available with the text.

– Sharron M. Graves
Stephen F. Austin State University

INCLUSION OF DERIVATIVES AND FINANCIAL INSTRUMENTS An appendix at the end of chapter 9 addresses derivatives (based upon the FASB Exposure Draft) reflecting the growing importance of these risky and often misunderstood investment vehicles. Immediately following the appendix is a supporting set of exercises specially designed to reinforce comprehension of this complex topic.

RECENT CHANGES IN GAAP The text has been modified to reflect changes to GAAP such as recent pronouncements for asset impairment, stock based compensation to employees, and earnings per share.

EXPANSION OF THE GAP IN GAAP Chapter 20, The Gap in GAAP, illustrates instances in which reporting in compliance with GAAP did not faithfully represent the underlying economic reality of the events in question. This chapter has been updated with current examples and is supported by additional cases and problems.

I found the opening vignettes very interesting. I've seen other texts try to do something similar but the ones in this book appear to be more understandable. . . and more useful as far as tying them to the content of the chapter.

– Penny Hanes
Mercyhurst College

The RCA Acquisition

One of GE's most intriguing moves to boost its net income was in its accounting for its $6.4 billion acquisition of RCA Corporation in 1986. Anytime an acquisition is made for a price exceeding the book value of the business, the premium over book value must be recorded on the buyer's books.

In the case of RCA, one former GE executive recalls that GE allocated a disproportionate amount of this so-called goodwill to ***NBC***, increasing the TV network's book value while reducing that of other RCA assets. GE's own annual reports appear to substantiate his recollection. In 1987, the year after the acquisition, GE raised NBC's book value to $3.8 billion from $3.4 billion. The higher book value for NBC and the resulting lower value for other RCA assets raised GE's profits on sales of RCA's non-NBC assets.

Source: Randall Smith, Steven Lipin and Amal Kumar Naj, "*Managing Profits,* How General Electric Damps Fluctuations in its Annual Earnings," *The Wall Street Journal,* November 3, 1994, pp. A1, 11.

IN FOCUS Included in more than half of the chapters are career profiles of young business professionals, most of them non-accountants, who use accounting information in their careers. These interesting interviews expose students to the cross-functional uses of accounting information in the business world.

EXCEL SPREADSHEET PROBLEMS Identified by the spreadsheet icon, selected problems can now be solved using Excel spreadsheet templates. Coupled with the Lotus templates introduced in the previous edition, the Excel templates provide instructors with added flexibility in teaching students the methods of computerized accounting.

CHECK FIGURES In this edition, check figures are available upon request. (ISBN 0-538-88067-8)

A SOLID FOUNDATION— PREVIOUS EDITION FEATURES RETAINED

INNOVATIVE PEDAGOGY

OPENING VIGNETTES Each chapter begins with an example of a real company or situation that illustrates the practical importance of the chapter's content.

I believe the concept/logic statements do a very good job of keeping the students focused on the underlying concept, or why, instead of the overworked how.

– Lola Dudley
Eastern Illinois University

CONCEPT/LOGIC STATEMENTS The underlying conceptual basis of each accounting issue is emphasized with this unique feature. These statements focus the student's attention on the conceptual basis of the various issues, such as revenue recognition or asset valuation.

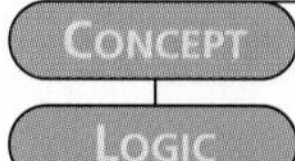

Revenue recognition.

Interest received on the bond investment is revenue and is recognized when earned in the current period. Amortization of the premium reduces the revenue recognized because the premium amount allocated over the life of the asset reduces the rate of return on the investment, thus reflecting the current market rate of interest at the time of purchase.

INTEGRATIVE CASES Twelve comprehensive cases, written specifically for this text by Philip Reiger of Arizona State University, add real world complexity by combining multiple topics in each case. These cases integrate accounting with other functions including marketing, production, and management and involve international, ethical, and financial issues that have confronted well-known companies such as GTE, Motorola, Dow Corning, and Ben & Jerry's Homemade, Inc.

ETHICS DECISION AND DISCUSSION CASES Each chapter features decision and discussion cases, many involving ethical or quality-based issues, that require students to analyze available information and exercise judgment in their decisions. These cases are ideally suited for class discussion, presentations, or written assignments.

SUPPLEMENTS FOR THE INSTRUCTOR

PRINTWARE

Instructor's Manual. Prepared by Jeannie Welsh (La Salle University) and Bart Hartman. Each chapter contains a list of key terms, a lecture outline, a selected bibliography of current readings, transparency masters, class participation ideas, supplemental examples and illustrations, alternative lectures and cases and selected group learning activities. (ISBN 0-538-87725-1)

Solutions Manual. Prepared by the text authors and checked by two independent problem solvers for accuracy, the manual contains answers to all questions, problems, and cases in the text. (ISBN 0-538-87727-8)

Test Bank. Prepared by Lola Dudley (Eastern Illinois University) and Barb Muller (Arizona State University-West). Revised to reflect the current edition, the Test Bank contains 1600 test short answer questions, problems, and discussion questions, with complete solutions. (ISBN 0-538-87730-8)

Transparency Acetates. Over 200 overheads feature solutions for all computational exercises, problems, and cases. Available upon request. (ISBN 0-538-87734-0)

SOFTWARE

WesTest. A computerized (Windows) version of the test bank allows instructors to quickly and easily customize tests for their students. (0-538-87731-6)

PowerPoint Lecture Presentations. Presentations enhance lecture quality and shorten preparation time. The 60+ slides per chapter outline chapter content and feature key exhibits from the text. (0-538-87732-4)

WestLaw. *Exclusive to Adopters!* Qualified adopters receive 10 free hours of WestLaw. Search more than 55 million documents in the Dow Jones News Retrieval System, which is the exclusive source of the Wall Street Journal.

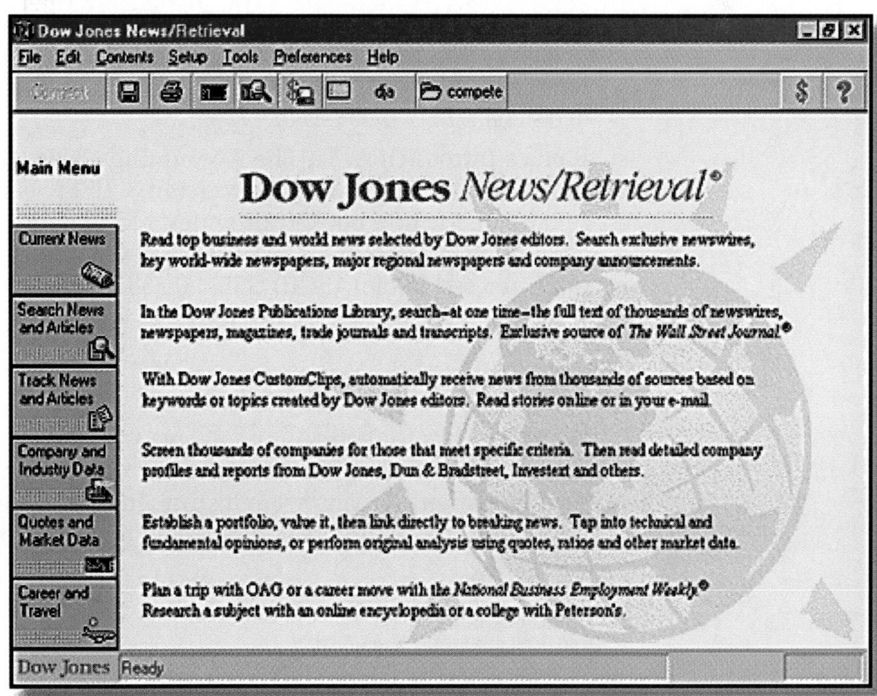

Excel/Lotus Spreadsheet Templates. Several problems in each chapter can be solved using these templates in either Excel or Lotus. (ISBN 0-538-87735-9)

SUPPLEMENTS FOR THE STUDENT

PRINTWARE

Study Guide. Prepared by Lola Dudley (Eastern Illinois University) and Barb Muller (Arizona State University-West). The study guide provides lecture outlines, extra problems, mastery problems, and study tips for additional study and review of chapter content. (ISBN 0-538-87728-6)

Student Solutions Manual. Prepared by the authors of the text, it includes solutions to even-numbered problems and exercises. (ISBN 0-538-87733-2)

Working Papers. Prepared by Bart Hartman. This volume provides accounting worksheets for end-of-chapter problems and exercises. (ISBN 0-538-87729-4)

SOFTWARE

Financial Accounting Simulation Analysis. Developed by Jamie Pratt (Indiana University) and Mike Groomer (Indiana University) for use with either Lotus or Excel, this flexible simulation provides students with the ultimate form of role-playing. Step-by-step instructions allow the student to build a set of financial statements and assess the effects of a variety of managerial, operating, investing, financing, and reporting decisions on these statements and related financial ratios over a three-year period. The decisions include (1) issuing stock and long-term debt under various terms, (2) purchasing and selling marketable securities, inventory, land, and equipment at various prices, (3) selling goods at various prices, (4) declaring cash and stock dividends, (5) employing different collection and payment strategies, and (6) choosing from among different methods of accounting for uncollectibles, inventory, depreciation, and amortizing debt premiums, and discounts. This unique simulation brings to life the economic consequences of accounting decisions. (ISBN 0-538-84107-9)

Rama's Introduction To The Accounting Cycle (A Computer Aided Instruction); CONTACCT II, Version 3. (ISBN 0-538-87584-4) This practice set and instruction booklet provides additional review and practice of the accounting cycle with an instructor's manual (ISBN 0-538-87586-0) and computerized test bank (ASCII) (ISBN 0-538-87588-7).

ACKNOWLEDGMENTS

We would like to thank all the people who have helped us during the preparation of this edition. The constructive comments and suggestions made by the following reviewers were instrumental in developing, rewriting, and improving the quality, readability, and student orientation of *Intermediate Accounting.*

Anne Lee Bain
St. Cloud State University

Bruce Busta
St. Cloud State University

Paul Chaney
Vanderbilt University

John Cheever
California State Poly University - Pomona

Corolyn Clark
St. Joseph's University

Alan Davis
Community College of Philadelphia

Lee Dexter
Moorhead State University

Lola Dudley
Eastern Illinois University

Don Edwards
University of Arkansas

Elaine Eikner
SW Texas State University

C. Patrick Fort
University of Alaska - Anchorage

Shelia Foster
The Citadel

Diane Franz
University of Toledo

Micah Frankel
California State, Hayward

Sharron Graves
Stephen F. Austin State University

Thomas Hogan
University of Massachusetts - Boston

Penny Hanes
Mercyhurst College

Linda Kistler
University of Massachusetts - Lowell

William Kross
Purdue University

Julia Karcher
University of Louisville

Vivek Mande
University of Nebraska - Omaha

Barb Muller
Arizona State University - West

Richard Murdock
Ohio State University

Dave Nichols
University of Mississippi

Al Oddo
Niagara University

Ralph Peck
Utah State University

Curt Penwell
Jamestown Business College

Larry Probert
Rider University

James Reburn
Samford University, Birmingham

Lynn Rees
Washington State University

Keith Richardson
Indiana State University

Sharon Salem
Westminster College

Richard Schmidt
Weber State University

Doug Sharp
Wichita State University

Kathleen Simons
Bryant College

Karen Smith
Arizona State University

Catherine Staples
Randolph-Macon College

Ian Stewart
Seattle Pacific University

Iris Stuart
Concordia College

Yaso Thiru
Alaska Pacific University

William Thomas
Gustavus Adolphus College

Linda Wade
Tarleton State University

Jeannie Welsh
La Salle University

PROBLEM CHECKERS

Many thanks to the following, who independently verified every exercise and problem in the text and supplements:

Anne Lee Bain
St. Cloud State University

Brindha Hariharan
St. Francis College

Don Loster
University of California - Santa Barbara

Barb Muller
Arizona State University - West

Denise Patterson
California State University - Fresno

Alice Sineath
Forsyth Technical Community College

Linda Wade
Tarleton State College

The authors also want to thank all the personnel at South-Western College Publishing for their efforts and assistance, including Rick Lindgren, Alex von Rosenberg, Mignon Worman, Jason Fisher, Matt Filimonov, Marci Dechter, Rebecca Glaab, and Katherine Meisenheimer. Special thanks are given to Philip Regier, Arizona State University for his assistance in the development of the Integrative Cases.

Bart P. Hartman

Robert M. Harper Jr.

James A. Knoblett

Philip M. Reckers

If you have questions or comments about this text please contact your ITP Sales Representative or the Accounting and Taxation Team at South-Western College Publishing directly:

Alex von Rosenberg
Acquisitions Editor
513-527-6148
Alex_Von_Rosenberg@swpco.com

Matt Filimonov
Marketing Manager
513-527-6107
mfilimon@swpco.com

South-Western College Publishing • 5101 Madison Road • Cincinnati, OH 45227

PART 1

BACKGROUND CORE

The Conceptual Framework and Objectives of Financial Reporting

The Accounting Process

Balance Sheet and Owners' Interests

1

The Conceptual Framework and Objectives of Financial Reporting

Learning Objectives

After studying this chapter, you should be able to:

1. Understand the relationship between accounting and the allocation of scarce resources.
2. Trace the evolution of Generally Accepted Accounting Principles (GAAP).
3. Relate the objectives of financial reporting as stated in the conceptual framework to the accounting process.
4. Interpret the meaning of the qualitative characteristics of accounting information enumerated in the conceptual framework.
5. Understand the assumptions and conventions underlying the recognition and measurement of accounting data for financial reporting.
6. Distinguish among the elements of the financial statements.
7. Develop an appreciation of ethical and moral considerations in business activity.

Cash Flows, Net Income, and Accrual Accounting

Our entire economy, like any free market, allocates the nation's collective wealth through a series of rational decisions about where it can best be invested to create more wealth. [As managers,] we base those decisions, above all, on what the bottom line provides.

We're making a big mistake. Reported earnings have become virtually worthless in terms of their ability to tell us what's really going on at a company. . . .

"As long as investors—including supposedly sophisticated institutions—place fancy valuations on reported 'earnings' that march steadily upward," wrote ***Berkshire Hathaway*** Chairman Warren Buffett to his shareholders last year, "you can be sure that some managers and promoters will exploit GAAP [Generally Accepted Accounting Principles] to produce such numbers, no matter what the truth may be."

Take ***Prime Motor Inns,*** for instance, which until a few months ago was the world's second largest hotel operator. Last year Prime reported a healthy net income of $77 million—18% of revenues—up nearly 15% from the year before.

In September Prime filed for Chapter 11 bankruptcy.

. . . Could the bankruptcy filing have been foreseen? Prime's problem was that it didn't have enough cash coming in. Much of its reported 1989 bottom line came from selling hotels. But outside financing for those sales had dried up, and Prime had to finance many of those deals itself—leaving it without enough cash to pay its debt service, including debt for the properties it had "sold." . . . Prime had a $15 million cash outflow from operations in 1989—the year it reported a $77 million profit—compared with a positive cash flow of $58 million the year before. . . .

As with hairdos and hemlines, fads in accounting come and go. In the 1920s, when stocks traded mostly on the basis of asset values (a foreshadowing of the 1980s!), accountants devoted their skills to inflating asset values. In the 1960s the focus was on revenues. Many franchisors, for example, would book "sales" immediately after signing a franchise agreement, even though many franchises failed ever to deliver any cash. In the 1980s the big problem was banks and savings and loans overstating the value of their assets.

Today, net income is making a comeback. So are what Berkshire Hathaway chairman Buffett likes to call "white lies" aimed at making reported profits look better than they really are.

Where did all this subjective judgment about the shape of the bottom line start? [T]he East India Trading Company, one of the first "joint stock" companies, was chartered by Queen Elizabeth I in 1600. Initially, the company distributed all profits (if any) at the end of each spice-trading voyage. But in 1661 the company's governor announced that future distributions would consist of periodic dividends paid out of retained earnings.

All of a sudden, measuring profits was a job for the accountants, who had to start making judgment calls. Assets and profits had to be apportioned among many voyages in different stages of completion.

In short, trading companies like the East India Company introduced accrual accounting, the bottom line, and most of the bookkeeping problems we face today.

Source: "Lies of the Bottom Line—Why Reported Earnings Don't Tell You What You Need to Know—and Why the East India Trading Company Is to Blame," *Forbes,* November 12, 1990.

ECONOMIC ENVIRONMENT AND FINANCIAL REPORTING

Understand the relationship between accounting and the allocation of scarce resources.

As the scenario in the preceding excerpt suggests, not all users of accounting information are entirely satisfied with the current rules and requirements of financial reporting. The principle of a free-enterprise economic system is that resources (collective wealth) will flow to the segments of the economy that will use those resources most efficiently in the creation of additional resources (wealth). This process takes place through a series of investment decisions made by the investing public after evaluation of alternative investment opportunities. But informed and intelligent evaluation of investment opportunities can be made only if the decision makers have access to relevant and reliable information—that is, information that permits them to effectively discriminate among alternative investment opportunities. Is the implied criticism of the accounting process in the *Forbes* article justified?

The accounting process provides some of the information necessary to evaluate alternative investment opportunities. In addition to accounting data, investors evaluate a host of other financial and economic factors that impact the future performance of any enterprise. The objective of the accounting process is to provide data that is useful in making those decisions. Accounting standards continue to evolve to achieve this objective, and while not perfect, the accounting system does provide a great deal of relevant and reliable information.

Unfortunately, not all of the information is being used as effectively as it could be. Mr. Buffett, for example, must have ignored the very information that he claims was lacking, information on cash flows. The statement of cash flows has been required since 1987. According to Buffett, the single most important number used in the decision-making process is annual earnings, or net income, which he believes may be a misleading indicator of true economic health, cash flow being much better. The example of ***Prime Motor Inns,*** a company that filed for bankruptcy immediately after reporting large profits in the preceding years, is presented as proof of his assertion. How can companies reporting healthy earnings be on the verge of bankruptcy? Buffett places at least part of the blame on certain accounting practices that he refers to as "white lies," or techniques that allow "management" of income. Several examples of these techniques follow.

ASSET IMPAIRMENT OR "THE BIG BATH"

One popular white lie is the so-called big-bath method of suddenly cleansing balance sheets of past sins after years of insisting that everything was just fine.[1] The big-bath theory stipulates that management thinks that users do not distinguish between a big loss and a small loss. Therefore, in periods when a loss is inevitable, management uses the opportunity to "write down" assets and thus clean up the balance sheet. The write-downs allow the company to show dramatic improvements in earnings growth and return on equity in the immediate future, encouraging investors to look favorably at the company in terms of future prospects.

The accounting standards regarding asset write-downs state that assets should be written down when they become "permanently impaired." This means that an asset valued at $20 million in 1990 could be worth only $5 million in

[1] "Lies of the Bottom Line," *Forbes,* November 12, 1990, p. 106.

1991, and it is left to the judgment of management and the accountant to determine when the write-down should occur. On the other hand, would it not be more misleading to carry the asset at its original value indefinitely? Until 1994, there were no specific accounting standards on asset write-downs, and even now, management has some discretion in determining if a loss has occurred and how much should be written off. Chapter 12 discusses asset impairments.

CONTINGENT LIABILITIES

Another "white lie," or income-management technique, often used is "managed" recognition of **contingent liabilities,** discussed more fully in Chapter 11. Accounting standards require recognition of the loss and related liability at the time the loss is probable and the amount is reasonably estimable. For example, a manufacturing company facing future costs for environmental cleanup may choose to accrue these expenses and related liabilities at opportune times. Buffett cites the oil companies as major players in this game, using as examples ***Amoco*** and ***Texaco.*** Amoco reported an extraordinary gain of $471 million in 1990 offset by a $477 million addition to the environmental damage fund. Similarly, Texaco reported a $362 million gain from the sale of a subsidiary offset by a $355 million charge to the environmental fund.[2] The timing of the recognition of the charge is, again, a matter of judgment for management and the accountant. The position of the profession is that recognition of these liabilities is preferable to nonrecognition, so is best left to the professional judgment of management and the accountant. The Securities and Exchange Commission has recently issued new rules related to environmental costs that are designed to bring about more consistent reporting of these liabilities.

AMORTIZATION AND DEPRECIATION

Still another of the "white lie" techniques sometimes used to manage earnings occurs with amortization and depreciation charges. These accounting issues involve allocating the cost of long-lived assets over some time period (a part of the accrual accounting process handed down by the East India Trading Company). They are important, however, in the determination of periodic earnings. What impact do these charges have on income?

Blockbuster Entertainment (the videotape rental chain) is required to amortize the cost of its video rental tapes. In 1988 Blockbuster changed the amortization period for its tapes "from a fast write-off over 9 months to a slow one over 36 months. That bookkeeping gimmick added $3 million, or nearly 20%, to Blockbuster's reported 1988 income."[3]

On a larger scale, ***General Motors (GM)*** and ***IBM*** also have benefited from changes in depreciation policies. In 1987 GM changed the depreciation rate on its tools and dies to make the rate comparable to those of ***Ford*** and ***Chrysler.*** This increased GM's reported earnings by $2.55 per share, bringing total earnings to $10.06 per share for the year. In 1984 IBM switched from an accelerated method to straight-line depreciation, increasing reported earnings by $375 million.[4]

[2]Ibid.

[3]"Earnings Helper," *Forbes,* June 12, 1989, p. 150.

[4]Ibid.

Are these practices wrong or misleading? Certainly they are permissible under Generally Accepted Accounting Principles (GAAP). In fact, the change made by GM is a recommended change because it made the company's financial statements more comparable to those of Ford and Chrysler. Changes in life expectancies of assets are referred to as changes in *accounting estimates*, while changes in depreciation methods are changes in *accounting principles*. Accounting principle changes are discussed in Chapter 6, and cost allocation for depreciation in Chapter 5.

We must recognize that accounting is a dynamic and ever-changing profession in which the rules and standards have evolved through the years in response to changes in the economic environment. As business evolved from trade-based economies to manufacturing and finally to the complex economies of today, accounting practices and rules have also changed in an effort to provide information useful for decisions about allocation of resources. Because accounting is a dynamic profession, accounting practices and rules will continue to change and evolve in response to changes in the economic environment, and in response to abusive practices.

For example, Statements of Financial Accounting Standards (SFAS) No. 95, "The Statement of Cash Flows," was adopted in 1987 to provide cash-based information to users of financial statements. Buffett's charge that net income is the wrong number on which to focus may, in some respects, be true. However, cash-based information has been required since the adoption of SFAS No. 95. Even before the adoption of SFAS No. 95, cash-based information was available. The accounting profession provides data for financial and economic decision making. Whether decision makers choose to use that information is up to them. The challenge to the profession is to provide the data in a format that is relevant, reliable, and useful for economic decision making.

In this chapter, we examine the development of accounting principles and practices, the organization and output of the major rule-making bodies, and other factors and influences that continue to play a part in the evolution of accounting principles. We will see that, at times, accounting is a *very politicized* process. We also study the conceptual framework, or theoretical basis, for the development of accounting standards. The conceptual framework identifies the objectives of financial reporting, the characteristics that make accounting data useful, the underlying assumptions, the principles and constraints of the accounting process, and the expected output of the accounting process.

GENERALLY ACCEPTED ACCOUNTING PRINCIPLES (GAAP)

Trace the evolution of Generally Accepted Accounting Principles (GAAP).

As the foregoing discussion implies, a possibility exists that accounting policies chosen for use by management may not always provide the most relevant and reliable information for investment decision making. Still, the accounting process tries to assist in identifying efficient versus inefficient users of economic resources. The role of accounting in the allocation of those resources is paramount, and the need for a comprehensive set of standards is crucial. Over the years, a set of such standards has been developed, called the **generally accepted accounting principles**, which govern U.S. accounting and reporting practices today.

Rule 203 of the American Institute of Certified Public Accountants (AICPA) Code of Professional Conduct provides that an auditor should not express an unqualified opinion on financial statements that contain a material departure from GAAP. There are four categories of pronouncements that make up GAAP.

The categories are arranged in a hierarchy, from most authoritative to least authoritative. This arrangement is reflected in Exhibit 1–1, GAAP Hierarchy Summary.

HISTORICAL DEVELOPMENT OF GAAP

The three main sources of U.S. GAAP have been the Committee on Accounting Procedure (CAP), the Accounting Principles Board (APB), and the Financial Accounting Standards Board (FASB). Groups that have influenced the development of accounting standards over the years include the Securities and Exchange Commission (SEC) and other regulatory bodies, the AICPA, private industry, the American Accounting Association (AAA), the Institute of Management Accountants (IMA), financial analysts, and other users of financial information. These groups of influential bodies have played a major role in the development of GAAP. The SEC has statutory authority from Congress to issue accounting standards but has allowed the profession to set its own standards to date.

EXHIBIT 1–1
GAAP Hierarchy Summary

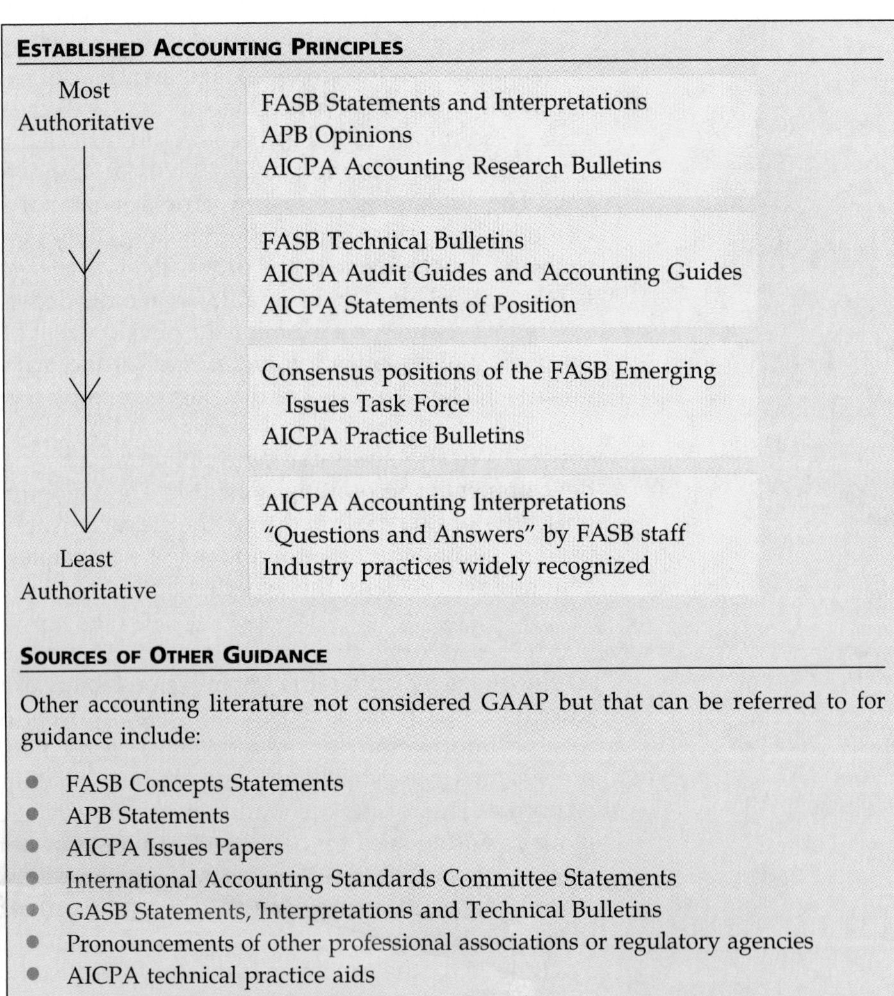

ESTABLISHED ACCOUNTING PRINCIPLES

Most Authoritative	FASB Statements and Interpretations APB Opinions AICPA Accounting Research Bulletins
↓	FASB Technical Bulletins AICPA Audit Guides and Accounting Guides AICPA Statements of Position
↓	Consensus positions of the FASB Emerging Issues Task Force AICPA Practice Bulletins
↓ Least Authoritative	AICPA Accounting Interpretations "Questions and Answers" by FASB staff Industry practices widely recognized

SOURCES OF OTHER GUIDANCE

Other accounting literature not considered GAAP but that can be referred to for guidance include:

- FASB Concepts Statements
- APB Statements
- AICPA Issues Papers
- International Accounting Standards Committee Statements
- GASB Statements, Interpretations and Technical Bulletins
- Pronouncements of other professional associations or regulatory agencies
- AICPA technical practice aids
- Accounting handbooks, textbooks, and articles

The **Committee on Accounting Procedure (CAP)** was the first private body concerned with writing accounting standards. Between 1939 and 1959 it issued 51 *Accounting Research Bulletins (ARBs)*. The members of CAP were practicing CPAs who dealt with accounting issues on an ad hoc, individual-problem basis, usually after a problem already had manifested itself. Because of dissatisfaction with this ad hoc, nonintegrated approach to problem areas, the **Accounting Principles Board (APB)** was appointed by the AICPA in 1959 to address accounting issues on a broader basis than the CAP.

The profession hoped that the APB would develop an overall conceptual framework that could be used as a reference point in resolving *emerging* problems. This would be considerably different from the ad hoc approach taken by the CAP. The membership of the APB was drawn primarily from public accounting, with some representation from industry and the academic community. The APB was an improvement over the ad hoc approach of the CAP in that the acceptable accounting alternatives were narrowed somewhat.

During the period of 1959 to 1973, the APB issued 31 *Opinions*. Unfortunately, the APB suffered a great deal of criticism, mainly for failure to act on a timely basis in dealing with emerging problems. Additionally, it met a great deal of opposition from both industry and public accounting over positions that it had taken on several controversial accounting issues. Finally, in 1971 the Wheat Committee (a study group on "Establishment of Accounting Principles") was appointed by the AICPA. The Wheat Committee was asked to investigate the organization and operations of the APB and to make recommendations for improvement. The Wheat Committee recommended replacing the APB with an entirely different standard-setting structure, consisting of three groups: the Financial Accounting Foundation (FAF), the Financial Accounting Standards Board (FASB), and the Financial Accounting Standards Advisory Committee (FASAC).

The **Financial Accounting Foundation (FAF)**, as its name implies, was to provide financial support for the new organization. The FAF funds the operations of the FASB through contributions from the private sector (industry and CPA firms) and, to a lesser extent, through the sale of the FASB publications. The FAF also appoints the members of the FASB and the **Financial Accounting Standards Advisory Committee (FASAC)**. The FASAC is charged with assisting the FASB on policy and technical issues and with choosing task-force members for special projects.

Establishment of the **Financial Accounting Standards Board (FASB)** was at the heart of the Wheat Committee recommendations. The FASB's stated purpose is to establish financial accounting and reporting standards for the guidance and education of the public. The "public" includes issuers, auditors, and users of financial data. The APB and the FASB differ in the following ways:

- *Smaller membership.* The FASB consists of seven members, compared to eighteen on the APB.
- *Paid, full-time members.* The APB members were part-time, unpaid members.
- *Independence of members.* Because the FASB members are full-time and highly compensated, they are expected to be more independent than members of the APB. Members of the FASB are required to sever all ties to their former firms.
- *Greater autonomy.* The FASB is appointed by and is responsible only to the FAF, whereas the APB was a committee of the AICPA.

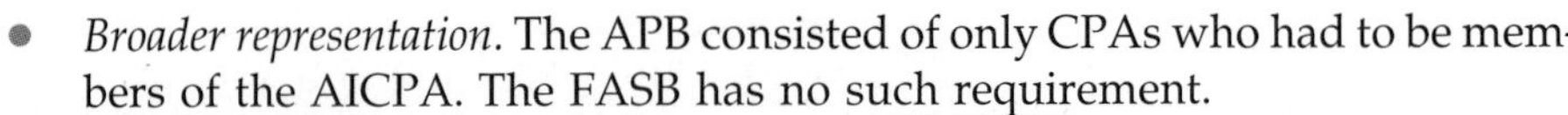

- *Broader representation.* The APB consisted of only CPAs who had to be members of the AICPA. The FASB has no such requirement.
- *Voting.* Passage of a standard by the FASB requires a super majority (five of seven), while the APB required a two-thirds approval vote.

By appointing a full-time, highly paid, independent group, the profession hoped to achieve a more effective process of setting accounting rules and standards.

STANDARD-SETTING PROCESS OF THE FASB

To ensure responsiveness to the needs and viewpoints of the entire economic community, the FASB is required to consist of a broad representation of the business community. A second requirement is a system of "due process" that gives all interested parties the opportunity to be heard. Thus, for all **Statements of Financial Accounting Standards (SFAS)** issued by the FASB, the following steps are taken:

1. A topic or project is placed on the board's agenda.
2. A task force of experts is appointed to define issues, alternatives, and problems related to the project.
3. The FASB technical staff researches the project.
4. A Discussion Memorandum is drafted and released to the public.
5. Public hearings are held approximately 60 days after the release of the Discussion Memorandum.
6. Public response is analyzed and evaluated.
7. An exposure draft is released to the public.[5]
8. Responses to the exposure draft are evaluated, and if necessary, the exposure draft is revised.
9. A vote is taken pursuant to issuing a new standard.

This rather lengthy process was designed to ensure that all interested constituencies would have ample opportunity to voice their concerns.

The *political aspects* of standard setting are very real, and the elaborate procedures outlined here were designed to accommodate the political process. In the beginning of this chapter, examples were given of how management can manipulate reported income by using various accounting techniques. These were referred to as "white lies" that potentially could mislead the investor. They are examples of situations in which some discretion is allowed in the implementation of accounting rules. Some in the investment community have criticized the accounting profession for allowing "excessive" discretion to exist in the standards.

Others charge that standards are overly restrictive. Some critics argue that the FASB has attempted to cover all situations with single statements, an objective they claim is unrealistic. For example, critics point to SFAS Nos. 87 and 106 as examples of very detailed standards. SFAS No. 87, "Employers'

[5]Occasionally the FASB will conduct a field test of the proposed standard, such as in the case of "Other Post-Employment Benefits." If the standard is likely to be particularly complex or difficult to implement, the FASB might ask for volunteer companies to test the standard to determine the impact it would have on their financial statements.

Accounting for Pensions," is 132 pages long and has received a great deal of criticism for narrowing the measurement and reporting options open to management. A positive result is that pension reporting now is much more consistent than prior to adoption of SFAS No. 87.

Still another problem area is addressed in SFAS No. 106, "Employers' Accounting for Postretirement Benefits Other Than Pensions." These postretirement benefits refer to the costs of insurance and benefits other than pensions that employees are entitled to receive after retirement. Prior to SFAS No. 106, companies did not accrue any liability for the future costs of these benefits but simply expensed them as they were paid. SFAS No. 106 requires companies to accrue liabilities for these future costs in much the same way that they are required to accrue liabilities for future pension benefits. Annual charges against income for these costs increased by 300% to 600%, and this standard has had significant social and economic consequences as firms have been forced to recognize the future costs of these benefits. Pensions and postretirement benefits are the topic of Chapter 16.

As seen in this brief discussion, many competing objectives and desires exist in the standard-setting process. To achieve better comparability between financial statements, users of financial statements—and investors in particular—want standards that restrict the number of acceptable alternatives. Conversely, issuers of financial statements are generally opposed to controls and restrictive standards, preferring more latitude and discretion in the preparation of financial statements. These competing objectives vie for the attention of the FASB in the standard-setting process.

POLITICAL INFLUENCES

The nine-step, due-process procedure outlined previously and followed by the FASB prior to issuing a standard was designed to accommodate this political process. The environment in which the FASB functions is one in which the competing interests of industry lobbying groups, major corporations, and public accounting practice are very vocal. In addition, the FASB must always be mindful of Congress, the SEC, and the public interest.

Congress and the SEC have the ultimate authority to mandate accounting standards. The Securities and Exchange Act of 1934 established the Securities and Exchange Commission and empowered it to prescribe accounting standards. The SEC's authority extends only to companies that must file statements with it—that is, all public companies, or those that sell stock to the public. Thus far, the SEC has generally allowed the accounting profession to set its own standards and rules, seldom interfering with the process. A notable exception occurred in 1978 when the SEC rejected SFAS No. 19[6] after holding public hearings. This unusual step by the SEC was attributed to aggressive lobbying in Congress by opponents of SFAS No. 19.[7] The SEC opposed the standard, and the lobbying efforts of the various groups provided the impetus for the commission to reject the standard.[8]

[6]FASB Statement of Financial Accounting Standards No. 19, "Accounting and Reporting by Oil and Gas Producing Companies," December 1977.

[7]Donald E. Gorton, "The SEC Decision Not to Support SFAS 19," *Accounting Horizons 5*, No. 1, March 1991, pp. 29–41.

[8]Ibid., p. 41.

Many of the most highly debated standards are those that would result in significant revisions or alterations to an existing rule. When the FASB reexamined the valuation of compensatory stock options in 1993 and 1994, the board received over 600 comment letters. Revisions of old or adoption of new standards are necessitated by changing economic circumstances and uncertainty in the economic environment. One way the FASB attempts to deal with uncertainty and the changing environment is through the **Emerging Issues Task Force (EITF).** This group is charged with identifying emerging issues for which a diversity of practices is likely to evolve. An issue is placed on the FASB agenda if 11 of 13 task-force members agree that it should be considered. The EITF receives input from various parties and evaluates current issues, paying attention to all factors that would affect a problem.

EFFICIENT-MARKETS HYPOTHESIS

A final factor affecting accounting reporting and disclosure requirements is the **efficient-markets hypothesis (EMH)**, which, in simple terms, means that stock prices continuously reflect all available and relevant information; therefore, stock prices will react only to unanticipated events. According to this theory, any publicly available information is very quickly impounded in stock prices. Attempts to generate abnormal returns (returns in excess of the overall market rate) based on public information will not be successful in the long run. At a minimum, the excess returns will not be commensurate with the extra costs necessary to produce those returns.

One implication of the EMH for accounting and financial reporting is that the use of alternative accounting methods would not significantly affect stock prices, particularly not the stock prices of those larger firms traded on the New York Stock Exchange (NYSE) that are closely followed by investment analysts. Analysts (who direct the investment policies of pension plans, trust funds, mutual funds, and insurance portfolios) should make adjustments for differences resulting from the accounting method alternatives used by these firms.

Another implication of the EMH for accounting and financial reporting is that investors would receive information from a variety of sources, not just from the financial accounting reports. For example, management has long been recognized as a primary source of information about the company, and the company's annual report contains a letter that is management's interpretation of the year's activity. Additionally, many newsletter services, brokerage firms, mutual funds, and other investment advisors provide information. The information from all of these sources, as well as the accounting data, is assimilated and used by the market.

Finally, we should note that market efficiency apparently is somewhat relative. Share prices of large NYSE companies that are closely followed by financial analysts seem to be more "efficient" than those of smaller companies that are not followed as closely by analysts. Many firms not traded on the NYSE do not have a following of analysts and may not exhibit the same degree of market efficiency.

Complicating the entire process of standard setting are the ongoing efforts at globalization and international standardization of accounting standards. Some generally accepted accounting principles of the United States differ from those in other countries. Companies that do not follow U.S. GAAP cannot be listed for trading on the stock exchanges of the United States. In general, U.S. GAAP is more restrictive than accounting standards used in other countries. The advantages of having foreign stocks listed and traded on domestic exchanges lie primarily in maintaining prominence in the world marketplace as the financial center of the world. The International Accounting Standards Committee (IASC) writes international rules, and the International Organization of Securities Commissions (IOSC) regulates securities markets. These two bodies have agreed to develop accounting standards by mid-1999 for companies seeking stock listing in global markets. The international In Practice excerpt contains a discussion of the importance associated with attracting foreign companies to the U.S. exchanges.

IN PRACTICE—INTERNATIONAL

Harmonization of Accounting Standards

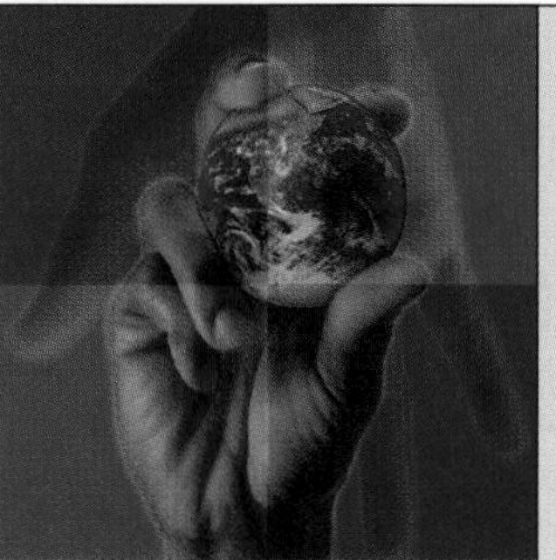

The major roadblock to foreign companies listing their overseas stock on U.S. exchanges has long been the vast differences between accounting standards in the U.S. and abroad. For decades, leading accounting theorists have advocated the harmonization of accounting principles worldwide to end the confusion and lack of comparability. But major foreign companies have resisted the move because they've felt that the tougher U.S. accounting rules would likely prevail in formulating global standards.

Suddenly, what seemed like an impossible dream appears a bit closer to reality with new moves by key accounting rulemakers—all with the goal of harmonizing disparate accounting rules worldwide.

The boards of the International Accounting Standards Committee (IASC), which makes international rules, and the International Organization of Securities Commissions have just agreed to develop accounting standards by mid-1999 for companies seeking stock listings in global markets to raise cross-border capital.

Even the Securities and Exchange Commission, which has long fought to maintain tough U.S. accounting standards, is easing the barriers somewhat.

Whatever the outcome, the stakes are enormous for both U.S. capital markets and the investment community. Big Board officials note that 55 million shares of nonregistered foreign stocks already trade in the Unites States, over the counter. They believe the U.S. stock market may lose world prominence to London and other European exchanges if foreign stocks aren't listed in New York.

Currently only 204 non-U.S. companies list on the New York Stock Exchange. To the Big Board, this seems like a pittance because there are 2,000 or more big foreign companies out there that could qualify for listing. So, the exchange has been working quietly to get regulators and rulemakers to permit another 200 or more big foreign companies to list here under international standards. This would almost double the Big Board's capitalization to close to $10 trillion from the current $5.4 trillion.

Source: Lee Burton, "All Accountants Soon May Speak the Same Language," *The Wall Street Journal*, August 29, 1995, p. A15.

The historical perspective of the role of the FASB is important in that the FASB was created to respond to accounting issues on a comprehensive, consistent, and timely basis. One of the specific charges of the FASB is to develop an overall framework that could serve as the theoretical basis of accounting rules and standards. This ongoing project is referred to as the **conceptual framework.**

CONCEPTUAL FRAMEWORK

Relate the objectives of financial reporting as stated in the conceptual framework to the accounting process.

The conceptual framework refers to the continuing series of statements of the FASB known as **Statements of Financial Accounting Concepts (SFACs).** The SFACs are intended to establish the objectives and concepts to be used by the FASB in developing standards for financial accounting and reporting. These statements set forth the FASB's position regarding the objectives of general-purpose financial statements; the characteristics of information that make it useful; the assumptions, conventions or principals, and constraints underlying the preparation of the information; and the elements included in the output of the process, that is, the financial statements. Exhibit 1–2 is a diagrammatic representation of the conceptual framework.

The conceptual framework project grew out of a necessity to establish a logical and cohesive set of interrelated concepts that would serve as a guide for

EXHIBIT 1–2
Conceptual Framework

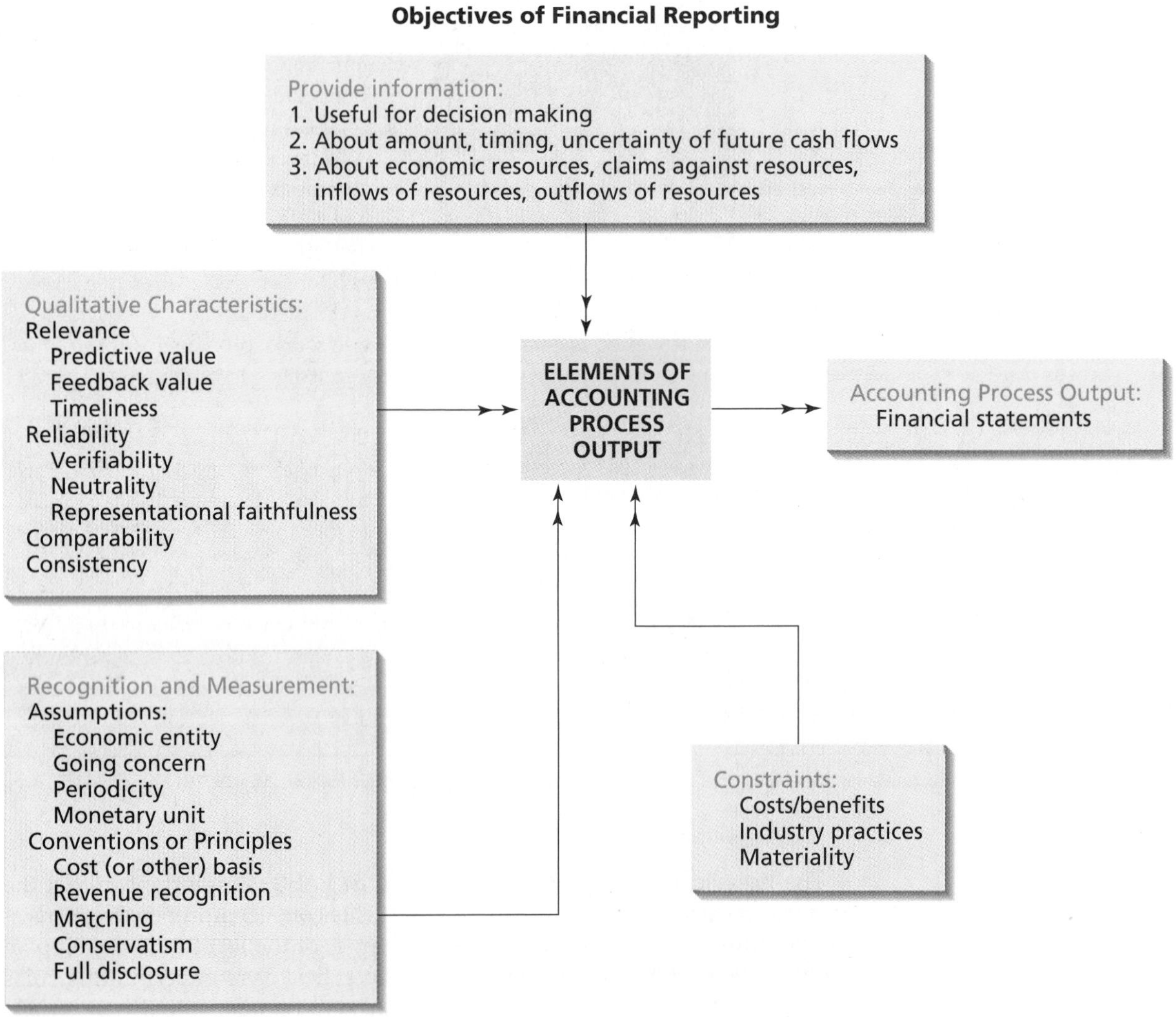

Objectives of Financial Reporting

Provide information:
1. Useful for decision making
2. About amount, timing, uncertainty of future cash flows
3. About economic resources, claims against resources, inflows of resources, outflows of resources

Qualitative Characteristics:
Relevance
- Predictive value
- Feedback value
- Timeliness

Reliability
- Verifiability
- Neutrality
- Representational faithfulness

Comparability
Consistency

ELEMENTS OF ACCOUNTING PROCESS OUTPUT

Accounting Process Output:
Financial statements

Recognition and Measurement:
Assumptions:
- Economic entity
- Going concern
- Periodicity
- Monetary unit

Conventions or Principles
- Cost (or other) basis
- Revenue recognition
- Matching
- Conservatism
- Full disclosure

Constraints:
- Costs/benefits
- Industry practices
- Materiality

the development of financial accounting and reporting standards. According to the FASB, the statements were intended to

> serve the public interest within the context of the role of financial accounting and reporting in the economy—to provide evenhanded financial and other information that, together with information from other sources, facilitates efficient functioning of capital and other markets and otherwise assists in promoting efficient allocation of scarce resources in the economy.[9]

To date, the FASB has issued six concepts statements. Statement No. 3 was replaced by Statement No. 6, and Statement No. 4 is concerned with nonbusiness organizations. Thus, Statement Nos. 1, 2, 5, and 6 contain the FASB's conceptual framework for financial reporting by business organizations.[10]

OBJECTIVES OF FINANCIAL REPORTING

In SFAC No. 1, the FASB identifies three major objectives of financial reporting (refer to Exhibit 1–2). First, financial reporting is to provide information *useful to present and potential investors and creditors and other users for making rational investment, credit, and similar decisions.* An explicit assumption made by the FASB is that the users of financial information possess a reasonable familiarity and level of competence in dealing with financial statements. An implicit assumption of this objective is that the information would assist in the allocation of scarce economic resources by enabling investors and creditors to better evaluate investment and lending opportunities. The emphasis of this first objective is to provide information *useful for decision making* and is consistent with the concept of scarce resource allocation discussed earlier in the chapter.

The second objective of financial reporting stated by the FASB is to *provide information about the amount, timing, and uncertainty of future cash flows.* Recall the emphasis on cash flow in the excerpt from the *Forbes* article at the beginning of the chapter. In that article, Buffett (as well as other investors) was dissatisfied with the exclusive use of the net income figure for evaluation of investment alternatives and advocated the use of cash flows in addition to net income. The proponents of using cash flow information believe it better enables them to form rational expectations about prospective cash flows and to assess the risk that the amounts and timing of those cash flows might be different from expectations. However, cash flow is a complement to income and not a replacement. An accrual-based income statement provides information not provided by a cash flow statement, and it should be used together with cash flow information to assess risk associated with future cash flow.

[9]FASB Statement of Financial Accounting Concepts No. 1, "Objectives of Financial Reporting by Business Enterprises," Foreword, November 1978.

[10]The six statements are

1. SFAC No. 1, "Objectives of Financial Reporting by Business Enterprises," November 1978.
2. SFAC No. 2, "Qualitative Characteristics of Accounting Information," May 1980.
3. SFAC No. 3, "Elements of Financial Statements of Business Enterprises," December 1980.
4. SFAC No. 4, "Objectives of Financial Reporting by Nonbusiness Organizations," December 1980.
5. SFAC No. 5, "Recognition and Measurement in Financial Statements of Business Enterprises," December 1984.
6. SFAC No. 6, "Elements of Financial Statements," December 1985.

The third objective of financial reporting stated by the FASB is to *provide information about enterprise resources, claims to those resources, and changes in those resources*. The purpose of this information is to help investors, creditors, and other users identify the strengths and weaknesses of an enterprise, as well as to assess its *liquidity, solvency, and financial flexibility*. Changes in those resources occur in response to enterprise performance and earnings. Therefore, part of this objective is to provide information to assess the *profitability* of an enterprise. Information about an enterprise's profitability performance is provided by measures of earnings and the components of earnings.

A close relationship exists between cash flow and profitability, as measured by accrual accounting. The objective of accrual accounting is to report the accomplishments (revenues) of a given period appropriately (called revenue recognition) and relate the efforts (costs) of that same period to those accomplishments (the matching principle). Over the life of an enterprise, net income from operations should equal total net cash inflows from operations excluding cash inflows from sales of stock. However, this relationship between cash flow and earnings will not hold for short periods, such as a year, because the *timing* of recognition of the components of earnings under the accrual basis differs from the timing of recognition under the cash basis.

Once the FASB set forth the overall objectives of financial reporting in SFAC No. 1, it next identified characteristics that make accounting information useful for economic decision making. These characteristics are defined in SFAC No. 2.

QUALITATIVE CHARACTERISTICS

Interpret the meaning of the qualitative characteristics of accounting information enumerated in the conceptual framework.

In SFAC No. 2, "Qualitative Characteristics of Accounting Information," the FASB continued its emphasis on providing useful information for decision making.

> The central role assigned here to decision making leads straight to the overriding criterion by which all accounting choices must be judged. The better choice is the one that, subject to considerations of cost, produces from among the available alternatives information that is most useful for decision making.[11]

SFAC No. 2 suggests that the characteristics could be viewed as a hierarchy of accounting qualities, with decision makers, or users of the accounting data, at the top of the hierarchy (see Exhibit 1–3). Each user must decide what information is of importance to the particular decision at hand, since the optimal information for one user may not be optimal for another.

Understandability provides a link between user characteristics and characteristics inherent in the information itself; it is the quality of information that enables users to perceive its significance. Even though information may be relevant and reliable, if the decision maker cannot understand it, the information is not useful.

Primary Decision Qualities. SFAC No. 2 identifies relevance and reliability as the two primary qualities that make accounting information useful for decision making.

[11]SFAC No. 2, par. 30.

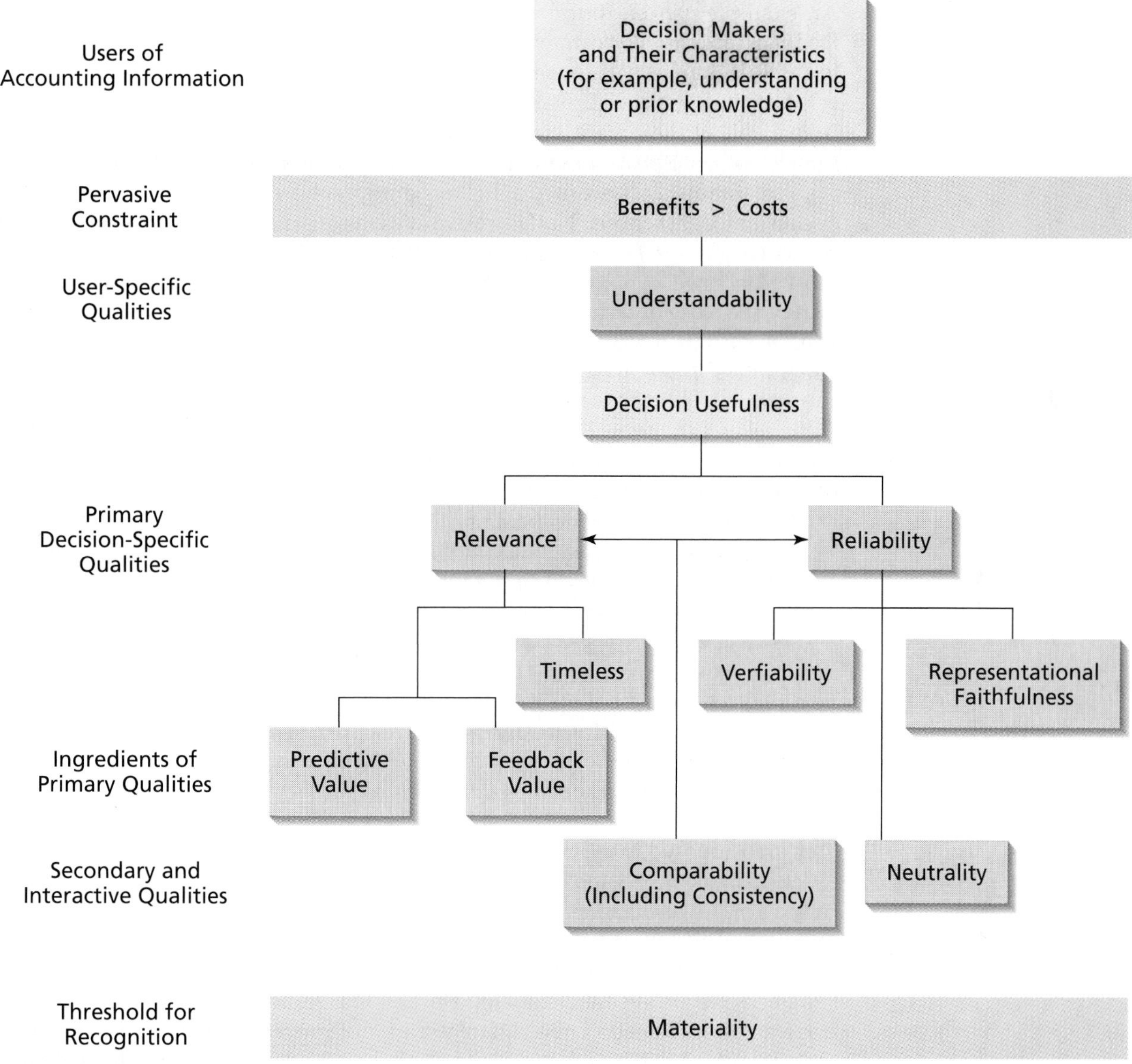

Source: Statement of Financial Accounting Concepts No. 2, "Qualitative Characteristics of Accounting Information," FASB, May 1980, p. 15.

EXHIBIT 1–3
A Hierarchy of Accounting Qualities

Relevance, the first primary quality, is defined as information that is "capable of *making a difference* in a decision by helping users form predictions about the outcomes of past, present, and future events or to confirm or correct prior expectations."[12] If information does not affect a decision outcome, or makes no difference to the decision, the information is not relevant.

Information can make a difference in a decision if it improves the decision maker's ability to predict outcomes of future events (**predictive value**) or if it confirms or corrects earlier expectations of past or present events (**feedback value**). Thus, predictive value and feedback value are components of relevance.

[12]SFAC No. 2, par. 47.

An example can be found in interim earnings reports, which provide both feedback on past performance and a basis for prediction for anyone wishing to forecast annual earnings before the year-end.[13]

The third aspect of relevance is timeliness, meaning that the information is available at the time it can affect the decision. Information that has become too old to be helpful in making a decision is no longer relevant.

Accounting is concerned with recognition and measurement of economic events and transactions. Not all relevant items are measured by the accounting process, however. For example, during the period 1990–1993, ***Intel Corporation*** enjoyed a huge competitive economic advantage as a computer chip manufacturer because of technological advantages. Intel was able to consistently generate net profit margins in excess of 25 percent. As a result, the marketplace valuation of Intel stock was second only to ***Microsoft*** among computer and software-related companies. Yet the *book value* of Intel stock was much less than the market valuation. This is because the accounting system at present does not incorporate technological and economic advantages, managerial expertise, or other seemingly relevant nonfinancial data in its valuation.

Reliability, the second primary quality, means that the information is objective, faithfully represents the underlying economic event, and is reasonably free from error and bias. Reliable information contains three essential characteristics–verifiability, representational faithfulness, and neutrality.

Verifiability implies a consensus among measurers; they arrive at the same result when using similar measurement methods. In other words, the data can be replicated because they are objective.

Representational faithfulness means a correspondence or agreement exists between a measure or description and the underlying economic event.[14] This means that the accounting numbers do, in fact, represent (or correspond to) the economic reality of the resources, obligations, or transactions and events they are supposed to represent. As an example, accounts receivable on a balance sheet purports to represent a sum collectible from customers. If a significant portion of the receivables is uncollectible, the information (accounts receivable number) would be unreliable.

Perhaps a more compelling example is the issuance in 1979 of SFAS No. 33, "Financial Reporting and Changing Prices." This standard required disclosure of current cost information about inventories and property, plant, and equipment for certain businesses and suggested several methods of compiling the information. Several years later, in 1984, SFAS No. 82, "Financial Reporting and Changing Prices: Elimination of Certain Disclosures," made these disclosures voluntary instead of mandatory. One of the reasons for this reversal by the FASB was the need to ensure the reliability of the data. In some cases, the methods used to obtain the data were suspect, lacking both verifiability and representational faithfulness.

Neutrality of accounting information means that it is free from bias intended to attain a particular result or mode of behavior. In both formulating and implementing accounting standards, the sole concern is the relevance and reliability of the information, without regard to the effect that the new rule may have on any particular interest. To be neutral, accounting information must report the economic transactions without attempting to influence behavior in some particular direction.

[13]Ibid., par. 42.
[14]SFAC No. 2, par. 63.

Recall the discussion earlier in the chapter about the political environment in which the FASB operates. Before a new rule or standard is adopted, all affected parties and economic interests have the opportunity to provide input, and many use that opportunity to make their views known. The FASB then must weigh all the evidence and formulate the standard without favoring a particular group, or trying to influence behavior in a particular direction. This, of course, will result in criticism of the board because not all affected parties will be satisfied with the provisions of the standard ultimately adopted.

Secondary Decision-Usefulness Qualities. Comparability and consistency are identified in SFAC No. 2 as secondary qualities necessary for information to be useful in decision making. Comparability is the quality of information that allows users to detect similarities in, and differences between, sets of data. The usefulness of information available from one enterprise is greatly enhanced if it can be compared with similar information from other enterprises.

Consistency refers to the use or application of the same accounting principles or methods to the same events over a span of time. This means that an enterprise should use the same accounting methods and principles from period to period unless a different method can be demonstrated as being preferable to the old. If a new method is adopted, its nature and effect must be disclosed in the notes to the financial statements.

Constraints. Exhibit 1–2 depicts three constraints in the preparation of accounting information: **costs/benefits, industry practices**, and **materiality**. As shown in Exhibit 1–3, SFAC No. 2 indicates that a pervasive constraint in the preparation of accounting data is **cost/benefits**. How the overall cost of compliance with a new standard compares with the overall benefits of the information provided is an issue that the board considers in its deliberations. When the board issued SFAS No. 106, "Employers' Accounting for Postretirement Benefits Other Than Pensions," a 17-page section was included justifying the rule on a cost-benefit basis. This was the first time such a section was included with a FASB pronouncement; it was a response to criticisms that the new rules were too costly and complex.

Another constraint recognized by the board can be referred to as **industry practices**. Certain industries have accounting practices peculiar to their particular business and different from GAAP. For example, revenue recognition is allowed at the endpoint of production in agricultural and mining operations as opposed to the point of sale, which is normally required for most other business activities.

In keeping with the concept of relevance, only those items material in amount should be separately reported or disclosed. **Materiality** and relevance are closely related in that an item must be large enough to impact a decision to warrant disclosure. Therefore, materiality provides a basic threshold for recognition in the financial statements.

Though the *concept* of materiality appears to be straightforward, in practice it is not. When the FASB included materiality as a constraint in the qualitative characteristics in SFAC No. 2, it was not defined, nor was a limit set. Instead, the board left it to the judgment of the accountant, stating "materiality judgments can properly be made only by those who have all the facts."[15]

[15]SFAC No. 2, par. 31.

The lack of a definition or a threshold limit creates a problem for both auditors and users because what is not considered material by one party might be very important to another. In other words, no consensus exists about what is material and what is not, and this lack of consensus could cause the accounting data to lack reliability.

An illustration of this divergence is found in a study in which auditors' judgments of materiality were compared with those of judges, corporate attorneys, bank loan officers, financial analysts, and credit managers.[16] The materiality judgments in the study concerned the timing of the write-off of obsolete inventory, the income statement treatment (ordinary versus extraordinary) of a gain resulting from a forced sale by eminent domain, the disclosure or nondisclosure of a lawsuit against the company, management's attempt to report a bribe paid as a normal operating expense, and the discontinuance of a product line. The findings reported a significant lack of consensus within the profession (among CPA respondents) as well as among the various other groups included in the study. These findings highlight the divergence possible as to what is considered material.

By leaving the interpretation of materiality to "professional judgment," a company's management can argue either against disclosure of unfavorable events or for the disclosure of unfavorable events, but in less conspicuous places, on the grounds of materiality. Such decisions can greatly erode the reliability of the data and the confidence of the financial statement users.

In sum, we can say that the primary purpose of accounting information is to assist users in decision making. To do so, it must be understandable to the user and be both relevant and reliable. Subject to the benefits outweighing the costs, and a materiality judgment, the information will be relevant if it makes a difference in the decision and reliable if the user can depend on its integrity. Relevant information will assist users in making predictions about the outcome of future events. It can also provide the users with feedback to correct or confirm anticipated events. It must be received in a timely manner. Reliable information will be verifiable by other measurers, will represent faithfully the economic events it purports to represent, and will be neutral in its presentation. When these qualities are present, the accounting information will be useful for decision making.

RECOGNITION AND MEASUREMENT IN FINANCIAL STATEMENTS

Understand the assumptions and conventions underlying the recognition and measurement of accounting data for financial reporting.

As seen in Exhibit 1–2, the output of the accounting process consists of financial statements, notes to the financial statements, supplementary information, and other means of financial reporting. A full set of financial statements would include the following:

- balance sheet at the end of the period (discussed in Chapter 3).
- income statement for the period (Chapter 6).
- statement of cash flows during the period (Chapter 7).
- statement of investments by and distributions to owners during the period (Chapter 19).

[16]Marianne Jennings, Dan C. Kneer, and Philip M.J. Reckers, "A Reexamination of the Concept of Materiality: Views of Auditors, Users, and Officers of the Court," *Auditing: A Journal of Practice and Theory* 6, No. 2 (Spring 1987), pp. 104–115.

These financial statements include or incorporate any individual elements of information that meet the criteria for recognition (or inclusion in the financial statements). **Recognition** is the process of formally incorporating an item into the financial statements of an entity as an asset, liability, revenue, expense, etc. **Measurement** is the amount at which the item is reported. The criteria for recognition and measurement of the information that should be formally incorporated into the financial statements are found in SFAC No. 5, "Recognition and Measurement in Financial Statements of Business Enterprises," issued by the FASB in 1984. The methods and procedures used to operationalize the recognition and measurement criteria for recording and classifying financial information are based on several assumptions, conventions, and constraints underlying the accounting process.

BASIC ASSUMPTIONS

We can identify four basic assumptions underlying the accounting process:

1. The **economic-entity assumption** presumes that the activities of each **economic entity** are separate and distinct from the activities of other economic units. For example, the financial affairs of an individual who owns a business are identified with the individual and are separate from the financial affairs that are identified with the business.
2. The **going-concern assumption** means that, in the absence of evidence to the contrary, we assume the enterprise will continue. This is a very important assumption because it provides the impetus for accrual accounting and the periodic reporting of earnings. In the discussion of the East India Trading Company at the beginning of the chapter, we saw that accounting problems developed when East India changed from its method of distributing profits at the end of each voyage (a completed-venture basis) to payment of periodic dividends before the venture was completed (an accrual-accounting basis). Accrual accounting is based on the going-concern assumption (i.e., the enterprise will continue indefinitely). This in turn, necessitates a further assumption, that of periodicity.
3. The **periodicity assumption** suggests that the economic activities of the enterprise can be divided into discrete time periods for reporting purposes (for example, one year or one quarter). Thus, when the East India Trading Company introduced the accrual-accounting concept, it forced accountants to divide the company's activities into artificial time periods. Costs and revenues were assigned to various voyages. Since most of the voyages lasted several years, allocation and recognition of revenues and expenses by time periods was necessary.
4. The **monetary unit assumption** means that currency—the dollar in the United States—is assumed to be an appropriate basis for measurement of economic activity. Implied in this assumption is that the dollar is a stable measurement unit and therefore is not adjusted for changes in purchasing power. In SFAC No. 5, the FASB recognized that the dollar is not a stable measurement unit; changes in purchasing power do occur and may be recognized in the future. At the present time, however, no adjustments for changes in price levels are made under GAAP.

BASIC CONVENTIONS OR PRINCIPLES

The assumptions underlying the accounting process lead to several conventions or principles used in recording and classifying financial information. These include the cost or other measurement basis, revenue recognition, matching, conservatism, and full disclosure.

Cost or Other Measurement Basis. The cost or other measurement basis is the amount at which an item is reported in the financial statements. According to SFAC No. 5, "Items currently reported in financial statements are measured by different attributes, depending on the nature of the item and the relevance and reliability of the attribute."[17] Five measurement bases currently are used in practice.

1. *Historical cost (historical proceeds).*
2. *Current cost.* Some inventories are reported at their current (replacement) cost, which is the amount of cash or its equivalent that would have to be paid if an equivalent asset were acquired currently.
3. *Fair value.* Securities that are classified as trading and available for sale are reported at fair value or current market value.
4. *Net realizable (settlement) value.* Short-term receivables and some inventories are reported at the amount of cash or its equivalent, into which an asset is expected to be converted in due course of business less direct costs, if any, necessary to make that conversion.
5. *Present (or discounted) value of future cash flow.* Long-term receivables are reported at their present value (discounted at an implicit or historical rate). This is the present or discounted value of future cash inflows into which an asset is expected to be converted in due course of business, less present values of cash outflows necessary to obtain those inflows.

An advantage historical cost has over the other measurement bases is that it is objective and verifiable; however, it is challenged frequently on the basis of relevance. For example, the historical cost of land acquired years earlier may be totally different from the current fair market value.

Revenue Recognition. The convention of revenue recognition involves two factors, (1) being either realized or realizable and (2) being earned.[18] *Realized* means that an exchange transaction has taken place—goods or services are exchanged for cash or claims to cash. Being *realizable* means that goods are readily convertible to a known amount of cash. That is, they are fungible (interchangeable) units with quoted prices available in an active market that can readily absorb the quantity of goods without affecting the price. Examples of fungible goods are agricultural products or mineral deposits.

Revenues are considered *earned* when the entity has substantially accomplished what it must do to be entitled to the benefits represented by the revenues.[19] For example, revenues for agricultural products are considered earned

[17]SFAC No. 5, par. 66.
[18]SFAC No. 5, par. 83.
[19]Ibid., par. 83b.

when harvested, and revenues from appliance sales are recorded when the appliance is delivered. Revenue is recognized (recorded) when revenue is both realized (or realizable) and earned. Revenue and expense recognition and the exceptions to the general rules are discussed in depth in Chapters 4 and 5.

Matching. The convention of matching is closely related to the going-concern assumption and revenue recognition. In brief, the matching convention requires that whenever reasonable and possible, the efforts (costs and expenses) required to generate revenues must be recognized in the same period that the revenues are recognized. For example, the cost of a machine is expensed through depreciation charges over its useful life—the time when it is contributing to the generation of revenue. Or as another example, consider a sailing vessel of the East India Trading Company. The cost of the vessel should be allocated to all the voyages that resulted in revenues being generated. Cost allocation is part of the accrual-accounting process.

Conservatism. The convention of conservatism means that when a choice of equally acceptable accounting methods is available, the method that is least likely to overstate income measurement and asset valuation should be chosen. The FASB has stated that the method selected should reflect the economic reality of the underlying event; that is, it must possess the qualitative characteristic of representational faithfulness. Conservatism influences revenue recognition, asset valuation, and recognition of gains and losses.

Full Disclosure. The convention of full disclosure requires presentation of any information important enough to influence the judgment of an informed decision maker. Disclosure may be either in the financial statements themselves, the notes to the financial statements, or supplementary information provided. An implied assumption is that all material items will be disclosed. However, recall our earlier discussion of materiality: Whether an item is disclosed, and how it is disclosed, is dependent on a preparer's judgment of whether or not it is material.

Basic Elements of Financial Statements

Distinguish among the elements of the financial statements.

Exhibit 1–2 shows that the objectives, qualitative characteristics, recognition and measurement principles, and cost/benefit constraints all interact to produce the elements of the accounting process output. The classes of items such as assets, liabilities, revenues, and expenses comprising the financial statements are referred to as the **elements**, or building blocks, of the financial statements. SFAC No. 6, "Elements of Financial Statements," defines ten such elements (see Exhibit 1–4).

The first three elements relate to the balance sheet. Assets and liabilities are defined in terms of *future economic benefits,* which gives the balance sheet a *prospective,* or forward-looking, emphasis. The balance sheet provides information relative to expected future cash flows of the enterprise. Elements 7 through 10 relate to the income statement. These items are defined in terms of inflows and outflows of assets—that is, future economic benefits. The income statement possesses feedback value for accounting information because it reports the results of operations for the period. The income statement helps make an assessment of whether expectations were met.

EXHIBIT 1–4
Elements of Financial Statements

1. ASSETS—probable future economic benefits obtained or controlled by a particular entity as a result of past transactions or events.
2. LIABILITIES—probable future sacrifices of economic benefits arising from present obligations of a particular entity to transfer assets or provide services to other entities as a result of past transactions or events.
3. EQUITY OR NET ASSETS—the residual interest in the assets of an entity that remains after deducting its liabilities. In a business enterprise, the equity is the ownership interest.
4. INVESTMENTS BY OWNERS—increases in equity of a particular business enterprise resulting from transfers to it from other entities of something valuable to obtain or increase ownership interests (or equity) in it.
5. DISTRIBUTIONS TO OWNERS—decreases in equity of a particular business enterprise resulting from transferring assets, rendering services, or incurring liabilities by the enterprise to owners.
6. COMPREHENSIVE INCOME—the change in equity of a business enterprise during a period from transactions and other events and circumstances from nonowner sources.
7. REVENUES—inflows or other enhancements of assets of an entity or settlements of its liabilities (or a combination of both) from delivering or producing goods, rendering services, or other activities that constitute the entity's ongoing major or central operations.
8. EXPENSES—outflows or other using up of assets or incurrences of liabilities (or a combination of both) from delivering or producing goods, rendering services, or carrying out other activities that constitute the entity's ongoing major or central operations.
9. GAINS—increases in equity (net assets) from peripheral or incidental transactions of an entity and from all other transactions, events, and circumstances affecting the entity except those that result from revenues or investments from owners.
10. LOSSES—decreases in equity (net assets) from peripheral or incidental transactions of an entity and from all other transactions, events, and circumstances affecting the entity except those that result from expenses or distributions to owners.

Items 4 through 6 represent the net change in residual interest or retained earnings. "Comprehensive income" includes all items that affect inflows and outflows of resources in the current period. The only items excluded from comprehensive income result from errors occurring in prior periods, and certain tax-related benefits that originated in prior periods, investments by or distributions to owners.

The definitions of the elements relate to economic transactions and events relevant to resource allocation decisions. The usefulness of the information provided depends upon its relevance and reliability and especially on its representational faithfulness.[20]

[20]SFAC No. 6, par. 10.

ETHICS IN ACCOUNTING AND CORPORATE AMERICA

Develop an appreciation of ethical and moral considerations in business activity.

"The secret of life is honesty and fair play—if you can fake that, you've got it made." While this quote is attributed to Groucho Marx, many students perceive this to be a recipe for success in business. It is not. However, widespread acceptance of this belief establishes a norm that, by itself, can serve to lower the level of ethical conduct practiced in business and the accounting profession. Too often, people use as guides for their own behavior what they believe others would do in like situations. Perceptions thus become critical. This type of ethical philosophy is called **cultural relativism.**

Cultural relativism is not only dangerous, it is a bankrupt philosophy. Cultural relativism relieves individuals from the need to *reason through ethical issues and justify choices* when confronted with ethical dilemmas. Justifying questionable forms of one's own behavior on the basis of another's questionable behavior is not an acceptable moral norm.

Philosophies of ethics that require fundamental analyses are **absolutism** (a rule-based theory) and **consequentialism** (or utilitarianism), each of which will be discussed here. Some knowledge of ethical philosophy is important to students of accounting because, inevitably, in the practice of their professional duties (which affect the financial wealth of other parties), ethical dilemmas *will* occur. A sound ethical framework to guide professional conduct is as essential as technical knowledge.

It is in the best interests of business and the accounting profession to expect ethical conduct by their employees and members. By maintaining high standards, corporate America can avoid excessive government regulation and *monitoring costs*—those costs incurred by stockholders (and society) to promote the ethical conduct of business leaders. For example, government regulations and watchdog agencies add cost but no value to the consumer's product. Thus, unethical business behavior increases the cost of doing business and consumer prices. As such, this behavior also reduces American industry's international competitiveness. To the extent that ethical behavior can reduce government regulation and other monitoring costs, everyone benefits, and resources can be directed to other productive activities. Corporations that look to the long-run value of ethical business conduct are better able to attract and retain customers, employees, suppliers, and distributors and to earn the public's goodwill. Public trust and confidence in the output of the accounting process is of critical importance to the accounting profession. A public accounting firm's reputation for integrity is its foremost asset.

ETHICS AND EDUCATION

Until about the last half-century, universities were acknowledged as providers of moral guidance as well as academic guidance. More recently, "value-neutral" education has been the norm, as teachers and instructors are hesitant to moralize for fear of offending some students. However, one might ask whether ethical behavior is simply a product of "good personal values" (or "good family training") or does it involve a cognitive element? Arguably, many students of business complete their collegiate education ill-prepared to confront ethical challenges. They lack a basic framework from which to approach an analysis of ethical issues.

FRAMEWORK FOR ETHICAL ANALYSIS

If cultural relativism does not provide a sound basis from which to evaluate an ethical dilemma, what other ethical philosophies are available? The American Accounting Association's Advisory Committee on Professionalism and Ethics suggests two: absolutism and utilitarianism.

Absolutism. One's ethics are those values by which one lives. Ethicists such as Aristotle and Kant believed that certain values are absolute, or unchanging across time and cultures. Some fundamental values are suggested in Exhibit 1–5.

Absolutism subscribes to the belief that the ends do not justify the means. A moral value such as honesty is critical to humanity because without it (that is, if everyone lied) society (and economic markets) would degenerate into chaos. Societies simply could not function in the absence of truthful representations of events. Thus, from these values spring certain citizen rights—rights to know (i.e., the truth), rights to respect, loyalty, and confidentiality. Implicit and explicit contractual rights also flow from these values. Pervasive in these values is a fundamental ethical standard: individuals may not act simply to secure their own self-interests.

Utilitarianism. Advocates of utilitarianism argue that absolutist philosophy does not always lead to clearly defined "right" actions. For example, loyalty to one party may conflict with loyalty to another. Or loyalty may conflict with duty; or one's right to confidentiality with another's right to know. In these instances, it is argued that ends may be responsibly considered. The decision maker is thus directed to consider alternative actions, the likely outcomes of

EXHIBIT 1–5
Fundamental Ethical Values

HUMAN WORTH	Human beings are important and should avoid harming others. Respect persons as ends, not means.
FAIRNESS	People ought to treat others fairly, justly, and equally.
LAWFULNESS	Laws should be respected and obeyed.
HONESTY	People should tell the truth and never cheat anyone.
FIDELITY	People should keep promises and act in good faith.
CONFIDENTIALITY	Betrayal is wrong. People ought to respect professional secrets and confidences.
DUTY	People should do their duty and fulfill the responsibilities of their role (parent, teacher, employee, manager, accountant, auditor, etc.)
INDEPENDENCE	People ought to act as they choose and not be coerced by others, so long as their acts do not violate other's independence.
COURAGE	People should not be afraid to speak out and defend what they know is right even in the face of adverse consequences.

Source: Adapted from Geoff Lantos, *Advanced Instructional Module* (St. Paul: West Publishing Co.) originally appearing in Edward J. Trunfio, *Enhancing Ethics in Business* (Boston: Vanguard Press, 1990), p.24.

these actions, and how these outcomes affect various stakeholders. Stakeholders are those affected by one's actions. Three types of stakeholders are

1. **individual stakeholders** (superiors, subordinates, peers, family, and so forth).
2. **corporate stakeholders** (stockholders, employees, management, labor unions, suppliers, distributors, competitors' stockholders, competitors' employees, and so forth).
3. **systemic stakeholders** (the accounting profession, government, citizens, taxpayers, consuming public, and investing public—potential stockholders or bondholders).

In utilitarian theory, ethical decisions (actions) are those that promote the greater good. Consistent with absolutism is the moral standard that the individual must go beyond personal interests to a universal standpoint in which everyone's interests are impartially considered equal. Accordingly, individuals serving in special fiduciary capacities (such as members of professions: doctors, lawyers, auditors) must go beyond equality and subordinate their personal interest to the interest of society and those they serve.

DECISION MODEL FOR ETHICAL DILEMMAS

In *Ethics in the Accounting Curriculum: Cases and Readings,* the American Accounting Association Advisory Committee on Professionalism and Ethics provides the following decision model to help guide sound analysis of an ethical dilemma:

1. Determine the facts:
   a. what happened,
   b. who the affected stakeholders are,
   c. where,
   d. when, and
   e. how.
2. Define the ethical issue.
3. Identify major values.
4. Specify the alternatives.
5. Compare values and alternatives (see if a clear decision emerges).
6. If a clear decision does not emerge, assess the consequences.
7. Make your decision.

Problems relying on application of this model are included in end-of-chapter problems throughout this book.

END-OF-CHAPTER REVIEW

SUMMARY

1. **Understand the relationship between accounting and the allocation of scarce resources.** The economic environment in which accounting operates has evolved over the centuries. Today the business environment is global in scope, and the accounting profession also operates in a global environment. To allocate resources effectively

and efficiently within this environment requires an accounting information system that provides financial information useful for decision making. Identification of the most efficient resource users encourages better allocations of those scarce resources.

2. **Trace the evolution of Generally Accepted Accounting Principles (GAAP).** Accounting principles have evolved over time in response to the changing business environment. Because of dissatisfaction with the CAP and the APB, the FASB was formed. A major ongoing project of the FASB is development of the conceptual framework, or a theoretical framework for the output of the accounting process.
3. **Relate the objectives of financial reporting as stated in the conceptual framework to the accounting process.** The overall objective of financial reporting is to provide information useful for decision making. This includes information about the amount, timing, and uncertainty of future cash flows and about economic resources, claims against those resources, and changes in those resources.
4. **Interpret the meaning of the qualitative characteristics of accounting information enumerated in the conceptual framework.** To be useful for decision making, accounting information must be relevant, reliable, comparable, and consistent. Relevant information makes a difference in a decision; therefore, it has predictive value, feedback value, and is timely. Information is considered reliable if it is verifiable, neutral, and faithfully represents the underlying economic events.
5. **Understand the assumptions and conventions underlying the recognition and measurement of accounting data for financial reporting.** For purposes of recognition and measurement, independent economic entities are presumed to exist. These entities are further presumed to be going concerns that will continue to operate in the future. To measure their results, periodic reporting is necessary, and monetary units are the basis of measurement. Assets typically are recorded at cost, and their cost is allocated to the periods in which revenues are derived. When choices exist, conservatism should be followed, and the choice of accounting policies must be disclosed.
6. **Distinguish among the elements of the financial statements.** The outputs of the accounting process are the financial statements and the accompanying notes to those statements. The financial statements consist of ten elements: assets, liabilities, equities, revenues, expenses, gains, losses, investments by owners, distributions to owners, and comprehensive income.
7. **Develop an appreciation of ethical and moral considerations in business activity.** Businesses and the accounting profession want and expect ethical conduct by their employees and members. One's ethics are those values by which one lives. Ethical actions are those that promote the greater good. Individuals serving in fiduciary capacities of society must subordinate their personal interests to the interests of society and those they serve.

KEY TERMS

Accounting Principles Board (APB) *9*
Committee on Accounting Procedure (CAP) *9*
consistency *19*
cost/benefits *19*
economic entity *21*
efficient-market hypothesis (EMH) *12*
Emerging Issues Task Force (EITF) *12*
feedback value *17*
Financial Accounting Foundation (FAF) *9*
Financial Accounting Standards Advisory Committee (FASAC) *9*
Financial Accounting Standards Board (FASB) *9*

generally accepted accounting principles *7*
industry practices *19*
materiality *19*
measurement *21*
neutrality *18*
predictive value *17*
recognition *21*
relevance *17*
reliability *18*
representational faithfulness *18*
timeliness *18*
verifiability *18*
understandability *16*

ASSIGNMENT MATERIAL

CASES

C1–1 Disclosure

CBX Industries is a genetic engineering research firm engaged in research, development, manufacturing, and sales of specialty drugs. John Miller, president of CBX Industries, and Colin P. Armon, the treasurer and chief financial officer, were discussing some information they had recently obtained from a regional sales manager. A competitor company had announced successful testing of a drug developed to prevent the spread of GRT disease. GRT is a disease similar to cancer, which, if left unchecked, causes rapid deterioration of bodily control and movement.

The successful testing of this drug was very important to CBX because CBX currently produces and markets the only FDA-approved drug available for GRT disease. Introduction of a new competitor drug could seriously undermine CBX's market position.

At the present time, CBX derives 30% of its revenue and 29% of its net profit from sales of this drug. Miller and Armon do not know what the effect on sales and profits will be if and when the new drug is approved, only that it will certainly have a negative impact, most likely severe.

Armon suggested that this should probably be mentioned in the annual report of CBX, due to be published in two months. Miller responded with a single word, "Why?"

Required:

A. Why would Miller oppose disclosure?
B. Is this information required to be disclosed by GAAP?
C. How does this decision situation relate to the conceptual framework?

C1–2 Generally Accepted Accounting Principles

Assume that you are the assistant controller for J. K. Tractor Company. You are preparing the financial statements at the end of the year when the marketing manager for the thresher division stops in to chat. In the course of your conversation, he asks you the meaning of the phrase "generally accepted accounting principles" that appears in the audit report of the financial statements.

Required:

A. Define the meaning of the term "generally accepted accounting principles."
B. How is the determination made as to whether or not an accounting principle is generally accepted? What are the sources of evidence?
C. Diversity in accounting practice will, and should, always exist among companies despite efforts to improve comparability. Discuss arguments that support this statement.
D. Discuss the role of materiality in financial reporting and disclosure.

C1–3 Integrative Conceptual Framework—R&D

SFAS No. 2, "Accounting for Research and Development Costs," generally requires that research costs be expensed in the period in which they were incurred unless there is tangible future benefit. If future benefit can be demonstrated (as in a building for research purposes), then the cost may be capitalized and allocated to future periods. Most industry groups opposed this standard.

Required:

A. What benefits do you see resulting from this standard? Frame your answer in terms of the conceptual framework considerations (objectives, qualitative characteristics of data, basic assumptions, principles, conventions).

B. On what grounds might industry groups oppose this standard? (Again, frame your answer in terms of the conceptual framework considerations.)

C1–4 Integrative Conceptual Framework—Inventory Valuation

FIFO (first-in, first-out) and LIFO (last-in, last-out) are two acceptable alternative methods of inventory valuation. Evaluate these two methods in relation to conceptual framework considerations (objectives, the qualitative characteristics of accounting information, recognition and measurement criteria in terms of assumptions, conventions).

C1–5 Integrative Conceptual Framework—Asset Valuation

Valuation of property, plant, and equipment for financial reporting requires the use of historical cost as the basis for valuation. If these assets become impaired (lose their productive value), they must be reduced in value. Similarly, inventories must be reported at the lower of cost or market value. Certain investment securities, however, are reported at fair value, which is market value.

Required: Discuss asset valuation in terms of (1) the qualitative characteristics of accounting information and (2) recognition and measurement criteria.

C1–6 Ethics—Confidential Information

The following scenario appeared in the November 15, 1993, issue of the *Arizona Republic.*

> When the ***Texas Instruments Inc.*** salesman settled into his seat on the airliner, he discovered a golden opportunity—and an ethical dilemma staring him in the face. Stuffed into the seatback pouch in front of him, among the in-flight magazines and instruction cards, was a document with a competitor's logo, stamped "confidential." What to do?
>
> No legal restrictions against using the information exist.

Required: Evaluate the situation in terms of the decision model presented in the chapter. What should the salesman do?

C1–7* Ethics and Expense Reports

Tom Waterman is a young management accountant at a large, diversified company. After some experience in accounting at headquarters, he has been transferred to one of the company's recently acquired divisions, run by its previous owner and president,

**Note:* The cases C1–7 and C1–8 are adapted from Steven Flory, Thomas Phillips, Eric Reidenbach, and Donald Robin, "A Multidimensional Analysis of Selected Ethical Issues in Accounting," *The Accounting Review* 67, No. 2 (April 1992), pp. 284–303.

Howard Heller. Heller has been retained as vice president of this new division, and Waterman is his accountant. With a marketing background and a practice of calling his own shots, Heller seems to play by a different set of rules than those to which Waterman is accustomed. So far, it is working, as earnings are up and sales projections are high.

The main area of concern to Waterman is Heller's expense reports. Heller's boss, the division president, approves the expense reports without review, and expects Waterman to check the details and work out any discrepancies with Heller. After a series of large and questionable expense reports, Waterman challenges Heller directly about charges to the company for typing that Heller's wife did at home. Although company policy prohibits such charges, Heller's boss again signed off on the expense. Waterman feels uncomfortable with this and tells Heller that he is considering taking the matter to the Board Audit Committee for review. Heller reacts sharply, reminding Waterman that "the board will back me anyway" and that Waterman's position in the company would be in jeopardy.

Required: What should Waterman do? Please evaluate this action using the decision model presented in the chapter.

C1–8 Ethics and Extension of Credit

Paul Tate is the assistant controller at Stern Electronics, a medium-sized manufacturer of electrical equipment. Tate is in his late fifties and plans to retire soon. His daughter has been accepted into medical school, and financial concerns are weighing heavily on his mind. Tate's boss is out of the office recuperating from health problems, and in his absence, Tate is making all the decisions for the department.

Tate receives a phone call from an old friend requesting a sizable amount of equipment on credit for his new business. Tate is sympathetic but cognizant of the risk of extending credit to a new company, especially under Stern's strict credit policy for such transactions. When Tate mentions this conversation to Warren, the general manager, he is immediately interested. Warren notes that the company needs an additional $250,000 in sales to meet the quarterly budget and thus assure bonuses for management, including Tate.

Required: What should Paul Tate do? Please evaluate this decision using the decision model for ethical dilemmas presented in the chapter.

C1–9 Ethics and Land Swap

Joyce Jackson is president and CEO of Tri-State Enterprises, a medium-sized real estate development company. Jackson owns several hundred acres of land that were inherited from her grandparents. Unfortunately, the land is situated adjacent to a commercial waste disposal facility, and the current market value is unknown because finding a buyer is questionable.

Tri-State Enterprises has recently acquired 20 heavily wooded acres on a large lake situated about 50 miles from a major population center. The cost of this parcel was $500,000. Jackson has proposed an exchange of her property for the Tri-State property.

Required: Assume that you are a member of the board of directors of Tri-State Enterprises. Prior to the meeting at which Jackson's proposal is to be discussed, she informs you that she is going to recommend that your firm receive an engineering contract worth $2,500,000. How would you react to Jackson's proposal about the land swap?

QUESTIONS

Q1–1 The excerpt from the *Forbes* article at the beginning of the chapter indicates that many economic decisions are made based on the bottom line, or earnings. Why is this a problem? How has the accounting profession already addressed the problem?

Q1–2 What is the relationship between net income and the "white lies" mentioned in the *Forbes* excerpt?

Q1–3 Give some examples of "white lies" that might be used to manage a company's income. What characteristics do they have in common?

Q1–4 How are the East India Trading Company's practices related to income management?

Q1–5 Why is accounting important to the functioning of a free enterprise economic system?

Q1–6 In the development of generally accepted accounting principles, both the APB and CAP received heavy criticism. Why?

Q1–7 Describe the differences between the FASB and the APB.

Q1–8 Why is the standard-setting process of the FASB like a political process?

Q1–9 What is the relationship of the efficient-markets hypothesis (EMH) to accounting?

Q1–10 An explicit assumption of the conceptual framework is that users of accounting data are relatively knowledgeable about business. How is this related to the efficient-markets hypothesis?

Q1–11 Why is the conceptual framework important for development of accounting standards?

Q1–12 What is the central theme of SFAC No. 1?

Q1–13 What is the central theme of SFAC No. 2, and how does it fit into the conceptual framework?

Q1–14 Describe how the going-concern assumption and the matching principle are related.

Q1–15 What is meant by relevance as a qualitative characteristic?

Q1–16 Describe the complementary relationship of relevance and reliability.

Q1–17 How does comparability differ from consistency?

Q1–18 Under what circumstances is it acceptable to recognize revenue prior to sale of the goods?

Q1–19 SFAC No. 5 identified five different measurement bases currently used in practice. Give an example of a financial statement element that uses (1) current cost as the valuation basis, (2) current market value as the valuation basis, and (3) net realizable value as the valuation basis.

Q1–20 How is a loss different from an expense?

Q1–21 What problems are associated with the monetary-unit assumption?

Q1–22 In the discussion of materiality in the chapter, it was stated that the FASB did not define materiality, nor did the FASB suggest guidelines for it. Instead, materiality was left to "professional judgment." Suppose that your employer asked you to define materiality. How would you respond?

Q1–23 The Committee on Accounting Procedures (CAP) produced 51 *Accounting Research Bulletins* between 1939 and 1959. Yet they were severely criticized for being ineffective as a rule-making body.

A. Describe the main problems encountered by the CAP that led to this criticism.

B. How are these problems handled today by the current rule-making body?

Q1–24 Why was the Wheat Committee appointed? Discuss its purpose, recommendations, and results.

Q1–25 In the excerpt from the *Forbes* article at the beginning of the chapter, net income was criticized for not providing relevant and reliable information for decision making. Buffett suggested that cash flow would be a better indicator of economic well-being than net income.

A. Why are cash flows different from net income?

B. How has the FASB recognized the importance of cash flows?

Q1–26 What role does the SEC play in setting accounting standards?

EXERCISES

E1–1 Conceptual Framework—Qualitative Characteristics

Identify the appropriate qualitative characteristic(s) of useful accounting information that best relate(s) to each concept below. A characteristic may be used more than once.

1. Relevance
2. Reliability
3. Feedback value
4. Predictive value
5. Understandability
6. Decision usefulness
7. Materiality
8. Timeliness
9. Verifiability
10. Neutrality
11. Representational faithfulness
12. Comparability
13. Consistency
14. Benefit exceeds cost

_____ **A.** A primary quality of accounting information that includes timeliness as an ingredient.

_____ **B.** The concept that accounting information may correct the decision maker's earlier expectation.

_____ **C.** The quality of information that enables users to confirm prior expectations.

_____ **D.** The characteristic dealing with having the information available *prior* to the decision date.

_____ **E.** The characteristic dealing with a high degree of consensus within a group.

_____ **F.** Two primary qualitative characteristics.

_____ **G.** The characteristic that ignores the economic consequences associated with a standard or rule.

_____ **H.** A qualitative characteristic essential for comparisons between companies in the same industry.

_____ **I.** Essential item for providing interperiod comparisons of a firm.

_____ **J.** A primary quality of accounting information that includes verifiability as an ingredient.

_____ **K.** Correspondence between underlying economic event and accounting measurement.

_____ **L.** The two overall or pervasive constraints developed in SFAC No. 2.

_____ **M.** The ingredient of the primary quality, relevance, that pertains to users making predictions about the outcome of future events.

E1–2 Principles and Assumptions

Following are the principles underlying GAAP, accounting assumptions, and the modifying conventions used in this chapter.

1. Going-concern assumption
2. Economic-entity assumption
3. Monetary-unit assumption
4. Periodicity assumption
5. Matching convention
6. Historical-cost convention
7. Full-disclosure convention
8. Cost-benefit restraint
9. Industry practices
10. Conservatism
11. Materiality

What concept is described or relates to each of the statements presented below?

_____ **A.** Permits expensing all expenditures for supplies that do not exceed a specified amount.

_____ **B.** Permits the use of market value determination in certain situations.

_____ **C.** Allocates expenses to revenues in the correct period.

_____ **D.** Ensures that all companies disclose such items as the amount of sales revenue.

_____ **E.** Indicates that market value changes subsequent to purchase are not recorded in the accounts.

_____ **F.** Explains why equipment is not reported at liquidation value. (*Hint:* the answer is not historical-cost principle.)

_____ **G.** Separates financial information into specific time periods for reporting purposes.

_____ **H.** Assumes that the dollar is the "measuring stick" used to report on financial performance.

_____ **I.** Indicates that the activity of a business should be kept separate from its owners.

E1–3 SFAC No. 2—Multiple Choice

1. Which of the following means that we choose the accounting alternative that is least likely to overstate income measurement and asset valuation?
   a. Benefits/cost
   b. Conservatism
   c. Timeliness
   d. Verifiability
2. Which of the following would prevent the accounting reports from showing favoritism to one economic interest over another?
   a. Conservatism
   b. Completeness
   c. Neutrality
   d. Representational faithfulness
3. According to SFAC No. 2, relevance and reliability are the two primary qualities that make accounting information useful for decision making. Timeliness is an ingredient of

	Relevance	*Reliability*
a.	No	No
b.	No	Yes
c.	Yes	Yes
d.	Yes	No

4. Information that constitutes significant input into the decision making process may be termed
   a. reliable.
   b. useful.
   c. relevant.
   d. reasonable.
5. In evaluating the reliability of data, which of the following need not be considered?
   a. Neutrality
   b. Verifiability
   c. Accessibility
   d. Representational faithfulness
6. The going-concern assumption indicates that
   a. the entity will not liquidate in the short run.
   b. historical cost is the most accurate measure of market value.
   c. expenses must be recognized as paid, regardless of the recognition of revenues.
   d. None of the above.

E1–4 Conventions and Assumptions

Identify the accounting conventions and assumptions in each of the following statements.

A. When two accounting treatments for a single transaction have equal theoretical weight, the treatment that precludes overstatement of reported income and/or net assets should be selected.

B. Significant economic events are the result of discrete transactions that can be separated as to their time of occurrence.

C. Each reporting entity can be identified and distinguished from all other entities for financial statement purposes.

D. Information that is not significant to users should not be included in financial statements.

E. Economic profits should not be reported on financial statements until the process of earning those profits is complete.

F. All financial statement users are seeking the same type of general purpose financial information.

E1–5 Elements of Financial Statements

SFAC No. 6, "Elements of Financial Statements," defined ten basic building blocks of the financial statements, which are listed below. You are to match the phrases with the appropriate building blocks (a building block may be used more than once).

1. Assets
2. Liabilities
3. Equity or net assets
4. Investments by owners
5. Distributions to owners
6. Comprehensive income
7. Revenues
8. Expenses
9. Gains
10. Losses

____3____ A. The residual interest in the assets of an entity after deducting its liabilities.
____5____ B. Transfer of company assets to its owners in the form of a cash dividend.
____7____ C. Inflows arising from primary operations.
____9____ D. Results from peripheral or incidental transactions of an entity.
____1____ E. Purchase of equipment to render services in the future.
____4____ F. An entity's receipt of cash in exchange for capital stock.
____6____ G. A positive change in equity in a period from nonowner sources.
____4____ H. An increase in ownership interest.
____2____ I. Probable future sacrifices of economic benefits arising from present obligations.

______ **J.** Decrease in assets during the period by abandoning assets not fully depreciated.
______ **K.** Increase in accounts receivable during a period through the sale of widgets.
______ **L.** Incurrence of a liability by purchasing supplies.
______ **M.** Decrease in equity arising from a severe hurricane.
______ **N.** Sale of machinery above book value.

E1–6 Conventions, Assumptions, Constraints

Listed below are the conventions underlying GAAP, accounting assumptions, and the constraints identified in this chapter.

1. Going-concern assumption
2. Economic-entity assumption
3. Monetary-unit assumption
4. Periodicity assumption
5. Matching convention
6. Historical-cost convention
7. Full-disclosure convention
8. Cost-benefit constraint
9. Industry practices constraint
10. Revenue recognition convention
11. Materiality
12. Conservatism

What concept is described or relates to each of the statements presented below?

______ **A.** Permits the use of current-cost valuation in certain situations.
______ **B.** Expenses the cost of a business vehicle by depreciating it over a five-year period.
______ **C.** Ensures that all companies disclose such items as the amount of sales revenue.
______ **D.** Has the primary advantage of a verifiable and objective measurement basis.
______ **E.** Explains why equipment is not reported at liquidation value. (*Hint:* The answer is not historical-cost principle.)
______ **F.** Assumes that the dollar is an appropriate measurement used to report on financial performance.
______ **G.** Indicates that the financial activity of a business should be kept separate from its owners' financial activity.
______ **H.** Allocates and recognizes revenues and expenses in specific time periods.
______ **I.** Indicates that revenue is usually recognized, as well as realized, at the point of sale.

E1–7 Cost or Measurement Basis for Recording Transactions

For each of the following transactions or situations, identify the cost or measurement basis that was used in the transaction.

A. One thousand shares of ***Intel*** are acquired as an investment on May 15 at a total cost of $55,600. The transaction is recorded initially at that amount.

B. With regard to the 1,000 shares of Intel in (A) above, assume that at the end of the year, the market price is now $60/share. This price ($60) is reflected in the financial statements at the end of the year.

C. A contract is signed to lease a machine for 10 years. The transaction is properly treated and recorded as a capital lease, which means that the present value of the long-term obligation is reflected as a liability on the balance sheet. What is the measurement base used for this liability?

D. Short-term notes and accounts receivable are reported on the balance sheet together with an allowance for doubtful accounts.

E. An automobile is purchased for use in the business.

F. Obsolete inventory is found in the warehouse. The cost of this inventory was $4,500. The balance sheet at the end of the period reflects a value of $1,000 for this merchandise.

E1–8 Stakeholders in Environmental Dispute

STG Microsystems purchased a building and 20 acres of land from Pixie Film Processing. Prior to the purchase, Pixie informed STG that a holding pond in the back of the building contained hazardous waste that resulted from the operations of the film processing. STG made the purchase with full knowledge of the hazardous waste but under the assumption that clean-up operations would amount to approximately $500,000. This amount was based on an estimate made by John Hutchins, an engineer with STG. Unfortunately, Hutchins seriously underestimated the cost of the clean-up, and the ultimate bill will approach $5 million.

Required: Identify the stakeholders affected by the error.

E1–9 Revenue Recognition, Cost Basis, and Representational Faithfulness

Three years ago, the TX Corporation purchased a tract of land, intending to expand its manufacturing facilities. The land cost $450,000 and was properly recorded at the time of purchase. TX has not expanded, because sales and profitability have declined. The tract of land, however, has increased in value significantly, and an appraisal indicates that it is now worth $2 million.

The TX president wants to increase the land value in the financial statement by making the following journal entry:

Land	1,550,000	
Gain From Land		1,550,000

Required: Discuss the appropriateness of this entry.

E1–10[*] Disclosure of Change in Accounting Principle

A. Why are accounting principles, once adopted, normally continued?

B. What is the rationale for disclosure of a change from one generally accepted accounting principle to another?

E1–11 Accounting Standards—True or False?

___ **A.** GAAP are determined by a corporation's elected board of directors and presented in the footnotes accompanying the corporation's financial statements.

___ **B.** The FASB is an agency of the federal government with responsibility to regulate the issuance of corporate debt and equity securities.

___ **C.** The SEC is an agency of the federal government empowered by Congress to establish both for-profit and not-for-profit auditing standards.

___ **D.** Compliance with GAAP ensures that corporate financial accounting systems capture all economically significant (material) and decision-relevant financial information relating to corporate transactions.

___ **E.** The FASB provides a very tight set of principles and procedures that American corporations must follow. To ensure interfirm comparability, corporations are allowed minimal choices among accounting procedures.

___ **F.** The role of the external auditor (CPA) is to prepare a firm's annual financial statements.

___ **G.** The ultimate authority for accounting practice in the United States is Congress.

[*]*Note*: E1–10 is adapted from the May 1990 CPA exam.

E1–12 Conceptual Framework—Multiple-Choice

1. In order for accounting information to be relevant to decision makers, it must be timely and it must possess
   a. representational faithfulness.
   b. predictive value.
   c. consistency.
   d. neutrality.
2. Components of reliability include all of the following except
   a. representational faithfulness.
   b. verifiability.
   c. comparability.
   d. neutrality.
3. When accountants depreciate the cost of a building, they are most concerned with
   a. the full-disclosure principle.
   b. the economic-entity assumption.
   c. reliability.
   d. the matching principle.
4. The efficient-markets hypothesis (EMH) states that
   a. analysts can beat the market by very detailed analysis of a public company.
   b. publicly available information obtained early is extremely valuable.
   c. stock prices react primarily to unanticipated events.
   d. some information, in addition to insider information, can be used to predict future stock prices better than the market itself.
5. Three major objectives of financial reporting identified in FASB SFAC No. 1 *do not* include which of the following:
   a. Providing information useful for decision making
   b. Providing information about the amount, timing, and uncertainty of future cash flows
   c. Providing information on management's intended use of resources
   d. Providing information useful in assessing a company's liquidity, solvency, and profitability

E1–13 Qualitative Characteristics

Identify the appropriate qualitative characteristic(s) or constraint(s) of useful accounting information that best relate(s) to each concept or phrase below. A characteristic or constraint may be used more than once.

1. Relevance	8. Timeliness
2. Reliability	9. Verifiability
3. Feedback value	10. Neutrality
4. Predictive value	11. Representational faithfulness
5. Understandability	12. Comparability
6. Decision usefulness	13. Consistency
7. Materiality	14. Benefits/costs

_____ A. The reliability characteristic that ignores the political consequences associated with accounting rules or standards.

_____ B. The quality of information that allows users to detect differences between multiple sets of data.

_____ C. The ingredient of a primary quality that pertains to making predictions about the outcome of past, present, and future events.

_____ **D.** The accurate depiction of an underlying economic event.
_____ **E.** A primary quality of accounting information that includes verifiability as an ingredient.
_____ **F.** The quality of information that confirms users' earlier expectations.
_____ **G.** Information that will make a difference in a decision.
_____ **H.** A primary quality of accounting information that includes timeliness as an ingredient.
_____ **I.** Characteristic dealing with a high degree of agreement among a group.
_____ **J.** Qualitative characteristic essential for comparisons between companies in the same industry.
_____ **K.** Accounting information that may correct or confirm the decision maker's earlier expectation.

E1–14 Political Influence on GAAP

Each of the following organizations has influenced GAAP in some specific form. Identify the appropriate organization that best relates to the statement or concept:

1. Financial Accounting Standards Board (FASB)
2. Accounting Principle Board (APB)
3. Committee on Accounting Procedure (CAP)
4. Securities and Exchange Commission (SEC)
5. Internal Revenue Service (IRS)
6. American Accounting Association (AAA)

_____ **A.** This organization dealt with accounting issues on an ad hoc basis and issued *Accounting Research Bulletins.*
_____ **B.** This organization existed from 1959 to 1973 and issued 31 opinions.
_____ **C.** This regulatory government agency has the authority to establish accounting rules but seldom does.
_____ **D.** The rules of this group are established by Congress and are mainly concerned with taxes.
_____ **E.** This organization influences accounting pronouncements through education and persuasion.
_____ **F.** This organization was formed as a result of the Wheat Committee recommendations. In addition, it is a highly paid, independent agency.

E1–15 Assumptions, Principles, Characteristics—Multiple-Choice

1. This assumption should not be made when a business is planning to file for bankruptcy.
   - **a.** Going-concern assumption
   - **b.** Economic-entity assumption
   - **c.** Periodicity assumption
   - **d.** Monetary-unit assumption
2. This assumption is the reason for adjusting entries.
   - **a.** Going-concern assumption
   - **b.** Economic-entity assumption
   - **c.** Periodicity assumption
   - **d.** Monetary-unit assumption
3. The matching principle indicates that
   - **a.** the entity will not liquidate in the short run.
   - **b.** historical cost is the most accurate measure of market value.

c. expenses must be recognized as paid, regardless of the recognition of revenues.
d. expenses must be recognized in the period that benefits are received from the expenses.

4. In evaluating the reliability of data, which of the following need not be considered?
   a. Neutrality
   b. Verifiability
   c. Timeliness
   d. Representational faithfulness
5. Information that costs significantly more to prepare than the benefits derived by users would violate which of the following?
   a. Reliability
   b. Usefulness
   c. Materiality
   d. Cost/benefit

PROBLEMS

P1–1 Comparison of FASB with APB—Report Preparation

The purpose of the FASB, according to Wheat Committee recommendations, is to establish financial accounting and reporting standards for users of financial statements. While the purpose of the FASB and its predecessor organization, the APB, was the same, the two organizations differ in several important ways.

Required: Prepare a short, concise report indicating how the APB and FASB differ along the following dimensions.

A. Size of membership
B. Remuneration of membership
C. Independence of membership
D. Autonomy of membership
E. Representation
F. Voting

P1–2 Relationship Between Cash Flow and Accrual Accounting—Memo Preparation

SFAC No. 1 indicates that the second objective of financial reporting is to provide information about the amount, timing, and uncertainty of future cash flows. The FASB also points out that cash flow is not a substitute for accrual-based accounting information but should be viewed as complementary to cash flows. An accrual-based income statement provides information not provided by cash flows, and it should be used together with cash flow information to assess risk associated with future cash flow.

George Gilday, the owner of Gilday's Group Software, believes that he understands cash flows. He would like to know the relationship between cash flows and the accrual basis of accounting.

Required: Prepare a memo to Gilday explaining the relationship between accrual accounting and cash flows.

P1–3 Elements of the Financial Statements

Several definitions and examples of the elements of financial statements are provided below.

Required: In each of the following, state which element of the financial statements is being referred to or defined.

A. The sale of machinery for less than its book value.
B. Issue of common stock at greater than the par value.
C. The residual interest in the assets of an entity that remains after deducting its liabilities.
D. Probable future economic benefit obtained or controlled by a particular entity as a result of past transactions or events.
E. Sale of merchandise on account.
F. Outflow or other using up of assets or incurrences of liabilities (or a combination of both) from delivering or producing goods, providing services, or carrying out other activities that constitute the entity's ongoing major or central operations.
G. The payment of dividends on common stock.
H. Assets less liabilities.
I. The sale of obsolete inventory at less than its cost.
J. The incurrence of a future obligation in exchange for receipt of management consulting services in the current period.

P1–4 Basic Conventions or Principles

One of the conventions used in recording and classifying financial information is the cost or measurement basis. Listed below are several items that are found in the financial statements of most companies.

Required: For each of the listed items, state the measurement basis that would be used to record and classify it.

A. Investment securities classified as trading securities.
B. Accounts receivable (net amount)
C. Accounts receivable (gross amount)
D. Land
E. Notes payable (due in three months)
F. Inventories reported at lower of cost or market
G. Bonds payable (long-term)
H. Accounts payable (short-term)
I. Machinery and equipment
J. Inventory considered obsolete

P1–5 Qualitative Characteristics—Memo Preparation

Jane Johnson has recently been appointed as the business editor of the local newspaper. She asks you to clarify some aspects of SFAC No. 2. Specifically, she is not sure of the meaning of the term "reliability" as it is used in the concepts statement.

Required: Prepare a memo to Johnson to help her understand the meaning of "reliability" as used in SFAC No. 2.

P1–6 SFAC No. 1, Purpose of Financial Reporting—Memo Preparation

You have been asked by the editor of the student newspaper to submit a short (four paragraphs at most) article about the importance of accounting and financial reporting.

Required: Prepare an article for the paper explaining the purpose of accounting and financial reporting as you understand it.

P1–7 Basic Assumptions and Principles of Financial Reporting

Below are statements and descriptions of situations related to financial reporting. For each of the statements, provide the assumption or principle that is appropriate.

A. ***Jacobsen Manufacturing*** (a U.S. corporation) reports the results of its operations and its financial position in dollars, while ***Unilever*** (a British corporation) uses pounds.
B. Both Jacobsen and Unilever (in [A] above) report results of operations and financial position on a quarterly basis.
C. Unilever has chosen to recognize revenues from licensing agreements over the life of the agreement instead of immediately recognizing the present value of the future cash inflows. Either method would satisfy GAAP.
D. Jacobsen has been named by the Environmental Protection Agency as one of eight companies that sent hazardous materials to a disposal site ten years ago. The operator of the site has closed it down, and the EPA regards the site as an environmental hazard. The EPA has asked the eight companies to pay for the clean-up operation. Jacobsen has chosen to discuss this development in its annual report.
E. Jacobsen depreciates equipment over the useful life of the equipment on a straight-line basis.
F. Jacobsen has four major divisions or subsidiaries. Each of these prepares separate financial statements, which are then combined for the corporate financial statements issued quarterly.
G. One of Jacobsen's customers is Alexander Co. Alexander Co. is wholly owned by Allison Alexander. Allison Alexander purchased a lawn mower directly from Jacobsen for her personal use but paid for it from the company account.
H. Jacobsen uses the allowance method for bad debts arising from credit sales.
I. Jacobsen provides detailed notes to the financial statements that explain the provisions of their pension program and their obligations under certain long-term lease arrangements.
J. Jacobsen reports certain short-term investments at their current market value on the balance sheet.
K. Jacobsen reports accounts receivable less the allowance for doubtful accounts on the balance sheet.

RESEARCH ACTIVITIES

R1–1 Violation of Accounting Principles

"Dial F for Fishy" is an article that appears in the November 25, 1992, issue of *Forbes* magazine. Using the referenced article as a starting point, develop answers to the following questions:

1. What accounting principles are involved in this article?
2. Explain how these accounting principles were violated in this example and what the proper method of accounting should have been.
3. One specific problem cited in the article is an extremely long collection period for the various revenues. To what does a collection period refer? Why is an extremely long period a problem?

R1–2 Investment Risk

In an article entitled "Sellers Beware," appearing in the January 21, 1991, issue of *Forbes* magazine, a discussion cautions naive buyers and sellers of junk bonds about investment opportunities in these securities. The article indicates that in some situations, junk bonds can become the real equity of the company, and it cites several examples of this occurring. The article further indicates that trading in these securities can be especially dangerous for most investors.

Using the referenced article as a starting point, develop answers to the following questions:

1. Why is trading in junk bonds more risky than trading in any other security?
2. Under what circumstances will junk bonds assume the characteristics of equity securities?
3. What regulatory bodies and agencies control trading in junk bond securities?
4. Explain how control of a company can be obtained through purchase of claims against the company.

R1–3 Accounting Data Usefulness

The article "Three Easy Steps," *Forbes,* October 30, 1989, p. 253, discusses three measures used by the author for analysis of investment opportunities.

1. What are those three measures?
2. Why are they important for investment analysis?
3. What accounting numbers and ratios are included in these measures?

R1–4 Representational Faithfulness

"An Eye on Fashion, Not the Books," *The New York Times,* February 11, 1993, and "Leslie Fay Replacing Officer in Fraud Inquiry," *The New York Times,* March 23, 1993, are two articles about fraud in the financial statements of ***Leslie Fay and Company.*** Locate these articles and answer the following questions:

1. In what way did the company misstate revenues?
2. Discuss the "representational faithfulness" of the financial statements of Leslie Fay.

R1–5 International Accounting Standards

The article "Wake-up Call to American Business: International Accounting Standards Are on the Way," *Journal of Accountancy,* July 1993, pp. 80–85, discusses the forward push for acceptance of international accounting standards. Locate the article and discuss the following points:

1. Why is there increasing emphasis being placed on international accounting standards?
2. What is the IOSCO? What role does it play in international accounting standards formulation?
3. What is the primary impediment to global allocation of resources?
4. What is the position of the SEC with regard to international accounting standards?
5. What is the position of the FASB with regard to international accounting standards?

R1–6 GAAP Hierarchy

Prepare a short report that summarizes the relationship of various pronouncements on GAAP as discussed in Statement on Auditing Standards No. 69 (SAS No. 69), "The Meaning of 'Present Fairly in Conformity with Generally Accepted Accounting Principles' in the Independent Auditor's Report." (This statement was printed in the March 1992 issue of *Journal of Accountancy.*) Include pronouncements of the FASB, AICPA, SEC, and other groups that may affect GAAP.

R1–7 International Considerations of Accounting Standards

The excerpt in the International Box in this chapter came from the article "All Accountants Soon May Speak the Same Language," which appeared in *The Wall Street Journal* on August 29, 1995, p. A15. Read this article in its entirety, and answer the following questions:

1. What does harmonization of accounting principles and standards worldwide mean?
2. Why is it important to U.S. securities markets that accounting standards be similar on a worldwide basis?
3. What are some dangers suggested in making U.S. standards "more flexible?"

2

The Accounting Process

Learning Objectives

After studying this chapter, you should be able to:

1. Analyze transactions based upon the accounting equation.
2. Interpret the four traditional financial statements.
3. Understand the accounting model, including the purpose of journals and ledgers.
4. Perform the steps in the accounting process, including adjusting, closing, and reversing entries, and preparation of an income statement and a balance sheet.
5. Identify types of research used to investigate and apply authoritative pronouncements.

Luca Pacioli, considered the father of double-entry accounting for describing accounting record-keeping practices, offered the following advice in his famous work, *Summa de Arithmetica, Geometrica, Proportioni et Proportionalita,* published in 1494:

> ### *Fifteenth Century Advice*
>
> A merchant must be a good bookkeeper and keep his affairs in an orderly way because where there is no order there is confusion. Affairs could be arranged in order, if all business transactions were recorded in a systematic way consisting of the debit (debito—owed to) and the credit (credito—owed by) method. Unless merchants follow this method they can have no rest in their minds and they will always be troubled. The important thing is to know the rules and then to apply them in particular cases.

Source: R. E. Taylor, *No Royal Road, Luca Pacioli and His Times,* University of North Carolina Press, Chapel Hill, N.C., 1980.

While the world today is far different than in Pacioli's time, businesses still must maintain records of their various transactions and summarize these transactions into financial reports. In this chapter, we examine the general accounting process for maintaining financial records and producing financial reports.

THE ACCOUNTING EQUATION

While reading the following discussion, you may wish to refer to Exhibit 1–4 of Chapter 1 for the definitions of various elements of financial statements. The heart of financial reporting is based upon the fundamental relationship between a company's resources and how these resources are financed. This relationship, called the **accounting equation**, states that

Assets = Liabilities + Owners' Equity

The left side of this equation represents the financial resources, *assets,* of an enterprise. The right side depicts the means by which the resources were financed, *liabilities* and *owners' equity.*

One view of this fundamental relationship is that it portrays the interests or *claims* of various parties on a company's assets. Creditors have claims on resources as indicated by the company's liabilities. Owners have claims to the residual resources as portrayed by owners' equity (also called *net assets*). To emphasize the residual nature of the claims of owners, the equation can be rearranged as follows:

Assets − Liabilities = Owners' Equity

Analyze transactions based upon the accounting equation.

TRANSACTION ANALYSIS BASED UPON THE ACCOUNTING EQUATION

As a company conducts business, the recorded amounts in the accounting equation change. Exhibit 2–1 illustrates the effect of four transactions on the

Assets	=	Liabilities	+	Owners' Equity

1. Receive $100,000 from original issue of shares of capital stock to shareholders.

	Assets	= Liabilities	+ Owners' Equity
	Cash		Capital Stock
1.	$100,000		$100,000

2. Purchase inventory of $20,000 on credit, payable in 30 days.

	Assets		= Liabilities	+ Owners' Equity
	Cash	Inventory	Accounts Payable	Capital Stock
1.	$100,000			$100,000
2.		$20,000	$20,000	
	$100,000	$20,000	$20,000	$100,000

3. a. Make a sale for $9,000 cash.
   b. The inventory that was sold cost $5,000 when purchased.

	Assets		= Liabilities	+ Owners' Equity		
	Cash	Inventory	Accounts Payable	Capital Stock	Revenue	Expense
1.	$100,000			$100,000		
2.		$20,000	$20,000			
3a.	9,000				$ 9,000	
3b.		(5,000)				$(5,000)
	$109,000	$15,000		$100,000	$ 9,000	$(5,000)
	$124,000		$20,000		$104,000	

4. Purchase additional inventory for $12,000 cash.

	Assets		= Liabilities	+ Owners' Equity		
	Cash	Inventory	Accounts Payable	Capital Stock	Revenue	Expense
1.	$100,000			$100,000		
2.		$20,000	$20,000			
3a.	9,000				$ 9,000	
3b.		(5,000)				$(5,000)
4.	(12,000)	12,000				
	$ 97,000	$27,000		$100,000	$ 9,000	$(5,000)
	$124,000		$20,000		$104,000	

EXHIBIT 2–1
The Accounting Equation and Transaction Analysis

accounting equation. Sample Company is established in the first transaction by selling shares of stock to investors, who become the owners of the corporation. The asset, cash, is increased, and capital stock is also increased. Inventory is purchased on credit in the second transaction; therefore, the asset inventory is increased by incurring debt. The company now has total assets of $120,000 financed by a $20,000 debt and owner contributions of $100,000.

In the third transaction, the company sells part of the inventory for cash. This is a revenue-generating transaction in which cash and sales are increased, and the inventory is reduced by the amount of the cost of the goods sold, which represents an expense. The last transaction reflects a cash purchase of inventory, reducing cash and increasing inventory. Note that total assets remain $124,000, while the individual balances for cash and inventory change. After this last transaction, the company controls assets of $124,000, which have been financed by a $20,000 debt, owner contributions of $100,000, and internally generated resources netting $4,000 for total shareholders' equity of $104,000.

A SET OF FINANCIAL STATEMENTS

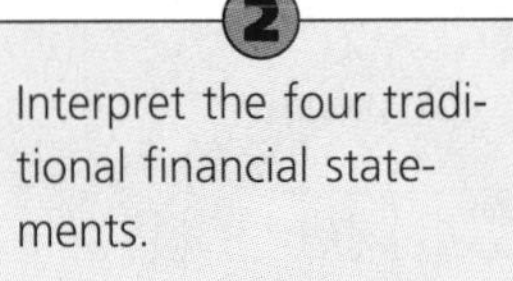
2
Interpret the four traditional financial statements.

Based upon these transactions, Exhibit 2–2 illustrates the four traditional financial statements of an enterprise: (1) the income statement, (2) the statement of changes in shareholders' equity, (3) the balance sheet, and (4) the statement of cash flows. Appendix C at the end of the textbook also illustrates these statements in the 1995 annual report of ***Motorola Corporation*** (see also the text's Internet site: *www.swcollege.com/hartman.html*).

The **balance sheet** is a report for a given *point in time,* in this case at year-end. The headings of the other three statements illustrate that they report activity for a *period of time,* in this case for a year. In addition to annual reports, *interim* financial statements are commonly prepared on a quarterly or monthly basis.

The **income statement** reports a company's periodic revenues, expenses, gains, and losses. Net income increases and net losses decrease the residual interest of owners, which is reflected in the **statement of changes in owners' (or shareholders') equity**. This statement identifies the transactions related to owners' equity during the period, such as additional investments from owners and distributions to owners. The addition of net income to retained earnings portrays the important link between the income statement and the balance sheet, called **articulation**.

For a given date, the balance sheet reports the status of the fundamental accounting equation. Note again that the income statement articulates with the balance sheet in that net income increases owners' equity (thereby increasing reported retained earnings).

SFAC No. 1 defines one objective of financial reporting as providing information about the amount, timing, and uncertainty of future cash flows. The conceptual framework project placed a great deal of importance on cash flows. A **statement of cash flows** categorizes cash changes into three types of cash flow activities: operating, investing, and financing. *Operating activities* refer to cash provided by or used for the operating cycle of a business—those activities directly related to the earnings process, such as buying and selling inventory.

Investing activities refer either to uses of cash for investing in a long-lived productive asset (such as equipment and machinery) or to cash provided from selling this type of asset. These assets are an integral part of the earnings process of an enterprise because they provide the capacity to generate revenues.

Financing activities refer either to cash provided by long-term debt and owner contributions (that is, financing to obtain funds) or to cash used for paying back long-term debt and for making owner distributions. In the example, Sample Company obtained financing from owners with the initial issuance of capital stock.

EXHIBIT 2–2
Financial Statements

SAMPLE COMPANY, INC.
Income Statement
For the Year Ended December 31, 1997

Sales revenue	$9,000
Expenses: Cost of goods sold	5,000
Net Income	$4,000

SAMPLE COMPANY, INC.
Statement of Changes in Shareholders' Equity
For the Year Ended December 31, 1997

	Capital Stock	Retained Earnings	Total
Balance 1/1/97	$ 0	$ 0	$ 0
Stock issuance	100,000		100,000
Net income		4,000	4,000
Balance 12/31/97	$100,000	$4,000	$104,000

SAMPLE COMPANY, INC.
Balance Sheet
December 31, 1997

Assets		Liabilities	
Cash	$ 97,000	Accounts payable	$ 20,000
Inventory	27,000		
		Shareholders' Equity	
		Capital stock	100,000
		Retained earnings	4,000
	$124,000		$124,000

SAMPLE COMPANY, INC.
Statement of Cash Flows
For the Year Ended December 31, 1997

Operating Activities:		
Cash from sales	$ 9,000	
Cash payments for purchases	12,000	
Net cash used by operations		$ (3,000)
Investing Activities:		0
Financing Activities:		
Issuance of capital stock	$100,000	
Net cash provided by financing		100,000
Net increase in cash		$ 97,000
Cash balance 1/1/97		0
Cash balance 12/31/97		$ 97,000

THE ACCOUNTING MODEL

Understand the accounting model, including the purpose of journals and ledgers.

Recall from Exhibit 2–1 how the fundamental accounting equation was used to record a limited number of transactions. Imagine trying to keep track of the tens of thousands of transactions of a major corporation with this structure. As the number of transactions for a company increases, the format used in the exhibit to capture transaction information would rapidly become unwieldy. Therefore, this section further develops the accounting model, beginning with a presentation of the account format for double-entry accounting.

THE ACCOUNT FORMAT

Exhibit 2–3 presents such a format with its more detailed breakdown of the accounting equation. As the previous discussion indicated, shareholders' equity typically arises from a combination of owner contributions and retained earnings. *Retained earnings* represent the cumulative resources provided by the undistributed income of an enterprise. Thus, in a given period, retained earnings are increased by net income (or decreased by net loss) for the period and decreased by dividends. Net income for a period is determined by the excess of periodic revenues and gains over periodic expenses and losses.

IN PRACTICE—GENERAL

Shareholders' Equity

Exhibit 2–3 highlights the basic elements of shareholders' equity. In practice, certain items can complicate the determination and presentation of these basic elements. Here are some examples.

1. Adjustments to contributed capital may be reported for stock repurchased and held by the corporation itself (called *treasury stock*), for unrealized holding gains and losses on certain investments, and for foreign currency translations. ***Walt Disney Company***, for instance, reduced shareholders' equity in its September 30, 1995, balance sheet by $1.6 billion for treasury stock, which was more than contributed capital of $1.2 billion. It also showed an increase of $37.3 million for cumulative translation and other adjustments.
2. Retained earnings at the start of a period may be adjusted to correct errors detected in prior periods (called *prior-period adjustments*).
3. Switching accounting methods may affect the determination of periodic net income with what is called the *cumulative effect* of an accounting change. For instance, many companies showed a cumulative effect on income in the early 1990s from adoption of SFAS No. 109, switching to a new method of accounting for income taxes.

These complexities are discussed later in the text.

The middle panel of Exhibit 2–3 extends the accounting equation into a columnar format, and a vertical line divides the left-hand side of the equation from the right. This provides the structure for the traditional account format of **double-entry accounting**. Since expenses (and losses) and dividends represent decreases to owners' equity, these are shifted to the left of the line.

The bottom panel of Exhibit 2–3 summarizes the use of the account format for the various elements of accounting. **Debits** are entries to the left-hand side

EXHIBIT 2–3
The Accounting Model

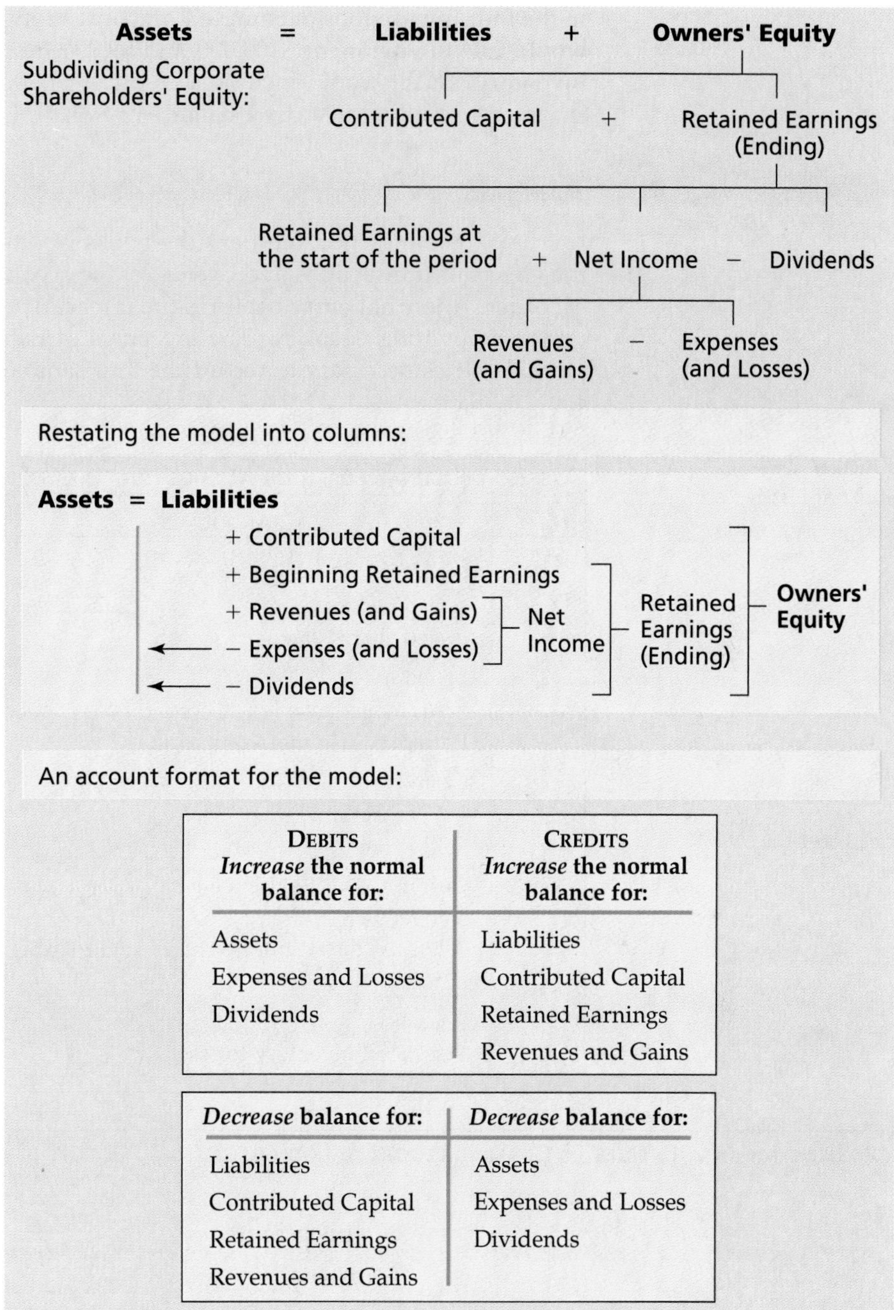

DEBITS *Increase* the normal balance for:	CREDITS *Increase* the normal balance for:
Assets	Liabilities
Expenses and Losses	Contributed Capital
Dividends	Retained Earnings
	Revenues and Gains

Decrease balance for:	*Decrease* balance for:
Liabilities	Assets
Contributed Capital	Expenses and Losses
Retained Earnings	Dividends
Revenues and Gains	

of the account format. Therefore, debits increase assets, expenses, losses, and dividends; they reduce liabilities, contributed capital, retained earnings, revenues, and gains. **Credits** are entries to the right hand side. Therefore, credits increase liabilities, contributed capital, retained earnings, revenues, and gains; they reduce assets, expenses, losses, and dividends.

Separate accounts are maintained for the various types of accounting elements. For instance, cash and inventory are the two types of assets included in the four transactions of Sample Company. From Exhibit 2–1, a cash account would include debits of $100,000 and $9,000 from issuing stock and selling inventory, and it would include a credit of $12,000 for the cash purchase of inventory, resulting in a debit balance of $97,000 (see Exhibit 2–4).

JOURNALS

Journals, or transaction files, are the books of original entry and summarize the effects of transactions and events on the accounting model in chronological order. A **journal entry** captures the impact of a single transaction or event on the accounting equation. The top panel of Exhibit 2–4 illustrates the five journal entries necessary to record the four sample transactions.

EXHIBIT 2–4
Journal Entries and Ledger Accounts

GENERAL JOURNAL FORM FOR ACCOUNTING TRANSACTIONS AND EVENTS:

DATE	ACCOUNTS	DEBITS	CREDITS
1.	Cash	100,000	
	Capital Stock		100,000
	Issued shares of stock for cash.		
2.	Inventory	20,000	
	Accounts Payable		20,000
	Purchased inventory on credit.		
3a.	Cash	9,000	
	Sales Revenue		9,000
	Sold inventory for cash.		
3b.	Cost of Goods Sold Expense	5,000	
	Inventory		5,000
	Allocated the cost of inventory sold to expense.		
4.	Inventory	12,000	
	Cash		12,000
	Purchased inventory for cash.		

POSTING JOURNAL ENTRIES TO GENERAL LEDGER ACCOUNTS:

CASH

Debit		Credit	
(1)	100,000		
(3a)	9,000		
		(4)	12,000
Bal.	97,000		

INVENTORY

Debit		Credit	
(2)	20,000		
		(3b)	5,000
(4)	12,000		
Bal.	27,000		

ACCOUNTS PAYABLE

Debit		Credit	
		(2)	20,000
		Bal.	20,000

CAPITAL STOCK

Debit		Credit	
		(1)	100,000
		Bal.	100,000

SALES REVENUE

Debit		Credit	
		(3a)	9,000
		Bal.	9,000

COST OF GOODS SOLD

Debit		Credit	
(3b)	5,000		
Bal.	5,000		

LEDGERS

While journal entries record transactions, they are not convenient for monitoring the activity and current balances of individual accounts. Any typical business enterprise may have hundreds or even thousands of transactions daily, and trying to examine cash, or any single account, would be very difficult if one relied on journal entries exclusively. To alleviate this problem, individual accounts are maintained in ledgers, or master files.

The process of transferring amounts from the journals into ledger accounts is called posting. The bottom panel of Exhibit 2–4 reflects the four sample transactions posted to **general ledger** accounts. A general ledger contains accounts for all the elements of the accounting system. Each account is illustrated here in a two-column format called a **T-account.**

With the framework of the accounting model in mind, the steps of the accounting process for a given accounting period are examined in the next section.

STEPS IN THE ACCOUNTING PROCESS

Perform the steps in the accounting process, including adjusting, closing, and reversing entries, and preparation of an income statement and a balance sheet.

Exhibit 2–5 summarizes the steps typically required to capture a given period's transaction information, create a set of periodic financial statements, and prepare the accounting records for the next period. For most companies, a significant portion of the process is accomplished with the aid of computerized software and other technological advancements.

THROUGHOUT THE ACCOUNTING PERIOD

Data Collection. Source documents provide evidence of transaction occurrence and facilitate processing in the accounting system. Sales invoices, shipping notices, remittance advices, purchase orders, and payment vouchers are

EXHIBIT 2–5
Steps in the Accounting Process

Throughout the accounting period:

1. **Data collection** for accounting transactions and events (create **source documents**).
2. **Data entry** into the accounting system (record transactions in **journals**).
3. **Posting** journal entries to **ledgers**.

End-of-period processing:

4. Prepare an **unadjusted trial balance**.
5. Journalize and post **adjusting entries**.
6. Prepare an **adjusted trial balance**.
7. Prepare **financial statements**.

(Steps 4–7: Use a **work sheet** to facilitate these steps (optional).)

8. **Closing process** (journalize and post **closing entries**).
9. Prepare a **post-closing trial balance**.

Beginning-of-next-period processing:

10. Journalize and post **reversing entries** (optional).

examples of common source documents. Specific types of documents, formats, and distributions vary from company to company.

Increasingly, the use of information technology makes data collection, document creation, and further processing of the data more efficient and effective. For example, **electronic data interchange (EDI)** is a technology using telecommunications for initiating, authorizing, executing, and documenting transactions electronically, without paper documents. When using EDI, companies collect and retain transaction data using electronic "images" of documents stored in computerized files. Regardless of the means, data collection and retention of transaction information form an integral part of the accounting process.

Data Entry. Data enters the accounting system through journal entries, which were illustrated in Exhibit 2–4. Depending upon the accounting system, transaction entry can occur simultaneously as data is collected or afterwards. Even in computerized systems, some companies accumulate source documents in batches, with data entry of these batches a separate step in the accounting process. Others use software and technology to make data entry into transaction files an automatic part of data collection. Many retail stores, for example, now use bar coding and scanning devices to simultaneously create sales documents and record sales in transaction files.

Posting to Ledgers. Like data entry into journals, the posting process is a separate step for some accounting systems; for others, transaction data is posted automatically to ledger accounts when data entry occurs. Many sophisticated

IN PRACTICE—GENERAL

Special Journals (Transaction Files) and Subsidiary Ledgers (Master Files)

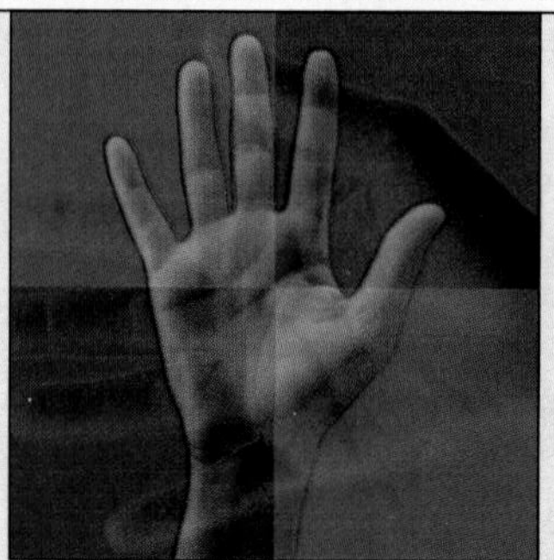

The primary focus of this text is on financial reporting. For explanation purposes, we depict journal entries in general journal form (as shown in Exhibit 2–4). In practice, though, many transactions would actually be recorded in *special journals* (also called *registers* or *transaction files*) rather than in a general journal. For example, sales are likely to be recorded in sales journals, and payroll is likely to be recorded in a payroll register. For efficiency, the form of these are typically not in general journal form. Whatever the form, all journals still must permit identification of debits and credits to respective accounts.

The text also concentrates on general ledger accounts (as shown in T-account form in Exhibit 2–4). However, businesses require more detailed account information than what general ledgers provide. For example, the general ledger maintains a single account for accounts receivable and another for salaries and wages. Yet, businesses must maintain individual accounts for each customer and for each employee. *Subsidiary ledgers* (also called *master files*) provide additional detail. Credit sales not only increase accounts receivable in the general ledger but also increase respective customer accounts maintained in an accounts receivable subsidiary ledger (customer master file). Payroll transactions increase employees' year-to-date balances in employee master files. Whenever detail accounts are needed for elements of financial statements, subsidiary ledgers are typically maintained—for example, accounts payable subsidiary ledger for vendors, cash subsidiary ledger for checking accounts, and inventory subsidiary ledger for inventory items.

database systems may not even maintain accounting information in traditional journal and ledger formats. Even so, these systems must have the capability to create journals and to determine account activity and balances.

END-OF-PERIOD PROCESSING

Unadjusted Trial Balance. A trial balance lists all the account balances in a company's general ledger as of a given date. An unadjusted trial balance is illustrated in Exhibit 2–6 and lists account balances prior to end-of-period adjusting entries. The purpose of the unadjusted trial balance is to check the equality of debits and credits.

Adjusting Entries. Significant transactions occur during the accounting period that typically remain unrecorded at year-end. For instance, wages and salaries may have been earned by employees but will not be paid until after year-end (the next payday). These events also probably have not been recorded, because normal recordkeeping relies upon identifiable transactions and events (for example, paying employees) to initiate entry into the accounting system. Since the wages clearly have been earned in the current accounting period, the

EXHIBIT 2–6
Example of Unadjusted Trial Balance

LEARNING TOOLS, INC.
Unadjusted Trial Balance
December 31, 1997

	DEBITS	CREDITS
Cash	$ 9,121	
Accounts Receivable	17,200	
Allowance for Bad Debts		$ 216
Notes Receivable	3,000	
Inventory (1/1/97)	20,700	
Prepaid Insurance	2,100	
Fixed Assets	64,500	
Accumulated Depreciation		5,500
Accounts Payable		3,212
Common Stock		20,000
Retained Earnings (1/1/97)		32,293
Dividends	12,000	
Sales Revenue		322,000
Sales Returns and Allowances	4,500	
Rent Revenue		12,000
Purchases	209,300	
Purchase Returns and Allowances		8,100
Freight-In	9,250	
Operating Expenses	10,365	
Wages and Salaries Expense	41,285	
	$403,321	$403,321

company is obligated to pay these wages. Thus, in preparing financial statements at the end of the period, the obligation should be included among the company's liabilities with the expense matched against the period's revenues.

Adjusting entries provide the mechanism for recognizing such previously unrecorded relationships. Adjusting entries bring the accounts up to date, properly recognizing revenues and expenses of the period, resulting in appropriate values for assets and liabilities at the end of the period.

CONCEPT Periodicity, revenue recognition, and matching.

LOGIC Many of the fundamental assumptions and conventions or principles discussed in Chapter 1 underlie the adjusting process. The need for the process arises because reports are prepared for distinct accounting periods. Revenue should be recognized in the period in which it is earned. Expenses incurred to generate revenues properly should be matched against those revenues in the period the revenue is recognized. Revenue recognition and matching are the basis of accrual accounting. Further, end-of-period adjustments are frequently necessary to properly reflect the company's resources and obligations and the changes to them.

This section addresses three major types of adjusting entries: (1) accruals, (2) deferrals, and (3) cost allocations and valuation adjustments. Exhibits 2–7, 2–8, 2–9, and 2–10 provide examples for Learning Tools, Inc.

Accruals. Revenues that have been earned but not yet received and expenses that have been incurred but not yet paid are **accruals**. That is, revenue or expense recognition *precedes* the exchange of cash, creating related receivables or payables. Exhibit 2–7 illustrates two examples: one for interest revenue earned on a note receivable and another for unpaid wages earned by employees.

Deferrals. Cash exchanges that occur before recognizing the related revenues and expenses are **deferrals**. A cash exchange occurs, but recognition of the associated revenue or expense is deferred. Cash *received* in advance for future services results in a liability for unearned revenue; cash *paid* in advance results in an asset for prepaid expenses. Exhibit 2–8 illustrates two examples of deferrals: one for rent *collected* in advance and another for insurance premiums paid at the start of insurance coverage.

Deferrals properly may be recorded initially two different ways. Cash received in advance may be recorded as revenue (prematurely, because it has not yet been earned) upon receipt of the cash in anticipation that the revenue ultimately will be earned. As an alternative, the cash received may be recorded as a liability—that is, unearned revenue. Similarly, cash paid in advance either may be recorded prematurely as an expense or as an asset—that is, prepaid expense. The required adjusting entry in each case will depend on the form of the original entry.

Exhibit 2–8 illustrates both methods of recording the original entry and the subsequent adjusting entry required. Note from the unadjusted trial balance for Learning Tools (Exhibit 2–6) that the company initially recorded rent received

EXHIBIT 2–7
Adjusting Entries: Accruals

Accruals are revenues or expenses to be recognized (i.e., accrued) in a given period *prior* to the respective cash receipt or cash payment. Adjusting entries for accruals generally result in related receivables or payables.

Revenue Example: Assume the $3,000 note receivable in the unadjusted trial balance in Exhibit 2–6 refers to an 8%, one-year note issued to Learning Tools by a customer on September 1, 1997, with principal and interest payable on September 1, 1998.

As of December 31, 1997, four months' interest has been earned but not yet received. The adjusting entry to accrue interest is:

12/31/97	Interest Receivable	80	
	Interest Revenue		80
	$3,000 × 8% × 4/12		

Expense Example: Assume that $865 in unrecorded wages for the last week of the year are to be paid on January 5, 1998.

As of December 31, 1997, the wage expense has been incurred but not yet paid. The adjusting entry to accrue wages is:

12/31/97	Wages and Salaries Expense	865	
	Wages and Salaries Payable		865

as revenue rather than a liability, so rent revenue has a balance and unearned rent does not. Further, the company initially recorded the insurance payment as an asset rather than expense, so prepaid insurance has a balance and insurance expense does not. Learning Tools would make the adusting entries shown in Exhibit 2–8 that are appropriate to the initial entries for these deferrals.

CONCEPT — Going concern, revenue recognition, and matching.

LOGIC — Because an enterprise's business activities cross time periods, adjusting entries are necessary to properly *recognize* revenue and to *match* expenses to related revenue. Therefore, in some cases revenue or expense must be *accrued* prior to the related cash transaction; in others, revenue or expense must be *deferred* until periods subsequent to the related cash transaction. In both situations, assets and liabilities must be adjusted to their appropriate values.

Cost Allocations and Valuation Adjustments. Some adjusting entries *allocate* the cost of assets to expense over one or more periods or *adjust the valuation* of reported assets, liabilities, or owners' equity. These **cost allocations** and **valuation adjustments** are based upon estimations of future events. As examples, depreciation is an important cost allocation of long-term assets over the periods of use; adjusting receivables for estimated bad debts is a valuation adjustment

Deferrals are elements ultimately *but not currently* to be recognized as revenue or expense (i.e., recognition is deferred) even though respective cash receipts or cash payments *have already occurred.* Deferrals typically result in related unearned revenue (liabilities) or prepaid expenses (assets).

Revenue Example: The entry for the initial transaction when cash is received can be recorded either as revenue *or* as a liability. The adjusting entry depends upon the initial entry. If initially recorded as revenue, the unearned portion at the end of the period must be recorded as a liability. If initially recorded as a liability, the earned portion must be recognized as earned revenue.

Assume the $12,000 rent revenue in Exhibit 2–6 applies to a full year's rent paid in advance to Learning Tools on June 1, 1997. The entries for both options follow:

	Recorded as Revenue			Recorded as a Liability		
Initial Transaction:						
6/1/97	Cash	12,000		Cash	12,000	
	Rent Revenue		12,000	Unearned Rent		12,000
Adjusting Entry:						
12/31/97	Rent Revenue	5,000		Unearned Rent	7,000	
	Unearned Rent		5,000	Rent Revenue		7,000
	Unearned Portion = $12,000 × 5/12			Earned Portion = $12,000 × 7/12		

In either case: Rent revenue reported on income statement = $7,000
Unearned rent reported on balance sheet = $5,000

Expense Example: The entry for the initial transaction when cash is paid can be recorded either as expense *or* as an asset. The adjusting entry depends upon the initial entry. If initially recorded as expense, the prepaid portion at the end of the period must be recorded as an asset. If initially recorded as an asset, the expired or used portion must be expensed.

Assume the $2,100 prepaid insurance in Exhibit 2–6 applies to a full year's insurance paid in advance by Learning Tools on November 1, 1997. The entries for both options follow:

	Recorded as Expense			Recorded as an Asset		
Initial Transaction:						
11/1/97	Insurance Expense	2,100		Prepaid Insurance	2,100	
	Cash		2,100	Cash		2,100
Adjusting Entry:						
12/31/97	Prepaid Insurance	1,750		Insurance Expense	350	
	Insurance Expense		1,750	Prepaid Insurance		350
	Prepaid Portion = $2,100 × 10/12			Expired Portion = $2,100 × 2/12		

In either case: Insurance expense reported on income statement = $ 350
Prepaid insurance reported on balance sheet = $1,750

EXHIBIT 2–8
Adjusting Entries: Deferrals

to estimate the net realizable value of accounts receivable. Both depreciation and bad debt expense adjustments result in *contra-asset accounts* (discussed shortly). Exhibit 2–9 illustrates three types of cost allocations or valuation adjustments.

EXHIBIT 2–9
Adjusting Entries: Cost Allocations and Valuation Adjustments

Estimating Bad Debts: Assume that, from previous experience, Learning Tools (Exhibit 2–6) estimates that 1% of its credit sales will prove uncollectible and that credit sales for 1997 were $200,000. The entry for adjusting the valuation of accounts receivable and matching bad debt expense with revenue generated is:

12/31/97	Bad Debts Expense	2,000	
	Allowance for Bad Debts		2,000
	200,000 × 0.01		

Depreciation: Assume that:

1. all of the $64,500 in fixed assets of Learning Tools (Exhibit 2–6) is depreciable,
2. the company uses straight-line depreciation based upon an estimated 10-year useful life and no salvage value.

The entry to allocate a portion of the cost of fixed assets to expense for 1997 is:

12/31/97	Depreciation Expense	6,450	
	Accumulated Depreciation		6,450
	$64,500/10 years		

Inventory and Cost of Goods Sold: Assume that a physical count by Learning Tools (Exhibit 2–6) on 12/31/97 determines that its remaining inventory has a cost of $26,000. Thus:

Inventory (1/1/97)		$ 20,700
Plus: Net purchases:		
Purchases	$209,300	
Freight-in	9,250	
Purchase returns and allowances	(8,100)	210,450
Goods available for sale		$231,150
Less: Inventory (12/31/97)		(26,000)
Cost of goods sold		$205,150

The adjusting entry for inventory and cost of goods sold is:

12/31/97	Inventory (increase)	5,300	
	Cost of Goods Sold	205,150	
	Purchase Returns and Allowances	8,100	
	Purchases		209,300
	Freight-In		9,250
	Inventory increase = $26,000 − $20,700		

Estimating Bad Debts. When credit is extended as a normal payment option, credit losses inevitably will occur. While a company cannot foresee exactly which receivables will be uncollectible (otherwise, of course, credit would not be granted in those cases), it can estimate the total amount of expected future bad debts. These estimates are usually based on percentages of credit sales, as shown in Exhibit 2–9, or on percentages of existing accounts receivable.

The adjusting entry recognizes as expense the estimated bad debts associated with the current period's revenue and reduces the estimated value of expected receivables. The accounts receivable are not reduced directly; instead an *Allowance for Bad Debts* account is used to depict expected reductions in receivables. This type of account is called a **contra account**, reflecting deductions from the associated primary account. The reported valuation on the balance sheet reflects the net amount of the primary account and contra-account balances. *Net* accounts receivable is the balance of accounts receivable less the balance of the allowance account. This net receivable is an estimate of the *net realizable value* expected from the collection of accounts receivable.

CONCEPT Matching and asset valuation.

LOGIC Bad debts result from generating revenue through the extension of credit. Anticipated expenses for bad debts should be matched with the revenue in the period of sale rather than in the period in which the debt is considered in default. Since assets represent expected future benefits, accounts receivable should be reported using an estimate of the expected future cash inflows (the net realizable value) and not at the gross amount receivable, because some portion is not expected to result in future cash inflows.

Depreciation. The costs of long-lived productive assets are **capitalized,** or recorded as assets because their expected future benefits span more than a single accounting period. Cost allocation is the mechanism for spreading portions of these costs to expense over multiple periods. **Depreciation** is the term used to allocate the costs of plant, property, and equipment (PP&E) such as machinery, equipment, and buildings. The cost of land is not depreciated, since presumed benefits continue indefinitely. **Depletion** is the term used to allocate the costs of natural resources like oil and mineral reserves. **Amortization** is the term used for allocating the costs of intangible assets like patents, copyrights, and goodwill.

Exhibit 2–9 presents an adjusting entry to record depreciation. In this example, the cost of fixed assets (also called plant, property, and equipment) is allocated using straight-line depreciation. A contra account is used for accumulated depreciation; fixed assets are reported net of accumulated depreciation to portray the costs that have not been depreciated. The net amount is their **book value**, or carrying value. When manufacturing companies record depreciation for assets related to production, depreciation is typically recorded as part of work-in-process inventory rather than as a separate depreciation expense.

CONCEPT Cost allocation and matching.

LOGIC Since long-lived productive assets provide benefits for multiple periods, portions of the cost are expensed in each of the periods in which they provide benefit. Thus, this type of cost allocation attempts to systematically match the portions expensed with the associated revenue in the period that the revenue is recognized.

Inventory and Cost of Goods Sold. The accounting model presented earlier in this chapter (Exhibits 2–1 through 2–4) illustrated the **perpetual system** for recording inventory. The inventory account is increased with purchases and decreased with sales. Thus, the account is continually updated with each associated transaction to maintain a current balance.

A **periodic system** is an alternative approach for inventory accounting that requires adjusting entries. All purchase activity for a period is recorded in purchase-related accounts (for example, Purchases, Purchase Discounts, Freight-In, and Purchase Returns and Allowances) rather than as direct entries to inventory accounts. Further, inventory accounts are not reduced for cost of goods sold at the time of sale.

For an illustration, refer to the sample journal entries in Exhibit 2–4. In a periodic inventory system, Sample Company would make the following entries:

2.	Purchases	20,000	
	Accounts Payable		20,000
3a.	Cash	9,000	
	Sales Revenue		9,000
3b.	No entry for Cost of Goods Sold		
4.	Purchases	12,000	
	Cash		12,000

Entries 2 and 4 would be debits to Purchases rather than to Inventory, and entry 3b to reduce inventory would not be made. When the entries are posted to ledgers, Inventory and Cost of Goods Sold would have zero balances, and Purchases would have a balance of $32,000.

In a periodic system, the balance maintained in the Inventory account throughout an accounting period is the beginning inventory balance (zero in the preceding example). At the end of the accounting period, the inventory account must be updated to reflect a proper ending balance and to recognize cost of goods sold as expense for the period. A physical count of the inventory remaining at the end of the period provides the proper ending balance. The cost of goods sold (*CGS*) can then be calculated as the beginning inventory (*BI*) plus the net purchases less the ending inventory *(EI) [BI + Net Purchases − EI = CGS]*.

Continuing the example, assume a physical count determined ending inventory costs to be $27,000 at year-end, there was no beginning inventory, and the purchases account had a balance of $32,000. Cost of goods sold would be $5,000 ($0 + $32,000 − $27,000). The adjusting entry to record the ending inventory, cost of goods sold, and to close the Purchases account would be

Inventory	27,000	
Cost of Goods Sold	5,000	
Purchases		32,000

As shown in the adjusted trial balance in Exhibit 2–6, Learning Tools, Inc., uses the periodic inventory method. This is evidenced by the inventory balance, which is the beginning 1997 balance, the purchase-related accounts, and the absence of a Cost of Goods Sold account. Exhibit 2–9 shows an adjusting entry for Learning Tools to adjust inventory and recognize cost of goods sold.

The cost of beginning inventory plus the net purchases equal the total cost of inventory available for sale during a period. The expense for cost of goods sold is the difference between the amount available for sale and the ending inventory as determined by the physical count. Essentially, the inventory adjusting entry shown in Exhibit 2–9 (1) records the change in inventory to bring the inventory account balance to year-end amounts, (2) recognizes the expense for cost of goods sold, and (3) transfers the net cost of purchases from purchase-related accounts to inventory and cost of goods sold.[1]

Income Tax Accrual. Corporations must pay income taxes based on the income earned. Therefore, expenses for income taxes are matched with the period in which the income is earned rather than the period in which the taxes are paid. An adjusting entry is necessary to accrue the income tax expense.

The adjusting entry for Learning Tools in Exhibit 2–10 illustrates a simplified example for accruing income taxes. Even though this entry is conceptually similar to the other accruals, it is shown separately because the previous adjustments are necessary to determine taxable income. The example is simplified by (1) assuming that all amounts for reported revenues and expenses are taxable

EXHIBIT 2–10
Adjusting Entries: Income Tax Accrual

For Learning Tools (Exhibit 2–6), assume a corporate income tax rate of 30% and that taxable amounts equal current revenues and expenses. The computation of income before taxes is:

Sales revenue	$322,000
Sales returns and allowances	(4,500)
Rent revenue	7,000
Interest revenue	80
Operating expenses	(10,365)
Wages and salaries expense	(42,150)
Insurance expense	(350)
Bad debts expense	(2,000)
Depreciation	(6,450)
Cost of goods sold	(205,150)
Income before taxes	$ 58,115

The adjusting entry to accrue income tax for the year is:

12/31/97	Income Tax Expense	17,435	
	Income Tax Payable		17,435
	$58,115 × 0.30		

[1]Textbooks vary in regard to the proper format for the inventory adjusting entry. Rather than a single debit or credit for the change in inventory, some texts portray both a credit to inventory for its beginning balance and a debit for its ending balance. Note that the net effect is the same.

Still others (particularly many introductory accounting texts) teach a bookkeeping routine of (1) debiting an account called income summary and crediting inventory for an amount equal to beginning inventory and then (2) debiting inventory and crediting income summary for an amount equal to ending inventory, (3) leaving nonzero balances in purchase-related accounts and (4) requiring a separate calculation with no account established for the cost of goods sold expense. Operationally, after all closing entries (which we later discuss in this chapter), the results are the same, but we feel this approach is conceptually unappealing.

items, (2) assuming a single tax rate for all income, and (3) assuming Learning Tools makes no contributions toward taxes during the year. Determination of actual income tax expense for a period is discussed in Chapter 17.

As a concluding comment regarding adjusting entries, many accounting software packages permit users to establish automatic and recurring entries. Some may be for fixed amounts every period (for example, using straight-line depreciation); others may be entries to the same accounts each period but for differing amounts, to be specified when the entry executes (such as the changing amounts for income taxes each period). Even when using this software convenience, users still must understand the purpose and use of adjusting entries.

Adjusted Trial Balance. An adjusted trial balance is prepared after all adjusting entries are made and posted. Exhibit 2–11 portrays the adjusted trial balance for Learning Tools, Inc. The reported amounts are for the unadjusted

EXHIBIT 2–11
Example of Adjusted Trial Balance

LEARNING TOOLS, INC.
Adjusted Trial Balance
December 31, 1997

	DEBITS	CREDITS
Cash	$ 9,121	
Accounts Receivable	17,200	
Allowance for Bad Debts		$ 2,216
Notes Receivable	3,000	
Interest Receivable	80	
Inventory (12/31/97)	26,000	
Prepaid Insurance	1,750	
Fixed Assets	64,500	
Accumulated Depreciation		11,950
Accounts Payable		3,212
Wages and Salaries Payable		865
Income Tax Payable		17,435
Unearned Rent		5,000
Common Stock		20,000
Retained Earnings (1/1/97)		32,293
Dividends	12,000	
Sales Revenue		322,000
Sales Returns and Allowances	4,500	
Rent Revenue		7,000
Interest Revenue		80
Operating Expenses	10,365	
Wages and Salaries Expense	42,150	
Insurance Expense	350	
Bad Debts Expense	2,000	
Depreciation	6,450	
Cost of Goods Sold	205,150	
Income Tax Expense	17,435	
	$422,051	$422,051

trial balance in Exhibit 2–6 modified to incorporate the adjusting entries in Exhibits 2–7, 2–8, 2–9, and 2–10. For example, the reported wage and salary expenses of $42,150 result from the $41,285 in Exhibit 2–6 plus the accrued wages of $865 in Exhibit 2–7. Also, the reported rent revenue of $7,000 results from the $12,000 in the unadjusted trial balance (Exhibit 2–6) reduced by the appropriate adjusting entry debiting rent revenue for $5,000 (Exhibit 2–8).

Financial Statements. An income statement and balance sheet can be prepared directly from the account balances listed in the adjusted trial balance. Exhibits 2–12 and 2–13 illustrate these two statements for Learning Tools.

The statement of cash flows and the statement of changes in shareholders' equity usually require other data besides the adjusted trial balance. For example, the adjusted trial balance in Exhibit 2–11 lists a $20,000 balance in common stock. This represents the balance at the end of 1997, but we do not know if that was the balance at the beginning of the year or if some stock was issued during the year. Any new issue of stock for cash would be shown on both a statement of cash flows and a statement of changes in shareholders' equity.

Work Sheets. A work sheet is an optional accountant's tool. As noted earlier in Exhibit 2–5, its purpose is to provide in one place all of the information used in adjusting the affected accounts in order to prepare an income statement and balance sheet. Exhibit 2–14 presents a work sheet for Learning Tools, Inc.

A thorough understanding of the steps involved to complete a work sheet such as the one shown in the exhibit is important in order to grasp the accounting process. As shown, adjusting entries are added to or subtracted from the unadjusted amounts to obtain the adjusted trial balance amounts, and those

EXHIBIT 2–12
Example of Income Statement

LEARNING TOOLS, INC.
Income Statement
For the Year Ended December 31, 1997

Revenue:		
Sales revenue	$322,000	
Sales returns and allowances	(4,500)	
Net sales		$317,500
Rent revenue		7,000
Interest revenue		80
Total revenue		$324,580
Expenses:		
Cost of goods sold	$205,150	
Operating expenses	10,365	
Wages and salaries expense	42,150	
Insurance expense	350	
Bad debts expense	2,000	
Depreciation expense	6,450	
Income tax expense	17,435	
Total expenses		283,900
Net income		$ 40,680

LEARNING TOOLS, INC.
Balance Sheet
December 31, 1997

Assets			Liabilities	
Current assets:			Accounts payable	$ 3,212
Cash		$ 9,121	Wages and salaries payable	865
Accounts receivable	$17,200		Income tax payable	17,435
Allowance for bad debts	2,216	14,984	Unearned rent	5,000
Notes receivable		3,000	Total liabilities	$ 26,512
Interest receivable		80		
Inventory		26,000	**Shareholders' Equity**	
Prepaid insurance		1,750		
Total current assets		$ 54,935	Common stock	$ 20,000
Long-term assets:			Retained earnings	60,973*
Fixed assets	$64,500		Total shareholders' equity	$ 80,973
Accumulated depreciation	11,950	52,550		
Total assets		$107,485	Total liabilities and shareholders' equity	$107,485

*Retained Earnings (1/1/97) + Net Income − Dividends = Retained Earnings (12/31/97)
$32,293 + $40,680 − $12,000 = $60,973

EXHIBIT 2–13
Example of Balance Sheet

are all totaled to ensure that the debits and credits balance. The adjusted amounts are extended to the respective columns as income statement amounts or balance sheet amounts. The difference between the credit amounts and debit amounts in the income statement columns represents net income (or loss). A balancing amount is placed at the bottom of the work sheet to "transfer" this difference from the income statement columns to the balance sheet columns because net income increases (net loss decreases) the retained earnings reported on the balance sheet. Notice that the balance sheet column contains amounts for beginning retained earnings, for dividends, and for the transferred net income. As the balance sheet in Exhibit 2–13 shows, these amounts typically would not be reported on the balance sheet, but they are included in the work sheet to provide the basis for determining the reported ending retained earnings.

A work sheet can be a useful tool for the adjusting and closing process, but it does not replace the previously described steps. Adjusting entries still must be entered into journals and posted to ledgers. An income statement and a balance sheet still must be prepared. The benefits of these types of work sheets are vanishing, since most companies use accounting software to assist in the accounting process. Users still must determine adjusting entries with such software, but the posting (updating) of these and the preparation of trial balances and financial statements are usually performed by the computer.

Closing Process. Balance sheet accounts are called **permanent (or real) accounts**. This means that the balances in the accounts at the end of the period "carry over" and remain the balances for the beginning of the next period. For example, the cash balance for Learning Tools, Inc., of $9,121 at the end of 1997 is the beginning cash balance of 1998.

EXHIBIT 2–14
Example of Work Sheet

LEARNING TOOLS, INC.
Work Sheet For the Year Ended December 31, 1997

ACCOUNT	UNADJUSTED TRIAL BALANCE		ADJUSTING ENTRIES		ADJUSTED TRIAL BALANCE		INCOME STATEMENT ACCOUNTS		BALANCE SHEET ACCOUNTS	
Cash	9,121				9,121				9,121	
Accounts Receivable	17,200				17,200				17,200	
Allowance for Bad Debts		216		2,000		2,216				2,216
Notes Receivable	3,000				3,000				3,000	
Inventory	20,700		5,300		26,000				26,000	
Prepaid Insurance	2,100			350	1,750				1,750	
Fixed Assets	64,500				64,500				64,500	
Accumulated Depreciation		5,500		6,450		11,950				11,950
Accounts Payable		3,212				3,212				3,212
Common Stock		20,000				20,000				20,000
Retained Earnings (1/1/97)		32,293				32,293				32,293
Dividends	12,000				12,000				12,000	
Sales Revenue		322,000				322,000		322,000		
Sales Returns and Allowances	4,500				4,500		4,500			
Rent Revenue		12,000	5,000			7,000		7,000		
Purchases	209,300			209,300						
Purchase Returns and Allowances		8,100	8,100							
Freight-In	9,250			9,250						
Operating Expenses	10,365				10,365		10,365			
Wages and Salaries Expense	41,285		865		42,150		42,150			
Interest Receivable			80		80				80	
Interest Revenue				80		80		80		
Wages and Salaries Payable				865		865				865
Unearned Rent				5,000		5,000				5,000
Insurance Expense			350		350		350			
Bad Debts Expense			2,000		2,000		2,000			
Depreciation Expense			6,450		6,450		6,450			
Cost of Goods Sold			205,150		205,150		205,150			
Income Tax Expense			17,435		17,435		17,435			
Income Tax Payable				17,435		17,435				17,435
	403,321	403,321	250,730	250,730	422,051	422,051	288,400	329,080		
Net Income							40,680			40,680
							329,080	329,080	133,651	133,651

In contrast, all other general ledger accounts are nominal (or temporary) accounts. Nominal account balances reflect the activity for the current time period only. Therefore, the balances at the beginning of each period are zero. For example, the sales revenue balance for Learning Tools, Inc., of $322,000 reflects the total sales for the year 1997. At the beginning of 1997, the sales account was zero, and to start 1998, the balance is also zero.

Essentially, nominal accounts such as revenues and expenses depict changes to stockholders' equity, which are recorded in retained earnings. The **closing process** ultimately transfers all nominal account balances to retained earnings. After closing, all nominal accounts will have a zero balance, retained earnings will have its proper ending balance, and the only accounts with nonzero balances will be the permanent, balance sheet accounts.

In computer accounting packages, the software generally performs this mechanical closing process at the request of the user. Even if the mechanics are performed by computer processing, understanding what is taking place with this process is extremely important. There can always be either human or software glitches, in which case someone must unravel the errors.

Exhibit 2–15 illustrates closing entries for Learning Tools, Inc., as a four-step process. First, all revenue-related accounts (and gains) are transferred, or "closed," to a temporary account called Income Summary. Second, all expense and loss accounts are closed to Income Summary. At this point, all temporary income statement account balances are zero, and the Income Summary account will have a credit balance equal to net income (or a debit balance equal to net loss). Third, the balance of Income Summary is closed to transfer net income (or loss) as an increase (decrease) to Retained Earnings. Fourth, Dividends are closed to reduce Retained Earnings. At the completion of this process, Retained Earnings reflects its ending balance, and all nominal accounts have a zero balance ready to begin the next period.

It is traditional to utilize Income Summary for closing entries. If desired, however, closing entries could be made directly to retained earnings, eliminating the third step above. Further, the entries can also be combined into a single entry, if desired.

A post-closing trial balance can be prepared as a final part of this process. This trial balance ensures that only permanent accounts have balances and that the closing entries have been posted properly, providing a summary of the beginning account balances for the next period.

BEGINNING OF NEXT-PERIOD PROCESSING

If used, *reversing entries* (discussed next) are made at the beginning of the next period, when the income statement accounts have a zero balance.

Reversing Entries. As the name implies, reversing entries "reverse" appropriate adjusting entries. They are an optional part of the accounting process, and only some adjusting entries may be reversed. Companies elect to use reversing entries to facilitate recording a future event.

For example, recall from Exhibit 2–7 that Learning Tools, Inc., made an adjusting entry to accrue $80 in interest revenue that established an Interest Receivable account. Exhibit 2–16 illustrates the subsequent entries related to this interest-bearing note, first assuming no reversing entry and then assuming

EXHIBIT 2–15
Example of Closing Entries

1. Close revenue related accounts (and gains) to Income Summary.

Date	Account	Debit	Credit
12/31/97	Sales Revenue	322,000	
	Rent Revenue	7,000	
	Interest Revenue	80	
	Sales Returns and Allowances		4,500
	Income Summary		324,580

2. Close expense (and loss) accounts to Income Summary.

Date	Account	Debit	Credit
12/31/97	Income Summary	283,900	
	Cost of Goods Sold		205,150
	Operating Expenses		10,365
	Wages and Salaries Expenses		42,150
	Insurance Expense		350
	Bad Debts Expense		2,000
	Depreciation Expense		6,450
	Income Tax Expense		17,435

3. Close Income Summary to Retained Earnings.

Date	Account	Debit	Credit
12/31/97	Income Summary	40,680	
	Retained Earnings		40,680

4. Close Dividends to Retained Earnings.

Date	Account	Debit	Credit
12/31/97	Retained Earnings	12,000	
	Dividends		12,000

INCOME SUMMARY

	Debit	Credit	
(2)	283,900	324,580	(1)
(3)	40,680	40,680	Temporary Bal.
		0	Ending Bal.

reversal. Without reversing, the company must know that $80 of the $240 is a reduction of the interest receivable. The remaining $160 is interest revenue for 1998. However, with the reversing entry, the entire $240 is recorded as interest revenue when the cash is received, which automatically leaves $160 as interest revenue for 1998. The reversing entry removed the receivable and temporarily established a "negative," or debit, balance of $80 in the Interest Revenue account. When the entire $240 is subsequently recorded as revenue, the balance for Interest Revenue in 1998 will be the proper $160.

As illustrated in Exhibit 2–16 for Learning Tools, Inc., two types of adjusting entries are appropriate to reverse: (1) accruals and (2) deferrals initially recorded as revenue or expense. With accruals, reversing entries remove any receivable or payable and temporarily set up a negative revenue or expense. Then, when cash is subsequently received or paid, revenue or expense is recorded for the

Accruals: Learning Tools, Inc., accepted an 8%, one-year $3,000 note receivable from a customer on September 1, 1997, with principal and interest receivable on September 1, 1998.

Adjusting Entry:	12/31/97	Interest Receivable	80	
		Interest Revenue		80
Closing Entry:	12/31/97	Interest Revenue	80	
		Income Summary		80

(Note that after closing, interest revenue = $0 and interest receivable = $80)

		WITHOUT REVERSING			WITH REVERSING		
Reversing Entry:	1/1/98	None			Interest Revenue	80	
					Interest Receivable		80
Subsequent Entry:	9/1/98	Cash	3,240		Cash	3,240	
		Notes Receivable		3,000	Notes Receivable		3,000
		Interest Revenue		160	Interest Revenue		240
		Interest Receivable		80			

Deferrals Initially Recorded as Revenue or Expense: Learning Tools, Inc., received $12,000 in advance for one year's rent on June 1, 1997.

Initial Entry:	6/1/97	Cash	12,000	
		Rent Revenue		2,000
Adjusting Entry:	12/31/97	Rent Revenue	5,000	
		Unearned Rent		5,000
Closing Entry:	12/31/97	Rent Revenue	7,000	
		Income Summary		7,000

(Note that after closing, rent revenue = $0 and unearned rent = $5,000)

		WITHOUT REVERSING			WITH REVERSING		
Reversing Entry:	1/1/98	None			Unearned Rent	5,000	
					Rent Revenue		5,000
Subsequent Entry:	5/31/98	Unearned Rent	5,000		None		
		Rent Revenue		5,000			

EXHIBIT 2–16
Example of Reversing Entries

full cash portion, leaving an appropriate balance for the period. With deferrals initially recorded as revenue or expense, reversing entries reestablish revenue or expense for the remaining portion; so, no subsequent entry is necessary to recognize revenue or expense expiration. Reversing entries for any other type of adjusting entries would be inappropriate and would only cause confusion and necessitate extra work to prevent errors. A very easy method of remembering which adjusting entries should be reversed is to follow this simple rule: *A reversing entry is appropriate only if the adjusting entry debits an asset account or credits a liability account.*

FINANCIAL RESEARCH

Identify types of research used to investigate and apply authoritative pronouncements.

To complete the entire accounting process successfully, professionals must frequently engage in research to find answers to accounting problems that result from new economic transactions. Two recurring types of financial research involve investigating (1) authoritative pronouncements and (2) reported financial information. Accounting professionals search authoritative sources to find the proper standards and regulations for such areas as financial accounting, auditing, and tax. They examine existing financial reports to determine how various companies report different financial elements. Reported financial information of different companies is also frequently analyzed for a variety of reasons, including investment analysis.

IN FOCUS

Wendy Wilson
Audit Senior Manager, Ernst & Young LLP

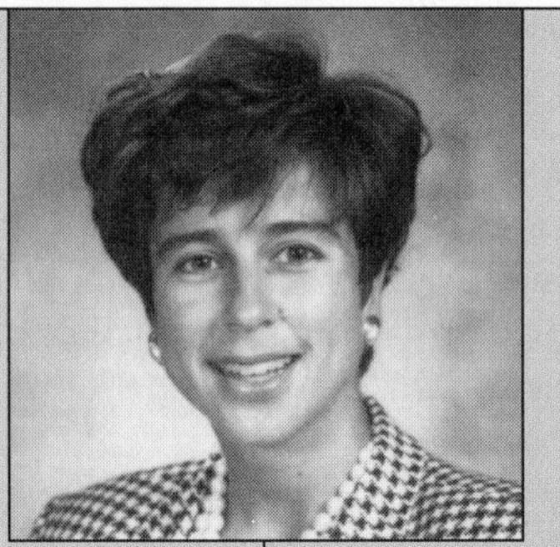

The preparation of financial statements is a huge industry. The in-house accounting departments of many large and small U.S. companies prepare their own, while CPA firms compile such statements for others. But then what? What purpose do they serve?

Setting aside the regulatory reasons for their preparation, there is a wide spectrum of uses of financial statements. A company that is trying to expand its operations may use them to demonstrate its financial condition to potential lenders or equity investors. Managers use them to make high-level decisions about operations, financing, and investing. Annual income statements and quarterly earnings reports of publicly traded firms drive investment decisions on Wall Street. And, of course, financial statements are an essential ingredient of shareholders' annual reports.

Because the balance sheet, income statement, statement of cash flows, and notes to financial statements are utilized by such a wide range of interested parties in making key financial decisions, the importance of meaningful data and adherence to generally accepted accounting principles is obvious. An investor interested in the telecommunications market, for instance, needs to know that the various companies she analyzes use the same accounting methods and standards, so that investment decisions are based on "apples-to-apples" comparisons.

CPAs like Wendy Wilson, Audit Senior Manager at Ernst & Young, help firms establish the reliability and credibility of the information in their financial statements through the audit process. Wilson manages a team that audits the statements of clients. "We certify that they are prepared in compliance with GAAP, are free of material misstatements, and fairly represent the financial standing of the company," she says. That opinion can then be used by her clients to support the financial statements in the annual report, when seeking new investors, or for other purposes.

While Wilson and her co-workers take a close look at the methods, procedures, and systems of their clients, they cannot possibly review all of the client's actual transactions. "The less sophisticated the client, the more likely we are to verify that individual transactions are properly recorded. With more sophisticated clients we test their systems of internal controls. When we're satisfied that the controls work, then we can reduce our look at individual transactions. But in any case, we could never look at *all* of the records of any client. That would be extremely time-consuming and expensive," Wilson adds.

While attention to detail and organization are important skills, Wilson accentuates the people side of her job. "Only about half of my time is on the technical side. The other half is managing and selling. I need good people skills for managing and motivating my team and for developing client relationships." Wilson, who is involved in college recruiting, adds that she always looks for well-rounded candidates who demonstrate a balance of skills, not just technical expertise.

Several sources provide information for financial research. Access to the various sources may be through printed hard copy, through telecommunication services to electronic databases, or through software utilizing CD-ROM databases. For example, professionals engaged in tax research might use telecommunications to search legal documents contained in LEXIS/NEXIS, an electronic database service provided by the ***Mead Company***. Financial accounting pronouncements (GAAP) are available (1) in hard-copy books, (2) as part of NAARS (National Accounting Automated Retrieval Service), which is maintained by the AICPA and available via LEXIS/NEXIS, and (3) through software that can be purchased from the AICPA. NAARS, Compustat, and DISCLOSURE are examples of computerized databases that provide financial reports for a large volume of companies. An increasingly popular telecommunications resource for financial research is the World Wide Web on the Internet. Many companies provide financial information through their Web sites. Throughout this text, we provide links to many Web sites through our homepage at *www.swcollege.com/hartman.html.*

Most chapters of this text provide a variety of research assignments. Some require examination of official accounting pronouncements to determine proper reporting for selected transactions. Others require analysis of financial statements and accompanying disclosures as well as other financial data. The sources for finding research material include the Internet and database services such as DISCLOSURE.

END-OF-CHAPTER REVIEW

SUMMARY

1. **Analyze transactions based upon the accounting equation.** The basic accounting equation is Assets = Liabilities + Owners' Equity. The owners' equity consists primarily of the owners' investments plus the earnings retained in the business. The earnings are revenues (and gains) minus expenses (and losses). All transactions affect the accounting equation.
2. **Interpret the four traditional financial statements.** The four statements are the income statement, balance sheet, statement of cash flows, and the statement of changes in shareholders' equity. The income statement reflects revenues and expenses for the period. The balance sheet portrays the asset, liability, and shareholders' equity balances at a point in time, typically the end of the accounting period. The statement of cash flows summarizes cash inflows and outflows from operating activities, investing activities, and financing activities for the period. The statement of changes in shareholders' equity reflects investments by owners, distributions to owners, and income or loss of the period.
3. **Understand the accounting model, including the purpose of journals and ledgers.** The steps in the accounting process ensure the accurate processing of economic data. The data represent the economic activities of the business. Accounting data are recorded in the journals and summarized in the ledgers.
4. **Perform the steps in the accounting process, including adjusting, closing, and reversing entries, and preparation of an income statement and a balance sheet.** The accounting process starts with journal entries to record transactions. The entries are posted to ledger accounts. At the end of the period, a trial balance is prepared.

Adjusting entries bring the accounts up to date and are posted to the ledgers. Then, an adjusted trial balance is prepared. The financial statements are prepared, and the temporary or nominal accounts closed. A post-closing trial balance is prepared, and, if desired, those adjusting entries in which an asset account was debited or a liability account credited are reversed.

5. **Identify types of research used to investigate and apply authoritative pronouncements.** Accounting professionals use many authoritative sources to research financial accounting standards, auditing standards, and tax laws. Access to the various sources may be through printed hard copy, through telecommunication services to electronic databases, or through software utilizing CD-ROM databases. In addition, NAARS, Compustat, and DISCLOSURE are computerized databases that provide financial reports for a large volume of companies. The Internet also provides access to abundant resources containing information useful to accounting professionals.

KEY TERMS

accounting equation *46*
accruals *56*
adjusted trial balance *63*
adjusting entries *56*
articulation *48*
balance sheet *48*
book value *60*
closing entries *67*
contra account *60*
cost allocations *57*
credits *51*
debits *50*
deferrals *56*
double-entry accounting *50*
income statement *48*
journals *52*
ledgers *53*
nominal (or temporary) accounts *67*
permanent (or real) accounts *65*
post-closing trial balance *67*
posting *53*
reversing entries *67*
statement of cash flows *48*
statement of changes in owners' (or shareholders') equity *48*
trial balance *55*
unadjusted trial balance *55*
valuation adjustments *57*
work sheet *64*

ASSIGNMENT MATERIAL

CASES

C2–1 Judgment and Decision—Income Taxes

For financial accounting purposes, revenues are recognized when earned in accordance with accrual accounting concepts, but small businesses and individuals typically follow a cash basis for determining income taxes. For 1997 Growth, Inc.'s reported revenues include $50,000 of credit revenues to be collected after year-end. These revenues under current law are not taxable until collected and therefore will not be included in Growth's tax return for 1997. Growth will not have to pay taxes on this revenue when it files its 1997 return in 1998. Instead, at the end of 1997, based upon Growth's current tax rate of 30%, Growth estimates that in 1999, it will have to pay an extra $15,000 in taxes when the 1998 return includes the $50,000 collected in 1998.

Required: Decide for yourself if Growth should include the estimated $15,000 as part of income tax expense for 1997 and report a liability for its ultimate payment. Do *not* consult current GAAP pronouncements to determine your answer. Instead, use logic and your understanding of the conceptual framework of accounting to make your decision.

C2–2 Judgment and Decision—Purchase Commitments

To ensure a ready supply of raw materials at a standard price, Hedgehog Company signed a purchase agreement on November 1, 1997, to buy from Standard Vendor Company over the next two years 200,000 tons of sludge at a set price of $30 per ton. In the event that Hedgehog does not purchase the full 200,000 tons, it still must pay for unpurchased sludge. By the end of 1997, Hedgehog had purchased 50,000 tons, leaving 150,000 tons remaining for the agreement. Clearly, Hedgehog is obligated to pay an additional $4,500,000 (150,000 × $30) to Standard Vendor in the future.

Required: Decide for yourself if Hedgehog should report at the end of 1997 a liability for the commitment to purchase the additional 150,000 tons. Do *not* consult current GAAP pronouncements to determine your answer. Instead, use logic and your understanding of the definition of a liability to make your decision.

C2–3 Judgment and Decision—Leases

The purchase price of equipment needed by Red Wave Company is $30,000. However, instead of purchasing the equipment, Red Wave Company leased it for five years. The terms of the noncancelable lease call for an initial $10,000 payment followed by 60 monthly payments of $500. At the end of the lease, Red Wave can pay $1 to purchase the used equipment.

Required: Decide for yourself how Red Wave should account for the lease. Is the lease essentially a rental agreement? If so, are the lease payments rent to be expensed in full as the equipment is utilized? Alternatively, has Red Wave essentially financed the purchase of the equipment? If so, is some portion of each lease payment interest and the remaining portion a reduction of the principal financed by the lease? Do *not* consult current GAAP pronouncements to determine your answer. Instead, use logic and your understanding of the conceptual framework to make your decision.

C2–4 Financial Analysis

Refer to the income statement and balance sheet for Learning Tools, Inc., in Exhibits 2–12 and 2–13, respectively.

Required:

A. What percentage of total assets is net income for 1997?

B. Do you think this percentage can be viewed as a return on the resources invested by the company? What weaknesses are there to such an interpretation?

C. From some current source, determine an approximate percentage for return on investments like U.S. Treasury notes, certificates of deposit, and savings accounts. How does the so-called "return" for Learning Tools compare? Would you advise investing in the company, given the opportunity?

QUESTIONS

Q2–1 What are the three primary ways a company can finance or obtain resources? How are these expressed as the fundamental accounting relation?

Q2–2 Explain the function of each of the four traditional financial statements.

Q2–3 What types of accounts do debits decrease and why?

Q2–4 What types of accounts do credits decrease and why?

Q2–5 Explain the purpose of journal entries, and give an example.

Q2–6 Explain the purpose of accounts in a ledger, and give an example.

Q2–7 Suppose you wanted to examine the impact upon the fundamental accounting relation of trading in an old vehicle for a new one by paying cash and financing the amount owed. Would you look in a journal or ledger? Why not the other?

Q2–8 Suppose you wanted to determine the amount of cash paid to vendors for credit purchases over some period. Would you look in a general journal or general ledger? Why not the other? Is there some other journal or ledger that might contain this information?

Q2–9 What does a trial balance portray? How is one useful?

Q2–10 What is the general purpose of adjusting entries?

Q2–11 Differentiate between accruals and deferrals.

Q2–12 Do accruals or deferrals typically result in receivables and payables? Explain.

Q2–13 Do accruals or deferrals typically result in unearned revenue and prepaid expenses? Explain.

Q2–14 If we pay six months' rent to our landlord in advance, why is it more expedient to record this as an expense at the time of payment? Why is recording the transaction as expense conceptually incorrect but still common practice?

Q2–15 What is the purpose of a contra account?

Q2–16 How can you tell by examining an unadjusted trial balance if a company is using perpetual or periodic inventory?

Q2–17 What were the three simplifying assumptions that were used to illustrate adjusting entries for income taxes?

Q2–18 What is the function of closing entries?

Q2–19 Assume that your accounting software performs the closing process for you. How can you tell if the process was done successfully?

Q2–20 What is the purpose of reversing entries? Are they a required part of the accounting process?

Q2–21 Exhibit 2–16 illustrated reversing entries for two of Learning Tools' adjusting entries, yet there are four adjusting entries that are acceptable to reverse. What are the other ones? How would the related subsequent events be recorded if they were reversed? if they were not reversed?

Q2–22 TRUE OR FALSE?

___ **1.** Financial statement footnotes should not be used to discuss material errors or omissions in the financial statements.

___ **2.** The assets of a firm include tangible and intangible resources to which the corporation has legal and enforceable title.

___ **3.** When a trial balance is found to be "in balance," the accountant can take comfort that all the information recorded in ledger accounts is true and accurate.

___ **4.** Closing entries set all nominal ledger accounts back to zero (at period end) and transfer prior account balances to the common stock accounts.

___ **5.** The calculation of ledger account balances and the listing of those balances in the trial balance is known as "posting."

___ **6.** The purpose of recording periodic depreciation is to ensure that the long-term, fixed-asset account balances reflect current market values.

___ **7.** The "net worth" of a firm is a term synonymous with the firm's "book value."

EXERCISES

E2–1 The Accounting Model

For each of the following accounts, indicate whether a debit would increase or decrease it:

1. Cash
2. Notes Payable
3. Accounts Receivable
4. Purchases
5. Trading Securities
6. Common Stock
7. Investment in Subsidiary
8. Accumulated Depreciation
9. Depreciation
10. Amortization of Patents
11. Sales Revenue
12. Social Security and Medicare Withholdings Payable
13. Retained Earnings
14. Bonds Payable
15. Loss on Sale of Fixed Assets
16. Wages and Salaries Expense
17. Land
18. General and Administrative Expenses
19. Bad Debts Expense
20. Sales Returns and Allowances

E2–2 The Accounting Model

For each of the following accounts, indicate whether a credit would increase or decrease it:

1. Service Revenue
2. Machinery
3. Supplies
4. Purchase Returns and Allowances
5. Allowance for Bad Debts
6. Interest Income
7. Accounts Payable
8. Dividends Payable
9. Goodwill
10. Income Tax Payable
11. Prepaid Insurance
12. Unearned Service Revenue
13. Gain on Sale of Securities
14. Patents
15. Merchandise Inventory

E2–3 The Accounting Model

Briefly describe a situation that would result in recording each of the following as part of a journal entry:

1. Credit to Cash
2. Credit to Land
3. Debit to Accounts Payable
4. Debit to Retained Earnings
5. Credit to Supplies Inventory
6. Credit to Common Stock
7. Credit to Prepaid Insurance
8. Debit to Unearned Service Revenue
9. Debit to Bad Debts Expense
10. Debit to Social Security and Medicare Withholdings Payable

E2–4 Journal Entries

Prepare journal entries for the following transactions in 1997:

1. April 1—sold merchandise on credit for $20,000 to a customer.
2. April 10—reduced a customer's account by $3,000 for returned merchandise previously sold.
3. May 5—received a $15,000 check from a customer as payment on account.
4. May 9—purchased on credit merchandise inventory from a vendor amounting to $2,000.
5. May 15—paid the vendor for the merchandise inventory obtained on May 9; by paying on a timely basis, received a 2% discount (use an account called Purchase Discounts for this).

6. May 29—purchased equipment for a price of $90,000 by paying 20% down and financing the remainder with a 7% installment note with monthly payments of $650 beginning June 30.
7. June 29—paid the first $650 payment for the note described in (6) of this exercise; $420 of the payment was interest.
8. July 29—paid the second $650 payment for the above note; $418.66 of the payment was interest.

E2–5 Ledger Accounts

Assuming a beginning cash balance of $30,000, prepare a T-account for cash, and post the relevant transactions from E2–4, concluding with an ending cash balance.

E2–6 Journal Entries

Prepare journal entries for the following transactions in 1997. There may be more than one way to record these transactions.

1. October 5—purchased merchandise inventory on credit for $120,000.
2. October 8—received advance payment of $8,000 for a new customer's order; preparation of the order and shipment will take approximately two weeks.
3. November 1— paid the lease for a year's rent of $14,400 in advance.
4. November 10—purchased supplies on credit amounting to $150.
5. December 1—declared and paid dividends of $20,000.

E2–7 Journals and Ledgers

The effects of five transactions are posted here (without dates) to ledger accounts. Construct the journal entries (including brief descriptions) for the transactions used to post these amounts. Since there are no dates, these can be in any order.

CASH		ACCOUNTS RECEIVABLE		EQUIPMENT	
80,000	80,000	120,000	30,000	250,000	
30,000	30,000				

ACCOUNTS PAYABLE		NOTES PAYABLE		SALES REVENUE	
30,000			170,000		80,000
					120,000

E2–8 Adjusting Entries

Prepare adjusting entries for each of the following situations assuming a December 31, 1997, year-end:

1. Wages and salaries earned but unpaid by year-end amounted to $33,333.
2. This company follows the procedure of recording supplies inventory when supplies are purchased. At year-end, the balance in the supplies inventory account was $122,222. A physical inventory determined that $100,000 of supplies remained on hand at the end of the year.
3. On September 1, 1997, the company borrowed $30,000 on a one-year, 8% promissory note with principal and interest payable on September 1, 1998.
4. On October 1, 1997, the company paid $160 to rent a Post Office box for a year, ending September 30, 1998. Rent expense was recorded when the cash was paid. Make the adjusting entry.

5. Credit sales for the year were $3,500,000. Bad debts are estimated as 1/2% of credit sales.
6. Machinery is depreciated using an estimated 10-year life and no residual value. The balances to start 1997 for machinery and associated accumulated depreciation were $700,000 and $140,000, respectively. No fixed assets were purchased or sold during 1997. Use straight-line depreciation.
7. Using periodic inventory, beginning inventory was $800,000, purchases were $1,500,000, and ending inventory was determined from a physical count as $600,000.

E2–9 Reversing Entries

For the adjusting entries in the previous exercise, E2–8, make reversing entries for those that are acceptable to reverse.

E2–10 Deferrals

When Novice User Company purchased computer equipment and software on March 31, 1997, it paid the vendor an extra $1,200 for a one-year maintenance contract effective April 1, 1997, through March 31, 1998.

Required:

A. Recording the initial payment as expense, journalize the initial entry, any adjusting entry required as of December 31, 1997, any reversing entry if acceptable, and any entry when the contract expires on March 31, 1998.

B. Repeat (A), but record the initial payment as a prepaid expense.

E2–11 Reversing Entries

Prepare the reversing entry for each of these adjusting entries that are acceptable to reverse.

12/31/97	Bad Debts Expense	23,200	
	Allowance for Bad Debts		23,200
12/31/97	Interest Expense	12,000	
	Interest Payable		12,000
12/31/97	Depreciation	45,600	
	Accumulated Depreciation		45,600
12/31/97	Prepaid Shipping Charges	300	
	Freight-In		300
12/31/97	Rental Expenses	1,200	
	Prepaid Rental Expenses		1,200
12/31/97	Subscriptions Revenue	66,000	
	Unearned Subscriptions Revenue		66,000

E2–12 Inventory and Cost of Goods Sold

The following selected account balances are taken from the December 31, 1997, unadjusted trial balance of Red Castle Company:

Inventory (1/1/97)	$ 88,000
Sales Revenue	1,900,000
Sales Returns and Allowances	200,000
Purchases	1,000,000
Purchase Returns and Allowances	30,000
Purchase Discounts	15,000
Freight-In	60,000

A physical inspection on December 31, 1997, of remaining inventory determined the ending cost of inventory to be $100,000.

Required:

A. Prepare a schedule to calculate cost of goods sold for 1997.
B. Prepare the adjusting entry related to inventory for December 31, 1997.

E2–13 Inventory and Cost of Goods Sold

The following selected account balances are taken from the December 31, 1997, unadjusted trial balance of Air Filter Company:

Inventory (1/1/97)	$ 950,000
Sales Revenue	22,000,000
Sales Returns and Allowances	800,000
Purchases	12,000,000
Purchase Returns and Allowances	900,000
Freight-In	200,000

A physical inspection on December 31, 1997, of remaining inventory determined the ending cost of inventory as $650,000.

Required:

A. Prepare a schedule to calculate cost of goods sold for 1997.
B. Prepare an adjusting entry related to inventory for December 31, 1997.

E2–14 Adjusting Entries—Depreciation

Prepare adjusting entries to record depreciation for each of the following situations assuming a December 31, 1997, year-end:

1. Machinery costing $450,000 is depreciated using the straight-line method (an equal amount each period), estimating a 15-year useful life and no residual value. The machinery was purchased six years ago.
2. Equipment costing $120,000 was purchased this year on July 1, 1997. Use straight-line depreciation and an estimated 5-year useful life with no salvage value.
3. Construction of a building that cost $2,000,000 was completed last year and is expected to be used for 20 years with a residual value of $200,000. Use straight-line depreciation.
4. A fleet of trucks (all purchased last year) cost $1,000,000. These are depreciated based upon a rate of $.30 per mile rather than on a straight-line basis. The total distance traveled in 1997 was 1,111,110 miles.

E2–15 Effects of Errors and Correcting Entries

Errors in accounting certainly occur and need to be corrected. Frequently these errors are detected at the end of the period, and adjusting entries are made to correct the errors. Prepare entries to correct the following errors occurring in 1997.

1. When $10,000 cash was received from a customer as payment on account, Sales was credited instead of reducing the customer's account.
2. A credit purchase was recorded when a purchase order was sent to a vendor to buy $12,000 of inventory. By the end of the year, the order had not arrived, nor had the vendor billed the company. The adjusting entry for inventory and cost of goods sold has *not* been made yet.

3. Apply the same facts as the previous correction except that the adjusting entry for inventory *has already* been made.

E2–16 Closing Entries

Based upon the following adjusted trial balance for Wrapping Up, Inc., prepare the closing entries to end 1997.

	DEBITS	CREDITS
Cash	$ 44,000	
Accounts Receivable	66,000	
Allowance for Bad Debts		$ 6,000
Inventory (12/31/97)	99,000	
Prepaid Rent	3,000	
Land	64,000	
Plant and Equipment	220,000	
Accumulated Depreciation		12,000
Accounts Payable		22,000
Income Tax Payable		35,000
Bonds Payable (long-term)		88,000
Common Stock		120,000
Retained Earnings (1/1/97)		91,000
Dividends	50,000	
Sales Revenue		800,000
Sales Returns and Allowances	16,000	
Rent Expense	7,000	
Interest Expense	8,000	
Miscellaneous Expenses	2,000	
Wages and Salaries Expense	88,000	
Bad Debts Expense	4,000	
Depreciation	8,000	
Cost of Goods Sold	440,000	
Income Tax Expense	55,000	
	$1,174,000	$1,174,000

E2–17 Income Statement and Balance Sheet

Using the adjusted trial balance sheet shown for the previous exercise, E2–16, prepare an income statement and balance sheet for Wrapping Up, Inc.

E2–18 Deferred Revenues

Winn Company sells subscriptions to a specialized directory that is published semiannually and shipped to subscribers on April 15 and October 15. Subscriptions received after the March 31 and September 30 cutoff dates are held for the next publication. Cash from subscribers is received evenly throughout the year and is credited to unearned subscription revenue. Data relating to 1997 are as follows:

Unearned subscriptions revenue (1/1/97)	$ 750,000
Cash receipts from subscribers	3,600,000

Determine the amount of subscription revenue to report for 1997 and the amount of unearned subscription revenue to report on the December 31, 1997, balance sheet. (AICPA adapted; MC29, Practice I, 11/91.)

E2–19 Deferred Revenues

Specialty Corporation requires advance payments from customers who make special orders. Payments received are credited to unearned revenue. The following pertains to activity related to special orders for 1997:

Unearned revenue (1/1/97)	$ 1,000,000
Collections for special orders	66,000,000
Special orders completed in 1997	60,000,000

Determine the amount of revenue to report for 1997 and the amount of unearned revenue to report on the 12/31/97 balance sheet.

E2–20 Financial Analysis

Selected information from the financial statements of MDB Company is shown here.

	1997	1996
Sales	$22,000,000	$20,000,000
Cost of goods sold	(15,000,000)	(12,500,000)
Gross profit	$ 7,000,000	$ 7,500,000
	12/31/97	**12/31/96**
Inventory	$ 8,000,000	$ 7,000,000
Accounts payable	3,000,000	2,400,000

Required:

A. Determine the amount of inventory purchased during 1997.
B. Determine the amount of cash paid during 1997 for inventory purchases.

E2–21 Financial Analysis

Selected information from the financial statements of Majestic, Inc., is shown here.

	1997	1996
Sales	$80,000,000	$70,000,000
Cost of goods sold	(50,000,000)	(30,500,000)
Gross profit	$30,000,000	$39,500,000
	12/31/97	**12/31/96**
Inventory	$ 4,000,000	$ 5,000,000
Accounts payable	3,000,000	3,400,000

Required:

A. Determine the amount of inventory purchased during 1997.
B. Determine the amount of cash paid during 1997 for inventory purchases.

E2–22 Financial Analysis

Selected information from the financial statements of King Company is shown here.

	1997	1996
Sales	$123,000,000	$120,000,000
Cost of goods sold	(43,000,000)	(35,000,000)
Gross profit	$ 80,000,000	$ 85,000,000
	12/31/97	**12/31/96**
Accounts receivable	$ 23,000,000	$ 20,000,000
Accounts payable	30,000,000	32,000,000

Required: Determine the amount of cash collected from customers during 1997.

E2–23 Financial Analysis

Selected information from the financial statements of Prince Company is shown here.

	1997	1996
Sales	$2,000,000	$1,400,000
Cost of goods sold	(1,000,000)	(700,000)
Gross profit	$1,000,000	$ 700,000
	12/31/97	**12/31/96**
Accounts receivable	$ 500,000	$ 800,000
Accounts payable	300,000	320,000

Required: Determine the amount of cash collected from customers during 1997.

PROBLEMS

P2–1 Cash Versus Accrual Accounting

New Company began operating in 1997. The only journal maintained for transactions was the company's checkbook register. The owner prepared the following as an "income statement" from this checkbook register.

NEW COMPANY
Income Statement
For the Year Ended December 31, 1997

Cash receipts from sales		$17,000
Less: cash expenditures for:		
Merchandise	$14,000	
Salaries	2,500	
Equipment	2,000	
Rent	2,000	
Insurance	1,200	21,700
Net Loss		$ (4,700)

Assume the owner hires you as an accountant to establish proper accounting records. Through consultation with the owner and various source documents, you determine the following:

1. The owner began the business with a cash investment of $40,000.
2. An additional $10,000 is owed by customers for credit sales.

3. The owner owes an additional $5,000 for merchandise purchased.
4. The owner owes $500 to the only employee for December's salary.
5. The cost of the equipment purchased at the beginning of the year was $5,000, for which $2,000 cash was paid down and the remainder financed at 10% with principal and interest payable in 18 months. The owner estimates the equipment can be used for five years with no residual value at the end of this period.
6. The rent paid at the beginning of the year was for two years' rent.
7. The insurance paid at the beginning of the year was for a three-year policy.
8. Inventory amounting to $4,000 remains at the end of the year.

Required: Prepare an income statement, a balance sheet, and a statement of cash flows. For owners' equity, use a single capital account that combines both contributed capital and retained earnings. There are no income taxes for this business. (*Hint:* Prepare entries to reconstruct events for the period.)

P2–2 Steps in the Accounting Process

An unadjusted trial balance (with accounts in alphabetical order) and information requiring adjustments are shown for ComBright, Inc.

COMBRIGHT, INC.
Unadjusted Trial Balance
December 31, 1997

	DEBITS	CREDITS
Accounts Receivable	$340,000	
Accumulated Depreciation		$ 22,000
Allowance for Doubtful Accounts		2,700
Capital Stock		100,000
Cash	213,000	
Furniture and Equipment	137,000	
Miscellaneous Office Expense	1,300	
Notes Payable		300,000
Office Salaries Expense	166,000	
Rent Expense	52,000	
Retained Earnings		5,300
Revenue From Consulting Fees		500,000
Supplies Inventory	11,000	
Unexpired Insurance	3,700	
Utilities Expense	6,000	
	$930,000	$930,000

Adjustments:

1. Fees received in advance from clients and recorded as revenue for which service has not been provided total $15,000.
2. Services performed for clients that were not recorded by December 31, 1997, total $20,000.
3. The allowance for doubtful accounts should be increased by 1% of total revenues (after considering [1] and [2] above).
4. Insurance expired during the year totals $1,300.

5. Furniture and equipment is being depreciated at 10% of cost per year.
6. On December 1, 1997, ComBright signed a 90-day note at 6% for $300,000, shown as Notes Payable. Accrue interest for this note.
7. Rent for the building is $4,000 per month. The rent for 1997 has been paid, as well as that for January 1998.
8. Office salaries earned but unpaid as of December 31, 1997, total $3,000.
9. Assume a 30% income tax rate and that amounts for all revenues and expenses are taxable.

Required: Prepare the following:

A. Adjusting entries
B. An adjusted trial balance
C. An income statement
D. A balance sheet
E. Closing entries
F. Where acceptable, reversing entries

P2–3 Work Sheets—to be used in conjunction with P2–2

Prepare a work sheet to assist with P2–2.

P2–4 Adjusting Entries

Prepare adjusting entries at December 31, 1997, for each of the following situations:

1. Wages and salaries accrued at December 31 amounted to $4,000.
2. A one-year note receivable in the amount of $1,000 with an interest rate of 10% was accepted March 31.
3. Cash of $180 was received for an 18-month subscription on April 1. The journal entry to record the transaction was a credit to Subscriptions Revenue.
4. Cash of $240 was received on June 1 for a 12-month service contract. The original entry credited Unearned Revenue for the amount.
5. Insurance Expense of $480 was debited on August 1 to record payment of a 12-month insurance premium.
6. Rent for a piece of machinery in the amount of $6,000 for a 12-month period was paid on August 1. The journal entry to record the transaction was as follows:

Prepaid Rent	6,000	
Cash		6,000

7. A note payable in the amount of $20,000 was issued on May 1. The note matures on April 30, 1998, and carries an interest rate of 10% payable annually on April 30.
8. The equipment account has a current balance of $38,000, and the related Accumulated Depreciation account has a current balance of $17,000. Depreciation is calculated using the straight-line method, for an estimated life of 12 years and an estimated salvage value of $2,000.
9. The physical count of the ending inventory amounted to $40,000. The beginning inventory was $35,000, purchases were $600,000, purchase returns were $3,000, and purchase discounts were $4,500. Freight charges to obtain the merchandise amounted to $7,000. The periodic inventory system is used.

P2–5 The Accounting Process

An unadusted trial balance for Stewart Corp. as of December 31, 1997, is shown at the top of the next page.

	DEBITS	CREDITS
Cash	$ 26,000	
Accounts Receivable	40,000	
Inventory (1/1/97)	14,000	
Equipment	200,000	
Accumulated Depreciation		$ 20,000
Accounts Payable		35,000
Notes Payable		50,000
Common Stock		100,000
Retained Earnings (1/1/97)		58,000
Sales Revenue		600,000
Purchases	200,000	
Purchase Returns and Allowances		2,000
Wages and Salaries Expense	220,000	
Rent Expense	15,000	
Other Expenses	150,000	
	$865,000	$865,000

Required:

A. Prepare adjusting entries required for each of the following:
   1. Stewart's equipment is depreciated using straight-line, a 10-year useful life, and no salvage value.
   2. On September 1, 1997, Stewart borrowed $50,000 on a one-year, 6% note.
   3. On April 1, 1997, Stewart paid $12,000 in advance for a year's rent on a warehouse.
   4. A physical count determines inventory on hand at December 31, 1997, of $10,000.

B. Prepare an income statement for 1997 and a balance sheet as of December 31, 1997. (Assume there are no income taxes.)

C. Prepare closing entries for 1997.

D. Prepare acceptable reversing entries for January 1, 1998.

P2–6 The Accounting Process

An unadusted trial balance for Sunshine Corporation as of May 31, 1998, is shown at the top of the next page. Take care to note the May 31 fiscal year-end.

Required:

A. Prepare adjusting entries required for each of the following:
   1. On October 1, 1997, Sunshine paid $54,000 for a one-year insurance policy effective from that date.
   2. A physical count determines inventory on hand at May 31, 1998, of $1,000,000.
   3. Sunshine's equipment is depreciated using straight-line, a 10-year useful life, and no salvage value.
   4. On January 1, 1998, Sunshine began renting a warehouse by paying a full year's rent of $240,000 for the calendar year 1998.
   5. The company's income tax rate is 25%.

B. Prepare an income statement for the year ended May 31, 1998, and a balance sheet as of May 31, 1998.

C. Prepare closing entries for May 31, 1998.

D. Prepare acceptable reversing entries for June 1, 1998.

	DEBITS	CREDITS
Cash	$ 50,000	
Accounts Receivable	63,000	
Inventory (6/1/97)	930,000	
Prepaid Insurance	54,000	
Equipment	4,000,000	
Accumulated Depreciation		$ 600,000
Accounts Payable		530,000
Common Stock		800,000
Retained Earnings (6/1/97)		400,000
Sales		9,470,000
Sales Returns and Allowances	40,000	
Purchases	5,200,000	
Purchase Returns and Allowances		120,000
Purchase Discounts		80,000
Freight-In	48,000	
Wages and Salaries Expense	1,220,000	
Rent Expense	240,000	
Other Expenses	155,000	
	$12,000,000	$12,000,000

P2–7 The Accounting Process

A trial balance for Turtle Company as of December 31, 1997, is shown below. This trial balance reflects all adjusting entries *except* those for the following:

1. Turtle determines that inventory on December 31, 1997, is $132,000.
2. The reported administrative expenses include $36,000 for a maintenance contract, effective for one year from the date the contract was paid on May 1, 1997.
3. The company has an income tax rate of 20%.

	DEBITS	CREDITS
Cash	$ 102,000	
Accounts Receivable	126,000	
Inventory (1/1/97)	114,000	
Equipment	324,000	
Accumulated Depreciation		$ 102,000
Accounts Payable		138,000
Wages and Salaries Payable		18,000
Common Stock		192,000
Retained Earnings (1/1/97)		150,000
Dividends	12,000	
Sales Revenue		480,000
Purchases	252,000	
Selling Expenses	96,000	
Administrative Expenses	54,000	
	$1,080,000	$1,080,000

Required:

A. Prepare the remaining necessary adjusting entries.
B. Prepare an income statement for 1997 and a balance sheet as of December 31, 1997.
C. Prepare closing entries for 1997.
D. Prepare acceptable reversing entries from (A) for January 1, 1998.

P2–8 Work Sheets

Complete the work sheet shown on the next page. Note that the adjusting entries are incomplete and that the applicable income tax rate is 25%.

P2–9 Statement of Changes in Owner's Equity

The following information is from Mystery Inc.'s records at the end of the 1997 year:

Current assets	$ 700,000
Current liabilities	400,000
Intangible assets	50,000
Long-term liabilities	200,000
Dividends declared	20,000
Income summary (credit balance)	144,000
Retained earnings (1/1/97)	?
Preferred stock (issued 7/1/97)	200,000
Common stock (none issued in 1997)	300,000
Paid-in capital in excess of par—common	700,000
Plant and equipment (net)	1,400,000

Required: From the above information prepare a statement of changes in shareholders' equity for 1997.

P2–10 Accounting Process

The following trial balance was taken from the books of Fast Freddy's Foods, Inc., on December 31, 1997.

	DEBITS	CREDITS
Cash	$ 12,000	
Accounts Receivable	90,000	
Allowance for Bad Debts		$ 3,000
Note Receivable	10,000	
Inventory (1/1/97)	62,000	
Unexpired Insurance	4,000	
Furniture and Equipment	52,000	
Accumulated Depreciation		4,000
Accounts Payable		20,000
Common Stock		66,000
Retained Earnings		38,000
Sales Revenue		301,000
Purchases	140,000	
Wages and Salaries Expense	50,000	
Rent Expense	12,000	
	$432,000	$432,000

THOMAS & THOMAS, INC.
Work Sheet
For the Year Ended December 31, 1997

ACCOUNT	UNADJUSTED TRIAL BALANCE		ADJUSTING ENTRIES		ADJUSTED TRIAL BALANCE		INCOME STATEMENT ACCOUNTS		BALANCE SHEET ACCOUNTS	
Cash	15,000									
Accounts Receivable	120,000									
Allowance for Bad Debts		20,000		(1) 4,000						
Inventory	350,000		(2) 25,000							
Plant, Property, and Equipment	975,000									
Accumulated Depreciation		175,000		(3) 75,000						
Notes Payable		400,000								
Common Stock		420,000								
Retained Earnings (1/1/97)		260,000								
Sales Revenue		999,000								
Purchases	???									
Miscellaneous Expenses	45,000									
Wages and Salaries Expense	210,000									
Rent Expense	75,000			(4) 25,000						
Interest Payable				(5) 20,000						
Interest Expense										
Prepaid Rent										
Bad Debts Expense										
Depreciation Expense										
Cost of Goods Sold										
Income Tax Expense (25%)										
Income Tax Payable										
Net Income										
								106,595		23,045

The following information needs to be incorporated into the records at year-end.

1. A full year's interest at 8% is receivable on the note.
2. Depreciable assets are assumed to have a 10-year life without any residual value.
3. Estimated bad debts are 0.5% of sales.
4. Insurance expired during the year was $2,000.
5. Accrued salaries and wages at December 31, 1997, total $3,500.
6. There is $8,000 of rent paid in advance at December 31, 1997.
7. The inventory on December 31, 1997, is $73,000.

Required:

A. Prepare all adjusting entries for the year.
B. Prepare an adjusted trial balance, a balance sheet, and an income statement. Ignore income tax.
C. Prepare closing and reversing entries.

P2–11 Work Sheet With Adjusting and Closing Entries

The trial balance for CJ Company is presented for the year ended December 31, 1997, along with some additional information you may need.

	DEBITS	CREDITS
Cash	$ 52,345	
Accounts Receivable	97,775	
Allowance for Bad Debts		$ 1,475
Inventory	144,888	
Prepaid Expenses	15,188	
Land	76,250	
Building	222,969	
Accumulated Depreciation		48,406
Furniture and Fixtures	38,750	
Accumulated Depreciation		17,500
Equipment	121,600	
Accumulated Depreciation		41,250
Intangible Assets	13,480	
Accounts Payable		66,438
Interest Payable		10,156
Taxes Payable		20,000
Short-Term Notes Payable		37,500
Long-Term Notes Payable		206,250
Common Stock (no par)		125,000
Retained Earnings		53,879
Sales Revenue		1,690,220
Cost of Goods Sold	1,067,085	
Selling Expense	234,150	
Administrative Expense	158,125	
Tax Expense	20,000	
Interest Expense	30,469	
Dividends	25,000	
	$2,318,074	$2,318,074

Additional Information: Assume that all adjusting and correcting entries have been made except for the following items:

1. A sales invoice in the amount of $9,500 and its related cost of goods sold was not recorded in the general ledger as of December 31, 1997. CJ sells its inventory at a 40% markup on cost and uses a perpetual inventory system.
2. CJ Company estimates bad debts such that the ending balance in the Allowance for Bad Debts account is equal to 6% of the ending Accounts Receivable balance. This is consistent with past experience in credit collections.
3. As of December 31, no accrual for electricity expense had been made. An electricity bill for the warehouse for $5,000 was received January 15, 1998, for electrical consumption from December 10, 1997, through January 10, 1998. The bill was paid on January 20, 1998, and debited to administrative expenses at that time.
4. CJ Company purchased a used delivery van on July 1, 1997, for $15,000 cash. This amount was debited to selling expenses in the general ledger. The van has an estimated useful life of three years and no salvage value.
5. A used copy machine was purchased on March 15, 1995, for $21,000 and debited to Equipment. It has a seven-year estimated useful life and no salvage value. Depreciation expense was not recorded for 1997.
6. Insurance on the delivery van was paid on January 31, 1997, for $2,000 for the time period of January 31, 1997, through January 31, 1998. The full amount was debited to administrative expenses at the time it was paid.
7. Wages for the time period of December 25, 1997, through January 7, 1998, were paid on January 15, 1998, in the amount of $8,000.
8. Total tax expense for 1997 should be 34% of income before taxes. Note that an entry for taxes was made previously.

Required: Using only the expense accounts in the existing trial balance and rounding to the nearest dollar:

A. Prepare adjusting and correcting entries for the additional information.
B. Prepare a work sheet for CJ Company.
C. Prepare closing entries for CJ Company for 1997.

P2–12 Adjusting, Closing, and Reversing Entries, Statement Preparation

The unadjusted trial balance for Maison, Inc., at December 31, 1997, appears on the next page:

Additional Information:

1. Included in the Sales account is $1,500 received for merchandise that is to be shipped in January.
2. Included in the Sales account is $4,000 received for rent on a building that Maison owns. The payment was received on July 1, 1997, and was for a period of eight months.
3. Maison estimates that 2% of the outstanding accounts receivable will be uncollectible.
4. On August 1, Maison paid $3,600 as advance payment for one year's rent.
5. Wages and salaries of $1,400 were accrued at December 31, 1997.
6. The purchases account erroneously included $4,000 for merchandise that Maison held on consignment. The physical count of the inventory at December 31, 1997, correctly totaled $147,000, excluding the merchandise held on consignment. Accounts Payable was credited for the consignment merchandise.
7. At December 31, 1997, $2,000 of advertising expenditures were applicable to 1998.

8. Maison uses the straight-line method to record depreciation expense on plant and equipment. Of the total $400,000, the equipment had an original cost of $150,000 and was expected to have a useful life of eight years with an estimated salvage value of $10,000. The plant had an original cost of $250,000, an estimated useful life of 20 years, and a salvage value of $30,000.
9. The note payable is a one-year, 12% note that was issued on March 1, 1997.
10. The bonds payable were issued at par on February 28, 1990, are due on July 1, 2014, and have semiannual interest payable dates of March 1 and September 1.
11. The income tax rate is 25%.

	DEBITS	CREDITS
Cash	$ 25,000	
Accounts Receivable	97,000	
Allowance for Bad Debts		$ 1,100
Inventory	177,000	
Prepaid Rent	3,600	
Prepaid Advertising	14,000	
Land	64,750	
Plant and Equipment	400,000	
Accumulated Depreciation		140,600
Accounts Payable		36,000
Notes Payable		10,000
Bonds Payable (9%)		100,000
Common Stock (20,000 shares outstanding)		200,000
Retained Earnings		40,900
Sales Revenue		585,000
Sales Returns and Allowances	3,000	
Interest Expense	5,250	
Wages and Salaries Expense	89,000	
Purchases	249,000	
Purchase Discounts		14,000
	$1,127,600	$1,127,600

Required:

A. Prepare the adjusting and correcting entries at December 31, 1997.
B. Prepare an income statement for the year ended 12/31/97.
C. Prepare a balance sheet at December 31, 1997.
D. Prepare closing entries at December 31, 1997.
E. Prepare reversing entries where appropriate at January 1, 1998.

RESEARCH ACTIVITIES

R2–1 GAAP Research—Donated Capital

The company for whom you were recently employed has received some land with an appraised value of $100,000. The land was contributed as incentive to open operations in the area by a nonprofit organization representing a special interest group. Your manager shows you her intermediate accounting text from when she had accounting at her university in the late 1980s. According to this text, the contribution should be recorded as a debit for the value of the asset received and as a credit to donated capital, which is considered a direct increase to contributed capital in shareholders' equity.

Required: The manager asks you to determine if the above accounting treatment for donated capital is still appropriate. Examine Statements of Financial Accounting Standards since SFAS No. 110, and prepare a brief memo describing proper accounting for the contribution.

R2–2 Accrual Decisions

The Oil Flow Company has had several of its former service stations declared as hazardous waste sites and is in the process of cleaning up the environmental damage. Future, yet unknown, events that are a direct result of today's activities will cost Oil Flow a significant sum of money as well. The accounting policy today is to record these events as they become known and the actual dollars are spent.

Required: Research your local newspaper(s) for events of this nature to determine the magnitude of these costs. (1) Provide arguments for continuing the present policy, and (2) provide an alternative way of reflecting the cost of these events.

R2–3 Financial Research

Use an electronic database to supply the information below for a well known company. To use the disk database that accompanies this text, follow instructions specific to your university to start the software. When prompted by the disk, select the *Easy Menu Search,* then *Begin a New Search,* followed by *Company Name,* and then finally *Full Company Name* in order to look at information for a company of your choice. After these selections, you will be asked for a few letters of a full company name; press any alphabetic character, and a list of firms appears. Then use the up and down arrows to highlight a company of your choice. When highlighted, press [Enter] to mark it and then the [F10] function key *When Done.* For the company you chose, select the *Display. . .* option and choose relevant *Display Formats* to answer the requirements shown. When finished, select *Quit Easy Menu Mode* and then *Return to DOS* to end the session. You can use the [F1] function key anytime for help and the [Esc] key for returning to previous selections.

Required: Provide the following information:

A. Company name
B. Company's auditor
C. Date for the most current financial statements
D. Number of years included of annual financial data
E. For the *two* most current years reported, determine

	MOST CURRENT	PREVIOUS PERIOD
1. Net income (loss)		
2. Earnings per share (EPS)		
3. Total assets		
4. Total liabilities		
5. Total shareholders' equity		
6. Cash provided by (used for) operations		

R2–4 Internet—Rutgers Accounting Web (RAW)

This Internet activity examines an extremely useful starting point for finding a vast array of useful accounting information, both educational and professional. This source is the Rutgers Accounting Web (RAW). Use your Web browser to find its homepage through *http://www.swcollege.com/hartman.html.*

From this homepage, find the section for *RAW Services.* From *Educational Materials,* select *Major Courses,* and then choose *Intermediate Accounting.* How many selections are there of material for intermediate financial accounting? Choose one of the course selections and determine if the requirements for the course are similar to those for your course.

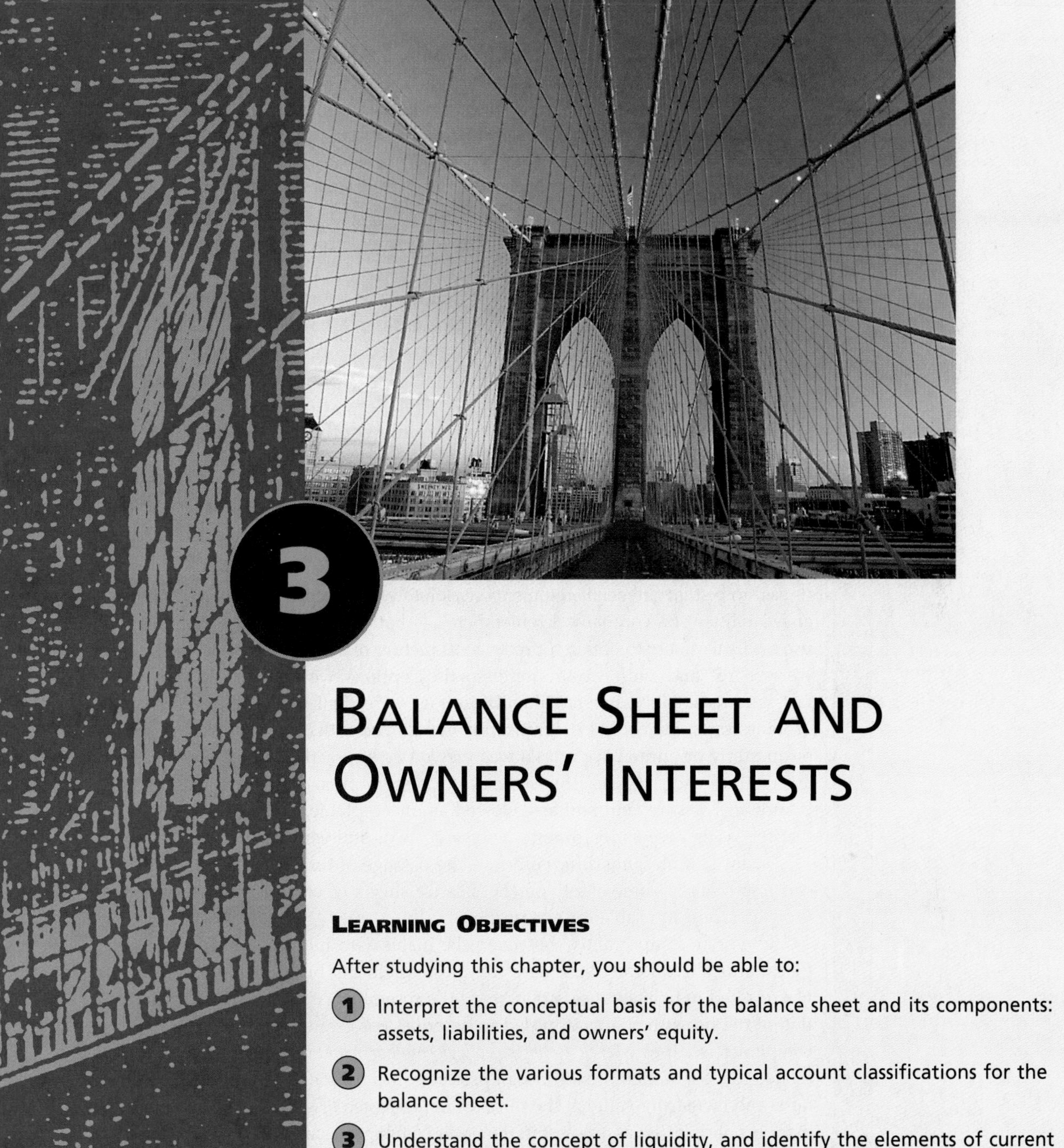

3

Balance Sheet and Owners' Interests

Learning Objectives

After studying this chapter, you should be able to:

1. Interpret the conceptual basis for the balance sheet and its components: assets, liabilities, and owners' equity.
2. Recognize the various formats and typical account classifications for the balance sheet.
3. Understand the concept of liquidity, and identify the elements of current assets and current liabilities that comprise an enterprise's working capital.
4. Understand the concept of solvency, and identify the noncurrent elements of a firm's balance sheet.
5. Distinguish among the various forms of entities, and interpret the traditional presentation of stockholders' equity by source: contributed capital and retained earnings.
6. Identify uses and limitations of traditional balance sheets for financial analysis.

The balance sheet reports the assets, liabilities, and owners' equity of an enterprise at *a given point in time.* What amounts should be assigned to the elements of the balance sheet and what the purpose of the balance sheet should be are somewhat controversial issues. Some of the purposes proposed for a balance sheet include portrayal of:

- The financial resources and obligations of an enterprise and the means by which the resources were financed.
- The aggregate effect of past transactions and events on an enterprise.
- Expected future cash receipts and payments (that is, assets and liabilities that describe the related amounts expected to be received or paid in the future).[1]

Existing accounting practice is complex and continues to evolve. The following excerpts highlight some difficulties associated with the balance sheet today.

Balance Sheets in Today's Economy

It used to be that financial statements reasonably and accurately reflected the assets and liabilities of a company. I remember. . . that we once believed that you could use a balance sheet to obtain a pretty good picture of a company. Most of the assets were "hard" and, with certain understood exceptions, were carried—as a matter of fact—at a reasonably current value. Of course, we recognized that the carrying value of some assets. . . could be significantly out of sync with current value, but the idea of quarterly or annual appraisals was viewed as impractical. Similarly, measuring asset values using indices of specific asset category price changes or market values if known. . . were, and still are, viewed as unacceptable. However, we all agreed that the system we had, although not perfect, was still very useful.

Today I think quite differently. . . the passage of time has made the historical carrying costs of some assets on the balance sheets of certain major corporations unrealistic and unusable for *any* purpose.

Even more importantly, however, the inability to recognize *at all* as assets on the balance sheet some of the new and most significant building blocks of business has resulted in balance sheets that bear little resemblance to the true financial position of the firms they are supposed to describe. For example, there are major drug companies, such as ***Merck*** (*www.swcollege.com/hartman.html*), that show no assets related to most of their breakthrough products. In addition, for example, the tremendous and increasing value of the ***Coca-Cola*** (*www.swcollege.com/hartman.html*) trademark is not reflected as an asset in the periodic financial statements of that company. Similarly, most intellectual property is not recorded as assets on the balance sheet of the firms that own the property. Finally, there are major software companies, like ***Microsoft*** (*www.swcollege.com/hartman.html*), whose stock is worth tens of billions of dollars with balance sheets that make them look like much smaller companies.

My concerns, then, are that there are a significant number of assets that are poorly measured through historical cost accounting and, more importantly, that we

[1]SFAC No. 6, par. 141.

> have entire categories of assets that are not recognized at all. And the problem is getting worse. In particular, it is the latter group of assets—those that are not even recognized—that are the fastest growing and most important parts of most of our new firms. In recent years, for example, service firms comprise the fastest growing segment of our economy. Yet, the most important assets of many of these firms—intellectual property and human assets—will not be found anywhere on the balance sheet of these entities.

Source: S. Wallman, "The Future of Accounting and Disclosure in an Evolving World: The Need for Dramatic Change," *Accounting Horizons,* September 1995, pp. 84–85.

The balance sheet is an integral part of financial reporting, providing information to a variety of users, including investors, creditors, employees, and government. This chapter presents a conceptual view of the balance sheet, and discusses classification of the elements of the balance sheet. Also described are the various legal forms of business and the owners' equity for each form. Particular emphasis is placed on the corporate form of reporting. The chapter concludes with a discussion of the uses and limitations of the balance sheet.

FINANCIAL POSITION—THE CONCEPT

Interpret the conceptual basis for the balance sheet and its components: assets, liabilities, and owners' equity.

As introduced in Chapter 1, SFAC No. 6 defines the basic elements of the balance sheet as follows:

- Assets are probable future economic benefits obtained or controlled by a particular entity as a result of past transactions or events.[2]
- Liabilities are probable future sacrifices of economic benefits arising from present obligations of a particular entity to transfer assets or provide services to other entities in the future as a result of past transactions or events.[3]
- Equity or net assets are the residual interest in the assets of an entity that remains after deducting its liabilities.[4] In a business enterprise, the equity is the ownership interest.[5]

In these definitions, the conceptual framework describes the financial resources and obligations of an enterprise in terms of probable future benefits and sacrifices. Accordingly, the conceptual framework describes accounting information as serving a *prospective,* or *future-oriented,* function.

As an example, amounts owed to a business by its customers for past credit purchases are assets (accounts receivable) valued at the expected future cash inflows. Likewise, machinery used in production is expected to yield future economic benefits as the output (product) ultimately is sold and cash is collected.

However, not all customers will pay their bills, so the expected benefits are not necessarily the total amounts receivable from these customers. Further, companies presumably expect the future benefits from production machinery

[2]Ibid., par. 25.
[3]Ibid., par. 35.
[4]Ibid., par. 49.
[5]Ibid., par. 60.

to equal or exceed the cost of the machinery. Given the wide range of possible future benefits and the accompanying uncertainty, machinery is valued at historical cost (assuming only cost recovery). As the expected benefits are received over time, the reported net asset (book value) is reduced through depreciation charges, and the remaining expected benefits are assumed to decline.

The preceding two examples highlight some complexities associated with prospectively viewing assets as future economic benefits—namely that of valuing assets in an amount equal to their future benefits (see the "In Practice" feature). Similarly, recognition and valuation of future economic sacrifices (or liabilities) can be equally complex.

IN PRACTICE—GENERAL

Commentary—What Is an Asset?

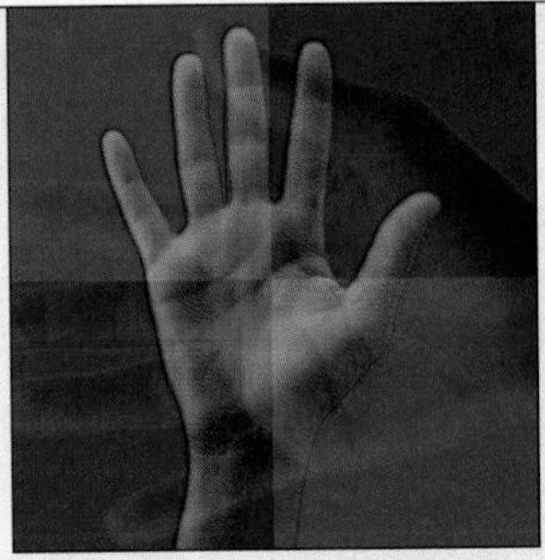

The FASB's definition [of an asset] is so complex, so abstract, so open-ended, so all-inclusive, and so vague that we cannot use it to solve problems. It does not require exchangeability, and therefore it allows all expenditures to be considered for inclusion as assets. The definition does not discriminate and help us to decide whether something or anything is an asset. That definition describes an empty box. A large empty box. A large empty box with sideboards. Almost everything or anything can be fit into it. Some even want to fit losses into the definition.

Remarks by Walter P. Schuetze, then chief accountant of the SEC, made at the AICPA's Twentieth Annual National Conference on Current SEC Developments (*Accounting Horizons,* September 1993, pp. 66–70).

Within the context of accrual accounting, issues related to recognition and valuation of assets and liabilities—as well as changes to assets and liabilities—are critically important to financial statement representations. Therefore, the next two chapters are devoted to the conceptual foundations of accrual accounting, with emphasis on these recognition and valuation issues.

BALANCE SHEET—FORMATS AND CLASSIFICATIONS

Recognize the various formats and typical account classifications for the balance sheet.

Balance sheet information can be presented in different ways. Exhibit 3–1 illustrates one possible format in the balance sheet from ***Motorola's*** 1995 annual report (also see this text's Web site: *www.swcollege.com/hartman.html*). Annual reports commonly present financial statements for multiple years (called **comparative financial statements**). For example, Motorola's 1995 annual report presents balance sheets for both the 1995 and 1994 year-end. **Consolidated financial statements** are prepared when a parent corporation owns controlling interests (greater than 50% of the voting stock) in one or more subsidiary companies.

Balance sheet information can be either classified or unclassified. Exhibit 3–1 is an example of a **classified balance sheet**, in which the respective assets and liabilities are classified into current and noncurrent categories. Exhibit 3–2 illustrates the classifications and accounts typically reported by many companies. Unclassified balance sheets list the assets and liabilities without the traditional current and noncurrent categories.

MOTOROLA, INC. & CONSOLIDATED SUBSIDIARIES
Consolidated Balance Sheets

(In millions, except per share amounts)

DECEMBER 31		1995	1994
Assets	*Current Assets*		
	Cash and cash equivalents	$ 725	$ 741
	Short-term investments	350	318
	Accounts receivable, less allowance for doubtful accounts (1995, $123; 1994, $118)	4,081	3,421
	Inventories	3,528	2,670
	Future income tax benefits	1,222	928
	Other current assets	604	847
	Total current assets	10,510	8,925
	Property, plant and equipment, net	9,356	7,073
	Other assets	2,935	1,538
	Total assets	$22,801	$17,536
Liabilities & Stockholders' Equity	*Current Liabilities*		
	Notes payable and current portion of long-term debt	$ 1,605	$ 916
	Accounts payable	2,018	1,678
	Accrued liabilities	4,170	3,323
	Total current liabilities	7,793	5,917
	Long-term debt	1,949	1,127
	Deferred income taxes	968	509
	Other liabilities	1,043	887
	Stockholders' Equity		
	Common stock, $3 par value		
	Authorized shares: 1995 and 1994, 1,400		
	Outstanding shares: 1995, 591.4; 1994, 588.0	1,774	1,764
	Preferred stock, $100 par value issuable in series		
	Authorized shares: 0.5 (none issued)	—	—
	Additional paid-in capital	1,813	1,415
	Retained earnings	7,461	5,917
	Total stockholders' equity	11,048	9,096
	Total liabilities and stockholders' equity	$22,801	$17,536

EXHIBIT 3–1
Example of Comparative and Consolidated Balance Sheets

In the United States and Canada, the assets and liabilities of most enterprises are presented in order of relative **liquidity**. That is, the most liquid assets and liabilities (those to be converted to cash most imminently) are presented first. In many European countries, the *least* liquid assets are presented first

EXHIBIT 3–2
Typical Balance Sheet Classifications and Accounts

Assets	Liabilities
Current assets	Current liabilities
Cash	Accounts payable
Short-term investments	Short-term notes payable
Accounts receivable	Accrued expenses/payables
Notes receivable	Unearned revenues
Inventory	Current maturing portion of long-term debt
Prepaid expenses	Long-term liabilities
Noncurrent assets	Notes or mortgages payable
Long-term investments	Bonds payable
Property, plant, and equipment	Lease obligations
Intangible assets	Deferred income taxes
Other assets	**Stockholders' Equity**
	Contributed capital
	Capital stock (at par)
	Additional paid-in capital
	Retained earnings
	Treasury stock

Note: This classification and related accounts are typical but *not* exhaustive. Each classification may have other accounts, and different account names may be used by various companies.

instead, followed by stockholders' equity, then liabilities. The In Practice example for ***Danco Company*** illustrates this method. In the United States, utility companies typically use this European format. In the United Kingdom, fixed or nonliquid assets are also listed first. Note from the In Practice example for the ***British Petroleum Company*** that current assets and current liabilities are combined to present net current assets. Then, liabilities are subtracted from assets to present net assets (owners' equity).

In the following sections, the major classifications of the balance sheet presented in Exhibit 3–2 are described and explained. Complexities associated with each of the major types of accounts are presented in subsequent chapters throughout this text.

CURRENT ASSETS

Understand the concept of liquidity, and identify the elements of current assets and current liabilities that comprise an enterprise's working capital.

Current assets are those assets expected to be converted to cash within the operating cycle or one year, whichever is longer. The **operating cycle** is the normal time necessary to purchase or manufacture inventory, sell the inventory, and collect the cash from the sale. The operating cycle of a department store is very short, perhaps two or three months, while the operating cycle of a winery may extend over several years. The classification of current versus noncurrent assets for the winery will differ from the department store because it is based on several years instead of one year.

Exhibit 3–2 lists the six major types of current assets most commonly reported by a business enterprise. Motorola, in Exhibit 3–1, uses most of these. Various conventions are used to establish the reported values for these assets.

IN PRACTICE—INTERNATIONAL

Example of Balance Sheet Typical of Many Countries Outside the United States

The following is a balance sheet for *Danco A/S*, a company in Denmark.

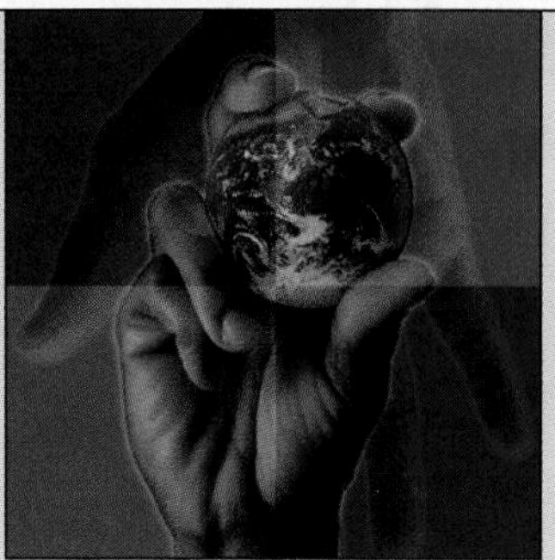

Notice how accounts are presented in essentially reverse order to that typically found in the United States. This framework is conventional in many European countries.

BALANCE SHEET
At December 31, 1988

ASSETS	(IN DKK 000S) 1988	1987	SHAREHOLDER'S EQUITY AND LIABILITIES	(IN DKK 000S) 1988	1987
Fixed assets:			Shareholder's equity		
Intangible fixed assets:			Capital stock (Note 6)	300	300
Deposits	198	145	Legal reserve	75	75
Tangible fixed assets:			Carried forward to next year (Note 7)	19,673	17,367
Equipment and motor vehicles (Note 4)	1,874	1,888	Total shareholder's equity	20,048	17,742
Total fixed assets	2,072	2,033	Provisions		
Current assets:			Deferred income tax (Note 3)	5,736	3,981
Finished goods inventories	10,532	8,741	Current liabilities:		
Receivables:			Owing to parent company	101	1,388
Trade receivables	28,700	32,612	Owing to affiliated companies	5,047	14,871
Owing by affiliated companies	—	181	Trade creditors	660	352
Other receivables	107	314	Income tax payable (Note 3)	4,531	2,399
Prepaid expenses	287	21	Other amounts payable (Note 8)	6,033	5,865
	29,094	33,128	Dividend proposed for the year	4,000	1,000
Cash (Note 5)	4,458	3,696	Total current liabilities	20,372	25,875
Total current assets	44,084	45,565			
Total assets	46,156	47,598	Total shareholder's equity and liabilities	46,156	47,598

Cash. Cash and cash equivalents are the most liquid assets. These include currency on hand, checking and savings accounts, and any other deposits that are available to meet current operating needs.

Short-Term Investments. Investments can be classified as short-term (current) assets or long-term (noncurrent) depending on management intent. Those intended to be temporary in nature are classified as current assets, while long-term investments are classified as noncurrent.

IN PRACTICE—INTERNATIONAL

Balance Sheets in the United Kingdom

The following is a balance sheet for ***British Petroleum Company (BP),*** a company in the United Kingdom. The balance sheet is for BP's consolidated group, which would be consistent with a set of consolidated financial state

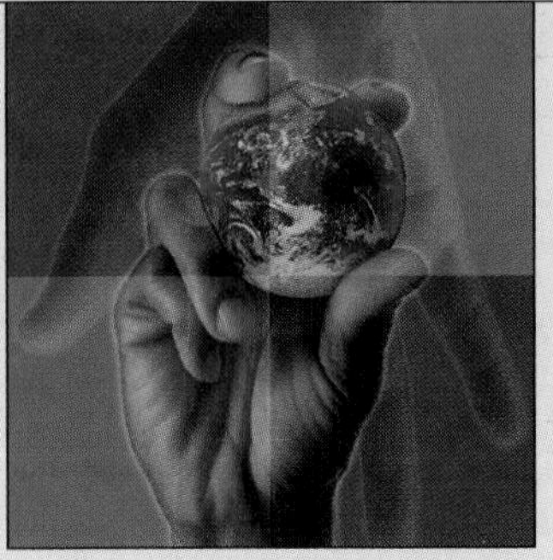

ments in the United States. Note that the British format is to present fixed assets first, followed by net current assets (i.e., current assets minus current liabilities), and finally to provide totals for net assets (i.e., shareholders' equity) rather than total assets.

	£ MILLION	
AT 31 DECEMBER	1993	1992
Fixed assets:		
Intangible assets	777	1,285
Tangible assets	19,954	20,864
Investments	1,975	2,104
	22,706	24,253
Current assets:		
Stocks	2,668	3,379
Debtor amounts falling due:		
Within one year	4,369	5,884
After more than one year	1,064	1,024
Investments	84	71
Cash at bank and in hand	126	179
	8,311	10,537
Creditor amounts falling due within one year:		
Finance debt	1,236	2,432
Other creditors	7,121	8,781
Net current assets	(46)	(676)
Total assets less current liabilities	22,660	23,577
Creditor amounts falling due after more than one year:		
Finance debt	7,144	7,827
Other creditors	2,055	2,459
Provisions for liabilities and charges:		
Deferred taxation	248	226
Other provisions	3,365	3,207
Net assets	9,848	9,858
Minority shareholders' interest	100	155
BP shareholders' interest	9,748	9,703
Represented by		
Capital and reserves:		
Called up share capital	1,375	1,367
Share premium account	1,812	1,756
Capital redemption reserve	197	197
Reserve	6,364	6,383
	9,748	9,703

Temporary investments of excess or idle cash include Treasury bills, certificates of deposit, and investments in equity securities (i.e., stock) and debt securities (i.e., bonds) of other companies. According to SFAS No. 115, short-term investments in debt and equity securities are designated by management as either *trading securities* or *available-for-sale securities* and are reported in the balance sheet at fair value. *Fair value* is the exchange price between two willing parties, other than in a forced or liquidation sale. Quoted market prices are considered fair value.

The distinction between trading and available-for-sale classification also depends upon management intent. Trading securities are those intended to be bought and sold with regularity, while available-for-sale securities are not intended for regular trading. Available-for-sale securities are also frequently classified as long-term investments, again depending on management's intentions with regard to the holding period.

Accounts Receivable and Notes Receivable. Accounts receivable arise from credit sale transactions and are reported at an estimate of their net realizable value. Net realizable value is face value less an estimated amount for uncollectible accounts. The uncollectible amount is estimated from past experience and is based on either a percentage of credit sales or a percentage of receivables. Notes receivable due in one year or less are also classified as current assets. They may arise from transactions in the normal course of business or may be accepted in place of overdue accounts receivable.

Inventory. Inventory represents merchandise that will be sold in the normal course of business operations. Valuation of inventory on hand and cost of goods sold can be determined using a variety of acceptable methods, such as a specific identification basis; first-in, first-out; last-in, first-out; average cost; or some combination of these. Whatever the method, it should be followed consistently from year to year and disclosed in the notes to the financial statements. Further, if costs based upon a selected method exceed the inventory's market value, the lower market value is reported instead. The consideration of market value is called lower of cost or market (lcm).

Prepaid Expenses. Prepaid, or unexpired, expenses that will be used up (or charged to expense) in the next year or operating cycle are classified as current assets. For example, insurance, rent, and advertising are expenses that may be paid in advance, with the benefits obtained in the next year or operating cycle. The future income tax benefits reported by Motorola in Exhibit 3–1 can be viewed as a type of prepaid income tax expense.

NONCURRENT ASSETS

4 Understand the concept of solvency, and identify the noncurrent elements of a firm's balance sheet.

Noncurrent assets are those resources whose benefits will be realized over more than one year or operating cycle. As depicted in Exhibit 3–2, investments; property, plant, and equipment; and intangible assets are the primary types of noncurrent assets.

Long-Term Investments. Long-term investments are typically securities of other corporations that management intends to hold for longer than one year. They may be the same general type of investments as those classified as temporary investments in the current assets section. The distinction for classification as current or noncurrent depends upon the intent of management with regard to their disposition. If management intends to hold them only temporarily, they are considered current assets. If management intends to hold them longer than one year, they are considered long-term assets.

Some investments in debt and equity securities that management intends to hold for longer than one year are classified as available for sale. Similar to short-term investments, these are also reported at fair value. Another classification category specified in SFAS No. 115 is *held to maturity* for debt securities investments. Since these investments are not intended for market trading, they are reported at amortized cost, not at fair value.

Investments in equity securities that provide significant influence over the policies of the investee (between 20% and 50% of the voting stock) are required to be accounted for under the equity method (see Chapter 9). Investments of greater than 50% of the voting stock require consolidated financial statements. Preparation of consolidated statements is the subject of advanced accounting courses and texts.

Property, Plant, and Equipment. Property, plant, and equipment (or fixed assets) represent a major resource commitment. These assets are recorded at cost upon purchase and remain on the books at historical cost. The original cost of plant and equipment is allocated or charged to expense over their expected useful life through depreciation charges. The carrying value, or book value, then becomes the historical cost less the accumulated depreciation recognized. Property, or land, is not depreciated.

While historical cost possesses the characteristic of reliability in that it is verifiable, it may lack representational faithfulness. The fair market value of the asset may be quite different from its book, or carrying, value. Assets purchased a number of years earlier and depreciated may have a book value significantly lower than the underlying economic value.

Intangible Assets. Intangible assets are resources with expected future economic benefits but lacking a physical substance. These include resources resulting from expenditures related to patents, franchises, goodwill, trademarks, copyrights, etc. Some costs incurred related to intangibles must be expensed immediately, while others are recognized as assets on the balance sheet.

LIABILITIES

Liabilities are classified as either current or long-term depending on their due date. Obligations due within one year or current operating cycle are classified as current, and obligations due thereafter are classified as long-term.

Current Liabilities. Current liabilities are those obligations expected to be settled through either the use of existing current assets or the creation of another current liability within the normal operating cycle or one year, whichever is longer. Obligations expected to be settled through some form of long-term financing arrangement are not classified as current obligations, even if their maturity date is within the year or operating cycle.

The major types of current liabilities are also depicted in Exhibit 3–2 and illustrated in Exhibit 3–1. Trade accounts payable are obligations arising from purchases of merchandise for resale. Both accrued expenses and unearned revenues were discussed in relation to adjusting entries in Chapter 2. Any portion of long-term debt maturing within the next period is classified as a current liability. Generally, current liabilities are reported at their **face value**—the full amount of the expected outflow of resources.

Long-Term Liabilities. Probable future sacrifices of economic benefits expected to occur subsequent to the next accounting period are termed **long-term liabilities**. Most are reported at the present (or discounted) value of their expected future cash outflows. For example, both leasehold obligations (for leased equipment) and bonds payable are reported at present value amounts. Deferred income taxes, in contrast, are reported at the full (undiscounted) face amount of anticipated future income tax payments.

Bonds payable, lease obligations, deferred income taxes, and other noncurrent liabilities are discussed in later chapters. They are briefly introduced here to highlight the significant valuation differences existing across accounts.

STOCKHOLDERS' EQUITY

Stockholders' (or shareholders') equity usually consists of contributed capital and retained earnings. **Contributed capital** includes investments made by stockholders for either preferred-stock shares or common-stock shares. The **par value** or **stated value** of the stock shares is the value set by the board of directors. The difference between the par or stated value and the issue price is typically reported in a separate account, such as Paid-In Capital in Excess of Par. **Retained earnings** represent the cumulative undistributed earnings of the business.

With this introduction to the structure and classification in the balance sheet, we now turn our attention to the different types of business entities and the ownership interest for each entity.

TYPES OF BUSINESS ENTITIES

Distinguish among the various forms of entities, and interpret the traditional presentation of stockholders' equity by source: contributed capital and retained earnings.

Exhibit 3–3 depicts the various types of entities. The ownership interests for proprietorships and partnerships are represented by capital accounts for each owner of the business. An owner's capital account is increased for contributions to the business and for the owner's share of periodic income. The account is decreased as distributions (that is, withdrawals) are made to the owner and for the owner's share of periodic losses. Exhibit 3–4 illustrates typical presentations of owners' equity for proprietorships and partnerships.

Today the corporate enterprise structure dominates the world of business. As Exhibit 3–3 depicts, there are many different types of corporations. However, some form of stock company is the most prevalent, and the most predominant of these is the private stock corporation. Private stock corporations report stockholders' (or shareholders') equity. The Motorola stockholders' equity presentation in Exhibit 3–1 is typical.

Exhibit 3–5 presents a balance sheet for ***Metropolitan Life Insurance Company***, a mutual company. (See *www.swcollege.com/hartman.html*) Since the policyholders are essentially the owners of this company, there are no stockholders and, thus, no stockholders' equity. Instead, the interest of the policy-

EXHIBIT 3–3
Various Types of Entities

I. PROPRIETORSHIPS—Enterprises with a single owner; typical of many small businesses; for a given business, a single equity account is maintained as the individual's ownership interests.
II. PARTNERSHIPS—Enterprises with multiple owners but which are not incorporated; typical of many small businesses and professional firms, such as public accounting firms and law firms; for a given partnership, separate equity accounts are generally maintained for each partner.
III. CORPORATIONS—Separate legal entities as established by applicable laws of incorporation; in the United States, a given company is incorporated in a single state and subject to that state's laws of incorporation.
   A. PRIVATE COMPANIES—Corporations privately owned by individuals or other institutions.
      1. STOCK COMPANIES—Profit organizations who issue shares of capital stock in exchange for certain contributions from shareholders.
         a. PUBLICLY HELD COMPANIES—Corporations whose stock is available for trade by the public and whose ownership is typically widespread; in the United States, publicly held corporations' stock and other securities are registered with the SEC, and these companies must report to and comply with the regulations of the SEC.
            i. LISTED COMPANIES—Corporations whose stock is actively traded on an organized stock exchange, such as the New York Stock Exchange (NYSE) and the American Stock Exchange (AMEX).
            ii. UNLISTED (OVER-THE-COUNTER) COMPANIES—Corporations whose stock is not traded on any organized stock exchange, but whose stock can still be bought and sold through registered securities dealers.
         b. CLOSELY HELD (NONPUBLIC) COMPANIES—Corporations with a limited numbers of shareholders whose stock is not available for purchase by the public; typical of many family-owned enterprises; a special type called a subchapter S corporation (as defined by the Internal Revenue Code) for tax purposes is treated as a partnership.
      2. NONSTOCK COMPANIES—Nonprofit organizations such as universities, charities, and churches
   B. PUBLIC COMPANIES—Corporations owned and established by governmental units; for example, the Federal Deposit Insurance Corporation (FDIC).
   C. MUTUAL COMPANIES—Corporations for whom its customers have ownership interests; for example, policy holders in many insurance companies and depositors in many savings and loan associations vote on corporate issues and receive profit distributions in such forms as reduced premiums or as dividends. These companies do not have shareholders' equity.

holders is reported as a surplus or reserve. Whatever terminology is employed, the residual interest represents the net assets of the business, similar to owners' equity for other forms of business. Also, mutual companies, like utilities, generally do not present assets in order of liquidity.

EXHIBIT 3–4
Typical Presentations of Proprietorship and Partnership Equity

Proprietorship Equity:

HERBIE'S SERVICE CENTER
Balance Sheet
December 31, 1997

Assets		Liabilities	
Cash	$ 2,000	Accounts payable	$10,000
Accounts receivable (net)	13,000	Notes payable	15,000
Fixed Assets (net)	35,000		$25,000
		Owners' Equity	
		Herb Jones, capital	$25,000
	$50,000		$50,000

Partnership Equity:

H & H SERVICE CENTER
Balance Sheet
December 31, 1997

Assets		Liabilities	
Cash	$ 2,000	Accounts payable	$10,000
Accounts receivable (net)	13,000	Notes payable	15,000
Fixed Assets (net)	35,000		$25,000
		Owners' Equity	
		Joan Hardin, capital	$14,000
		John Hind, capital	11,000
	$50,000		$50,000

CORPORATE FORM OF BUSINESS

The corporate form of business has several advantages over proprietorships and partnerships. These include:

1. the potential to accumulate large amounts of capital.
2. limited liability for the owners.
3. unlimited life and relative ease of transferability of ownership.

Perhaps the greatest single advantage is the ability of corporations to accumulate large amounts of capital for acquisition and maintenance of operating resources. Capital is accumulated through the issuance of stock and bonds to the public. A second major advantage is that because a corporation is a legal entity separate from its owners, the owners' liability for corporate obligations is generally limited to their investment in the stock of the corporation. A third is that the use of capital stock enables corporations to have an unlimited life, because ownership interests are transferred as shares of stock are traded or transferred. Shares of stock are personal property of the owners, who may trade the shares without consent of the corporation in most instances.

EXHIBIT 3–5
Example of Balance Sheet for Mutual Corporations

METROPOLITAN LIFE INSURANCE COMPANY
Balance Sheets

DECEMBER 31 (IN MILLIONS)	1995	1994
Assets		
Bonds	$ 70,955	$ 65,592
Stocks	3,646	3,672
Mortgage loans	14,211	14,524
Real estate	9,470	10,417
Policy loans	3,956	3,964
Cash and short-term investments	1,923	2,334
Other invested assets	2,480	2,262
Premiums deferred and uncollected	1,568	1,250
Investment income due and accrued	1,589	1,440
Separate account assets	31,707	25,424
Other assets	627	298
Total Assets	$142,132	$131,177
Liabilities		
Reserves for life and health insurance and annuities	$ 76,249	$ 73,204
Policy proceeds and dividends left with the company	4,482	3,534
Dividends due to policyholders	1,371	1,407
Premium deposit funds	12,891	14,006
Interest maintenance reserve	1,148	881
Other policy liabilities	3,882	3,364
Investment valuation reserves	1,860	1,981
Separate account liabilities	31,226	25,159
Other liabilities	2,459	1,337
Total Liabilities	$135,568	$124,873
Surplus		
Special contingency reserves	$ 754	$ 682
Surplus notes	1,400	700
General contingency reserves	4,410	4,922
Total Surplus	$ 6,564	$ 6,304
Total Liabilities and Surplus	$142,132	$131,177

There are also potential disadvantages of the corporate form of business:

1. Double taxation
2. Limited control by the owners
3. Additional regulatory and reporting requirements

Double taxation occurs because corporate earnings are subject to corporate income taxes. Distribution of corporate earnings to the owners in the form of dividends triggers income taxes for the owners on the dividends received.[6] Thus, corporate earnings are taxed twice. Proprietorships and partnerships do not incur taxes on earned income. Rather, tax on this income is paid exclusively by the owners.

Limited control occurs because shareholders delegate that control to the corporation's board of directors, and the board of directors further delegates control to the management of the corporation. Ideally, management, as agents of the owners, will operate and make decisions in the owners' interest. To encourage such behavior, management compensation programs often pay bonuses for achievement of certain goals. Where these goals are income-related (such as percentage increases in income), problems of income management may occur. Management has the ability to influence accounting practices of the firm without direct owner involvement. Management may select from acceptable reporting alternatives at times simply to achieve "desired" results, even if those results lack representational faithfulness and are not consistent with underlying economic reality. Standard setters, auditors, regulators, and users in general must be alert to such potential manipulation of financial results in analyzing financial performance. Thus, this limited-control feature of the corporate form has significant accounting ramifications.

Finally, most corporations are subject to a variety of regulatory and reporting requirements. For example, all stock corporations have certain regulations and restrictions regarding distributions to shareholders. Also, publicly held corporations in the United States must report to and comply with the regulations of the Securities and Exchange Commission (SEC).

ACCOUNTING FOR STOCKHOLDERS' INTERESTS

In many ways traditional accounting for stockholders' equity is based upon legal concepts as established by state law. Generally, state corporate laws include details about two important aspects of stockholders' equity: (1) minimum contributions from shareholders when issuing stock and (2) restrictions upon distributions to shareholders. Because of these two aspects, stockholders' equity usually is reported by source of capital as contributed or earned. Contributed capital is typically (but not necessarily) further subdivided into par or stated value and additional paid-in capital. Earned capital is reported as retained earnings. Motorola's balance sheet in Exhibit 3–1 portrays the traditional reporting of common stock at par, additional paid-in capital, and retained earnings.

The number of shares and the different classes of stock that a corporation is authorized to issue are established by its articles of incorporation. At a minimum, all stock corporations have common stock. As Exhibit 3–1 illustrates, common stock is the only class of stock issued by Motorola.

Par Value, Stated Value, and Legal Capital. When first authorized, shares of capital stock usually are assigned a par value. If no par value is assigned, the

[6]In the United States, an exception to corporate taxation applies to the earnings of a subchapter S corporation. Further, when one domestic corporation owns shares of stock in another domestic corporation, a large portion of earnings distributions from the latter corporation to the former corporation is generally not subject to corporate income taxes again by the former. Details regarding subchapter S corporations and dividend exclusions are beyond the scope of this chapter.

stock may be given a stated value. Some states have established legal capital as minimum equity, which is typically the par value of a corporation's stock. In those states, if the investor pays less than the legal capital amount (par or stated value), the investor may be required to pay the difference between the purchase price and full par value in case of financial difficulty. Further, a company may not make distributions to owners that would reduce shareholders' equity below its legal capital.

Thus, the traditional reporting distinction for contributed capital into an amount equivalent to par and an amount for additional paid-in capital at first appears useful in that legal capital is reported separately. In the current business environment, however, this distinction is probably artificial.

> In this century, almost all common stock issued with par value has been low par or nominal par stock—stock issued with a par value deliberately chosen well below any potential market price of the stock issuance.[7]

To illustrate nominal par values, ***Sierra On-Line,*** a computer software company based in California, reported as of March 31, 1990, common stock of $35,100 and paid-in capital of $13,539,700 as contributed capital for its 3.51 million shares of $0.01 par common stock. The par value is an insignificant and trivial amount of the total contributed capital.

Current standards do not require that contributed capital be reported separately as par or stated value amounts and additional paid-in capital amounts. For example, ***Walt Disney Company's*** (see *www.swcollege.com/hartman.html*) common stock has a $0.025 par (see Exhibit 3–6); yet, Disney reports contributed capital for 575.4 million shares as a single amount totaling $1,226.3 million as

EXHIBIT 3–6
Stockholders' Equity Without Additional Paid-In Capital

THE WALT DISNEY COMPANY AND SUBSIDIARIES
(Dollar amounts in millions)

SEPTEMBER 30	1995	1994
Shareholders' Equity		
Preferred stock, $0.10 par value		
Authorized—100.0 million shares		
Issued—none		
Common stock, $.025 par value		
Authorized—1.2 billion shares		
Issued—575.4 and 567.0 million shares	$1,226.3	$ 945.3
Retained earnings	6,990.4	5,790.3
Cumulative translation and other adjustments	37.3	59.1
	8,254.0	6,794.7
Less treasury stock, at cost—51.0 million shares and 42.9 million shares	1,603.2	1,286.4
	$6,650.8	$5,508.3

[7] P. McGough, "The Legal Significance of the Par Value of Common Stock: What Educators Should Know," *Issues in Accounting Education,* Fall 1988, pp. 330–331.

of September 30, 1995. If it reported at par, the $1,226.3 million would be split into common stock of $14.4 million and additional paid-in capital of $1,211.9 million. Even Sierra On-Line, as of March 31, 1995, started combining common stock and paid-in capital into a single reported amount of $70.1 million for its 18.7 million shares of $0.01 par stock.

Retained Earnings. Retained earnings generally represent a corporation's undistributed income since its inception. That is, retained earnings represents an accumulation of net earnings reduced by net losses and dividends. Just as current standards do not require the separation of par from additional paid-in capital, current standards also do not require reporting shareholders' equity by source. Some companies, therefore, do not distinguish between contributed capital and retained earnings on their balance sheets. Exhibit 3–7, for example, portrays a partial balance sheet for ***Minnesota Mining and Manufacturing Company (3M)*** (see *www.swcollege.com/hartman.html*). Notice that stockholders' equity is reported as a single amount without the traditional source classifications. These classifications, and changes to them, are typically reported in a separate statement of changes in shareholders' equity or disclosed in footnotes, as depicted for 3M in Exhibit 3–8.

Other Shareholders' Equity Accounts. Both Motorola (Exhibit 3–1) and Walt Disney (Exhibit 3–6) are authorized to issue preferred stock. Preferred stock has certain preferential rights relative to common stock, typically with regard to dividend distributions and resource distributions upon liquidation. In return,

EXHIBIT 3–7
Unclassified Stockholders' Equity

MINNESOTA MINING AND MANUFACTURING COMPANY AND SUBSIDIARIES (3M COMPANY)
Partial Consolidated Balance Sheet

AT DECEMBER 31 (DOLLARS IN MILLIONS)	1995	1994
LIABILITIES AND STOCKHOLDERS' EQUITY		
Current Liabilities		
Accounts payable	$ 762	$ 820
Payroll	298	279
Income taxes	214	110
Short-term debt	822	917
Other current liabilities	1,628	1,130
Total current liabilities	3,724	3,256
Other liabilities	2,372	2,047
Long-term debt	1,203	1,031
Stockholders' Equity—net	**6,884**	**6,734**
Shares outstanding—1995: 418,702,754; 1994: 419,793,702		
Total	$14,183	$13,068

EXHIBIT 3–8
Statement of Shareholders' Equity

MINNESOTA MINING AND MANUFACTURING COMPANY (3M)
Stockholders' Equity

Common stock, without par value, of 500,000,000 shares is authorized, with 472,016,528 shares issued in 1995, 1994 and 1993. Treasury shares at year-end totaled 53,313,774 in 1995, 52,222,826 in 1994 and 42,537,890 in 1993. This stock is reported at cost. Preferred stock, without par value, of 10,000,000 shares is authorized but unissued. All share and per-share data reflect a two-for-one common stock split effective March 15, 1994.

(DOLLARS IN MILLIONS)	COMMON STOCK	RETAINED EARNINGS	TRANSLATION AND FAIR VALUE ADJUSTMENTS	ESOP UNEARNED COMPENSATION	TREASURY STOCK	TOTAL
Balance, December 31, 1992	$296	$8,012	$(198)	$(498)	$(1,013)	$6,599
Net income		1,263				1,263
Dividends paid ($1.66 per share)		(721)				(721)
Reacquired stock (13,161,736 shares)					(706)	(706)
Issuances pursuant to stock option and benefit plans (4,572,274 shares)		(54)			245	191
Amortization of unearned compensation				19		19
Translation adjustments			(133)			(133)
Balance, December 31, 1993	$296	$8,500	$(331)	$(479)	$(1,474)	$6,512
Net income		1,322				1,322
Dividends paid ($1.76 per share)		(744)				(744)
Reacquired stock (13,136,376 shares)					(689)	(689)
Issuances pursuant to stock option and benefit plans (3,451,440 shares)		(39)			188	149
Amortization of unearned compensation				19		19
Translation and fair value adjustments			165			165
Balance, December 31, 1994	$296	$9,039	$(166)	$(460)	$(1,975)	$6,734
Net income		976				976
Dividends paid ($1.88 per share)		(790)				(790)
Reacquired stock (5,879,092 shares)					(351)	(351)
Issuances pursuant to stock option and benefit plans (4,788,144 shares)		(61)			273	212
Amortization of unearned compensation				23		23
Translation and fair value adjustments			80			80
Balance, December 31, 1995	$296	$9,164	$ (86)	$(437)	$(2,053)	$6,884

preferred shareholders usually have no voting rights in the management of the corporation.

Any issuance of preferred stock is recorded and reported in a manner similar to common stock. That is, corporations may use a separate classification for par (or stated) value and capital in excess of par or may record the proceeds in a single preferred stock account. Generally, separate accounts are reported for each class of stock, preferred and common.

For a variety of reasons, corporations may purchase their own stock in the open market. This is called treasury stock, and its cost is reported as a reduction of shareholders' equity. Walt Disney in Exhibit 3–6 illustrates typical reporting of treasury stock. Other accounts portray various forms of additional equity and reductions to equity (e.g., foreign currency translation and valuations adjustments, as shown for Walt Disney and 3M in Exhibits 3–6 and 3–8).

Changes in Stockholders' Equity. Changes to the stockholders' equity during a period can occur for a number of reasons. Each period, the firm will have income or loss, dividends may be declared, and additional stock may be issued. Additionally, treasury stock may be bought or sold, or a number of other events affecting stockholders' equity may take place. The effects of these events are summarized and reported in a separate statement called the statement of changes in stockholders' equity, or statement of shareholders' equity. An example appears in Exhibit 3–8 from the footnotes of 3M Company. The statement covers a three-year period from 1993 through 1995.

We next discuss how balance sheet information can be used for financial analysis. Potential investors and creditors look to the balance sheet for information related to liquidity and solvency.

USEFULNESS AND LIMITATIONS OF THE BALANCE SHEET

Identify uses and limitations of traditional balance sheets for financial analysis.

The balance sheet provides evidence about an enterprise's liquidity and solvency. Elements of a balance sheet may be compared for a given firm over a number of years or with competitors and industry averages. When an enterprise borrows funds, creditors frequently place restrictions in loan agreements or covenants that are based upon balance sheet relationships (for example, upper limits on the percent of debt to total assets).

FINANCIAL ANALYSIS

Several popular ratios facilitate analysis and comparison between firms. We present many of these popular ratios throughout this text. Further, elements of financial statements are frequently expressed in terms of changes or percentages. The use of ratios, changes, and percentages helps indicate trends over time or unusual conditions.

Working Capital and Liquidity. Working capital is usually defined as the excess of current assets over current liabilities:[8]

Working Capital = Current Assets − Current Liabilities

[8]Some professionals view current assets as working capital and current assets minus current liabilities as *net* working capital.

Working capital thus represents those current resources not required to meet current, existing obligations from which a business can draw to meet unexpected needs, opportunities, or contingencies.

At the end of 1995, Motorola's (see Exhibit 3–1) current assets ($10,510 million) exceeded its current liabilities ($7,793 million) by $2,717 million. Normally it is desirable for current operating cash inflows to at least cover current operating cash outflows. Working capital, the excess of current assets over current liabilities, provides a cushion if the timing of cash inflows and outflows do not precisely coincide. Note from the earlier presentation of the In Practice example for British Petroleum Company that balance sheets in the United Kingdom typically portray net current assets (or working capital).

Thus, the current assets and current liabilities of an enterprise provide an indication of its liquidity, or ability to pay current debt and continue to operate. A frequently used indicator of liquidity is the current ratio (sometimes called the *working capital ratio*), which is the ratio of current assets to current liabilities:

$$\text{Current Ratio} = \frac{\text{Current Assets}}{\text{Current Liabilities}}$$

Motorola's current ratio at the end of 1995 is 1.35 (10,510/7,793). Any ratio greater than 1.00 indicates positive working capital, or current assets in excess of current liabilities.

For a ratio to be useful, there must be a standard for comparison. Comparison may be made to ratios from previous periods, to ratios for competitors or other firms, to industry averages, or to some benchmark or targeted ratio. A common rule of thumb used by some analysts is approximately 2.0 as a "desirable" current ratio, but caution is advised in relying too heavily on such rules of thumb. Each industry is different in terms of its liquidity requirements. For example, the median current ratio for manufacturers of electronic components and accessories is 1.8. This contrasts sharply with the median of 2.6 for manufacturers of aircraft engines and engine parts, and with 0.8 for motion picture theaters.[9]

The current ratio is only a snapshot of liquidity at the point in time when the balance sheet is prepared. Obligations are incurred continuously, so cash must be generated from operations, not only to pay existing obligations but to pay future operating-cycle obligations as well. For this reason, one should not place too much emphasis on the current ratio to reflect a firm's liquidity. Any indicator of liquidity is best used in conjunction with some expectation of future net cash flows from operating activities.

Noncurrent Components and Solvency. Solvency refers to the long-term financial status of an enterprise. It requires that a company be able to meet its long-term obligations as well as its current obligations. A company whose financial obligations (liabilities) exceed its financial resources (assets) is considered insolvent.[10]

[9]As reported by Robert Morris Associates (1993).

[10]A strict legal definition of insolvency depends upon state corporate law. In some states, insolvency occurs when a company's assets are less than the sum of its liabilities and legal capital. In others, insolvency results when a company's assets are less than its liabilities; and in some cases, current market values rather than book values may provide the basis for this valuation. See the section on the corporate form of business in this chapter and the chapter on distributions to shareholders.

Noncurrent components of an enterprise's financial condition are critical elements in its continued ability to meet obligations and remain profitable. Noncurrent assets portray the mix of long-term commitments for resources devoted to continued operations. Noncurrent liabilities depict the financial obligations that must be met in the future.

One useful indicator of solvency is the proportion of resources financed by liabilities. A frequently used solvency indicator is the debt ratio, the proportion of total liabilities to total assets.

$$\text{Debt Ratio} = \frac{\text{Total Liabilities}}{\text{Total Assets}}$$

Motorola's (Exhibit 3–1) 1995 year-end total liabilities are $11,753 million ($7,793 + $1,949 + $968 + $1,043), resulting in a debt ratio of 51.5% (11,753/22,801). As with the current ratio, judgment is required to interpret the debt ratio. Experts generally agree that financing some proportion of assets with liabilities is sound economic business practice, but just how much debt to incur is debatable. Some basis for comparison, such as previous periods' ratios, industry averages, or some targeted benchmark, is important in making any judgment regarding a company's solvency as reflected in the debt ratio. For example, manufacturers of electronic components have a median debt ratio of 56.5%, compared to the medians of 44.4% for manufacturers of aircraft engines and engine parts and of 69.7% for motion picture theaters.[11]

Some analysts use a debt-to-equity ratio, which is total liabilities divided by owners' equity. The two ratios are interchangeable. For example, a debt ratio of 0.5 (50%) is the same as debt-to-equity of 1.00—a situation where total liabilities equal owners' equity.

Part 4 of this text addresses solvency concerns and focuses upon noncurrent components of an enterprise's financial condition. Many of the more controversial issues in accounting concern these noncurrent components.

Horizontal Analysis. One method of analysis is based on changes or percentage changes in accounts or account classifications over time. For example, Exhibit 3–9 illustrates the changes in the balance sheet accounts of Sound Financial Enterprises. The beginning reported value (the end of the prior-period balance) represents the base, or denominator, for determining the percentage changes. Analysis based upon account increases and decreases is called horizontal analysis.

Vertical Analysis. Another analysis technique is to express accounts or categories as a percentage of some total or base. Balance sheet amounts can be expressed as percentages of total assets. Exhibit 3–10 presents percentages of total assets on the balance sheets for Sound Financial Enterprises. Income statement items are frequently expressed as percentages of net sales revenue. Elements expressed in this form are often called common-size financial statements information; analysis based upon these percentages is known as vertical analysis.

[11]Based upon reported debt-worth ratios by Robert Morris Associates (1993).

SOUND FINANCIAL ENTERPRISES
Balance Sheet
(Dollar Amounts in Thousands)

	12/31/97	12/31/96	INCREASE (DECREASE)	PERCENT INCREASE (DECREASE)
Assets				
Current assets:				
Cash	$ 500	$ 525	$ (25)	(4.8)%
Accounts receivable (net)	1,280	1,200	80	6.7%
Inventory	6,000	5,670	330	5.8%
Other current assets	720	605	115	19.0%
	$ 8,500	$ 8,000	$500	6.3%
Property, plant, and equipment (net)	5,000	4,910	90	1.8%
Other assets	650	290	360	124.1%
Total Assets	$14,150	$13,200	$950	7.2%
Liabilities				
Current liabilities:				
Accounts payable	$ 3,000	$ 2,350	$650	27.7%
Current maturing portion of long-term debt	800	1,050	(250)	(23.8)%
	$ 3,800	$ 3,400	$400	11.8%
Mortgages payable	1,800	2,000	(200)	(10.0)%
	$ 5,600	$ 5,400	$200	3.7%
Shareholders' Equity				
Common stock	$ 4,000	$ 4,000	$ 0	0.0%
Retained earnings	4,550	3,800	750	19.7%
	$ 8,550	$ 7,800	$750	9.6%
Total Liabilities and Shareholders Equity	$14,150	$13,200	$950	7.2%

EXHIBIT 3–9
Horizontal Analysis

Ratio analysis is a convenient and widely used tool for evaluating complex financial information. Earlier in the chapter, two ratios were introduced, the current ratio and the debt ratio. While potentially valuable, caution is advised regarding ratio analysis. First, meaningful comparison among firms may be hindered for a variety of reasons. Firms from different industries can face different economic factors influencing ratio values. Therefore, differences from average industry ratios may be more meaningful than raw ratios. Even firms within the same industry may use different accounting techniques, such as the use of different cost-flow assumptions for valuing inventory. Thus, ratio differences can be due to alternative values from different accounting techniques rather than different economic factors.

Second, ratios should not be the only means of financial evaluation, and decisions should not be based upon any one single financial indicator. All ratios should be used in concert with other indicators of financial status and performance.

EXHIBIT 3–10
Common-Size Statements and Vertical Analysis

SOUND FINANCIAL ENTERPRISES
Balance Sheet
(Dollar Amounts in Thousands)

	12/31/97		12/31/96	
Assets				
Current assets:				
Cash	$ 500	3.5%	$ 525	4.0%
Accounts receivable (net)	1,280	9.0%	1,200	9.1%
Inventory	6,000	42.4%	5,670	43.0%
Other current assets	720	5.1%	605	4.6%
	$ 8,500	60.1%	$ 8,000	60.6%
Property, plant, and equipment (net)	5,000	35.3%	4,910	37.2%
Other assets	650	4.6%	290	2.2%
Total Assets	$14,150	100.0%	$13,200	100.0%
Liabilities				
Current liabilities:				
Accounts payable	$ 3,000	21.2%	$ 2,350	17.8%
Current maturing portion of long-term debt	800	5.7%	1,050	8.0%
	$ 3,800	26.9%	$ 3,400	25.8%
Mortgages payable	1,800	12.7%	2,000	15.2%
	$ 5,600	39.6%	$ 5,400	40.9%
Shareholders' Equity				
Common stock	$ 4,000	28.3%	$ 4,000	30.3%
Retained earnings	4,550	32.2%	3,800	28.8%
	$ 8,550	60.4%	$ 7,800	59.1%
Total Liabilities and Shareholders' Equity	$14,150	100.0%	$13,200	100.0%

SUPPLEMENTAL NOTES AND DISCLOSURES

A complete set of financial statements includes a set of accompanying notes and disclosures. These provide information pertaining to significant accounting policies and other factors to assist in interpretation of the statements. For example, a corporation's annual report contains a summary of significant accounting policies. Other notes describe pertinent information about long-term debt, outstanding classes of capital stock, long-term assets, and depreciation. Also included are commitments and contingencies, post-employment benefits, deferred taxes, and post-balance sheet events. An unresolved debate among professionals involves footnote disclosure versus recognition in actual financial statements. Some argue that disclosure cannot be used as a replacement for recognition; others argue that as long as information is provided to users in disclosure, recognition is not always necessary. Regardless, any meaningful analysis of a balance sheet, or any other financial statement, should include a study of these supplemental disclosures.

Loss Contingencies. Loss contingencies are potential future obligations that can be either short-term or long-term. Because their outcomes are uncertain, recognition and valuation of these items requires discretion and judgment. The general rules for recognition state that if the outcome is a probable loss and the amount of the loss can be reasonably estimated, the loss and related liability should be recorded at the estimated amount. If the loss is deemed possible but not probable, it must be disclosed in the notes to the financial statements. If the loss is only remotely possible, no action is required. Loss contingencies are a prime example of the conservatism convention. Gain contingencies, continuing with a conservative approach to accounting, are not recognized in financial statements.

Subsequent Events. Several months often elapse between the end of the reporting period and the date the financial statements are issued. The delay between the reporting date and issue date is caused by compilation of the data, audit procedures, and printing of the annual report. Events occurring during this period that are not part of the normal operating activities of the enterprise are referred to as subsequent events. They can be of two types: (1) those events originating prior to the statement date and resolved during the subsequent period and (2) those events originating during the subsequent period. Visually, they are as shown in Exhibit 3–11.

Type 1 subsequent events require adjustment of the financial statements. These events originate in the period for which the statements are prepared and are resolved prior to their issuance. Therefore, the financial statements for that period must reflect the effects of these events. For example, a loss contingency such as a lawsuit may originate during the 1997 fiscal year. As of the closing date, December 31, 1997, the outcome may be uncertain. Prior to the issuance of financial statements, however, either the case might be settled or enough information may become available to estimate the probable loss. If so, the loss and related liability should be reflected in the 1997 financial statements.

Type 2 subsequent events require disclosure in the notes to the statements. These events originate after the closing date but will affect future financial statements: thus, disclosure in the notes is warranted. For example, because a stock or bond issuance during this period will materially affect future financial statements, it must be disclosed in the notes.

EXHIBIT 3–11
Two Types of Subsequent Events

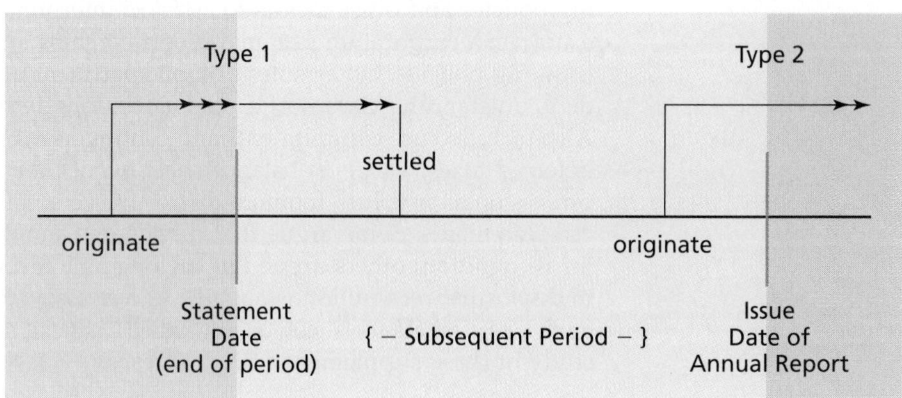

Some events require no disclosure at all, namely, those related to general business conditions, such as strikes, competitor product developments, and others of similar nature.

Limitations. The balance sheet does not reflect all the resources and obligations of an enterprise. For example, a company's human capital, both management and its work force, provide expected future benefits, but these are not reported as assets on the balance sheet. Controversy continues as to which transactions and events should be recognized as assets. This dilemma is highlighted in a recent American Accounting Association report:

> The most general criticism to be leveled at financial statements in their present form is that they are seriously *incomplete.*[12]

The committee cites internally generated intangibles as examples of omission. Internally generated goodwill and benefits resulting from research and development activities are not recognized as assets.[13] Both the introductory vignette at the beginning of this chapter and the "In Practice" feature here elaborate on the incompleteness of financial statements.

IN PRACTICE—GENERAL

Commentary—Financial Statements Are Incomplete

One respect in which financial statements are now incomplete is that, because they are substantially transaction-based, they fail to recognize some value changes occurring during a period that are not associated with a transaction. . . . If relative price changes between the time that resources are acquired and the balance sheet date (assuming that they have not already been sold), the value of resources to the enterprise is misrepresented if they continue to be carried at historical cost. . . . The problem is exacerbated if the general level of prices is also changing. For these reasons the balance sheet has little claim to being a statement of financial position at the accounting date. It does not realistically represent the resources employed in the business. Even its name is obsolete.

Source: M. Barrett, W. Beaver, W. Cooper, J. Milburn, D. Solomons, D. Tweedle, "American Accounting Association Committee on Accounting and Auditing Measurement, 1989–90," *Accounting Horizons,* September 1991, pp. 83 and 92.

Even when the results of past transactions and events are included in a balance sheet, the prospective nature of accounting complicates the decision on what amounts should be reported regarding these results. For example, the current practice of reporting fixed assets based upon their historical cost and allocation of cost through depreciation is frequently criticized. Many critics propose instead the use of some form of market price or current value. The "In Practice" feature discusses the richness of market values.

[12]M. Barrett, W. Beaver, W. Cooper, J. Milburn, D. Solomons, D. Tweedle, "American Accounting Association Committee on Accounting and Auditing Measurement, 1989–90," *Accounting Horizons,* September 1991, p. 83.
[13]Ibid., pp. 83–89.

IN PRACTICE—GENERAL

Commentary on Market Prices

The market prices of assets and liabilities potentially capture the multidimensional features of future events. Market prices reflect the market's assessment of the uncertain nature of future events and an assessment of the time value of money. . . .

Other than market values, no other measure is viewed conceptually as being rich enough to collapse the multidimensional aspects of future cash flows into a single number. Once market values are discarded, the conceptual basis for other measures of performance is unclear. From this perspective, the accrual process can be viewed as a system for reflecting future benefits and sacrifices when the market price data are not used to perform this role. Ambiguities arise in this system because there is not a unique, conceptually defensible method for reducing uncertain future cash flows into a single number.

Source: W. Beaver, "Problems and Paradoxes in the Financial Reporting of Future Events," *Accounting Horizons,* December 1991, pp. 128–9.

Authorities opposed to reporting assets based on some form of market value argue that such treatment would recognize gains from asset appreciation before they are realized. They also contend that many market values are not verifiable and are thus unreliable. The opportunity for income manipulation is reduced by use of objective and verifiable (historical cost) figures for valuation.

SFAS No. 115 recently required reporting of some investments at fair value. Many reported current assets and current liabilities are approximately equal to their respective market values. Thus, working capital and liquidity analysis based upon reported current assets and liabilities are reasonable reflections of existing financial conditions. As the time horizon broadens, however, uncertainty related to noncurrent elements can increase dramatically, and economic conditions can be radically altered. Thus, reported amounts for these noncurrent components of financial condition are less closely aligned with market values than are current ones.

END-OF-CHAPTER REVIEW

SUMMARY

1. **Interpret the conceptual basis for the balance sheet and its components: assets, liabilities, and owners' equity.** To provide information useful for decision making, the balance sheet presents the assets, liabilities, and owners' equity of an enterprise. From a prospective view, assets and liabilities are perceived as future economic benefits and sacrifices. Owners' equity is the residual interest in the enterprise's net assets.
2. **Recognize the various formats and typical account classifications for the balance sheet.** A balance sheet may be presented in various forms. Classified balance sheets subdivide assets and liabilities into classifications, primarily current and noncurrent

components. In the United States, accounts typically are presented in order of liquidity.

3. **Understand the concept of liquidity, and identify the elements of current assets and current liabilities that comprise an enterprise's working capital.** The current components provide an indication of an enterprise's liquidity—that is, its ability to meet upcoming cash obligations and continue to operate. Working capital is the excess of current assets over current liabilities, and the current ratio is the proportion of current assets to current liabilities. Working capital and the current ratio provide an indication of liquidity but should be used in concert with other measures of financial analysis.
4. **Understand the concept of solvency, and identify the noncurrent elements of a firm's balance sheet.** Noncurrent components of a balance sheet assist in appraising a company's solvency, or long-term financial status. A debt ratio indicates the proportion of an enterprise's resources financed by incurring liabilities. Noncurrent assets provide an indication of resources devoted to continuing operations, and long-term liabilities indicate obligations that must be met in the distant future.
5. **Distinguish among the various forms of entities, and interpret the traditional presentation of stockholders' equity by source: contributed capital and retained earnings.** There are multiple ownership formats for various entities, the stock corporation being the most predominant. Stock corporations report stockholders' or shareholders' equity. The traditional reporting of stockholders' equity is based upon a fading concept of legal capital; subdividing contributed capital into par and additional paid-in capital has little relevance. Reporting equity based upon the relative claims of the various stakeholders is more relevant to sound financial analysis.
6. **Identify uses and limitations of traditional balance sheets for financial analysis.** The balance sheet is useful in assessing the liquidity and solvency of an enterprise. Contractual agreements may be based upon maintenance of certain relationships among balance sheet accounts (e.g., minimal current ratios and limits upon the proportion of current debt to total debt). Several popular ratios used for financial analysis are based upon reported balance sheet components.

   Yet the balance sheet does not portray all of a firm's resources and obligations expected to provide economic benefits and sacrifices. And even for those elements recognized and reported on a balance sheet, reported valuations can be difficult and controversial. Uncertainty associated with the prospective nature of accrual accounting creates such difficulties.

KEY TERMS

ASSIGNMENT MATERIAL

CASES

C3–1 Corporate Form of Business, Report Preparation

Assume that you are a key employee for a proprietor that has been very successful in recent years with the business essentially outgrowing itself. The proprietor is asking your opinion about incorporating.

Required: Prepare a report for the proprietor addressing the following issues:

A. What are the advantages and disadvantages of incorporation?

B. If incorporated, what advantages are there of going public?

C3–2 Reporting by Source of Equity

This graph portrays, for ***Walt Disney*** and ***Sierra On-Line***, proportions of contributed capital and retained earnings in shareholders' equity. How would you interpret this graph? Do you feel reporting by source, which is criticized by some professionals, has any usefulness? Support your view.

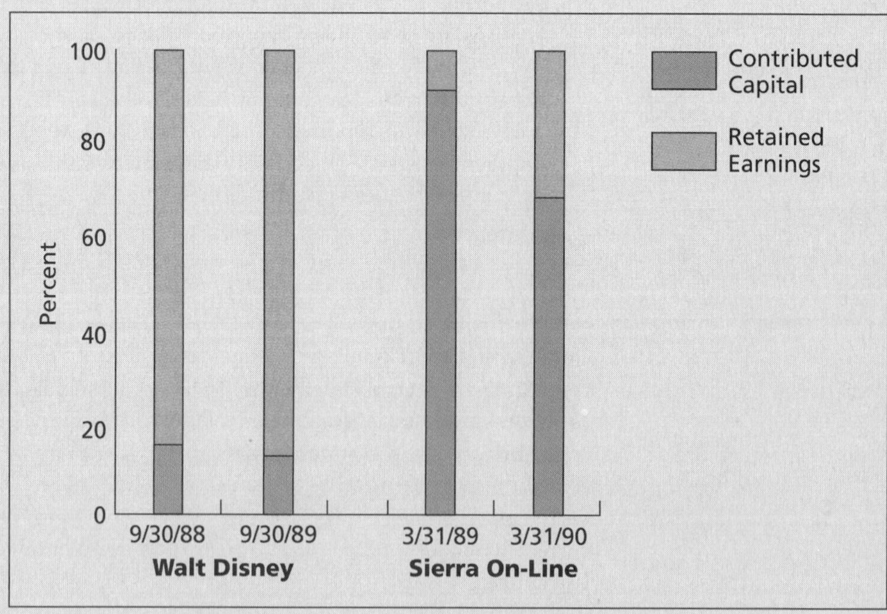

C3–3 Subsequent Events, Judgment, and Ethics

Assume that during December 1997 *The Wall Street Journal* reported a story about the financial difficulties of Stormy Weather, Inc., a customer of your firm with receivables amounting to $25,000. In the normal course of preparing adjusting entries, you are still uncertain (and hopeful) regarding the collection of these receivables. Thus, the receivables are maintained on your books and not written off. Then, late in January 1998, subsequent to the balance sheet date of December 31, 1997, but before the 1997 financial statements have been issued, you find that Stormy Weather, Inc., has declared bankruptcy. After some inquiries, you become certain that your firm will not be able to collect any of these receivables.

Required:

A. What is the proper accounting treatment for the 1997 annual report currently being prepared regarding these receivables?
B. Would there be any temptation to overlook this new information? What harm is there, if any, to overlooking it?

C3–4 Current Values and Ethics

Criticisms are noted in this chapter regarding the use of historical cost as a basis for reporting most fixed assets. For example, the citation below from ***Hilton Hotels'*** 1988 annual report regarding the Waldorf-Astoria illustrates that historical costs can bear little relation to current expected benefits. Thus, many professionals advocate the use of some form of current market value for reporting fixed assets.

> There are several ways to define value. We provide three measures in this report. The first, "stockholder's equity per share," gives the book or historical accounting basis for our assets. . . . The deficiencies of stockholder's equity per share are apparent. For a hotel such as the Waldorf-Astoria that was acquired many years ago, the historical accounting basis bears little relationship to its value today. Therefore, since 1976 we also have presented supplementary information on the current value of our assets and liabilities. . . . A third measure of value is reflected in the public securities markets. . . . The distortion of historical cost has never been more evident than today.

Assume that GAAP permitted the use of current market values for reporting fixed assets and that the company employing you as an internal auditor hires independent appraisers to estimate the current values for your firm's sizable real estate holdings. It is upper management's responsibility to select these appraisers.

Required:

A. If real estate values have significantly increased resulting in substantial appreciation, how would you recommend reporting this appreciation?
B. What incentives does upper management likely have to report these assets at higher amounts, perhaps even higher than true market values?
C. What problems could you expect regarding the use of "independent" appraisers?
D. Would you think that purposefully hiring appraisers who historically appraise property higher than other appraisers violates ethical standards?
E. Do you think auditors' functions should include examination of appraisers' independence and quality of judgments?

C3–5 Balance Sheet Interpretation

Assume that you are explaining the balance sheet shown here to a new manager with no accounting background.

YOUR COMPANY
Balance Sheet
December 31, 1997

Assets		Liabilities	
Cash	$ 50,000	Accounts payable	$ 75,000
Accounts receivable (net)	90,000	Notes payable	100,000
Inventory	110,000		$175,000
Fixed assets (net)	300,000		
Other assets	50,000	**Shareholders' Equity**	
		Common stock, $1 par	$ 50,000
		Paid-in capital	300,000
		Retained earnings	75,000
			$425,000
	$600,000		$600,000

You explain that the balance sheet portrays the company's financial resources and how the resources were financed. The manager says, "So the company received $50,000 when it issued its stock?" You respond that the company actually received resources totaling $350,000 when common stock was issued. The manager then asks, "What resources were acquired or financed by the $350,000 stock issuance?"

Required: Answer the manager's question and explain your answer.

C3–6 Balance Sheet Amounts—The Appearance of Certainty

Based on the following excerpt, discuss the validity and implications regarding the usefulness of the balance sheet. Are there alternative financial statement formats that could perhaps alleviate the appearance of certainty?

> Given that the current financial statement format essentially assigns a single number to each account, there will be some degree of arbitrariness in selecting that number. A *major feature of current financial reporting is that it is accounting for assets and liabilities with uncertain future benefits and sacrifices in terms of a format that is very deterministic in appearance.* . . . [A] single number creates the appearance of certainty when it does not exist. [W. Beaver, "Problems and Paradoxes in the Financial Reporting of Future Events," *Accounting Horizons,* December 1991, p. 126.]

C3–7 The Statement of Financial Position

Discuss the validity and relevance of using the statement of financial position as an alternative name for the balance sheet. In your discussion, consider the commentaries located in the opening vignette, Balance Sheets in Today's Economy, and in the two In Practice features of the limitations section of this chapter: Commentary—Financial Statements are Incomplete and Commentary on Market Values.

QUESTIONS

Q3–1 A stated objective of financial reporting is to provide information about enterprise resources, claims to those resources, and changes in those resources. Which of these is depicted in an enterprise's balance sheet?

Q3–2 Consider the perspectives that (1) the balance sheet summarizes the aggregate effect on an enterprise of *past* transactions and events and (2) it portrays expected *future* benefits and sacrifices. Can a balance sheet conceptually fit both perspectives or are these competing and mutually exclusive?

Q3–3 What is meant by the contention that accounting information serves a prospective, or future-oriented, purpose?

Q3–4 What are comparative financial statements?

Q3–5 What criterion is used to determine the order of presentation for accounts in a balance sheet? How is this order changed in many European countries?

Q3–6 What is working capital, and, conceptually, what does it portray?

Q3–7 With respect to financial analysis, distinguish between the concepts of liquidity and solvency.

Q3–8 What is meant by the net assets of an enterprise? What are some other terms used synonymously with net assets?

Q3–9 Distinguish between the use of "capital" in the following statements.

1. How much capital stock does XYZ Corporation have?
2. To pay for this venture, we would have to raise some capital.
3. What is the capital structure of XYZ Corporation?
4. For GAAP, some expenditures may be capitalized and others may not.
5. The automotive industry is a highly capital-intensive industry.

Q3–10 Distinguish among reporting the owners' equity for proprietorships, partnerships, mutual corporations, and stock corporations.

Q3–11 What are the predominant distinctions for sources of capital by shareholders?

Q3–12 What features make the existence of par value for common stock of little significance in today's corporate world?

Q3–13 Differentiate horizontal analysis from vertical analysis.

Q3–14 What are common size financial statements, and how might they prove useful for financial analysis?

Q3–15 What are some of the criticisms leveled at the current reporting requirements of the balance sheet? How is the effectiveness of the balance sheet limited if these criticisms are valid?

EXERCISES

E3–1 Balance Sheet Classifications

Major balance sheet classifications are as follows:

- **A.** Current assets
- **B.** Investments
- **C.** Property, plant, and equipment
- **D.** Intangible assets
- **E.** Other assets
- **F.** Current liabilities
- **G.** Long term liabilities
- **H.** Stockholders' equity—contributed capital
- **I.** Stockholders' equity—retained earnings

For each of the following items, indicate the letter code associated with the category in which that item would traditionally be classified on a balance sheet. Use a code of "X" for any items that would not appear on a balance sheet. Place parentheses () around contra accounts.

1. Merchandise inventory
2. Capital in excess of par
3. Supplies
4. Bonds payable
5. Building
6. Purchases
7. Trade accounts payable
8. Advances from customers
9. Deposits advanced to a vendor
10. Land
11. Prepaid insurance
12. Dividends payable
13. Dividends paid
14. Unamortized bond discount
15. Real estate property (by a realty company)
16. Patents
17. Allowance for bad debts
18. Stock investment to be sold in two months
19. Ownership interest in a subsidiary
20. Amortization of goodwill
21. Checking account balance
22. Short-term loans to employees
23. A 90-day note payable
24. Deferred revenue
25. Sales returns and allowances
26. Income taxes payable
27. Deferred income taxes
28. Marketable securities
29. Federal income taxes withheld for employees
30. Goodwill

E3–2 Balance Sheet Classifications

Major balance sheet classifications are as follows:

A. Current assets
B. Investments
C. Property, plant, and equipment
D. Intangible assets
E. Other assets
F. Current liabilities
G. Long-term liabilities
H. Stockholders' equity—contributed capital
I. Stockholders' equity—retained earnings

For each of the following items, indicate the letter code associated with the category in which that item would traditionally be classified on a balance sheet. Use a code of "X" for any items that would not appear on a balance sheet. Place parentheses () around contra accounts.

1. Marketable securities
2. Preferred stock
3. Discount on bonds payable
4. Purchase discounts
5. Franchises
6. Cost of goods sold
7. Current maturing portion of long-term debt
8. Advances to employees
9. Unearned rent revenue
10. Unexpired insurance
11. Magazine subscriptions collected in advance
12. Amortization of patents
13. Bonds payable
14. Investment in bonds
15. Certificates of deposit
16. Income tax refund due
17. Accumulated depreciation
18. Depreciation
19. Withdrawals for a proprietorship
20. Sales returns and allowances
21. Equipment
22. Prepaid advertising
23. Donated capital
24. Leasehold improvements
25. Research & development costs
26. Treasury stock
27. Organizational costs
28. Consignments from suppliers
29. Deferred gross profit
30. Cash surrender value of life insurance

E3–3 Asset Classifications

Rogo Corporation's trial balance reflected the account balances shown here in alphabetical order at December 31, 1997:

Accounts Receivable (net)	$ 80,000
Accumulated Depreciation	75,000
Cash	55,000
Equipment and Furniture	125,000
Land	90,000
Merchandise Inventory	150,000
Patent	20,000
Prepaid Expenses	5,000
Trading Securities	25,000

Required: Prepare the asset section of a balance sheet for Rogo using a classified balance sheet format. (AICPA adapted, Accounting Practice—Part I, MC#1, May 1989.)

E3–4 Asset Classifications

Pocket Corporation's trial balance reflected the following account balances, shown here in alphabetical order, at December 31, 1997:

Accounts Receivable	$ 210,000
Accumulated Depreciation	175,000
Allowance for Bad Debts	4,200
Cash	110,000
Goodwill	200,000
Inventory	450,000
Machinery	1,375,000
Trading Securities	165,000
Prepaid Advertising	10,000
Retained Earnings	440,000
Unearned Rent Revenue	220,000
Unexpired Insurance	40,000

Required: Prepare Pocket's asset section using a classified balance sheet format.

E3–5 Current Liabilities

Kelly Corporation's trial balance reflected the credit balances shown here in alphabetical order at December 31, 1997. For the notes payable, $500,000 in principal, plus interest, must be paid every June 30. The bonds mature in the year 2000.

Accounts Payable	$ 250,000
Accumulated Depreciation	1,000,000
Additional Paid-In Capital	30,000,000
Allowance for Doubtful Accounts	180,000
Bonds Payable	8,000,000
Common Stock	12,500,000
Interest Payable	160,000
Notes Payable	4,000,000
Purchase Returns and Allowances	350,000
Rent Revenue	1,200,000
Retained Earnings	9,000,000
Sales Revenue	99,999,999
Unearned Rent Revenue	120,000

Required: Prepare the current liabilities section of the balance sheet for Kelly Corporation at December 31, 1997.

E3–6 Liabilities and Shareholders' Equity

Robin Corporation's trial balance reflected the credit balances shown here in alphabetical order at December 31, 1997. Interest and principal for the note are to be paid in 1998. The bonds mature in the year 2010.

Accounts Payable	$ 500,000
Accumulated Depreciation	750,000
Allowance for Doubtful Accounts	80,000
Bonds Payable	5,000,000
Capital in Excess of Par	4,000,000
Common Stock	20,000,000
Consulting Fees	1,200,000
Interest Payable	60,000
Notes Payable (short-term)	600,000
Purchase Discounts	50,000
Retained Earnings (1/1/97)	2,000,000
Sales Revenue	9,999,999
Unearned Rent Revenue	320,000

Required: Reported net income for 1997 was $4,000,000, and no dividends were declared or paid. Prepare the liabilities and stockholders' equity sections of a balance sheet for Robin Corporation at December 31, 1997.

E3–7 Balance Sheet Classifications and Preparation

Below is the adjusted trial balance of Shaw Corporation at December 31, 1997:

SHAW CORPORATION
Trial Balance
December 31, 1997

	DEBITS	CREDITS
Cash	$ 675,000	
Accounts Receivable (net)	2,695,000	
Inventory	2,185,000	
Fixed Assets (Net)	7,366,000	
Accounts Payable and Accrued Liabilities		$ 1,801,000
Income Tax Payable		654,000
Deferred Income Tax Payable		85,000
Common Stock		2,300,000
Additional Paid-In Capital		3,680,000
Retained Earnings, 1/1/97		3,350,000
Net Sales and Other Revenues		13,360,000
Costs and Expenses	11,180,000	
Income Tax Expense	1,129,000	
	$25,230,000	$25,230,000

Required:

A. Determine the following amounts for Shaw as of December 31, 1997:
   1. Current assets
   2. Current liabilities
   3. Working capital
   4. Retained earnings (12/31/97)
   5. Current ratio
   6. Debt ratio

B. Prepare an unclassified balance sheet for Shaw as of December 31, 1997. (AICPA adapted, Accounting Practice—Part I, MC#2, 3, 4, May 1989.)

E3–8 Balance Sheet Classifications and Preparation

The following is the adjusted trial balance of Straw Corporation at December 31, 1997:

STRAW CORPORATION
Trial Balance
December 31, 1997

	DEBITS	CREDITS
Cash	$ 3,375,000	
Accounts Receivable	13,475,000	
Allowance for Bad Debts		$ 800,000
Inventory	10,925,000	
Plant, Property, and Equipment	36,830,000	
Accumulated Depreciation		6,000,000
Accounts Payable		9,000,000
Unearned Revenue		430,000
Bonds Payable		3,270,000
Common Stock		11,500,000
Retained Earnings, 1/1/97		35,150,000
Sales Revenue		60,000,000
Cost of Goods Sold	55,900,000	
Other Expenses	5,645,000	
	$126,150,000	$126,150,000

Required:

A. Determine the following amounts for Straw as of December 31, 1997:
   1. Current assets
   2. Current liabilities
   3. Working capital
   4. Retained earnings (12/31/97)
   5. Current ratio
   6. Debt ratio

B. Prepare an unclassified balance sheet for Straw as of December 31, 1997.

E3–9 Horizontal Analysis

For this exercise, refer to the exhibit in the chapter for Motorola, Inc. (Exhibit 3–1).

Required:

A. Determine the change and the percentage change in each account and category in the balance sheet.
B. Identify the account with the largest change for the year.
C. Identify the account with the largest percentage change for the year.
D. What do you think are the most significant changes, if any, for the year? Why?

E3–10 Vertical Analysis

For this exercise, refer to the exhibit in the chapter for Motorola, Inc. (Exhibit 3–1).

Required:

A. For each date portrayed, prepare common-size balance sheets based upon total assets.
B. From the common size information, summarize what you think are important proportions.

E3–11 Financial Analysis

For this exercise, refer to Exhibit 3–5 for Metropolitan Life Insurance company.

Required:

A. Determine the debt ratio for each date.
B. How do these ratios compare with those of the previous exercise? What factors justify the extreme nature of these ratios?
C. Notice that the first liability depicted is a reserve for anticipated obligations to make ultimate payments to policyholders. Since policyholders are essentially the "owners" of a mutual company, could this reserve be considered owners' equity instead of a liability?
D. If we assume that this reserve is owners' equity, determine what the debt ratio would be for each date.

E3–12 True or False?

1. In the United States, GAAP requires that all assets be measured at their historical cost.
2. Par value is an important indicator of firm performance over the life of the corporation.
3. Treasury stock is voting common stock held by a parent corporation in a subsidiary corporation.
4. Dividends and interest are "costs of capital" and are thus reported as expenses in the income statement.
5. The balance sheet is instrumental in assessing a firm's solvency, liquidity, and financial flexibility.

E3–13 Multiple Choice

1. Acme Consolidated Enterprise purchased a desk, computer, and other office equipment for its new regional office building in Dallas. How should the expenditure be entered in the accounting books?
   a. Inventory
   b. Office supplies
   c. A period expense

d. Fixed assets
e. Intangible assets
f. Prepaid expenses
g. Other

2. To what does the term "par value" frequently refer?
   a. The market value at which the state (of incorporation) authorized the sale of stock.
   b. The portion of a corporation's owners' equity that may not be distributed in the form of an ordinary cash dividend.
   c. The market value of the common stock (or preferred stock) at the end of the accounting period.
   d. The average market value of the common stock (preferred stock) for the most recent 12-month accounting period.
3. To what does the term "treasury stock" refer?
   a. Short-term, U.S. Treasury bills.
   b. Redeemable preferred stock—that is, preferred stock exhibiting more characteristics of debt than equity ownership.
   c. Authorized but unissued stock.
   d. Common voting stock of a less than wholly owned subsidiary corporation that is held by the parent corporation.
   e. Stock has been previously issued by a corporation and subsequently reacquired (but not formally retired).

E3–14 CPA Exam Questions

Determine the best answer.

1. (11/92, MC#6) Rice Co. was incorporated on January 1, 1991, with $500,000 from the issuance of stock and borrowed funds of $75,000. During the first year of operations, net income was $25,000. On December 15, Rice paid a $2,000 cash dividend. No additional activities affected owners' equity in 1991. At December 31, 1991, Rice's liabilities had increased to $94,000. In Rice's December 31, 1991, balance sheet, total assets should be reported at:
   a. $598,000
   b. $600,000
   c. $617,000
   d. $692,000
2. (11/92, MC#7) On September 1, 1992, Hyde Corp., a newly formed company, had the following stock issued and outstanding:
   - Common stock, no par, $1 stated value, 5,000 shares originally issued for $15 per share.
   - Preferred stock, $10 par value, 1,500 shares originally issued for $25 per share.
   - Hyde's September 1, 1992, statement of stockholders' equity should report:

	Common Stock	Preferred Stock	Additional Paid-In Capital
a.	$ 5,000	$15,000	$92,500
b.	$ 5,000	$37,500	$70,000
c.	$75,000	$37,500	$ 0
d.	$75,000	$15,000	$22,500

3. (11/93, MC#1) Mill Co.'s trial balance included the following account balances at December 31, 1992:

Accounts Payable	$15,000
Bonds Payable, due 1993	25,000
Discount on Bonds Payable, due 1993	3,000
Dividends Payable 1/31/93	8,000
Notes Payable, due 1994	20,000

What amount should be included in the current liabilities section of Mill's December 31, 1992, balance sheet?

a. $45,000
b. $51,000
c. $65,000
d. $78,000

E3–15 Effects of Errors

On its unaudited balance sheet for December 31, 1997, Shabby Inc. reported current assets of $850,000, total assets of $2,850,000, and retained earnings of $1,200,000. However, the following two errors were discovered in the audit of Shabby.

1. Supplies purchased for $220,000 and still on hand were recorded as expense.
2. A purchase of machinery (a fixed asset) for $150,000 was debited to Purchases. This amount was *not* included in the amount reported for ending inventory. Depreciation of $30,000 should have been (but was not) recorded for the machinery.

Required: Determine the correct amounts to report for current assets, total assets, and retained earnings as of December 31, 1997.

E3–16 Error Correction

After closing the books for 1997, Tack, Inc., had a retained earnings balance of $150,000. Late in January 1998, before the 1997 financial statements have been prepared, Tack discovered that merchandise costing $40,000 had not been included in inventory at December 31, 1997. This inventory had been recorded properly as a purchase. Tack has a 30% tax rate.

Required:

A. Prepare necessary entries to correct this oversight.
B. When corrected, how will current assets, total assets, current liabilities, shareholders' equity, and net income change for the 1997 financial statements? (AICPA adapted, 11/92 MC #8.)

E3–17 Shareholders' Equity

Wawona Corp. had net income of $500,000 for 1997. The following depicts shareholders' equity for Wawona Corp.:

DECEMBER 31	1997	1996
Common stock, $1 par; 100,000 shares authorized; issued 60,000 and 50,000 shares respectively	$ 60,000	$ 50,000
Additional paid-in capital	240,000	190,000
Retained earnings	1,200,000	800,000
	$1,500,000	$1,040,000

Required: Prepare a statement of changes in shareholders' equity for 1997.

E3–18 Shareholders' Equity

Spamona Corp. declared and paid dividends of $3,750,000 for 1997. The following depicts shareholders' equity for Spamona Corp.:

DECEMBER 31	1997	1996
Common stock, $0.01 par; 10,000,000 shares authorized; issued 7,500,000 and 6,000,000 shares respectively	$ 75,000	$ 60,000
Additional paid-in capital	112,000,000	72,000,000
Retained earnings	89,175,000	80,940,000
	$201,250,000	$153,000,000

Required: Prepare a statement of changes in shareholders' equity for 1997.

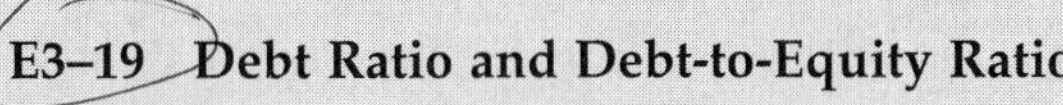

E3–19 Debt Ratio and Debt-to-Equity Ratio

Required:

A. Convert the following debt ratios into debt-to-equity ratios:
 1. 0.3333
 2. 0.40
 3. 0.75

B. Convert the following debt-to-equity ratios into debt ratios:
 1. 0.25
 2. 0.50
 3. 1.50
 4. 7.00

E3–20 Subsequent Events

State the proper accounting treatment for the following subsequent events that occurred after the end of the report date but prior to issuing financial statements for the report date.

1. Employees at a plant site went on strike, causing a shut-down of the plant, which is anticipated to cost the company lost revenue during the period of nonoperation.
2. Issued additional shares of common stock.
3. Settled a lawsuit against the company for damages of $2.5 million. In anticipation of a probable loss of this suit, the company had already recorded an estimated loss and contingent liability for $3 million.
4. Settled a lawsuit against the company for damages of $2.5 million. The lawsuit was in existence prior to the report date, but a contingent liability for the suit had not been recorded because the company had previously estimated a low probability of losing the suit.

E3–21 Subsequent Events

State the proper accounting treatment for the following subsequent events that occurred after the end of the December 31, 1997, report date but prior to issuing financial statements for the report date.

1. Purchased 1,000 shares of treasury stock for $50 per share as part of a repurchase plan announced in November 1997.

2. The CEO and several other top executives suddenly quit the company and announced new positions with a major competitor.
3. Lost a lawsuit filed against a competitor for copyright infringement. The suit had been filed early in 1997, and the company was seeking $10 million in damages. The company does not plan to appeal the decision.
4. Received an insurance payment of $2 million for losses incurred by a fire in November 1997. The company had previously been unsure of the amount to be awarded by the insurance company and had recorded a loss of $2.2 million for the incident.

Type 1

PROBLEMS

P3–1 Effect of Transactions

For each event below, state the effect on working capital, total assets, and net income. (Assume the use of periodic inventory.)

1. Sell merchandise for $50,000 cash.
2. Sell merchandise on credit for $100,000.
3. Receive $100,000 payment on account from a customer.
4. Purchase merchandise for $20,000 cash.
5. Purchase merchandise on credit for $30,000.
6. Pay vendor $30,000 for credit purchase.
7. Purchase a vehicle for $30,000 by paying $10,000 down and signing a long-term note for the remainder.
8. Issue common stock for $200,000.
9. Declare dividends of $50,000.
10. Pay dividends declared.
11. Make a loan payment of $3,000 of which $2,000 is interest. The principal is classified as a current portion of notes payable.
12. Receive advance payment of $40,000 from a customer for a special order.
13. Complete and ship the above special order.
14. Pay advertising costs of $12,000.
15. Record an adjusting entry for depreciation.
16. Record an adjusting entry for accrued wages.
17. Record an adjusting entry for periodic inventory and cost of goods sold. Inventory increased over the period.
18. Sign a purchase commitment with a vendor to buy $30,000 in merchandise in the next year.
19. Receive an order from a customer for merchandise with a sales price of $10,000.
20. Send a purchase order to a vendor to buy machinery for $40,000.

P3–2 Balance Sheet Preparation

Presented here is a single-column adjusted trial balance (that is, debit balances are positive and credit balances are negative) for Kyle Industries as of December 31, 1997. Regarding the notes payable, a payment of $100,000 is due December 1, 1998; $60,000 of this payment will be interest and the remainder a reduction of principal.

Accounts Payable	$ (63,000)
Accounts Receivable	233,753
Accumulated Depreciation	(7,840)
Allowance for Bad Debts	(14,170)
Bad Debts Expense	13,365

Common Stock	(540,000)
Cash	355,990
Cost of Goods Sold	1,008,363
Depreciation	2,350
Fixed Assets	523,500
Income Tax Payable	(37,404)
Interest Expense	5,000
Interest Payable	(5,000)
Inventory	168,000
Notes Payable (15% rate)	(400,000)
Office Supplies Expense	7,160
Operating Expense	31,364
Payroll Tax Expense	5,566
Payroll Withholding and Taxes Payable	(2,388)
Provision for Income Tax	37,404
Rent Expense	24,530
Retained Earnings (1/1/97)	(63,491)
Sales Revenues	(1,410,504)
Sales Discounts	11,900
Sales Returns	62,056
Wages and Salaries Expense	53,496
	$ 0

Required: Prepare a classified balance sheet for Kyle Industries as of December 31, 1997.

P3–3 Balance Sheet Preparation

The following trial balance of Nong Corp. at December 31, 1997, has been adjusted except for income taxes.

	DEBITS	CREDITS
Cash	$ 1,500,000	
Accounts Receivable, net	8,750,000	
Inventory	4,000,000	
Prepaid Income Taxes	1,000,000	
Property, Plant, and Equipment (net)	5,250,000	
Accounts payable		$ 4,250,000
Note Payable, due 1999		5,000,000
Common Stock, $1 par		1,500,000
Paid-In Capital		7,750,000
Retained earnings (deficit)	3,500,000	
Revenues		17,500,000
Expenses	12,000,000	
	$36,000,000	$36,000,000

Required:

A. The company has made estimated prepayments of income taxes throughout 1997, its applicable tax rate is 30%, and all income statement items are also taxable items. Prepare the adjusting entry for income taxes.

B. Prepare a 12/31/97 classified balance sheet.

C. Determine the company's current ratio and debt ratio.

P3–4 Balance Sheet Correction and Preparation

Presented here is the unaudited balance sheet as of December 31, 1997, prepared by the bookkeeper of Zeus Manufacturing Corporation.

ZEUS MANUFACTURING CORPORATION
Balance Sheet For the Year Ended December 31, 1997

Assets	
Cash	$ 225,000
Accounts receivable (net)	345,700
Inventories	560,000
Prepaid expenses	40,000
Investments	57,700
Land	450,000
Building	1,750,000
Machinery and equipment	1,964,000
Goodwill	37,000
	$5,429,400
Liabilities & Stockholders' Equity	
Accounts payable	$ 133,800
Mortgage payable	900,000
Notes payable	500,000
Wages and payroll taxes payable	80,000
Income taxes payable	61,200
Deferred tax liability	28,000
Accumulated depreciation (total)	420,000
	$2,123,000
Common stock, $50 par; 40,000 shares issued	$2,231,000
Retained earnings	1,075,400
	$3,306,400
	$5,429,400

Your firm has been engaged to perform an audit, during which the following data are found:

1. Checks totaling $14,000 in payment of accounts payable were mailed on December 30, 1997, but were not recorded until 1998. Late in December 1997, the bank returned a customer's $2,000 check, marked "NSF" (nonsufficient funds), but no entry was made.
2. Included in accounts receivable is a $30,000 note due on December 31, 1999, from Zeus's president.
3. Treasury stock was recorded at cost when Zeus purchased 200 of its own shares for $32 per share in May 1997. This amount is included in investments.
4. On December 30, 1997, Zeus borrowed $500,000 from a bank in exchange for a 10% note payable maturing December 30, 2002. Equal principal payments are due December 30 of each year, beginning in 1998.

5. The mortgage payable requires $10,000 principal payments, plus interest, at the end of each month.
6. The company was authorized to issue 100,000 shares of its $50 par value common stock.

Required: Prepare a corrected classified balance sheet as of December 31, 1997. This financial statement should include a proper heading, format, and necessary descriptions. (AICPA adapted; Accounting Practice—Part I, Number 4, Nov. 1990.)

P3–5 Book Value of Equity

Refer back to the excerpt in case C3-4 from the 1988 annual report of Hilton Hotels. As indicated, financial analysts sometimes refer to *book value per share* of corporations. Book value per share for a given date is calculated as common shareholders' equity divided by the number of outstanding shares of common stock. For this exercise, refer to the respective exhibits in the chapter for Motorola, Walt Disney, and 3M.

Required:

A. Determine the book value per common share of each company for each date reported.
B. What complicates this determination for Walt Disney?
C. Which company has the highest book value per share? the lowest?
D. Determine the percentage change in book value per share for each company. Which company had the largest percentage increase?
E. Of what relevance, if any, is book value per share?

P3–6 Issue Price of Stock

For this exercise, refer to the exhibits in the chapter. Estimate the average issue price per share of common stock for:

1. Motorola as of December 31, 1995 and 1994 (Exhibit 3–1).
2. Walt Disney as of September 30, 1995 and 1994 (Exhibit 3–6).
3. 3M as of December 31, 1995 and 1994 (Exhibit 3–8).
4. Why can the average issue price not be determined from the balance sheet for 3M (Exhibit 3–7)?
5. Determine the average cost of treasury stock for Walt Disney and 3M on the report dates. How do these costs compare to the average issue prices for the respective companies?
6. Determine the average issue price for the shares issued by Walt Disney during the year ended September 30, 1995. How does this average price compare to the average cost of treasury stock?

P3–7 Balance Sheet Preparation

Incomplete account information for Lopes Corporation, as of December 31, 1997, is provided here.

	Account Balance	
	Debits	Credits
Common Stock		$ 6,400,000
Bonds Payable		31,000,000
Paid-In Capital		3,700,000
Prepaid Assets	$ 2,000,000	

	ACCOUNT BALANCE	
	DEBITS	CREDITS
Building	$ 8,000,000	
Accounts Payable		$ 6,000,000
Inventory	25,300,000	
Land	6,400,000	
Cash	700,000	
Equipment	29,100,000	
Notes Payable (long-term)		4,100,000
Accounts Receivable	?	
Allowance for Depreciation		15,000,000
Treasury Stock	1,900,000	
Current Bond Maturities		8,000,000
Retained Earnings		?

Current Ratio = 3
Debt Ratio = ?

Required: Prepare a balance sheet.

P3–8 Classification

Incomplete balance sheet information for Michele Corporation at 12/31/97 is as follows:

Cash	$ 12,000	
Accounts receivable	125,000	
Allowance for bad debts	(12,000)	
Inventory	100,000	
Total current assets		$225,000
Land	$ 50,000	
Plant and equipment	400,000	
Allowance for depreciation	(80,000)	
Intangibles (net)	30,000	
Total long-term assets		400,000
Total assets		$625,000
Total liabilities		$350,000
Capital stock	$100,000	
Retained earnings	175,000	
Total equity		275,000
Total liabilities and equity		$625,000

Additional Information:

1. Accounts Receivable includes a credit balance of $4,000, representing an overpayment by one customer.
2. Included in the cash account is a check from a customer in the amount of $2,000 that was returned by the bank because the customer's account had no money in it.
3. Plant and Equipment contained $3,000 of supplies that were recorded in the account.
4. The liabilities include accounts payable in the amount of $200,000, a short-term note payable of $20,000, income tax payable of $10,000, and long-term bonds payable of $120,000.

5. The capital stock has a par value of $1 per share, the company is authorized to issue 150,000 shares, and 20,000 shares have been issued.

Required: Prepare a corrected classified balance sheet for the end of the year.

P3–9 Classification

Incomplete balance sheet information for Newline Corporation as of 12/31/97 is as follows:

Cash	$?	
Accounts receivable	162,000	
Allowance for bad debts	(12,000)	
Inventory	100,000	
Total current assets		$300,000
Land	$ 50,000	
Plant and equipment	400,000	
Allowance for depreciation	(80,000)	
Intangibles (net)	80,000	
Total long-term assets		450,000
Total assets		$750,000
Total liabilities		$?
Capital stock	$275,000	
Retained earnings	75,000	
Total equity		350,000
Total liabilities and equity		?

Additional Information:

1. The liabilities include accounts payable in the amount of $200,000, a short-term note payable of $20,000, income tax payable of $10,000, and long-term bonds payable of $170,000.
2. The capital stock has a par value of $1 per share, the company is authorized to issue 500,000 shares, and 100,000 shares are issued.

Required:

A. Calculate the current ratio.
B. Calculate the debt ratio.
C. Prepare a corrected classified balance sheet for the end of the year.

P3–10 Statement of Shareholders' Equity

The following equity transactions took place for Capital Corp. after it was incorporated in 1995:

1. Issued 30,000 shares of $3 par common stock for $30 each on 3/1/95.
2. Issued another 10,000 common shares on 6/1/95 for $33 per share.
3. Paid a $1-per-share dividend on 9/1/96.
4. Issued 10,000 shares of $50 par preferred stock at par on 10/1/96.
5. Issued 15,000 common shares on 6/1/97 for $40 per share.
6. Paid dividends of $25,000 on preferred stock and $55,000 on common stock on 9/1/97.

Capital Corp. had a net loss of $50,000 in 1995, net income of $100,000 in 1996, and net income of $200,000 in 1997. The company is authorized to issue 100,000 shares of common stock and 50,000 shares of preferred stock.

Required:

A. Prepare a statement of shareholders' equity for the period 1/1/95 to 12/31/97.
B. Prepare comparative shareholders' equity sections of the balance sheet for Capital Corp. as of December 31, 1995, 1996, and 1997.

P3–11 Financial Statement Analysis

Balance sheets for Clover Corporation appear as follows:

CLOVER CORPORATION
Balance Sheet

(DOLLARS IN THOUSANDS, EXCEPT PAR VALUE)	12/31/97	12/31/96
Assets		
Cash	$ 4,000	$ 3,000
Accounts receivable (net)	20,000	16,000
Inventory	40,000	37,000
Property, plant, and equipment (net)	65,000	59,000
Intangible assets	4,000	3,000
Total assets	$133,000	$118,000
Liabilities		
Accounts payable	$ 22,000	$ 14,000
Mortgages payable: Current portion	10,000	10,000
Mortgages payable: Long-term portion	16,000	20,000
	$ 48,000	$ 44,000
Shareholders' Equity		
Common stock, $1 par; 500,000 shares issued	$ 500	$ 500
Additional paid-in capital	19,500	19,500
Retained earnings	65,000	54,000
	$ 85,000	$ 74,000
Total liabilities and shareholders' equity	$133,000	$118,000

Required:

A. Determine the percentage change in current liabilities during 1997.
B. Determine the percentage of current assets to total assets for each year-end.
C. Determine the current ratio for each year-end.
D. Determine the debt ratio for each year-end.
E. Determine the average issue price for the company's stock.
F. During 1997, the company paid dividends of $2 per share. Determine net income for 1997.
G. Clover Corporation wants to obtain additional capital of $10,000,000 for plant expansion. Does the expansion seem like a good idea? How would you suggest the company raise the money?

P3–12 Financial Statement Analysis

Here are financial statements for Crimson Corporation. All notes are current.

CRIMSON CORPORATION
Balance Sheet

	12/31/97	12/31/96
Assets		
Cash	$ 130,000	$ 100,000
Accounts receivable (net)	896,000	832,000
Notes receivable	652,000	548,000
Inventory	640,000	400,000
Property, plant, and equipment (net)	5,440,000	5,171,000
Total assets	$7,758,000	$7,051,000
Liabilities and Owners' Equity		
Accounts payable	$ 552,000	$ 576,000
Notes payable	608,000	480,000
Bonds payable	500,000	500,000
Common stock, $10 par; 400,000 shares issued	4,000,000	4,000,000
Retained earnings	2,098,000	1,495,000
Total liabilities and owners' equity	$7,758,000	$7,051,000

CRIMSON CORPORATION
Income Statement

	For the Year Ended December 31,	
	1997	1996
Sales	$24,000,000	$21,600,000
Cost of goods sold	15,220,000	13,760,000
Gross margin	$ 8,780,000	$ 7,840,000
Other expenses	6,177,000	5,880,000
Net income	$ 2,603,000	$ 1,960,000

Required:

A. Determine and compare the percentage changes in revenue, net income, and total assets for 1997.
B. Determine the current ratio for each year-end.
C. Determine the debt ratio for each year-end.
D. Determine the percentage of resources invested in fixed assets for each year-end.
E. Determine the amount of cash collected from customers during 1997.
F. Determine the amount of dividends paid for 1997. If you owned 1,000 shares of stock, how much would you have received in dividends?
G. Make a brief analysis regarding the company's liquidity and solvency.

RESEARCH ACTIVITIES

R3–1 Research Case

Examine past issues of *The Wall Street Journal* or some other source to determine the market prices of the three firms' common stock in P3–5 at the close of each report date. Then, using the results from P3–5 concerning book values, answer the following:

1. Did the same firm have both the highest book value per share and market value per share?
2. For each firm, determine the ratio of book value to market value for each report date. Do you detect any patterns concerning this ratio?

R3–2 Financial Research

Find a current annual report (within the last two years) and use it for the following activities:

1. Prepare an analysis of the firm to determine its liquidity and solvency.
2. Determine which comparative years are given.
3. If comparative years are provided, prepare both horizontal and vertical analyses for the income statement.
4. Read the footnotes and find an example of one estimated amount that may affect net income.
5. Are any loss contingencies reported? If so, what are they?
6. Are any subsequent events reported? If so, what are they?

R3–3 What Is an Asset?

Consider the commentary in the In Practice feature, "What Is an Asset?" These remarks were made by Walter P. Schuetze, then chief accountant of the SEC, made at the AICPA's Twentieth Annual National Conference on Current SEC Developments (*Accounting Horizons*, September 1993, pp. 66–70).

Required: Study the full text of the remarks made by Schuetze as printed in *Accounting Horizons*. Prepare a report that summarizes FASB's definition of an asset, problems in practice with using this definition, and the alternative proposed by Schuetze.

R3–4 Par Value and Paid-In Capital

Viewing owners' equity as a residual interest is fairly straightforward. However, traditional reporting of stockholders' equity can appear quite complex, thus clouding the interpretation of stockholders' equity as a residual interest. Some question the usefulness of the traditional framework used to report stockholders' equity.

The pertinent questions are: (1) Can any benefit be gained from separating contributed capital into two categories of par value and contributed capital in excess of par, and (2) Does any benefit exist in separating contributed capital from retained earnings?

Required: Prepare a report to address these questions. Some possible sources of material can be found in the following:

- P. McGough, "The Legal Significance of the Par Value of Common Stock: What Accounting Educators Should Know," *Issues in Accounting Education*, Fall 1988, pp. 330–350.
- M. Roberts, W. Samson, and M. Dugan, "The Stockholders' Equity Section: Form Without Substance," *Accounting Horizons*, December 1990, pp. 35–46.

R3–5 Motorola—Segment Reporting

As part of their supplemental reporting, companies must disclose information about major segments of their business. Appendix C at the end of the text provides Motorola's 1995 annual report.

Required: Identify Motorola's major segments. For each segment, identify the net sales and operating profit for 1995 and the assets as of December 31, 1995. What do the percentages in the operating profit section of the segment information represent? Which segment appears to be the most profitable? Why do you think this is so?

R3–6 Motorola—Financial Analysis

Refer to Motorola's annual report in Appendix C at the end of the text.

Required: From the statement of consolidated stockholders' equity, determine when Motorola issued stock in a public offering. For this offering, what amount was received, how many shares were issued, and what was the average issue price per share?

R3–7 Internet—SEC's EDGAR

Open the homepage for the text (*www.swcollege.com/hartman.html*), and select the Chapter 3 EDGAR site. Next, select *Important Information About EDGAR (Read This First!).* After scanning this important information, go back to the EDGAR homepage. From this homepage, select *Search the EDGAR Database... Search the EDGAR Archives...* Then, in the keyword area, enter *Microsoft*, and a list of filings by this company should be found. Notice the difference in the size of the files for the annual filings (10K) and quarterly filings (10Q). You can get any of these listed; when selected, the files are transferred to your computer. These files can even be saved and edited. Because the transfer for the relatively large 10Ks can take some time, let's examine a 10Q instead. From the Microsoft list, click and retrieve the most recent 10Q. From this 10Q, determine the following:

- Report date
- Balance sheet
- Current assets
- Total assets
- Current liabilities
- Total liabilities

PART 2

PROFITABILITY AND OWNERSHIP INTERESTS

Conceptual Foundations of Accrual Accounting—Revenue Recognition

Conceptual Foundations of Accrual Accounting—Allocations

The Income Statement and Measures of Performance

Statement of Cash Flows

4

Conceptual Foundations of Accrual Accounting—Revenue Recognition

Learning Objectives

After studying this chapter, you should be able to:

1. Understand the concept of recognition.
2. Interpret the recognition criteria for assets and liabilities.
3. Interpret the recognition criteria for revenues.
4. Apply various revenue-recognition points to appropriate situations.
5. Understand the concepts of income and capital maintenance.

THE CONCEPT OF RECOGNITION

Understand the concept of recognition.

Accounting recognition focuses on real-world events that change an entity's assets, liabilities, or equity. Determining whether an economic event that affects an entity has occurred, identifying and measuring its effects on the real-world assets, liabilities, and equity of the entity, and deciding when those effects should be formally reported or incorporated into the entity's financial statements constitute the essence of accounting recognition.[1]

Recognition issues, the principal topic of this chapter, have always been among the most controversial issues in accounting. It is the job of the Securities and Exchange Commission (SEC) and the Financial Accounting Standards Board (FASB) to maintain a watchful eye over matters relating to revenue and expense recognition. The opening vignette, entitled "Revenue Recognition and Area Development Rights," testifies to that vigilance.

Revenue Recognition and Area Development Rights

In February 1988, ***Jiffy Lube International*** (*www.swcollege.com/hartman.html*), a Baltimore-based franchiser of quick-oil-change centers (fiscal 1988 revenues, $78 million), was ordered by the Securities and Exchange Commission to change its accounting. The surprise order resulted in a staggering earnings hit for the first quarter of Jiffy's 1989 fiscal year: net income of $95,000, less than 25% of what Jiffy would have reported. Why the SEC order? Because the commission said Jiffy was claiming income it hadn't yet earned.

Over the previous two years, the SEC had made similar charges against about a half a dozen other fast-growing startups in the franchise field. Among them: ***Moto Photo, Inc., Swensen's, Inc.,*** and ***Le Peep Restaurants, Inc.***

The accounting issue involves the tricky problem of revenue recognition from the sale of so-called area development rights. These are contracts that are sold by the company granting the developer the exclusive rights to open franchises in a particular territory. In return, the developer traditionally pays the company a *nonrefundable* fee *up front*.

The SEC's position is based on two long-held accounting principles: *Revenue* must be earned in order to be *recognized;* and *costs* must be *matched* with revenue as they are earned.

In publishing, for example, magazines collect fees for subscriptions up front, but until the magazine publishes those future issues, the money cannot be recognized as revenue. Instead, the funds must be recorded as a balance sheet liability, often labeled "unearned income." When the issues are published, the revenues are taken into income and the cost of publishing deducted.

In the case of area development fees, the SEC argues that the companies have not *truly earned* the revenues until the franchise units are open and operating."

Source: Penelope Wang, "Claiming Tomorrow's Profits Today," *Forbes,* October 17, 1988, p. 78.

[1] L. T. Johnson and R. K. Storey, "Recognition in Financial Statements: Underlying Concepts and Practical Conventions," *Research Report,* Financial Accounting Standards Board, Stamford, Connecticut (1982).

This article relates to revenue recognition by franchisors. Retail franchise sales in the United States nearly doubled in the 1980s and today clearly dominate some industries. A major controversy arising in this industry is *when* the franchisor should recognize revenue relating to the initial franchise fee. A franchisor earns income from two sources: (1) the initial franchise fee paid by the franchisee and (2) continuing periodic fees (paid for continuing services). In return for the initial franchise fee, only a portion of which need be paid up front, the franchisor may commit to assisting with a variety of startup problems: site selection, construction, employee training, sales promotion, selection and installation of computing and accounting systems, and so forth. The question is, when should the revenue be recognized?

Franchisors traditionally have sought to recognize initial franchise fees up front, when the package of services is sold to the franchisee. Alternatively, these revenues might be recognized when cash collections are made, *as* the services are performed, or *after* all services are performed. In part, the preference for early recognition may be because the ability to sell additional franchises may depend on the franchiser's financial statements showing increasing (possibly sharply increasing) profits as soon as possible.

Ideally, of course, revenue should be recognized only when it has been "truly earned," to use the language of the excerpted article: not before, but also not after. But when is it "truly earned?"

THE DEFINITION OF RECOGNITION

Recognition can be defined as the process of formally recording or incorporating an item into the financial statements of an entity. Information may be included in either the statement itself or in the footnotes to the statement. Information contained in footnotes is an integral part of the financial statements, and specific disclosures are required under generally accepted accounting principles (GAAP). Still, the focus of this chapter and the subject of most accounting controversies are the criteria for including items in the body of the financial statements. Thus, recognition *hereafter is defined to include "depiction of an item in both words and numbers, with the amount included in the totals of the financial statements."*[2]

To be included in the financial statements, an item must satisfy the following requirements:

1. It must possess the characteristics of an element of the financial statements as defined by SFAC No. 6. That is, an item must exhibit the characteristics of an asset, liability, revenue, expense, gain, or loss.
2. It must be measurable, relevant, and reliable.

These characteristics will be discussed later in the chapter.

ACCRUAL- VERSUS CASH-BASED ACCOUNTING

Careful selection of what to report in financial statements is necessary to meet the established objectives of financial reporting. The determination of appropriate

[2]SFAC No. 5, Recognition and Measurement in Financial Statements, FASB, par. 6.

recognition criteria is therefore critical. Criteria attempt to promote the goals of financial reporting. As discussed in Chapter 1, SFAC No. 1 established three broad purposes for financial reporting:

1. To provide information that is useful to present and potential investors and creditors and other users in making rational investment, credit, and similar decisions.
2. To supply information to help investors, creditors, and others assess the amounts, timing, and uncertainty of the prospective cash flows of the related enterprise because *their prospects* for receiving cash from investments in, loans to, or other participation in the enterprise *depend on its cash-flow prospects*.
3. To provide data about economic resources of an enterprise, the claims to those resources . . . and the effects of transactions, events, and circumstances that change resources and claims to those resources.[3]

The emphasis placed on the amount, timing, and uncertainty of future cash flows has focused increased attention on the statement of cash flows, one of four statements required by GAAP. However, statements of cash flows present few, if any, recognition problems, because all cash receipts and disbursements are recognized when they occur. Reporting cash flows involves no estimates or allocations; that is, it is a very objective process. The same is true of cash-basis income statements. So why do we not use cash-basis income statements in the United States? The answer is that U.S. standard setters believe that

> "Interest in an enterprise's future cash flows and its ability to generate favorable cash flows leads primarily to an interest in information about its earnings rather than information directly about its cash flows. . . . Information about enterprise earnings and its components measured by accrual accounting *generally* provides a better indication of enterprise performance than information about current cash receipts and payments [emphasis added]."[4]

Accrual-based accounting is different from cash-basis accounting in that accrual-based accounting attempts to *recognize* (record) changes in financial statement elements in the period in which the transactions and events occur rather than in the period in which cash changes hands. Financial statement users focus on the *process* by which cash expended on resources and activities is returned (and, it is hoped, increased), "not just with beginning and end of the process" when cash is invested or cash is collected.[5] The emphasis is on the process because *the process is what is recurring and is the source of future cash flows.*

The measurement of periodic accrual-based income involves periodicity, the relating to periods of the benefits and costs of operations not necessarily started and completed in that same period. The practice of reporting income periodically (customarily annually) relates to users' needs for timely and systematic information. Frequently, normal operating cycles begin and end in different years. On this point, SFAC No. 1 observes:

[3]SFAC No. 1, Objectives of Financial Reporting, FASB, pars. 34–40.
[4]Ibid., pars. 43–44.
[5]Ibid., par. 44.

"Modern business activities are largely conducted on credit and often involve long and complex financial arrangements or production or marketing processes. An enterprise's receivables and payables, inventory, investment, property, plant, equipment, and other noncash resources and obligations are the links between its operations and other transactions, events, and circumstances that affect it and its cash receipts and outlays. For example, labor is often used by an enterprise before it is paid for, requiring that salaries and wages payable be accrued to recognize the obligation and to measure the effects on earnings in the period the labor is used rather than when the payroll checks are issued. Conversely, resources such as raw materials and equipment may be paid for by an enterprise in a period that does not coincide with their use, requiring that the resources on hand be recognized and the effect on earnings be deferred until the period the resources are used. Similarly, receivables and the related effects on earnings must often be accrued before the related cash is received, or obligations must be recognized when cash is received and the effects on earnings must be identified with the periods in which goods or services are provided. *The goal of accrual and deferral of benefits and sacrifices is to relate the accomplishments and their efforts so that reported earnings measure an enterprise's performance during the period instead of merely listing cash receipts and outlays* [emphasis added]."[6]

Determination of accrual-based periodic income involves estimates and allocations. Estimating the uncertain results of incomplete transaction cycles is costly and involves risks. Still, the business community traditionally has weighed the benefits of timely financial reporting, based on sales and other observable events, as more relevant than reporting on cash receipts and disbursements

ETHICS IN PRACTICE

Recognition Before Performance

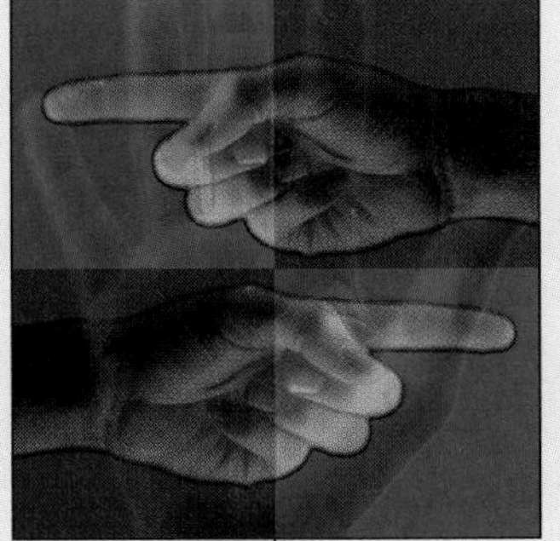

Policy Management Systems Corp., in a filing in federal court, acknowledged that it recognized on its financial statements some revenue from license agreements before the agreements were formally signed. Particularly, it had recognized revenue in the fourth quarter of 1992 from license agreements that were not formally signed by the parties until the first quarter of 1993.

In April 1993, Policy Management disclosed that first-quarter results would fall well below the company's expectations because several contracts hadn't closed as expected. That news prompted Policy Management's share price to fall 43%. The accuracy of the Blythwood, S.C., company's financial reporting became the subject of federal and internal investigations.

In the court filing, the company also said that, on occasion, its employees agreed with customers that the customer would receive future services in exchange for payment of certain invoices. In those cases, the company said, it recognized the revenue from the invoices in quarters before the customer received the services, according to the filing . . . A company spokesman said that the statements in the filing are "not an admission that the company broke any accounting rules."

Source: Helene Cooper, "Policy Management Says It Booked Revenue Before Completion of Accords," *The Wall Street Journal*, January 24, 1994, p. A9.

[6] Ibid., par. 45.

only. *The final results of incomplete accounting cycles usually can be reliably measured at some point of substantial completion.* It is not always necessary to totally delay recognition to the point of full completion or cash recovery. However, flexible revenue recognition standards can tempt firms to follow aggressive accounting practices as, arguably, ***Policy Management*** did in the In Practice box "Recognition Before Performance." (See prior page.)

RECOGNITION CRITERIA—ASSETS AND LIABILITIES

Interpret the recognition criteria for assets and liabilities.

An asset is a probable future economic benefit obtained or controlled by a particular entity as a result of a past transaction or event. A liability is a probable future sacrifice of economic benefits arising from present obligations of a particular entity to transfer assets or provide services to other entities in the future as a result of past transactions or events.

An event, transaction, or circumstance giving rise to an asset, liability, or change in an asset or liability should be recognized when four criteria are met. The item must (1) meet the definition of an asset or a liability and be (2) relevant, (3) reliable, and (4) measurable.

There are also two constraints to which recognition is subject. The first is the pervasive cost/benefit concept, which mandates that the perceived benefits from information recognition and use must exceed the expected costs of recognition and use. The second constraint is that of materiality. Materiality provides that recognition of an item is not necessary if the individual item is not large enough to be material and if the aggregate of individually immaterial items is not so large that their omission or misstatement would likely cause the judgment of a reasonable person to be changed or influenced.

RELEVANCE

Relevance implies that an item of information must have the capacity to influence the decisions of investors, creditors, or other financial statement users. It must be timely and have either incremental feedback value or predictive value, or both, in the context of a full set of financial statements.[7] Recall that one of the objectives of financial reporting is to assist in the prediction of a firm's future cash flows, their timing, and the uncertainty surrounding them.

RELIABILITY

Reliability implies that the accounting data are verifiable, neutral, and represent faithfully the underlying economic event. Numerous critics of accounting have charged that decisions made in the name of maintaining high levels of reliability have been spurious and detrimental to the progress of the profession. There is no denying that reliability concerns clearly have had a pervasive effect on the timing of recognition in the past. In their landmark work of 1940, *An Introduction to Corporate Accounting Standards,* Paton and Littleton praised the historic U.K. emphasis on *objectivity* and *verifiability* as an important contribution to the development of accounting in the United States.[8] And so it was. Frequently,

[7]SFAC No. 5, Recognition and Measurement in Financial Statements, FASB, par. 74.
[8]American Accounting Association, Monograph No. 3.

the first available information about an event that may have resulted in a change in an asset or liability has been rejected as too uncertain to allow recognition.

Controversy regarding the appropriate measurement attribute for a class of accounts often reduces to a trade-off between relevance and reliability. SFAC No. 5 observes that "unavailability or unreliability of information may delay recognition of an item, but waiting for virtually complete reliability or minimum cost may make the information so untimely that it loses its relevance."[9] One challenge facing the accounting profession is to balance the certainties of cash-basis accounting with the uncertainties associated with accrual accounting. The profession does not wish to eliminate the timeliness advantages of accrual-based accounting compared with cash-basis accounting. At the same time, the profession does not wish to lose public confidence by engaging in what, at least in hindsight, might be viewed as baseless speculation. Many of the "strict" recognition criteria that still persist today were developed in the reform-minded aftermath of the stock market crash of 1929 and the following depression. This may in part explain the historical emphasis of the profession on reliability over relevance.

MEASURABILITY

The **measurability** of an item must be considered simultaneously with relevance and reliability. That is, to be recognized, it is not enough that an asset or liability be quantifiable in monetary units. Rather, a *relevant* attribute must be quantifiable or measurable with sufficient *reliability*.[10] Items currently appearing in financial statements exhibit one of five relevant measurability attributes. **Historical cost** is the basis of measurement of property, plant, and equipment. **Current cost**, or **replacement cost**, is frequently the measurement basis for inventory under the lower-of-cost-or-market method. **Fair value** is used for investments in marketable securities classified as trading or available for sale. **Net realizable** (settlement) **value** is used with short-term receivables. **Present** (or discounted) **value of future cash flows** is the measurement basis for leases, pension obligations, and certain other long-term receivables and payables. These measurability attributes were defined in Chapter 1 and are discussed in subsequent chapters as they apply to specific elements of the financial statements.

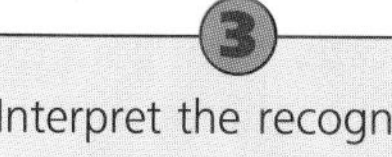

Interpret the recognition criteria for revenues.

In addition to the criteria just cited for recognition of assets and liabilities, further guidance is provided for recognition of transactions, events, or circumstances affecting **revenues**. Revenues are defined as:

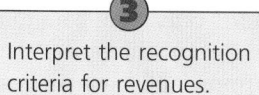

> "inflows and other enhancements of assets of an entity or settlement of its liabilities (or a combination of both) from delivering or producing goods, rendering services, or other activities that constitute the entity's ongoing major or central operations."[11]

If a transaction, event, or circumstance involves two elements of financial statements, say an asset and a revenue, the characteristics of both elements must be satisfied. To be recognized, revenues must also be (1) realized or realizable

[9]SFAC No. 5, Recognition and Measurement in Financial Statements, FASB, par. 77.
[10]Ibid., par. 65.
[11]SFAC No. 6, Elements of Financial Statements, FASB, 1985, par. 78.

and (2) earned. While specifically defined by SFAC No. 5, these terms are very difficult to interpret operationally, a problem contributing to controversy within the profession over specific applications. Revenue is said to be **realized** "when products (goods or services), merchandise, or other assets are exchanged for cash or claims to cash." Revenues are **realizable** "when related assets received or held are readily convertible to known amounts of cash or claims to cash."[12] **Readily convertible** assets, in turn, are defined as assets that have (1) interchangeable units and (2) quoted prices available in an active market that can readily absorb the quantity held by an entity without significantly affecting the price.

The **earned** criterion is defined thus: "Revenues are considered to be earned when the entity has *substantially* completed what it must do to be entitled to the benefits represented by the revenues."[13] Interpretation of the "earned" criterion must be made with the objectives of accrual-based accounting in mind. This criterion should not be used to delay revenue recognition and eliminate the claimed advantages of accrual-based accounting. SFAC No. 5 states that the profession traditionally has considered that the benefits of timely financial reporting based on sales and *other more relevant events,* rather than on cash receipts and disbursements, outweigh the costs and risks of estimating uncertain results of incomplete cycles.[14] The final results of incomplete accounting cycles usually can be reliably measured at some point of substantial completion of the process. Thus, it is not necessary to totally delay recognition to the point of full completion or cash recovery. Critics of the current accounting model, however, contend that, regardless of original intentions, the conventional application of revenue recognition criteria is tantamount to postponing revenue recognition until cycle completion.

VALUE-ADDING PROCESS

The value-creating activities of an enterprise may be compared to the magician's black box—you see what goes in, you see what comes out, but you're uncertain what goes on inside the box. In business operations, you also see what goes in; that is, transactions occur to acquire the factors of production (material, labor, and capital) at costs that are observable and verifiable. At the end of the value-adding process, you see what comes out; that is, the product is sold and cash is received. However, the sale did not create the value; it only confirms that value was added in the process of combining the factors of production. What goes on in the black box is that value is added: assets appreciate. That process is measured internally by the enterprise with its cost accounting system.

Why are the assets not written up during the process and revenue recognized when value is really added? Because the current accounting model, in most instances, treats the value-adding process as a black box. And in a black box, you cannot see what is going on inside! If that is so, one can only assume what might have happened. If that is not so, other opportunities discussed in the following section become available. However, first consider the possibility that what we really have is a black box into which we cannot peer.

[12]SFAC No. 5, Recognition and Measurement in Financial Statements, FASB, par. 83a.
[13]Ibid., par. 83b.
[14]Ibid., pars. 36–37.

Among available assumptions suggested by the FASB Research Report, *Recognition in Financial Statements: Underlying Concepts and Conventions,* are the three graphically depicted in Exhibit 4–1 (Box A, Box B, and Box C). In Box A it is assumed that no value is added during the process. In Box B value is assumed to be added in a straight-line increment. In Box C value is assumed to be added at a compounding rate.

The revenue-postponement alternative (Box A) is the one most widely used in accounting today. It "is known *not* to represent faithfully the asset-creating and consuming activities of the enterprise."[15] So why is it used? Although revenue recognition is in many instances deferred until after the value-adding process is complete, the deferral is not the result of ignorance. It is instead the result of caution in evaluating evidence of the existence of income. However, in most instances, revenue recognition does follow other patterns as found in boxes B and C. These instances are discussed in later sections of the chapter.

ROLE OF CONSERVATISM

Conservatism has long been believed by many accountants to be appropriate in making accounting decisions. In 1964, the Accounting Principles Board (APB) wrote,

> "Frequently, assets and liabilities are measured in a context of significant uncertainties. Historically, managers, investors, and accountants have generally preferred that possible errors in measurement be in the direction of understatement rather than overstatement of net income and net assets. This has led to the convention of conservatism."[16]

EXHIBIT 4–1
Available Value-Added Options

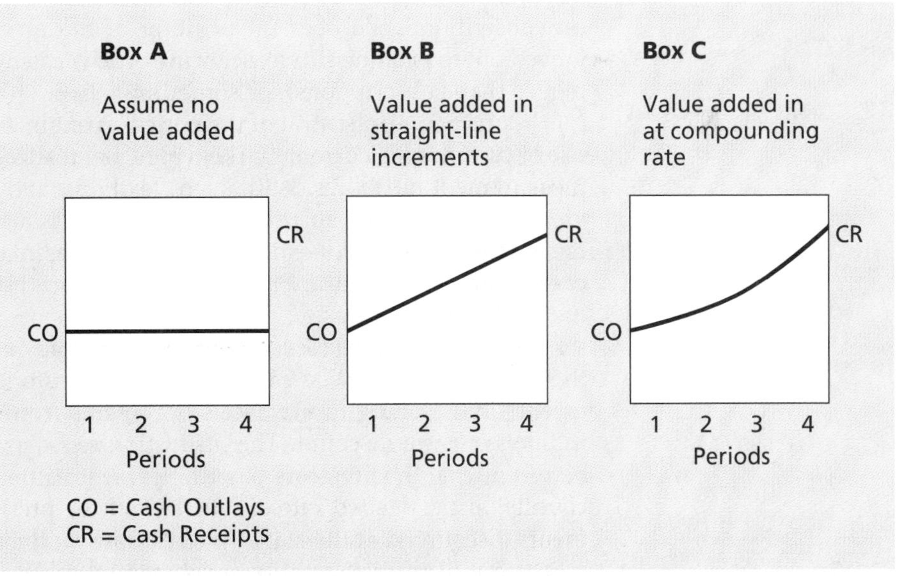

[15]FASB Research Report, Recognition in Financial Statements: Underlying Concepts and Practical Conventions, p. 163.
[16]Accounting Principles Board, Opinion No. 4, par. 171.

Nonetheless, more recently in 1980, members of the FASB in SFAC No. 2 observed,

> "Conservatism in financial reporting should no longer connote deliberate, consistent underreporting of net assets and profits. The Board emphasizes that point because conservatism has long been identified with the idea that deliberate understatement was a virtue. . . . The convention of conservatism, which was once expressed in the admonition to "anticipate no profits but anticipate all losses," developed during a time when balance sheets were considered the primary financial statement and details of profit or other operating results were rarely provided outside business enterprises. Conservatism no longer requires deferring recognition of income beyond the time that adequate evidence of its existence becomes available."[17]

Note, however, that Statements of Financial Accounting Concepts (SFACs) do not change current practice. Instead, they describe concepts and relations that will underlie future financial accounting standards and practices and, in due course, serve as a basis for evaluation of existing standards and practices.

THE CRITICAL EVENT

The term "substantial completion" (the definition of "earned") has had a number of interpretations. One suggests that profit is earned at the moment the most critical decision is made in the cycle of a transaction. This critical decision, or **critical event**, signals substantial completion. But what is the critical event for a business? Making this determination can be difficult. Is there, truly, only one critical event that determines ultimate success or failure for an enterprise? In the oil business, is it the discovery of the oil, the sale of the end products, or both? In the magazine business, is it the sales of subscriptions, cash collections on subscriptions, subsequent printing of the magazine (which is frequently jobbed out to printing firms), securing of advertising (a source of revenue much bigger than subscriptions), or something else?

In practice, application of the critical event interpretation might rely on the use of current cost, current market value, net realizable value, and present value measurement attributes. With such flexibility and discretion allowed to individual firms, it is not surprising that the SEC is a busy policeman. It is almost inevitable that some questionable applications may arise, as seems to be the case regarding Chemical Bank, as discussed in the *Forbes* article abstracted in the In Practice feature.

Chemical Bank (*www.swcollege.com/hartman.html*) provides an illustration of the securitization practice followed by some institutions. The financial institution essentially is selling future assets (payments from credit cards or mortgages) to investors at a discount. The institution recognizes income as the difference between what the investors pay (the present value of the future payments discounted at the desired rate of return) and the present value of the future payments discounted at the stated interest rate on the asset. This is an example of a financial institution creating a substantial profit.

Thus, while interpreting "substantially complete" to mean "beyond the critical events" allows recognizing revenue on a far more timely basis than is conventional in most U.S. businesses, it also invites some uncustomary applications.

[17]SFAC No. 2, pars. 93, 95.

IN PRACTICE—GENERAL

Chemical Bank

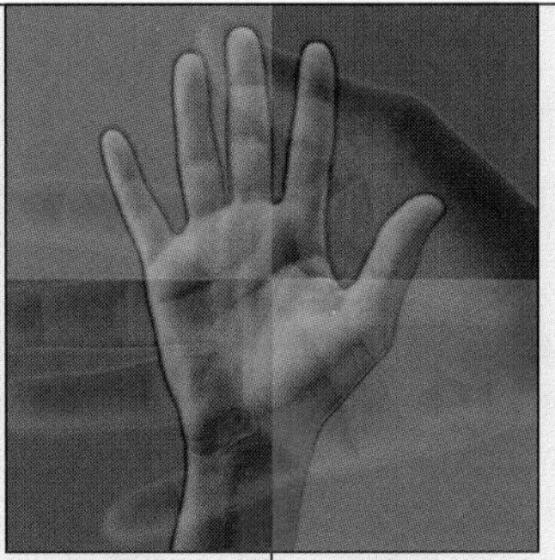

Buried in the $465 million or so ***Chemical Bank*** reported as pretax income in 1988 (excluding nonrecurring items) was some $15 million that the giant bank had not yet earned.

Flimflam? No, what this $70 billion (assets) bank was doing was perfectly legal—Chemical had joined the swelling ranks of banks and finance companies that sell their balance sheet assets, transforming them into securities. This "securitization" (excluding that of mortgages) would top $13 billion in 1988, up from some $10 billion in 1987, according to ***First Boston,*** which keeps track of such things.

What kinds of assets? Credit card receivables are the biggest, fastest growing part of the nonmortgage, asset-backed security market; about $6.5 billion were securitized in 1988, up from virtually zero in 1986. The figure has continued to grow throughout the 1990's.

How are these asset-backed securities creating profits? Chemical packaged $850 million of balances outstanding on its consumer credit cards. The balances have been packaged into two, two- to three-year trusts, issued at $350 million and $500 million, each yielding 9.3%, and sold to institutional investors. Chemical calculated the present value of the difference between the 17% or so consumers pay on credit cards and the 9.3% that trust investors get, minus service costs of the portfolio. The very substantial difference is booked as profit—even though not a penny of that interest has yet been paid by the cardholders.

That is permissible under current accounting rules, but a lot of accountants don't like the idea. Neither does the Securities and Exchange Commission, which in August 1988 asked the Financial Accounting Standards Board to review the accounting procedures for credit card receivables deals. A big problem is that credit card balances, on average, stay unpaid for only six months or so. And the trusts last much longer. This means that some banks have taken profits on the sale of assets that have not been created. "We could not believe that people would recognize a gain on receivables that don't yet exist," says Christopher Lynch, project manager at the accounting board.

Source: L. Jereski, "If It Moves, Package It?" *Forbes,* November 28, 1988, p. 134.

The issue of revenue recognition involves the bigger issues of equity and ethics in business. The accountant must expect to be continually confronted with these challenges. Commenting on this point, the managing partners of the then "Big Eight" accounting firms observed in unison in their combined 1989 white paper that

> "The ability to apply decision rules embodied in the accounting model is only part of the goal [of education]. Accountants must be able to use the data, exercise judgments, evaluate risks, and solve real-world problems. . . . Practitioners must also be able to identify ethical issues and apply a value-based reasoning system to ethical questions."[18]

Some suggest that deficient accounting practices contributed significantly to the debacle in the savings and loan and banking industries in the late 1980s and early 1990s. Others suggest that the causes were rooted in many other factors, including government regulatory changes, general economic conditions and circumstances, and in some cases, less than ethical behavior by individuals motivated by the desire for self-enrichment.

[18] *Perspectives in Education: Capabilities for Success in the Accounting Profession,* Arthur Andersen & Co., Arthur Young, Coopers & Lybrand, Deloitte Haskins & Sells, Ernst & Whinney, Peat Marwick Main & Co., Price Waterhouse, Touche Ross, 1989, pp. 6, 8.

POINTS OF REVENUE RECOGNITION

Apply various revenue-recognition points to appropriate situations.

GAAP today allows revenue recognition using various measurement attributes at several points in the production cycle. The selection of the appropriate option depends on the facts of the case. Common revenue recognition points used today are defined in Exhibit 4–2. Conventional practice as to when revenue is recognized has evolved and continues to evolve. In many older industries, what is done this year is largely determined by what was done last year and the year before. In other instances, such as the Chemical Bank case referred to earlier, new industries are emerging, new commercial instruments are appearing, and new business practices are developing. These changes, and changes in user needs in the 1990s and beyond, continue to challenge the accounting profession. Timely, relevant information regarding revenue generation is central to user needs. Reliable information is also paramount, and the controversy over revenue recognition likely will continue.

REVENUE RECOGNITION AT THE TIME OF SALE

In current practice, revenue is most frequently recognized at the point of sale. There are several reasons for this. Certainly among those reasons are convenience and objectivity. The point of sale is an observable event often accompanied by dated documents (e.g., signed contracts, receipts) *that confirm value has been added in preceding manufacturing and/or retailing processes. No assumption regarding value*

EXHIBIT 4–2
Points of Revenue Recognition

a. *Time of Sale* (usually operationalized as time of delivery).
b. ***Time of Production (Before Time of Sale).*** If products or other assets are readily salable without significant effort (as may be the case with various metals, commodities, and securities), revenues may be recognized at completion of production or *when the prices of the assets change* (assuming reliably determined market prices or market value—that is, windows in the black box exist).
c. ***Time of Production (After Time of Sale, Before Delivery).*** If the product is contracted before production, collectibility is probable, and production requires an extended period of time (as may be the case with long-term construction contracts), revenue may be recognized *during production* (assuming reasonable measures of progress—that is, windows in the black box exist).
d. ***Time of Production or Delivery.*** If sales and cash receipts precede production and delivery (as may be the case with magazine subscriptions), revenue is recognized *at the point of production and/or delivery.*
e. ***Time of Service.*** If contracted in advance, revenues for continuously rendered services (or rights to use assets) may be recognized *as the service is rendered.*
f. ***Time of Expiration of Return Privileges or Guarantees.***
g. ***Time of Cash Collection.*** If collectibility of receivables received for a product, service, or other assets is doubtful, revenues must be deferred and recognized on the basis of cash received (i.e., *cash and accounting cycle completion).*
h. ***Passage of Time*** (as in the case of interest, or rent, which conceptually is a function of time. Interest is paid for the use of money over time; rent is paid for the use of tangible assets over time.)
i. ***Time of Exchange.*** If products, services, or other assets are exchanged for noncash, nonmonetary assets (such as property, plant, and equipment) that are not readily convertible into cash (i.e., revenue is realizable), revenue may still be recognized *at the point of exchange* if fair values can be determined within reasonable limits.

accretions are necessary. It is a point that auditors can verify; thus, revenue recognition is less easily manipulated by the unscupulous. Another reason for the popularity of revenue recognition at the point of sale is that it produces results (i.e., revenue figures) very similar to results generated by other revenue recognition methods that may be more costly to implement and/or less objective (or verifiable by auditors). For example, the production process for many items is very short and those items are sold quickly after production. In these instances, if revenue is recognized consistently at the point of sale, the annual revenues will vary little from the income results that would have been obtained if revenue had been recognized during production or at the end of production. Similarly, in many cases, cash is received at the point of sale or shortly thereafter. Accordingly, in these instances recognizing revenue at the point of sale is the same as or closely approximates revenue recognized at the point of cash collection.

The time of sale and the time of delivery are frequently the same in the retail industry. For example, if you purchase clothing at ***Sears,*** you likely take possession and accept the quality of the goods at the point of sale. However, this is not always the case. If you purchase a large-screen television set, it is unlikely that the TV you see in the store will be the TV that you receive (you only observe a representative floor model). Plus, delivery may not take place until the week following the sale. In these cases, two possibilities for the timing of revenue recognition exist: recognition at the point of sale or recognition at the point of product acceptance/delivery. It is likely that both methods will generate very similar results. However, this may not be the case in all instances. Auditors must insist that the method chosen be used consistently to avoid manipulation of earnings figures in specific years. Documents are generated to record each event (sale and delivery), so that both are documented and easily verified. Orders for nonconsumer goods, however, are frequently placed by one company with another by telephone or other electronic means. Customarily, these revenues are recorded at the point of delivery. It is at the point of delivery that the quality/size/color of the ordered goods is checked and accepted. It is not infrequent for some or all goods to be returned. Recognizing revenue at the point of delivery in industry thus takes into consideration the likelihood that full acceptance may not occur. If full acceptance does not occur, revenue recognition at the point of product ordering may be premature.

In industry, revenue at the point of delivery is typically recorded in the following manner:

RCA delivers 20 television sets to a retail customer. The agreed-upon price is $500 each. RCA's cost to manufacture the items was $250 each, and total delivery costs borne by RCA is $275.

Accounts Receivable	10,000	
Sales Revenue		10,000
To record sale and receivable at point of delivery.		
Delivery Expense	275	
Delivery Payable		275
To record expense in the same year as revenue.		
Cost of Goods Sold	5,000	
Inventory		5,000
To record expense in the same year as revenue and to reduce asset inventory.		

Recognizing revenue at the documented point of delivery, however, does not guarantee reliable results. See the In Practice box "Trade Loading."

IN PRACTICE—GENERAL

Trade Loading

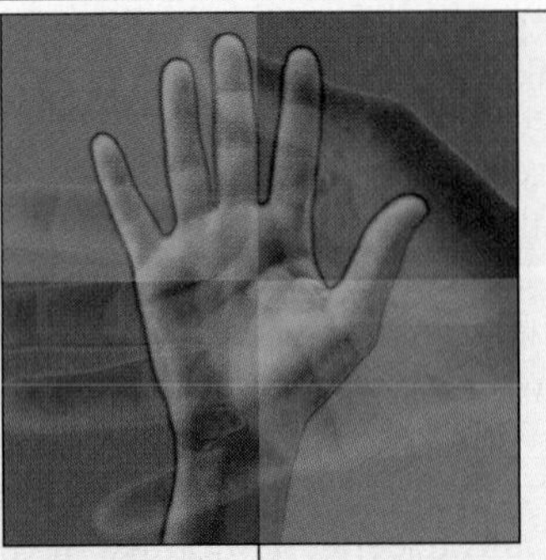

RJR Nabisco. It looked like just one more announcement in a year of many. In September 1989, ***RJR Nabisco*** (*www.swcollege.com/hartman.html*) declared that it would end the practice in domestic cigarette distribution known as trade loading. A startling number was attached to the statement. The company, as a result, would forgo $340 million in operating profits this year. Trade loading is a crazy, uneconomic, insidious practice through which manufacturers—trying to show sales, profits, and market share they didn't actually have—induce their wholesale customers, known as the trade, to buy more product than they can promptly resell. RJR engaged in this practice aggressively enough over the previous few years to overstate operating profits in its tobacco division by an estimated $250 million. RJR executives do not deny that the practice of trade loading was misguided. That's why new managment has stopped the game.

The shame of trade loading is that so many businesspeople accept it as necessary. Whether this acute case of managed earnings amounts to a violation of the securities laws is another question. The management of earnings can be smelly but permissible —or just plain illegal. The uncertainty in this instance brings to mind a Michael Knisley line in the *New Republic:* "When wrongdoing is exposed, the real scandal is what's legal."

Bausch & Lomb, Inc. ***Bausch & Lomb, Inc.*** (*www.swcollege.com/hartman.html*) said its board named a committee of four independent directors to review internal investigations conducted in 1994 of corporate sales and accounting practices.

Bausch & Lomb began investigating its sales and accounting practices in the summer of 1994 after the company said it had oversupplied distributors with $75 million of sunglasses and contact lenses. At the time, the company said some of those shipments were "inappropriately recorded as sales." To address the problem, the company drastically reduced shipments and established a $20 million reserve to buy back inventory and cover the cost of slashing prices to clear remaining product.

Sources: Carol Loomis, "The $600 Million Cigarette Scam," *Fortune,* December 4, 1989, pp. 89–90; "Bausch Says It Named Panel to Review Probe of Sales, Accounting," *The Wall Street Journal,* October 26, 1995, p. C21.

REVENUE RECOGNITION AT THE TIME OF PRODUCTION

Delaying revenue recognition to the point of product sale, however, may not be necessary or appropriate in selected circumstances. Two examples follow that relate to accounting for commodities and accounting for long-term construction or long-term service contracts.

Commodities. Because the environment surrounding business operations that produce or extract actively traded commodities (such as farm grains, chemicals, or metals) is sufficiently different from the preceding retail and manufacturing examples, point-of-sale revenue recognition methods typically are not used. *Uniquely objective measurement of the value-adding process is possible during the production or extraction of commodities (or commodity-like items). No assumptions regarding value accretions are necessary.* Instead, windows to the process are opened by the existence of reliable and objective market prices (market values) for intermediate and/or final products. Inventory may be revalued at intermediate stages using current market values as the relevant measurement attribute.

In some cases, marketable intermediate products may not exist, but reliable market prices for the end products do exist. If reliable estimation of the remaining costs in the process is possible, then net realizable values may be used as the relevant measurement attribute. The use of net realizable value would allow recognition of the value added (asset appreciation) and revenue. Exhibit 4–3 illustrates accounting for commodities.

EXHIBIT 4–3
Commodities

During 1995, Gerard Polanski produced 10,000 bushels of grain. The costs of production included the following:

Materials (seed grain, fertilizer, etc.)	$12,000
Labor	36,000
Overhead (equipment depreciation)	15,000
Overhead (crop insurance)	5,000

At the end of the harvest, the grain was selling at $8 per bushel in the market. Costs of transportation to market and other incidental selling costs were estimated to be an additional $.50 per bushel. Polanski decided not to sell the grain in 1995 but to wait until after year-end for higher winter prices. The grain was sold in February at $9 per bushel.

	Debit	Credit
1995 Entries:		
1. Inventory of Grain	68,000	
Cash (and/or Wages Payable)		36,000
Farm Supplies Inventory		12,000
Accumulated Depreciation		15,000
Cash (and/or Prepaid Insurance)		5,000
To record costs of grain production in 1995.		
2. Inventory of Grain	12,000	
Cost of Farm Production	68,000	
Farm Revenue		80,000
(10,000 bushels @ $8)		
Estimated Selling and Transportation Costs	5,000	
Inventory of Grain		5,000
To recognize revenue earned and matching expenses associated with farm production. Asset (Inventory of Grain) revaluation based on estimates of net realizable values. Net Realizable Value = $80,000 − $5,000 = $75,000		
1996 Entry:		
3. Cash (or Accounts Receivable)	90,000	
Inventory of Grain		75,000
(Speculatory) Grain Holding Gain		10,000
Cash (or Transportation Payable)		5,000
To record sale of 1995 crop at $9 per bushel less transportation costs to market.		

The practical utility of an accounting model that recognizes revenue only at the point of sale/delivery is highly questionable in the case of the production or extraction of commodities. Practical utility is the simplicity, efficiency (cost savings), and faithfulness with which a method represents underlying economic phenomenon. In the case of commodities, one can reliably measure value added and, thus, reliably recognize revenue continuously throughout the process, or at least at process end. Delaying revenue recognition to the point of product sale will generate significantly different annual income figures and reports. One must ask, "Why should I wait to a later date to report the reliable results of past actions?" The accounting profession acknowledges that to do so risks reporting important information too late for its effective use.

Long-Term Construction Contracts. Recognizing revenue at the end of production versus during production is itself an important choice in certain cases. Significantly different income figures may well develop based on this choice. The difference between the two can be especially great when accounting for long-term construction (or service) contracts. These are instances when the product is contracted before production, collectibility is probable, and production requires an extended period of time.

Imagine a contract that calls for the construction of a trans-Alaskan pipeline or a new urban business and cultural complex that will take more than one year to complete. Suppose a firm devotes all of its efforts to these activities and completes the project on January 10 of the third year. If revenue can be recognized only at completion, the pattern of recognized income would be no income in Year 1, no income in Year 2, and aggregate project income in Year 3. This result does not represent underlying economic reality, especially if the project is concluded in the third year, on January 10. In such instances, the practical utility of single-point revenue recognition is so obviously diminished that it necessitates other solutions. Accordingly, in such circumstances the **percentage-of-completion method** of revenue recognition has developed.

In this case, value is assumed to be added in proportion to an activity basis, as measured by costs incurred divided by total estimated costs for the project. That is, the arbitrary assumption that no value is added until project completion is replaced by the arbitrary assumption that value is added (and revenue recognized) proportionately with cost incurrance. A variation of alternative Assumption B in Exhibit 4–1 is selected over Assumption A. Both are approximations of economic value added, and in these circumstances, the percentage of completion represents a better approximation of revenue earned than does point of sale.

What is meant by "arbitrary" is that no one method (assumption) can be definitively defended against all others; in other words, not all accountants agree on any one method as best. This inability to develop consensus in many areas of accounting practice is one reason why GAAP frequently permits more than one way to account for a transaction, event, or circumstance. Exhibit 4–4 contains an example of revenue recognition for long-term construction contracts. The exhibit compares the completed-contract method to the percentage-of-completion method.

EXHIBIT 4–4
Long-Term Construction Contracts

Flanigan Construction signed a contract with Loyland Enterprises to construct an apartment complex beginning April 15, 1995. The completion date is established as December 31, 1997. The total contract price is $10,000,000, and the total projected costs are $9,000,000. Assume that the project is completed on time, and the following information is related to the construction period.

A. Data for Contract

	1995	1996	1997
Accumulated costs at 12/31	$2,000,000	$6,500,000	$ 9,300,000
Estimated costs to complete	7,000,000	2,700,000	0
Progress billings to 12/31	1,000,000	6,000,000	10,000,000
Cash collections to 12/31	700,000	4,000,000	10,000,000

B. Percentage-of-Completion Method of Revenue Recognition

(1) Costs and gross profit:

	1995	1996	1997
Contract price	$10,000,000	$10,000,000	$10,000,000
Less: Costs			
Accumulated cost at 12/31	$ 2,000,000	$ 6,500,000	$ 9,300,000
Estimated costs to complete	7,000,000	2,700,000	0
Total estimated costs	$ 9,000,000	$ 9,200,000	$ 9,300,000
Estimated gross profit	$ 1,000,000	$ 800,000	$ 700,000

*(2) Gross profit to be recognized:**

	1995	1996	1997
$\frac{\$2,000,000}{\$9,000,000} \times \$1,000,000 =$	$222,222		
$\frac{\$6,500,000}{\$9,200,000} \times \$800,000 =$		$565,217	
			$700,000
Less: Gross profit recognized in prior year		(222,222)	(565,217)
		$342,995	$134,783

*(3) Revenue to be recognized:***

	1995	1996	1997
$\frac{\$2,000,000}{\$9,000,000} \times \$10,000,000 =$	$2,222,222		
$\frac{\$6,500,000}{\$9,200,000} \times \$10,000,000 =$		$7,065,217	
			$10,000,000
Less: Prior-year revenue		(2,222,222)	(7,065,217)
Revenue to be recognized		$4,842,995	$ 2,934,783

*Percent complete × Estimated total project profit − Profit recognized in prior periods
**Percent complete × Estimated total project contract price − Revenue recognized in prior periods

C. Journal Entries—Percentage of Completion

	1995		1996		1997	
Construction in Progress	2,000,000		4,500,000		2,800,000	
Material, Cash, etc.		2,000,000		4,500,000		2,800,000
To record construction costs.						
A/R—Construction in Progress	1,000,000		5,000,000		4,000,000	
Billings on Construction in Progress		1,000,000		5,000,000		4,000,000
To record progress billings.						
Cash	700,000		3,300,000		6,000,000	
A/R—Construction in Progress		700,000		3,300,000		6,000,000
To record collections.						
Construction in Progress	222,222		342,995		134,783	
Cost of Construction in Progress	2,000,000		4,500,000		2,800,000	
Construction Revenue		2,222,222		4,842,995		2,934,783
To recognize profit.						
Billings on Construction in Progress					10,000,000	
Construction in Progress						10,000,000

Construction in Progress is an inventory account.

Billings on Construction in Progress is a contra account to Construction in Progress. It reflects the customers' equity in the inventory. A liability (to provide construction) occurs when the billings exceed the construction in progress.

Cost of Construction in Progress is an expense account and appears on the income statement as a deduction from the Construction Revenue account. The difference between the Cost of Construction and Construction Revenue represents the gross profit recognized during the period. The gross profit is added to the Construction in Progress account.

The final entry closes out the asset (Construction in Progress) and the contra asset (Billings on Construction in Progress) at the end of the contract.

EXHIBIT 4–4
(Continued)

Exhibit 4–4 illustrates the case where net profit is generated each year. Exhibit 4–5 illustrates the recognition of a loss on a contracted project. In this revised example, it became apparent for the first time in 1996 that the project would yield a net loss (total costs exceed contracted selling price). When losses are probable and can be estimated reliably, the entirety of the loss (rather than a percentage thereof) must be recognized immediately in the year of estimation (in this case, 1996). This treatment of estimates of future losses is consistent with the conservative traditions found frequently in current practice. Current practice also requires the entirety of the projected loss to be recognized in 1996 under the completed-contract method. The loss recognized in 1996 under the completed-contract method would be less than that recognized in 1996 under the percentage-of-completion method because the completed-contract method would not have recognized any profit in 1995 that would have required reversal in 1996.

A loss in 1996 also would have been recognized under the percentage-of-completion method (but not the completed-contract method) if estimated costs to complete the project were $3,300,000 (instead of the originally estimated $2,700,000 in Exhibit 4–4 or the $3,700,000 in Exhibit 4–5). In this additional instance, an overall profit still would have been anticipated for the project as a whole. The contracted selling price of $10,000,000 still would exceed total

EXHIBIT 4–4
(Concluded)

D. Financial Statement Disclosures—Percentage of Completion

BALANCE SHEET

	1995	1996
Current assets:		
(1) Receivables from construction in progress	$ 300,000	$2,000,000
(2) Inventories—construction in progress	2,222,222	7,065,217
Less: Progress billings	(1,000,000)	(6,000,000)
Equity in construction in progress	$1,222,222	$1,065,217

(1) Receivables = Billings − Collections
(2) Construction in progress:
1995: ($2,000,000 + $222,222)
1996: ($2,000,000 + $222,222 + $4,500,000 + $342,995)

INCOME STATEMENT

	1995	1996	1997
Construction revenue	$2,222,222	$4,842,995	$2,934,783
Cost of construction	2,000,000	4,500,000	2,800,000
Gross profit on construction	$ 222,222	$ 342,995	$ 134,783

E. Completed-Contract Method of Revenue Recognition

Under the completed-contract method, no profit is recognized on the contract until the year of completion. The journal entries for Flanigan are the same each year except for the entry to recognize the gross profit. That entry would be omitted until 1997, at which time an entry would be made to recognize the entire profit at the completion of the contract. Entries follow:

Each Year

Construction in Progress	XXX,XXX	
Materials, Cash, etc.		XXX,XXX
To record construction costs.		
A/R—Construction in Progress	XXX,XXX	
Billings on Construction in Progress		XXX,XXX
To record progress billings.		
Cash	XXX,XXX	
A/R—Construction in Progress		XXX,XXX
To record collections.		

1997

Billings on Construction in Progress	10,000,000	
Construction in Progress		9,300,000
Gross Profit on Construction Projects		700,000
To close out accounts and record profit.		

EXHIBIT 4–5
Long-Term Construction Contracts

A. Data for Contract

	1995	1996	1997
Accumulated costs at 12/31	$2,000,000	$6,500,000	$10,200,000
Estimated costs to complete	7,000,000	3,700,000	0
Progress billings to 12/31	1,000,000	6,000,000	10,000,000
Cash collections to 12/31	700,000	4,000,000	10,000,000

B. Percentage-of-Completion Method of Revenue Recognition

Costs and gross profit:

	1995	1996	1997
Contract price	$10,000,000	$10,000,000	$10,000,000
Less: Costs			
Accumulated cost at 12/31	$ 2,000,000	$ 6,500,000	$10,200,000
Estimated costs to complete	7,000,000	3,700,000	0
Total estimated costs	$ 9,000,000	$10,200,000	$10,200,000
Estimated gross profit	$ 1,000,000	$ (200,000)	$ (200,000)

*Gross profit to be recognized:**

	1995	1996	1997
$\frac{\$2,000,000}{\$9,000,000} \times \$1,000,000 =$	$222,222		
$\frac{\$6,500,000}{\$10,200,000} = 63.725\%$		$(200,000)	
			$(200,000)
Less: Gross profit recognized previously		(222,222)	(200,000)
		$(422,222)	$ 0

*Revenue to be recognized:***

	1995	1996	1997
$\frac{\$2,000,000}{\$9,000,000} \times \$10,000,000 =$	$2,222,222		
$\frac{\$6,500,000}{\$10,200,000} = 63.725\%$		$6,300,000*	
			$10,000,000
Less: Prior-year revenue		(2,222,222)	(6,300,000)
Revenue to be recognized		$4,077,778	$ 3,700,000

*100% of estimated losses must be recognized in 1996. Thus, no loss (nor any gain) is deferred to 1997. Accordingly, remaining revenue is set to equal remaining estimated expenses (estimated costs of $3,700,000) to yield a zero profit figure for 1997 (unless year-end 1996 estimates prove incorrect.)
**Percent complete × Estimated total project profit − Profit recognized in prior periods
***Percent complete × Estimated total project contract price − Revenue recognized in prior periods

estimated costs of $9,800,000 ($6,500,000 plus $3,300,000 costs to complete) by $200,000. However, profit in the amount of $222,000 already had been recognized in 1995. The revenue recognition entry in 1996 would change as follows (other entries would remain the same in 1996):

C. Journal Entries—Percentage of Completion

	1995		1996		1997	
Construction in Progress	2,000,000		4,500,000		3,700,000	
Materials, Cash, etc.		2,000,000		4,500,000		3,700,000
To record construction costs.						
A/R—Construction in Progress	1,000,000		5,000,000		4,000,000	
Billings on Construction in Progress		1,000,000		5,000,000		4,000,000
To record progress billings.						
Cash	700,000		3,300,000		6,000,000	
A/R—Construction in Progress		700,000		3,300,000		6,000,000
To record collections.						
Construction in Progress	222,222			422,222		
Cost of Construction in Progress	2,000,000		4,500,000		3,700,000	
Construction Revenue		2,222,222		4,077,778		3,700,000
To recognize profit.						
Billings on Construction in Progress					10,000,000	
Construction in Progress						10,000,000

EXHIBIT 4–5
(Concluded)

Costs of Construction in Progress	4,500,000	
Construction Revenue		4,410,431
Construction in Progress		89,569*

*Calculations follow:

Contracted selling price	$10,000,000
Accumulated costs (12/31/96)	$ 6,500,000
Estimated costs to complete	3,300,000
Total estimated costs	$ 9,800,000
Residual profit	$ 200,000

Percent complete ($6,500,000/$9,800,000) = 66.3265%

Profit to be recognized to 12/31/96	$132,653
Profit recognized in 1995	222,222
Loss to be recognized in 1996	$ (89,569)

REVENUE RECOGNITION AT THE TIME OF DELIVERY

Some short- and intermediate-term contracts also provide for monthly, periodic, or progress billings, as in the above discussed case of long-term construction contracts; others require customers to pay in advance. Subscribers to magazines frequently pay in advance. However, it is generally considered inappropriate to recognize revenue at the point of cash receipt when the cash is received before the product is received or the service rendered. It is reasoned that until the provider engages in the value-adding function, revenue has not been earned. Of course, a magazine has several sources of revenue (frequently advertising revenue exceeds subscription revenue) and arguably engages in several value-adding activities. Next we consider only the example of subscriptions revenue. Revenue from subscriptions may be recorded at the end of production, or at point of delivery, or for convenience, at week- or month-end, if the results substantially reflect the same earnings process.

Accounting Age magazine receives $38 for a one-year subscription to its magazine on July 1, 1997. By paying in advance, the customer qualifies for a free subscription premium: a solar calculator. The cost of the calculator to *Accounting Age* is $1; its cost of mailing and handling is also $1.

Cash	38	
Premium Inventory		1
Postage Payable		1
Deferred Subscriptions Revenue		36
To record magazine subscription on July 1 and accompanying receipt of cash. Premium was taken from inventory and mailed to customer.		
Deferred Subscriptions Revenue	3	
Subscriptions Revenue		3
To record monthly revenue at July (and every) month-end from prepaid subscriptions.		

REVENUE RECOGNITION AT TIME OF SERVICE

Term contracts also are common in the service area. The controversy surrounding when to record long-term franchisor services was addressed at the beginning of this chapter. Other types of services contracted on terms of varying lengths include those for advertising, bookkeeping and payroll, legal counsel, warranties, and building and equipment maintenance. An example of accounting for a janitorial services contract follows:

J&W Janitorial Services signs a 36-month janitorial services contract with the state of Arizona for the state's new legislative office building. The contract is for $72,000. The contract begins November 1, 1997. Appropriate entries for 1997 follow:

Cash (or Contracts Receivable)	72,000	
Deferred Contract Revenue		72,000
To record contract and any advance.		
Deferred Contract Revenue	2,000	
Services Revenue		2,000
To record monthly revenue at November month-end.		
Deferred Contract Revenue	2,000	
Services Revenue		2,000
To record monthly revenue at December month-end.		

REVENUE RECOGNITION AT TIME OF EXPIRATION OF RETURN PRIVILEGES

Most firms extend their customers certain merchandise return privileges. Extending these privileges promotes greater sales, as wholesale and retail consumers know they can return unsold or unused items. Privileges vary by industry and may be for 30 days or more. Aggressive sales representatives may rely on these privileges to secure sales of new product lines. In these instances providing adequate allowances for revenue-offsets is critical to providing reliable financial reports. In Practice boxes "What Did KnowledgeWare Know?" and "How Good Was Intellicall's Call?" note the temptation NOT to provide adequate allowances.

IN PRACTICE—GENERAL

What Did KnowledgeWare Know?

While details of the lawsuits weren't available, questions about ***KnowledgeWare's*** (*www.swcollege.com/hartman.html*) [accounting] practices are fueling a growing controversy over how small high-tech companies report sales. Critics say that such companies are often tempted to inflate sales in order to keep their stocks buoyant and creditors at bay. Such companies as ***Kendall Square Research Corp., Cambridge Biotech Corp., Policy Management Systems Corp.,*** and ***Kurzwell Applied Intelligence, Inc.*** have acknowledged booking sales too aggressively.

As recently as June 1984, KnowledgeWare said it expected revenue of $156 million for the fiscal year ended June 30. Actual revenue was $132.5 million. In a news release, the company blamed the discrepancies on its inexperience in distributing its products through software industry resellers. KnowledgeWare said the rate of return for unsold products was much higher than it had anticipated and said it would now revise its accounting procedures to take such rates of return into account.

Source: Timothy O'Brian, "KnowledgeWare Accounting Practices Are Questioned," *The Wall Street Journal,* September 7, 1994, p. 62.

IN PRACTICE—GENERAL

How Good Was Intellicall's Call?

Intellicall, Inc., (*www.swcollege.com/hartman.html*) of Dallas, runs a profitable business. Revenues have increased tenfold in the last three years . . . [however] Intellicall's accounting for ordinary sales looks aggressive. The list price of a "smart" phone is $1,000, payable up front, plus $500 payable over five years as monthly $8.33 "license fees." When are the five years of license fees reported as revenue? On day one, when the phone is sold.

This is permissible under generally accepted accounting principles if full collection is reasonably assured. But, for Intellicall, full collection is doubtful. In fact, *Forbes* spoke to several dealers who have stopped paying the license fees and who say they know of a few dozen others who have done the same. Why? The dealers explain that Intellicall misled them on the economics of owning "smart" phones, so they've disabled the circuit boards of their phones and made them "dumb" again. Their estimates of phones on which license fees are not being paid already range as high as 10,000—out of a total of about 91,000 shipped . . . to *Forbes* this hot little company begins to look more than a little warmed over.

Source: D. W. Linden, "Dial F for Fishy," *Forbes,* November 25, 1991, pp. 158–160.

Under certain circumstances, it may be so difficult to estimate the likely amount of returns (and, thus, ultimate sales revenues) that revenue recognition should be deferred to that point at which return privileges expire. This treatment, however, is the exception, not the norm, and seldom occurs without pressure from auditors, if not regulators.

It is typical, however, to defer recognition of service revenues until the service is provided. It is at that point that accountants most commonly argue the revenue is "earned" (the critical event is providing the service at less than the contracted price). Arguably, in the case of Intellicall, no additional effort or cost is incurred to "provide the service," as the service is simply use of the provided "smart" feature. Similar issues arise in other industries such as the motion picture business: When should revenue be recognized on a contract signed between a studio and a TV network? Such contracts typically grant the network the right for a given number of years to televise a given motion picture(s) that were produced in the past. Given that the studio has to incur no additional effort or costs, can the studio recognize the revenue when the contract is signed or must the revenue be spread over future periods? No consensual agreement among accountants has developed. In these and similar cases where diversity of practice becomes too great, the FASB may feel compelled to intercede with a standard specifying one or a limited number of options. However, standards themselves frequently change over time as the popularity of different options shift.

REVENUE RECOGNITION AT TIME OF CASH COLLECTION

Goods and services are frequently sold on account (i.e., credit is extended rather than demanding immediate cash payment). Most firms extend credit even though they know that they will not collect from all credit customers. Some acceptable level of bad debts is reasoned simply to be the cost of the increased volume of sales made possible by more liberal credit policies. When the expected number of noncollectible accounts is small relative to total receivables and a reasonably reliable estimate, based on past experience, can be made, the following entries are appropriate.

Candem Manufacturing Corporation sold $400,000 of product in the month of May on account. Based on past experience, Candem projects that 2% will prove noncollectible. Subsequently, on June 30, Parker Enterprises, a customer who owes $4,000, concedes insolvency and declares bankruptcy. Candem expects no recovery. Related entries follow:

Accounts Receivable	400,000	
Sales Revenues		400,000
To record sales in May.		
Bad Debts Expense	8,000	
Allowance for Bad Debts		8,000
To record bad debts expense in May, thus matching revenues and enabling costs (expenses).		
Allowance for Bad Debts	4,000	
Accounts Receivable—Parker Enterprises		4,000
To write down specific receivables known to no longer be collectible.		

Income is not affected by this last entry; only asset and contra-asset accounts are involved.

However, the above illustrated treatment is not appropriate in circumstances in which there exist large uncertainties surrounding the collectibility of receivables. Arguably, this is the situation in which Sequoia Systems found itself in the In Practice box *Phantom Sales*.

ETHICS IN PRACTICE

Phantom Sales

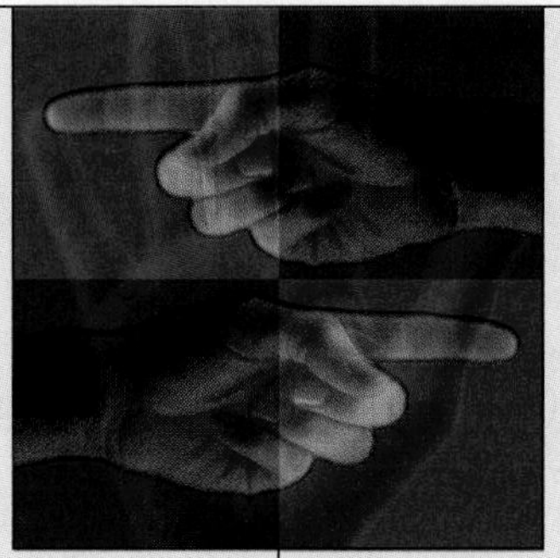

Sequoia Systems, Inc. (*www.swcollege.com/hartman.html*) seemed to have everything going for it. It was a hot company in a hot market selling "fault tolerant" computers designed to keep running even if a component failed. While others in the industry faltered, Sequoia's sales were soaring.

Or so it seemed. In fact, to keep up its rapid growth, Sequoia was booking questionable sales. In at least one case, it recorded the sale of a computer that the customer says it decided not to buy and never received. In other cases, it booked sales of computers on liberal terms to buyers who haven't yet been able to pay. Indeed, at one point, the company had receivables equal to almost half of its annual revenue, a level nearly double that of its competitors.

As a result, it forecast in May 1992 that it would post sales of $85 million for its fiscal year ended June 30, then in August reported sales of $71 million, restated them to $65.7 million, and now will have to restate them again, meaning that sales might be even lower than fiscal 1991's $63.2 million. The Securities and Exchange Commission has begun an investigation . . . "Like an old pinball machine, the situation you had was a 'tilt,'" concedes Richard Goldman, Sequoia's new chief financial officer, who was named acting co-chief executive officer last week.

Source: John Wilke, "Sequoia Systems Remains Haunted by Phantom Sales," *The Wall Street Journal,* October 30, 1992, p. B8.

If reliable estimates of bad debts cannot be made, revenues are not recognized until cash is collected. Even then, two methods are possible, as illustrated below.

Country Scouts, Inc., sold 42 pop-up tent trailers for $3,600 each. No down payments were required. Terms require customers to pay $300 per month, plus 12% interest on any unpaid balance. Country Scouts bought the trailers from the manufacturer for $1,800 each. Significant uncertainty exists which precludes reliable estimates of uncollectibles. The sales were recorded as follows:

Accounts Receivable	151,200	
Inventory		75,600
Deferred Installment Revenue		75,600

Jerome Thomas purchased one of the trailers. Under the installment sales method, revenue would be recognized as follows when Thomas's first- and second-month payments are received.

Cash	336	
Interest Revenue		36
Accounts Receivable		300
To record receipt of payment plus $36 interest ($3,600 × 12% × 1/12 year = $36).		
Deferred Installment Revenue	150	
Installment Revenue		150
To recognize installment revenue: Cash collected on account ($300) × gross profit margin (50%).		
Cash	333	
Interest Revenue		33
Accounts Receivable		300
To record receipt of second payment plus $33 interest ($3,300 × 12% × 1/12 year = $33).		

Deferred Installment Revenue	150	
Installment Revenue		150
To recognize installment revenue related to second payment: Cash collected on account ($300) × gross profit margin (50%).		

Country Scouts thus recognizes 50% of every dollar received (excluding interest) when received as revenue.

A second and still more conservative method (which is seldom used because of its extreme conservatism) would recognize no revenue until after all costs are fully recovered. Thus, the first $1,800 in collections on account (i.e., the first six payments) would prompt no recognition of revenue. However, after collecting the first $1,800, all collections, dollar for dollar, would be recognized as revenue.

REVENUE RECOGNITION WITH PASSAGE OF TIME

The preceding section noted that the percentage-of-completion method assumes value is added proportionately to cost incurrence. In cases where the interest rate is significantly less than the current market rate, the interest revenue on notes receivable is recognized under Assumption C of Exhibit 4–1. The assets (notes receivable) are assumed to appreciate at a compounding rate. This is called the *effective-interest method* and is illustrated in Exhibit 4–6. The **effective interest** is the interest revenue recognized on the book value of the asset at a constant rate (effective rate) over the life of the asset.

EXHIBIT 4–6
Recognizing Interest Revenue Over Time

On January 1, 1995, Ace Corporation accepted a $10,000,000, 3-year, 2% interest-bearing note from Beta Industries in full payment for the purchase of a piece of property that Ace had purchased in 1990 for $5,000,000, The current rate of interest for notes of similar risk is 10%. Annual payments of $200,000 occur on January 1.

Cash Flows and Present Values:

YEAR	CASH FLOWS	INTEREST FACTOR	PRESENT VALUE
1	$ 200,000	.9091	$ 181,820
2	200,000	.8264	165,280
3	200,000	.7513	150,260
3	10,000,000	.7513	7,513,000
			$8,010,360

Amortization Table:

DATE	BOOK VALUE	10% INTEREST	CASH PAID	AMOUNT DUE
1/1/95	$ 8,010,360	$ 801,036	$200,000	$ 601,036
12/31/95	8,611,396	861,139	200,000	661,139
12/31/96	9,272,535	927,465*	200,000	727,465
12/31/97	10,000,000*			
		$2,589,640	$600,000	$1,989,640

*Rounding differences to $10,000,000, due to use of 4-decimal interest factors.

EXHIBIT 4–6
(Concluded)

Date	Account	Debit	Credit
Jan. 1, 1995	Notes Receivable	8,010,360	
	Property		5,000,000
	Gain on Sale of Property		3,010,360
	To record sale of property at net present value.		
Dec. 31, 1995	Notes Receivable	601,036	
	Interest Receivable	200,000	
	Interest Revenue		801,036
	To record interest earned in 1995.		
Jan. 1, 1996	Cash	200,000	
	Interest Receivable		200,000
	To record partial payment of interest receivable in 1995 (12/31); remaining interest to be collected at maturity.		
Dec. 31, 1996	Notes Receivable	661,139	
	Interest Receivable	200,000	
	Interest Revenue		861,139
	To record interest earned in 1996.		
Jan. 1, 1997	Cash	200,000	
	Interest Receivable		200,000
	To record partial payment of interest receivable in 1996 (12/31); remaining interest to be collected at maturity.		
Dec. 31, 1997	Notes Receivable	727,465	
	Interest Receivable	200,000	
	Interest Revenue		927,465
	To record interest earned in 1997.		
Jan. 1, 1998	Cash	200,000	
	Interest Receivable		200,000
	To record partial payment of interest receivable in 1997; remaining interest to be collected at maturity.		
	Cash	10,000,000	
	Notes Receivable		10,000,000
	To record collection of note at maturity.		

In the effective-interest method (which is discussed in detail in a future chapter and only illustrated here), the asset (notes receivable), is recorded at the present value of the future cash inflows ($8,010,360, or what a bank might pay now for certain secured promises to pay in the future). In Exhibit 4–6, each of the future payments to which Beta commits is "deflated" or "discounted" for interest. Ace Corporation is engaged in two revenue-generating activities: (1) the sale of property and (2) financing (money lending). Ace determines that Beta's commitments to future payments are currently worth $8,010,360; the rest is interest ($2,589,640: payments of $10,600,000 less present value of $8,010,360). (The discount rate used is the current market rate of interest (10%). The present-value factors are found in Appendix A, Table A–2, "Present Value of a Single Sum." The interest revenue ($2,589,640) must be spread over the time of the loan (three years). The prescribed method to allocate interest revenue to different periods is the effective-interest method.

Each period, the effective interest earned is calculated by multiplying the carrying (book) value of the asset by the effective-interest rate. The difference between the effective-interest amount due and the annual cash interest amount received is the amount due which is added to the book value of the asset. Thus, the book value (or amount of claim) increases (compounds) each period by the difference between the cash interest received and the effective interest due. Value is thus added to the asset on a compounding basis.

COMPLEX APPLICATIONS IN THE "REAL WORLD"

When and how revenue should be recognized are often contentious issues between firms and their auditors and/or regulators. The complexity of intertwining value-adding processes and transactions is reflected in the case of Manufactured Homes (see In Practice box). This case is illustrative of a vertically integrated firm that may engage in several sequential value-adding processes: manufacturing, retailing, and financing.

If a firm manufactures a product, when should the revenue from the manufacturing process be recognized? The standard answer is when the revenue is realized (or realizable) and when the revenue is earned. As discussed above, this may be at various stages during production or at the end of production in the case of commodity-like products (e.g., precious metals, livestock, or grains), which can be sold at objectively determined prices on established markets. That is, revenue is recognized before actual sale because the ability to sell at set prices is assumed/guaranteed by the existence of an organized trading exchange. The sale is not the critical event; production at less-than-established market prices is the critical event. Revenue may also be recognized during or at end of production in the case of long-term construction projects under fixed price contracts. The sale in this case is also not the critical event. The sale precedes production. Again, the critical event arguable is production at a cost less than the contracted price.

Neither of these conditions, however, applies in the case of a manufacturer of prefabricated or mobile homes. These items are not commodity-like goods, and sales typically occur after production, not in advance, with the sales not ensured at any particular price. The manufacturer may know at what price it wishes to sell the item, but actual selling price will depend on various market conditions, including competitors' prices. So, when should revenue be recognized? When is the revenue "earned"? And, what is the "critical event" that ensures profit has developed?

When is revenue "realized"? Ordinarily, a manufacturer must wait until the product is sold to a retailer (or wholesaler) or to another manufacturing firm if the item is used in a larger product (e.g., a radio used in an automobile). But conditions are more complicated if the firm is a vertically integrated firm. This is the case when a manufacturer retails part or all of its output to the ultimate consumer. A retailer provides value by locating a willing buyer (via advertising or other means) and providing the product at the right place and the right time. The value added by the retailer is reflected in the spread between the price the retailer pays for the product and the price at which the retailer sells it. The critical event is the successful bringing together of the product and a willing buyer, at a particular price, place, and time. This achievement is reflected in a consumated sale. Typically, retailers recognize revenue at the point of sale. But what if the firm is both a manufacturer and a retailer? When is revenue recognized? And, should it be recognized at only one point?

IN PRACTICE—GENERAL

Manufactured Homes

"Disappearing Act: How Manufactured Homes' Profit Vanished." Several weeks ago, North Carolina-based ***Manufactured Homes,*** which sells primarily low-priced mobile homes to customers in seven southeastern states, released [its] 10K report. . . . It doesn't make pretty reading. In fact, the financial disclosure document reveals that the company's efforts to obfuscate its dismal financial condition and operating results are headed toward an inglorious conclusion. . . . It discloses among other things that the SEC's "informal inquiry" is into Manufactured Homes' "method of accounting for sale of receivables with recourse."

More specifically, the commission's staff is taking issue with the company's accounting for the transfer of receivables with recourse under provisions of Statement of Financial Accounting Standards (SFAS) No. 77.

Traditionally, at least through 1987, the company sold—with recourse—its customers' retail installment credit agreements to financial institutions at a price based on an agreed upon interest rate that was below the rate to be paid by the customer. The difference was dubbed the company's financial participation income.

When it sold its retail installment sales contract, Manufactured Homes would receive immediate payment for its stated principal amount and a portion of the finance participation resulting from the interest rate differential. The financial institution would keep the rest of this differential as security against credit losses and pay it to the company only in proportion to customer payments received. But Manufactured Homes would account for these transactions as sales of receivables, under SFAS No. 77, recognizing up front virtually all the potential finance participation income.

Source: Abraham Briloff, "Disappearing Act: How Manufactured Homes' Profit Vanished," *Barrons,* May 29, 1989, pp. 46–47.

Consider the case of a manufacturer who produces 100 mobile homes at a cost of $20,000 each and sells half to a national retailer of mobile homes for $30,000 each and keeps the other half of production to retail directly to ultimate consumers. It is expected that the selling price to the ultimate customer will be $40,000 per unit. Vertically integrated firms that (1) sell part of their output to other manufacturers or retailers and (2) retail part of their output directly are common in the petroleum, distillery, forestry, and various manufacturing industries. A challenging question is whether value added during production should be recognized as revenue when the opportunity to sell is objectively confirmed (in this case, by sale of 50% of output at $30,000) or whether revenue and value added can only be recognized on the portion actually sold. What are the vital distinctions between the opportunity to sell, confirmed by the existence of an organized commodity exchange, and the opportunity to sell confirmed by partial sale or documented offers to buy? These and similar issues continue to challenge accountants. Accountants still disagree as to when a value-adding process is complete, when revenue has been earned, and, very importantly, when revenue has been realized or is realizable. Recall that "realized" is defined as "when products, merchandise, or other assets are exchanged for cash or claims to cash." Realizable is defined as "when related assets received *or held* are readily convertible to known amounts of cash or claims to cash." Conservative traditions discourage "premature" revenue recognition; however, corporate America often poses challenging arguments as to when revenue is *realizable.*

The example of Manufactured Homes shows vertical integration extending beyond manufacturing operations and retailing operations to include financing operations. In this example, consumer purchases of mobile homes might be financed by a bank or by the retailer, or some by the bank and other sales by the retailer. In these instances, a question that must be addressed with regard to revenue recognition is whether revenue can only be recognized for cash sales (i.e., sales financed by banks). Has revenue only been technically *realized* with respect to cash sales? Must recognition of the value added during the production process as well as value added during the retailing process be postponed until eventual receipt of cash? Typically, the answer is no. Revenue is realized when assets are exchanged for cash *or claims to cash.* As discussed in the section entitled *"Time of Cash Collection"*, barring great uncertainty regarding collectibility of accounts, the installment method, which recognizes revenue only upon receipt of cash, is *not* used. Normally, revenue is recognized at the point of sale, and an estimate is provided to reduce revenue for some expected percentage of noncollectible accounts.

When Manufactured Homes receives cash from retail customers who finance with Manufactured Homes, however, the total cash collected will exceed the selling price. It will include interest. Thus, if a mobile home is sold for $40,000, eventual payments by the customer may exceed $60,000 (the difference being interest.) Thus, still another revenue recognition question arises. When should interest income be recognized? Typically, the accounting profession directs that interest be a function of time and must be recognized over time. The value-earning process is the sacrifice of other uses for funds by lending them to the customer. Thus, if a ten-year mortgage is provided, interest revenue is recognized over that ten-year period. However, in the In Practice article, it is noted that Manufactured Homes did not always choose to wait the full period. Rather, it chose to "sell" the receivables in some cases to a financial institution. The "sales" to the financial institution were at more than the recorded amount of Accounts Receivable but less than the aggregate amount of cash to be collected over the ten years (for example, for one sale, more than $40,000 but less than $60,000). The financial institution may be willing to pay more than $40,000 because the $20,000 of interest charged to the customer is more than required by the bank. The practice that the SEC challenged was the immediate recognition of any excess paid by the financial institution in excess of $40,000. When the difference should be recognized as revenue depends on one's perspective.

If the point of view is taken that receivables are just like any other asset (say, a truck) and the firm is simply selling one of its assets above book value, immediate revenue recognition seems defensible. If, however, the asset is sold with certain significant rights of return (as discussed on page 166 in the section entitled "Revenue Recognition at Time of Expiration of Return Privileges") or similarly with significant rights of recourse, as in the Manufactured Homes example, cogent arguments can be made for postponing revenue recognition. Rights of recourse mean that if the customer fails to pay the accounts (mortgages) payable, the seller of the receivables (in this case, Manufactured Homes) would have to reimburse the financial institutions for those defaults. If significant questions about collectibility exist, conservative traditions could argue to delay revenue recognition until the customer actually makes payments.

Similarly, revenue recognition should be delayed if the perspective taken is that the transaction between Manufactured Homes and the financial institution is not a sale at all but a collateralized loan. The issue, then, is the substance of the transaction versus form. Authoritative accounting pronouncements insist that accountants look to substance over form. It could be contended in the case of Manufactured Homes that the cash extended by the financial institution was simply a loan against which the borrower provided collateral, in this case, some amount of its accounts receivable. The "with recourse" provisions of the transaction give some enhanced credibility to this interpretation. If the events were viewed as a loan, Manufactured Homes would have to (1) recognize interest revenue from the customer over the mortgage period and (2) recognize interest expense to the financial institution over the same mortgage period. That is, recognition of any net profit would be deferred rather than recognized immediately. Challenging real world cases such as these are frequent, and their resolutions demand considerable professional judgment. The Chemical Bank case featured in an In Practice box earlier in this chapter refers to a similar instance of receivables sales, with Chemical Bank opting for immediate revenue recognition, much to the displeasure of accountants and regulators. Issues of revenue recognition remain among the most difficult confronted by professional accountants.

CONCEPTS OF INCOME AND CAPITAL MAINTENANCE

Understand the concepts of income and capital maintenance.

Comprehensive income is defined as "the change in equity of a business enterprise, during a period, from transactions and other events and circumstances, from nonowner sources."[19] As such, it includes all changes in equity during a period except those resulting from investment or disinvestment by owners.

The concept of **income** is essentially one of "better-offness." The question is, "How much better off is an entity today than twelve months earlier?" An entity is better off to the extent that its revenues are adequate to pay all expenses and that it has something left over. A concept of **maintenance of capital**, or *recovery of cost*, is a prerequisite for separating a **return *on* capital** from a **return *of* capital**. Only revenue inflows in excess of amounts necessary to maintain the preexisting status contribute to a change in equity and owner better-offness.

Three concepts of capital maintenance are considered today: maintenance of nominal financial wealth, maintenance of real financial wealth (or purchasing power), and maintenance of physical (or resource) wealth. A simple example may serve to illustrate these three concepts. Assume that a young couple purchased a home in Anytown, USA, in 1985 for $100,000. During the course of the ensuing 10 years, the nation experienced significant inflation, with the consumer price index rising from 100 to 160—that is, a 60% aggregate inflation. In 1995 the couple sold the home for $180,000 and purchased a comparable home on the other side of town to be geographically nearer to their work. How much better off are they in 1995 than 1985? Using a capital-maintenance concept focusing on nominal financial wealth, the couple is better off by $80,000 (the $180,000 sale price minus the $100,000 purchase price).

Using a capital-maintenance concept focusing on purchasing-power change, $160,000 of the $180,000 sale price of the home was necessary to maintain the purchasing power sacrificed when the home was purchased (60% appreciation is needed to keep pace with inflation, or a diminished dollar value). Thus, the couple's return *of* equity is $160,000, and only $20,000 represents a return *on* equity (or income). They are better off by $20,000.

Using a capital-maintenance concept focusing on physical wealth, the couple is not better off at all because of the sale, since all the proceeds of the sale ($180,000) were needed to purchase a comparable replacement home that would maintain their presale living condition. Further, on which income measure should income taxes be assessed?

[19]SFAC No. 6, Elements of Financial Statements, FASB, 1985, par. 70.

The current monetary unit or measurement scale used in U.S. financial statements is the nominal dollar, unadjusted for changes in purchasing power over time. Accordingly, *current practice does not accommodate a capital-maintenance concept that focuses on purchasing power or real wealth.* In the balance sheet, current practice adds together dollars expended on assets acquired in different years as if the dollars were stable. Thus, preparation of financial statements is simpler with nominal dollars than with either of the other methods. The disadvantages of the nominal-dollar, capital-maintenance concept are discussed in later chapters when ratio analyses related to specific long-term accounts and inventory are the focus of attention.

IN FOCUS

Celeste Rooney
Assistant Controller, Dinsmore & Shohl

Unlike manufacturers or retailers that sell tangible products, service companies generally cannot tie revenue recognition to easily identified events such as delivery or installation. Service providers must use other criteria, which vary from industry to industry and even project to project. Celeste Rooney, assistant controller of the law firm ***Dinsmore & Shohl*** and former controller of an architectural firm, has seen how the special characteristics of these firms shape the accounting techniques they use.

For instance, differences between architecture and law mean differences in the timing of revenue recognition. While both firms use cash-basis accounting and recognize revenue when it is billed and received, the nature of their work has a big impact on when billing can take place. The architectural firm normally sets a fixed fee for a project and invoices the client as the project progresses. For instance, if the project is contracted to be complete in one year, payment may be made in monthly installments as long as it stays on schedule. In other cases, payment may be tied to specified milestones, such as 25% payment due at the end of the design phase. "The key in this case," says Rooney, "is that you typically know in advance what the total fee is, even though you bill it and recognize the revenue in phases. And because you're working toward a tangible result, such as a new office building, you can identify when one phase is done and the next one is starting."

Contrast these billing arrangements with a contingent fee in the legal environment. Contingent fees, used in wrongful death suits, for example, mean that the plaintiff's law firm is paid only when the client receives a judgment or out-of-court settlement from the defendant. Because it can never be known with certainty whether a case will be won or what the awarded damage amount may be, it is impossible to recognize revenue as the case progresses even though expenses for depositions and other activities are incurred along the way. "If you look at the financial statements before a case is complete, you would only see the impact of expenses," Rooney explains. "We basically go in the hole until the case is concluded and an award is made. We don't know what the revenue will be, so there's no way to recognize it earlier." And, of course, if the plaintiff is not awarded damages, revenue is never received or recognized, similar to a manufacturer that produces a product that never sells.

Revenue recognition is just one of many functions Rooney is involved in. She emphasizes the importance of attention to detail in all of her responsibilities. "Most entry-level accounting positions require what seems at the time to be 'grunt work,'" Rooney describes. "But that kind of work where you get into the finest level of detail in the financial statements and systems is where you really learn about how minor errors can snowball into major problems. Without that experience, it's easy to lower your standards for accuracy and detail. When that happens, you can't place much faith in the numbers being used to make decisions about the operations of the firm."

Current practice does accommodate a physical capital-maintenance concept. In some instances, and for some financial statement elements (to be discussed in later chapters), replacement cost is the measurement attribute favored by current practice; thus, no single capital-maintenance concept is pervasive, although the nominal-dollar financial concept is dominant.

END-OF-CHAPTER REVIEW

SUMMARY

1. **Understand the concept of recognition.** Recognition is the process of formally recording or incorporating an item into the financial statements of an entity. As such, the process of accounting recognition must identify and measure those events, transactions, and circumstances that should be captured in the accounting information system.
2. **Interpret the recognition criteria for assets and liabilities.** Recognition of an asset or liability should take place when an item (1) exhibits the characteristics of an asset or a liability, and when it is (2) measurable, (3) relevant, and (4) reliable.
3. **Interpret the recognition criteria for revenues.** Revenue should be recognized when it is realized or realizable and earned. Revenue is said to be realizable and earned when the earnings or value-adding process is substantially complete, meaning that the event critical to the ultimate economic success of an entity has occurred.
4. **Apply various revenue-recognition points to appropriate situations.** Revenue is recognized when it is realized or realizable and earned. Long-term construction contracts can be accounted for under the percentage-of-completion method or the completed-contract method. The revenue-recognition points depend on the method used, during the construction process for the former, or at the end of the project for the latter. Interest revenue follows the effective-interest method, which provides recognition of a constant rate of return on the book value over the life of the investment. Commodities are an example of revenue recognition at the completion of the production cycle as opposed to the point of sale.
5. **Understand the concepts of income and capital maintenance.** Comprehensive income is the change in equity between balance sheet dates arising from nonowner sources: basically revenues minus expenses. The economic concept of income is that of better-offness at one point in time compared to another.

KEY TERMS

ASSIGNMENT MATERIAL

CASES

C4–1 Judgment and Materiality

A pervasive recognition constraint is the materiality of an item. In fact, Statements of Financial Accounting Standards (SFAS) only prescribe treatments for "material" items. It has been charged, nonetheless, that materiality suffers a serious definitional problem. For example, in court cases involving the issue of materiality, the following definitions have appeared:

1. Any fact that would affect the investor's decision to buy, sell, or retain.
2. Any fact that would materially affect the judgment of the other party to the transaction.
3. Any fact that would influence the reasonable and prudent person in an investment decision.
4. Any fact having a "significant propensity" to influence the investment decision.
5. Any fact a recipient would be likely to regard as important.
6. Materiality standards that vary according to situations, contexts, and companies.
7. Any omission of facts that has a substantial likelihood of affecting the average prudent investor's decision.

On pages 179–180 are two cases, A and B, involving liability and revenue-recognition issues. In each, "recognition versus nonrecognition" may turn on whether the item is material. Each case requires you to determine at what level an item becomes material. Consider that jury members who probably have no more accounting knowledge than you (and most frequently less) must decide these and similar matters in court. Consider each case independently.

Both cases presented assume a firm of identical financial dimensions. That is, the following financial information applies to each case:

BALANCE SHEET

(IN THOUSANDS OF DOLLARS)	YEAR 1	YEAR 2	YEAR 3
Cash & receivables	$ 22,842	$ 14,213	$ 13,236
Receivables	47,485	50,284	50,933
Inventories	73,955	75,418	75,075
Other current assets	13,343	7,162	3,336
Long-term assets	224,353	283,869	284,273
Total assets	$381,978	$430,946	$426,853
Short-term liabilities	$ 76,496	$ 75,141	$ 86,959
Long-term liabilities	107,653	149,218	124,973
Stockholders' equity	197,829	206,587	214,921
Total liability and equity	$381,978	$430,946	$426,853

INCOME STATEMENT

(IN THOUSANDS OF DOLLARS)	YEAR 1	YEAR 2	YEAR 3
Sales	$585,133	$698,456	$780,172
Cost of sales	(526,028)	(639,462)	(713,795)
Selling and administrative expenses	(26,747)	(29,299)	(36,471)
Other expenses	(5,150)	(4,859)	(6,725)
Income taxes	(7,316)	(6,909)	(7,777)
Extraordinary items and discontinued operations	(3,500)	0	0
Net income	$ 16,392	$ 17,927	$ 15,404

Financial Ratios:

	YEAR 1	YEAR 2	YEAR 3
Current ratio	2.1/1	1.96/1	1.6/1
Debt-to-equity ratio	.93/1	1.08/1	.98/1
Earnings per share	$2.22	$2.42	$2.07
Income to assets	4.3%	4.1%	3.6%
Income to equity	8.3%	8.6%	7.2%
Net margin	2.8%	2.6%	2.0%

Case A (for C4–1)

Certified Products Company is a medium-sized, publicly traded, U.S. corporation founded in 1958. It engages in the manufacture and wholesale distribution of ceramic tile products and cleaning products for use in the home and industry. During the current annual audit, pursuant to the firm's publication of its annual financial statements, the auditors and management have arrived at an impasse as to whether a certain contingent loss must be disclosed. The contingency relates to a lawsuit filed against Certified Products by another corporation. Knowledge of the pending court action is not widespread; that is, the suit has not been reported in the financial press.

Current accounting standards issued by the FASB require footnote disclosure of contingent lawsuits if the probability of loss occurring is "reasonably possible" and if the loss is also "material." A loss must be recognized and a liability reported if the likelihood of the loss occurring is "probable" and if the loss is "material." Independent legal counsel, who are specialists in this type of case, were engaged by the auditor and advise that the likelihood of loss is about 75%, that is, "probable." The general question is at what size loss *you* would find the item "material." The materiality would cause the auditor to insist on management's disclosure of the item in the annual statements and report to stockholders, or disclose the item in the auditor's opinion, which is published as part of the annual financial report to stockholders. Management is strongly opposed to recognizing any loss currently, stating, "We still have a good chance to win this thing!" They further argue that recognizing the loss now will hurt their case in court.

As you reflect on the materiality issue and examine the financial data presented for this case, what factors do you feel should be considered in making this decision? Evaluate the relative significance that you believe should be given to each of the following items. A choice of "1" indicates "No Importance," and a choice of "10" indicates "Critical." Also discuss which items you believe to be most important and why. What other items might be relevant?

The contingent loss as a percentage of

1. working capital 1..2..3..4..5..6..7..8..9..10
2. total revenues 1..2..3..4..5..6..7..8..9..10
3. total assets 1..2..3..4..5..6..7..8..9..10
4. net income 1..2..3..4..5..6..7..8..9..10
5. long-term liabilities 1..2..3..4..5..6..7..8..9..10
6. the earnings trend impact 1..2..3..4..5..6..7..8..9..10

Lastly, specify the specific dollar threshold amount at which you would deem the contingent loss "material."

Case B (for C4–1)

Damber Industries is a medium-sized, and until recently, a privately held, U.S. corporation founded in 1959. Damber engages in the manufacture and wholesale distribution of ceramic tile products and cleaning products for use in the home industry. During the current audit, pursuant to the firm's filing of stock registration documents with the SEC and issuance of new stock to the public, the auditors and management have arrived at an impasse. Early last year, management decided to expand their product line with a new form of glazed tile. The new tile was rushed into production and then distributed nationally to building suppliers and contractors. The much touted new product, unfortunately, was subsequently found to suffer from a severe application defect. Production has been halted, but Damber holds a large inventory of returned defective tiles. As no buyer could be found during the last half of the year, management has decided to crush the existing inventory next year and reuse it as raw material in the production of conventional tile products. This reuse of the product base naturally will result in an accounting loss.

The auditors, reasoning per GAAP that the inventory is permanently impaired and overstated in value, argue that the asset should be written down immediately on the balance sheet and the loss charged against income this period on the income statement. The inventory would then better reflect market value. Management, on the other hand, strongly prefers to delay the write-off of the asset and the reporting of the loss to current and prospective shareholders. Disclosure of the loss so soon after the product's much touted introduction would prove embarrassing. The disagreement ultimately may be resolved on the basis of "materiality." As all accounting standards apply only to "material" items, the recognition of the loss (inventory write-down) this period is mandated only if the matter is material. The general question is at what size loss the item should be found material. If the item is determined to be material, the auditor must insist on either management's recognition of the loss this period or the disclosure of the matter in the auditor's opinion, which is published as part of the stock registration.

As you reflect on the materiality issue and examine the financial data presented for this case, what factors do you feel should be considered in making this decision? Evaluate the relative significance you believe should be given to each of the following items. A choice of "1" indicates "No Importance," and a choice of "10" indicates "Critical." Also discuss which items you believe to be most important and why. What other items might be relevant?

The contingent loss as a percentage of

1. working capital 1..2..3..4..5..6..7..8..9..10
2. total revenues 1..2..3..4..5..6..7..8..9..10
3. total assets 1..2..3..4..5..6..7..8..9..10
4. net income 1..2..3..4..5..6..7..8..9..10
5. long-term liabilities 1..2..3..4..5..6..7..8..9..10
6. the earnings trend impact 1..2..3..4..5..6..7..8..9..10

Lastly, name the specific dollar threshold amount at which you would deem the inventory loss material.

Additional Questions:

A. Were your answers the same in both cases? Why or why not?

B. If you discussed these cases in groups, how closely did members of the group agree? Do you believe that members of the profession would come to consensual answers? What answers do you believe professional accountants would come to? If not the same as your answers, why not?

C. As these same cases actually have been previously addressed by U.S. judges, attorneys, and Big Six audit managers and partners, comparisons of your responses to those of others is possible. Your instructor has summary data. After examining this data (published in *Securities Law Review*, 1986, pp. 37–86), how consensual do you believe accountants are with respect to interpreting the concept "material"?

C4–2 Revenue Recognition and Measurement

The Eddie Bender Pool Company sells and constructs residential swimming pools in Ahwatukee, Arizona. During a sales campaign conducted in late 1997, Bender contracted to build 300, 35-foot, kidney-shaped pools for individual customers by May 1, 1998. One hundred of these customers paid the total contract price in advance, to secure a 10% discount; their net price was $9,000. The other 200 customers provided the minimum down payment of $1,000; their balance due on completion of the pool was $9,000. Construction of these pools was scheduled for January through April of 1998.

Construction of the pools was to be done by a Bender crew in part or entirety and/or by subcontractors. Bender frequently finds he has secured more contracts than he can complete on a timely basis. Routinely when this occurs, Bender assigns the actual construction tasks to subcontractors with whom he has worked before. Since Bender is the dominant pool contractor in Ahwatukee, several smaller contractors have come to rely on work from Bender. Eddie Bender has found these subcontractors to be highly reliable; further, if completion of assigned construction is delayed, the subcontractors, who are fully bonded, must bear a $100 per day penalty for late completion of the job.

Bender has found that construction costs can be reliably estimated as follows:

CONSTRUCTION TASK	BENDER CREW	SUBCONTRACTORS
Digging and earth removal	$ 900	$1,000
Framing	800	1,000
Electrical & plumbing	700	850
Equipment & installation	700	900
Concrete shell	1,400	1,800
Plaster	1,200	1,200
Decking	1,000	1,300
	$6,700	$8,050

In only rare instances have actual costs deviated from these estimates by more than 3% for any aspect of the construction.

Actual construction occurred between January and April 1998. Bender crews, operating at full-time capacity, provided for 200 of the contracted sales; subcontractors attended to the other 100 contracts (50 of which were among those contracts prepaid in full). Subcontracted costs were true to estimate except for decking costs, which in aggregate ran over by $2,000, and plaster, which ran over by $1,400.

Required:

A. Discuss the economic substance of the Bender operation; what is it that Bender does that contributes to its success or failure? Does Bender do one thing or several things that "earn" profit and add value?

B. The accounting profession attempts to provide users with information that is both reliable and relevant. To meet those ends, when do you believe profit should be recognized in this case and in what amount(s)? Discuss different ways of measuring the value added (income earned) by Bender, and evaluate the reliability of each approach.

C. If you were a December college graduate entertaining offers for an entry-level accounting position at two construction companies (Bender and one other), would the number of signed contracts that each firm had in hand at year-end be relevant and timely information to your decision? Discuss the trade-off between information relevance and reliability.

C4–3 Sale of Future Revenue

Early in January 1997 a successful rock star completed recording for a new release on CD and cassette tape. This recording is to be released in October 1997. All indications are that the recording should be a huge success. The star will receive royalties from the recording company based upon a percentage of CD and cassette sales. The musician has no further obligations regarding promotion of the new release. The recording company assumes all liabilities and costs to market the release.

Desiring an immediate return, the rock star sells to an independent third party the right to receive a portion of her future royalties from the release. The buyer pays the star in March 1997 a total of $3 million; in return, the buyer is to receive 10% of the star's royalties from the release for the five-year period from 1998 through 2002. All projections are that the buyer should receive a generous return on the $3 million investment, but these returns are not guaranteed. The star is not obligated to guarantee any minimum royalties; the buyer is entitled only to the specified percentage of royalties, no matter what amount. Further, the rock star is not prevented from selling additional percentages of her royalties, either for the upcoming release or for other recordings.

Required:

A. First, ignore the sale of future royalties to the third party.
   1. Identify alternative approaches to the rock star's recognition of revenue for royalties from the new release. Which alternative do you prefer and why?
   2. How would your response change (if at all) if the rock star was contracted to help promote the release through the creation of videos for MTV and through concert tours?

B. Now consider the sale of future royalties to the third party.
   1. Identify alternative approaches to the rock star's recognition of revenue for the $3 million. Which do you prefer and why?
   2. How would your response change (if at all) if the buyer was to pay the $3 million in three installments: $1 million in March for the next three years beginning with the first installment paid up front in 1997?
   3. How would your response change (if at all) if the rock star guaranteed the buyer would receive a minimum of $3.5 million from the specified percentage of royalties by the end of the year 2002? Any amount less than the $3.5 million would have to be paid by the rock star.

C4–4 Sale of Products With Other Considerations

Middleman Enterprises purchases surgical supplies in volume from manufacturers and resells these supplies to hospitals at a price below that at which the hospitals could secure them individually. Among the products for which they do a large volume of sales are Capper model #312 surgical kits. These kits contain disposable products used with Capper surgical pumps. Capper's sales recently have increased markedly in the local market due to the distribution efforts of Middleman Enterprises. It is in Capper's interest to support Middleman Enterprises, which promotes Capper products in preference to those of other manufacturers. Capper would also like to introduce a new surgical kit, model #810. The new kit is both cheaper to produce (thus allowing increased profits) and technologically superior. The model #810 kit, however, may be used only in conjunction with a newly designed Capper pump. Capper's primary profits are derived from sales of the disposables, not sales of the pumps. Still, the initial outlay for the new pumps is significant enough to cause many hospitals to pause.

To achieve both their ends (to get the new pumps into the hospitals and to support Middleman Enterprises), Capper "sells" 10 of the new pumps (which retail at $20,000) to Middleman for $10,000 each in 1997. Capper's regional sales manager, however, simultaneously agrees to provide free "samples" of the old model #312 and new model #810 kits in an equivalent amount, $100,000 (about 120 days' sales).

Middleman Enterprises subsequently sells the pumps at deeply discounted figures. In 1998 one pump is sold to St. Mary Hospital for $10,000 cash. Another is sold to City General for $10,000. These hospitals are quoted a price for the disposables of $200 each for the next three years. This allows Middleman a $50 markup over the $150 price guaranteed by CAPPER. A third hospital, Mercy Hospital, needs two pumps but lacks current funds. In 1998 Middleman agrees to sell Mercy two pumps at $1,000 each; Mercy agrees (contracts) for a disposable surgical kit up-charge of 10% over the next three years. That is, Mercy agrees to pay $220 per kit over the next three years and agrees to purchase at least 1,000 kits. Thus, Mercy does not have to pay $18,000 currently but instead can pay in the future as surgeries are performed, and the costs can be passed on to the patient. (The $20,000 contracted minimum allows for interest in addition to cost.)

Required:

A. Discuss how Middleman should record the "purchase" of the pumps in 1997.

B. Explain how Middleman should record the delivery of the $100,000 in "samples."

C. Discuss how Middleman should record the sales to St. Mary and City General Hospitals of two pumps in 1998 and the sale to Mercy Hospital of two other pumps in the same year.

C4–5 Sale of Contract Rights

Rojo Inc. is the franchised U.S. distributor of Highland scotch whiskey. In January 1997, Rojo Inc. was experiencing serious negative cash flows. The problem was deemed to be only a short-term problem, however. To secure needed cash, Rojo sold contracts to customers providing rights to purchase up to 100,000 gallons of product over the next four years at $8.50 per gallon or 15% below prevailing wholesale market prices, whichever was lower. In January 1997 the product was selling at $10 per gallon wholesale. Klareden Clubs, Inc., Topper Clubs International, Hamilton Entertainment Group, and R. R. Enterprises each contracted with Rojo on July 1, 1997, for these rights, each paying $50,000 in cash. The contracted rights were transferrable.

Rojo had a five-year, fixed-price contract from the distiller to purchase up to 1,000,000 gallons over the next five years at $5 per gallon. Additional purchases would be at the prevailing distillery market price (currently $6). Transportation in to Rojo facilities, handling costs, and shipping costs to Rojo's customers typically ran about $.50 per gallon.

Required:

A. Discuss whether Rojo should recognize any revenue from the sale of the four fixed-price contracts to its customers at the point of sale.

B. On December 15, 1997, Klareden Clubs sold (assigned) its contractual rights to Palace Clubs, Inc., for $90,000. When may Klareden Clubs recognize these revenues?

C4–6 Ethical Considerations

In late 1997 Ashley-Kristin Products was preparing for a public-stock offering in early 1998. Sales had been somewhat sluggish in 1997. A push was on to increase sales in the last quarter to facilitate obtaining a good price for the new stock in early 1998.

To that end, on December 15, 1997, the Ashley-Kristin Products sales force solicited sales of 100,000 model A-12 compact disc (CD) players to Philips Home Appliances. Delivery was made December 27 to a public warehouse rented by Philips exclusively for the purpose of receiving these goods, at a cost of $20,000 per month. The sales price of the goods was discounted by Ashley-Kristin by $20,000. Terms did not require cash payment for 180 days; normal terms in the industry are 60 to 90 days. Philips was guaranteed right of return at any time within the 180 days; defective merchandise could also be returned subsequently. In the immediately preceding year, total model A-12 CD player sales of Philips Home Appliances had been 60,000 units.

In early January, Ashley-Kristin's external auditor is examining this transaction. Would the interests of the public be best served by recording sales revenue in 1997, or should an alternative procedure be followed? Discuss the alternatives and the possible consequences of the alternatives. Would it make a difference if Ashley-Kristin Products had been the short-term lessee of the warehouse rather than Philips?

C4–7 General Electric: Earnings Management

On November 3, 1994, *The Wall Street Journal* published an article entitled "Managing Profits: How General Electric Damps Fluctuations In Its Annual Earnings" (*www.swcollege.com/hartman.html*). The following is an excerpt from that article.

> The debacle at ***Kidder, Peabody & Co.*** might ruin the year for most companies. But the roughly $750 million in losses and after-tax charges that ***General Electric Co.*** will incur this year before finally unloading Kidder will barely dent GE's smooth, consistent earnings growth. Despite those losses, some analysts believe, GE may be able to match or top last year's profit of $5.13 billion.
>
> In the past decade, GE's earnings have risen every year, although net income fell in 1991 and 1993 because of accounting changes related to post-retirement benefits. The gains, ranging between 1.7% and 17%, have been fairly steady—especially for a company in a lot of cyclical businesses. As a result, GE almost seems able to override the business cycle.
>
> How does GE do it? One undeniable explanation is the fundamental growth of its eight industrial business units. "We're the best company in the world," declares Dennis Dammerman, GE's chief financial officer.
>
> But another way is "earnings management," the orchestrated timing of gains and losses to smooth out bumps and, especially, avoid a decline. Among big companies, GE is "certainly a relatively aggressive practitioner of earnings management," says Martin Sankey, a ***CS First Boston, Inc.*** analyst.

To smooth out fluctuations, GE frequently offsets one-time gains from big asset sales with restructuring charges; that keeps earnings from rising so high that they can't be topped the following year. GE also times sales of some equity stakes and even acquisitions to produce profit gains when needed.

Asked several times about earnings management, Dammerman declined to discuss directly whether GE engages in the practice. Asked whether offsetting one-time gains with one-time charges could be considered earnings management, he said, "I've never looked at it in that manner." He also declined to say whether other companies use such tactics.

Most U.S. companies do try to smooth profit growth. ***Walt Disney Co.*** (*www.swcollege.com/hartman.html*), for example, can decide when it wants profits from a videocassette re-release of "Snow White." Banks and insurance companies do a lot of smoothing by adjusting the level of their reserves, and many companies time write-offs carefully.

A look at GE illustrates how analysts say one giant corporation manages earnings. They add that few companies have maneuvered so successfully for so long on so large a scale. GE's size and diversity give it an unusual array of opportunities, of course. Moreover, Chairman Jack Welch relentlessly monitors GE's profit growth.

Last April, when announcing that a bond-trading scheme at Kidder had generated false 1993 profits and triggered a $210 million first-quarter charge, Welch said investors prize GE's ability "to deliver strong, consistent earnings growth in a myriad of global economic conditions. Having this reprehensible scheme . . . break our more-than-decade-long string of 'no surprises' has all of us damn mad."

His dislike of surprises extends beyond what GE's operating executives tell him to what GE tells Wall Street. Russell Leavitt, a ***Saloman Brothers*** analyst, says GE executives "give you some guidance" on what other analysts' estimates are and how reasonable they are. The result, says Ben Zacks of ***Zacks Investment Research,*** is that analysts' GE estimates fall in a "very, very tight range."

GE especially prizes consistent growth because it has so many different businesses that most analysts can't track them all. For example, GE is followed by electrical equipment analysts, most of whom have a loose grasp of financial services.

GE's two major parts are an industrial conglomerate and a financial services conglomerate, and both segments outdo their market peers. According to an analysis of data from ***Morgan Stanley & Co.,*** industrial conglomerates sold at an average 20% discount to the market as of Sept. 30, based on their multiple of price to next year's anticipated earnings, while financial services companies—banks, finance, and insurance—were at a 35% discount. But partly because of its consistent earnings growth, GE sold at a discount of only 11%.

Required: Develop responses to the following questions preparatory to a class discussion. Consider each question from the point of view of (1) current investors, (2) potential investors, (3) creditors, (4) financial analysts, and (5) the FASB.

A. GE's chairman states that investors prize a firm's ability "to deliver strong, consistent earnings growth." Do you believe that financial statement users would value earnings increases over a period of time that occur evenly more highly than the same increases that occur unevenly? Why or why not?

B. Would the nature of the industry involved influence your response to the above question?

C. What reasons would incline financial statement users to approve of income smoothing? to disapprove of it? Explain.

QUESTIONS

Q4–1 A major national fast-food franchisor signs a franchise agreement with a local franchisee on January 1, 1997. Under the terms of the contract, an initial franchise fee of $200,000 must be paid by the franchisee ($50,000 due each January 1 beginning in 1998 through January 1, 2001). The fee is compensation for assistance in site location, facility design, computerized information-systems implementation and initial employee training. A site is selected and acquired in June of 1998; construction is completed by November 1998. The facility opens for business on January 1, 1999. Initial employee training is conducted throughout the first two years of operations. Discuss issues of revenue recognition and measurement with respect to when the franchisor may recognize initial franchise fee revenue.

Q4–2 An event, transaction, or circumstance giving rise to an asset, liability, or change in an asset or liability should be recognized when what four criteria are met?

Q4–3 A revenue should be recognized when what six recognition criteria are met?

Q4–4 What is the distinction between when a revenue is realizable and when it is realized? What is the significance of the difference?

Q4–5 When is an asset readily convertible?

Q4–6 Revenues are "earned" when the entity has substantially completed what it must do to be entitled to the benefits represented by the revenues. Many professionals interpret this guidance to mean revenue should be recognized when the critical event (or events) occurs. In magazine publishing, two major sources of revenue exist—advertising fees (usually the larger) and subscription revenue. Significant activities undertaken by a magazine relate to procurement of advertising contracts, procurement of subscriptions, composition of articles, production/printing, and distribution. Discuss the value-adding process in publishing and when revenue might be recognized under the critical-event interpretation.

Q4–7 The application of the six revenue-recognition criteria is subject to two pervasive constraints. What are they?

Q4–8 Discuss the concept of conservatism as it relates to revenue recognition in accounting.

Q4–9 Windows to the value-adding process are said to appear in many industries but especially in vertically integrated firms. Consider the case of a vertically integrated rubber company that produces its own rubber, manufactures tires, and sells the tires both wholesale (via private labeling and through national chains such as ***Sears***) and through firm-owned retail tire stores. Discuss the availability of reliable value-added measures and the conceptual propriety of multi-point revenue recognition versus the practical utility of single-point revenue recognition.

Q4–10 When is an item considered "material'?

Q4–11 How does the completed-contract method differ from the percentage-of-completion method with respect to revenue recognition?

Q4–12 How does revenue recognition for commodities differ from revenue recognition for manufactured products?

Q4–13 Explain the distinction between a return on capital and a return of capital.

Q4–14 How is income related to maintenance of capital?

EXERCISES

E4–1 True or False?

___ 1. The calculation of cash-basis income is very subjective in that it requires the use of many estimates and judgments.

___ 2. The use of revenue-recognition criteria and the matching concept under U.S. GAAP allows firms a fair amount of discretion in their decisions on when to recognize revenue in some instances.

___ 3. When firms combine various "factors of production" to make a saleable product, they are creating value. Thus, the actual sale of the product does not actually create value.

___ 4. The role of the accountant in producing financial statements for external users is to protect these users by providing them with conservative financial statements, where great care is taken to recognize all possible expenses and liabilities but never to "anticipate revenues" (i.e., recognize revenue before the cash is received).

___ 5. Cash-basis accounting will provide financial statement users with income statements that are more useful for predicting income for future periods than will the use of accrual-basis accounting.

___ 6. Revenue may be recognized when it is realizable, not merely when it is realized.

___ 7. If a construction firm uses the completed-contract method of revenue recognition, it will end up, over the life of the firm, recognizing more revenue than it would if it had used the percentage-of-completion method.

___ 8. Cash-basis accounting recognizes transactions only if the transactions are complete and will have no further impact on the firm.

___ 9. An advantage of accrual accounting with respect to cash-basis accounting is that accrual accounting does not necessitate the delay of revenue recognition to the point of full business cycle completion (or cash recovery).

___ 10. Firms that produce coal can recognize revenue as the coal is placed into inventory. Firms that produce toothbrushes can also do this.

E4–2 Multiple Choice/Matching

1. Which of the following quantitative attributes of financial statement elements are not acceptable in any instances under GAAP?
   a. Historical cost
   b. Current cost
   c. Current market value
   d. Net realizable value
   e. Present value of future cash flows
   f. All of the above are acceptable in certain instances
2. U.S. GAAP provides for revenue to be recognized at various points in the value-adding process, depending on attendant circumstances. Which of the following is not a point at which revenue is customarily recognized?
   a. At the completion of production
   b. When the prices of readily salable assets change
   c. At the point of delivery
   d. At the beginning of production
   e. With the passage of time
   f. During production
3. Match the account and the measurement attribute(s) most commonly used in its measurement.

ACCOUNT	ATTRIBUTE
____ Accounts Receivable	**a.** Historical cost
____ Equipment	**b.** Current cost
____ Trading Securities	**c.** Current market value
____ Pension Obligations	**d.** Net realizable value
____ Leases	**e.** Present value of future cash flows
____ Patents	

E4–3 Point of Production Revenue Recognition—Net Realizable Value

Bandeman Construction Company signed a long-term construction contract committing to build a 30-mile stretch of highway over the next three years. The contracted price was $60,000,000. During the first year of construction, Bandeman incurs the following expenditures:

Material	$6,000,000
Labor	7,000,000
Equipment	3,500,000

Of the $6,000,000 expended for materials (cement, stone, etc.), $1,000,000 remains unused at year-end. Equipment costs of $3,000,000 were incurred at the start of the first year for the purchase of new earth-moving equipment, which is expected to have a six-year life. The other $500,000 of equipment costs was for the rental of other equipment used in the project. At the end of the year, total future costs to complete the project are estimated at $39,000,000.

Required: Calculate how much income should be recognized in the first year, and make all necessary entries under the percentage-of-completion method. Assume the firm will expense the full cost of the equipment in equal amounts in each of the six years.

E4–4 Revenue Allocation Using Compounding Assumption

On January 1, 1997, Ashley Corporation accepted a $10,000, 4-year, noninterest-bearing note from a customer in full payment of outstanding receivables in the amount of $6,355. The current interest rate for notes of similar risk was 12%, yielding a net present value of $6,355. Thus, interest revenue to be allocated over the ensuing four years was $3,645 (i.e., $10,000 repayment minus $6,355 original investment).

Required: Determine how much interest income should be allocated to each of the four years using the effective-interest method.

E4–5 Alternative Revenue—Recognition Points

On December 1, 1997, Sci-Fi Flicks, Inc., signed a contract with CineVision for the right to show a package of 30 films that Sci-Fi Flicks has produced over the past 12 years. CineVision received the exclusive right to show these films during the period of December 1, 1997, to December 31, 2002, and has signed a contract to pay Sci-Fi Flicks $5,000,000 immediately (December 1, 1997) and $4,000,000 per year for 1998–2002 (payable December 1 of each year beginning in 1998).

Required:

A. Identify possible alternatives for Sci-Fi Flicks regarding the recognition of the $25,000,000 as revenue.

B. Which alternative do you prefer and why?

E4–6 General Recognition Issues

Discuss the following proposed accounting treatments:

1. A retailer purchases washing machines from the manufacturer for $10,000 and records the transaction by crediting cash for $10,000 and debiting an expense.
2. The owner of a strip mall signs an 18-month rental agreement with a tenant on July 1, 1997, receiving the first six months' rent in advance. The transaction is recorded by debiting the cash received and crediting Rent Revenue. The owner of the mall uses a calendar-year accounting period.
3. Acton Industries made sales of merchandise in the amount of $120,000 in the current year with installment terms calling for the buyer to make equal payments of $10,000 over the 12 months beginning next January 1. The financial viability of the customer, however, is an open question, as they are currently in Chapter 11 bankruptcy reorganization proceedings. Acton records the transaction by debiting Accounts Receivable and crediting Sales for $120,000.
4. Shelbee, Inc., reacquired 3,000 shares of its own $5 par value common stock for $30,000. The stock when first issued was issued for $12 per share. Shelbee recognizes revenue of $6,000—the difference between the initial sale price of the stock ($36,000) and the reacquisition price. Does the $6,000 difference qualify as revenue?
5. Colleen Cosmetics, Inc., expanded its manufacturing facility by adding a new plant wing. The least expensive bid for the job received by an outside contractor was $12,000,000. Using its own employees, the firm built the wing itself, at a cost of $11,000,000. In recording the new construction, the firm debited Plant Assets for $12,000,000, credited Cash for $11,000,000 and recognized a $1,000,000 gain on construction.

E4–7 Critical Event for Revenue Recognition

For each of the following independent cases, indicate when revenue should be recognized in the income statement.

1. On December 15, 1997, $10,000 of merchandise was sold, with $1,000 received and payments agreed to in the amount of $100 per month plus interest until fully paid.
2. Cash of $1,500 was received on December 28, 1997, for merchandise that will be delivered on January 5, 1998.
3. A wheat crop planted in April 1997 was harvested in August 1997. The crop was stored until sale in February 1998.
4. Merchandise was sold and delivered on December 20, 1997. Payment for the merchandise was received on January 15, 1998.

E4–8 Revenue Received in Advance

Weist Publishing Company recognizes revenue as its monthly magazine is mailed to subscribers and newsstands. Robert Weist, the owner of Weist, has expressed a desire to record revenue on these subscriptions when the cash is received, at the beginning of the subscription period. What problems exist in Weist's proposal?

E4–9 Comparison of Valuation Methods

WWW is a specialty retailer of electronics. Wendy Watson, the owner of the company, is considering the use of different methods of valuation for internal purposes. She is considering the following three methods of valuation:

1. Fair market value
2. Net realizable value
3. Discounted present value

Required:

A. How could these methods be used by Watson?
B. How would the information provided by each of the valuation methods be helpful to Watson?

E4–10 Revenue Recognition at Various Points

For each of the following independent cases indicate under current GAAP the point at which revenue should be recognized and why.

1. Black Jack Distillery produces an expensive and highly regarded bourbon. The company uses an old secret recipe and ages its bourbon for eight years. In 1998 Black Jack puts $1,000,000 of bourbon in barrels to age for eight years, after which it will be bottled and sold. It is expected that the bourbon will increase in value at a compound annual rate of 20%.
2. Strike-It-Rich Mining Company mines gold. During the current year, 2,000 ounces of gold were recovered. Strike-It-Rich delivered 1,500 ounces of the gold to Exclusive Jewelers Inc. during the year at prices averaging $400 per ounce, the average market price of gold during the year.
3. The East India Trading Company builds oil tankers. Each tanker takes four years to complete and is built on contract to specific customers. East India receives 20% of the contract price on each ship at the time of signing of the contract and progress payments in increments of 20% at various stages of completion.

E4–11 Long-Term Construction

During 1998, Mitchell Corporation started a two-year construction job with a total contract price of $600,000. Additional data at the end of 1998 include the following:

Actual costs incurred	$150,000
Estimated remaining costs	300,000
Billed to customer	240,000
Received from customer	210,000

Under the percentage-of-completion method, what amount should Mitchell recognize as revenue and gross profit in 1998?

E4–12 Percentage-of-Completion

Jordan Construction is in the midst of a highway project expanding a 20-mile stretch of highway. Revenue contracted for this project is $200 million. Construction is estimated to take three years. By the end of the first year, construction costs were $30 million, and another $90 million in costs were estimated for the project.

Jordan used the percentage-of-completion method and recognized $50 million in revenue for this first year. Construction costs escalated during the second year. Costs for the project in the second year were $80 million, and at the end of this second year, Jordan expected remaining costs to total another $60 million.

Required:

A. How did Jordan determine the $50 million in revenue for the first year? What gross profit should be recognized for Year 1?
B. What percentage of the project is complete by the end of the second year?
C. How much revenue should Jordan recognize for the second year? What gross profit should be recognized for Year 2?

D. How should the project be reported on the balance sheet at the end of the second year if Jordan has billed the client a total of $50 million to date?

E. How should the project be reported on the balance sheet at the end of the second year if Jordan has billed the client a total of $120 million to date?

E4–13 Commodities

FreshLand Farms produces apples that are sold fresh to wholesalers during the months of January, February, and March. During 1997, the firm spent $50,000 on fertilizer, labor, and other production expenses. As of the first of September, all the fruit had been harvested and warehoused awaiting sale. Given the market price for apples on September 1, the crop could sell for $65,000. While the apples are waiting to be sold, they must be kept cold and surrounded by a gas that slows deterioration of the apples. Given expected inventory levels, the firm will spend $1,000 before sale for this storage.

Required:

A. If FreshLand wishes to recognize the revenue for the apple crop before it is actually sold, what entries will it have made during 1997?

B. If the value of the apples increases between September 1 and December 31 by $10,000, what entry should be made on December 31?

C. If the value of the apples declines by $10,000 before sale due to an unexpectedly large harvest (i.e., is expected to be a permanent decline), what December 31 entry should be made?

E4–14 When Is It Revenue?

1. Close-Out Kings, Inc., purchases overstocked and discontinued items at a discount, and it sells them to small wholesalers in several overseas underdeveloped countries. These items are sold on credit, and Close-Out Kings has agreed to receive payment for its merchandise after the wholesalers have succeeded in selling it. When should Close-Out Kings recognize revenue for these items? Why?
2. Tom's Tourist Stop, Inc., pays local teenagers for a particular kind of attractive rock found in the area, which it then polishes and sells to tourists. The area has been a prime tourist attraction for years, and Tom's has a large repeat clientele. The store has never had any difficulty selling all of the polished rocks it can obtain. It sells the rocks for a price of $5 each. Can Tom's, under GAAP, recognize the revenue for these rocks as they are polished? Why or why not?
3. Wandering River Ranch, Inc., operates as a vacation spot for city dwellers who want to "get away from it all" during the summer and fall months. The ranch provides all food and lodging for its guests during their stay. It takes reservations beginning January 1 of every year and has all its available cabins reserved by the end of March. All reservations must be paid in full by the middle of April. The actual vacationers arrive beginning May 1, and the last leaves by October 15. When should Wandering River Ranch recognize revenue?

E4–15 Is It Revenue?

1. A credit card company requires all of its cardholders to provide it with a deposit of $500 before opening an account. This money can be used to cover interest or charges made by the customer that are not paid for within the required period of time. Does the receipt of these $500 payments constitute revenue for the credit card company?

2. Weather Wise, Inc., a firm that installs aluminum windows and screens, requires its customers to pay for one-half of their order before the work is done. This money is used to purchase the materials required for the installation jobs the firm does. Weather Wise has signed a contract with Joe Williams for the installation of storm windows. The contract price is $1,200, and the firm received a check from Joe for $600 on August 20. Should this money be considered revenue? What entry should Weather Wise make for the receipt of this check?
3. A credit union provides advances to its members for income tax refunds due to these customers. The credit union charges its members interest at the rate of 10% per year on these advances. When should the credit union recognize the interest revenue for these advances?

E4–16 Installment Sales

Bell Tractor and Equipment sold a tractor to Meadowland Milk Producers for $75,000. The sale was on an installment basis with payments of $25,000 due at the end of years 2000, 2001, and 2002. The cost to Bell of the tractor was $60,000. Show the entries that Bell would make for this sale for 2000 using the installment sales method.

PROBLEMS

P4–1 Long-Term Construction

Mejia Company signed a long-term construction contract agreeing to build a mass transit rail system (trolley system) for the central business corridor of Phoenix, Arizona. The contracted price was $100,000,000. Work began January 1, 1997, with an estimated completion date of December 31, 2001.

During 1997 Mejia incurred the following costs related to the contract.

Payroll	$ 1,200,000
Insurance	800,000
Materials (cement, steel, etc.)	6,000,000
New equipment	10,000,000

The new equipment has a five-year expected life and will be used exclusively on this contract. Equal use of the equipment is expected each year, and one-fifth of the equipment cost will be expensed in each year.

At the end of 1997 Mejia estimated that the remaining costs to be incurred amounted to $40,000,000, including the $8 million of undepreciated equipment cost remaining.

During 1998 Mejia incurred the following additional costs relating to the contract:

Payroll	$3,000,000
Insurance	800,000
Materials	8,200,000

At the end of 1998, Mejia estimated that the remaining costs to be incurred amount to $36,000,000 including the remaining undepreciated equipment costs.

Required: Calculate the amount of revenue, expense, and net income to be recognized in 1997 and 1998.

P4–2 Interest-Bearing Note

Marlin Equipment Manufacturers accepted a $150,000, five-year, 5% interest-bearing note on January 1, 1998, from ReelTime Enterprises in full payment for merchandise that Marlin has manufactured at a cost of $80,000. The prevailing interest rate for notes of similar risk was 10%.

Make appropriate accounting entries on the books of Marlin Equipment Manufacturers for 1998 and 1999. Assume that interest for each year is due on the first day of January in the following year. Assume the firm uses the perpetual inventory method.

P4–3 Various Points of Revenue Recognition

Discuss when revenue should be recognized in the following cases.

- **Case A:** Polanski manufactures and sells patented switching devices for which it owns the patent. The product sells for $50 per item. Polanski's costs to manufacture the item average $23. These same products have been produced by Polanski for the last eight years in large volumes. Manufacturing costs have been extremely stable. Polanski has fixed-price contracts with suppliers of components and raw materials; a new multiyear labor contract recently has been signed. The company frequently works at or near the capacity of its manufacturing facility. When demand for the product exceeds productive capacity, Polanski frequently subcontracts out the manufacture of the product to E. L. Faris Corporation, with which it maintains a very good relationship. Faris Corporation has a very reliable supply record and charges $28 per unit, delivery guaranteed.

  In December 1997, Polanski signs a sales contract with Ford Motor Company to deliver 50,000 switching devices in 1998 and 50,000 units in 1999. Polanski's president wishes to recognize revenue from the sale in 1997. He argues that the creditworthiness of the customer is without question, the volume and selling price are fixed, and the costs to manufacture are highly predictable. When should revenue be recognized and why?

  If Polanski's facilities are working at capacity, and the new contract is also subcontracted in December 1997 with Faris at a price of $28 per unit for 50,000 units in 1998 and 50,000 in 1999, may Polanski then recognize any profit? Why or why not?
- **Case B:** On January 1, 1997, Hargraves and Company signed a 50-year lease on an office building at Broadway and Main Streets in Denver, Colorado. GAAP required Hargraves to treat the lease as a capital lease (capital acquisition). Accordingly, the lease rights were recorded as an asset at the present value of future contracted payments, $25,000,000. A long-term liability was established for a like amount.

  Later in 1997 Hargraves sublet the same property for the full term of the initial lease to a major Fortune 500 retail firm. Recent commercial development (groundbreaking by a major regional mall) had caused the value of the property to significantly appreciate. The present value of the scheduled future cash receipts under the sublease is $35,000,000. The sublessee assumes all risks of maintenance and ownership. May Hargraves recognize any revenue in 1997? Why or why not?
- **Case C:** C. J. Blevin, Inc., purchased patent rights in 1997 for $10,000,000. On January 1, 1998, Blevin assigned those patent rights in a noncancelable contract to Mendel Brothers Corporation, a firm of sound financial condition, for $1 per unit of sales of the patented product for 10 years. Mendel forecasts annual sales of 2,000,000 units. May Blevin recognize any revenue in 1998? Why or why not?
- **Case D:** Assume the same data as in Case C except that the forecast of annual sales is 3,000,000 units and that Mendel guarantees annual sales over this period of 2,000,000 units. May Blevin recognize any revenue in 1998? Why or why not?

P4–4 Revenue Recognition for Heavy Equipment Leases

Mammoth Machinery is a large manufacturer of heavy equipment. It has historically leased its equipment to customers. Mammoth then recognizes as revenue the payments from the customers as the payments are received. Thus, if the terms of the lease are for a five-year period, revenue from the equipment leased is recognized over the five-year contract period.

In 1997, Mammoth's company president changed the manner of revenue recognition on these contracts. Beginning in this year, it recognized all the revenue from the contract in the year that the contract was signed. You have just been hired by Mammoth as controller.

Required: Which method of revenue recognition can you justify? How should this be explained to the company president? Under what circumstances could either method be appropriate?

P4–5 Revenue Recognition

Oil Miners' Inc. pumps crude oil out of the ground and then sells it to Refinery Inc., which refines the oil, making gasoline. The gasoline is sold to U-Pump-It Inc., which distributes and sells gasoline at its local service stations. Assume that all sales are for cash.

The following events occurred over a three-year period:

- Oil Miners' Inc.
  1. **Year 1**—Pumps 100,000 barrels of crude oil at a cost of $10/barrel. Record as Crude Oil Inventory, and for simplicity, record the credit as "Various Credits."
  2. **Year 1**—Sells the crude to Refinery Inc. for $15 per barrel. (Record both the sale and the cost of goods sold.)
- Refinery Inc.
  3. **Year 1**—Purchased the crude oil mentioned above from Oil Miners' Inc. Record as either Crude Oil Inventory or Raw Materials.
  4. **Year 2**—Spends an additional $500,000 to refine the oil into 80,000 barrels of gasoline. (Create an account called either Gasoline Inventory or Finished Goods. For simplicity, record the $500,000 credit as "Various Credits.')
  5. **Year 2**—Sells the gasoline to U-Pump-It Inc. for $30 per barrel. (Record both the sale and the cost of goods sold.)
- U-Pump-It Inc.
  6. **Year 2**—Purchased the gasoline mentioned above from Refinery Inc. Record it as Gasoline Inventory.
  7. **Year 3**—Sells the gasoline at its pumps for $1.25 per gallon, totaling $5,000,000. (Record both the sale and the cost of goods sold.)

Required:

A. Journalize the transactions for each of these three independent companies. Then determine the amount of revenue and gross profit to be recognized by each company each year.

B. Now suppose that instead of three separate companies, these entities are different divisions of the same company.

1. If the company recognizes revenue at the traditional point of sale, how much revenue and gross profit would be recognized each year?
2. If the company recognizes revenue at points of production for products with intermediate markets, how much revenue and gross profit would be recognized each year?
3. Which of these alternatives do you prefer and why?

P4–6 Long-Term Construction Contract

Best Builders Corporation signs a long-term contract to build a factory and office complex for a local manufacturer. The contract price is $250,000,000. Work is scheduled to begin on April 1, 1998, with an estimated date of completion of December 31, 2002.

Best Builders began work on the site in 1998 and by year-end had incurred costs as follows:

Materials	$20,000,000
Labor	30,000,000
Overhead (insurance, equipment costs, etc.)	10,000,000

Best Builders has estimated the remaining costs on the project at $140,000,000.

Required: Prepare journal entries for 1998 using:

A. The completed-contract method.
B. The percentage-of-completion method.

P4–7 Recognition of Revenue on Warranties

On January 1, 1997, Eagle-American sold 10,000 trucks. The average price was $20,000. The buyers of 8,000 of the trucks also purchased a five-year maintenance contract at $2,000. Gross proceeds were $216,000,000. The average cost of the trucks was $16,000; the selling price thus yielded a margin of 20% of selling price. Estimated costs to service the warranty were as follows:

Year 1	$100
Year 2	150
Year 3	250
Year 4	300
Year 5	400

These costs have been highly stable over the last five years; no major design changes have occurred over that period to the trucks sold and warranteed. A normal markup for nonwarranty service is 25% over cost. Discuss the appropriate method to recognize warranty revenues.

P4–8 Utility Revenues

Center City Utility Corporation is operating at near capacity. Nonetheless, it contracts with Center City University to provide electrical power for the next five years at an off-peak-hour rate. Center City University's electrical needs have been highly stable over the last five years.

The utility corporation shortly thereafter enters into a five-year contract with Northern Electric to purchase electrical power equivalent to Center City University's needs. The contracted price with Northern Electric is 20% below the price charged Center City University. Northern Electric has significant excess capacity and had been soliciting business at the reduced rates for some time.

Center City Utility adroitly recognizes the opportunity to contract with the two parties and secures a handsome profit at no cost to itself. Its cost related to the arrangement over the next five years is immaterial. When should Center City recognize the related revenue and profits?

P4–9 Shipment of Goods to a Warehouse Awaiting Delivery

On December 15, 1998, Pilsman Corporation of Washington, D.C., ordered 100,000 model #C611 containers from BranForm Container Corporation of Chicago at $87 each. BranForm had 300,000 of the items in stock; their cost was $55, and estimated delivery costs would be $12 each. Pilsman, however, directs BranForm to delay normal delivery until after January 1 but before January 3, 1999. Normally shipping requires five to seven days. Pilsman agrees to pay for any special shipping costs incurred.

On December 22, BranForm ships the goods to a public warehouse in Baltimore, Maryland, 35 miles from Pilsman's facility. Pilsman agrees to pick up the goods from the rented warehouse on January 2. BranForm pays the rental fee for the warehouse and passes it on to Pilsman in the form of a special delivery cost. Discuss when BranForm should recognize the sales revenue.

P4–10 Effective Interest

On January 1, 1997, Kensington Corporation sold equipment to Heart Inc. that had a book value of $60,000 (original cost was $100,000). In payment, Kensington accepted 100, 10-year, 8% bonds of $1,000 par value. The market value of the equipment given and the bonds received was $87,710. This price provides a 10% internal rate of return (rate of interest). Interest is payable annually at year-end.

Required: Prepare an amortization schedule for the life of the 10-year bonds, using the effective-interest method.

P4–11 Effective Interest

On January 1, 1998, Moline Manufacturing Corporation sold merchandise (manufactured finished good inventory) to Spenser Corporation. The inventory had a carrying cost of $90,000. In payment, Moline Manufacturing accepted a 10-year, $100,000 face value note receivable with a stated rate of interest of 12%. The market value of the inventory sold and the note received was $112,289. This price provided a 10% yield or internal rate of return. Interest is payable annually at year-end.

Required:

A. Prepare a schedule allocating interest revenue over the life of the 10-year note, using the effective-interest method.

B. Prepare the journal entries necessary for all the related transactions for 1998, 1999, and 2000 for Moline Manufacturing.

P4–12 Long-Term Construction Contract*

London, Inc., began operation of its construction division on October 1, 1997, and entered into contracts for two separate projects. The Beta project contract price was $600,000 and provided for penalties of $10,000 per week for late completion. Although during 1998 the Beta project had been on schedule for timely completion, it was completed four weeks late in August 1999. The Gamma project's original contract price was $1,000,000. Change orders during 1999 added $40,000 to the original contract price. The following data pertain to the separate long-term construction projects in progress:

*Adapted from CPA exam, November 1993, Practice—Part I, Number 5.

	BETA	GAMMA
As of September 30, 1998:		
Costs incurred to date	$360,000	$410,000
Estimated costs to complete	40,000	410,000
Billings	315,000	510,000
Cash collections	275,000	365,000
As of September 30, 1999:		
Costs incurred to date	450,000	720,000
Estimated costs to complete	—	180,000
Billings	560,000	710,000
Cash collections	560,000	625,000

Additional Information:

1. London accounts for its long-term construction contracts using the percentage-of-completion method for financial reporting purposes.
2. London's income before income taxes from all divisions, before considering revenues from long-term construction projects, was $300,000 for the year ended September 30, 1998.

Required:

A. Prepare a schedule showing London's gross profit (loss) recognized for the years ended September 30, 1998, and 1999, under the percentage-of-completion method.

B. Prepare a schedule showing London's balances in the following accounts at September 30, 1998, under the percentage-of-completion method:
   1. Accounts receivable
   2. Costs and estimated earnings in excess of billings
   3. Billings in excess of costs and estimated earnings

P4–13 Commodities

Fairfield Enterprises is a large, vertically integrated food manufacturer. It owns farms that produce wheat for its use in baking. During 1997, these farms produced 100,000 bushels of hard red wheat (current market price is $9 per bushel). The firm plans to use all of this wheat in its own production processes during 1998. Production expenses included $140,000 for materials (fertilizer, chemical, seed, etc.), $400,000 for labor, $120,000 for equipment depreciation costs, and $20,000 for administrative expenses. Storage of the wheat until use is expected to cost $.30 per bushel.

Required:

A. Provide reasons for recognizing the revenue for the wheat crop at the completion of the harvest. Provide reasons for delaying recognition until the end products (baked goods) are sold. Which do you feel is preferable?

B. If the firm recognizes the revenue at the completion of the harvest, how much revenue would it record for the production of the crop and for its "sale"?

C. If the firm delays recognition of the revenue for the wheat until it is used in baked goods and the baked goods are sold, how will this influence the financial statements?

P4–14 The Purpose of Reporting

Return to the information provided for Problem 4–13. Assume that this firm has habitually recognized the grain revenue upon harvest. However, this year (1997) the firm is doing unusually well and expects to report record profits even without the grain revenue. The firm's top management does not expect that earnings can be maintained at this level in the future and would like to delay the recognition of the grain revenue until the sale of the final products (1998). This choice would present readers of the firm's financial statements with a less volatile earnings trend. Is this a reasonable and allowable thing to do? Discuss with attention to the management of the firm, the stockholders, other external users, and the auditors.

P4–15 Long-Term Construction Contract

Monumental Construction Co. began operations on January 1, 1998. It signed contracts to build three major projects, all of which are expected to take over one year to complete. Information on these projects is given below:

	PROJECT 1	PROJECT 2	PROJECT 3
Total contract amount	$500,000	$800,000	$450,000
Costs incurred during 1998	300,000	200,000	0
Estimated additional costs to complete	110,000	460,000	350,000

Monumental has received payments of $200,000 on the first project, $220,000 on the second project, and $50,000 on the third project.

Required:

A. What revenues and expenses would be recognized during 1998 using the completed-contract method?

B. What revenues and expenses would be recognized during 1998 using the percentage-of-completion method?

C. What revenues and expenses would be recognized during 1999 if the firm completes Project 1 with costs exactly as projected, spends $480,000 to complete Project 2, and spends 100,000 on Project 3 with an estimated $260,000 remaining to be spent? Use the percentage-of-completion method.

RESEARCH ACTIVITIES

R4–1 Up-Front Revenue Recognition

Harvey Speer Industries, having need of cash, "sold" $1,000,000 in customer's notes receivable to AIM Financial Services, Inc., for $1,048,000. Speer has found that historically, about 5% of notes receivable prove uncollectible. AIM Financial Services was willing to pay a premium for the receivables (even though 5% were unlikely to be collectible) because the customers' notes carried an interest provision of 20% on the 24-month notes; AIM's charge to Speer was considerably less (12%). The notes receivable are sold with recourse. AIM advances $990,000 to Speer at the transaction date, with the balance due at the end of 24 months. Speer recognizes all the revenue at the date of the transaction—that is, contract price ($1,048,000) minus asset book value ($1,000,000 less $50,000 estimated uncollectible). Discuss the propriety of this up-front revenue recognition. For guidance, see SFAS No. 77, pars. 1, 5–6, 9—Reporting by Transferrers for Transfers of Receivables with Recourse.

R4–2 Motorola—Financial Analysis

Refer to management's discussion and analysis and the supplemental segment information in Motorola's 1995 annual report in Appendix C of this Text.

Required: Discuss the growth rates of various Motorola segments. How important to continuing growth is the international market?

R4–3 Financial Research Using Disclosure Data

Find the annual reports for a firm in the airframe manufacturing business and a company in the restaurant business. Compare their reported revenues.

Required: Describe how revenue recognition would differ between these two types of industries.

5

Conceptual Foundations of Accrual Accounting—Allocations

Learning Objectives

After studying this chapter, you should be able to:

1. Explain the relationship between expense recognition and revenue recognition.
2. Allocate costs of long-lived tangible assets to periods benefited.
3. Differentiate between cost allocations for intangible assets and tangible assets.
4. Apply the principles of allocation to the cost-of-debt funds.

No Accounting For It!

America's 500 biggest industrial companies barely broke even in 1992, largely because of a new rule on how businesses must account for retiree benefits, *Fortune* magazine said in its annual ranking. . . . Altogether, after taking the accounting rule into consideration, the top 500 companies earned $10.5 *million*—less than what some top executives earn in a year. It was the lowest earnings total since *Fortune* began the rankings in 1955. . . . The new accounting rule, known as Financial Accounting Standard No. 106, masked some signs of health, *Fortune* said. Without the rule, earnings of the *Fortune 500* would have risen to $70.5 *billion*. "If it weren't for this aberrational accounting setaside, profits would have advanced quite substantially," said Marshal Loeb, *Fortune*'s managing editor.

Source: P. Lamiell, *Fortune*, The Associated Press, New York, March 31, 1993.

The Associated Press article reports the effects of SFAS No. 106 on the 500 largest industrial companies in the United States. SFAS No. 106 established new guidelines regarding the years to which retiree health benefits are allocated. Prior to SFAS No. 106, postretirement health benefits were expensed when paid, that is, *on a cash basis* after retirement. The U.S. accounting system, however, is predominantly an accrual based system. An *accrual-based accounting system* requires expenses to be **matched** against (that is, reported in the same year as) revenues generated. In an effort to better match costs and benefits, SFAS No. 106 requires that postretirement health benefits be allocated to and expensed in the years in which employees worked, not to those years in which they did not work.

As seen in the excerpted news article, allocation rules can have very significant effects. Arbitrary expense allocations can mask true underlying economic developments and lead to misinterpretation of financial performance reports if not thoroughly understood. The focus of this chapter is **cost allocation** in general. Cost allocation is the process of assigning costs incurred either to assets produced or to periods in which produced assets are consumed, generating net revenues.

EXPENSE RECOGNITION

Explain the relationship between expense recognition and revenue recognition.

Recognition and measurement of economic events in the accrual accounting system are based on the assumptions, principles, and constraints identified in SFAC No. 5, "Recognition and Measurement in Financial Statements of Business Enterprises." The matching principle allows the accountant to determine when expenses should be recognized. SFAC No. 6 defines **expenses** as

> outflows or other using up of assets or incurrences of liabilities (or a combination of both) from delivering or producing goods, rendering services, or carrying out other activities that constitute the entity's ongoing major or central operations.[1]

[1]SFAC No. 6, par. 80.

Under the matching principle, expenses are usually recognized in the same period (or periods) in which the benefits derived from those costs are recognized.

Extensive criteria for when expenses are recognized do not exist in the same sense that they exist for revenues. *Recognition of expenses is dictated by when related revenues are recognized under revenue-recognition criteria.* Thus, the task of expense recognition is to establish associations between revenues and costs. This is a difficult task in many instances. See the In Practice box "The Matching Principle."

IN PRACTICE—GENERAL

The Matching Principle

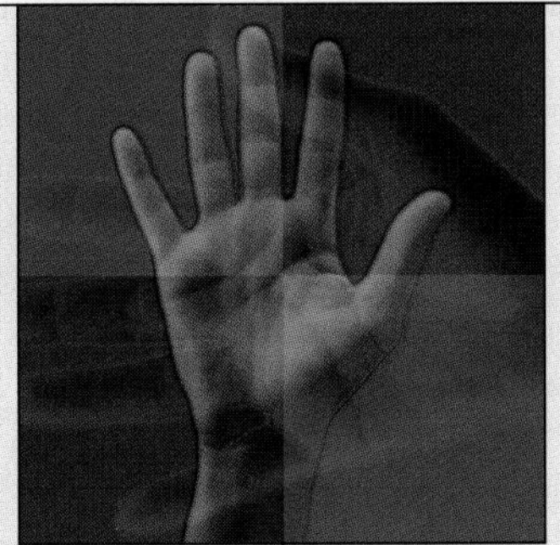

A few months ago ***Chambers Development, Inc.*** (*Forbes,* Oct. 21, 1991), was the darling of Wall Street. Then on March 17, the developer of landfills dropped a bombshell. Chambers said it would start expensing indirect costs related to developing landfill sites. The company had been capitalizing these costs, which include public relations and legal costs to obtain permits for landfills.

The charge resulted in a $27 million charge to earnings, wiping out more than half the company's 1991 net income. . . . The debate whether to expense or defer costs is one of the biggest in accounting. And it's heating up in the wake of the Chambers write-off. The general rule is that companies can capitalize costs only when the costs provide benefits beyond the year in which they are incurred. But, it's often difficult to determine if work done today will bring future revenue, and when.

Robert Willens, an accounting expert at ***Shearson Lehman Brothers,*** thinks Chambers' capitalization was perfectly valid. Why? Because, he argues, Chambers was simply matching the costs of obtaining permits against future landfill revenues. "There's a belief that conservative accounting is accurate accounting," says Willens, "but there's a larger principle you have to adhere to, and that's to match revenues with expenses."

Source: Roula Khalaf, "Fuzzy Accounting," *Forbes,* June 22, 1992, p. 96.

In some instances, a cause-and-effect association between costs and revenues may be obvious. For example, if an automobile salesperson sells a car for $20,000 in 1997, and the revenue is recognized in 1997, then the sales commission paid by the auto dealership to the salesperson also should be recognized as an expense in 1997. This would be the case regardless of whether the commission was actually paid to the salesperson in 1997 or 1998. Commissions presumably are a direct result of sales, and thus, the cost and the benefit must be recognized in the same period. **Direct costs** are those costs traceable to an object, product, or process. Another cost that can be directly associated with the 1997 sales revenue is the price paid by the dealership to the manufacturer for the car. The cost of the car should not be expensed when the dealer purchases the car, nor when the dealer pays for the car, but when the car is sold. This is the point at which those costs yield recognized benefit and the earnings process is substantially completed.

A direct cause-and-effect association, however, is not always apparent or easily measured. For example, it may be difficult to ascertain whether any (or what percentage) of the benefits of a late-year advertising campaign remain at year-end. How should the costs of the campaign be allocated? Should the cost be completely expensed at the end of the current year or matched against benefits and expensed across future periods? Does the cost incurred meet the definition of a continuing asset? Is the information *relevant* to users, and can it be *measured* in a *reliable* fashion (refer back to Chapter 4 for a discussion of these terms)? Similarly, a retail showroom may be instrumental in generating sales revenues for many years. Yet determining how much of the showroom's original costs should be allocated to and expensed in each year is an approximation at best.

Advertising and showroom costs are examples of **joint costs**. They are allocation dilemmas because costs are incurred that benefit multiple accounting periods. Joint costs also are incurred in the production of multiple outputs. An example of multiple product output would be allocation of the cost of crude oil to the several products (gasoline, kerosene, aviation fuel, and so on) that result from the refining process. The question is how to allocate the total costs of production (material costs, labor costs, equipment and facilities costs, and so on) to the different products—how to match the costs and benefits, i.e., the expenses and revenues.

Faced with dilemmas such as the lack of direct, measurable cause-and-effect relationships, the accountant has but one choice: arbitrary allocation. The costs must be allocated to the different products produced or years benefited. If allocated to years, the costs may be arbitrarily allocated to one year or multiple years. This is much the same choice faced by accountants in recognizing revenue (as discussed in the preceding chapter) when the revenue-generating cycle spans two or more years.

The dilemma confronted in revenue recognition most frequently has been resolved by allocating revenue to one year. All value added throughout the production process is recognized in the year of sale. Revenue is recognized predominately at the point of sale because it purportedly avoids unreliable allocations that might distort reported income from operations. However, this is not entirely true. Reed Storey, one of the authors of the FASB Research Report, "Recognition in Financial Statements," observes:

> The arbitrary choice of the sale as the point of revenue recognition is one of the major contributing factors of the difficulties of periodic income determination. . . .
>
> The realization convention [sale basis of revenue recognition] does not eliminate or decrease the effects of uncertainty and subjectivity in accounting; it merely shifts the problem from the revenue to the cost side. . . . The accountant has turned his attention from revenue accounting, where he considers the problem largely solved, to the problem of cost allocation, wherein he faces his greatest difficulties. In reality, the cost-allocation problem is caused by the revenue-accounting solution.[2]

Thus, revenue recognition necessitates arbitrary allocations of expenses. Many expenses, including most selling and administrative salaries and costs incurred in research and development, are allocated to one year—the year in

[2]Reed K. Storey, Matching Revenues with Costs: An Analysis of Accounting Adaptation to Uncertainty (PhD dissertation, University of California, 1958), p. 15. Cited in Research Report, Recognition in Financial Statements: Underlying Concepts and Practical Conventions, Reed Storey, FASB, 1982, p. 191.

which the cost is incurred or liabilities created. These conventions of practice, however, are continually being challenged and changing. The In Practice box "A Different Bottom Line" notes that ***America Online*** (*www.swcollege.com/hartman.html*) is one firm who challenges the general position that marketing and research and development (R&D) costs should be recognized immediately.

IN PRACTICE—GENERAL

A Different Bottom Line

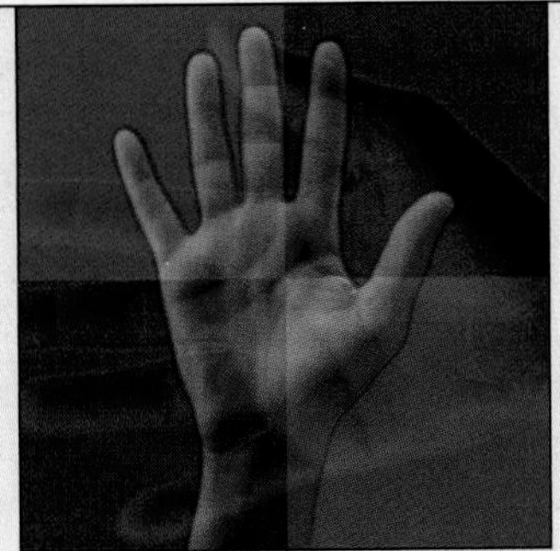

When it comes to technology companies, the stock market's current mania, it's hard to top ***America Online***. Technology stocks are up about 50 percent on average this year, but AOL is positively scalding, up about 135 percent. . . . But look closely and you see that AOL is as much about accounting technology as it is about computer technology.

Accounting is terribly important to AOL. The better the numbers look, the more Wall Street loves it and the easier AOL can sell new shares to raise cash to pay its bills. By my analysis, the company is running a cash deficit of about $75 million a year, covering up the shortfall with perfectly legal accounting techniques and covering its cash deficit with money from stock sales. . . . So what about the high-tech accounting that transmutes AOL's operating losses into profits? "The SEC received our 10K [annual report] and blessed it," said AOL's chief financial officer. . . . But the point isn't that AOL violates the rules—it clearly doesn't. The point is to show how you can satisfy the rules and still make it incredibly difficult for investors to know what's going on.

One of AOL's hidden assets is the brilliant accounting decision to treat its marketing and R&D costs as capital items rather than expenses. It's really neat. A capital item—something long-lived like a power plant—gets charged to your expenses over a long period. That's because you want to match the cost of a long-lived asset to its long life. AOL says marketing and R&D created long-lived customer accounts. By my math, these capitalized expenses totaled about $130 million last year, a lot of money for a $400 million company.

Even though AOL shells out the cash immediately, it charges R&D to expenses over a five-year period, a very long period in the online business. In July, AOL began charging off marketing expenses over two years, up from 15 months. Had the new policy been in effect in 1995, AOL would have reported operating profits of about $50 million rather than $23 million.

Why change to 24 months from 15? Leader [AOL's chief financial officer] said it's because the average life of an AOL account has climbed to 41 months from 25 in 1992. How many AOL customers have been around for 41 months? Almost none. . . . AOL has added virtually all its customers in the past 36 months. Leader says the 41-month average life number comes from projections. Of course, it will take years to find out if he is right. What happens to the costs AOL defers? Funny you should ask. Using standard accounting, AOL turns them into "product development costs" and "deferred subscriber acquisition costs," which become assets on its balance sheet. These totaled $96 million as of June 30. That's up from $34 million a year earlier. Translation: AOL's profit would have been $62 million lower if it charged off these expenses as incurred, rather than treating them as capital items.

Source: Allan Sloan, "Online's Bottom Line," *Newsweek*, October 30, 1995, p. 66.

Facing the uncertainty about whether future benefits will exist after year-end and the difficulty of measuring those future benefits, the arbitrary assumption typically is made for marketing and R&D costs that no future benefit exists. Costs incurred for which there is no assumed future value must be expensed, as they no longer meet the definition of an asset. America Online, as noted in the In Practice box, is one firm who challenges this position.

For other assets such as property, plant, and equipment, future benefits are routinely assumed. In these instances, the costs incurred are recognized as assets in the year the cash is spent or liabilities incurred. The economic benefits of the asset are used up in delivering products or rendering services in future years. As a result, revenue is recognized and costs are allocated to these periods to effect a matching of revenues and expenses. The basis of this allocation process is tenuous. Applying specific numbers (percentages of asset cost) to specific years leads to further arbitrary choices. Are the benefits received from a building or new technology greater in those years when it is new, and if so, how much greater? Or is equal benefit truly derived each year, as many firms represent through straight-line depreciation? These and other questions related to the cost allocation process are addressed in this chapter.

ALLOCATING COSTS OF LONG-LIVED ASSETS

Allocate costs of long-lived tangible assets to periods benefited.

Long-lived tangible assets such as equipment and buildings represent some of the largest costs incurred by manufacturing firms. These assets are purchased with the intent of gaining economic benefits over multiple accounting periods. Accordingly, the matching concept requires a systematic and rational allocation of the **historical costs** of buildings and equipment to the years of benefit. *Systematic* and *rational* imply that costs must be allocated in a relatively consistent manner across time and in a fashion free of bias. This allocation process for plant and equipment is called **depreciation**, which will be discussed here in detail. Depreciation, therefore, is a method of historical cost allocation and not a method of asset valuation. Depreciated historical costs do not equate to current market values.

UNITS OF PRODUCTION

Ideally, the matching concept would be satisfied if the cost of the asset could be identified specifically with the output of (benefits derived from) the asset. For example, if a piece of machinery cost $20,000, produced 5,000 units of product or inventory, and had no salvage value at the end, the allocated machine cost would be $4 per unit. This method of cost allocation is quite sensible and is consistent with matching. This method of allocation is known as the **units-of-production method** because it allocates the asset cost over the units of output of the asset.

The units-of-production method is used extensively in the extractive industries in calculating **depletion**. In these industries equal portions of asset cost (such as the cost of an oil field or silver mine) are allocated to the inventory of natural resources extracted (such as barrels of oil or ounces of silver). This method has some intuitive appeal in that it mirrors an economic concept of depreciation if we assume that usage (wear and tear) of the asset affects its economic value. The units-of-production method is illustrated in Exhibit 5–1.

Unfortunately, this method is not always practically expedient. Measuring outputs frequently is difficult. Often, too, an enterprise will have many machines, and many assets producing a wide variety of products. Allocating costs on an individual basis would prove very costly and would not avoid the joint-cost problem where one machine produces a variety of products. As a result, other practical, low-cost allocation patterns have developed. They are discussed in the next sections.

EXHIBIT 5–1
Units-of-Production Depreciation

Alpha Industries invested $100,000 in new equipment. The new equipment was expected to produce 50,000 units over its productive life. The following data relate to the equipment.

Equipment cost	$100,000
Equipment life	five years
Salvage value	$0
Projected capacity (volume of units that might be produced or hours operated)	50,000 units

Formula for Units-of-Production (or Usage) Annual Depreciation:

(Asset Cost − Salvage) × Percentage of Capacity Consumed

Schedule of Depreciation:

YEAR	UNITS PRODUCED	PERCENT OF TOTAL	DEPRECIATION
1	12,500	25%	$ 25,000
2	20,000	40	40,000
3	7,500	15	15,000
4	10,000	20	20,000
	50,000	100%	$100,000

ACCELERATED, DECELERATED, AND STRAIGHT-LINE DEPRECIATION

Three other patterns of cost allocation for long-term assets that are common today are (1) accelerated depreciation methods, (2) decelerated depreciation methods, and (3) the straight-line method. Each of these specific allocation methods is arbitrary in the sense that it cannot be logically and definitively defended as the single best method. Different operating environments among firms may very appropriately lead to different depreciation methods. Equally competent accountants acting in good faith may prefer different methods for different reasons. Recognizing that one best method does not exist, standard setters continue to allow a variety of methods in practice.

Accelerated Depreciation Methods. The sum-of-the-years'-digits and declining-balance methods, illustrated in Exhibit 5–2, are examples of **accelerated-depreciation methods**. They charge decreasing amounts of depreciation to the later years benefiting from the use of the asset. One rationale for allocating larger amounts of depreciation to earlier years of the asset's life and progressively less in later years is the assumption that assets generate greater benefits in years when they are relatively newer. This may be especially true with regard to equipment subject to technological obsolescence.

The **sum-of-the-years'-digits method** uses original cost less salvage value as the depreciable cost or basis of the asset. The **declining-balance method** uses book value as the depreciable basis. Salvage value is ignored because the declining-balance method applies the depreciation percentage to progressively smaller book values and, as such, will never reach zero. The last year's charge

EXHIBIT 5–2
Accelerated Depreciation Methods

Alpha Industries invested $100,000 in new equipment. The investment was undertaken with the expectation of generating a combination of additional revenues and/or cost savings of $26,379 per year for five years. These are incremental cash inflows or economic benefits from the investment.

Equipment cost	$100,000
Equipment life	five years
Salvage value	$0
Projected annual benefit	$26,379

Formula for Sum-of-the-Years'-Digits Depreciation:

$$\text{Depreciable Value}^{a} \times \frac{\text{Remaining Number of Years}}{\text{Sum of Digits}^{b}}$$

[a]Depreciable Value = Original Cost − Salvage Value
[b]Sum of Digits = 15 (5 + 4 + 3 + 2 + 1)
or $n(n + 1)/2$ where n = number of years
$5(5 + 1)/2$

Schedule of Depreciation:

YEAR	DEPRECIABLE VALUE	REMAINING YEARS	SUM OF DIGITS	DEPRECIATION
1	$100,000	5	15	$33,333
2	100,000	4	15	26,667
3	100,000	3	15	20,000
4	100,000	2	15	13,333
5	100,000	1	15	6,667

Formula for Double-Declining-Balance:

Book Value = 2 (100%/Life of Asset)

Schedule of Depreciation:

YEAR	BOOK VALUE	STRAIGHT-LINE RATE[a]	DOUBLE RATE	DEPRECIATION
1	$100,000	20%	40%	$40,000
2	60,000	20	40	24,000
3	36,000	20	40	14,400
4	21,600	20	40	8,640
5	12,960	20	40	12,960

[a]Straight-Line Rate = 100%/Life of Asset

for declining-balance depreciation amounts to the remaining depreciable cost. In Exhibit 5–2, the remaining cost at the beginning of Year 5 was $12,960, and this amount was charged to depreciation expense in that year.

Accelerated depreciation methods may also be defended when it is assumed the asset will generate equal benefits in each accounting period. It may be argued that the total costs of asset use should be considered in attempting to match costs and benefits, and depreciation is only one cost. A second cost, frequently significant, is maintenance cost. If maintenance costs increase progressively across time as an asset gets older, then a progressively decreasing depreciation charge may be necessary to achieve a relatively constant *total* charge to periods of equal benefit.

Decelerated Depreciation Methods. Representative of decelerated depreciation methods is the effective-interest method (the annuity and sinking fund methods). An example of an effective-interest method is illustrated in Exhibit 5–3. Decelerated methods allocate increasing amounts of depreciation to sequential years benefiting from the use of the asset. This method provides a constant return on the asset investment. The return is equal to the effective interest rate at the time of the investment.

EXHIBIT 5–3
Effective-Interest Method of Depreciation

Alpha Industries invested $100,000 in new equipment. The investment was undertaken with the expectation of generating incremental cash flows of $26,379 per year for five years, thus providing a 10% return on investment.

Equipment cost	$100,000
Equipment life	five years
Salvage value	$0
Incremental projected annual cash flow	$26,379
Effective interest rate of return	10%[a]

[a]Calculated as follows:

Present Value	=	Future Cash Flows	×	Five-Year Ordinary Annuity at 10%
$100,000	=	$26,379	×	?
$100,000	=	$26,379	×	3.791

3.791 = Present value of ordinary annuity of 10% for five periods.

Formula for Effective-Interest Depreciation:

Cash Flow − Asset Book Value × Rate of Return

Schedule of Depreciation:

YEAR	INCREMENTAL CASH FLOW	−	(BOOK VALUE	×	RATE OF RETURN)	=	INCREMENTAL DEPRECIATION
1	$26,379	−	($100,000	×	10%)	=	$ 16,379
2	26,379	−	(83,621	×	10%)	=	18,017
3	26,379	−	(65,604	×	10%)	=	19,819
4	26,379	−	(45,785	×	10%)	=	21,801
5	26,379	−	(23,984	×	10%)	=	23,984
							$100,000

[a]Book value:
Year 1 = original cost
Year 2 = $100,000 − $16,379 = $83,621
Year 3 = $ 83,621 − $18,017 = $65,604
Year 4 = $ 65,604 − $19,819 = $45,785
Year 5 = $ 45,785 − $21,801 = $23,984

In the effective-interest method of depreciation, the amount of depreciation expense recognized is based on the difference between the incremental cash flow generated by the asset and the rate of return on the current book value of the asset. The incremental cash flows are the cost savings and/or the incremental revenues from the asset investment. These incremental cash flows ($26,379 in Exhibit 5–3), discounted at the anticipated rate of return on the investment (10% in Exhibit 5–3), are equal to the present value (or book value) of the investment at the beginning of each year. The change in present value (book value) each year represents the amount of depreciation expense for that year.

This is called the effective-interest method because the discount rate (10%) multiplied by the book value represents the return on the asset each period. The discount rate is the effective interest rate. Each year the depreciation expense recognized will increase because the change in the book value increases. As the depreciation expense increases, net income recognized will decrease.

Straight-Line Depreciation. Straight-line depreciation arbitrarily allocates the depreciable cost of the asset evenly over the expected useful life of the asset. Exhibit 5–4 illustrates this method. The original cost less salvage value (if any) is simply divided by the expected useful life.

EXHIBIT 5–4
Straight-Line Depreciation

Alpha Industries invested $100,000 in new equipment. The investment was undertaken with the expectation of generating additional revenues of $26,379 per year for five years, thus providing a 10% return on investment.

Equipment cost	$100,000
Equipment life	five years
Salvage value	$0
Projected annual benefit	$26,379

Formula for Annual Straight-Line Depreciation:

(Asset Cost − Salvage Value) × (100%/Life of Asset)
($100,000 − 0) × (100%/5)
$100,000 × 20% = $20,000/yr.

Comparison of Reporting Effects for Financial Analysis. The different methods of depreciation result in differential reported rates of return on assets. One argument in favor of effective-interest depreciation is that it provides a constant rate of return (return on assets) to be reported across an asset's life. That is (as in our example given in Exhibit 5–3), if a firm invests in an asset with the expectation of earning a 10% return, and events (cash inflows or cost savings) occur as expected, the firm will report a 10% return in each year. A constant rate of return will not be reported under these conditions with other depreciation methods. Other depreciation methods, in fact, will contribute to the reporting of progressively larger and larger return-on-assets ratios as the assets get older. Exhibit 5–5 compares the results of the four depreciation methods and indicates how each method affects rate-of-return measures.

An understanding of this feature of straight-line and accelerated depreciation methods is important. Lacking such an understanding, financial statement users might easily misinterpret return-on-assets (ROA) ratios. Otherwise comparable firms will report different earnings and ROA figures simply because they use different allocation methods. Further, with two otherwise comparable firms, a greater ROA will be reported by the firm with older equipment, even

EXHIBIT 5–5
Comparison of Reporting Effects

Schedule of Reporting Effects: Sum-of-the-Years'-Digits Method:

YEAR	BOOK VALUE	RATE OF RETURN[a]	NET INCOME[b]	ECONOMIC BENEFIT	DEPRECIATION
1	$100,000	(6.9)%	$(6,954)	$26,379	$ 33,333
2	66,667	(0.43)	(288)	26,379	26,667
3	40,000	15.9	6,379	26,379	20,000
4	20,000	65.2	13,046	26,379	13,333
5	6,667	295.6	19,712	26,379	6,667
					$100,000

[a]Rate of Return = Net Income/Book Value
[b]Net Income = Economic Benefit − Depreciation

Schedule of Reporting Effects: Double-Declining-Balance Method:

YEAR	BOOK VALUE	RATE OF RETURN[a]	NET INCOME[b]	ECONOMIC BENEFIT	DEPRECIATION
1	$100,000	(13.6)%	$(13,621)	$26,379	$ 40,000
2	60,000	3.9	2,379	26,379	24,000
3	36,000	33.3	11,979	26,379	14,400
4	21,600	82.1	17,739	26,379	8,640
5	12,960	103.5	13,419	26,379	12,960
					$100,000

[a]Rate of Return = Net Income/Book Value
[b]Net Income = Economic Benefit − Depreciation

Schedule of Reporting Effects: Effective-Interest Method:

YEAR	BOOK VALUE	RATE OF RETURN[a]	NET INCOME[b]	INCREMENTAL CASH FLOW	DEPRECIATION
1	$100,000	10%	$10,000	$26,379	$ 16,379
2	83,621	10	8,362	26,379	18,017
3	65,604	10	6,560	26,379	19,819
4	45,785	10	4,578	26,379	21,801
5	23,984	10	2,395[c]	26,379	23,984
					$100,000

[a]Rate of Return = Net Income/Book Value
[b]Net Income = Incremental Cash Flow − Depreciation
[c]Rounded by $3.

(continued)

EXHIBIT 5–5
(Concluded)

Schedule of Reporting Effects: Straight-Line Method:

YEAR	BOOK VALUE	RATE OF RETURN[a]	NET INCOME[b]	ECONOMIC BENEFIT	DEPRECIATION
1	$100,000	6.4%	$6,379	$26,379	$ 20,000
2	80,000	8.0	6,379	26,379	20,000
3	60,000	10.6	6,379	26,379	20,000
4	40,000	15.9	6,379	26,379	20,000
5	20,000	31.9	6,379	26,379	20,000
					$100,000

[a]Rate of Return = Net Income/Book Value
[b]Net Income = Economic Benefit − Depreciation

if both use the same depreciation methods—if those methods are either straight-line or accelerated depreciation methods.

Why, then, do the majority of U.S. firms use straight-line depreciation methods for most of their assets? (In 1990, *Accounting Trends and Techniques* surveyed corporations to find the extent to which different methods are used. Straight-line depreciation was reported as a method used by 562 of 745 respondents.) Two reasons seem apparent. First, the straight-line method is the simplest to calculate. In earlier periods, before the general availability of computers, this reason was more important. Today, it is probable that many use straight-line depreciation because they did so last year and the year before and are simply reluctant to change.

However, another important reason also exists. Straight-line depreciation contributes to a relatively stable, smoother earnings trend across time because it provides a constant dollar charge against income. Accelerated methods provide a progressively decreasing depreciation charge, which contributes to an increasing income trend and a sharply increasing return-on-assets ratio. Decelerated depreciation (which is seldom used in practice) provides progressively increasing charges against income and thus declining income trends but stable return-on-assets ratios.

The choice of allocation (depreciation) method used by firms may contribute to significantly different income figures, income trends, and ROA ratios. It is important to recognize that these differences may result not because of underlying real economic differences but because of arbitrary choices made among allowable allocation methods or stages in the asset's life.

Complicating Conditions—Estimating Asset Life. Income figures, income trends, and ROA and other performance ratios also can be significantly affected by varying estimates of assets' lives. The In Practice box "A Tall Tale" illustrates how even some financial analysts can be confused by corporate decisions regarding asset lives. The In Practice box "The Truth Shall Set You Free" observes how analysts value honesty . . . or is it conservatism?

Additional confusion regarding asset depreciation exists because rules for depreciation for tax purposes vary significantly from rules for depreciation for financial reporting purposes. The same asset may be depreciated very differently

In Practice—General

A Tall Tale

If you love growth stocks and you are not too fussy about depreciation schedules, you will love ***Hollywood Entertainment Corp.***, the fast-paced video rental chain from Beaverton, Oreg. From a standing start a mere seven years ago, it has grown to 240 superstores and a fabulous $800 million market value. . . . Analysts love the company. It can sustain 50% earnings-per-share growth over the next three to five years, announces ***Raymond James'*** Scott Barry. Bo Cheadle at ***Montgomery Securities*** adds, in a July 6 report, "This company, like all great retailers, has a history of experimenting with new concepts and will continue to test new formats and products for future growth."

So far, the analysts are looking smart. . . . Public appetite for the stock seems justified by published numbers. Hollywood Entertainment reported $39 million in revenues and $4.2 million, or 12 cents a share, in earnings in its September quarter. . . .

What's wrong with the picture? Accounting. The biggest single expense in running a video rental store is buying tapes from the studios. That makes earnings extremely sensitive to the depreciation rate chosen by the store. Hollywood's depreciation rate is on the sluggish side. Videos are a very perishable product. The store pays $65 to $75 for each copy of a hot new release—say, *Pulp Fiction* or *Batman Forever*. In its first few months, that tape cranks out revenue of $3 every time that it leaves the store. After a few months, the tape isn't worth much. There will be some traffic for movies a couple years old, even those thirty years old, but nothing like the demand immediately after the video release. One Hollywood Entertainment store in Mountain View, Calif., has 140 copies of *Pulp Fiction* on its shelf. How much are those copies going to be worth in a year?

Hollywood says it writes off its tapes in from nine months to three years, depending on the title and how many copies it's buying. The average is close to two years. . . . Once a store is stocked up, it doesn't get any bigger, so depreciation charges should just about equal outlays for new tapes. . . . But Hollywood isn't writing off old tapes as fast as it's buying new ones. In the most recent quarter, it charged off only $11.7 million in depreciation on tapes, while spending almost twice as much on new tapes—$21.1 million. The difference is not something you can shrug off in a company netting $4.2 million.

Contrast ***Blockbuster*** (*www.swcollege.com/hartman.html*). In its last quarterly report as an independent company, it charged off $235 million in tape depreciation and spent just $229 million on new tapes. Is there some magic that makes old tape worth more in Hollywood's hands than in Blockbuster's?

Source: Rita Koselka, "Tall Story," *Forbes*, December 18, 1995, pp. 46–47.

for tax and financial reporting purposes. For tax purposes, MACRS (Modified Accelerated Cost Recovery System) is mandatory for most tangible depreciable assets placed in service after December 31, 1986. Under MACRS, the cost of eligible property is depreciated over a period of 3, 5 , 7, 10, 15, 20, 27.5, 31.5, or 39 years, depending on the type of asset. For example, three-year property includes special tools; five-year property includes light trucks, automobiles, computer equipment, copiers, and assets used in research and development; and seven-year property includes office furniture and fixtures and most other equipment. For assets of less than 15 years' life, MACRS typically allows double (i.e., 200%)-declining-balance depreciation. The 150%-declining-balance method is applied to assets with lives of 15 years or longer. Numerous specific other rules (or IRS interpretations of legislation) apply—rules that are frequently challenged by taxpayers. See the case of musician Brian Liddle featured in the In Practice box "Fiddling With Depreciation."

ETHICS IN PRACTICE

The Truth Shall Set You Free

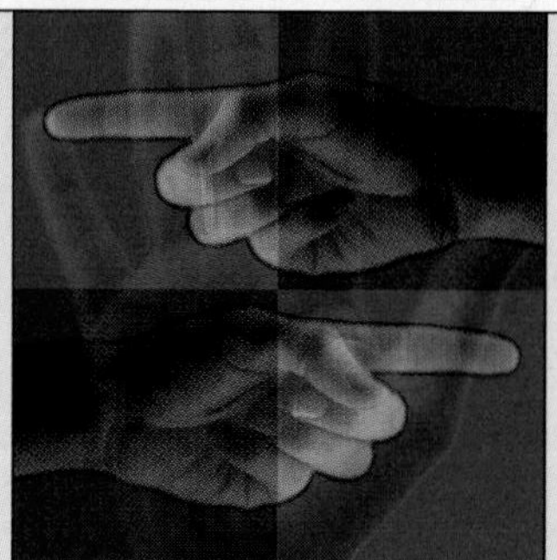

Last September ***U.S. West, Inc.*** took a $5.4 billion pretax charge against earnings. That worked out to $7.45 per share . . . and wiped out a little over one-third of the stockholders' equity. Wall Street's response was equally stunning. Within hours of the announcement, Colorado-based U.S. West's stock rose 4%.

In bidding up U.S. West's stock, Wall Street was sending two messages. One, that U.S. West should be rewarded for honest bookkeeping. Two, that its bookkeeping—like that of the other ***Bell*** companies—has not been very honest in recent years.

U.S. West's huge one-time charge resulted mainly from the way it carried its investments into equipment—copper wire, switches, software, and other tools of the telephone trade. Telecommunications technology and legal barriers to entry into the industry are changing so rapidly these days that telephone companies should depreciate their equipment rapidly. Yet until U.S. West took its big charge, the company had been using depreciation schedules that stretched for some equipment to 30 years. This method resulted in skimpy depreciation charges to earnings and higher reported earnings.

Source: Riva Atlas, "Honesty Isn't Such a Bad Policy," *Forbes,* July 4, 1994, p. 118.

IN PRACTICE—GENERAL

Fiddling with Depreciation

A federal appeals court in Philadelphia ruled that a professional musician may depreciate the cost of his 17th century bass violin, in much the same way as a company routinely depreciates its plant and equipment. . . . The victor in the Philadelphia case is Brian Liddle. In 1984, after a season with the Philadelphia Orchestra, Mr. Liddle paid $28,000 for a bass violin made by Francesco Ruggieri. He and his wife filed a joint tax return for 1987 and claimed a depreciation deduction . . . for the Ruggieri bass under the " accelerated cost recovery system." . . . The Internal Revenue Service . . . strongly disagrees. It rejected the deduction, saying that the Ruggieri bass will appreciate in value, not depreciate . . . A three-judge panel said the musician could depreciate the valuable bass violin, since it was used as a tool of the trade, even though it actually increased in value while he owned it.

Source: Tom Herman, "Federal Appeals Court Rules a Musician May Depreciate the Cost of a Bass Violin," *The Wall Street Journal,* September 14, 1995, p. B2.

IRS rules and interpretations of tax legislation are so frequent, indeed, that *The Wall Street Journal* runs a weekly front-page column to address pending tax cases and controversial tax issues. Differences between financial reporting and tax practices give rise to many complicated issues facing accountants. These issues are discussed in Chapter 17, "Accounting for Income Taxes."

Complicating Conditions—Estimating Salvage Value. For simplicity, the above illustrations assumed no salvage value. Exhibit 5–6 illustrates comparative depreciation schedules if the equipment purchased by Alpha Industries had a $10,000 salvage value. Thus, the amount to be depreciated (i.e., the Base) is $90,000. Note in each instance, except the double-declining method, the depreciable Base changes to reflect a $10,000 reduction for salvage. A modified effective-interest method is not provided, because of the complexity of the adjustments.

The double-declining method ignores salvage, except that total depreciation cannot exceed the depreciable base. Thus, only depreciation in the final years of an asset's life will be affected. Once total depreciation reaches a figure equal to the depreciable base, no further depreciation is taken.

Complicating Conditions—Partial-Year Depreciation. For simplicity, the preceding illustrations also have provided depreciation figures for only full

EXHIBIT 5–6
Depreciating With Salvage Values

Schedule of Depreciation:
Units-of-Production Output Method:

YEAR	BASE	PERCENT OF TOTAL CAPACITY	DEPRECIATION
1	$90,000	25%	$22,500
2	90,000	40	36,000
3	90,000	15	13,500
4	90,000	20	18,000
			$90,000

Sum-of-the-Years'-Digits Method:

YEAR	BASE	REMAINING YEARS	SUM OF DIGITS	DEPRECIATION
1	$90,000	5	15	$30,000
2	90,000	4	15	24,000
3	90,000	3	15	18,000
4	90,000	2	15	12,000
5	90,000	1	15	6,000
				$90,000

Straight-Line Method:

Asset Base/Asset Life: ($100,000 − $10,000)/5 years = $18,000

Double-Declining-Balance Method:

YEAR	BASE	DOUBLE RATE	DEPRECIATION
1	$100,000	40%	$40,000
2	60,000	40	24,000
3	36,000	40	14,400
4	21,600	40	8,640
5	2,960*	40	2,960
			$90,000

*Remaining depreciable cost, i.e., cost less salvage and previous depreciation.

years. This is appropriate if an asset is acquired at the very beginning of the year. However, most assets are not purchased on the first day of the year. When assets are acquired during the year, the accountants can (1) modify depreciation schedules to provide for partial-year depreciation or (2) make simplifying assumptions.

Exhibit 5–7 provides depreciation schedules if the equipment purchased by Alpha Industries had $10,000 in salvage value and was acquired on July 1, 1997. The units-of-production method is not illustrated because it is not based on units of time (i.e., time periods) but units of output, and thus is unaffected.

To avoid the extra work associated with providing for partial-year depreciation, many accountants follow simplifying procedures. Among those simplifications is the practice of (1) recording no depreciation in the year of purchase or (2) providing a full year of depreciation irrespective of the time during the year the asset is purchased. If applied on a consistent basis by a firm making numerous acquisitions throughout the year and across years, this simplifying convention is acceptable when it does not lead to materially different results than using the more detailed approach.

Accordingly, the schedules in Exhibit 5–6 represent relative simplications of procedures used by some firms. Frequently, however, firms record a full year's depreciation on an asset purchased during the first half of the year and a half-year depreciation on assets acquired during the second half of the year, rather than resort to more detailed (and costly) calculations. Again, if applied on a consistent basis, these simplifying assumptions usually provide acceptable cost allocations across time.

EXHIBIT 5–7
Partial-Year Depreciation

Sum-of-the-Years'-Digits Method:

CALENDAR YEAR	PORTION OF CALENDAR YEAR		YEAR OF LIFE	LIFE YEAR DEPRECIATION	CALENDAR-YEAR DEPRECIATION
1997	½	×	1	$30,000	$15,000
1998	½	×	1	30,000	$15,000
	½	×	2	24,000	12,000
					$27,000
1999	½	×	2	24,000	$12,000
	½	×	3	18,000	9,000
					$21,000
2000	½	×	3	18,000	$ 9,000
	½	×	4	12,000	6,000
					$15,000
2001	½	×	4	12,000	$ 6,000
	½	×	5	6,000	3,000
					$ 9,000
2002	½	×	5	6,000	$ 3,000

(*continued*)

EXHIBIT 5–7
(Concluded)

Straight-Line Method:

CALENDAR YEAR	PORTION OF CALENDAR YEAR		YEAR OF LIFE	LIFE YEAR DEPRECIATION	CALENDAR-YEAR DEPRECIATION
1997	½	×	1	$18,000	$ 9,000
1998	½	×	1	18,000	$ 9,000
	½	×	2	18,000	9,000
					$18,000
1999	½	×	2	18,000	$ 9,000
	½	×	3	18,000	9,000
					$18,000
2000	½	×	3	18,000	$ 9,000
	½	×	4	18,000	9,000
					$18,000
2001	½	×	4	18,000	$ 9,000
	½	×	5	18,000	9,000
					$18,000
2002	½	×	5	18,000	$ 9,000

Double-Declining-Balance Method:

CALENDAR YEAR	PORTION OF CALENDAR YEAR		YEAR OF LIFE	LIFE YEAR DEPRECIATION	CALENDAR-YEAR DEPRECIATION
1997	½	×	1	$40,000	$20,000
1998	½	×	1	40,000	$20,000
	½	×	2	24,000	12,000
					$32,000
1999	½	×	2	24,000	$12,000
	½	×	3	14,400	7,200
					$19,200
2000	½	×	3	14,400	$ 7,200
	½	×	4	8,640	4,320
					$11,520
2001	½	×	4	8,640	$ 4,320
	½	×	5	2,960	1,480
					$ 5,800
2002	½	×	5	2,960	$ 1,480

Other Depreciation Methods. *Group and Composite Methods.* Accounting efficiencies may be gained from the depreciation of pools of assets rather than each individual item. Group and composite methods of depreciation provide these efficiencies. Illustrated in Exhibit 5–8, these methods differ only in the type of assets included in the depreciation pools. Group depreciation relates

EXHIBIT 5–8
Group and Composite Depreciation

	ITEM 1		ITEM 2		ITEM 3		ITEM 4		TOTAL
Equipment cost	$20,000		$36,000		$40,000		$15,000		$111,000
Equipment life	4 years		6 years		5 years		7 years		
Salvage value	–0–		$ 6,000		–0–		$ 1,000		$ 7,000
Straight-line	$ 5,000	+	$ 5,000	+	$ 8,000	+	$ 2,000	=	$ 20,000

Group or Composite Rate:

$$\frac{\text{Annual Straight-Line Charge}}{\text{Total Cost of Assets}} = \frac{\$20{,}000}{\$111{,}000} = 18.02\%$$

Group or Composite Life:

$$\frac{\text{Total Cost} - \text{Total Salvage}}{\text{Annual Straight-Line Charge}} = \frac{\$104{,}000}{\$20{,}000} = 5.2 \text{ years}$$

Group or Composite Formula for Annual Depreciation:

Total Cost of Assets[a] × Depreciation Rate = Annual Depreciation

[a]The total cost of assets may change as items are added or removed from the pool of assets considered a relevant group or composite.

Sale of Group or Composite Depreciated Asset:
The steps in making the accounting entry include:

1. Debit value received.
2. Credit original cost of specific asset sold.
3. Debit or credit the difference between (1) and (2) to Accumulated Depreciation in order to balance entry.
4. No gain or loss is to be recognized on disposition of group or composite depreciated asset.

to pools of similar assets, while **composite depreciation** relates to pools of dissimilar assets. Efficiencies are achieved by allowing individual assets to be added or removed from the pools without making changes to depreciation rates.

Retirement and Replacement Methods. Retirement and replacement depreciation methods (illustrated in Exhibit 5–9) are used in such industries as utilities or railroads for assets that are systematically retired and replaced on a regular schedule. In **retirement depreciation**, none of the cost of the old asset is charged to depreciation expense until the old asset is removed from service. At that time, the full cost is charged to expense. The cost of the new asset then is added to the account when acquired. Thus, this method provides a more current cost for asset valuation on the balance sheet, while charging to expense the older costs.

In contrast, **replacement depreciation** charges all the cost of the new (replacement) asset to depreciation expense when it is acquired. The cost of the

EXHIBIT 5–9
Retirement and Replacement Depreciation

Equipment cost	$500,000
Equipment life	20 years
Salvage value	$0

Retirement schedule: 5% of assets retired and replaced regularly each year.
Cost of replacement assets in current year: $30,000

Formula for Retirement Depreciation:
The asset is recorded at cost. No depreciation is recorded until the asset is retired. Full cost of the asset is charged to depreciation expense in the year of retirement.

New Asset	30,000	
Cash		30,000
Depreciation Expense	25,000	
Old Asset		25,000

Formula for Replacement Depreciation:
Asset replacement cost is fully depreciated (charged to depreciation expense) in year of replacement. Initial cost of asset being replaced remains on the books.

Depreciation Expense	30,000	
Cash		30,000

The cost of the old assets stays on the books.

original assets remains in the asset account long after their disposition. This method more closely matches current revenue with current costs for income determination. But the original (older) costs of the assets are used then for asset valuation on the balance sheet.

Residual Allocations. All costs of buildings and equipment must be allocated over their productive lives. Much of this cost allocation takes the form of annual depreciation expense charges. However, a **residual allocation** is made in the year of asset disposition (sale or abandonment). Any residual costs (costs not recognized as depreciation expense over the asset's life) will affect income in the period of disposition. The difference between the fair market value and book value is recognized as a gain or loss on the sale in that period. See the In Practice box "Reel Revenues That Lead to 'Unreal' Losses!"

If a piece of equipment originally was purchased at a cost of $10,000 and five years later sold for $3,000 cash, the amount of the gain or loss reported in the year of sale will depend on the amount of depreciation charged during the interim. If the accumulated depreciation charged was $6,000, a loss of $1,000 would be recognized as follows:

Cash	3,000	
Accumulated Depreciation	6,000	
Loss on Equipment Sale	1,000	
Equipment		10,000

ETHICS IN PRACTICE

Reel Revenues That Lead to "Unreal" Losses

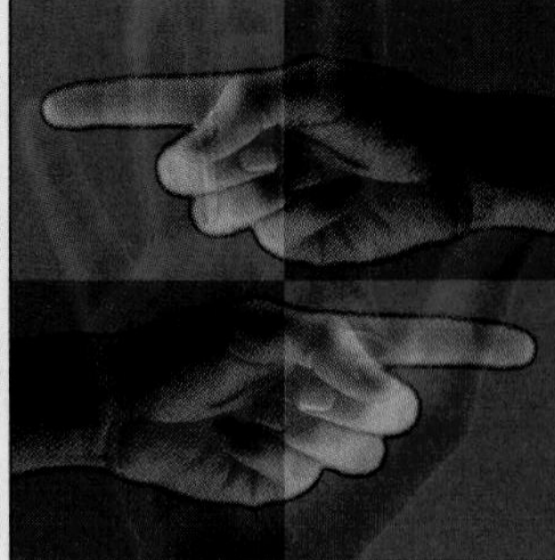

Hollywood may not want to clean up its movies and TV programs, but some studio bosses do want to sanitize their industry's financial statements. Representatives of the major studios began getting together two years ago under the auspices of the California Society of CPAs. Last month they proposed changes to rules governing how entertainment companies keep their books. . . .

The main changes in rules the Hollywood group is now advocating involves limiting the number of years over which studios can amortize the costs of making movies. This is a sensitive area for the studios; these numbers can be enormous. Most of a movie company's expenses involve the costs of making films—***Time Warner*** (www.swcollege.com/hartman.html), for example, carried $1.7 billion in unamortized film costs on its balance sheet last year.

There is ample scope for abuse here. . . . Say a studio spends $100 million to make "Gone With the Winos." If a studio executive predicts it will earn $500 million over 30 years, who's to say the studio executive is wrong? But when the first year's revenues come in at a mere $10 million, management charges only one-fiftieth—$2 million—of the bomb's cost against earnings. The other $98 million remains as an asset on the balance sheet, to be dealt with later.

There's a related problem. When estimating a film's earnings potential, management can include in the projections the film's earnings in ancillary markets—TV, cable, videocassette, pay-per-view, CD-ROM, plus licensing revenues from products tied to the film. These are important revenues sources. . . . Today domestic box office accounts for just 21% of revenues.

Source: Riva Atlas, "Reel Numbers," *Forbes,* August 29, 1994, pp. 61–62.

If the accumulated depreciation was $8,000, a gain of $1,000 would be recognized instead of the loss.

The amount of depreciation charged in prior years, and reflected in the accumulated depreciation balance, depends, of course, on the firm's arbitrary choice of depreciation method. Thus, a reported gain on a sale of a long-lived asset does not necessarily reflect a favorable economic development in the current year; nor does a loss necessarily reflect an unfavorable economic development in the current year. It may simply reflect that too much or too little depreciation was charged in prior years. Too much or too little depreciation charged may be attributable to the use of different depreciation methods or inaccurate estimates of the salvage value or the life of the asset.

The eccentricities of the tax law and the required use of the Modified Accelerated Cost Recovery System (MACRS) can also lead to sub-optimal decision making within a firm. The In Practice box "The IRS Says Your PC Is Not Obsolete!" illustrates how seemingly benign rules may not really be so.

The problem, however, is not restricted to tax depreciation. Anxiety over writing off assets with significant remaining book values (or selling them at nominal figures) and the depressing effect of recognizing these losses on financial earnings statements deter many CEOs from otherwise prudent operating decisions.

Secondary Allocations: Product Versus Period Costs. Product costs are production costs that become part of inventory cost; they include materials, labor,

IN PRACTICE—GENERAL

The IRS Says Your PC Is Not Obsolete!

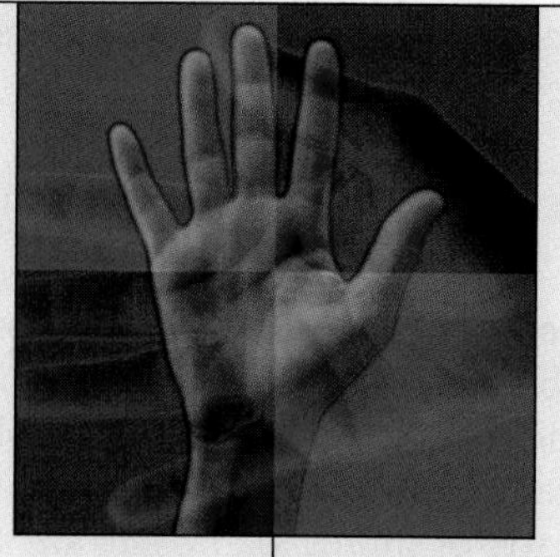

Mark Hauf recalls a two-year stretch when his previous employer, a large telecommunications company, barred him from buying several thousand 486-based PCs for his IS department. Why? The 386-machines they were meant to replace were only partway through their five-year tax depreciation cycle.

The bean counter's ban meant Hauf had to delay modernizing a vast and vital customer support operation. Hauf's predicament was typical of one bedeviling many IS executives and financial officers. Although federal tax code mandates five-year depreciation cycles for computer hardware, the technology advances far more rapidly.

Source: "Another IRS Insanity," *Forbes,* August 28, 1995, pp. 26 and 28.

and factory overhead. **Period costs** are those costs that are expensed immediately in the period incurred. Although the matching concept seeks to match revenues and expenses, depreciation is not always expensed in the year to which it is first allocated. For example, in an enterprise that manufactures products, the entry to record depreciation on manufacturing equipment is not charged directly against periodic revenues by a debit to Depreciation Expense. Instead, it becomes part of (is allocated to) the asset account Inventory; thus, it is treated as a product cost instead of a period cost. This is similar to direct labor and direct material costs; they are also charged to the cost of the inventory.

In general, *all* necessary costs incurred to produce inventory are capitalized, not expensed. These product costs include all necessary costs of material, labor, and factory overhead. Overhead is an **indirect cost**. Indirect costs are not traceable to an object, product, or process. Depreciation on manufacturing equipment and facilities is part of overhead. Costs allocated to inventory subsequently will be charged to expense in the year of recognized benefit—typically the year in which the inventory is sold and revenue is recorded. Thus, a matching of revenue with costs incurred to produce revenues (that is, expenses) is accomplished.[3]

However, questions do remain as to the worth of the numbers ultimately derived from such a system. How reliable are such derived measures of income in any year? Allocation of material, labor, and overhead costs to specific inventory products may entail many joint-costing problems (alluded to in the introduction of this chapter) and many systematic and rational (albeit arbitrary) allocations.

Treated somewhat differently is depreciation on equipment and other assets used for selling or administrative purposes as opposed to manufacturing. Depreciation on this equipment is expensed in the year incurred. It is argued that the required steps to (1) identify the "products" developed from selling and administrative efforts, (2) allocate selling and administrative costs to multiple products, and (3) trace those costs to potentially multiple years of future benefit

[3]An exception to this general rule is found in the horse industry, where the costs incurred while the horse grows are expensed instead of capitalized.

are simply "too complex" and "too arbitrary" to warrant the accounting effort. In recognition of the practical limitations and cost-benefit trade-offs inherent in this process, selling and administration costs are simply treated as period costs and expensed as incurred.

ALLOCATING COSTS OF LONG-LIVED INTANGIBLE ASSETS

Differentiate between cost allocations for intangible assets and tangible assets.

In concept and purpose, the allocation of costs of intangible assets is quite similar to tangible assets. In practice, a number of differences exist. One difference is that only the cost of purchased intangibles is capitalized; costs of internally developed intangibles are expensed as incurred. A minor difference is terminology: allocated costs of intangible assets are called **amortization**, whereas allocated costs of tangible assets are called **depreciation** (or **depletion** for natural resources). Two representative intangible items are discussed in this chapter: (1) research and development and (2) goodwill. These and other intangible assets are further addressed in Chapter 13.

ALLOCATING COSTS OF RESEARCH AND DEVELOPMENT

As noted above, perceptions regarding appropriate expense allocations can vary significantly. Costs can be allocated on a direct cause-and-effect basis when a direct relationship is obvious and measurable. In the absence of a direct relationship, arbitrary allocation may be made to (1) a point in time, or one year, or (2) multiple points over time, or several years.

Another significant example of allocation of costs to one year (in addition to depreciation on selling and administrative equipment/facilities) are costs that qualify as research and development (R&D) costs. SFAS No. 2, "Accounting for Research and Development Costs," requires that all *noncapital expenditures* for R&D be allocated to (expensed in) the year the cost is incurred or the liabilities created. This is the case regardless of whether the research leads to a patentable product or process design. Exhibit 5–10 illustrates accounting for R&D. Chapter 13 discusses which costs technically qualify as R&D costs and which do not.

The arbitrary allocation to one year rather than multiple years is required by the FASB for two reasons: (1) the FASB is not convinced that R&D costs satisfy the characteristics of an asset, and (2) the FASB is not convinced that future benefits are demonstrable and measurable. (Assets, recall, are defined as probable future economic benefits obtained or controlled by a particular entity as a result of past transactions or events.) That is, the board believes that any allocation pattern of R&D costs over future years would be excessively arbitrary because a definitive method of determining to which years R&D costs provided benefits (in the form of increased revenues) could not be established. This is mainly a measurement problem; few believe there are no future benefits. The method selected, immediate recognition, is just as arbitrary as the method rejected, deferred recognition.

The FASB also wanted to improve comparability across firms in the way in which similar events were reported. The FASB's requirement that all R&D costs be allocated to the year incurred is meant to provide consistency in treatment. Prior to adoption of the current standard, firms followed a variety of practices, much as they still do with respect to other expenses, including depreciation.

EXHIBIT 5–10
Research and Development Costs

A. Internally Conducted R&D

Alpha Industries incurred the following research and development costs in 1997:

Materials and supplies	$ 50,000
Salaries of research staff	360,000
Depreciation on research facility	140,000

During 1997, eleven research projects were undertaken. Two projects developed patentable products; additional legal and patent fees were $35,000 for each product. Nine projects did not lead to economically feasible products, and related research was discontinued.

1997 journal entries were as follows:

Research and Development Expense	550,000	
Inventories of Materials and Supplies		50,000
Cash and/or Salaries Payable		360,000
Accumulated Depreciation		140,000
To expense all R&D incurred during 1995.		
Patents	70,000	
Cash		70,000
To capitalize costs of patent; costs to be amortized over future years of benefit.		

B. Externally Contracted R&D

Alpha Industries contracted with Clarion Laboratories for R&D services related to eleven projects in 1997. The fee Alpha agreed to pay was $600,000. Alpha, in return, received all rights to research results. That is, Alpha bore all risks (costs) and retained all rights (benefits). As a result of Clarion's research efforts, two projects developed patentable products for Alpha; additional legal and patent fees were $35,000 for each product. Nine projects did not lead to economically feasible products, and related research was discontinued.

1997 journal entries for Alpha were as follows:

Research and Development Expense	600,000	
Cash		600,000
Patents	70,000	
Cash		70,000

C. Acquisition of Externally Developed Patents

During 1997, Alpha Industries purchased two patents from Eta Enterprises for $670,000. Eta Enterprises had conducted noncontracted research on eleven projects during 1997, two of which resulted in products that Eta patented. That is, Eta incurred all risks of success or failure during the research stage. Specific costs incurred by Eta during 1997 were as follows:

Materials and supplies	$ 50,000
Salaries of research staff	360,000
Depreciation on research facility	140,000
Patent fees	70,000

(*continued*)

EXHIBIT 5–10
(Concluded)

Eta sold the two patented products to Alpha at a price to allow full recovery of all R&D costs plus a profit margin of $50,000.

A 1997 journal entry by Alpha Industries was as follows:

Patents	670,000	
Cash		670,000
To record costs of acquired patents; costs to be amortized over future years of benefit.		

Other commentators view the FASB's claim of greater interfirm comparability (consistency) with skepticism. They point out that while internally conducted R&D must be fully expensed in the year incurred, all costs of patents acquired from sources external to the firm (whose prices can be expected to include a recovery of R&D expenditures) are not to be expensed, but rather must be capitalized and allocated to future years of benefit. Thus, significant differences

IN PRACTICE—INTERNATIONAL

Goodwill Around the World

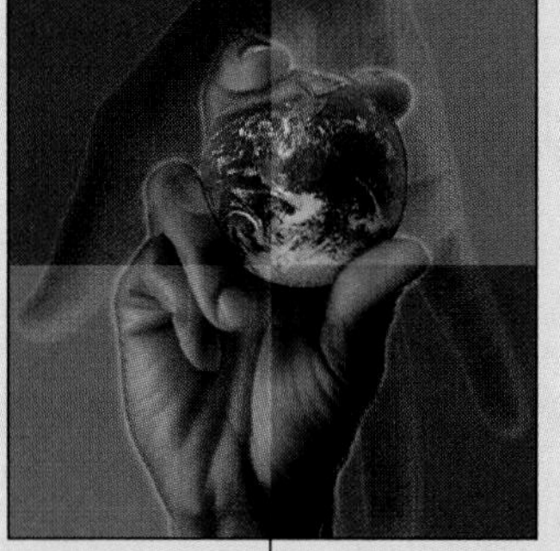

Costs incurred internally to develop goodwill or positive customer and public relations must be fully expensed in the year incurred, similar to the treatment accorded research and development costs. Externally acquired goodwill, however, may be capitalized (recorded as an asset) in the United States in the year acquired and the costs subsequently allocated (amortized, or expensed) over the future years of benefit. As the costs are expensed, both the asset (goodwill) and the equity (retained earnings) of the firm are reduced. Externally acquired goodwill is measured as the difference between the purchase price of an entity and the fair value of its tangible and intangible assets less the fair value of its liabilities. Global treatment of goodwill, however, varies significantly. In some countries, the option exists to write off goodwill directly to equity and thus not affect reported income numbers. In other countries, the costs are capitalized but then subsequently allocated over varying periods of assumed benefit. The chart shown here indicates the practices followed by a number of major U.S. trading partners:

NATION	MAY CHARGE DIRECTLY TO EQUITY	MAY EXPENSE ENTIRELY IN YEAR ACQUIRED	MAXIMUM AMORTIZATION PERIOD
Australia	No	No	20
Canada	No	No	40
France	Yes	No	20
Italy	Yes	Yes	10
Japan[a]	No	Yes	5
Netherlands	Yes	Yes	5
U.K.	Yes	No	0[a]
U.S.	No	No	40

[a]Rarely amortized.

exist between internally conducted research and development and the acquisition of the fruits of externally conducted R&D.

In addition, international practices in this area are not consistent with U.S. practices, though business more than ever is operating in a global market. For example, Japan, a principal competitor of the United States, allows capitalization of R&D costs. This topic is taken up in more detail in Chapter 13.

ALLOCATING COSTS OF GOODWILL

In the United States, goodwill is another example of a long-lived intangible asset whose accounting treatment is similar to that of R&D. In the United States all costs of internally generated goodwill must be expensed as incurred. Internally generated goodwill might arise from a superior brand image or name recognition. On the other hand, goodwill is recorded in the United States upon the purchase of one company by another. If the purchase price exceeds the sum of the fair market values of the net assets acquired, the difference is recorded as goodwill. If goodwill is capitalized and recorded as an asset, it is allocated to expense (amortized) over its economic life (but not a period greater than 40 years).

International practice with respect to goodwill recognition varies markedly. Generally, when comparing financial statements across nations, instances where goodwill is written off over shorter periods of time provide for lower asset value representations and lower income figures in early years and higher income and ROA (return on asset, or investment) figures in later years. In some instances, goodwill is charged directly to equity, providing the highest income figures initially and across time.

IN PRACTICE—INTERNATIONAL

International Treatments of Goodwill

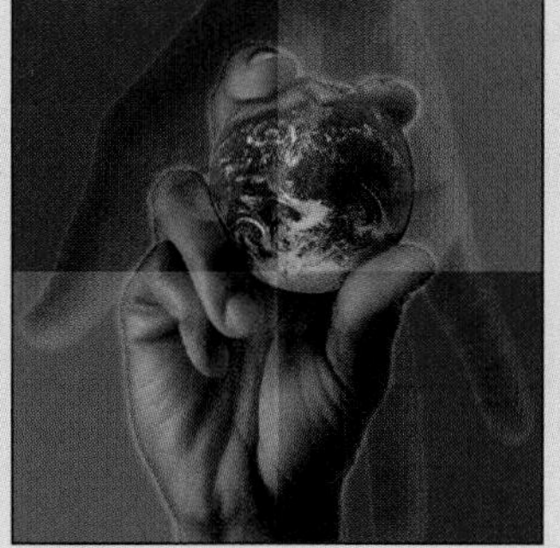

Assume Corporation A purchases from existing stockholders all the stock of Corporation B for cash in the amount of $100,000,000. Corporation B lists the following assets and liabilities at market value: Accounts Receivable ($8,000,000), Inventory ($30,000,000), Equipment ($30,000,000), and Bonds Payable ($8,000,000). The additional $40,000,000 paid by Corporation A beyond the current value of the net assets of Corporation B relates to goodwill: certain brand names and brand recognition, secret recipes, and locational advantages. Other Corporation A balance sheet accounts include:

Cash	$ 17,000,000
Accounts Receivable	3,000,000
Inventory	20,000,000
Investment in B	100,000,000
Equipment	60,000,000
Bonds Payable	(90,000,000)
Stockholders' Equity	(110,000,000)

(continued)

Unrelated net earnings amount to $7,000,000 annually. Balance sheet and results-of-operations figures for the year after acquisition under three assumptions are as follows.

(1) Goodwill charged to Stockholders' Equity (U.K., France):

Accounts Receivable	8,000,000	
Inventory	30,000,000	
Equipment	30,000,000	
Stockholders' Equity	40,000,000	
Bonds Payable		8,000,000
Investment in B		100,000,000
To record consolidation.		

BALANCE SHEET	
Cash	$ 17,000,000
Accounts receivable	11,000,000
Inventory	50,000,000
Equipment	90,000,000
Bonds payable	(98,000,000)
Stockholders' equity	(70,000,000)

RESULTS OF OPERATIONS	
Net income	$7,000,000
Return on net assets	10%*

*$7,000,000/$70,000,000

(2) Goodwill capitalized as asset and amortized over ten years (Italy):

Accounts Receivable	8,000,000	
Inventory	30,000,000	
Equipment	30,000,000	
Goodwill	40,000,000	
Bonds Payable		8,000,000
Investment in B		100,000,000
To consolidate operations.		
Amortization Expense	4,000,000	
Goodwill		4,000,000
To record amortization for year.		
Retained Earnings	4,000,000	
Amortization Expense		4,000,000
To close nominal accounts at year-end.		

BALANCE SHEET	
Cash	$ 17,000,000
Accounts receivable	11,000,000
Inventory	50,000,000
Equipment	90,000,000
Goodwill	36,000,000
Bonds payable	98,000,000
Stockholders' equity†	106,000,000

†Includes Retained earnings

RESULTS OF OPERATIONS	
Net income	$3,000,000*
Return on net assets	2.8%**

*$7,000,000 – $4,000,000
**$3,000,000/$106,000,000

(continued)

(3) Goodwill capitalized as asset and amortized over 40 years (U.S., Canada):

Accounts Receivable	8,000,000	
Inventory	30,000,000	
Equipment	30,000,000	
Goodwill	40,000,000	
Bonds Payable		8,000,000
Investment in B		100,000,000
To consolidate operations.		
Amortization Expense	1,000,000	
Goodwill		1,000,000
To record amortization for year.		
Retained Earnings	1,000,000	
Amortization Expense		1,000,000
To close nominal accounts at year-end.		

BALANCE SHEET	
Cash	$ 17,000,000
Accounts receivable	11,000,000
Inventory	50,000,000
Equipment	90,000,000
Goodwill	39,000,000
Bonds payable	98,000,000
Stockholders' equity†	109,000,000

†Includes Retained earnings

RESULTS OF OPERATIONS	
Net income	$6,000,000*
Return on net assets	5.5%**

*$7,000,000 − $1,000,000
**$6,000,000/$109,000,000

ALLOCATING COSTS OF BORROWED FUNDS

Apply the principles of allocation to the cost-of-debt funds.

Today nearly all corporations finance a major portion of their operations with borrowed funds. They do so to take advantage of *leverage,* a concept discussed in Chapter 6. A debt-to-equity ratio of 2:1 is not uncommon and would signify that twice as many of a corporation's assets are financed with borrowed funds as with invested capital. The cost of borrowing funds to finance operations is interest, and like all costs, interest must be allocated to years of presumed benefit (to achieve matching)—not expensed when the loan is paid back.

Except in selected instances of self-constructed assets, GAAP further prescribes that interest is to be considered a period cost and expensed or allocated to the period in which it is incurred. Unlike the treatment accorded other factors of production (material, labor, and overhead), no efforts are made to allocate interest costs to associated products or output. This is the case even if the interest costs are related to the financing of manufacturing operations. As with selling and administrative costs, interest costs are allocated only to accounting periods, not products (inventory).

Allocation of interest costs can take two forms, the straight-line method and the effective-interest method. However, while straight-line depreciation methods dominate practice and effective-interest depreciation methods are seldom used, just the opposite condition prevails with interest. In fact, GAAP prohibits the straight-line allocation of interest except where it does not depart materially from allocations established using the effective-interest method.

As might be expected from the earlier discussions of depreciation methods, the *straight-line method of interest allocation produces equal charges against income* each period. It also results in *varying financial rates* across the various years of the borrowing. The *effective-interest method,* on the other hand, *produces different (unequal) annual charges against income but results in a constant rate of interest.* Which is correct? Neither and both. As with depreciation, the matters at hand are not matters of valuation, but allocation—and choices are arbitrary. However, different results are obtained from the two methods, and in this instance, standard setters have sought to provide greater uniformity in practice by explicit endorsement of only one method.

As noted, the cost of borrowing is interest. The period of benefit is deemed to be the period of time during which the company has the use of the borrowed money. It is hoped that the firm will invest borrowed funds wisely (in plant and equipment, inventory, and research) and earn a return greater than its cost. The aggregate cost of borrowing (using funds) is simply the difference between the funds received and the funds paid back later.

However, this concept is often confusing because of the terminology involved. For example, assume a corporation issues 10-year bonds with a par value of $1,000,000. The bonds require the corporation to pay 8% "interest" annually, at year-end, and are sold to the public for $877,068. The public was unwilling to pay $1,000,000 for these bonds. Why? The answer is because other, comparable debt securities are yielding a higher than 8% return, which in this case is a 10% return. The $877,068 amount is the present value (*PV*) of future cash flows (*FCF*), which the corporation has committed to make over the next 10 years, discounted at 10%. Those cash flows are $1,000,000 at maturity (10 years hence) and $80,000 annually, at year-end (8% of par or face value). An investment by the lender of $877,068 allows the lender to earn a 10% return. The present value is computed as follows:

PV = [(Principal) × (PV of SS, 10%, 10 periods)] + [(Interest) × (PVOA, 10%, 10 periods)]
PV = ($1,000,000 × .3855)[a] + ($80,000 × 6.1446)[b]
PV = $877,068

[a].3855 is the present value discount factor for a payment of $1 to be received or paid at the end of 10 periods at 10%.
[b]6.1446 is the present value discount factor for an annuity of $1 to be received or paid at the end of the 10 successive periods at 10%.

Aggregate interest expense to be allocated over the 10-year life of the bond is thus $922,932 and is computed as follows:

Cash Payments	−	Cash Received	=	Interest Cost
[($80,000 × 10) + $1,000,000]	−	877,068	=	$922,932

Interest ($922,932) is the difference between cash inflows to the corporation ($877,068) and cash outflows ($1,800,000). Thus, $922,932 of interest must be allocated to the 10 years during which the corporation has use of the money. Exhibits 5–11 and 5–12 illustrate straight-line and effective-interest allocation. Note that in no year is interest expense $80,000. The $80,000 figure is simply an annual cash flow. As such, $80,000 would be the annual interest expense under a cash-basis accounting system but not under an accrual-based system.

EXHIBIT 5–11
Straight-Line Interest Allocation—With Discount

Brianco Industries issued $1,000,000 par value, 10-year, 8% bonds on January 1, 1997. Interest is payable annually at year-end at a rate of 8%. The bonds were sold for $877,068, providing investors an internal rate of return of 10%, determined as follows:

Present Value of $80,000 at 10%, 10*n*	$80,000 × 6.1446 = $491,568
+ Present Value of Single Sum of $1,000,000 at 10%, 10*n*	$1,000,000 × .3855 = 385,500
Present Value	$877,068

Total interest cost to be allocated thus is $922,932, determined as follows:

Cash Outflows	−	Cash Inflows	=	Interest Cost
$1,800,000	−	$877,068	=	$922,932

Allocation Formula:

$$\frac{\text{Total Interest Cost}}{\text{Period of Borrowing}} = \frac{\$922{,}932}{10 \text{ years}} = \$92{,}293$$

To Issue Bonds:

	Debit	Credit
Cash	877,068	
Discount on Bonds Payable	122,932	
Bonds Payable		1,000,000

Annual Entry:

	Debit	Credit
Interest Expense	92,293	
Cash		80,000
Discount on Bonds Payable		12,293

At Maturity:

	Debit	Credit
Bonds Payable	1,000,000	
Cash		1,000,000

Exhibits 5–13 and 5–14 illustrate how interest cost is allocated when a bond sells initially above face value.

Residual Allocation. All costs of buildings and equipment are allocated over their productive lives. Likewise, all costs of borrowing are allocated over the life of the loan (borrowing). Much of this cost allocation takes the form of annual interest charges. However, a residual allocation may occur if a bond is called or retired (repurchased in the bond market) prior to maturity.

Any difference between the book value of the bond liability and the cash required to retire the debt will be recognized as a gain or loss. That is, the accounting entry will (1) credit cash expended, (2) debit the liability at book value, and (3) balance the entry by recording any required debits as losses or credits as gains *in the year of retirement*. Thus, the amount of gain or loss reported in the year of debt retirement will depend on the book value of the debt, and the book value of the debt will depend on whether the straight-line or effective-interest amortization method is used.

EXHIBIT 5–12
Effective-Interest-Rate Allocation—Discount

Effective Interest Allocation Formula:

Liability Book Value × Effective Interest Rate = Annual Expense

Amortization Schedule:

LIABILITY BOOK VALUE	EFFECTIVE INTEREST RATE	INTEREST EXPENSE	CASH PAYMENT	AMORTIZATION (INCREASE IN BOOK VALUE)
$877,068	10%	$ 87,707	$ 80,000	$ 7,707
884,775	10	88,477	80,000	8,477
893,252	10	89,325	80,000	9,325
902,577	10	90,258	80,000	10,258
912,835	10	91,283	80,000	11,283
924,118	10	92,412	80,000	12,412
936,530	10	93,653	80,000	13,653
950,183	10	95,018	80,000	15,018
965,201	10	96,520	80,000	16,520
981,721	10	98,279[a]	80,000	18,279
		$922,932	$800,000	$122,932

[a]Rounding difference.

To record bond issue:

	Cash	877,068	
	Discount on Bonds Payable	122,932	
	Bonds Payable		1,000,000

Accrual entries for interest:

1997	Interest Expense	87,707	
	Cash		80,000
	Discount on Bonds Payable		7,707
1998	Interest Expense	88,477	
	Cash		80,000
	Discount on Bonds Payable		8,477

Entry at maturity to retire bonds:

	Bonds Payable	1,000,000	
	Cash		1,000,000

The amount of the gain or loss also depends on the market price of the debt—that is, the cost to retire (repurchase) the bonds. The market price of debt is affected by many influences, including general economic conditions. The market price of a bond will seldom equal its book value because our system of accounting is not valuation-based, but rather allocation-based. A reported gain on the retirement of long-term debt, therefore, does not necessarily reflect a favorable economic development of the current year; nor does a loss necessarily reflect an unfavorable economic development of the current year. The value

EXHIBIT 5–13
Straight-Line Allocation of Interest—With Premium

Brianco Industries issued $1,000,000 par value, 10-year, 12% bonds on January 1, 1997. Interest is payable annually at year-end at a rate of 12%. The bonds sold for $1,122,852, which allows investors an internal rate of return of 10%, determined as follows:

Present Value of "interest" @ 10%, 10*n*	$120,000 × 6.1446 =	$ 737,352
+ Present Value of maturity value @ 10%, 10*n*	$1,000,000 × .3855 =	385,500
Present Value		$1,122,852

Total interest cost to be allocated thus is $1,077,142, determined as follows:

Cash Outflows	–	Cash Inflows	=	Interest Cost
$2,200,000	–	$1,122,852	=	$1,077,148

Allocation Formula:

$$\frac{\text{Total Interest Cost}}{\text{Period of Borrowing}} = \text{Annual Interest Expense}$$

$$\frac{\$1{,}077{,}148}{10 \text{ years}} = \$107{,}715$$

Entry to record bond issue:

Cash	1,122,852	
Bonds Payable		1,000,000
Premium on Bonds Payable		122,852

Accrual entries for interest and premium amortization:

Interest Expense	107,715	
Premium on Bonds Payable	12,285	
Cash		120,000

To retire bonds at maturity:

Bonds Payable	1,000,000	
Cash		1,000,000

of the bond may have been changing for several years, but the accounting system in the United States does not recognize value changes as they occur, even though they may be measurable and verifiable (as with the case of actively traded corporate bonds). Accordingly, the difference between book value and market value observed at the time of debt retirement may be attributable to value changes occurring in several prior years.

Reflecting several years' value changes in one year as income (loss) poses the danger of misleading financial statement users. For this reason, gains and

EXHIBIT 5–14
Effective-Interest Amortization With Premium

Allocation Formula:

Liability Book Value × Effective Rate = Annual Interest Expense

Amortization Schedule:

LIABILITY BOOK VALUE	EFFECTIVE INTEREST RATE	INTEREST EXPENSE	CASH PAYMENT	AMORTIZATION INCREASE (DECREASE) IN BOOK VALUE
$1,122,852	10%	$ 112,285	$ 120,000	$ (7,715)
1,115,137	10	111,514	120,000	(8,486)
1,106,650	10	110,665	120,000	(9,335)
1,097,315	10	109,732	120,000	(10,268)
1,087,047	10	108,705	120,000	(11,295)
1,075,752	10	107,575	120,000	(12,425)
1,063,327	10	106,333	120,000	(13,667)
1,049,660	10	104,966	120,000	(15,034)
1,034,626	10	103,463	120,000	(16,537)
1,018,089	10	101,911[a]	120,000	(18,089)
		$1,077,149	$1,200,000	$(122,851)

[a]Rounding difference.

Entry to issue bonds:

	Cash	1,122,852	
	Bonds Payable		1,000,000
	Premium on Bonds Payable		122,852

Annual entries for interest:

1997	Interest Expense	112,285	
	Premium on Bonds Payable	7,715	
	Cash		120,000
1998	Interest Expense	111,514	
	Premium on Bonds Payable	8,486	
	Cash		120,000

To retire bonds at maturity:

	Bonds Payable	1,000,000	
	Cash		1,000,000

losses recognized in the year of debt retirement are designated as *extraordinary items.* Labeling these items as extraordinary helps focus greater user attention on them and thus somewhat removes temptations for corporations to "manage" (manipulate) income trends by selective and timely reacquisition of debt securities.

Opportunity Costs. Nonrecognition of value changes also results in misrepresentation of the true costs of borrowing in years subsequent to the first. For example, if $1,000,000 of 10-year, 8% bonds is sold for $877,068, a 10% rate of interest is incurred and recognized in Year 1. However, unless the market value of the bond in Year 2 changes to $884,775 (see Exhibit 5–12), the rate of interest is no longer 10% from an opportunity cost perspective.

That is, at the beginning of Year 2, management is confronted with two uses for their funds. The first alternative is that the funds can be used to retire their debt at the existing market price. This will earn a 10% return if the bonds can be reacquired at a price of $884,775. The second alternative is that the firm can retain the funds and invest them elsewhere. The cost of the second alternative is the return forgone—the 10% return from retirement of the bonds at $884,775. Stated otherwise, the opportunity cost of alternative use (retention of funds) is 10%. However, this opportunity cost will be 10% only if the market value of the bonds in Year 2 is $884,775. Any other price for the bonds results in a different opportunity cost.

Why should one care about opportunity cost? It is because management's performance should be evaluated based on resources actually available to them. The real choice confronting management is whether to (1) retain use of the borrowed funds or (2) surrender them. The cost of retention (of continued borrowing) is the opportunity cost. Or, stated otherwise, the return earned on retained funds should exceed the opportunity costs forgone. This, then, is simply one more disadvantage of an allocation-based accounting system; it does not necessarily provide accurate performance measures with which to judge management's performance.

Allocating Costs of Labor. Unlike the treatment accorded R&D costs and interest costs, but similar to the treatment accorded depreciation, GAAP requires the costs of labor engaged in manufacturing to be allocated first to the products produced (inventory) and then later, via a second reallocation, to the accounting period of ultimate benefit. This is typically the year of inventory sale. Labor costs related to selling and administrative efforts, however, are charged to the year the service is provided. These labor costs are not assumed to "attach" to any "product" that might be easily and reliably traceable to future years of benefit.

Included in labor costs are not only current cash disbursements but also pension costs and postretirement health benefit costs. Measurement of pension costs and postretirement health benefit costs is based on the present value of projected future cash flows—cash flows that typically are very difficult to estimate and that sometimes will be made many years in the future.

To be consistent with the matching concept, all the costs of labor should be recognized in those years in which the benefits of labor are recognized (through increased revenue). Logically, it is further argued, an entity does not gain benefit from an employee when that employee is retired, but when that employee is working. Accordingly, all costs of labor, whether costs of current salaries, vacation pay, retirement pay, or pre- and postretirement health coverage, must be allocated, tenuous as the allocations may be, to periods in which the employees work. Pension costs are discussed in depth in Chapter 16.

END-OF-CHAPTER REVIEW

SUMMARY

1. **Explain the relationship between expense recognition and revenue recognition.** Recognition and measurement in accrual-based accounting systems are based on the assumptions, principles, and constraints identified in the conceptual framework. The matching principle indicates that expenses are usually recognized in the same period in which the benefits derived from those costs are recognized. Extensive criteria for when expenses are recognized do not exist. Recognition of expenses is dictated by when related revenues are recognized under revenue-recognition criteria.
2. **Allocate costs of long-lived tangible assets to periods benefited.** The matching principle indicates that the cost of long-lived assets should be allocated over their useful lives in a systematic and rational manner. The allocation process for long-lived tangible assets is called depreciation. Various depreciation methods are used and are acceptable, including the accelerated, decelerated, and straight-line methods. The choice of depreciation methods may contribute to significantly different income figures, income trends, and return-on-assets (ROA) ratios for different firms. These differences may not result from underlying real economic differences, but rather from the depreciation method and assumptions of the method selected.
3. **Differentiate between cost allocations for intangible assets and tangible assets.** In concept and purpose, the allocation of costs of intangible assets is quite similar to tangible assets. However, significant differences exist in determination of capitalizable cost for allocation between intangible and tangible assets. Many costs that have a future benefit are expensed instead of being capitalized as intangible assets.
4. **Apply the principles of allocation to the cost-of-debt funds.** The cost of borrowed funds is interest. Interest is allocated to expense over the time the debt is outstanding. The amount of expense recognized each period depends on the issue price of the debt and the method of allocation used. The difference between the par or face value and the issue price must be allocated to expense along with the interest over the life of the debt. The method of allocation prescribed by GAAP is the effective-interest method. The straight-line method can be used if the difference in results is not material.

KEY TERMS

ASSIGNMENT MATERIAL

CASES

C5–1 Direct and Arbitrary Cost Allocations

Clarke Manufacturing Co. began operations in 1997 and incurred the following costs:

Costs related to production:	
Materials	$ 40,000
Labor	100,000
Equipment depreciation	40,000
Rental of building	50,000
Utilities and insurance	20,000
Selling and administrative costs:	
Salaries	27,000
Equipment depreciation	10,000
Rental of building	14,000
Research and development	19,000

Clarke produced 15,000 tables and sold half of them for $200,000; the other half remains in inventory. The matching concept requires that costs be matched and expensed in the year in which they yield benefit. Which (and how much) of the above costs should be expensed in the current year?

C5–2 Cost Allocation Practices for Oil and Gas Versus R&D

1. International Energy Resources, Inc., incurs $1,000,000 in costs (materials, $270,000; labor, $630,000; utilities, insurance, and depreciation, $100,000) related to oil exploration conducted at ten sites. Each project used about the same amount of materials and labor. Nine projects failed to discover commercially viable oil deposits and were abandoned. One project discovered significant oil reserves. It was expected that a pumping well put in place subsequent to discovery, at a cost of $50,000, would be productive for the next ten years. Statistics indicate that only about one in ten explorations find commercially viable deposits and International Energy was aware of this when it undertook the exploration of the ten sites. One commercially viable well can be expected to yield revenues of $1,500,000 over its life. Provide arguments pro and con for each of the following three cost allocation alternatives:
   - **A.** All costs should be expensed in the current year as incurred.
   - **B.** The $900,000 attributable to the abandoned explorations should be expensed currently; the remaining costs should be expensed over the next ten years.
   - **C.** All costs ($1,050,000) should be expensed over the next ten years.
2. Inter-Galactic Industries incurs $1,000,000 in costs (materials, $270,000; labor, $630,000; utilities, insurance, and depreciation, $100,000) related to research conducted on ten projects. Each project used about the same amount of materials and labor. Nine projects failed to produce commercially viable products and were abandoned. One project resulted in a project that was patented at a cost of $50,000. Future benefits from this patent are expected to span the next ten years.

Required:

- **A.** How much of the $1,050,000 in costs incurred must be allocated (expensed) in the current year?
- **B.** Contrast the R&D treatment with that afforded the exploration costs in the first part (1) of this case. Is the difference justified?

C5–3 Warranty Cost Allocations

In 1997 Perfection Industries manufactured (at a cost of $100 per unit) and sold (at a price of $200 per unit) 30,000 commercial-grade juice extractors. The products carry a two-year limited warranty. Estimates of warranty costs, based on past experience, are about $10 per year per unit. Comment on this approach and Perfection Industries' proposed entries that follow.

Accounts Receivable	6,000,000	
Sales Revenue		6,000,000
Cost of Goods Sold	3,000,000	
Inventory		3,000,000
Warranty Expense	600,000	
Estimated Warranty Obligation		600,000

C5–4 Asset/Expense

During 1997, Harridan Enterprises Inc. (a firm with annual sales exceeding $1 billion) purchased new wastebaskets for all of its shop offices at its Cleveland manufacturing facility. The total cost was $360. Although the wastebaskets are expected to serve for many years, the accountant fully expensed all the costs in 1997. The accountant notes the firm has a policy of expensing all costs incurred under $1,000. Is there any sound basis for such a policy?

C5–5 Arbitrary Joint-Cost Allocation

Theil Grocery Market purchased three head of cattle. The costs of the cattle inclusive of slaughtering costs and delivery were, respectively, for the three, $400, $500, and $450. The $400 carcass weighed 400 pounds, and Theil butchers cut it into the following four cuts:

CUTS	SELLING PRICE	TOTAL WEIGHT
Steaks	$5.00 per pound	120 pounds
Roasts	4.00 per pound	80 pounds
Hamburger	3.00 per pound	140 pounds
Scrap	0.25 per pound	60 pounds

Other costs incurred included:

Butcher labor (5 hours @ $20)
Vacation pay[a]
Utilities for meat department[b]

[a]Employees work 2,000 hours per year and receive two weeks (80 hours) paid vacation.
[b]The bill for the current 30-day month was $556. The meat department takes up about 1,200 square feet of the grocery, which is 10,000 square feet. Assume 8 hours per day of operations.

Required: Discuss which costs should be allocated to which meat products and in what amounts.

C5–6 Product Versus Period Costs

Diversified Industries purchased two assets on January 1, 1997. Each cost $35,000 and had a five-year expected life, with a salvage value of $5,000. One was a forklift to be used on the floor of the manufacturing facility to move products between fabrication processes. The other was a car to be used by Craig Stone, one of the sales staff, when visiting customers. In 1997 the manufacturing facility produced the following output:

PRODUCTION	VALUE PER UNIT
300,000 units of item U-2	$10
100,000 units of item B-4	14
100,000 units of item K-9	21

Each unit of item U-2 requires approximately 8 hours of manufacturing time; each unit of B-4, approximately 4 hours; and each unit of K-9, about 3 hours. Respective weights of the products are 10 pounds, 20 pounds, and 32 pounds for items of U-2, B-4, and K-9.

Fifty thousand units of U-2 and B-4 were sold in 1997; only 10,000 units of K-9 were sold.

During 1997, Craig Stone visited 30 client locations and procured contracts for the sale of 12,000 units of U-2 and 50,000 units of K-9. Ten thousand of the U-2 units were delivered to customers this period. Ten thousand of the K-9 units were also delivered in 1997.

Required: Discuss the relative merits of alternative methods of allocating the equipment costs.

C5–7 Ethical Dilemma

Drew Isler, a plant's chief accountant, is having a friendly conversation with Leo Sullivan, operations manager and old college buddy, and Fred LaPlante, the sales manager. Sullivan tells Isler that the plant needs a new computer system to increase operating efficiency. LaPlante interjects that with the increased efficiency and decreased late deliveries their plant will be the top plant next year.

However, Sullivan wants to bypass the company policy which requires that items greater than $5,000 receive prior board approval and be capitalized. Sullivan would prefer to generate purchase orders for each component part of the system, each being under the $5,000 limit, and thereby avoid the approval "hassle." Isler knows this is clearly wrong from a company and an accounting standpoint, and he says so. Nevertheless, he eventually says that he will go along with the plan.

Six months later, the new computer system has not lived up to its expectations. Isler indicates to LaPlante that he is really worried about the problems with the computer and that the auditors will disclose how the purchase was handled in the upcoming visit. LaPlante acknowledges the situation by saying that production and sales are down and his sales representatives are also upset. Sullivan wants to correct the problems by upgrading the system (and increasing the expenses) and urges Isler to "hang in there."

Required: Feeling certain that the system will fail without the upgrade, Isler agrees to approve the additional expense. Please evaluate this action of Drew Isler using the decision model for ethical dilemmas presented in Chapter 1, right before the chapter summary.

Source: This scenario was taken from "A Multidimensional Analysis of Selected Ethical Issues in Accounting," by Steven Flory, Thomas Phillips, Eric Reidenbach, and Donald Robin, *The Accounting Review*, 67, No. 2 (April 1992), pp. 284–303.

C5–8 "Move to Become Nimbler!"

Read the following excerpt from *The Wall Street Journal* (Friday, November 10, 1995, p. B6) by Gautam Naik:

GTE Planning to take charge of $4.7 billion.

New York's ***GTE Corp.*** will take a one-time charge of $4.7 billion in the fourth quarter for accelerating depreciation of phone equipment, triggering a large loss for the quarter and the year.

Like the seven Baby ***Bells*** that have taken similar charges, GTE (*www.swcollege.com/hartman.html*) is moving to become nimbler as it prepares to take on a slew of new local phone rivals . . .

The $4.7 billion noncash charge will reduce earnings by about $4.83 per share for the fourth quarter and for all of 1995 . . . In 1994, GTE earned $2.4 billion, or $2.55 a share . . .

Because of the accounting changes, GTE's balance sheet will better reflect the financial condition of an unregulated entity rather than a regulated one. [Regulators have long required GTE to depreciate its equipment over periods that may extend beyond the assets' actual economic lives.] In the past this has caused GTE's assets to be higher than would have been recorded if it were an unregulated company . . .

GTE and other big phone companies are going up against younger players such as ***MFS Communications*** and ***Teleport***, which have newer equipment and shorter depreciation schedules on their network gear.

Required:

A. How does the GTE action help it become nimbler?

B. Why would regulators require firms to depreciate assets over longer periods of time than would be used by unregulated companies?

C. How will these noncash charges help GTE compete more effectively with other firms in the market? Will any future cash flows be affected?

QUESTIONS

Q5–1 The allocation dilemma is said to lie with "joint costs." What is meant by the term "joint costs"?

Q5–2 Discuss the concept of conservatism as it relates to recognition in accounting for expenses.

Q5–3 Why is units-of-production depreciation sometimes the most sensible of the depreciation methods? Why is it not required in all instances?

Q5–4 Paul's Pork Market faces the classic joint-cost problem. The enterprise purchases the whole animal carcass, cuts it into various cuts of steak, ribs, bacon, ham, etc. How can the firm determine at what price to sell the different cuts so as to produce a profit on each? How should the firm determine income for the period if not all the meat is sold during the period and different amounts of the different cuts remain in inventory at year-end? How is this cost allocation problem similar to the problem of allocating the cost of a building over its expected life?

Q5–5 True or False?

____ **1.** The matching concept directs that interest expense should be recorded in the year in which the interest is paid out.

____ **2.** Depreciation on manufacturing equipment is a period cost.

____ **3.** Interest related to manufacturing operations is usually considered a product cost.

____ **4.** Composite depreciation provides a cost-effective method for calculating depreciation on assets of similar lives and physical nature.

____ **5.** Current GAAP requires that, in the name of conservatism, goodwill should be expensed in the year funds are expended to acquire it.

____ **6.** Examples of accelerated depreciation are the double-declining-balance and sum-of-the-years'-digits methods.

____ **7.** Gains and losses experienced on retirement of debt are classified as extraordinary items on the income statement to apprise the user of their unusual and nonrecurring nature.

____ **8.** Gains and losses experienced on the retirement and sale of manufacturing equipment are classified as extraordinary items on the income statement to apprise the user of their unusual and nonrecurring nature.

____ **9.** All necessary material, labor, and overhead costs associated with the manufacture of inventory are included in the cost of the inventory and expensed when the inventory is sold (or revenue otherwise recognized.)

____ **10.** All necessary material, labor, and overhead costs associated with research and development efforts leading to patentable designs are capitalized (i.e., included in the cost of the patent) and subsequently allocated to (expensed over) the life of the patent.

____ **11.** Current GAAP allows the use of either the straight-line or effective-interest methods for allocation of the costs of long-lived assets.

____ **12.** Current GAAP allows both the straight-line and effective-interest methods for allocation of the costs of borrowing.

____ **13.** Relatively uniform international practices exist for accounting for goodwill.

____ **14.** The use of straight-line depreciation provides for a constant return on assets, whereas accelerated depreciation is associated with trends of increasing return on assets.

____ **15.** The use of effective-interest depreciation provides for a constant return on assets over an asset's life.

____ **16.** No gain or loss may be recognized on the sale or abandonment of a group or composite-depreciated asset.

____ **17.** Retirement and replacement depreciation, while common in the United States before World War II, is no longer acceptable.

____ **18.** GAAP requires that internally developed goodwill must be expensed as incurred, but externally acquired goodwill should be capitalized and amortized over multiple periods of benefit.

____ **19.** Contracted research and development performed by external laboratories for the benefit of the contracting firm may be capitalized.

____ **20.** The United States, Japan, and Western Europe all provide similar accounting treatment for research and development.

EXERCISES

E5–1 Comparing Depreciation Methods

Explico Maintenance Services was formed in 1997. It purchased its only asset, a piece of equipment, on January 1, 1998, for $100,000. The equipment is expected to have a 15-year life, with a salvage value of $10,000. All other facilities and equipment were leased.

Required:

A. Calculate depreciation for years 1998 through 2002 using the straight-line, 150%-declining-balance, and sum-of-the-years'-digits methods.

B. If income before depreciation was constant at $12,000 for years 1998–2002, calculate return on assets (ROA) for each year under each depreciation method. Which depreciation method yields the highest ROA in 2000? Which depreciation method yields the most rapidly increasing ROA trend?

E5–2 Allocating Manufacturing Costs

In 1997 Allbright Manufacturing Company produced 50,000 pieces of inventory (all identical). The firm sold 35,000 pieces in 1997, 10,000 pieces in 1998, and the remaining inventory in 1999. Allbright incurred the following costs to produce the inventory:

Material	$ 60,000
Labor:	
Current wages	40,000
Pension benefits earned	10,000
Overhead:	
Depreciation on equipment	80,000
Interest on debt financing of equipment (current period)	12,000
Inspections	10,000
Total	$212,000

Required: Allocate the $212,000 in expenses to the appropriate years.

E5–3 Group and Composite Depreciation

Vandiver Industries purchased four pieces of equipment in 1997. The firm decided to apply group-depreciation methods. Relevant information follows:

ITEM	COST	LIFE	SALVAGE
1	$10,000	6 yrs.	$1,000
2	21,000	8 yrs.	1,000
3	7,000	7 yrs.	0
4	16,000	4 yrs.	0

Required:

A. Determine the annual group depreciation rate.

B. If Item 3 is sold in 1999, what gain or loss should be recorded on the sale if it sold for $5,000 (alternatively, if it sold for $9,000)?

C. Determine group depreciation in 2000 if the group depreciation rate was not revised after the sale of Item 3.

E5–4 Retirement and Replacement Depreciation

Medford Utility Company replaces approximately 2% of its 80,000 telephone poles each year. This means that the poles have an expected life of 50 years (salvage value is minimal and can be ignored). The cost of the poles is $50 each. Assume that this cost has remained constant since the firm began operations.

Required:

A. Determine annual depreciation for the poles using the straight-line, replacement, and retirement methods.

B. If the current price changes today to $60 per pole, determine the annual depreciation expenses for this year using both the replacement and retirement methods.

E5–5 Depletion: Allocation of Costs of Natural Resources

The Arlington Mining Company purchased a tract of land with mineral rights for \$500,000. A geological study of the land indicates that Arlington will be able to mine 1,000,000 tons of iron ore from this tract. Federal and state laws mandate the reclamation of the land after the mining is completed. This restoration is expected to cost \$150,000. After restoration, the market value of the land is expected to be \$30,000. During 1997, 200,000 tons of ore were extracted and sold.

Required:

A. Calculate the depletion cost that should be expensed in 1997.
B. If only half of the ore extracted in 1997 was actually sold, how much depletion should be expensed in that year?

E5–6 Comparing Interest Allocation Methods

Longstride Industries issued \$1,000,000 in 10-year, 10% bonds on January 1, 1997, for \$791,356, yielding an effective rate of 14%. Under the bond contract, annual payments of \$100,000 are to be made at each year-end (December 31), starting December 31, 1997. The bonds are to mature on December 31, 2006.

Required:

A. Determine aggregate interest to be recognized over the life of the borrowing.
B. Provide an interest amortization schedule using the effective-interest amortization method.
C. Provide an interest amortization schedule using the straight-line amortization method.
D. Which method provides a constant rate of interest (i.e., cost of borrowing)?

E5–7 Comparing Interest Allocation Methods

Shortstep Enterprises issued \$1,000,000 in 10-year, 10% bonds on January 1, 1997, for \$1,134,202, yielding an effective rate of 8%. Under the bond contract, annual payments of \$100,000 are to be made at each year-end (December 31), starting December 31, 1997. The bonds are to mature on December 31, 2006.

Required:

A. Determine aggregate interest to be recognized over the life of the borrowing.
B. Provide an interest amortization schedule using the effective-interest amortization method.
C. Provide an interest amortization schedule using the straight-line amortization method.
D. Which method provides a constant rate of interest (i.e., cost of borrowing)?

E5–8 Direct Versus Indirect Costs

Which of the following expenses can be directly associated (DA) with related revenues on a cause-and-effect basis, and which must be arbitrarily allocated (AA)?

1. Research and development
2. Advertising to create a favorable company image
3. Labor to produce inventory
4. Salary of the factory manager
5. Externally acquired goodwill

6. Salary of the company president
7. Payments to an advertising agency for developing advertisements
8. Legal fees for registering a patent

E5–9 Period Versus Product Costs

Which of the following are period costs and which are product costs?

1. Interest on debt-financed manufacturing equipment.
2. Cost of labor incurred in the manufacturing process.
3. Research and development.
4. Costs of raw materials included in manufactured inventory.
5. Costs of selling inventory.
6. Interest on debt-financed administrative facilities.
7. Depreciation on manufacturing facilities and equipment.
8. Depreciation on selling equipment.

E5–10 Declining-Balance Depreciation

A plant asset purchased for $105,000 at the beginning of the year has an estimated life of 10 years and a residual value of $12,000. Using the double-declining-balance method, determine depreciation for the second year.

E5–11 Sum-of-the-Years'-Digits Depreciation

A plant asset purchased for $20,000 at the beginning of the year has an estimated life of 5 years and a residual value of $2,000. Using the sum-of-the-years'-digits method, determine depreciation for the fourth year.

E5–12 Residual Allocations

A truck that cost $19,000 on May 1, 1997, is "totaled" in an accident on July 1, 1999, and has become worthless. The insurance company paid damages on September 1, 1999, of $10,000. If the company used straight-line depreciation, a useful life of 5 years, and a salvage value of $4,000, what gain or loss, if any, should be recognized from the accident in 1999? Assume depreciation is recorded at the end of each month.

E5–13 Residual Allocations

In creating a revolutionary new product, Jones Company spent $50,000,000 for research and development and then an additional $30,000 for registration and legal fees for a patent for the product. Immediately after obtaining the patent, and before amortizing any of it, the company, facing possible bankruptcy, was forced to sell the patent rights for this product to a competitor for $25,000,000.

Required:

A. What amount of gain or loss would Jones Company recognize from selling the patent rights?
B. In your opinion, would Jones Company consider this gain or loss an accurate reflection of the economic reality of the patent sale? Why or why not?

E5–14 Depreciation Methods

Assume the cost of machinery is $200,000, its residual value is $50,000, and its estimated life is 5 years.

Required:

A. Prepare a schedule of depreciation in the format shown here, using the straight-line, sum-of-the-years'-digits, and double-declining-balance methods.

END OF YEAR	COMPUTATION	DEPRECIATION EXPENSE	ACCUMULATED DEPRECIATION	BOOK VALUE
0	—	—	—	$200,000
1				
2				
3				
4				
5				

B. Assume straight-line depreciation recorded at year-end, that the machinery was purchased on January 1, 1997, and then sold on May 1, 1999, for $140,000. Prepare the journal entries required on May 1, 1999, to record depreciation and to record the sale.

C. Assume sum-of-the-years'-digits depreciation and that the machinery was purchased on October 1, 1997. Determine the amount of depreciation to allocate for 1997 and 1998.

E5–15 Patents

A. Firm A has been conducting research to create a new drug. This research has cost the firm $100,000 in salaries, $25,000 in equipment depreciation, and $200,000 in other costs (laboratory expenses, payments to subjects, etc.) during 1997 and 1998. The firm also spent $25,000 in legal and patent fees to register the patent in December 1998. The firm now has a drug that has FDA approval, and a registered patent. What entries should Firm A have made on its books to account for this entire process? Assume that one half of the research expenses were spent in each of 1997 and 1998.

B. Firm B discovers that Firm A has created a drug that fits well in Firm B's own product line. Firm B negotiates with Firm A to purchase the patent. The two firms agree on a price of $1,000,000 for ownership of the patent. What entries should Firm A make for this transaction? What entries should Firm B make?

C. Firm B now owns the patent. The patent is for 17 years beginning December 31, 1997. Firm B uses straight-line depreciation for intangibles, and it expects some other firm to come up with a better drug for this ailment within about ten years. How much amortization should Firm B recognize each year? Why?

E5–16 Allocation of the Cost of Long-Lived Assets

Ramirez Realty, Inc., just purchased a large, modern apartment building for $230,000. The firm has been in business for many years, owns and operates numerous apartment and office buildings in the area, and is very familiar with property values and trends in neighborhood conditions. Ramirez Realty takes excellent care of the buildings it purchases with regard to proper maintenance, and it always carries good insurance coverage. It has bought and sold numerous buildings in the past thirty years and has never sold one for less than original purchase price. Can the firm, under GAAP, decide to carry the newly purchased building on its books at purchase price, allocating none of the purchase cost to operations? Why or why not?

E5–17 Allocation of the Cost of Long-Lived Assets

The Blue Bayou Restaurant uses replacement depreciation for its silverware and dishes. It has just purchased $500 worth of silverware on January 12, 1997, to replace items that have been "appropriated" by souvenir seekers. What entry should the firm make for this purchase?

E5–18 Replacement of an Asset

Murphy's Magnificent Pizzeria installed new larger windows five years ago. The cost of these windows was capitalized (original cost, $4,000; accumulated depreciation to date, $3,000). The restaurant has just replaced these windows on February 5, 1997, with thermal glass windows in an attempt to lower the heating bills. These new windows cost $6,500. The old windows were sold for $400. What entries should the firm make?

PROBLEMS

P5–1 Interest Allocation

Carmody Industries issued 1,000 10-year, 8%, $1,000 bonds on January 1, 1997. Interest is payable annually at year-end at a rate of 8%. The bonds sold for $773,991, which allows investors an internal rate of return of 12%, determined as follows:

Annual Payments × 12% Annuity Factor: ($80,000 × 5.650223)	$452,018
+ Maturity Payment × 12% Discount Factor: ($1,000,000 × .321973)	321,973
= Present Value	$773,991

Required:

A. Determine total interest to be allocated.
B. Prepare an interest amortization schedule using the straight-line method.
C. Prepare an interest amortization schedule using the effective-interest method.
D. Calculate the cost of funds (rate of interest) for years 1997–2006 using both methods.
E. Prepare journal entries for interest expense in years 1997–1999 for both methods.

P5–2 Interest Allocation

Harmony Enterprises issued 1,000 10-year, 8%, $1,000 bonds on January 1, 1997. Interest is payable annually at year-end at a rate of 8%. The bonds sold for $1,231,652, which allows investors an internal rate of return of 5%, determined as follows:

Annual Payments × 5% Annuity Factor: ($80,000 × 7.721735)	$ 617,739
+ Maturity Payment × 5% Discount Factor:	613,913
= Present Value	$1,231,652

Required:

A. Determine total interest to be allocated.
B. Prepare an interest amortization schedule using the straight-line method.
C. Prepare an interest amortization schedule using the effective-interest method.
D. Calculate the cost of funds (rate of interest) for years 1997–2006 using both methods.
E. Prepare journal entries to record interest expense in years 1997–1999.

P5–3 Group Depreciation

Mobile Earth Moving Equipment Manufacturers, Inc., purchased three pieces of manufacturing equipment on January 1, 1997. The firm decided to use group depreciation methods with regard to these assets. Relevant information regarding these assets follows:

	ITEM 1	ITEM 2	ITEM 3
Equipment cost	$64,000	$90,000	$20,000
Equipment life	8 years	10 years	6 years
Salvage value	none	5,000	2,000

Required:

A. Calculate the group depreciation rate.
B. Calculate the group depreciation life.
C. Record the proper depreciation for 1997.
D. Record the sale of Item 3 on January 1, 1998, for $16,000.
E. Record depreciation for 1998 (assuming no group rate changes and rounding to the nearest dollar).

P5–4 Bond Retirement

Phoenix Aviation Corporation issued 10%, 20-year bonds with a face value of $1,000,000 for $735,075 to yield 14% on January 1, 2000. The interest expense was calculated annually using the effective-interest method. On January 1, 2010, Phoenix reacquired the bonds at a market price of $700,000.

Required:

A. Prepare an interest amortization schedule using the effective-interest method.
B. Record the bond reacquisition.

P5–5 Depreciation Methods

Nash & Williams, Inc., purchased an asset on January 1, 1998, for $896,000. The asset had an expected useful life of 18 years and a salvage value of $50,000. Contrary to the firm's expectations, the market value of this asset increased from 1998 to 2001. Nash & Williams, pressed for cash, sold the asset on December 31, 2001 for $1,090,000. Net income from other operations *excluding* the sale of this asset and this year's depreciation was a loss of $300,000.

Required:

A. Assume the firm used straight-line depreciation. Make the entry to record the sale of the asset.
B. Assume the firm used double-declining balance depreciation. Make the entry to record the sale of the asset.
C. Calculate the firm's 2001 net income under each of the above conditions and under the condition the asset was *not* sold (and straight-line depreciation was used). Which income figure best assists the user of the income statement in forecasting future cash flows from this business?

P5–6 Effects of Allocation Methods on Performance Measures

Phillips and Jamison Amalgamated Enterprises started business on January 1, 2000. Stockholders invested $1,000,000 in the firm, and these funds were used to purchase equipment ($800,000) and provide working capital ($200,000). The equipment was estimated to have a 10-year life, with zero salvage, and produce annual revenues of $153,375 (i.e., approximately a 14% rate of return). On January 1, 2005, Phillips and Jamison sought to significantly expand operations. To do so, they needed to secure additional funding.

Required: Calculate the income trend and the trend of return on assets from 2000 through 2004 under straight-line, double-declining-balance, and sum-of-the-years'-digits depreciation methods. Which trend, if any, is reflective of actual performance? Which trend would appear more attractive to potential new investors?

P5–7 Depreciation Conventions in Practices

Abrams Corporation purchased new equipment costing $200,000, with a 6-year estimated life and salvage value of $20,000 on August 1, 2000.

Required: Calculate depreciation for 2000 and 2001 under each of the following conditions.

A. Abrams (1) consistently uses straight-line depreciation, and (2) consistently charges a whole year's depreciation in the year of asset acquisition, irrespective of when during the year the asset is acquired.

B. Abrams (1) consistently uses straight-line depreciation, and (2) consistently charges a whole year's depreciation in the year of asset acquisition if the asset is acquired during the first half of the year, and one-half year's depreciation if acquired after July 1.

C. Abrams (1) consistently uses straight-line depreciation, and (2) consistently charges a whole year's depreciation in the year of asset acquisition if acquired in the first half of the year, but no depreciation if the asset is acquired after July 1.

D. Abrams (1) consistently uses straight-line depreciation, and (2) applies the straight-line method on a fractional year (monthly) basis.

E. Abrams (1) consistently uses sum-of-the-years'-digits depreciation, and (2) applies the depreciation method on a fractional year (monthly) basis.

P5–8 Comparison of Interest Amortization Methods

Ashley Industries issued 1,000 10-year, 12%, $1,000 bonds on January 1, 2000. Interest is payable annually at year-end at a rate of 12%. The bonds sold for $1,268,403, which allows investors an internal rate of return of 8%, determined as follows:

Annual Payments × 8% Annuity Factor: ($120,000 × 6.710081)	$ 805,210
+ Maturity Payment × 8% Discount Factor: ($1,000,000 × .463193)	463,193
= Present Value	$1,268,403

Required:

A. Determine total interest to be allocated.

B. Prepare an interest amortization schedule using the straight-line method.

C. Prepare an interest amortization schedule using the effective-interest method.

D. Calculate the cost of funds (rate of interest) for years 2000–2009 using both methods.

E. Prepare journal entries to record interest expense in years 2000–2002.

P5–9 Point of Production Revenue and Expense Recognition

The Moline Construction and Paving Company signed a long-term contract committing it to build two bridges over the next two years. The contracted price was $40,000,000. During the first year of construction, the firm incurred the following costs:

Material	$8,000,000
Labor	500,000
Equipment	2,000,000

Of the $8,000,000 expended on materials, $2,000,000 remains unused as of year-end. Equipment costs consisted of $1,500,000 spent for a piece of bridge-building equipment (useful life of 5 years, no salvage, straight-line depreciation), and the rest for equipment rental. At the end of the year, estimated costs to complete the project were $21,900,000.

Required: Calculate how much income should be recognized in the year just ended, and make all necessary entries under the percentage-of-completion method.

P5–10 Depreciation Methods

On July 1, 1999, UA Corporation purchased a new machine that would produce circuit boards to be used in its new computers. The machine cost $500,000. The company estimates that the machine will be worth $50,000 after a useful life of five years. The machine is expected to produce 1 million boards during that time. Actual production data are as follows:

Year 1 (7/1/99–12/31/99)	80,000
Year 2	200,000
Year 3	250,000
Year 4	200,000
Year 5	150,000
Year 6 (1/1/04–6/30/04)	120,000

A. Indicate the depreciation expense for Years 1 and 4 using straight-line, sum-of-years' digits, and double-declining depreciation methods.

B. Which method would you recommend that UA use? Why? If the "best" method requires underlying assumptions, clearly state those assumptions.

P5–11 Depreciation Choice and Operating Results

Assume that a firm has a choice between retirement and replacement depreciation methods for a category of assets. Discuss the effect that this choice would have on the firm's balance sheet and income statements in times of rising prices.

P5–12 "Masking" or "Revealing"?

Reread the Associated Press article on SFAS No. 106 at the beginning of this chapter. The text, at the end of that section, says: "Arbitrary expense allocations can mask true underlying economic developments and lead to misinterpretation of financial performance reports if not thoroughly understood." Consider what the FASB is trying to do with SFAS No. 106 and the likely impact of the 1992 financial statements mentioned in the article on investors, and answer the following:

Required:

A. In what way does SFAS No. 106 *mask* "true underlying economic developments"?
B. In what way does SFAS No. 106 *reveal* "true underlying economic developments'?
C. In your judgment, was the effect of this pronouncement beneficial (made financial statements more representative of true firm conditions) in the short run? in the long run?

P5–13 Alternative Choices of Depreciation

A. Modern Manufacturing, Inc., purchased a piece of manufacturing equipment for $160,000 on January 1, 1997. The firm decided to use straight-line depreciation and a 6-year life, with depreciation being recorded at the end of each year. The salvage value of the equipment was estimated as $40,000. On January 1, 2000, the firm sold the equipment for $80,000.
   Provide the appropriate entries for Modern Manufacturing over this entire period, from purchase through sale.
B. More Modern Manufacturing, Inc., purchased an identical piece of equipment for the same price on the same day. However, this firm decided to use double-declining-balance depreciation and a 5-year life. This firm also sold the equipment on January 1, 2000, for $80,000.
   Provide appropriate entries for More Modern Manufacturing over this entire period, from purchase through sale.
C. Compute the actual after-the-fact cost of using this machine from January 1, 1997, through January 1, 2000, for each firm. Compare the figures obtained, and discuss why they have the relationship you found.

P5–14 Research and Development Costs

Consider the following statement:

> "Any R&D project that a firm is currently working on must be useful. If it didn't have positive expected future benefits, the firm would abandon the research. Therefore, firms should be allowed to capitalize R&D costs as long as they are continuing to work on the project. When they quit working on it, then the accumulated costs should be expensed if the project is abandoned or capitalized permanently if the project leads to a new product."

Required:

A. Explain whether you agree or disagree with the above statement and why.
B. Are some kinds of firms likely to suffer more ill consequences than others from the requirement that R&D be expensed immediately? Why?

P5–15 Asset Replacement

K.C. Railroad follows a policy of preventive replacement with respect to its railroad ties. The expected life of these ties is 20 years, so the firm systematically replaces 5% of its ties each year. The firm has followed this practice for over 80 years. The price of the ties has increased consistently by 3% per year. The current price for one tie is $90. K.C. Railroad has 200,000 ties in place currently.

Required:

A. Record the replacement of 10,000 ties (5% of the total) using both the replacement and the retirement methods. (*Hint:* you will need to determine the price at which ties were purchased twenty years ago.)

B. Discuss the magnitude of the effect of using these different methods on the income statement and balance sheet this year.

C. Discuss the difference between these methods and straight-line (20-year) depreciation of *all* ties during the last 5 years. Provide a schedule for each method for depreciation for the last 5 years.

D. What is the greatest advantage of retirement and replacement depreciation?

E. Discuss how the solution to (C) above would have been different if prices of ties had generally increased at a rate of 8% per year.

RESEARCH ACTIVITIES

R5–1 Research and Development

Kendall Laboratories contracted with Morris Industries to conduct specific research for a fee of $600,000. Kendall began the research in November 1998; it was completed in March 1999. All commercial applications flowing from the research, by contract, belonged to Morris. During 1998 Kendall incurred $200,000 in costs ($60,000 for material, $100,000 for labor, and $40,000 in overhead). At the end of 1998, how should Kendall report the costs incurred during the year? Do they constitute an expense, or are they an asset? See SFAS No. 2, Accounting for Research and Development Costs, pars. 2 and 29.

R5–2 Motorola—Financial Analysis

Answer the following based on ***Motorola's*** 1995 Proxy Statement. This can be found in the SEC's Edgar Database (*http://www.sec.gov/edgarhp.htm*, followed by selecting the Edgar database, selecting the Edgar Archives, using Keyword Motorola, and choosing the document denoted DEF14A).

1. What percentage is depreciation of net sales for each year reported? Is this percentage relatively stable over time? Do you think depreciation is a significant component of Motorola's periodic expenses? For what type of business might depreciation be an insignificant component of periodic expenses?
2. What depreciation method does Motorola primarily use for property, plant, and equipment?
3. Determine the reported costs (i.e., gross amounts prior to accumulated depreciation) and accumulated depreciation for Motorola's property, plant, and equipment at 1994 and 1995 year-ends. (Note that this information is not available in the 1995 10-K or in the 1995 Proxy Statement. You must obtain an annual report for 1995. One possible source is Motorola's home page at *http://www.mot.com*, and another is your library.) For each date, what percentage of cost is accumulated depreciation? Does this percentage provide an approximate average age for Motorola's fixed assets? Explain.

R5–3 Financial Research

Identify an industry in which you think depreciation of fixed assets would be a rather insignificant segment of periodic expenses, and another industry in which depreciation is extremely significant. Then, find an annual report for a company in each industry to see if your opinion is valid. For each company, determine the percentages of depreciation to net sales and of net fixed assets to total assets.

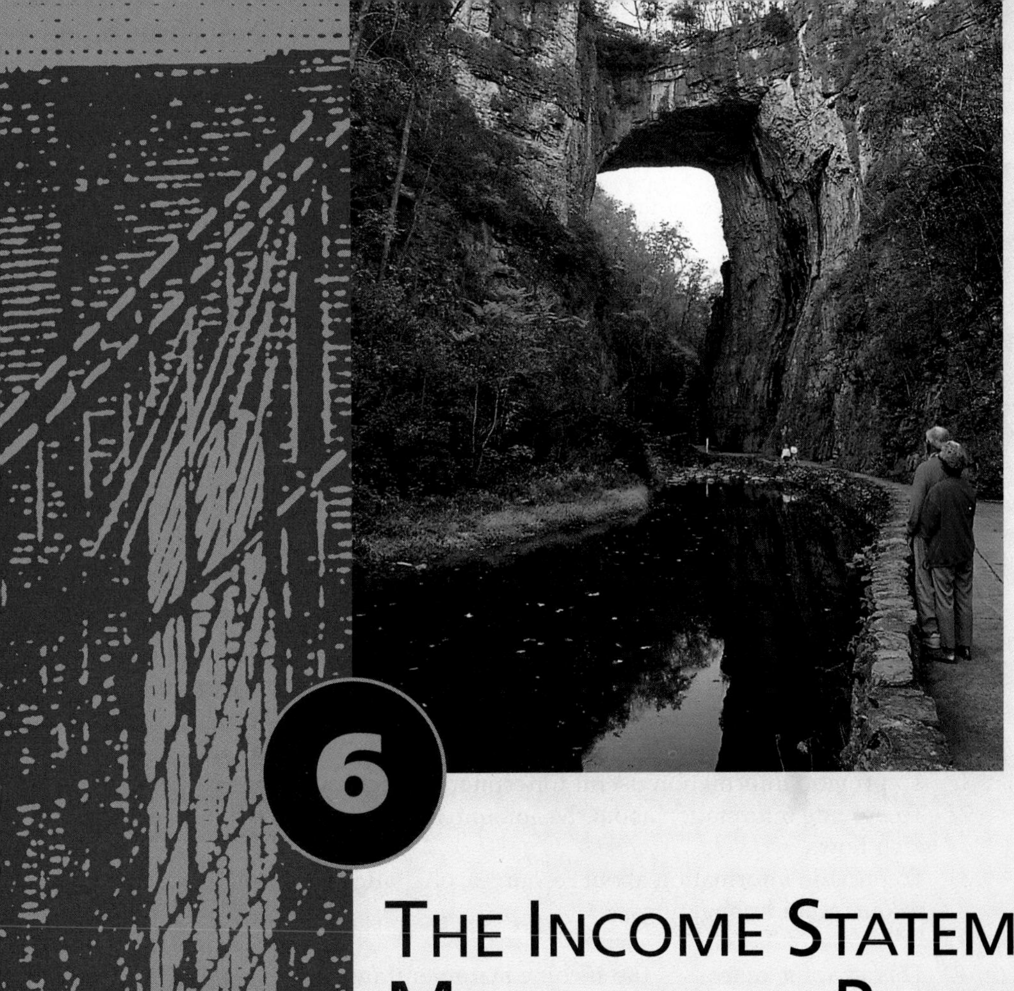

6

THE INCOME STATEMENT AND MEASURES OF PERFORMANCE

LEARNING OBJECTIVES

After studying this chapter, you should be able to:

1. Explain the different concepts of income: cash, economic, and accrual-based income measures.
2. Demonstrate the format of the income statement.
3. Specify which circumstances qualify as special reporting items, and explain how to measure and report those special items on the income statement.
4. Specify which circumstances qualify as prior-period adjustments, and explain how to measure, account for, and report those adjustments in the financial statements.
5. Illustrate the computations and reporting requirements for earnings-per-share presentations.
6. Understand corporate risk and profitability analysis using the basic ratios and categories of ratios.

> Almost all external users of financial information reported by profit-oriented firms are involved in efforts to predict the earnings of the firm for some future period. The net earnings of the firm is considered to be the most important single item of information relevant to the prediction of future earnings. It follows from this that past earnings should be measured and disclosed in such a manner as to aid the user in making this prediction with a minimum of uncertainty.

Source: American Accounting Association, 1966, p. 23.

Recognition and measurement of assets, liabilities, revenues, and expenses, as discussed in Chapters 4 and 5, provide the conceptual basis for the accrual-based accounting system. This chapter and the next discuss two profitability reports that are outputs of the accounting system—the income statement and the statement of cash flows. Both statements provide information about inflows and outflows of resources. Both are essential to meeting the objectives of accounting information as stated in SFAC No. 1:

1. To provide information useful for economic decision making.
2. To provide information about the amount, timing, and uncertainty of future cash flows.
3. To provide information about resources, obligations, and changes to those resources and obligations.

This chapter discusses the income statement and demonstrates that the elements of the income statement provide information that is relevant and reliable, and therefore useful for economic decision making.

INCOME STATEMENT

The primary vehicle used in the United States to communicate earnings information is the **income statement**. It is the starting point for most corporate financial analysis and the focus of this chapter. The composition and format of the income statement is important for clear and accurate communication of earnings information to users.

CONCEPT OF INCOME

> 1
> Explain the different concepts of income: cash, economic, and accrual-based income measures.

Income may be defined and measured in a variety of ways. While **cash-basis income** was commonly used in the past, *cash-basis measures of performance* currently are not consistent with generally accepted accounting principles (GAAP). However, current practice does recognize the importance of cash flow information to users in facilitating accurate predictions of the amount, timing, and uncertainty of future cash flows. Both the income statement and the statement of cash flows, which is discussed in Chapter 7, provide significant cash flow information.

Income also may be defined in the economic sense of "well-offness." **Economic income** is the maximum amount of *value* that a person can consume during a period and still be as well off at the end of the period as at the beginning. Thus, economic income relates to *changes in economic value* during a period. To measure income in this fashion, a firm must assess its financial position periodically in terms of current (real) value and discern whether it has increased over a period of time. That is, the elements of the balance sheet require valuation at market value figures. Historically, the accounting profession in the United States has found this task untenable because of the lack of objectivity, as well as cost-benefit considerations.

A third measure of income, consistent with U.S. GAAP, is **accrual-based income.** Accrual-based income is the product of the accrual-based accounting system described in Chapters 4 and 5. Principles of revenue recognition and applications of the matching concept direct the amount and timing of revenue and expense recognition. Essentially, this system is based on historical cost. Specifically, accrual-based income is the net figure derived from subtracting period expenses and losses from period revenues and gains. As noted in the opening quotation from the American Accounting Association, the accrual-based measure of *net income* is generally considered to be the most important single item of information relevant to the prediction of future earnings.

However, no single number adequately provides all the information that users want and need. If it did, the value of the income statement would be greatly reduced. The income statement provides much more information than a single index of performance or change in resources. Users are interested not only in the amount of change (or income), but also in information about *why* those changes occurred. Different sources of income and different causes of change in resources may or may not recur. Information regarding the elements of income is crucial to the reliable prediction of the amount, timing, and uncertainty of future cash flows. In this chapter, we will also be attentive to potential abuses of the trust placed in the corporate financial statement and address how to deal with these concerns. See the In Practice box "More Than the Bottom Line" for one critic's view of the usefulness of the sole "bottom line" net income figure.

IN PRACTICE—GENERAL

More Than the Bottom Line

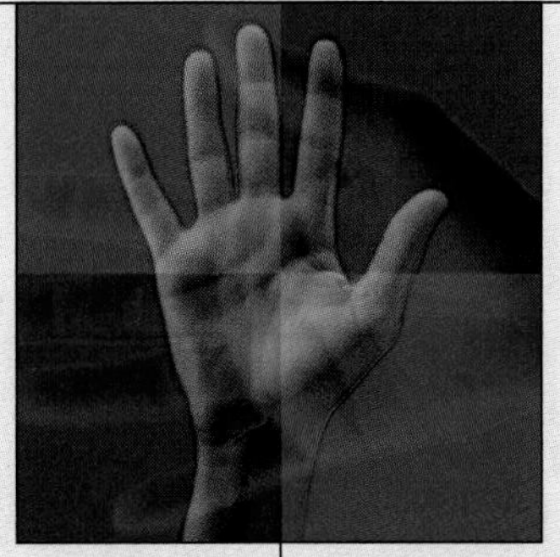

For decades the most fundamental and far-reaching economic decisions have been made on the basis of that supposedly magic number, the bottom line.

Investors buy and sell stocks depending on whether a company's earnings are growing or shrinking . . . They could be making a big mistake. Reported earnings have become virtually worthless in terms of their ability to reveal what's really going on at a company. This is partly due to a business environment in which managers, obsessed with how investors will react to the quarterly numbers, are tempted to fiddle. But, blame must also go to the accountants, who in their well meaning attempts to cure abuses, have in many cases made it even easier for companies to "hide the ball."

Source: Dana Linden, "Lies of the Bottom Line," *Forbes*, November 12, 1990, pp. 106 and 112.

FORMAT OF INCOME STATEMENT

Demonstrate the format of the income statement.

In 1940 Paton and Littleton, in their landmark monograph, *An Introduction to Corporate Accounting Standards*, offered the following advice:

> A particular form for the enlarged income statement need not be specified in a discussion of standards because accounting skill and the doctrine of clear disclosure will no doubt develop several satisfactory arrangements of data. It seems inescapable, however, that the statement will need to have two sections, or else the distinction between recurring and nonrecurring items will not be clearly reported.[1]

Current practice still follows this advice. Accordingly, today GAAP permits both **single-step** and **multi-step income statement** formats. Preparers decide which is the most useful arrangement of data for their firms. With either format, APB Opinion No. 30 requires that results of nonrecurring items (i.e., discontinued operations, extraordinary gains and losses, and the cumulative effects of changes in accounting principles) be presented after income from continuing operations, as illustrated in Exhibits 6–1 and 6–2. Each of these must be presented net of (or after) income tax effects.

EXHIBIT 6–1
Simplified Single-Step Income Statement

Revenues:	
Sales revenue	$ xxx
Interest income	xxx
Dividend revenue	xxx
Gain on sale of equipment	xxx
Other income	xxx
Total revenue	$ xxx
Expenses:	
Cost of goods sold	$(xxx)
Selling and administrative expense	(xxx)
Interest expense	(xxx)
Loss on sale of land	(xxx)
Other expense	(xxx)
Provision for income taxes	(xxx)
Total expenses	$(xxx)
Income from continuing operations	xxx
Discontinued operations (net of tax)	xxx
Income before extraordinary items and cumulative effect of change in accounting principle	$ xxx
Extraordinary items (net of tax)	xxx
Cumulative effect of a change in accounting principle (net of tax)	xxx
Net income	$ xxx

[1]W. A. Paton and A. C. Littleton, "An Introduction to Corporate Accounting Standards," *American Accounting Association*, 1940, p. 102.

EXHIBIT 6–2
Simplified Multi-Step Income Statement

Sales revenue	$ xxx	
Cost of goods sold	(xxx)	
Gross profit		$ xxx
Operating expenses:		
Selling and administrative expenses	$ xxx	
Other operating expenses	xxx	
Operating expenses		(xxx)
Income from operations		$ xxx
Other revenue and gains:		
Interest revenue	$ xxx	
Dividend revenue	xxx	
Gain on sale of equipment	xxx	xxx
Other expenses and losses:		
Loss on sale of land	$(xxx)	
Other expenses	(xxx)	
Other revenue (expense)		(xxx)
Net income before taxes		xxx
Provision for income taxes		(xxx)
Income from continuing operations		xxx
Discontinued operations (net of tax)		xxx
Income before extraordinary items and cumulative effect of change in accounting principle		xxx
Extraordinary items (net of tax)		xxx
Cumulative effect of a change in accounting principle (net of tax)		xxx
Net income		xxx

The distinction between recurring and nonrecurring items is relevant given the user's need for information to help predict the amount, timing, and uncertainty of future cash flows. Exhibit 6–1 illustrates a simplified single-step statement. Exhibit 6–2 illustrates a simplified multi-step statement.

Although a multi-step statement facilitates calculation of many financial ratios and trend analyses, many firms continue to use a single-step statement. As shown in the exhibits, a single-step format combines revenues and gains in one category and expenses and losses in a second category. The difference in these two categories is income from continuing operations. A multi-step format divides the income statement into operating and nonoperating sections. The operating section includes sales, cost of goods sold, and operating expenses. The nonoperating section includes revenues, gains, expenses, and losses stemming from activities that are not part of the main activity of the business.

While items included in income from continuing operations are used for predictive purposes, all the income statement items, including the nonrecurring items, provide feedback about past predictions. This is consistent with the conceptual framework's discussion of the predictive and feedback value of financial statements.

ELEMENTS OF INCOME STATEMENT

Elements of the multi-step income statement include sales and operating revenues, cost of goods sold, other operating expenses, nonoperating items, provision for income taxes, and special items. It should be kept in mind, however, that these income statement elements relate to U.S. financial statements prepared under U.S. GAAP. Accounting principles do continue to vary significantly worldwide. See the In Practice box "Harmonization of International Standards."

IN PRACTICE—INTERNATIONAL

Harmonization of International Standards

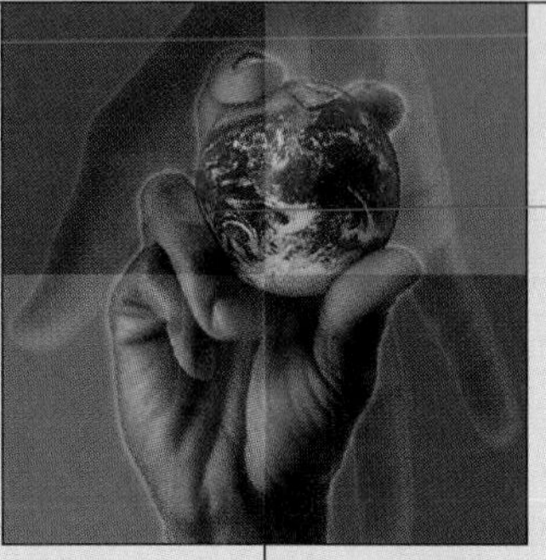

What's all this talk about harmonizing accounting rules across Europe? So far, mostly talk. A study by the U.K. arm of ***Deloitte & Touche*** adapted one multinational's accounts to seven different European countries' domestic accounting standards. Net profit for the company ranged from the equivalent of $153 million in Spain to $225 million in the United Kingdom.

More than 200 European companies trade in the United States as sponsored depository receipts. The exchange-listed firms offer reconciliation of their books to U.S. accounting principles. But about two-thirds of the companies trade here over-the-counter and thus need only present their books figured "homestyle."

Source: Roula Khalaf, "Buyer Beware," *Forbes,* June 20, 1994, pp. 204–205.

Sales and Operating Revenues. Sales and operating revenues include revenues from sales of goods or services to customers less any discounts, returns, or allowances. Operating revenues may also include royalties, lease revenues, or other revenues, depending on the principal operations of the firm.

Cost of Goods Sold. Cost of goods sold, for a retailer, includes beginning inventory plus purchases (net of discounts, returns, and allowances but including transportation costs) minus ending inventory. For a manufacturer, cost of goods manufactured is used instead of purchases in the computation of cost of goods sold.

Operating Expenses. Operating expenses normally consist of administrative and selling expenses. Administrative expenses include (but are not limited to) administrative salaries, depreciation and insurance on administrative facilities and equipment, related utility costs, and bad debts expense. Selling costs typically include sales personnel costs for salaries, commissions and benefits, promotional and advertising costs, depreciation and insurance on selling facilities and equipment, and supplies used in the selling efforts.

Nonoperating Items. Nonoperating items include revenues, expenses, gains, and losses incurred in activities of the enterprise not directly related to normal operations. Usually listed among these items (except for financial institutions) are interest and dividend revenues, interest expense, and gains and/or losses on the sale of plant and equipment or investments. Also included in this category are gains and losses resulting from transactions that are either unusual in nature or infrequent in occurrence, but not both.

For example, write-downs of assets could be included in this category. During the early 1990s, many companies recognized losses in asset value (impairment) as part of restructuring, or simply following changes in management. By reducing asset values, management expected the company to be situated well for future growth. Not all members of the investment community are pleased with such management conduct. The excerpt from *Forbes* in the In Practice box "Taking a 'Big Bath'" provides an example of these types of write-offs. See also the In Practice box "Managing Income Around the World."

IN PRACTICE—GENERAL

Taking a 'Big Bath' (or Cleaning up Future Income Statements)

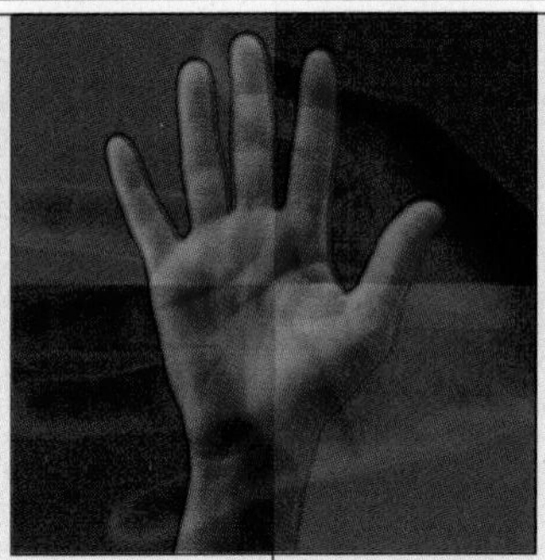

Earlier this year ***Federal Express Corp.*** (*www.swcollege.com/hartman.html*) wrote off $250 million for its ill-fated overseas expansion. The big write-off resulted in a $3.58-per-share loss in the third quarter of the fiscal year. But the very next quarter the courier service posted a $36 million profit. That was 14% higher than in the year earlier.

Solid growth in the underlying business? Or fancy bookkeeping? These days it's hard to tell. When companies take big write-offs, they can later reinject some of the reserves into operating income if the initial write-off estimate turns out to have been larger than what was actually required. Also, because the disclosure rules are so vague in this area, these hidden "earnings" need not be flagged as nonrecurring.

"The problem [for investors] is that you can get an accounting turnaround when you don't necessarily get a business turnaround," says John C. Burton, a former Securities and Exchange Commission chief accountant.

Serious money is probably sitting on corporate balance sheets as hidden reserves available to bolster earnings. According to ***Goldman, Sach's*** (*www.swcollege.com/hartman.html*) Patricia Shangkuan, last year alone S&P 500 companies wrote off a record $42 billion. It's a good bet that some of that money will find its way back into earnings reports.

Source: Mary Beth Grover, "Generally Vague Accounting Principles," *Forbes*, September 14, 1992, p. 218.

Provision for Income Taxes. Income taxes (federal, state, and local) related to the preceding items are usually reported in a separate section of a multi-step income statement. Accounting for income taxes is discussed in Chapter 17. Income taxes related to the special reporting items discussed next are not included in the income taxes section of the income statement. These special items are reported net of (or after) the effect of income taxes.

The process of associating income taxes with related items is called **intraperiod tax allocation**. Five items require intraperiod tax allocation: (1) income from continuing operations, (2) discontinued operations, (3) extraordinary items, (4) cumulative effects of accounting changes, and (5) prior-period adjustments. The first four are reported on the income statement; prior-period adjustments are made to retained earnings and are reported on the statement of shareholders' equity.

IN PRACTICE—INTERNATIONAL

Managing Income Around the World

"For a long time U.S. investors were fed the line that European stocks were cheap because European companies understate their earnings. They had hidden reserves or unconsolidated subsidiaries or overstated depreciation schedules. "It's a myth that European companies understate earnings," says Christopher Nobes, an accounting professor at Reading University. "It depends what country, what industry, and what year you're in."

Yes, there are hidden reserves in Switzerland, Germany, and Sweden. But that doesn't mean that there is more to these companies than meets the eye. Loosey-goosey reserves cut both ways. Reserves tucked away in earlier years could have been used to paper over last year's losses.

Daimler-Benz (*www.swcollege.com/hartman.html*), the auto maker, had a horrendous 1993. So it simply released $1.6 billion in contingency reserves back into income. This fictitious income would never pass muster in the United States. *Or would it?*

The debacle at ***Kidder, Peabody & Co.*** might have ruined the year for most companies. But the roughly $750 million in losses and after-tax losses that ***General Electric Co.*** incurred in 1994 before finally unloading Kidder barely made a dent in GE's smooth, consistent earnings growth. How does GE do it? "We're the best company in the world," declares Dennis Dammerman, GE's chief financial officer. But another way is "earnings management," the orchestrated timing of gains and losses to smooth out bumps and, especially, avoid a decline. Among big companies, GE is "certainly a relatively aggressive practitioner of earnings management," says Martin Sankey, a ***CS First Boston, Inc.*** analyst. Most U.S. companies do try to smooth profit growth.

Sources: Roula Khalaf, "Buyer Beware," *Forbes*, June 20, 1994, pp. 204–205; "How General Electric Damps Fluctuations in Its Annual Earnings," *The Wall Street Journal*, November 3, 1994, pp. A1, A8.

Specify which circumstances qualify as special reporting items, and explain how to measure and report those special items on the income statement.

Special Reporting Items. Three items require special treatment on the income statement according to APB Opinion No. 30: discontinued operations, extraordinary items, and accounting changes. These **special reporting items** are reported separately to provide a distinction between the income (loss) derived from normal and recurring operations and the income (loss) attributable to nonrecurring, special events recognized in the current period.

DISCONTINUED OPERATIONS

APB Opinion No. 30 specifies that the results of **discontinued operations** and any gains or losses realized on the disposal of the net assets of the discontinued line of business (i.e., segment) must be reported in the income statement separately from income from *continuing* operations. Related issues are (1) what constitutes a discontinued operation, (2) what special principles of revenue recognition (if any) apply to accounting for discontinued operations, and (3) how results of discontinued operations are disclosed in the financial statements. Each of these issues is addressed in turn.

What Constitutes a Discontinued Operation? APB Opinion No. 30 defines a business segment as:

a component of an enterprise whose activities represent a major line of business or class of customer. A segment may be in the form of a subsidiary, a division, or a department, and in some cases a joint venture or other nonsubsidiary investee, provided that its assets, results of operations, and activities can be clearly distinguished, physically and operationally and for financial reporting purposes, from the other assets, results of operations, and activities of the enterprise.[2]

In a subsequent interpretation of APB Opinion No. 30, the AICPA provided illustrative examples of what constitutes a segment of a business (and what does not) as supplemental guidance. See Exhibit 6–3.

A discontinued operation exists when management commits the firm to a formal plan to dispose of a segment of the business via sale or abandonment. The date of this formal commitment is designated the **measurement date** (MD). The plan must include as a minimum the following items:

1. Identification of the major assets to be disposed.
2. Identification of the principal method of disposition.
3. Identification of the expected period required for disposition.
4. Adoption of an active program to find a buyer if sale is planned.
5. An estimate of the results of forthcoming operations if operations will continue through the disposition period.
6. An estimate of proceeds (or salvage) to be realized on disposition of the business segment.[3]

EXHIBIT 6–3
Discontinued Operations

Disposals that **should** *be classified as discontinued operations:*

A. A sale by a diversified enterprise of a major division that represents the enterprise's only activities in the electronics industry. The assets and results of operations of the division are clearly segregated for internal financial reporting purposes from the other assets and results of operations of the enterprise.
B. A sale by a meat-packing enterprise of a 25 percent interest in a professional football team that has been accounted for under the equity method. All other activities of the enterprise are in the meat-packing business.
C. A sale by a communications enterprise of all its radio stations that represent 30 percent of gross revenues. The enterprise's remaining activities are three television stations and a publishing enterprise. The assets and results of operations of the radio stations are clearly distinguishable physically, operationally, and for financial reporting purposes.
D. A food distributor disposes of one of its two divisions. One division sells food wholesale primarily to supermarket chains, and the other division sells food through its chain of fast food restaurants, some of which are franchised and some of which are owned by the enterprise. Both divisions are in the business of distributing food. However, the nature of selling food through fast food outlets is vastly different from that of wholesaling food to supermarket chains. Thus, by having two major classes of customers, the enterprise has two segments of its business.

(continued)

[2] APB Opinion No. 30, par. 13.
[3] APB Opinion No. 30, par. 14.

EXHIBIT 6–3
(Concluded)

Disposals that* should not *be classified as discontinued operations:

A. The sale of a major foreign subsidiary engaged in silver mining by a mining enterprise that represents all of the enterprise's activities in that particular country. Even though the subsidiary being sold may account for a significant percentage of gross income of the consolidated group and all of its revenues in the particular country, the fact that the enterprise continues to engage in silver-mining activities in other countries would indicate that there was a sale of a *part* of a line of business.

B. The sale by a petrochemical enterprise of a 25 percent interest in a petrochemical plant that is accounted for as an investment in a corporate joint venture under the equity method. Since the remaining activities of the enterprise are in the same line of business as the 25 percent interest that has been sold, there has not been a sale of a major line of business but rather a sale of *part* of a line of business.

C. A manufacturer of children's wear discontinues all of its operations in Italy that designed and sold children's wear for the Italian market. In the context of determining a segment of business by class of customer, the nationality of customers or slight variations in product lines in order to appeal to particular groups are not determining factors.

D. A diversified enterprise sells a subsidiary that manufactures furniture. The enterprise has retained its other furniture manufacturing subsidiary. The disposal of the subsidiary, therefore, is not a disposal of a segment of the business but rather a disposal of *part* of a line of business. Such disposals are incidental to the evolution of the entity's business.

E. The sale of all the assets (including the plant) related to the manufacture of men's wool suits by an apparel manufacturer in order to concentrate activities in the manufacture of men's suits from synthetic products. This would represent disposal of a product line as distinguished from the disposal of a major line of business.

Source: AICPA, AIN-APB No. 30, pars. 503 and 504.

In short, before classifying charges as "discontinued," the accountant must verify that assets have been specifically identified for disposal and that an active program is in place to find a purchaser.

What Special Revenue Recognition Principles Apply? APB Opinion No. 30 stipulates that if a loss is expected to occur as a result of a discontinued operation, the estimated amount of the loss should be recognized at the measurement date (the date of adoption of the formal plan of disposition). However, if a gain is expected, it must be deferred until it is realized. That is, the gain should not be recognized at the measurement date, but rather, recognition should be made only upon actual realization of the gain. This treatment is consistent with many other accounting standards that also exhibit conservatism regarding the timing of gain and loss recognition.[4]

[4]Throughout this text, we will see other examples of the underlying effects of conservatism on recognition and measurement in accounting standards.

The gains and losses estimated from a discontinued segment include both (1) expected net gains or losses on the sale or abandonment of the net assets of the discontinued business segment and (2) expected gains or losses from operating activities by the business segment after the measurement date and during the disposition process. Both types of gains and losses (from the sale of the assets and from operations during disposition) are combined into a single "net" figure. If the net amount is a loss, it is recognized at the measurement date. If the net amount is a gain, it must be deferred and recognized as it is realized. Note that income or loss from operations from the beginning of the year until the measurement date is always reported in the first year separately, regardless of what happens after the measurement date. For example, consider the following instance:

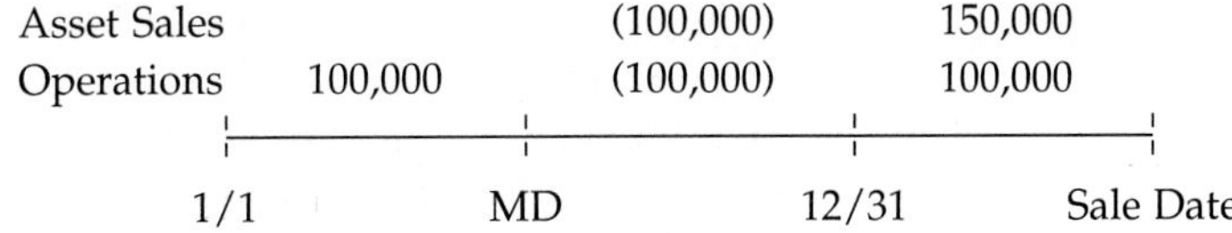

In Year 1, the $100,000 income from operations from January 1, Year 1, until the measurement date (MD) is reported in Year 1 net of tax (40% rate), or $60,000. Combining the other four figures obtains a net gain of $50,000. However, this net gain will not be realized until Year 2, when the sale is complete. Therefore, the gain cannot be recognized in Year 1 but must be deferred until Year 2. If the combined other four figures result in a net loss, the loss is reported net of tax in Year 1 and nothing is reported in Year 2. These different possible combinations of gains and losses are illustrated in Exhibit 6–4.

EXHIBIT 6–4
Reporting Results of Discontinued Operations

Each of the following cases is independent (40% assumed tax rate).

	CASE A	CASE B	CASE C	CASE D
Realized results of operations from beginning of year (1/1) to measurement date.	$ 100,000	$100,000	$ 100,000	$ 100,000
Realized results of operations from measurement date to end of year (12/31).	100,000	100,000	(100,000)	(100,000)
Realized gains or losses on the disposition of assets (or liquidation of liabilities) from measurement date to end of year.	100,000	100,000	(100,000)	(100,000)
Expected (forecasted) results of operations during phase-out, after end of year.	100,000	100,000	100,000	100,000
Expected (forecasted) gains or losses on disposition of net assets during phase-out, after end of year.	(150,000)	(50,000)	(50,000)	150,000

(continued)

EXHIBIT 6–4
(Continued)

Case A:

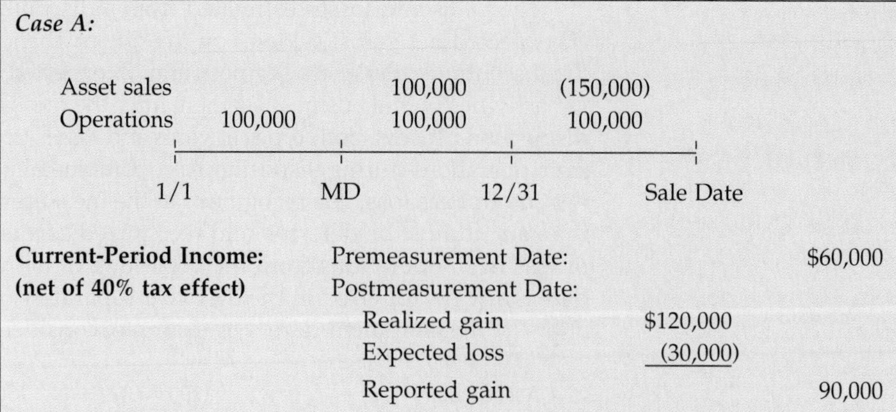

	1/1	MD	12/31	Sale Date
Asset sales		100,000	(150,000)	
Operations	100,000	100,000	100,000	

Current-Period Income:	Premeasurement Date:		$60,000
(net of 40% tax effect)	Postmeasurement Date:		
	Realized gain	$120,000	
	Expected loss	(30,000)	
	Reported gain		90,000

Explanation: Realized results of operations before the measurement date must be reported net of income taxes (i.e., $100,000 × [1 − tax rate] = $60,000).

After-year-end forecasts predict a net loss of $50,000 ($100,000 in income from operations less a $150,000 loss from net asset dispositions). Consistent with conservative tradition, this net forecast charge against income (i.e., loss) of $50,000 must be recognized in the current year. Thus, the $200,000 in credits to income arising before year-end, but after the measurement date, is combined with the net after-year-end loss of $50,000 to equal a figure of $150,000. After tax, the figure is further reduced to $90,000. If next year's results match predictions, no further gain or loss from discontinued operations is recognized.

Case B:

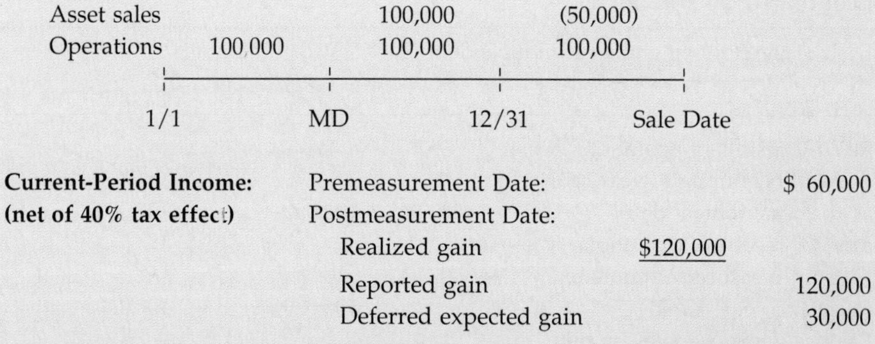

	1/1	MD	12/31	Sale Date
Asset sales		100,000	(50,000)	
Operations	100,000	100,000	100,000	

Current-Period Income:	Premeasurement Date:		$ 60,000
(net of 40% tax effect)	Postmeasurement Date:		
	Realized gain	$120,000	
	Reported gain		120,000
	Deferred expected gain		30,000

Explanation: Realized results of operations before the measurement date must be reported net of income taxes (i.e., $100,000 × [1 − tax rate] = $60,000).

After-year-end forecasts predict a net credit to income of $50,000 ($100,000 in income from operations less a loss of $50,000 from net asset dispositions). Consistent with conservative tradition, this net forecast credit (increase) of $50,000 to income cannot be recognized in the current year but must be deferred until actually realized. Thus, the $200,000 in credits to income arising before year-end, but after the measurement date, is not increased by forecasted events of the following year. After a 40% tax, the $200,000 figure is reduced to $120,000. If the results match predictions next year, the net gain of $30,000 ($50,000, net of tax) is recognized next year.

(continued)

EXHIBIT 6–4
(Continued)

Case C:

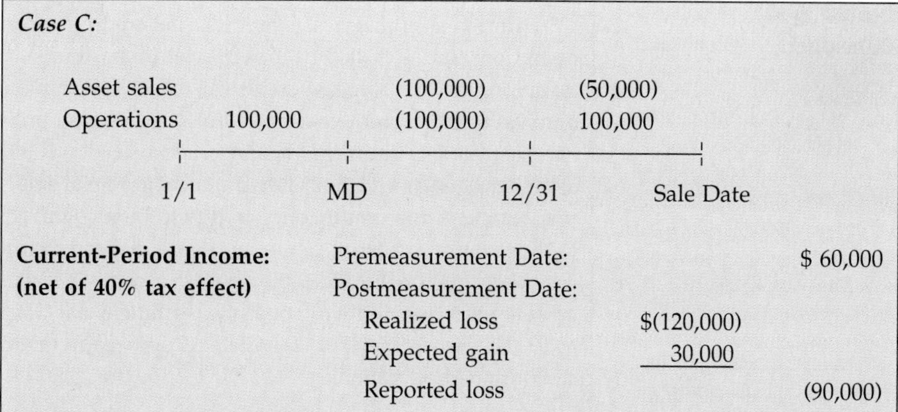

Current-Period Income:	Premeasurement Date:		$ 60,000
(net of 40% tax effect)	Postmeasurement Date:		
	Realized loss	$(120,000)	
	Expected gain	30,000	
	Reported loss		(90,000)

Explanation: Realized results of operations before the measurement date must be reported net of income taxes (i.e., $100,000 × [1 − tax rate] = $60,000).

After-year-end forecasts predict a net credit to income of $50,000 ($100,000 in income from operations less a loss of $50,000 from net asset dispositions). Consistent with conservative tradition, this net forecast credit (increase) to income ordinarily would not be recognized in the current year but would be deferred until actually realized. However, an exception arises in this instance because $200,000 in charges to income (losses) arise before year-end but after the measurement date. APB Opinion No. 30 allows post-year-end forecast income credits to be recognized in this instance, but limited to the amount of post-measurement-date realized charges (losses). In this case, that means that the $50,000 forecast income credits should be recognized in the current year, thus reducing post-measurement-date losses from $200,000 by $50,000 to $150,000. After tax, the $150,000 loss figure is further reduced by tax effects to $90,000.

In other words, combining all the predicted gains and losses after the measurement date resulted in a net loss. That loss (net of tax) is recognized immediately. No gain or loss would be recognized in the following year(s) as long as the results matched the predictions.

Case D:

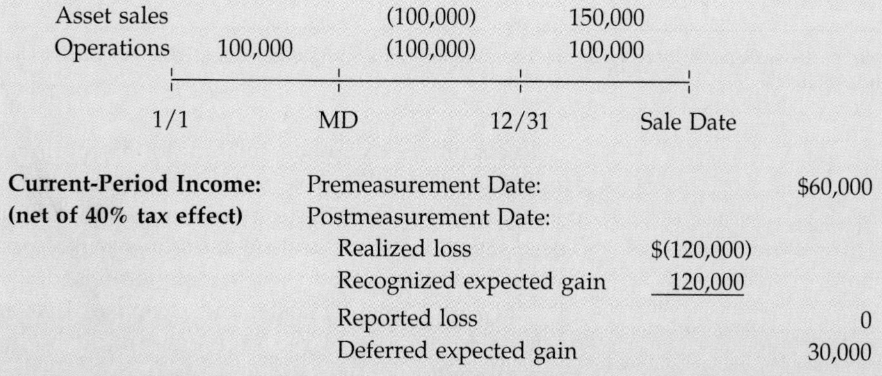

Current-Period Income:	Premeasurement Date:		$60,000
(net of 40% tax effect)	Postmeasurement Date:		
	Realized loss	$(120,000)	
	Recognized expected gain	120,000	
	Reported loss		0
	Deferred expected gain		30,000

Explanation: Realized results of operations before the measurement date must be reported net of income taxes (i.e., $100,000 × [1 − tax rate] = $60,000).

(continued)

EXHIBIT 6–4
(Concluded)

After-year-end forecasts predict a net credit to income of $250,000 ($100,000 from operations and $150,000 from net asset dispositions). Consistent with conservative tradition, this net forecast credit (increase) to income ordinarily would not be recognized in the current year but would be deferred until actually realized. However, an exception arises in this instance because $200,000 in charges to income (losses) arise before year-end but after the measurement date. APB Opinion No. 30 allows post-year-end forecast income credits to be recognized in this instance, but limited to the amount of post-measurement-date realized charges (losses) of $200,000. In this case, $200,000 of the $250,000 forecast income credits should be recognized in the current year, thus reducing post-measurement-date losses from $200,000 by $200,000 to $0. The remaining $50,000 will be recognized in the following year as income from discontinued operations.

The above discussion and Exhibit 6–4 examples suggest that accounting for discontinued operations is a very precise matter. The In Practice box "Timing Write-Offs" may suggest too much artistry is still allowed within current standards in the minds of some.

IN PRACTICE—GENERAL

Timing Write-Offs

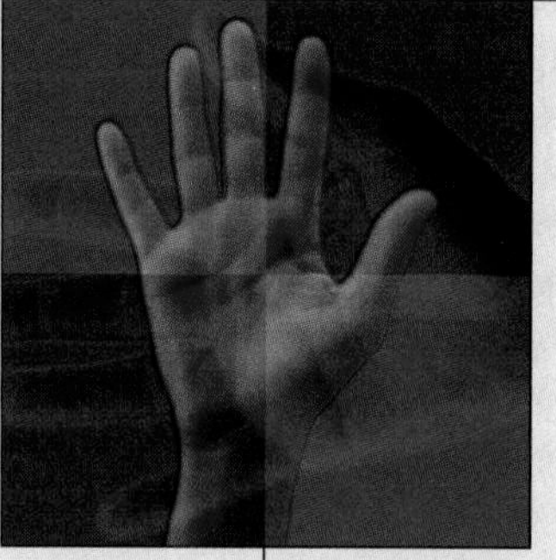

In the past decade, GE's earnings have risen every year. How does GE (*www.swcollege.com/hartman.html*) do it?

The clearest way GE manages earnings is through restructuring charges. When GE sells a business at a profit or takes an unusual gain, it generally takes an offsetting restructuring charge of roughly equal size. In six of the years since 1983, GE has taken charges totaling $3.95 billion in this way.

When GE booked a $1.43 billion pretax gain on the sale of its aerospace business, for example, it took a $1.01 billion charge to cover costs of "closing and downsizing and streamlining of certain production, service and adminstrative facilities worldwide." After tax, the gain and the charge matched up exactly.

Source: "How General Electric Damps Fluctuations in Its Annual Earnings," *The Wall Street Journal*, November 3, 1994, pp. A1 and A8.

Recognition of losses related to discontinued operations is limited to amounts that can be projected with reasonable accuracy. However, estimates usually will need periodic revision as new information becomes available. These revisions of accounting estimates will affect the reported income of the enterprise in the period the estimate is revised.

Only adjustments, costs, and expenses that are directly the result of the decision to dispose of the segment should be included in gains and losses from discontinued operations. These would be items such as severance pay to employees, additional pension costs, employee relocation expenses, future lease rentals under noncancelable leases (if not offset by subrentals), and gains and losses on the sale of specific plant assets.

Financial Statement Disclosures. The form of disclosure of gains and losses from discontinued operations on the income statement is illustrated in Exhibits 6–1 and 6–2. The results of discontinued operations must be shown separately from results of continuing operations, extraordinary items, and the effects of changes in accounting principles. The gains and losses also are to be reported net of their tax effects.

In addition to disclosures in the financial statements, the footnotes to the financial statements must disclose the following items:

1. The identity of the segment of the business being discontinued.
2. The expected disposal date if known.
3. The expected manner of disposition.
4. A description of the remaining assets and liabilities subject to disposition.
5. Separation of income or loss derived from (a) operations and (b) disposition of the net assets of the segment during the period from the measurement date to the date of the balance sheet.

EXTRAORDINARY ITEMS

The caption of **extraordinary item** is reserved for those events and transactions distinguished by both their unusual nature and by their infrequency of occurrence. These criteria are explicitly defined in APB Opinion No. 30 as follows:

- **Unusual nature:** The underlying event or transaction possesses *a high degree of abnormality* and is of a type clearly unrelated to, or only incidentally related to, the ordinary and typical activities of the enterprise, *taking into account the environment* in which the enterprise operates.
- **Infrequency of occurrence:** The underlying event or transaction is of a type that *would not reasonably be expected to recur in the foreseeable future*, taking into account *the environment* in which the enterprise operates.[5]

APB No. Opinion 30 further explicitly states that "an event or transaction may be unusual in nature for one enterprise but not for another because of differences in their respective environments."[6] That is, a firm's environment is a primary consideration in determining if an event or transaction is truly abnormal and significantly different from the typical activities of the business. Relevant environmental factors include characteristics of the industry, the geographic location, and the nature and extent of government regulation. Whether the event or transaction was voluntary or beyond the control of management, however, is not a criterion useful in discerning whether the item is unusual in nature.

An event or transaction is considered to occur "infrequently" if it is "of a type not reasonably expected to recur in the foreseeable future."[7] The history of occurrence of such events provides evidence to assess the probability of future occurrence. However, the changing environment in which a firm finds itself also is relevant.

[5]Ibid., par. 20.
[6]Ibid., par. 21.
[7]Ibid., par. 22.

The APB stated that certain events and transactions should not be reported as extraordinary because they customarily fail to satisfy one or both criteria in the U.S. business environment. Explicit examples cited in the standard include the following:

1. The write-down of receivables, inventories, equipment leased to others, or intangibles.
2. Gains or losses from (a) exchange or (b) translation of foreign currencies (including those related to major devaluations).
3. Gains or losses from sale or abandonment of property, plant, or equipment used in the business operations.
4. Adjustments of gross profit accruals on long-term contracts.

Professional Judgment. Determination of whether an item is extraordinary requires informed, objective, professional judgment. Estimation of the costs or revenues associated with extraordinary events also requires informed, objective, professional judgment. Specifically, APB Opinion No. 30 observes,

> Circumstances attendant to extraordinary items frequently require estimates, for example, of associated costs and occasionally of associated revenues, based on judgment and evaluation of the facts known at the time of the first accounting for the event.[8]

To facilitate determination of what constitutes an extraordinary item, the APB provided a list of examples (see Exhibit 6–5). However, there remains no substitute for experience and integrity in arriving at estimates of gains and losses.

Since the promulgation of APB Opinion No. 30, the FASB has defined several additional specific items as extraordinary. Notable among these are gains and losses realized on retirement of debt. Accordingly, current GAAP classifies all material gains and losses on early retirement of debt as extraordinary and reported net of tax on the income statement. Why did the FASB require gains and losses on extinguishment of debt to be reported as extraordinary? The FASB specifically wanted to preclude "management of income" by selectively retiring debt obligations early as market rates of interest changed.[9]

Extraordinary items is one area in which the philosophy of U.S. GAAP differs from the philosophy of the European Community (EC). The EC takes a more long-range view with respect to evaluation of company performance, which some consider more permissive. The different outlook results in several differences in what would be considered extraordinary. See the In Practice feature "Extraordinary Items: U.S. Versus EC Style."

ACCOUNTING CHANGES

APB Opinion No. 20 requires special treatment for **accounting changes** also. Accounting changes are of three types:

1. A change from one generally acceptable accounting principle or method to another.

[8] Ibid., par. 25.
[9] Extinguishment of debt is discussed further in Chapter 14.

EXHIBIT 6–5
Extraordinary Gains and Losses

Events that would be both unusual and infrequent:

A. A large portion of a tobacco manufacturer's crops are destroyed by a hail storm. Severe damage from hail storms in the locality where the manufacturer grows tobacco is rare.

B. A steel fabricating enterprise sells the only land it owns. The land was acquired 10 years ago for future expansion, but shortly thereafter the enterprise abandoned all plans for expansion and held the land for appreciation.

C. An enterprise sells a block of common stock of a publicly traded enterprise. The block of shares, that represent less than 10% of the publicly held enterprise, is the only security investment the enterprise has ever owned.

D. An earthquake destroys one of the oil refineries owned by a large multinational oil enterprise.

Events that would not be both unusual and infrequent:

A. "A citrus grower's Florida crop is damaged by frost. Frost damage is normally experienced every three or four years. The criterion of infreq iency of occurrence taking into account the environment in which the enterprise operates would not be met."

B. "An enterprise that operates a chain of warehouses sells the excess land surrounding one of its warehouses. When the enterprise buys property to establish a new warehouse, it usually buys more land than it expects to use for the warehouse with the expectation that the land will appreciate in value. In the past five years, there have been two instances in which the enterprise sold such excess land. The criterion of infrequency has not been met."

C. "A large diversified enterprise sells a block of shares from its portfolio of securities that it has acquired for investment purposes. This is the first sale from its portfolio of securities. Since the enterprise owns several securities for investment purposes, it should be concluded that sales of such securities are related to its ordinary and typical activities in the environment in which it operates and thus the criterion of unusual nature would not be met."

D. "A textile manufacturer with only one plant moves to another location. It has not relocated a plant in 20 years and has no plans to do so in the foreseeable future. Notwithstanding the infrequency of occurrence of the event as it relates to this particular enterprise, moving from one location to another is an occurrence that is a consequence of customary and continuing business activities, some of which are finding more favorable labor markets, more modern facilities, and proximity to customers and suppliers. Therefore, the criterion of unusual nature has not been met."

2. A change from one "good faith" estimate to another (prompted by environmental changes or availability of new information).
3. A change in reporting entity (such as a change in financial statement presentation from an individual-firm basis to a consolidated-entity basis).

Changes in reporting entities (i.e., [3] above) occur when the financial statements reflect information for a different reporting entity than reflected on previous statements. Changes in reporting entities are beyond the scope of this book. Accounting for changes in principle and for changes in estimates will be

IN PRACTICE—INTERNATIONAL

Extraordinary Items: U.S. Versus EC Style

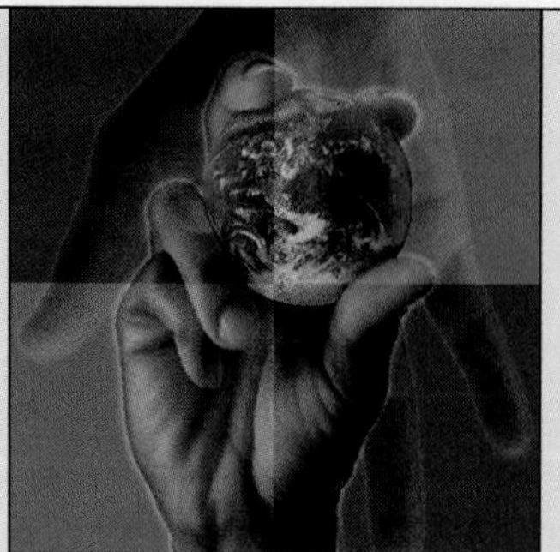

A philosophy of financial reporting in the European Community (EC) is that "long-term performance is much more relevant than annual results." Less emphasis in the EC on an accurately calculated annual profit results in several other differences between EC and U.S. reporting. One such difference pertains to extraordinary items:

[A]s stated in the EC's fourth directive, extraordinary items "arise otherwise than in the course of the company's ordinary activities." Therefore, some items will be labeled extraordinary that to the U.S. CPA seem nonextraordinary.

As examples, a British company might classify as extraordinary any "profit on sale of unlisted investments held as fixed assets" and "compensation received for breach of patent held by the group."

Source: L. Sundby and B. Schweiger, "EC, EZ?" *Journal of Accountancy*, March 1992, p. 75.

discussed. Accounting changes can greatly impact a firm's reported earnings. Thus, it is critically important that financial statement users understand the nature and impact of accounting changes and not rely exclusively on the bottom line (i.e., net income). See the In Practice box "Using Accounting Changes to Tidy Up the Bottom Line."

Changes in Accounting Principle or Method. To ensure the consistency of accounting data, a firm cannot arbitrarily change from one method of financial reporting to another, even if GAAP acknowledges multiple acceptable methods to report an event or transaction. APB Opinion No. 20 permits a **change in accounting principle** "only if the enterprise justifies the use of an alternative acceptable accounting principle on the basis that it is preferable."[10] Acceptable reasons include (1) improved matching of expenses and revenues, (2) improved asset valuation, or (3) compliance with newly adopted Statements of Financial Accounting Standards (SFAS). Other common reasons include the desire to minimize accounting costs or conform to industry practice. It was the latter reason along with (1) that ***GTE*** (*www.swcollege.com/hartman.html*) argued when it switched depreciation methods in the mid-1990s and took a $4.7 billion charge against income. In a short period of time the regulatory environment for phone companies changed markedly (e.g., they were no longer required by regulators to write off installed copper lines over 20–30 years using the straight-line method) and many new competing firms entered the market place (firms that used accelerated depreciation processes). Large industrywide changes were made to accelerated depreciation methods by ***GTE*** and many regional ***Bell*** companies.

If a change in accounting principle or method—such as a change from straight-line to accelerated methods for depreciation or from FIFO to LIFO methods of accounting for inventory—is deemed preferable, two specific means of disclosing these changes to users are prescribed. These treatments are known as the current approach and the retroactive approach.

[10]APB Opinion No. 20, par. 16.

ETHICS IN PRACTICE

Using Accounting Changes to Tidy Up the Bottom Line

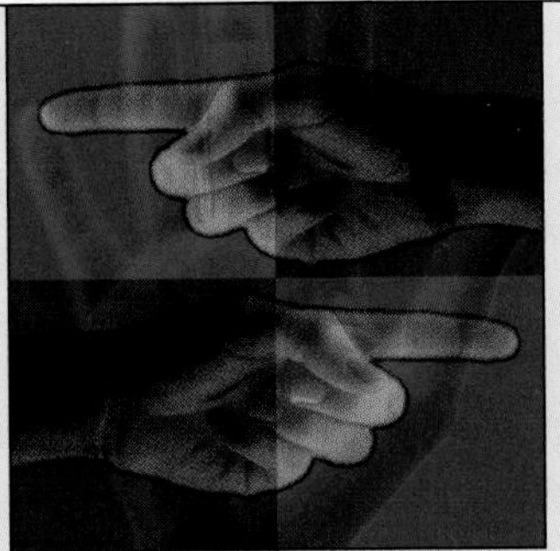

As usual, hard times are producing soft earnings. Accounting rules, precise and objective as they may seem, actually give executives a lot of leeway when it comes to deciding which dollars find their way to the bottom line. Companies are likely to use every inch of maneuvering room when business turns sour.

The results can dazzle or confound even the most experienced analyst. So this season, a ***Merrill Lynch*** (*www.swcollege.com/hartman.html*) executive is fighting back. He is sponsoring a contest: Dinner for two at a top New York restaurant goes to the analyst on his staff who spots the best example of balance sheet artistry in this season's crop of financial reports.

The winner has not yet been announced. But based on the sightings so far, it is already possible to identify the likely losers. They will be anyone in the investment community who takes this season's earnings reports at face value, without looking behind the bottom line.

For a closer look at accounting changes, review the table below for how a change in accounting procedures affected net income of three companies.

	BEFORE CHANGE	AFTER CHANGE
K-MART (*www.swcollege.com/hartman.html*)	$967.0 million	$1,146.2 million
Continental Mortgage & Equity Trust	−$574,000	$926,000
National Income and Realty Trust	−$6.3 million	−$3.1 million

Source: Diana B. Henriques, "Tidying Up That Old Bottom Line," *New York Times,* April 7, 1991, p. C4.

The **current approach** is used for most changes in accounting principle. Under the current approach the following directives of APB Opinion No. 20 apply:

1. Prior-year financial statements—including the income statement, the statement of retained earnings, and the balance sheet—when republished, even for comparative purposes, remain unchanged (that is, they are not restated).
2. The cumulative income difference between the two methods for all affected prior periods is reported as an element of income in the year of change. This amount, net of tax, is reported in the income statement as illustrated in Exhibits 6–1 and 6–2.
3. The new accounting method is effective as of the beginning of the year. That is, the current income statement reflects the new method, and prior years' income statements reflect the old.
4. To facilitate trend analysis, the effects of the new accounting method on the income in the year of change must be disclosed (in the notes or elsewhere).
5. To facilitate trend analysis, certain income and per-share figures for all prior years presented must be disclosed as if the new accounting principle were in effect during those periods. These *pro forma* (as if) figures may be disclosed on the face of the statements or prominently noted in supplemental schedules.
6. In any future year in which statements are provided for the year of change, the preceding disclosures must be repeated.

As an example, assume the following set of circumstances. Parker Products, a two-year-old firm, switches its inventory accounting methods from FIFO to a weighted-average method on January 1, 1997. The company had reported net income of $200,000 in both 1995 and 1996. The following information is also available:

CURRENT APPROACH

	FIFO		
	1995	1996	TOTAL
Purchases	$100,000	$100,000	$200,000
Cost of goods sold	30,000	30,000	60,000
Ending inventory	70,000	140,000	140,000

	AVERAGE COST		
	1995	1996	TOTAL
Purchases	$100,000	$100,000	$200,000
Cost of goods sold	40,000	40,000	80,000
Ending inventory	60,000	120,000	120,000

The entry to record the change would be as follows (assuming a 30% tax rate):

Cumulative Effect of Change in Accounting for Inventory	14,000	
Tax Refund Receivable	6,000	
Inventory		20,000

Of the $200,000 in goods purchased in prior periods, FIFO had expensed (via cost of goods sold) only $60,000, while the weighted-average method would have expensed $80,000. Therefore, $20,000 in additional income (pretax) would have been reported and closed to retained earnings in 1995 and 1996 under FIFO ($10,000 each year). The cumulative effect of the accounting change is $20,000 before income tax considerations.

However, under the current approach, income from operations for prior years is *not* restated (reduced in this case) when statements for those years are republished; they remain the same. Likewise, income tax expense will not be restated for prior years, although the entity will apply for a tax refund. Adjusted net income for 1995 and 1996 thus would remain $200,000 each year.

In the retained earnings statement, retained earnings at the beginning of 1996 and 1997 also remains unadjusted. At the end of 1997, the Retained Earnings balance sheet account will be adjusted, in that the income statement account, Cumulative Effect of a Change in Accounting for Inventory, will be closed to Retained Earnings. The Inventory account, as of January 1, 1997, is adjusted to the figure that would have prevailed if the weighted-average method had always been in place ($120,000, on January 1, 1997).

The **retroactive approach** is applied in only a small, select set of cases, including the following:

1. A change *from* LIFO inventory accounting methods to some other inventory method.
2. A change to or from the full-cost method in extractive industries.

3. A change to the equity method of accounting for equity investments in the stock of other firms.
4. A change in the method of accounting for long-term construction (or service) contracts from the completed-contract method to the percentage-of-completion method, or vice versa.
5. A change from retirement/replacement accounting to other depreciation methods in the railroad industry.
6. All accounting changes made in conjunction with an initial public stock offering.
7. A change to a new accounting method adopted by the FASB or other authoritative body that specifically requires retroactive application.

The retroactive approach requires the following steps:

1. In the year of change, the cumulative income difference (between the two accounting methods) for all affected prior periods *must be shown as an adjustment* to the beginning retained earnings in the earliest year shown. For single-year presentations, this would be to the beginning retained earnings for the current year. For multiple-year or comparative presentations, the catchup adjustment would be to the opening retained earnings balance of the first year presented. Each subsequent year, retained earnings must reflect the cumulative after-tax effect of the change attributable to all affected prior periods.
2. In the year of change, affected balance sheet accounts must be adjusted by the cumulative income difference.
3. Whenever reissued (often for comparative purposes in annual reports), prior-period financial statements must reflect account balances restated to conform to the new accounting principle.
4. The effects of the change on earnings and per-share figures for all periods presented must be disclosed in the notes to the financial statements.

As an example, assume the following set of circumstances. Parker Products, a two-year-old firm, switches its inventory accounting methods from LIFO to FIFO on January 1, 1997. The company had reported net income of $200,000 in both 1995 and 1996. The following information is also available:

RETROACTIVE APPROACH

	LIFO		
	1995	1996	TOTAL
Purchases	$100,000	$100,000	$200,000
Cost of goods sold	50,000	50,000	100,000
Ending inventory	50,000	100,000	100,000

	FIFO		
	1995	1996	TOTAL
Purchases	$100,000	$100,000	$200,000
Cost of goods sold	30,000	30,000	60,000
Ending inventory	70,000	140,000	140,000

The ending inventory is $40,000 greater for FIFO than LIFO, and cost of goods sold is correspondingly $40,000 less for FIFO. Thus, FIFO-based income for the two periods combined would be $40,000 greater before considering income tax. This is reflected by an adjustment made to retained earnings. The entry to record the change would be as follows (assuming a 30% tax rate):

Inventory	40,000	
Retained Earnings		28,000
Deferred Taxes Payable		12,000
(30% × 40,000)		

Of the $200,000 in goods purchased in prior periods, FIFO would have expensed (via cost of goods sold) only $60,000, while LIFO had expensed $100,000. Therefore, $40,000 in additional income (pretax) would have been reported and closed to retained earnings in prior years under FIFO ($20,000 each year). Income from operations before taxes for prior years thus must be restated (increased) by $20,000 in each year whenever statements for those years are republished on a FIFO basis.

As income is restated upward, income tax expenses in those years also must be adjusted upward, and additional tax liability recognized. The restated net income for 1995 and 1996 thus would be $214,000 each year, i.e., {[i.e., $200,000 + [$20,000 × (1 − .30)]}. Retained earnings at the beginning of 1996 and 1997 also must be adjusted for the net effect of these income and expense adjustments ($14,000 in 1996 and $28,000 in 1997), because all revenues and expenses are periodically closed to retained earnings. The 1997 beginning Retained Earnings balance sheet account would require adjustment in the amount of $28,000.

The Inventory account, as of January 1, 1997, also must be adjusted to reflect the amount using the FIFO method ($140,000 on January 1, 1997). Thus, both the current book accounts must be adjusted (via the entry presented earlier), and selected figures appearing on financial statements of prior periods must be restated.

The APB limited the use of the retroactive approach to these relatively few accounting changes for disclosure purposes. To provide useful information to users of financial statements, the impact of most accounting changes is disclosed in a separate section of the income statement as a part of the current year's net income.

Discussion of Retroactive Versus Current Approach. The requirement of APB Opinion No. 20 to use the current approach for most changes in accounting principle is based on two arguments. First, the current approach is consistent with an all-inclusive income statement concept. The merit of this concept is that it requires most earnings-related events and transactions to appear on the income statement, thereby reducing opportunities to manipulate financial statement results. In this way, management is prohibited from selectively reporting "good news" type items on the income statement while charging "bad news" type matters directly to retained earnings—a problem that allegedly reached epidemic proportions in the 1960s and led to the current standard.

The second argument is based on a consideration of the public's confidence in and perception of financial statements and the accounting system. To require restatement of financials every time a material change in accounting method occurred could cause an erosion of that confidence. A realistic fear exists that the public will make the evaluation that "if you keep changing it, it can't be too good."

The other side of the argument suggests that the current approach significantly distorts measures of current performance. Even though the adjustments are reported separately, they are still included on the income statement. A problem arises because of the size of these adjustments, and because of the fact that some statistical services report only a single number—net income. For example, ***Value Line, Standard and Poor's,*** and a number of others report only net income. This single profitability figure then is reflected in return on equity, growth rate calculations, and assorted other ratios and averages. In 1985, when SFAC No. 5, "Recognition and Measurement in Financial Statements of Business Enterprises," was issued, the FASB recommended that the cumulative effect of changes in accounting principles not be included in earnings for the year of change. However, to date no GAAP revision has been made.

Discussion of All-Inclusive Income Statement Concept. Interpretational issues created by adoption of an all-inclusive income statement philosophy are not limited to the effects of changes in accounting method. Including other events such as extraordinary items and discontinued operations on the income statement is a policy inconsistent with the policies of many other nations. Inclusion of items unrelated to the "core business" or items "related" to other periods on the income statement has been the subject of significant discussion, as reflected in the excerpted *Forbes* article in the In Practice feature titled "Unusual Items."

Use of Changes by Management. A related issue of significance to the accounting profession is the questionable motivation of management for accounting changes. Acceptable reasons under GAAP for selection of one accounting method over another and acceptable arguments for changes in accounting principles were discussed earlier. However, evidence from researchers suggests that changes in accounting methods frequently are made simply to avoid the unfavorable economic consequences of reporting accounting losses or diminished income. An example of the many research studies on this matter is that of Ken Schwartz, reported in the *Journal of Accounting, Auditing, and Finance.* Schwartz found that approximately twice as many firms exhibiting financial stress change accounting methods as do firms exhibiting solid financial performance. Further, over four times as many changes *increase* income and/or other related measures of performance. On this point Professor Revsine of Northwestern University proposes the following explanation:

> As business and society grew more complex, it became difficult to make financial decisions by directly observing the important variables. This complexity gave rise to financial reporting, since "abstractions" (or surrogates) became necessary to summarize events and to provide information for more complex analyses. . . . Today virtually all financial decisions in both the private and the public sector use accounting surrogates rather than directly observed events as the basis for action. Not surprisingly, managers . . . gradually learned that while the events that affect performance often cannot be controlled, the way that people *perceive* these events can be controlled. Manipulating the surrogates provides decision makers with a means for influencing people's perceptions of managerial performance.

IN PRACTICE—GENERAL

Unusual Items

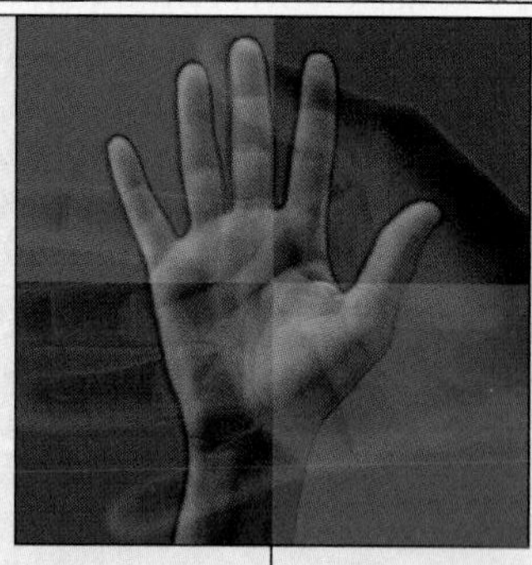

Suppose your metal-bending company owns an old desk. It's on the books for $100. One day you discover the old desk belonged to Ben Franklin. Sotheby's auctions it off for $50,000.

The end of the year rolls around and you're calculating your company's operating earnings from bending metal. Question: Should you include the $49,900 profit from selling that old desk?

Don't laugh. In their reported operating earnings, lots of big companies include gains (and losses) from "once-only" events. As a result, says David Hawkins, professor of accounting at Harvard Business School, "investors cannot just take the bottom-line numbers before or after extraordinary items and assume that they understand what is going on." Doing so, Hawkins warns, "can be dangerous to your wealth."

Consider ***Time, Inc.*** (*www.swcollege.com/hartman.html*) For 1986, the august publisher reported income, before taxes, of $626 million. After-tax net came to $376 million, $5.95 per share, up 89% from 1985. With earnings momentum like that, maybe Time was worth the $100-plus a share it was selling for before Bloody Monday ripped it to $81.

But did Time's ongoing, operating businesses really earn $376 million? Is the figure a good basis from which to project 1987's earnings and buy its stock? Not necessarily.

Look at the $376 million reported profit, and you'll see it includes the equivalent of Ben Franklin's desk. To wit: In 1986, when the stock market was hot, Time sold 20% of a cable television subsidiary, ***American Television Communications Corp.***, to the public for a pretax gain of $318 million. Time booked this one-time gain as operating earnings—even though the only way it might realize a comparable gain next year would be to sell off yet another 20%.

Time also threw a $33 million profit on another investment, and $113 million in one-time expenses from relocating offices and reducing staff, into pretax earnings. Eliminate these once-only gains from selling off investments, and Time's after-tax operating earnings from ongoing businesses was around $129 million last year, down over 35% from 1985.

What's going on here? We called John Shank, professor of accounting at Dartmouth's Tuck School. "Don't blame Time Inc.," said Shank. "Blame the accountants. Their rules make companies include such unusual items as stock sale profits and office relocation expenses in income, even though they are unrelated to current, or future, operations."

Source: Subrata N. Chakravarty, "Unreal Accounting," *Forbes,* November 16, 1987, pp. 74–75.

> Virtually all U.S. companies have management compensation plans tied to reported earnings numbers; consequently, managers have a natural incentive to increase reported profit since higher profit means higher compensation.[11]

Corporate management also has influence over the number of GAAP alternatives available. Managers desire flexible accounting rules because the result is a latitude in representing their performance, and they actively lobby the FASB to this end. To the extent that flexible rules do exist, greater ethical challenges confront accountants and corporate leaders to resist temptations to artificially distort results of financial performance. When some individuals fall prey to these temptations, the whole accounting profession loses some measure of credibility, and users approach published financial data with greater and greater skepticism. Members of the profession must vigilantly monitor the ethics of its members.

[11]Lawrence Revsine, *Accounting Horizons,* December 1991, pp. 16–17.

Earnings Quality. Earnings quality is a matter of high interest to financial analysts and other users of financial statements. Earnings quality can be defined in various ways. Generally, the term relates to the overall permanence of earnings. High-quality earnings are sustainable earnings. The stock market tends to reward firms having high earnings quality and high management integrity with high price/earnings (P/E) multiples (that is, the firm's stock, per share, sells at a higher multiple of earnings per share than the stock of firms with low perceived quality). Managers often thus need to consider the trade-off between reporting higher earnings and the possible negative perceptions of earnings quality that may accompany certain choices of accounting practices or operations. Some research has found that P/E ratios systematically differ among firms in relation to the method of depreciation used. Firms using straight-line depreciation, which tends to produce higher earnings (and earnings per share) figures, have lower P/E ratios than firms using accelerated depreciation methods.

The ethics of selected "earnings management" practices is also uncertain, if not controversial. The In Practice box "Managing Short-Term Earnings" (page 278) reports the results of a survey conducted by Professors William Bruns (of Harvard) and Ken Merchant (of University of Southern California) of 649 corporate managers. These researchers were admittedly "troubled" by the inability of these managers to agree on the types of earnings-management activities that are acceptable. To the degree that the acceptability of different conduct varies, practice can also be assumed to vary, placing the financial statement user at risk of more untoward behavior. Clear "norms of conduct" may not exist.

Changes in Accounting Estimate. Environmental changes or newly available information might warrant a change in accounting estimate. Examples would be changes in the estimated useful life of a depreciable asset or the estimated percentage of uncollectible credit sales. APB Opinion No. 20 prescribes the prospective method for treating changes in accounting estimates. Under this method, no cumulative effect on income for prior years is calculated for changes in accounting estimates; only the current and future periods are affected by the change in the accounting estimate. The income statement of the current year simply reflects revenues or expenses based on the revised estimate. Prior financial statements, including income statements and statements of retained earnings, are unchanged. No cumulative effect of a change in accounting estimate appears on the income statement. Exhibits 6–6 and 6–7 contrast the accounting treatment accorded changes in accounting principle and accounting estimate.

Only changes in estimates made in good faith may use the prospective treatment. Estimates that were known to be made erroneously (for purposes of manipulating financial performance measures) are treated differently. Changes made to such "bad-faith" estimates are considered to be *corrections of accounting errors* or *prior-period adjustments* and are discussed in the following section of this chapter. Likewise, changes of original estimates exhibiting gross negligence (that is, gross disregard of available information) are treated as *corrections of accounting errors.*

Unfortunately, the motivation of management cannot always be definitively established by the accountant. Accordingly, significant changes in accounting estimates often make headlines in the financial press. Management's motives are openly questioned, and the accounting treatment of those changes is challenged, as related in the excerpt in the Ethics In Practice feature "Changes in Accounting Estimates."

EXHIBIT 6–6
Changes in Accounting Principle

Control Corporation purchased equipment in 1993 for $100,000. The equipment was estimated to have a 10-year life with zero salvage value. The equipment was depreciated using the straight-line method. In 1997 Control changed the method of accounting for this equipment from straight-line depreciation to sum-of-the-years'-digits depreciation. Relevant information follows:

	Alternate Depreciation Schedules	
Period	Straight-Line	Sum-of-the-Years'-Digits
1993	$10,000	$18,182
1994	10,000	16,364
1995	10,000	14,545
1996	10,000	12,727
	$40,000	$61,818
1997		$10,909

The cumulative effect of using different depreciation methods in prior years is thus $21,818 ($61,818 − $40,000). Had the sum-of-the-years'-digits method always been used, $21,818 more would have been credited to Accumulated Depreciation and debited to Depreciation Expense (which in turn would have been closed at year-end to Retained Earnings.) To effect the switch from straight-line depreciation to sum-of-the-years'-digits depreciation, the following entry is required to adjust book balances:

Cumulative Effect of Change in Depreciation Method (net of 40% tax effect)	13,091	
Income Tax Refund Receivable	8,727	
Accumulated Depreciation		21,818

The cumulative effect of the change in accounting method is reported net of tax on the current year's (1997) income statement, reducing net income by $13,091. If prior tax returns are amended, a tax refund of $8,727 is expected, as less income is attributable to prior taxable years. The Cumulative Effect account is closed to Retained Earnings at year-end.

Depreciation for the current year (1997) is computed using the sum-of-the-years'-digits method and is reported in the appropriate operating section of the income statement. The following adjusting entry is made at year-end:

Depreciation Expense	10,909	
Accumulated Depreciation		10,909

Specify which circumstances qualify as prior-period adjustments, and explain how to measure, account for, and report those adjustments in the financial statements.

PRIOR-PERIOD ADJUSTMENTS

SFAS No. 16 provides authoritative guidance as to what constitutes a **prior-period adjustment** and how such adjustments are to be reported in financial statements. By definition, these are adjustments (1) required to correct an error in the financial statements of a prior period, (2) needed to recognize as income any tax-loss carryforwards of purchased subsidiaries, or (3) specified as prior-period adjustments by the FASB. The second item is beyond the scope of this book, and the third is self-explanatory, so the following discussion focuses on the first item.

EXHIBIT 6–7
Change in Accounting Estimate

Control Corporation purchased equipment in 1993 for $100,000. The equipment was estimated to have a 10-year life with zero salvage value. The equipment was depreciated using the straight-line method. In 1997 Control estimated the equipment actually had a 20-year life, with 16 years remaining. Relevant information follows:

	ALTERNATE DEPRECIATION SCHEDULES	
PERIOD	10-YEAR LIFE	20-YEAR LIFE
1993	$10,000	$ 5,000
1994	10,000	5,000
1995	10,000	5,000
1996	10,000	5,000
	$40,000	$20,000

The cumulative effect of using different estimates of the asset's life in prior years is thus $20,000. Had a 20-year life always been estimated, $20,000 less would have been credited to Accumulated Depreciation and debited to Depreciation Expense during years 1993–1996. Under current GAAP, this cumulative difference, however, is irrelevant. Changes in accounting estimates are accorded a prospective treatment. That means, unlike changes in accounting principles, no adjustments to book balances are required to effect the change. Accumulated Depreciation remains at $40,000, as do the former charges to Depreciation Expense (since closed to Retained Earnings).

The charge against operating income in 1997 for depreciation will be $3,750 (a significant decline from prior years). This figure is derived by spreading the remaining unadjusted book value over the remaining asset life as revised (i.e., $60,000 undepreciated book value divided by 16 remaining years). The appropriate year-end adjusting entry would be as follows:

Depreciation Expense	3,750	
Accumulated Depreciation		3,750
($60,000 book value ÷ 16 years = $3,750)		

An accounting error can originate from several underlying causes, including:

1. Intentional use (that is, "bad faith" application) of unrealistic accounting estimates for purposes of manipulating key financial statement measures of performance.
2. Use of unrealistic accounting estimates because of gross negligence or disregard of available, relevant information.
3. Arithmetic mistakes.
4. Application of non-GAAP principles (for example, capitalization of research and development costs even though current authoritative standards require immediate expensing).
5. Classification errors (for example, classifying an extraordinary item as an element of operating income).

Accounting errors also might be classified by their effects on the financial statements. First, some errors made in prior periods affect the financial statements but do not affect net income. An example is the misclassification of an

ETHICS IN PRACTICE

Managing Short-Term Earnings

	Proportion of Managers That Judge the Practice as:		
	Ethical	Questionable, or a Minor Infraction	Unethical, or a Serious Infraction
1. Managing short-term earnings by changing or manipulating operating decisions or procedures:			
a. When the result is to reduce earnings	79%	19%	2%
b. When the result is to increase earnings	57%	31%	12%
2. Managing short-term earnings by changing or manipulating accounting methods:			
a. When the change to earnings is small	5%	45%	50%
b. When the change to earnings is large	3%	21%	76%
3. Managing short-term earnings by deferring discretionary expenditures into the next accounting period:			
a. To meet an interim quarterly budget target	47%	41%	12%
b. To meet an annual budget target at year-end	41%	35%	24%
4. Increasing short-term earnings to meet a budget target:			
a. By selling excess assets and realize a profit	80%	16%	4%
b. By ordering overtime work at year-end to ship as much as possible	74%	21%	5%
c. By offering customers special credit terms to accept delivery without obligation to pay until the following year	43%	44%	15%

Source: "The Dangerous Morality of Managing Earnings," *Management Accounting,* August 1990, pp. 22–25.

extraordinary item as an operating item on the income statement. No entry is required to correct the accounting records because, irrespective of whether the gain or loss was reported as extraordinary or ordinary (operating), the item would have been closed at year-end to retained earnings. Thus, current account balances, including the retained earnings figure, are correct. However, the classification error should be corrected whenever the previously published statement is reissued or presented in comparative schedules. A note also should discuss the nature of the error.

A second type of error is one that does affect income reported in prior years but has already "self-corrected." For example, recognition of revenue in the wrong period may cause net income of one prior period to be underreported and net income of another period to be overreported. Current account balances, including the Retained Earnings account, will be correct; so no correcting entry is necessary. As before, the error should be corrected whenever the previously published financial statements are reissued or presented in comparative schedules.

ETHICS IN PRACTICE

Changes in Accounting Estimates

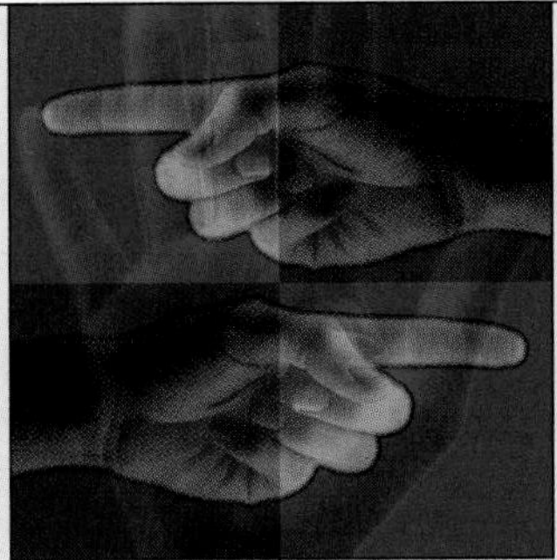

No one ever said accounting was an exact science. How inexact it can be has been illustrated in two recent cases: ***Cineplex Odeon*** (*www.swcollege.com/hartman.html*) and ***Blockbuster Entertainment*** (*www.swcollege.com/hartman.html*). Both companies minimized the amortization of assets to the benefit of reported earnings.

In the case of Cineplex Odeon, the movie theater circuit amortizes its leasehold improvements—seats, carpet, equipment and the like—over an average of 27 years, despite the fact that many of these assets will almost certainly be on the scrap heap long before 27 years have elapsed.

In the Blockbuster case, the aggressive videotape rental store chain recently spread the amortization period for its tapes from a fast write-off over 9 months to a slow one over 36 months. That bookkeeping gimmick added $3 million, or nearly 20%, to Blockbuster's reported 1988 income. One report has it that ***Bear Stearns*** (*www.swcollege.com/hartman.html*), critical of Blockbuster's accounting, sliced $226 million off the company's market value within two days.

Questions about proper amortization and depreciation schedules even involve companies that have never been accused of dubious accounting practices, as Cineplex and Blockbuster have. Consider ***General Motors*** (*www.swcollege.com/hartman.html*). Until 1987, GM wrote off tools and dies at by far the fastest rate in the car business. But in that year the company slowed amortization of its tools and dies down to a level comparable with those of ***Ford*** (*www.swcollege.com/hartman.html*) and ***Chrysler*** (*www.swcollege.com/hartman.html*). GM was in no way cooking the books, but the move did increase GM's reported earnings by $2.55 per share; total earnings came to $10.06 per share that year.

In 1984 ***IBM*** (*www.swcollege.com/hartman.html*) shifted from accelerated depreciation to the straight-line method for its rental machines, plant and other property. According to Thornton O'Glove, author of the "Quality of Earnings Report," the change increased IBM's reported earnings by $375 million, or 37 cents a share.

What's going on here? When it comes to amortization and depreciation, generally accepted accounting principles provide only the vaguest of guidelines. Why doesn't the SEC insist upon more conformity? As Howard Hodges, chief accountant for the SEC's corporate finance division, once said: "We try to be observant, but when a company says it's depreciating its plant over 30 to 40 years, we don't know the intimate details. And there's no practical way we could. I'd like the accountants to take more responsibility for it."

For their part, the accountants retort that they're doing the best they can—that when reviewing depreciation, they look at engineering reports, industry practices, and the company's historical use of assets. Even so, they say, it's difficult to pass judgment on how much value can be squeezed from the assets. As a result, the corporation's auditors will probably go along with management's judgment as long as the write-off period doesn't diverge too much from general industry practice. Yet the permissible variations are so great as to make it difficult to compare two companies' earnings without intimate knowledge of their accounting practices.

Source: Dana Weschler, "Earnings Helper," *Forbes*, June 12, 1989, pp. 150, 153.

A final type of error is one that has affected income reported in prior years but has not "self-corrected." An example would be the failure to record depreciation expense. For these types of errors, not only must previously published financial statements be corrected (whenever reissued or presented in comparative schedules), but an entry is required to adjust current account balances in the firm's accounting records. The correcting entry normally involves at least three accounts: the Retained Earnings account (to which the erroneous nominal accounts have been closed), the related balance sheet account, and either an Income Tax Payable or Receivable account, if income tax effects exist. Exhibit 6–8 illustrates representative examples.

Note that prior-period adjustments of current account balances do not affect current-period income and are not reported on the income statement in the year of correction. Instead, adjustments are made directly to the Retained Earnings account. In the year of correction these appear as adjustments to the beginning balance of retained earnings on a **statement of retained earnings**, as illustrated in Exhibit 6–9. In the year of correction, the beginning balance of retained earnings is adjusted for each year presented. The nature of the error should also be discussed in a note to the statement. Subsequent financial statements, however, need not repeat the disclosures. The statement of changes in stockholders' equity and adjustments to it are discussed in Chapter 19.

EXHIBIT 6–8
Examples of Prior-Period Adjustments

Case A

Sparkle Enterprises purchases equipment in 1995 at a cost of $100,000. The equipment was estimated to have a 10-year life and zero salvage. Customarily, Sparkle uses the straight-line method to depreciate its equipment. Due to an oversight, no depreciation was recognized in 1995 and 1996. Depreciation expense of $10,000 should have been properly recognized in each year. The income tax rate in 1995 and 1996 was 40%. If the error was uncovered in January 1997, the following entry would be required:

Retained Earnings	12,000	
Income Tax Refund Receivable	8,000	
Accumulated Depreciation		20,000

Case B

The 1995 and 1996 income statements of Tempe Time Inc. reported the following cost of goods sold figures:

	1995	1996
Beginning inventory	$ 100,000	$ 130,000
Plus: Purchases	400,000	350,000
Goods available	$ 500,000	$ 480,000
Less: Ending inventory	(130,000)	(100,000)
Cost of goods sold	$ 370,000	$ 380,000

Subsequently it was discovered in 1997 that the physical ending inventory count for 1995 had mistakenly excluded $20,000 in inventory held at an overseas site. The physical ending inventory count for 1996 was correct.

No entry to correct the accounting books is necessary in 1997 because (1) inventory is currently correctly valued based on an accurate 1996 year-end inventory count and (2) retained earnings is correct. Retained earnings is correct because the inventory error is self-correcting. Because the ending inventory in 1995 was understated, the beginning inventory in 1996 was likewise undervalued. Accordingly, the cost of goods sold in 1995 was overstated (income was understated) and in 1996 was understated (income was over stated) by the same $20,000 figure.

(continued)

EXHIBIT 6–8
(Concluded)

Case C

In 1996 Fashionplate Industries incurred costs of $400,000 to remodel one of its leased retail outlets. The firm generally remodels about every five years. Fashionplate erroneously expensed all $400,000 in 1996, whereas the cost should have been capitalized and amortized (depreciated) over the five-year expected life (using the straight-line method). The external audit discovered the error at the end of 1997. The prevailing tax rate is 30%. The correcting entry would be as follows:

Leasehold Improvements	400,000	
Depreciation Expense	80,000	
Accumulated Depreciation		160,000
Retained Earnings		224,000
Income Taxes Payable		96,000

The correcting entry performs the following:

1. It adjusts the asset account to its full value of $400,000.
2. It records depreciation expense for 1997.
3. It adjusts accumulated depreciation to reflect two years' charges (at $80,000 per year).
4. It adjusts the beginning balance in 1997's retained earnings for prior-period errors net of tax ($400,000 of 1996 charges made in error minus $80,000, the proper 1996 charges for depreciation times 1 minus the tax rate).
5. It recognizes a tax liability on the additional $320,000 in income that properly should have been recognized in 1996.

EXHIBIT 6–9
Statement of Retained Earnings With Prior-Period Adjustment

SPARKLE ENTERPRISES
Statement of Retained Earnings
For the Year Ended December 31, 1997

Retained earnings, January 1, 1997 (as previously reported)	$500,000
Correction of error in depreciation expense charged in prior periods (net of $8,000 tax)	12,000
Adjusted balance, January 1, 1997	$488,000
Add: Net income, 1997	100,000
Deduct: Dividends declared on	
Preferred Stock ($3 per share)	(30,000)
Common Stock ($1 per share)	(40,000)
Retained earnings, December 31, 1997	$518,000
Less: Appropriations for plant expansion	(300,000)
Unappropriated balance	$218,000

A summary of the accounting required for accounting changes, error corrections, and changes in estimates is presented in Exhibit 6–10.

EXHIBIT 6–10
Summary of Accounting Changes, Error Corrections, and Changes in Estimates

APPROACH	FEATURES	USE
Retroactive (past-period changes)	Adjust beginning Retained Earnings (net of taxes) and other balance sheet accounts. When presented, restate prior-year statements. Adjustment does *not* affect current-period earnings.	Prior-period adjustments (to Retained Earnings), for error corrections and "certain" accounting changes.
Current (current-period changes)	Adjust beginning balance sheet accounts *except* Retained Earnings to reflect balances under new method. Report cumulative impact from prior periods (net of taxes) as a charge or credit to current-period earnings. Use the new method for the current period. When presented, *do not* restate prior-year statements *but* disclose "pro forma" accounts as *if* new method had been used.	Cumulative effect (on income) for *most* accounting principle changes.
Prospective (future-period changes)	*No* adjustments to beginning balance sheet accounts or current-period earnings. Use revised estimate for current and future periods based upon estimated *remaining* future amounts and estimated periods, *given* that past estimates remain intact. When presented, *do not* restate prior-year statements. If material, "pro forma" impact or some notice of estimate change *may be* disclosed (but is not required).	Changes in accounting estimates.

USING INCOME STATEMENT DATA

EARNINGS PER SHARE

Earnings per share (EPS) are also a required part of the income statement. To assist users in economic decision making, separate EPS figures are required for (1) income from continuing operations, (2) income before extraordinary items and accounting changes, (3) the cumulative effect of an accounting change, and (4) net income.

Illustrate the computations and reporting requirements for earnings-per-share presentations.

EPS for income from continuing operations and net income are calculated after the effects of any required distributions to preferred shareholders. An example of EPS calculations and presentation for Jay's Barbeque appears in Exhibit 6–11. Distributions to preferred shareholders are deducted from income because users are interested in the earnings that will be available to the corporation to distribute to the common shareholders or to reinvest in the business. Obligations to the preferred shareholders represent distributions of resources that will not be available for reinvestment or distribution to common shareholders. EPS computations can become quite complex. These are explained and illustrated in Appendix B of the text.

As discussed in Chapter 3, various approaches to financial statement analysis are used. In some instances, the absolute amount of an item may be highly

EXHIBIT 6–11
Earnings-Per-Share Computations

1. Data: Assume that Jay's Barbecue has the following:

Income from continuing operations	$10,000,000
Loss on discontinued operations (net of tax)	(200,000)
Net extraordinary gain from early extinguishment of debt (net of tax)	2,000,000
Net loss from change in accounting principle (net of tax)	(2,500,000)
Net income	$ 9,300,000

Preferred stock, 1,000,000 shares of 8%, $10 par, issued and outstanding. Common stock, 2,000,000 shares of no-par stock, issued and outstanding.

2. Earnings-per-share presentation on income statement:

(A) Income from continuing operations	$4.60
Discontinued operations (net of tax)	(.10)*
(B) Income before extraordinary items	$4.50
Extraordinary gain (net of tax)	1.00*
(C) Loss from change in accounting principle	(1.25)
(D) Net income per share	$4.25

*Optional disclosure

3. Computations:

(A) $$\frac{\$10{,}000{,}000 - (.08 \times \$10 \text{ par} \times 1{,}000{,}000 \text{ shares})}{2{,}000{,}000 \text{ shares}} = \$4.60$$

$$\frac{\$200{,}000}{2{,}000{,}000} = (.10)$$

$$\frac{\$2{,}000{,}000}{2{,}000{,}000} = 1.00$$

(C) $$\frac{(\$2{,}500{,}000)}{2{,}000{,}000} = (1.25)$$

(D) $$\frac{\$9{,}300{,}000 - (.08 \times \$10 \text{ par} \times 1{,}000{,}000 \text{ shares})}{2{,}000{,}000} = 4.25$$

relevant. More often, the relative size of a current account or ratio compared to prior years' figures or compared to other firms in the same industry is more relevant. It is also relevant to consider the nation in which the firm reports its financial statements, as international differences exist, as noted in the In Practice feature "Performance Ratios Around the World."

IN PRACTICE—INTERNATIONAL

Performance Ratios Around the World

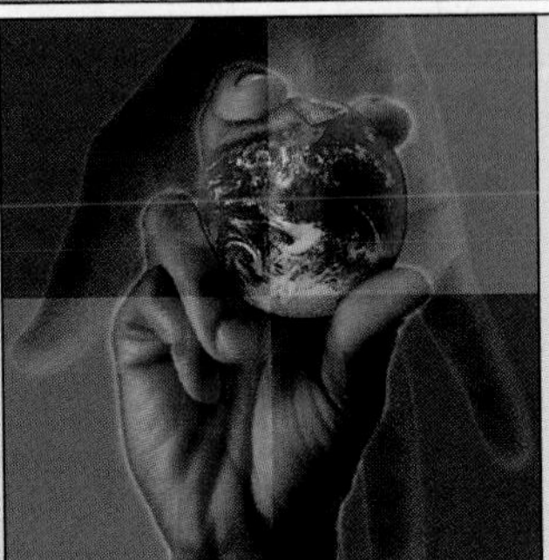

Daunting in one country, investor difficulties in valuing companies multiply abroad. In theory, investors buy equity to have a share in companies' earnings.

Even within the accounting rules of one country, companies find plenty of ways to adjust their earnings up or down. Untroubled by the threat of takeover, German and Japanese companies tend to understate profits and so escape taxes; British and American firms are sufficiently nervous of their shareholders to prefer the opposite approach. Some recent work by ***Smithers & Co.***, a London-based research boutique, attempts to tackle these (and similar) distortions.

Smithers (also) sets out to explain Japan's (high) price/earnings (p/e) ratios by adjusting them for the effect of cross-holdings (Column 3 in the following table). On his reckoning, 45% of the shares in Tokyo's market are beneficially owned by another quoted company. To own the market, therefore, an investor needs only to buy 55% of it: Tokyo is really 45% cheaper than its market capitalization. To build on this start, Smithers considers the different accounting procedures by which firms calculate their profits. One big variable is the rate at which capital is depreciated. Many German firms write off their capital quickly, during which time their profits are misleadingly small; subsequently, they are artificially inflated. In America and Britain, firms tend to mislead in the opposite direction.

The last step towards internationally comparable ratios is to reflect economic cycles (Column 2 in the following table). The results are summarized in the table.

International Price/Earnings Ratios:

	PUBLISHED P/E 12 FEB. 92	CYCLICALLY ADJUSTED P/E	RATIO OF TRUE TO PUBLISHED PROFITS	FULLY ADJUSTED P/ES
Japan	36.7	37.3	1.69	22.1
United States	25.6	20.4	.77	26.5
Britain	15.5	14.7	.75	19.6
France	11.2	12.2	.84	14.5
Germany	15.9	19.1	1.00	19.1

Source: "All the World's a Ratio," *The Economist*, February 22, 1992, p. 73.

Ratio analysis at the most fundamental level tends to be directed in two areas: profitability analysis and risk analysis. This is because the purpose of financial reporting is to provide information that facilitates (1) the prediction of future cash flows and (2) an assessment of the surrounding uncertainty of those predictions. **Profitability analysis** attempts to capture an understanding of the operating process and trends of the business. Operating processes and trends are important because they generate future profitability and cash flows.

Risk analysis helps assess potential obstacles to the continuity of operations. While many ratios are suggested and used by various analysts within these catagories, no definitive method exists to quantitatively and objectively aggregate all profitability and risk measures. Financial statement analysis will always be somewhat of an art and involve forecast error. Nonetheless, understanding as much as possible about the accounting methods and procedures that go into producing the financial reports will reduce unnecessary risk. See the In Practice feature "Financial Statement Analysis."

IN PRACTICE—GENERAL

Financial Statement Analysis

Your broker just recommended two stocks: XYZ Inc., which just reported a 134% surge in earnings, and ABC Corp., which just posted a big loss, sharply reversing a solid profit in the previous year. Which do you buy?

XYZ's annual report shows that its hefty profits of $327 million included a one-time, after-tax gain of $240 million from the sale of 80% of the company's U.S. business. Earnings actually fell 11%. A closer investigation into ABC's financial statements shows its drop in earnings was largely the result of a big charge for restructuring. Which stock do you now buy?

Careful reading of annual reports can be crucial in making investment decisions.

Balance Sheet. A quick way to determine the financial strength of a company is to compare shareholders' equity to the total debt. This key ratio can be a warning that the company's borrowing is excessive. A normal corporate balance has 75% equity and 25% debt. A weak balance sheet, on the other hand, might have 80% debt and 20% equity.

Another important number is working capital—the difference between a company's current assets and current liabilities. A company low on working capital might have trouble paying its bills. In general, the greater the working capital, the more secure the business.

An improving cash position suggests a company has been socking money away successfully—a sign of prosperity. A trend of declining long-term debt is also a sign of prosperity.

Investors should also make sure nothing on the balance sheet is ballooning out of proportion. With a manufacturer or a retailer, an inventory buildup is a bad sign.

Income Statement. One of the first things investors should look for is the trend of revenue over a period of years. A steady gain is usually a sign of an expanding firm. The growth in revenue should ideally be accompanied by a corresponding increase in net earnings. If revenues are growing faster than earnings, the company may be failing to control expenses.

The most common extraordinary items are gains and losses from sales of assets and discontinued operations. Most important to the reader of financial statements is net earnings before extraordinary items.

Source: Sandra Santedicola, "Make Sure to Get Whole Picture," *The Financial Post*, March 30, 1992, p. 16.

6 Understand corporate risk and profitability analysis using the basic ratios and categories of ratios.

PROFITABILITY ANALYSIS

Possibly the most common index of profitability is the rate of *return on assets* (or ROA). This performance measure is defined as follows:

$$\text{ROA} = \frac{\text{Net Income} + [\text{Interest Expense} \times (1 - \text{Tax Rate})]}{\text{Average Total Assets}}$$

The numerator measures operating profits after income taxes and excludes interest costs. That is, ROA is a measure of operational performance only; it ignores the means of financing used by the business.

The desire to exclude financing costs is why interest expense (net of tax effects) is added back. Interest is the cost of debt financing. This does not mean that the method of financing is unimportant. Quite to the contrary, the method of financing assets (operations) may significantly affect the volatility, or *uncertainty,* of future net income and cash flow streams; it is accordingly evaluated as a part of risk analysis, discussed later.

An enterprise's ROA ratio may be compared to past performance or to other firms. To most effectively and reliably evaluate profitability, the ROA figure should be divided into its constituent parts: net profit margin and asset turnover. The relationship of these components to ROA is best described by the following formula:

$$\text{ROA} = \text{Net Profit Margin} \times \text{Asset Turnover}$$

That is,

$$\frac{\text{Net Income} + [\text{Interest Expense} \times (1 - \text{Tax Rate})]}{\text{Average Total Assets}} = \frac{\text{Net Income} + [\text{Interest Expense} \times (1 - \text{Tax Rate})]}{\text{Sales}} \times \frac{\text{Sales}}{\text{Average Total Assets}}$$

The **net profit margin** indicates how much operating profit is derived from each dollar of sales. **Asset turnover** measures the efficiency with which assets are used to produce the sales. These figures tend to vary significantly by industry, so they should be evaluated by comparisons within the industry for a particular company.

Capital-intensive firms, those firms that rely more heavily on plant and equipment than labor, are said to exhibit a high degree of operating leverage. These firms will experience greater increases in operating income as sales increase. This is because, as sales increase, the fixed costs of plant and equipment do not. Alternatively viewed, as sales increase, fixed costs are spread over the larger number of units sold, thus reducing average unit cost. When sales decrease, however, the opposite occurs, and the firm experiences sharper decreases in profit. Consequently, firms with a relatively high operating leverage display greater variability in net profit margin and ROA as short-term economic conditions change. Capital-intensive industries such as utilities usually display high operating leverage.

Changes in Asset Turnover. The stage of the economic life of the firm's principal product(s) may affect asset turnover (i.e., sales/average total assets). Asset turnover may be relatively low in the early stages of a product's life cycle because sales may be modest, but the book value of newly acquired manufacturing equipment will likely be high. As the product achieves wider acceptance, sales can be expected to grow. Asset turnover should also increase, not only because of increased sales (that is, a larger ratio numerator), but also because the depreciated book value of manufacturing equipment is lower (that is, a smaller ratio denominator). In the declining stage of a product's life, asset turnover will begin to decline at that point where sales decrease at a faster rate than depreciated-asset book value.

Changes in Net Profit Margin. The profit margin may also vary with product life stage and relative competition. For example, when a product is first introduced, competition may be limited. High selling prices and large gross profit margins (one element of net profit margin) are possible; however, specific pricing strategies may vary with perceived demand for the product. As product acceptability increases, large gross profit margins remain viable if adequate entry barriers exist to restrict competition. As competition increases from (1) other firms or (2) substitute products (in the declining stages of a product's life), however, profit margins will decline.

Net profit margin will also change as expenses other than cost of goods sold change. Accordingly, analysis of changes in the net profit margin also requires analysis of trends in other expenses such as advertising, marketing research, or administrative costs as a percentage of sales.

RISK ANALYSIS

We noted before that the Return-on-Assets (ROA) ratio ignores the means by which operations are financed. To rectify this omission, some analysts calculate the ratios for *return on equity* (ROE) or *return on common equity* (ROCE). Total return on assets thus can be separated into a return to each of the sources by which the assets were financed—creditors, preferred shareholders, and common shareholders. Creditors receive interest; preferred shareholders receive dividends (which are not tax-deductible expenses for the enterprise, hence no tax effect); and the residual is left for the residual owners (the common shareholders). The relationship of ROCE to ROA is as follows:

RATIO	=	NUMERATOR	÷	DENOMINATOR
Return on Assets		Net Income + Interest Expense (1 − Tax Rate)		Average Total Assets
− Return to Creditors[12]		Interest Expense (1 − Tax Rate)		Average Total Liabilities
− Return to Preferred Shareholders		Preferred Dividends		Average Preferred Equity
= Return to Common Shareholders		Net Income − Preferred Dividends		Average Common Equity

Changes in Return on Common Equity do not correlate precisely with changes in Return on Assets. Rather, the relationship depends on the amount of financial leverage—that is, the amount of non-common-equity financing. For

[12]The return to the creditors is actually the interest they receive. The cost to the company is the interest reduced by the tax savings (1 − Tax Rate).

example, consider two firms, A and B, equal in every dimension except for the amount of debt financing used. The firm with greater debt will experience less stable or more uncertain future net profits and cash flows as environmental conditions change. Exhibit 6–12 illustrates the effects of financial leverage, as measured by the debt-to-equity ratio.

When conditions cause revenues to increase, the net income of a more highly leveraged firm will increase proportionately more than the net income of a less leveraged firm. Likewise, when conditions cause revenues to decrease, a greater relative decrease in net income of a highly leveraged firm will result. Thus, the future income stream of a more highly leveraged firm will display more uncertainty, or risk. One measure of relative financial leverage is the debt-to-equity ratio, illustrated in Exhibit 6–12.

Finally, we should observe that there is still a great deal of discussion concerning the current financial accounting model. Some argue that the current model simply does not provide information adequate to satisfy the needs of users. These arguments are summarized in the *Journal of Accountancy* article which follows.

Understanding the needs of users of financial information and the limitations of the current accounting model is critical to the accounting profession if it is to fulfill its fiduciary responsibility to the public. Therefore, throughout this text, emphasis will be placed on the value and meaning of accounting data.

EXHIBIT 6–12
Financial Leverage

Consider two firms, equal in every way, except for the amount of debt and equity financing:

FINANCIAL POSITION	FIRM A	FIRM B
Assets	$1,000,000	$1,000,000
Debt (12% interest-bearing)	700,000	300,000
Equity	300,000	700,000
Debt-to-equity ratio:	2.33	.43
Condition #1		
Operating income before interest expense	$160,000	$160,000
Less: Interest expense	84,000	36,000
Operating income	$ 76,000	$124,000
Condition #2: Revenues increase 20%		
Operating income before interest expense	$192,000	$192,000
Less: Interest expense	84,000	36,000
Operating income	$108,000	$156,000
	(42% increase)	(26% increase)
Condition #3: Revenues decrease 30%		
Operating income before interest expense	$112,000	$112,000
Less: Interest expense	84,000	36,000
Operating income	$ 28,000	$ 76,000
	(63% decrease)	(39% decrease)

IN PRACTICE—GENERAL

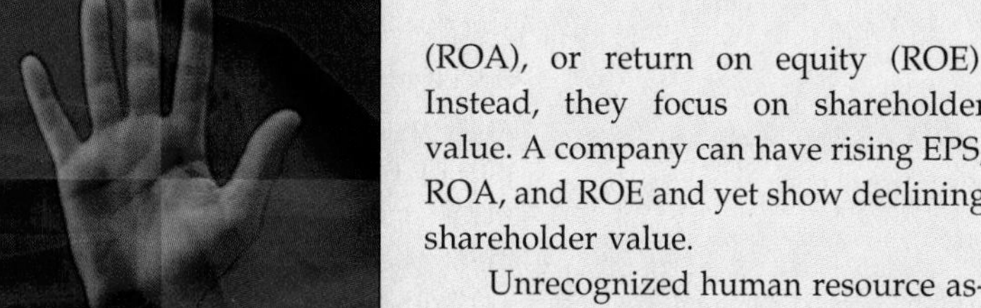

Limitations of the Current Accounting Model

The U.S. financial accounting model is important to the country's national competitiveness. The model is broken, however, and needs to be fixed. Its periodic, historical, cost-basis financial statements served the bygone industrial era well but are not sufficient for evaluating information-era companies. Worse, they discourage companies from departing from the obsolete industrial era while competitors (principally Japan and Germany) are moving forward.

New accounting models are needed to measure rates of change in resources and processes and to account for the off-balance-sheet assets so vital to the information-era enterprise. Management today would benefit from continuous measures of business activity in place of summaries prepared after the fact. Companies adapting to the information era are aware their accounting systems do not provide the types of information they need to manage. Some are experimenting with systems that measure not only traditional financial attributes but also attributes such as customer satisfaction, internal processes (productivity, quality, and cycle time), and capacity for innovation (learning curves and conversion of research to salable products).

A key difference is that the financial measures do not focus on earnings per share (EPS), return on assets (ROA), or return on equity (ROE). Instead, they focus on shareholder value. A company can have rising EPS, ROA, and ROE and yet show declining shareholder value.

Unrecognized human resource assets, for example, can tempt management to take a short-term earnings lift by dismissing or discouraging skilled personnel, which could be expensive when shortages in skills and deficits in experience hamper future growth and profitability. Economist Lester Thurow has said that the United States, where R&D is charged straight to income, alone among major competitors has an R&D curve that rises and falls with the business cycle. This suggests that R&D providing future economic benefits should be capitalized, rather than automatically charged against earnings.

In evaluating the tradeoffs between the relevance and reliability of information to be presented to users, the FASB should consider not only the relevance and reliability of the data that might newly be required but also whether investors are depending on less reliable sources of information. The comparison to historical cost may make the new information seem soft, but the comparison to other, even softer, information investors are forced to rely on might make it seem relatively hard. It would also throw light on investors' needs—the FASB will be judged by its service to users of financial reports.

Source: Robert Elliott and Peter Jacobson, "U.S. Accounting: A National Emergency," *Journal of Accountancy,* Vol. 172, 1991, pp. 54–57.

END-OF-CHAPTER REVIEW

SUMMARY

1. **Explain the different concepts of income: cash, economic, and accrual-based income measures.** Accrual-based income is consistent with GAAP. Principles of revenue recognition and applications of the matching concept direct the amount and timing of revenue and expense recognition. Accrual-based income is determined by subtracting period expenses and losses from period revenues and gains. Economic income is the amount of value that may be consumed during a period and leave the firm as well off at the end as at the beginning of the period. This measure of income is based on real or current values of resources. Cash-based measures of performance are based on inflows and outflows of cash. Cash-based income and economic income are not consistent with GAAP.

2. **Demonstrate the format of the income statement.** The income statement can be presented in a single-step or a multi-step approach. The difference between the two is in the format and method of aggregation of the various elements of the statement. The special reporting items are presented in the same manner for both approaches.
3. **Specify which circumstances qualify as special reporting items, and explain how to measure and report those special items on the income statement.** Three special reporting items appear on the income statement: discontinued operations, extraordinary items, and accounting changes. Discontinued operations represent disposal of a segment or line of business. Extraordinary items are those events and transactions that are both unusual in nature and infrequent in occurrence, given the environment in which the entity operates. Accounting changes can be either changes in accounting principles or changes in estimates. Most changes in principle are reported by presenting the cumulative effect of the change on the income statement. Changes in estimates are treated as prospective changes in that they will affect reporting in future periods.
4. **Specify which circumstances qualify as prior-period adjustments, and explain how to measure, account for, and report those adjustments in the financial statements.** A prior-period adjustment is either (1) an adjustment required to correct an error in the financial statements of a prior period or (2) an adjustment necessary to recognize as income any tax-loss carryforwards of purchased subsidiaries. If accounting errors are discovered in subsequent periods, and if the effects of these errors have not self-corrected, an adjustment to the beginning retained earnings is made. A footnote explaining the error and correction is also required.
5. **Illustrate the computations and reporting requirements for earnings-per-share presentations.** Earnings per share (EPS) are part of the income statement. EPS must be presented for income from continuing operations, earnings before extraordinary items and accounting changes, the cumulative effect of an accounting change, and net income. Any distributions required for preferred shareholders are subtracted from income available to common shareholders.
6. **Understand corporate risk and profitability analysis using the basic ratios and categories of ratios.** Profitability analysis is measured commonly by return on assets (ROA). ROA is a function of profit margin and asset turnover. Profit margin is measured by income as a percentage of sales, while asset turnover is measured by sales as a percentage of assets. Firms with a relatively high degree of fixed assets are said to exhibit a relatively higher degree of operating leverage. That means that as sales increase, the cost per unit will tend to decrease and thereby improve profit margins and ROA.

KEY TERMS

accounting changes *266*
accrual-based income *253*
asset turnover *286*
cash-basis income *252*
change in accounting principle *268*
change in accounting estimate *275*
current approach (treatment) *269*
discontinued operations *258*
earnings per share *282*
economic income *252*
extraordinary item *265*
income *252*
income statement *252*
intraperiod tax allocation *257*
measurement date *259*
multi-step income statement *254*
net profit margin *286*
prior-period adjustment *276*
profitability analysis *284*
prospective method (treatment) *275*
retroactive approach (treatment) *270*
risk analysis *285*
single-step income statement *254*
special reporting items *258*
statement of retained earnings *280*

ASSIGNMENT MATERIAL

CASES

C6–1 Ethics: Materiality and Sale of Property to State

Associated Products Incorporated is a medium-size, publicly traded, U.S. corporation founded thirty years ago. It engages in the manufacture and wholesale distribution of ceramic tile products and cleaning products for use in the home and by industry.

During the current annual audit, pursuant to the firm's publication of its annual financial statements, the auditors and management have arrived at an impasse. During the current year management was required to sell certain properties by cause of eminent domain to the state for construction of a new highway. This transaction resulted in an accounting gain on the sale. The auditors, correctly reasoning per GAAP that the event was "unusual in nature" and "infrequent in occurrence," noted that the item should be disclosed as extraordinary and nonrecurring, in a special section of the financial report, and not as part of ordinary operating income. Management, however, has chosen to report the gain in its annual report in its operating income section of the statement.

The disagreement ultimately must be resolved on the basis of materiality. As all accounting standards apply only to "material" items, separate disclosure of the item is not required unless the item is material. The general question, therefore, is at what size the item in this instance would be material. If considered material, the auditor should either (1) insist on management's presentation of the item in the extraordinary section of the statements or (2) disclose the special nature of the item itself in the "auditor's opinion" (which is published as part of the annual report to stockholders) and highlight the deficiency of management's statements. Additional information about the firm's performance follows:

BALANCE SHEET (IN THOUSANDS OF DOLLARS)

	YEAR 1	YEAR 2	YEAR 3
Cash and securities	$ 22,842	$ 14,213	$ 13,236
Receivables (net)	47,485	50,284	50,933
Inventories	73,955	76,418	72,075
Other current assets	13,343	7,162	3,336
Long-term assets (net)	224,353	283,869	287,273
Total assets	$381,978	$431,946	$426,853
Short-term liabilities	$ 76,496	$ 75,141	$ 86,959
Long-term liabilities	107,653	149,218	124,973
Stockholders' equity	197,829	207,587	214,921
Total liabilities and equity	$381,978	$431,946	$426,853

Required:

A. Calculate for Year 2 and Year 3 the current ratio, debt-to-equity ratio, return on assets, net margin, and asset turnover.

SUMMARIZED INCOME STATEMENT (IN THOUSANDS OF DOLLARS)

	YEAR 1	YEAR 2	YEAR 3
Sales	$ 585,133	$ 698,456	$ 759,946
Cost of goods sold	(526,028)	(639,462)	(713,795)
Selling and administrative expenses	(26,747)	(29,299)	(33,254)
Interest taxes expense	(5,150)	(4,859)	(6,725)
Income taxes expense	(7,316)	(6,909)	(2,067)
Extraordinary items and discontinued operations	(3,500)		
Net income	$ 16,392	$ 17,927	$ 4,105

B. Consider the general materiality issue posed in the problem. Specify the dollar amount at which you believe the extraordinary item in this case would constitute a "material" item and compel compliance with GAAP. Include the following in your response:
   1. What is meant by material.
   2. The factors you feel should be considered in the assessment.
   3. The weights you gave to the effect of the extraordinary item on the earnings trend and to the extraordinary item as a percentage of (a) working capital, (b) total revenues, (c) total assets, (d) income, and (e) long-term liabilities in arriving at your determination of the materiality threshold.

C. Discuss the fiduciary responsibilities of corporate management, the corporate accountant, and the independent public accountant (auditor) to the various stakeholders who may be affected by the reporting decisions. Included among the stakeholders would be (1) corporate management, (2) the auditor, (3) current stockholders, (4) the public and potential stockholders, (5) current and potential creditors, and (6) current and potential employees. How would the financial well-being of these stakeholders be affected by a decision to report the increase in income as (1) ordinary income or (2) extraordinary income? How does the issue of materiality relate to ethical responsibility? What is meant by the term "material"?

C6–2 Ethics: Materiality and "Bribes" to Foreign Governments

Associated Products Incorporated is a medium-size, publicly traded U.S. corporation founded in 1960. It engages in the manufacture and wholesale distribution of ceramic tile products and cleaning products for use in the home and by industry.

During the current annual audit, pursuant to the firm's publication of its annual financial statements, the auditors and management have arrived at an impasse. The auditors have discovered that Associated Products has made certain "sensitive payments" to officials of foreign governments and companies to secure contracts. These "bribes" are deemed illegal by the Foreign Corrupt Practices Act enacted by the U.S. Congress. Management admits that such payments have been made in small amounts over the past several years. It further concedes that such activity increased during the current audit year.

Management reports these payments as "miscellaneous expenses" in the annual financial statements. Management is resistant to any special disclosure of the practice, which, they argue, is simply part of doing business in overseas markets. The firm also wishes to avoid any embarrassment and loss of corporate image that public disclosure might bring. The auditors are nevertheless concerned that this form of "burying" the item may be unacceptable practice.

The resolution of the impasse may eventually rest with the concept of *materiality*. All accounting standards apply only to material items; separate disclosure of an item is not required unless the item is "material to users' decisions." The general question, therefore, is at what size the item in this instance would be material. If deemed material, the auditor should either (1) insist on management's presentation of the item as a separate item of the income statement or (2) disclose the special nature of the item itself in the auditor's opinion (which is published as part of the annual report to stockholders) and highlight the deficiency of management's statements. For additional information about the firm's recent performance, use the financial statement data provided in C6–1.

Required:

A. Consider the general materiality issue posed in the problem. Specify the dollar amount at which you believe the "sensitive payment" in this case would constitute a "material" item and compel compliance with GAAP. Or do you believe that matters such as this, which reflect the integrity of management, "are always germane to the public's interests" and thus are always material irrespective of amount? What other factors did you consider in making your assessment?

B. Discuss the fiduciary responsibilities of corporate management, the corporate accountant, and the independent public accountant (auditor) to the various stakeholders who may be affected by the reporting decisions. Included among the stakeholders would be (1) corporate management, (2) the auditor, (3) current stockholders, (4) competing firms, (5) the public and potential stockholders, (6) current and potential creditors, and (7) current and potential employees. How would the financial well-being of these stakeholders be affected by a decision to report the increase in income as (1) ordinary income or (2) extraordinary income? How does the issue of materiality relate to ethical responsibility?

C6–3 Report Presentation, Prior-Period Adjustment

Mary Polchinski is an accountant for Deisen Corporation. She has worked for the firm for eight years; it was her first job after college. Polchinski is currently being considered for promotion to corporate controller upon retirement of the present controller. She has an appointment with the president of the corporation next week. In addition to the possible promotion, she knows a second matter, a financial reporting issue, is on the agenda.

The management of Deisen Corporation is under attack by a vocal minority stockholder group that has initiated a proxy fight, hoping to replace senior management. The president of the firm has been looking for ways to improve the profit picture and thus improve his position in the proxy fight. One avenue has been suggested by Bill Harris, another candidate for the open controller position. Harris suggests that Deisen Corporation do the following two things. First, make a change in the estimated lives of certain of the corporation's assets. The assets in question were purchased 8 years ago and have been depreciated on the basis of a 40-year estimated life, with zero salvage. Harris suggests changing the estimated life to 10 years and treating the change as a prior-period adjustment. The rationale he offers for treating the change as a prior-period adjustment is that the retiring controller could be said to have been grossly negligent in establishing such long lives in the first place. Treating the change as a prior-period adjustment would allow the charge (debit) to be made directly to retained earnings and thus not affect (reduce) net income by the cumulative effect. Second, with the book value of the assets thus reduced to very low figures, the assets might be sold with very large gains reported on the income statement, boosting net income significantly.

Polchinski knows that she must take a position on the recommendation when she meets with the president. She also knows that some firms in the industry do depreciate similar assets over a period shorter than 40 years, but she has never heard of a period as short as 10 years being used.

Required: If you were Mary Polchinski, what recommendation would you make to the president of the company? Prepare a presentation to "sell" your position to the president.

C6–4 Report Preparation, Evaluation of Alternatives

Clarke County Bank & Trust Company (CCB&T) is entering its 100th year of service to the local community. CCB&T serves a small rural community in central Iowa. It is by far the largest of the three financial institutions serving the community. Carl Williams, the bank president, knows the area residents well, and they know and respect him. Currently, the bank, like many other financial institutions, is suffering from a protracted recession. In fact, federal examiners have placed CCB&T in their "troubled bank" category of banks to watch. The federal examiners note that CCB&T is undercapitalized and is not in compliance with reserve requirements.

Carl Williams believes three options exist for the bank: (1) secure new equity investment, (2) boost equity with sharply improved earnings, or (3) submit to a forced merger with a larger New York banking syndicate. Williams is very doubtful, given the hard times, that the first option is a viable one. And he knows that if the third option is taken, not only will he lose his job and community stature, but bank stockholders (of whom he is one) will suffer significant financial losses. He also fears that the people of Clarke County will receive far poorer service from a large, out-of-state banking corporation. Williams thus has placed his hope in finding some way to increase accounting income and, in turn, retained earnings and equity.

After much thought, Williams has come up with a "bank saving" idea, which he has shared with Peter Marple, the bank controller. The problem, Williams suggests, is the lack of economic reality in accounting. "They make me write all my assets down when they go down in value, but they don't let me write any up when they go up in value, unless I sell them." So Williams proposes to sell the bank building (which book value has a far below market value) and then buy it back. "This will let me show the income and equity boost that we need to keep the wolves away until this recession is over. And the auditors surely can't complain, because we will actually sell the building and transfer title, the whole bit! And then we will buy it back." Further, Williams is confident that he can find some "friends" of the bank in the community who will be sympathetic to the problem and be glad to help. "After all, we don't have to receive cash when we sell the bank," Williams observes. "We will accept a note receivable upon sale, and then offset that claim against our obligations when we repurchase the building."

Required: Taking the role of Peter Marple, the bank controller, prepare a report with your reasoned reaction to Williams' proposal.

C6–5 Financial Analysis (Big-Bath Phenomenon)

Harold Newbein is the new president of Reves Industries. Shortly after taking over management of Reves Industries, Newbein instructed the corporate controller to do several things. First, plant asset book values were to be written down by 20% and patents by 50%. Second, manufacturing equipment was to be written down by 35%. Third, estimates of contingent losses related to current litigation were to be increased to the maximum possible figures.

Required: What effect will these actions, if carried out, have on current and future income figures and return on assets? Why would the new president choose to follow this course of action? Should the controller agree to all? to part? How would you determine the "proper" course of action?

QUESTIONS

Q6–1 Discuss three concepts of income.

Q6–2 The income statement, the balance sheet, and the statement of shareholders' equity are said to be articulated statements. This means they tie together. Accordingly, does the all-inclusive income statement concept mean that all events and transactions that cause changes to balance sheet accounts between balance sheet dates are reflected in the income statement? Does GAAP result in an all-inclusive income statement? Explain.

Q6–3 APB Opinion No. 20 mandates that results of discontinued operations, extraordinary gains and losses, and the cumulative effects of changes in accounting principles must be presented after income from continuing operations (in that order). Does this prescription apply only if a multi-step format is adopted for the income statement? Explain.

Q6–4 To constitute a formal plan of disposition of a segment of a business, the plan must, at a minimum, include what six elements?

Q6–5 Define a "business segment."

Q6–6 GAAP requires that gains and losses related to discontinued operations should *not* include adjustments, costs, and expenses associated with normal business activities, i.e., costs of a going-concern. Provide examples of costs that would and would not qualify for inclusion among gains and losses from discontinued operations.

Q6–7 Describe the necessary characteristics that distinguish an extraordinary item.

Q6–8 What are the seven instances in which changes in an accounting principle should be accorded retroactive treatment?

Q6–9 Describe the steps to be taken into account for a change in accounting principle when a retroactive approach is deemed appropriate.

Q6–10 Describe the steps to be taken into account for a change in accounting principle when a current approach is deemed appropriate.

Q6–11 Discuss the advantages and disadvantages of the all-inclusive income statement concept.

Q6–12 Discuss appropriate and inappropriate motives that management might have for changes in accounting principles.

Q6–13 Discuss the ethics of corporate lobbying and other management involvement in financial accounting standards formulation.

Q6–14 Accounting errors may originate from five sources. Name these sources.

Q6–15 Accounting errors may be of three types (based on their effects). Name the three types. Which type(s) require correcting "entries"?

Q6–16 Discuss the relationship between financial leverage and risk.

Q6–17 Discuss the relationship between return on assets (ROA) and return on common equity (ROCE). What additional dimension does ROCE consider that ROA does not consider?

Q6–18 Discuss the relationship between return on assets, net profit margin, and asset turnover.

Q6–19 Define the following ratios and describe how each can be useful:

- Return on assets
- Net profit margin
- Asset turnover
- Accounts receivable turnover
- Inventory turnover
- Return on common equity
- Current ratio
- Quick ratio
- Defensive interval
- Times interest earned

EXERCISES

E6–1 Multi-Step Income Statement

Indicate in which section of the income statement the following items will be found, using the following codes for income statement sections:

R	Revenue section
CGS	Cost of goods sold section
OP	Operating expenses section
NOP	Nonoperating items section
SP	Special items section
X	Not in income statement

_____ **1.** Sales returns and allowances
_____ **2.** Extraordinary items
_____ **3.** Administrative salaries
_____ **4.** Purchases of raw materials for production
_____ **5.** Advertising
_____ **6.** Cumulative effect of change in accounting principle
    a. If current approach is appropriate
    b. If retroactive approach is appropriate
_____ **7.** Ending inventory
_____ **8.** Gain on sale of manufacturing equipment
_____ **9.** Depreciation on administrative offices
_____ **10.** Supplies used in selling
_____ **11.** Discontinued operation
_____ **12.** Sales commissions

E6–2 Discontinued Operations

Which of the following would qualify for inclusion among gains and losses related to discontinued operations?

1. Normal, "going-concern" write-down of inventory to reflect lower-of-cost-or-market value.
2. Employee relocation costs for employees of the discontinued operations.
3. Future lease payments on long-term lease commitments (net of expected subrentals) related to discontinued operations.

4. Write-down of plant and equipment to reflect depreciation preceding adoption of formal plan of disposition.
5. Severance pay to employees of discontinued operations.
6. Loss on sale of plant and equipment (that would not have been sold had segment operations not been discontinued).

E6–3 Discontinued Operations

State which of the following disposals should be classified as discontinued operations and which should not be so classified. Explain why for each case as well.

1. A sale by a diversified enterprise of a major product line that represents one of the enterprise's three product lines in the electronics industry. The assets of the three electronics' product lines are combined at one manufacturing location.
2. A sale by a brewery/snack food enterprise of its 25 percent interest in a professional baseball team that has been accounted for under the equity method. All other activities of the enterprise are in the brewery/snack food business.
3. A diversified enterprise sells its North Carolina subsidiary that manufactures cherry furniture. The enterprise has retained its other West Coast furniture manufacturing subsidiary, which builds using other types of wood.
4. A sale by a communications enterprise of all its radio stations (representing a major percentage of gross revenues). The enterprise's remaining activities are six television stations. The assets and results of operations of the radio stations are clearly distinguishable physically, operationally, and for financial reporting purposes.
5. The sale of a major foreign subsidiary engaged in copper mining by a mining enterprise that represents all of the enterprise's activity in that particular country.
6. A food distributor disposes of one of its two divisions. One division sells food wholesale primarily to supermarket chains, and the other division sells food through its chain of fast-food restaurants, some of which are franchised and some of which are owned by the enterprise.
7. A manufacturer of menswear discontinues all of its operations in Brazil. These operations designed, manufactured, and sold menswear in the Brazilian market. Similar operations continue in North America and Europe.
8. The sale of all the assets (including the physically separate plant) related to the manufacture of men's wool suits by an apparel manufacturer in order to concentrate activities in the manufacture of men's suits from synthetic products.
9. A sale by a diversified enterprise of a major division that represents the enterprise's only activities in the electronics industry. The assets and results of operations of the division are clearly segregated for internal financial reporting purposes from the other assets and results of operations of the enterprise.

E6–4 Extraordinary Item Classification

State which of the following items should be classified as extraordinary, and which should not be so classified.

1. The write-down of leased equipment because of unexpectedly early obsolescence.
2. The loss on sale of an office building because of an excess supply of office space in metropolitan area.
3. The write-down of inventory of children's toys because of an unexpected change in consumer preferences.
4. A loss on sale of an office building because of a decreased demand for office space in the area because of racial tension and rioting. The city has never before experienced race-related rioting.

5. A loss on exchange of foreign currency acquired and held prior to a major and unexpected currency devaluation by a South American nation.

E6–5 Extraordinary Item Classification

State which of the following items should be classified as extraordinary and which should not be so classified. Briefly justify each classification.

1. A large portion of a tomato manufacturer's crops are destroyed by a hailstorm. Severe damage from hailstorms in the locality where the manufacturer grows its crop is rare.
2. A textile manufacturing enterprise sells the only land it owns. The land was acquired 10 years ago for future expansion, but shortly thereafter the enterprise abandoned all plans for expansion at that location and held the land for appreciation.
3. An enterprise redevelops downtown urban areas, building convention centers and upscale retail centers in the renovated area. When the enterprise buys property to establish a new urban civic center, it usually buys more land than it expects to use, with the expectation that the extra land will appreciate in value. In the past five years, there have been two instances in which the enterprise sold such excess land at a significant profit.
4. An enterprise sells a block of common stock of a publicly traded enterprise. The block of shares, which represents less than 10% of the publicly held enterprise, is the only security investment the enterprise has ever owned.
5. A large diversified enterprise sells a block of shares from its portfolio of securities that it has acquired for investment purposes. The portfolio includes stock in 34 U.S. corporations. This is the first sale from its portfolio of securities.
6. An electronics manufacturer with only one plant moves to another location, where labor is less expensive. It has not relocated a plant in 20 years and has no plans to do so in the foreseeable future.
7. An earthquake partially destroys an office building located in downtown Los Angeles.
8. A citrus grower's Florida crop is damaged by frost. Frost damage is normally experienced in this locality every three or four years.

E6–6 Statement of Retained Earnings

Prepare a statement of retained earnings for Midland Manufacturing Corporation for 1998 using the following information:

Preferred dividends declared in 1998	$ 60,000
Common stock dividends paid in 1998	80,000
Cumulative credit effect of an accounting change (net of tax, switch from LIFO to FIFO)	15,000
Unappropriated retained earnings, 1/1/98	820,000
Prior-period adjustment (depreciation not accrued in prior periods, net of tax)	75,000
Net income in 1998	300,000
Extraordinary loss (net of 30% tax)	80,000
Common stock dividends declared in 1998	100,000
Unappropriated retained earnings, 12/31/98	650,000
Appropriation for plant expansion, 12/31/98	250,000
Preferred dividends paid in 1998	60,000

E6–7 Research and Development

Jason Electronics Corporation, established January 1, 1997, expended $500,000 in 1997 and $700,000 in 1998 in research and development (R&D). These large expenditures were necessary given the competitiveness of the industry and the nature of the firm's electronic products. Jason recorded these costs as assets and used straight-line methods to amortize the costs over 10 years (the expected period of benefit). Accordingly, amortization expense of $50,000 was recorded in 1997 and $120,000 in 1998.

In 1999 Jason hired a new chief accountant. The new chief accountant immediately informed management that GAAP, throughout the period of relevance, prohibited the capitalization and amortization of R&D costs: Statements of Financial Accounting Standards require that all research and development costs be expensed immediately as incurred. Accordingly, all $800,000 in new R&D costs incurred in 1999 were expensed.

Required: What entry (if any) is required in 1999 to deal with prior-period R&D costs?

E6–8 Change in Accounting Principle

In 1997 Garman Oil Company expended $400,000 to drill 10 oil wells at a cost of $40,000 per well. Two drillings led to discovery of commercially viable oil deposits; eight are abandoned as "dry holes." GAAP allows two methods to account for these exploration costs: successful-efforts accounting and the full-costing method. Garman uses the full-costing method, which allows all $400,000 to be capitalized as an asset (i.e., no costs are expensed in 1997; expenses are to be recorded as the oil is extracted and sold). In 1998 Garman Oil Company adopts the successful-efforts method of accounting for exploration costs. This is the more prevalent method in the industry.

Required:

A. Make any entry required to record the switch from full-costing to successful-efforts accounting.

B. Discuss the definitions of assets and expenses as they relate to this case.

E6–9 Financial Analysis

Which of the following ratios relate to profitability analysis, and which to risk analysis?

1. Return-on-assets ratio
2. Debt-to-equity ratio
3. Net profit margin ratio
4. Asset turnover ratio
5. Current ratio

E6–10 Financial Leverage

Consider two firms, ABC Corporation and XYZ Corporation, which are equal is every way except for the relative amount of debt financing used. Each reports assets equal to $4,000,000. However, ABC Corporation has financed its operations with $3,000,000 in debt and $1,000,000 in equity, while XYZ Corporation reports $1,000,000 in debt and $3,000,000 in equity. Each firm reports operating income before interest or tax expense of $400,000. Interest accrues at a rate of 10% for both firms. The effective tax rate is 40%.

Required:

A. Calculate the debt-to-equity ratio for each firm.

B. Determine the percentage change in net income for each firm if each firm experiences a 10% increase in revenues.

C. Determine the percentage change in net income for each firm if each firm experiences a 10% *decrease* in revenues.

D. For which firm is the uncertainty (risk) surrounding projected future cash flows the greatest?

E6–11 Earnings per Share—Special Reporting Items

A partial income statement for Jaffey Manufacturing Company is shown below:

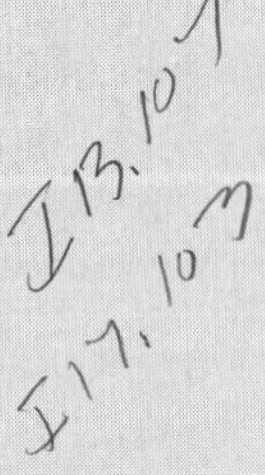

Income from continuing operations	$ 1,080,000
Discontinued operations, net of tax	(105,000)
Income before extraordinary gain	$ 975,000
Extraordinary gain (net of tax)	37,500
Net income	$ 1,012,500

Jaffey had 150,000 shares of common stock outstanding throughout the year.

Required: Calculate the mandatory earnings-per-share figures.

E6–12 Earnings per Share—Continuing Operations

The earnings per share for Allied National Corporation for net income were as follows:

1997	$8.00
1998	7.00
1999	8.10
2000	9.90
2001	8.70
2002	8.50

Allied National had 200,000 common shares outstanding throughout the entire time period. The firm's tax rate was 40%. The following information is also available:

1. In 1998, a tornado destroyed a warehouse and its inventory for an uninsured extraordinary loss of $400,000 before tax.
2. In 2000, Allied National sold a division, which qualified as a discontinued operation, for a gain of $400,000 after applicable tax of $200,000.
3. In 2002, the firm reported a loss (after tax) due to an accounting change of $200,000.

Required: Calculate total firm income from continuing operations for each year.

E6–13 Change in Accounting Principle

On January 2, 1997, to better reflect the variable use of its only machine, Holly, Inc., elected to change its method of depreciation from the straight-line method to the units-of-production method. The original cost of the machine on January 2, 1995, was $50,000, and its estimated life was 10 years with no salvage value. Holly estimates that the machine's total life is 50,000 machine hours. Machine hours usage was 5,500 during 1996 and 3,500 during 1995. Holly's income tax rate is 30%. How should Holly report the accounting change in its 1997 financial statements? (AICPA adapted, November 1993, p. 1.)

E6–14 Special Reporting Items

The unaudited income statement of Zymol for year-end December 31, 1997, included the following items in the section entitled "Extraordinary Items."

1. A gain of $550,000 from the early retirement of bonds payable.
2. An uninsured fire loss in the amount of $700,000.
3. A loss in the amount of $150,000 related to the write-down of obsolete inventory.
4. A loss in the amount of $200,000 from the sale of land to the city. The city expropriated the land for future highway construction.
5. A gain of $1,000,000 related to the sale of a subsidiary company. The subsidiary was engaged in the pipe fabrication business, and Zymol has no other operations in that business.
6. A gain of $300,000 resulting from a change in depreciation method. Zymol changed from double-declining-balance to straight-line depreciation.

Income from continuing operations before tax is $2,000,000.

Required: Assume a 40% income tax rate.

A. What is the proper disposition of each of the items in this case? Explain.
B. Prepare the "Special-Reporting Items" section of the income statement.

E6–15 Reporting Revenues

A firm has the following choices for reporting revenues:

CHOICE 1—DETAILED	CHOICE 2—SUMMARY
Gross sales	Net sales
Less:	
Returns	
Allowances	
Discounts	
Net sales	

Which presentation better meets the needs of investors who want to evaluate the quality of management of the firm? Why?

E6–16 Is It Extraordinary?

APB No. 30 states that "an event or transaction may be unusual in nature for one enterprise but not for another because of differences in their respective environments." Read the following scenarios, and describe one set of surrounding circumstances that would result in considering the item as extraordinary and another set that would result in considering the item as part of the operating income section of the income statement. Assume the amounts are material.

1. A loss of a large part of one year's crop due to a hailstorm.
2. A gain from the sale of a piece of equipment.
3. A loss of profits due to an earthquake.

E6–17 Change in Accounting Estimate

A firm purchased a molding machine on January 1, 1997 (cost, $50,000; estimated useful life, 5 years; estimated salvage value, $5,000). The firm used straight-line depreciation for 1997 and 1998 for this piece of equipment. On January 1, 1999, the firm's engineers conducted an examination of all equipment and decided that this particular piece of equipment had an expected useful future life of four years (the salvage estimate remained the same). On January 1, 1999, the firm made all needed entries for all changes decided upon by the engineering group. The firm records depreciation 12/31/XX. What entry or entries were made for the molding machine during 1999?

E6–18 Correction of an Error

A firm made the following errors. The firm has a 12/31/XX year-end and records all depreciation at year-end. For each, describe the effect on the firm's financial statements and provide any needed entries to correct the error. Assume the date when the errors were discovered was June 1, 1999. Ignore any tax effects.

1. The firm neglected to record depreciation of $5,000 for a piece of equipment on 12/31/97.
2. The firm expensed the purchase (1/1/97) of a new vehicle (original cost, $25,000; estimated useful life, 4 years; estimated salvage value, $5,000; double-declining-balance method of depreciation) by mistake in 1997.
3. The firm made a mistake when counting inventory at year-end 1997 (12/31/97). The inventory was understated by $3,000. The count was correct in 1998.

PROBLEMS

P6–1 Single-Step Statement

Given the following information for Hartley Corporation for 1998 (year ended 12/31/98), prepare a simplified single-step income statement.

Loss on the sale of land*	$ 21,000
Cost of goods sold	130,000
Other income	15,000
Interest income	11,000
Provision for income taxes	23,000
Dividend revenue	18,000
Dividends declared and paid	21,000
Extraordinary gain ($25,000 gross/$15,000 net of tax)	15,000
Cumulative credit effect of change in accounting principle ($45,000 gross/$27,000 net of tax)	27,000
Administrative expense	17,000
Sales revenue	200,000
Gain on the sale of equipment**	28,000
Loss on discontinued operations ($16,000 gross, $10,000 net of tax)	(10,000)
Interest expense	6,000
Selling expenses	31,000
Other expense	9,000

*A site adjacent to manufacturing facility, previously used for parking.
**A part of the normal process of replacement.

P6–2 Multi-Step Statement

Given the information provided in P6–1, prepare a multi-step income statement.

P6–3 Discontinued Operations

In each of the following cases, determine net period income (loss) from discontinued operations and note the portion attributable to premeasurement date performance and postmeasurement date events. In each case assume a 30% tax rate.

Case A

\$ 190,000	Realized results of operations before measurement date.
\$ 130,000	Realized results of operations after measurement date but before year-end.
\$ (60,000)	Realized gains or losses on the disposition of assets (or liquidation of liabilities) after the measurement date but before year-end.
\$ 99,000	Expected (forecast) results of operations during disposition phase-out after year-end.
\$(110,000)	Expected (forecast) gains or losses on disposition of net assets during phase-out after year-end.

Case B

\$ 190,000	Realized results of operations before measurement date.
\$ 130,000	Realized results of operations after measurement date but before year-end.
\$ (60,000)	Realized gains or losses on the disposition of assets (or liquidation of liabilities) after the measurement date but before year-end.
\$ (50,000)	Expected (forecast) results of operations during disposition phase-out after year-end.
\$ (10,000)	Expected (forecast) gains or losses on disposition of net assets during phase-out after year-end.

Case C

\$ 190,000	Realized results of operations before measurement date.
\$ 130,000	Realized results of operations after measurement date but before year-end.
\$ (60,000)	Realized gains or losses on the disposition of assets (or liquidation of liabilities) after the measurement date but before year-end.
\$ (50,000)	Expected (forecast) results of operations during disposition phase-out after year-end.
\$ (80,000)	Expected (forecast) gains or losses on disposition of net assets during phase-out after year-end.

P6–4 Discontinued Operations

In each of the following cases, determine net period income (loss) from discontinued operations for Year 1 and Year 2 for the portion attributable to postmeasurement date events. In each case assume a 50% tax rate.

Case A

\$ 199,000	Realized results of operations before measurement date.
\$ (99,000)	Realized results of operations after measurement date but before year-end.
\$ 100,000	Realized gains or losses on the disposition of assets (or liquidation of liabilities) after the measurement date but before year-end.

$ 100,000	Expected (forecast) results of operations during disposition phase-out after year-end.
$ (50,000)	Expected (forecast) gains or losses on disposition of net assets during phase-out after year-end.

Case B

$ 100,000	Realized results of operations before measurement date.
$(100,000)	Realized results of operations after measurement date but before year-end.
$(100,000)	Realized gains or losses on the disposition of assets (or liquidation of liabilities) after the measurement date but before year-end.
$ 100,000	Expected (forecast) results of operations during disposition phase-out after year-end.
$ (50,000)	Expected (forecast) gains or losses on disposition of net assets during phase-out after year-end.

Case C

$ 100,000	Realized results of operations before measurement date.
$ (50,000)	Realized results of operations after measurement date but before year-end.
$ (60,000)	Realized gains or losses on the disposition of assets (or liquidation of liabilities) after the measurement date but before year-end.
$ 80,000	Expected (forecast) results of operations during disposition phase-out after year-end.
$ 40,000	Expected (forecast) gains or losses on disposition of net assets during phase-out after year-end.

P6–5 Change in Accounting Principle

Lofton Inc. began business on January 1, 1997, and used FIFO as its inventory accounting method until December 31, 1998. The firm switched to average costing on January 1, 1999. The firm had reported net income of $320,000 in 1997 and $450,000 in 1998. The following information also is available:

	FIFO	AVERAGE COST
1997:		
Purchases	$210,000	$210,000
Cost of goods sold	90,000	110,000
Ending inventory	120,000	100,000
1998:		
Purchases	$180,000	$180,000
Cost of goods sold	160,000	180,000
Ending inventory	140,000	100,000

Required: Prepare the journal entry to record the change (assume a 40% tax rate).

P6–6 Change in Accounting Principle

Frotian Enterprises, a two-year-old firm, switches its inventory accounting methods from FIFO to average costing on January 1, 1999. The company had reported net income of $217,000 in 1997 and $221,000 in 1998. The following information also is available:

	FIFO	AVERAGE COST
1997:		
Purchases	$ 99,000	$ 99,000
Cost of goods sold	40,000	50,000
Ending inventory	59,000	49,000
1998:		
Purchases	$200,000	$200,000
Cost of goods sold	90,000	110,000
Ending inventory	169,000	139,000

Required: Make the journal entry to record the change (assume a 30% tax rate).

P6–7 Change in Accounting Principle

Darnell Corporation purchased equipment on January 1, 1997, for $130,000. The equipment was estimated to have a 12-year life, with $10,000 salvage value. It was depreciated using the straight-line method. In 2000 Darnell changed the method of accounting for this equipment from straight-line to sum-of-the-years'-digits depreciation. All depreciation is recorded at year-end (12/31). Relevant information follows:

Alternative Depreciation Schedules:

PERIOD	STRAIGHT-LINE	SUM-OF-THE-YEARS'-DIGITS
1997	$10,000	$18,462
1998	10,000	16,923
1999	10,000	15,385
	$30,000	$50,770
2000		$13,846

Required: Make the accounting entry required (if any) to effect the change in accounting method. Also make any other depreciation-related entries required in 2000. Ignore income taxes.

P6–8 Change in Estimate

Greengage Manufacturing purchased equipment on January 1, 1997, for $320,000. The equipment was estimated to have a 10-year life, with a $20,000 salvage value. It was depreciated using the straight-line method. Depreciation is recorded on December 31 of each year. On January 1, 2001, Greengage engineers estimated the equipment still had an estimated remaining useful life of 10 years and a salvage value of $5,000.

Alternative Depreciation Schedules:

PERIOD	10-YEAR LIFE	14-YEAR LIFE
1997	$30,000	$22,143
1998	30,000	22,143
1999	30,000	22,143
2000	30,000	22,142

Required: Make any depreciation-related entries required during 2001. Ignore any income tax effects.

P6–9 Correction of Error

Sprinkle Products Corporation purchased equipment in 1997 at a cost of $150,000. The equipment was estimated to have a 10-year life, with a salvage value of $30,000. Customarily Sprinkle uses the straight-line method to depreciate its equipment. Due to an oversight, no depreciation was recognized in 1997 and 1998. Depreciation expense of $12,000 should have been properly recognized in each year. The income tax rate in 1997 and 1998 was 40%.

Required:

A. If the error was uncovered in January 1999, what entry (if any) would be required?

B. Describe the effect on book value of the equipment and net income in 1997 and 1998 when presented in comparative financial statements.

P6–10 Correction of Error

ABC Industries began operations on January 1, 1995. Among the assets acquired at that time was equipment costing $900,000. At the direction of Homer Spencer, the CEO and principal stockholder, the equipment was depreciated on a straight-line basis, assuming a 40-year life and $100,000 in salvage value. On June 1, 2005, it was estimated that the remaining life of the equipment was only 5 years (with zero salvage), not another 30 years (with $100,000 in salvage).

Further inquiries revealed that both Spencer, who had since left the company, and the chief accountant knowingly overestimated the asset life (and salvage) so as to reduce depreciation charges and thus improve reported income figures.

Required: Record any depreciation-related entries required in 2005. Ignore income tax. Depreciation is recorded at year-end (12/31).

P6–11 Correction of Error

The 1997 and 1998 income statements of Spotlight Industries reported the following cost of goods sold figures:

	1997	1998
Beginning inventory	$ 200,000	$ 150,000
Plus: Purchases	300,000	350,000
Goods available for sale	$ 500,000	$ 500,000
Less: Ending inventory	(150,000)	(100,000)
Cost of goods sold	$ 350,000	$ 400,000

It was discovered in early 1999 that the physical ending inventory count for 1997 had mistakenly counted $30,000 in inventory held on consignment, which was the property of the consignor, not Spotlight. Thus, 1997's ending inventory had been overstated. The physical ending inventory count for 1998, however, was correct. Ignore income taxes.

Required:

A. Make any adjusting and correcting entries necessary upon discovery of the prior-period error.

B. If the error had been discovered in the middle of 1998, what adjusting and correcting entries (if any) would have been required?

P6–12 Financial Analysis

A balance sheet and income statement of Hermosa, Inc., are shown. Given this data, calculate the following ratios:

1. Return on assets
2. Net profit margin
3. Asset turnover
4. Return to creditors
5. Return to preferred shareholders
6. ROCE
7. Current ratio
8. Quick ratio

Some of the relevant formulas can be found on pp. 286–287 of the text. Be sure to take into account the treasury stock when computing ROCE.

COMPARATIVE BALANCE SHEET

	1/1/97	12/31/97
Assets:		
Cash	$ 40,000	$120,000
Receivables	60,000	70,000
Inventory	80,000	75,000
Plant and equipment	200,000	240,000
Accumulated depreciation	(60,000)	(80,000)
Land	60,000	100,000
Total assets	$380,000	$525,000
Liabilities and Equity:		
Accounts payable	$ 80,000	$140,000
Notes payable	60,000	20,000
Current bond maturities	40,000	10,000
Bonds payable	60,000	125,000
Common stock	80,000	120,000
Preferred stock	20,000	50,000
Retained earnings	60,000	90,000
Less: Treasury stock*	(20,000)	(30,000)
Total liabilities and equity	$380,000	$525,000

*Common stock

INCOME STATEMENT
For the Year Ended December 31, 1997

Revenues	$ 270,000
Cost of goods sold	(80,000)
Gross margin	$ 190,000

(continued)

Selling and Administrative Expenses:	
Rental expense	$ (40,000)
Commissions	(20,000)
Depreciation	(20,000)
	$ (80,000)
Other Expenses:	
Interest expense	(30,000)
Income tax (50%)	(40,000)
	$(150,000)
Net income	$ 40,000
Beginning retained earnings	$ 60,000
Plus: Net income	40,000
Preferred dividends	(2,000)
Common dividends	(8,000)
Ending retained earnings	$ 90,000

P6–13 Accounting Errors and Their Correction

1. Enter the following data in the template, and follow the additional instructions found there.

   On January 1, 1997, ABC Company purchased a piece of equipment. Due to a miscalculation, depreciation expense was erroneously recorded as $2,000. Depreciation expense of $7,000 should have been recorded. The error was repeated at the end of 1998 and 1999. It was discovered early in 2000. Assume a corporate tax rate of 30%.
2. What was the erroneous entry made on the books of ABC at the ends of 1997, 1998, and 1999? What entries should have been made at the end of each of those years?
3. For each year, 1997 through 1999, what effect (overstatement/understatement) does the error have on each of the following?
   a. Net income before taxes
   b. Income tax expense
   c. After-tax net income
   d. Retained earnings
4. What entry should be made in 2000 to correct these errors?
5. If the error had been in the opposite direction (i.e., recorded expense = $7,000, actual expense = $2,000), would you, as owner of ABC, be more or less concerned? Why? Discuss in terms of both tax effects and the financial statement impacts.

P6–14 Discontinued Operations Disclosure

Matlin Manufacturing Corporation has decided to discontinue a major line of business and has made the following disclosure in its financial statements for 1998:

> Management has decided to discontinue a segment of its business due to continuing deterioration of profit margins in that area. This decision was made on June 12, 1998 and a customer has been located for the assets that will be eliminated. A contract for disposal has been signed.

Does the above satisfy the requirements for disclosure of a segment of a business? Why or why not?

P6–15 Discontinued Operations

A firm has decided to discontinue its operations in a particular line of business (the manufacture and sale of small household appliances, which employs 1,500 people). Some employees will take early retirement, some will be relocated to other operations, and the rest will be laid off. The decision was made this year, and the disposition of assets is expected to take place this year as well. Which of the following should be included in the entry on the income statement for discontinued operations at year-end? Why should each be included? not included?

1. The firm will be laying off 2,000 employees, including both employees in the discontinued operations (900) and in ongoing operations, and will incur expenses for unemployment insurance and severance pay, which average $3,000 per employee.
2. Five hundred employees in the discontinued unit will be taking early retirement, and this will result in increased pension costs.
3. One hundred employees in the discontinued unit will be relocated to other installations owned by the firm, resulting in relocation costs.
4. The firm will incur expenses and losses on the sale of the equipment involved.
5. The firm will have to pay lease expenses for the buildings for the discontinued operations for one additional year.

P6–16 Financial Analysis

Financial statements are supposed to provide information for economic decision making by people outside the firm. Consider the following set of income statements from the point of view of a prospective bondholder. What figures would you examine? Why?

	YEAR 1	YEAR 2	YEAR 3
Revenues	$40,000	$42,000	$44,000
Cost of goods sold	20,000	22,000	24,200
Gross margin	$20,000	$20,000	$19,800
Selling expenses	$ 2,000	$ 2,100	$ 2,200
Administrative expenses	1,500	1,600	1,700
Advertising expense	1,500	1,700	2,000
Interest expense	1,000	2,000	3,000
Research and development expense	2,000	2,200	2,000
Gross profit	$12,000	$10,400	$ 8,900
Income taxes	4,800	4,160	3,560
Profit after tax	$ 7,200	$ 6,240	$ 5,340

P6–17 Measures of Performance

George Westover has invested in several firms and is trying to compare the performance of his various investments. He wants to decide where to increase his investment in a firm and where to decrease it. Westover is using the published financial statements of these firms for comparison purposes.

Required:

A. What things might cause differences in the financial statements that do not reflect real performance differences?

B. What things might cause differences in the financial statements that will *not* carry over to future performance?

RESEARCH ACTIVITIES

R6–1 Cumulative Effect of Accounting Changes

Corporations frequently report a cumulative effect of an accounting change in the period in which the provisions of a new standard are adopted. For example, ***McDonnell Douglas*** reported in 1992 such a large decrease in earnings for adopting SFAS No. 106 regarding postretirement benefits that the company reported a net loss.

Required: Find a recent annual report for a company that reports a large increase in earnings for a cumulative effect of an accounting change. Examine this report to determine what change resulted in the large increase. How would such large increases and decreases for accounting changes affect financial analysis? Do these reported amounts reflect economic results of performance for a reporting period?

R6–2 Professional Research and Decision Making

Mary Campbell is a member of the internal audit department of Patricoll Corporation. While examining the preliminary, unaudited income statement for the current year, Campbell observes a significant increase in R&D expense. She correctly recalls that current GAAP requires all R&D expenses to be expensed as incurred but also knows the firm has never spent large amounts on R&D. This year it appears to be up more than 120% from last year.

After much checking and cross-checking, she discovers that included in what has been classified as R&D this year are large expenditures for repairs of defective equipment sold to customers. The defective equipment came primarily from a new product line that the company rushed into production to meet competitive challenges. When confronted with what Campbell sees as a possible misclassification of expenses, operating personnel argue that the costs do relate to R&D in the sense that "we always learn from our mistakes and we learned how to make the product better next time."

Required:

A. Are these costs properly classified as R&D costs? See SFAS No. 2, "Accounting for Research & Development Costs."

B. What is the danger, if any, posed by this classification?

R6–3 Earnings per Share, Market Efficiency Project

Note: The objective of this activity is to familiarize students with common uses of price-earnings ratios and earnings-per-share numbers. The activity requires access to back issues of the *Value Line Investment Survey* and *The Wall Street Journal*.

Introduction:

Earnings per share (EPS) is the single most important ratio derived from the financial statements. It is the only ratio shown on the face of the financial statements. This activity focuses on how EPS is used in common applications. Specifically, this activity is designed to expose you to two topics in investment analysis that utilize the EPS ratio: The price-earnings ratios (and pitfalls in relying on them) and the effect of new information on share prices.

Choosing a Company:

First, select a domestic company covered by the *Value Line Investment Survey*. This is a ready source of investor information on more than 1,100 companies. *Value Line* is published weekly, with firms categorized into one of 13 weekly editions. Consequently, each firm is reviewed once each quarter. (For example, after the 13 weekly editions have been issued that comprise the first quarter, *Value Line* begins issuing editions 1 through 13 for the second quarter, 1 each week for 13 weeks.) The following guidelines will help in completion of this project.

- Don't choose a utility, bank, thrift, or insurance company. Companies in these regulated industries often behave differently than nonregulated companies.
- Select a company in a clearly defined industry (i.e., not one in the "miscellaneous firms" classification).
- The company should be covered in editions 6 through 13. (This makes it easier to obtain the appropriate earnings forecasts and earnings figures for the requirements that follow.)

Once you have selected a company, obtain the fourth-quarter *Value Line* ratings and reports on your firm for the most recent fiscal year-end. To answer the following questions, use a narrative form; don't assume that your instructor knows what the question is when he or she is reading the report. If you have to make calculations, clearly show your computations.

Segment 1: Price-Earnings Ratios

It doesn't take much exposure to investment analysis before one encounters the price-earnings (P/E) ratio. This is the ratio between the price per share of the company's common stock and the earnings per share reported on an annual basis. Analysts often refer to these ratios, and each day *The Wall Street Journal* publishes recent P/E ratios for every listed firm. *Value Line* reports P/E ratios in each quarterly report on each firm. To begin exploring how accounting earnings are used in investment analysis, think about and respond to the following questions.

1. What is the P/E ratio for your company as reported by *Value Line* during the fourth quarter of the most recently completed fiscal year?
2. For the week your firm is covered, calculate the median P/E ratio of all companies in the same industry as the firm you picked.
3. Why do some firms have P/E ratios that are above the median for the other firms in the industry? Does a high P/E ratio tell something about investor expectations for the firm? Can P/E ratios be affected by accounting policies within firms or industries? If a conservative accounting policy is one that understates income, what is the effect of a conservative accounting policy on the ratio? To help answer these, you may also want to examine the Standard and Poor's tear sheets for relevant firms (available at most libraries).
4. For the firm you chose, comment on differences between the individual company P/E ratio and the industry median P/E ratio. If possible, address the role of accounting in causing differences in these two P/E ratios.

Segment 2: Earnings Forecasts, Actual Earnings, and the Market's Reaction to Earnings Announcements

To gauge the importance of earnings forecasts and deviations of actual earnings from the forecasts, one need look no further than *The Wall Street Journal.* Each day the *Journal* publishes a list of companies reporting earnings on the previous day that substantially exceeded or fell short of analysts' projections. (The listing is in a box entitled "Quarterly Earnings Surprises" on the same page as the "Digest of Earnings.") *Value Line* reports earnings forecasts for the remaining quarters of the current year and for each quarter of the next year. Note that these forecasts are typically projections of earnings per share, not "bottom line" accounting earnings.

1. For your company, what EPS figure did *Value Line* project for the fourth quarter? For the year?

2. In forecasting EPS, what does it appear that *Value Line* includes in its computations?
3. Using *The Wall Street Journal,* find the actual fourth-quarter earnings announcement for your firm. For December year-end companies, this announcement is generally made in January or February and carried in *The Wall Street Journal*'s "Digest of Earnings" the following day. (Because companies generally issue these announcements on or about the same day each year, you might find when the announcement was made for the fourth quarter in the previous year by consulting that year's *Index*. This should expedite your search.)
4. What was the size of the earnings "surprise"? That is,

   Actual EPS − Projected EPS = Earnings "surprise"

   This amount represents the "new information" in the earnings announcement. Assuming the market had already incorporated its expectation of earnings in the share price, what impact would you expect the new earnings information to have on the share price on the day earnings are announced? Would the price of a share increase or decrease?

   To find out whether your prediction is accurate, it will be necessary to find out what happened to your company's common stock price during the two-day period surrounding the fourth-quarter earnings announcement (*The Wall Street Journal* stock pages). However, the company's stock price is affected by *marketwide* as well as *firm-specific* (i.e., earnings) information. The earnings announcement is firm-specific information that could move the price of the stock in the same direction, or a different direction, from the marketwide information. Marketwide information includes information on interest rates, inflation, the money supply, and other information that affects all companies in the market.

   To find out how the firm-specific earnings information affected the stock price of your company, determine the total return over two days and subtract the portion due to marketwide factors.

Required:

A. Calculate the percentage change in the share price of your company's stock over the two-day period including the day before the earnings announcement appeared in *The Wall Street Journal* and the day of the announcement. (Announcements occur the day prior to publication, hence the need for a two-day return period.) The return can be calculated as:

$$\frac{\text{Ending price} - \text{Beginning price}}{\text{Beginning price}}$$

   where the ending price is the price at the end of the day the earnings were published in *The Wall Street Journal,* and the beginning price is the opening price on the previous day. This return is the *total return.*

B. Next, figure out how much the market moved as a whole. This requires some measure of the *market return.* One measure of the market return is the change in the S&P 500 Index for the two-day period including the day before and the day of *The Wall Street Journal* earnings announcement. Information on changes in the S&P 500 Index are contained in section C of *The Wall Street Journal.*

C. The final step is to subtract the market return from the total return to provide the *firm-specific* return. This is the return for your company after information that affected the market as a whole has been factored out. If the earnings announcement contained new information, the effect of the new information on the share price should be contained in the firm-specific return. Based on your analysis, is the direction of the firm-specific return the same as predicted?

R6–4 Segment Earnings Reports: Motorola

The information needed for this question may be found in ***Motorola***'s 1995 Proxy Statement, footnote 7 (Information by Industry Segment and Geographic Region).

Motorola's 1995 Proxy Statement may be found in the SEC's Edgar database (*http://www.sec.gov/edgarhp.htm* followed by selecting Search the Edgar Database, selecting Search the Edgar Archives, using the Keyword Motorola and choosing the document denoted DEF14A) or on Motorola's home page in the 1995 Annual Report, footnote 3 (*http://www.mot.com* and select Inside Motorola).

Note the Statements of Consolidated Earnings found in the body of the report and the Information by Industry Segment and Geographic Region found in the Notes to the Financial Statements.

Required:

A. Given that the Statements of Consolidated Earnings are included, what additional information is gained by the inclusion of the segment and geographic information?

B. How might investors in Motorola benefit by the inclusion of this additional information?

7

Statement of Cash Flows

Learning Objectives

After studying this chapter, you should be able to:

1. Understand how the statement of cash flows assists users in the evaluation of firm performance.
2. Interpret the format and content of the statement of cash flows.
3. Derive cash flow information analytically from accrual information.
4. Differentiate between the direct and indirect method of presentation.
5. Prepare a statement of cash flows.
6. Analyze the effects of several statement implementation issues that affect comparability among firms.

Cash Flow and Small- To Medium-Size Businesses

Most of the financing secured by small- to medium-sized businesses is initially provided by owners and a lending institution, typically a bank. The primary financial concern from the inception of these businesses to their dissolution is cash flow management. Cash flow management involves understanding the sources and timing of cash flows, as well as various needs within the business competing for the cash flow generated. This information is not directly provided by the balance sheet or income statement, each of which has its own utility, but rather by the statement of cash flows.

Source: Leonard J. Sliwoski, "Using the Statement of Cash Flows to Understand a Closely Held Business," *Journal of Commercial Bank Lending,* May 1991, p. 53.

Cash Flow and Large Corporate Enterprises

In the decade of debt financing (1980s), cash was trash. It wasn't smart to sit with it... But in the last 12 months, everything except cash has come crashing down to earth. Mergers and acquisitions are off nearly 50% because few corporations can borrow the money to swing a deal... Cash is king, but how long will this uncompromising sovereign reign? Says James Grant, editor of *Grant's Interest Rate Observer* and an early prophet of the dash to cash: "I think a long time, because of the extreme indebtedness built up in the 1980s... Corporations are deep in debt..." The ascendancy of cash implies that credit will be tighter in the Nineties than in the Eighties... Compare ***Nordstrom*** (*www.swcollege.com/hartman.html*), the well financed Seattle-based department store chain that is steadily expanding with ***R.H.Macy,*** which is selling equity and trying to shed assets to pay down debt.

Source: B.D.F., "Cash: Once Trash, Now Treasure," *Fortune,* January 14, 1991, p. 54.

The focus of attention in prior chapters primarily has been on the accrual-based accounting system used in the United States, and the two fundamental financial statements that flow *directly from accrual accounts,* the balance sheet and income statement. A balance sheet is prepared by listing the system's permanent accounts and their balances in the prescribed format. The system's nominal (or temporary) accounts, when presented in the proper format, constitute the income statement. Prior chapters emphasized the format of these statements and the uses of the information contained in them. Some limitations of the accrual system and the arbitrary nature of some accrual practices were also discussed. Still, the system has served users' interests well for many years.

The excerpts presented here indicate, however, that the objectives of financial reporting will be served only partially if other *derived* cash flow information is not also provided. The purpose of this chapter is to discuss those other user needs, to show how the statement of cash flows (the newest of the FASB-prescribed statements) serves those needs, and to illustrate how the statement is generated. The figures on a cash flow statement (unlike the figures on the balance sheet and income statement) do not represent period-end, accrual-system account balances. Instead, the figures must be analytically derived (or separately computed) because the statement of cash flows is essentially a cash-basis statement, and a cash-basis statement cannot flow directly from records maintained on an accrual basis. Nonetheless, the statement of cash flows is an **articulated statement** in that the figures can be calculated using information contained in the other statements, as will be illustrated in this chapter.

Before addressing such operational issues as (1) what information is provided in the statement of cash flows, (2) in what format, and (3) how the information is derived from the other statements, attention is directed to why GAAP requires a statement of cash flows. That is, we address the purpose of the statement: meeting user needs.

USER NEEDS

Understand how the statement of cash flows assists users in the evaluation of firm performance.

CURRENT OPERATING CASH FLOWS (COCF)

A firm's **current operating cash flows (COCF)** is of profound interest to users of financial accounting information. COCF is defined as cash available from normal operations. COCF includes cash inflows from sales less cash outflows for all necessary costs incurred to produce sales, such as cash outflows related to inventory purchases, salaries, rent, utilities, interest, taxes, and so forth. User interest in COCF is acute, because COCF provides the wherewithal for continued existence and prosperity. For an enterprise to be successful, COCF must be sufficient to provide for five corporate needs:

1. Permanent working capital
2. Seasonal working capital
3. Net fixed (and other long-term) assets
4. Repayment of debt principal and interest
5. Payment of dividends[1]

In the short run, exceptions occur. New debt may be used to retire old debt, and expansion of the asset base may be funded by debt. However, in the longer run, COCF is the critical wherewithal for continued existence and prosperity.

Permanent working capital is a firm's permanent investment in net operating assets, which are the investments in receivables and inventory less the amount of this investment financed by trade creditors through accounts payable. This investment may be considered permanent in the sense that while individual accounts receivable or items of inventory turn over, the overall level of receivables and inventory tends to remain constant (permanent). Seasonally increased demands for the firm's product or service may require temporary increases in inventory levels carried or accounts receivable outstanding. These temporary increases are called investments in **seasonal working capital**. Enterprise needs for other noncurrent assets to support operations are called investments in *net fixed assets.*

To avoid forced bankruptcy, *interest* on outstanding debt must be paid when due and the *principal* must be refinanced or paid at maturity. These debt-related demands on corporate cash constitute the fourth corporate need. The fifth need, *payment of dividends,* represents a return on investment that must be paid to equity investors to maintain the continued support of stockholders.

[1]Leonard J. Sliwoski, "Using the Statement of Cash Flows to Understand a Closely Held Business," *Journal of Commercial Bank Lending,* May 1991, p. 56.

Without making regular dividends payments, a corporation may find it difficult to raise new funds through stock issuance, and to elect a board of directors that will be friendly to management at the annual stockholders' meeting.

ADEQUACY RATIOS

In the long run, firms must be able to finance their entire operations from COCF. Exhibit 7–1 illustates several ratios, called adequacy ratios, that can help assess the adequacy of COCF to meet these needs. The capital-acquisition ratio discloses whether COCF is adequate to fund current capital acquisitions. If not, other sources of financing must be found. The capital-financing ratio tells the reader the extent to which capital acquisitions are financed with new debt. The reinvestment ratio reveals the degree to which assets are being replaced as consumed.

The cash-interest-coverage ratio highlights the firm's ability to pay current cash-interest payments from operations and thus helps measure the risk of short-run failure. If a firm fails to make interest payments when due, creditors can "call the loans" (that is, demand immediate payment of principal as well as interest), which may lead to bankruptcy. The debt-coverage ratio may be interpreted as a measure of long-run credit risk or, if inverted, as the debt payback period. The dividend-coverage and dividend-payout ratios are similar and address the firm's ability to continue paying dividends at current levels and thus attract new equity investments. The cash-flow-adequacy ratio is a composite ratio measuring the ability of COCF to meet aggregate investment, debt, and dividend needs.

EXHIBIT 7–1
Selected Common Adequacy Ratios

Capital Acquisition	$\frac{\text{Current Operating Cash Flows}}{\text{Current Acquisitions of PP\&E}}$
Debt Coverage	$\frac{\text{Current Operating Cash Flows}}{\text{Debt}}$
Dividend Coverage	$\frac{\text{Current Operating Cash Flows}}{\text{Common Stock (or total) Dividends}}$
Cash Flow Adequacy	$\frac{\text{Current Operating Cash Flows}}{\text{PP\&E Acquisitions + Debt + Dividends}}$
Other Related Ratios:	
Capital Financing	$\frac{\text{Net Cash Flows for Investing}}{\text{Net Cash Flows from Financing}}$
Reinvestment	$\frac{\text{Cash Acquisitions of Long-Term Assets}}{\text{Depreciation + Amortization}}$
Cash-Interest Coverage	$\frac{\text{COCF + Interest + Taxes}}{\text{Cash Interest Payments}}$
Dividend Payout	$\frac{\text{Current Dividends}}{\text{Current Operating Cash Flows}}$

EXHIBIT 7–2
Selected Common Performance and Quality Ratios

Ratio	Formula
Cash Flow Return on Assets	$\frac{\text{COCF before Interest and Taxes*}}{\text{Average Total Assets}}$
Cash Flow Return on Equity	$\frac{\text{COCF} - \text{Preferred Dividends}}{\text{Average Stockholders' Equity}}$
Quality-of-Sales Ratio	$\frac{\text{Cash from Sales}}{\text{Sales}}$
Quality-of-Income Ratio #1	$\frac{\text{Current Operating Cash Flows}}{\text{Operating Income}}$
Quality-of-Income Ratio #2	$\frac{\text{COCF before Interest and Tax}}{\text{Income before Interest, Taxes, Depreciation}}$
Cash Flow per Share	$\frac{\text{COCF} - \text{Preferred Dividends}}{\text{Weighted-Average Common Shares}}$

*Inclusion of taxes in numerator varies in practice.

PERFORMANCE MEASURES

While both creditors and investors are interested in various adequacy (risk) ratios, investors are also interested in **performance (or efficiency) ratios**. Several performance ratios are provided in Exhibit 7–2. The quality-of-sales ratio shows the percentage of each dollar of sales currently collected in cash. Cash flow return on assets is another measure of efficiency. It is frequently compared with accrual return on assets to assess the effects of the various accrual methods used and estimates made by the reporting corporation. Other common ratios that help assess the impact of "arbitrary" accrual practices are the quality-of-income ratios, such as cash-return-on-equity and cash-flow-per-share. The return on assets and the return on equity cash flow per share have accrual counterparts, discussed in Chapter 6. In each instance COCF is replaced by net income in the numerator. Many users prefer cash flow ratios because figures taken from the statement of cash flows are arguably more reliable than those taken from the income statement. Indeed, the FASB (in SFAS No. 95) acknowledges,

> "The measurement of cash flows is perceived as being more reliable and more objective than the measurement of income because the latter involves more judgment about accruals, allocations, and valuations."[2]

Nonetheless, to avoid user confusion, SFAS No. 95 explicitly prohibits disclosure of cash-flow-per-share figures in the annual report.

CASH FLOW STATEMENT CONTENT AND FORMAT

The statement of cash flows may be presented in either a direct or indirect format. Compare Exhibits 7–3 and 7–4. The **direct cash flow method** presented in Exhibit 7–3 has three principal sections (the operating section, the investing section, and the financing section) and two ancillary sections (the noncash investing/financing section and the reconciliation section). Only the operating

[2] C. Carslaw and J. Mills, "Developing Ratios for Effective Cash Flow Statement Analysis," *Journal of Accountancy*, November 1991, p. 67.

EXHIBIT 7–3
Direct Format of Cash Flow Statement

EAST-WEST INDUSTRIES
Statement of Cash Flows for the Year Ended June 30, 1997

Cash Flows From Operating Activities:		
Collections from customers	$200,000	
Payments to vendors (for inventory and supplies)	(60,000)	
Payments to employees (for labor services)	(40,000)	
Payments to creditors (of interest)	(20,000)	
Payments to utilities (for services)	(20,000)	
Payments to governmental agencies (of taxes and fees)	(30,000)	
Net cash flow from operations		$ 30,000
Cash Flows From Investing Activities:		
Proceeds from sale of PP&E	$100,000	
Proceeds from sale of land	110,000	
Proceeds from sales of patents	70,000	
Payments to purchase PP&E	(200,000)	
Payments to purchase land	(50,000)	
Payments to acquire intangibles	(20,000)	
Net cash flow from investing activities		10,000
Cash Flows From Financing Activities:		
Proceeds from issuance of stock	$ 30,000	
Proceeds from issuance of bonds	100,000	
Payments to repurchase stock	(90,000)	
Payments to retire debt	(10,000)	
Payments of dividends	(20,000)	
Net cash flow from financing activities		10,000
Net Increase in cash		$ 50,000
Balance, June 30, 1996		120,000
Balance, June 30, 1997		$170,000
Noncash Investing and Financing Activities:		
Conversion of bonds to common stock		$ 90,000
Reconciliation of Net Income and Net Operating Cash Flow:		
Net income		$ 97,000
Adjustments for noncash accrual items:		
Depreciation expense	$ 48,000	
Amortization of patents	4,000	
Depletion of natural resources	6,000	
Deferred income taxes	17,000	
Noncash interest expense charges	19,000	
Gain on sale of land	(47,000)	
Loss on sales of PP&E	12,000	
Gain on retirement of debt	(40,000)	19,000
Decrease in accounts receivable		9,000
Increase in allowance for bad debts		3,000
Increase in inventory		(60,000)
Decrease in accounts payable		(30,000)
Decrease in wages payable		(12,000)
Increase in utilities payable		4,000
Net cash flow from operations		$ 30,000

EXHIBIT 7–4
Indirect Format of Cash Flow Statement

EAST-WEST INDUSTRIES
Statement of Cash Flows
For the Year Ended June 30, 1997

Cash Flows From Operating Activities:		
Net income		$ 97,000
Adjustments for noncash accrual items:		
Depreciation expense	$ 48,000	
Amortization of patents	4,000	
Depletion of natural resources	6,000	
Deferred income taxes	17,000	
Noncash interest expense charges	19,000	
Gain on sale of land	(47,000)	
Loss on sales of PP&E	12,000	
Gain on retirement of debt	(40,000)	19,000
Decrease in accounts receivable		9,000
Increase in allowance for bad debts		3,000
Increase in inventory		(60,000)
Decrease in accounts payable		(30,000)
Decrease in wages payable		(12,000)
Increase in utilities payable		4,000
Net cash flow from operations		$ 30,000
Cash Flows From Investing Activities:		
Proceeds from sale of PP&E	$100,000	
Proceeds from sale of land	110,000	
Proceeds from sales of patents	70,000	
Payments to purchase PP&E	(200,000)	
Payments to purchase land	(50,000)	
Payments to acquire intangibles	(20,000)	
Net cash flow from investing activities		10,000
Cash Flows From Financing Activities:		
Proceeds from issuance of stock	$ 30,000	
Proceeds from issuance of bonds	100,000	
Payments to repurchase stock	(90,000)	
Payments to retire debt	(10,000)	
Payments of dividends	(20,000)	
Net cash flow from financing activities		10,000
Net increase in cash		50,000
Balance, June 30, 1996		120,000
Balance, June 30, 1997		$170,000
Noncash Investing and Financing Activities:		
Conversion of bonds to common stock		$ 90,000

section differs in the **indirect cash flow method**. Further, the reconciliation section provided in the direct format is essentially the operating section of an indirect-format section. Thus, the readers of a direct-format statement have the advantage of an operating section cast in both a direct and an indirect form.

CASH FLOWS FROM OPERATING ACTIVITIES

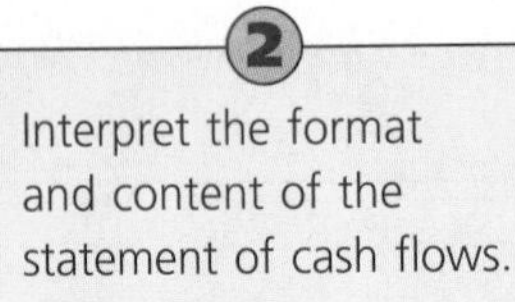

2
Interpret the format and content of the statement of cash flows.

The Cash Flows from Operating Activities section includes the increases and decreases resulting from normal recurring **operating activities** of the business. These are activities in which the entity is engaged on a regular basis and are not classified as investing or financing activities.

CASH FLOWS FROM INVESTING ACTIVITIES

Transactions investing corporate funds (however secured) in *noncurrent* assets are reported as **investing activities**. Purchases and sales of tangible and intangible assets are included here. Other cash transactions relating to the normal conduct of the business are included in the operating section.

CASH FLOWS FROM FINANCING ACTIVITIES

Financing activities include all cash transactions involving *nontrade short-term debt, all long-term debt, and stockholders' equity*. That is, it reports on transactions relating to long-term corporate debt and equity instruments. Significant funds are raised by corporate enterprises through debt and equity security offerings. The first appendix to this chapter includes a detailed list of items that may appear in each of the three primary sections.

NONCASH INVESTING AND FINANCING ACTIVITIES

The noncash investing and financing section includes those *noncash* transactions that jointly affect both investing accounts (long-term assets) and financing accounts (long-term debt or equity accounts). This section is included in the statement for completeness. Transactions of comparable substance might be affected in different ways, and were it not for this section, some, but not others, would be reported within the statement. For example, funds raised through the issuance of bonds might be invested in property, plant, and equipment (PP&E) creating a source of funds in the financing section and a use of funds in the investing section. Alternatively, the PP&E might be acquired in direct exchange for the debt securities, thus involving no cash flow. Unless a special noncash section was provided, this transaction would not be reported in the statement of cash flows. The FASB is of the opinion that this and similar noncash transactions should be reported on the statement of cash flows when no substantive difference exists between the resulting economic effects of transactions framed in different ways.

The last section of the direct cash flow statement is the reconciliation section. This section is included to ease the transition of users to the new direct format preferred by the FASB and illustrated in Exhibit 7–3. The reconciliation also ties cash flows from operations to net income reported on the income statement.

DERIVING CASH FLOW INFORMATION

Since the items appearing on the statement of cash flows do not represent account balances within the accounting records, they must be analytically derived from the available accrual information. Exhibits 7–5, 7–6, and 7–7 illustrate how some of the more common elements of the operating section are calculated. Note the source of the information required to perform the calculations.

EXHIBIT 7–5
Derivation of Cash Collections From Customers

ANALYTICAL RELATIONSHIP	DATA SOURCE
Beginning accounts receivable	Prior-period balance sheet*
+ Current-period sales	Current-period income statement
− Accounts written off	To be derived—see below.
− Ending accounts receivable	Current-period balance sheet
= Cash collections from customers	

Derivation of Receivable Write-Offs:

ANALYTICAL RELATIONSHIP	DATA SOURCE
Beginning allowance for bad debts	Prior-period balance sheet
+ Current bad debts expense	Current-period income statement
− Ending allowance for bad debts	Current-period balance sheet
= Accounts written off	

*Prior period's ending accounts receivable balance.

DERIVING CASH FLOW FROM OPERATING ACTIVITIES

Derive cash flow information analytically from accrual information.

Collections of Accounts Receivable. Cash collections from customers may be calculated by analyzing the Accounts Receivable account (see Exhibit 7–5). At the beginning of a period some balance likely is due from customers. This amount due will increase if the firm provides other products or services to its customers (that is, sales or service revenue). By the end of the period, these receivables will have been either (1) collected (the figure sought for the cash flow statement), (2) written off as uncollectible, or (3) reported on the balance sheet as still receivable. By subtracting items (a) and (3) from total receivables (sales plus beginning balance), cash collections can be isolated. The ledger account is as follows:

ACCOUNTS RECEIVABLE	
Beginning balance	
Sales	(1) Receipts from customers
	(2) Bad debts written off
(3) Ending balance	

It is easiest to use aggregate sales (not just credit sales) in this analysis because this figure is readily available from most income statements. Likewise, it is easiest to derive gross receipts from customers (not just cash payments on account) because this is the figure needed for the statement of cash flows. If the reader prefers, however, to use only credit sales and cash collections on account in this analysis (amounts actually debited and credited to the Accounts Receivable account), care must be taken to remember to subsequently add to the derived figure proceeds from cash sales. Both methods yield the correct answer.

Payments on Accounts Payable. Similarly, at the beginning of the accounting period, the firm usually owes money to suppliers for past purchases, reported as accounts (or notes) payable (see Exhibit 7–6). The amount owed increases if further purchases are made. Some of these obligations may be paid immediately, some later. But by the end of the accounting period, the amounts owed will either (1) have been paid (the figure sought for the cash flow statement) or (2) remain as an account payable. By subtracting the amount still owed from total payables (beginning balance plus purchases), one can isolate cash payments to suppliers.

ACCOUNTS PAYABLE	
	Beginning balance
(1) Payments to suppliers	Purchases
	(2) Ending balance

Alternatively viewed, payments to suppliers equal purchases plus any net decrease in the Accounts Payable account, or purchases minus any net increases in the Accounts Payable account over the course of the year's operations.

Collections and Payments From Other Operating Activities. Other accounts, such as Wages Payable, Interest Payable, Utilities Payable, or Property Taxes Payable, also arise through operating activities. Exhibit 7–7 illustrates specifically the derivation of cash payments to employees, but the same process applies to the other items as well.

EXHIBIT 7–6
Derivation of Cash Payments to Suppliers of Inventory

ANALYTICAL RELATIONSHIP	DATA SOURCE
Beginning accounts payable	Prior-period balance sheet*
+ Purchases	To be derived—see below.
− Endings accounts payable	Current-period balance sheet
= Cash payments to suppliers	

Derivation of Purchases:

ANALYTICAL RELATIONSHIP	DATA SOURCE
Ending inventory balance	Current-period balance sheet
+ Cost of goods sold	Current-period income statement
= Goods available for sale	Subtotal
− Beginning inventory balance	Prior-period balance sheet
= Purchases	
Beginning inventory balance	Prior-period balance sheet

*Prior period's ending accounts payable balance.

WAGES PAYABLE	
(1) Payments to employees	Beginning balance Wages earned
	(2) Ending balance

By subtracting the ending payable balance from the beginning payable balance plus wages earned (expense), cash payments to employees may be derived.

Alternatively viewed, payments to employees equals wages earned (wages expense) plus any net decrease in the Wages Payable account, or wages earned minus any net increase in the Wages Payable account over the course of the year's operations.

EXHIBIT 7–7
Derivation of Cash Payments to Suppliers of Labor Services

ANALYTICAL RELATIONSHIP	DATA SOURCE
Beginning wages payable	Prior-period balance sheet*
+ Purchases of labor services	Income statement wages expense
− Ending wages payable	Current-period balance sheet
= Cash payments to employees	

*Prior period's ending wages payable balance.

DERIVATION OF CASH FLOWS FROM INVESTING ACTIVITIES

Exhibit 7–8 illustrates the derivation of a representative investment section item. Specifically, Exhibit 7–8 considers the derivation of cash proceeds on the sale of PP&E. The journal entry to record the cash sale of an asset essentially involves three elements: (1) the cash received, (2) the net book value of the asset sold, and (3) the difference, which is recorded as a gain or loss. Knowledge of any two items allows calculation of the third. Note, however, that while the accrual-based income statement focuses on the gain or loss, the statement of cash flows focuses on the proceeds of the transaction.

Derivation of amounts in the investing section, however, may require additional information beyond the data contained in the balance sheet and income statement because of two conditions. First, the balance sheet and the income statement usually combine many accounts into just a few. For example, many buildings and much equipment may be collectively reported as one

EXHIBIT 7–8
Derivation of Cash Proceeds From Sale of PP&E

ANALYTICAL RELATIONSHIP	DATA SOURCE
Net book value of asset	Prior-period balance sheet
− Current year's depreciation expense on assets sold	Current-period income statement
+ Gain on sale or − Loss on sale	Current-period income statement
= Cash proceeds from sale	

account, Property, Plant, & Equipment. And, second, multiple cash flow transactions may occur that involve these aggregate control accounts during the span of the year. For example, several pieces of equipment may be sold and others purchased. Of course, the corporate accountant in preparing the statement of cash flows has access to all the firm's accounting records, not just the summarized data reflected in the balance sheet and the income statement. Accordingly, while Exhibit 7–8 reflects an important relationship existing between accrual-based and cash-based accounting systems, other data sources may be necessary as well in the actual derivation of cash flow statement items.

DERIVATION OF CASH FLOW FROM FINANCING ACTIVITIES

Exhibits 7–9 and 7–10 illustrate the underlying relationships for derivation of selected financing section items. Usually the amount of cash dividends declared and paid during the period can be easily obtained from an inspection of the statement of retained earnings. Two fundamental items affecting retained earnings are (1) net income (which increases retained earnings) and (2) dividends (which reduce retained earnings). Later in this text, other events that affect retained earnings will be discussed.

Exhibit 7–10 illustrates that, when considering the retirement of bonds, it is once again the cash flow involved in the transaction, not the accrual gain or loss, that is of interest. For example, if bonds exhibited a net book value at the time of retirement of $100,000 but were reacquired in the bond market for $80,000, it is the $80,000 of cash outflow upon which the statement of cash flows focuses, not the $20,000 gain reported on the accrual income statement.

EXHIBIT 7–9
Derivation of Cash Dividend Payments

ANALYTICAL RELATIONSHIP	DATA SOURCE
Beginning retained earnings	Prior-period balance sheet
+ Net income	Current-period income statement
− Ending retained earnings	Current-period balance sheet
= Cash dividend payments	

Note: Chapters 18 and 19 discuss other transactions that affect Retained Earnings and thus affect these analyses slightly.

EXHIBIT 7–10
Derivation of Cash Payments Made in Retirement of Bonded Debt

ANALYTICAL RELATIONSHIP	DATA SOURCE
Beginning debt book value	Prior-period balance sheet
+ Current year's discount amortization on bonds retired, or	Current-period income statement, or other accrual-system records
− Current year's premium amortization on bonds retired	Current-period income statement, or other accrual-system records
− Gain on retirement or + Loss on retirement	Current-period income statement, or other accrual-system records
= Cash retirement payments	

INDIRECT METHOD FOR CASH FLOW STATEMENT

Differentiate between the direct and indirect method of presentation.

The discussion thus far has focused on the elements of the statement of cash flows using the direct method. However, the statement may be (and most frequently still is) presented using the indirect method, illustrated in Exhibit 7–4. The investing, financing, and noncash investing and financing sections of the cash flows statement prepared under both methods are the same. As mentioned before, the difference between the methods lies in the format of the operating activities section, although both methods arrive at the same balance for net cash flows from operations.

The indirect method is so named because this essentially cash-basis accounting statement starts with the accrual-basis net income figure and then cancels out (by add-backs or subtractions) all noncash items appearing on the income statement. For example, depreciation, amortization, and depletion charges are added back to net accrual income because they were subtracted in arriving at net income and yet they do not represent cash outflows. Likewise, any gains or losses on the sale of equipment or retirement of debt are respectively subtracted or added back because it is not the gain or loss that reflects cash flows but rather the cash payments or receipts (which are reported in the investing and/or financing activities sections). Any and all noncash accrual revenues and expense (many of which are discussed in subsequent chapters) require reversal.

In addition, the operating activities section under the indirect method also must deal with the changing account balances of current assets and liabilities. (Changing long-term assets, you will recall, are reported in the investing section, and the financing section deals with period transactions involving long-term liabilities and equity.) In a method found less than satisfying by those preferring the direct method (including the FASB, itself), all increases in noncash current assets and decreases in current liabilities are listed as outflows or uses of funds. Conversely, all decreases in noncash current assets and increases in current liabilities are listed as inflows or sources of funds (see Exhibit 7–4). A basic logic motivates these treatments. For example, all decreases in accounts receivable may be considered to reflect cash collections from customers, and all payable increases may be considered as borrowing of funds from various sources.

COMPREHENSIVE ILLUSTRATION OF CASH FLOW STATEMENT

Prepare a statement of cash flows.

Exhibit 7–11 presents the 1996 and 1997 balance sheets and the 1997 income statement for James Feniman & Company. From these accrual statements, the 1997 statement of cash flows can be derived. In this example, the only additional information necessary pertains to a noncash investing and financing activity, the purchase of land in exchange for $25,000 in bonds payable.

A three-step process may be used to derive the statement of cash flows. First, the first chapter appendix (page 340) may be used as a guide for items to be included in the operating activities section. Not all items listed in this appendix will necessarily be relevant to all firms. In the Feniman & Company example, operating items include only:

- Receipts from customers
- Payments to suppliers
- Payments to employees
- Payments to creditors

EXHIBIT 7–11
Comprehensive Illustration: Income Statement and Comparative Balance Sheets

An income statement and comparative balance sheets for James Feniman & Company appear below. Given this data, prepare a statement of cash flows for 1997 using the direct method.

COMPARATIVE BALANCE SHEETS

	12/31/96	12/31/97
Assets		
Cash	$ 50,000	$ 75,000
Receivables	80,000	95,000
Less: Allowance for bad debts	(5,000)	(10,000)
Inventory	190,000	160,000
Plant & Equipment	180,000	90,000
Accumulated depreciation	(50,000)	(30,000)
Land	70,000	120,000
Total assets	$ 515,000	$ 500,000
Liabilities & Equities		
Accounts payable	$ 80,000	$ 110,000
Commissions payable	10,000	20,000
Interest payable	30,000	20,000
Bonds payable	255,000	160,000
Common stock (no par)	90,000	100,000
Retained earnings	50,000	90,000
Total liabilities and equities	$ 515,000	$ 500,000

INCOME STATEMENT
For the Year Ended December 31, 1997

Revenues	$ 300,000
Cost of goods sold	(150,000)
Depreciation of retail facility	(20,000)
Sales commissions	(30,000)
Bad debts expense	(10,000)
Interest expense	(24,000)
Other expenses (all paid in cash)	(40,000)
Gain on the sale of equipment	30,000
Gain on retirement of bonds	20,000
Net income	$ 76,000

The first step in deriving the statement of cash flows is identification of the relevant types of operating cash flows and their calculation. The second and third steps relate to the investing and financing sections.

OPERATING CASH FLOWS

Receipts From Customers. Receipts from customers, the first operating cash inflow in our example, can be derived from an analysis of the Accounts Receivable ledger T-account, presented later in this section. Accounts receivable had a beginning balance of $80,000 on the December 31, 1996, balance sheet and an ending balance of $95,000 on the December 31, 1997, balance sheet. Entries of three kinds typically occur during a year and would account for this change in the account balance. First, credit sales increase Accounts Receivable and are recorded as follows:

Accounts Receivable	300,000	
Sales		300,000

The sales during the year can be found on the income statement. No distinction need be made between credit sales and cash sales because no such distinction is sought with respect to the source of cash receipts from customers in the statement of cash flows. It is easiest to visualize all sales as credit sales.

The second type event that may affect the Accounts Receivable account is the writing off of specifically identified uncollectible accounts (bad debts). This event requires a credit to Accounts Receivable.

Allowance for Bad Debts	5,000	
Accounts Receivable		5,000

Last, the Accounts Receivable account is reduced upon receipt of customer payments. The general form of this entry is as follows:

Cash	?	
Accounts Receivable		?

The amount of the cash receipts from customers is an operating cash flow. This number may be accessed directly from a computerized accounting system or derived by an analysis of the Accounts Receivable account as follows. (The T-account reflects the posting of the above entries.)

ACCOUNTS RECEIVABLE	
80,000 Beginning balance	
300,000 Sales	5,000 Bad debts write-offs
	? Receipts from customers
95,000 Ending balance	

The receipts of cash from customers thus can be determined to be $280,000. This figure appears in the statement of cash flows in Exhibit 7–12.

While the beginning and ending account balances can be obtained from the balance sheet and the sales figure can be found on the income statement, a determination of the amount of bad debt write-offs may require an analysis of the Allowance for Bad Debts T-account. During the year, the allowance

EXHIBIT 7–12
Comprehensive Illustration: Cash Flow Statement

JAMES FENIMAN & COMPANY
Statement of Cash Flows
For the Year Ended December 31, 1997

Cash Flows From Operating Activities:		
Cash collections from customers	$ 280,000	
Cash payments to suppliers	(90,000)	
Cash payments to sales personnel	(20,000)	
Cash payments of interest	(34,000)	
Other miscellaneous cash expenses	(40,000)	
Net cash flow from operations		$ 96,000
Cash Flows From Investing Activities:		
Sale of equipment	$ 80,000	
Purchase of land	(25,000)	
Net cash flow from investing activities		55,000
Cash Flows From Financing Activities:		
Issued common stock	$ 10,000	
Retired bonds payable	(100,000)	
Paid dividends	(36,000)	
Net cash flow from financing activities		(126,000)
Net increase in cash		$ 25,000
Cash at beginning of year		50,000
Cash at end of year		$ 75,000
Noncash Investing and Financing Activities:		
Purchased land by issuing bonds payable		$ 25,000

account will be credited for the annual expense provision and debited for write-offs. The specific entries in this case are as follows:

Bad Debt Expense	10,000	
Allowance For Bad Debts		10,000
To record annual provision for uncollectible accounts.		
Allowance For Bad Debts	?	
Accounts Receivable		?
To record write-off of specifically identified bad debts.		

The posted T-account would appear as follows:

ALLOWANCE FOR BAD DEBTS	
	5,000 Beginning balance
? Bad debts write-offs	10,000 Bad debts expense
	10,000 Ending balance

Bad debts written off during the period thus are found to be $5,000.

Payments to Suppliers. The amount of cash payments to suppliers is an operating cash flow. It may be accessed directly from a computerized accounting system or may be derived by analyzing the Accounts Payable ledger T-account presented later in this section. The beginning balance of Accounts Payable on December 31, 1996, was $80,000, and the ending balance was $110,000 at December 31, 1997. Entries of two kinds typically occur during a year and account for this change in account balance. Credit purchases of inventory and supplies increase Accounts Payable and are recorded as follows:

Inventory	120,000	
Accounts Payable		120,000

The amount of purchases made during the year may not be immediately available (since in only some instances do purchases appear on the income statement). When purchases do not appear on the income statement, this figure may be derived via an analysis of the Inventory account.

The second type event affecting the Accounts Payable account is the payment of accounts due. The general form of this entry is as follows:

Accounts Payable	?	
Cash		?

The amount of the cash payments to suppliers may be derived by analyzing the Accounts Payable account as follows:

ACCOUNTS PAYABLE	
	80,000 Beginning balance
? Payments to suppliers	? Purchases
	110,000 Ending balance

As noted earlier, while the beginning and ending account balances can be obtained from the balance sheet, a determination of the amount of purchases may require an analysis of the Inventory T-account. During the year, the Inventory account will be debited for purchases and credited for cost of goods sold. The specific entries in this case are as follows:

Inventory	?	
Accounts payable		?
To record purchases of inventory on account.		
Cost of Goods Sold	150,000	
Inventory		150,000
To record reduction of inventory accompanying sale.		

The posted T-account appears as follows:

INVENTORY	
190,000 Beginning balance	
? Purchases	150,000 Cost of goods sold
160,000 Ending balance	

The amount of purchases made during the year thus can be calculated to be $120,000. This amount now can be entered as a credit in the Accounts Payable account, and finally, payments to suppliers can be determined to be $90,000. This payment to suppliers of $90,000 is entered in the operating activities section of the statement of cash flows provided in Exhibit 7–12.

ACCOUNTS PAYABLE	
	80,000 Beginning balance
? Payments to suppliers	120,000 Purchases
	110,000 Ending balance

Payments to Employees. The amount of cash payments to employees is an operating cash flow. It may be accessed directly from a computerized accounting system or by analyzing the Commissions (or Wages) Payable ledger T-account. Commissions payable exhibited a (beginning) balance of $10,000 on the December 31, 1996, balance sheet and an ending balance of $20,000 at December 31, 1997. Entries of two kinds typically occur during a year and account for this change in account balance. Commissions earned by employees would increase Commissions Payable and be recorded as follows:

Sales Commissions Expense	30,000	
Commissions Payable		30,000

The amount of commissions earned by employees during the year appears on the income statement.

The second type event that affects the Commissions Payable account is the payment of commissions due. The general form of this entry is as follows:

Commissions Payable	?	
Cash		?

The amount of the cash payments to employees may be derived by an analysis of the Commissions Payable account as follows:

COMMISSIONS PAYABLE	
	10,000 Beginning balance
? Payments to employees	30,000 Commissions earned
	20,000 Ending balance

Payments to employees thus can be determined to be $20,000. This figure is entered in the operating activities section of the statement of cash flows provided in Exhibit 7–12.

Payments to Creditors. The FASB requires that the amount of cash payments to creditors for interest be classified as an operating cash flow. This is the case irrespective of whether the interest is paid to a supplier (for short-term credit) or a bondholder (for long-term debt). Thus, the borrowing and repayment on long-term debt are considered financing cash flows, but the payment of interest on long-term debt is considered an operating cash flow. The FASB took this position primarily for purposes of simplicity and consistency.

The cash interest paid figure may be accessed from a computerized accounting system or may be derived by analyzing the Interest Payable ledger account shown later in this section. Interest Payable exhibited a balance of $30,000 on December 31, 1996, and a balance of $20,000 at December 31, 1997. Entries of two kinds typically occur during a year and account for this change in year-end balance. First, accruing interest increases Interest Payable and is recorded as follows:

Interest Expense	24,000	
Interest Payable		24,000

The amount of interest accrued during the year appears on the income statement.

The second type event affecting the Interest Payable account is the payment of interest due. The general form of this entry is as follows:

Interest Payable	?	
Cash		?

The amount of the cash payments for interest may be derived by an analysis of the Interest Payable account as follows:

INTEREST PAYABLE	
	30,000 Beginning balance
? Payments to creditors	24,000 Accrued expense
	20,000 Ending balance

Payments to creditors, therefore, can be determined to be $34,000. This balance is entered in the operating activities section of the statement of cash flows provided in Exhibit 7–12. The income statement and the statement of cash flows also reveal $40,000 of other miscellaneous cash expenses during the period. For simplicity, our illustration assumes these miscellaneous expenses have been paid in cash. Normally they may not appear as such on the income statement, and other sources might have to be sought.

Excluded from the operating activities section of the statement of cash flows prepared under the direct method are such items as depreciation of capital equipment and amortization of intangibles. These noncash items appear in the indirect format as adjustments (not flows) to the income figure.

INVESTING ACTIVITIES

Cash flows of an investing nature can be determined by examining a firm's long-term asset accounts. In this instance, James Feniman & Company owns two long-lived assets, PP&E and land.

Property, Plant, & Equipment. The Property, Plant, & Equipment account exhibited a balance of $180,000 on the December 31, 1996, balance sheet and a balance of $90,000 at December 31, 1997. The account should be affected by asset purchases and/or sales. The related Accumulated Depreciation account exhibited a balance of $50,000 on the December 31, 1996, balance sheet and a balance of $30,000 at December 31, 1997. Entries of two kinds typically occur during a year and account for the change in the Accumulated Depreciation account: periodic depreciation and asset disposition (sale or abandonment). Representative entries follow. The first relates to periodic depreciation.

Depreciation Expense	20,000	
Accumulated Depreciation		20,000

The amount of depreciation accruing during the year appears on the income statement.

The second type event that may affect the Accumulated Depreciation account is the sale of an asset. The general form of this entry is as follows:

Cash	?	
Accumulated Depreciation	40,000	
Property, Plant, & Equipment		90,000
Gain on Sale of Equipment		30,000

It is the cash figure that is required for the statement of cash flows. The credit to PP&E may be inferred from the decline in that account from $180,000 to $90,000. The amount of the gain on the sale may be obtained from the income statement, and the debit to Accumulated Depreciation may be derived from an analysis of that account.

ACCUMULATED DEPRECIATION	
	50,000 Beginning balance
? Sale of asset	20,000 Accrued depreciation
	30,000 Ending balance

The necessary balancing debit is $40,000.

The cash receipts figure for statement purposes is $80,000, and this figure is entered in the investing section of the statement of cash flows, as shown in Exhibit 7–12.

Land. The Land account exhibited a balance of $70,000 on the December 31, 1996, balance sheet and a balance of $120,000 at December 31, 1997. In addition, it is known that land in the amount of $25,000 was acquired in a noncash investing and financing activity. An analysis of the Land account thus permits one to analytically establish that a second cash purchase in the amount of $25,000 must also have occurred. Accordingly, this figure is entered in the statement of cash flows as an investing outflow in Exhibit 7–12.

LAND	
70,000 Beginning balance 25,000 *Noncash* Purchase 25,000 *Cash* Purchase	
120,000 Ending balance	

FINANCING ACTIVITIES

Cash flows from financing events can be determined by examining a firm's long-term liability and equity accounts. In this instance, James Feniman & Company has one long-term liability (bonds payable) and two equity accounts (common stock and retained earnings).

Bonds Payable. Typical events that affect the Bonds Payable account are the issuance of new bonded debt or the retirement of old debt. Further, retirement of debt prior to maturity normally will give rise to either a gain or loss. In this instance, we already know that new debt in the amount of $25,000 was issued in a noncash purchase of land. The related entry follows:

Land	25,000	
Bonds Payable		25,000

Further analysis of the Bonds Payable T-account allows one to conclude that $120,000 in bonds were also retired.

BONDS PAYABLE	
? Debt retirement	255,000 Beginning balance 25,000 Purchase of land
	160,000 Ending balance

However, the $120,000 debit to the liability does not represent a cash flow. A reconstruction of the retirement entry is necessary to derive the cash flow figure. That reconstructed entry is:

Bonds Payable	120,000	
Cash		?
Gain on Retirement of Bonds		20,000

Accordingly, the cash outflow from financing activities appearing on the statement of cash flows is $100,000, as shown in Exhibit 7–12.

Common Stock. A second account relevant to determining financing cash flows is Common Stock. In this instance, a comparison of beginning and year-end balances reveals an increase of $10,000. While a variety of events to be explored later in this text might account for this change, we will assume here that the change was brought about by the cash sale of $10,000 of additional stock, inclusive of any premium. (Frequently premiums are accounted for in separate accounts such as Paid-In Capital in Excess of Par.) Accordingly, $10,000 appears in Exhibit 7–12 as a financing section cash inflow.

Retained Earnings. Finally, Retained Earnings also is a source of financing activity cash flow. While a number of events may affect this account, the two most common items are (1) entries to close net income to Retained Earnings and (2) payments of cash dividends. These entries are presented below:

Income Summary	76,000	
Retained Earnings		76,000
To close nominal (temporary) accounts at year-end.		
Retained Earnings	?	
Cash		?
To record payment of dividends.		

An analysis of the Retained Earnings T-account allows the derivation of the amount of dividends.

RETAINED EARNINGS	
	50,000 Beginning balance
? Dividends	76,000 Net income
	90,000 Ending balance

Thus, dividends of $36,000 may be imputed. This final financing cash outflow is reflected in Exhibit 7–12.

ISSUES OF INTERFIRM COMPARABILITY

Analyze the effects of several statement implementation issues that affect comparability among firms.

There are several implementation matters that affect the comparability of the statement of cash flows across entities, namely,

- cash equivalents,
- classification of activities,
- netting of amounts, and
- discontinued operations.

CASH EQUIVALENTS

In SFAS No. 95, Statement of Cash Flows, cash is defined to include cash equivalents. **Cash equivalents,** in turn, are defined to include very short-term, highly liquid assets that meet two tests:

1. They are readily convertible into cash of a known amount; that is, they are highly marketable.
2. They are so close to maturity that any risk of change in interest rate is insignificant.

To satisfy the second criterion, a 90-day test is generally applied. Any temporary investment that is purchased with a maturity date of 90 days or less is normally considered to be a cash equivalent. The rationale for this treatment is that it is common practice to invest cash in excess of current operating needs in temporary securities rather than letting the cash remain idle. These investments typically are very liquid. Thus, a certificate of deposit maturing within 90 days would qualify as a cash equivalent but a bond maturing within 30 years would not.

An issue of substance versus form, however, has arisen in recent interpretations of the 90-day rule. Short-term investments in Treasury bills that mature within 90 days of purchase qualify as a cash equivalent at statement date. However, an original long-term investment that now matures within 90 days of the purchase date or year-end does not qualify, regardless of the intent or purpose of the investment. If management fully intends to use the proceeds of such soon-to-mature investments to meet operating needs during the ensuing period, arguably the item should be treated as a cash equivalent. Nonetheless, current GAAP requires that an original long-term investment due within 90 days of purchase date or year-end does not qualify as a cash equivalent.

Somewhat different rules also apply to financial institutions. Financial institutions that routinely invest temporary excess cash holdings as part of their earnings process are not required to classify these temporary investments as cash equivalents. The individual entity may establish its own policy in regard to the classification of cash equivalents and short-term investments. Any subsequent change of policy, however, must be accounted for as a change in accounting principle (with all disclosures required of a change in principle including restatement of prior-period financial statements). This permitted flexibility, however, is restricted to financial institutions.

CLASSIFICATION OF ACTIVITIES

Some theoretical inconsistencies also seem to emerge in how activities are grouped into the various classifications of the statement of cash flows. For example, interest revenues, dividend revenues and interest expenses are all classified as operating activities, while dividends paid are classified as financing activities. This different treatment for dividends paid relates, in part, to the fact that dividends paid do not appear in the accrual income statement, whereas dividend and interest revenues, and interest expense do. Excluding dividends paid from the operating activities section simplifies the reconciliation of operating cash flows with net income.

However, there is a cost to this operational compromise. A case can easily be made that interest and dividend revenues and interest and dividend payments are inflows and outflows associated with investment and financing activities and should be classified as such. Cash invested in long-term investments, such as marketable securities, reflects investing activities; the return on these investments (interest and/or dividend revenues) arguably also should be considered investment activities. GAAP, however, requires all interest and dividend revenues to be reported as operating cash flows.

Likewise, an argument can be made that interest paid should be classified as a financing activity. Because interest is a cost of borrowing, it can logically be considered a financing activity. Current GAAP nonetheless mandates that all interest paid be considered an operating cash flow. Dividends paid, however, are classified as financing activities. Many professionals find these differing treatments of interest and dividends (and dividends received versus dividends paid) inconsistent and hard to defend.

Undefined terms also remain a problem. For example, SFAS No. 95 in paragraph 24 indicates that "certain cash receipts and payments may have aspects of more than one class of cash flows. . . . a cash payment may pertain to an item that could be considered either inventory or a productive asset." The standard goes on to reason that if the general purpose in purchasing or producing the asset is "to be used by the enterprise or rented to others for a short period and then sold, . . . the acquisition or production and subsequent sale shall be considered operating activities." That is, the asset is treated as inventory. While this seems reasonable, among interesting questions subsequently raised are: "What is meant by short term?"

NETTING OF AMOUNTS

SFAS No. 95 states in paragraph 11 that "generally, information about gross amounts of cash receipts and cash payments during a period is more relevant than information about net amounts. . . ." The standard then indicates, however, that there are exceptions, as outlined in paragraphs 12, 13, and 28. "Items that qualify for net reporting because their turnover is quick, their amounts are large, and their maturities are short are cash receipts and payments pertaining to (a) investments (other than cash equivalents), (b) loans receivable, and (c) debt (providing that the original maturity of the asset is three months or less)."

If *gross reporting contains more relevant information*, then why have expedient exceptions been provided that further erode the main purpose of the intent of the statement? Today a consistency in reporting is lacking because firms are permitted a degree of latitude in reporting certain cash flows at either gross or net amounts. While the policy choice must be footnoted and any change in policy must be disclosed as an accounting principle change, this does not fully restore comparability among firms using different policies. Finally, netting the amounts has the potential to disguise the actual variances of activities that may be important and that may affect related ratios.

DISCONTINUED OPERATIONS

Separate disclosure for discontinued operations is not required but is permitted under SFAS No. 95. Again, disparate treatments emerge.

In addition, in those cases in which the firm elects to report discontinued operations separately, the associated income tax effect is not permitted to be shown. The argument given by the FASB is that the issues are so complex and arbitrary that it is not cost-justified. This treatment and logic, however, are inconsistent with the fact that the accrual income statement requires net-of-tax reporting for discontinued operations. An obvious question that arises is "If it is not cost-prohibitive and excessively arbitrary in one instance (the income statement), why is it so in the other (the statement of cash flows)?" If it is deemed to have value in one case, why not the other?

The preceding are some issues statement readers should be aware of prior to calculating and analyzing certain ratios.

APPENDIX: CASH FLOW CATEGORIES AND ELEMENTS

Operating Activities

Sources of Cash:

- Receipts from customers:
  - *For past sales and/or services*
  - *For current sales and/or services*
  - *For future sales and/or services (advances from customers)*
- Refunds:
  - *From suppliers of deposits*
  - *From suppliers for sales return and/or allowances*
  - *From suppliers for overpayments*
  - *From IRS for carryback benefits, amended returns or overpayments*
- Proceeds from successful litigation
- Proceeds from insurance claims
- Receipts of interest
- Receipts of dividends

Uses of Cash:

- Payments to suppliers for operating materials and inventory
  - *Provided in the past, provided currently, or to be provided*
  - *Prospectively (advances to suppliers)*
- Payments to employees for labor services
  - *Provided in the past, provided currently, or to be provided*
  - *Prospectively (advances to employees)*
- Payments for postretirement employee pension and health benefits
- Operating lease payments
- Payments of unsuccessful litigation damages, fines, and penalties
- Payments to creditors for the uses of funds (i.e., interest)
- Payments to government taxing agencies
- Charitable corporate giving

Investing Activities

Sources of Cash:

- Proceeds from the sale of long-lived tangible assets
  - *Including sale of buildings, equipment, land, patents, copyrights, leasehold rights, etc.*
- Proceeds from the sale of debt and equity securities of other firms
  - *If not cash equivalents*
- Collection of principal on loans made to noncustomers

(continued)

Uses of Funds:

Payments to purchase long-lived tangible and intangible assets

Payments incurred to construct long-lived facilities or equipment

Including capitalizable interest

Payments to purchase debt and equity securities of other firms

If not cash equivalents

Payments to extend noncustomer loans

Financing Activities

Sources of Cash:

Proceeds from issuance of debt securities

Loan proceeds

Proceeds from the issuance of equity securities

Uses of Cash:

Payments to buy back (retire) firm's outstanding debt securities

Principal payments of loans

Principal payments on capital leases

Payments to buy back firm's outstanding equity securities

Payments of dividends to stockholders

APPENDIX: ADDITIONAL REPORTING REQUIREMENTS

Additional reporting requirements beyond those illustrated in the text exist for both the indirect and direct methods of reporting activities from operations. They are discussed below.

Use of the direct method to calculate cash flows from operating activities requires the reporting entity to provide at a minimum the amount of cash collected from:

1. customers
2. licensees, lessees, and other similar groups
3. interest or dividends
4. any other cash receipts from operations

In a similar fashion, certain cash disbursements also must be reported such as the following cash payments:

1. to employees and other suppliers of goods and/or services.
2. for other services such as insurance, advertising, etc.
3. for income taxes, interest, and any other operating cash disbursements.

INFREQUENT AND/OR UNUSUAL ITEMS

Several transactions that occur infrequently or are peculiar in nature also may require inclusion in the statement of cash flows. Some of these items are:

1. Other noncash expenses and revenues
2. Additional working capital items
3. Extraordinary items

4. Pensions
5. Leases and interest
6. Insurance
7. Stock options
8. Effects of foreign exchange rates
9. Significant noncash transactions
10. Exemptions
11. Amendments

OTHER NONCASH EXPENSES AND REVENUES

All revenue and expense amortizations are noncash adjustments to accrual income under the indirect method. Accordingly, amortization of the costs of intangible assets is treated in the same manner as depreciation expense. Depletion of natural resources and amortization of bond premiums and bond discounts also fall in this category.

Likewise, adjustments for income tax expense take into consideration the difference between the reported expense(s) on the income statement and the actual cash outflow as reflected in remaining liability (deferral) account(s).

The recognition of investment income under the equity method requires a deduction from cash flows from operations under the indirect method. While income has been recognized, cash flow has not necessarily occurred. When and if dividends are received, they do increase cash flow.

ADDITIONAL WORKING CAPITAL ITEMS

Some changes in working capital items do not affect net income. For instance, although investments in short-term marketable securities (or short-term nontrade receivables) use cash, they do not affect net income. This transaction should be shown in the investing section of the statement of cash flows.

The same is true of short-term nontrade loans. These borrowings provide cash but do not affect net income and are reflected in the financing section of the statement. Bank overdrafts are similar in nature and represent short-term financing.

A similar type of current liability is dividends payable. When dividends are declared but not paid, they affect neither net income nor cash; thus, they are not shown on the statement and require separate disclosure.

EXTRAORDINARY ITEMS

Transactions classified as extraordinary must be carefully analyzed to determine if they belong in either investing activities or financing activities rather than operating activities. Early extinguishment of debt for less than the carrying value of the debt is an example. If the transaction results in a gain, the gain is deducted from net income under the indirect method and the cash outlay appears as an outflow in the financing section.

STOCK OPTIONS

Entities with stock option or stock appreciation plans may report compensation expenses without any actual cash outlays. In such cases, the noncash expenditure must be accorded the same treatment as any other noncash expenditure. That is, it is added back to net income under the indirect method to find cash provided from operations, and is excluded under the direct method.

PENSIONS

Many pension plans are not funded (cash deposited in the plan) at the same level as the amount recognized as an expense during a period. As a result, the actual cash outlay is different from the recorded expenses and an appropriate adjustment must be made in the operating section of the statement.

LEASES AND INTEREST

Operating and capital leases are treated differently in the statement of cash flows. Operating lease payments appear in the operating section, while capital lease payments are divided between the operating and investing activities sections. The interest portion of payments made under capital leases is reported in the operating section and the payment toward the principal is included in the financing activities section. Another interest transaction that requires unusual treatment is interest that is capitalized as part of the cost of self-constructed assets. This interest is included in the investing section of the statement.

INSURANCE

Payments toward life insurance on key employees also may have two parts. When the employer pays the premium for key employee insurance, the cash payment is an operating activity outflow. However, if there is an increase in the cash surrender value of the policy, a pro rata share of the outflow should be reported as an investment activity.

EFFECTS OF FOREIGN EXCHANGE RATES

SFAS No. 95 requires that the effects of foreign exchange rates be indicated in a separate section of the statement. This section follows the financing activities section and appears as a separate amount to be added or deducted to determine the change in cash.

SIGNIFICANT NONCASH TRANSACTIONS

SFAS No. 95 also requires that all material transactions not cash-related be reported separately so that the statement user can determine what possible effect these types of transactions might have on the entity in the future. A common example would be the purchase of an asset such as land in which a mortgage is given to the seller.

EXEMPTIONS

SFAS No. 102 supersedes SFAS No. 95 in part and exempts certain enterprises from the requirement of providing a statement of cash flows as part of the entity's reporting requirements. Specifically, while it is encouraged, it is not required for defined-benefit plans that meet the reporting requirements of SFAS No. 35. Also, certain investment companies and trust funds maintained by an insurance company, bank, or other entity acting as a trustee, administrator, or a guardian are exempt from reporting if they meet the specific criteria as outlined in paragraph 7 of SFAS No. 102.

AMENDMENTS

SFAS No. 104 amends SFAS No. 95 and permits the netting of certain cash receipts and cash payments for some financial institutions and certain hedging transactions of all entities.

APPENDIX: INDIRECT METHOD CASH FLOW STATEMENT

A statement of cash flows can be prepared by the indirect method from consecutive balance sheets and supplemental information derived by analyzing transactions that effect changes in the account balances. The analysis is performed in the same fashion as that discussed throughout this chapter. The only different portion of the statement is the operating activities section. The other sections are the same as the direct method.

In preparing the operating section of the statement of cash flows, accrual net income for the period is adjusted to provide a cash-basis net income. This is accomplished partly by adding back the noncash accrual charges such as depreciation, amortization, and losses and by deducting premium amortization and gains. Other major adjustments include adding decreases in current asset account balances for the period and increases in current liabilities. The increases in current asset balances for the period and the decreases in current liability accounts are deducted. An illustration follows.

	12/31/98	12/31/97	CHANGE
Assets			
Cash	$ 14,000	$ 10,500	$ 3,500
Accounts receivable	76,000	68,000	8,000
Inventory	32,000	34,000	(2,000)
Prepaid rent	20,000	15,000	5,000
Equipment	209,000	215,000	(6,000)
Accumulated depreciation	(61,000)	(54,500)	(6,500)
Total assets	$290,000	$288,000	$ 2,000
Liabilities and Owners' Equity			
Accounts payable	$ 29,000	$ 28,500	$ 500
Accrued expenses	18,000	16,500	1,500
Notes payable	0	10,000	(10,000)
Common stock	86,000	86,000	0
Retained earnings	157,000	147,000	10,000
Total liabilities and owners' equity	$290,000	$288,000	$ 2,000

Assume that the firm had net income of $48,000 for the year, sold equipment (original cost, $6,000, accumulated depreciation, $2,000) for $3,000 cash, repaid a note payable of $10,000, and paid cash dividends of $38,000. These are the only transactions that cannot be derived analytically from the data provided.

The objective is the same for both the direct and the indirect methods. We want to explain the change in the cash position from one period to another. Note that the change column provides most of the information for the adjustments as well as the change in cash.

STATEMENT OF CASH FLOWS
For the Year Ended December 31, 1998

Operating Activities:		
Net income	$ 48,000	
Depreciation	8,500	
Loss on sale	1,000	
Increase in accounts receivable	(8,000)	
Decrease in inventory	2,000	
Increase in prepaid rent	(5,000)	
Increase in accounts payable	500	
Increase in accrued expenses	1,500	
Net cash flows from operating activities		$ 48,500
Investing Activities:		
Sale of equipment		3,000
Financing Activities:		
Payment of note payable	$(10,000)	
Payment of dividends	(38,000)	
Net cash flows from financing activities		(48,000)
Increase in Cash		$ 3,500
Cash at beginning of the period		10,500
Cash at end of the period		$ 14,000

Note that the amount of depreciation expense is not apparent without an income statement. The amount of the depreciation charge can be determined by analyzing the effect of the sale of equipment on the account balances. The entry made at the time of the sale is as follows:

Cash	3,000	
Accumulated Depreciation	2,000	
Loss on Sale	1,000	
Equipment		6,000

The effect of this transaction on the account balances is to reduce the balance of the Equipment account by $6,000, which explains the change to that account. The contra account of Accumulated Depreciation is also reduced by $2,000. Thus, the charge for depreciation is $8,500 and the ending account balance of Accumulated Depreciation is $61,000 ($54,500 − $2,000 + $8,500).

EQUIPMENT			
Beginning balance	215,000	6,000	Sale of equipment
Ending balance	209,000		

ACCUMULATED DEPRECIATION			
		54,500	Beginning balance
2. Decrease in accumulated depreciation	2,000	8,500	Expense
		61,000	Ending Balance

END-OF-CHAPTER REVIEW

SUMMARY

1. **Understand how the statement of cash flows assists users in the evaluation of firm performance.** An item of profound interest to users in evaluation of entity performance is current operating cash flows (COCF). These are the cash flows made available from normal operations, that is, cash inflows from sales revenues less cash outflows for all necessary costs to produce revenues. For an enterprise to be successful, COCF must provide for permanent and seasonal working capital, long-term assets, repayment of debt, and payment of dividends.
2. **Interpret the format and content of the statement of cash flows.** The statement of cash flows can be prepared on a direct or an indirect basis. The two methods differ in the cash flows from the operating activities section; the investing and financing sections are the same. The reconciliation section prepared with the direct format provides essentially the same information as found in the operating activities section of the indirect format.
3. **Derive cash flow information analytically from accrual information.** The items on the statement of cash flows must be analytically derived from the available accrual information. This involves analysis of the changes in the relevant accounts and their balances.
4. **Differentiate between the direct and indirect method of presentation.** The indirect method is said to be indirect because it starts with accrual-based net income in the operating activities section. It then proceeds to cancel out (by add-backs or subtractions) all noncash items appearing on the income statement. Likewise, any gains or losses on the sale of assets or retirement of debt are also added back or subtracted.
5. **Prepare a statement of cash flows.** A three-step process may be followed to derive the statement of cash flows. First, the relevant types of operating cash flows must be identified and calculated. Second, the relevant cash flows from investing activities must be identified and calculated. The long-term asset accounts contain this data. Third, the relevant cash flows from financing activities must be identified and calculated. The long-term liability and equity accounts contain this information.
6. **Analyze the effects of several statement implementation issues that affect comparability among firms.** Cash equivalents are defined differently for financial institu-

tions compared to other entities. There are also some inconsistencies in how various activities are grouped in particular classification categories on the statement of cash flows. Additionally, while the standard states that gross amounts are more relevant than net amounts, it allows several exceptions. Finally, separate disclosure of the effects of discontinued operations is permitted but not required. All of these issues may have an impact on the comparability of the financial data across firms.

KEY TERMS

adequacy ratios *318*
articulated statement *317*
current operating cash flows *317*
direct cash flow method *319*
financing activities *322*
indirect cash flow method *321*
investing activities *322*
operating activities *322*
performance ratios *319*
permanent working capital *317*
seasonal working capital *317*

ASSIGNMENT MATERIAL

CASES

C7–1 Financial Analysis

The following are summarized statements of cash flows for Start-Up Company for its first two years of operations:

	1997	1996
Cash provided by (used for):		
Operating activities	$ (500,000)	$ (3,000,000)
Investing activities	(6,000,000)	(9,000,000)
Financing activities	7,000,000	15,000,000

Most of the $15,000,000 raised from financing activity in 1996 was from the initial issuance of capital stock. Most of the $7,000,000 raised in 1997 was from long-term borrowings.

Required: In your opinion, is Start-Up Company in danger of future cash flow problems? For Start-Up Company to be successful, what pattern of cash activity would you expect as time passes?

C7–2 Discussion—Accrual- Versus Cash-Based Accounting

Consider the following assertion:

> What's the big emphasis all of a sudden on cash flow statements? Research generally suggests that accrual-based accounting measures are better predictors of future cash flows than are cash-based measures. The FASB acknowledges this relative predictability in the conceptual framework when supporting its stance on the continued use of accrual accounting.

Required: Discuss the relative merits of the statement of cash flows vis-à-vis the accrual-based income statement and balance sheet.

C7–3 Interpretation—Group Presentation

Divide the class into two teams of equal size. Each team is to prepare an answer to both of the following scenarios with a spokesperson selected for each scenario. Each team is to critique the other's presentation. Use the following cash flow information from the operating activities section.

Cash Flows From Operating Activities:

Net income	$ 200,000
Adjustments for noncash accrual items:	
Depreciation expense	15,000
Increase in accounts receivable	(150,000)
Increase in inventory	(200,000)
Increase in accounts payable	110,000
Net cash flow from operations	(25,000)

Required: Each team is to provide a scenario that represents "good news" to investors and a scenario that represents "bad news" to investors. To do so, discuss what the cash flow from investing activities and the cash flow from financing activities sections would look like under these two scenarios.

QUESTIONS

Q7–1 What is the purpose of the statement of cash flows (SCF) in relation to the other statements required for reporting purposes?

Q7–2 What are the three major sections of the SCF?

Q7–3 What information is provided in the three sections of the SCF?

Q7–4 What is meant by the terms *cash* and *cash equivalents?*

Q7–5 What types of information are necessary in order to prepare a SCF?

Q7–6 What are the major sources of cash inflows (1) in the operating section, (2) in the investing section, and (3) in the financing section of the SCF?

Q7–7 What are the major outflows by section?

Q7–8 What are the basic differences between the direct method and the indirect method in the operating activities section of the SCF?

Q7–9 Explain the major adjustments that are made to net income in the indirect method.

Q7–10 Which section(s) of the balance sheet is (are) most useful in adjusting net income to the cash basis of accounting under the indirect method?

Q7–11 Assume sales are $200,000 and accounts receivable decreased by $40,000 with no bad debts. Under the direct method of presentation, how much cash from accounts receivable would be reported?

Q7–12 In determining cash flows from operating activities using the indirect method, indicate whether the following items would be treated as cash inflows, cash outflows, adjustments, or ignored.

1. An increase in accounts payable
2. An increase in accounts receivable
3. Gain on the sale of equipment
4. Amortization of goodwill
5. Depreciation expense
6. An increase in the dividends payable
7. Amortization of premium on bonds payable
8. Gain on the sale of cash equivalents
9. Bad debts expense

Q7–13 Analyze all the items in Q7–12 in terms of the direct method, and indicate the effect.

Q7–14 Classify the following activities as operating, investing, financing, or other significant events. Also indicate whether they are inflows or outflows.

1. Sale of additional shares of common stock
2. Purchases of short-term marketable equities
3. Trade-in allowance on the purchase of new equipment
4. Extraordinary gain on the restructuring of debt
5. Acquisition of treasury stock
6. Proceeds from sale of treasury stock that exceed cost
7. Proceeds from life insurance on a key executive
8. Amortization of discount on bonds payable
9. Land donated by the county
10. Payment of stock dividends

Q7–15 Where should gains and/or losses from foreign exchange transactions be indicated in the SCF?

Q7–16 The fourth section of the cash flow statement, noncash investing and financing activities, does not involve cash transactions. Why is this section included in the cash flow statement? Be sure to include examples in your answer.

Q7–17 The cash flow statement is divided into four sections: (1) cash from operating activities, (2) cash from investing activities, (3) cash from financing activities, and (4) noncash investing and financing activities. How does this division into four sections help the investor in his/her analysis of the firm's results?

EXERCISES

E7–1 Ratio Analysis

Describe conditions in which the following ratios could be misleading for the investor if they were used alone to compare firms in the same industry. The ratios may be found in Exhibits 7–1 and 7–2.

1. Capital acquisition ratio
2. Quality-of-sales ratio
3. Dividend payout ratio

E7–2 Different Points Of View

Examine the ratios presented in Exhibits 7–1 and 7–2.

Required:

A. Which of these ratios would least interest a person considering a stock purchase and why?

B. Which of these ratios would least interest a person considering the purchase of a 5-year bond and why?

E7–3 Alternative Presentations

A firm decides to purchase new equipment for one of its manufacturing facilities. The equipment will cost $3,500,000. The firm can choose to pay for this equipment by (1) selling bonds in the corporate bond market or (2) giving the seller of the equipment a long-term note.

Required:

A. Show how each of these alternatives would appear on the cash flow statement. (List name(s) of the section(s) in which it would appear and the dollar figures.)

B. What are some of the factors the firm might consider in making a choice between these two alternatives?

E7–4 Indirect Method

Information concerning the BSMB Company is provided below.

BSMB COMPANY
Comparative Balance Sheet
December 31, 1997

	1997	1996	DIFFERENCE
Assets			
Cash	$ 3,250	$ 1,640	$ 1,610
Accounts receivable (net)	12,500	13,200	(700)
Inventory	8,330	4,540	3,790
Prepaid insurance	500	200	300
Equipment	30,000	15,000	15,000
Accumulated depreciation	(6,000)	(3,000)	(3,000)
Total assets	$48,580	$31,580	$17,000
Liabilities and Equities			
Accounts payable	$ 5,000	$ 4,500	$ 500
Accruals payable	700	400	300
Notes payable	15,000	5,000	10,000
Retained earnings	27,880	21,680	6,200
Total	$48,580	$31,580	$17,000

Additional Information: The BSMB Company paid dividends of $15,000 during the year. There were no gains or losses from transactions involving noncurrent accounts during the year.

Required: Prepare a statement of cash flows using the indirect method.

E7–5 Direct Method

Given the income statement shown at the top of next page, prepare the operating-activities section of the statement of cash flows using the direct method.

Additional Information:

	12/31/97	12/31/96
Accounts receivable	$12,000	$13,000
Inventory	26,000	29,000
Accounts payable	24,000	20,000

INCOME STATEMENT
For the Year Ended December 31, 1997

Sales		$148,000
Cost of goods sold		78,000
Gross profit		$ 70,000
Expenses:		
Salaries	$22,000	
Building rental	12,000	
Depreciation—Equipment	9,000	
Supplies	3,000	
Insurance	1,800	
Interest on notes payable	1,000	
Total expenses		48,800
Net income		$ 21,200

E7–6 Indirect Method

Information concerning the Apparel Company is provided below.

APPAREL COMPANY
Comparative Balance Sheet
December 31, 1997

	1997	1996	DIFFERENCE
Assets			
Cash	$ 7,000	$ 4,500	$ 2,500
Accounts receivable (net)	37,000	38,000	(1,000)
Inventory	37,000	35,000	2,000
Prepaid insurance	500	600	(100)
Equipment	100,000	85,000	15,000
Accummulated depreciation—Equipment	(47,500)	(34,000)	(13,500)
Total assets	$134,000	$129,100	$ 4,900
Liabilities and Equities			
Accounts payable	$ 35,000	$ 32,000	$ 3,000
Accruals payable	800	1,200	(400)
Notes payable	9,000	10,000	(1,000)
Common stock	50,000	25,000	25,000
Retained earnings	39,200	60,900	(21,700)
Total	$134,000	$129,100	$ 4,900

Additional Information: The Apparel Company paid dividends of $25,000 during the year. There were no gains or losses from transactions involving noncurrent accounts during the year.

Required: Prepare a statement of cash flows using the indirect method.

E7–7 Direct Method

Using the information from E7–6 and the income statement shown here for the Apparel Company, prepare the operating activities section of the statement of cash flows using the direct method.

APPAREL COMPANY
Income Statement
For the Year Ended December 31, 1997

Sales		$226,500
Cost of goods sold		120,000
Gross profit		$106,500
Expenses:		
Salaries	$58,000	
Building rental	24,000	
Depreciation—Equipment	13,500	
Supplies	4,500	
Insurance	2,400	
Interest on notes payable	800	
Total expenses		103,200
Net income		$ 3,300

E7–8 Analysis

From the information that follows, determine the cash payments to suppliers for Home Grocery Store.

Cost of goods sold:	
Beginning inventory	$ 84,000
Purchases	40,000
Goods available for sale	$124,000
Less: Ending inventory	55,000
Cost of goods sold	$ 69,000

Additional Information: The accounts payable beginning balance was $10,000, and the ending balance was $24,000.

E7–9 Analysis

From the information given below for the Jot 'em Down Store, determine the cash payments to suppliers.

Cost of goods sold:	
Beginning inventory	$25,000
Purchases	40,000
Goods available for sale	$65,000
Less: Ending inventory	30,000
Cost of goods sold	$35,000

Additional Information: The accounts payable beginning balance was $40,000, and the ending balance was $18,000.

E7–10 Direct Method

Given the income statement and additional information shown below, prepare the operating activities section of the statement of cash flows using the direct method.

INCOME STATEMENT
For the Year Ended December 31, 1997

Sales		$310,000
Cost of goods sold		190,000
Gross profit		$120,000
Expenses:		
Salaries	$32,000	
Building rental	21,000	
Depreciation—Equipment	10,000	
Uniforms rental	3,000	
Supplies	15,000	
Utilities	4,000	
Insurance	2,000	
Interest on notes payable	3,000	
Total expenses		90,000
Net income		$ 30,000

Additional Information:

	12/31/97	12/31/96
Accounts receivable	22,000	25,000
Inventory	31,000	29,000
Accounts payable	18,000	14,000

E7–11 Analysis

From the information that follows, determine the cash payments to suppliers for the Maximum Fitness Store. Note that the accounts payable beginning balance was $30,000 and the ending balance $26,000.

Cost of goods sold:	
Beginning inventory	$110,000
Purchases	580,000
Goods available for sale	$690,000
Less: Ending inventory	120,000
Cost of goods sold	$570,000

E7–12 Analysis

From the information given below for The Bath Boutique, determine the cash payments to suppliers. The accounts payable beginning balance was $65,000, and the ending balance was $72,000.

Cost of goods sold:	
Beginning inventory	$ 85,000
Purchases	780,000
Goods available for sale	$865,000
Less: Ending inventory	88,000
Cost of goods sold	$777,000

E7–13 Analysis

Bishop Co. reported cost of goods sold of $235,000 for 1996. The firm had a beginning balance of $19,000 and an ending balance of $22,000 in inventory. It had a beginning balance of $39,000 and an ending balance of $31,000 in accounts payable.

Required: If Bishop uses the direct method, what amount should the firm report as cash paid to suppliers in 1996 in its statement of cash flows?

E7–14 Interpretation

Given the following cash flow statement, provide an interpretation of its meaning from the point of view of a stockholder. The organization involved is a mature corporation in the pharmaceutical industry. Net income in the previous year was $195,000.

Cash flows from operating activities:	
Net income	$ 200,000
Adjustments for noncash accrual items:	
Depreciation expense	70,000
Amortization expense	20,000
Decrease in accounts receivable	40,000
Decrease in inventory	30,000
Increase in accounts payable	60,000
Net cash flow from operations	$ 420,000
Cash flows from investing activities:	
Proceeds from sale of PP&E	$ 80,000
Proceeds from sale of patent	110,000
Payments to purchase PP&E	(70,000)
Net cash flow from investing activities	$ 120,000
Cash flows from financing activities:	
Payments to retire bonds	$(150,000)
Payments of dividends	(400,000)
Net cash flow from financing activities	$(550,000)
Net decrease in cash	$ (10,000)
Balance, 12/31/95	50,000
Balance, 12/31/96	$ 40,000

E7–15 CPA Exam Questions (Part I, MC, November 1993)

Lino Company's work sheet for the preparation of its 1992 statement of cash flows included the following:

	DECEMBER 31	JANUARY 1
Accounts Receivable	$29,000	$23,000
Allowance for Uncollectible Accounts	1,000	800
Prepaid Rent Expense	8,200	12,400
Accounts Payable	22,400	19,400

Required: Lino's 1992 net income is $150,000. What amount should Lino include as net cash provided by operating activities in the statement of cash flows?

E7–16 CPA Exam Questions (Part I, MC, November 1993)

During 1992 Xan Inc. had the following activities related to its financial operations:

Payment for the early retirement of long-term bonds payable (carrying amount, $370,000)	$375,000
Distribution in 1992 of cash dividend declared in 1991 to preferred shareholders	31,000
Carrying amount of convertible preferred stock in Xan, converted into common shares	60,000
Proceeds from sale of treasury stock (carrying amount at cost, $43,000)	50,000

Required: In Xan's 1992 statement of cash flows, net cash used in financing operations should be what amount?

E7–17 CPA Exam Questions (Part I, MC, November 1993)

Duke Co. reported cost of goods sold of $270,000 for 1992. Additional information is as follows:

	DECEMBER 31	JANUARY 1
Inventory	$60,000	$45,000
Accounts payable	26,000	39,000

Required: If Duke uses the direct method, what amount should be reported as cash paid to suppliers in its 1992 statement of cash flows?

E7–18 CPA Exam Questions (Part I, MC, November 1993)

Karr Inc. reported net income of $300,000 for 1992. Changes occurred in several balance sheet accounts as follows:

Equipment	$25,000 increase
Accumulated Depreciation	40,000 increase
Note Payable	30,000 increase

Additional Information: During 1992, Karr sold equipment costing $25,000, with accumulated depreciation of $12,000, for a gain of $5,000. In December 1992, the company purchased equipment costing $50,000 with $20,000 cash and a 12% note payable of $30,000. Depreciation expense for the year was $52,000.

Required:

A. In Karr's 1992 statement of cash flows, net cash provided by operating activities should be what amount?

B. In Karr's 1992 statement of cash flows, net cash used in investing activities should be what amount?

PROBLEMS

P7–1 Statement of Cash Flows—Indirect Method

Below are comparative balance sheet data for the Argo Company.

	As of December 31,	
	1998	**1997**
Assets		
Cash	$ 15,000	$ 4,000
Trading securities	22,000	25,000
Accounts receivable	45,000	40,000
Inventory	50,000	35,000
Property, plant, and equipment	300,000	280,000
Accumulated depreciation	(120,000)	(100,000)
Total assets	$ 312,000	$ 284,000
Liabilities and Stockholders' Equity		
Accounts payable	$ 50,000	$ 45,000
Short-term notes payable	22,000	22,000
Long-term notes payable	40,000	42,000
Common stock, $10 par	100,000	100,000
Paid-in capital in excess of par	25,000	25,000
Retained earnings	75,000	50,000
Total liabilities and stockholders' equity	$ 312,000	$ 284,000

Additional Information:

Trading securities are considered cash equivalents for this problem. Cash dividends of $20,000 were paid in 1998. There were no other changes to retained earnings for 1998 other than net income.

Required: Prepare a statement of cash flows for the year ended 1998, using the indirect method.

P7–2 Statement of Cash Flows—Direct Method

Use the financial statements for Argo in P7–1 and the income statement data shown on the next page for Argo Company for the year ended December 31, 1998.

Additional Information:

Equipment with an original cost of $40,000 and a book value of $10,000 was sold for $12,000. Trading securities with a value of $3,000 were sold for $3,000. Cash dividends were paid in the amount of $20,000.

Required: Prepare a statement of cash flows using the direct method for year-end 1998. Do not prepare a reconciliation schedule.

Sales revenue		$ 625,000
Cost of goods sold		(343,750)
Gross profit		$ 281,250
Operating expenses:		
Selling expenses	$84,000	
Administrative expenses	91,000	
Depreciation expense	50,000	
Total operating expenses		225,000
Income from operations		$ 56,250
Other revenues/expenses:		
Gain on sale of equipment	$ 2,000	
Dividend revenue	500	
Interest expense	(4,200)	
Total other revenue and expenses		(1,700)
Net income before taxes		$ 54,550
Income tax expense		(9,550)
Net income		$ 45,000

P7–3 Statement of Cash Flows—Indirect Method

Shown here are data for a comparative balance sheet for Justin Inc. at December 31.

	As of December 31,	
	1998	1997
Assets		
Cash	$ 9,000	$ 12,000
Certificates of deposit	15,000	20,000
Accounts receivable	65,000	50,000
Inventory	40,000	42,000
Prepaid expenses	4,000	2,000
Property, plant, and equipment	400,000	350,000
Accumulated depreciation	(120,000)	(100,000)
Total assets	$ 413,000	$ 376,000
Liabilities and Stockholders' Equity		
Accounts payable	$ 42,000	$ 35,000
Short-term notes payable	0	25,000
Long-term notes payable	50,000	35,000
Common stock ($10 par)	200,000	150,000
Paid-in capital in excess of par	60,000	60,000
Retained earnings	61,000	71,000
Total liabilities and stockholders' equity	$ 413,000	$ 376,000

Additional Information:

The certificates are considered cash equivalents. Old equipment costing $50,000 with a book value of $10,000 was sold for $5,000, and new equipment was purchased for $100,000. Cash dividends of $20,000 were paid during the year. The only other change to retained earnings was from net income.

Required: Prepare a statement of cash flows using the indirect method.

P7–4 Statement of Cash Flows—Direct Method

Below are income statement data for Justin Inc. for the year ended December 31, 1998.

Sales revenue		$ 500,000
Cost of goods sold		(250,000)
Gross profit		$ 250,000
Operating expenses:		
Selling expenses	$84,000	
Administrative expenses	80,000	
Depreciation	60,000	224,000
Income from operations		$ 26,000
Other revenues and expenses:		
Loss on sale of equipment	$ (5,000)	
Dividend revenue	3,600	
Interest expense	(4,000)	(5,400)
Net income before taxes		$ 20,600
Income tax expense		(10,600)
Net income		$ 10,000

Required: Using the above information and data from P7–3, prepare a statement of cash flows using the direct method for the year ended 1998 for Justin Inc. Do not prepare a reconciliation schedule.

P7–5 Statement of Cash Flows—Indirect Method

Below are comparative balance sheet data for the Metcalfe Company.

	As of December 31	
	1997	1996
Assets		
Cash	$ 20,000	$ 28,000
Treasury bills	10,000	12,000
Accounts receivable	52,000	50,000
Inventory	45,000	46,000
Property, plant, and equipment	260,000	220,000
Accumulated depreciation	(95,000)	(86,000)
Total assets	$292,000	$270,000
Liabilities and Stockholders' Equity		
Accounts payable	$ 42,000	$ 30,000
Short-term notes payable	10,000	10,000
Bonds	60,000	65,000
Common stock, $5 par	110,000	110,000
Paid-in capital in excess of par	20,000	20,000
Retained earnings	50,000	35,000
Total liabilities and stockholders' equity	$292,000	$270,000

Additional Information:
Treasury bills are considered cash equivalents for this problem. Cash dividends of $15,000 were declared and paid in 1997. There were no other changes to Retained Earnings for 1997 other than net income.

Required: Prepare a statement of cash flows using the indirect method.

P7–6 CPA Exam Questions (Part I, MC9–13, November 1992)

Flax Corporation uses the direct method to prepare its statement of cash flows. Flax's trial balances at December 31, 1991, and December 31, 1990, are as shown.

	12/31/91	12/31/90
Debits:		
Cash	$ 35,000	$ 32,000
Accounts receivable	33,000	30,000
Inventory	31,000	47,000
Property, plant, and equipment	100,000	95,000
Unamortized bond discount	4,500	5,000
Cost of goods sold	250,000	380,000
Selling expenses	141,500	172,000
General and administrative expenses	137,000	151,300
Interest expense	4,300	2,600
Income tax expense	20,400	61,200
	$756,700	$976,100
Credits:		
Allowance for uncollectible accounts	$ 1,300	$ 1,100
Accumulated depreciation	16,500	15,000
Trade Accounts payable	25,000	17,500
Income taxes payable	21,000	27,100
Deferred income taxes	5,300	4,600
8% Callable bonds payable	45,000	20,000
Common stock	50,000	40,000
Additional paid-in capital	9,100	7,500
Retained earnings	44,700	64,600
Sales	538,800	778,700
	$756,700	$976,100

Flax purchased $5,000 in equipment during 1991. It allocated one-third of its depreciation expense to selling expenses and the remainder to general and administrative expenses.

Required: Determine the amounts Flax should report in its statement of cash flows for the year ended December 31, 1991, for the following:

A. Cash collected from customers?
B. Cash paid for goods to be sold?
C. Cash paid for interest?
D. Cash paid for income taxes?
E. Cash paid for selling expenses?

P7–7 CPA Exam Questions (Part I, MC5–7, November 1991)

The differences in Beal Inc.'s balance sheet accounts at December 31, 1990, and December 31, 1989, are shown here.

	INCREASE (DECREASE)
Assets	
Cash and cash equivalents	$ 120,000
Short-term investments	300,000
Accounts receivable (net)	—
Inventory	80,000
Long-term investments	(100,000)
Plant assets	700,000
Accumulated depreciation	—
Total assets	$1,100,000
Liabilities and Stockholders' Equity	
Accounts payable and accrued liabilities	$ (5,000)
Dividends payable	160,000
Short-term bank debt	325,000
Long-term debt	110,000
Common stock ($10 par)	100,000
Additional paid-in capital	120,000
Retained earnings	290,000
Total liabilities and stockholders' equity	$1,100,000

Additional Information:

The following information relates to 1990:

- Net income was $790,000.
- Cash dividends of $500,000 were declared.
- A building costing $600,000 and having a carrying amount of $350,000 was sold for $350,000.
- Equipment costing $110,000 was acquired through issuance of long-term debt.
- A long-term investment was sold for $135,000. There were no other transactions affecting long-term investments.
- 10,000 shares of common stock were issued for $22 a share.

Required: Calculate the following items in Beal's 1990 statement of cash flows:

A. Net cash provided by operating activities.
B. Net cash used in investing activities.
C. Net cash provided by financing activities.

P7–8 Deriving Cash Flows

1. Given the following information, solve for cash collections from customers:

Beginning accounts receivable	$ 50,000
Ending accounts receivable	60,000
Current sales	2,000,000
Accounts written off	0

2. Given the following information, solve for receivable write-offs:

Ending allowance for bad debts	$ 5,000
Beginning allowance for bad debts	10,000
Bad debts expense	100,000

3. Given the following information, solve for cash payments to suppliers:

Purchases	$800,000
Beginning accounts payable	130,000
Ending accounts payable	90,000

4. Given the following information, solve for purchases:

Beginning inventory	$ 90,000
Ending inventory	57,000
Cost of goods sold	200,000

5. Given the following information, solve for proceeds from sale of property, plant, and equipment:

Beginning book value of asset	$400,000
Loss on sale	100,000
Current depreciation expense	100,000

6. Given the following information, solve for cash dividend payments:

Net income	$ 60,000
Ending retained earnings	70,000
Beginning retained earnings	270,000

7. Given the following information, solve for cash payments made for retirement of debt:

Beginning debt book value	$120,000
Unamortized discount	80,000
Loss on retirement	40,000

P7–9 Deriving Cash Flows

1. Given the following information, solve for cash collections from customers:

Beginning accounts receivable	$ 75,000
Ending accounts receivable	80,000
Current sales	2,250,000
Accounts written off	5,000

2. Given the following information, solve for receivable write-offs:

Ending allowance for bad debts	$ 18,000
Beginning allowance for bad debts	22,000
Bad debts expense	103,000

3. Given the following information, solve for cash payments to suppliers:

Purchases	$970,000
Beginning accounts payable	165,000
Ending accounts payable	145,000

4. Given the following information, solve for purchases:

Beginning inventory	$ 37,000
Ending inventory	42,000
Cost of goods sold	235,000

5. Given the following information, solve for proceeds from sale of property, plant, and equipment:

Beginning book value of asset	$320,000
Gain on sale	24,000
Current depreciation expense on asset	35,000

6. Given the following information, solve for cash dividend payments:

Net income	$ 45,000
Ending retained earnings	660,000
Beginning retained earnings	670,000

7. Given the following information, solve for cash payments made for retirement of debt:

Beginning book value of debt	$250,000
Unamortized discount	50,000
Loss on retirement	10,000

P7–10 Direct Method

Shown here is an income statement and a comparative balance sheet for JRSK Inc.

INCOME STATEMENT
For the Year Ended December 31, 1998

Sales revenue	$ 750,000
Cost of goods sold	(375,000)
Depreciation expense	(23,000)
Bad debts expense	(15,000)
Franchise amortization	(20,000)
Salary and wages expense	(125,000)
Administrative expenses	(80,000)
Other expenses	(5,000)
Interest revenue	4,000
Interest expense	(20,000)
Income tax expense	(28,000)
Net income	$ 63,000

COMPARATIVE BALANCE SHEET

	As of December 31, 1998	As of December 31, 1997	Increase (Decrease)
Debits			
Cash	$ 45,000	$ 38,000	$ 7,000
Trading securities	69,000	50,000	19,000
Accounts receivable	56,000	42,000	14,000
Inventory	158,000	120,000	38,000
Prepaid insurance	2,100	1,800	300
Accrued interest receivable	1,400	600	800
Investments (long-term)	60,000	40,000	20,000
Land	50,000	25,000	25,000
Building	250,000	250,000	0
Furniture and fixtures	65,000	50,000	15,000
Franchise	80,000	100,000	(20,000)
	$836,500	$717,400	$119,100
Credits			
Allowance for bad debts	$ 2,300	$ 2,100	$ 200
Accumulated depreciation—Building	20,000	10,000	10,000
Accumulated depreciation—Furniture	23,000	10,000	13,000
Accounts payable	45,000	38,000	7,000
Accrued wages payable	3,000	2,400	600
Income taxes payable	6,000	4,500	1,500
Notes payable (long-term)	200,000	200,000	0
Common stock, $15 par	405,000	375,000	30,000
Paid-in capital in excess of par	70,000	50,000	20,000
Retained earnings	62,200	25,400	36,800
	$836,500	$717,400	$119,100

Additional Information:

1. Cash dividends of $26,200 were paid during the year.
2. Bad debts were written off in the amount of $14,800.
3. There were 2,000 shares of common stock sold for $50,000.

Required: Prepare a statement of cash flows using the direct method. (Do not prepare a reconciliation schedule.)

P7–11 Financial Analysis

Use the data for JRSK from P7–10.

A. Prepare as many adequacy ratios as possible.
B. Prepare as many performance and quality ratios as possible.
C. Provide a brief interpretation of these ratios.

P7–12 Direct Method

The income statement and balance sheet data for the TJ & KA Clothing Store are shown here.

COMPARATIVE BALANCE SHEETS

	1998	1997	INCREASE (DECREASE)
Debits			
Cash	$ 40,000	$ 48,000	$ (8,000)
Certificates of deposit	75,000	60,000	15,000
Accounts receivable	75,000	50,000	25,000
Inventory	200,000	175,000	25,000
Prepaid insurance	2,400	1,500	900
Accrued interest receivable	1,500	1,000	500
Investments (long-term)	80,000	60,000	20,000
Land	75,000	50,000	25,000
Building	300,000	300,000	0
Furniture and fixtures	90,000	70,000	20,000
Franchise	120,000	150,000	(30,000)
	$1,058,900	$965,500	$ 93,400
Credits			
Allowance for bad debts	$ 3,700	$ 2,500	$ 1,200
Accumulated depreciation—Building	24,000	12,000	12,000
Accumulated depreciation—Furniture	32,000	14,000	18,000
Accounts payable	70,000	50,000	20,000
Accrued wages payable	3,600	3,000	600
Income taxes payable	7,000	5,000	2,000
Mortgage payable (long-term)	300,000	300,000	0
Common stock ($25 par)	500,000	500,000	0
Paid-in capital in excess of par	50,000	50,000	0
Retained earnings	68,600	29,000	39,600
	$1,058,900	$965,500	$ 93,400

INCOME STATEMENT

Sales revenue	$ 820,000
Cost of goods sold	(410,000)
Depreciation expense	(30,000)
Bad debts expense	(16,000)
Franchise amortization	(30,000)
Salary and wages expense	(140,000)
Administrative expenses	(75,000)
Other expenses	(10,000)
Interest revenue	8,000
Interest expense	(30,000)
Income tax expense	(27,400)
Net income	$ 59,600

Additional Information:

1. Cash dividends of $20,000 were paid.
2. Bad debts write-offs were $14,800.
3. Certificates of Deposit are cash equivalents.
4. Long-term investments were paid with cash.

Required: Prepare a statement of cash flows using the direct method. Do not prepare a reconciliation schedule.

P7–13 Indirect Method

Using the information in P7–12, prepare a statement of cash flows using the indirect method.

P7–14 Direct Method

An income statement and comparative balance sheets for Erica Pullman & Company appear here. Given this data, prepare a statement of cash flows for 1997 using the direct method. Dividends were declared and paid in the amount of $20,000. Also calculate for Pullman & Company the cash flow ratios illustrated in this chapter (ignore income taxes).

COMPARATIVE BALANCE SHEETS

	12/31/97	12/31/96
Assets		
Cash	$ 94,000	$ 60,000
Receivables	85,000	102,000
Less: Allowance for bad debts	(9,000)	(12,000)
Inventory	160,000	150,000
Plant and equipment	90,000	180,000
Accumulated depreciation	(40,000)	(50,000)
Land	120,000	70,000
Total assets	$500,000	$500,000
Liabilities & Equities		
Accounts payable	$110,000	$ 80,000
Commissions payable	20,000	10,000
Interest payable	4,000	30,000
Bonds payable	160,000	240,000
Common stock (no par)	100,000	90,000
Retained earnings	106,000	50,000
Total liabilities and equities	$500,000	$500,000

INCOME STATEMENT
For the Year Ended December 31, 1997

Revenues	$ 300,000
Cost of goods sold	(150,000)

(continued)

Depreciation of retail facility	(20,000)
Sales commissions	(30,000)
Bad debt expense	(10,000)
Interest expense	(24,000)
Other expenses (all paid in cash)	(40,000)
Gain on sale of equipment	30,000
Gain on retirement of bonds	20,000
Net income	$ 76,000

P7–15 Cash Flows From Selected Sources

1. Given the following information, solve for cash collections from customers:

Beginning accounts receivable	$ 22,000
Ending accounts receivable	30,000
Current sales	190,000
Accounts written off	10,000

2. Given the following information, solve for receivable write-offs:

Ending allowance for bad debts	$ 7,000
Beginning allowance for bad debts	17,000
Bad debts expense	40,000

3. Given the following information, solve for cash payments to suppliers:

Purchases	$300,000
Beginning accounts payable	300,000
Ending accounts payable	200,000

4. Given the following information, solve for purchases:

Beginning inventory	$400,000
Ending inventory	300,000
Goods available for sale	700,000

5. Given the following information, solve for proceeds from sale of property, plant, and equipment:

Beginning book value of asset	$400,000
Gain on sale	30,000
Current depreciation expense	60,000

6. Given the following information, solve for cash dividend payments:

Net income	$ 60,000
Ending retained earnings	120,000
Beginning retained earnings	100,000

7. Given the following information, solve for cash payments made for retirement of debt:

Beginning debt book value	$1,200,000
Discount amortization	40,000
Gain on retirement	100,000

P7–16 Cash Flows From Selected Sources

1. Given the following information, solve for cash collections from customers:

Beginning accounts receivable	$ 18,000
Ending accounts receivable	21,000
Current sales	210,000
Accounts written off	7,000

2. Given the following information, solve for receivable write-offs:

Ending allowance for bad debts	$15,000
Beginning allowance for bad debts	13,000
Bad debts expense	33,000

3. Given the following information, solve for cash payments to suppliers:

Purchases	$480,000
Beginning accounts payable	275,000
Ending accounts payable	208,000

4. Given the following information, solve for purchases:

Beginning inventory	$270,000
Ending inventory	230,000
Goods available for sale	570,000

5. Given the following information, solve for proceeds from sale of property, plant, and equipment:

Beginning book value of asset	$510,000
Loss on sale	28,000
Current depreciation expense on asset	75,000

6. Given the following information, solve for cash dividend payments:

Net income	$ 55,000
Ending retained earnings	165,000
Beginning retained earnings	120,000

7. Given the following information, solve for cash payments made for retirement of debt:

Beginning book value of debt	$2,250,000
Discount amortization	50,000
Gain on retirement	67,000

P7–17 Analysis of Cash Flows

1. Given the following information, solve for cash collections from customers:

Beginning accounts receivable	$ 43,000
Ending accounts receivable	61,000
Current sales	157,000
Accounts written off	9,000

2. Given the following information, solve for receivable write-offs:

Ending allowance for bad debts	$ 25,000
Beginning allowance for bad debts	30,000
Bad debts expense	100,000

3. Given the following information, solve for cash payments to suppliers:

Purchases	$2,000,000
Beginning accounts payable	400,000
Ending accounts payable	200,000

4. Given the following information, solve for purchases:

Beginning inventory	$300,000
Ending inventory	400,000
Cost of goods sold	300,000

5. Given the following information, solve for proceeds from sale of property, plant, and equipment:

Beginning book value of asset	$400,000
Loss on sale	70,000
Current depreciation expense	40,000

6. Given the following information, solve for cash dividend payments:

Net income	$ 60,000
Ending retained earnings	40,000
Beginning retained earnings	150,000

7. Given the following information, solve for cash payments made for retirement of debt:

Beginning book value of debt	$500,000
Premium amortization	40,000
Loss on retirement	40,000

P7–18 Indirect Method

The income statement and balance sheet data for Rondol Inc. are on the next page.

Additional Information:

1. New machinery with a value of $100,000 was purchased for $70,000 cash and a trade-in of old equipment with a book value of $40,000. At the time of the exchange, the accumulated depreciation was $10,000 and the original cost was $50,000.

BALANCE SHEET

	1998	1997	INCREASE (DECREASE)
Debits			
Cash	$ 60,000	$ 80,000	$ (20,000)
Accounts receivable	175,000	110,000	65,000
Inventory	335,000	275,000	60,000
Prepaid insurance	2,400	1,500	900
Accrued interest receivable	1,500	1,000	500
Investments (long-term)	80,000	60,000	20,000
Land	100,000	50,000	50,000
Building	250,000	250,000	0
Equipment	200,000	150,000	50,000
Copyrights	120,000	150,000	(30,000)
	$1,323,900	$1,127,500	$196,400
Credits			
Allowance for bad debts	$ 3,900	$ 3,000	$ 900
Accumulated depreciation—Building	20,000	10,000	10,000
Accumulated depreciation—Equipment	70,000	30,000	40,000
Accounts payable	58,500	40,000	18,500
Accrued wages payable	4,000	4,500	(500)
Income taxes payable	6,000	7,000	(1,000)
Bonds payable	300,000	250,000	50,000
Premium on bonds payable	27,500	24,000	3,500
Common stock, $25 par	700,000	650,000	50,000
Paid-in capital in excess of par	60,000	50,000	10,000
Retained earnings	74,000	59,000	15,000
	$1,323,900	$1,127,500	$196,400

INCOME STATEMENT

Sales revenue	$1,134,000
Cost of goods sold	(500,000)
Depreciation expense	(60,000)
Bad debts expense	(20,000)
Copyrights amortization	(40,000)
Salary and wages expense	(270,000)
Administrative expenses	(100,000)
Other expenses	(12,500)
Interest revenue	8,000
Interest expense	(28,500)
Loss on equipment	(10,000)
Income tax expense	(30,000)
Net income	$ 71,000

2. Cash dividends of $56,000 were paid during the year.
3. Legal fees of $10,000 were paid for a successful defense against copyright infringement.
4. Ten-year, 10% bonds with a face value of $50,000 were issued in January 1998 for $55,000. The old bonds were 25-year, 10% bonds, issued in January 1997. Straight-line amortization is used for both bond issues.
5. Assume all other changes in the balance sheet accounts are self-explanatory.

Required: Prepare a statement of cash flows using the indirect method.

P7–19 Direct Method

Using the information in P7–18, prepare a statement of cash flows using the direct method and adding any necessary explanatory footnotes. Also, prepare a schedule to reconcile the operating section to accrual net income.

RESEARCH ACTIVITIES

R7–1 Report Preparation

Research the background that led to the adoption of the present statement of cash flows. Prepare a report that includes a brief history of the developments leading to the current statement of cash flows. Discuss the similarities and differences between the old statement of changes in working capital and the current statement of cash flows. What were the disadvantages of the old statements, and what are some of the criticisms of the presently required statement of cash flows? What improvements do you think could be made to the statement of cash flows?

R7–2 SFAS No. 95

What was the FASB's rationale for adopting SFAS No. 95? What are the main purposes of SFAS No. 95? Why does the statement prohibit the calculation of earnings per share on a cash basis? In your discussion of this prohibition, provide support for the position taken by the FASB on this matter, and also mention some of the weaknesses of this position.

R7–3 Financial Research

Find an annual report for a company that has negative cash flows from operations for all years reported (i.e., cash *used* for operations). Provide a statement showing how this company has managed to finance its operations. In your opinion, is the viability of this company as a going concern in jeopardy? Support your conclusion.

R7–4 Internet Exercise

Search the internet for information concerning cash flows. One method is to uses a search engine and type in key words relevant to this chapter such as cash flows. How does this location relate to the material in this chapter?

R7–5 Motorola—Financial Analysis

Examine the statement of cash flows in ***Motorola's*** (*www.swcollege.com/hartman.html*) annual report in Appendix C. To summarize this statement, list the net operating, investing, and financing activities for each period reported. Next to each net amount, place a plus sign if there was significant cash provided, a minus sign for significant cash used, or a zero if the amount is insignificant (in your opinion). Based upon these symbols, provide a brief statement that summarizes Motorola's cash activities for each period.

Refine this for financing activity to indicate whether the principal activity involved creditors or shareholders (or both). Were there any significant differences over the periods? If so, what do you think were the causes of these differences?

INCOME STATEMENT	
Sales revenue	$ 820,000
Cost of goods sold	(410,000)
Depreciation expense	(30,000)
Bad debts expense	(16,000)
Franchise amortization	(30,000)
Salary and wages expense	(140,000)
Administrative expenses	(75,000)
Other expenses	(10,000)
Interest revenue	8,000
Interest expense	(30,000)
Income tax expense	(27,400)
Net income	$ 59,600

PART 2

INTEGRATIVE CASES

TWO COMPUTER COMPANIES

INTRODUCTION

Similar financial statements of firms in the same industry can often mask dramatically different share-price performance. For example, Exhibits 1, 2, and 3 show balance sheet, income statement, and cash flow information for ***Apple Computer*** and ***Compaq Computer.*** The common-size financial statements at the lower sections of Exhibits 1 and 2 indicate that the gross margin and asset structure of both companies are similar. However, Exhibit 4 indicates that during 1994 and 1995 the returns to investors in the two companies differed dramatically. The purpose of this case is to "tease out" some financial statement signals that would help explain the different return performances of the two companies.

EXHIBIT 1 Comparative and Common-Size Income Statements

	APPLE COMPUTER			COMPAQ COMPUTER		
	1995	1994	1993	1995	1994	1993
Net sales	$11,062	$ 9,189	$ 7,977	$ 14,755	$10,866	$ 7,191
Cost of sales	(8,204)	(6,846)	(5,249)	(11,367)	(8,139)	(5,493)
Selling, general, and administrative	(1,583)	(1,384)	(1,632)	(1,594)	(1,235)	(837)
Other income and expenses	(553)	(419)	(944)	(560)	(271)	(202)
Operating income	$ 722	$ 540	$ 152	$ 1,234	$ 1,221	$ 659
Interest expense	(48)	(40)	(12)	(46)	(49)	(43)
Provision for taxes	(250)	(190)	(53)	(399)	(305)	(154)
Net income	$ 424	$ 310	$ 87	$ 789	$ 867	$ 462
Common-size income statements:						
Sales	100.0	100.0	100.0	100.0	100.0	100.0
Cost of sales	(74.2)	(74.5)	(65.8)	(77.0)	(74.9)	(76.4)
Selling, general, and administrative expenses	(14.3)	(15.1)	(20.5)	(10.8)	(11.4)	(11.6)
Other income and expenses	(5.0)	(4.6)	(11.8)	(3.8)	(2.5)	(2.8)
Operating income	6.5	5.9	1.9	8.4	11.2	9.2
Interest expense and other income	(0.4)	(0.4)	(0.2)	(0.3)	(0.5)	(0.6)
Provision for taxes	(2.3)	(2.1)	(0.7)	(2.7)	(2.8)	(2.1)
Net income	3.8	3.4	1.1	5.3	8.0	6.4

EXHIBIT 2
Comparative and Common-Size Balance Sheets

	APPLE COMPUTER		COMPAQ COMPUTER	
	1995	**1994**	**1995**	**1994**
Assets				
Current assets	$5,224	$4,476	$6,527	$5,158
Property, plant, and equipment	711	667	1,110	944
Other assets	296	160	181	64
Total assets	$6,231	$5,303	$7,818	$6,166
Liabilities and equity				
Current liabilities	$2,325	$1,944	$2,680	$2,013
Long-term debt	303	305	300	300
Deferred taxes	702	671	224	179
Total liabilities	$3,330	$2,920	$3,204	$2,492
Contributed capital	$ 437	$ 287	$ 890	$ 739
Retained earnings	2,464	2,096	3,724	2,935
Total equity	$2,901	$2,383	$4,614	$3,674
Total liabilities and owners' equity	$6,231	$5,303	$7,818	$6,166
Common-size balance sheets:				
Assets				
Current assets	83.8	84.4	83.5	83.7
Property, plant, and equipment	11.4	12.6	14.2	15.3
Other assets	4.8	3.0	2.3	1.0
Total assets	100.0	100.0	100.0	100.0
Liabilities and equity				
Current liabilities	37.3	36.7	34.3	32.6
Long-term debt	4.9	5.8	3.8	4.9
Deferred taxes	11.3	12.7	2.9	2.9
Total liabilities	53.4	55.1	41.0	40.4
Contributed capital	7.0	5.4	11.4	12.0
Retained earnings	39.5	39.5	47.6	47.6
Total equity	46.6	44.9	59.0	59.6
Total liabilities and owners' equity	100.0	100.0	100.0	100.0

EXHIBIT 3
Statement of Cash Flows

	APPLE COMPUTER			COMPAQ COMPUTER		
	1995	1994	1993	1995	1994	1993
Cash flows from operating activities:						
Net income ($000,000)	$ 424	$ 310	$ 87	$ 789	$ 867	$ 462
Adjustment to reconcile net income to cash from operations:						
Depreciation and amortization	127	168	166	214	169	156
Tax benefit associated with stock options				60	53	44
Loss on disposal of assets	6	11	13	2	2	2
Changes in asset and liabilities (net)	(797)	248	(917)	(122)	(1,192)	(424)
Cash provided by (used in) operations	$(240)	$ 737	$(651)	$ 943	$ (101)	$ 240
Cash flows from investing activities:						
Purchases of property, plant, and equipment	(159)	(160)	(213)	(391)	(357)	(145)
Other, net	(243)	158	706	(312)	(51)	0
Cash provided by (used in) investing	$(402)	$ (2)	$ 493	$(703)	$ (408)	$(145)
Cash flows from financing activities:						
Issuance of common stock	86	82	85	79	100	142
Increase (decrease) in long-term borrowings	(2)	297	(11)		300	
Increase in short-term borrowings	169	(531)	639			
Cash dividends	(58)	(56)	(56)			
Other			(321)			
Cash provided by (used in) financing	$ 195	$(208)	$ 336	$ 79	$ 400	$ 142
Effect of exchange rate changes on cash				$ (45)	(47)	$ 33
Change in cash	$(447)	$ 527	$ 178	$ 274	$ (156)	$ 270

EXHIBIT 4
Apple Computer and Compaq, Incorporated Cumulative Returns to Shareholders, 1993–1995

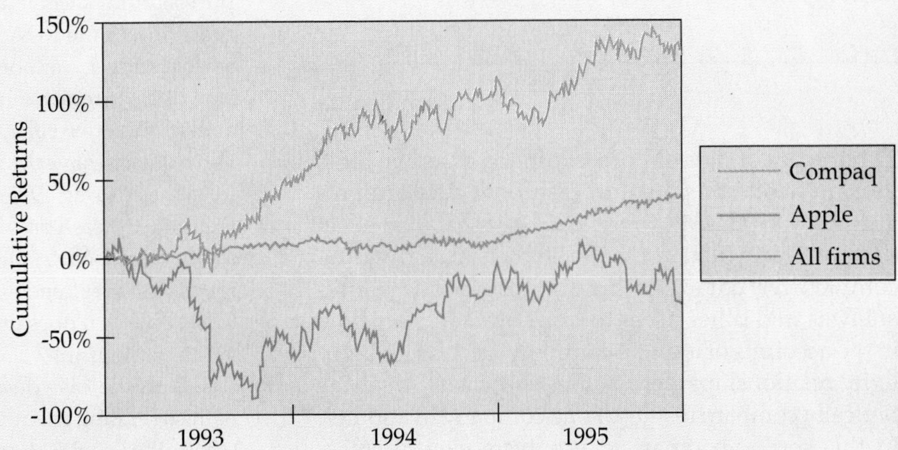

Company Descriptions

Compaq Presario

Compaq Computer Corporation produces *IBM*-compatible personal computers (PCs) and peripheral equipment which utilize MS-DOS® or Microsoft Windows® operating systems. Incorporated in 1982, the company is the largest supplier of personal computers in the world, maintaining an approximate 10 percent share of the worldwide PC market. The company's 1995 sales were distributed among commercial desktop PCs (45 percent of sales), PC system products and options (22 percent), portable PCs (17 percent), and PCs for the consumer and home office market (16 percent).

Apple Computer is another large producer of personal computer hardware, however, its computers utilize the Macintosh operating system (Mac OS). The company is a partner, with IBM and Motorola, in providing hardware and computing systems based on the PowerPC® system architecture. In early 1995 the company began to license the Mac OS to other vendors to stimulate demand for Mac OS-based systems. Substantially all of the company's net sales come from the sale of Macintosh computers and peripherals.

Other Information

Three types of data are present in the exhibits. First, income statement data and cash flow data are provided for 1993, 1994, and 1995, and balance sheet data are provided for 1994 and 1995. Providing comparative data over a range of periods allows analysts and other users to detect trends over time in the accounts of a single company. Second, to highlight relationships across the two firms, analysts typically compare results of one company to another. In this sort of comparison, analysts view a cross-section of firms at a single point in time. For example, comparing the net property and equipment of the two firms at the end of 1995 is an example of a cross-sectional comparison. Finally, to provide a more meaningful comparison for firms that differ in size, users often restate the balance sheet accounts as a percentage of total assets, and the income statement accounts as a percentage of sales. The resulting data can be used to make "common size" financial statements. Without correcting for these differences in size, users will not be able to make valid judgements regarding financial relationships. For example, it would be difficult to infer anything about the operating success of ***GM*** and ***Chrysler*** simply by comparing the two companies' annual net sales figures: GM is a much larger company and historically has had higher levels of sales than Chrysler.

Required

A. Describe the trend in net income and profit margin for Apple Computer from 1993 through 1995. Based on this trend, how would you expect the stock price to behave during the period?

B. Compare Apple and Compaq's return on assets (ROA) for 1995. (To calculate the average tax rate, divide the provision for income taxes by income before taxes.) Break down the ROA into its net profit margin and asset turnover components. What does this comparison of asset return tell you about the relative profitability of the two companies? Which company would you expect to have the most favorable stock price performance during 1995?

C. Examine the cash provided by operating activities for the two companies. Over the three-year period, how much cash was generated by operation for each firm? What potential does this difference have to affect the value of the firm?

D. Based on the case description and your knowledge of the operating environment of these two companies, what other explanations not present in the financial statements might account for the stock return pattern of Exhibit 4?

Revenue and Expense Recognition for the IRIDIUM® System (Motorola)

"Our philosophy is to manage for long-term growth and profitability, while consistently and appropriately investing in technology to maintain competitive leadership."

From Motorola's 1996 Annual Report

It's late in 1993, and Barbara Barnwell, an accountant in Motorola's Satellite Communication Division (SATCOM), is mulling over a memo she has just received from the division's chief accountant. The memo asks Barnwell to develop the division's response to two challenging accounting issues faced by ***SATCOM.***[1] Both issues arise from the company's involvement in the IRIDIUM® System, and the potential financial statement impact of each issue is significant.[2] Barnwell wants to be sure that she carefully prepares her response.

International Communications

Background on the IRIDIUM System

Motorola, Inc., is one of the world's leading providers of electronic equipment, systems, components and services. The company, headquartered in Schaumburg, Illinois, had over $27 billion dollars in sales and employed over 140,000 people worldwide in 1995. At the end of that year, Motorola was the world's largest provider of wireless communications equipment (cellular telephones, pagers, and two-way radios), and a world leader in semiconductors; these two business segments accounted for 60% and 29% of total sales in 1995. Exhibit 1 shows that over the past six years Motorola has continually increased sales; the total return on its stock over the six-year period from 1990 through 1995 has been over 270%, compared with just over 75% for the market as a whole.

However, maintaining technological leadership in its core businesses requires extensive investment in research and development and a commitment to innovation. This commitment follows naturally from the company's long history of risk-taking. Founded in 1928 by Paul Galvin, the company first flourished by manufacturing car radios, an innovative product for the time, and invented the hand-held walkie-talkie for use during World War II. In 1949, the company moved into the emerging semiconductor industry, and twenty-five years later sold its color television division to a Japanese company in order to focus exclusively on semiconductors and wireless devices.

Consistent with this history of risk-taking and innovation, Motorola in 1993 officially embarked on what *The Wall Street Journal* described as the company's, "most ambitious project ever." The IRIDIUM System is a satellite-based, wireless communications network designed to offer high-quality, voice, paging, fax, and data transmission to its subscribers anywhere on earth. The heart of the network is a constellation of 66 satellites in low earth orbit approximately 400 miles above the earth's surface, as opposed to conventional communications satellites, which orbit 22,000 miles above the earth. The relatively low orbit allows the satellites to receive cellular phone signals from the surface, and the large number of satellites allows them to maintain contact so that telephone signals from earth may be easily passed from one satellite to the next until the signal reaches its destination.

[1]Barabara Barnwell is a fictional character.
[2]IRIDIUM is a registered trademark and service mark of ***Iridium, Inc.***

EXHIBIT 1
Motorola Sales:
Cumulative Returns

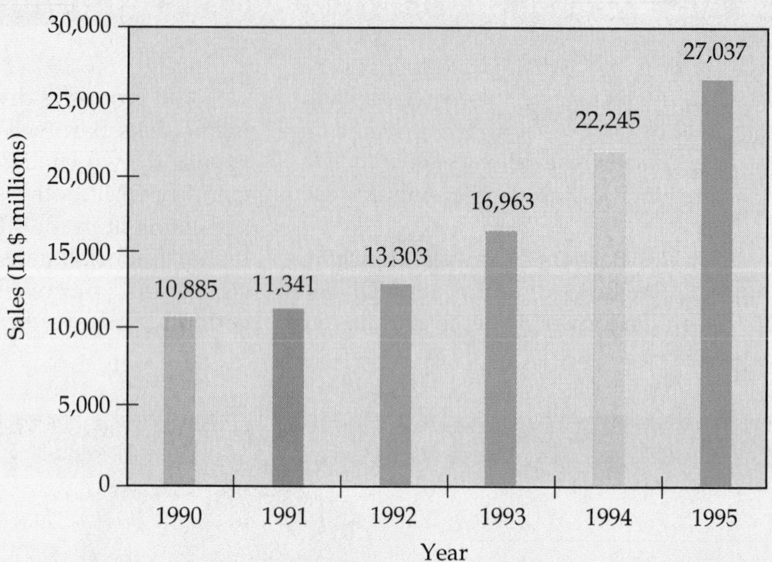

Cumulative Equity Returns,
1990–1995

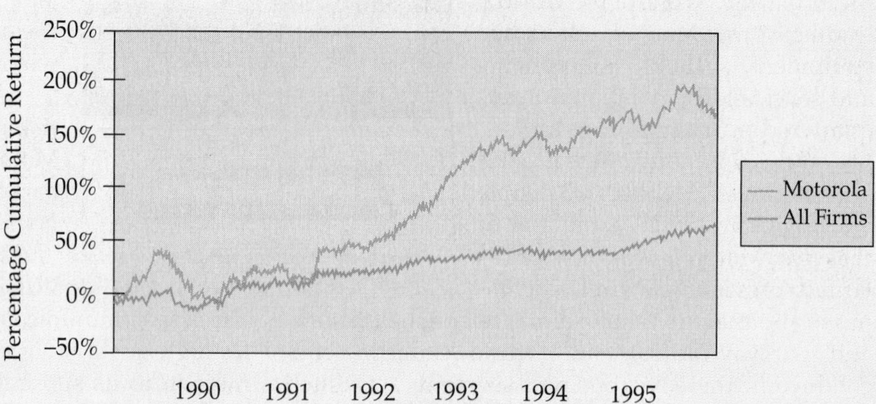

While the market for such a system may not be obvious to U.S. citizens long accustomed to ready access to both domestic and international phone service, consider that currently over half the world's population lives more than two hours from a phone. *The Economist* paints this picture of an IRIDIUM System user:

> Standing on a rocky strip of land, somewhere in the middle of the lone and level Pacific, you pull a chunky little telephone from an inside pocket, extend an aerial, and dial a number. Soon the radio signals bearing your call are dancing direct from your telephone to a necklace of satellites 500 miles or so above the earth, and then back down to where your great-aunt Madge sits on the other side of the world dispensing sensible advice. Desert islands will never be the same again—nor will political dissidents, remote third-world villages or peripatetic businessmen.

To finance the system, Motorola formed a consortium called Iridium, Inc., which consists of seventeen international investors. In July 1993 Iridium, Inc., signed a $3.4 billion contract with Motorola to purchase the IRIDIUM System from Motorola's Satellite Communication Division (SATCOM). This agreement is referred to as the Space System Contract. Additionally, the consortium has committed to a $2.8 billion maintenance contract with Motorola commencing in 1998 and running for a five-year period; this contract is referred to as the Operations and Maintenance (O&M) Contract. At the time of signing, Motorola's portion of the joint venture was over 30 percent; the company anticipates retaining no more than 15 percent ownership over the term of the contract. Assume for purposes of the case that the anticipated cost to develop, construct, and deploy the IRIDIUM System to Motorola is approximately $3.0 billion.

Thus, Motorola has two somewhat independent roles in the IRIDIUM project. First, Motorola's SATCOM Division is the lead contractor, responsible for development, construction, deployment, and delivery of the system. Second, Motorola, Inc., has a substantial investment in Iridium, Inc.[3]

Although SATCOM is the lead contractor in the IRIDIUM System, key elements of the system will be provided by some of the largest engineering and high-technology firms in the world, including ***Lockheed, Raytheon, Siemens, Bechtel,*** and ***Scientific Atlanta.*** The satellites themselves will be placed into orbit by three subcontractors: ***McDonnell Douglas*** will launch satellites using its Delta 2 rocket; ***Khrunichev Enterprise*** of Russia will provide launch services using its Proton launch vehicle; and ***China Great Wall Industry*** will provide services using its Long March IIc vehicle.

The contract schedule calls for satellite launches to begin in 1996, with commercial service commencing in 1998. The system will be accepted by Iridium, Inc., when it is complete and functioning according to specifications.

Revenue and Expense Recognition Challenges for Motorola

This case focuses on two income statement challenges faced by SATCOM as the lead contractor for the IRIDIUM project.

For SATCOM, the arrangement with Iridium is a long-term construction and maintenance agreement that must be accounted for in a way that matches benefits and expenditures. Assume for purposes of the case that the Space System Contract is structured as follows: It contains a schedule of 50 project milestones, which SATCOM is required to reach on specific dates. Exhibit 2 provides examples of these milestones. The milestones were established to provide a set of readily verifiable construction progress points. The $3.4 billion purchase price was allocated to the construction milestones; as the milestones are completed, the Iridium consortium is required to make progress payments to SATCOM. The milestones are spaced roughly one month apart; however, there are months when there are no milestones, and some milestones are more difficult to achieve than others. The contract cash flows reflect these variations, ranging in amounts from $20 million to $100 million per milestone.

Exhibit 2
Space System Contract Milestone Examples

- Complete the design of the satellite antenna.
- Perform a ground test of the satellite communications module.
- Complete the first launch.
- Finish construction of the ground control facility.

[3]Assume for purposes of the case that the company accounts for its investment in Iridium, Inc., using the equity method due to its substantial, nonmajority influence in the consortium.

Iridium, Inc., may withhold payment to SATCOM if milestones are not achieved.

What Triggers Revenue Recognition?

One of the first accounting challenges was to determine the procedure used to recognize portions of **revenue earned** during the Space System Contract. While it was clear that the contract would require some form of percentage of completion, a variety of options existed regarding how to calculate what percentage of the contract was complete. Basically, Motorola executives considered the implications of the following three options:

1. *Cost-to-cost.* This method is commonly used in long-term construction contracts, and it relies on assessing what percent of the total *estimated cost* was incurred during a given period. That period expense is then matched with the calculated percentage of total revenue. For example, if during 1993 $450 million (or 15 percent of the total anticipated $3.0 billion cost to complete) of cost was incurred related to the Space System Contract, $510 million (15 percent of $3.4 billion) of revenue would be recognized.
2. *Earned value.* This method is based on a measure of *total work* required to complete a project, e.g., labor hours or labor dollars). The procedure is often used in government contracting, where large projects are broken into small work packages. At the end of each period, an estimate of total work completed on each work package is made, which allows an estimate of the percent of total work complete on the project. Revenue is then recognized in proportion to total work achieved during the period.
3. *Milestone recognition.* A third alternative is to recognize revenue based on the milestones achieved. In the Space System Contract, revenue equal to the *construction milestone* billings (see Exhibit 2) could have been recognized when the milestones (production outputs) were complete.

One Contract or Two?

A second accounting issue faced by Motorola affected the timing of **expense recognition** for certain expenditures made to develop the IRIDIUM System. A considerable amount (assume greater than $300 million) of design and development expenditures will be incurred early in the project. These design and development expenditures will benefit both the Space System Contract and the O&M Contract. In determining how to allocate the design and development expenditures, Motorola executives had to address a fundamental issue: Whether the Space System Contract and O&M Contract were in substance two separate contracts, or whether the economic events surrounding the contracts made them in essence a single contract.

The accounting implications of the decision are substantial: If the contracts are viewed as a single undertaking, these costs would be recognized over the roughly eleven-year period (from mid-1993 through 2003) over which both contracts extend. If the contracts are viewed as separate, the expenditures would be matched with revenue over the duration of the Space System Contract, and no expenditures would be capitalized and recognized during the period of the O&M Contract. Therefore, the timing of profit recognition is critically dependent upon the perspective taken in regard to these contracts: Viewing the items as a single contract spreads the expenses and makes profit in the initial years much higher than it would be if all the design and development costs are front-loaded to the Space System Contract.

In addressing this issue, Motorola executives were aware of the guidance provided in paragraphs 34 through 38 of the AICPA's Statement of Position (SOP) 81–1, *Accounting for Performance of Construction-Type and Certain Product-Type Contracts.* Paragraph 37 reads in part:

> A group of contracts may be combined for accounting purposes if the contracts . . .
>
> a. Are negotiated as a package in the same economic environment with an overall profit margin objective . . .
> b. Constitute in essence an agreement to do a single project.
> c. Require closely interrelated construction activities with substantial common costs . . .
> d. Are performed concurrently or in a continuous sequence under the same project management . . .

e. Constitute in substance an agreement with a single customer . . .

Contracts that meet all of these criteria may be combined for profit recognition . . .

Required

Now place yourself in the position of an accountant at SATCOM.

A. First, consider the options available to the chief accountant of SATCOM in regard to the timing of revenue recognition. From the alternative percentage-of-completion methods presented, supply the chief accountant with reasoned arguments which favor one procedure over the other two.

B. Second, after considering both sides of the issue, assume a position in regard to whether Motorola should account for the Space System Contract and O&M Contract as one or two contracts. Write a brief memo to the chief accountant of SATCOM (your accounting superior), which:

1. Explains the alternatives, and the potential balance sheet and income statement effects of the alternatives;
2. Sets forth your position;
3. Provides reasons in favor of your position.

Political Costs and Financial Statement Information: Did Pfizer Inc. Manage Its Income?

In this case students analyze selected financial statement information for ***Pfizer Inc.*** to arrive at a position regarding whether Pfizer reduced 1993 earnings to avoid potential government regulation.

"The company did the politically prudent thing at the beginning of the debate over health-care reform. They managed down the numbers."[1]

(***PaineWebber*** drug analyst Ronald M. Nordmann, commenting on Pfizer's 1993 financial statements)

Managed Care and the Drug Industry

Health Care Reform and the Drug Industry

In September 1993, the Clinton Administration initiated Congressional debate on health care by introducing the Health Security Act. Two provisions within the Health Security Act threatened the income of drug manufacturers. First, the proposed legislation contained provisions requiring discounts of around 15 percent for drugs used by Medicare recipients; second, it allowed the secretary of Health and Human Services to exclude certain drugs from the Medicare market if the price was deemed excessive.

Drug companies vehemently opposed these provisions. In discussing these features of the legislation, *The Wall Street Journal* reported:

> Those facets "are price controls, no matter what you call them," said Charles Sanders, chairman and chief executive officer of the U.S. unit of the huge British drug maker, ***Glaxo Holding PLC.*** "They are real show-stoppers for our ability to do innovative Research and Development." . . .

[1]J. Weber, "Did Pfizer Doctor Its Numbers?" *Business Week*, February 14, 1994, p. 34.

Those two regulations weren't unexpected, since the administration has been criticizing drug prices of double the rate of consumer inflation during the 1980s.[2]

Analysts following drug companies were quick to understand that excessive drug company earnings could jeopardize drug industry efforts to derail the Clinton health care proposal. For example, in a 1993 second quarter round-up of industry news, *The Wall Street Journal* characterized one analyst's view of drug company stocks as follows:

> D. Larry Smith at ***Hambrecht & Quist*** came in second (in selecting drug company stocks), with gains in such stocks as Pfizer and ***Alza.*** He still likes Pfizer because he thinks its new-product array looks strong. . . . (But) don't expect brand-name drug companies in general to show much earnings growth soon, he warns. The unfavorable political climate gives the big drug companies little incentive to show earnings growth, he believes. "Showing earnings now is like casting pearls before swine."[3]

As the health care example shows, there are times when companies "in the public eye" may wish to *reduce* earnings in order to avoid or avert government regulation. This is contrary to firms' usual preference of reporting earnings growth to their shareholders and other interested parties. Analysts and academics have long recognized that highly visible firms in the center of public policy debates may adopt accounting procedures that reduce reported net income in order to avoid political costs (such as higher taxes and increased regulation) associated with excessive income.

Pfizer Inc. and Income Management

Pfizer Inc. is an international, research-based health care company. In 1993, the company had four primary divisions: Health Care, which includes prescription pharmaceuticals and hospital products; Consumer Health Care, which includes nonprescription drugs; Animal Health; and Food Science. The company sold the Food Science segment in 1995. In 1993, the Health Care segment comprised 83 percent of the company's sales and 109 percent of the segments' consolidated income. The company's chief executive officer, William Steere, Jr., was chairman of the Pharmaceutical Manufacturers' Association, which is the drug industry's principal Washington lobbying group.

Pfizer reported 1993 income on January 19, 1994. While sales rose from year-earlier levels, net income was down almost 20 percent from 1992 levels. (Sales and income from continuing operations for a ten-year period as reported in 1995 are depicted in Exhibit 1. As the quote at the beginning of this case suggests, analysts suspected that the company had taken steps to reduce earnings in order to avoid possible political consequences of reporting high earnings growth.

Pfizer's comparative income statement and selected cash-flow information as reported in 1993 appear in Exhibit 2; selected information from the notes is contained in Exhibit 3.

[2]M. Waldholz, "Angry Drug Makers Say Rules Would Strangle R&D," *The Wall Street Journal*, September 13, 1993, A6.

[3]E. Tanouye and R. McGough, *The Wall Street Journal*, September 15, 1993, p. R3.

Required

A. Examine Pfizer's income statement. Based upon the readings in Part II of this text, distinguish between income statement revenue and expense items over which management may exercise relatively high degrees of discretion, either in terms of amount or timing.

B. Compute the impact of those items you identified in (**A**) on net income. Discuss the trend in operating income before and after consideration of these items. Also, describe the trend in operating income and operating cash flow (as reported in 1993). Identify possible causes for changes in trends in the two items.

C. Determine whether Pfizer did or did not "manage down the numbers" in 1993. Prepare a brief report explaining your position referring to items identified in (**A**) above.

D. Regardless of the position that you adopted in (**C**), assume that Pfizer did manage its income to provide lower earnings in 1993.

1. Identify stakeholders who may be affected by such income management. What are the potential consequences of such income management to these stakeholders?

2. Would you consider such income management to be ethical? What stakeholders in the firm should Pfizer's management consider prior to arriving at a decision regarding income management? Would your answer to either of these questions change if you held 1,000 shares of Pfizer's common stock?

EXHIBIT 1
Pfizer Inc. Net Sales and Income from Continuing Operations, 1985–1995

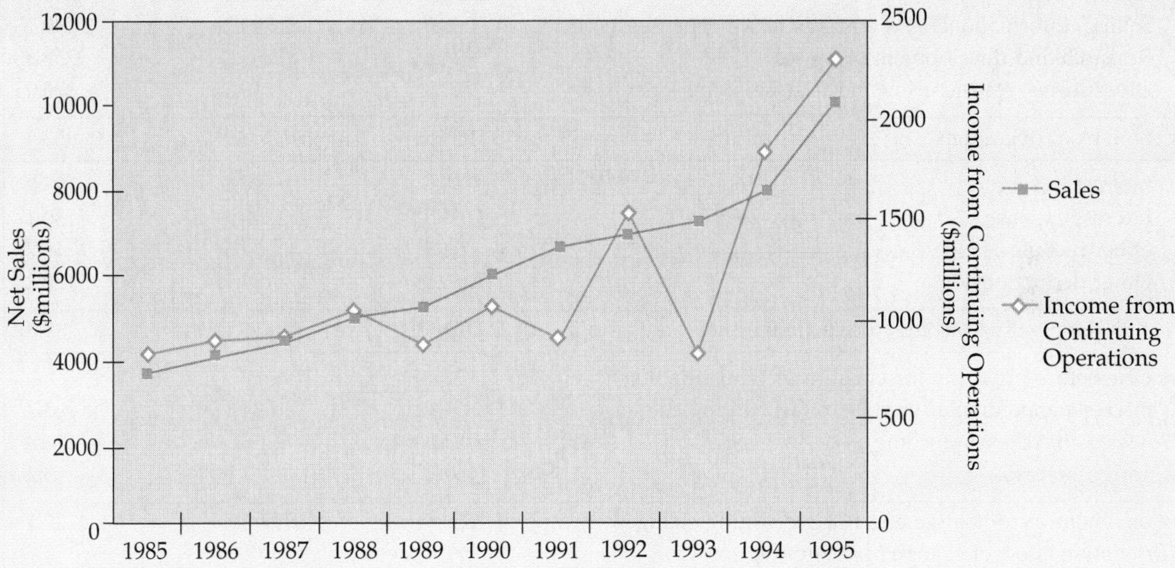

EXHIBIT 2

PFIZER INC.
Consolidated Statement of Income
(in millions of dollars)

	YEAR ENDED DECEMBER 31:		
	1993	1992	1991
Net sales	$7,477.7	$7,230.2	$6,950.0
Operating costs and expenses			
Costs of sales	1,722.0	2,024.3	2,200.6
Selling, informational and administrative expenses	3,066.0	2,899.3	2,739.1
Research and development expenses	974.4	863.2	756.8
Divestitures, restructuring and unusual items—net	752.0	(110.5)	300.0
Income from operations	$ 913.5	$1,553.9	$ 953.5
Interest income	163.5	184.6	193.8
Interest expense	(106.5)	(103.4)	(130.1)
Other income	34.6	34.6	46.7
Other deductions	(153.5)	(134.9)	(120.2)
Nonoperating income/(deductions)—net	$ (61.9)	$ (19.1)	$ (9.8)
Income before provision for taxes on income, minority interests and cumulative effect of accounting changes	851.4	1,534.8	943.7
Provision for taxes on income	191.3	438.6	218.4
Minority interests	2.6	2.7	3.2
Income before cumulative effect of accounting changes	$ 657.5	$1,093.5	$ 722.1
Cumulative effect of change in accounting for:			
Postretirement benefits, net of taxes		(312.6)	
Income taxes		30.0	
Net income	$ 657.5	$ 810.9	$ 722.1

ADDITIONAL SELECTED CASH-FLOW INFORMATION

	1993	1992	1991
Adjustments to reconcile net income to net cash provided by operating activities (selected):			
Divestitures, restructuring and unusual items	$ 752.0	$(110.5)	300.0
Deferred income amortization	(28.3)	(74.3)	(99.9)
Net cash provided by operating activities	1,263.0	807.0	847.6

Exhibit 3

Selected Information from the Financial Statement Notes and the Financial Review

From the notes:

Divestitures, restructuring and unusual items

Income from operations for 1993 includes a charge of $750 million to cover a worldwide restructuring program as well as unusual items. The restructuring is expected to generate substantial savings and, over several years, lead to a worldwide workforce reduction of approximately 3,000 employees. The charge is related to such worldwide actions as consolidation of manufacturing, distribution and administrative infrastructures and staff realignments. Unusual items include the writedown of goodwill [$124.4 million] and anticipated losses associated with certain tangible assets. The writedown of goodwill relates to a business evaluation, where it has now been determined that revenue and profitability levels are not meeting previously estimated levels and unamortized goodwill will not be recovered through future cash flows of the business. . .

Income from operations for 1992 includes a restructuring credit of $110.5 million relating to the divestiture and restructuring of certain of the company's businesses. This consists of a $54.0 million credit representing the gain on the sale of businesses, offset by charges for restructuring, consolidation and streamlining of certain businesses. In addition, curtailment gains of $56.5 million associated with postretirement benefits other than pensions of divested operations were recognized.

Income from operations for 1991 was reduced by a charge of $300 million ($195 million after tax) for potential future ***Shiley*** Convexo/Concave (C/C) heart valve fracture claims . . .

From the Financial Review (Management's Discussion and Analysis)

Health Care Reform Proposal

. . . The Health Security Act includes provisions that would form an Advisory Council on Breakthrough Drugs, require rebates on pharmaceuticals reimbursed under the Medicare program and authorize the Secretary of Health and Human Services to exclude from coverage under Medicare, or require prior authorization for, drugs the Secretary considers to be excessively priced. While these provisions could have an adverse impact on the Company's pharmaceutical business in the U.S., other bills that have been introduced do not contain such provisions. It is uncertain whether legislation will be enacted in 1994 or, if legislation is enacted, whether it will have a significant adverse effect on the Company.

In 1993, the Company's average pharmaceutical price increases in the United States were below the U.S. Consumer Price Index. In addition, the Company has announced that its weighted average U.S. pharmaceutical price increase will be less than 2.5% for 1994.

PART 3

LIQUIDITY AND FINANCIAL FLEXIBILITY

8

Cash and Receivables

Learning Objectives

After studying this chapter, you should be able to:

1. Understand the composition and control of cash.
2. Record and value accounts receivable.
3. Demonstrate how accounts receivable are used as the basis for financing.
4. Record and value notes receivable.
5. Calculate and interpret key liquidity and asset management ratios.

As Its Borrowing Expenses Grow, IBM Plans New Measures to Raise, Save Cash

Now as its stock has recovered from a low, the computer giant is shying away from public offerings and instead plans to raise about $3 billion through a series of novel financing programs. These quick-fix moves are intended to bolster the company's sagging balance sheet and conserve badly needed cash.

The flood of employee departures is greater than IBM planned, increasing the pressure for cash. The company has had to cope with an additional 25,000 unexpected departures, as employees rushed to seize generous benefits before they were curtailed in June; on top of that, the company will shed 35,000 more workers by the end of 1994. To meet these employee obligations, IBM will have to come up with an additional $4.6 billion over the next 16 months, according to the company's second-quarter filings with the Securities and Exchange Commission. A solution outlined by Jerome B. York, IBM's new senior vice-president and chief financial officer, in a July 27 conference with analysts, is intended to raise cash cheaply and conserve it wherever possible.

IBM has already cut its dividend to 25 cents from 54 cents a quarter. Now it will step up the pace of "securitizing" its receivables, selling $1 billion of its uncollected bills in the form of a triple-A rated security. It also will issue new stock for the employee purchase plan, rather than buying on the open market, and will contribute stock to the pension fund instead of cash. These share issuances combined will add more than $1 billion to IBM's shrunken equity.

Source: Laura Jereski, "As Its Borrowing Expenses Grow, IBM Plans New Measures to Raise, Save Cash," *The Wall Street Journal,* September 7, 1993, pp. C1, C2.

Cash and receivables are important components of assets in that they provide the liquidity necessary for an enterprise to carry on its daily operations. Converting receivables into cash through efficient collection procedures is essential to the survival of the enterprise. Without the liquidity provided by cash, even a fundamentally sound business will find it extremely difficult to survive in the short term.

Even old, well-established companies must pay attention to their liquidity position. ***IBM*** (*www.swcollege.com/hartman.html*) was long considered to be one of the very best companies, but during the early 1990s it had some very serious business problems. To deal with these problems and provide a basis for the future, IBM was forced to take several steps to conserve existing cash and improve future cash flows. These steps are described in the accompanying excerpted article.

Revenue generation is important to an enterprise. Turning that revenue into cash is critical if the business is to meet the going-concern assumption. The focus of this chapter is on cash and receivables and on the part they play in the liquidity of an enterprise.

COMPOSITION AND CONTROL OF CASH

COMPOSITION OF CASH

Cash generally means money, the coin and currency used as the medium of exchange in the country in which the enterprise does business. This is in

Understand the composition and control of cash.

keeping with the monetary-unit assumption, but each country measures its monetary units in a different denomination. These different denominations (or currencies) can themselves be freely traded and be a source of profit or loss. As the internationalization of business increases, the monetary units and denominations of different countries become increasingly important, as indicated in the accompanying In Practice excerpt.

IN PRACTICE—INTERNATIONAL

International Monetary Units

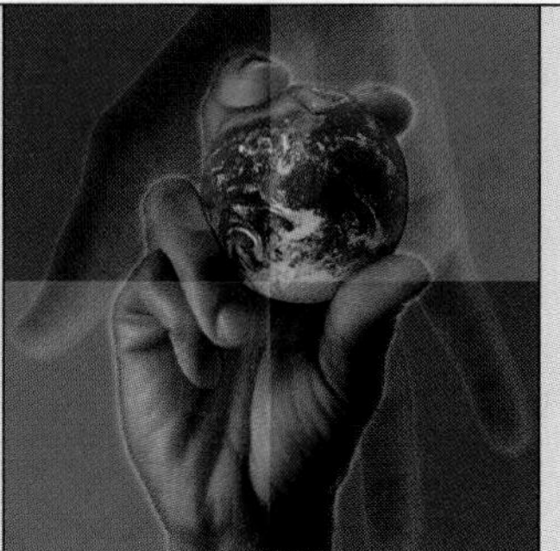

London, November 23—Europe's monetary system looked more shaky than ever as governments and central banks battled to head off another full-fledged currency crisis.

Spain, Ireland, and Norway all raised interest rates to bolster their currencies, and Denmark said it would raise rates if necessary. There was some pressure on currencies generally considered strong. The Bank of France, for example, felt compelled to intervene in the market to support the franc.

The European Community sought to ease the strains in the system by devaluing the Spanish peseta and the Portuguese escudo. But the continuing vulnerability of a number of currencies and the defensive measures adopted by central banks illustrated the skittishness gripping the currency markets.

The monetary system had been designed as a precursor to European monetary union and served as the centerpiece of European cooperation, before being battered by waves of speculative selling. Britain and Italy, unable to defend the values of their currencies, were forced at that time to withdraw entirely from the system of semifixed exchange rates.

"The history of fixed exchange rate systems is that they give way under the pressure of prolonged recessions," said David Morrison, an economist at ***Goldman, Sachs & Company*** in London.

Central banks can seek to support their currencies by buying them on the open market, but this crisis showed just how quickly foreign exchange reserves can be exhausted in the face of huge speculative capital flows.

Source: Richard W. Stevenson, "Europe's Monetary System Is Staring at Another Crisis," *The New York Times*, November 24, 1992, pp. D1 and D15.

Because cash is a medium of exchange, it is the most liquid of all assets and is used to acquire other assets and liquidate debt. In accounting, cash also includes demand deposits (checking accounts), cashiers' checks, certified checks, money orders, personal checks, bank drafts, petty cash, and any foreign currency that is freely convertible and usable. Savings accounts technically are short-term investments but frequently are classified as cash.

Other current assets are *near cash*, but they are not included as part of cash because they lack instant liquidity. Such items as postage stamps, postdated checks, certificates of deposit (CDs), and IOUs are examples of these near-cash items. Cash funds restricted for special uses are not considered cash, since they can be used only for specific purposes. These are either current or long-term assets depending on the date the funds become available for use.

Many companies use a balance sheet classification of *cash and cash equivalents*. Frequently companies invest temporarily in-excess cash as part of their cash management policy and fully intend to use the cash proceeds from these investments to meet current operating needs. **Cash equivalents** are short-term investments with very high liquidity that must meet two tests:

1. They are readily converted into a certain sum of cash.
2. They are so close to maturity that any change in interest rate is remote.

Treasury bills, commercial paper, and certificates of deposit purchased within 90 days of maturity are considered cash equivalents.

CONTROL OF CASH

Because of its liquid nature and vulnerability to theft or misappropriation, cash usually is subject to many internal controls. Some of these controls and their accounting implications are discussed here.

Petty Cash Funds. Most companies have a petty cash account for small-dollar purchases and transactions, either a petty cash checking account or an imprest petty cash fund. In a *petty cash checking account,* individual checks are limited to a relatively small amount, depending upon the size of the company. The types of transactions covered by the use of these funds usually are restricted by specific policies of the company. A more common type of petty cash fund is an imprest system.

Imprest petty cash funds provide a means of paying for small expenditures and purchases evidenced by vouchers or receipts. The size of the fund is limited to relatively small amounts in relation to the size of the organization. Some fund balances may be less than $100, while others may be $1,000 or more. The amount is determined by how often the fund is to be replenished, the estimated number of transactions per period, and the average expenditure. The fund is established with a fixed sum and periodically replenished based upon an approved request by the person responsible for administering the fund. The request to bring the fund back to its authorized cash balance is supported by signed vouchers or receipts, which provide control. As an example, assume that Craft Industries establishes a petty cash fund for $200 on October 1, 1998, and makes the following disbursements out of the fund during October:

Supplies	$ 40
Postage stamps	29
Delivery charges	35
Blacktop repair	65
Total disbursements	$169

The journal entries to establish the fund and, subsequently, to replenish it are as follows:

1998			
Oct. 1	Petty Cash	200	
	Cash		200
	To establish fund.		
31	Supplies Expense	40	
	Postage Expense	29	
	Delivery Expense	35	
	Repairs Expense	65	
	Cash		169
	To replenish fund.		

Occasionally the amount of cash on hand and the receipts and vouchers total to an amount different from the authorized fund balance. The difference is either debited or credited to a Cash Short or Over account, which is reported as a miscellaneous expense or revenue.

Bank Checking Accounts. Checking accounts provide an excellent means of cash control. After cash funds are deposited in the bank account, disbursal is made through prearranged procedures such as authorized single or dual signatures on checks. Today electronic transfers of funds are also becoming more common.

As an example, *lock boxes* are increasingly being used to speed up the availability of funds that have been remitted to a company. To set up a lock-box system, a bank is authorized to collect checks remitted to a company's post office box address in the customer's geographic region. The address could also be that of the bank. Daily the bank deposits the funds and makes electronic transfers to the company's central banking account. This procedure reduces the time in the mail (*mail float time*), makes the funds received by the bank immediately available to the company, and increases the interest earned on these funds.

Bank Statement Reconciliation. Each month a bank statement is typically sent to depositors of demand accounts. Upon its receipt, a bank reconciliation of the differences (if any) between the cash balance as shown by the bank and the cash balance reflected on the books of the organization should be made. For most organizations the Cash account has more activity than any other account, making the reconciliation process extremely important, since it helps maintain control of cash.

The proper method of reconciliation is to bring both balances up to date, reflecting the correct cash amount, a point at which the book balance and bank balance should be the same. This method highlights the adjustments required to bring the book balance to the true cash position at the date of reconciliation. The book balance also could be reconciled to the bank balance or the bank to the books. Neither of these procedures, however, will provide the correct cash balance at the financial statement date.

Exhibit 8–1 illustrates a **bank reconciliation** in which both the bank balance and the book balance are brought to the true cash-available position. To adjust the bank balance, any checks outstanding are deducted and deposits in transit added. Any errors made by the bank also must be corrected. The most frequent adjustments to the book balance are for bank service charges, interest earned on the account, errors made in the books, and checks returned by the bank as **nonsufficient funds (NSF) checks**. These are customer checks deposited in an account that have been returned to the depositor's bank because they failed to clear the customer's bank. Note that any correction to the book balance requires an adjusting entry to correct the Cash account. Any adjustments to the bank balance will be made by the bank and do not require adjusting entries on the company books.

There are other controls for cash as well. They are part of the company's normal system of internal control and are topics for auditing and systems courses.

EXHIBIT 8–1
Bank Statement Reconciliation

Data:

1. Balance per books, 9/30/95 $3,185
2. Balance per bank statement, 9/30/95 3,254
3. Checks not cleared by bank at 9/30/95:

CHECK NO.	AMOUNT
10087	$ 8
10094	24
10097	30
10098	68
10099	52

4. Customer check returned by bank as NSF ($25)
5. Bank service charge for September ($5)
6. Interest earned on account credited by bank ($16)
7. Deposits not yet credited by bank ($100)
8. Posting error made on Check No. 10089, written as $58 but posted as $59 to Supplies Expense.

Bank Reconciliation

Balance per books, September 30, 1995		$3,185
Adjust for items on bank statement, not on books:		
Add: Interest earned during September	$16	
Check No. 10089 written as $58 but recorded as $59	1	17
		$3,202
Deduct: Bank service charges	$ 5	
Check deposited September 25 and returned NSF	25	30
Corrected book balance		$3,172
Balance per bank statement		$3,254
Adjust for items on books, not on bank statement:		
Add: Deposits in transit (September 30)		100
		$3,354
Deduct: Outstanding checks		
No. 10087	$ 8	
No. 10094	24	
No. 10097	30	
No. 10098	68	
No. 10099	52	182
Corrected bank balance		$3,172

Adjusting entry to bring the Cash account to the proper balance.

Accounts Receivable	25	
Service Charge Expense	5	
Interest Income		16
Supplies Expense		1
Cash		13

ACCOUNTS RECEIVABLE

Accounts receivable are current assets that result from sales or services rendered to another person or company in the normal course of business. Accounts receivable facilitate the process of doing business between entities. Rather than wait for the actual transfer of cash to consummate a deal, the company making the sale or rendering the service agrees, by prior arrangement, to make an unsecured short-term loan to the customer. While steps such as credit checks and investigations before credit is extended are taken to minimize possible losses from such practices, some risk of nonpayment always is present. The capital markets and lenders frequently look to the quality of a company's accounts receivable in assessing risk in relation to the market price of the stock and interest rates for loans. The In Practice excerpt illustrates the importance of the quality of accounts receivable.

To increase the quality of their receivables, firms frequently offer sales terms that include some inducement for early payment. Terms such as *2/10, n/30* indicate that a 2% discount will be allowed if payment is made within 10 days of the sale, with the balance due in 30 days. As a practical matter, if the discount is not taken, the likelihood of receiving the funds within 30 days drops drastically. Failure to take such discounts is extremely costly to the buyer and is an indication that the buyer may have cash flow problems, bad management, or both. Companies that habitually forgo discounts seem to be of higher credit risk, and some firms have adopted the policy of refusing credit to those companies that regularly fail to take discounts.

RECORDING ACCOUNTS RECEIVABLE

2 Record and value accounts receivable.

Accounts receivable are similar to other assets in that they represent future economic benefits to the company. Two acceptable methods of initially recording accounts receivable, the gross method and the net method, are presented in Exhibit 8–2. The gross method records the sale at the invoice price without taking into consideration any possible discounts for early payment. If the buyer pays within the discount period, a Sales Discounts account reflects the difference between the cash received and the recorded receivable. The Sales Discount account appears as a *contra account to sales revenue.* If the buyer forfeits the discount, there is no record that the sales discount has not been taken.

In contrast, the net method records the sale at the invoice price less the amount of the discount. If the buyer pays within the discount period, both Cash and Accounts Receivable are recorded at the amount received. If the buyer forfeits the discount, the discount not taken is recorded and accumulated in an account called Sales Discounts Forfeited.

Although the gross method is common in practice, conceptually, the net method is more appealing. The cash selling price (net of discount) is the sales price of the product. Companies that fail to make payment within the discount period are in substance paying interest for the use of money. If the credit terms are 2/10, n/30, the buyer is paying 2% interest to use the money for the extra days from the 10th day to the 30th day (an extra 20 days). This is equivalent to an annual percentage rate of 36.5% (365 days/20 days × 2%).

If payment is made after the discount period, Sales Discounts Forfeited is credited and treated as a separate revenue account in the "Other Revenue and

IN PRACTICE—GENERAL

The Importance of Accounts Receivable

For an entire generation of Americans, Brooklyn's ***Topps Company, Inc.,*** had the sports card market to itself. But competitors weighed in during the 1980s when collectors were paying thousands of dollars for old baseball cards, thereby helping create new interest in baseball and other sports cards. Today as many as 100 competitors vie for pieces of the $1.4 billion (annual retail sales) sports and entertainment card market.

With a 32% market share, Topps remains the biggest player. . . .

But trouble may be brewing for Topps. The card publishing business is inherently risky because sales to wholesalers and retailers—which account for about 70% of cards shipped by Topps—can be returned to the manufacturer. (Only hobby dealers have no right to make returns.)

Ominously, for four consecutive quarters Topps' accounts receivable have risen steadily. In the past two quarters, receivables have risen over 50% while sales have gone down. Says Howard Schilit, American University accounting professor who looked at Topps' books, "When I see receivables going up so much faster than sales, I'm very suspicious."

Is Topps having trouble collecting from its wholesalers? Are some wholesalers waiting to see how the cards sell before they pay? And will they end up "burying" Topps in unwanted inventory? John Perillo, Topps chief financial officer, says no. He says that Topps still gets paid every 21 days. He adds that receivables appear to be rising only because Topps has been shipping nearly 50% of its cards in the final few weeks of each quarter, leaving huge receivables on the books at quarter's end. The increased receivables are really just an accident of bookkeeping timing, says Perillo, who adds that Topps changed its shipping schedules in the past year.

Some of Topps' competitors find this explanation hard to swallow. And Lou J. Biggs, senior buyer for ***Weeke Wholesale Company*** in Fairview Heights, Illinois, says that in 1990 his Topps cards sold out in six months. This year, he says, it has taken him eight months to get rid of 74%, and he's returning the balance—around 30% more of the 55-cent cards than last year, and 5% to 10% more of Topps's premium priced cards.

Topps books its sales, less a reserve for returns, as soon as it ships its products. Topps is not required to disclose its reserves in its quarterly reports, and any charges accumulated over the year are deducted from the reserve at year-end. If the actual returns are higher than the amount reserved, the difference is charged against earnings.

Perillo insists Topps' overall returns won't increase as a percentage of sales this year. But shareholders won't really know the score until after Topps' current fiscal year ends, on February 27. . . .

Many security analysts who follow Topps say they expect no sizable write-off this year. They predict fiscal 1993 earnings of $1.35 a share, versus $1.15 in 1992. But if Topps' reserves against returns prove inadequate, the company's stock, recently trading at $15 per share, will take a pounding. . . .

Since January, Topps' insiders have unloaded over 700,000 shares—1.5% of the company's outstanding stock —at prices from $15\frac{5}{8}$ to $19\frac{1}{2}$. They may know something.

Source: Roula Khalaf, "Card Glut," *Forbes,* December 21, 1992, p. 39.

Expense" section of the income statement. Recording Sales Discounts Forfeited as a separate revenue account properly reflects the sources of income from the business transaction. One part of the transaction results in revenue from the sale of a product or service, and the other part results in interest from extending additional credit.

As previously indicated, the collectibility of an account deteriorates if the discount is not taken. As the account gets older, the probability of collection diminishes. Estimating uncollectible accounts receivable is discussed next.

EXHIBIT 8–2
Gross Versus Net Method of Recording Accounts Receivable

	(a) Gross Method		(b) Net Method	
1. To record sales of $100, terms, 2/10, n/30				
Accounts Receivable	100		98	
Sales		100		98
2. Collection within discount period				
Cash	98		98	
Sales Discounts	**2**			
Accounts Receivable		100		98
3. Collection after discount period expires				
Cash	100		100	
Accounts Receivable		100		98
Sales Discounts Forfeited				**2**

(a) Assumes discounts will not be taken and thus captures Sales Discounts taken (a contra-revenue account).
(b) Assumes discounts will be taken and thus captures Sales Discounts Forfeited (a miscellaneous revenue account).

VALUATION OF ACCOUNTS RECEIVABLE

Accounts receivable normally are reported at *net realizable value* (the amount expected to be realized at the time of collection). Net realizable value for accounts receivable is approximated by establishing an Allowance for Bad Debts account with a corresponding charge to bad debts expense in an adjusting entry at the end of the period. At issue is the amount to charge in the entry. Two generally recognized methods of estimating bad debts are the percentage-of-sales method and the percentage-of-accounts-receivable method, both of which will be discussed. The percentage-of-sales method is based on sales revenue and reflects an income statement approach. The percentage-of-receivables method is based on an asset (accounts receivable) and reflects a balance sheet approach.

Percentage-of-Sales Method. The percentage-of-sales method is consistent with the matching principle. The expense for the credit losses is recognized in the same period that the sales are made, thus achieving a proper matching of revenue and expense. The percentage of sales estimated to be uncollectible is based on past experience or industry averages. The percentage is multiplied by the sales for the period to obtain an estimate of bad debts.[1] As an example, assume that historically 3% of sales proved uncollectible. If the sales for the current period are $1,000,000, then the adjusting entry for estimated bad debts is:

Bad Debts Expense	30,000	
Allowance for Bad Debts		30,000
(3% × $1,000,000)		

[1]If the company separates credit and cash sales, the credit sales amount would be used as the basis for determination of bad debts. Most companies use total sales because they do not distinguish between cash and credit sales.

CONCEPT Expense recognition and matching.

LOGIC The matching principle attempts to match costs incurred in the period that associated revenues are generated. Bad debts are a result of revenues generated by the extension of credit. These costs should be matched to the period in which the credit is extended and the sales are reported.

The Bad Debts Expense account is an income statement expense item, while the Allowance for Bad Debts account is a balance sheet account contra to Accounts Receivable. Assume that $600,000 of the credit sales remain uncollected at the end of the period and the balance in Allowance for Bad Debts is $30,000 after this adjusting entry. Net receivables then would be reported on the balance sheet at their estimated net realizable value of $570,000. The net realizable value provides an estimate of future cash flows that will be generated from accounts receivable and reflects management's assessment of the risk inherent in providing credit.

Percentage-of-Receivables Method. The percentage-of-receivables method of estimating bad debts relies on an examination of the asset, accounts receivable, through a process referred to as *aging*. The usual method of aging accounts receivable, illustrated in Exhibit 8–3, is to place each customer's account into a group or partition based on the age of the transactions. The total of each group represents all unpaid transactions in that age category. The age category total is multiplied by a percentage estimated from experience or perhaps from industry averages in order to determine an estimate of bad debts. The percentage generally increases as the accounts get older because older accounts are more difficult to collect. The total estimated uncollectible accounts of each of the separate age categories represent the estimated desired balance for the Allowance for Bad Debts account. Any difference between the estimated desired balance and the current balance is the required adjustment to the Allowance account. This adjustment is the bad debts expense for the period.

As shown in Exhibit 8–3, the balance before adjustment (or current balance) in the Allowance account is $3,000, and the estimated amount necessary to absorb future write-offs per the accounts receivable aging schedule is $15,500.

A simpler version of the aging method treats the entire balance of accounts receivable as a single age group and estimates the allowance as a single percentage of total accounts receivable. For example, assume that 9% of all receivables is estimated as uncollectible. Then $16,200 (.09 × $180,000) of the total receivables shown in Exhibit 8–3 would be the required balance for the Allowance account (rather than $15,500). The amount for the adjusting entry becomes $13,200 ($16,200 − $3,000).

Both the percentage-of-sales and percentage-of-receivables methods intend to match revenue and expense in the proper period, and both methods intend to properly report net realizable value for financial statement purposes. The main conceptual difference between the two is the basis for calculation and resulting statement orientation. The sales method is based on a revenue account (sales) and is income statement oriented in that the main focus is matching the expense of uncollectible accounts to the period in which revenues from sales are generated

EXHIBIT 8–3 Aging Accounts Receivable

NAME	AMOUNT	CURRENT	30 TO 60 DAYS OLD	61 TO 90 DAYS OLD	91 TO 180 DAYS OL	
J. Adams	$ 500	$ 400	$ 100			
B. Bang	800		300	$ 500		
S. Crane	300	100	200			
W. Duck	1,200		300	400	$ 500	
O. Eider	1,000		500	300	200	
.	.	.	.	.	.	.
.	.	.	.	.	.	.
T. Zyke	900	500	400			
(1) Totals[a]	$180,000	$70,000	$40,000	$30,000	$30,000	$10,000
(2) Likelihood of default[b]		0	.05	0.1	0.25	0.3
(3) Amount expected to be uncollectible[c]	$ 15,500	$ 0	$ 2,000	$ 3,000	$ 7,500	$ 3,000

ALLOWANCE FOR BAD DEBTS

	3,000 Balance before adjustment
	12,500 Adjusting entry*
	15,500 Required ending balance

[a]Total of age group.
[b]Likelihood of default is based on prior experience of company or on industry average.
[c]Amount expected to be uncollectible is the product of row (1) × row (2).
*Adjusting Entry:

Bad Debts Expense	12,500	
Allowance for Bad Debts		12,500

Balance sheet presentation:

Accounts receivable	$180,000	
Less: Allowance for bad debts	(15,500)	$164,500

and recognized. That is, a relatively stable relationship between bad debts expense and sales is maintained, but the relationship between accounts receivable and the allowance for bad debts can fluctuate. The percentage-of-receivables method is based on an asset (accounts receivable) and is balance sheet oriented in that the main focus is the proper valuation of the accounts receivable balance. The relationship between accounts receivable and the allowance is maintained, but the relationship between bad debts expense and sales can fluctuate.

Many firms use both methods. During the year, the sales method is used for interim reporting, and the aging method is used to determine year-end values for financial statement purposes. Regardless of which method is used for estimating bad debts expense, the actual write-off of an uncollectible account is the same. The Allowance account is reduced (debited) and the Accounts Receivable account is also reduced (credited) for the amount determined uncollectible. For example, assume that the balance of O. Eider's account from Exhibit 8–3 is deemed to be uncollectible in the amount of $1,000. The entry to write it off is as follows:

Allowance for Bad Debts	1,000	
Accounts Receivable—Eider		1,000

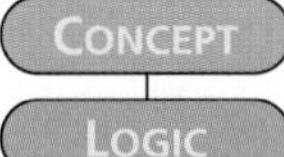

Expense recognition and matching.

The asset has no value and is written off. The expense was recognized previously when the adjusting entry for bad debts was made at the end of the period.

Note that the charge in this entry is to the allowance account, not to an expense account. The net receivables are unchanged. The expense for the bad debt was recognized in the same period the sale was made via the adjusting entry for bad debts, thus achieving a proper matching of revenue and expense. If O. Eider subsequently pays the amount written off, the entry will be reversed to reestablish the account, and the normal entry, debiting cash and crediting Accounts Receivable, will be made.

An alternative to the allowance methods illustrated here is the direct write-off method, which is not accrual-based. For the same reasons that cash-basis accounting is not consistent with GAAP, neither is the direct write-off method. Any bad debts are charged directly to expense and removed from the receivables account at the time the account becomes uncollectible in this method. No attempt is made to match the expense with the period in which the sales revenue was recognized. An example of the direct write-off method is:

Bad Debts Expense	1,000	
Accounts Receivable—Eider		1,000

FINANCING WITH RECEIVABLES

Some firms use their receivables as an immediate source of cash, either by *assigning* them as collateral for a loan or by *factoring* (selling) them. If the receivables are sold, they can be sold either with or *without recourse*. Recourse refers to the ultimate responsibility for payment of the debt. If the receivable is transferred without recourse, the buyer of the receivable assumes all responsibility in the event of default. If the receivable is transferred with recourse, the seller of the receivable is liable for payment in the event of default, which creates a contingent liability for the seller.

Demonstrate how accounts receivable are used as the basis for financing.

ASSIGNMENT OF RECEIVABLES

Accounts receivable used as collateral for loans are referred to as accounts receivable assigned. The amount of the loan is usually a percentage of the face value of the assigned receivables, with interest charged by the lender at an agreed-upon rate on the outstanding balance of the loan. Both the interest rate charged and the percentage of the assigned receivables loaned are a function of the lender's assessment of risk. The higher the perceived risk, the higher the interest rate and the lower the percentage loaned on the assigned receivables. The arrangement typically calls for the borrower to collect the receivables in the normal course of business and to remit the collections to the lender.

Assume that on April 1, 1998, Dean Corporation arranges an $80,000 loan at 12% interest using receivables with a face value of $100,000 as collateral. At the time the loan is received, a fee of $1,200 is charged to process the loan by the lender. Dean would make two journal entries on April 1. One entry would record the cash received, the financing charge, and the liability. The second entry would reclassify the pledged accounts receivable.

1998			
Apr. 1	Cash	78,800	
	Financing Expense	1,200	
	Notes Payable		80,000
1	Accounts Receivable Assigned	100,000	
	Accounts Receivable		100,000

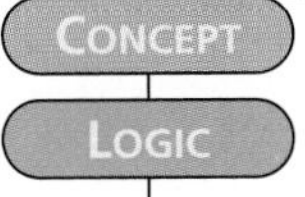

Proper classification of assets.

Future benefits of this asset (accounts receivable) are no longer available to use. By reclassifying the accounts receivable, Dean is disclosing to statement readers that cash inflows from Accounts Receivable Assigned will be used to reduce collateralized debt and will not be available for other corporate uses.

Exhibit 8–4 illustrates the balance sheet presentation of assigned accounts receivable. Notice that the note payable is reported as a contra account to reduce the reported book value of assigned accounts; it is not reported with other liabilities. This is an unusual classification of a liability. The note payable is classified in this manner because the asset (assigned accounts receivable) must be reported at the value of the future benefit. That value is the face amount of the receivables less the amount of the note.

As the receivables subsequently are collected, Dean must periodically remit the proceeds to the lender. After the entire loan is repaid with interest, any remaining accounts receivable assigned will be reclassified to accounts receivable. To illustrate, assume that Dean uses the gross method and that $60,000 of the

EXHIBIT 8–4
Partial Balance Sheet of Dean Corporation

DEAN CORPORATION
Partial Balance Sheet
April 1

Accounts receivable		$250,000
Accounts receivable assigned	$100,000	
Less: Notes payable	80,000	
Equity in accounts receivable assigned		20,000
Total accounts receivable		$270,000

assigned receivables are collected during April, half of which are subject to a 2% sales discount. Assume also that sales returns are $1,000. During May, an additional $30,000 is collected without any discounts or returns. Funds collected are remitted to the lender on the 1st of the following month. The note is fully paid on June 1. The journal entries to record these transactions in April, May, and June follow.

During April	Cash	58,400	
	Sales Returns and Allowances	1,000	
	Sales Discounts	600*	
	Accounts Receivable Assigned		60,000
	To record collections in April.		
	\$60,000 × .5 × .02 = \$600		
May 1	Interest Expense	789*	
	Notes Payable	57,611**	
	Cash		58,400
	To record remittance on May 1.		
	*(\$80,000 × .12 × 30)/365 = \$789		
	**\$58,400 − \$789 = \$57,611		
During May	Cash	30,000	
	Accounts Receivable Assigned		30,000
	To record collections in May.		
June 1	Interest Expense	228*	
	Notes Payable	22,389**	
	Cash		22,617
	To record remittance on June 1.		
	*(22,389 × .12 × 31)/365 = \$228		
	**\$80,000 − \$57,611 = \$22,389		
	Accounts Receivable	10,000	
	Accounts Receivable Assigned		10,000
	To reclassify remaining accounts.		

FACTORING ACCOUNTS RECEIVABLE

A second method of obtaining cash from receivables is by transferring them to a *factor*. This process is known as **factoring receivables**, and the key accounting issue is to determine whether the transaction results in the sale of an asset. The In Practice excerpt from ***Black Enterprises*** relates how a company regularly transferred its receivables to a third party. The question at issue is whether the company in this instance sold an asset (the receivables) or simply borrowed money by pledging some of the firm's assets as collateral. Should a revenue-generating asset sale be recognized or should a liability be recognized?

Transfer of a receivable without recourse usually is treated as a sale, but transfer with recourse can result in treatment as either a sale or a borrowing, depending on the conditions of the transfer. Exhibit 8–5 provides a general framework of accounting for factoring of accounts receivable; the next sections describe this framework.

Factoring Without Recourse. Factoring without recourse is normally treated as a sale of the receivables because the factor bears the risk and benefits from the collection of the receivables. Because an asset has been sold, the difference between the sales price and the book value is gain or loss. Historically, firms

IN PRACTICE—GENERAL

CAPITAL IDEAS—Alternative Financing

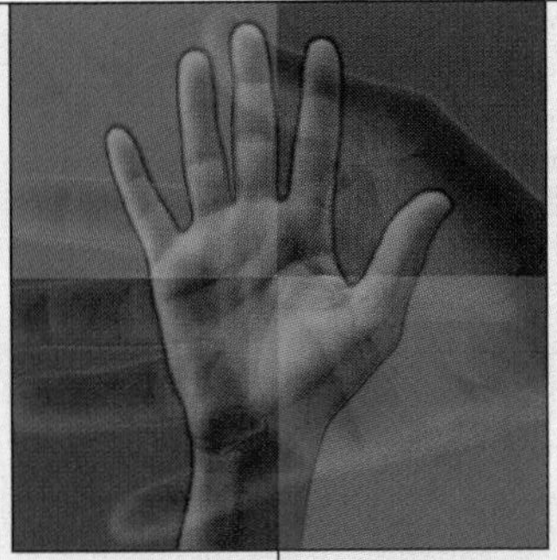

Factoring Your Way Out of a Cash Crunch. "As sales increase, the cost to pay for the goods increases. If we don't get paid for 45 to 60 days after a shipment, then there's a big gap [in our cash flows]," says company president Spencer L. Perry Jr. To help remedy this problem, ***Young Nation*** entered into an agreement with a factor. So, instead of having to wait more than 30 days to get paid on a product already delivered, the company sold its receivables to a third party investor or factor.

Companies typically known for factoring have been in the textile and apparel industries. But today, "just about any type of business has the potential to benefit from factoring," says Anthony Jones, a certified factor specialist and president of ***International Fidelity Mortgage Co.*** in Dewitt, N.Y. A typical business that extends credit will have 10% to 20% of its annual sales tied up in accounts receivables at any given point in time, adds Jones. "Just think for a moment about how much money is tied up in 60 days' worth of receivables. You can't pay the electric bill or this week's payroll with a customer's invoice. But you can sell that invoice for the cash to meet those obligations.

Source: C.M.B., *Black Enterprises,* September 1994, p. 28.

in the garment industry have used the factoring process to obtain cash for operating purposes while avoiding the burden of collecting the receivables. The factor pays some percentage of the face value of the receivables to the seller. Either party may *service* the account, that is, collect the receivables.

The seller usually receives less than the face amount of the receivables from the factor, resulting in a loss to the seller. However, when receivables that have interest charges, like credit card receivables, are factored, a gain is possible. The factor is purchasing not only the face value of the receivables but future interest charges on them as well.

Frequently the factor withholds some of the proceeds due the seller in order to absorb any adjustments for sales discounts, returns, and allowances. As an example, assume that Olin Inc. factors $100,000 of accounts receivable without recourse to Financo. The finance charge is 15% of the face amount of the receivables, an additional 10% is withheld for sales adjustments, and Financo will service the accounts. The journal entries to record these events on both sets of books follow:

Olin Books:

Account	Debit	Credit
Cash	75,000	
Loss on Sale of Receivables	15,000*	
Receivable From Financo	10,000**	
Accounts Receivable		100,000

**$100,000 × 15% = $15,000*
***$100,000 × 10% = $10,000*

Financo Books:

Account	Debit	Credit
Accounts Receivable	100,000	
Payable to Olin		10,000
Financing Revenue		15,000
Cash		75,000

EXHIBIT 8–5
Factoring of Accounts Receivable

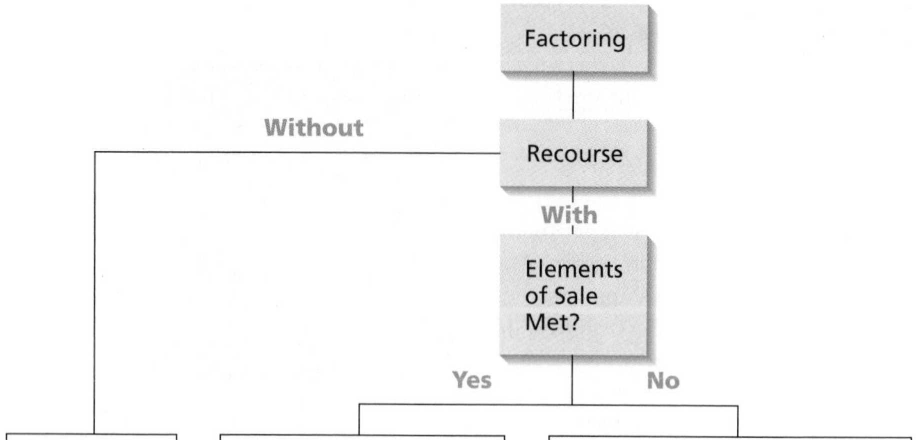

Factoring → Recourse
Without → Treat as sale. No contingent liability exists.
With → Elements of Sale Met?
Yes → Treat as sale. Even though Contingent liability exists.
No → Treat as borrowing. Contingent liability exists.

	Without recourse	With recourse — Yes	With recourse — No
Accounting Treatment	Treat as sale. No contingent liability exists.	Treat as sale. Even though Contingent liability exists.	Treat as borrowing. Contingent liability exists.
Entries: At Factor date	Cash Loss on Sale A/R	Cash Loss on Sale A/R	Cash Interest Expense Liability for Transferred A/R
Collection of Accounts Receivable	No entry	No entry	Liability for Transferred A/R A/R
Default on Accounts Receivable	No entry	Allowance for Bad Debts or A/R—Defaulted Cash	Allowance for Bad Debts or A/R—Defaulted Cash Liability for Transferred A/R Accounts Receivable

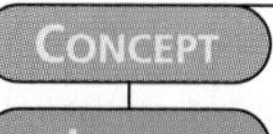

Recognition of loss at completion of earnings process.

The earnings process is completed because Olin sold the asset (receivables) for cash. The sale was for less than book value; therefore, a loss is recognized at the time of the transfer of the receivables. A loss is recognized instead of financing expense because Olin could have held the asset until the full amount was paid; instead, Olin chose to sell the receivables and settle for less money, thus incurring a loss on the sale. Financo treats this as revenue because Financo is in the business of extending credit. This is part of its normal business operations.

Assume that the factor (Financo) collects all of the accounts receivable except $3,000 that are uncollectible and $1,000 of sales discounts that are taken. Assume also that sales returns and allowances on the factored accounts amount to $2,000, and Financo remits the balance of $7,000 to settle the account with Olin. The entries to record these events are:

Financo Books:

	Debit	Credit
Cash	94,000	
Bad Debts Expense*	3,000	
Payable to Olin	3,000	
Accounts Receivable		100,000
**Or Allowance for Bad Debts if previously established ($1,000 + $2,000).*		
Payable to Olin	7,000	
Cash		7,000

Olin Books:

	Debit	Credit
Cash	7,000	
Sales Returns and Allowances	2,000	
Sales Discounts	1,000	
Receivable From Financo		10,000

Factoring With Recourse. When accounts receivable are factored with recourse, uncollectible accounts are absorbed by the transferor. However, under current GAAP (SFAS No. 77), the transfer is treated as a sale if all the following conditions of a sale are met:

1. The risk, rewards, and benefits are transferred.
2. The future cash outflows and inflows are reasonably estimable at the date of the transfer.
3. The transferee cannot require the transferor to repurchase the receivables except pursuant to recourse provisions.

Factoring With Recourse Treated as Sale. As shown in Exhibit 8–5, if the transfer of the receivables meets the conditions of a sale, the transaction will be treated the same as a transfer of receivables without recourse except for the bad debts expense. There is no difference, because if the conditions of the sale are met, the seller (Olin) has given up the rights of ownership. These rights and risks of ownership have been assumed by the factor (Financo). Olin (the transferor) will be liable for any uncollectible receivables, and this should be disclosed in the notes to the financial statements.

As shown in Exhibit 8–5, when uncollectible receivables occur, the expense or loss is borne by the seller. Thus, unlike the previous example, Financo would not record bad debts expense and would reduce the amount payable to Olin:

Financo Books:

	Debit	Credit
Cash	94,000	
Payable to Olin	6,000*	
Accounts Receivable		100,000
**$3,000 + $1,000 + $2,000 = $6,000*		
Payable to Olin	4,000	
Cash		4,000

Olin Books:

	Debit	Credit
Cash	4,000	
Bad Debts Expense*	3,000	
Sales Returns and Allowances	2,000	
Sales Discounts	1,000	
Receivable From Financo		10,000
**or Allowance for Bad Debts*		

Factoring With Recourse Treated as Borrowing. If the transfer of the receivables does not meet the conditions of a sale, then it is treated as a borrowing. As indicated in Exhibit 8–5, there are two differences in the accounting treatment: (1) instead of crediting the Accounts Receivable account upon the transfer of the receivables, an account called Liability on Transferred Accounts Receivable is credited; and (2) instead of recognizing a loss on the sale of the receivables, an expense account called Interest Expense or Discount on Transferred Accounts is used. Factoring of accounts receivable with recourse treated as a borrowing is illustrated using the same example as the Olin and Financo example for transfer without recourse. The journal entries on both sets of books assuming a borrowing instead of a sale upon the transfer of the receivables follow:

Olin Books:			
	Cash	75,000	
	Discount on Transfer of Receivables	15,000	
	Receivable From Financo	10,000	
	Liability for Transferred Receivables		100,000
Financo Books:			
	Accounts Receivable	100,000	
	Payable to Olin		10,000
	Financing Revenue		15,000
	Cash		75,000

Because the accounts receivable are transferred with recourse, Olin must record the liability for the transferred receivables instead of simply removing the receivables. The Liability for Transferred Receivables account *is reported as a current liability* on Olin's balance sheet. As Financo collects the receivables, it periodically notifies Olin of the collections, and Olin then reduces both the liability and the related receivables remaining.

NOTES RECEIVABLE

Record and value notes receivable.

Notes receivable are written promises to pay certain sums at specific future dates. Notes are negotiable instruments in that they can be transferred to another party in exchange for other considerations. Notes receivable provide legal evidence of debt, can be either short-term or long-term, and may be either interest-bearing or noninterest-bearing. While short-term notes receivable are considered liquid assets because they can be readily converted to cash, long-term notes are classified as noncurrent assets on the balance sheet. At the time of receipt, the proper *valuation of notes receivable is the present value of the future cash inflows from the note.* The present value of the note is based upon an effective interest rate at the time the notes are issued.

Most notes are interest-bearing; that is, they explicitly state the amount of interest to be paid by the lender to the borrower. Noninterest-bearing notes do not state the amount of interest. Some notes include an interest rate that is unreasonable relative to the current market rate and/or the credit standing of the borrower. Other notes are exchanged for noncash assets. The problems that arise in recording transactions involving these different types of notes are discussed in the following sections.

SHORT-TERM NOTES RECEIVABLE

Short-term notes mature within one year or operating cycle, whichever is longer. They are valued at face value less any allowance for bad debts. Because they are short-term, the assumption is made that there is no material difference between the discounted present value of the future cash inflows (principal plus interest) and the face value of the note. Notes receivable are often obtained in exchange for past-due accounts receivable, for other assets, or for the provision of services in the normal course of business. As an illustration, assume that on March 1, 1998, Sellco accepts a note receivable from Johnco in the amount of $1,000. The note is due in six months, at an interest rate of 10%, and in exchange for a past-due account receivable of $1,000. The entry on Sellco's books to record this transaction follows:

1998			
Mar. 1	Notes Receivable—Johnco	1,000	
	Accounts Receivable—Johnco		1,000

When the note is paid on September 1, 1998, interest is recognized on the books of the holder of the note (Sellco), and the note is removed as follows:

1998			
Sept. 1	Cash	1,050	
	Interest Revenue		50*
	Notes Receivable—Johnco		1,000
	\$1,000 × 10% × 6/12 = \$50		

Interest-Bearing Versus Noninterest-Bearing Notes. The previous illustration is an example of an *interest-bearing note,* in which an effective interest rate is explicitly stated as part of the note agreement. The carrying (or book) value of an interest-bearing note is the note receivable plus any interest receivable accrued at the statement date.

In contrast, *noninterest-bearing notes* are written with a zero interest rate. The note is recorded at its face value, an amount that is more than the fair market value. The difference between the fair market value of the obligation and the face value amount of the note is unearned interest and is recorded in an account called **Discount on Notes Receivable**. This account appears as a contra account to notes receivable on the balance sheet. As the interest is earned, the discount account is reduced. Thus, the carrying (or book) value of a noninterest-bearing note is the note receivable less the balance in the Discount on Notes Receivable account.

Notes of this nature date back to antiquity when most societies had usury laws. Lenders would write the note for an amount greater than the amount of cash given to the borrower. Without any stated rate of interest on the note, charges of usury were avoided.

If a note is accepted for cash and no other considerations, the present value of the note is the cash amount exchanged. The present value of the future payments is equal to the cash exchange amount at the time of issue. This is the case if the note has no interest rate stated or if the rate appears unreasonably low.

Exhibits 8–6 and 8–7 compare the accounting for a noninterest-bearing note with the accounting for an interest-bearing note. If the note in these exhibits had been written as an interest-bearing note, the face of the note would be $38,100, the same as the fair market value. The 8% interest rate and payment terms would be stated in the note. If the note had been written as a noninterest-bearing note, the face of the note would specify four $10,000 future cash payments totaling $40,000, with no interest rate stated. Still, the amount of the loan (or fair market value) remains $38,100—the present value of the $10,000 future payments (annuity) at an effective 8% annual interest rate (2% quarterly).

As each payment is received, the carrying value, or balance of the note, is reduced by an amount equal to the reduction in principal. The interest-bearing note is reduced directly by the difference between the $10,000 cash payment and accrued interest. This difference represents a reduction of the principal of the note. However, the noninterest-bearing note is reduced by the full cash payment, and the discount on notes receivable is reduced by the amount of interest earned.

In substance, the two notes are identical. Sales revenue and subsequent interest revenue each quarter are the same, as is the carrying (or book) value of the note receivable balance. This carrying (or book) value is the basis used to compute the following period's interest revenue.

Notes Receivable With Interest Rates Lower Than Current Market Rate. For notes with an interest rate less than the current market rate (or with no interest rate), an effective interest rate must be assigned to the note. If the fair market value of the assets surrendered in exchange for the note is known, the *fair market value* is used to assign an implicit interest rate to the note. If the fair market value of the asset is not known, the market rate of interest assigned is the borrower's incremental borrowing rate or the current market rate for equivalent loans at equivalent risk.

EXHIBIT 8–6 Interest-Bearing vs. Noninterest-Bearing Notes: Data and Amortization Schedule

Data:

On January 1, 1998, YourCo sells machinery to a customer for no money down and four quarterly payments of $10,000 each. The cash price for the machinery is $38,100. The difference between the total $40,000 in payments and cash price of $38,100 represents interest of $1,900 and is based upon an effective annual interest rate of 8%.

Amortization Schedule

DATE	CASH PAYMENT	INTEREST (2% PER QUARTER)	PRINCIPAL REDUCTION	DISCOUNT BALANCE	FUTURE PAYMENTS	CARRYING VALUE
1/1/98				$1,900	$40,000	$38,100
3/31/98	$10,000	$762[a]	$9,238[b]	1,138[c]	30,000[d]	28,862[e]
6/30/98	10,000	577	9,423	561	20,000	19,439
9/30/98	10,000	389	9,611	172	10,000	9,828
12/31/98	10,000	172[f]	9,828	0	0	0

[a]$38,100 × 0.02 = $762
[b]$10,000 − $762 = $9,238
[c]$1,900 − $762 = $1,138
[d]$40,000 − $10,000 = $30,000
[e]$38,100 − $9,238 = $28,862
[f]$24 rounding difference

EXHIBIT 8–7 Interest-Bearing vs. Noninterest-Bearing Notes: Journal Entries

Date	Recorded as Interest-Bearing	Debit	Credit	Recorded as Noninterest-Bearing	Debit	Credit
1998						
Jan. 1	Notes Receivable	38,100		Notes Receivable	40,000	
	Sales		38,100	Discount on Note Rec.		1,900
				Sales		38,100
Mar. 31	Cash	10,000		Cash	10,000	
	Interest Revenue		762	Discount on Note Rec.	762	
	Notes Receivable		9,238	Interest Revenue		762
	(Note Balance = $28,862)			Notes Receivable		10,000
				(Note Balance = $30,000		
				Discount Bal. = 1,138		
				Net Balance = $28,862)		
June 30	Cash	10,000		Cash	10,000	
	Interest Revenue		577	Discount on Note Rec.	577	
	Notes Receivable		9,423	Interest Revenue		577
	(Note Balance = $19,439)			Notes Receivable		10,000
				(Note Balance = $20,000		
				Discount Bal. = 561		
				Net Balance = $19,439)		
Sep. 30	Cash	10,000		Cash	10,000	
	Interest Revenue		389	Discount on Note Rec.	389	
	Notes Receivable		9,611	Interest Revenue		389
	(Note Balance = $9,828)			Notes Receivable		10,000
				(Note Balance = $10,000		
				Discount Bal. = 172		
				Net Balance = $ 9,828)		
Dec. 31	Cash	10,000		Cash	10,000	
	Interest Revenue		172	Discount on Note Rec.	172	
	Notes Receivable		9,828	Interest Revenue		172
				Notes Receivable		10,000

Fair Market Value Known. If the fair market value of the assets surrendered is known, it is considered to be the present value of the future cash inflows from the note. The amount of the discount on the note is the difference between the fair market value of the assets and the face amount of the note. As an example, assume that Arledge Inc. accepts a 3-year, noninterest-bearing note with a face value of $10,000 on December 31, 1998, in exchange for land with a fair market value of $7,120 and an original cost of $5,000. The difference between the face value of the note and the fair market value of the land is the discount on the note. This difference represents the interest implied in the transaction. Arledge would make the following journal entry to record the exchange:

Date	Account	Debit	Credit
1998			
Dec. 31	Notes Receivable	10,000	
	Discount on Notes Receivable		2,880*
	Land		5,000
	Gain on Sale of Land		2,120**

**$10,000 − $7,120 = $2,880*
***$7,120 − $5,000 = $2,120*

The discount must be amortized over the life of the note and recognized as interest revenue using the effective-interest method. The effective interest rate is the rate used to discount the face value of the note ($10,000) to the present value of the note ($7,120) at the time of the exchange.[2] Yearly journal entries for the amortization of the interest and payment of the note at maturity follow:

1999			
Dec. 31	Discount on Notes Receivable	854*	
	Interest Revenue		854
	**$7,120 × 0.12*		
2000			
Dec. 31	Discount on Notes Receivable	957*	
	Interest Revenue		957
	$7,120 + $854) × 0.12		
2001			
Dec. 31	Discount on Notes Receivable	1,069*	
	Cash	10,000	
	Interest Revenue		1,069
	Notes Receivable		10,000
	**[($7,120 + $854 + $957) × 0.12 = $1,072; $2,880 − $854 − $957 = $1,069] $3 difference in amortization total due to rounding.*		

At the end of each of the three years, Arledge recognizes revenue in the amount of the imputed interest on the note. The carrying value of the note (face value less the unamortized discount) increases each year until maturity.

Fair Market Value Unknown. If the fair market value of the assets surrendered is unknown, the interest rate assigned or implicit in the transaction is based on either (1) the incremental rate at which the borrower is able to obtain other loans or (2) the current rate at which other loans of similar risk are being offered. As an example, assume that Jenkins Company accepts a 3-year note receivable dated December 31, 1998, with a face value of $5,000 and a stated interest rate of 12% paid annually, in exchange for land that cost $2,000 and has an uncertain fair market value.

In this example, the 12% stated rate on the note is considered too low, or "unreasonable," because the borrower's incremental rate is 15%. That is, if the borrower were to obtain the funds from a third party, the interest rate would be 15%. Therefore, the present value of the note discounted at 15% is equal to the fair market value of the land. The difference in interest rates represents a discount provided to the buyer.

[2]The discount rate can be found by locating the present-value factor of 0.7120 ($7,120/$10,000) in the "Present Value of a Single Sum" table in Appendix A for three years. The rate is almost 12 percent, since the factor found is .7118.

[3]The present value of the note is found as follows:

Present value of principal (single sum):	
discounted at 15%, 3 periods: $5,000 × 0.6575	= $3,288
Present value of interest (annuity = $5,000 × 12% = $600):	
discounted at 15%, 3 periods: $600 × 2.2832	= 1,370
Total present value of note	$4,658

At 15%, the present value of this note is $4,658.[3] Jenkins would make the following journal entry to record the exchange:

1998			
Dec. 31	Notes Receivable	5,000	
	Land		2,000
	Discount on Note Receivable		342*
	Gain on Sale of Land		2,658**

\$5,000 − \$4,658 = \$342
***\$5,000 − \$2,000 − \$342 = \$2,658*

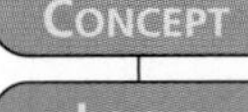

Recognition of gain and valuation of asset.

The earnings process is complete for the asset, land. The fair market value of the land at the time of sale was $4,658, the present value of the note receivable discounted at the incremental rate of the maker, 15%. The gain is the difference between the carrying value ($2,000) and the fair market value.

The discount is the difference between the face value and the present value of the note and represents the difference in the current market rate of interest (15%) and the stated interest rate on the note (12%) discounted over three years. The incremental interest is recognized over the life of the note as the discount is amortized. Exhibit 8–8 presents an amortization table for this note, and Exhibit 8–9 shows the journal entries required at the end of each year.

FINANCING WITH NOTES RECEIVABLE

Because notes are negotiable instruments, they can be used to obtain cash in a fashion similar to that of accounts receivable. These transactions are referred to as *discounting* of notes. SFAS No. 77 is used to determine if notes receivable

EXHIBIT 8–8
Interest When Fair Market Value Is Unknown: Data and Amortization Table

Data:
3-Year, $5,000, 12%, note receivable discounted at 15%

Amortization Table

DATE	CASH INTEREST 12%	EFFECTIVE INTEREST 15%	DISCOUNT AMORTIZED	UNAMORTIZED DISCOUNT BALANCE	BOOK VALUE OF NOTE
1/1/97				$342	$4,658
12/31/97	$600[a]	$699[b]	$ 99[c]	243[d]	4,757[e]
12/31/98	600	714	114	129	4,871
12/31/99	600	729[f]	129	0	5,000

[a]$5,000 × 12% = $600
[b]$4,658 × 15% = $699
[c]$699 − $600 = $99
[d]$342 − $99 = $243
[e]$4,658 + $99 = $4,757
[f]$2 rounding difference

EXHIBIT 8–9
Interest When Fair Market Value is Unknown: Journal Entries

Date	Account	Debit	Credit
1997			
Jan. 1	Notes Receivable	5,000	
	Land		2,000
	Discount on Notes Receivable		342
	Gain on Sale of Land		2,658
Dec. 31	Cash	600	
	Discount on Notes Receivable	99	
	Interest Revenue		699
1998			
Dec. 31	Cash	600	
	Discount on Notes Receivable	114	
	Interest Revenue		714
1999			
Dec. 31	Cash	600	
	Discount on Notes Receivable	129	
	Interest Revenue		729
2000			
Dec. 31	Cash	5,000	
	Notes Receivable		5,000

have been sold or simply used as collateral for a loan. Notes receivable can be discounted (sold) either with or without recourse. The process of discounting notes receivable follows:

1. Determine the maturity value of the note:

Maturity Value = Principal + Interest
Maturity Value = Principal + (Principal × Interest Rate × Time)

2. Determine the amount of the discount.
   a. Multiply the maturity value by the discount rate.
   b. Multiply the result of step 2a by the number of discount days divided by 365 days (or 360).
3. Calculate the proceeds of the sale of the note. (Subtract the discount from the maturity value.)
4. Determine the book value, or carrying value, of the note:

Note Principal + Accrued Interest = Book Value

5. Determine if there is a gain or loss by comparing the book value (carrying value) to the proceeds.[4]

[4]If the note is sold without recourse or with recourse and meets the three conditions for a sale, a gain or loss is recognized. Otherwise, the transaction is treated as a borrowing, and interest revenue or expense is recognized instead of a gain or loss.

Discounting Notes Receivable Without Recourse. If a note is discounted without recourse, the transaction is treated as a sale of an asset. The seller of the note has no further responsibility with regard to the note, and the note is removed from the seller's books. The buyer assumes responsibility for collecting the note and bearing the loss in the event of default. To illustrate a sale without recourse, assume that Arrington Corporation holds a $1,000, 10%, 6-month note receivable dated March 1, 1998. On July 1, 1998, Arrington discounts the note at Second National Bank at a discount rate of 12%. The journal entry to record the sale to the bank would be

1998			
July 1	Cash	1,029	
	Loss on Sale of Notes Receivable	4	
	Notes Receivable		1,000
	Interest Revenue		33
	Maturity value: $1,000 + ($1,000 × .10 × 6/12)	*$1,050*	
	Discount: $1,050 × .12 × 2/12	*21*	
	Proceeds: $1,050 − $21		*$1,029*
	Accrued interest: $1,000 × .1 × 4/12	*$ 33*	
	Principal	*1,000*	
	Book value: 1,000 + 33		*1,033*
	Loss ($1,029 − $1,033)		*$ 4*

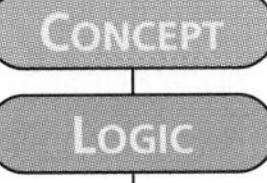

Recognition of gains and losses on the sale or disposal of an asset.

The earnings process is complete upon receipt of cash for assets that have been sold. The fair market value of the note at the time of sale is $1,029, and the book or carrying value is $1,033. The difference of $4 is a loss recognized at the time of sale. The bank becomes the owner of the note and has no recourse to the seller (Arrington) in the event of default.

Notes Receivable Discounted With Recourse. Notes receivable discounted with recourse are not treated as the sale of an asset because the buyer has recourse to the seller in the event of default on the note. Using the same Arrington example, we can see that the journal entry made by Arrington to discount the note would be the same as the entry illustrated earlier. The only differences are that the Notes Receivable Discounted account would be credited instead of Notes Receivable, and Interest Expense would be debited instead of Loss on Sale of Notes Receivable. In the event that the debtor defaults on the note, Arrington would be liable to the bank for the full amount of the note, plus the interest, plus any fees charged by the bank. Notes receivable discounted may appear on the balance sheet contra to the notes receivable. If the notes receivable are reported net (that is, net of the discounted notes receivable), then the notes to the financial statements would indicate the existence of a contingent liability.

When the maker of the note pays the holder, the bank (holder) will notify Arrington, and Arrington will eliminate both the Notes Receivable and Notes Receivable Discounted accounts as follows:

Notes Receivable Discounted	1,000	
Notes Receivable		1,000

This entry removes both the contingent liability and the original Notes Receivable account, since the note has been paid. However, in the event that the maker defaults on the note, Arrington would be immediately notified by the bank to make payment. Assume that the maker defaulted on the note in our example and the bank charges a $20 protest fee. The entries on Arrington's books would be as follows:

Notes Receivable Discounted	1,000	
Notes Receivable		1,000
Accounts Receivable	1,070*	
Cash		1,070

**$1,000 + $50 + $20 = $1,070*

When a discounted note is *dishonored* (the maker defaults on the due date), the note is no longer negotiable; therefore, both the Notes Receivable and the Notes Receivable Discounted accounts are removed from the books of Arrington. An account receivable is established for the total due, including the principal, interest, and protest fee. Notice that the $20 protest fee is not charged to expense, but rather it is included in the amount due from the maker of the original note.

REPORTING CONSIDERATIONS

Unrestricted cash is reported in the current assets section of the balance sheet, while restricted cash accounts are properly reported as current assets, investments, or other assets, depending on the availability for disbursement. Accounts receivable are normally reported at net realizable values after deducting allowances for bad debts. Current notes receivable also are reported net of allowances, along with any notes receivable discounted amounts. Any future obligations for notes receivable discounted must also be reported. Exhibit 8–10 provides an illustration of reporting for cash and receivables.

FINANCIAL ANALYSIS

A primary concern of an analyst is *liquidity,* the ability to meet short-term obligations with current assets, and the composition of *working capital* (current assets). While projected cash budgets provide insights to a firm's liquidity, comparing cash and other current assets to current obligations is also helpful. These relationships are liquidity ratios.

LIQUIDITY RATIOS

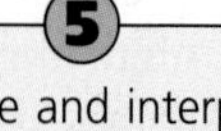

Calculate and interpret key liquidity and asset management ratios.

Two of the most frequently used liquidity ratios are the current ratio and the quick ratio, or acid-test ratio. They are illustrated in Exhibit 8–11.

Current Ratio. The *current ratio* (sometimes referred to as the *working capital ratio*) is found by dividing current assets by current liabilities. Prepaid items, if material, sometimes are deducted in the numerator by some analysts because of their relative nonliquidity. The argument is that the immediate cash value of prepaid items is substantially less than the carrying value of these assets; hence, they should be excluded. The current ratio is an indicator of the ability

EXHIBIT 8–10
Reporting for Cash and Receivables

FORM COMPANY
Partial Balance Sheet—Current Sections
December 31, 1998

Assets		
Current assets:		
Cash		$ 266,300
Investments in trading securities		73,100
Accounts receivable (net of allowance for bad debts of $19,900)		644,300
Accounts receivable assigned	$240,000	
Less: Notes payable	(200,000)	40,000
Notes receivable	$150,400	
Less: Notes receivable discounted	(100,000)	50,400
Inventories		680,000
Interest receivable		8,000
Prepaid items		15,000
Total current assets		$1,777,100
Liabilities		
Current liabilities:		
Short-term debt		$ 15,600
Trade and other payables		940,000
Income taxes		42,600
Current portion of long-term debt		20,000
Capitalized lease obligations		13,200
Accrued liabilities		15,500
Total current liabilities		$1,046,900

to meet current obligations. If a firm begins to pay its current obligations more slowly than in the past, causing payables to rise faster than current assets, the current ratio decreases—a possible indicator of liquidity problems.

Quick or Acid-Test Ratio. The *quick ratio,* also called the *acid-test ratio,* is an adjustment to the current ratio and is calculated by subtracting inventories and prepaid expenses from the current assets in the numerator. Many analysts believe that the quick ratio is a better indicator of liquidity because of the removal of both inventories and prepaid items from the ratio. In an economic downturn, decreases in sales result in an unwanted buildup of inventory. If inventory increases, the current ratio also increases (other things held equal), which in distressed times is a false indicator.

The quick ratio does not suffer from this deficiency and is a more stringent measure of liquidity. For example, ***McDonnell Douglas*** (*www.swcollege.com/hartman.html*) reports for December 31, 1992, current assets of $10,178 million and current liabilities of $6,518 million. The current ratio, then, is 1.56. However, current assets other than inventory (which includes contracts in process of $7,230 million) are less than half of its current liabilities. The quick ratio is only 0.45.

EXHIBIT 8–11

FORM COMPANY
Financial Analysis
December 31, 1998

These calculations are based upon data in Exhibit 8–10 for Form Company, as of December 31, 1998, and on the following information:

Sales for the year	$4,100,500
Accounts receivable, beginning of year	550,000

$$\text{Current Ratio} = \frac{\text{Current Assets}}{\text{Current Liabilities}} = \frac{\$1{,}777{,}100}{\$1{,}046{,}900} = 1.697$$

$$\text{Quick Ratio} = \frac{(\text{Current Assets} - \text{Inventory} - \text{Prepaid Items})}{\text{Current Liabilities}}$$

$$= \frac{\$1{,}777{,}100 - \$680{,}000 - \$15{,}000}{\$1{,}046{,}900} = 1.034$$

$$\text{A/R Turnover} = \frac{\text{Sales}}{\text{Average Accounts Receivable}}$$

$$= \frac{\$4{,}100{,}500}{(\$550{,}000 + \$644{,}300)/2} = 6.867$$

$$\text{Average Collection Period} = \frac{365 \text{ days}}{\text{Accounts Receivable Turnover}} = 53.15 \text{ days}$$

This company appears to be in fairly good shape from a liquidity standpoint. While the current ratio is not high, the quick ratio is above 1:0, indicating the ability to pay all of the current debt on a timely basis. Once the product is sold, it takes about 53 days to collect cash. If the company can reduce its average collection period to 45 days, the accounts receivable turnover would equal 8.11 (365/45).

ASSET MANAGEMENT RATIOS

Asset management ratios indicate how well management is managing its assets. Two closely related ratios in this group, illustrated in Exhibit 8–11, are accounts receivable turnover and average collection period (ACP). *Accounts receivable turnover* is determined by dividing credit sales by average accounts receivable. The *average collection period (ACP)* is the average number of days required to collect a receivable. ACP is found by dividing the number of days in the year (365) by the accounts receivable turnover.

Both ratios are measures of how effectively accounts receivable are turned into cash. Exhibit 8–11 provides examples of these calculations. As with all ratios, the values determined should be interpreted by comparisons with the company's own past values, current industry norms, and management expectations. For example, comparison is fruitless between ***Wal-Mart***, (*www.swcollege.com/hartman.html*) with a turnover of 117.6, or ACP of three days (for the year ended January 31, 1993) and ***Orion Pictures***, with a turnover of 1.71, or ACP of 213 days (for the year ended February 28, 1993).

These ratios provide an indication of credit policies used by the firm. A very high turnover (and very low collection period) compared to other firms in the industry might indicate rather stringent credit policies. That is, extension of credit may be granted only to the very highest-rated customers. If the firm chooses to relax the credit extension policy a little, an increase in sales may result. Conversely, a very low turnover (high collection period) might mean that the receivables are overdue. The quality of the receivables may be suspect.

APPENDIX: FOUR-COLUMN PROOF OF CASH

A four-column proof of cash is sometimes referred to as a comprehensive bank reconciliation. It is primarily an audit tool that is an effective means of detecting errors whenever internal controls are considered weak. Basically, the procedure reconciles the ending cash bank balance of a previous period to the ending cash bank balance of the current period and the ending book balance of cash for the previous period to the ending book balance of the current period. Both actual cash balances should then be the same.

Four columns are used, hence the name. There are two basic sections to the reconciliation. One section contains data effecting the bank balance of cash, and the other section is comprised of data effecting the book balance of cash. The first column contains the prior period's bank reconciliation with the bank's cash balance brought to the actual cash balance in the upper section. The lower section contains the book's reconciliation to the actual cash balance at the end of the previous period.

The second column for both sections starts with the total receipts for each entity. The total receipts for the bank are those indicated on the bank statement, and the total receipts for the company are those recorded in its books. These starting totals are adjusted for timing difference and discovered errors so that the ending balance of receipts is the same at the end of the period. The third column starts with total disbursements for the period, as indicated by both entities' books which are similarly reconciled to each other by timing differences and discovered errors.

The final column is similar to being the bank reconciliation for the current period with the bank amounts in the top section and the book amounts in the lower section, both of which are brought to the correct current cash balance.

Figure 8A–1 contains an illustration of a four-column proof of cash. The illustration is based on the following data. Fryman's bank reconciliations for the months of April and May and the pertinent data to prepare them are at the top of the next page.

The following additional information from Fryman's May bank statement was used to prepare the bank reconciliation for the month of May. Fryman's discovered that a deposit recorded as $500 cleared the bank as $550 with an appropriate credit memo included with the bank statement. Fryman's also discovered that Check No. 483, recorded in the books at $100, was written for $135 and cleared the bank. Other information is presented following the bank reconciliation on the next page.

As can be seen from the illustration in Exhibit 8A–1, the four-column proof of cash, besides including bank reconciliations for two consecutive periods, is really a reconciliation of the receipts and disbursements for the two entities so that the ending balances of the receipts and disbursements agree and reflect the true condition. This reconciliation of receipts and disbursements is an excellent means of discovering kiting as well as honest mistakes.

FRYMAN'S FISHERIES
Bank Reconciliations
For April and May 1998

	APRIL 30	MAY 31
Cash per bank statement	$6,843	$6,500
Deposits in transit:		
April 30	365	
May 31		245
Outstanding checks:		
April 30	(1,820)	
May 31		(2,020)
Actual cash balance at end of month	$5,388	$4,725
Cash per books	$5,153	$4,480
Error in deposit		50
Note and interest collected	250	340
Bank service charges	(15)	(20)
NSF check returned		(40)
Charge for new checks		(50)
Error in recording Check No. 483		(35)
Actual cash balance at end of month	$5,388	$4,725

	PER BANK	PER BOOKS
Balance, May 1	$6,843	$5,153
May deposits	2,829	2,949
May checks	(3,442)	(3,622)
June note collected		
($40 interest)	340	
June bank charges:		
Service	(20)	
New checks	(50)	
Balance, May 31	$6,500	$4,480

ANALYTICS FOR ADJUSTMENTS

The additions and deductions to the columns for receipts and disbursements are based upon logic. For instance, look at the adjustment to the bank's May receipts. The deposit in transit at the end of April will clear the bank in May and therefore must be deducted to arrive at the real May receipts. Similarly, deposits in transit at the end of May must be added to bring the banks receipt column in agreement with Fryman's receipts for the month.

In a similar fashion, adjustments must be made to Fryman's receipts. Assuming that the note collected by the bank for Fryman's during April was recorded by Fryman's during May, that amount would need to be deducted

EXHIBIT 8A–1 Four-Column Proof of Cash Illustration

FRYMAN'S FISHERIES
Four-Column Proof of Cash
For May 1998

	APRIL 30 BALANCE	MAY RECEIPTS	MAY DISBURSEMENTS	MAY 31 BALANCE
Per bank statement	$6,843	$3,169	$3,512	$6,500
Deposits in transit:				
April 30	365	(365)		
May 31		245		245
Outstanding checks:				
April 30	(1,820)		(1,820)	
May 31			2,020	(2,020)
Correct amounts	$5,388	$3,049	$3,712	$4,725
Per books	$5,153	$2,949	$3,622	$4,480
Error in deposit recorded		50		50
Note and interest collected by bank				
April	250	(250)		
May		340		340
Bank service charge				
April	(15)		(15)	
May			20	(20)
NSF check		(40)		(40)
Charge for new checks			50	(50)
Error in recording Check No. 483			35	(35)
Correct amounts	$5,388	$3,049	$3,712	$4,725

The entries that Fryman's makes to bring the books to the proper balances are:

Service Charges	20	
Supplies Expense	50	
Cash		70

The increase of $50 for the deposit and the deduction for the checks could be made by correcting the original entries or by making the following entry:

Cash	15	
Expense	35	
Revenue or Accounts Receivable		50

from Fryman's receipts unless it was recorded at the end of the previous month. The amount collected by the bank in May would need to be added, since it has not been recorded by Fryman's at this point in time. The NSF check returned by the bank to Fryman's must be deducted, since this amount would be included in Fryman's starting balance of receipts. Also, the deposit incorrectly recorded by Fryman's must be added for the difference of $50 because that was included in the bank receipts and was not included in Fryman's receipts. Otherwise, Fryman's receipts for the month would be understated.

The reconciliation for disbursements follows a similar logic. April's outstanding checks would clear the bank during May, and the outstanding checks at the end of May need to be added to bring the bank's ending disbursements in agreement with the books of Fryman's.

The disbursement column of Fryman's also will need to be adjusted based on information obtained from the bank statement. If the April service charge is recorded by Fryman's in May, it will need to be deducted from Fryman's disbursements since, it properly belongs as part of April's disbursements. (If the adjustment was made by Fryman's at the end of the previous month, no adjustment would be necessary, since the amount would not be included in the starting total of disbursements.) The May service charge by the bank needs to be added to Fryman's May disbursements. In a similar fashion, the bank charges for new checks would need to be added. Since Check No. 483 was written for $35 more than was recorded by Fryman's and cleared the bank, Fryman's would need to include this $35 difference as an additional disbursement.

END-OF-CHAPTER REVIEW

SUMMARY

1. **Understand the composition and control of cash.** Cash is the most liquid asset of any enterprise. Without the liquidity provided by efficient collection of cash, the well-being of a business may be impaired. Cash controls discussed in this chapter include petty cash funds, checking accounts with dual signatures, and reconciliation of bank statements for checking accounts.
2. **Record and value accounts receivable.** Accounts receivable are valued at net realizable value, with a contra account called Allowance for Bad Debts used to determine this value. The allowance account can be determined either by the percentage-of-sales method or the percentage-of-receivables method. The sales method is based on sales, while the receivables method focuses primarily on the asset, accounts receivable, for balance sheet purposes.
3. **Demonstrate how accounts receivable are used as the basis for financing.** Receivables can be used for instant liquidity by assigning them as collateral for loans (assignment) or selling them (factoring). Factoring of accounts receivable can be either with or without recourse. Factoring receivables without recourse is an outright sale, and a loss is recognized at the time of sale. Receivables factored with recourse are also treated as a sale if the factor can only force a buy-back through the recourse provisions of the contract; otherwise, they are treated as a borrowing. If the factored receivables are treated as a borrowing, the seller has a contingent liability on the receivables until collection is complete.
4. **Record and value notes receivable.** Short-term notes receivable include both interest-bearing and so-called noninterest-bearing notes. The interest rate on a noninterest-bearing note is not stated on the face of the instrument. It must be determined either through the fair market value of the asset received or by assuming that the marginal borrowing rate of the buyer applies.

Notes receivable can be used as a source of cash by discounting (or selling) the notes. The proceeds from the sale are compared with the book value (carrying value) of the note (principal plus the accrued interest at the date of sale) to determine the gain or loss on the transaction. Notes can be discounted (sold) either with or without recourse.

5. **Calculate and interpret key liquidity and asset management ratios.** Two key financial liquidity ratios are the current ratio and the quick ratio, and two asset management ratios are accounts receivable turnover and average collection period. These ratios are interrelated and, as with all ratios, should be interpreted only by comparisons over time, or to industry norms, or against management expectations. The current and quick ratios provide indications of current debt-paying ability. The receivables turnover and average collection period indicate the amount of time required to collect an average receivable.

KEY TERMS

accounts receivable *393*
accounts receivable assigned *398*
allowance for bad debts *395*
asset management ratios *414*
bank reconciliation *391*
cash *388*
cash equivalents *389*
direct write-off method *398*
factoring receivables *400*
gross method *393*
liquidity ratios *412*
net method *393*
nonsufficient funds (NSF) check *391*
notes receivable discounted *411*
percentage-of-receivables method *396*
percentage-of-sales method *395*
petty cash *390*
recourse *398*

ASSIGNMENT MATERIAL

CASES

C8–1 Ratios, GAAP, and Ethics

The Finagle Company desires to obtain a $25,000, short-term loan from its bank to meet current operating needs. From past history, management knows that the bank views as critical hurdles a minimum current ratio of 2:1 and a quick ratio of 1:1 in making its decision to lend money. Finagle's current balance sheet is presented on the next page.

Finagle's accountant and the president discussed the current balance sheet and decided to take the following actions before applying for a loan from the bank:

1. Sell the trading securities for $27,750.
2. Factor $55,000 of accounts receivable with recourse and receive 95% of the face value.
3. Reclassify the long-term, available-for-sale securities to short-term trading securities.
4. Use the proceeds from (1) and (2) to pay off $80,000 of accounts payable.
5. Prepare the balance sheet shown on the following page.

Required:

A. What were the current and quick ratios on November 1, 1998?
B. What were the current and quick ratios on November 2, 1998?
C. Did Finagle's president and accountant follow GAAP?
D. Are there any ethical considerations here?
E. Are there any other issues that you think should be discussed?

FINAGLE COMPANY
Balance Sheet
November 1, 1998

Assets			
Current assets:			
Cash		$ 2,000	
Investments—Trading securities		25,000	
Accounts receivable		105,000	
Inventories		100,000	
Prepaid items		2,500	
Total current assets			$234,500
Noncurrent assets:			
Investments, available-for-sale			25,000
Property, plant, and equipment			
Land		$ 50,000	
Plant and equipment	$350,000		
Less: Accumulated depreciation	50,000	300,000	350,000
Total assets			$609,500
Liabilities			
Current liabilities		$150,000	
Long-term debt		200,000	
Total liabilities			$350,000
Stockholders' Equity			
Paid-in capital		$200,000	
Retained earnings		59,500	
Total stockholders' equity			259,500
Total liabilities and stockholders' equity			$609,500

FINAGLE COMPANY
Balance Sheet
November 2, 1998

Assets		
Current assets:		
Cash	$ 2,000	
Investments—Trading securities	25,000	
Accounts receivable	50,000	
Inventories	100,000	
Prepaid items	2,500	
Total current assets		$179,500

(continued)

Noncurrent assets:			
Property, plant, and equipment:			
Land		$ 50,000	
Plant and Equipment	$350,000		
Less: Accumulated depreciation	50,000	300,000	350,000
Total assets			$529,500
Liabilities			
Accounts Payable (short-term)			$ 70,000
Long-term debt			200,000
Stockholders' Equity			
Paid-in capital		$200,000	
Retained earnings		59,500	
Total stockholders' equity			259,500
Total liabilities and stockholders' equity			$529,500

C8–2 Financial Analysis and Decision Making, Report Preparation

MKK Inc. wishes to obtain a short-term loan from Turfway Bank. Turfway uses the classical 2:1 current ratio as a threshold for granting loans. Use MKK's balance sheets for the past two years and the current income statement.

MKK INC.
Balance Sheet
December 31, 1997

Assets			
Current assets:			
Cash		$ 42,000	
Investments—Trading securities		150,000	
Accounts receivable		250,000	
Inventories		225,000	
Prepaid items		8,000	
Total current assets			$675,000
Noncurrent assets:			
Investments:			
Land		$225,000	
Investment in subsidiary		100,000	325,000
Property, plant, and equipment:			
Land		$150,000	
Plant and equipment	$700,000		
Less: Accumulated depreciation	100,000	600,000	750,000
Total assets			$1,750,000

(continued)

Liabilities			
Current liabilities:			
Accounts payable		$600,000	
Accrued taxes		25,000	
Total current liabilities			$ 625,000
Long-term debt			200,000
Total liabilities			$ 825,000
Stockholders' Equity			
Paid-in capital		$500,000	
Retained earnings		425,000	
			925,000
Total liabilities and stockholders' equity			$1,750,000

MKK INC.
Balance Sheet
December 31, 1998

Assets			
Current assets:			
Cash		$300,000	
Investments—Trading securities		200,000	
Accounts receivable		450,000	
Inventories		275,000	
Prepaid items		6,000	
Total current assets			$1,231,000
Noncurrent assets:			
Investments:			
Land		$225,000	
Investment in subsidiary		100,000	325,000
Property, plant and equipment:			
Land		$150,000	
Plant and equipment	$700,000		
Less: Accumulated depreciation	150,000	550,000	700,000
Total assets			$2,256,000
Liabilities			
Current liabilities:			
Accounts payable		$800,000	
Accrued taxes		30,000	$ 830,000
Long-term debt			200,000
Total liabilities			$1,030,000
Stockholders' Equity			
Paid-in capital		$500,000	
Retained earnings		726,000	
			$1,226,000
Total liabilities and stockholders' equity			$2,256,000

MKK INC.
Income Statement
For the Year Ended December 31, 1998

Sales	$1,500,000
Less: Sales returns and allowances	(30,000)
Net sales	$1,470,000
Cost of goods sold	(750,000)
Gross profit	$ 720,000
Selling and administrative expenses	(260,000)
Net income before taxes	$ 460,000
Income taxes	(90,000)
Net income after taxes	$ 370,000

Required:

A. Determine the current and quick ratios.
B. Determine the asset management ratios.
C. What do you think Turfway will do in regard to the loan request? Are there any actions that could be taken by MKK before seeking a loan to improve the likelihood of being successful? Prepare a presentation that you would make to the loan officer.

C8–3 Financial Analysis and Discussion

Presented here are the current assets and current liabilities (in thousands $) of Wal-Mart Stores, Inc., and Subsidiaries:

	JAN. 31, 1993	JAN. 31, 1992
Current assets:		
Cash and cash equivalents	$ 12,363	$ 30,649
Receivables	524,555	418,867
Recoverable costs from sale/leaseback	312,016	681,387
Inventories	9,268,309	7,384,299
Prepaid expenses	80,347	60,221
Total	$10,197,590	$8,575,423
Current liabilities	$ 6,754,286	$5,003,775

Required:

A. Determine Wal-Mart's current ratio and quick ratio for each year-end.
B. Discuss whether Wal-Mart is in danger of not being able to pay its upcoming bills (i.e., current liabilities). What other sources not listed as current assets might the company have available to meet its current obligations?

C8–4 Financial Analysis (Management Ratios) Group Project—Communication

In discussing asset management ratios, the chapter notes a wide disparity between the accounts receivable turnover and average collection period for Wal-Mart and Orion Pictures. Discuss the nature of these companies' respective business environments and how they contribute to the observed ratios. Locate two other industries and choose two companies from each industry and report the relevant ratios. You may wish to locate some trade publications associated with the industries chosen and report the norms of these ratios for your selected industries.

C8–5 Ethics Report

The following was taken from "A Multidimensional Analysis of Selected Ethical Issues in Accounting," by Steven Flory, Thomas Phillips, Eric Reidenbach, and Donald Robin, *The Accounting Review* 67, No. 2 (April 1992): pp. 284–303.

> Anne Devereaux, company controller, is told by the chief financial officer, Jane Seth, that the company "has to meet its earnings forecast, is in need of working capital, and that's final." Unfortunately, Devereaux does not see how additional working capital can be raised, even through increased borrowing, since income is well below the forecast sent to the bank. Seth suggests that Devereaux review bad debts expense for possible reduction and hold sales open longer at the end of the month. Seth also brushes off the management-letter request from the outside auditors to write down the spare parts inventory to reflect its "true value."
>
> At home on the weekend, Devereaux discusses the situation with her husband, Larry, a senior manager of another company in town. "They're asking me to manipulate the books," she says. "On the one hand," she complains, "I'm supposed to be the conscience of the company, and on the other, I'm supposed to be absolutely loyal." He tells her that companies do this all the time and that when business picks up again, she'll be covered. He reminds her how important her salary is to help maintain their comfortable lifestyle and that she shouldn't do anything drastic that might cause her to lose her job.

Required: Evaluate Devereaux's situation using the decision framework for ethical dilemmas presented in Chapter 1 and make a recommendation to her as to what she should do.

C8–6 Financial Analysis Report Preparation

The CEO of Bruce Company has found out that accounts receivable can be used to raise quick cash. He has proposed that his company either assign or factor Bruce Company's receivables, which are currently $1 million. He also tells you that the minimum amount of cash he expects to raise from this transaction is $990,000 and that he does not have a preference for either factoring or assignment. (He is willing to pay a $10,000 fee for this transaction.)

Required:

A. Prepare a report to explain to the CEO the problems with trying to assign the receivables to raise the $990,000.

B. Suppose you have convinced the CEO that assignment would be undesirable for this transaction and that factoring is the way to go. Explain the basics of factoring accounts receivable. In your discussion, include the roles of recourse and financing charges.

C. Considering your answers to the first two questions, what is your final recommendation to the CEO concerning the possibility of using Bruce Company's $1 million receivables to raise $990,000 in quick cash? Prepare a memo to explain your position.

C8–7 Four-Column Proof of Cash

A four-column proof of cash is another method of preparing a bank reconciliation. It frequently is used by auditors as a test of internal control. The four-column proof of cash uses data from the bank reconciliation at the beginning of the period as well as data from the bank reconciliation at the end of the period.

Another feature of the four-column proof of cash is the reconciliation of the cash receipts and disbursements reported on the bank statements with the cash receipts and disbursements reported in the books. If there is a discrepancy between the bank and book-adjusted total receipts and total disbursements, further investigation is warranted.

John Smith has been the treasurer of his church for the past two years. The church books are audited every two years. In preparation for the audit this year, Smith finds a four-column proof of cash prepared by Sally Mills, the previous treasurer. Smith decides that he also should prepare a four-column reconciliation as part of his preparation for the audit. Besides Mills' four-column bank reconciliation for two years, Smith found the following supporting documents that Mills used as well as all the bank statements for that period of time.

ST. HUBERT'S CHURCH
Four-Column Proof of Cash
For the Years 1992 and 1993
March 1, 1994

	DECEMBER 31, 1991	ANNUAL RECEIPTS	ANNUAL DISBURSEMENTS	DECEMBER 31, 1993
Balance per Bank	$12,716.17	$172,597.10	$178,478.87	$6,834.40
Add:				
Deposit in Transit				
12/31/91	309.00	(309.00)		
12/31/93		320.00		320.00
Deduct:				
Outstanding Checks				
12/29/91	(3,388.81)		(3,388.81)	
12/29/93			1,046.83	(1,046.83)
Corrected Bank Balance	$ 9,636.36	$172,608.10	$176,136.89	$6,107.57
Balance per Books	$ 9,636.37	$172,510.10	$176,038.89	$6,107.58
Deduct Error	(0.01)			(0.01)
Corrected Book Balance	$ 9,636.36	$172,510.10	$176,038.89	$6,107.57

OUTSTANDING CHECKS, 12/31/91

NO.	AMOUNT
578	$1,317.50
579	1,800.00
580	212.37
581	19.75
582	39.19
	$3,388.81

OUTSTANDING CHECKS, 12/31/93

NO.	AMOUNT
590	$ 12.32
835	15.00
858	25.00
910	100.00
924	20.00
925	56.90
926	23.25
927	63.41
928	42.00
930	218.95
931	75.00
932	270.00
933	125.00
	$1,046.83

Smith used Mills' working papers to develop the following data:

Bank balance, 12/31/95	$5,641.63
Deposit in transit to bank	1,393.00

OUTSTANDING CHECKS, 12/31/95

No.	Amount
1297	$ 150.00
1301	262.60
1302	227.75
1303	197.60
1304	12.00
1305	1,000.00
1306	325.00
1307	125.00
Total	$2,299.95

TOTALS PER BANK STATEMENTS

1994	Deposits	Disbursed
January	$ 6,483.90	$ 2,305.66
February	2,701.56	1,481.32
March	5,292.50	10,619.38
April	3,156.10	2,269.43
May	2,219.61	5,486.49
June	1,713.00	4,798.40
July	3,732.35	2,004.89
August	7,538.68	2,414.16
September	3,047.74	4,027.54
October	2,117.58	3,271.35
November	3,675.50	5,099.37
December	4,262.91	5,196.25
Totals	$ 45,941.43	$ 48,974.24
1995	**Deposits**	**Disbursed**
January	$ 14,647.00	$ 10,526.05
February	14,702.51	18,809.13
March	5,035.15	3,541.26
April	4,855.00	4,048.94
May	3,177.47	5,130.98
June	19,291.00	12,485.66
July	6,590.91	9,901.59
August	3,548.59	3,348.25
September	10,133.06	12,209.31
October	4,402.00	3,326.73
November	2,792.00	4,087.37
December	4,661.02	4,580.40
	$ 93,835.71	$ 91,995.67
Totals	$139,777.14	$140,969.91

TOTALS PER BOOKS

1994	Deposits	Disbursed
January	$ 6,606.95	$ 2,215.08
February	2,258.10	1,736.63
March	5,863.50	10,774.20
April	2,585.10	4,734.17
May	2,727.61	5,200.96
June	3,132.00	2,593.76
July	2,104.28	1,284.34
August	7,822.73	5,361.41
September	3,211.87	1,934.61
October	2,539.58	2,624.30
November	3,593.65	6,048.91
December	4,358.25	4,643.37
Totals	$ 46,803.62	$ 49,151.74
1995	**Deposits**	**Disbursed**
January	$ 13,254.00	$ 12,626.38
February	14,702.51	16,410.55
March	5,875.15	5,021.90
April	4,741.00	2,271.05
May	13,211.47	15,440.90
June	8,244.00	10,019.96
July	7,057.10	2,880.70
August	2,359.40	3,803.94
September	10,133.06	9,824.31
October	4,292.00	6,346.73
November	3,537.00	2,449.72
December	5,002.72	4,338.04
	$ 92,409.41	$ 91,434.18
Totals	$139,213.03	$140,585.92

In reviewing Mills' working papers, Smith noticed that she had discovered debits with offsetting credits of $98 representing bank corrections. In developing his own data, he noticed that this same offsetting of debits and credits occurred when the church's bank was bought out and the new bank first took over the operations.

Required: Prepare a four-column proof of cash based on the data that was developed by Smith. Provide explanations for any discrepancies that you note.

QUESTIONS

Q8–1 What is included in the cash account?

Q8–2 What is meant by the phrase "near-cash items"?

Q8–3 What is the meaning of the phrase "cash and cash equivalents"?

Q8–4 What purpose(s) does a petty cash fund serve and how is such a fund established?

Q8–5 Why is control of cash so important to a firm? What are some important controls other than bank reconciliations?

Q8–6 Name the three methods of reconciling cash. Which method do you consider to be the best and why?

Q8–7 Name four typical items on a bank reconciliation that reconciles the book balance to the correct balance and vice versa. Explain why each item is a reconciling item.

Q8–8 Why do companies have accounts receivable? Explain the difference in the net method and the gross method as they affect receivables.

Q8–9 How are accounts receivable valued for statement purposes?

Q8–10 Why is an Allowance for Bad Debts account used?

Q8–11 Name the two major methods of establishing and maintaining an Allowance for Bad Debts account. What are the differences between these two methods? To which statement is each oriented?

Q8–12 How can receivables be used to obtain cash quickly?

Q8–13 The terms "assigning" and "discounting" are used with both accounts receivable and notes receivable. Define each term, explaining any differences between them.

Q8–14 Why do firms factor accounts receivable? "Recourse" is a term that drives the accounting treatment for factoring receivables. Explain the difference between factoring with and without recourse. Why would a company factor its receivables with recourse?

Q8–15 When is factoring deemed a sale? What criteria are used to determine if a sale took place?

Q8–16 How are the proceeds to be received from discounting notes determined?

Q8–17 How is the gain or loss on discounting notes receivable determined?

Q8–18 What does the term "noninterest-bearing note" mean? Why is it necessary to determine the effective interest on such notes? How is the effective interest rate on these notes determined?

Q8–19 Explain the difference between the fair-market-value method and the incremental-interest-rate method. Which is the preferred method?

Q8–20 How are accounts receivable assigned normally presented on the balance sheet?

Q8–21 What is the difference in information provided by the current and quick ratios?

Q8–22 What were the two asset management ratios discussed in this chapter? How are the values for these ratios determined? What information do they provide?

Q8–23 There are two basic criteria used in evaluating all ratios. What are they? Why are they important?

EXERCISES

E8–1 Cash Items

The cash account of Henco Inc. has a balance of $36,540. Your examination of the account reveals that the total is comprised of the following items:

1. $20,100 in a checking account.
2. $150 in a petty cash account that contains $50 currency.
3. $3,000 in a savings account.
4. $10,000 in certificates of deposits that mature in three days and were purchased six months ago.
5. A demand IOU from the company president for $3,000.
6. Postage stamps worth $290.

Required: Determine the correct cash balance. Make the necessary entries to obtain this balance. Use miscellaneous expenses to replenish the petty cash fund.

E8–2 Cash Items

The cash balance of Rasco Inc. is currently shown as $47,430. Your examination of the account reveals the total is comprised of the following items:

1. $32,300 in the checking account.
2. $200 in a petty cash account that contains $10 in currency.
3. $5,000 in certificates of deposits that mature in 21 days that were purchased 45 days ago.
4. $2,500 in a savings account.
5. $3,400 in a money market account.
6. An IOU from the president in the amount of $4,000.
7. Postage stamps in the amount of $30.

Required: Determine the correct cash balance and provide the necessary entries.

E8–3 Petty Cash Fund

On November 1, 1997, Fast Freddy Co. established a petty cash fund in the amount of $300. On November 20, 1997, the custodian requested that the fund be replenished and submitted vouchers and receipts as follows:

Postage	$ 32
Supplies purchased	75
Federal Express service	60
Travel reimbursement	120

Required: Prepare the entries to establish the fund and to replenish the fund. Also give the entry to increase the fund to $450.

E8–4 Petty Cash Fund

On June 1, 1998, KYPA Inc. established a $200 petty cash fund. On June 15, 1998, the custodian of the fund requested that the fund be replenished and submitted vouchers and receipts as follows:

Postage	$29
IOU from the company president	75
Supplies purchased	45
U.S. Postal Service (overnight)	42

Required: Provide the entries to establish and replenish the fund. Also give the entry to increase the fund to $400.

E8–5 Bank Reconciliation

The cash records of Core Products indicate the following:

Ending cash balance, per bank statement	$16,900
Ending balance, per books	15,525
Outstanding checks	3,400
Deposit in transit	4,200
Service charge	10
Charge for new checks	25
Bank collection of $2,000 note with interest	2,210

Required: Prepare a bank reconciliation bringing both the bank and the book balance to the actual cash position. Give the required entry to correct the book balance.

E8–6 Bank Reconciliation

The cash records of Simco indicate the following:

Ending cash balance, per bank statement	$12,400
Ending balance, per books	11,500
Outstanding checks	3,600
Deposits in transit	5,300
Service charge	25
Charge for new checks	30
Bank collection of $2,500 note with interest	2,750
NSF check from Cold Storage Inc.	95

Required: Prepare a bank reconciliation for Simco. Give the entry required to correct the bank balance.

E8–7 Recording Trade Receivables

Texas Inc.'s credit sales for May 1998 are $800,000, with credit terms of 2/10, n/30. Fifty percent of the customers took the discount; the remaining customers paid within 30 days.

Required:

A. Prepare the journal entries to record the above activities using each of the following:
   1. The gross method of recording sales and receivables.
   2. The net method of recording sales and receivables.

B. Explain why a company would choose one method over the other.

E8–8 Receivables With Discounts

The following events occurred in June 1998 for Arkansas, Inc.

1998	
June 1	Credit sales of $600,000 with terms 2/10, n/30.
10	Payments received for one-half the uncollected sales for June 1.
21	Credit sales of $200,000 with terms 2/10, n/30.
30	Payments received for one-half the uncollected sales for both June 1 and June 21.

Required:

A. Use the gross method of recording sales and receivables to
   1. Record the transactions.
   2. Determine amounts to report on a June income statement and June 30, 1998, balance sheet (assuming no beginning receivables).

B. Repeat (A) using the net method.

C. Explain any differences in reported revenues and receivables between the two methods.

E8–9 Allowance for Bad Debts

Chemical Inc. has credit sales for the month of March totaling $450,000 and collections on account for the month totaling $200,000. The balances in Accounts Receivable and Allowance for Bad Debts on March 1, 1998, were $1,000,000 and $50,000, respectively.

Required:

A. Past experience indicates that 2% of credit sales will become uncollectible. Prepare the adjusting entry for estimated bad debts using the percentage-of-sales method.

B. Based upon past experience, the company estimates that 5% of accounts receivable will become uncollectible. Prepare the adjusting entry for bad debts using the percentage-of-receivables method.

E8–10 Allowance for Bad Debts

Manufacturers Inc. began 1998 with accounts receivable and allowance for bad debts of $2.5 million and $0.12 million, respectively. During 1998 the company had credit sales of $5.6 million, collections on account of $6 million, and wrote off $0.1 million for accounts identified as uncollectible.

Required:

A. Past experience indicates that 1% of credit sales will become uncollectible. Prepare the adjusting entry for the sales method.

B. Based upon past experience, the company estimates that 4% of accounts receivable will become uncollectible. Prepare the adjusting entry for the percentage-of-receivables method.

E8–11 Accounts Receivable Assigned

Heavy Products needed operating cash. The company arranged a $90,000 loan at 12% and assigned $100,000 of accounts receivable to FinCo as collateral. FinCo charged a fee of $2,700. Heavy Products collected $80,000 of the assigned receivables and remitted these funds to FinCo one month after the loan origination. There were no sales discounts.

Required: Prepare the entries for both companies for the transactions.

E8–12 Accounts Receivable Assigned

Frozen Foods Inc was experiencing cash flow problems and needed operating cash. On June 1, the company arranged to borrow $150,000 at 10% interest and assigned $200,000 of accounts receivable as collateral to Fourth Third Bank. Fourth Third charged a fee of $3,000. On July 1, Frozen Foods collected $125,000 of the assigned receivables and remitted the funds to Fourth Third. $100,000 of the receivables collected received a 2% discount.

Required: Provide the entries for both companies for the above transactions.

E8–13 Factoring Without Recourse

Miller Corporation factored $320,000 of accounts receivable without recourse to Top$ Inc. and received proceeds of $240,000 on June 1, 1998. Of the $80,000 difference, $32,000 is withheld for sales adjustments. On November 30, 1998, Top$ sent $25,000 to Miller Corporation, indicating that sales returns were $4,000, sales discounts were $3,000, and the remainder of the receivables had been collected.

Required: Provide the entries for both sets of books for the transactions. Miller uses the gross method to record receivables.

E8–14 Factoring with Recourse Treated as Sale

The Needy Company factored $360,000 of accounts receivable with recourse to Ready Cash Company. However, Ready Cash can return receivables only under conditions outlined in the factoring agreement. Ready charges a 5% factor fee and withholds 10% for contingencies.

Assume that Ready Cash subsequently collects $333,000 of Needy's factored receivables. The difference is comprised of $7,000 of uncollectible accounts, sales discounts taken of $5,000, and $15,000 of sales returns and allowances.

Required: Prepare the entries for both companies to record the following:

A. The factoring transaction.
B. Collection of the receivables.
C. Settlement to close out the factoring arrangement.

E8–15 Notes Receivable Discounted Without Recourse

Industry Wholesalers sold $25,000 of merchandise to Retail Company on account. Retail experienced cash-management problems and agreed to pay $10,000 on the account. Retail issued a 12% interest-bearing note dated June 1, 1998, with a maturity date of December 1, 1998, for the remainder. On September 1, 1998, Industry discounted Retail's note without recourse at 15% to Security Bank.

Required:

A. Prepare the entries for Industry Wholesalers to record these transactions.
B. Assume the note was discounted with recourse. Prepare all the entries under each of the following assumptions.
   1. The discounted note was paid by Retail.
   2. The discounted note was dishonored by Retail, and the bank charged a $100 protest fee.

E8–16 Discounting Notes Receivable With and Without Recourse

P. Regier accepts a note receivable as a replacement of accounts receivable in the amount of $10,000. The note is dated March 1, 1998, has an interest rate of 8%, and a maturity date of December 1, 1998. Regier discounts the note on July 1, 1998, to Security Savings. Security charges a discount rate of 12%.

Required:

A. Assume that the note is discounted without recourse. Prepare the entries for Regier to record these events.
B. Assume that the note is discounted with recourse. Prepare the entry for Regier to discount the note on July 1, 1998. Then prepare the entries necessary on December 1, 1998, under the following assumptions.
   1. The note is paid at maturity.
   2. The note is defaulted at maturity, and Security charges a $50 protest fee.

E8–17 Noninterest-Bearing Notes

On October 1, 1998, Peabody Inc. gave Johnson Corp. a 6-month, noninterest-bearing note with a face value of $3,300 for a used truck. Johnson is on a calendar-year basis. The note was paid in a timely fashion.

Required: Provide the entries for Johnson's books on October 1, 1998, December 31, 1998, and April 1, 1999, under the following conditions:

A. The fair market value of the truck at the time of sale was $3,000, the cost was $6,000, and accumulated depreciation was $2,000.
B. The fair value of the truck was unknown, but Peabody's incremental borrowing rate is 18% per annum.

E8–18 Noninterest-Bearing Notes

On November 1, 1998, Holston Inc. gave Turner Corp. a 6-month, noninterest-bearing note with a face value of $15,000 for equipment. Turner is on a calendar-year basis and the note was paid by Holston Inc. when due.

Required: Provide the entries on Turner's books on November 1, 1998, December 31, 1998, and May 1, 1999, under the following conditions:

A. The equipment at the time of the sale was being sold for $14,000 cash and cost $11,000.
B. The equipment had a carrying value on Turner's books for $12,000, and the fair market value of similar-type equipment was $13,000.

E8–19 Liquidity Ratios

The data presented were extracted from Paragon's 1998 annual report.

	1998	1997	1996
Current assets:			
Cash	$ 25,000	$ 17,000	$ 18,000
Investments—Trading securities	25,000	8,000	4,000
Accounts receivable (net)	40,000	36,000	20,000
Inventories	80,000	85,000	60,000
Prepaid items	4,000	5,000	3,000
Total current assets	$174,000	$151,000	$105,000
Current liabilities	$ 90,000	$ 75,000	$ 50,000

Required: Calculate the current and quick ratios for each of the three years. Has the company's liquidity position improved? Explain.

E8–20 Asset Management Ratios

Refer to the information in E8–19 and the following table:

	1998	1997	1996
Credit sales	$266,000	$168,000	$95,000

Required: Calculate the accounts-receivable turnover and the average collection period for Paragon in 1997 and 1998. Is the company improving in its asset management? Why or why not? What cash management strategies would you recommend?

PROBLEMS

P8–1 Bank Reconciliation

The May bank statement for Harry's Hat Shop indicated an ending balance of $13,440. A May 31 deposit for $3,500 was not included in the statement. Harry's also had outstanding checks in the amount of $6,400. The bank statement included the following:

1. A canceled check for $400 charged against Harry's account that belonged to Happy the Glass Man.
2. A service charge for $15 and a collection fee of $25 for collecting $3,200 on a $3,000 face-value note plus interest.
3. A check written by Cool Co. for $350, included in a May 15 deposit and returned marked "Nonsufficient Funds."

On May 31 Harry's book balance of cash was $8,130.

Required: Prepare a bank reconciliation for Harry's Hat Shop and the adjusting entry to bring the cash balance up to date.

P8–2 Bank Reconciliation

Happy the Glass Man's bank statement for May indicated an ending balance of $23,680. A May 31 deposit for $6,500 was not included in the statement. Happy also had outstanding checks totaling $8,600. The bank statement included a canceled check for $600 that belonged to Harry's Hat Shop. Also charged against Happy's account was a service charge for $15 and a collection fee of $20 for collecting $2,200 on a $2,000 face-value note plus interest. A check written by Cool Company for $150, included in a May 15 deposit, was returned marked "Nonsufficient Funds." On May 31, Happy's book balance of cash was $20,165.

Required: Prepare a bank reconciliation for Happy the Glass Man and the adjusting entry to bring the cash balance up to date.

P8–3 Estimating Bad Debts

The data shown here were taken from the 1998 records of Fire Sales Company.

Cash sales	$125,000
Credit sales	900,000
Accounts receivable, 1/1/98	158,000
Accounts receivable, 12/31/98	170,000
Allowance for bad debts, 1/1/98	16,000

Fire Sales wrote off $30,000 of accounts receivable during 1998.

Required: Provide the year-end adjusting entries assuming the following situations.

A. 3% of credit sales is used to estimate bad debts.

B. 10% of the ending balance of accounts receivable is used to estimate bad debts.

Why would a company choose the method in (A)? in (B)?

P8–4 Estimating Bad Debts

During the year, Cereal Company estimates bad debts by using the percentage-of-sales method for interim reporting purposes and the percentage-of-receivables method at year-end. The totals of Cereal's aging schedule appear as shown.

AGE	PERCENT BAD DEBTS	AMOUNT
Under 30 days	0%	$180,000
Between 30 and 60 days	3	140,000
Between 61 and 120 days	5	90,000
Between 121 and 180 days	10	50,000
Between 181 and 365 days	15	40,000
Over 1 year	50	20,000
Total accounts receivable		$520,000

Required:

A. Prepare adjusting entries under the assumption that the allowance account has the following balances:

1. $2,300 debit
2. $4,500 credit
3. $28,000 credit

B. Why is aging of accounts receivable performed? That is, how does an aging analysis add to a company's ability to manage its accounts-receivable collection process?

P8–5 Estimating Bad Debts

During the year, Can Company estimates bad debts by the percentage-of-sales method for interim reporting purposes and uses the aging method at year-end. The totals of Can's aging schedule appear as follows:

AGE	PERCENT BAD DEBTS	AMOUNT
Under 30 days	0%	$280,000
Between 30 and 60 days	3	180,000
Between 61 and 120 days	6	100,000
Between 121 and 180 days	12	80,000
Between 181 and 365 days	18	60,000
Over 1 year (on an individual basis)		20,000
Total accounts receivable		$720,000

Short Company has an $8,000 balance that is over two years old and is considered uncollectible. Hathaway Company agreed to sign a 6-month note at 15% to replace its balance of $12,000, which is 14 months old.

Required:

A. Prepare the journal entries to dispose of the accounts that are more than one year old.

B. Prepare adjusting entries under the assumption that the allowance account has the following balances before the entries in (A) were recorded.

1. A $3,200 debit balance.
2. A $5,400 credit balance.
3. A $32,000 credit balance.

P8–6 Accounts Receivable Assigned

Strange & Associates assigns $50,000 of its accounts receivable to the bank. The bank charges 6% of the face value of the accounts receivable as a fee. The collateralized loan, dated June 1, 1998, is for 80% of the assigned receivables at 10% interest per annum.

The proceeds are reduced by the fee. During June, Strange collects $45,000 of the assigned receivables, half of which were given a 2% sales discount. Strange uses the gross method to record receivables. Cash received also was reduced by $500 for sales returns allowed. Funds collected are remitted to the bank on the first of the following month.

Required: Provide all the entries for Strange & Associates to record these transactions. Explain why Strange & Associates might have decided to assign its receivables.

P8–7 Accounts Receivable Assigned

Herby & Associates assigns $80,000 of its accounts receivable to the bank. The bank charges 5% of the face value of the accounts receivable as a fee. The collateralized loan, dated September 1, 1998, is for 80% of the assigned receivables at 12% interest per annum. During September, Herby collects $50,000 of the assigned receivables, half of which were given a 2% sales discount. Herby uses the gross method. Cash collected was reduced by $400 for sales returns allowed. During October, Herby collects an additional $20,000 of the assigned receivables without any discounts or returns. Funds collected are remitted to the bank on the first of the following month.

Required: Provide all entries on both sets of books to record these transactions.

P8–8 Factoring Accounts Receivable Without Recourse

On December 1, 1997, Electronic Sales Co. enters into a financial arrangement with Second Finance Company in which the receivables from all credit sales are sold to Second Finance. Second Finance pays 84% of the face value of the factored receivables and withholds 5% of the face value to provide for any sales adjustments. The receivables are transferred to Second Finance at the time of the sale. Electronic uses the gross method to record sales. The data for the month of December follow:

Electronic Sales Co.:	
Credit sales	$200,000
Credit sales returned	3,000
Second Finance Company:	
Collections	$120,000
Sales discounts	1,000

Required: Provide all entries for both sets of books for the month of December.

P8–9 Factoring Accounts Receivable With Recourse, Treated as a Sale

On December 1, 1997, Fancy Dress Makers entered into a financial arrangement in which all credit sales would be sold to Quick Finance. Fancy Dress has the option to repurchase receivables. Quick Finance pays 90% of the face value of the factored receivables and withholds an additional 8% to provide for any sales adjustments. Fancy Dress estimates that 3% of the credit sales is uncollectible, 3% will be returned, and 50% will take a 2% sales discount. Fancy Dress uses the gross method. Data for the month follow:

Fancy Dress Makers:	
Credit sales	$100,000
Credit sales returned	1,500
Quick Finance:	
Collections	$ 70,000
Sales discounts	600
Cash sent to reduce payable	3,000

Required:

A. Would this factoring arrangement be treated as a sale or a borrowing according to SFAS No. 77? Explain.

B. Prepare the entries for both sets of books.

P8–10 Factoring Accounts Receivable Without Recourse

On January 1, 1998, Appliance Sales Company entered into a financing arrangement in which all credit sales are sold without recourse to Fast Finance Company. Fast Finance pays 85% of the face value of the factored receivables and withholds 10% of the face value to provide for any sales adjustments. The receivables are transferred to Fast Finance at the time of sale. Appliance uses the gross method to record sales. Data for the first two months of 1998 are presented.

	JANUARY	FEBRUARY
Appliance Sales Company:		
Credit sales	$180,000	$125,000
Credit sales returned	3,700	2,400
Fast Finance Company:		
Collections:		
January receivables	$ 90,000	$ 60,000
February receivables		64,000
Sales discounts	1,400	1,500
Cash sent to Appliance to reduce payable		$ 12,900

Required: Provide all entries for both sets of books for the first two months of the arrangement.

P8–11 Factoring Accounts Receivable With Recourse, Treated as Sale

On January 1, 1998, Electronic Products entered into a financing arrangement in which all credit sales are sold with recourse to Ready Cash Company. Electronic has the option to repurchase receivables. Ready Cash pays 95% of the face value of the factored receivables and withholds an additional 10% to provide for any sales adjustments. Electronic estimates that 2% of credit sales is uncollectible, 4% of the sales will be returned, and 50% will take a 2% sales discount. Electronic uses the gross method. Data for the first two months of 1998 are presented.

	JANUARY	FEBRUARY
Electronic Products:		
Credit sales	$180,000	$125,000
Credit sales returned	4,800	7,500
Ready Cash Company:		
Collections:		
January receivables	$ 90,000	$ 60,000
February receivables		64,000
Sales discounts	1,400	1,500
Cash sent to Electronic to reduce payable		7,500

Required:

A. Would this factoring arrangement be treated as a sale or a borrowing arrangement according to SFAS No. 77? Explain.

B. Would Electronic Products prefer to structure this arrangement as a sale or a borrowing arrangement? Consider the balance sheet and income statement impacts of each accounting treatment in your answer.

C. Prepare the journal entries for both sets of books for the first two months of the arrangement.

P8–12 Notes Receivable

During 1998, Shank's Supplies entered into the following transactions:

Feb. 1	Accepted a 12%, $4,000, 30-day note for a past-due account from Smith.
Mar. 2	Smith paid the note and interest due.
15	Sold $3,000 of supplies to Hank's and received a noninterest-bearing $3,200 note due in three months.
April 15	The bank agreed to discount Hank's note at 15% without recourse.

Required:

A. Provide the above entries for Shank's Supplies.

B. Why would both parties agree to accept Hank's note?

P8–13 Notes Receivable

During 1998, Fayette Feeds entered into the following transactions:

May 1	Accepted a 12%, $3,000, 60-day note from Jones for a past-due account.
15	Sold $2,500 of grain to McDonald Farms and received a $2,750 noninterest-bearing note due in six months.
June 1	The bank agreed to discount Jones's note at 15% with recourse.
30	Jones dishonored the note held by the bank, and the bank notified Fayette and assessed a protest fee of $25.

Fayette Feeds' fiscal year ends on June 30.

Required:

A. Provide the relevant journal entries for Fayette Feeds during this period to record the transactions.

B. Why would Fayette Feeds want to discount the Jones note?

P8–14 Financial Management

The management of King Corporation prefers to buy long-term assets with cash rather than borrowing to finance these purchases. Because of this desire for cash, the company's credit policy is very strict. Customers' payments for their credit purchases must be received within 20 days of the purchase. This policy is strictly enforced.

Required:

A. The president of King Corporation has been studying the financial analysis you have prepared for her. She believes that the company's credit policy translates into a desirable accounts-receivable turnover of 12 because there are 20 business days each month. Is she correct? Explain.

B. If the company's accounts-receivable turnover is 12, is the company enforcing its collection policy strictly or loosely? Explain.

C. The president has proposed to you that one way to improve the company's current ratio would be to change the collection period from 20 days to 30 days. Would King Corporation's current ratio be higher if such a change were made? Explain.

P8–15 Interest-Bearing Versus Noninterest-Bearing Notes

On January 1, 1998, Barney Company lends $85,500 to a borrower who agreed to pay $100,000 on December 31, 2000, to retire the debt. The present value of $100,000 at 4% for four years is $85,500. A partial amortization table follows:

DATE	INTEREST REVENUE	UNAMORTIZED DISCOUNT	FUTURE PAYMENT	CARRYING VALUE
1/1/98		$14,500	$100,000	$85,500

Required:

A. Complete the amortization schedule shown above. Round all amounts to the nearest dollar.
B. Prepare all entries assuming the note is recorded as interest-bearing.
C. Prepare all entries assuming the note is recorded as noninterest-bearing.

P8–16 Interest-Bearing Versus Noninterest-Bearing Notes Receivable

On July 1, 1998, Clipper sells equipment to a customer. The cash price of the equipment is $113,650. The terms of the sale are a $25,000 cash down payment plus four semiannual payments of $25,000 each beginning on 1/1/99.

Required:

A. Determine the effective interest rate on the note.
B. Prepare an amortization schedule for the note.
C. Prepare the journal entries for Clipper to record the sale and collect the payments assuming the note is recorded as a noninterest-bearing note. (Ignore the adjusting entries to accrue interest on December 31 of each year.)
D. Prepare the journal entries for Clipper to record the sale and collect the payments assuming the note is recorded as an interest-bearing note. (Ignore the adjusting entries to accrue interest on December 31 of each year.)

P8–17 Uncollectible Accounts (CPA Exam Question, Part I, 4(b), May 1992)

Sigma Company began operations on January 1, 1990. On December 31, 1990, Sigma provided for uncollectible accounts based on 1% of annual credit sales. On January 1, 1991, Sigma changed its method of determining its allowance for uncollectible accounts by applying certain percentages to the accounts receivable aging as shown in the accompanying table.

DAYS PAST INVOICE DATE	PERCENT DEEMED TO BE UNCOLLECTIBLE
0–30	1%
31–90	5
91–180	20
Over 180	80

In addition, Sigma wrote off all accounts receivable that were over one year old. The following additional information relates to the years ended December 31, 1991, and 1990:

	1991	1990
Credit sales	$3,000,000	$2,800,000
Collections	2,915,000	2,400,000
Accounts written off	27,000	—
Recovery of accounts previously written off	7,000	—

DAYS PAST INVOICE DATE AT 12/31		
0–30	$ 300,000	$ 250,000
31–90	80,000	90,000
91–180	60,000	45,000
Over 180	25,000	15,000

Required:

A. Prepare a schedule showing the calculation of the allowance for uncollectible accounts at December 31, 1991.

B. Prepare a schedule showing the computation of the provision for uncollectible accounts for the year ended December 31, 1991.

P8–18 Four-Column Proof of Cash

The MGT Co. deposits all cash receipts and makes all payments by check. The following data were taken from MGT's records:

From the bank reconciliation of July 31:

Deposits in transit	$3,000
Outstanding checks	2,400

August data:

	PER BANK	PER BOOKS
Balance, August 1	$ 8,200	$ 8,800
August deposits	13,100	14,000
August checks	13,300	12,100
August note collected	1,000	
August bank charges:		
Service	20	
New checks	40	
Balance, August 31	$ 8,940	$10,700

Included with the August bank statement was a credit memo indicating that a deposit slip made out by MGT for $800 was actually $900.

Required: Prepare a four-column proof cash based on the above information.

P8–19 Determining Deposits in Transit and Outstanding Checks From a Four-Column Proof of Cash

The Tearney Co., as a matter of policy, deposits all cash receipts and makes all payments by check. The following data were taken from the cash records of the company:

From the bank reconciliation of May 31:

Deposits in transit	$2,200
Outstanding checks	1,400

June data:

	PER BANK	PER BOOKS
Balance, June 1	$ 5,000	$ 5,800
June deposits	10,600	12,300
June checks	14,500	13,900
June note collected (including interest of $200)	2,200	
June bank charges	10	
Balance, June 30	$ 3,290	$ 4,200

Required:

A. Compute the deposits in transit and the outstanding checks as of June 30.
B. Prepare a bank reconciliation using the four-column proof of cash.

RESEARCH ACTIVITIES

R8–1 Financial Analysis

Examine Motorola's 1995 annual report provided in Appendix C.

Required:

A. Determine the cash collected from customers for 1995.
B. Determine the company's receivables turnover and average collection period for 1995.
C. What type of entity is Motorola's primary customer?
D. Given the nature of the company's primary customers, does the average collection period seem a reasonable one? Why or why not?

R8–2 Financial Research

The chapter noted the extremely short average collection period for Wal-Mart Stores. Find an annual report for another company that you think would have a similar business environment to Wal-Mart's. For this company, determine its receivables turnover and average collection period. How do these compare with Wal-Mart's?

R8–3 Financial Research

A current ratio of 2.0 or higher is sometimes recommended as a desirable "rule of thumb." This suggests that many successful companies would have current ratios of 2.0 or higher. Choose a financial database of corporations (such as the DISCLOSURE database accompanying this text) and guess what proportion of the companies in the database would have a current ratio of 2.0 or higher. Then, search the database to determine the actual proportion. How close was your guess? Based upon your results, what is your opinion of the popular "rule of thumb"?

Next, find a sample of two companies with relatively large current ratios (e.g., higher than 3.0). For these firms, prepare a brief analysis stating the major element(s) on the balance sheet contributing to the high ratios.

Would you say that firms with higher current ratios more effectively manage current resources than do firms with lower ones? Why or why not?

R8–4 Report Preparation

Obtain a current (1997 or later) annual report. Prepare a summary of the impact of accounts receivables on the current income statement, balance sheet, and the statement of cash flows. (*Hint:* Calculate all applicable ratios that include accounts receivable, then deduct the accounts receivable amount(s) and calculate the ratios again.)

R8–5 Internet Exercise Factoring

Search the Internet for information concerning factoring. One source of information can be found at *http/www.infi.net/~ibsva/CFFOV/factor.htm.* Another method is to use a search engine and type in key words relevant to this chapter, such as factoring. How does this location relate to the material in this chapter?

R8–6 Financial Research

Examine annual reports for two retail businesses.

Required:

A. Determine the accounts receivable turnover and the average days to collect for each firm for as many years as possible from the data given.
B. Calculate the current ratios and quick ratios.
C. Compare the two companies as to their liquidity and their cash flow from operations.
D. Which company would you consider to be in the better cash position?

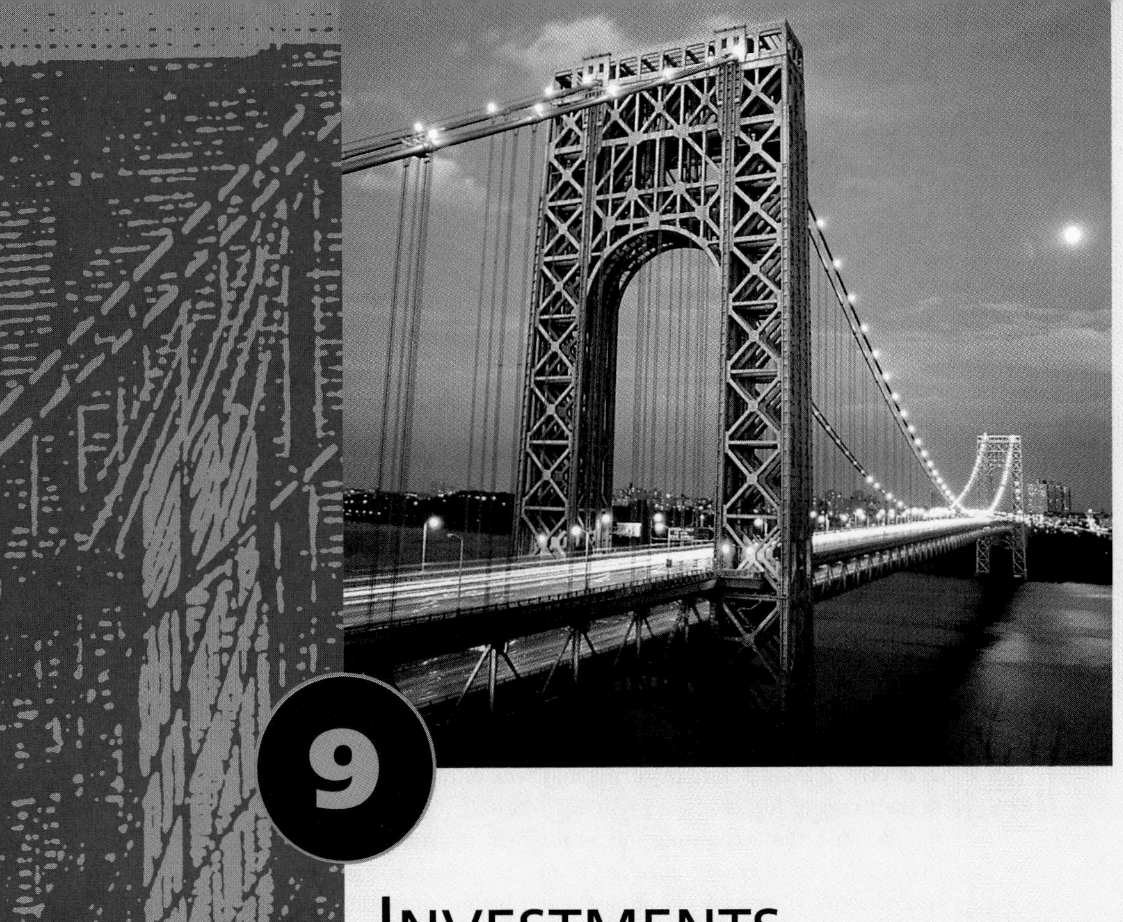

9

Investments

Learning Objectives

After studying this chapter, you should be able to:

1. Explain the recognition and measurement issues associated with investments.
2. Record and report transactions for debt-security investments and equity-security investments of less than 20 percent.
3. Record and report equity-security investment transactions of greater than 20 percent and less than 50 percent.
4. Record and report transactions for funds and life insurance investments.
5. Analyze the impact of the different accounting methods for investments on profitability and liquidity measures.
6. Understand the concepts and complexities associated with derivative financial instruments.

FASB No. 115: It's Back to the Future for Market Value Accounting

Like time travel, comprehensive market value accounting still lies in the future. In an era of deregulated interest rates and massive losses from thrift and bank failures, a debate has raged over the accounting for financial instruments. Market value accounting has been called a panacea by some and a placebo by others. The Financial Accounting Standards Board, under intense pressure from the Securities and Exchange Commission and others to resolve the issue, accelerated part of its financial instruments project to focus on accounting for debt securities. In May 1993, the FASB issued Statement No. 115, "Accounting for Certain Investments in Debt and Equity Securities."

New Business Environment

The business strategies of financial institutions and other investors have become more dynamic since interest rates were deregulated over a decade ago. At one end of the spectrum are investors that manage a part of their investment portfolios as a trading account. At the other end are those that purchase debt instruments, rarely (if ever) sell them before maturity, and seek only to earn an interest spread relative to their cost of funds.

Because the accounting model for debt instruments was designed in simpler times, its continued relevance has been questioned, particularly in the case of portfolios carried at cost. Accounting standards that allow financial statements to overstate significantly a business enterprise's underlying economic value—as was the case with many failed banks and savings and loans—are fair game for criticism. Many believe market value accounting is the best way to move the accounting model into the future.

Source: James T. Parks, "FASB No. 115: It's Back to the Future for Market Value Accounting," *Journal of Accountancy*, September 1993, pp. 49–56.

The excerpt from the article by James T. Parks in the *Journal of Accountancy* addresses the historical background for the accounting and reporting requirements for investments in debt and equity securities. The principal standards for these securities are prescribed in SFAS No. 115 and APB Opinion No. 18. SFAS No. 115 was enacted for several reasons. First, there were perceived inconsistencies in income measurement and asset valuation when following the precepts of APB Opinion No. 18 and SFAS No. 12. These inconsistencies were addressed in SFAS No. 115. Second, during the mid to late 1980s and early 1990s, there was a growing movement in the financial community toward current-market valuation of asset holdings. This shift was triggered to some degree by the many failures of banks and savings and loan institutions, referred to in the press as the S&L crisis. SFAS No. 115 applies to those financial statements issued after December 15, 1993. The provisions of SFAS No. 115 require that investments in bonds be carried at fair value, or market value, unless the investor has the intent and ability to hold the bonds until they mature. Equity securities are also to be carried and reported at fair value. This chapter discusses the accounting and reporting requirements for debt and equity investment securities.

RECOGNITION AND MEASUREMENT

Explain the recognition and measurement issues associated with investments.

Investments are assets; they represent economic resources owned or controlled by the firm, from which the firm expects to receive future economic benefits. The nature of these expected future economic benefits could be long-term or short-term (or both) depending on the timing of the revenue-generating process of the investment.

Conceptually, accounting for investments depends on this underlying revenue-generating process. The accountant's ability to monitor or measure this process is crucial to recognition of the revenue derived from the assets as well as the proper classification and valuation of the investment assets. Revenues derived from an investment expected over a number of future periods are classified differently from those expected in the current period only. That is, if the benefits of the asset are expected to be entirely realized in the current period, proper classification and valuation would be as a current asset. Conversely, if benefits are expected to be realized in current and future periods, proper classification and valuation would be as a long-term asset.

Proper accounting for investments depends on the intentions of management with regard to the holding period for investments in debt and equity securities, the ownership percentage represented by a stock investment, and the marketability of the investment. SFAS No. 115 applies to all debt securities and to those equity investments that have "readily determinable fair values" and are not accounted for using the equity method (generally less than 20 percent ownership). Readily determinable **fair value** refers to the sales price or bid-and-ask quotations that are currently available on a securities exchange registered with the SEC or the National Association of Securities Dealers. APB Opinion No. 18 applies to those equity investments accounted for using the equity method (generally greater than 20 percent ownership interest). Exhibit 9–1 provides a summary of accounting requirements for securities investments.

DEBT SECURITY AND EQUITY SECURITY INVESTMENTS OF LESS THAN 20 PERCENT OWNERSHIP

Record and report transactions for debt-security investments and equity-security investments of less than 20 percent.

SFAS No. 115, "Accounting for Certain Marketable Securities," superseded SFAS No. 12 and became effective for fiscal years beginning after December 15, 1993. SFAS No. 115 applies to all investments in debt securities and to passive investments in equity securities that have readily determinable fair values. A *passive investment* is one in which the investor has no ability to exercise "significant influence" over the policies of the investee. Significant influence is presumed to exist with ownership of 20 percent to 50 percent of the voting stock of the investee. Prior to the adoption of SFAS No. 115, U.S. GAAP was consistent with international accounting standards.

CLASSIFICATION OF INVESTMENT SECURITIES

Three classification categories are designated in SFAS No. 115: held-to-maturity securities, trading securities, and available-for-sale securities. **Held-to-maturity securities** are debt securities that the entity has the positive intent and ability to hold to maturity.[1] **Trading securities** are those debt and equity securities bought and held principally for the purpose of sale in the near term. They are purchased with the intent of generating profit on short-term changes in price.[2] **Available-for-sale securities** are those debt and equity securities neither clas-

[1]SFAS No. 115, FASB, May 1993, par. 12.
[2]Ibid., par. 7.

EXHIBIT 9–1 Summary of Accounting Requirements for Investments

APPROPRIATE GAAP	SFAS NO. 115	APB OPINION NO. 18	
OWNERSHIP	0% ◄——► 20%	20% ◄——► 50%	50% ◄——► 100%
	Accounting Method: Fair value or Amortized cost	**Accounting Method:** Equity method	**Accounting Method:** Consolidated financial statements
	Where applicable: 1. Debt investments 2. Equity investments of < 20% voting interest	**Where applicable:** Equity securities investments with significant influence (20%–50% of voting stock)	**Where applicable:** Equity security investments with more than 50% of voting stock
	Classes of Investments: 1. Trading securities 2. Available-for-sale 3. Held-to-maturity		
	Accounting Required for Each Class: 1. Trading securities a. Changes in market value recognized as gain or loss in current-period income b. Securities reported at market value 2. Available-for-sale a. Changes in market value recognized as separate component of shareholders' equity until realized b. Securities reported at market value 3. Held-to-maturity a. Changes in market value not recognized b. Securities reported at amortized cost	**Accounting Required:** a. Investment recorded at cost b. Investment account increased for proportionate share of income c. Investment account decreased for: 1. Dividends received 2. Extra depreciation 3. Amortization of goodwill	**Accounting Required:** Beyond scope of text

IN PRACTICE—INTERNATIONAL

Equity Method

International accounting standards for investments were consistent with U.S. GAAP prior to adoption of SFAS No. 115. IAS No. 25, "Accounting for Investments," requires lower-of-cost-or-market treatment for investments with less than significant influence. IAS No. 28, "Accounting for Investments in Associates," requires use of the equity method for investments in which significant influence exists. Similar to U.S. GAAP, a cutoff of 20 percent is used in determining the existence of significant influence.

Several European countries, among others, do not require the use of the equity method. Germany expressly prohibits its use. And although permitted, the equity method is rarely used in Belgium, Greece, Ireland, Italy, Luxembourg, Portugal, and Spain.

Source: L. Sundby and B. Schwieger, "EC, EZ?" *Journal of Accountancy,* (March 1992), p. 73.

sified as trading securities nor as held-to-maturity securities.[3] The available-for-sale classification is intended for securities that management declares are not for trading purposes or realization of profit on short-term changes in price. Available-for-sale and held-to-maturity investments may be classified as either short-term or long-term investments, depending on the maturity dates of the investment and intention of management.

Proper classification of the investment into these designated categories is important. The assumed revenue recognition is different for each category. The revenue to be recognized stems from changes in fair value of the security, the dividend or interest income, gains or losses on the sales of the investments, and the amortization of discount or premium on available-for-sale and held-to-maturity debt securities. Exhibit 9–2 provides an illustration of the classification process.

HELD-TO-MATURITY SECURITIES

Held-to-maturity securities are debt securities that the entity has the intent and ability to hold until they mature and are redeemed by the issuing entity. Valuation for balance sheet reporting purposes does not consider fair value; instead, they are reported at amortized cost. *Amortized cost* is the original cost plus or minus any unamortized portion of the discount or premium on the purchase. Interest revenue (cash received plus discount amortized, or cash received minus premium amortized) is reported as income.

Debt Securities Purchased at a Premium or Discount. Investments in debt securities are recorded at cost, including all acquisition costs and fees. The market price of the bond at acquisition represents a composite of the market's assessment of the risk associated with the debt security, and the stated interest rate of the bond in relation to the current market rate (or yield) for securities of similar risk and maturity.

If the stated interest rate on the bond is exactly equal to the current market rate, the bonds will sell at par (face) value. If the stated interest rate is below the current market rate, the bonds will sell at a **discount**, or less than par value. If the stated interest rate is above the current market rate, the bonds will sell at a **premium**, or above the par value. The discount or premium on the selling price exists because of the difference between the stated interest rate and the current market rate. This results in a **yield**, or **return on the investment,** equal to the current market rate.

Computing Market Prices of Bond Investments. The market price of a bond is the sum of the present values of the future interest payments and the present value of the face amount or maturity value. The interest rate used in the present value calculation is the current market rate of interest. For example, the current market price for 100, 10-year, 10%, $1,000 bonds, with interest payable annually and discounted to yield the current market rate of 8%, would be:

Present value of face: $100,000 × .4632	= $ 46,320
Present value of interest payments: $100,000 × 10% × 6.71	= 67,100
Current market price at 8% yield	$113,420

[3]Ibid.

EXHIBIT 9–2
Investment Classification Decisions

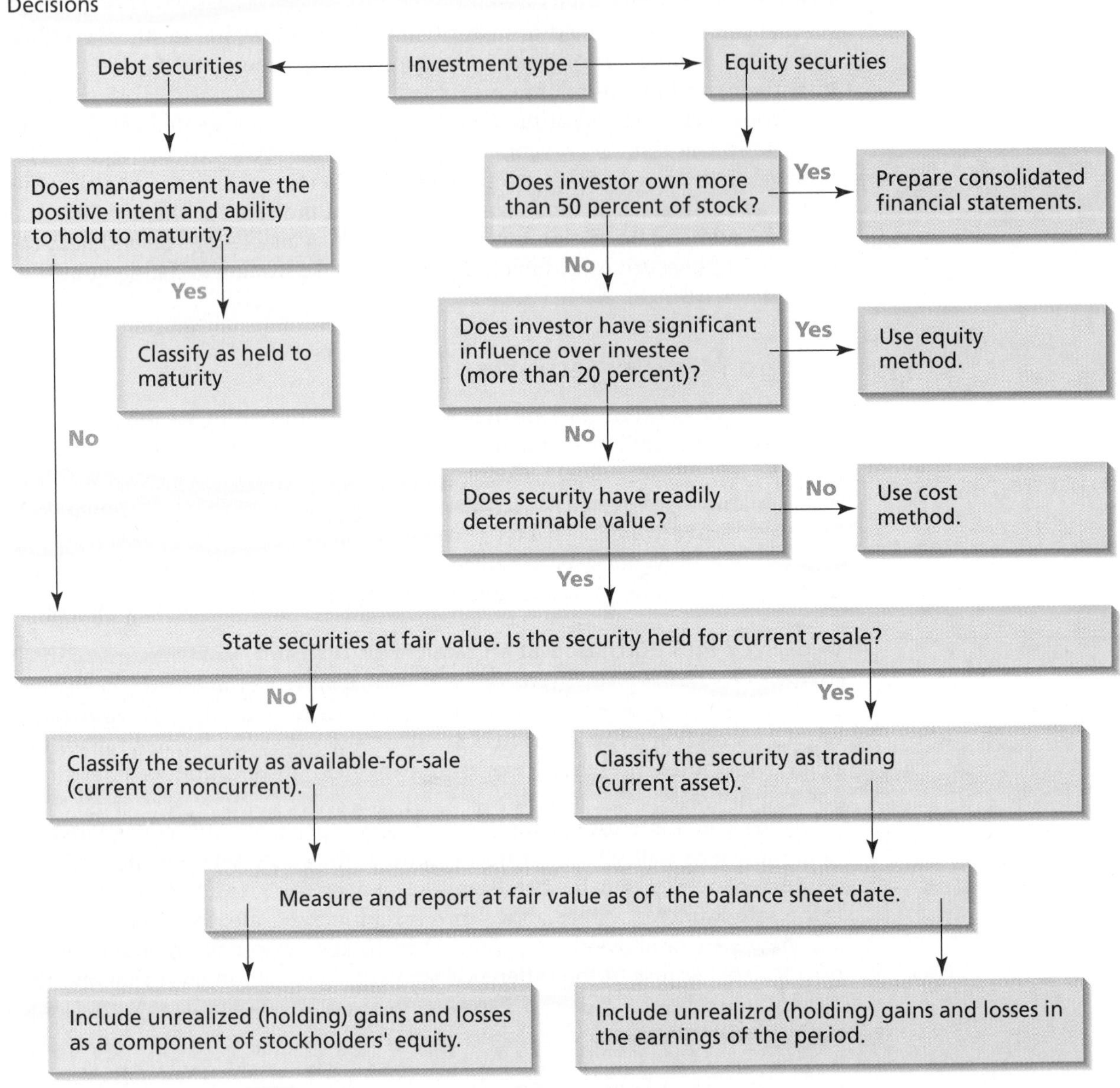

This market price represents a premium of $13,420 that an investor is willing to pay because the annual "interest" payments on these bonds (10%) is greater than the current market rate of interest (8%). If the current market rate were to increase, the price of these bonds would decrease so that the yield would always be equivalent to the current market yield. *The market prices of bonds move in the opposite direction of interest rate changes.*

Assuming that the interest payments are made at December 31 of each year, and the purchase of $100,000 in face value of these bonds is made at January 1, 1995, the journal entry to record the investment would be as follows:

Investment in Debt Securities	113,420	
Cash		113,420

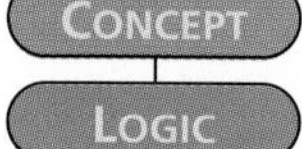

Asset valuation at cost.

Investments are assets and are recorded at cost. Cost (the amount paid) in this case is derived from the present value of future cash inflows discounted at the current market rate of interest.[4]

The economic substance of this transaction is that, for an investment of $113,420, the investor will receive in return $200,000 ($100,000 in maturity value at the end of 10 years plus 10 annual interest payments of $10,000). That is, the 10-year, revenue-generating process will add value in the amount of $86,580 ($200,000 − $113,420). The difference between what one invests ($113,420) and what one gets back ($200,000) is interest revenue. A fundamental revenue recognition issue is *when* the revenue should be recognized. Revenue could be recognized (1) during the value-adding process, (2) as it is "earned," or (3) at one point at the end when it can be definitively verified.

GAAP currently dictates that revenue is to be recognized during the 10-year, value-adding process. Thus, a second question emerges: *how* should the revenue be recognized? One set of options for recognition of the revenue would be to *assume* value is added (1) in a straight-line process ($8,658 per year; that is, one-tenth of $86,580 per year), (2) in a compounding incremental process, or (3) some other process. To ensure comparability of treatment across firms, although not necessarily representational faithfulness to economic reality, GAAP prescribes the effective-interest method,[5] which is discussed next.

Amortization of Bond Premiums and Discounts. Amortization of bond premiums and discounts follows the effective-interest method, which results in a constant rate of return on the book value of the investment from period to period. Exhibit 9–3 illustrates amortization of the bond premium of $13,420, which assumes the purchase of $100,000 par value bonds at a price of $113,420.

On each interest payment date, the carrying value (or book value) of the bonds is adjusted to amortize the premium or discount on the investment. The amortization amount is found by using an 8% discount rate, the market rate of interest prevailing at the time the investment was made. The current interest rate is not used, and so the adjusted book values do not reflect current market values. Since the bonds were purchased at January 1, 1995, the first interest

[4]Note that, by convention, a separate discount or premium account is established for investments in bonds—unlike the treatment for bonds payable.

[5]GAAP allows use of the straight-line method of amortization if the results are not significantly different from the effective-interest method.

payment date is December 31, 1995. The journal entry to record the receipt of interest and amortize the premium would be

Cash	10,000*	
Investment in Debt Securities		926
Interest Revenue		9,074**

To record interest received of $10,000 cash and amortization of premium of $926 (see Exhibit 9–3).

\$100,000 × 10%
***\$113,420 × .08*

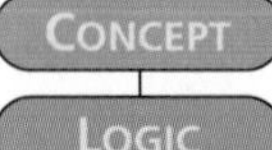

Revenue recognition.

Interest received on the bond investment is revenue and is recognized when earned in the current period. Amortization of the premium reduces the revenue recognized because the premium amount allocated over the life of the asset reduces the rate of return on the investment, thus reflecting the current market rate of interest at the time of purchase.

Thus, interest revenue is $9,074, an 8% yield rate multiplied by the book value (8% × $113,420). The premium amortization is the difference between the cash interest and the interest revenue ($10,000 − $9,074 = $926). In 1996

EXHIBIT 9–3
Amortization of Bond Premium

Data:
Assume the purchase of $100,000 par value bonds that pay 10% annual interest on December 31 of each year. The bonds mature on 12/31/04, and were purchased on 1/1/95 at a total cost of $113,420, providing a yield or effective interest rate of 8%.

The amortization table for these bonds follows:

(1) DATE	(2) ANNUAL PAYMENT	(3)* INTEREST REVENUE	(4)** PREMIUM AMORTIZATION	(5)*** BOOK VALUE
1/1/95				$113,420
12/31/95	$10,000	$9,074	$ 926	112,494
12/31/96	10,000	8,999	1,001	111,493
12/31/97	10,000	8,919	1,081	110,413
12/31/98	10,000	8,833	1,167	109,246
12/31/99	10,000	8,740	1,260	107,985
12/31/00	10,000	8,639	1,361	106,624
12/31/01	10,000	8,530	1,470	105,154
12/31/02	10,000	8,412	1,588	103,567
12/31/03	10,000	8,285	1,715	101,852
12/31/04	10,000	8,148	1,852	100,000

*8% of column (5) from previous year
**Column (2) − column (3)
***Column (5) of previous year minus column (4) of current year

and every year thereafter, interest revenue again reflects an 8% yield on the beginning book value (8% × $112,494 = $9,000 for 1996).

The book value of the Bond Investment account is the present value of the principal plus the present value of the interest payments. The discount rate used is the market rate of interest at the time of purchase. Another determination of the new book value is the par plus the unamortized premium (or minus the unamortized discount). The amortization required is the change in the book value from the previous amortization date, or the difference between the cash received and the interest revenue recognized. The resulting interest revenue is that portion of the $86,580 in lifetime interest allocated to the current year. The journal entries to record the interest and amortize the premium over the life of an investment classified as held-to-maturity are illustrated in Exhibit 9–4. If the bonds were purchased at a discount, the amortization would represent an increase in interest revenue and therefore an increase in the Investment account.

Sale of Held-to-Maturity Debt Securities Before Maturity Date. If debt securities are sold before the maturity date, the premium or discount must be amortized and interest must be accrued up to the date of sale. The difference between the sales price and the carrying (book) value of the investment after premium/discount amortization represents a realized gain or loss on the investment. The realized gain or loss on the investment subsequently appears as "Other revenue" or "Other expense" on the income statement.

EXHIBIT 9–4
Journal Entries at Each Interest Payment Date

Date	Account	Debit	Credit
1995			
Dec. 31	Cash	10,000	
	Investment in Bonds*		926
	Interest Revenue		9,074
1996			
Dec. 31	Cash	10,000	
	Investment in Bonds		1,001
	Interest Revenue		8,999
1997			
Dec. 31	Cash	10,000	
	Investment in Bonds		1,081
	Interest Revenue		8,919
⋮	⋮		
2004			
Dec. 31	Cash	10,000	
	Investment in Bonds		1,852
	Interest Revenue		8,148

*Note that the Investment in Bonds account is directly reduced at each interest payment date rather than a separate premium account.

To illustrate, assume the bonds in Exhibits 9–3 and 9–4 are sold on June 30, 2001, at a price of $101,000 plus accrued interest. The sale necessitates the following journal entries:

Interest Revenue	735*	
Investment in Bonds—HTM		735
To amortize premium 1/1/01 to 6/30/01.		
**$1,470 × 6/12*		

Interest Receivable	5,000*	
Interest Revenue		5,000
To accrue interest 1/1/01 to 6/30/01.		
**$100,000 × 10% × 6/12*		

Cash	106,000*	
Loss on Sale	4,889	
Interest Receivable		5,000
Investment in Bonds		105,889**
**$101,000 + $5,000*		
***$106,624 − $735*		

Computation of the loss:	
Carrying value at 1/1/01	$106,624
Less: Premium amortization	(735)
Book value at time of sale	$105,889
Sales price (101% of Par)	(101,000)
Loss on sale	$ 4,889

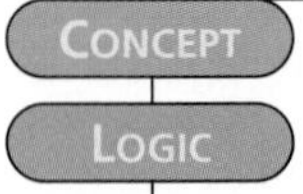

Recognition of gain/loss at completion of earnings process.

The earnings process for these assets (debt securities) has been completed. The periodic revenue from the interest is recognized to the date of sale, and the premium is amortized. The loss on the sale is the difference between the price received and the amortized cost (carrying or book value) of the asset.

The individual debt-security investments require this periodic amortization of premium or discount if they are classified either as held-to-maturity or available-for-sale. The amortization amounts, together with the interest received, are reflected in current-period income. The held-to-maturity debt securities are reported at amortized cost on the balance sheet and do not reflect changes in fair values, whereas available-for-sale debt securities are reported at "fair value" on the balance sheet. Accounting for available-for-sale debt securities is discussed next.

Accounting for Available-for-Sale Debt Securities. Available-for-sale debt securities are recorded initially at cost. Subsequent to purchase, the premium or discount must be amortized in a fashion similar to held-to-maturity debt securities, and *the securities are carried on the investor's books at amortized cost. The securities are reported, however, at fair value on the investor's balance sheet.* An Adjustment to Market account is used for the difference between the carrying value (amortized cost) and the fair value used for reporting purposes. The total of the Investment account and the Adjustment to Market account is the fair market value of the securities at the reporting date.

For securities classified as available-for-sale, the changes in fair values from one reporting period to the next are reported as a separate component of equity. Only the net interest revenue (after amortization of the discount or premium) is reported in periodic income. The bonds in Exhibit 9–3 can be used to illustrate the basic accounting requirements.

Suppose that the bonds acquired in Exhibit 9–3 were classified by management as available-for-sale at acquisition on January 1, 1995. At the end of each reporting period (assume one year), adjusting entries would be required to (1) record interest revenue and premium amortization and (2) mark the bonds to fair value. To illustrate, assume these year-end fair values:

12/31/95	$115,000
12/31/96	112,500

In 1995 the following journal entries would be recorded:

1/1	Investment in Debt Securities—AFS*	113,420	
	Cash		113,420
	To record the purchase.		
12/31	Cash	10,000	
	Investment in Debt Securities—AFS		926
	Interest Income		9,074
	To record interest and premium amortization.		
	Adjustment to Market—AFS	2,506**	
	Unrealized Holding Gain (Loss) AFS—Equity		2,506

**AFS refers to Available For Sale in this and following examples.*
***$115,000 − ($113,420 − $926)*

The Adjustment to Market amount ($2,506) is the difference between the market value at year-end ($115,000) and the amortized cost of the investment ($113,420 − $926).

The total of the Adjustment to Market account ($2,506) and the Investment account ($112,494) is the market value ($115,000) at year-end. The Unrealized Holding Gain (Loss) account is reported as a separate account in the equity section.

At the end of the next period (1996), the premium is amortized, interest revenue recorded, and the fair market value again reported. The Adjustment to Market and the Unrealized Holding Gain (Loss) accounts are increased or decreased to again equal the difference between market value and amortized cost. The adjusting entries at the end of 1996 would be as follows:

12/31	Cash	10,000	
	Investment in Debt Securities—AFS		1,001
	Interest Revenue		8,999
	To record interest and amortization.		

Unrealized Holding Gain (Loss) AFS—Equity		1,499*	
Adjustment to Market—AFS			1,499
* Required balance:			
Current market value	$112,500		
Amortized cost ($112,494 − $1,001)	111,493		
Balance required	$ 1,007		
Current balance in adjustment account	2,506		
Adjustment required (reduction)	$ (1,499)		

The book value of the bonds (amortized cost) at December 31, 1996, is $111,493 ($112,494 − $1,001). The market value at year-end is $112,500; therefore, the required balance in the Adjustment to Market account is the difference, $1,007. The existing previous balance was $2,506, so the balance must be reduced by the difference, $1,499. Each period thereafter, the adjustments are made in a similar fashion.

Sale of Available-for-Sale Debt Securities. If these bonds were sold before the maturity date, the difference between the carrying value and the proceeds of the sale is recorded as a realized gain or loss. At the same time, the Adjustment to Market account and the Unrealized Holding Gain or Loss account are removed from the books if these were the only securities that were held in the available-for-sale category. To illustrate, assume these bonds were sold at 1/1/97 for $112,500 and were the only securities in this category. The journal entries to record the sale would be:

Cash	112,500	
Realized Gain on Sale of Debt Securities—AFS		1,007
Investment in Debt Securities—AFS		111,493
Unrealized Holding Gain (Loss) AFS—Equity	1,007	
Adjustment to Market—AFS		1,007

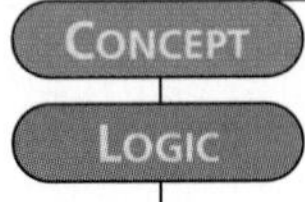

Recognition of gain on sale of asset.

When the asset (investment) is sold, the difference between the sales price and the carrying (book) value is recognized as a gain or loss.

If other securities were held in the available-for-sale category, the second entry above to remove the Unrealized Holding Gain and Adjustment to Market accounts would not be made. Instead, at the end of the period, these accounts would again be adjusted to reflect the difference between the carrying value and the current fair value of the remaining securities in the available-for-sale category.

Accounting for Debt Securities Classified as Trading. Purchases of debt securities that management intends to hold for only short periods are recorded at cost and classified as trading securities. Because they will be held for only short periods, amortization of premiums and discounts will not be material and is therefore ignored. Changes in fair value of these investments are reported in current-period income.

To illustrate, we can use the same bonds that were used to illustrate the available-for-sale classification. Assume that the bonds are purchased on November 15, 1998, at a price of $113,420 and that the market price at December 31, 1998, is $115,000. The journal entries to record the purchase and adjust to fair value follow:

1998			
Nov. 15	Investment in Debt Securities—TS*	113,420	
	Cash		113,420
Dec. 31	Adjustment to Market—TS	1,580**	
	Unrealized Holding Gain (Loss) TS—Income		1,580

**TS refers to trading securities in this and following examples.*
***$115,000 – $113,420*

This investment would be reported on the balance sheet at the fair market value of $115,000. The change in market value would be reported as a part of income. No amortization of premium or discount is necessary, since the bonds will be sold very quickly.

When the bonds are sold, gains and losses already recognized will not be recorded; only those gains and losses that arise after the most recent financial statement date must be recognized. Assume that the bonds are sold at $115,000 on January 2 of the next year. The entry to record the sale would be as follows:

1999			
Jan. 2	Cash	115,000	
	Investment in Debt Securities—TS		113,420
	Adjustment to Market—TS		1,580

If the same bonds were sold on a later date at a price other than $115,000, a gain or loss would be recognized at the time of sale. Suppose that these bonds were sold on March 15, 1999, at a price of $115,400. The journal entry to record this transaction would be:

1999			
Mar. 15	Cash	115,400	
	Investment in Debt Securities—TS		113,420
	Adjustment to Market—TS		1,580
	Gain on Sale of TS		400

In this instance, the total gain on the transaction is $1,980, which is the difference between the cost ($113,420) and the sales price ($115,400). Of the total gain, $1,580 had already been recognized in the adjustment to market at the end of 1998. The remaining price change of $400 is recognized at the time of the sale.

REPORTING CHANGES IN FAIR VALUE FOR EQUITY SECURITIES

Changes in fair value refer to changes in the current market price compared to cost or the last measured market price. Prior to SFAS No. 115, declines in market value were recognized, but increases in market value above cost were not. Hence, lower-of-cost-or-market accounting was followed for equity investments. The FASB deemed this inconsistent, and SFAS No. 115 now prescribes that both increases and decreases be recognized either in income or in equity, depending on the classification category of the investment.

Equity Trading Securities. Similar to other assets, equity trading securities are recorded initially at cost. Realized gains and losses from sale of these securities are included in income. Unrealized holding gains and losses on these securities are also included in income. Holding gains and losses stem from price fluctuations in the security. Any dividend and/or interest income received is also included in income. Valuation of these securities is at fair value for balance sheet reporting purposes and can be accomplished either by use of an Adjustment to Market account, or by adjusting the investment account directly. SFAS No. 115 does not prescribe a particular treatment. Using an Adjustment to Market account is consistent with the treatment accorded securities classified as available-for-sale. Adjustment of the investment account directly is justifiable on the basis that trading securities are sold soon after purchase and are not held for long periods.

To illustrate accounting for trading securities, assume that the following information relevant to the Kay Stevens Inc. portfolio of trading securities is available at 12/31/98.

	TOTAL COST	FAIR VALUE AT 12/31/97	FAIR VALUE AT 12/31/98
1,000 shares Teradyne	$ 23,000	$ 28,500	$ 37,000
2,000 shares Intel	100,000	142,500	96,500
2,000 shares Brunswick	46,000	39,000	42,000
Total equity securities	$169,000	$210,000	$175,500

Assume that all the stock was purchased during 1997. Further assume that Stevens sold 1,000 shares of Intel for a net price of $81,000 during 1998 and received dividends of $20,000 in each year. The journal entries to record all these transactions follow.

1997	Investment in Equity Securities—TS	169,000	
	Cash		169,000
	To record the purchase of the securities		
	Cash	20,000	
	Dividend Income		20,000
	To record receipt of dividends during 1997.		

If we assume that Kay Stevens uses an Adjustment to Market account for its trading securities, at December 31, 1997, Stevens would make the following entry to adjust the trading securities portfolio to fair value and to recognize the unrealized holding gain/(loss) as part of income.

1997			
Dec. 31	Adjustment to Market—TS	41,000*	
	Unrealized Holding Gain on TS—Income		41,000

$210,000 − $169,000

Alternatively, if Stevens did not use an Adjustment account, the adjustment instead would be made directly to the investment account.

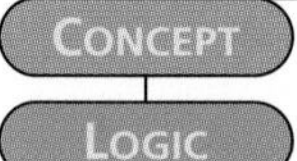

Representational faithfulness.

Since trading securities are purchased with the intention of realizing profit from short-term price fluctuations, recognition of unrealized gains and losses in current-period income is representative of the underlying economic event.

To record the receipt of dividends in 1998, Stevens would make the following entry.

Cash	20,000	
Dividend Income		20,000

The sale of trading securities results in a realized gain or realized loss at the time of sale. The amount of the gain or loss is the difference between the most recently recorded market price and the sales price of the securities. During 1998, the sale of 1,000 shares of Intel at a price of $81,000 results in a realized gain of $9,750 ($81,000 − $71,250). The following entry is made assuming that Stevens uses an Adjustment account.

Cash	81,000	
Investment in Equity Securities—TS		50,000
Adjustment to Market—TS		21,250*
Realized Gain on TS		9,750

**$71,250 − $50,000*

At the end of 1998, the trading securities portfolio must again be adjusted to the current market price with any unrealized gain or loss on the portfolio reported in income.

Adjustment to Market—TS	36,750*	
Unrealized Holding Gain on TS—Income		36,750

*Equity securities fair value	$ 175,500
Equity securities cost ($169,000 − $50,000)	(119,000)
Adjustment account balance required	$ 56,500
Current balance in account ($41,000 − $21,250)	(19,750)
Adjustment amount required	$ 36,750

If Stevens did not use the Adjustment to Market account, $36,750, would be added to the Investment account instead.[6] The trading securities would be reported on the balance sheet at the end of 1997 and 1998 at fair market values of $210,000 and $175,500, respectively. The notes to the financial statements would reflect the original cost, the realized and unrealized gains and losses.

[6]Either method of accounting for the trading securities investment is acceptable. The exercises and problems at the end of this text, and the supplemental problems posted on the Internet site (*www.swcollege.com/hartman.html*), use the Adjustment to Market account method unless otherwise stated. While this is not as straightforward as the direct method, it is more consistent with the treatment accorded available-for-sale securities.

Accounting for available-for-sale equity securities is exactly the same as trading securities for initial acquisition and any dividends or interest received. Reporting changes in fair values at the end of the reporting period is slightly different, as the unrealized gains and losses are reported in stockholders' equity instead of the income statement.

Available-for-Sale Securities. Available-for-sale equity securities are recorded at cost initially. Any **realized** gains or losses on the sale of these securities are included in current-period income, as are dividends received. Dividends are also included in current-period income.

Net unrealized holding gains and losses from price fluctuations are **excluded** from earnings, however, and reported as a separate component of shareholders' equity until realized. Since management has not designated these securities as trading, price fluctuations are not recognized in current-period income. These assets were not purchased with the intent of realizing profit from short-term price fluctuations; therefore, recognition of income or loss from short-term price changes would not be appropriate. Valuation for balance sheet purposes, however, is at fair value similar to trading securities. The Adjustment to Market account appears on the balance sheet along with the Investment account and contains the net difference between the cost and the year-end market value of the equity securities classified as available-for-sale.

To illustrate the journal entries required for investments in available-for-sale securities, assume that 2,000 shares of Microsoft were purchased in 1997 at $80 per share. The price at the end of 1997 was $100/share, and it was $180/share by the end of 1998. In 1998, 500 shares were sold at $120/share. The relevant journal entries follow:

	Investment in Equity Securities—AFS	160,000*	
	Cash		160,000
	To record the purchase during 1997.		
	*$2,000 × $80		
1997			
Dec. 31	Adjustment to Market—AFS	40,000*	
	Unrealized Holding Gain on AFS Securities—Equity		40,000
	To adjust to market.		
	*$200,000 − $160,000		
1998	Cash	60,000*	
	Investment in Equity Securities—AFS		40,000**
	Realized Gain on Sale		20,000
	To record the sale of 500 shares during 1998.		
	*$500 × 120		
	**500 × 80		
1998			
Dec. 31	Adjustment to Market—AFS	110,000*	
	Unrealized Holding Gain on AFS Securities—Equity		110,000
	To adjust to market.		

*1,500 shares at $180	$270,000
1,500 shares at $80	120,000
Amount required in Adjustment account	$150,000
Current balance in Adjustment account	40,000
Adjustment amount required	$110,000

The unrealized holding gains on the equity securities are treated as an equity account until the gains are realized, not as current-period income. This account appears in the Shareholders' Equity section of the balance sheet at the net amount of the unrealized gains and losses. The Adjustment to Market account contains the net difference between the cost of the securities and the market value at year-end. This account appears on the balance sheet along with the Investment account to reflect the securities at fair value.

TRANSFERS BETWEEN CATEGORIES

The initial classification, or category assignment, of an investment security at the time of purchase can change in the future as a result of changes in circumstances or management intent. SFAS No. 115 requires that all transfers between categories be effected at fair value at the time of transfer. The fair value at the time of transfer is then treated as the cost of the security for future valuation purposes.

Any unrealized holding gain or loss at the time of transfer will be recognized in earnings immediately or as a separate component of shareholders' equity. For securities transferred *from* the trading category, the unrealized holding gain or loss already will have been recognized in earnings, so no further adjustment is necessary. For any securities transferred *into* the trading category, the unrealized holding gain or loss should be recognized in earnings immediately.[7]

For debt securities transferred into the available-for-sale category from the held-to-maturity category, the unrealized holding gain or loss is recognized as a separate component of shareholders' equity. For debt securities transferred into held-to-maturity from available-for-sale, the unrealized holding gain or loss continues to be reported as a separate component of shareholders' equity. The unrealized holding gain or loss on the newly transferred held-to-maturity security is then treated as premium or discount and amortized over the remaining life of the security.[8] Exhibit 9–5 illustrates transfers of securities between categories.

IMPAIRMENT OF SECURITIES

Impairment applies to securities held in the available-for-sale and held-to-maturity categories. These securities are said to be impaired when they suffer a probable loss in value that is other than temporary,[9] that is, permanent. If it cannot be shown that the loss in value is temporary, the individual security must be written down to fair value, and the amount of the write-down must be included in earnings as a realized loss. Any subsequent changes in fair value of available-for-sale securities are reported as a separate component of shareholders' equity.

Determination of "permanent" declines in market value, as opposed to "temporary" declines, is difficult. For example, consider the difficulty in determining impairment of asset value or recognition of liability for environmental cleanup charges. Chapter 1 mentioned some of these difficult areas of judgment. The timing of recognition of the loss is left to the judgment of management

[7]Ibid., par. 15.
[8]Ibid.
[9]Ibid., par. 16.

EXHIBIT 9–5
Transfers Between Categories of Securities (Investor Holdings of Less Than 20% for Equity Securities)

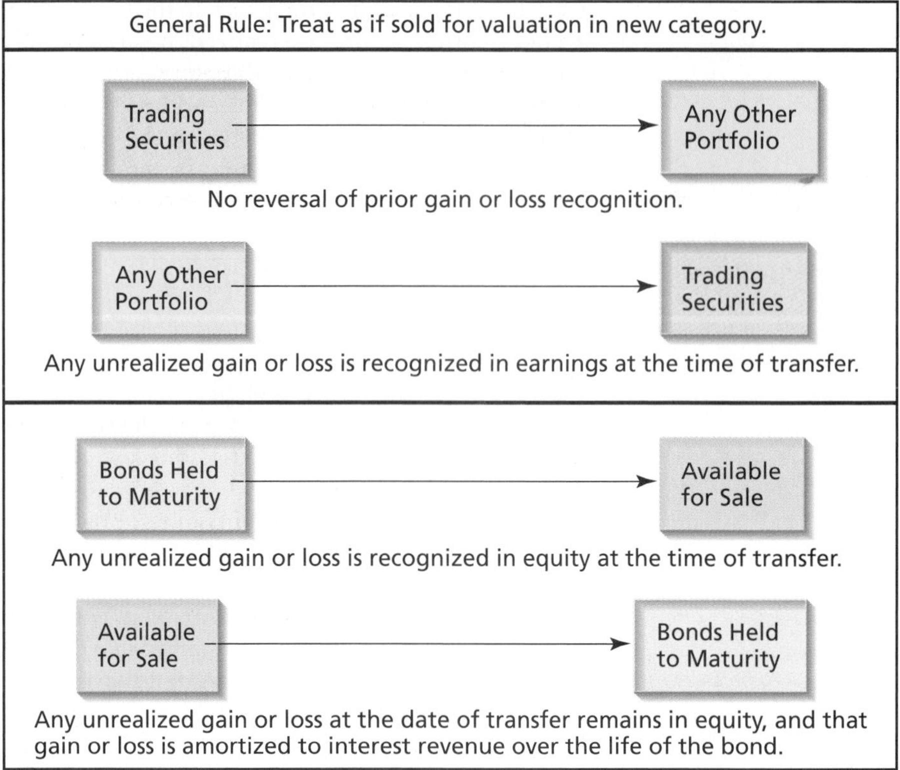
General Rule: Treat as if sold for valuation in new category.
Trading Securities
Any Other Portfolio
No reversal of prior gain or loss recognition.
Any Other Portfolio
Trading Securities
Any unrealized gain or loss is recognized in earnings at the time of transfer.
Bonds Held to Maturity
Available for Sale
Any unrealized gain or loss is recognized in equity at the time of transfer.
Available for Sale
Bonds Held to Maturity
Any unrealized gain or loss at the date of transfer remains in equity, and that gain or loss is amortized to interest revenue over the life of the bond.

ETHICS IN PRACTICE

Impairment of Securities

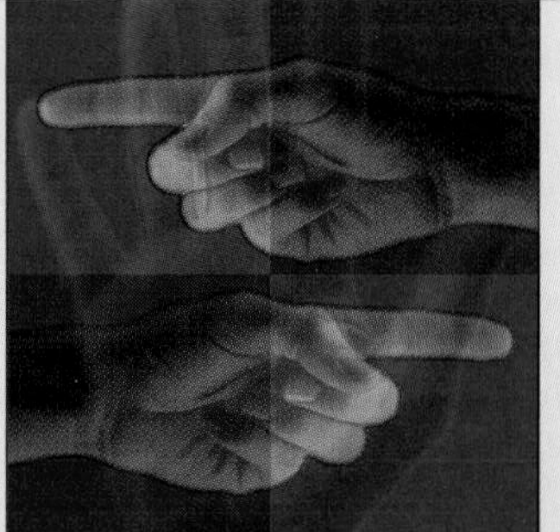

Impairment of an asset means a permanent loss in value and requires recognition of a loss on the income statement with a corresponding reduction in the asset value on the balance sheet. How does one determine when to write down the value of an investment? If the decision is left to management, is it wrong for management to wait until a period in which a large income is available to offset the loss?

During the 1980s, so-called *junk bonds* were issued as financing tools to provide capital for purchasing other companies. These bonds were typically unsecured and very high-risk instruments. Investors were attracted to them because of their very high yield. As predicted, some of the bonds became worthless. In other cases, the market values declined drastically but eventually recovered. Should management have written down the carrying values of the junk bonds held as investments only to see them increase in value several years later? The issue raised here is the income management opportunity afforded management by the great latitude allowed in determining the timing of write-downs.

(and the auditor). The problem with leaving these issues to individual discretion is the lack of comparability that results. Also, an opportunity is provided for managing income by the inclusion or exclusion of these items in income determination.

FINANCIAL STATEMENT PRESENTATION

The financial statement presentation of investments is consistent with management intent with respect to the holding period. Those securities designated as trading securities are classified as current assets on the balance sheet. Securities classified as available-for-sale could be classified either as current assets or as long-term assets. If individual securities are expected to be realized (sold) in the current period, they are classified as current assets. Similarly, if the maturity date of an available-for-sale or held-to-maturity debt security is within the current period, that debt security is classified as a current asset.[10]

DISCLOSURES

At the end of the period, separate disclosure in the notes to the financial statements is required for the aggregate fair value of both the available-for-sale and the held-to-maturity securities. For both these categories, the gross unrealized holding gains and losses must also be disclosed. For the held-to-maturity securities, the amortized cost basis of each security and information about the maturity dates should also be disclosed.[11]

Disclosures relative to the income statement include the following:

1. Proceeds from sales of available-for-sale securities and gross realized gains and losses on the sale.
2. The cost basis used to determine the realized gains and losses.
3. Gross gains and losses included in earnings from transfers from available-for-sale to trading.
4. Changes in net unrealized holding gains or losses on available-for-sale securities that have been included as a separate component of shareholders' equity.
5. The change in net unrealized holding gains or losses on trading securities included in earnings.

UNRESOLVED CONTROVERSIES

SFAS No. 115 reduced some of the inconsistency associated with accounting for investments, but not all. Companies can still engage in "gains trading" by moving securities between portfolios. Leaving the classification of individual investments to the discretion of management makes an income management option available. Through the timely transfers of individual securities between the portfolios, winners can be moved to the trading-securities portfolio and losers to the available-for-sale portfolio.

At the same time, it is not clear how the earnings process of the trading portfolio differs from that of the available-for-sale portfolio. It is argued that temporary changes in market values may not be as relevant to financial statement users, due to differing classifications and durations of various investments. If an investor is not pressed to liquidate an investment quickly, market losses may not be realized. Thus, changes in the fair value of the portfolio of available-for-sale investments are not included in the determination of income. Instead,

[10]Ibid., par. 17.
[11]Ibid., pars. 19–20.

these changes in value are reported in the stockholders' equity section as a separate amount. The effect of this treatment is to provide a smoother stream of reported income over time, an advantage that management finds important.

EQUITY SECURITY INVESTMENTS OF GREATER THAN 20 PERCENT OWNERSHIP

APB Opinion No. 18 prescribes accounting and reporting requirements for investments in equity securities providing more than 20% ownership. The use of the equity method is required for situations in which 20% or more of the voting stock is owned. If more than 50% of the stock is owned, consolidated financial statements are prepared.

Record and report equity-security investment transactions of greater than 20 percent and less than 50 percent.

SIGNIFICANT INFLUENCE

An ownership position of 20% or more of the voting stock presumes an ability to exercise "significant influence" over the policies of the investee. Sometimes significant influence can be exercised over the financial and operational policies of an investee with less than 20% ownership interest. Likewise, it is possible to own 20% or more of the voting stock of an investee yet be unable to exercise significant influence over the investee's financial and operating policies.

The ability to exercise significant influence over operating and financial policies is often a matter of judgment. Some indications of significant influence are the following:[12]

1. Representation on the board of directors.
2. Participation in policy-making processes.
3. Material intercompany transactions.
4. Interchange of managerial personnel.
5. Technological dependency.

Because it is difficult to determine an investor's ability to exercise significant influence, and each investment situation requires a separate assessment, or judgment, of the existence of significant influence, the APB chose 20% ownership of voting shares as the threshold for significant influence. Seeking a reasonable degree of uniformity in application of the rule, the APB decided that 20% or more would lead to a presumption of an ability to exercise significant influence unless evidence to the contrary could be presented.

The basis of the equity method is that, since the investor has the ability to exercise significant influence over the policies of the investee, the investor has the ability to influence the timing of the distribution of the earnings of the investee. Thus, the equity method requires the investor to report as income the investor's proportionate share of the investee's earnings without regard to distributions of dividends. As the investee's income and net assets increase, the investor's claims increase also, and the carrying value (book value) of the investment increases as well.

The initial investment is recorded at cost. The Investment account then is increased by the investor's share of income and decreased by any dividends received from the investee company. Dividends represent a net decrease of assets by the investee; therefore, the Investment account is decreased by the

[12]Account Principles Board Opinion No. 18, par. 17

amount of the dividend received. Because the investor is presumed to exercise significant influence over the investee, that influence is assumed to extend to dividend and other financial policies. Theoretically, the investor can influence the investee to pay dividends and allow the investor to *realize* earnings accrued in the investment account. The purpose is to recognize income as it is "earned," or when the earnings process is "substantially complete."

APPLYING THE EQUITY METHOD

Conceptually, the equity method of accounting for investments is reasonably straightforward. Purchase of a proportion of the investee stock entitles the investor to a proportionate share of the investee's business, including the net assets, and future returns (the net earnings or losses) on those assets. The investment price represents the investor's proportion of the fair market value of the net assets (assets minus liabilities) acquired, plus any premium paid for the excess earning power of those assets. The premium paid is referred to as **goodwill** (see Chapter 13, "Intangible Assets").

The fair market value of the net assets acquired sometimes is greater than the book value of those assets. In these cases, the depreciation expense recorded by the investee is less than if the depreciation had been based on the purchase price (fair market value of the assets) paid by the investor. Net income reported by the investee, then, is greater than if depreciation had been based on fair market values of the assets. Accordingly, the investor, in keeping with the equity method, must adjust the Investment and the Investment Income accounts for the difference between depreciation based on book values and fair market values.

In a similar fashion, if the investor pays extra for excess earning power of the assets (that is, purchases goodwill), the goodwill must be amortized over a period not exceeding 40 years. The Investment Income and Investment accounts must be reduced to reflect the amortization.

The equity method can be summarized as follows:

1. Record investment at cost.
2. Record investor's share of income as an increase in the Investment account and as Investment Income.
3. Record investor's share of investee's loss as a decrease to the Investment account and as Loss on Investments.
4. Record dividends as increases in the Cash or Dividends Receivable account and as decreases in the Investment account.
5. Amortize differences between the book value and the fair market value of the investee depreciable assets over the remaining useful lives of the assets by decreases to the Investment account and to the earnings from the investee (investment income).
6. Reduce investment income and the Investment account by the amortization of any goodwill.
7. Report as extraordinary or as an accounting principle change the investor's share of any extraordinary items or changes in accounting principle.

Exhibit 9–6 and Exhibit 9–7 illustrate application of the equity method. Exhibit 9–6 presents the data, and Exhibit 9–7 the journal entries.

EXHIBIT 9–6
Application of the Equity Method Data

1997

Jan. 1	Purchased 40,000 shares (20%) of the voting stock of Bushong Barbecue for $200,000. The book value of the net assets on this date was $500,000, and the fair market value was $800,000, with 10 years remaining of useful life.
Dec. 31	Bushong reports earnings of $250,000 for 1997.
31	Bushong declares and pays dividends of $100,000.

1998

Dec. 31	Bushong reports a net loss of $80,000 for 1998.
31	Because of the net loss of 1998, Bushong decides to cut the dividend in half. Bushong declares and pays a dividend of $50,000 for 1998.

Goodwill is amortized over 15 years.

EXHIBIT 9–7
Application of Equity Method Journal Entries

1997			
Jan. 1	Investment in Bushong Barbecue	200,000	
	Cash		200,000
Dec. 31	Investment in Bushong Barbecue (20% × $250,000)	50,000	
	Investment Income		50,000
31	Cash (20% × $100,000)	20,000	
	Investment in Bushong Barbecue		20,000
31	Investment Income	8,667	
	Investment in Bushong Barbecue		8,667

*Amortization of the difference between the fair market value of the net assets and the price paid.

20% × $800,000	= $160,000 equity
	200,000 investment
Excess cost (goodwill)	$ 40,000
	÷ 15 yrs.
	$ 2,667 per year

Amortization of Excess Depreciation: FMV of $800,000 − BV of $500,000 = $300,000 excess depreciation. Assume 10 years of remaining life.

20% of FMV $800,000	= $160,000
20% of BV 500,000	= 100,000
Difference	= $ 60,000
	= ÷ 10 yrs.
	= $ 6,000 per year
Total = $6,000 + $2,667	= $ 8,667 per year

1998			
Dec. 31	Investment Income (20% × $80,000)	16,000	
	Investment in Bushong Barbecue		16,000
31	Cash (20% × $50,000)	10,000	
	Investment in Bushong Barbecue		10,000
31	Investment Income	8,667*	
	Investment in Bushong Barbecue		8,667

*Amortization of excess cost over net asset value acquired $2,667 plus excess depreciation of $6,000 as computed above.

CHANGING TO AND FROM EQUITY METHOD

It is commonplace to change the level of investment in a particular equity security. An investor may increase or decrease the amount of the investment either to include or exclude a pro rata portion of the earnings of the investee. By increasing the investment to obtain significant influence, the investor must change to the equity method. By decreasing the investment to a level at which significant influence no longer exists, the investor must change from the equity method to fair value, in accordance with SFAS No. 115 (as explained earlier in this chapter).

Changes to Equity Method. Changing from fair value to the equity method is an accounting change and requires that the equity method of accounting be applied on a *retroactive* basis. The investor must calculate the amount *that would have been in the investment account at the beginning of the period if the equity method had been applied consistently* to the investment using the percentages of ownership in effect during the ownership period. This amount is then compared to the actual amount currently in the Investment account, and an adjusting entry is made to the Investment and Retained Earnings accounts at the beginning of the period.

To illustrate, assume that Lin Corporation had these transactions with PKR Inc.:

1997	
Jan. 1	Purchased 10,000 shares (10%) of PKR voting stock for $200,000. The book value of the net assets at this date was $1,500,000, and the fair market value was $2,000,000. The assets had an estimated useful life of 10 years.
Dec. 31	PKR reports income of $500,000.
31	PKR declares dividends of $300,000.
1998	
Dec. 31	PKR reports income of $700,000.
31	PKR declares dividends of $400,000.
1999	
June 1	Lin purchases 20,000 shares (20%) of the voting stock at a cost of $580,000. The book value of the net assets on this date was $2,000,000, and the fair market value was $2,600,000.
Dec. 31	PKR reports income of $600,000.
31	PKR declares dividends of $200,000.

Lin followed SFAS No. 115 and correctly classified this investment as available-for-sale from January 1, 1997, until June 1, 1999, at which time Lin switched to the equity method and applied it retroactively with an adjusting entry at the beginning of 1999. Assume the following. PKR's stock price was $21 per share at January 1, 1999. Lin's investment account reflected the original cost of $200,000. The Adjustment to Market—Available-for-Sale account and the Unrealized Gain on Equity Securities—Available-for-Sale accounts both had balances of $10,000.

To change to the equity method, Lin must recompute the Investment account balance as of January 1, 1999, to reflect the investment as if it always had been carried under the equity method. The computation is as follows:

1/1/97	Original investment	$200,000
12/31/97	10% income (10% × $500,000)	50,000
	10% dividends (10% × $300,000)	(30,000)
	Excess depreciation:	
	($2,000,000 − $1,500,000) × 10% × 1/10	(5,000)
12/31/98	10% income (10% × $700,000)	70,000
	10% dividends (10% × $400,000)	(40,000)
	Excess depreciation:	
	($2,000,000 − $1,500,000) × 10% × 1/10	(5,000)
1/1/99	Investment balance using equity method	$240,000
	Current balance in Investment account	200,000
	Adjustment required for Investment account	$ 40,000

At June 1, 1999, when Lin purchases the additional 20 percent of PKR, Lin would make the following entries to restate retroactively retained earnings and to remove the adjustment to market and unrealized gain accounts:

Investment in PKR	580,000	
Cash		580,000
Investment in PKR	40,000*	
Retained Earnings		40,000
*$240,000 − $200,000		
Unrealized Holding Gain on AFS Securities—Equity	10,000*	
Adjustment to Market—AFS		10,000

*Original investment	$200,000
Fair market value at 1/1/99	210,000
Balance in adjustment account	$ 10,000

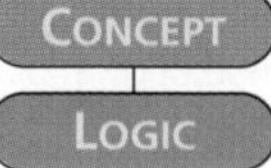

Accounting change requiring retroactive restatement.

Lin has changed to the equity method of accounting for this investment as prescribed in APB Opinion No. 18. This is one of the exceptions to the all-inclusive income concept that requires an adjustment of prior-period income and is reported in retained earnings. Therefore, Retained Earnings is credited, because this is an adjustment for prior periods.

Subsequently, Lin continues to use the equity method and makes the following entries at the end of 1999:

Cash	60,000*	
Investment in PKR		60,000
To record receipt of dividends.		
*30% × $200,000		

Investment in PKR	130,000*	
Investment Income		130,000
To record share of income.		

*10% × $600,000 × 5/12	= $ 25,000
30% × $600,000 × 7/12	= 105,000
Total Income	$130,000

Investment Income	19,208*	
Investment in PKR		19,208
To record excess depreciation and amortize goodwill.		

*Excess depreciation:

($2,000,000 − $1,500,000) × 10% × 1/10 × 5/12		= $ 2,083
($2,600,000 − $2,000,000) × 30% × 1/8 × 7/12		= 13,125
Total excess depreciation		$15,208
Goodwill amortization:		
First purchase:		
10% × $2,000,000	= $200,000	
Purchase price	200,000	
Goodwill	$ 0	
Second purchase:		
20% × $2,600,000	= $520,000	
Purchase price	580,000	
Goodwill	60,000	
Amortize over	÷ 15 yrs.	
Amortization per year		4,000
Total excess depreciation and goodwill amortization		$19,208

In subsequent periods, Lin continues to recognize 30% of the net income of PKR as an increase to the Investment account and 30% of the dividends as a decrease to the Investment account. The income recognized is decreased by the amortization of the excess depreciation (30% of $600,000) and amortization of the goodwill ($60,000 over 15 years).

Changes From Equity Method. As prescribed by SFAS No. 115, an investor must change from the equity method to fair value if the investment is reduced to a level that no longer provides significant influence to the investor. The current balance in the Investment account becomes the cost basis of the investment, and no retroactive adjustments are necessary.

DISCLOSURES REQUIRED FOR EQUITY METHOD

The importance of an investment to an investor's financial position and results of operations influences the extent and manner of disclosures about the investee. Separate disclosure may be appropriate if an investment is highly significant to the investor, while disclosures on a combined basis may be appropriate for investments not as significant. In general, the following disclosures are applicable.

1. The name of each investee and percentage of ownership.
2. The accounting policies of the investor with respect to investments in common stock. In addition, the investor must disclose the reasons for not using the equity method for any investments of 20 percent or more and for using the equity method for investments of less than 20 percent.
3. The difference, if any, between the carrying amount of the investment and the amount of the underlying equity in net assets and the accounting treatment of the difference.
4. The market value of each investment in common stock for which a quoted market price is available. This disclosure is not required for investments in common stock of subsidiaries (investments of greater than 50% of outstanding stock).
5. If equity method investments in joint ventures or other business arrangements are material to the investor, summarized information relative to the assets, liabilities, and results of operations of the investee may be necessary. These disclosures may be made either separately or in groups.

CASH FLOWS

The dividend cash flows to the investor are the same regardless of the accounting method used. The cash flows originating from purchases, sales, and maturities of trading securities are classified as cash flows from *operating activities* on the statement of cash flows. Cash flows from purchases, sales, and maturities of available-for-sale and held-to-maturity securities are classified as cash flows from *investing activities*. They should be reported gross for each security classification in the statement of cash flows.[13]

Cash flows are affected either directly or indirectly by interest revenue and amortization of premiums/discounts, realized gains and losses on investment sales, unrealized holding gains and losses, dividends from equity investment, and earnings from equity method investees. These are summarized in Exhibit 9–8.

FAIR VALUE VS. EQUITY METHOD ISSUES

There are two major issues involved in setting accounting practices with regard to use of the equity method versus the fair value method. First, is a fundamentally different earnings process present in a relatively small, short-term investment compared to a long-term investment that allows significant influence? Second, when should the events leading to asset value changes be recognized as revenue?

The equity method, much like the percentage-of-completion method in long-term construction accounting, attempts to recognize revenue as it is earned (or as value is being added) rather than recognizing revenue exclusively at some point after completion of the entire multiyear process. The fair value method relies on the availability of market prices to effect a more timely recognition of asset value changes in the short-term revenue recognition process.

[13]Ibid., par. 18.

EXHIBIT 9–8
Investments and the Statement of Cash Flows

INTEREST REVENUE

1. Direct Method: Cash Received for Interest Revenue
   a. Interest revenue recognized
   b. Plus premium (minus discount) amortized
   c. Plus the decrease (minus the increase) in Interest Receivable
2. Indirect Method: Adjust net income by
   a. Subtracting premium (adding discount) amortized
   b. Subtracting increase (adding decrease) in Interest Receivable

EARNINGS FROM EQUITY METHOD INVESTEE

1. Direct Method: Cash received from equity method investment = Cash dividends received
2. Indirect Method: Adjust net income by subtracting the excess of revenue recognized over the amount of cash dividends received.

REALIZED GAINS AND LOSSES ON THE SALE OF INVESTMENTS

1. Direct Method:
   a. Cash flow from operations: Do not include realized gains and losses but do include net cash flows from sales and purchases of trading securities.
   b. Investing activities: Include net cash flows from the actual sales and purchases of available-for-sale and held-to-maturity investments.
2. Indirect Method:
   a. Cash flow from operations: Adjust net income by adding back any loss (subtracting any gain) on the sale of Investments and include net cash flows from sales and purchases of trading securities.
   b. Investing activities: Include net cash flows from the actual sales and purchases of available-for-sale and held-to-maturity investments.

UNREALIZED HOLDING GAINS AND LOSSES

1. Direct Method: Do not include unrealized holding gains or losses in the statement of cash flows.
2. Indirect Method: Adjust net income by adding back any unrealized holding loss (subtracting any gain) on trading security investments only.

STOCK DIVIDENDS AND SPLITS

Stock dividends and stock splits result in the receipt of additional shares by the investor. The number of additional shares received is proportional to the original number of shares owned. Neither stock dividends nor stock splits affect the total carrying value of the investment on the investor's books. Receipt of the additional shares requires no journal entry but only a memorandum entry, indicating the receipt of the additional shares and a lower cost per share for subsequent accounting purposes.

STOCK RIGHTS

Stock rights refer to the right to purchase shares of newly issued stock. Two types of stock rights are common: preemptive rights and stock warrants. Stock rights stipulate an exercise (purchase) price, the number of shares that may be purchased with each right, and an expiration date. They are classified as assets because they are a source of future economic benefit to the investor and are considered similar to equity investment securities since their value is derived from equity securities.

Preemptive Stock Rights. Preemptive stock rights allow existing shareholders to purchase additional shares in proportion to their current holdings. Exercise of these rights prevents the possible dilution of ownership interests. Usually one right is issued for each share of stock outstanding, and the terms of the new issue indicate the number of rights required for each new share of stock.

Stock rights trade independently of the stock after they are issued and before the expiration date. The original shareholder who receives rights may (1) sell them at current market value, (2) exercise them, or (3) allow them to expire. Because stock rights have no cost, the book value of the original investment is allocated between the stock rights and the shares of stock, using the relative fair market value method.

For example, assume the Carruth Investment Corporation owns 100,000 shares of Home Depot purchased at an average cost of $50 per share, or $5,000,000. Home Depot issues one stock right for each share of stock owned. Five rights plus $60 cash enables the shareholder to purchase one additional share of stock. Carruth receives 100,000 rights, entitling Carruth to purchase 20,000 additional shares at $60 cash plus five rights. The market price of the common stock immediately after the rights issue is $80. Thus, we may assume that each right is worth $4: ($80 − $60)/5. Carruth would assign cost to the rights in the following manner:

Market value of stock:	$80 × 100,000 =	$8,000,000
Market value of rights:	$ 4 × 100,000 =	400,000
Total market value		$8,400,000

Cost allocation:

To stock: $\frac{\$8,000,000}{\$8,400,000} \times \$5,000,000 = \$4,761,905$

To rights: $\frac{\$400,000}{\$8,400,000} \times \$5,000,000 = \$\ 238,095$

Carruth would make the following journal entry:

Investment in Home Depot Stock Rights	238,095	
Investment in Home Depot Stock		238,095

If Carruth sold the rights, the difference between the proceeds realized from the sale and the allocated cost would be recognized as a gain or loss on the transaction. For example, assume Carruth sells the rights for $280,000.

Cash	280,000	
Investment in Home Depot Stock Rights		238,095
Gain on Sale of Rights		41,905

CONCEPT Recognition of gain or loss.

LOGIC The stock rights were assets because they possessed future benefits. The benefits are realized upon the sale; therefore, the gain or loss on the sale should be recognized.

If Carruth exercised the rights, the following entry would be appropriate:

Investment in Home Depot Stock	1,438,095	
Investment in Home Depot Stock Rights		238,095
Cash		1,200,000*

**$60 × 100,000/5*

CONCEPT Valuation of asset at cost.

LOGIC Valuation of assets at the time of purchase is at cost or the value of the consideration given up. The book value of the stock rights was $238,095, and the cash given was $1,200,000; therefore, the acquisition cost is the total, $1,438,095.

Finally, if the rights expire, Carruth must recognize a loss:

Loss on Expiration of Home Depot Stock Rights	238,095	
Investment in Home Depot Stock Rights		238,095

CONCEPT Recognition of loss.

LOGIC Upon the expiration of the rights, the future benefits cease to exist. Therefore, a loss must be recognized.

Purchased Stock Warrants. Stock warrants are similar to preemptive rights in that they provide the right to purchase new shares at a set price. Warrants sometimes are attached to bond or preferred-stock issues as "sweeteners" to make the securities more attractive to investors. They may also be sold separately by the issuing corporation. In either case, these types of warrants are referred to as *detachable warrants* and trade separately in the marketplace. *Nondetachable warrants* require the surrender of the attached security and are discussed in Chapter 14.

Investors treat detachable warrants the same as other investments, recording them at acquisition cost and designating them as trading securities for subsequent valuation and accounting. If the warrants are attached to another security at the time of issue, the investor allocates the costs to the warrant and the other security using the relative-market-value method. When the warrants are exercised, the cost basis of the new shares is equivalent to the cash paid (exercise price) plus the book value of the warrants exercised. If the warrants are sold, recognition of a gain or loss for the difference between the sales price and book value is appropriate.

Investments Providing Control

Ownership interests in excess of 50 percent are assumed to provide control over the operating and financial policies of the investee. These are normally referred to as *parent-subsidiary relationships* and viewed as a single economic entity. Because the parent and subsidiary are considered a single economic entity, they combine, or *consolidate,* their financial statements. Thus, the financial statements of the two individual companies are presented as if they pertained to a single economic entity. To prepare consolidated financial statements, the Investment account of the parent company is eliminated against the stockholders' equity accounts of the subsidiary. The remaining assets, liabilities, and equities of the two companies are combined and intercompany transactions eliminated. Consolidated financial statements are beyond the scope of this text and are found in advanced accounting texts.

Other Long-Term Investments

Other long-term investments include various types of funds (often referred to as *sinking funds*) and the cash surrender value of life insurance policies. Funds may be created for many reasons, such as retirement of long-term debt or plant expansion. Whole life insurance policies provide a cash value in the event of cancellation or expiration of the policy.

Record and report transactions for funds and life insurance investments.

Accounting for Funds

Each special-purpose fund should be accounted for separately because each is a separate asset, with separate cash flows and economic benefits. As an example, a bond indenture (contract) may require a sinking fund to retire the debt. The terms of the indenture might require deposits each year to accumulate sufficient funds to retire the bonds at maturity.

Suppose the Ballard Corporation makes annual deposits to a sinking fund to retire $1,000,000 of bonds at the end of 10 years. Assume that Ballard can earn a return of 10% on all deposits to the fund. The annual deposit required would be calculated using the future value of an annuity (Table 3 in Appendix A at the end of the text) as follows:

$$\$1{,}000{,}000/15.9374 = \$62{,}745$$

Exhibit 9–9 illustrates the typical journal entries associated with a sinking fund.

Cash Surrender Value of Life Insurance

Life insurance on key executives is often purchased by a business. A whole life insurance policy provides death protection and a cash surrender value (as well as a loan value). The premium paid represents an expense portion (the death protection) and an asset (cash surrender portion). For example, if Holland

EXHIBIT 9–9
Accounting for a Sinking Fund—Ballard Corporation

Assumptions:
a. $1,000,000 bond issue to be retired at the end of 10 years
b. 10% rate of return on deposits to the fund

Account	Debit	Credit
Sinking Fund Cash	62,745	
Cash		62,745
To record annual contribution.		
Sinking Fund Investments	50,000	
Sinking Fund Cash		50,000
To record purchase of securities for $50,000.		
Sinking Fund Cash	5,000	
Sinking Fund Revenue		5,000
To record receipt of sinking fund income (dividends).		
Sinking Fund Expense	500	
Sinking Fund Cash		500
To record payment of trustees' expenses.		
Sinking Fund Cash	40,000	
Sinking Fund Investments		25,000
Gain on Sale of Sinking Fund Investments		15,000
To record sale of one-half of sinking fund investment.		

Assume the fund contains $1,200,000 at the end of ten years. The bonds are retired, and the excess cash is returned to the general cash account.

Account	Debit	Credit
Bonds Payable	1,000,000	
Cash	200,000	
Sinking Fund Cash		1,200,000

Company pays an annual premium of $1,500 for a $50,000 whole life insurance policy on its president, and the cash surrender value increases from $12,000 to $12,700 during the year, Holland makes the following journal entry:

Account	Debit	Credit
Life Insurance Expense	800	
Cash Surrender Value of Life Insurance	700	
Cash		1,500

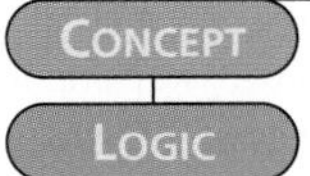

Expense recognition and cost allocation.

Part of the $1,500 increases the cash surrender value of the insurance policy; hence, it is capitalized as an asset. The remainder is recognized as an expense as it applies to the protection or insurance part of the plan.

If the president died at the beginning of the next year, and Holland collected the $50,000 face value of the policy, the journal entry would be:

Account	Debit	Credit
Cash	50,000	
Cash Surrender Value of Life Insurance		12,700
Gain on Life Insurance		37,300

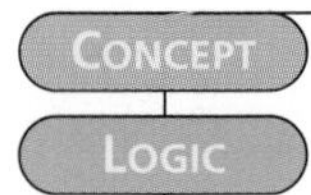

Recognition of gain.

The total received is in excess of the asset value. The difference is a gain. The gain is not considered extraordinary, nor is it taxable as income, because the premiums paid are not tax-deductible.

FINANCIAL ANALYSIS

Analyze the impact of the different accounting methods for investments on profitability and liquidity measures.

The excerpt in the In Practice—General feature "Abuse of the Equity Method" emphasizes the importance of the method of accounting for investments to users of financial information. Specifically, it points out one allegedly abusive application of the equity method. This "abuse" typifies the problems faced by accounting standard-setting boards, in this case the Accounting Principles Board (APB). In attempting to stem one abusive practice, the door is often left open to another. One purpose of the equity method of accounting for investments is to thwart the income manipulation possible when one firm obtains significant influence over another—significant influence over dividend payments, among other things. If accounting standards allowed recognition of investment revenue only at the end of the revenue-generating process with the receipt of cash dividends, a firm with significant influence could easily manipulate its income.

IN PRACTICE—GENERAL

Abuse of the Equity Method

Managements once again have found a way to get more smoke out of their earnings chimneys even though there isn't much fire in their stoves. The smoke—smoke screen might be a better term—comes from what accountants call equity earnings. Equity earnings are profits earned by another company but carried on one's P&L statement as well as on the other company's.

Under a 1971 Accounting Principles Board (APB) ruling, if Company A owns between 20% and 50% of Company B, A is required to report a portion of B's earnings—equal to A's percentage of ownership. Nevertheless, B continues to show 100% of its earnings. It's called equity accounting.

This use of equity accounting brings in alleged earnings, not corresponding revenues. So it can throw off all the common measures of success: profit margin, return on equity, even price-earnings multiples.

Take a modest example of the resulting confusion: ***Giant Bendix Corporation*** ($3.8 billion revenues) has a 21% interest in ***ASARCO***, a metals producer. Bendix adds onto its income statement some $25.5 million from ASARCO, driving up its earnings to $163 million. This deflates Bendix's current P/E from 8.2 to 6.9, inflates its profit margin from 3.6% to 4.2%, and blows up its return on equity from 15% to a more impressive 18%.

Mark this, however: When ASARCO was losing money, Bendix carefully kept its interest below 20%. But it became apparent that ASARCO was going to make money. So, Bendix signed an anti-takeover agreement with ASARCO. It then picked up more stock and started to pick up earnings.

Bendix is not doing anything shady. It is simply complying with generally accepted accounting principles (GAAP).

Sources: "Equity Earnings," *Forbes*, March 31, 1980, pp. 100–104; "Equity Accounting Isn't Equitable," *Forbes*, March 31, 1980, pp. 104–105.

It is very difficult to root out all abuse, and we should not wholly condemn the accrual methods discussed in this chapter simply because certain parties take advantage of specific features; the alternatives are often equally flawed. The standard-setters continually try to plug loopholes, but high professional integrity simply is not universal. In the end, one's best safeguard is a thorough understanding of GAAP; an understanding that allows one to detect the manipulation of standards.

As pointed out in the In Practice excerpt, *the method of accounting for marketable equity securities could have an impact on measures of profitability* such as earnings, price-earnings ratios, profit margins, and return on equity. Also affected, however, is the Investment account in the asset section. We have seen how the Investment account is affected by use of the equity method by the investor, as compared to the fair value approach of SFAS No. 115. We compare the two methods in Exhibits 9–10, 9–11, and 9–12.

Assume that the Coates Corporation purchases 10,000 shares of Zenith Inc. at a price of $70 per share, and this represents just under a 20% interest in Zenith. At the end of the year, Zenith reports income of $600,000, and the market price of Zenith is $100 per share. Coates could designate the investment as trading, available-for-sale as a current asset, or available-for-sale as a long-term asset. If the investment is 20% and provides significant influence, Coates could use the equity method. Assume Coates had the account balances shown in Exhibit 9–10 immediately after the investment and before consideration of the effects of the investment in Zenith. Assume that Coates has zero income of its

EXHIBIT 9–10
Alternative Accounting Methods for Investment Account Balances After Purchase

COATES CORPORATION
Balance Sheet

	TRADING	AVAILABLE-FOR-SALE CURRENT	AVAILABLE-FOR-SALE LONG-TERM	EQUITY METHOD
Current assets	$1,000	$1,000	$1,000	$1,000
Investment in Zenith	700	700	0	0
Total current assets	$1,700	$1,700	$1,000	$1,000
Long-term assets:				
Investment in Zenith	$ 0	$ 0	$ 700	$ 700
Other long-term assets	3,300	3,300	3,300	3,300
Total long-term assets	$3,300	$3,300	$4,000	$4,000
Total Assets	$5,000	$5,000	$5,000	$5,000
Current liabilities	$1,000	$1,000	$1,000	$1,000
Long-term liabilities	2,500	2,500	2,500	2,500
Total liabilities	$3,500	$3,500	$3,500	$3,500
Stockholders' equity	1,500	1,500	1,500	1,500
Total liabilities and stockholders' equity	$5,000	$5,000	$5,000	$5,000

EXHIBIT 9–11 Alternative Accounting Methods for Investment Account Balances After One Year

COATES CORPORATION
Balance Sheet

	TRADING	AVAILABLE-FOR-SALE CURRENT	AVAILABLE-FOR-SALE LONG-TERM	EQUITY METHOD
Current assets	$1,000	$1,000	$1,000	$1,000
Investment in Zenith	1,000	1,000	0	0
Total current assets	$2,000	$2,000	$1,000	$1,000
Long-term assets:				
Investment in Zenith	$ 0	$ 0	$1,000	$ 820
Other long-term assets	3,300	3,300	3,300	3,300
Total long-term assets	$3,300	$3,300	$4,300	$4,120
Total assets	$5,300	$5,300	$5,300	$5,120
Current liabilities	$1,000	$1,000	$1,000	$1,000
Long-term liabilities	2,500	2,500	2,500	2,500
Total liabilities	$3,500	$3,500	$3,500	$3,500
Stockholders' equity:				
Beginning	$1,500	$1,500	$1,500	$1,500
Increase in FMV	0	300	300	0
Income recognized	300	0	0	120
Total	$1,800	$1,800	$1,800	$1,620
Total liabilities & equity	$5,300	$5,300	$5,300	$5,120

own and 500,000 shares of stock outstanding with a current market price of $12 per share. If Coates designates this investment as trading securities, the change in market value of the Zenith shares (10,000 shares × $30/share = $300,000) is recognized in current earnings and the investment is reported at current market value. If Coates designates this investment as available-for-sale as a current or long-term asset, the change in market value of the Zenith shares is recognized as a separate item in stockholders' equity and the investment is reported at current market value, either current or long-term. If this investment provides significant influence and Coates uses the equity method of accounting, Coates would recognize 20% of the Zenith income (20% × 600,000 = $120,000) in current-period earnings. The Investment account would be increased by the same amount. The new balance sheet for Coates would appear as shown in Exhibit 9–11.

The ratios in Exhibit 9–12 illustrate the effect of the accounting method on various measures of profitability for Coates: These results illustrate the point made in the In Practice excerpt. Measures of liquidity and profitability can vary significantly with the method of accounting used even when cash flows and

EXHIBIT 9–12 Profitability Measures and Choice of Accounting Method

COATES CORPORATION				
	TRADING	AVAILABLE-FOR-SALE CURRENT	AVAILABLE-FOR-SALE LONG-TERM	EQUITY METHOD
Current ratio	2,000/1,000	2,000/1,000	1,000/1,000	1,000/1,000
Net earnings	300,000	0	0	120,000
Earnings per share	$ 0.60	$ 0.00	$ 0.00	$ 0.24
Market price per share	$12.00	$12.00	$12.00	$12.00
Price/earnings	20	0	0	50
Return on equity:				
300,000/1,800,00	16.67%			
0/1,800,000		0.00%		
0/1,800,000			0.00%	
120,000/1,620,000				7.41%

other conditions remain the same. SFAS No. 115 has brought consistency to treatments of changes in fair value for securities intended for trading purposes. It also has brought consistency to valuation of investments with less than significant influence on the investee. However, the issues that are left open to management discretion still have the potential for inconsistent treatment across firms.

The final topic considered in this chapter will be **derivative financial instruments**. These complex instruments are the subject of an FASB Exposure Draft that is currently being debated. We examine the issues in the next section.

DERIVATIVE FINANCIAL INSTRUMENTS

Understand the concepts and complexities associated with derivative financial instruments.

Large losses were suffered by individuals and institutions related to derivative financial instruments in the early 1990s. One such loss ($2 billion) caused the collapse of ***Barings Bank***, one of Britain's oldest and most prestigious institutions. In the United States, Orange County, California, also lost close to $500 million because of trading in derivatives. Trading in derivatives and accounting for them has been likened to the wild frontier where adventure and danger are constant companions. Accounting standards only now are emerging. The FASB recently issued an exposure draft that contains proposed standards for accounting for derivative financial instruments.

Entities use derivative financial instruments to manage financial risk. Financial risk originates from three basic sources: changes in fair values, changes in cash flows, and foreign currency exposures. Reducing the exposure to financial loss stemming from these risks is the motivation for using derivatives.

As an example, suppose that ABC Corporation borrows $100,000 from Core States Bank and agrees to pay interest based on market rates; that is, the loan would have a variable interest rate attached. If market interest rates decrease, ABC would have low interest debt. However, if market interest rates increase, the cost of the funds also increases. To protect itself from increasing interest rates, ABC may enter into a hedge contract with a third party (Nations Bank) to pay Nations Bank 8 percent fixed interest and receive from Nations Bank interest at a variable rate. This hedge contract would be based on the underlying $100,000 bank loan (referred to as the **notional amount**).

A hedge contract requires only that the two parties (ABC and Nations Bank in this case) "settle" the differential interest amount at the end of each period. That is, the difference between the 8 percent fixed rate and the current market rate would be paid or received (settled) between ABC and Nations Bank. ABC thus would be able to offset the variable cash flows from the hedge against the variable interest owed to Core States. This is an interest rate swap. The value of the swap is the present value of the projected differential net cash flows. Increases and decreases in the value of the swap are dependent on the market interest rates.

This hedge contract between ABC and Nations Bank is a form of derivative. On June 20, 1996, the FASB issued the exposure draft, "Accounting for Derivative and Similar Financial Instruments and for Hedging Activities." The purpose of the Exposure Draft is to propose accounting and reporting standards for derivative financial instruments. The statement applies to all entities and to all derivative financial instruments and similar financial instruments that have both cash instrument and derivative characteristics.

DEFINITION

The Exposure Draft defines a derivative financial instrument as follows:

> A financial instrument that by its terms, at inception or upon the occurrence of a specified event, provides the holder (or writer) with the right (or obligation) to participate in some or all of the price changes of an underlying (that is, one or more referenced financial instruments, commodities, or other assets, or other specific items to which a rate, an index of prices, or another market indicator is applied) and, except as noted below, does not require that the holder or writer own or deliver the underlying. A contract that requires ownership or delivery of the underlying is a derivative financial instrument if (a) the underlying is another derivative, (b) a mechanism exists in the market (such as an organized exchange) to enter into a closing contract with only a net cash settlement, or (c) the contract is customarily settled with only a net cash payment based on changes in the price of the underlying.[14]

In the definition, "underlying" refers to the financial instrument upon which the derivative is based. In the preceding example, the $100,000 loan from Core States Bank to ABC is the "underlying" financial instrument. The derivative in that example is the hedge contract between ABC and Nations Bank.

The proposal in the Exposure Draft would standardize accounting for these financial instruments by requiring that derivative financial instruments be recognized as assets or liabilities and measured in the financial statements at fair value.[15] The Exposure Draft also proposes that (under certain conditions)

[14]"Accounting for Derivative and Similar Financial Instruments and for Hedging Activities" *Proposed Statement of Financial Accounting Standards,* FASB, June 20, 1996, par. 6.
[15]Ibid., par. 3.

an entity may designate a derivative financial instrument or other similar financial instrument as one of the following:

a. A hedge of the exposure to changes in the fair value of a recognized asset or liability or a **firm commitment** (referred to as a **fair value hedge**).
b. A hedge of the exposure to variable cash flows of a **forecasted transaction** (referred to as a **cash flow hedge**).
c. A **hedge of the foreign currency exposure** of a net investment in a foreign operation.

RECOGNITION AND MEASUREMENT

According to the Exposure Draft, "An entity shall recognize all derivatives in the statement of financial position as assets (or liabilities) depending on the rights (or obligations) under the contracts and measure all derivatives at fair value."[16] The change in fair value (gain or loss) of an asset or liability refers to the difference between its fair value at the beginning of the period and at the end of the period, after adjustments to exclude payments received in recovering the asset or payments have been made in settling the liability. Accounting for changes in fair value would depend on the intended use of the derivative, as follows.

a. For a fair value hedge, the gain or loss would be recognized in earnings in the period of change (together with an offsetting loss or gain on the hedged asset or liability).
b. For a cash flow hedge, the gain or loss would be reported as a component of "other comprehensive income" outside of earnings and recognized in earnings on the projected date of the forecasted transaction.
c. For a hedge of the foreign currency exposure of an investment in a foreign operation, the portion of the change in fair value equivalent to a foreign currency transaction (gain or loss) would be reported in other comprehensive income (outside of earnings) as part of the cumulative translation adjustment with any remaining changes in fair value recognized in earnings.
d. For a derivative not designated as a hedge, the gain or loss shall be recognized in earnings in the period of change.

Two examples are adapted from the Exposure Draft and illustrated in the appendix to this chapter. One is an example of accounting for a fair value hedge, and the other is an example of accounting for a cash flow hedge. The Exposure Draft contains other examples for other types of derivatives as well.

At the time this text was being prepared, the FASB was soliciting comments on the Exposure Draft from any interested party. The final standard was scheduled to be issued in October 1997. If adopted, the standard would become effective for fiscal years beginning after December 15, 1997. To find the current status, check the Internet homepage for this text at *www.swcollege.com/hartman.html.*

[16]Ibid., par. 10.

IN FOCUS—INTERNATIONAL

Patrick J. Burke
Managing Partner
Burke & Company/PLL
BS, University of Dayton
JD, University of Cincinnati

"It's like solving a puzzle because every portfolio has its own special circumstances."

What is the value of an investment portfolio containing a variety of corporate and government bonds, a few thousand shares of GE and Xerox, and a 60% stake in a software business? Financial statements prepared in accordance with GAAP, including appropriate application of the amortized cost or equity methods, would provide one answer.

But if this portfolio is subject to division in a divorce settlement, the value provided by financial statements may be unsatisfactory to one or both parties. That's when CPAs are often called upon to help the divorcing parties (and in some cases, the court) set a fair value. Pat Burke, Managing Partner of Burke & Company, has been involved in many such cases.

"The financial statements rarely tell the whole story," says Burke, a graduate of the University of Dayton. While some marital assets, such as publicly traded stocks, have fairly clear market values, bond values must be updated to reflect the current market rate for bonds of similar risk. And in the case of (generally privately held) bonds of struggling companies, Burke may examine the warrants associated with the bonds that entitle bondholders to assume possession of firm assets if coupon payments cannot be made. "In that case we have to look beyond the bonds and consider the value of the underlying business and its assets," says Burke.

There's still more work to do when the portfolio includes full or partial interest in a small business. "We generally use a multiple of earnings as an estimate of a firm's value, usually 4-6 times earnings," says Burke. These earnings can be determined through examination of tax returns or financial statements. But it's rarely that simple. For instance, if the income statement shows earnings of $30,000 a year after the owner pays him or herself a $350,000 salary, logic dictates that much of that salary be added back into the earnings stream before the multiple is applied.

If the divorcing parties can't come to agreement on their own, Burke may testify in court where the goal is to communicate his findings in such a way that they are meaningful to the judge, who is not normally a financial expert. "It's very interesting and challenging work," says Burke, "It's like solving a puzzle because every portfolio has its own special circumstances and there are so many potential variables to consider in finding the true value."

In addition to his hands-on client work, Burke has owned and managed Burke & Company for 13 years. "It's definitely a people job," he says. "My inventory is people's time, so my job is to maximize the value of that time. We want to find the niches where we can stand out from the competition, and therefore charge a premium rate."

Asked about advice for current accounting students, Burke described an important lesson that all new accountants must learn—ninety-nine percent correct may earn an A+ in class, but making careless errors on one percent of a real client assignment can create huge problems for the client and the accountant. "There's no replacement for doing it right the first time," he says.

APPENDIX[17]: DERIVATIVE FINANCIAL INSTRUMENTS

In this appendix, two examples from the Exposure Draft are illustrated and explained. The first is a cash flow hedge of a variable interest rate attached to interest bearing debt. The second is a fair value hedge of a fixed interest rate on interest bearing debt. Other examples of hedges are presented in the exposure draft, and many other types of hedges and derivative instruments exist in the

[17]Source: "Accounting for Derivative and Similar Financial Instruments and for Hedging Activities," *FASB Exposure Draft*, Appendix B, June 20, 1996.

financial world. These two serve as examples of the complexities encountered in the computation and accounting for these financial instruments.

The first example from the Exposure Draft is the hedge of a forecasted transaction, or a cash flow hedge. According to the Exposure Draft, the changes in fair value of a derivative designated as a hedge of a forecasted transaction would be reported as *a component of comprehensive income outside of earnings and recognized in earnings on the date on which the forecasted transaction is expected to occur*. The FASB has a separate project related to comprehensive income.

Comprehensive income was defined in SFAC No. 6 as "the change in equity (net assets) during a period from transactions and other events and circumstances from nonowner sources. It includes all changes in equity during a period except those resulting from investments by owners and distributions to owners." This project is related to hedging and derivatives in that it would allow a means of displaying certain gains and losses on these instruments that are not reported in earnings. Related to comprehensive income, the FASB has decided (among other items) the following:

1. Comprehensive income should be divided into two broad display categories: net income and other comprehensive income.
2. The total of other comprehensive income for a period should be transferred to a separate component of equity in the statement of financial position at the end of an accounting period. The accumulated balances for each classification in the separate component of equity should be disclosed on the face of the statement of financial position, in the statement of changes in equity, or in notes accompanying the financial statements.

The final statement on comprehensive income is scheduled to be issued in the first quarter of 1997. (To find the current status of this statement, check the Internet homepage for this text at *www.swcollege.com/hartman.html*.)

The facts used in the first example follow.

Example 1: Cash Flow Hedge—Variable Rate Interest-Bearing Debt. On January 1, 19X1, ABC Company borrows $10,000 from XYZ at a variable rate of interest for four years. Interest will be paid annually to XYZ on December 31, and the $10,000 principal is due on December 31, 19X4. According to the agreement, the market interest rate on each January 1 establishes the variable interest rate for that period and the amount of interest to be paid to XYZ on the following December 31. At this point, ABC has obligated itself to a four-year loan with a variable interest rate.

To protect itself from fluctuations in interest rates, ABC hedges the variable interest rate. Assume that on January 1, 19X1, ABC Company enters into a four-year agreement with Ajax Corporation to *receive* variable interest payments and to *pay* a fixed interest rate. This is a **receive-variable, pay-fixed interest rate swap.** The objective for ABC in this second agreement is to offset the variable interest rates paid to XYZ against the variable interest received from Ajax. The interest rate swap is based on a notional[18] amount of $10,000 and will result in a cash settlement to be paid to or received from Ajax Corporation by ABC Company on each December 31. The cash settlement amount is the difference

[18]The "notional amount" refers to the underlying amount of the debt, in this case, the $10,000 loan.

between the 8 percent fixed-rate interest payment and the variable-rate interest received. Assume that ABC Company designates this interest rate swap as a cash flow hedge of the variability in the interest payments on the variable-rate debt.

Each of the December 31 variable interest rate cash flows is considered a separate forecasted transaction designated by ABC as hedged. Therefore, the swap itself is viewed as a *series* of individual forward contracts, with each individual contract designated for (or related to) an individual forecasted transaction (the interest payment/receipt).

Accounting for the swap as a hedge requires (1) recognition of the swap as an asset or liability measured at fair value and (2) reporting periodic changes in fair value in "Other comprehensive income."[19] The gains and losses related to the changes in fair value would be included in earnings at the projected date for each forecasted transaction (the interest payment/receipt date). The amount recognized in current earnings would be the amount of gain or loss related to the particular forward contract for that specific date.

Assume that on January 1, 19X1 (the inception of the hedge), the market rate of interest is 8 percent. Further assume that market interest rates rise to 10 percent on December 31, 19X1, 11 percent on December 31, 19X2, and remain at 11 percent through December 31, 19X4. The net cash settlement amounts at each interest payment date for ABC would be as follows:

	12/31/X1	12/31/X2	12/31/X3	12/31/X4
Pay 8% fixed	$(800)	$ (800)	$ (800)	$ (800)
Receive variable	800	1,000	1,100	1,100
Interest rate swap settlement amount	$ 0	$ 200	$ 300	$ 300

These settlement amounts represent the net difference between the 8% fixed rate and the variable rate in the interest rate swap, based on an underlying (notional) amount of $10,000. The interest rate swap thus allows ABC to pay a fixed rate of interest at 8%. The cash interest receipts (payments) on the variable-rate debt and interest rate swap by ABC Company are as follows:

Cash Interest Receipts (Payments):

	12/31/X1	12/31/X2	12/31/X3	12/31/X4
Variable-rate debt	$(800)	$(1,000)	$(1,100)	$(1,100)
Interest rate swap net	0	200	300	300
Net cash payment	$(800)	$ (800)	$ (800)	$ (800)

The interest rate swap is either an asset (if the market interest rate exceeds the fixed interest rate) or liability (if the market interest rate is below the fixed rate) and is measured at fair value. Fair value measurements are based on the present value of the future cash flows. For this example, the fair values, and changes in fair value, of the variable-rate debt and interest rate swap at each December 31 are as follows:

[19]Other comprehensive income is part of the equity section of the balance sheet and includes the changes in fair value of investment securities classified as available-for-sale.

Fair Value—Asset (Liability):				
Variable-rate debt	$(10,000)	$(10,000)	$(10,000)	$ 0
Interest rate swap	497[20]	514[21]	270[22]	0
Changes in Fair Value—Gain (Loss):				
Variable-rate debt	$ 0	0	0	0
Interest rate swap	497	217[23]	56[24]	30[25]

The fair value of the variable-rate debt is $10,000 each year because the present value of the principal and the interest is discounted at the market rate of interest (the variable rate). The fair value of the interest rate swap each year reflects the present value of the net difference in interest amounts (the net settlement amount above). Thus, $497 is equal to the present value of an ordinary annuity of $200 discounted at 10% for three periods. The amount $514 is the present value of an ordinary annuity of $300 discounted for two periods at 11%, and $270 is $300 discounted at 11% for one period. These amounts are reported as assets/liabilities on the statement of financial position, respectively, in Years 1, 2, and 3.

The changes in fair value of the swap, adjusted for settlement receipts during the period would be reported as "Other Comprehensive Income" as part of the equity section of the balance sheet. The changes in fair value of the swap that relate to the current period's forecasted transaction would be recognized in earnings on the projected date for each forecasted transaction (December 31).

Accounting for the variable-rate debt and interest rate swap results in the following balances and effects on annual earnings:

	12/31/X1	**12/31/X2**	**12/31/X3**	**12/31/X4**
Balances—debit (credit):				
Cash	$ 10,000	$ 10,000	$ 10,000	$ 0
Variable-rate debt (liability)	(10,000)	(10,000)	(10,000)	0
Interest rate swap (asset)	497	514	270	0
Other comprehensive income (equity section of balance sheet)	(497)	(514)	(270)	0
Earnings:				
Variable rate debt:				
Interest expense	(800)	(1,000)	(1,100)	(1,100)
Interest rate swap:				
Deferred gains from other comprehensive income[26]	0	200	300	300
Net interest expense	$ (800)	$ (800)	$ (800)	$ (800)

[20]$497 = Present value of ordinary annuity of $200 at 10% for three periods.
[21]$514 = Present value of ordinary annuity of $300 at 11% for two periods.
[22]$270 = Present value of $300 discounted at 11% for one period.
[23]$217 = $514 − $497 + $200
[24]$ 56 = $270 − $514 + $300
[25]$ 30 = $0 − $270 + $300
[26]For illustrative purposes, changes in the value of the swap have been classified as an adjustment of interest expense. However, this statement does not prescribe the classification of gains and losses on derivative financial instruments in the statement of financial performance.

This amount reflects recognition of gains previously deferred in other comprehensive income on the projected date of the hedged cash flow.

The Exposure Draft does not provide examples of the journal entries, but conceptually, these would follow:

Date	Account	Debit	Credit
19X1			
Jan. 1	Cash	10,000	
	Note Payable		10,000
	To record the original loan from XYZ to ABC.		
Dec. 31	Interest Expense	800	
	Cash		800
	To record payment of interest to XYZ.		
31	Interest Rate Swap (Asset)	497	
	Change in Fair Value of Swap—Equity		497
	To record the fair value of swap as an asset and the Deferred Gain as Other Comprehensive Income outside of earnings. This is an equity account on the balance sheet.		
19X2			
Dec. 31	Interest Expense	1,000	
	Cash		1,000
	To record the variable interest paid to XYZ on the note.		
31	Cash	200	
	Interest Rate Swap—Asset		200
	To record the cash received from Ajax for the settlement difference on the hedge.		
31	Change in Fair Value of Swap—Equity	200	
	Deferred Gain From Other Comprehensive Income (earnings)		200
	To recognize the deferred gain on the swap on the forecast date in earnings of current period.		
31	Interest Rate Swap (Asset)	217	
	Change in Fair Value of Swap—Equity		217
	To record the change in fair value of swap as a deferred gain in other comprehensive income in stockholders' equity section of the balance sheet.		
19X3			
Dec. 31	Interest Expense	1,100	
	Cash		1,100
	To record the variable interest paid on the note to XYZ.		
31	Cash	300	
	Interest Rate Swap—Asset		300
	To record the cash received from Ajax for the settlement difference on the hedge.		
31	Change in Fair Value of Swap—Equity	300	
	Deferred Gain From Other Comprehensive Income (earnings)		300
	To recognize deferred gain on the swap on the forecast date in earnings of current period.		
31	Interest Rate Swap (Asset)	56	
	Change in Fair Value of Swap—Equity		56
	To record the change in fair value of swap as a deferred gain in other comprehensive income in the stockholders' equity section of the balance sheet.		

19X4			
Dec. 31	Interest Expense	1,100	
	Cash		1,100
	To record the variable interest paid to XYZ on the note.		
31	Cash	300	
	Interest Rate Swap—Asset		300
	To record the cash received from Ajax for the settlement difference on the hedge.		
31	Change in Fair Value of Swap—Equity	300	
	Deferred Gain From Other Comprehensive Income (earnings)		300
	To recognize deferred gain on swap on the forecast date in earnings of current period.		
31	Interest Rate Swap (Asset)	30	
	Change in Fair Value of Swap—Equity		30
	To record the change in fair value of swap as a deferred gain in other comprehensive income in the stockholders' equity section of the balance sheet.		

The Deferred Gain From Other Comprehensive Income recognized in earnings each year partially offsets the interest expense for the period. The Interest Rate Swap—Asset account is offset by the equity account, Change in Fair Value of Swap—Equity, on the statement of financial position. These two accounts appear as follows at the end of each year:

	12/31/X1	12/31/X2	12/31/X3	12/31/X4
Interest Rate Swap—Asset	$497	$514	$270	$0
Change in Fair Value of Swap—Equity	497	514	270	0

The account Change in Fair Value of Swap—Equity is reported in "Other comprehensive income" as part of stockholders' equity on the balance sheet. The "Other comprehensive income" section of stockholders' equity also includes gains and losses on changes in fair value of investment securities classified as available-for-sale.

Example 2: Fair Value Hedge—Fixed-Rate Interest-Bearing Debt. The second example presented and explained here is one of the fair value hedge examples from the Exposure Draft.

The conceptual basis for these types of derivatives is that they are hedges of risk in a fixed contractual amount. For example, debt bearing a fixed interest rate is subject to changes in fair value because of variability in the market rate of interest. To protect against changes in market value, a company may enter into a hedge contract similar to the one described below.[27]

Assume that on January 1, 19X1, DEF Company borrows $10,000 from LUM at an 8 percent fixed rate of interest, with interest to be paid annually to LUM on December 31 and the $10,000 principal to be repaid on December 31, 19X4.

[27]This example is adapted from Example No. 2 from Appendix B of the Exposure Draft "Accounting for Derivative and Similar Financial Instruments and For Hedging Activities," FASB, June 20, 1996.

On January 1, 19X1, DEF Company enters into a four-year, receive-fixed, pay-variable interest rate swap with ACME Corporation and designates the interest rate swap as a hedge of the fair value of the fixed-rate debt. The interest rate swap, based on a notional amount of $10,000, will result in a cash settlement to be paid to or received from ACME by DEF company on each December 31. The cash settlement is the net of a variable interest payment based on the market rate of interest and an 8 percent fixed interest receipt. The market interest rate on January 1 determines the variable portion of the swap settlement on the following December 31.

The Exposure Draft prescribes that changes in fair value of the underlying debt (net of the amortization amounts) be reported in earnings to the extent of the changes in fair value of the derivative, with corresponding adjustments to the carrying amount of the debt. The Exposure Draft also prescribes the effective-interest method to be used based on the balance of the debt at the beginning of the period. The derivative is to be measured at fair value. Changes in the fair value (adjusted for any settlement payments/receipts during the period) are to be reported in earnings.

Market interest rates are 8 percent on January 1, 19X1, 10 percent on December 31, 19X1, and 11 percent on December 31, 19X2, through December 31, 19X4. The interest payments on the fixed-rate debt to LUM and the interest rate swap to ACME by DEF Company are as follows:

	12/31/X1	12/31/X2	12/31/X3	12/31/X4
Fixed-rate debt	$ (800)	$ (800)	$ (800)	$ (800)
Interest rate swap	0	(200)	(300)	(300)
Net cash payment	$ (800)	$(1,000)	$ (1,100)	$(1,100)

The fair values, and changes in fair value, of the fixed-rate debt and interest rate swap at each December 31 are as follows:

Fair Value—Asset (Liability):				
Fixed-rate debt[28]	$(9,503)	$(9,486)	$ (9,730)	$ 0
Interest rate swap	(497)[29]	(514)[30]	(270)[31]	0
Changes in Fair Value—Gain (Loss):				
Fixed-rate debt[32]	$497	$167	$ 0	$ 0
Interest rate swap	(497)	(217)[33]	(56)[34]	(30)[35]

[28]Fair value of debt at end of period:
$9,503 = PVSS (10,000, 3n, 10%) + PVOA (800, 3n, 10%)
$9,486 = PVSS (10,000, 2n, 11%) + PVOA (800, 2n, 11%)
$9,730 = PVSS (10,000, 1n, 11%) + PVOA (800, 1n, 11%)

[29]$497 = Present value of ordinary annuity of $200 at 10% for three periods.

[30]$514 = Present value of ordinary annuity of $300 at 11% for two periods.

[31]$270 = Present value of 300 discounted at 11% for one period.

[32]Change in fair value—debt
$497 = $9,503 − $10,000
$167 = $514 − $497 + $150
$(0) = $270 − $514 + $244

[33]$217 = $514 − $497 + $200

[34]$ 56 = $270 − $514 + $300

[35]$ 30 = $0 − $270 + $300

Present value of debt (1/1)	$(9,503)	$ (9,486)	$ (9,730)
Present value of debt (12/31)	(9,653)	(9,730)	(10,000)
Amortization amount	$ (150)	$ (244)	$ (270)

The interest rate swap is measured at fair value, and changes in fair value, which are adjusted for settlement payments made during the period, are reported in earnings. The fair value of the fixed-rate debt is equal to the present value of the future obligation. The changes in the fair value of the fixed-rate debt, which are adjusted for any yield adjustments recorded during the period, are reported in earnings only to the extent of the change in fair value of the derivative, with corresponding adjustments to the carrying amount of the debt.

Accounting for the fixed-rate debt and interest rate swap as a hedge results in the following balances and effect on annual earnings:

	12/31/X1	**12/31/X2**	**12/31/X3**	**12/31/X4**
Balances—debit (credit):				
Fixed-rate debt	$(9,503)	$(9,486)	$(9,730)	$ 0
Interest rate swap	(497)	(514)	(270)	0
Earnings (changes in net assets):				
Fixed-rate debt:				
Interest expense	$ (800)	$ (800)	$ (800)	$ (800)
Change in fair value	497	167	0	0
Amortization amount	0	(150)	(244)	(270)
Interest rate swap:				
Change in fair value	(497)	(217)	(56)	(30)
Net interest expense	$ (800)	$(1,000)	$(1,100)	$(1,100)

The Exposure Draft does not provide sample journal entries, nor does it prescribe the account titles. Conceptually, the following entries would result:

19X1			
Jan. 1	Cash	10,000	
	Note Payable		10,000
	To record the issue of the note to LUM.		
19X1			
Dec. 31	Interest Expense	800	
	Cash		800
	To record the interest paid to LUM on the note.		
31	Note Payable	497	
	Change in Fair Value of Note Payable		497
	To record the change in fair value of the note. The change in fair value is reported in earnings.		
31	Change in Fair Value of Swap	497	
	Interest Rate Swap (liability)		497
	To record the change in fair value of the swap and the swap as a liability. The change in fair value is reported in earnings and offsets the change in fair value of the note payable.		

Date	Account	Debit	Credit
19X2			
Dec. 31	Interest Expense	950	
	Note Payable		150
	Cash		800
	To record payment of interest to LUM and amortization of the discount on the note payable using the effective-interest method.		
31	Note Payable	167	
	Change in Fair Value of Note Payable		167
	To record the change in fair value of the note. The change in fair value is reported in earnings.		
31	Change in Fair Value of Swap	217	
	Cash		200
	Interest Rate Swap (liability)		17
	To record the change in the fair value of the swap net of the settlement amount paid to ACME. The change in fair value is reported in earnings and offsets the change in fair value of the note payable.		
19X3			
Dec. 31	Interest Expense	1,044	
	Note Payable		244
	Cash		800
	To record payment of interest to LUM and amortization of the note payable using the effective-interest method.		
31	Change in Fair Value of Swap	56	
	Interest Rate Swap (Liability)	244	
	Cash		300
	To record the change in the fair value of the swap net of the settlement amount paid to ACME. The change in fair value is reported in earnings.		
19X4			
Dec. 31	Interest Expense	1,070	
	Note Payable		270
	Cash		800
	To record payment of interest to LUM and amortization of the discount on the note payable using the effective-interest method.		
31	Interest Rate Swap (Liability)	270	
	Change in Fair Value of Swap	30	
	Cash		300
	To record the change in the fair value of the swap net of the settlement amount paid to ACME. The change in fair value is reported in earnings.		
31	Note Payable	10,000	
	Cash		10,000
	To record repayment of the note to LUM.		

The Note Payable account would contain the following balances:

1/1/X1	Balance	$10,000
12/31/X1	Change in fair value	(497)
	Balance	$ 9,503
12/31/X2	Amortization of discount	150
	Change in fair value	(167)
	Balance	$ 9,486
12/31/X3	Amortization of discount	244
	Balance	$ 9,730
12/31/X4	Amortization of discount	270
	Balance	$10,000

The Interest Rate Swap account would contain the following:

12/31/X1	Balance	$(497)
12/31/X2	Change in fair value in X2	(17)
	Balance	$(514)
12/31/X3	Change in fair value in X3	244
	Balance	$(270)
12/31/X4	Change in fair value in X4	270
	Balance	$ 0

The change in fair value of the note is reported in earnings to the extent of the change in fair value of the interest rate swap. Here, the entire amount of the fair value change in the note is offset by the change in fair value of the swap.

END-OF-CHAPTER REVIEW

SUMMARY

1. **Explain the recognition and measurement issues associated with investments.** Investments represent economic resources owned or controlled by the firm and from which the firm expects to receive future economic benefits. The benefits can be long- or short-term depending on the timing of the revenue-generating process. Accounting for investments depends on the underlying revenue-generating process. Short-term benefits from the revenue-generation process result in short-term or current asset classification. Long-term benefits result in noncurrent asset classification.
2. **Record and report transactions for debt-security investments and equity-security investments of less than 20%.** SFAS No. 115 applies to all investments in debt securities and to passive investments in equity securities. Three classification categories are designated in SFAS No. 115: trading securities, held-to-maturity securities, and available-for-sale securities. SFAS No. 115 requires reporting investments at fair value for trading and available-for-sale securities and at amortized cost for held-to-maturity securities. Changes in fair value for trading securities are reflected in earnings of the current period, while changes for available-for-sale securities are reflected as a separate reporting item in shareholders' equity. If debt securities are purchased at a premium or discount, the premium or discount must be amortized using the effective-interest method.

3. **Record and report equity-security investment transactions of greater than 20 percent and less than 50 percent.** APB Opinion No. 18 prescribes accounting and reporting requirements for investments in equity securities with greater than 20 percent ownership interest. The ability to exercise significant influence over the policies of the investee is presumed to exist in this type of investment. APB Opinion No. 18 requires the use of the equity method to account for these investments. The investment is recorded at cost, increased for the investor's proportionate share of income of the investee, and reduced by the dividends received from the investee.

4. **Record and report transactions for funds and life insurance investments.** Each special-purpose fund should be accounted for separately, because each is a separate asset with separate cash flows and economic benefits. Special funds can be used for retirement of debt, plant expansion, or any other special purpose designated by the entity.

   Whole life insurance policies on key executives provide death protection and a cash surrender value. The premium paid represents an expense portion (for the death protection) and an asset (for the cash surrender value).

5. **Analyze the impact of the different accounting methods for investments on profitability and liquidity measures.** The fair value method of accounting for investments results in different income-recognition amounts depending on which category management designates as the investment classification. The trading-securities category recognizes as current-period income changes in fair value during the current period, but the available-for-sale method does not. The equity method recognizes a proportionate share of the investee income as income of the investor. These all affect profitability.

   The fair value method reports the Investment account at fair values except for held-to-maturity securities, which are reported at amortized cost. The equity method reports the investment account at original cost adjusted for the investor's proportionate share of investee income, less any dividends received. These affect asset valuation and, in turn, liquidity measures.

6. **Understand the concepts and complexities associated with derivative financial instruments.** Derivative financial instruments are used to reduce financial risk stemming from changes in fair values, cash flows, or foreign currency exposures. Accounting standards for these instruments are currently being developed, and the proposals call for recognition of these instruments as assets or liabilities at fair values in the statement of financial condition. The changes in fair values are included in either other comprehensive income as part of stockholders' equity or current-period earnings depending on the type and purpose of the derivative financial instrument.

KEY TERMS

amortization *449*
available-for-sale securities *445*
discount *447*
derivative financial instruments *477*
effective-interest method *449*
equity method *462*
fair value *445*
goodwill *463*
held-to-maturity securities *445*
impairment *459*
notional amount *478*
preemptive stock rights *470*
premium *447*
stock rights *470*
stock warrants *471*
trading securities *445*
yield *447*

ASSIGNMENT MATERIAL

CASES

C9–1 Role Play With Ethics

On January 15, 1998, Sunrise Technology purchased a 10% interest in Laseroptics Research Corporation for $25 million in cash. Sunrise manufactures and sells lasers used for corrective eye surgery, and Laseroptics holds several patents for products and processes used in the correction of astigmatism.

Additionally, Laseroptics had another process in the final stages of clinical trials for approval by the FDA. Approval of this process was expected, and its licensing was expected to generate significant future revenue and profit. This was reflected in the very high price-earnings ratio (150/1) of Laseroptics' stock price. At the time of Sunrise's investment, the market price of Laseroptics was $100 per share with earnings of $.67 per share. Both companies' stocks are traded over the counter.

Sunrise recorded the investment at cost, and management designated the shares as available-for-sale. On the financial statements for December 31, 1998, the investment was included at the market value of $42 million on the balance sheet and an unrealized gain of $17 million in the shareholders' equity section.

Late in 1999, the FDA rejected Laseroptics' application for the new process, indicating the long-term effects were uncertain. The price of the stock immediately plummeted from $225 to $20 and was still falling when trading was halted by the NASDAQ. By the end of 1999, trading in the shares of Laseroptics had not resumed.

Also late in 1999, Sunrise was in the midst of some delicate negotiations with its bankers regarding the renewal of some short-term debt and the borrowing of an additional $20 million on a long-term basis. Sunrise desperately needed the funding from the banks, since it had no alternative source of funding.

The banks were concerned about the prospects for Sunrise. Over the last three years, Sunrise had struggled to barely break even, and the trend of earnings had been downward and included a loss in the last year. In addition, a competitor company had recently introduced a product that performed the same functions as the Sunrise main laser product but was priced at 25 percent below the Sunrise product.

At the end of 1999, the Sunrise auditors wanted to write down the value of the Laseroptics investment and report a loss of approximately $37 million on the income statement. Sunrise's management was adamantly opposed to the write-down.

Required:

A. Assume the role of the auditors and negotiate your position with management.

B. Assume the role of management and negotiate your position with the auditor.

C9–2 Equity Trading and Available-for-Sale Securities—Report Preparation

Vane Company has two portfolios of marketable equity securities. One is classified as trading securities, and the other is classified as available-for-sale. Vane does not have the ability to exercise significant influence over any of the companies in either portfolio. Some securities from each portfolio were sold during the year. One of the securities in the trading portfolio was reclassified to the available-for sale portfolio when its market value was less than cost. At the beginning and end of the year, the aggregate cost of each portfolio exceeded its aggregate market value by different amounts.

Required: Prepare a report that addresses the following:

A. How should Vane measure and report the income statement effects of the securities sold during the year from each portfolio?

B. How should Vane account for the security that was reclassified from the trading portfolio to the available-for-sale portfolio?

C. How should Vane report the effects of investments in each portfolio on its balance sheet as of the end of the year and its income statement for the year? Why? (*Note:* Do not discuss the securities sold.)

C9–3 Classification of Securities

Houston Company has three portfolios of securities: trading, available-for-sale, and equity method investments. The equity method investment securities reflect an ownership of 20% in each of the three separate investments.

Sam Houston, president of Houston Company, wants to reclassify two of the three stocks from the equity method to trading securities because the market prices of both are significantly above the carrying value of the investment account. Sam Houston proposes to sell a nominal number of shares of each to reduce the ownership proportion to just under 20%, allowing use of the fair value method of accounting as opposed to the equity method. He has heard that this change would allow Houston Company to report the difference between the market values of the stocks and the current carrying values of the investment accounts as current-period income, and this is quite appealing to him because his bonus is based on reported income each period.

Required:

A. What are the accounting implications of the change?

B. Is this a legitimate change to make?

C. Will Sam Houston achieve the objective of increasing income by making this change?

C9–4 Equity Method

Leasco Inc., an investment corporation, owns 3% of the voting stock of Reliance Group. Leasco is taking in 3% of the earnings of Reliance, claiming that Leasco effectively has control of Reliance. Similarly, Bangor Punta is the owner of 7% of the stock of Lone Star Industries, bringing in 7% of the earnings of Lone Star under the equity method. This contributed over $3 million to Bangor Punta's earnings.

Required: What circumstances could justify use of the equity method in these two cases?

C9–5 International Accounting Standards and Investments—Report Preparation

Freeport McMoran is a large company with worldwide holdings in timber, mining, and manufacturing operations. One of the investments that Freeport holds is a 10% interest in Poly-X LTD, a gold mine in Malaysia. The shares of Poly-X are traded on the Singapore Stock Exchange, and the financial statements are prepared in conformance with international accounting standards. Freeport reports this investment in compliance with SFAS No. 115.

Required: If Freeport were to report this investment in conformity with international accounting standards instead of SFAS No. 115, prepare a report indicating what, if anything, would change.

QUESTIONS

Q9–1 What is the difference between recognition and realization of gains and losses?

Q9–2 What is meant by the phrase "ability to exercise significant influence'?

Q9–3 How is the investor's ability to exercise significant influence related to the realization of future economic benefits of the investment?

Q9–4 Explain the relationship between the proper classification of investment securities and revenue recognition.

Q9–5 Briefly summarize the differences in accounting requirements for investments in securities classified as trading versus those classified as available-for-sale and those classified as held-to-maturity.

Q9–6 What is the distinction between investment securities classified as current assets and those classified as noncurrent assets?

Q9–7 Explain the difference in revenue recognition resulting from classification of an investment as trading versus available-for-sale.

Q9–8 Explain the difference in revenue recognition resulting from using the equity method to account for an investment as opposed to the fair value method as outlined in SFAS No. 115.

Q9–9 Assume an investment is made that results in no significant influence. Would it be possible for the management of the investor corporation to manipulate, or manage, income by classification of the investment as either trading or available-for-sale? If yes, how? If not, why not?

Q9–10 Why are the holding gains and losses on the portfolio of trading securities treated differently from those of available-for-sale securities?

Q9–11 How do we know if a decline in the market value of an equity security is permanent rather than temporary? What significance does it have?

Q9–12 What is the rationale for using the equity method of accounting for investments in equity securities?

Q9–13 When an investment is made in debt securities that will be classified as held-to-maturity, what does the purchase price represent?

Q9–14 In reference to an investment in bonds, what is a premium? What is a discount?

Q9–15 Why is the effective-interest method of amortization of premium and discount required? What qualitative characteristic of accounting data does this requirement help to achieve? Are there alternative methods of amortization that would be suitable?

Q9–16 Explain how amortization of premiums and discounts is related to revenue recognition.

Q9–17 Explain why the effective-interest method of amortization of premiums and discounts does not reflect current market values for the bond investment.

Q9–18 How is U.S. GAAP different from international accounting standards for investments?

Q9–19 What measures of liquidity are affected by valuation of investments?

Q9–20 How are measures of profitability affected by valuation of investments?

Q9–21 How are cash flows affected by valuation of investments?

Q9–22 What are the economic purposes of derivative financial instruments?

Q9–23 How can derivative financial instruments be used to reduce risk?

Q9–24 What types of financial risk can be managed with derivatives?

EXERCISES

E9–1 Journal Entries for Trading Investments

Record the following transactions for the Welch Corporation in general journal format. Assume these are the only investments Welch has and that they are classified as trading securities.

1998		
Jan.	10	Purchased 200 shares of Xdent at $30/share.
Feb.	12	Purchased 400 shares of Nugent at $25/share.
Mar.	1	Received $1/share cash dividends from Xdent Corp.
May	14	Purchased 600 shares of TROP Corp. at $20/share.
June	1	Received notice that Nugent stock had split two for one.
	15	Sold 200 shares of Nugent at $15/share.
Sep.	22	Sold all the Xdent stock for $5,500 including commissions.
Oct.	12	Received a cash dividend of $.50/share from TROP Corp.
Dec.	1	Transferred the Nugent stock to the available-for-sale portfolio. The market price at the time of transfer was $10/share.
	31	The market price of Nugent was $8/share, and TROP was $18/share.

E9–2 Portfolio Valuation

SCA Corporation had the following portfolio of trading securities purchased during 1997.

	SHARES	COST	12/31/97
Jordan Inc.	400	$ 8,500	$12,000
Pippen Co.	300	7,200	8,500
Ewing Inc.	500	15,000	11,200
Johnson's Magic	1,000	25,000	7,800
Barkley's Best	800	20,000	16,400
LL Bird	2,000	30,000	20,000
SQ O'Neal	900	27,000	35,000

Required:

A. Prepare the adjusting entry at 12/31/97 for the SCA Corporation to properly reflect the investment portfolio at fair value.

B. Without regard to part **(A)**, suppose that SCA management wanted to transfer the Jordan, Ewing, and O'Neal shares to the available-for-sale portfolio. Prepare the journal entries to effect the transfer at 12/31/97.

E9–3 Short-Term Investments, Journal Entries, Income Statement, and Balance Sheet

The Agudelo Corporation's balance sheet at 12/31/96 after all adjustments were made included the following balance for investments:

Investment in equity securities—Trading	$165,000
Adjustment to market—Trading securities	(12,000)
Fair market value, 12/31/96	$153,000

During the year 1997, Agudelo had the following transactions affecting the investment account:

- Sold 1,000 shares of Hammer Corp. for $30,000, cost of $20,000.
- Sold 2,000 shares of ICT for $40,000, cost of $65,000.
- Purchased 1,000 shares of Metallica for $35,000.

At the end of 1997, the aggregate market value of the investment portfolio was $120,000.

Required:

A. Prepare the journal entries required in 1997 for the Investment account.
B. Prepare the descriptions and amounts that should be presented on Agudelo's income statement for 1997.
C. Prepare the descriptions and amounts that should be reported on the balance sheet for 1997.

E9–4 Trading and Available-for-Sale Securities

The investment portfolio of Jennings Company at 12/31/97 included the following:

COMPANY	SHARES	COST	MARKET VALUE AT 12/31/96	MARKET VALUE AT 12/31/97
A	500	$90	$80	$100
B	1,000	60	50	40
C	2,000	15	20	25
D	4,000	20	30	25

Assume the following occurs in 1998.

1. The stock of A splits 4 for 1.
2. Cash dividends of $1.00 per share are received from B.
3. A 10% stock dividend is received from C.
4. Stock D was sold for $18 per share.
5. At the end of 1998, the market value of A was $30/share, B was $30/share, and C was $20/share.

Required:

A. Prepare the adjusting entry required at the end of 1997 assuming the securities were designated as (1) trading and (2) available-for-sale.
B. Prepare the journal entries to record these transactions in 1998 assuming the securities were designated as (1) trading and (2) available-for-sale.

E9–5 Trading Securities and Available-for-Sale

The investment portfolio of Smith consists of the following securities at 12/31/98:

STOCK	ACQUISITION DATE	NUMBER OF SHARES	ACQUISITION PRICE	MARKET PRICE 12/31/97	MARKET PRICE 12/31/98
GM	1/6/95	2,000	$ 35	$40	$42
Ford	2/8/95	4,500	42	45	50
GE	4/5/96	3,200	50	40	38
IBM	5/7/96	2,000	100	90	75
Xerox	6/1/97	3,000	80	60	50

No changes in the portfolio occurred during 1998 other than the price changes.

Required:

A. Assume that Smith treats these as trading security investments. Prepare the adjusting entry at 12/31/98 to reflect fair value.

B. Assume that Smith treats these as available-for-sale investments. Prepare the adjusting entry at 12/31/98 to reflect fair value.

C. Explain the differences (if any) between **(A)** and **(B)** in terms of income determination, balance sheet presentation, and cash flows.

E9–6 Equity Method, Two Years

On February 1, 1997, Dugan Inc. purchased 25% of the outstanding voting stock of MacGuigan for $150,000. The book value and the fair market value of the net assets on this date were both $600,000. Dugan purchased the stock to establish a long-term relationship with MacGuigan, which was one of Dugan's principal suppliers.

MacGuigan paid a cash dividend of $20,000 on June 1 and reported earnings of $80,000 for the year 1997. In 1998, MacGuigan omitted the cash dividend because the company was experiencing financial difficulty. For the year 1998, MacGuigan reported a net loss of $100,000.

Required:

A. Prepare the journal entries on the books of Dugan to record the investment in MacGuigan and the entries required in 1997 and 1998.

B. Determine the balance in the Investment account at the end of 1998.

E9–7 Equity Method, Correction of Error

JMH is a producer of high-quality expensive components for specialized machinery. In 1997, JMH had purchased 200,000 shares of EXCED as an investment at a total cost of $1,200,000. This represented 40% of EXCED's total shares outstanding. At the time of the purchase, EXCED had total assets of $6 million and total liabilities of $3 million. Assume that the fair market value of the assets was equal to the book value. EXCED had the following results in the ensuing years:

	Dividends Paid	Net Income (Loss)
1997	$100,000	$600,000
1998	120,000	400,000
1999	50,000	(200,000)

The Investment in EXCED account on the JMH books reflects a current balance of $1,512,000 after recording the dividends received in 1999 and its share of the loss for the year.

Required: Calculate the correct amount that should be in the Investment in EXCED account on the JMH books at the end of 1999, and prepare a correcting entry. Assume that the books have been closed for 1999.

E9–8 Equity Method, Goodwill Amortization, Excess Depreciation

On 1/1/97, A. Reinstein purchased 20% of the voting stock of Brister Inc. for a total price of $750,000. At the time of purchase, Brister had net assets of $3,000,000 at book value and $3,600,000 at fair market value. Brister had the following results for 1997 and 1998:

	Dividends Paid	Net Income (Loss)
1997	$80,000	$200,000
1998	80,000	40,000

At the time of purchase, Reinstein estimated that the depreciable assets had 12 years of remaining life. Reinstein amortized goodwill over 15 years.

Required:

A. Prepare the journal entry to record the investment at January 1, 1997.
B. Prepare the journal entries required in 1997 and 1998 to record the income, dividends, excess depreciation, and amortization of goodwill.
C. Calculate the balance in the Investment account at January 1, 1999.

E9–9 Change to Equity Method

Alford Investments made the following investments in Hazeltine:

1/1/97	12,000 shares (12% of total)	$480,000
6/1/98	3,000 shares (3% of total)	150,000
3/1/99	10,000 shares (10% of total)	550,000

These were designated as available-for-sale until March 1, 1999. Hazeltine has reported the following results during this time:

	MARKET PRICE AT 12/31	DIVIDENDS PAID 12/31	NET INCOME (LOSS)
1997	$45	$ 0	$100,000
1998	52	50,000	200,000
1999	60	50,000	100,000

Assume that Alford followed proper accounting procedures for its investment in Hazeltine.

Required:

A. Prepare the journal entries that Alford would have made in each of the first two years.
B. Calculate the amount of unrealized gain in shareholders' equity from this investment at 12/31/98.
C. Calculate the correct amount that would have been in the Investment account at January 1, 1999, if the equity method had been used (assume that fair market value and book value of the net assets are the same and that the purchase price is equal to book and fair market value).
D. Prepare the journal entry to retroactively restate the Investment account at January 1, 1999.
E. Prepare the entry to record the final purchase.

E9–10 Stock Rights

R. Young currently owns 10,000 shares of Whiteco common stock. Young purchased this stock over a period of time at an average cost of $40 per share. Whiteco is planning a major new stock offering, equivalent to twenty percent of the shares currently outstanding. The existing shareholders will have the right to purchase one new share of the stock at $80 per share for each five shares currently owned. The stock of Whiteco is currently trading at $110 per share.

Young does not wish to purchase any of the additional shares and sells her rights for a total of $51,400, less commissions and fees of $700.

Required: Prepare the journal entry to record the sale of the rights by Young.

E9–11 Investment in Debt Trading Securities

J. Ruhl purchased 200 bonds with a face value of $1,000 each on March 1, 1996. The bonds have a stated interest rate of 8%, and the interest payment dates are January 31 and July 31. Ruhl paid cash of $197,000, which included accrued interest at the time of purchase. The bonds were sold on August 1, 1996, for a total cash price of $202,000. Ruhl designated these as trading securities.

Required: Prepare the journal entries necessary at March 1, 1996, July 31, 1996, and August 1, 1996.

E9–12 Investment in Debt Trading Securities

C. Copp Corp. purchased 10 bonds with a face value of $1,000 each on April 1, 1998. Copp paid cash of $11,200 for the bonds including accrued interest. The stated interest rate on the bonds is 12% and is paid semiannually on February 1 and August 1. Copp sold the bonds on September 1 for $11,000 cash including accrued interest.

Required: Prepare all the journal entries necessary in 1998 to properly account for these bonds assuming they are designated as trading securities.

E9–13 Calculate Purchase Price of Bond

D. Deis purchased 20 bonds with a face value of $1,000 each on January 1, 1990. The bonds had a stated interest rate of 12%, payable semiannually on June 30 and December 31. The bonds had a maturity date of December 31, 1999. At the time of purchase, the market rate of interest was 10%.

Required:

A. How much did Deis pay for these bonds?

B. Supposing the market rate was 12%, what was the purchase price?

E9–14 Purchase and Sale of Bonds

Assume the purchase of twenty $1,000, 16% bonds on July 31 at a price of 104 plus accrued interest and commission of $1,500 as trading securities investments. The interest payment dates are March 31 and September 30. The bonds are sold November 1 at 109 plus accrued interest, less a sales commission of $1,000.

Required: Prepare the journal entries to record the purchase, the receipt of interest on September 30, and the sale of the bonds, assuming they were designated as trading securities.

E9–15 Preparation of an Amortization Table

K. Klingler purchased bonds with a face value of $100,000 on January 1, 1990. The bonds paid interest annually at 8% on December 31. The maturity date is December 31, 1996. Klingler purchased the bonds to obtain a yield of 12%.

Required: Prepare a schedule to show the amortization of the bonds.

E9–16 Journal Entries for a Sinking Fund

Memorex has a $5,000,000 bond issue that must be retired at the end of 5 years. Memorex is required to make five deposits to a sinking fund that will earn 10% compounded annually to retire the bonds. The first deposit must be made immediately.

Required:

A. Prepare the journal entry necessary to record the initial deposit.

B. Prepare the journal entry to record the earnings on the sinking fund after the first year.

C. Assume that the sinking fund ends up with $5,100,000 because it earns more than was expected. Prepare the journal entry to retire the bonds and dissolve the fund.

E9–17 Equity Method, Differences Between Purchase Price and Book Value

Merck Corporation purchased a 40 percent interest in the voting stock of Biotronics, a genetics research company on April 21, 1998, for $4 million. At the time of purchase, the book value of the net assets was $6 million, with an average life expectancy of ten years. The fair market value of these assets at the time of purchase was $9 million.

Biotronics reported a net loss of $500,000 for the year 1998. Merck follows a policy of taking a full year's depreciation/amortization in the year of asset purchase.

Required:

A. Prepare the journal entries for 1998 to record Merck's (1) purchase, (2) accrual of income, (3) amortization of excess depreciation, and (4) amortization of goodwill over 15 years.

B. Calculate the amount in the Investment in Biotronics account at December 31, 1998, after the books have been closed.

E9–18 Life Insurance

Larry Latuso is the president and CEO of Landmark Mining. Landmark purchased a $100,000 whole life insurance policy on Latuso at the time he was elected president and CEO, five years ago. The annual premium on the policy is $6,500. The current cash value of the policy is $21,000 and will increase to $25,500 with the premium payment on June 1 of this year. The cash value earns interest at a current rate of 4%.

Required:

A. Prepare the journal entry to record the premium payment on June 1.

B. Prepare the adjusting entry necessary at December 31.

C. Unfortunately, Latuso was inspecting one of Landmark's mines on January 1 of the next year and was killed in an accident. Prepare the journal entry.

E9–19 Held-to-Maturity Investment

On January 1, 1998, G. Hosch purchased $100,000 par value, 10% bonds when the market rate of interest was 8%. The bonds mature on January 1, 2008, and pay interest semiannually on July 1 and January 1, with the first payment due July 1, 1998. Assume there were no acquisition fees and that Hosch classifies the bonds as held-to-maturity.

Required:

A. Calculate the purchase price of the bonds.

B. Prepare the journal entries necessary on the following dates:

1. January 1, 1998, to record purchase.
2. July 1, 1998, to record interest received and to amortize the premium.
3. December 31, 1998, to accrue interest and to amortize the premium.
4. January 1, 1999, to record interest received.

EXERCISES RELATED TO APPENDIX: DERIVATIVE FINANCIAL INSTRUMENTS

***E9–20**

On January 1, 1995, ABC signs a 5-year note payable to borrow $100,000 from ACE Finance at a fixed interest rate of 9%. ABC enters a second agreement with Main Line Bank for an interest rate swap. ABC is to receive a fixed interest rate of 9% and pay a variable rate that would be determined by the current market rate on January 1 of each year. ABC designates this as a hedge of the change in fair value of the $100,000 note payable.

Required: Determine the cash flow amounts that ABC must account for related to the note and swap over the life of the note. Assume the interest rates are 9%, 10%, 11%, 11%, and 11% respectively for the next five years.

***E9–21**

On January 1, 1995, ABC signs a 4-year note payable to borrow $100,000 from ACE Finance at a variable interest rate determined by the market rate of interest on January 1 of each year. ABC enters a second agreement with Main Line Bank for an interest rate swap. ABC is to receive a variable interest rate and pay a fixed rate of 9% each year over the life of the note payable. ABC designates this interest rate swap as a hedge of the cash flows of the interest rate. Assume the interest rates are 9%, 10%, 11%, and 11% over the next four years.

Required: Determine the cash flow amounts that ABC must account for related to the note and swap over the life of the note.

***E9–22**

On January 1, 1995, ABC signs a 4-year note payable to borrow $100,000 from ACE Finance at a variable interest rate determined by the market rate of interest on January 1 of each year. ABC enters a second agreement with Main Line Bank for an interest rate swap. ABC is to receive a variable interest rate and pay a fixed rate of 9% each year over the life of the note payable. ABC designates this interest rate swap as a hedge of the cash flows of the interest rate. Assume the interest rates are 9%, 8%, 8%, and 7% over the next four years.

Required: Determine the cash flow amounts that ABC must account for related to the note and swap over the life of the note.

***E9–23**

On January 1, 1995, ABC signs a 5-year note payable to borrow $100,000 from ACE Finance at a fixed interest rate of 9%. ABC enters a second agreement with Main Line Bank for an interest rate swap. ABC is to receive a fixed interest rate of 9% and pay a variable rate that would be determined by the current market rate on January 1 of each year. ABC designates this as a hedge of the change in fair value of the $100,000 note payable.

Required: Determine the cash flow amounts that ABC must account for related to the note and swap over the life of the note. Assume the interest rates are 9%, 8%, 8%, 7%, and 8% respectively for the next five years.

*Refers to material in chapter appendix.

PROBLEMS

P9–1 Short-Term Investments

At December 31, 1998, Texas Utilities' portfolio of investments in equity securities included the following:

SECURITY	ACQUISITION DATE	NO. OF SHARES	COST PER SHARE	MARKET VALUE AT 12/31/98
A	2/1/98	3,000	$25	$30
B	4/1/98	2,000	30	32
C	6/1/98	4,000	20	11
D	8/8/98	1,000	48	42

During 1999, the following events take place.

1. Received a 20 percent stock dividend on 3/1/99 from C.
2. Received cash dividends of $1.00 and $1.50 per share for A and B, respectively, on 6/1/99.
3. Sold 500 shares of D on 8/1/99 for $35 per share.
4. Purchased 1,500 shares of E at $40 per share on 9/4/99 and designated it as a part of the trading securities portfolio.
5. At the end of 1999, the market values were: A, $40; B, $35; C, $25; D, $20; and E, $50.

At 12/31/98, Securities A and B are designated as trading, while C and D are designated as available-for-sale current assets.

Required:

A. Prepare the adjusting entries required at 12/31/98 to record fair values.
B. Prepare the journal entries required in 1999.
C. What is the net effect of the transactions in 1999 on income in 1999?

P9–2 Investment Effect on Income Statement

On June 1, 1997, GSU invests its temporarily idle cash in the following securities:

SECURITY	NO. OF SHARES	COST/SHARE	MARKET VALUE AT 12/31/97
A	1,000	$55	$55
B	2,000	45	50
C	1,000	60	70

In 1998, the following events take place:

1. Received cash dividends of $2 and $2.50 per share from B and C, respectively.
2. Received a 10% stock dividend from A.
3. At December 31, 1998, the market values per share were $40 for A, $44 for B, and $61 for C.

In 1999, the following events take place:

1. Received cash dividends of $2 per share from B.
2. Sold all the shares of C at $65 per share.
3. Purchased 3,000 shares of D at $20 per share.
4. The stock of A split 2 for 1.
5. The market values per share at 12/31/99 were $25 for A, $40 for B, and $19 for D.

Required: Prepare all the journal and adjusting entries required for 1998 and 1999 to properly record and reflect the investments at fair value. Assume all the investments are designated as trading securities.

P9–3 Available-for-Sale vs. Trading

Wheeler Corporation's investment portfolio at December 31, 1997, consisted of the following:

Security	Date of Acquisition	Acquisition Price	Market Price at 12/31/97
100 shares AA	4/10/96	$40	$70
400 shares BB	5/11/96	50	55
1,000 shares CC	8/12/97	30	32
500 shares DD	9/15/97	60	55

During 1998, the following events occurred:

Feb.	5	Purchased 100 additional shares of AA at $75/share.
July	1	Received a 20 percent stock dividend from CC.
Sep.	1	Sold 200 shares of BB at 45/share.
Dec.	31	The market values per share were $60 for AA, $30 for BB, $25 for CC, and $150 for DD.

Required:

A. Assume these investments are designated as trading securities. Prepare the adjusting entry at 12/31/98 to reflect the investments at fair value.

B. Assume that these investments are designated as available-for-sale securities. Prepare the adjusting entry at 12/31/98 to reflect the investments at fair value.

P9–4 Trading and Available-for-Sale Securities

Netterville Inc. provides you with the following information about the cost and market values of its short- and long-term investments at the end of years 1997 and 1998.

Trading Securities Investments:

Stock	Cost	Market Value at 12/31/97	Market Value at 12/31/98
A	$30,000	$27,000	$23,000
B	21,000	25,000	27,000
C	52,000	55,000	Sold at 50,000
D	35,000	42,000	38,000
E	26,000	27,000	30,000
F	15,000	18,000	Sold at 19,000
G	30,000	26,000	25,000
Available-for-Sale Investments (Noncurrent):			
H	$50,000	$55,000	$52,000
I	40,000	47,000	Sold at 45,000
J	60,000	62,000	65,000

Required:

A. At what amounts would the trading investments be reported on the balance sheets for 1997 and 1998?

B. At what amounts would the available-for-sale investments be reported on the balance sheets for 1997 and 1998?

P9–5 Equity Method

On March 15, 1997, Brooks purchased 20 percent of the outstanding stock of Caldwell for $2 million. At the time of the purchase, Caldwell had total assets with a book value and fair market value of $15 million and total liabilities of $6 million. Goodwill is amortized over 15 years.

In July 1997, Caldwell paid cash dividends of $250,000 and reported net income for the year of $1.2 million. Included in the income was an extraordinary loss of $300,000 from tornado damage to one of its facilities.

In July 1998, Caldwell paid cash dividends of $150,000 and reported a net loss for the year of $1 million.

Brooks sold all its shares in Caldwell on March 1, 1999, for a total price of $1 million.

Required: Prepare all the necessary journal entries related to the investment in Caldwell and its subsequent sale.

P9–6 Trading vs. Available for Sale, EPS and P/E Ratios

WWW Corp. invested $2,000,000 in the common stock of Jonesboro on August 18, 1997. The investment represented a ten percent interest in the stock of Jonesboro. At the time of the purchase, the Jonesboro stock was selling at a price of $20 per share. Jonesboro reported dividends and net income in the following amounts for a three-year period, and WWW's income before consideration of any dividends or income from Jonesboro was as follows:

	JONESBORO		WWW
	DIVIDENDS	INCOME	INCOME
1997	$400,000	$3,000,000	$5,000,000
1998	500,000	4,500,000	2,000,000
1999	600,000	4,000,000	6,000,000

WWW has 2,000,000 shares of stock outstanding, and the market price at the end of each year for the two companies' stock was as follows:

	JONESBORO	WWW
1997	$25/share	$45/share
1998	$18/share	$30/share
1999	$15/share	$57/share

Required:

A. Assume that WWW is unable to exercise significant influence on Jonesboro and treats the investments as trading securities.

1. Prepare all the journal entries necessary on WWW books relative to the investment.

2. Calculate earnings per share (EPS) and the price/earnings (P/E) ratio for WWW for all three years. (The price/earnings ratio is calculated as the market price per share of the stock divided by earnings per share.)

B. Assume that WWW accounts for the investment as available-for-sale. Calculate the EPS and the P/E ratio for WWW for all three years.

C. Which reporting method is most advantageous to WWW? Why?

P9–7 Dividends, Splits, Fair Value, and Equity Method

Nellcor Investment Co. has both short-term and long-term investment accounts. At the beginning of 1999, the short-term portfolio included the following securities:

	COST	MARKET
Trading Securities:		
1,000 shares AT&T	$ 90,000	$115,000
5,000 shares Chrysler	100,000	85,000
3,000 shares DuPont	90,000	78,000
Available-for-Sale Securities:		
2,000 shares Citicorp	50,000	55,000
2,000 shares Microsoft	142,000	150,000

The long-term portfolio included only one security:

	COST	MARKET
Available-for-Sale Securities:		
3,000 shares Mobil Oil	$120,000	$ 91,000

Since Nellcor is unable to influence any of these companies, both portfolios are accounted for at fair value.

In addition to these investments, Nellcor also owns 25 percent of the stock of Biosphere Ltd., a newly emerging environmental science company. Nellcor purchased 100,000 shares of Biosphere in 1997 at a total cost of $500,000. Nellcor uses the equity method to account for Biosphere, and the current balance at the beginning of 1999 is correctly stated at $395,000.

During 1999, the following events took place relative to these investments:

1. The stock of AT&T split three for one.
2. Received dividends from the following:

CASH	STOCK
ATT, $1 per share (after the split)	Microsoft, 10%
Mobil, 1.40 per share	
Dupont, 1.50 per share	

3. Purchased 1,000 shares of Chrysler at $30 per share.
4. Biosphere reported its first-ever income, in the amount of $200,000, and declared a stock dividend of 10%.
5. The market values at the end of the year 1999 were:

AT&T	$40
Chrysler	25
DuPont	27

Citicorp	$18
Microsoft	80
Mobil	25

Required:

A. Prepare all the journal entries for 1999 to record these events and to state the short- and long-term portfolios at fair value.

B. Calculate the ending balance in the Biosphere account. (Assume the book value and purchase price were equal.)

P9–8 Changing From Fair Value to Equity

Cincom Corp. is a medium-sized closely held computer software vendor with a total of 100,000 shares of common stock outstanding at January 1, 1997. The stock is traded over the counter. Cincom has been a profitable company over the years and has paid a cash dividend of $1 per share each year on August 1.

Cincinnati Milling is a customer of Cincom and has been investing in Cincom stock since 1997, making the following purchases:

DATE	SHARES	PRICE PER SHARE
1/1/97	10,000	$25
3/1/98	5,000	18
3/1/99	10,000	20

The earnings and stock prices of Cincom follow:

	1997	1998	1999
Income for year	$300,000	$400,000	$600,000
Stock price per share (12/31)	18	15	30

At the time of the first purchase by Cincinnati Milling, the appraisal value (fair market value) of the total net assets of Cincom was $2.1 million. Assume that the appraisal values of the net assets were equal to the purchase price at the time of the second and third purchases. Also assume that there is no difference between the book values and appraisal values of the assets of Cincom. Goodwill is amortized over 15 years.

Required: Cincinnati Milling follows GAAP in accounting for the investment in Cincom. The initial purchase was designated as available-for-sale.

A. Prepare all the journal entries necessary relative to the Investment in Cincom account from January 1, 1997, through December 31, 1998.

B. Calculate the fair value of the Cincom investment at December 31, 1998.

C. Calculate the basis for the equity method as of January 1, 1999, and the amount of the adjustment required to the Retained Earnings account.

P9–9 Equity Method, Correction of Errors

P. Escobar owns a 40 percent interest in G&E Laundering and Cleaning Inc. The balance in this account at 12/31/98 is $1.2 billion. Escobar also owns a 30 percent interest in Poppy Productions Inc., which has a current account balance at 12/31/98 of $1.5 billion, and a 40 percent interest in S&D Corporation, which is a sales and distribution network. The investment account for S&D has a balance of $2.1 billion at 12/31/98.

In 1999, Escobar was forced to hire a new bookkeeper because the previous bookkeeper had suddenly contracted a fatal case of lead poisoning. The new bookkeeper, I. L. Egit (a former CPA who lost his license to practice for ethics code violations) was reviewing the transactions for the three investment accounts. He found a number of transactions that he believes were recorded incorrectly.

1. On 4/15/95, a cash dividend in the amount of $50 million received from G&E Laundering was recorded as Cash and credited to Dividend Income. After further investigation, Egit finds that the same thing happened on the same dates in 1996 and 1997 for the same amounts.
2. On 6/12/96, Escobar provided S&D Corporation with $40 million to pay sales commissions to M. Noriega. This transaction had been recorded by the previous bookkeeper by charging (debiting) the G&E Investment account and crediting Cash.
3. Dividends from S&D of $200 million were not recorded in 1997. This led to the former bookkeeper's untimely demise.
4. In 1996, the total income of Poppy Production was $1.2 billion. However, the bookkeeper picked up only $200 million for the Investment account.
5. In 1998, the income of each investment company had not been recorded because of the previous bookkeeper's untimely death. The amounts were G&E, $800 million; Poppy Production, $600 million; and S&D, $700 million.

Required:

A. Prepare correcting and adjusting entries to correctly state the account balances at 12/31/98.

B. Prepare a schedule to determine the proper balances in each of the three investment accounts at the end of 1998.

C. What is Escobar's total investment in each company at 12/31/98.

P9–10 Stock and Bond Investments

Betsy's Boatinq is a dealer for skiboats and sailboats. This has been a very successful business and has accumulated a large investment portfolio. At January 1, 1997, the investment accounts contained the following:

	Price Per Share	
	Cost	Market
Trading securities:		
2,000 shares Glaxo Corp	$ 80	$ 95
1,000 shares Syntex	70	50
3,000 shares Avon	45	30
$5,000 par value GSU 8% bonds	4,200	4,500
Available-for-sale securities:		
$60,000 par value 6% bonds issued by city of Chicago.	60,000	59,000

The GSU bonds pay interest semiannually on April 1 and October 1. They were purchased on February 1, 1993, and have a maturity date of April 1, 2025. The city of Chicago bonds were purchased June 1, 1991, at par plus accrued interest. There were no commissions paid. These bonds have a maturity date of December 31, 1999, and pay interest annually on December 31.

During 1997, the following events took place:

Jan.	20	Purchased 500 shares of Phelps Dodge at $40/share and classified them as available-for-sale.
Feb.	25	Purchased 1,000 shares of Brown Shoe at $20/share and classified it as available-for-sale.
Apr.	1	Received the semiannual interest from GSU.
June	1	Sold the Syntex shares at $45/share.
Aug.	15	Received a cash dividend of $.50/share from Avon.
Oct.	1	Received semiannual interest from GSU.
Nov.	1	Sold 500 shares of Glaxo at 90.
Dec.	31	Received annual interest from city of Chicago.

The year-end values for each investment are:

	1997
Glaxo	$ 98
Avon	32
Phelps Dodge	35
Brown Shoe	27
GSU	5,000
City of Chicago	50,000

Required:

A. Calculate the investment balances in the trading and available-for-sale accounts at December 31, 1997.

B. Calculate realized and unrealized gains and losses on trading securities in 1997.

C. Calculate realized and unrealized gains and losses on available-for-sale securities in 1997.

P9–11 Fair Value and Cash Flow

On December 31, 1997, Lee Inc. reported the following equity securities as noncurrent available-for-sale:

Dale Corp., 5,000 shares of common stock (1% interest)	$110,000
Ewing Corp., 10,000 shares of common stock (2% interest)	150,000

Additional Information:

1. On May 1, 1998, Dale issued a 10% stock dividend, when the market price of its stock was $24 per share.
2. On November 1, 1998, Dale paid a cash dividend of $0.75 per share.
3. On August 5, 1998, Ewing issued, to all shareholders, stock rights on the basis of one right per share. Market prices at date of issue were $13.50 per share (ex-rights) of stock and $1.50 per right. Lee sold all rights on December 16, 1998, for net proceeds of $18,800.
4. Market prices per share of the marketable equity securities, all listed on a national securities exchange, were as follows:

	DEC. 31, 1997	DEC. 31, 1998
Dale Corp.—common	$22	$23
Ewing Corp.—common	15	14

Required: Assume the balance in the Adjustment to Market—Available-for-Sale account at 12/31/97 was zero.

A. Prepare a schedule setting forth for each investment the transactions and computations necessary to determine the ending balance in Lee's December 31, 1998, balance sheet for investments carried at fair value.

B. Prepare a schedule showing all income, gains, and losses relating to Lee's investments for the year ended December 31, 1998.

C. Prepare a schedule to determine the amounts reported on the statement of cash flows for 1998 assuming use of the indirect method.

P9–12 Available-for-Sale Debt Securities, Premium

Mustang Inc. purchased $100,000 par value bonds of Pinto Inc. on January 1, 1997, at a total cost of $112,642, providing an effective yield of 6%. The coupon rate on the bonds is 9%, paid annually on December 31. The bonds mature on December 31, 2001. Assume the market prices on these dates were as follows:

12/31/97	$105,000
12/31/98	109,000
12/31/99	106,000

Required: Assume the bonds are classified as available-for-sale.

A. Prepare the journal entry to record the purchase.

B. Prepare the adjusting entries required at the end of each of the first two years to:

1. record interest.
2. amortize premium.
3. recognize changes in market value.

C. Prepare the relevant portions of the balance sheet at December 31, 1997, and December 31, 1998.

P9–13 Available-for-Sale Debt Securities, Discount

Black purchased $100,000 par value bonds of Red on January 1, 1997, at a total cost of $88,702 providing an effective yield of 12%. These bonds mature on December 31, 2006, and pay interest annually on December 31 at the rate of 10%. The year-end market values are $96,500 for 1997 and $91,000 for 1998.

Required: Assume the bonds are classified as AFS.

A. Record the purchase at January 1, 1997.

B. Prepare the adjusting entries at December 31, 1997, and 1998.

C. Prepare the relevant portions of the balance sheet at December 31, 1997, and 1998.

D. Assume the bonds are sold on January 1, 1999, for $90,800. Ignore commissions and tax. Prepare the journal entry to record the sale.

P9–14 Available-for-Sale Equity Securities

The following information is provided:

1997

Jan.	1	Purchased 5,000 shares of Mallory at $12 per share and 4,000 shares of Delta at $20 per share.
Dec.	31	Market values were $10 per share for Mallory and $21 per share for Delta.

1998

June	30	Market value of Mallory decreased to $7 per share, a decline that was considered a permanent impairment.
Sep.	5	Sold 1,000 shares of Delta at $24 per share, net.
Dec.	31	Market values were $6 per share for Mallory and $22 per share for Delta.

Required: Prepare the journal entries to record these events.

P9–15 Accounting for Equity Security Investments

ESI had the following year-end (reporting date) balances in the indicated equity security investment portfolios:

		AVAILABLE-FOR-SALE	
	TRADING	CURRENT	NONCURRENT
Year 1:			
Cost	$100,000	$ 80,000	$120,000
Fair value	125,000	76,000	114,000
Year 2:			
Cost	150,000	110,000	115,000
Fair value	135,000	105,000	110,000
Year 3:			
Cost	140,000	170,000	130,000
Fair value	160,000	190,000	145,000

As part of its equity security investment activity in Year 1, ESI purchased an available-for-sale (current) security for $30,000 and sold a trading security for $15,000 (original cost of $12,000).

At the end of Year 2, a trading security with original cost of $20,000 was transferred to the available-for-sale (noncurrent) category. On this date, the fair value of this security was $25,000. In the information above, this security is included in the trading dollar amounts (i.e., before recognizing the transfer).

Required:

A. What entries would ESI make at year-end for each year to account for cost and fair value differences, during Year 1 to account for the securities purchased and sold, and at the end of Year 2 to account for the reclassified security?

B. How would ESI's equity security investment information impact its financial statements in Years 1, 2, and 3?

C. What does the FASB's adoption of SFAS No. 115 say about the accounting profession's commitment to the "conservatism" perspective? What does it imply, if anything, about moving toward a fair-value-oriented accounting system? Discuss.

RESEARCH ACTIVITIES

R9–1 Motorola's Financial Statements

Required: Examine the ***Motorola*** financial statements in Appendix C of the text to answer the following:

A. How does Motorola classify its investment securities?
B. Does Motorola have investments accounted for by the equity method? If so, what is their impact on reported income?
C. Locate the footnote that describes the investment securities and determine the amount of realized and unrealized gains reported by Motorola.

R9–2

Obtain a current (1995 or later) annual report. Prepare a summary of the impact of investments on the income statement, balance sheet, and statement of cash flows.

R9–3 Economic Consequences of Accounting Standards

Required: Prepare a report that summarizes the following:

A. Similarities in accounting for investments in debt securities.
B. Differences in accounting for investments in debt securities.
C. Effects on income of market fluctuations for the three categories of securities.

R9–4 Internet Activity

Access one of the financial databases available on the Internet, or the Disclosure database. Find several companies in the same industry and compare the level of investment between them. Your comparison should contain the following:

1. Investments as a percentage of current assets.
2. Investments as a percentage of total assets.
3. Unrealized holding gains (loss) reported in income as a percentage of total income.
4. Unrealized holding gains (losses) reported in stockholders' equity as a percentage of stockholders' equity.
5. Realized gains (losses) reported in income as a percentage of total income.

R9–5 Internet Activity

Access a company home page and prepare a short report about any current items reported on that home page.

R9–6 Internet Activity

Access the South-Western home page for this text. Find any current updates related to this chapter on this home page.

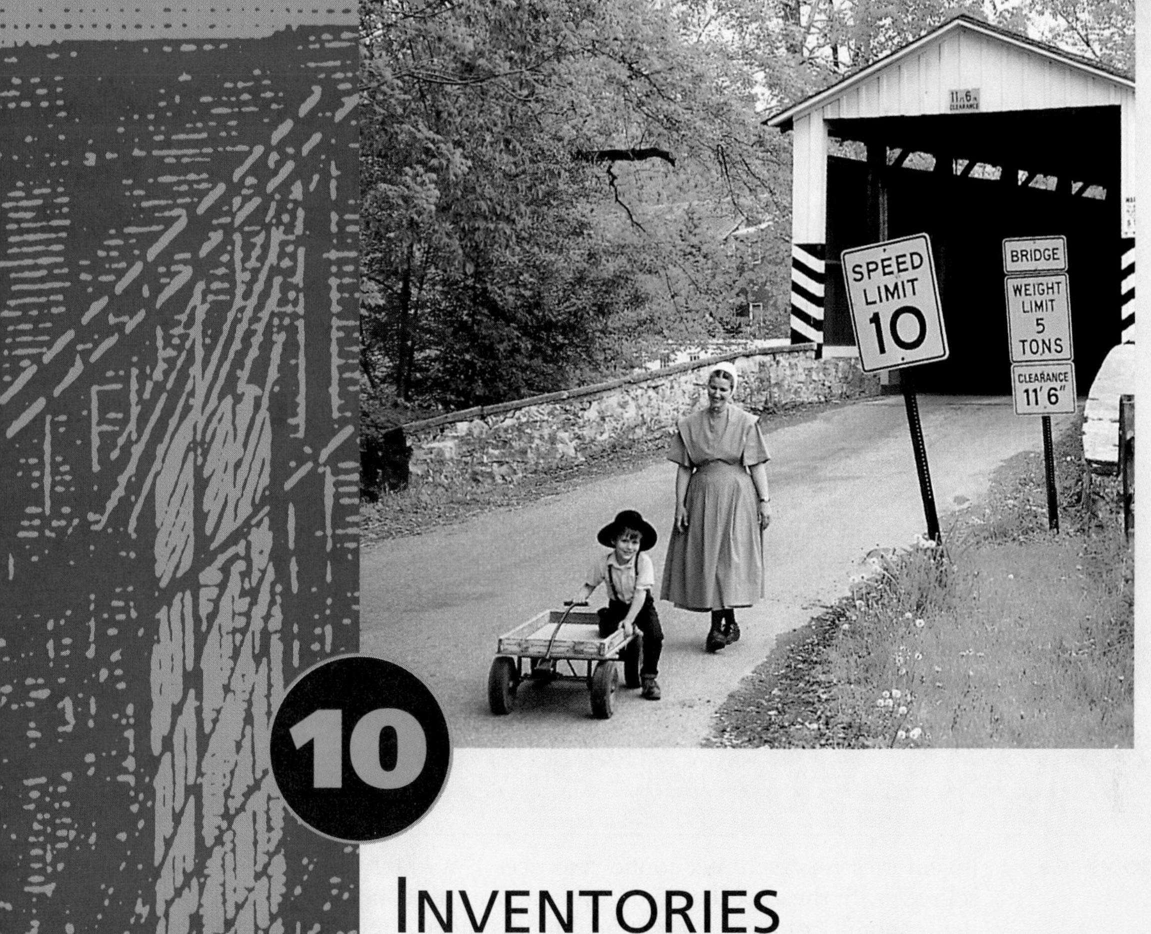

10

INVENTORIES

LEARNING OBJECTIVES

After studying this chapter, you should be able to:

1. Explain the importance of inventory for asset valuation and income measurement.
2. Understand the nature of inventory and what is included in it.
3. Differentiate between perpetual and periodic inventory measurement systems.
4. Record and report inventories for different valuation systems.
5. Estimate inventories using various methods.
6. Analyze the impact of inventory valuation on liquidity and profitability analysis.

ust how important is inventory in the financial statements and to the price of the stock? The accompanying excerpt helps answer that question.

Inventory and Stock Prices

Motorola Inc., in a rare stumble, said its inventory of cellular phones has swollen in the United States, a problem that will crimp earnings growth in coming quarters.

The news jolted Motorola's stock, which slid $6.375, or 9.9%, to close at $57.875 in New York Stock Exchange composite trading.

The company said that it doesn't expect a write-down in the first quarter, which ends April 1. However, a Motorola spokesman said that the problem would hamper profit gains in the period, although the company still expects "good" profit growth compared with last year.

Several analysts said the bloated inventories could shave as much as 10 percent off Motorola's earnings over the next two quarters, and many cut their profit forecasts.

Source: "Motorola, Citing Swollen Inventory of Cellular Phones, Sees Damage to Net," *The Wall Street Journal*, February 21, 1995, p. B6.

IMPLICATIONS OF CONCEPTUAL FRAMEWORK

Explain the importance of inventory for asset valuation and income measurement.

Inventories represent economic resources. An enterprise owns economic resources with the expectation of receiving future economic benefits. The cost of the economic resource commitment to inventory often represents a significant portion of the total asset investment by the enterprise. A major question for management is: At what level is the allocation of resources to inventory too great (or too small) for the enterprise? Could those same resources be used more efficiently if they were invested in other types of assets? Providing information that assists with difficult decisions regarding resource allocation is an important aspect of the accounting function.

One factor of importance to investor decision making is the method used for valuation of a company's inventories. Inventories are assets, or future economic benefits, of the enterprise. As the enterprise realizes the benefits of these assets through their sale, the related cost of these benefits is expensed and affects reported earnings. The inventory valuation method selected by the enterprise determines the amount of expense reported on the income statement and the asset value reported on the balance sheet. Several valuation methods are acceptable, though each may result in dramatically different earnings and asset values. As an example, last-in, first-out (LIFO) produces earnings figures that capture the current cost of sales but values unsold inventory at older (often lower) prices. On the other hand, first-in, first-out (FIFO) provides more recent asset valuation but charges older (often lower) costs to expense. (Both methods will be discussed further.)

Because inventories are a critical element of the cash flow cycle, investment decisions must take into account the *trend* of inventory levels, or the relationship between inventories and sales measured by the inventory turnover. Inventories increasing at a rate faster than sales (a lower turnover) could indicate potential future problems. It may signal obsolete merchandise or depressed sales for the enterprise, which could lead to reduced earnings and cash flow in the future.

On the other hand, inventories and sales increasing at approximately the same rate sends a positive signal, indicating potential future growth in earnings and cash flow.

According to SFAC No. 1, the objective of financial reporting is to provide information useful for decision making. The information should assist the user in assessing the amount, timing, and uncertainty of future cash flows. Inventories are a critical element of the cash flow cycle as they represent investment of cash upon purchase and receipt of cash upon sale.

THE NATURE OF INVENTORY

Understand the nature of inventory and what is included in it.

Inventories are assets of two general types: (1) those held for sale (or resale) in the ordinary course of business and (2) those used or consumed in the production of goods to be sold in the ordinary course of business. A retail business (such as ***Wal-Mart*** or ***K-Mart***), which purchases merchandise from a manufacturer or a wholesaler ready for immediate resale to the public, has just one type or class of inventory—purchased goods. This kind of business is a *trading concern*. In contrast, a *manufacturer* (such as ***Exxon*** or ***IBM***) produces a product from raw materials. The production process transforms the raw materials into a finished product commonly called *finished goods inventory*. Materials that have not completed the production process, *work-in-process inventory*, require additional processing before reaching a salable state. Stockpiles of raw materials awaiting entry to the production process are the *raw materials inventory*. Measurement and valuation of these various inventories using several valuation methods for a single enterprise is not uncommon. The enterprise may use LIFO for part of its inventory and FIFO for the remainder. For convenience, the discussions in this chapter refer to a single inventory account similar to that for a trading enterprise.

COMPOSITION OF INVENTORY

Determination of ownership for inventory purposes is very important because misstatements of inventories, accounts payable, and accounts receivable have a direct impact on the financial statements of the enterprise. The general rule is that title to the merchandise provides evidence of ownership, and the owner includes the merchandise in its inventory.

Goods in Transit. Following the general rule that title to the merchandise is evidence of ownership, any goods in transit belong to whomever has title or legal ownership. When merchandise is in transit between buyer and seller, title or legal ownership is dependent on the shipping terms between the buyer and seller. If the goods are shipped F.O.B. shipping point, title passes to the buyer at the time the goods are loaded on the common carrier. The buyer assumes the responsibilities of ownership, including freight charges, insurance, and risk of loss or damage, and includes the merchandise in inventory. When the terms of the sale are F.O.B. destination, title transfers to the buyer at the time the goods are off-loaded to the buyer from the common carrier. In this case, the seller assumes responsibility for the freight charge, insurance, and risk of loss, and includes the merchandise as part of inventory until the buyer takes possession.

Occasionally, the terms of the agreement will designate an intermediate point between the buyer and seller. For example, the shipping terms may be *F.O.B.*

ETHICS IN PRACTICE

Audit Report Details Fraud at Leslie Fay

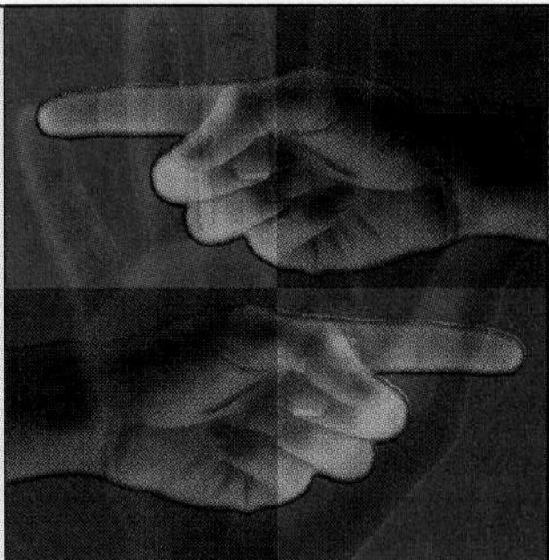

The accounting fraud at troubled apparel maker Leslie Fay Companies was far more pervasive than previously revealed, according to a board audit committee report that sharply criticized top management.

It would have been difficult for senior management not to spot the extensive inventory and sales fraud, the previously sealed report says.

The report shows that at least 15 financial and operational managers orchestrated sales to reach a preset budget. These managers also set budgets for revenues and profits in advance of actual sales, according to the report. It notes that many of the reported sales actually involved goods prematurely shipped to retailers before the goods were expected. Some items later were returned.

The document describes numerous ways in which Leslie Fay sought to ensure that quarterly sales met preestablished budgets. When sales fell short, the report alleges, the company "shipped" goods to trailers near a Wilkes-Barre, Pa., facility.

To boost sales and lower costs, the report claims, mid-level company officials forged inventory tags, ignored expected inventory shrinkage, multiplied the value of items in inventory, improperly inflated sales and made up phantom inventory. These officials, it adds, also constantly altered records to meet sales targets.

The report alleges Leslie Fay inflated sales and profits and improperly reduced its costs in several other ways. One example included invoicing goods to be shipped in the final day of a quarter even though the goods were shipped in the following quarter, a deviation from generally accepted accounting principles.

Source: "Audit Report Details Fraud at Leslie Fay," *The Wall Street Journal*, March 28, 1995, pp. B1, B4.

St. Louis for a buyer and seller in Chicago and New Orleans, respectively. This means title passes at the location named in the agreement.

Consignment Merchandise. Consignments are a marketing arrangement in which the owner of the merchandise (the **consignor**) places it with another party (the **consignee**) for sale. The consignee acts as a sales agent and earns a commission on any merchandise sold. Upon the sale of the consigned merchandise, the consignee remits the proceeds of the sale (less any commission) to the consignor.

Any merchandise on consignment remains the property of the consignor and is included in the consignor's inventory and excluded from the consignee's inventory. If the amount of merchandise on consignment is materially large in relation to the total inventory, the consignor might include a separate category of inventory for the consigned merchandise or include a note to the financial statements indicating the cost and location of the merchandise on consignment.

Special Sales Agreements. At times, the general rule of title providing evidence of ownership may not match the economic realities of the transaction. For example, assume that in a *product-financing arrangement,* the seller, Company S, sells merchandise to a buyer, Company B, and agrees to buy it back at a specified (higher) price in the future. Company B borrows the money to purchase the merchandise using the merchandise as collateral. Later, when Company S repurchases the merchandise from B, S pays a price high enough for B to repay the loan plus earn a return. The advantage gained by S in this transaction is removal of inventory (and liability) from its books, perhaps decreasing its property taxes and improving the financial statements by recording a "sale" of merchandise. However, the reality of the transaction is that S is simply financing its inventory. SFAS No. 49, "Accounting for Product Financing Arrangements," addresses this situation, stating that the merchandise should be included as part of the inventory of the "seller," and no sale should be recorded.

A similar situation occurs with **sales with right of return**, an arrangement where the buyer has a right to return the merchandise within a specified period after the sale. Recall the Topps Company trading card example from Chapter 8. Topps customarily ships trading cards to its dealers who have the right to return any unsold cards. In Chapter 8, the point was made that Topps was recording revenue at the time of shipment, even though the dealers expected to send large quantities back. Topps indicated that it had made adequate provisions for the returns. The question remains, at which point should the sale be recorded? Revenue recognition and inventories in this situation are addressed in SFAS No. 48, which specifies six conditions that must be met before a sale may be recorded. If any one of the conditions is not met, sales and cost of sales may be recognized either when the return privilege has substantially expired or if those conditions subsequently are met.[1]

In an **installment sale**, the buyer takes possession of the merchandise, but the seller retains title until all the payments have been made. An example of an installment sale would be a car dealer's sale of a new car that is financed by the dealership. In these types of transactions, the seller normally removes the merchandise from inventory even though title may not have passed to the buyer.

PURCHASE COMMITMENTS

A **purchase commitment** is a noncancellable, long-term executory contract to purchase materials or merchandise. An enterprise enters into a transaction of this nature to assure itself of a long-term source of supply of raw materials or perhaps to protect itself against future price increases. The essence of the transaction is the incurrence of a long-term obligation to purchase assets at a fixed price. This type of contract insulates the buyer from price changes in the future, because the long-term purchase price is fixed. However, an accounting issue arises in the proper treatment of differences between market prices and the contract price prior to the completion of the contract.

At the time of contract signing, no asset or liability recognition is appropriate because neither party has fulfilled its part of the contract; that is, the contract is totally executory. If material, disclosure of the details of the contract in the notes to the financial statements of the buyer is required. Further accounting for purchase commitments depends on any price changes between the contract inception date and the execution date.

Subsequent accounting follows conservatism, matching, and revenue-recognition principles. Consistent with the conservatism convention and matching principle, material price declines occurring between the contract inception and execution dates must be recognized as losses during the period in which they occur. On the other hand, price increases above the contract price before execution of the contract must be deferred and not recognized until they are

[1] *SFAS No. 48*, "Revenue Recognition When Right of Return Exists," FASB, 1981, par. 6.

realized. This is in accordance with both the conservatism convention and revenue recognition but inconsistent with the matching principle. Finally, if a price decline is followed by a recovery, the initial amount of the loss recognition limits the amount of the recovery that may be recognized.

These requirements pose a question about consistency. If losses in market value are recognized at the time of price decreases, why not recognize price increases above contract prices as well? SFAS No. 115 prescribes recognition of holding gains for certain investment securities (see discussion in Chapter 9). However, purchase commitments and inventory holding gains are not recognized until realized at the time of sale. Exhibit 10–1 illustrates the journal entries required for purchase commitments.

EXHIBIT 10–1
Accounting for Purchase Commitments

Data

On June 1, 1998, SCS Company signs a contract to purchase 400,000 pounds of sugar cane at $1.20 per pound. The contract execution date is April 1, 1999. The following prices are in effect at December 31, 1998, and April 1, 1999:

	PRICE PER POUND				
DATE	CASE A	CASE B	CASE C	CASE D	CASE E
12/31/98	$1.20*	$1.00	$1.00	$1.00	$1.00
4/1/99	1.20	1.00	.90	1.05	1.40

Journal Entries

Case A:			
12/31/98	No entry required		
4/1/99	Purchases (400,000 @ $1.20)	480,000	
	Accounts Payable		480,000
Case B:			
12/31/98	Estimated Loss on Purchase Commitment	80,000	
	Estimated Liability for Loss on Purchase Commitment		80,000
4/1/99	Purchases (400,000 @ $1.00)	400,000	
	Estimated Liability for Loss on Purchase Commitment	80,000	
	Accounts Payable		480,000
Case C:			
12/31/98	Estimated Loss on Purchase Commitment	80,000	
	Estimated Liability for Loss on Purchase Commitment		80,000
4/1/99	Purchases (400,000 @ $.90)	360,000	
	Estimated Liability for Loss on Purchase Commitment	80,000	
	Loss on Purchase Commitment	40,000	
	Accounts Payable		480,000

(continued)

EXHIBIT 10–1
(Concluded)

Case D:			
12/31/98	Estimated Loss on Purchase Commitment	80,000	
	Estimated Liability for Loss on Purchase Commitment		80,000
4/1/99	Purchases (400,000 @ $1.05)	420,000	
	Estimated Liability for Loss on Purchase Commitment	80,000	
	Accounts Payable		480,000
	Recovery of Loss on Purchase Commitment		20,000
Case E:			
12/31/98	Estimated Loss on Purchase Commitment	80,000	
	Estimated Liability for Loss on Purchase Commitment		80,000
4/1/99	Purchases (400,000 @ $1.20)	480,000	
	Estimated Liability for Loss on Purchase Commitment	80,000	
	Accounts Payable		480,000
	Recovery of Loss on Purchase Commitment		80,000*

*Recovery limited by loss recorded at 12/31/98.

QUANTITY MEASUREMENT

Differentiate between perpetual and periodic inventory measurement systems.

Quantity measurement refers to the physical flow of the merchandise recorded using either a *periodic* or *perpetual* inventory system. The physical flow is not necessarily the same as the cost flow or dollar flow assumption used to value the inventory. The physical flow relates to the actual movement of the inventory. The cost flow relates to assumptions underlying the inventory valuation method selected by the company, such as FIFO or LIFO. The cost flow and physical flow may be totally unrelated.

A **periodic inventory system** records all merchandise purchases in a Purchases account and determines the inventory quantity and value periodically (usually at the time of preparation of the financial statements) by actual physical count. This system makes no attempt to maintain a current balance in the Inventory account.

In contrast, a **perpetual inventory system** does maintain a current balance in the Inventory account. Increases to the Inventory account occur with each new purchase, while decreases are made with each sale. Compared to the periodic system, the perpetual system requires more record keeping, but it affords greater control over the inventory.

Exhibit 10–2 illustrates the difference between the two systems. Note that because all inventory units cost $5, the results are the same under both systems; the cost of goods sold is $1,800, and the inventory is valued at $450. This results only when prices do not change during the period. When prices are changing, results can differ for periodic and perpetual systems and for the valuation method used. Historically, businesses used periodic inventory systems for items that were somewhat inexpensive and had a high turnover rate. Perpetual systems were used for items with higher unit values and slower turn-over. Today, most

EXHIBIT 10–2 Periodic and Perpetual Inventory Systems

Data

Date	Transaction	Units
1/1	Beginning inventory	100 @ $5
1/2	Purchase	150 @ $5
1/3	Returned 20 units purchased	@ $5
1/5	Sale	220 @ $8
1/10	Sales returns of 40 units sold	@ $8
1/15	Purchase	200 @ $5
1/22	Sale	140 @ $8
1/31	Ending inventory	110 @ $5

	JOURNAL ENTRIES FOR PERIODIC INVENTORY			JOURNAL ENTRIES FOR PERPETUAL INVENTORY		
1/1	Inventory	No entry		No entry		
1/2 (Purchase)	Purchases	750		Inventory	750	
	Accounts Payable		750	Accounts Payable		750
	(150 @ $5)					
1/3 (Return)	Accounts Payable	100		Accounts Payable	100	
	Purchase Returns		100	Inventory		100
1/5 (Sale)	Accounts Receivable	1,760		Accounts Receivable	1,760	
	Sales		1,760	Sales		1,760
	(220 @ $8)					
	No inventory entry			Cost of Goods Sold	1,100	
				Inventory		1,100
				(220 @ $5)		
1/10 (Return)	Sales Returns	320		Sales Returns	320	
	Accounts Receivable		320	Accounts Receivable		320
	No inventory entry			Inventory	200	
				Cost of Goods Sold		200
				(cost = $5 × 40)		
1/15 (Purchase)	Purchases	1,000		Inventory	1,000	
	Accounts Payable		1,000	Accounts Payable		1,000
	(200 @ $5)					
1/22 (Sale)	Accounts Receivable	1,120		Accounts Receivable	1,120	
	Sales		1,120	Sales		1,120
	(140 @ $8)					
	No inventory entry			Cost of Goods Sold	700	
				Inventory		700
				(140 @ $5)		
1/31 (adjusting)	Cost of Goods Sold	1,600		No adjusting entry		
	Purchase Returns	100				
	Inventory	50				
	Purchases		1,750			

businesses use a perpetual system for inventory because product scanners and computers make it easier to maintain a perpetual system than once was the case.

INVENTORY VALUATION

Record and report inventories for different valuation systems.

Valuation of inventory can be a complex undertaking. In general, historical cost (or some modification of historical cost) is the basis for valuation. Sometimes, though, estimates of inventory value are made instead of determining the actual cost. Because inventory is a current asset (one expected to be used or liquidated in the next period or operating cycle), market value also must be considered during the valuation process. In this section, we explore various cost flow methods of valuation in addition to lower-of-cost-or-market (LCM) valuation, the gross profit and retail methods of estimating inventory values, and a special LIFO method known as dollar-value LIFO.

COST-BASED MEASUREMENTS

Cost-based measurements of inventory values include specific identification, FIFO, LIFO, and average cost. Ideally, the inventory valuation method selected for use would be the one that provides the most relevant and reliable information for financial statement preparation. However, as a practical matter, the choice of method depends on several other factors, such as the financial position of an individual entity, its profitability and type of product, general economic conditions, and the entity's tax status. For example, a highly profitable, growing entity may choose a measurement method that minimizes tax payments, while a marginally profitable organization may not worry about tax consequences. If prices were stable, the valuation method used would not matter, because all would provide the same result. Prices, however, are not stable; thus, the inventory valuation method is very important.

Specific Identification. The **specific-identification method** matches unit cost and unit physical flow exactly. The cost of goods sold includes the actual cost for each unit sold, while the ending inventory includes the actual cost of each unit on hand. Entities with somewhat small unit flows of high-cost items (such as car dealerships) might use this costing method.

First-In, First-Out (FIFO). The **first-in, first-out (FIFO)** inventory method expenses the earliest costs of merchandise while maintaining the most recent costs in inventory. Asset valuation on the balance sheet reflects the most current inventory costs, but the cost of goods sold in the income statement includes the costs from the beginning inventory and the purchases from earlier in the period.

Cost of goods sold, therefore, includes prior-period costs from the beginning inventory that are matched against current-period revenue, resulting in a slight mismatching of expense and revenue. FIFO inventory valuation produces exactly the same results using either a perpetual or periodic system, as illustrated in Exhibit 10–3. Note in the exhibit that under the periodic method, ending inventory of $7,600 is determined using the FIFO cost flow assumption and then subtracted from the cost of goods available for sale to determine the cost of goods sold expense of $13,400. Using the perpetual method, cost of goods sold for the period is the balance in the Cost of Goods Sold account.

EXHIBIT 10–3
Example of FIFO Inventory System: Periodic and Perpetual Method

Presented here are the July transactions for Jay Company

	Units	Cost per Unit
Beginning inventory	1,000	$5.00
7/3 Purchase	1,500	6.00
7/7 Sale	900	
7/11 Sale	700	
7/20 Purchase	1,000	7.00
7/21 Sale	600	
7/29 Sale	200	
Ending inventory	1,100	

Periodic Method

	Units	Costs	
Beginning inventory	1,000	$ 5,000	
Purchases	2,500	16,000	
Available for sale	3,500	$21,000	
Sales	(2,400)		
Ending inventory	1,100	7,600	1,000 @ $7
			100 @ $6
Cost of goods sold		$13,400	

Perpetual Method

Date	Purchase	Cost of Goods Sold		Balance	
7/1				1,000 @ $5 = $5,000	
7/3	1,500 @ $6			1,000 @ $5 = $5,000	
				1,500 @ $6 = 9,000	$14,000
7/7		900 @ $5 =	$ 4,500	100 @ $5 = $ 500	
				1,500 @ $6 = 9,000	$ 9,500
7/11		100 @ $5 =	500		
		600 @ $6 =	3,600	900 @ $6 = $5,400	5,400
7/20	1,000 @ $7			900 @ $6 = $5,400	
				1,000 @ $7 = 7,000	$12,400
7/21		600 @ $6 =	3,600	300 @ $6 = $1,800	
				1,000 @ $7 = 7,000	$ 8,800
7/29		200 @ $6 =	1,200	100 @ $6 = $ 600	
				1,000 @ $7 = 7,000	$ 7,600
		Cost of goods sold =	$13,400		

Last-In, First-Out (LIFO). The last-in, first-out (LIFO) inventory system is the exact opposite of FIFO. LIFO allocates the most recent costs to cost of goods sold and maintains the earliest costs in ending inventory. LIFO achieves a close matching of current costs with current revenues for purposes of income determination because cost of goods sold includes the most recent costs. However, asset valuation on the balance sheet consists of older costs that may not reflect current values.

EXHIBIT 10–4
Example of LIFO Inventory System: Periodic and Perpetual Methods

Presented here are the July transactions for Jay Company.

Data

		UNITS	COST PER UNIT
Beginning inventory		1,000	$5.00
7/3	Purchase	1,500	6.00
7/7	Sale	900	
7/11	Sale	700	
7/20	Purchase	1,000	7.00
7/21	Sale	600	
7/29	Sale	200	
Ending inventory		1,100	

Periodic Method

	UNITS	COSTS	
Beginning inventory	1,000	$ 5,000	
Purchases	2,500	16,000	
Available for sale	3,500	$21,000	
Sales	(2,400)		
Ending inventory	1,100	5,600	1,000 @ $5
			100 @ $6
Cost of goods sold		$15,400	

Perpetual Method

DATE	PURCHASE	COST OF GOODS SOLD	BALANCE	
7/1			1,000 @ $5 = $5,000	
7/3	1,500 @ $6		1,000 @ $5 = $5,000	
			1,500 @ $6 = 9,000	$14,000
7/7		900 @ $6 = $ 5,400	1,000 @ $5 = $5,000	
			600 @ $6 = 3,600	$ 8,600
7/11		600 @ $6 = 3,600		
		100 @ $5 = 500	900 @ $5 = $4,500	$ 4,500
7/20	1,000 @ $7		900 @ $5 = $4,500	
			1,000 @ $7 = 7,000	$11,500
7/21		600 @ $7 = 4,200	900 @ $5 = $4,500	
			400 @ $7 = 2,800	$ 7,300
7/29		200 @ $7 = 1,400	900 @ $5 = $4,500	
			200 @ $7 = 1,400	$ 5,900
		Cost of goods sold = $15,100		

The primary reason for using LIFO is minimization of income tax liability. Current income tax regulations require that LIFO be used for financial reporting if it is used for tax purposes (this is called the *LIFO conformity rule*). Historically, the general trend of prices is upward, and during periods of rising prices, LIFO results in lower income (and therefore lower tax liability) than FIFO because the most recent (highest) costs are matched against current revenues. In periods of falling prices, the opposite effect occurs. Exhibit 10–4 illustrates the use of LIFO for both the periodic and perpetual inventory systems using the same Jay Company data as used in the FIFO example, Exhibit 10–3. Like the FIFO exhibit, cost-of-goods sold using the periodic method is the difference between the cost-of-goods available for sale and ending inventory. In the perpetual method, cost of goods sold is again reflected as the account balance.

The LIFO results are different for perpetual and periodic methods because the measurements are made at different points in time. The measurement for the periodic method is made at the end of the period, and the perpetual measurement is made at each sale date.

Average Costing. The use of **average costing** provides inventory values and income amounts between FIFO and LIFO. In a periodic system, the average cost per unit is a weighted average derived from the cost of the beginning inventory plus all the purchases during the period, divided by the total units available for sale. The average cost per unit is used for asset valuation on the balance sheet and in cost of goods sold for income determination.

In a perpetual system, each new purchase requires calculation of a new weighted average cost, resulting in a moving average. Exhibit 10–5 illustrates average costing for both the periodic and perpetual inventory systems, again using the data from Jay Company. And again, the results are different for the perpetual and periodic systems because the measurements are made at different points in time.

LOWER OF COST OR MARKET (LCM)

Inventory market values may fall below cost in response to changing price levels, damage, obsolescence, or other factors, indicating that a loss in utility has occurred. The term **lower of cost or market (LCM)** implies recognition of the loss in utility during the period in which the loss occurs.[2] The ending inventory is reduced to current cost value. Recognition of the loss in the period in which it occurs and reduction of the carrying value to current market is consistent with both the matching principle and the conservatism convention.[3]

Accounting Research Bulletin (ARB) No. 43 defines market in terms of *current replacement cost,* either by purchase or manufacture, constrained by upper (ceiling) and lower (floor) limits, defined as follows:

[2]Valuation of inventory when a loss in utility has occurred is addressed in *Accounting Research Bulletin No. 43.*

[3]Theoretical justification for this treatment is found in *Accounting Research Bulletin No. 43,* Ch. 4, par. 7, which states that "a departure from the cost basis is required when the utility of the goods is no longer as great as its cost. . . . the difference should be recognized as a loss of the current period. This is generally accomplished by stating such goods at a lower level, commonly designated as market."

EXHIBIT 10–5
Example of Average Costing Inventory System: Periodic and Perpetual Methods

Presented here are the July transactions for Jay Company.

Data

		UNITS	COST PER UNIT
Beginning inventory		1,000	$5.00
7/3	Purchase	1,500	6.00
7/7	Sale	900	
7/11	Sale	700	
7/20	Purchase	1,000	7.00
7/21	Sale	600	
7/29	Sale	200	
Ending inventory		1,100	

Periodic Method

	UNITS	COST
Beginning inventory	1,000	@ $5 = $ 5,000
Purchases	1,500	@ $6 = 9,000
	1,000	@ $7 = 7,000
Available for sale	3,500	@ $6 = $21,000*
Sales (cost of goods sold)	(2,400)	@ $6 = 14,400
Ending inventory	1,100	@ $6 = $ 6,600

*$21,000/3,500 units = $6/unit

Perpetual Method

		TRANSACTION			BALANCE		
DATE		UNITS	UNIT COST	TOTAL COST	UNITS	UNIT COST	TOTAL COST
7/1	Inventory				1,000	$5.00	$ 5,000
7/3	Purchase	1,500	$6.00	$9,000	2,500	5.60*	14,000
7/7	Sale	900	5.60	5,040	1,600	5.60	8,960
7/11	Sale	700	5.60	3,920	900	5.60	5,040
7/20	Purchase	1,000	7.00	7,000	1,900	6.337**	12,040
7/21	Sale	600	6.337	3,802	1,300	6.337	8,238
7/29	Sale	200	6.337	1,267	1,100	6.337	6,971

Cost of goods sold:

7/7	900 @ $5.60 =	$ 5,040
7/11	700 @ $5.60 =	3,920
7/21	600 @ $6.337 =	3,802
7/29	200 @ $6.337 =	1,267
	Cost of goods sold =	$14,029

*$5.60 Average cost = $14,000/2,500 units
**$6.337 Average cost = $12,040/1,900 units

- Ceiling—the net realizable value; the estimated selling price in the ordinary course of business, less reasonably predictable costs of completion and disposal.
- Floor—the net realizable value reduced by a normal profit margin.

These ceiling and floor constraints on the market value prevent overstatement or understatement of the inventory value. The ceiling ensures that the reduction is sufficient to include the current and any future losses in value. The floor constraint prevents the recognition of excessive losses in the current period that would lead to recognition of excessive profits in the future. Consider the following:

Selling price		$10
Less: Freight	$2	
Handling	1	(3)
Net realizable value (ceiling)		$ 7
Less: Normal profit		(2)
Floor		$ 5

If the replacement cost is $8 per unit and is used to value the inventory, the inventory value would be overstated by $1 per unit, because $7 is the net realizable value. Overstating the inventory values results in an overstatement of net income this period.

On the other hand, assume a replacement cost of $3.50 per unit. If the inventory is valued at $3.50, we would understate the inventory value by $1.50 per unit and recognize a smaller profit (or larger loss) in the current period than justified. In effect, assigning a value of $3.50 to the inventory (understating its value) understates expenses by $1.50 in a future period when the inventory is sold.

The ceiling and floor are tests of the reasonableness of the replacement cost figure in determination of market value used for comparison with cost. Once the replacement cost is determined, it is compared with the ceiling value and floor values. The value that lies between the other two values is deemed the market value. The market value is then compared with the original cost of the inventory, and the lower of the two is chosen for valuation purposes.

Methods of Applying Lower of Cost or Market (LCM). The LCM rule can be applied to the overall inventory valuation in three different ways: (1) to each inventory item separately, (2) to each category or classification of items in the inventory, or (3) to the inventory as a whole. The method chosen should be the one that most clearly reflects periodic income, i.e., the one that provides the most relevant and reliable data for income measurement. Exhibit 10–6 illustrates the three alternatives for application of LCM.

Recording Reductions of Inventory Cost to Market. Valuation of the inventory at LCM each period creates a discrepancy between the original cost of the merchandise and LCM when LCM falls below the cost. This difference arises because the merchandise on hand can be replaced for less than the original cost; it is called a *holding loss*. Consistent with the conservatism convention and the matching principle, a holding loss should be recognized in the period in

EXHIBIT 10–6
Application of Lower of Cost or Market

Data

ITEM	QUANTITY	CURRENT REPLACE-MENT COST	NET REALIZABLE VALUE	NET REALIZABLE VALUE LESS NORMAL MARKUP	MARKET	ORIGINAL COST
Category 1						
A	500	$11	$12	$ 8	$11	$14
B	400	22	20	15	20	27
C	1,000	4	8	7	7	6
Category 2						
D	2,500	7	11	8	8	9
E	600	36	41	35	36	25

Calculation of LCM based on individual items, category, and the inventory as a whole

ITEMS	COST	MARKET	(A) INDIVIDUAL ITEMS	(B) MAJOR CATEGORIES	(C) INVENTORY TOTAL
Category 1					
Item A	$ 7,000	$ 5,500	$ 5,500		
Item B	10,800	8,000	8,000		
Item C	6,000	7,000	6,000		
Total	$23,800	$20,500		$20,500	
Category 2					
Item D	$22,500	$20,000	20,000		
Item E	15,000	21,600	15,000		
Total	$37,500	$41,600		37,500	
Inventory					
Total	$61,300	$62,100	$54,500	$58,000	$61,300

Note that Column A is always less than or equal to Column B, and Column B is always less than or equal to Column C. This occurs because aggregation of the gains and losses in Column B and Column C allows the holding gains and losses to be offset by each other while each loss is counted in Column A. The amount of aggregation in Column B, the major categories method, is less than the aggregation occurring in Column C.

which it occurs, that is, the period in which the value falls below the original cost. This may be accomplished by using the *allowance* method to record the loss, as illustrated in Exhibit 10–7.

In the allowance method, the loss is charged to a separate Holding Loss account and credited to an Allowance account. The holding loss is closed to Income, and the Allowance account appears on the balance sheet as a contra account to the Inventory account (see Exhibit 10–8 for the financial statement treatment). The allowance method has the advantage of preserving the original

EXHIBIT 10–7 Allowance Method of Lower of Cost or Market

Data

DATE	COST	MARKET VALUE	REQUIRED FOR ALLOWANCE ACCOUNT
1/1/1997	$75,000	$75,000	$ 0
12/31/1997	77,000	65,000	12,000
12/31/1998	74,000	70,000	4,000
12/31/1999	78,000	80,000	0

Assume that purchases each year equal $500,000.

Journal Entries

12/31/97			
Close beginning inventory and purchases.	Cost of Goods Sold	575,000	
	Inventory		75,000
	Purchases		500,000
Record ending inventory.	Inventory	77,000	
	Cost of Goods Sold		77,000
Record holding loss.	Inventory Holding Loss	12,000	
	Allowance to Reduce Inventory to LCM		12,000
12/31/98			
Close beginning inventory, purchases, and allowance accounts.	Cost of Goods Sold	565,000	
	Allowance to Reduce Inventory to LCM	12,000	
	Inventory		77,000
	Purchases		500,000
Record ending inventory.	Inventory	74,000	
	Cost of Goods Sold		74,000
Record holding loss.	Inventory Holding Loss	4,000	
	Allowance to Reduce Inventory to LCM		4,000
12/31/99			
Close beginning inventory, purchases, and allowance account	Cost of Goods Sold	570,000	
	Allowance to Reduce Inventory to LCM	4,000	
	Inventory		74,000
	Purchases		500,000
Record ending inventory	Inventory	78,000	
	Cost of Goods Sold		78,000

cost data and reporting the inventory at market value. The Allowance account is closed at the end of each year as part of the Inventory adjusting entry. This allows recognition of the full amount of the holding loss in the current year and reduces the Cost of Goods Sold account by the amount charged as a loss in the previous period. In Exhibit 10–8, the cost of the beginning inventory charged to Cost of Goods Sold in 1998 is $65,000 because the $12,000 holding loss had been charged in 1997. In a similar manner, the cost of the beginning

EXHIBIT 10–8
Partial Financial Statements for Lower of Cost or Market

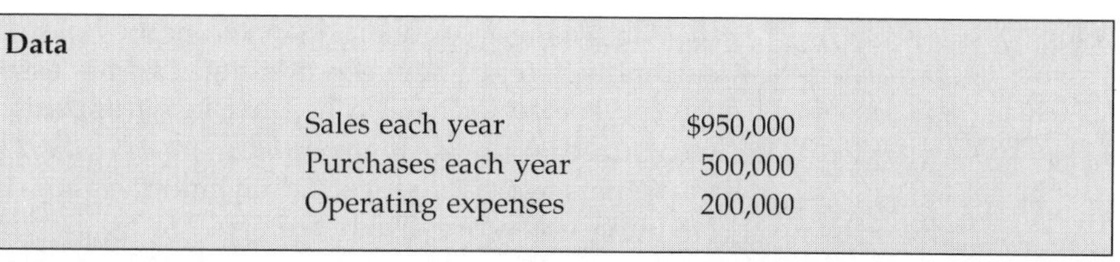

Data	
Sales each year	$950,000
Purchases each year	500,000
Operating expenses	200,000

INCOME STATEMENTS

(IN THOUSANDS OF DOLLARS)	1997	1998	1999
Sales	$ 950	$ 950	$ 950
Cost of goods sold:			
Beginning inventory (at cost)	$ 75	$ 77	$ 74
Less: Holding loss of prior period		(12)	(4)
Purchases	500	500	500
Available for sale	575	565	570
Ending inventory	(77)	(74)	(78)
Cost of goods sold	498	491	492
Add: Holding loss from inventory	12	4	0
Adjusted cost of goods sold	510	495	492
Gross profit	440	455	458
Operating expenses	(200)	(200)	(200)
Income from operations	240	255	258

BALANCE SHEETS

(IN THOUSANDS OF DOLLARS)	1997	1998	1999
Inventory	$ 77	$ 74	$ 78
Less: Allowance to reduce inventory to market	(12)	(4)	0
	$ 65	$ 70	$ 78

inventory charged to Cost of Goods Sold in 1999 is $70,000 because the $4,000 holding loss had been expensed in 1998.

In the third year, 1999, the market value increased above cost to $80,000, creating a holding gain of $2,000. However, the gain must be deferred until the merchandise is sold. Deferral of holding gains is inconsistent with the immediate recognition of holding losses but is consistent with revenue recognition.

There are several acceptable methods used other than the allowance method. Although less desirable conceptually, they are supported on the grounds of materiality and convenience. For example, some would merely adjust the Allowance account at the end of the period to bring it to the corrected balance. If the correct balance calls for a decrease in the Allowance account, this would require the recognition of a gain or recovery of a loss. However, the balance in the Allowance account originates from the holding loss of the prior period. The current difference between cost and LCM is associated with the inventory of the current period, and a holding loss from this current inventory should be recognized in the current period.

Others would reduce the inventory value directly, recording a loss and crediting inventory. This is referred to as the *direct method*. Use of the direct method does not, however, preserve the original cost of the inventory for reporting purposes.

Evaluation of LCM. The LCM rule emanates from the conservatism convention. The LCM rule reduces the asset value in the balance sheet and recognizes a loss in the income statement when a decline in value has occurred. This prevents the overstatement of asset value and charges the loss to the period in which it occurs. Probable losses that are reasonably estimable are recognized currently; therefore, if a decline in inventory value has occurred, it should be recognized currently.

Some accountants would argue that this practice merely allows the company to engage in income shifting. Recognizing an inventory market decline that occurs in 1998 during 1998 will increase cost of goods sold and reduce income in 1998, but it will decrease cost of goods sold and increase income for 1999, when the inventory is sold. In effect, this procedure shifts the loss from the period of sale to the prior period when the decline in value took place.

Some also criticize the LCM rule for recognizing losses immediately but not allowing the recognition of holding gains. If the inventory value increases above cost, the inventory still must be reported at cost. This is consistent, however, with the revenue recognition principle, which requires recognition of gains only upon completion of a transaction (sale). Critics would argue that if losses are recognized, then gains also should be recognized on the grounds of consistency. As we saw in Chapter 9, SFAS No. 115 allows recognition of holding losses and gains in current-period earnings for certain classes of investment securities. Prior to the adoption of SFAS No. 115, marketable securities were valued at LCM and thus were consistent with inventory. Now that SFAS No. 115 has been adopted, that consistency is gone, and two current assets have different bases of valuation.

Finally, LCM has been criticized because three different values can be used to determine the market value. This practice has been criticized on the grounds of comparability for investment decision making because the financial statement reader cannot compare one company to another without knowing the value used to determine the market value. The same reasoning is used to criticize the alternative methods of applying the LCM rule because the method of application (individual item, category, or total) potentially could have a material effect on the inventory value.

ESTIMATING INVENTORY VALUES

At times it may be desirable or necessary to estimate the amount of inventory. For example, if a fire destroys the inventory, the damage claim to the insurance company requires an estimate of the loss suffered. Also, for interim reporting purposes, estimation of the inventory is often more cost effective than taking a physical count.

GROSS PROFIT METHOD

Estimate inventories using various methods.

The **gross profit method**, illustrated in Exhibit 10–9, is one way of preparing estimates. This method requires information from the current year's records of purchases, beginning inventory, and sales. Prior years' records of sales, cost of goods sold, and gross profit provide the data to estimate the composite gross profit percentage (rate).

EXHIBIT 10–9
Gross Profit Method of Estimating Inventory

Data for Alexandria's Seasonings

Beginning inventory	$ 40,000
Purchases	480,000
Sales (total)	700,000
Historical gross profit margin	30%

Sales Detailed by Product Line

Tabasco sauce	$200,000
Red pepper	200,000
Lemon pepper	300,000
Total	$700,000

Estimate value of ending inventory:

Beginning inventory		$ 40,000
Purchases		480,000
Goods available for sale		$ 520,000
Sales	$ 700,000	
Gross profit ($700,000 × 30%)	(210,000)	
Cost of goods sold (70%)		(490,000)
Estimated ending inventory (at cost)		$ 30,000

An alternative method:

Sales		$ 700,000
Cost of goods sold:		
Beginning inventory	$ 40,000	
Purchases	480,000	
Goods available for sale	$ 520,000	
Estimated ending inventory	(c)	
Cost of goods sold		(b)
Gross profit		$ (a)

(a) Gross Profit = 30% × $700,000 = $210,000
(b) Cost of goods sold = 70% × $700,000 = $490,000
(c) Estimated ending inventory = $520,000 − $490,000 = $30,000

Calculation of Gross Profit Percentage. The sales price of a product consists of two elements, the cost and the markup (or the gross profit). The **markup** may be stated either in terms of selling price or cost, and the accountant should be familiar with both and understand the relationship between them. The following example illustrates the computation of the gross-profit (markup) percentage.

	CASE A	CASE B
Sales price	$100	$100
Cost	80	75
Gross profit	$ 20	$ 25
Markup percent based on sales price	20%	25%
20% = 20/100		
25% = 25/100		
Markup percent based on cost	25%	33%
25% = 20/80		
33% = 25/75		

Evaluation of Gross Profit Method. The gross-profit method is useful in situations where a physical inventory is not practical, such as a fire loss or a suspected theft loss. The gross-profit method is not acceptable for financial reporting purposes (except during interim reporting periods), because it provides only an estimate of the inventory. A physical count must be taken for annual financial reporting purposes.

Two major assumptions underlie the gross-profit method: (1) the *rate* of gross profit is constant from one period to the next, and (2) the *sales mix* of products is constant from one period to the next. The historical records of the company provide the information necessary to use the gross profit method. The rate of gross profit is based on the weighted average of the gross profit rates of all the individual products. This assumes that the gross profit rates of the individual products are constant from one period to the next and that the mix of products sold is constant from one year to the next. Finally, the gross profit method assumes that if any changes in the gross profit rates or the product mix sold did occur, the changes would offset each other with no resulting differences in the composite gross profit rate. If any of these assumptions is violated, the gross profit method gives a faulty estimate of the inventory value.

RETAIL METHODS OF ESTIMATION

The **retail inventory method** is commonplace in the retail industry. As purchased merchandise is received, it is displayed immediately for sale at the retail price. Most retail concerns follow a consistent, observable pattern of markup on the cost of the merchandise, thereby allowing the use of the retail method to estimate the cost of the ending inventory.

The records required for the retail method include beginning inventory, purchases at cost and retail, total sales, and any changes in selling price resulting from additional markups and markdowns. A cost-to-retail ratio is calculated from these data and then applied to the ending inventory at retail to estimate the ending inventory at cost. The following example illustrates the basic concepts:

	COST	RETAIL
Beginning inventory	$ 6,000	$ 10,000
Purchases	48,000	80,000
Goods available for sale	$54,000	$ 90,000
Deduct sales		(70,000)
Ending inventory at retail		$20,000
Cost-to-retail ratio:		
($54,000/$90,000)		× 60%
Ending inventory at cost		
($20,000 × 60%)		$ 12,000

The retail method can be used in conjunction with the FIFO, average costing, or LIFO cost flow assumptions and has been approved by the accounting profession and the Internal Revenue Service. The primary advantage of this method is that it provides an estimate of the inventory without requiring a physical count. Consequently, it is especially useful for interim reporting purposes. A physical inventory is necessary annually, but interim amounts can be estimated. A second advantage is that it serves as a control device. Any discrepancies between the end-of-year physical count and the estimated amount are highlighted for investigation. A third advantage is the simplification of the year-end inventory procedure. Retailers simply use the retail amounts from the merchandise when the physical count is taken and are not required to trace the merchandise to the original invoice sheets to find the original cost.

Two underlying assumptions form the basis of the retail method: (1) the relationship between cost and selling price is constant for the goods in the inventory, and (2) the mix of goods in the ending inventory reflects the mix of goods purchased. These assumptions are similar to the assumptions of the gross profit method.

Terminology. The preceding illustration of the retail method assumed no changes in the retail prices after they were first established. Obviously, this is unrealistic, as sales prices frequently change, both upward and downward. To understand and use the retail methods, we must be familiar with the terminology associated with price changes. The most important terms follow:

- Markup—the amount by which the original sales price exceeds the cost. This is also called the *normal profit.*
- Additional markup—the amount added to the original sales price.
- Markup cancellation—cancellation of all or part of the additional markup. The amount of the markup cancellation cannot exceed the amount of the additional markup.
- Net markup—additional markups less the markup cancellations.
- Markdown—amount subtracted from the original sales price.
- Markdown cancellation—cancellation of part or all of the markdown. The markdown cancellation cannot exceed the amount of the markdown.
- Net markdown—the difference between the total markdowns and the markdown cancellations.

To illustrate the use of these terms, assume that the AAA Auto Parts Store purchases a large supply of floor mats for cars at a cost of $15 each. The mats are priced for sale at $20, a *markup* or *normal profit* of $5. Subsequently, because of heavy demand, the price increases to $24, an *additional markup* of $4. Several weeks later, AAA puts the mats on sale at $21, resulting in a *markup cancellation* of $3 and leaving a *net markup* of $1. Some of the floor mats do not sell and are placed in a clearance sale at a reduced price of $17, which represents a *markup cancellation* of $1 and a *markdown* of $3. At this point, the *net markup* is zero for the unsold floor mats. After the clearance sale, the remaining floor mats are priced at $19, a *markdown cancellation* of $2, leaving a *net markdown* of $1.

Application of Retail Method. The retail method of valuation can be used with FIFO or FIFO on an LCM basis, average costing or average costing on an LCM basis, or LIFO. Average costing on an LCM basis is the method preferred by retailers and is sometimes referred to as the "conventional method." Regardless of the cost flow method chosen for use, the same three computations are made in calculating the cost of the ending inventory:

1. Calculate the retail value of the ending inventory.
2. Calculate the cost-to-retail ratio for the particular cost flow assumption being used.
3. Multiply the retail value of the ending inventory by the cost-to-retail ratio to find the cost of the ending inventory.

The cost-to-retail ratio is the basis for differentiation among the various cost flow methods, as it is slightly changed for each method (see Exhibit 10–10). The cost-to-retail ratios for FIFO and LIFO use identical calculations because both are concerned with costing only current-period purchases. FIFO assumes that the beginning inventory has been sold, and thus the ending inventory consists solely of current-period purchases. With LIFO, the prior-period cost of the beginning inventory is carried forward as a separate amount. The layer added in the current period is based on the cost of the current-period purchases.

Note in Exhibit 10–10 that purchases are included in the numerator at cost, and the denominator at retail, for all four methods. The numerator also includes any freight charges and subtracts any discounts and any returns and allowances. The denominator does not consider freight or discounts. The net markups are included in the denominator at retail for all four methods as well. The ratio changes depending on the treatment of two items: beginning inventory and net markdowns.

The beginning inventory is excluded from the FIFO and LIFO cost-to-retail computations. On the other hand, consistent with the average cost flow assumption, the beginning inventory is included in both the numerator and denominator of the cost-to-retail ratio for average costing.

The net markdowns are excluded from the LCM cost-to-retail ratios because net markdowns are reductions of the normal profit margins. In the earlier AAA Auto Parts example, the floor mats had an original cost of $15, a markup or normal profit of $5, and a selling price of $20. When the price dropped to $19, this became the net realizable value (or the "ceiling" price in LCM computations). Also, with a selling price of $19, the net markdown is $1, the difference between the original selling price of $20 and the net realizable value of $19. The LCM

	COST METHODS		LOWER OF COST OR MARKET	
	FIFO/LIFO	AVERAGE COST	FIFO	AVERAGE COST
Beginning inventory	**Exclude**	**Include**	**Exclude**	**Include**
Purchases	Include	Include	Include	Include
Net markups	Include	Include	Include	Include
Net markdowns	**Include**	**Include**	**Exclude**	**Exclude**

$$\text{FIFO and LIFO} = \frac{\text{Purchases} - \text{Purchase Returns} - \text{Purchase Discounts} + \text{Freight}}{\text{Purchases} - \text{Purchase Returns} + \text{Net Markups} - \textbf{Net Markdowns}}$$

$$\text{Average Costing} = \frac{\textbf{Beg. Inv.} + \text{Purchases} - \text{Purchase Returns} - \text{Purchase Discounts} + \text{Freight}}{\textbf{Beg. Inv.} + \text{Purchases} - \text{Purchase Returns} + \text{Net Markups} - \textbf{Net Markdowns}}$$

$$\text{FIFO, LCM} = \frac{\text{Purchases} - \text{Purchase Returns} - \text{Purchase Discounts} + \text{Freight}}{\text{Purchases} - \text{Purchase Returns} + \text{Net Markups}}$$

$$\text{Average Costing LCM} = \frac{\textbf{Beg. Inv.} + \text{Purchases} - \text{Purchase Returns} - \text{Purchase Discounts} + \text{Freight}}{\textbf{Beg. Inv.} + \text{Purchases} - \text{Purchase Returns} + \text{Net Markups}}$$

Note: (1) Numerator items are at cost.
(2) Denominator items are at retail.
(3) Items that change are in **bold print.**

EXHIBIT 10–10
Cost-to-Retail Calculations

value for the floor mats would be the floor value of $14 ($19 net realizable value less normal profit of $5). The net markdown from $20 to $19 is already included in the LCM floor value, therefore, it is excluded from the cost-to-retail ratio. Exhibit 10–11 illustrates the retail method computations for finding the cost of the ending inventory using FIFO, average costing, FIFO based on LCM, average costing based on LCM, and LIFO.

Special Items. Several additional factors frequently enter the retail method computations and may affect the calculation of the ending inventory at retail as well as the cost-to-retail ratio:

- *Freight-in*—This is considered part of the cost of purchases and should be added to the numerator in the cost-to-retail ratio.
- *Purchase discounts*—These are considered a reduction in the purchase cost and are subtracted in the numerator of the cost-to-retail ratio.
- *Purchase returns and allowances*—These items reduce both the cost and the retail amount of purchases. They should be subtracted from purchases in determining the ending inventory at retail and also subtracted in both the numerator (at cost) and denominator (at retail) of the cost-to-retail ratio.
- *Sales returns and allowances*—These are reductions of sales and are subtracted from sales in calculating the ending inventory at retail.
- *Sales discounts*—These are considered financing expenses when using the gross method of recording sales and are not included in the calculation of either the ending inventory or the cost-to-retail ratio.

EXHIBIT 10–11 Ending Inventory Retail Method Computations

Data

	COST	RETAIL
Beginning inventory	$ 5,000	$ 8,000
Purchases	85,000	160,000
Purchase discounts	4,000	
Purchase returns	1,000	2,000
Freight-in	5,000	
Net markups		14,000
Net markdowns		15,000
Sales		125,000

Ending Inventory at Retail:

Beginning inventory	$ 8,000
Purchases	160,000
Purchase returns	(2,000)
Net markups	14,000
Goods available	$ 180,000
Net markdowns	(15,000)
Net sales	(125,000)
Ending inventory @ retail	$ 40,000

Estimated Ending Inventory at Cost:

$$\text{FIFO} = \frac{\text{Purchases} - \text{Purchase Discounts} - \text{Purchase Returns} + \text{Freight}}{\text{Purchases} - \text{Purchase Returns} + \text{Net Markups} - \text{Net Markdowns}} \times \text{End. Inv. @ Retail}$$

$$= \frac{\$85{,}000 - \$4{,}000 - \$1{,}000 + \$5{,}000}{\$160{,}000 - \$2{,}000 + \$14{,}000 - \$15{,}000} \times \$40{,}000 = \underline{\underline{\$21{,}656}}$$

$$\text{Average Costing} = \frac{\text{Beg. Inv.} + \text{Purchases} - \text{Purchase Discounts} - \text{Purchase Returns} + \text{Freight}}{\text{Beg. Inv.} + \text{Purchases} - \text{Purchase Returns} + \text{Net Markups} - \text{Net Markdowns}} \times \text{End. Inv. @ Retail}$$

$$= \frac{\$5{,}000 + \$85{,}000 - \$4{,}000 - \$1{,}000 + \$5{,}000}{\$8{,}000 + \$160{,}000 - \$2{,}000 + \$14{,}000 - \$15{,}000} \times \$40{,}000 = \underline{\underline{\$21{,}818}}$$

$$\text{FIFO, LCM} = \frac{\text{Purchases} - \text{Purchase Discounts} - \text{Purchase Returns} + \text{Freight}}{\text{Purchases} - \text{Purchase Returns} + \text{Net Markups}} \times \text{End. Inv. @ Retail}$$

$$= \frac{\$85{,}000 - \$4{,}000 - \$1{,}000 + \$5{,}000}{\$160{,}000 - \$2{,}000 + \$14{,}000} \times \$40{,}000 = \underline{\underline{\$19{,}767}}$$

$$\text{Average Costing LCM} = \frac{\text{Beg. Inv.} + \text{Purchases} - \text{Purchase Disc} - \text{Purchase Ret} + \text{Freight}}{\text{Beg. Inv.} + \text{Purchases} - \text{Purchase Returns} + \text{Net Markups}} \times \text{End. Inv. @ Retail}$$

$$= \frac{\$5{,}000 + \$85{,}000 - \$4{,}000 - \$1{,}000 + \$5{,}000}{\$8{,}000 + \$160{,}000 - \$2{,}000 + \$14{,}000} \times \$40{,}000 = \underline{\underline{\$20{,}000}}$$

(continued)

EXHIBIT 10–11 (Concluded)

Retail LIFO

A. Ending inventory at retail = $40,000

B. Cost-to-retail ratio:

$$\text{LIFO} = \frac{\text{Purchases} - \text{Purchase Returns} - \text{Purchase Discounts} + \text{Freight}}{\text{Purchases} - \text{Purchase Returns} + \text{Net Markups} - \text{Net Markdowns}}$$

$$= \frac{\$85{,}000 - \$1{,}000 - \$4{,}000 + \$5{,}000}{\$160{,}000 - \$2{,}000 + \$14{,}000 - \$15{,}000} = \underline{\underline{0.5414}}$$

C. Calculate inventory at cost:

	RETAIL	COST
Beginning inventory	$ 8,000	$ 5,000
Layer added	32,000*	17,325*
Ending inventory	$40,000	$22,325

*$32,000 = $40,000 − $8,000; $17,325 = $32,000 × 0.5414

D. Now assume the ending inventory at retail is $6,000. What is the value at cost using LIFO?

The ending inventory of $6,000 is less than the beginning inventory of $8,000 at cost; therefore, the inventory has decreased during the period. The cost of the ending inventory will have the same cost-to-retail ratio as the beginning inventory because it was added in the prior period.

$$\text{Estimated ending inventory at cost} = \frac{\$5{,}000}{\$8{,}000} \times \$6{,}000$$

$$= \underline{\underline{3{,}750}}$$

- *Employee discounts*—If sales to employees are recorded "net" of discounts, these are subtracted from the goods available for sale when calculating the inventory at retail but ignored in the cost-to-retail ratio. Otherwise, they are treated like sales discounts.
- *Normal shortages*—These are subtracted from the goods available for sale when calculating the ending inventory at retail but ignored in the cost-to-retail ratio.

LIFO INVENTORY

Advantages of LIFO. There are two primary reasons for using LIFO: (1) matching current costs with current sales and (2) taking advantage of the income tax effects during periods of rising prices. Because LIFO expenses the most recent purchase costs first, the cost of goods sold approximates replacement cost. During inflationary periods, this matching results in a lower taxable income and, hence, reduced tax payments. Reduction of the tax payments leaves cash in the enterprise, which may be reinvested in the business, used for creditor payments, or paid as dividends to the owners. The potential tax savings of LIFO are substantial. For many areas of accounting, tax laws permit different accounting methods for financial reporting and income tax reporting. However, to take advantage of the LIFO method for tax purposes, companies also must use LIFO for financial reporting.

Disadvantages of LIFO. Using LIFO creates three potential problems: (1) it can distort asset valuation on the balance sheet, (2) it can become cumbersome and complex very quickly, and (3) it can affect income if early low-cost layers are liquidated. Because the stated inventory value on the balance sheet consists of the earliest costs, it is not representative of the current inventory value. Any ratio or other analysis that incorporates inventory values may thus be distorted and provide faulty comparisons across companies.

Perhaps more serious is the second problem, involving the application of LIFO. It is necessary to maintain complete records of all purchases and their associated costs as well as the costs of each unit in the beginning inventory. This is a very cumbersome task for an enterprise with a high turnover of inventory or a large variety of items in inventory.

The third problem occurs if the inventory level is reduced during the accounting period. As the inventory is decreased, the most recently added layers are eliminated (expensed) first, and if the reduction is large enough, early low-cost layers are sold. Matching these earlier, lower costs with current revenues can reduce cost of goods sold and increase income. If this **LIFO-layer liquidation** is permanent, an increased tax liability results. If the LIFO-layer liquidation is only temporary, and if management intends to replace the inventory *before* the end of the annual accounting period (that is, the temporary liquidation occurs at a quarterly date), the difference between the LIFO cost and the current cost of the merchandise may be credited to a temporary liability account.

When the inventory is replenished, the temporary liability is removed, and the new merchandise is placed in inventory at the original LIFO cost. At the quarterly reporting date, the temporary liability account appears on the balance sheet as a current liability, even though it does not meet the SFAC No. 6 definition of a liability. There is no probable future sacrifice of economic benefit of the entity to transfer benefits or provide services to another entity, so the definition is not met.

If the LIFO layers are not restored by the end of the year, a permanent liquidation is assumed and the low costs from earlier periods are matched with revenues in the current period. The increased income triggers a larger tax liability. Management may try to prevent the increased tax by purchasing additional inventory to restore the layers before the end of the year. This may not always be a wise decision, however, as it may be more beneficial for the company to carry a smaller inventory.

LIFO Pools. To help prevent liquidation of layers and to ease record-keeping requirements, LIFO can be applied to groups (called *pools*) of similar items that are treated as a single unit for costing purposes. The items in each pool are treated as if all had been purchased at the same time for the same amount. As an example, consider a shoe store that carries men's, women's, and children's shoes, plus a line of work shoes. Each line of shoes is treated as a pool for LIFO inventory purposes. The first-year inventory of men's shoes would consist of all the men's shoes at the average purchase cost for the year. If the inventory of men's shoes increased in the second year, the layer added would be priced at the average purchase cost of the second year. The same thing would be true for all the other lines of shoes. Exhibit 10–12 illustrates the pooled-quantity approach for LIFO for a shoe store and a single pool for the men's line.

Note that within the men's pool, the individual styles may increase or decrease in quantity, but the beginning inventory level is determined by the total quantity of the combined styles. That is, the beginning inventory consisted of 500 units, and the ending inventory of 850 (the 500-unit beginning layer plus an added layer of 350 units). The advantage of this pooled approach is that decreases in one style are offset by increases in other styles, thus preserving the integrity of the layer.

The pooled-quantity approach illustrated in Exhibit 10–12 overcomes some problems associated with individual-unit LIFO. However, the pooled-quantity method also creates some problems. The product mix of most companies changes and evolves continually. The shoe company in Exhibit 10–12, for example, may expand the sports shoe line or create a separate pool exclusively for running shoes. As the product mix changes, the pools must be redefined and parts of the layers replaced with different products. Some advantages of the LIFO method are therefore lost because the changing product mix liquidates the base layers.

Dollar-Value LIFO. The dollar-value LIFO method alleviates some of the problems of erosion of the layers and changing product mix in the pools. In this method, the pools consist of dollars instead of unit quantities. Each succeeding

EXHIBIT 10–12
LIFO Pools

PRODUCT	WING-TIPS	LOAFERS	CASUAL	SPORTS	TOTAL
Beginning inventory:					
Units	100	200	100	100	500
Price	× $60	× $40	× $25	× $35	× $40*
Total	$ 6,000	$ 8,000	$ 2,500	$ 3,500	$ 20,000
Purchases:					
Units	400	600	800	1,200	3,000
Price	× $75	× $55	× $30	× $45	× $47*
Total	$30,000	$33,000	$24,000	$54,000	$141,000
Unit sales	400	750	720	780	2,650

Ending Inventory Units = 500 Beg. Inv. + 3,000 Purchased − 2,650 Sold = 850

Ending inventory @ LIFO			
	Beginning inventory	500 units @ $40 =	$ 20,000
	Layer added	350 units @ $47 =	16,450
		850	$ 36,450

*$40 = $20,000/500 units
$47 = 141,000/3,000 units

year after the base year (the year of LIFO adoption), layer increases and decreases stem from total dollar changes in the pool instead of quantity changes. The advantage of this approach is that the pools may contain a much broader array of products, and new items may be added to the pool or substituted for discontinued products in the pool without changing the layers. Because the pool and the layers of inventory in the pool are considered to be comprised of dollars instead of units of products, the layers in the pool change only as the dollar value in the pool changes. The dollar-value LIFO method may be used either at cost—*the dollar-value LIFO cost method*—or combined with the retail method as a *dollar-value retail LIFO method.* We discuss and illustrate the cost method first.

Dollar-Value LIFO Cost Method. Because the layers consist of dollars instead of units, any layer increase or decrease in a given year means dollars are added to or subtracted from the inventory value. Conceptually, this is an easy method to apply, as illustrated in Exhibit 10–13.

No Inflation. The first part of Exhibit 10–13 assumes that prices are constant. The base layer of inventory at the end of 1997 was $20,000, as measured in terms of 1997 prices. The ending inventories of 1998 and 1999 were $23,100 and $27,250, respectively. The prices in each of those years were also the same as 1997 prices (that is, there was no inflation). The ending inventory for 1998 and 1999 would consist of the base layer of $20,000 plus the layers added in each year as follows:

	LAYERS	TOTAL
1997 base layer at 1997 prices	$20,000	
1998 layer added (1998 prices = 1997 prices)	3,100	$23,100
1999 layer added (1999 prices = 1997 prices)	4,150	$27,250

In each succeeding year, if the prices stay at 1997 levels, increases in inventory would form new layers in the year the increase occurred. If a decrease in inventory occurred, the most recently added layer(s) would be removed.

Inflation. Unfortunately, prices do change. Exhibit 10–13 also illustrates the layering concept with price changes of 5% and 4% in 1998 and 1999, respectively. The 1998 ending inventory of $23,100 at 1998 prices must be allocated between the 1997 base layer at 1997 prices and the 1998 layer at 1998 prices. To separate the layers, we first restate the inventory into 1997 (base year) prices with the following calculation:

$$\frac{\$23{,}100}{105\%} = \$22{,}000$$

This first calculation removes the price increase that occurred in 1998. The $22,000 consists of the $20,000 base layer from 1997 and $2,000 (at 1997 prices) added in 1998. The 1998 layer must be stated in terms of 1998 prices, so that $2,000 layer is multiplied by 105%.

$$\$2{,}000 \times 105\% = \$2{,}100$$

EXHIBIT 10–13
Dollar-Value LIFO With and Without Price Changes

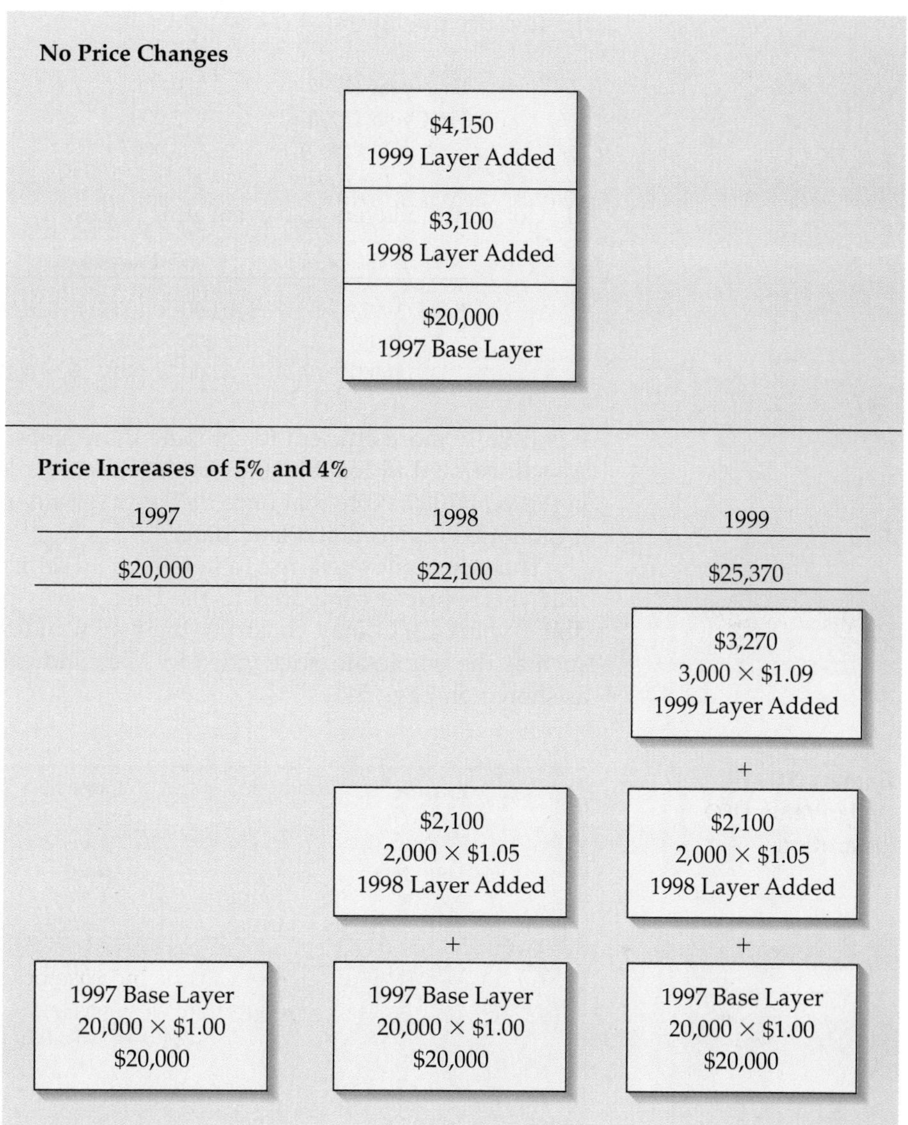

Thus, the dollar value inventory for 1998 is

$$\$20{,}000 + \$2{,}100 = \$22{,}100$$

In 1999 assume that a further price increase of 4% occurs, so that the total increase between 1997 and 1999 is 9%. That means that 1999 prices are equivalent to 109% of 1997 prices. The ending inventory in 1999 prices is $27,250. Following the same procedures as above, the dollar-value LIFO inventory is found by the following procedure:

I. Restate to base-year prices:

$$\$27{,}250/109\% = \$25{,}000$$

II. Identify the layers:

Base year (1997)	$20,000
First year (1998)	2,000
(1999)	3,000

III. Convert the layers to current-year prices:

	LAYERS	TOTAL
Base (1997)	$20,000 × 100% = $20,000	$20,000
(1998)	2,000 × 105% = 2,100	22,100
(1999)	3,000 × 109% = 3,270	25,370

It is usually more efficient to combine these steps, as shown in Exhibit 10–14. Also illustrated in Exhibit 10–14 is the effect of a layer decrease that occurred in the year 2000. Note that once the layer (or any portion thereof) is removed, it cannot be replaced at a later date.

The price index referred to in Exhibit 10–14 is a ratio that reflects the current year's prices compared to the base year's prices. Those entities using dollar-value LIFO may construct their own index or use a published index such as the wholesale price index for their industry. An index is constructed as shown on page 541.

EXHIBIT 10–14
Dollar-Value LIFO Illustration

YEAR	ENDING INVENTORY AT CURRENT-YEAR PRICES	÷	PRICE INDEX	=	ENDING INVENTORY AT BASE-YEAR PRICES	LAYERS × PRICE INDEX =	DOLLAR-VALUE LIFO
1997	$20,000		$1.00		$20,000	$20,000 × $1.00 =	$20,000
1998	23,100		1.05		22,000	20,000 × 1.00 =	20,000
						2,000 × 1.05 =	2,100
							$22,100
1999	27,250		1.09		25,000	20,000 × 1.00 =	$20,000
						2,000 × 1.05 =	2,100
						3,000 × 1.09 =	3,270
							$25,370
2000	27,600		1.15		24,000	20,000 × 1.00 =	$20,000
						2,000 × 1.05 =	2,100
						2,000 × 1.09 =	2,180
							$24,280
2001	32,400		1.20		27,000	20,000 × 1.00 =	$20,000
						2,000 × 1.05 =	2,100
						2,000 × 1.09 =	2,180
						3,000 × 1.20 =	3,600
							$27,880

$$\frac{\text{Current Year's Quantities} \times \text{Current Year's Prices}}{\text{Current Year's Quantities} \times \text{Base Year's Prices}}$$

This is referred to as the *double-extension method.* Note that the quantity factor is the same but the prices used are different, which has the effect of isolating the price-change factor. With a published index, the denominator is always the price index in the year of LIFO adoption:

$$\frac{\text{Current Year's Index}}{\text{Index from Year of LIFO Adoption}}$$

As an example, assume the wholesale price index in the year of adoption was 140 and the current year's index was 168. The price index would become

$$\frac{168}{140}, \text{ or } 120\%.$$

Dollar-Value LIFO Retail Method. Dollar-value LIFO can be applied to the retail method very easily. In the retail method, all the calculations are at the retail price; therefore, the conversion to cost is made by using the cost-to-retail ratio from the year in which each layer was added. The appropriate cost-to-retail ratio is the same ratio calculated earlier when using the retail FIFO method on a cost basis. To apply this method, first find the retail value of the ending inventory at current year-end prices, and then follow the steps outlined above for dollar-value LIFO. A final computation converting each layer from retail price to cost is necessary. Exhibits 10–15, 10–16, and 10–17 illustrate the dollar-value retail LIFO method.

EXHIBIT 10–15
Dollar-Value Retail LIFO Calculations

	1996		1997		1998		1999	
	COST	RETAIL	COST	RETAIL	COST	RETAIL	COST	RETAIL
Inventory, 1/1	$12,000	$ 25,000		$ 30,240		$ 40,250		$ 36,600
Purchases	80,000	150,000	$95,000	180,000	$110,000	198,000	$121,000	224,000
Purchase returns	(2,200)	(4,000)	0	0	(1,600)	(3,000)	(600)	(1,000)
Freight-in	2,000		4,000		5,000		3,000	
Net markups		23,000		25,000		35,000		37,000
Net markdowns		(4,760)		(5,000)		(6,000)		(3,000)
Sales		(160,000)		(191,000)		(235,000)		(250,000)
Sales returns		1,000		1,010		7,350		4,500
Inventory, 12/31		$ 30,240		$ 40,250		$ 36,600		$ 48,100
Price Index (Assumed) (1/1/96 = 100%)		1.08		1.15		1.22		1.30

EXHIBIT 10–16
Dollar-Value Retail LIFO Calculations: Calculation of Cost-to-Retail Ratios

Beginning Inventory = $12,000/$25,000 = .480

$$\frac{\text{Purchases} - \text{Purchase Returns} + \text{Freight}}{\text{Purchases} - \text{Purchase Returns} + \text{Markups} - \text{Markdowns}} = \text{cost-to-retail ratio}$$

$$1996 = \frac{80{,}000 - 2{,}200 + 2{,}000}{150{,}000 - 4{,}000 + 23{,}000 - 4{,}760} = \frac{79{,}800}{164{,}240} = .486$$

$$1997 = \frac{95{,}000 + 4{,}000}{180{,}000 + 25{,}000 - 5{,}000} = \frac{99{,}000}{200{,}000} = .495$$

$$1998 = \frac{110{,}000 - 1{,}600 + 5{,}000}{198{,}000 - 3{,}000 + 35{,}000 - 6{,}000} = \frac{113{,}400}{224{,}000} = .506$$

$$1999 = \frac{121{,}000 - 600 + 3{,}000}{224{,}000 - 1{,}000 + 37{,}000 - 3{,}000} = \frac{123{,}400}{257{,}000} = .480$$

EXHIBIT 10–17
Dollar-Value Retail LIFO Calculations

YEAR	INVENTORY 12/31 RETAIL	PRICE INDEX	INVENTORY BASE-YEAR PRICE	LAYERS	PRICE INDEX	COST-TO-RETAIL RATIO	DOLLAR-VALUE LIFO	TOTAL
1996	$30,240	1.08	$28,000	$25,000	1.00	0.480	$12,000	
				3,000	1.08	0.486	1,575	
				$28,000				$13,575
1997	40,250	1.15	35,000	$25,000	1.00	0.480	$12,000	
				3,000	1.08	0.486	1,575	
				7,000	1.15	0.495	3,985	
				$35,000				$17,560
1998	36,600	1.22	30,000	$25,000	1.00	0.480	$12,000	
				3,000	1.08	0.486	1,575	
				2,000	1.15	0.495	1,138	
				$30,000				$14,713
1999	48,100	1.30	37,000	$25,000	1.00	0.480	$12,000	
				3,000	1.08	0.486	1,575	
				2,000	1.15	0.495	1,138	
				7,000	1.30	0.480	4,368	
				$37,000				$19,081

FINANCIAL ANALYSIS

EVALUATION OF INVENTORY METHODS

Accounting Research Bulletin No. 43 indicates that the primary basis of accounting for inventories is cost, unless the market value of the goods is less than

Analyze the impact of inventory valuation on liquidity and profitability analysis.

their cost. Most companies use lower of cost or market (LCM) to price all or some portion of their inventories. Many companies use more than one method to determine the total cost of their inventory. The principal methods used are FIFO, LIFO, and average costing, or some combination of LIFO with some other method.

If prices were stable and did not change, the method of inventory valuation would not matter, because all would yield the same results. However, the long-term trend of prices has been upward. The different inventory valuation methods provide different amounts not only for inventory on the balance sheet but also for income determination on the income statement. As seen in the earlier discussion and illustrations, during periods of rising prices, FIFO results in the largest asset valuation on the balance sheet and LIFO the smallest. For income determination, the results are the same: FIFO gives the largest income because the earliest (lower) costs are expensed through cost of goods sold, and LIFO reports the smallest income, since the latest (highest) costs are expensed through cost of goods sold. Average costing provides results between FIFO and LIFO for both the balance sheet and income statement. In periods of falling prices, the results would be just the opposite.

LIQUIDITY CONSIDERATIONS

Inventory is classified as a current asset and is part of working capital. Inventory management and costing methods are very important to the analyst because inventories often comprise significant portions of the current assets regardless of the method used to value them.

Liquidity is generally regarded as the ability to match cash inflows with cash outflows. Principal measures of liquidity are working capital, the current ratio, and the quick (or acid-test) ratio. Like most ratios, these should be compared with industry standards.

Inventory is related to cash flows through sales in that sales are often a primary determinant of the size of inventory. Traditionally, as sales increase, investment in inventories also increases to support the higher level of sales. During the late 1980s, management began thinking in terms of carrying much smaller inventories, recognizing the costs involved with large inventory levels. More attention was paid to efficient inventory management, with the objective of increasing turnover of the inventory. *Inventory turnover* is calculated as the cost of goods sold divided by the average inventory, as follows:

$$\text{Inventory Turnover} = \frac{\text{Cost of Goods Sold}}{(\text{Beginning Inventory} + \text{Ending Inventory})/2}$$

A higher turnover results in a smaller inventory value and indicates more efficient management of inventory. At the same time, if the inventory value is smaller, it becomes less important as a factor in working capital and the current ratio. If fewer funds are required for investment in inventory, additional funds will be available for investment in other assets, reduction of debt, or distribution to the owners. A low inventory turnover could indicate the existence of old merchandise or obsolescence.

An indication of the relative age of the inventory is found by calculating the average number of days required to sell the inventory. This is sometimes referred as the "number of days' sales in inventory" and indicates approximately how many days on average that an inventory unit will be on hand before sale.

$$\text{Days' Sales in Inventory} = \frac{365}{\text{Inventory Turnover}}$$

To a certain extent, future cash inflows depend on the profit margins generated by the sales of inventory. Certainly, if frequent markdowns are necessary to sell the merchandise, the profit margins will shrink and future cash inflows will suffer. An indication of potential problems in this regard is often found in the inventory turnover ratio. A decrease in the turnover ratio usually means that the inventory remains on hand for a longer period of time, increasing the potential for obsolescence, theft, spoilage, or other forms of loss in value.

Use of the inventory turnover ratio is complicated somewhat by the alternative methods of inventory valuation. LIFO costing does not provide ratios relevant for analysis purposes. The LIFO values may be so old that they bear no relationship to the current values of the inventory. Further, comparing two companies, even if both use LIFO, may be impossible because the layers of inventory may have been added during periods when vastly different prices were in effect.

PROFITABILITY CONSIDERATIONS

Inventory valuation methods affect profitability because they result in different net income figures. Exhibits 10–18 and 10–19 compare FIFO, LIFO, and average costing methods in periods of rising and falling prices. These exhibits reflect the effects of the different costing methods on inventory value and the subsequent effects on income tax and net income. When evaluating profitability and using measures such as return on investment or return on shareholders' equity (illustrated in Chapter 6), it is very important for the user to know the method of inventory valuation used.

In sum, inventory is a principal component of working capital. The required investment in inventory is related to sales levels and efficient management of the inventory. Comparison and evaluation of inventory policies across companies is made more difficult by the various methods of valuation used by different companies.

INVENTORY ERRORS

Inventory errors were discussed in Chapter 6. This section explores the source of inventory errors, the impact on asset valuation and income determination resulting from the errors, and the proper methods of correction. Errors originate because of one or more of the following: (1) incorrect quantities, (2) incorrect values, or (3) improper accounting. An incorrect quantity error occurs if an item of merchandise is either included or excluded from the inventory count by mistake. For example, merchandise owned but on consignment at a customer location could be excluded from the owner's inventory and mistakenly included with the inventory of the holder. Merchandise in transit between buyer and seller is another frequent source of incorrect quantity error because it is easily

Data

Assume the following, plus rising prices.

Sales	$160,000
Beginning inventory	15,000
Purchases	120,000
Other expenses	20,000
Tax rate	40%

Ending values assumed for different cost flow methods. The following table shows the effects of the inventory cost flow assumptions on values of ending inventory, income tax, and the net income after tax.

FIFO, LIFO, and Average Costing

	FIFO		LIFO		AVERAGE	
	PERIODIC	PERPETUAL	PERIODIC	PERPETUAL	PERIODIC	PERPETUAL
Net sales	$160,000	$160,000	$160,000	$160,000	$160,000	$160,000
Cost of goods sold						
Beginning inventory	$ 15,000	$ 15,000	$ 15,000	$ 15,000	$ 15,000	$ 15,000
Purchases	120,000	120,000	120,000	120,000	120,000	120,000
Available for sale	$135,000	$135,000	$135,000	$135,000	$135,000	$135,000
Ending inventory	**40,000**	**40,000**	**30,000**	**32,000**	**35,000**	**37,000**
Cost of goods sold	$ 95,000	$ 95,000	$105,000	$103,000	$100,000	$ 98,000
Gross profit	$ 65,000	$ 65,000	$ 55,000	$ 57,000	$ 60,000	$ 62,000
Other expenses	20,000	20,000	20,000	20,000	20,000	20,000
Income before tax	$ 45,000	$ 45,000	$ 35,000	$ 37,000	$ 40,000	$ 42,000
Income tax (40%)	**18,000**	**18,000**	**14,000**	**14,800**	**16,000**	**16,800**
Income after tax	**$ 27,000**	**$ 27,000**	**$ 21,000**	**$ 22,200**	**$ 24,000**	**$ 25,200**

EXHIBIT 10–18
Inventory Cost Flow Assumptions

overlooked by both the buyer and the seller. Misstated values or valuation errors can also occur simply by recording the incorrect amount for purchases or using an incorrect figure from an invoice. An example of a common accounting error is failure to record a purchase. Improper treatment of a purchase discount is another common error.

If any of these errors is not discovered in the current period, it will affect calculations of asset value and income during the current and succeeding periods. The effect of the error in the second period exactly offsets the effect in the first period; therefore, retained earnings will be correct after two periods. If the error is discovered prior to the end of the second period, it should be treated as a prior-period adjustment to retained earnings. Discovery of an inventory error after the second year requires no correction, since the accounts are correctly stated after two years. If the statements are reissued in comparative format, though, they should be corrected.

EXHIBIT 10–19 Inventory Cost Flow Assumptions Compared

FIFO, LIFO, and Average Costing in Periods of Rising Prices

	FIFO		LIFO		AVERAGE	
	PERIODIC	PERPETUAL	PERIODIC	PERPETUAL	PERIODIC	PERPETUAL
Ending inventory value	1	1	5	4	3	2
Income tax	1	1	5	4	3	2
Income after tax	1	1	5	4	3	2

FIFO, LIFO, and Average Costing in Periods of Falling Prices

	FIFO		LIFO		AVERAGE	
	PERIODIC	PERPETUAL	PERIODIC	PERPETUAL	PERIODIC	PERPETUAL
Ending inventory value	5	5	1	2	3	4
Income tax	5	5	1	2	3	4
Income after tax	5	5	1	2	3	4

Note: 1 = highest or greatest amount; 5 = lowest or least amount.

ETHICS IN PRACTICE—"COOKING THE BOOKS"

"How Pressure to Raise Sales Led MiniScribe to Falsify Numbers"

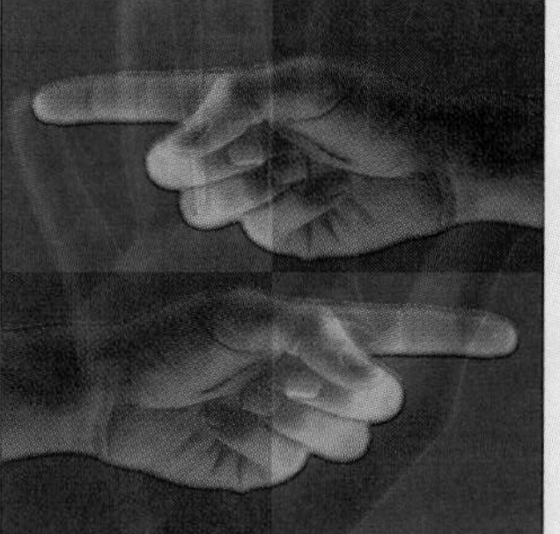

Last October, as other computer-disk drive companies were laying off hundreds of employees, ***MiniScribe Corporation*** announced its 13th consecutive record-breaking quarter. This time, however, the surge in sales sent a shiver of apprehension through MiniScribe's board.

"The balance sheet was scary," says William Hambrecht, one of the directors.

What worried Hambrecht was a sudden, three-month run-up in receivables to $173 million from $109 million, a 59% increase. Inventories were similarly bloated, swelling to $141 million from $93 million—a dangerous development because disk drives can become obsolete from one quarter to the next.

Seven months later, the portents that had worried Hambrecht generated grim headlines: MiniScribe's spectacular sales gain had been fabricated. In fact, the company acknowledged, it didn't know whether it could produce accurate financial statements for the prior three years.

Virtually all of MiniScribe's top management has been dismissed, and layoffs have shrunk worldwide employment to 5,700, from a peak of 8,350 a year ago. MiniScribe might have to write off as much as $200 million in bad inventory and uncollectible receivables.

Sales objectives became the company's driving force, . . . financial results became "the sole determinant" of whether bonuses were awarded. . . .

Hitting the number became a companywide obsession. Although many high-tech manufacturers accelerate shipments at the end of a quarter to boost sales,—a practice known as "stuffing the channel"—MiniScribe went several steps beyond that. On one occasion, an analyst relates, it shipped more than twice as many disk drives to a computer manufacturer as had been ordered; a former MiniScribe sales manager says the excess shipment was worth about $9 million. MiniScribe later said it had shipped the excess drives by mistake. The extras were returned—but by then MiniScribe had posted a sale at the higher number.

Source: "Cooking the Books: How Chief's Pressure to Raise Sales of Disk Drives Led MiniScribe to Falsify Data," *The Wall Street Journal*, September 11, 1995, pp. A1, A12.

IN FOCUS

Michael Ridgeway

VP—System Development
MKS, Inc.
BS, State University of New York at Albany
MS, Villanova University

"The client has to balance its information needs with the operational and cost issues."

Selection of the appropriate method for accounting for inventory is difficult because of the complex tradeoffs involved. For instance, LIFO provides income tax advantages during periods of rising prices but at the same time tends to understate inventory on the balance sheet by using the oldest units' costs.

These financial analysis tradeoffs are tricky enough, but practical and operational factors must be considered as well. Computer analyst and programmer Mike Ridgeway of MKS, Inc., has helped many firms grapple with these issues. MKS provides a computer package that automates the purchasing, warehousing, accounting, and other functions of companies with sales in the range of 10–100 million dollars.

"Our system can handle whatever inventory method the client intends to use. I can't make that decision for them, but I can tell them about the experiences of other clients," says Ridgeway. "For our clients that use LIFO, our system tracks the cost layers and so on. But it turns out that for most of our clients, the Average Cost method is a lot more manageable at the operational level." Using LIFO often means having one or more people on the payroll just to keep track of all of the purchase transactions and the related costs. These record-keeping expenses may be significant in high-volume operations. "Of course, the client has to balance its information needs with the operational and cost issues," Ridgeway adds.

The companies that use the MKS package are generally not large or sophisticated enough to keep programmers on staff, so in many cases Ridgeway acts as the client's MIS department, coordinating the system's installation and then working by phone and modem to address whatever needs may arise. "Every client's business is unique," he says. "They all buy our standard package, and then I work with them to customize it to their specific operations. I need to really understand how they do business and make decisions, so when they call and describe some new process or report, I can deliver what they need right away."

One current client—a book distributor—illustrates the unique character of different industries. This firm tracks the value of its inventory several different ways for different purposes. Because the entire book industry revolves around cover price, the company calculates the value of its inventory on cover price and then deducts the discount it conveys to retailers. It also tracks inventory on the actual costs incurred. Other clients, including a firearm distributor, have their own unique vocabularies and information needs.

Ridgeway's programming skills and understanding of accounting and other business issues are essential to his success, but he says many people would be surprised how much he relies on communication skills. "Most people probably think of programmers as working alone most of the time, but I probably spend at least four hours a day on the phone with clients."

END-OF-CHAPTER REVIEW

SUMMARY

1. **Explain the importance of inventory for asset valuation and income measurement.** Accounting for inventories potentially has a dramatic impact on the financial statements. Inventories are a substantive portion of current and total assets. Asset valuation, income determination, income tax liability, and financial analysis are all affected by the method selected to account for inventory.
2. **Understand the nature of inventory and what is included in it.** Inventories represent goods purchased for resale or used in the manufacture of goods for resale.

Inventory ownership, in general, follows title to the merchandise. Those items to which the entity has title should be included in the inventory.

3. **Differentiate between the perpetual and periodic inventory measurement systems.** Perpetual and periodic measurement systems refer to the method of tracking inventory quantities and costs. A perpetual system always maintains a current balance in the inventory account, while a periodic system does not. A perpetual system is most commonly used because it provides an element of control over the inventory.
4. **Record and report inventories for different valuation systems.** Inventory valuation systems include FIFO, LIFO, average costing, and specific identification. Inventories are reported at the lower of cost or market on the balance sheet.
5. **Estimate inventories using various methods.** The gross profit method and the retail methods are used to estimate the value of inventory. These methods are based on the assumptions that the markup percentages remain constant and that the mix of products in the ending inventory is representative of the mix of products purchased throughout the period.
6. **Analyze the impact of inventory valuation on liquidity and profitability analysis.** The LIFO method of valuation provides better measures of income, while FIFO provides better measures for asset valuation. LIFO also is favored because it reduces tax liability during periods of rising prices. Average costing produces results that fall between LIFO and FIFO.

   The choice of an inventory valuation method by an enterprise is dependent on its short- and long-term objectives. Whatever method is selected, the enterprise must fully disclose the basis for valuation in the notes to the financial statements.

   Because inventory is such an important part of the cash flow cycle, particular attention is paid to it by users of accounting information. Inventory is a large part of the current assets and plays a prominent role in liquidity and profitability ratios.

KEY TERMS

ASSIGNMENT MATERIAL

CASES

C10–1 Profitability—Investigate Inventories and Oral/Written Report

Howe's Electronics manufactures small components for radios. Ben Howe, the owner, is confused by the fact that although sales have increased, net income has decreased. After spending many hours poring over the financial statements and the supporting data, he has asked you to help him understand how this situation could occur.

Howe tells you that he is fairly certain that the selling and administrative expenses are reasonable for the level of operations. He is not as certain that the production expenses are reasonable. He has determined that the gross profit percentage has decreased from 55% to 45% in the course of one year. In addition, the prices paid for the raw materials have stayed constant because of long-term purchase commitments he had made several years ago. His labor costs are also constant, since there were no scheduled raises in the labor contract. Finally, he indicates that the shop has worked no overtime, his utility bills have been approximately the same as last year, and he has no reason to believe that the other overhead expenses are any different from last year.

Required: Howe has asked you to investigate the production expenses and ascertain why the gross profit percentage has changed so drastically. Records of sales, purchases, inventories, shipments, and anything else you need will be provided. He has asked you to submit a written report to him detailing:

1. Your method of investigation.
2. The probable cause of the change in the gross profit rate.
3. Your suggestions for changes in operations to restore the profitability rates to their former levels.

C10–2 Decision—Proper Accounting Treatment, Sales on Layaway

Sally Smith opened a small dress shop in a strip shopping center only one week ago. She has been very busy ordering merchandise, setting up displays, hiring sales clerks and training them, and making the other arrangements necessary for a successful business. Smith graduated from State University 12 years ago with a degree in accounting. After graduation, she immediately accepted a position with a large hotel and stayed with them until last year, when she decided to open her shop. She has purchased an accounting software package to help record her purchases, sales, and other operating expenses.

During the second week of business, one of the clerks came to Smith and indicated that a customer wanted to make a layaway purchase. Smith indicated that would be fine. That evening, as Smith was reviewing the day's activities, she found a notation regarding the layaway. The note indicated that the customer had made a cash deposit of $20 and intended to pay $20 per week for the next seven weeks until the dress was fully paid. The note also indicated that the clerk had not recorded the layaway in any way, because she was not sure how to do so.

Smith also was unsure of the proper accounting treatment for a layaway. She did not know if it would be proper to record the transaction as a sale and recognize the revenue or not. Further, she was unsure what to do about the merchandise in terms of inventory. Was it still part of her inventory or was it the property of the customer?

Required: Discuss the proper accounting treatment of a layaway sale. Discuss recognition of revenue and ownership of the merchandise.

C10–3 User-Oriented, Written/Oral Report—Lower of Cost or Market

Jon Horton, owner of Horton Plastics Company, is confused by the inventory treatment recommended at the end of the period by his accountant. Horton realizes that the value of the inventory has declined during the year; however, he does not think that he should have to charge that loss against his income for the period. He states, "You accountants tell me that I have to wait for a sale to take place before I can record a profit on the inventory, but now you say that I have to record a loss before I sell the inventory. Besides that, I don't see what difference it makes if I use this allowance method or some other method to record the change in inventory value. Won't the income be the same in any case?"

Required: Prepare a response for Horton. Include in your response an explanation of the LCM rules, why he must charge the loss against income, and why the allowance method is the preferred method compared to the direct write-off method.

C10–4 LIFO Purchasing and Ethical Considerations

Sean Meares, the head of industrial parts purchasing for Breaux Wholesale Supply, is puzzled. She recently received a directive from the controller's office indicating that she is to defer purchases of inventory for any parts that were sold in the current quarter. Meares thinks that this is very unusual because the company policy has always been to keep adequate inventory on hand.

Breaux Wholesale uses LIFO inventory valuation. Breaux also has had several consecutive quarters that were not profitable. This is of concern to the chief financial officer because several moderately large bank loans are up for renewal at the end of the quarter.

Required:

A. What could be the reason for deferral of inventory purchases?

B. Explain the relationship of the CFO's concerns and LIFO purchasing policies.

C10–5 Report Preparation—Inventory Valuation Methods

Johnson Products is a small wholesaler of paper goods to restaurants. The owner, Ed Johnson, asks you to explain the impact of using different inventory valuation methods on the balance sheet, income statement, and income tax.

Required: Prepare a report that summarizes the impact of the following inventory valuation methods on the balance sheet, income statement, and income taxes.

A. FIFO

B. LIFO

C. Average cost

C10–6 Report Preparation—Dollar Value LIFO

Prepare a report that explains how dollar-value LIFO simplifies use of LIFO for companies that have high turnover and/or new or different products frequently added to their product line.

QUESTIONS

Q10–1 What factors contribute to a loss in value of inventory? How should the loss be recognized?

Q10–2 How is the inventory "market value" determined by *Accounting Research Bulletin No. 43*? What constraints are placed on "market value" and why?

Q10–3 What are the methods of applying LCM to inventory? Which method results in values furthest removed from cost and why?

Q10–4 How should reductions of inventory cost to market be recorded? Accounting generally follows the historical cost principle in the United States. The lower-of-cost-or-market rule appears to violate this principle. Why is the lower-of-cost-or-market rule allowed if it violates historical cost?

Q10–5 What are purchase commitments? How do purchase commitments differ from ordinary purchase orders?

Q10–6 Explain how a retailer using the specific-identification method to value inventory could manipulate income.

Q10–7 What are the underlying assumptions of the gross profit method of estimating inventory? Why are they important?

Q10–8 How are the net markups and net markdowns incorporated into the cost-to-retail ratios?

Q10–9 What are some common inventory errors? When must they be corrected?

Q10–10 Explain the role of inventory in financial analysis.

Q10–11 What is a purchase commitment? How are purchase commitments related to conservatism and revenue recognition?

Q10–12 If allowing different inventory costing methods also enables income manipulation, why do the accounting standards allow more than one inventory costing method? Would it not be better to require one standard costing method?

Q10–13 (M90, T4 AICPA adapted)

1. What are the advantages of using the dollar-value LIFO method as opposed to the traditional LIFO method?
2. How does the application of the dollar-value LIFO method differ from the application of the traditional LIFO method?

Q10–14 (M89, T3 AICPA adapted) In general, why is the lower-of-cost-or-market rule used to report inventory values?

Q10–15 (M89, T3 AICPA adapted) In general, what criteria should be used to determine which costs should be included in inventory?

Q10–16 (M89, T3 AICPA adapted) Steel Company, a wholesaler that has been in business for two years, purchases its inventories from various suppliers. During the two years, each purchase has been at a lower price than the previous purchase.

Steel uses the lower-of-FIFO-cost-or-market method to value inventories. The original cost of the inventories is above replacement cost and below the net realizable value. The net realizable value less the normal profit margin is below the replacement cost.

Required:

A. At what amount should Steel's inventories be reported on the balance sheet? Explain the application of the lower-of-cost-or-market rule in this situation.
B. What would have been the effect on ending inventories and net income for the second year had Steel used the lower-of-average-cost-or-market inventory method instead of the lower-of-FIFO-cost-or-market inventory method? Why?

EXERCISES

E10–1 FIFO, LIFO, Average Cost

Junge Inc. provides the following information relative to its inventory:

Balance at 1/1	100 @ $25
Purchases:	
1/5	150 @ $30
1/11	200 @ $35
1/21	200 @ $40
Sales:	
1/4	60 @ $85
1/14	100 @ $90
1/17	210 @ $90
1/24	130 @ $80

Required:

A. Calculate the value of the ending inventory assuming a periodic inventory system and
  1. FIFO.
  2. LIFO.
  3. Average costing.

B. Repeat **(A)**, but assuming a perpetual inventory system.

C. Why would a company choose each of the three methods in **(A)** to value its inventory?

E10–2 FIFO, LIFO, Average Costing

Assume the following purchases and sales for Zaleski Inc., with a beginning inventory of 1,000 @ $10.

PURCHASES	SALES (AT VARIOUS DATES)
2,000 @ $9	$ 500
1,500 @ $10	1,400
1,600 @ $11	3,000

Required:

A. Assume a periodic inventory system. What is the value of the ending inventory if Zaleski uses
  1. LIFO.
  2. FIFO.
  3. Average costing.

B. Why would a company choose to use a periodic rather than perpetual inventory accounting system?

C. Is it true that a company that uses a periodic inventory accounting system has no idea of how much inventory it has during the year? Why or why not?

E10–3 Inventory Quantity Determination

The physical count of the inventory of the Zymol Company at December 31 was determined as a total cost of $34,500 without considering any of the following items. Zymol uses a perpetual inventory system.

1. Merchandise in transit with a cost of $2,000 was shipped F.O.B. destination and had been excluded from the inventory value. Zymol had recorded the sale for $3,000.
2. Merchandise in transit with a cost of $3,600 had been shipped F.O.B. destination. This merchandise had been excluded from the inventory by Zymol, and Zymol had recorded the sale of the merchandise for $5,400.
3. Purchases of raw materials by Zymol were in transit on December 31. These materials had a cost of $4,700 and were shipped F.O.B. destination. Zymol had not recorded the purchase nor included these items in its inventory.
4. Zymol had $2,500 of merchandise out on consignment with F. Johnson, a manufacturer's representative. This merchandise was not included in Zymol's physical inventory count.
5. During the physical count, certain items of inventory on hand had been double-counted. These items had a total cost of $1,500 but had been added to the physical count at $3,000, and no entry has been made for the difference.
6. On December 30, Zymol received $2,300 in merchandise that had been ordered by another company with a similar name. This merchandise was not included in the inventory; nevertheless, a purchase has been recorded.

Required:

A. Calculate the proper value of the ending inventory.
B. Prepare any adjusting entries necessary to correct the books and bring the accounts up to date.

E10–4 Gross Price versus Net Price

Recording purchases at gross or net amounts is the other side of the credit-sale transaction reported at gross or net amounts discussed in Chapter 8.

On July 1, Jorgenson buys $50,000 of merchandise from Dees Corporation on account. Terms granted Jorgenson are 2/10, n/30. Assume that payment in full is made on July 10.

Required:

A. Assume Jorgenson uses a periodic inventory system, and prepare the journal entries necessary on July 1 and 10 to record the purchase using (1) the net price method and then (2) the gross price method.
B. Assume Jorgenson uses a perpetual inventory system, and prepare the journal entries necessary on July 1 and 10 to record the purchase using (1) the net price method and then (2) the gross price method.
C. Different information is available to a company that uses the net method for recording purchases than is available under the gross method. Describe this difference.

E10–5 Inventory Quantity Determination

The following transactions of Marshall Inc. have not been recorded at year-end.

1. A purchase of $4,000 being shipped F.O.B. shipping point but still in transit.
2. Merchandise on consignment to Nelson Company with a cost of $400 was sold by Nelson for $750 cash. Under the consignment agreement, Nelson is to receive a 10 percent sales commission.
3. Merchandise with a cost of $2,500 and a retail price of $3,500 was shipped to Brown, the buyer on December 28. The shipping terms were 2/10, n/30, and shipped F.O.B. shipping point. Prior to their arrival at Brown (on December 30), Marshall received notification that Brown had filed for bankruptcy. Marshall immediately halted the

shipment and reclaimed the merchandise. Marshall had recorded the sale at the time of shipment but has not recorded anything for the reclaimed merchandise. Marshall uses the net method to record sales.

Required:

A. Assume Marshall uses the periodic inventory system. Prepare any correcting entries necessary at year-end. Assume the books have not been closed and that the adjusting entries for inventory and cost of goods sold have not been made.

B. Assume Marshall uses the perpetual inventory system. Prepare any adjusting entries necessary at year-end. Assume the books have not been closed.

E10–6 Lower of Cost or Market

Dee Dee's Inc. is a gourmet food store that also sells cooking supplies. The accompanying data relate to inventory.

Item	Units	Current Replacement Cost	Net Realizable Value	Net Realizable Value Less Normal Profit	Original Cost
Skillets	100	$12.00	$16.00	$12.50	$10.00
Woks	25	25.00	32.00	22.00	22.00
Trays	130	6.00	8.00	6.00	8.00
Tea kettles	10	10.00	14.00	12.00	13.50
Candy jars	125	9.00	8.00	6.50	7.00
Knife sets	35	28.00	36.00	26.00	29.00
Pitchers	24	10.00	18.00	13.00	15.00
Tureens	8	56.00	52.00	40.00	36.00

Required:

A. Calculate the inventory on an item-by-item basis using the lower-of-cost-or-market method.

B. Calculate the inventory on an aggregate basis using the lower-of-cost-or-market method.

C. Explain why the lower-of-cost-or-market rule for inventory places a "floor" and "ceiling" around the market value that is allowable for valuation of inventory rather than just using the market value.

E10–7 Lower of Cost or Market

Red-Stick Sports had the following inventory on hand on December 31, 1998:

Item	Cost	Market
T-shirts	$ 750	$ 820
Running shorts	600	540
Tennis rackets	1,020	995
Squash rackets	1,150	1,320
Handballs	245	325
Volleyballs	250	180
Basketballs	285	325

Required: Calculate the inventory value, LCM basis as follows:

A. Item-by-item.
B. Grouped into three categories: clothing, rackets, and balls.
C. Total inventory.

E10–8 LCM Journal Entries

The records of Carla's Knick-Knack Shop reflected inventory as shown here. Assume that purchases each year were $5,000.

DATE	COST	LCM	DIFFERENCE
January 1, 1998	$1,000	$1,000	$ 0
December 31, 1998	1,100	975	125
December 31, 1999	950	950	0

Required: Prepare the journal entries to reduce inventory to LCM using the allowance method at the end of 1998 and 1999.

E10–9 LCM Allowance Method

The inventories for Brady Soap Company are shown here for 1998 through 2000.

DATE	CURRENT REPLACEMENT COST	NET REALIZABLE VALUE	NET REALIZABLE VALUE LESS NORMAL PROFIT	ORIGINAL COST
January 1, 1998	$10,000	$12,000	$ 8,000	$10,000
December 31, 1998	14,000	15,000	12,000	18,000
December 31, 1999	18,000	16,000	14,000	16,500
December 31, 2000	16,000	18,000	15,000	17,000

Required:

A. Calculate LCM inventory for each year.
B. Prepare journal entries using the allowance method and assuming purchases of $50,000 each year.

E10–10 Purchase Commitment

On October 1, 1997, Gorton Bookbindery Inc. contracted for the purchase of binding materials in the amount of $120,000 on various dates in 1997 and 1998. At December 31, 1997, the market price had fallen to $100,000. One-half of the contracted materials were purchased on November 1, 1998, when the market price was $45,000. The market price of the remaining materials was $50,000 on December 31, 1998. The contract is noncancellable.

Required:

A. Prepare the required journal entry for December 31, 1997.
B. Prepare the journal entry for November 1, 1998.
C. Prepare the journal entry for December 31, 1998.
D. Assume the final purchase is made on January 30, 1999, when the market price is $65,000. Prepare the journal entry.

E10–11 Gross Profit

The De Luna Cheese Shop provided the following information for its merchandise:

PRODUCT	UNIT SALES	SELLING PRICE	GROSS PROFIT
Brie	250	$45	60%
Gruyere	175	38	55
Gouda	400	20	46
Swiss	350	25	50
Cheddar	500	25	40

Required: Calculate the composite gross profit rate.

E10–12 Gross Profit Rate

Seoul-Mate Imports Corporation's largest store crumbled in a severe earthquake on October 6, 1999. Because most merchandise was fragile, the salvageable goods will sell for only $1,000. The records show the following information before the earthquake:

Inventory at June 30, 1999	$ 45,000
Purchases July 1 through October 6	400,000
Sales, third quarter to date	500,000
Gross profit rate on sales	25%

Required: Estimate the earthquake loss for insurance purposes.

E10–13 Gross-Profit Rate

Chapman Guitar Manufacturing Company wants to compute the composite gross profit rate. Its records provide the following pertinent information:

PRODUCT	UNIT SALES	UNIT COST	SALES PRICE
Six-string Acoustic	15,000	$150	$175
Twelve-string Acoustic	7,500	225	300
Six-string Electric	12,000	200	300
Twelve-string Electric	6,000	275	350

Required: Calculate the following rates, rounding to two decimal places.

A. Each item's gross profit rate based on sales.

B. The composite rate based on sales.

E10–14 Dollar-Value LIFO

Chandler's Sporting Goods is in the process of preparing the 1998 year-end financial statements. Chandler's adopted dollar-value LIFO as of December 31, 1997, when the price index was 1.00. Chandler's provides the following information relative to the inventory:

Ending inventory, 1997	$ 12,500
1998 purchases	452,000
Cost of goods sold, 1998	444,700

Chandler's indicates that the relevant price index is 110% of the base index at the time of adoption of dollar-value LIFO.

Required: Calculate the value of the ending inventory at December 31, 1998 using dollar-value LIFO.

E10–15 Retail Inventory

Anthony's Seafood Market was established in 1983. Since the opening of the store, Anthony's has developed a steady clientele who are particularly pleased with the products carried. Anthony's business has grown steadily over the years and is now one of the largest seafood retailers in the Northeast. The owner has asked you to help with the end-of-year inventory and provides the following information from his records:

	COST	RETAIL
Inventory, 1/1	$ 30,000	$ 70,000
Purchases	220,000	355,000
Purchase returns	1,000	2,000
Freight-in	6,000	
Net markups		7,000
Net markdowns		3,000
Sales		350,000

Required: Calculate the cost of the ending inventory using the following retail methods: FIFO, FIFO LCM, average costing, lower of average cost or market, and retail LIFO.

E10–16 Retail Inventory

Norman's Nourishing Niblets is a wholesaler of junk foods. The products are sold in vending machines at universities and high schools throughout the Southwest. Norman started the business years ago when he was in college and would take orders for snacks in the evening in his dormitory. He filled the orders at the local 24-hour supermarket adjacent to campus. Eventually, he began stocking the more popular items in his room for resale and soon was engaged in a large operation. After graduation, he contracted with several dormitories to stock his merchandise in vending machines. From that point, the business grew rapidly. You find the following information in the accounting records:

	COST	RETAIL
Inventory, 1/1	$ 40,000	$ 90,000
Purchases	330,000	620,000
Purchase returns	7,000	17,000
Freight-in	16,000	
Net markups		4,000
Net markdowns		21,000
Sales		650,000

Required: Calculate the cost of the ending inventory at retail average cost and retail average cost LCM.

E10–17 LIFO-Layer Liquidation

Assume the Hallman Company uses dollar-value LIFO for reporting purposes. Further assume that Hallman has a temporary-layer liquidation in the third quarter of 100 units at a LIFO cost of $500 per unit. Hallman replenishes these units in the fourth quarter at a cost of $500 per unit.

Required: Prepare the journal entries necessary for the third and fourth quarters.

E10–18 Self-Constructed Price Index

Breck's Candy Company uses dollar-value LIFO for inventory valuation. Breck's uses self-constructed indexes and is in the process of constructing the price index for the current year. It has the following data available:

Product	Quantity	Unit Cost, Base Year	Unit Cost, Current Year
A	600	$ 50	$ 80
B	1,100	90	100
C	800	100	120
D	900	60	80

Required: Calculate the current year's price index using the double-extension method.

E10–19 Dollar-Value LIFO Inventory

Peterborough uses the dollar-value LIFO method to value its inventory. Peterborough has provided you with the following data:

	1998	1999
Inventory, 1/1	$30,000	
Inventory, 12/31	39,200	$50,000
Current price index	1.12	1.25
(January 1, 1998 = 1.00)		

Required: Use the data to calculate the value of the ending inventory in the years 1998 and 1999.

E10–20 Dollar-Value Retail LIFO

Trey's Fishing and Camping Store uses the dollar-value retail LIFO method to value its inventory. Trey's adopted this method on January 1, 1998, when the price index was 1.00. During 1998, its sales were $390,000, and in 1999 they were $430,000. The price index was 1.10 at the end of 1998 and 1.20 at the end of 1999. Trey's was forced to mark down its merchandise $7,000 in 1998 and $10,000 in 1999. The following information can be obtained from the records:

	1998		1999	
	Cost	Retail	Cost	Retail
Inventory, 1/1	$ 16,000	$ 24,000		
Purchases	250,000	400,000	$280,000	$440,000
Net markups		6,000		20,000

Required: Find the cost of the ending inventory in each of the years 1998 and 1999 using the dollar-value retail LIFO method.

E10–21 Dollar-Value Retail LIFO—Base Index Not Equal To 1.0

Bret's Backpacker Shop is a retailer of camping equipment. Bret opened his business about four years ago and has been very successful. At the beginning of 1998, his accountant suggested that he switch to dollar-value retail LIFO inventory valuation. At that time, Bret had inventories on hand with total retail prices of $86,000, for which he had paid $45,000. The price index on January 1, 1998, was 1.20.

Required: Use the following data to calculate the value of the inventory in the years 1998 and 1999. (Round to four decimal places.)

	1998		1999	
	COST	RETAIL	COST	RETAIL
Purchases	$210,000	$595,000	$280,000	$607,000
Net markups		1,000		13,000
Net markdowns		12,000		11,000
Sales		620,000		590,000
Current price index		1.4		1.5

E10–22 Errors

Hap Hazard, Inc., made several errors in accounting for inventory over a two-year period. In 1998, a $12,000 purchase was correctly recorded, but the inventory was not included in the inventory count. In 1999, $3,000 of goods held by Hap Hazard on consignment were included in the inventory count. No correcting entries have been made. Assume a periodic inventory system.

Required:

A. By how much is the 1999 income under- or overstated?
B. By how much is the 1999 ending inventory under- or overstated?

E10–23 Errors

Jerry L's Superstore uses a periodic inventory system. Jerry has one superstore and one superwarehouse, where all excess inventory is stored. At year-end, inventory is counted at each location to arrive at the total ending inventory. The following errors were made in the count:

1. Inventory of $40,000 was in transit from the warehouse to the store, and it was left out of both counts.
2. Inventory of $25,000 was shipped from the warehouse to the store overnight, and it was included in both counts.
3. Inventory of $15,500 was included in the count at the warehouse, but because of a billing delay, the purchase had not been recorded.
4. Inventory of $45,000 was purchased F.O.B. shipping point. Neither the merchandise nor the bill had arrived yet, so the transaction was not recorded. However, the merchandise was in transit during the count.

Required:

A. The ending inventory was calculated to be $75,000. What is the correct ending inventory?

B. The net income for the year was stated at $1,450,000. Ignore income taxes and determine the correct net income.

E10–24 Inventory Valuation Methods Compared

As of January 1, 1998, after West Products had been in operation for two years, the beginning inventory for its sole product was determined for FIFO and LIFO. Those amounts are shown below:

FIFO			LIFO		
UNITS		COST	UNITS		COST
2,000	@	$90 = $180,000	1,000	@	$85 = $ 85,000
1,000	@	$95 = 95,000	2,000	@	$90 = 180,000
		$275,000			$265,000

During 1998, West Products purchased 5,000 units at a cost of $100 per unit. A physical inventory on December 31, 1998, determined that 3,500 units remained in ending inventory. West uses a periodic inventory system.

Required:

A. For each of the methods above, determine amounts for the December 31, 1998, ending inventory and for cost of goods sold in 1998.

B. Repeat **(A)** assuming the company had 2,800 units of ending inventory instead of 3,500 units.

E10–25 Financial Analysis

Use the information shown here to compute the inventory turnover and days'-sales-in-inventory ratios for Company A and Company B.

	1997 ENDING INVENTORY	1998 ENDING INVENTORY	1998 GOODS SOLD
Company A	$100,000	$190,000	$435,000
Company B	350,000	680,000	800,000

Required:

A. Based only on these two ratios, which company appears to manage its inventory better? How did you decide?

B. What factors other than these ratios can help assess whether a company manages its inventory well? Be specific.

E10–26 Dollar-Value LIFO

Expansion Company uses dollar-value LIFO for reporting inventory. The reported inventory for January 1, 1997, and associated index for each reported layer are shown below. Note that these are the reported amounts for the layers, not the amounts at base year prices. During 1997, the company made inventory purchases totaling $10,000,000. At the end of 1997, the current cost of its ending inventory and associated price index were determined to be $1,440,000 and 1.20, respectively.

INDEX	REPORTED INVENTORY
1.00	$250,000
1.02	306,000
1.10	440,000
	$996,000

Required: Determine the amounts to report for ending inventory on December 31, 1997, and for cost of goods sold in 1997.

E10–27 Dollar-Value LIFO

South Company uses dollar-value LIFO for reporting inventory. The reported inventory for January 1, 1997, and associated index for each reported layer are shown below. Note that these are the reported amounts for the layers, not the amounts at base year prices. During 1997, the company purchased 5,000 units of its sole inventory product at a cost of $100 per unit. At the end of 1997, the current cost of its ending inventory and associated price index were determined to be $370,000 and 120, respectively.

INDEX	REPORTED INVENTORY
100	$ 85,000
110	165,000
	$250,000

Required:

A. Determine the amounts to report for ending inventory on December 31, 1997, and for cost of goods sold in 1997.

B. Repeat **(A)** assuming the amount of ending inventory at 120 above is $270,000 instead of $370,000.

PROBLEMS

P10–1 LCM Ceiling and Floor

Bayou Bargain Audio-Video Company was flooded, and some of its uninsured merchandise was damaged. The inventory will be sold after repairs are made. The following per-unit data pertain to the merchandise:

ITEM	REPAIR COST	SELLING COST	ESTIMATED SALES PRICE
Turntables	$ 45	$10	$150
CD players	100	25	385
Speakers	30	18	100
Televisions	50	20	190
VCRs	70	12	250

Desired profit is 18% of sales.

Required: Calculate floor and ceiling values for each item.

P10–2 LCM Applications

Moonman Company is a hardware distributor that groups inventory into three categories as shown. The inventory on hand on December 31, 1999, is as follows:

ITEM	UNITS	CURRENT REPLACEMENT COST	NET REALIZABLE VALUE	NET REALIZABLE VALUE LESS NORMAL PROFIT	ORIGINAL COST
Category 1:					
Hammers	400	$ 5.00	$ 6.50	$ 4.50	$ 4.00
Wrenches	850	4.25	6.00	5.00	5.50
Pliers	560	8.50	8.00	7.50	7.00
Clamps	220	11.00	14.00	11.25	12.00
Category 2:					
Sanders	50	70.00	88.00	75.00	72.00
Drills	65	45.00	56.00	42.00	50.00
Circular saws	40	120.00	110.00	94.00	125.00
Category 3:					
Caulking	325	8.00	12.00	6.00	5.00
Paint	500	4.00	8.00	4.00	6.00
Plywood	1000	17.00	15.00	10.00	8.00

Required:

A. Compute inventory value, applying LCM, item by item.
B. Compute inventory value, applying LCM to categories.
C. Compute inventory value, applying LCM to the total inventory.

P10–3 LCM Adjusting Entries

B. Johnson Drug Emporium values its inventory at the lower of cost or market. The inventory is grouped into three categories for accounting purposes. The records on December 31, 1999, revealed the following information:

ITEM	UNITS	CURRENT REPLACEMENT COST	NET REALIZABLE VALUE	NET REALIZABLE VALUE LESS NORMAL PROFIT	ORIGINAL COST
Category 1:					
A	1200	$1.50	$2.00	$1.75	$1.50
B	1550	.75	.65	.62	.62
Category 2:					
C	3250	.80	.75	.70	.95
D	800	1.20	1.55	1.18	1.45
Category 3:					
E	2000	.55	.63	.52	.50
F	2400	.25	.40	.30	.28

Inventory at January 1, 1999, had a cost of $10,000 and market value of $8,500, with the appropriate $1,500 allowance for reduction to LCM. Purchases for 1999 were $60,000.

Required:

A. Determine inventory, on an LCM basis, by category.
B. Prepare the adjusting entries required for the allowance method.

P10–4 LCM—Unit and Total Inventory, Adjusting Entries

The following records for Virginia Henry Camping Supplies have been made available to you:

ITEM	MESS KITS	CANTEENS	FLASHLIGHTS	LANTERNS
Selling price	$25	$15	$5.00	$50
Cost	20	9	3.00	35
Freight	3	2	0.25	7
Selling expense	2	2	0.05	4
Replacement cost	18	10	2.50	28
Units	50	60	75	30

Required:

A. Calculate the item-by-item inventory value, LCM, assuming the normal profit is 20% on each item.

B. Assuming beginning inventory was $3,000 and purchases were $10,000, prepare the adjusting entries required at year-end using the allowance method.

C. Prepare the adjusting entries as in (**B**) but using LCM on a total-inventory basis.

P10–5 Journal Entries—Income Statement

Luken Lore Corporation completed the following transactions during the first quarter of 1999:

Jan.	1	Had inventory on hand with a cost of $25,000, which was below the market value.
	1	Purchased inventory on credit with a quoted price of $100,000. Terms were 2/10, n/30, and purchases are recorded net.
	15	Paid $8,000 in cash for freight on the new merchandise.
Feb.	15	Paid the invoice for the merchandise.
	28	Returned defective merchandise and received a $3,000 refund.
Mar.	2	Sold merchandise for $58,000 on credit.
	15	Sold merchandise for $63,000 cash.
	18	Refunded $6,500 cash for returned defective merchandise.
	19	Repaired defective merchandise at a cost of $1,500 and returned it to the inventory to be sold as "new."
	25	Received full payment on accounts receivable.
	31	Inventory on hand had a cost of $40,000 and a market value of $38,000. Operating expenses incurred for the quarter were $18,000. Luken Lore uses the allowance method. The applicable tax rate is 25%.

Required:

A. Prepare journal entries, including adjusting entries. (Assume use of the periodic inventory method.)

B. Prepare an income statement for the first quarter.

P10–6 LCM—Unit Basis, Adjusting Entry

Hot Wax Company, a Texas record store, lost electricity for 72 hours in mid-July, and some of its merchandise was somewhat warped. Because Hot Wax specializes in hard-to-find items, however, management is confident that a slightly damaged record will not stop collectors from buying. The inventory will be sold, but at a reduced price. The following per-unit data pertain to the merchandise:

ITEM	UNITS	ORIGINAL COST	ESTIMATED SELLING COST	ESTIMATED SALES PRICE	REPLACEMENT COST
ABC	3	$ 32	$ 3	$ 18	$ 15
DEF	2	125	35	150	95
GHI	4	25	4	22	20
JKL	2	250	80	250	200
MNO	5	16	2	15	10

Desired profit is 20% of sales.

Required:

A. Calculate floor and ceiling values for each item.

B. Calculate the LCM on an item-by-item basis.

C. Make the appropriate journal entry for December 31 using the allowance method. Assume the beginning inventory was $8,000, with no accrued loss, the undamaged inventory had a cost of $5,000 and a market value of $5,400, and purchases were $50,000.

D. What if the records had been severely damaged? What entry would Hot Wax make for this inventory?

P10–7 Markups

Lacey's Hosiery, Inc., sells three types of products. Their sales prices and costs are quoted below:

ITEM	SALES PRICE	COST
N	$ 6	$ 4
Q	8	6
X	16	10

Required:

A. Calculate the markup rate for each item based on sales.

B. Calculate the markup rate for each item based on cost.

P10–8 Gross Profit

You are preparing the preliminary year-end financial reports for Morgan-Harding Company, but the inventory count has been delayed at some locations. The records do provide the following information to assist you in estimating the inventory in lieu of an actual count:

Gross sales	$250,000
Beginning inventory	40,000
Purchases	200,000
Freight-in	10,000
Purchase returns	5,000
Sales returns	25,000

Historical gross profit rate is 30% of net sales.

Required:

A. Calculate the ending inventory and cost of goods sold.

B. After completing your preliminary reports, management informs you that a new pricing policy was in effect this year. The profit rate was cut significantly to increase sales volume, and you are provided with a new estimated gross profit rate of 18%. Recalculate ending inventory and cost of goods sold.

P10–9 Gross Profit—Estimation of Loss

Rin-Tin-Tin Sheet Metal Company manufactures an ultra-thin aluminum sheeting. Unfortunately, a large batch awaiting shipping was left outdoors during an unexpected hailstorm, and much of it was dented. The aluminum was returned to raw materials inventory at a salvage value of $2,500. The accounting records provided this additional information:

Beginning inventory	$ 25,000
Items manufactured and transferred to inventory	150,000
Sales	200,000
Ending inventory in warehouse, undamaged by storm	40,000
Gross margin on sales	40%

Required:

A. Estimate the hailstorm loss.

B. What conditions would alter your answer?

P10–10 Markups

The books of Meyer Clothiers Company provide the following information:

- Item 1: Cost is $250; gross profit on sales is 45 percent.
- Item 2: Cost is $175; markup on cost is 60 percent.

Required:

A. Compute the markup on cost for Item 1.

B. Compute the sales price of Item 1.

C. Compute the sales price of Item 2.

D. Compute the gross profit, in dollars, of Item 2.

E. Compute the markup on sales, as a percentage, for Item 2.

F. What factors does a company consider when deciding how much markup over cost to charge its customers?

P10–11 Markups

Calculate the following:

1. Given: Cost is $225; markup on cost is 75 percent. Compute the sales price and the gross profit.
2. Given: Cost is $30; markup on cost is 85 percent. Compute the sales price and gross profit.
3. Given: Cost is $100; sales price is $145. Compute the markup on cost and gross profit percentage.
4. Given: Cost is $75; gross profit on sales price is 25 percent. Compute the gross profit percentage of cost.

P10–12 Fire Loss

The Boston Pops Fireworks Brigade got careless on July 4, and a fire destroyed all inventory on hand. The accounting records provided this additional information:

Beginning inventory	$ 2,000
Purchases	125,000
Sales	100,000
Markup percentage on cost	250%

Required:

A. Calculate the gross profit percentage based on sales.
B. Estimate the amount of the fire loss.

P10–13 Retail Inventory

The Hawksters are a chain of delicatessens that cater to sporting event parties. They were started five years ago by a former basketball player who could not compete any longer because of injuries. Hawksters provides you with the following data for the current year, which were obtained from the accounting records.

	COST	RETAIL
Inventory, 1/1	$ 46,000	$ 78,000
Purchases	256,000	347,000
Purchase returns	3,400	6,000
Freight-in	10,000	
Net markups		11,000
Net markdowns		4,000
Sales discounts		2,000
Sales		396,000

After discussing the operations with the owner, you learn that of the $10,000 charged to the Freight-In account, $3,600 was for delivery expenses. All the other amounts are correct.

Required: Determine the cost of the ending inventory using

A. Retail FIFO method.
B. Retail average costing method.
C. Retail FIFO LCM method.
D. Retail average costing LCM method.
E. What are the assumptions that underlie the use of the retail method of inventory estimation? Are these assumptions likely to be violated by many companies? Why is the retail method of inventory estimation a useful tool?

P10–14 Retail Inventory

Trey's Treasurehouse is a retailer of specialty merchandise. Unfortunately, its record keeping is not very good. You learn that the inventory on January 1 of the current year had a cost of $37,000 and a retail value of $56,000. You also learn that Trey's made additional markups of $28,000 during the year and subsequently had to cancel $10,000 of those additional markups. Trey's also informs you that $10,000 of markdowns were made and $1,000 of those markdowns canceled at a later date. Employee sales are recorded net of discounts. From the records, you are able to find the additional following information:

	COST	RETAIL
Purchases	$348,000	$521,000
Purchase returns	11,000	17,000
Freight-in	12,000	
Sales discounts		13,000
Sales		524,000
Employee discounts		1,000

Required: Calculate the cost of the ending inventory using the following methods:

A. Retail FIFO.
B. Retail average costing.
C. Retail FIFO LCM.
D. Retail average costing LCM.

P10–15 Inventory Costing Methods

Nouveau Corporation began business in 1998, so it had no beginning inventory that year. The following information pertains to purchases and sales for 1998 and 1999.

Purchases:

1998	UNITS	1999	UNITS
March	8 @ $100 = $ 800	February	4 @ $115 = $ 460
June	4 @ 110 = 440	June	10 @ 111 = 1,110
September	12 @ 105 = 1,260	August	15 @ 110 = 1,650
December	8 @ 112 = 896	October	9 @ 115 = 1,035

Ending inventories:

1998	1999
12 units	14 units

Required:

A. Assume a periodic inventory system. Determine the reported values for ending inventory and cost of goods sold for both years using FIFO, LIFO, and average costing.

B. The following additional information relates to the timing of company sales in 1998. (Sales price of each unit is $150.)

1998	
May	6 units
August	6 units
October	8 units

Assuming a perpetual inventory system, determine the reported values for ending inventory and cost of goods sold in 1998 using FIFO, LIFO, and average costing.

C. Explain the results in (**B**).

P10–16 Dollar Value LIFO

Jackson Manufacturing uses the dollar-value LIFO method to value their inventory. Jackson provides the following information:

	1995	1996	1997	1998
Inventory, Jan. 1	21,000			
Inventory, Dec. 31	25,200	34,200	36,000	42,900
Current price index	1.05	1.14	1.2	1.3
(Jan. 1, 1995 = 1.00)				

Required: Use the data above to calculate the value of the ending inventory in each of the years 1995 through 1998.

P10–17 Retail Dollar-Value LIFO

The Memphis Warehouse Corporation uses the dollar-value retail LIFO method to value its inventory. You have found the following data in its records. Memphis began using LIFO on January 1, 1997, when the price index was 1.00.

	1997		1998		1999	
	COST	RETAIL	COST	RETAIL	COST	RETAIL
Inventory, Jan. 1	$ 5,000	$ 8,000				
Purchases	118,014	180,000	$146,060	$221,000	$152,460	$240,000
Net markups		4,500		3,000		2,000
Net markdowns		2,940		6,000		0
Sales		175,000		178,110		206,850
Current price index		1.12		1.21		1.28
(Jan. 1, 1997 = 1.00)						

Required: Use the above data to find the value of the ending inventories for the years 1997, 1998, and 1999, respectively, using the dollar-value retail LIFO method.

P10–18 Errors And Their Effects

Williams is a new employee at Baker Furniture Co. Williams has been familiarizing himself with Baker's accounting by reviewing some prior-months working papers, including the estimation of inventory for October and November 1999. Baker uses a calendar year-end.

In his review, Williams found that Baker inadvertently computed ending inventory for both October and November using an incorrect cost-to-retail percentage for each month. The employee who had done the computations had computed a retail-to-cost percentage rather than a cost-to-retail percentage in each month.

Williams has gone to his supervisor with the error after computing the amount by which inventory was wrong in each month. She told Williams that the error did not matter, even though Williams thinks that the amount of error is material for Baker.

Required:

A. Is inventory as of October 31, 1999, over- or understated? What about November 30, 1999, ending inventory? How can you tell?

B. Is Williams' supervisor correct when she states that the error does not matter? Why or why not?

P10–19 Retail Dollar Value LIFO—Layer Liquidation

The Texas Produce Corporation uses the dollar-value retail LIFO method to value inventory. Over the last few years, its business has been growing steadily. Sales have increased each year over the last year, but inventories have fluctuated erratically. The results are shown below:

	1995		1996		1997	
	COST	RETAIL	COST	RETAIL	COST	RETAIL
Inventory, Jan. 1	$ 15,000	$ 20,000				
Purchases	140,000	220,000	$150,000	$241,000	$187,200	$290,000
Net markups		3,000		5,000		2,000
Net markdowns		13,000		6,000		4,000
Sales		180,000		250,000		260,000
Current price index (Jan. 1, 1995 = 1.00)		1.12		1.25		1.28

Required: Using the data, calculate the value of the ending inventory in 1995, 1996, and 1997, respectively. (Use two decimal places in the cost-to-retail ratio.)

P10–20 Retail Dollar Value LIFO—Layer Liquidation

The Mississippi River Barge Company is a wholesaler of products used in river transportation. At the beginning of 1995, it switched to the dollar-value retail LIFO method of inventory valuation. Operating results for the last three years are shown here:

	1995		1996		1997	
	COST	RETAIL	COST	RETAIL	COST	RETAIL
Inventory, Jan. 1	$ 35,000	$ 47,000				
Purchases	160,000	275,000	$180,000	$275,000	$225,000	$310,000
Net markups		14,000		4,000		15,000
Net markdowns		11,000		6,000		5,000
Sales		260,000		268,000		280,000
Current price index (Jan. 1, 1995 = 1.00)		1.12		1.25		1.32

Required: Using the data, calculate the value of the ending inventories for the years 1995, 1996, and 1997, respectively. (Use four decimal places in the cost-to-retail ratio.)

P10–21 Retail LIFO—Price Index Not Equal To 1.00

Lush Landscaping Corporation uses the dollar-value retail LIFO method to value inventory. It adopted this method in 1995 when the price index was 1.10.

	1997		1998		1999	
	COST	RETAIL	COST	RETAIL	COST	RETAIL
Inventory, Jan. 1	$ 15,000	$ 25,000				
Purchases	114,000	180,000	$135,000	$215,000	$150,000	$252,000
Net markups		3,000		4,000		3,000
Net markdowns		1,000		9,000		5,000
Sales		175,000		195,000		215,000
Current price index		1.34		1.42		1.49
Base price index = 1.1						

Required: Calculate the ending inventory values at the end of 1997, 1998, and 1999 using the dollar-value retail LIFO. (Use four decimal places in the cost-to-retail ratio.)

P10–22 Retail LIFO—Price Index Not Equal To 1.00

Sam's Surfing and Sails was established in 1995. It has always used the dollar-value retail LIFO method to value its inventory. At the end of 1995 when it prepared its first set of financial statements, the relevant price index was 1.12. Sam's provides the following data for the last three years.

	1997		1998		1999	
	COST	RETAIL	COST	RETAIL	COST	RETAIL
Inventory, Jan. 1	$ 40,000	$ 80,000				
Purchases	325,000	450,000	$350,000	$477,000	$350,000	$480,000
Net markups		0		12,000		22,000
Net markdowns		10,000		4,000		12,000
Sales		430,000		460,000		465,000
Current price index		1.18		1.24		1.32
Base price index = 1.12						

Required: Determine the cost of the ending inventories for each of the three years using the dollar-value retail LIFO. (Use four decimal places in the cost-to-retail ratio.)

P10–23 Errors

Presented here is an abbreviated income statement for Mr. Wrong Robotics Corporation:

MR. WRONG ROBOTICS CORPORATION
Income Statement
For the Year Ending December 31, 1998

Sales revenue		$2,000,000
Cost of goods sold:		
Beginning inventory	$ 400,000	
Add: Purchases	1,000,000	
Cost of goods available for sale	$1,400,000	
Less: Ending inventory	(250,000)	
Cost of goods sold		1,150,000
Gross margin on sales		$ 850,000
Operating expenses		400,000
Income before taxes		$ 450,000
Income taxes (40% rate)		180,000
Net income		$ 270,000

However, the following errors were made in the records:

1. $100,000 of purchases were recorded, but the inventory was in transit and was not counted. The shipping terms are FOB shipping point.
2. Mr. Wrong was selling items for May-Bee Sewing Co. on consignment. This inventory was valued at $20,000 and included in the inventory.
3. The market value of one particular robot in the ending inventory, having a cost of $6,000, soared to $15,000. The junior accountant thought that this holding gain was "too significant not to write up the value of the inventory," so he did.
4. New inventory of $10,000 was included in the count, but only a 10 percent down payment was recorded in the purchases.

Required: Prepare the corrected income statement.

RESEARCH ACTIVITIES

R10–1 Ethics and Research—LIFO Purchasing and Ethics (CMA Adapted) Nason Corporation manufactures and distributes a line of toys for adolescent boys and girls, preschool children, and infants. As a consequence, the corporation has large seasonal variations in sales. Nason issues quarterly financial statements, and first-quarter earnings were down from the same period last year.

During a visit to the preschool and infant division, Nason's president expressed dissatisfaction with the division's first-quarter performance. As a result, John Kraft, the division manager, felt pressure to report higher earnings in the second quarter. Kraft was aware that Nason Corporation uses the LIFO inventory method, and he instructed the purchasing manager to postpone several large inventory orders scheduled for delivery in the second quarter. Kraft knew that the use of older inventory costs during the second quarter would cause a decline in the cost of goods sold and thus increase earnings.

During a review of the preliminary second-quarter income statement, Donna Jensen, division controller, noticed that the cost of goods sold was low relative to sales. Jensen analyzed the Inventory account and discovered that the scheduled second-quarter material purchases had been delayed until the third quarter. Jensen prepared a revised income statement using current replacement costs to calculate cost of goods sold. She submitted the income statement to John Kraft, her superior, for review. Kraft was not pleased with these results, insisting that the second-quarter income statement remain unchanged. Jensen tried to explain to Kraft that the interim inventory should reflect the expected cost of the replacement of the liquidated layers when the inventory is expected to be replaced before the end of the year. Kraft did not relent and told Jensen to issue the income statement using the LIFO costs. Jensen is concerned about Kraft's response and is contemplating what her next action should be.

Required:

A. Determine whether or not the actions of John Kraft, division manager, are ethical, and explain why or why not.

B. Referring to specific standards of *Statements on Management Accounting Number 1C (SMA1C),* "Standards of Ethical Conduct for Management Accountants,"

1. Describe the specific standards that would apply in Donna Jensen's evaluation of the actions of her superior, John Kraft.
2. Recommend a course of action that Donna Jensen should take in proceeding to resolve this situation.

R10–2 Decision—Accounting Method for Consignment Merchandise

Linden Corporation is a retailer of specialty products used in oil field operations. Its products are sold through a network of representatives and dealers who take the products on a consignment basis from Linden. In addition, Linden carries a substantial inventory of its own.

Required: Assume that the merchandise on consignment owned by Linden represents a material portion of its total inventory. What is the proper method of accounting for these inventories and their subsequent sale?

R10–3 Financial Research

Find a recent annual report for ***McDonald's Corporation.*** From this report, determine the company's inventory turnover and average days to sell. In your opinion, does McDonald's have a relatively high or low turnover? What aspects of its business contribute to this turnover? Briefly explain your answers.

R10–4 Motorola—Financial Analysis

Examine the 1995 annual report for ***Motorola*** in Appendix C.

Required:

A. What inventory valuation method does Motorola use?
B. Determine the company's inventory turnover and average days to sell.
C. Does the turnover seem reasonable, given Motorola's business environment? Why or why not?

R10–5 Database Financial Analysis

Using a financial database, choose one industry. Determine the inventory valuation method used by the companies in that industry. For each company in the industry, calculate the inventory turnover ratio and compare it to the average of all the companies in the industry. Answer the following questions:

Required:

A. Do all companies use the same valuation method? Which methods are predominant?
B. For those companies that do not use the predominant method in the industry, how would the inventory turnover ratio change if they switched to the predominant method for the industry?
C. What reasons can you suggest for the individual companies to use a method other than the predominant one for the industry?

R10–6 Financial Research

Identify the large retail firms in any financial database (i.e., those with SIC codes that start with 5, except eating and drinking firms). For each firm, list the most recent quick ratio, current ratio, inventory balance, current asset balance, and percentage of inventory to current assets. What impact does inventory have on the liquidity of this industry?

R10–7 Internet Activity

Access the SEC database EDGAR. Identify four companies that use the same inventory valuation method. Compare the inventory turnover for all the companies, and suggest reasons why they may be different.

R10–8 Internet Activity

Access any financial database with which you have become familiar. Select any five companies, and calculate the current ratio for each. Then, calculate the percentage of current assets represented by the inventory for each company. Then, calculate the percentage of total assets represented by the inventory of each company. Suggest some reasons why these percentages should differ among the companies.

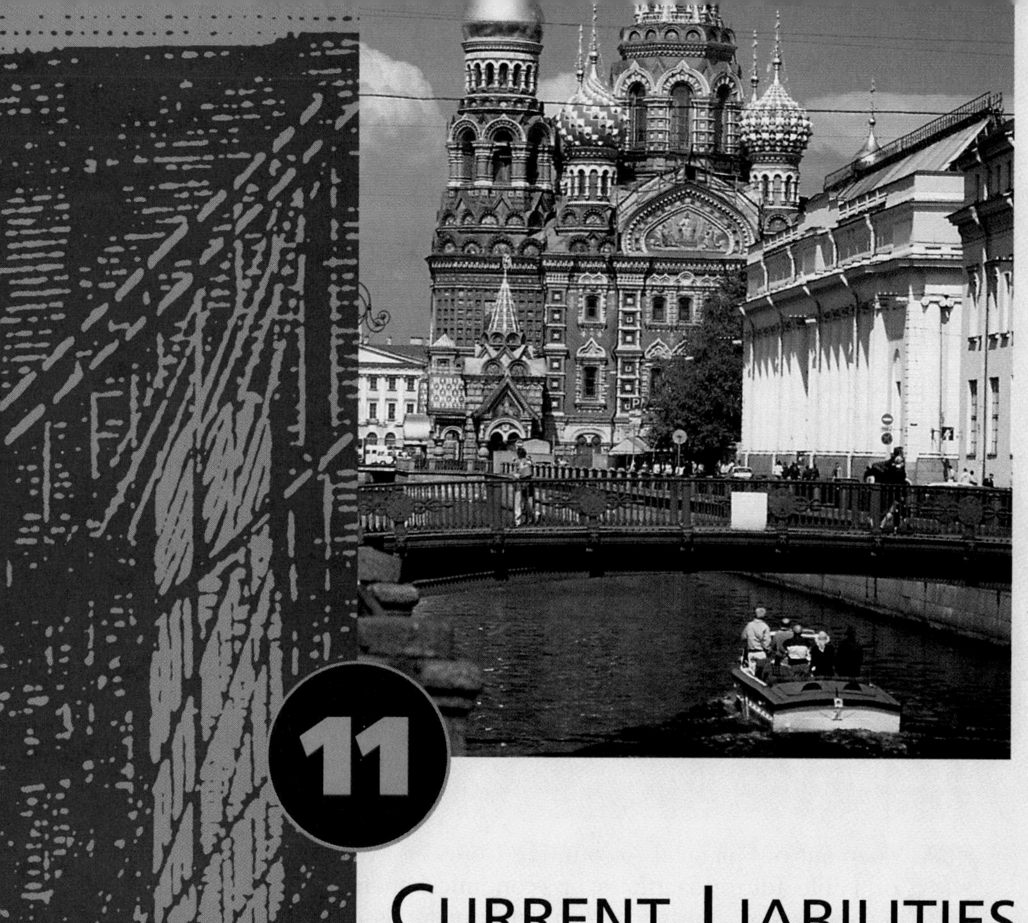

11

CURRENT LIABILITIES

LEARNING OBJECTIVES

After studying this chapter, you should be able to:

1. State the criteria for proper classification of current liabilities.
2. Explain the basis of measurement of current liabilities.
3. Apply the various methods of accounting for contingent liabilities.
4. Illustrate the accounting requirements for determinable current liabilities.
5. Use current liabilities in financial analysis and liquidity considerations.

Contingent Liabilities—Actual Liabilities

A Nevada jury added $10 million in punitive damages to $4.1 million in compensatory damages it assessed against Dow Chemical Company in the first silicone breast-implant trial Dow Chemical had faced on its own.

Dow Chemical, a co-owner of longtime implant manufacturer Dow Corning Corporation, had previously gone on trial with Dow Corning. But Dow Corning now is in federal bankruptcy-reorganization proceedings, and thousands of women now are bringing their lawsuits solely against Dow Chemical.

Dow Chemical shares fell 87.5 cents to $69.875 in New York Stock Exchange trading yesterday.

If the verdict stands, it opens up a new and potentially costly front in the silicone breast-implant litigation. Since Dow Corning is in Chapter 11 proceedings, it is essentially protected from the full brunt of the litigation. However, Dow Chemical had been regarded as relatively tenuous because it didn't manufacture the devices.

Source: Thomas M. Burton, "Dow Chemical is Ordered to Pay Punitive Damages in Implant Trial," *The Wall Street Journal,* October 31, 1995, p. B7.

Statement of Financial Accounting Concepts No. 6 defines **liabilities** as probable future sacrifices of economic benefits arising from present obligations of a particular entity to transfer assets or provide services to other entities in the future as a result of past transactions or events.[1] The FASB further identified three essential characteristics of a liability:

1. There is a present duty or responsibility to one or more entities that requires settlement by a probable future transfer or use of assets at a specified or determinable date, or occurrence of a specified event, or on demand.
2. The enterprise has little or no discretion to avoid the future sacrifice.
3. The underlying transaction or event causing the obligation has already occurred.

Put another way, a liability exists when (1) an entity has a probable obligation to transfer assets to another entity on demand or on a specified date, (2) the obligation realistically cannot be avoided, and (3) the obligation arose as a result of a past transaction or event. Recognition of a liability does not require that the recipient of the transfer be known, but merely that an obligation exists. For example, the specific recipients of future warranty benefits may be unknown at the time of sale of warranted products, but a liability is deemed to exist.

Further, the obligation need not be absolute, only probable. Given such arguable terms as "probable," it is not surprising that implementation of these concepts raises many questions, most notably, questions regarding the measurement and timing of liability recognition.

[1]*Statement of Financial Accounting Concepts No. 6,* "Elements of Financial Statements," FASB, December 1985, par. 35.

The opening excerpt from *The Wall Street Journal* concerning ***Dow Chemical*** and its potential liability for silicone breast implants is an example of recognition and measurement of a liability. Dow Chemical was thought to be immune from litigation because it did not actually manufacture the implants. However, if Dow is held liable, it could prove to be very costly. Some questions regarding liabilities are clearly answered in the authoritative literature. But many, such as in the Dow case, continue to require a great deal of judgment by management and the accountant. In this chapter, we discuss liabilities of various origins and the special accounting problems posed.

NATURE AND CLASSIFICATION OF LIABILITIES

State the criteria for proper classification of current liabilities.

Liabilities can be classified as either current or noncurrent, depending on their settlement date. **Current liabilities** require settlement within one year or one operating cycle, whichever is longer. Furthermore, classification as a current liability requires that settlement be from existing current assets or the creation of new current liabilities. An **operating cycle** is the length of time that it takes to obtain or manufacture a product, sell it, and collect the proceeds of the sale. The cycle may be relatively short, as in a retail department store, or relatively long, as in a liquor distillery. **Noncurrent liabilities** include those obligations whose settlement extends beyond one year or operating cycle.

Classification of a liability as current or noncurrent is very important; it affects the computation of net working capital, as well as various liquidity ratios such as the current ratio and the acid-test (or quick) ratio. The classification also provides a very different signal or message to users of financial statements relative to prediction of future cash flows.

Classification of a liability as *current* decreases net working capital and liquidity ratios and implies greater short-term corporate risk. This could negatively affect the firm's ability to borrow on a short-term basis. Conversely, if some obligations are classified as *noncurrent,* solvency ratios may be negatively affected. Thus, proper classification and measurement of liabilities is extremely important to financial statement users.

MEASUREMENT OF CURRENT LIABILITIES

Explain the basis of measurement of current liabilities.

In theory, liabilities should be measured at the present value of the future transfers of assets required to settle an obligation. However, in practice, current liabilities are often recorded at face value (or maturity value) because of their short-term nature. The difference between the face value and the present value of most current liabilities usually is not material.[2]

The existence and amount of some liabilities may be uncertain. These are referred to as **contingent liabilities** and are resolved when one or more future events occur or fail to occur. When both the existence and amount of a liability are definite, it is known as a **determinable current liability**. In the following sections, we discuss recognition and measurement of both contingent and determinable liabilities.

[2]Paragraph 3 of *APB Opinion No. 21,* "Interest on Receivables and Payables," indicates that payables arising from transactions with suppliers in the normal course of business are exempted from measurement on a present value basis.

CONTINGENT LIABILITIES

Apply the various methods of accounting for contingent liabilities.

A *contingency* is defined in SFAS No. 5 as "an existing condition, situation, or set of circumstances involving uncertainty as to possible gain (**gain contingency**) or loss (**loss contingency**) to an enterprise that ultimately will be resolved when one or more future events occur or fail to occur."[3] The accounting issues involved with contingencies are related to the measurement and the timing of their recognition.

Gain contingencies are not recognized until (and if) the gains are realized. Loss contingencies may be related to asset impairments or may result in the incurrence of a liability. Impairment of an asset means a loss in its value, such as the inability to collect a receivable, or the expropriation of property. These types of loss contingencies result in decreased asset value and not in a liability to a third party; therefore, no liability is recorded when the loss is recognized. However, loss contingencies resulting in obligations to third parties result in liabilities.

Determination of the existence and the amount of the liability is difficult and requires judgment. An example can be found in the case of ***Union Carbide*** and the Bhopal, India, chemical plant disaster in 1984. Over $3 billion in damages were claimed in numerous lawsuits pending against Union Carbide as a result of the accident; yet no accruals for damage awards were made by Union Carbide.

While it was clear that Union Carbide would suffer some amount of financial loss because of the Bhopal accident, the amount of the loss was not certain, and therefore none was recognized and accrued prior to 1987. Even the amounts recognized in 1987 and 1988 were for litigation expenses, not

IN PRACTICE—GENERAL

Contingent Liabilities at Union Carbide

Note 17 of the 1984 annual report of Union Carbide discussed the contingent liability resulting from the chemical plant disaster as follows: "While it is impossible at this time to determine with certainty the outcome of any of the lawsuits described above, in the opinion of management, based in part on the advice of counsel, they will not have a material adverse effect on the consolidated financial position of the Corporation. In the opinion of management, based in part on the advice of counsel, *no charge or accrual is required for any liabilities or any impairment of assets that may result from lawsuits described above relating to the Bhopal plant.*"

On November 2, 1987, *The Wall Street Journal* reported, Union Carbide Corp. and the Indian government appeared near a settlement in their bitter legal wrangling over compensation of victims of the 1984 Bhopal poison gas disaster. Sources close to both sides indicated that the settlement is likely to call for Carbide to pay the victims between $500 million and $600 million. The Indian government had sued for $3 billion in compensation. Last year, Carbide offered to pay $350 million.

Further, on January 13, 1988, *The Wall Street Journal* reported that Union Carbide Corp. planned an $85 million pretax charge against 1987 fourth-quarter earnings for possible litigation costs, primarily related to the Bhopal disaster. Carbide took a litigation-contingency charge of $185 million before taxes in 1985. . . . The charges reflect reserves for litigation expenses but not possible damage awards.

[3] *Statement of Financial Accounting Standards No. 5,* "Accounting for Contingencies," FASB, 1975, par. 1.

for damage awards. Apparently, in the judgment of management, no further accruals were necessary.

SFAS No. 5 provides for three possible methods of accounting for loss contingencies: (1) accrual of a liability, (2) disclosure in the notes to the financial statements, or (3) no disclosure. The correct method of accounting depends upon the likelihood of the future, confirming event occurring and the ability to reasonably estimate the amount of the liability. In SFAS No. 5, the FASB stated that "the likelihood that a future event or events will confirm the loss or impairment of an asset or the incurrence of a liability can range from probable to remote."[4] The FASB used the following definitions:

- **Probable**—The future event(s) is likely to occur.
- **Reasonably Possible**—The chance of the future event(s) occurring is more than remote but less than likely.
- **Remote**—The chance of the future event(s) occurring is slight.

A loss contingency should be recognized and accrued by a charge to expense and a liability recorded only if both of the following conditions are met:

1. Information available prior to the issuance of the financial statements indicates that it is *probable* that a liability has been incurred at the date of the financial statements.
2. The amount of the loss can be reasonably estimated.

If a range of possible loss amounts exists and the liability is deemed probable, a liability and loss must be recorded in an amount equal to the most likely amount in the range. If all figures within the range are equally likely, the lower bound of the range must be recorded. It is not necessary that the exact date or the exact recipient of the obligation be known, but it must be probable that a liability has been incurred and that the amount can be reasonably estimated.

If a loss is only reasonably possible instead of probable, then footnote disclosure is required. If the probability of the loss is remote, no disclosure is required. Interpretations of the terms *probable, reasonably possible,* and *remote* require a great deal of judgment by management and the accountant. Write-downs of assets (especially those resulting from impairment) require judgment in the determination of both the amount and the timing of the loss recognized.

Exhibit 11–1 indicates the three possible ways of dealing with contingent losses: (1) accrual as a liability, (2) footnote disclosure only, or (3) ignoring them. If the loss is probable and can be reasonably estimated, it should be accrued. A reasonable estimate can mean a range as well as a specific amount.

We should point out here that it is becoming increasingly difficult and dangerous both to the company and to the accountant not to disclose a contingent liability. As society has become more litigation-conscious, even remotely possible loss contingencies are candidates for disclosure. The authors are of the opinion that all material events that may affect a company's performance should be disclosed, so that the users of the financial statements will have information to make more informed judgments and decisions.

[4]Ibid., par. 5.

EXHIBIT 11–1
Accounting for Contingencies

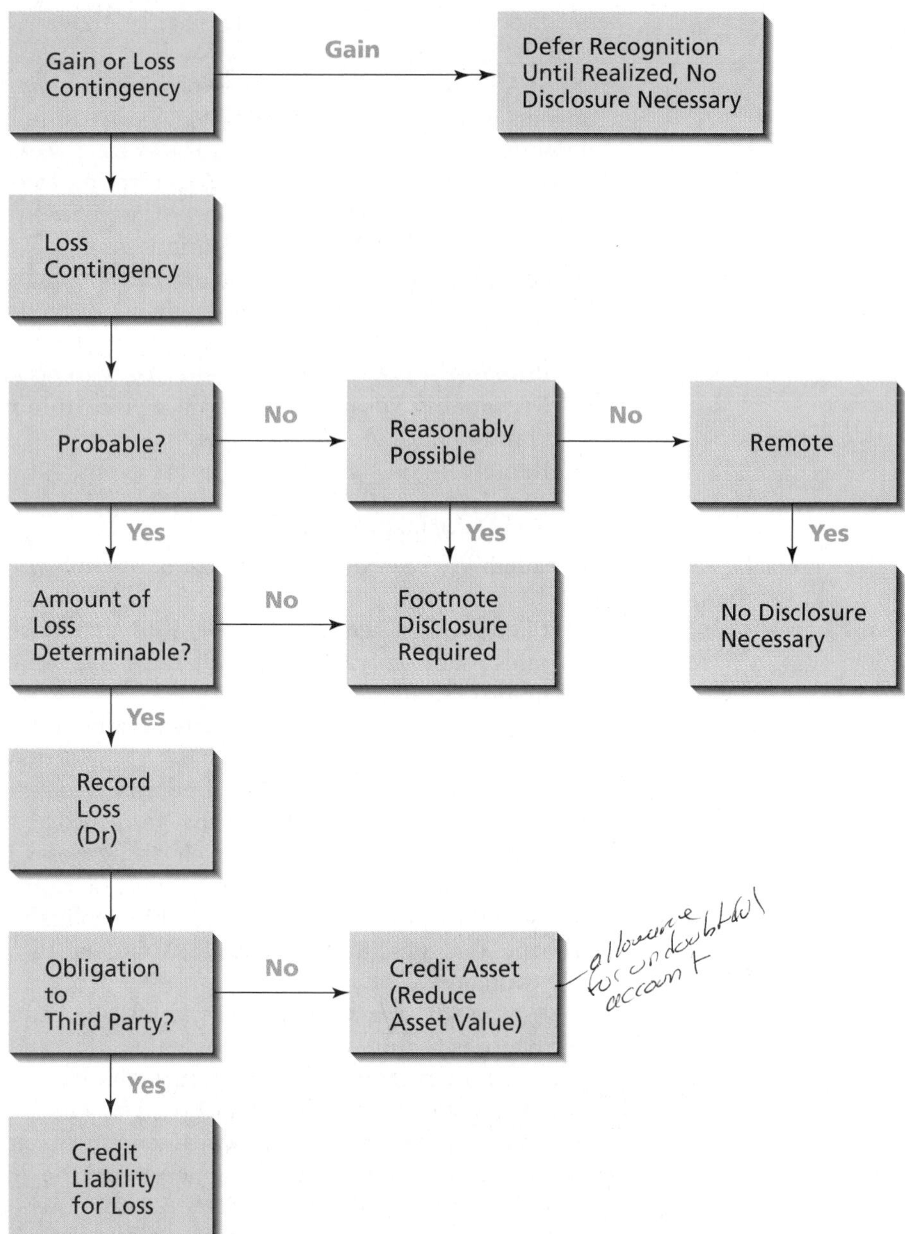

CONTINGENT LIABILITIES THAT ARE ACCRUED AS EXPENSES

Other types of contingent losses that are probable and can be reasonably estimated are accrued in the normal course of business. These include losses related to receivables, product warranties, and premiums offered to customers. In these cases, the probability of the loss is fairly certain, and the amount of the loss is typically estimable.

ETHICS IN PRACTICE

Loss Contingencies

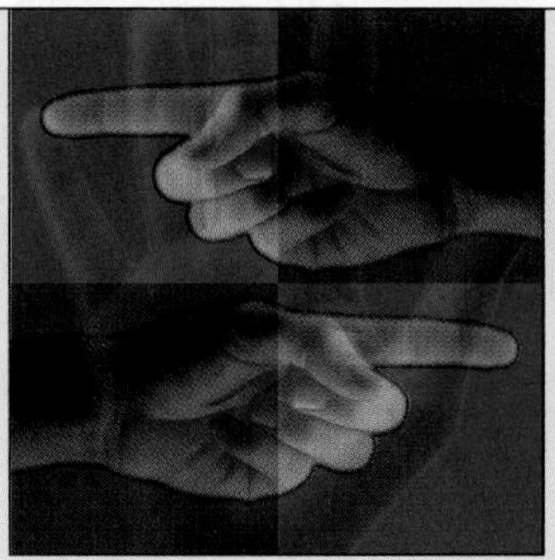

Valuation of the accounting for and disclosure of litigation, environmental liabilities, pending and potential product liability claims, and other loss contingencies often present difficulties to the accountant. These contingencies pose difficulties because of the judgment required and the lack of information available for (1) assessing the probability of loss, and (2) making a reasonable estimate of the amount. In cases that are borderline, management will frequently opt for disclosure in the most favorable light.

CONCEPT Expenses versus losses.

LOGIC Although these typically accrued contingencies fit the concept of loss contingencies, they are usually recorded as operating **expenses** rather than losses in an attempt to match costs with associated revenues.

Thus, bad debts expenses, warranty expenses, and premium expenses are recorded for contingent losses related to receivables, product warranties, and premium offers, respectively. Classification as expenses rather than losses is primarily semantic and focuses upon classification of income statement items. The impact on net earnings is not affected. Recognition of contingent bad debts relates to asset impairment and was discussed in Chapter 8. Recognition of warranty and premium expenses relates to contingent liabilities and is discussed in the following sections.

While the above contingencies are usually accrued and recorded as expenses, other loss contingencies may also be recognized depending upon the circumstances. These include threats of expropriation, guarantees of indebtedness of others, actual or possible assessments, obligations of commercial banks under "standby letters of credit," and agreements to repurchase receivables (or other property) that have been sold. The impact of these events are recognized as losses (not expenses) when they meet the accrual requirements portrayed in Exhibit 11–1. Otherwise, they warrant either footnote disclosure or nonrecognition.

Product Warranties and Guarantees. A warranty or guarantee is a promise by a manufacturer (or other seller) of a product to ensure the quality or performance of the product for a specified period of time. Most familiar are warranties for automobiles, appliances, and other similar products. The In Practice feature about ***Chrysler Corporation's*** warranty costs illustrates how significant these costs can be. Warranties entail future costs that are loss contingencies. There are two methods of accounting for warranty costs, the cash basis and the accrual basis. The accrual basis is required by GAAP unless the difference between the two methods is not material.

IN PRACTICE—GENERAL

Chrysler Warranty Costs

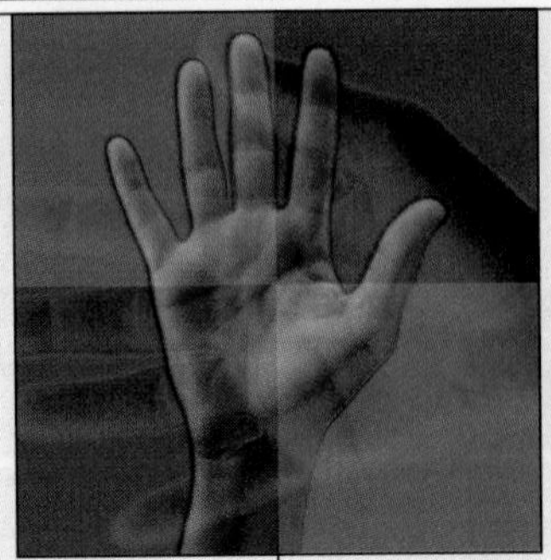

Chrysler planning documents indicate that ***Chrysler Corporation's*** costs for providing warranty-covered repairs have shot up 48% per vehicle over the past two years.

... This year Chrysler expects to spend $2.38 billion, or $959 for each vehicle it sells in 1995, on warranty repairs. That is up from $1.91 billion, or $763 a vehicle, last year and $1.45 billion, or $647 a vehicle, in 1993. . . .

Jerome B. York, the vice chairman of ***Tracinda Corporation***, has made an issue of Chrysler's warranty costs, arguing that more effective management of them would free cash that the car company could use to enhance shareholder value. Tracinda, the investment vehicle of investor Kirk Kerkorian, is Chrysler's biggest shareholder, with a 14.1% stake. York, a former Chrysler chief financial officer, was hired as Kerkorian's chief strategist in a possible bid for control of the No. 3 automaker.

Source: Angelo B. Henderson and Oscar Suris, "Chrysler Documents Show Sharp Rise in Costs for Warranty-Covered Repairs," *The Wall Street Journal*, October 23, 1995, pp. A4–5.

The cash-basis method of accounting for warranty costs recognizes warranty costs as expenses in the period in which the costs are incurred. The cash method is justified on the basis of materiality and convenience. It is used in cases where the warranty costs are immaterial or when the warranty period is less than a year. The cash-basis method is required for income tax purposes. Differences in income for tax purposes and income for financial reporting purposes may arise if the cash-basis method is used for tax purposes, while the accrual-basis method is used for financial reporting.

The accrual-basis method of accounting for warranty costs is consistent with the matching concept and revenue-recognition principle. This method requires recognition of the estimated liability in the period in which the product is sold. The accrual-basis method follows either (1) the expense method or (2) the sales method. The **expense method** is used when the warranty and the sales price are considered inseparable. The **sales method** is used when the sales price can be separated into sales revenue and warranty revenue. The sales method is appropriate for all warranties that are sold separately. For example, extended warranties on autos, stereo equipment, or appliances should be accounted for using the sales method. The expense method assumes all profit is earned from selling the product. The sales method assumes some profit is from sale of the warranty.

The expense and sales warranty treatments are illustrated in Exhibit 11–2. With the expense method, estimated future warranty costs are charged to current operating expense in the period of sale in conformity with the matching principle. The warranty and the sales price are considered inseparable, and the warranty expense is matched against the sales revenue in the period of sale. If all benefits (revenues) from a sales transaction are recorded in one year, then all expenses also must be recorded in that same year to effect revenue-expense matching. This results in an estimated future liability for the warranty being recognized in the period of sale. As the warranty work is performed, the cost is offset against the liability account. At the expiration of the warranty period, all future obligations for warranty repairs and work expire. Any balance remaining in the Warranty Liability account should be transferred to a revenue account and recognized as income. This is illustrated as entry number 5 in Exhibit 11–2.

EXHIBIT 11–2 Accrual Method of Accounting for Warranty Costs

Assumed Data

1. One hundred computers were sold at $2,000 each in 1997.
2. Warranty repairs made in 1997, $2,500.
3. Estimated future liability for warranty costs of 1997 sales, $22,500.
4. Warranty repairs made in 1998 on 1997 sales, $15,000.

EXPENSE WARRANTY METHOD			SALES WARRANTY METHOD*		
1. One hundred computers were sold at $2,000 each in 1997.					
Cash or Accounts Receivable	200,000		Cash or Accounts Receivable	200,000	
Sales		200,000	Sales		175,000
			Unearned Warranty Revenue		25,000
2. Warranty repairs made in 1997.					
Warranty Expense	2,500		Warranty Expense	2,500	
Cash, Various Accounts		2,500	Cash, Various Accounts		2,500
			Unearned Warranty Revenue	2,500	
			Warranty Revenue		2,500
3. Recognize future estimated liability for warranty costs of 1997 sales.					
Warranty Expense	22,500				
Estimated Liability Under Warranty		22,500			
4. Warranty repairs made in 1998 for 1997 sales.					
Estimated Liability Under Warranty	15,000		Warranty Expense	15,000	
Cash, Various Accounts		15,000	Cash, Various Accounts		15,000
			Unearned Warranty Revenue	15,000	
			Warranty Revenue		15,000
5. Recognize remainder of warranty revenue at end of 1998.					
Estimated Liability Under Warranty	7,500		Unearned Warranty Revenue	7,500	
Warranty Revenue		7,500	Warranty Revenue		7,500

*Assumes computers are sold for $1,750 each and warranty contracts are valued at $250 each.

In the sales method, the selling price is separated into sales revenue and unearned warranty revenue. The unearned warranty revenue is a deferred revenue or liability. As the warranty service is performed (that is, as costs are incurred), the warranty revenues are considered realized and are therefore recognized. This is consistent with revenue recognition and matching. Revenue earned and the expense incurred to generate the revenue are recognized when the revenue is realized. At the end of the warranty period, any deferred warranty revenue that has not been expensed should be recognized as earned. In many industries, such as the automobile industry, profit is generated not only from the sale of the product but also from the sale and servicing of the warranty contract. In those instances, deferred warranty revenue recognized at the point of sale may exceed estimated future warranty costs.

The two methods result in the same aggregate net income across time. Note, however, that although net income is the same, the sales method reports less revenue and correspondingly less expense on the income statement in the first year. In the second year, the sales method reports more revenue and a correspondingly greater amount of expense on the income statement.

Premiums and Coupons. Premiums and coupons are used by manufacturers to increase sales and market share of their products. A **premium** may be the right to obtain products such as silverware or pots and pans. **Coupons** usually entitle the buyer to a cash discount at the time of purchase. A variation of the cash discount coupon is a cash rebate from the manufacturer, which entitles the buyer to a refund when he or she sends in the rebate coupon, the Universal Product Code symbol from the product's packaging, and the store receipt.

The purpose of all these offers is to stimulate sales. To achieve proper matching of revenue and expense, the cost associated with premium or coupon offers should be included as an expense of the period in which the sale is made and revenue recognized. All premiums and coupons redeemed in the same period in which the sales are made are properly expensed in that period. However, all anticipated redemptions arising from the sales also should be included as expenses in the period of sale. Anticipated redemptions are loss contingencies that are probable and reasonably estimable. Therefore, an expense should be recognized and a liability established in the period of sale.

Exhibit 11–3 illustrates accounting for premium offers. The cost of the premiums is treated like another inventory account. The premiums (utensils, towels, etc.) are purchased and stored until redemptions occur. As the redemptions occur, premium expense is recorded to reflect the cost of the premium issued. At the end of the period, the estimated liability for future redemptions is charged to expense and a liability established. The liability is decreased as redemptions occur in future periods.

Accounting for premiums in this manner allows recognition of the revenue and the premium expense in the period in which the sale is made, which is consistent with the matching principle. The estimated liability account appears as a current liability on the balance sheet.

The examples for warranties and premiums (Exhibit 11–3) record a liability for estimated future costs as an adjusting entry at the end of the period. Costs incurred in the year of sales are thus charged to expense. Alternatively, the expense and liability could be recognized at the time of the sale instead of at the end of the year. Then, as costs are actually incurred, the liability would be

EXHIBIT 11–3
Accounting for Premium Offers

Assumed Data:

Sunburst Orange Juice Co. offers a premium of a paring knife in exchange for $.50 and two can labels. The knives cost $.60 each, and Sunburst expects a redemption rate of 40%. Sunburst also expects to incur $.30 in postage costs for each knife sent out. Sunburst sells 50,000 cans of juice at $1.10 each, purchases 10,000 knives, and redeems 16,000 labels in the first year. Sunburst expects redemption of an additional 4,000 labels in the second year.

1. To record the sale of 50,000 cans of orange juice at $1.10 each:

Cash	55,000	
Sales		55,000

2. To record the purchase of 10,000 knives at $.60 each:

Inventory of Knives	6,000	
Cash		6,000

3. To record redemption of 16,000 can labels:

Cash	4,000*	
Premium Expense	800**	
Inventory of Knives		4,800***

**[(16,000/2) × .50] = $4,000*
***[(16,000/2) × (.60 − .50)] = 800*
****[(16,000/2) × .60] = $4,800*

Postage Expense (or Premium Expense)	2,400*	
Cash		2,400

**[(16,000/2) × .30¢] = $2,400*

4. To record estimated liability for premium offers outstanding:

Premium Expense	800	
Estimated Liability for Premiums		800

Unit sales in 1995	50,000
Estimated redemption rate	× 40%
Estimated total units redeemed	20,000
Actual redemptions to date	16,000
Estimated future redemptions	4,000

Estimated future claims value:
[(4,000/2) × ($0.60 + $0.30 − $0.50)] = $800
or (60¢ + 30¢ − 50¢)] = $800

reduced. For example, in Exhibit 11–3, the total estimated cost for premium redemptions is $4,000 [(20,000/2 × (.90 − .50)]. A $4,000 expense and liability could be recorded at the time of sale. Then, the $3,200 charge (debit) when the 16,000 labels are redeemed would reduce the liability.

DETERMINABLE CURRENT LIABILITIES

Illustrate the accounting requirements for determinable current liabilities.

In contrast to contingent liabilities, determinable current liabilities are definite in amount. The amount of the payment necessary to settle the obligation is certain, although the exact timing of the payment may be uncertain. Determinable current liabilities are recorded and settled at their face value. The matching concept is again the underlying principle. Included in these liabilities are accounts payable, short-term notes payable, advances and deposits received, accrued liabilities, dividends payable, collections for third parties, revenues received in advance, compensated absences, current maturities of long-term debt, and obligations refinanced.

ACCOUNTS PAYABLE

Accounts payable are amounts owed for the purchase of goods and services on open account. These liabilities arise because of the time lag between the delivery of the goods and services and settlement of the account. Payment terms vary in practice, although suppliers frequently allow cash discounts for early payments. Discount terms of 2/10, n/30, or some variation, are fairly common. Measurement of the amount of the liability poses no particular problem. Opportunities for errors occur mainly with the purchase of merchandise at or near the end of an accounting period. Transactions for inventory purchases near the cutoff date should be examined carefully to determine ownership of merchandise in transit.

NOTES PAYABLE

Current liabilities for *notes payable* include trade notes, short-term loan notes, and current maturities of long-term debt.

Trade Notes Payable. Suppliers of goods and services sometimes require *trade notes payable* instead of open accounts for purchases. Trade notes usually are interest-bearing and reported at face value.

Determination of whether to record a note at its face value or present value depends on the difference between the stated rate of interest and the current market rate of interest, and the term of the note. If the difference between the stated interest rate and the market rate is not material, the note is recorded at its face value. If the interest rate stated on the note departs significantly from the market interest rate, the liability should be recorded at its present value. The difference between the present value of the note and the face value is the *discount,* and it is recorded as a contra account to the note payable called *Discount on Note Payable.* The discount is amortized over the life of the note using the effective-interest method. This process is similar to the amortization of discount described in Chapter 8 for notes receivable.

In firms that have operating cycles longer than one year (such as shipbuilding and distilleries), notes with maturities of two to three years could be classified as current liabilities. Since there can be a material difference between the present value and the face amount of the note, these liabilities should be reported at their present value.

Short-Term Loan Notes Payable. Noninterest-bearing notes payable to financial institutions are recorded slightly differently. The financial institution usually remits cash to the borrower in an amount less than the face value of the note. This is referred to as discounting the note payable.[5]

To illustrate, assume that Carnes Inc. has its one-year, $10,000, noninterest-bearing note discounted at Hibernia Bank at 8% on October 1. Carnes records the following journal entry:

Cash	9,200	
Discount on Notes Payable	800	
Notes Payable		10,000

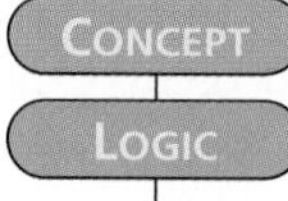

Recognition and measurement of a liability.

Carnes incurs a liability in the amount of $10,000. The liability is measured at the present value of future obligations. That present value is the cash value received, $9,200.

While the stated rate of interest is 8%, the effective rate is actually 8.696% ($800/$9,200), because Carnes has available for use only $9,200, not $10,000. Assuming no material difference between the straight-line and effective-interest methods, the choice is made to record the interest expense by amortizing the discount on a straight-line basis in monthly increments of $66.67 with the following journal entry:

Interest Expense	66.67*	
Discount on Notes Payable		66.67

**$800 ÷ 12 months = $66.67*

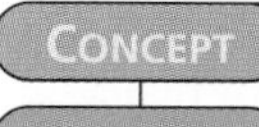

Recognition of expense.

The discount of the note is a prepaid expense (interest) that is allocated to expense in a systematic and rational manner over the life of the note. In this example, the allocation method used is the straight-line method.

At December 31, the balance in the Discount on Notes Payable account is $600 [$800 − (3 × $66.67)], and it is deducted from notes payable in the "Current Liabilities" section of the balance sheet:

Current liabilities:		
Notes payable	$10,000	
Less: Discount on notes payable	600	$9,400

[5]Notice the different usage of the terms *discount* and *discounting* for these different types of notes payable. For trade notes payable, the discount refers to the difference between the face of the note and the present value of the note. The discount is a contra account that is amortized over the life of the note.

For short-term loan notes payable, *discounting of the note* is the practice of the bank or other financial institution. The lender withholds the full amount (like prepaid interest) and remits to the borrower the face value of the note less the amount of the discount.

CURRENT MATURITIES OF LONG-TERM DEBT

Long-term debt that is due within the next 12 months is classified as a current liability unless one of the following conditions exists:

1. It is to be retired using assets that have been classified as noncurrent.
2. It is to be refinanced from the proceeds of a long-term debt issue.
3. It is to be converted into capital stock.

If one of the above three conditions exists, then the liability should remain in the "long-term liability" classification with either parenthetical or footnote disclosure of the plan for liquidation. The underlying rationale for this treatment is that these debts will be settled without using existing current assets.

REFINANCING SHORT-TERM OBLIGATIONS

Current liabilities are expected to be settled by use of current assets during the next year or operating cycle. Accordingly, financial statement users try to decide whether expected future cash flows from operations and current assets will be adequate to meet these needs. This is an element of short-term corporate risk analysis. If, instead, current liabilities are intended to be refinanced with long-term debt or equity-security offerings, these liabilities should be excluded from the current liability section. Exclusion from the current liability section is proper only if the following criteria are met:

1. The enterprise intends to refinance on a long-term basis.
2. The enterprise has the ability to refinance on a long-term basis, evidenced by the following:
   a. The long-term debt or equity securities are issued after the balance sheet date but before the balance sheet is issued, or
   b. A financing agreement is entered that permits the enterprise to refinance the short-term obligation on a long-term basis.[6]

If the long-term debt or equity securities are issued in the post-balance-sheet period (after the balance sheet date but before the balance sheet is issued), as in (2a) in the preceding list, the amount excluded from the current liability section may not exceed the proceeds of the new securities offering. For example, assume Carnes Corporation had $10 million of long-term debt currently due and intended to refinance $8 million of this debt through the issue of preferred stock. If the refinancing occurred in the post-balance-sheet period, $2 million of the debt would be classified as current and the other $8 million as long-term.

If a financing agreement is relied upon to demonstrate ability to refinance, as in (2b) in the preceding list, all of the following conditions must be met:

1. The agreement must be noncancellable and must not expire within one year of the balance sheet date or one operating cycle, whichever is longer.
2. The company must not be in violation of any provisions of the agreement at the balance sheet date or issue date.
3. The lender or investor must be financially capable of honoring the agreement.

[6]*Statement of Financial Accounting Standards No. 6,* "Classification of Short-Term Obligations Expected to Be Refinanced," FASB, 1975, par. 11.

The amount excluded from current liabilities and classified as long-term cannot exceed the amount available under the financing agreement.[7]

DIVIDENDS PAYABLE

Dividends can be in the form of cash, stock, or property. Once declared, cash and property dividends are current liabilities because they require distribution of resources of the enterprise within the current operating cycle. The liability is created by the board of directors on the date of declaration and settled on the date of payment. Stock dividends do not require distribution of enterprise resources but rather a distribution of additional shares of stock, representing a reclassification of retained earnings to permanent capital. Stock dividends distributable are in a transition stage of the reclassification process and appear as part of shareholders' equity, not in the liability section.

Dividends do not accrue and are not considered liabilities until declared by the board of directors. Cumulative preferred stock requires that all *dividends in arrears* (accumulated but undeclared dividends) be settled (paid) before any dividends may be paid to the common shareholders. Dividends in arrears are disclosed in the footnotes or parenthetically in the capital stock section but are not liabilities. Dividends are discussed in depth in Chapter 19.

ACCRUED LIABILITIES

Accrued liabilities represent expenses incurred but not yet paid. A familiar example would be for wages earned through the end of the accounting period but paid in the following period. An adjusting entry at the end of the accounting period is necessary to properly match revenue and expense of the current period. Other examples of accrued liabilities include compensated absences (vacation, sick leave, holidays), payroll taxes, and interest. *Compensated absences* are absences from employment for which the employee will be paid. SFAS No. 43, "Accounting for Compensated Absences," requires employers to accrue a liability for compensation for future employee absences if the following conditions are met.

1. The employer's obligation relating to employees' rights to receive compensation for future absences is attributable to employee services already rendered.
2. The obligation relates to rights that vest or accumulate.
3. Payment of the compensation is probable.
4. The amount can be reasonably estimated.[8]

[7]Any restrictions or limitations on the funds obtained in the refinancing indicating that the full amount will not be available to retire the short-term obligations requires a corresponding reduction of the amount reclassified as a long-term liability. Finally, the amount of short-term debt excluded from current liabilities may not exceed a reasonable estimate of the minimum amount expected to be available for refinancing. If the amount expected to be available is a fluctuating amount, then the minimum available must be used. This could occur if the financing agreement was based on inventory or receivables pledged as collateral for the loan. Because the pledged assets fluctuate in value, the minimum loan value must be used as the basis for reclassification of current liabilities as long-term.

[8]*Statement of Financial Accounting Standards No. 43*, "Accounting for Compensated Absences," FASB, 1980, par. 6.

If the amount cannot be reasonably estimated (condition no. 4 above) but the other conditions are met, the obligation should be disclosed in a note to the financial statements.

SFAS No. 43 requires accrual of a liability for sick pay that is vesting. Vested rights require payment of unused sick pay upon termination of employment and are not contingent upon future illness and absence from employment. If the sick pay is nonvesting, employees receive the benefit only in the event of illness. If the sick pay is not used, it is forfeited. The FASB allows, but does not require, accrual of a liability in this instance, even though the number of sick days is usually subject to a reasonable estimate based upon prior experience. Accordingly, employers are still allowed to charge the sick pay to expense as it is incurred if it is nonvesting.

Exhibit 11–4 illustrates accrual of liabilities for compensated absences for vacation and vesting sick pay. Note that the liability was accrued in 1997 at the wage rate ($100 per day) prevailing in 1997. When the vacation and sick days are used in 1998, the required payment is at 1998 wage rates of $120 per day. This necessitates an additional expense of $20 per day in 1998.

ADVANCES AND DEPOSITS

Payments in advance from customers create obligations to provide goods or services in the future. Accrual accounting does not record revenue when cash is received (as does the cash-basis method of accounting), but rather revenue is recognized when it is earned (typically upon delivery of the goods or services). If the goods or services are not provided, then there is an obligation to return the advance. When the advance is received, an Unearned Revenue account is usually credited as the liability.

Cash	4,000	
Unearned Revenue		4,000

CONCEPT Recognition of liability.

LOGIC A future obligation for goods or services is incurred upon the receipt of the cash; therefore, a liability is recognized.

When the revenue is earned, the following entry is recorded:

Unearned Revenue	4,000	
Revenue Earned		4,000

CONCEPT Recognition of revenue.

LOGIC Revenue is recognized when the goods or services are provided.

Deposits are received from customers to ensure against loss or damage to property held by the customer. An obligation is created to return the deposit

EXHIBIT 11–4
Accounting for Compensated Absences

Assumptions

1997	a.	Ten new employees paid $100 per day.
	b.	Each employee earns two weeks of vacation beginning after first full year.
	c.	Each employee earns five vested sick days beginning after first full year.
1998	a.	Rate changes to $120 per day.
	b.	All ten employees take two-week vacations.
	c.	Thirty sick days used.

Journal Entries Required for 1997

12/31	Wage & Salary Expense	15,000	
	Vacation Pay Payable		10,000*
	Sick Pay Payable		5,000**
	To accrue vacation and sick pay.		

**$100 × 10 days × 10 employees*
***$100 × 5 days × 10 employees*

Journal Entries Required for 1998

During Year	Vacation Pay Payable	10,000	
	Sick Pay Payable	3,000	
	Wage and Salary Expense*	2,600	
	Cash		15,600
	To pay vacation and sick days earned in 1997, but paid at 1998 rates.		

Computations:
*Sick Days: ($120 − $100) × 30 = $ 600
Vacation days: ($120 − $100) × 100 = 2,000
Total = $2,600

$100 × 10 × 10 = $10,000
30 days × $100/day = $3,000
$120 × 130 days = $15,600

12/31	Wage & Salary Expense	18,000	
	Vacation Pay Payable		12,000*
	Sick Pay Payable		6,000**
	To accrue vacation and sick pay.		

*$120/day × 10 days × 10 employees = $12,000
**$120/day × 5 days × 10 employees = $6,000

upon return of the property in an undamaged state. If the customer forfeits the deposit because of damages to the property, the liability is offset against the cost of repairs. For example, if Smith were holding a $5,000 deposit from Black, and Black forfeited the deposit because equipment was damaged resulting in $6,000 of repairs, Smith would make the following journal entry:

Accounts Receivable—Black	1,000	
Liability for Deposits	5,000	
Cash, Various Accounts		6,000

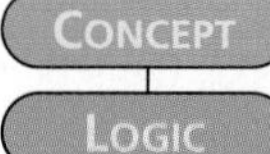

CONCEPT Settlement of a liability.

LOGIC If a deposit is forfeited because of damages, the liability is settled in that the deposit is applied to repair the damages. Further, Smith would attempt to collect the extra $1,000 in repair damage from Black and therefore recognize a receivable from Black.

COLLECTIONS FOR THIRD PARTIES

Taxes collected from customers and amounts withheld from employees create liabilities until those amounts are remitted.

Sales Taxes. Sales taxes collected from customers must be remitted monthly or quarterly to local or state governments. Sales tax may be separated at the time of sale or may be included in the total sales figure until remitted to the taxing authority.

As an example, assume Irwin Inc. has sales for the month of June of $150,000. The state sales tax rate is 4 percent, and the local sales tax rate is an additional 4 percent. If Irwin records the sales tax separately, the following entry is appropriate:

Cash or Accounts Receivable	162,000	
State Sales Tax Payable		6,000
City Sales Tax Payable		6,000
Sales		150,000

When the tax is remitted to the proper authorities, Irwin will remove the liabilities and credit Cash.

If Irwin includes the sales tax as part of the sale, the journal entry to record sales would be as follows:

Cash or Accounts Receivable	162,000	
Sales		162,000

When Irwin remits the tax to the proper authorities, sales will be reduced as follows:

Sales	12,000*	
Cash		12,000

**$162,000 ÷ 1.08 = $150,000;*
$162,000 − $150,000 = $12,000

Payroll-Related Taxes and Withholdings. Employers are liable for certain payroll taxes on all wages paid to employees and also for any amounts withheld from employees to be paid to a third party. Payroll taxes include the employer's share of the Federal Insurance Contribution Act (FICA), state unemployment insurance, and federal unemployment taxes. These taxes are expenses of the current period and, consistent with the matching principle, are accrued when the payroll is incurred. Periodically, they are remitted to the proper authority.

Under the current laws, employers and employees each must make FICA contributions of 7.65% of the first $62,700 in wages earned after which the rate drops to 1.45%. The current Federal Unemployment Tax Act (FUTA) requires a tax equivalent to an effective rate of 0.8% of the first $7,000 in wages paid to each employee. The federal tax rate is 6.2% less a credit for state unemployment tax paid at a standard rate of 5.4%. The state unemployment rates differ based on the unemployment patterns in each state.

Federal and state income tax and FICA tax are required to be withheld from employees' salaries. Other amounts withheld, such as union dues, insurance premiums paid by employees, or any other authorized payroll deduction, create liabilities at the time they are deducted from the payroll. The liability is settled at the time the funds are remitted to the proper agency.

As an example, suppose Brown has a total payroll of $30,000 for six employees. Brown withholds $3,000 in federal income tax, $2,500 in state income tax, $2,295 (7.65% × $30,000) in FICA tax, and $185 in union dues. In addition, Brown would recognize additional payroll tax expense for FICA tax, FUTA tax, and state unemployment tax for the payroll tax amounts that must be paid. Assuming that none of the employees exceeds the limit on any of the taxes, the proper journal entries would be

Account	Debit	Credit
Payroll Expense	30,000	
Federal Income Tax Payable		3,000
State Income Tax Payable		2,500
FICA Tax Payable		2,295
Union Dues Payable		185
Cash		22,020
Payroll Tax Expense	4,155	
FICA Tax Payable		2,295*
FUTA Tax Payable		240**
State Unemployment Tax Payable		1,620***

**7.65% × $30,000 = $2,295*
***.8% × $30,000 = $240*
****5.4% × $30,000 = $1,620*

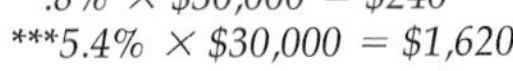

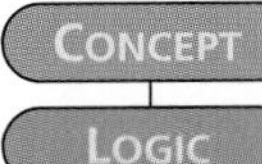

Concept: Recognition of expense and liability.

Logic: Payroll provides benefits in the current period; therefore, expense is recognized in the current period. The amounts withheld from employees are liabilities that must be remitted to the proper authorities. The payroll taxes apply to wages earned in the current period and are therefore recognized as expense in the current period. These taxes are obligations to an outside party until they are remitted. Both the payroll taxes and the amounts withheld from employees are classified as current liabilities because they are payable within one year.

LIABILITIES DEPENDENT ON OPERATIONS

Determinable liabilities dependent on periodic income include income taxes, bonus arrangements, and profit-sharing plans. These liabilities are usually measured as percentages of annual income or some other measure of operating results.

Income Taxes Payable. A corporation's liability for income taxes is based on periodic taxable income following government tax regulations. To the extent these obligations are not paid, the income taxes payable should be reported as current liabilities. Determination of this liability is complicated by many factors, including previous estimated prepayments for income taxes and temporary differences between taxable income and income for financial reporting. Chapter 17 is concerned with income tax.

Proprietorships and partnerships are not taxable entities, and thus, tax liabilities do not appear on the proprietorship and partnership statements. Instead, the individual owners and partners are subject to personal income tax on their share of the entity income.

Bonus and Profit-Sharing Arrangements. Many enterprises reward key employees with bonuses or profit sharing at year-end. These arrangements can take many forms, but they frequently are based on some form of income, and the accountant often is requested to determine the proper amount of the distribution.

Bonuses and profit sharing are additions to wages and salaries of the enterprise and are treated as expenses in determination of periodic income. The amount of the payment is dependent on the terms of the agreement. Several examples of bonus plans are illustrated in Exhibit 11–5.

For any bonus or profit-sharing plan, the calculated amount is recorded as an expense of the current period, and a liability is established and reported on the balance sheet as a current liability. The proper journal entry would be

Bonus and Profit-Sharing Expense	XXX	
Bonus and Profit-Sharing Payable		XXX

When the bonus is paid, the proper journal entry would be

Bonus and Profit-Sharing Payable	XXX	
Cash		XXX

FINANCIAL ANALYSIS

Use current liabilities in financial analysis and liquidity considerations.

Recognition and measurement of current liabilities is very important to corporate risk analysis and specifically to analysis of liquidity and financial flexibility. Because current liabilities are used to determine net working capital, they also affect two important liquidity ratios, the current ratio and the quick (acid-test) ratio. *Net working capital* is defined as current assets minus current liabilities. The *current ratio* and *acid-test* (or quick) *ratio* are computed as follows:

EXHIBIT 11–5
Bonus Plan Examples

Assumptions

Income before bonus and tax is $100,000.
Income tax rate is 30%.
Bonus rate is 10%.

Examples:

Case 1: Bonus based on income before tax, before bonus.

$$B = .10 \times 100{,}000 = \underline{\underline{\$10{,}000}}$$

Case 2: Bonus based on income before tax, after bonus.

$$\begin{aligned} B &= .10\,(100{,}000 - B) \\ B &= 10{,}000 - .1B \\ 1.1B &= 10{,}000 \\ B &= 10{,}000/1.1 = \underline{\underline{\$9{,}091}} \end{aligned}$$

Case 3: Bonus based on income after tax, before bonus.

$$\begin{aligned} B &= .10\,(100{,}000 - T) \\ T &= .30\,(100{,}000 - B) \\ B &= .10\,[100{,}000 - .30\,(100{,}000 - B)] \\ B &= .10\,[100{,}000 - 30{,}000 + .3B] \\ B &= 7{,}000 + .03B \\ .97B &= 7{,}000 \\ B &= 7{,}000/.97 = \underline{\underline{\$7{,}216}} \end{aligned}$$

Case 4: Bonus based on income after tax, after bonus.

$$\begin{aligned} B &= .10\,(100{,}000 - B - T) \\ T &= .30\,(100{,}000 - B) \\ B &= .10\,[100{,}000 - B - .30\,(100{,}000 - B)] \\ B &= .10\,[100{,}000 - B - 30{,}000 + .3B] \\ B &= 7{,}000 - .07B \\ 1.07B &= 7{,}000 \\ B &= 7{,}000/1.07 = \underline{\underline{\$6{,}542}} \end{aligned}$$

Net Income Calculations for Each Case:

	CASE 1	CASE 2	CASE 3	CASE 4
Income before bonus	$100,000	$100,000	$100,000	$100,000
Bonus	(10,000)	(9,091)	(7,216)	(6,542)
Income before tax	$ 90,000	$ 90,909	$ 92,784	$ 93,458
Income tax (30%)	(27,000)	(27,273)	(27,835)	(28,037)
Net income	$ 63,000	$ 63,636	$ 64,949	$ 65,421

$$\text{Current Ratio} = \frac{\text{Current Assets}}{\text{Current Liabilities}}$$

$$\text{Quick Ratio} = \frac{\text{Current Assets} - \text{Inventories} - \text{Prepaids}}{\text{Current Liabilities}}$$

Both of these ratios are used as measures of current debt-paying ability and short-term risk. Existing and potential creditors, for example, use these ratios in decisions to extend short-term credit. Normal standards for the current ratio and the quick ratio vary with the industry. Revenue streams in the utility industries are more stable than those for certain manufacturers and retailers of seasonal or cyclical products. Consequently, these ratios for the utility industry may be significantly lower than for such manufacturers or retailers.

For any given company, creditors may be reluctant to extend short-term credit (or increase short-term credit lines) if these ratios do not meet industry standards. If this source of borrowing is closed, financial flexibility is reduced and the borrower may be forced to seek alternative financing such as long-term notes or even equity financing.

Enterprises at times have made efforts to "clean up" their balance sheets at the end of the period. This may include an attempt to improve the current ratio by reduction of short-term debt. As an example, assume that the Ward Oil Company had current assets of $20 million and current liabilities of $12 million as follows:

CURRENT ASSETS:		CURRENT LIABILITIES:	
Cash	$4,000,000	Accounts payable	$8,000,000
Trading securities	3,000,000	Notes payable	4,000,000
Receivables	4,000,000		
Inventory	8,000,000		
Prepaids	1,000,000		

Ward's current ratio is

$$\text{Current Ratio} = \frac{\$20,000,000}{\$12,000,000} = 1.667$$

Assume that the norm in Ward's industry is 2:1. If Ward is concerned about being below the standard, Ward might consider paying some of the liabilities with the cash and securities on hand. If Ward paid $5 million of the liabilities, the ratio would become

$$\text{Current Ratio} = \frac{\$20,000,000 - \$5,000,000}{\$12,000,000 - \$5,000,000} = 2.14$$

This same result could be accomplished if Ward were able to classify some of the current liabilities as long-term liabilities. That is one reason why it is so important to properly classify short- and long-term liabilities.

END-OF-CHAPTER REVIEW

SUMMARY

1. **State the criteria for proper classification of current liabilities.** Liabilities are probable future sacrifices of economic benefits arising from present obligations to transfer assets or provide services in the future as a result of past transactions. Liabilities can be either current or noncurrent. Current liabilities require settlement within one year or the operating cycle, whichever is longer, and the settlement must be made by using existing current assets or by creating new current liabilities.

2. **Explain the basis of measurement of current liabilities.** Current liabilities are typically recorded at their face value because the difference between the present value and face value is usually not material. Some current liabilities are definite or certain in amount (determinable), and others may be uncertain in amount and timing of payment (contingencies and estimated items).

3. **Apply the various methods of accounting for contingent liabilities.** Contingent liabilities are those for which the amount, timing, and perhaps the existence are uncertain. These liabilities are dependent on the occurrence or nonoccurrence of a future event to establish the amount or timing of their payments. The accounting issues involved relate to the manner and timing of recognition. Loss contingencies are recognized if the loss is probable and the amount of the loss can be reasonably estimated. If the loss is reasonably possible, note disclosure is required. If the probability of the loss is remote, no disclosure is required.

   Contingent liabilities that require recognition and accrual of a liability include product warranties and guarantees and premium and coupon offers. Accounting for product warranties can be on a cash basis or an accrual basis. The cash-basis method charges the warranty costs to the period in which the cost occurs, and it is justified on the basis of materiality and convenience. The accrual-basis method requires recognition of the estimated expense and estimated liability in the period in which the product is sold. The accrual-basis method can follow either the expense method or the sales method. The sales method is proper when a portion of the total selling price can be attributed to the warranty. The expense method is proper if the sale and warranty are considered inseparable. Premium and coupon offers are contingent liabilities that also require accrual of a liability.

4. **Illustrate the accounting requirements for determinable current liabilities.** Determinable current liabilities include accounts payable, notes payable, current maturities of long-term debt, dividends payable, accrued liabilities, advances and deposits, collections for third parties, and amounts withheld from employees. The amount of the obligation for each of these is certain, and in most cases, the timing of the payment is also certain. Other determinable current liabilities are dependent on operations of the business to establish the amount of the obligation. Examples of these include income taxes, bonus arrangements, and profit-sharing plans.

5. **Use current liabilities in financial analysis and liquidity considerations.** Current liabilities affect net working capital, the current ratio, and the quick ratio. Proper classification between current and noncurrent liabilities is important. If current liabilities are understated, the appearance of greater liquidity results. If current liabilities are overstated, the appearance of poor liquidity may result, thereby removing a source of funding from the enterprise.

KEY TERMS

accrual-basis method of accounting for warranty costs *582*
cash-basis method of accounting for warranty costs *582*
contingent liabilities *577*
coupons *584*
current liabilities *577*
determinable current liability *577*
gain contingency *578*
liabilities *576*
liquidity ratios *594*
loss contingency *578*
noncurrent liabilities *577*
operating cycle *577*
premium *584*
warranty *581*

ASSIGNMENT MATERIAL

CASES

C11–1 Ethical Considerations

Washburn Enterprises has current liabilities of $40 million to be reported on its 1997 balance sheet. Mary Johnson, the head of financial accounting, is concerned because the current ratio will be less than 2:1 and thus violate one of the covenants of a long-term note payable in the amount of $30 million. Violation of this debt covenant would enable the holder of the note to demand immediate payment in full, and the lender has indicated its intention to exercise this right.

Johnson has discussed the situation with the chief financial officer (CFO), who has instructed her to take the following actions:

1. Reclassify $5 million of long-term investment as short-term.
2. Immediately liquidate $10 million of short-term debt by using existing cash and certificates of deposit.
3. Reclassify an existing note due in 1998 from current to long-term notes payable. The amount of the note is $4 million.

Johnson is not entirely comfortable with these actions, but the CFO has become impatient with her. During their last discussion, he alluded to "team players" and mentioned changing the roster if necessary. Because of a variety of factors, Johnson's alternative employment opportunities are limited.

Required:

A. What are the issues?
B. Who are the stakeholders?
C. What are Johnson's alternatives?
D. What would you recommend?

C11–2 Ethical Considerations—Classification of Debt

John Travis is in the midst of a heated discussion with his CPA concerning bonds that are due within the next year. The CPA has advised him that these obligations must be classified as current liabilities, but Travis does not wish to do so. "Doggone it, Parks," he says to the CPA, "you know very well I can't take the financial statements to the bank like that. The current liabilities would be so large, they would violate the terms of the loan package we just negotiated. Besides, we've had those bonds on the balance sheet as long-term liabilities for over 10 years. There's absolutely no reason to change them now."

Parks patiently explained (again) that while these particular bonds indeed had always been classified as long-term, the classification had to change this year because the maturity date was on June 1 of the following year.

Required:

A. Is it possible to exclude these bonds from classification as a current liability? If so, under what circumstances?
B. If it is possible to exclude these bonds from the current liabilities, does Parks have an obligation to tell Travis how it would be possible to do so?
C. If you do not think Parks has an *obligation* to tell Travis how to have these bonds excluded from current liabilities, do you believe that he *should* tell Travis how to have them excluded?
D. Do you think Parks has any obligation to the bank?

C11–3 Ethical Considerations—Propriety of Loans

Wendy Cantrelle is a senior accountant with a large CPA firm. She is currently participating in the audit of a large contractor and thus reviewing several financing arrangements between the contractor and a local bank. The loans that concern her seem to be quite complex. For example, in one loan arrangement, the contractor borrowed $2 million by signing an 18%, five-year note payable at Capital Bank. The loan was to purchase property for development. The property was subsequently purchased for a total of $1.1 million. Cantrelle has asked several times why the contractor borrowed $2 million for a $1.1 million purchase, but she has not yet received a satisfactory answer.

She also questioned another transaction that occurred at the same time as the property purchase. The contractor purchased two apartment buildings for a total of $700,000 from an individual named Allison Bogus. Bogus is the vice-president for Commercial Lending of Capital Bank. Similar apartment buildings were currently selling at less than $100,000 each when buyers could be found. When Cantrelle asked the contractor about the apartment buildings, he simply said it was "poor judgment" on his part.

Required:

A. Is there a problem here about which Cantrelle should be concerned?
B. How would you advise Cantrelle?

C11–4 Financial Analysis—User-Oriented

SFAS No. 6 permits a short-term obligation to be excluded from current liabilities provided that the enterprise has the ability and intent to refinance the obligation on a long-term basis. The existence of a financing agreement that clearly allows the short-term obligation to be refinanced on a long-term basis is one means of demonstrating that ability.

Assume that in 1996 ***Blockbuster Video*** has in place a financing arrangement with Suncoast Financial Corporation that will allow Blockbuster to replace $20 million of short-term financing with long-term notes payable. The long-term notes would mature in $1 million increments beginning at the end of the fifth year.

Among the various standard clauses of this financing arrangement is one that allows Suncoast to demand payment in full on the entire balance of the notes. This clause indicates that Suncoast can demand payment in full if Blockbuster misses an interest or principal payment, or if Suncoast otherwise has reason to believe that Blockbuster is financially insecure. Suncoast insists on these terms in all of its financial arrangements. It also has occasionally demanded acceleration of the payment schedule, as when the borrower was on the verge of bankruptcy.

Required: Discuss the ramifications of this clause on the classification of the liabilities on Blockbuster's balance sheet at December 31, 1996.

C11–5 Financial Analysis—Communication, Written Report

Expert Systems is a fast-growing computer software company that is very labor-intensive. Most of its growth in revenue has been financed through debt, because the founder of the company has steadfastly refused to relinquish any control or to issue any equity securities. As a result, Expert's debt classified as current is approximately $30 million in 1997, and its long-term debt is approximately $70 million. Expert has approximately $20 million in current assets, including about $5 million in inventory, $2 million in cash or near-cash items, and the remainder in receivables.

Expert's annual sales last year were $180 million, and net income of $5 million was reported. Included in the income were charges for depreciation of $10 million, and amortization of $15 million. Expert has an immediate problem for 1998. A note payable currently included in the $70 million of debt in the amount of $25 million will be due and payable on March 15, 1999. Expert would like to refinance this obligation on a long-term basis, but finding a source of financing is proving difficult.

Required:

A. Why would prospective lenders be reluctant to provide financing?

B. Assume you are the chief financial officer of Expert. Prepare a loan proposal that you believe will be satisfactory to a prospective lender.

C11–6 Financial Analysis—Report Preparation

Pagach Corporation has $30 million of long-term bonds payable that mature in the next year. Pagach intends to retire $5 million and refinance the remaining $25 million. Pagach has entered a financing agreement with Seminole Securities for the placement of $25 million in 14% bonds that will mature in 10 years. Pagach expects to issue the new bonds and retire the old ones on March 1, which is in the post-balance-sheet period.

One of the clauses in the financing agreement states that Pagach "will maintain net working capital of $12 million. Violation of this provision at any time during the period the bonds are outstanding will give Seminole the right to accelerate payment at Seminole's option."

Required: Prepare a report that addresses the following:

A. Of what significance is this clause to the financing agreement? to the financial statements of Pagach?

B. Suppose that Pagach has net working capital of $14 million at the present time. How should the $30 million of long-term bonds appear on the 1995 balance sheet?

C. Suppose that Pagach has net working capital of only $8 million. How should the $30 million of long-term bonds appear on the 1996 balance sheet?

C11–7 Integrative Liquidity Case

The following page shows financial data items that apply to Woodrow Wilson Wholesalers.

Wilson wants to borrow $2,500,000 with a two-year note payable at your bank. Wilson has offered to pay 15% annual interest. Your cost of funds is currently 5%, and your prime lending rate is 8%.

Required: Based on the above information, should you make the loan? Justify your position. What other information would be useful?

WOODROW WILSON FINANCIAL DATA

(IN THOUSANDS OF DOLLARS)	1997	1998
Cash	$ 1,200	$ 2,500
Investments—Trading securities	0	5,000
Accounts receivable (net)	5,000	3,200
Notes receivable (short-term)	800	2,000
Inventories (average LCM)	5,000	2,300
Total current assets	$12,000	$15,000
Property, plant & equipment (net)	$ 4,000	$ 3,200
Intangible assets	1,000	1,300
Total assets	$17,000	$19,500
Trade accounts payable	$ 2,400	$ 4,500
Accrued interest payable	100	100
Other accrued liabilities	500	1,400
Notes payable	5,600	4,700
Current maturities of long-term debt	1,400	300
Total current liabilities	$10,000	$11,000
Long-term notes payable	$ 500	$ 2,000
Long-term bonds payable	2,500	5,000
Total long-term liabilities	$ 3,000	$ 7,000
Total liabilities	$13,000	$18,000
Total equity	$ 4,000	$ 1,500
Total liabilities and equity	$17,000	$19,500
Sales	$18,000	$19,000
Cost of goods sold	15,000	16,900
Gross profit	$ 3,000	$ 2,100
Operating expenses	3,600	4,700
Income from operations	$ (600)	$ (2,600)
Interest expense	(1,100)	(1,900)

QUESTIONS

Q11–1 At what value are current liabilities recorded and why?

Q11–2 What conditions are necessary for classification as a current liability?

Q11–3 Explain why proper classification of a liability is important.

Q11–4 What distinguishes determinable current liabilities from contingencies and estimated liabilities?

Q11–5 How does a trade note payable differ from a short-term loan note payable?

Q11–6 Distinguish between *effective* interest rate and the *stated discount* rate for a short-term bank loan.

Q11–7 Under certain circumstances, long-term debt that is due within the next year or operating cycle continues to be classified as long-term debt. What are those circumstances? Explain the rationale that allows classification as long-term liabilities instead of current liabilities.

Q11–8 Explain the difference between vesting and nonvesting sick pay. Why are they treated differently for accounting purposes?

Q11–9 Why are gain contingencies accounted for differently than loss contingencies?

Q11–10 Why do advances and deposits from customers result in liabilities?

Q11–11 Why should there be a difference in taxable income compared to accounting income? Provide several examples that may cause these differences.

Q11–12 Loss contingencies may or may not result in liabilities. Explain.

Q11–13 Suppose that your client has a material loss contingency from a lawsuit and the client is discussing the proper accounting treatment. You are having some difficulty explaining the options and requirements for each option. To help the client see all the options and requirements in one place, prepare a table that clearly indicates the various accounting options and the conditions for each to be used.

Q11–14 What is the essential difference between the cash-basis method of accounting for warranties and the accrual-basis method?

Q11–15 Why does the sales warranty method result in exactly the same net income as the expense warranty method?

Q11–16 Why do manufacturers use premium and coupon offers?

Q11–17 Explain why (how) proper accounting for premiums and coupons achieves a proper matching of revenue and expense.

Q11–18 What is important for liquidity considerations?

Q11–19 Your client comes to you with an unusual request; the liquidity position does not look favorable. The total current assets are $3,000,000, and the total current liabilities are $2,000,000. Included in current assets are inventories of $1,200,000. Your client asks you to suggest some steps that might be taken to improve the liquidity position. Is that proper, or ethical, for you to do?

Q11–20 Explain the relationship between liquidity and financial flexibility.

Q11–21 Why are estimated costs related to uncollectible receivables, warranties, and premium offers treated as expenses rather than losses? Is the distinction important? Why or why not?

EXERCISES

E11–1 Journal Entries

Prepare journal entries for Smyth Corporation to record the following transactions. If no journal entry is necessary, indicate the proper disposition of the transaction.

1. Purchased merchandise on account for $10,000 (assume periodic inventory).
2. Signed a promissory note with Mellon Bank on June 1. The note was in the amount of $100,000 for 12 months with an interest rate of 12%. Smyth received $100,000 cash.
3. Guaranteed payment of Jackson's loan at Chase Bank. Jackson's loan is a six-month note in the amount of $50,000, with an interest rate of 10%.
4. Received notice that a dissatisfied customer had filed suit against Smyth in the amount of $2,000,000. Smyth's attorneys indicate that some amount of loss is possible.
5. Discounted a noninterest-bearing, six-month note with First State Bank. The note had a face value of $20,000, and the bank charged a discount rate of 15%.

E11–2 Classification of Current Liabilities

The balances in selected ledger accounts at December 31, 1997, for Taylor Company follow:

1. Trade accounts payable of $22,000 (including a debit balance in the subsidiary ledger of Mattel of $3,000).
2. Notes payable of the following:
   a. $15,000, 10%, 12 months, dated June 30, 1997, with interest payable at maturity.
   b. $20,000, 8%, five years, dated April 1, 1997, with interest payable annually on April 1.
3. A deposit of $3,000 from Alexander received as a down payment for an order placed in November and scheduled for delivery in February of 1998.
4. Unpaid utility bills for December of $4,000.
5. Unpaid vested sick leave of $14,000.
6. Sales taxes collected that will be submitted in January in the amount of $6,000.

Required: Calculate the correct amount of current liabilities that should be reported at December 31, 1997, for Taylor's balance sheet.

E11–3 Short-Term Loan Notes Payable

Tiffany borrows $10,000 from Chase Manhattan Bank on March 1, 1997.

Required:

A. Assume that Tiffany signs a one-year, 15% note payable. Prepare the journal entries on Tiffany's books necessary on March 1, 1997, December 31, 1997, and February 28, 1998, the due date. Assume the accrued interest is recorded at the end of the year.
B. Without regard to the information in (1), assume that Chase Manhattan discounts Tiffany's noninterest-bearing note on March 1, 1997, at 15%. Prepare the journal entries on Tiffany's books necessary on March 1, 1997, December 31, 1997, and February 28, 1998. Assume the discount is amortized at the end of the year.
C. Explain the difference in the two sets of entries. Include in your explanation the effective interest rate in each case.

E11–4 Short-Term Loan Notes Payable

Coates Candies obtains a one-year, $50,000 loan from Sunburst Financial. To obtain the loan, Coates executed a noninterest-bearing note payable that Sunburst discounted at 18% on July 1, 1997. Coates amortizes the discount on a monthly basis.

Required: Prepare a table that illustrates the monthly amortization and the balance in the Discount account.

E11–5 Current Maturities of Long-Term Debt

Jason has a total of $42 million of debt classified as current liabilities at December 31, 1997. As you review the financial information, you discover the following details:

1. Included in the $42 million are three notes payable in the amount of $3 million each. Each of these notes originally had been classified as long-term. The maturity dates are June 1, 1998, October 1, 1998, and December 1, 1998. The notes carry interest rates of 12% each, payable annually on the maturity date anniversary. No interest has been accrued at December 31, 1997.
2. Included as part of the $42 million is $500,000 (a debit balance) that Jason paid to Jones, a supplier, as a down payment on special-order merchandise that will be delivered in July of 1998.
3. You discover that $10 million of bonds payable mature on June 30, 1998. Jason has classified these as long-term because he intends to refinance them when they mature. Upon further investigation, you learn that Jason has been diligently trying

to arrange the refinancing for at least six months. However, as of December 31, 1997, he has no commitments from any lender.

4. No liability for unused sick leave has been recorded. Employees earned 600 days of sick leave in 1997 but used only 250. Each day is equivalent to $100, and the unused days accumulate to a maximum of 180 days for each employee. No employee has reached the 180-day maximum. Any unused sick leave is paid to the employees in cash at retirement or when they leave the company.

Required:

A. Calculate the correct amount of current liabilities that should be included in the balance sheet at December 31, 1997.

B. Prepare any journal entries necessary to correct the accounts.

E11–6 Sales Taxes

Braun Shoe Stores began operations on July 1, 1997. Braun has the following monthly sales totals:

	SALES	TAX	TOTAL
July	$10,000	$ 500	$10,500
August	18,000	900	18,900
September	21,000	1,000	22,000
October	15,000	750	15,750
November	14,000	700	14,700
December	18,000	900	18,900

Assume that Braun remits the sales taxes to the city on a quarterly basis (October 1 and January 1).

Required: Prepare the journal entries to record the sales and to remit the sales taxes to the city under the following assumptions.

A. Braun records the sales taxes as part of the sale.

B. Braun records the sales taxes separately.

E11–7 Bonuses

Chris Vordick owns five yogurt parlors. He has hired a store manager for each of the five stores. As part of the managers' compensation agreement, Vordick has offered each a bonus plan. The bonus is calculated differently in each of the stores, reflecting the results of negotiations between Vordick and the various store managers. For each of the managers, the bonus rate is 10% and the tax rate is 40%.

	STORE 1	STORE 2	STORE 3	STORE 4	STORE 5
Sales	$128,000	$210,000	$170,000	$205,000	$190,000
Expenses	80,000	150,000	45,000	155,000	120,000
Operating income	$ 48,000	$ 60,000	$ 25,000	$ 50,000	$ 70,000

The bonus for Store 1 is based on income after tax and before bonus. Bonuses for Stores 2 and 5 are based on income after tax and after bonus. Bonus for Store 3 is based on income before tax and before bonus, and Store 4 is based on income before tax but after the bonus.

Required: Calculate the amount of the bonus in each of the five stores.

E11–8 Warranties

ABC Company reported net income of $90,000 for the year 1999. During a discussion with management, you realized that the company used the cash-basis method of accounting for warranty expenses. You want to restate net income using the accrual-basis method of accounting. Management estimates that the warranty cost on all 1999 sales will be $3,000, of which $1,000 has been incurred and recorded in the books.

Required: Recalculate net income for 1999 using the accrual-basis method of accounting for warranties.

E11–9 Bonuses

Jillson provides a bonus plan for its president. The president receives a bonus equal to 10% of income in excess of $200,000 after deduction of bonus and tax. If tax is 40% and income before bonus and tax is $900,000, what is the amount of the bonus?

E11–10 Deposits

AAA Rental routinely requires the customer to either pay a damage insurance premium for equipment rented or to leave a deposit at the time the equipment is rented. The deposit is returned in its entirety when the equipment is brought back undamaged. If the equipment is returned with damage or otherwise needing repairs (other than normal maintenance), the cost of the repairs is deducted from the deposit.

During July, AAA had rentals of $28,000, received $870 in insurance payments by the customers, paid insurance premiums of $620, received damage deposits of $2,200, and refunded $2,050 of the deposits. No equipment remains outstanding. One customer was assessed $150 for damages.

Required: Prepare journal entries to record these July events.

E11–11 Contingencies

The Alert Watchdog Company markets home security systems. As part of its marketing effort, it encourages customers to purchase its 24-hour monitoring service. While this service is fairly expensive, Watchdog guarantees response time to be within 10 minutes of the alarm.

Watchdog began operations in 1997 and recorded revenues of $2,000,000 from the sales of its basic system, plus $1,500,000 from customers who purchased the 24-hour monitoring service. During 1997, only one instance occurred in which Watchdog failed to respond to an alarm within the advertised 10 minutes. Unfortunately, this incident occurred at the home of an elderly couple and resulted in a severe heart attack for the homeowner.

The homeowner had filed suit for recovery of valuable paintings ($300,000), jewelry ($50,000), medical expenses ($75,000), and pain and suffering ($500,000).

Required:

A. What are the possible methods of accounting for this lawsuit?
B. Under what circumstances is each method appropriate?
C. Suppose that Watchdog's attorney indicates that a loss in the range of $250,000 to $700,000 is likely. What should Watchdog do?

E11–12 Warranties—Cash Basis and Accrual Basis

Datacom manufactures circuit boards used in electronic equipment. During 1997, the following results were obtained:

Sales	$15,000,000
Warranty repairs made relating to 1997 sales	1,000,000
Estimated total warranty claims relating to 1997 sales	1,400,000

Required:

A. Prepare journal entries for 1997 to record the above information assuming that Datacom uses the cash basis of accounting for warranty repairs.

B. Prepare journal entries for 1997 to record the above information assuming that Datacom uses the accrual-based expense warranty method of accounting for warranty repairs.

E11–13 Warranties—Accrual Basis

Assume the following data for 1997 and 1998:

	1997
Sales	$600,000
Warranty repairs made in 1997 for 1997 sales	20,000
Estimated future liability for warranties at 12/31/97	10,000
Warranty repairs made in 1998 for 1997 sales	8,000

Warranties expire at end of 1998.

Required:

A. Prepare the journal entries necessary in 1997 and 1998 for the warranties using the expense warranty method.

B. Prepare the journal entries necessary in 1997 and 1998 for the warranties using the sales warranty method. Assume 5% of the sales price is related to the warranties.

E11–14 Compensated Absences

E. D. White has a sick-pay policy that allows employees 15 sick days annually but only 5 days of vacation annually. All employees use all 20 days per year because any unused sick leave is forfeited. The vacation days do not accrue until after the employee has worked one full year, and employees are not eligible for sick leave until after one full year of employment. White has a work force of 20 full-time employees, earning an average daily wage of $150 per day in 1998 and $160 per day in 1999. All the employees have been with the company at least four years.

Required: Prepare the journal entries to

A. Accrue vacation and sick pay earned in 1998.

B. Record payment of sick pay and vacation time used in 1999.

E11–15 Compensated Absences

Assume the following:

	1997	1998
Vacation days earned	700	760
Sick days earned	240	250
Vacation days used	680	720
Sick days used	200	170
Wage rate	$15/hr.	$16/hr.

Assume also that there were no unused vacation days or sick days at the beginning of 1997. Each work day is eight hours long.

Required: Prepare journal entries in 1997 and 1998 to accrue and to pay the vacation and the sick pay.

E11–16 Profit Sharing

A. Cuccia has a profit-sharing plan that provides for a distribution of profit to eligible employees. The profit sharing is equivalent to 10% of net income after tax and after the profit sharing, and this amount is deposited with a trustee who uses the funds to purchase outstanding company stock in each eligible employee's name.

In 1998, Cuccia had income of $3,540,000 before income taxes or profit sharing. The tax rate is 30% for Cuccia, and there are 40 eligible employees. The stock is currently trading at $20 per share on the American Stock Exchange.

Required: Calculate the number of shares of stock that each eligible employee will receive.

E11–17 Premium Offers

Copp Cereal Corporation has developed a new multigrain cereal that is very low in fat and has no sugar. To introduce this new product, Copp is enclosing a coupon in each box. Each coupon plus $2.00 entitles the redeemer to a coffee mug. Copp has purchased 50,000 mugs in 1997 at $4.50 each. The corporation expects 35,000 coupons to be redeemed in 1997 and 15,000 in 1998. It also anticipates sales of 100,000 boxes of cereal in 1997 and 110,000 boxes in 1998, all at $2.54 per box.

Required: Assume that all Copp's expectations are correct. Prepare all the journal entries in 1997 and 1998 to record these events.

E11–18 Bonuses in Japan

Yoshira Film Company has operations in the United States and in Japan. Yoshira routinely pays bonuses to officers and directors of its company in Japan. In 1997, six corporate officers and four directors received bonuses of $20,000 each. GAAP in Japan allows bonuses to be charged to stockholders' equity instead of operating expenses as in U.S. GAAP.

Required:

A. Prepare the journal entry to record the bonuses under GAAP in Japan.

B. Suppose the American subsidiary also had six corporate officers and four directors. Assume the same bonuses were paid to its American subsidiary officers and directors. Prepare the journal entry to record the bonus payments in the United States.

E11–19 Coupon Redemptions

Peter's Pastries is a new bakery trying to establish a customer base. Peter's decided to try two promotion ideas.

1. A $1 coupon is included in each of 1,000 boxes of a dozen cookies. Each coupon may be redeemed at the store for cash or a credit on a purchase of bakery goods. These coupons expire in two weeks.
2. 400 coupons were distributed to nearby residents offering a two-for-one sale. Each coupon entitles the holder to an additional item of equal or lesser value with the purchase of a first item. These coupons expire in one week.

Peter's has the following results:

1. Of 1,000 coupons offering $1 in cash or credit, 450 are redeemed. Of these, 200 are cash redemptions and 250 are applied to purchases of cookies. Coupon-related sales amounted to $1,850.
2. Of the 400 coupons offering two packages of cookies for the price of one, 120 were presented for redemption. The average sale was $4.
3. Other than coupon sales, Peter also had regular sales of $2,400 per week for the first three weeks of operation.

Required: Prepare the journal entries to record the transactions.

E11–20 Financial Analysis

Assume the following information is available from the records of Jorgenson:

Cash	$450,000
Accounts receivable	600,000
Trading securities	150,000
Inventories	300,000
Accounts payable	400,000
Notes payable (short-term)	600,000
Notes payable (long-term)	200,000
Mortgage payable	300,000
Bonds payable	800,000

The mortgage payments begin in three years and are therefore long-term. None is due currently. However, the bonds are serial bonds with $200,000 due in the next year. Interest accrued on all the debt equals $100,000.

Required:

A. Calculate the total working capital.
B. Calculate the net working capital.
C. Calculate the current ratio.
D. Calculate the acid-test ratio.
E. Make a determination of the liquidity status of Jorgenson.

E11–21 Financial Analysis

The following information is available to you:

Current assets:	
Cash	$150,000
Trading securities	150,000
Accounts receivable (net)	200,000
Inventories (FIFO, LCM)	700,000
Current liabilities:	
Accounts and notes payable	500,000
Accrued interest payable	40,000
Liability for premium redemptions	60,000
Current portion of long-term debt	200,000

You discover that (1) accounts receivable include $50,000 that is more than two years old and will probably not be collected, (2) the inventories include merchandise with a book value of $150,000 that is obsolete, and (3) a product liability lawsuit against the company has been decided in favor of the plaintiff in the amount of $100,000. The company plans to appeal the verdict.

Required: Assume you are a commercial loan officer at Union National Bank. This company is applying for a short-term loan in the amount of $500,000. Will you recommend making the loan to the loan committee? Justify your position.

E11–22 Premium Offers

On November 14, 1998, Company Z redeemed 20,000 labels and shipped 10,000 sets of spoons to its customers. Customers sent $1 with each label submitted for redemption. The spoons cost $5 per set, and the cost of shipping was $1 per set. The Estimated Liability for Premiums account had a balance of $30,000 prior to recording the transaction.

Required: Prepare the journal entry to record the transaction.

E11–23 Notes Payable

Management of your company is considering two alternatives to financing its current demand for cash.

1. A local bank offer of $19,250 in exchange for a 3-month, noninterest-bearing note with a face value of $20,000.
2. A national bank offer of $20,000 in exchange for a 3-month, 14% note with a face value of $20,000.

Required: Assuming that both offers can fully meet the current cash needs of the company, which alternative should the company adopt and why?

E11–24 Notes Payable

Lemma Co. purchased a piece of land on January 1, 1998, in order to expand its parking lot. The fair market value of the land on that date was $500,000. The company issued a 3-year noninterest-bearing note with a face value of $665,500 in exchange for the land.

Required:

A. Prepare the journal entry to record the transaction.

B. Prepare the journal entries to record the amortization of the discount at the end of each of the three years prior to payment.

PROBLEMS

P11–1 Refinancing Arrangement

Beck Inc. has $100 million in long-term debt outstanding that matures next year. Beck intends to refinance this debt by issuing common stock and obtaining a new five-year secured loan. The company has signed an agreement with Darryl Lynch and Company, an underwriter, for the issue of 2 million shares of common stock at a price of $25 per share. Because the current market price of Beck's stock is $35 per share, the underwriter fully expects the offering to be completely sold out. The fees and expenses associated with the offering amount to $5 million.

In a separate transaction, Beck has arranged to borrow up to $50 million from Fast Financial using the inventory as collateral. The terms of this arrangement state that Fast will lend 80% of the inventory value reported at December 31. Beck's normal inventory level fluctuates between $40 million and $45 million. At December 31, the inventory value was $45 million.

Required: Determine the amount of the $100 million that may be excluded from the current liabilities at December 31. Indicate how it would be classified and why. Fully explain your answer.

P11–2 Footnote for Deferred Revenues

Affiliated Publications Inc. sells commercial magazines and newspapers and provides you with the following list of liabilities at December 31, 1997:

Current maturities of long-term debt	$ 2,379,000
Dividends payable	4,198,000
Accounts payable	36,728,000
Deferred subscription revenue[d]	10,780,000
Accrued expenses:	
Payroll & vacation	10,825,000
Federal income tax	8,393,000
State income tax and other taxes	1,099,000
Other	13,327,000
Notes payable (due on 1/15/98)	8,000,000
Unamortized discount on notes payable	800,000
Long-term bonds payable	100,000,000
Unamortized premium on long-term bonds	5,000,000

Assume that the deferred subscription revenue is related to subscriptions for the following two years. Affiliated records the gross amount of revenue received (less the commissions paid) as the liability and amortizes it over the life of the subscriptions. A total of $8,000,000 in subscriptions is due in the next year, and the remainder in the year after.

Required:

A. Prepare footnote "d" (for "Deferred Subscription Revenue").
B. Prepare the "Current Liabilities" section of the balance sheet.

P11–3 Warranties

XYZ Company uses the accrual-basis method of accounting for warranty costs. In reviewing the books, you found the following entries recorded in 1998 and 1999.

February 1998:		
Cash	400,000	
Sales		350,000
Unearned Warranty Revenue		50,000
June 1998:		
Warranty Expense	5,000	
Cash		5,000
Unearned Warranty Revenue	5,000	
Warranty Revenue		5,000
March 1999:		
Warranty Expense	30,000	
Cash		30,000
Unearned Warranty Revenue	30,000	
Warranty Revenue		30,000
August 1999:		
Unearned Warranty Revenue	15,000	
Warranty Revenue		15,000

Required:

A. Which form of the accrual-basis method of accounting for warranty costs did the company use?

B. Prepare the journal entries, including the adjusting entries, assuming that: (1) you use the alternative form of the accrual-basis method of accounting for warranty costs; and (2) an adjustment for the estimated liability under warranty is made at the end of each fiscal period.

C. Compare the effect both forms have on the income statement for 1998 and 1999.

P11–4 Journal Entries

The V-shop is an automobile repair shop that has the following transactions during December.

Dec. 2 Purchased $2,000 of repair parts on account.

4 Repaired two Volvos, a 1990 model and a 1994 model. The 1990 model was an extensive repair, for which the customer was billed $1,800. The customer had made arrangements to pay in two installments, 50 percent upon completion of the repairs and the balance in three months. The 1994 model was a routine servicing, for which the customer paid $357 in cash. (Sales taxes are 5%, and the V-shop does not record them separately.)

5 Purchased $1,400 of repair parts on account.
Received the utility bill in the amount of $350.

6 Repaired three Volvos and two Volkswagens. Total cash received was $1,680.

8 Paid wages to Sandy and Tom, the two full-time mechanics. Sandy worked 50 hours at $15 per hour, and Tom worked 40 hours at $12 per hour. The federal income tax withholding is 20%, and FICA rate is 6.2%.

Dec. 10 Borrowed $2,000 at City S&L by signing a 60-day note discounted by City at 10%.
17 Purchased $3,000 of parts on account.
20 Delivered four repaired autos to their owners. Total amount billed and collected was $2,625, including sales taxes.
30 Paid the accounts payable from November in the amount of $4,200. No discounts were allowed or taken.
31 Submitted the sales tax to the city.

Required: Prepare journal entries to record the transactions.

P11–5 Journal Entries

The following transactions for Burgard's Bakery took place in December.

1. On December 10, Burgard's received $500 as a deposit on bakery goods for the annual Christmas party sponsored by M. A. Hanna Corporation. The total order is $2,500, and the party is scheduled for December 23.
2. During December, cash sales totaled $24,720 including the $2,500 order by Hanna. This included a 3% sales tax that must be remitted to the city on January 15.
3. During December, Burgard's purchased baking supplies in the amount of $15,000 on account. Terms of the purchases provide for a 2% cash discount when paid by the 15th of the following month. Since Burgard's always pays within the discount period, all purchases are recorded using the net method.
4. Burgard's purchased baking supplies in the amount of $10,000 in November. These were paid in December, less the 2% discount.
5. At the end of December, accrued wages amounted to $3,000.
6. Burgard's has a $10,000, 8% note payable outstanding with the local bank that was issued three years ago. The note is due next June, and interest is payable annually on January 1.

Required:

A. Prepare all the journal entries necessary to record the transactions as they occurred as well as the adjusting entries required at December 31.
B. From this information, determine the total current liabilities of Burgard's.

P11–6 Notes Payable

At December 31, 1997, Globe Inc. had four notes payable outstanding. They included the following:

1. A noninterest-bearing note with a face value of $25,000, issued at a discount of 12% on June 1, 1997, and maturity date of May 30, 1998. Globe amortizes the discount on a monthly basis.
2. A noninterest-bearing two-year note with a face value of $96,800. This note was issued on July 1, 1997, to State National Insurance Company, which charged a 10% discount rate.
3. An 8%, six-month note issued to Travelers Company, on August 31, 1997, in the amount of $50,000.
4. A 10%, eight-month note in the amount of $40,000, dated December 1, 1997, and payable to John Logan.

Required:

A. Prepare the journal entries to record the issue of these notes.

B. Prepare the adjusting entries at December 31, 1997, to accrue the interest and to amortize the discount. (Use straight-line amortization.)

C. Determine the total amount of the current liabilities resulting from these notes.

P11–7 Bonuses

Pat Stack is the president and CEO of Stack's Stitchery, a chain of fabric stores. Stack receives an annual salary of $125,000, and a bonus each year. In 1997, operating income before bonus and before income tax was $500,000. The tax rate is 40%, and the bonus rate is 10%.

Required: Calculate the total compensation of Stack if the bonus is based on income

A. before tax and before bonus.

B. before tax but after bonus.

C. after tax but before bonus.

D. after tax and after bonus.

P11–8 Bonus

O'Neal is negotiating a bonus clause in his employment contract with the LA Streamers. The bonus will be based on the Streamers' net income after deduction of all expenses, including the bonus and income tax. The bonus will be equal to 5% of the net income in excess of $2,000,000 and less than $20,000,000, and thus can vary between zero and $900,000. The income tax rate is 40%.

Required:

A. If O'Neal earns a bonus of $100,000 in 1997, what is the Streamers' income

1. after tax and after bonus?
2. before tax and before bonus?

B. In 1998, if O'Neal earned a bonus of $400,000, what is the Streamers' income

1. after tax and after bonus?
2. before tax and before bonus?

C. How much must the Streamers' earn before tax and before bonus for O'Neal to collect $900,000 in bonus?

P11–9 Bonus

Assume the same facts as in P11–8. Also assume the Streamers' income before bonus and before tax is $32,000,000 in 1997.

Required: Calculate the following for 1997.

A. The amount of O'Neal's bonus.

B. The amount of income tax liability.

C. The net income after tax and after bonus for the Streamers.

P11–10 Premium Offers

Cooker is introducing a new product, a dinner entree that is microwavable. To stimulate interest in this product, Cooker is offering a set of potholders in exchange for two UPC labels from the dinners and $1.00. The dinners sell for $4.29 each. Cooker expects a 70% redemption rate. During 1997 and 1998, the following events related to this offer take place:

1997

1. Sold 120,000 entrees.
2. Purchased 40,000 sets of potholders at $2.00 each.
3. Redeemed 70,000 UPC labels and shipped 35,000 sets of potholders. The shipping costs were $.60 per set.

1998

1. Sold 26,000 entrees at $4.29 each.
2. Purchased an additional 10,000 sets of potholders at $2.00 each.
3. Redeemed 22,000 UPC labels and shipped 11,000 potholders. Shipping costs were $.60 per set.
4. No additional redemptions were anticipated, so the remaining potholders were donated to the Salvation Army and various other charitable organizations.

Required:

A. Prepare the journal entries for 1997 and 1998 to record these events.
B. Determine the amounts to be found on the balance sheet at December 31, 1997, related to these transactions.

P11–11 Vacation and Sick Pay

Charity Hospital employs 100 nurses who each work eight-hour shifts, five days a week. The nurses are able to accumulate five vested sick days and ten vested vacation days annually. Data for 1997 and 1998 follow:

PER NURSE	1997	1998
Average hourly rate	$15	$16
Average vacation days earned	10 days	10 days
Average vacation days used	4	10
Average sick days earned	5	5
Average sick days used	3	3

Required: Prepare journal entries for 1997 and 1998.

P11–12 Warranty Costs

Eglin Electronics manufactures a variety of products. All of its products include a two-year manufacturer's warranty. The warranty repairs are made at various authorized centers around the country. The repair centers then bill Eglin for their services.

During 1997, Eglin had sales of products with two-year warranties of $5,000,000. The total estimated cost of warranty repairs on these products is $600,000, which will be spread throughout 1997, 1998, and 1999 when the warranty period expires. Also during 1997, a total of $80,000 in repairs were made related to these product warranties and paid by Eglin to the repair centers. In 1998, an additional $250,000 in claims were paid, and in 1999, $200,000 in warranty claims were paid.

Required: Prepare journal entries for all three years under the following assumptions.

A. Eglin uses the cash-based method of accounting for warranty costs.
B. Eglin uses the accrual-based expense method of accounting for warranty costs.
C. Eglin uses the accrual-based sales method of accounting for warranty costs.

P11–13 Financial Analysis and Judgment

The following selected account balances are provided for a two-year period:

(IN THOUSANDS OF DOLLARS)	1998	1997
Cash	$ 150	$ 400
Trading securities	100	300
Accounts receivable (net)	450	400
Inventories (FIFO, LCM)	500	500
Total current assets	$1,200	$1,600
Accounts payable	$ 100	$ 200
Notes payable	130	300
Current portion of long-term debt	100	50
Accrued liabilities	50	150
Other current liabilities	120	200
Total current liabilities	$ 500	$ 900

Required:

A. For each year, calculate
1. Net working capital
2. Current ratio
3. Acid-test ratio

B. Is the liquidity position better or worse in 1998 than 1997? Why? Support your conclusion.

P11–14 Integrative Liquidity Analysis

The following account balances for the Delta Corporation include two years of data:

(IN THOUSANDS OF DOLLARS)	1998	1997
Cash	$1,800	$1,200
Trading securities	1,600	2,300
Accounts receivable (net)	1,750	1,600
Inventories (LCM—average cost)	900	840
Other current assets	1,550	1,060
Total current assets	$7,600	$7,000
Accounts payable	$1,050	$1,200
Notes payable	800	1,000
Dividends payable	250	250
Accrued liabilities	600	700
Estimated future warranty liability	700	800
Other current liabilities	0	50
Total current liabilities	$3,400	$4,000
Sales (all on credit)	$6,475	$5,600
Cost of goods sold	3,626	3,360

Required:

A. Evaluate the liquidity position for 1997 and 1998.

B. Has the liquidity position improved for 1998 compared to 1997? Why or why not?

P11–15 Notes Receivable and Notes Payable

On April 1, 1997, SaleCo Inc. sold equipment to BuyIt Company for a purchase price of $2,500,000. BuyIt Company paid $614,000 down and signed a note with SaleCo for the remaining $1,886,000. The terms of the note call for BuyIt to make two semiannual payments of $1,000,000 each, the first on October 1, 1997, and the second on April 1, 1998. These payments are based upon an 8% effective annual interest rate.

Required:

A. For the note, complete the amortization schedule.

DATE	INTEREST	PAYMENT	REDUCTION OF PRINCIPAL	CARRYING VALUE
4/1/97	0	0	0	
10/1/97				
4/1/98				

B. Assume that BuyIt Company records the note as an interest-bearing note. Prepare BuyIt's journal entries to record the following:

1. Purchase on April 1, 1997.
2. First payment on October 1, 1997.
3. Adjusting entry for the note on December 31, 1997.
4. Second payment on April 1, 1998.

C. Assume that SaleCo Inc. records the note as a noninterest-bearing note. Prepare SaleCo's journal entries to record the following:

1. Sale on April 1, 1997 (the sale only—not the reduction of inventory and recognition of cost of goods sold).
2. Receipt of the first payment on October 1, 1997.
3. Adjusting entry for the note on December 31, 1997.
4. Second payment on April 1, 1998.

P11–16 Premium Offers

Management of a retail toy company enjoying market power in a small town in Texas decided to price-discriminate among its customers in order to increase sales and profitability. The controller of the company proposed that the company use premiums to implement this new policy. The proposal was adopted by management and involved offering a coffee mug to customers at a price of $3 per mug plus the return of 4 labels. The following transactions occurred in 1998 and 1999.

1998

1. Cash sales of 200,000 toys at $10 each.
2. Purchased on account 25,000 mugs at $5 each and paid an additional $25,000 in cash to have the company's name and trademark placed on the mugs.
3. Redeemed 60,000 labels and shipped mugs to customers at a shipping cost of $1 per unit.
4. Estimated redemption rate was 40%.

1999

1. Cash sales of 300,000 toys at $11 each.
2. Purchased 30,000 mugs at $6 each and paid an additional $60,000 in cash to have the company's name and trademark placed on the mugs.
3. Redeemed 140,000 labels and shipped mugs to customers at a shipping cost of $1.50 per unit. Of the 140,000 labels redeemed, 20,000 were related to 1998 sales.
4. Estimated redemption rate was 50%.

Required:

A. Prepare the journal entries to record the above transactions, including year-end adjustments for 1998 and 1999. Use the LIFO cost-flow assumption in determining the cost of shipping the mugs.

B. Assume that further redemptions will take place in the year 2000. What amounts will be reported for the inventory of mugs and the estimated liability for premium on the balance sheet at December 31, 1998 and December 31, 1999?

P11–17 Vacation And Sick Pay

The collective agreement between the management and union of Al-Mesh Manufacturing Enterprises entitles each employee to a vacation and vested sick pay. There are three classifications of employment in the company, namely administrative, supervisory and shop floor. Information relating to vacation and sick pay is summarized as follows for the years 1998 and 1999.

	ADMINISTRATIVE		SUPERVISORY		SHOP FLOOR	
	1998	**1999**	**1998**	**1999**	**1998**	**1999**
Number of employees	10	8	5	8	100	120
Average hourly rate ($)	30	35	20	25	10	18
Average vacation days earned	10	10	8	8	6	7
Average vacation days used	8	10	5	8	4	5
Average sick days earned	5	5	4	4	3	4
Average sick days used	1	2	3	4	2	4

Required:

A. Prepare the journal entries for 1998 and 1999 to record all transactions related to vacation and sick pay. Prepare separate entries for the use and earning of vacation and sick pay. Assume that payment for vacation and sick pay is customarily made some time before the end of the fiscal period. There was no unused vacation or sick pay outstanding at the beginning of 1998.

B. Determine the amount of the payables for vacation and sick pay that will be reported on the balance sheet for December 31, 1998 and December 31, 1999.

P11–18 Financial Analysis

You are reviewing a loan application of a small company operating in the Mesa, Arizona, area. The company has provided you with a summary report of its working capital position. The reported figures include current assets of $200,000, current liabilities of $100,000, and net working capital of $100,000. You decide to conduct an investigation of the reported figures and the following transactions that were not taken into account in the determination of the reported figures that have been brought to your attention.

1. Merchandise purchased on account from J&J Co. is still in transit. The shipping terms are F.O.B. shipping point. The purchase price of the merchandise is $4,000.
2. The uncollectible amount of credit sales made during the year is estimated to be $1,000.
3. Estimated warranty expense and premium expense for the period are $5,000 and $7,500, respectively.
4. Three months of interest on a 10%, $100,000 note payable was not recorded.
5. A $10,000 long-term liability expected to mature in six months is classified as non-current, and management has neither the intention nor the ability to renew the loan or defer its payment.

Required:

A. Recalculate the net working capital position of the company.
B. Calculate the current ratio using the new figures for the working capital elements.
C. Assuming that the correct value of merchandise inventory is $20,000 and there are no prepayments, calculate the quick ratio.

P11–19 Multiple Choice CPA-Adapted Questions

1. Case Cereal Company frequently distributes coupons to promote new products. On October 1, 1991, Case mailed 1,000,000 coupons for $0.45 off each box of cereal purchased. The company expects 120,000 of these coupons to be redeemed before the December 31, 1991, expiration date. It takes 30 days from the redemption date for Case to receive the coupons from the retailers. Case reimburses the retailers an additional $ .05 for each coupon redeemed. As of December 31, 1991, it had paid retailers $25,000 related to these coupons and had 50,000 coupons on hand that had not been processed for payment. What amount should Case report as a liability for coupons in its December 31, 1991, balance sheet?
   A. $35,000
   B. $29,000
   C. $25,000
   D. $22,500
2. Regal Department Store sells gift certificates, redeemable for store merchandise, that expire one year after their issuance. Regal has the following information pertaining to its gift certificates sales and redemptions:

Unredeemed at December 31, 1990	$ 75,000
1991 sales	250,000
1991 redemptions of prior-year sales	25,000
1991 redemptions of current-year sales	175,000

   Regal's experience indicates that 10% of gift certificates sold will not be redeemed. In its December 31, 1991, balance sheet, what amount should Regal report as unearned revenue?
   A. $125,000
   B. $112,500
   C. $100,000
   D. $50,000

3. On April 1, 1992, Ash Corporation began offering a new product for sale under a one-year warranty. Of the 5,000 units in inventory at April 1, 1992, 3,000 had been sold by June 30, 1992. Based on its experience with similar products, Ash estimated that the average warranty cost per unit sold would be $8. Actual warranty costs incurred from April 1 through June 30, 1992, were $7,000. At June 30, 1992, what amount should Ash report as estimated warranty liability?
   A. $9,000
   B. $16,000
   C. $17,000
   D. $33,000
4. Pam Inc. has $1,000,000 of notes payable due June 15, 1989. At the financial-statement date of December 31, 1988, Pam signed an agreement to borrow up to $1,000,000 to refinance the notes payable on a long-term basis. The financing agreement called for borrowing not to exceed 80% of the value of the collateral Pam was providing. At the date of issue of the December 31, 1988, financial statements, the value of the collateral was $1,200,000 and was not expected to fall below this amount during 1989. In its December 31, 1988, balance sheet, Pam should classify the notes payable as what?

	SHORT-TERM OBLIGATIONS	LONG-TERM OBLIGATIONS
A.	$ 0	$1,000,000
B.	40,000	960,000
C.	200,000	800,000
D.	1,000,000	0

5. During 1989 Tedd Company became involved in a tax dispute with the IRS. At December 31, 1989, Tedd's tax advisor believed that an unfavorable outcome was probable. A reasonable estimate of additional taxes was $400,000 but could be as much as $600,000. After the 1989 financial statements were issued, Tedd received and accepted an IRS settlement offer of $450,000. What amount of accrued liability should Tedd have reported in its December 31, 1989, balance sheet?
   A. $400,000
   B. $450,000
   C. $500,000
   D. $600,000
6. In May 1985 Croft Company filed suit against Walton, Inc., seeking $950,000 damages for patent infringement. A court verdict in November 1988 awarded Croft $750,000 in damages, but Walton's appeal is not expected to be decided before 1990. Croft's counsel believes it is probable that Croft will be successful against Walton for an estimated amount in the range between $400,000 and $550,000, with $500,000 considered the most likely amount. What amount should Croft record as revenue from the lawsuit in the year ended December 31, 1988?
   A. $750,000
   B. $500,000
   C. $400,000
   D. $0

RESEARCH ACTIVITIES

R11–1 Financial Research

Examine recent annual reports for two retail businesses.

Required:

A. Prior chapters presented receivables and inventory-turnover ratios. From these, average days to collect and average days to sell are determined. In a similar manner, how do you think payables turnover and an average days to pay vendors could be determined?
B. Calculate the average days to pay vendors for each of the two retail businesses.
C. Calculate the sum of the average days to sell and average days to collect for each company.
D. Based upon these results, make a short statement about each company's average cash needs regarding purchases of inventory. Compare and contrast the two companies.

R11–2 Database Financial Comparisons

1. Select an industry from a database that you are able to access. Calculate the following industry average ratios from the company data for your selected industry:
   a. Liquidity ratios
   b. Profitability ratios
   c. Receivables and inventory-turnover ratios
   d. Debt ratios
2. Divide the companies in the industry into two groups: One group with ratios below the industry averages and the other group with ratios above the industry averages. Are there companies that do not fall into either group? Why?
3. If there are companies that do not fall into either group, how would you classify them with regard to investment risk and potential for profitability?
4. Is there a tradeoff between some of the ratios? (Are some better at the expense of others?)

R11–3 Financial Research

Search a database with which you are familiar and print a list of firms with a current ratio less than one. Next to each firm's name, write the value for the most recent current ratio. Would you say that these firms are in financial difficulty because their current liabilities exceed their current assets?

For the firm with the smallest current ratio, identify the major element(s) contributing to such a low ratio. Has the major element(s) historically contributed to low current ratios for this firm? Is there a liquidity problem?

R11–4 Internet Activity

Access the SEC database EDGAR. Find one company that reports a significant contingency in its footnotes. Prepare a report that explains the nature and amount of the contingency.

R11–5 Internet Activity

Access any database with which you have become familiar. Identify five companies in the same industry in the database. Calculate the current ratio and the quick ratio for each of the companies. Prepare a ranking of the companies based on the calculated ratios.

R11–6 Internet Activity

Access the South-Western Home page for Intermediate Accounting for this text at *www.swcollege.com/hartman.html* and find out if anything has been posted for current liabilities.

PART 3

INTEGRATIVE CASES

LIQUIDITY AND PROFITABILITY ANALYSIS: BEN & JERRY'S HOMEMADE, INC.

INTRODUCTION

Early in 1996, Maria, your best friend from college, calls you for some investment advice. Maria was a management major who wanted to start her own business—something small and socially conscious, but with big growth potential.

After her first business folded, Maria took a job as a sales representative for a pharmaceutical company and found she had a knack for sales. She quickly ascended within the company and, after eight years, has a sizeable income and a penchant for investing. She still seeks out the sort of companies she wanted to start when she left college. Social responsibility is as important as ever, but she's careful not to invest in companies that aren't fiscally responsible as well.

Her latest investment pick is an ice cream company, ***Ben & Jerry's Homemade, Inc.*** The company has received high marks for social responsibility, but Maria is concerned that the company is so concerned about increasing everyone else's wealth that it might be forgetting its own investors. She wants you to examine the financial statements and make a recommendation to her regarding whether to invest or not.

COMPANY DESCRIPTION

Ben & Jerry's Homemade, Inc. is a leading producer of super premium ice cream and frozen yogurt. The company's 1995 10–K filing stated that the company

> . . . began active operations in May 1978, when Ben Cohen, now the Company's Chairperson, and Jerry Greenfield, now the Company's Vice Chairperson, opened a retail store in a renovated gas station in Burlington, Vermont. The store featured homemade ice cream made in an antique rock salt ice cream freezer. That ice cream parlor continues to make its own ice cream in the same freezer in a larger location in Burlington . . .

BEN & JERRY'S HOMEMADE, INC.

The company's marketing strategy emphasizes a down-home, made-in-Vermont image in addition to its products' gourmet quality and natural ingredients. Pictures of Ben and Jerry appear on most ice-cream cartons. In addition, the company has developed a reputation as a socially conscious employer and manufacturer; in 1995 the company donated approximately 7½ percent of its pretax profits to nonprofit charitable groups in Vermont and elsewhere. The company has been a strong advocate of the Children's Defense Fund, an advocacy group for poor and underprivileged children.

Financial Analysis

Comparative balance sheets and income statements from the company's 1995 annual report are shown in Exhibits 1 and 2. Additionally, industry standard financial statement ratios are provided for the 1994–1995 period to provide a benchmark in comparing Ben & Jerry's performance against other firms in the industry.

Part 1

Using only the financial statements provided for Ben & Jerry's, calculate for 1995 the liquidity, asset management, and profitability ratios shown in the

Exhibit 1

Ben & Jerry's Homemade, Inc.
Consolidated Balance Sheet
For Period Ending:

	December 30, 1995	December 31, 1994
	(000 omitted)	
Current assets:		
Cash and cash equivalents	$ 35,406	$ 20,778
Trade accounts receivable, net	11,660	9,902
Other receivables	854	2,003
Inventories	12,616	13,463
Deferred income taxes	3,599	3,146
Income taxes receivable	2,831	2,098
Prepaid expenses	1,097	534
Total current assets	$ 68,063	$ 51,924
Property, plant, and equipment (net)	$ 59,600	$ 57,981
Investments	1,000	8,000
Other assets	2,411	2,391
	$131,074	$120,296
Current liabilities:		
Accounts payable and accrued expenses	$ 16,592	$ 13,915
Current portion of long-term debt	448	553
Total current liabilities	$ 17,040	$ 14,468
Long-term debt and lease obligations	$ 31,977	$ 32,419
Deferred income taxes	3,526	907
Total liabilities	$ 35,503	$ 33,326
Stockholders equity:		
$1.20 noncumulative Class A preferred stock	$ 1	$ 1
Class A common stock	209	208
Class B common stock	30	31
Additional paid-in capital	48,521	48,336
Retained earnings	31,264	25,316
Cumulative translation adjustment	(114)	
Treasury stock, at cost	(1,380)	(1,420)
Total stockholders' equity	$ 78,531	$ 72,502
	$131,074	$120,296

EXHIBIT 2

BEN & JERRY'S HOMEMADE, INC.
Consolidated Statement of Income
Years Ended:

	DECEMBER 30, 1995	DECEMBER 31, 1994 (000 OMITTED)	DECEMBER 25, 1993
Net sales	$155,333	$148,802	$140,328
Cost of sales	109,125	109,760	100,210
Gross profit	$ 46,208	$ 39,042	$ 40,118
Selling, general and administrative expenses	(36,362)	(36,253)	(28,270)
Asset write-down		(6,779)	
Other income (expenses):			
Interest income	1,681	1,034	757
Interest expense	(1,525)	(295)	(104)
Other	(597)	(511)	(456)
Income (loss) before income taxes	$ 9,405	$ (3,762)	$ 12,045
Income taxes (benefit)	3,457	(1,893)	4,844
Net income (loss)	$ 5,948	$ (1,869)	$ 7,201
Net income per common share	$ .83	$ (.26)	$ 1.01
Weighted average number of common and common equivalents outstanding	7,222	7,148	7,138

industry standards table. To calculate the turnover ratios, use the average of the beginning and ending accounts receivable and inventory.

Based on your analysis, provide a brief written summary to Maria discussing the liquidity, current asset management, and profitability of Ben & Jerry's relative to the industry as a whole.

PART 2

As part of your analysis in Part 1, you should have noted areas of concern in which Ben & Jerry's does not appear to perform as well as other firms in the industry. The discussion of "Risk Factors" contained in Management's Discussion and Analysis from the 1995 10–K is provided in Exhibit 4. Does information contained in that discussion affect your decision regarding the health of Ben & Jerry's summarized in Part 1? After reading this section, would your investment advice to a friend be the same as it was before reading it? If the information is needed to make an informed investment decision, why isn't the information contained in the financial statements or notes to the financial statements? Should the information be contained in the financial statement footnotes?

Exhibit 3
Industry Standards

	Industry Standard, 1994–1995
Liquidity:	
Current ratio (times)	2.3
Quick ratio (times)	1.1
Average receivable collection period (days)	31.9
Average number of days inventory on hand (days)	50.0
Current asset management:	
Accounts receivable turnover (times)	11.4
Inventory turnover (times)	7.3
Profitability:	
Net profit margin (%)	4.3
Return on equity (%)	10.5
Return on total assets (%)	5.2

Exhibit 4
Risk Factors

Dependence on Independent Ice Cream Distributors. The Company is dependent on maintaining satisfactory relationships with independent ice cream distributors that now generally act as the Company's exclusive or master distributor in their assigned territories. While the Company believes its relationships with Dreyer's and its other distributors generally have been satisfactory and have been instrumental in the Company's growth, the Company has at times experienced difficulty in maintaining such relationships. Available distribution alternatives are limited. Accordingly, there can be no assurance that difficulties in maintaining relationships with distributors, which may be related to actions by the Company's competitors or by one or more of the Company's distributors themselves (or their controlling persons), will not have a material adverse effect on the Company's business. The loss of one or more of the Company's principal distributors or termination of one or more of the related distribution agreements could have a material adverse effect on the Company's business. . . .

Growth in sales and earnings. In 1995, net sales of the Company increased 4.4% to $155 million from $149 million in 1994. Pint volume decreased 1.5% compared to 1994. The Company believes this decrease is consistent with the recent performance in the super premium category overall excluding sorbet, which contributed more growth than the total increase in the super premium category from 1994 to 1995. Given these overall domestic super premium industry trends, the successful introduction of innovative flavors on a periodic basis has become increasingly important to any sales growth by the Company. Accordingly, the future degree of market acceptance of the Company's sorbet line, which is being introduced February through May 1996, and which will be accompanied by a significant increase in promotional expenditures is likely to have an important impact on the Company's 1996 and future financial results. . . .

(*continued*)

EXHIBIT 4
(Concluded)

Competitive Environment. The super premium frozen dessert market is highly competitive with the distinctions between the super premium category, and the "adjoining" premium category less marked than in the past and with the domestic super premium frozen dessert category showing a recent decline in industry sales, except for sorbet. And, as noted above, the ability to successfully introduce innovative flavors on a periodic basis that are accepted by the marketplace is a significant competitive factor. In addition, the Company's principal competitors are large, diversified companies with resources significantly greater than the Company's. The Company expects strong competition to continue, including competition for adequate distribution and competition for the limited shelf space for the frozen dessert category in supermarkets and other retail food outlets. . . .

The Company's Social Mission. The Company's basic business philosophy is embodied in a three-part "mission statement," which includes a "social mission" to "operate the Company. . . to improve the quality of life of our employees and a broad community: local, national and international." The Company believes that implementation of its social mission, which is integrated into the Company's business, has been beneficial to the Company's overall financial performance. However, it is possible that at some future date the amount of the Company's energies and resources devoted to its social mission could have a material adverse financial effect on the Company's business. . . .

COLUMBIA GAS SYSTEM: READING BETWEEN THE LINES OF A FOOTNOTE

In this case, students evaluate the adequacy of disclosure in a commitment footnote, and become familiar with the role played by financial analysts in reading and reporting on financial statements.

INTRODUCTION

At the end of 1990, ***Columbia Gas System*** was a solid buy on many brokers' lists of recommended stocks. The natural gas supply company served over eight million customers and operated a transmission system consisting of over 18,000 miles of pipeline. By 1990, the company was delivering over one trillion cubic feet of gas annually to its customers in fifteen states, and it was one of the companies included in the Dow Jones Utility Average.

If there was a dark cloud on the company's horizon, it was the combination of long-term gas purchase commitments and declining natural gas prices. The commitments, most of which had been entered prior to 1980, forced the company to buy gas at relatively high contract prices, while its transmission unit was transporting gas sold by other companies at cheaper prices. If the company did not accept delivery of the gas under the commitments, it was still obligated to pay the purchase price; hence, the obligations were referred to as take-or-pay contracts. In 1985, the company thought it had put many of the contract problems behind it by restructuring many of the contracts, reducing the contract price to around $3 per thousand cubic feet of gas. However, the price of gas had continued to decline. By the beginning of 1991, the price was about $2.00 per thousand cubic feet, and few analysts saw any chance of rebound in the near future.

The take-or-pay contracts were no secret in the industry. Many suppliers were obligated under similar commitments, and analysts realized that declining prices were going to further squeeze the obligated companies. Still, the outlook of most analysts was that the natural gas market was robust and poised for a recovery. The Gulf War further bolstered the opinion of most industry observers regarding the future prospects for natural gas.

GAAP for Take-or-Pay Contracts

Take-or-pay contracts are one form of a more general class of contract called *unconditional purchase obligations*, which the FASB defines as:

> . . . an obligation to transfer funds in the future for fixed or minimum amounts or quantities of goods or services at fixed or minimum prices. (paragraph 6, *Statement of Financial Accounting Standards No. 47—Disclosure of Long-Term Obligations*)

Columbia Gas System

In *Statement No. 47* the FASB required extensive disclosure in the footnotes of such obligations provided that the obligations were (1) essentially noncancelable, (2) negotiated as part of a financing arrangement for the facility that will provide the goods, and (3) have a remaining term in excess of one year. The second criterion appears to exclude Columbia Gas's take-or-pay obligations from the disclosure requirement of *Statement No. 47*.

Part 1: Financial Highlights and Adequacy of Disclosures

Financial highlights of Columbia Gas System's 1990 balance sheet and income statement are provided in Exhibit 1.

During 1990, the company reported net income of $104.7 million on sales of over $1.8 billion; dividends were $2.20 per share, providing a yield on

Exhibit 1
Financial Highlights

Columbia Gas System
Financial Highlights
At and For the Year Ending December 31, 1991

Balance sheet information:	
Gas inventories (millions)	$ 435.5
Total current assets	1,461.6
Total assets	6,196.3
Total current liabilities	1,932.8
Total other liabilities and long-term debt	2,505.7
Total equity	1,757.8
Income statement information:	
Total operating revenues	2,357.9
Total operating expenses	2,095.8
Net income	104.7
Earnings per share	2.21
Dividends per share	2.20

investment over 6 percent. While sales and income were down from the previous year, the company noted that:

> . . . extremely warm weather experienced in Columbia Transmission's operating territory during 1990 and 1991, significantly reduced sales volumes and, in turn, purchases from producers. Management currently expects that recoupable take-or-pay obligations of up to $100 million may be incurred in 1991.

In December of 1990, the company had a public offering of its stock, selling the securities at $49 per share, and in January, 1991, Columbia raised its dividend by 5 percent. During this period, the spot price of natural gas continued to drift downward. By late February, the spot price dropped to $1.23 per thousand cubic feet. In the company's first quarter report filed with the SEC about May 15, the following discussion of the take-or-pay commitments was included, but not in the footnotes to the financial statements. The discussion was included in the section of the report entitled "Management's Discussion and Analysis" under the heading "Transmission Operations—Supply Matters".

> The 1990–1991 heating season was the second warmest in Transmission's history. The warm weather increased the amount of winter capacity available on interstate pipelines which provided distribution customers more opportunities to purchase low-cost spot market gas and transport it on the pipelines. Reduced heating demand in much of the country contributed to the weak spot market prices, resulting in a depressed market for the sale of higher-priced, pipeline-owned gas supplies held under firm, long-term contracts with producers. These conditions have created problems for Columbia Transmission in meeting minimum contractual purchase obligations with producers. One result has been the need to maintain a larger than normal inventory of gas in storage, which was more than 100 Bcf [billion cubic feet] above planned levels at the end of the first quarter. . . .
>
> Actions to minimize supply management costs in the summer of 1991 and provide additional operating flexibility, together with higher carrying costs due to the excess storage position, are estimated to cost Columbia Transmission approximately $30 million after-tax. Despite these efforts, Columbia Transmission may incur approximately $65 million of recoupable take-or-pay liabilities in 1991.
>
> In the third quarter of 1990, Columbia Transmission announced that it would attempt to renegotiate certain high-cost gas supply contracts. Using recently revised gas price projections, Columbia Transmission's cost of gas is now projected to be higher than generally anticipated gas price levels, even assuming the successful completion of the announced renegotiations. Consequently, gas sales are projected to be insufficient to avoid future gas supply management costs. In addition, Columbia Transmission may not be able to meet the test of price comparability with other pipe-lines which is required to permit it to collect its gas inventory charge to reimburse it for gas supply management costs. Therefore, Columbia Transmission has concluded that actions beyond the previously announced renegotiations of certain producer contracts are necessary. The parameters of the problem and the costs and feasibility of various possible responses, . . . are under intense study in light of current and prospective market conditions and the impact of final deregulation of gas prices in 1993.

There was little movement of the company's stock price from the time of this 10–Q filing until mid-June.

However, before the start of trading on June 19 the company disclosed the extent of its supply problems under take-or-pay contracts. It indicated that many of the contracts required it to pay as much as $6.70 per thousand cubic feet at a time when retail residential customers were paying rates averaging only $5.38 per thousand cubic feet. The company disclosed that it was obligated to purchase as many as 200 billion cubic feet a year at these above market prices, and the potential loss from such contracts could exceed $1 billion. The company anticipated recognizing this loss during the second quarter of 1991. It also warned that unless suppliers renegotiated the take-or-pay contracts, the company might be forced to seek protection under the bankruptcy code.

When trading in the stock opened around 12:30 p.m., the stock opened at $20 per share, down 42 percent ($14.50) from the previous day's closing price.

REQUIRED:

Place yourself in the place of the chief accounting officer of the company. Considering all aspects of the situation, how would you defend the extent of disclosure the company supplied in the financial statement footnotes at the end of 1990? If you were the chief accounting officer, would you have supplied additional information? Why?

PART 2: THE ROLE OF THE ANALYST

Although the first quarter 10–Q was issued in May, weeks before the June 19 announcement, few analysts reacted to the disclosure shown. According to *The Wall Street Journal*, one of the few who did was Joseph Egan, an analyst for the tiny brokerage firm of ***Pforzheimer & Co.*** Egan read the 10–Q disclosure and realized that the gas supply situation was a fundamental problem—one going beyond the warm weather of a single winter. Egan advised his clients to sell the stock.

Few other analysts took this step. As the *Journal* relates:

> ... a closer look suggests that Columbia may rank as one of the Street's most glaring blown calls. Besides Egan, most other analysts picked up on Columbia's distress signals, and some weakened their recommendations prior to its June 19 announcement. But for varying reasons, they failed to do the one thing that would have saved their clients' money—put out a straightforward recommendation to sell . . .
>
> But the failure of most analysts to make the right call when it really counted goes to the heart of the trouble with much of Wall Street's research. Analysts are wonderful at crunching numbers, but the job also entails making judgments—seeing the puzzle's basic shape in spite of its missing pieces. "One job of Wall Street is to look beyond the numbers," says ***Prudential Securities Inc.'s*** David Fleischer. . . .
>
> Many analysts feel subtle pressure not to be explicitly negative. Columbia, for instance, was given a neutral rating of "hold" by most analysts. And some brokers, having promoted Columbia's stock in a public offering at $49 a share last December, may have been reluctant to abandon ship soon after. ***Morgan Stanley Group Inc.***, the lead underwriter, said in April that Columbia's "secure dividend should limit any price correction." Columbia has suspended its 58-cent quarterly payout. . . .
>
> Among Wall Street's brokerage analysts, "Joe [Egan] was the only one who critically read the 10–Q and determined that their [prior] take-or-pay settlement was limited," says David Zimmerman of ***Loomis, Sayles & Co.***, a money manager in Boston.

REQUIRED:

Reread the first quarter 10–Q disclosure. What "red-flags" do you note with the benefit of hindsight?

Place yourself in the position of a financial analyst following the firm for a brokerage company. In your position, was the disclosure made by the company at the end of 1990 adequate? If it met the requirements of GAAP, would you be satisfied, or would you have wanted additional information? What sort of information would you want? Why would you want the information?

Place yourself in the position of an individual who had relied on an analyst's buy recommendation and purchased a substantial amount of Columbia's stock. Do you think the analyst "blew the call," as indicated in the article above, or is the problem with the extent and amount of disclosure? In other words, who is at fault? the analysts? the accountants who prepare the financial statements or auditors who attest to their fairness? or the bodies that regulate accounting disclosure such as the SEC and FASB? Who, if anyone, would you blame for your loss and why?

Changes in Accounting for Extended Warranty Contracts: Best Buy's Change from Partial Revenue Recognition to Full Deferral

Accounting for Extended Warranty Contracts

Extended warranty contracts are a form of future service liability that have changed the way in which retailers of consumer electronics do business. These warranty contracts are sold along with individual units of electronic equipment, and they extend the manufacturer's original warranty for a specified period of time. In 1990, sales of extended warranties accompanied approximately 40 percent of the unit sales in the consumer electronics industry, and the average profit margin was approximately 70 percent. The high profit margin allows retailers to establish a lower selling price and increase volume sales of their electronic equipment.

There are three methods available to account for extended warranty contracts. Before 1989, most companies followed an immediate recognition policy, which recognized all of the revenue associated with the extended warranty at the time of sale, matching an estimate of future expenses with the revenue at that time. In 1990, responding to events at a meeting of the Emerging Issues Task Force, many consumer electronics companies changed to a method of partial recognition. Under this method, the total sales and total expenses related to sale of both the product and warranty are calculated. In the period of the sale a portion of the total revenue is deferred; the amount deferred is equal to the total revenue times the ratio between the estimated expense associated with the extended warranty and total expenses. Following the meeting of the Emerging Issues Task Force, the FASB issued *FASB Technical Bulletin 90–1* which required a third method of accounting for extended warranty contracts beginning in 1991. The third method is a full deferral method, which requires all of the extended warranty contract revenue to be capitalized on the balance sheet and amortized over the contract period, preferably using a straight-line procedure.

The three methods are illustrated in Exhibit 1. In this illustration, assume that a video camera costing $900 is sold for $1000 at the end of Year 1, along with a two-year, $100 extended warranty contract. The company anticipates that, on average, services performed under the extended warranty have a total cost of $20. The exhibit illustrates that partial recognition does not differ materially from immediate recognition for most companies because the expenses of the extended warranties are generally small relative to the cost of the underlying unit.

Impact of Full Deferral on Best Buy Co., Inc.

Best Buy Co., Inc., will be used to illustrate the impact of the different accounting methods on a company's financial statements. Since the late 1980s, Best Buy Co., Inc., has been one of the country's fastest-growing specialty retailers (see Exhibit 2). Its stores offer name brand consumer electronics, home office equipment, appliances, and entertainment software. At the end of the company's 1996 fiscal year, it operated 251 stores in 29 states. The company offers extended warranty contracts on most of its consumer electronic products.

Best Buy Co., Inc.

The impact of Best Buy's change from partial recognition to the full deferral method can be seen in Exhibits 3 and 4, which contain the income statement and balance

EXHIBIT 1 Accounting for Extended Warranty Contracts

FULL RECOGNITION			PARTIAL RECOGNITION			FULL DEFERRAL		
Year 1:			*Year 1:*			*Year 1:*		
Cash	1100		Cash	1100		Cash	1100	
Revenue		1100	Revenue		1076.10	Revenue		1000
			Warranty Liability		23.90	Warranty Liability		100
CGS	900							
Inventory		900	CGS	900		CGS	900	
			Inventory		900	Inventory		900
Warranty Expense	20							
Warranty Liability		20						
Years 2 and 3:								
Warranty Liability	10		Warranty Liability	11.95		Warranty Liability	50	
Cash		10	Revenue		11.95	Warranty Revenue		50
			Warranty Expense	10.00		Warranty Expense	10	
			Cash		10.00	Cash		10

Financial Statement Effects, Year 1:

FULL RECOGNITION: INCOME STATEMENT		BALANCE SHEET		PARTIAL RECOGNITION: INCOME STATEMENT		BALANCE SHEET		FULL DEFERRAL: INCOME STATEMENT		BALANCE SHEET	
Revenue	$1,100	W. liability	$20	Revenue	$1076.10	W. liability	$23.90	Revenue	$1000	W. liability	100
Expense	920			Expense	900.00			Expense	900		
Gross profit	$ 180	(Includes only future service costs)		Gross profit	$ 176.10	(Includes future service costs and deferred profit)		Gross profit	$ 100		

Years 2 (and 3)

FULL RECOGNITION: INCOME STATEMENT		BALANCE SHEET		PARTIAL RECOGNITION: INCOME STATEMENT		BALANCE SHEET		FULL DEFERRAL: INCOME STATEMENT		BALANCE SHEET	
		W. liability	$10	Revenue	$11.95	W. liability	$11.95	Revenue	$50	W. liability	$50
None			(0)	Expense	10.00		(0)	Expense	10		(0)
				Gross profit	$ 1.95			Gross profit	$40		

sheet for Best Buy Co., Inc., for fiscal years 1991 and 1990. Because the company changed from partial recognition to full deferral on March 4, 1990, the column headed "March 2, 1991" provides financial results in the year of Best Buy's accounting change. Additionally, the income statement contains pro forma amounts for both years indicating what revenues and income would have been had full deferral been in use prior to 1990. After examining the statements, answer the following questions.

REQUIRED:

1. Best Buy, along with other large retailers such as *Circuit City, Inc.,* opposed the change from partial

recognition to full deferral. If all three methods recognize the same amount of total expense over the life of the warranty contract, why would Best Buy oppose the change?

2. What is the effect in fiscal 1991 (year ending March 2, 1991) of the accounting change on (1) income, (2) total shareholders' equity, and (3) return on beginning equity?

3. What theoretical justifications can you provide for (1) immediate recognition of all extended warranty revenue, and (2) full deferral of all extended warranty revenue?

EXHIBIT 2 Best Buy Sales and Operating Income Series, 1986–1995

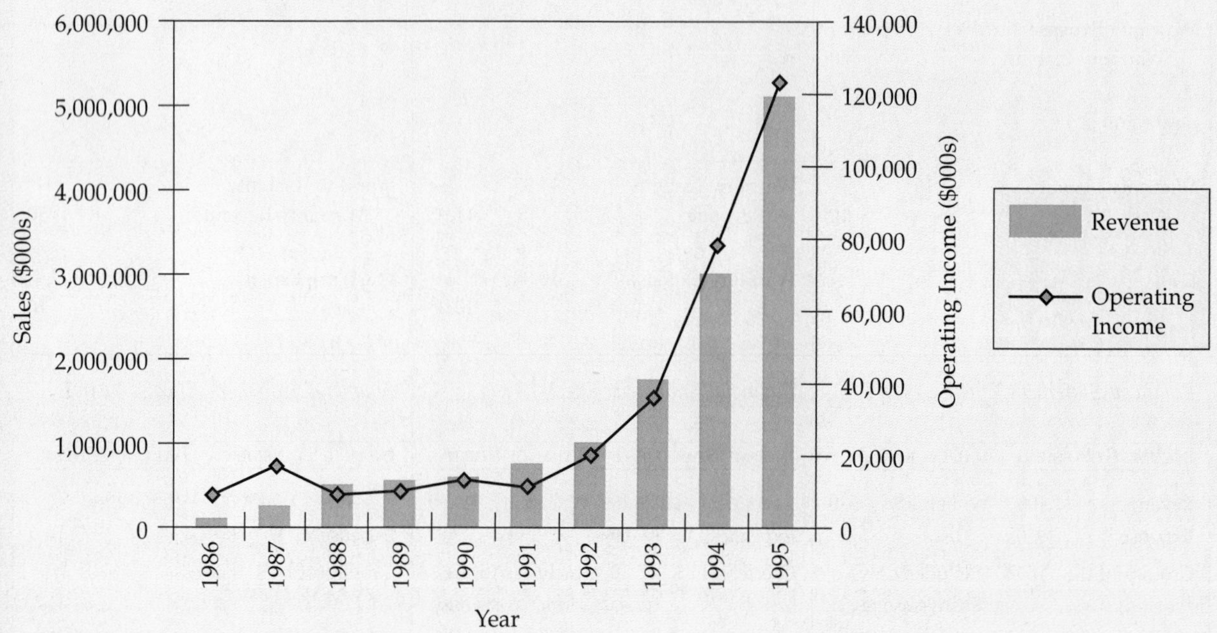

EXHIBIT 3
Best Buy's Income Statement

BEST BUY CO., INC.
Statements of Consolidated Income
For Period Ending:

	MARCH 2, 1991	MARCH 3, 1990
Revenues (in $000)	$664,823	$512,850
Cost of goods sold	523,166	392,509
Gross profit	$141,657	120,341
Selling, general, and administrative	130,681	107,194
Operating income	10,976	13,147
Interest expense	3,586	3,674
Earnings from continuing operations before income taxes	7,390	9,473

(continued)

Exhibit 3
(Concluded)

	March 2, 1991	March 3, 1990
Income tax expense	2,850	3,790
Earnings from continuing operations	4,540	5,683
Cumulative effect of change in accounting principle	(13,997)	
Net earnings (loss)	$ (9,457)	$ 5,683
Pro forma amounts assuming the change in accounting was applied retroactively:		
Revenues	$664,823	$509,175
Net earnings (loss)	4,540	3,935

Exhibit 4
Best Buy's Consolidated Balance Sheets

Best Buy Co., Inc.
Consolidated Balance Sheets

	March 2, 1991	March 3, 1990
Current assets (in $000):		
Cash and cash equivalents	$ 27,063	$ 23,830
Accounts receivable, net	8,716	7,318
Inventory	95,684	92,991
Prepaid income taxes	7,602	3,224
Prepaid expenses	$ 541	642
Total current assets	$139,606	$128,005
Tangible assets (net)	39,572	27,359
Prepaid income taxes	5,682	821
Other assets	668	602
Total assets	$185,528	$156,787
Current liabilities:		
Obligations under financing arrangements	$ 4,444	$ 2,598
Accounts payable	41,900	29,710
Accrued salaries	5,029	4,882
Accrued liabilities	6,741	5,066
Deferred service plan revenue	14,377	3,944
Accrued income tax	2,178	3,223
Current portion of long-term debt	314	184
Total current liabilities	$ 74,983	$ 49,607
Deferred service plan revenue—long term	$ 18,423	$ 5,931
Long-term debt	35,381	35,099
Total paid-in capital	42,214	42,166
Retained earnings	14,527	23,984
Total shareholders' equity	$ 56,741	$ 66,150
Total liabilities and shareholders' equity	$185,528	$156,787

PART 4

Solvency and Operational Capacity

12

Property, Plant, and Equipment

Intangible Assets

Long-Term Liabilities

Accounting for Leases

12

Property, Plant, and Equipment

Learning Objectives

After studying this chapter, you should be able to:

1. Calculate the cost basis of a productive asset acquired through a monetary exchange.
2. Explain the conceptual and accounting differences between dissimilar and similar assets for nonmonetary asset exchanges.
3. Account for assets obtained through exchanges for stock or by donation.
4. Account for costs incurred after the initial acquisition of assets.
5. Record the final disposition of property, plant, and equipment assets.
6. Interpret the fixed-asset-utilization and the return-on-assets ratios.

The Johnsons' Balance Sheet

Detailed Audit to Public Puts 'Capital' at $3,484,098, on Original-Cost Basis; Current Value Believed Higher

Washington—President Johnson acknowledged that the private wealth his family has acquired during his years in public office will be a campaign issue, by making public what appeared to be an unprecedented detailed accounting of assets and liabilities. . . .

The document released by the White House declares the Johnson "capital" to be $3,484,098. But Lady Bird broadcasting stock, Lyndon's ranch lands and the family's other properties are essentially figured on the basis of original cost rather than current market values.

"The amounts . . . are not intended to indicate the values that might be realized if the investments were sold."

To see what difference this makes, glance at the TV and radio empire that was formerly known as the LBJ Co. and currently is called Texas Broadcasting Corp. Industry experts estimate the company's broadcast holdings alone (not counting extensive real estate investments) would be worth some $7 million on the open market nowadays, which would place the Johnson family's 84% stock interest at nearly $6 million. But the White House document, even when including the real estate, states the family's interest in the company to be $2,445,830. . . .

The financial declaration mentions, but assigns zero value to the broadcasting company's 50% stock option plan in an Austin community, TV cable system. Some experts figure this option's likely worth $5 million when exercised—but the bookkeeping is defensible because the Johnson company acquired the valuable option without putting up a cent.

Source: Louis M. Kohlmeier, "The Johnson's Balance Sheet," *The Wall Street Journal,* August 20, 1964, p. 2.

GAAP requires valuation of long-term assets at historical cost less a contra-asset account for depreciation. The excerpt shown here, though approximately 30 years old, illustrates the dilemmas still posed by balance sheet values that reflect historical cost.

This is indeed a classic dilemma of relevance versus reliability. These primary qualitative characteristics were identified in SFAC No. 2 as necessary to make accounting data useful for decision making. Valuation of fixed assets at historical cost is objective and verifiable and thus meets the reliability criterion, but it may not meet the criterion of relevance. As illustrated in the excerpt, the assets valued at historical cost do not portray the underlying economic reality and thus lack representational faithfulness.

COST BASIS OF PRODUCTIVE OR CAPITAL ASSETS

Productive assets, also called **capital assets**, are long-term tangible assets used in the process of manufacturing goods and delivering services. This process generates revenues that eventually result in net cash inflows. Other titles for such assets are *property, plant and equipment, fixed assets,* and *long-term assets.* Unlike other revenue-generating assets such as inventory items and investments, productive (or capital) assets are not held for resale in the normal course of business but instead are utilized in the production process. As a result, their future economic benefit and service potential are diminished.

ACQUISITION COST TO BE CAPITALIZED

Productive assets can be acquired in several ways. The most frequent method of acquisition is by purchase from another entity, either by the transfer of assets (usually cash) or the promise to surrender assets or deliver services in the future. Other means of acquisition include leasing, self-construction, trading of assets, and donations. Regardless of the method of acquisition, two common issues must be addressed from an accounting standpoint: classification and valuation.

An asset is *classified* as a capital asset if the production of goods and services provides benefits longer than one operating cycle or one year. *Valuation* of the asset refers to cost capitalization. All costs incurred in acquisition and the preparation of the asset for its intended use are capitalized. The capitalized costs are subsequently allocated in a systematic manner over the asset's useful life in an attempt to match cost with periodic revenues. The main issue in this chapter is the determination of the initial cost to be capitalized. Cost allocation was discussed in Chapter 5.

There are several measurement problems concerning assets. What is the value of an asset? In the case of productive assets, does the value remain fixed over the life expectancy of that asset or does it change in response to market pressures? If the value changes, how should those changes be recognized in the financial statements? Additionally, how should the initial cost of the asset be allocated to achieve a proper matching of revenue and cost associated with the asset? Finally, at what point in the revenue-generation process is the revenue realized and recognized as income?

Current GAAP prescribes that the initial acquisition cost be used for asset valuation and as the basis of cost allocation. Conceptually, the value of any asset is the sum of the future net cash inflows discounted at the market-determined rate of return. Competitive buyers will bid the price of the asset to the point at which the acquisition cost will provide future cash inflows equal to the desired rate of return. Thus, in an arm's-length transaction, the marketplace will provide the fair value of assets.

IN PRACTICE—INTERNATIONAL

Revaluation of Assets

Several European countries either require or permit companies to revalue assets periodically to reflect changing prices. Generally, the companies use replacement cost as a basis for their write-ups. Germany and Luxembourg are the only countries in the European Community that prohibit write-ups to current costs.

"Since 1984, because of severe inflation, Mexican accounting principles have required all nonmonetary assets to be valued at current replacement cost or at restated historical cost" (that is, restated to reflect changing prices based on some index). Of these two alternatives, companies listed with the Mexican equivalent of the SEC are required to use current replacement cost.

Sources: L. Sundby and B. Schieger, "EC, EZ?," *Management Accounting,* March 1992, pp. 72–73; *Doing Business in Mexico,* Price Waterhouse, 1993.

Theoretically, on the acquisition date, all the values—current cost, either exit value or replacement cost, historical cost, and discounted cash flows—are equal. Valuation difficulties arise, however, in subsequent reporting periods because an efficient unbiased measuring tool such as the marketplace does not always exist. Accordingly, under current GAAP, long-lived assets are reported at historical cost. In many regards, the reported values of productive assets are the least relevant for current valuation purposes of any items on the balance sheet. Reporting long-lived assets at historical cost is one area in which current U.S. GAAP is at odds with the accounting standards of several other nations.

This is a problem recognized by the profession and by the Securities and Exchange Commission (SEC). The chief accountant of the SEC spoke to this point in 1992, indicating that problems associated with valuation of assets were indeed under consideration by the profession.

IN PRACTICE—GENERAL

Cost Capitalization

The following excerpt addresses the current awareness of problems in the way assets are valued.

> Walter P. Schuetze, the Securities and Exchange Commission's new chief accountant, is a precise man. He chooses his words carefully and speaks in measured phrases. He does not, however, mince words. In a *Journal* interview shortly after he took office in January, he clearly defined his top priorities upon assuming his position. When asked about the profession's problem areas, he said, "I do not think the users of financial statements have been well served over the last 10 to 15 years. As a result, I think financial accounting and reporting have lost some of their credibility, and we need to improve this relevance."
>
> Schuetze also has firm ideas on how financial reporting can regain its credibility. He said, "I know where to begin the process of improving financial accounting and reporting. We need to get debt and equity securities marked to market. . . ." He, however, goes on to say, "I think getting to market value on fixed assets is a long way away. . . ."

Source: Gene R. Barrett, "The SEC's New Chief Accountant Sets Some Clear Goals," *Journal of Accountancy*, June 1992, p. 102.

MONETARY EXCHANGES

Calculate the cost basis of a productive asset acquired through a monetary exchange.

EQUIPMENT COSTS

In general, costs associated with obtaining new assets and placing them in operation are capitalized. These *equipment costs* include the initial purchase price, transportation costs, and placement and installation costs. The costs of trial runs and spoilage or defective products resulting from such runs also are capitalized.

LAND COSTS

Land costs include the initial acquisition cost and all expenditures necessary to prepare it for its intended use. Commissions paid, costs incurred in grading and clearing, drainage, and any such similar costs are capitalized as part of the land cost. If existing structures must be demolished to prepare the land site, these costs (less any proceeds from salvage) also are capitalized and included as part of the carrying cost of the land.

Costs of improvements providing permanent benefits toward the service potential of the land are included in the Land account because the property benefits from these improvements last indefinitely. Examples are assessments for sewage, sidewalks, curbs, and lights. None of these expenditures is depreciated, because (1) the future service potential is generally not affected by the use of land as a building site, and (2) maintenance of these is usually the responsibility of the government body involved.

Improvements with limited lives, however, are given the same status as any other long-lived asset, and a separate account (Land Improvements) is maintained with an attendant contra-asset account for depreciation. Examples of this type of improvement are parking lots, private roads, sidewalks, fences, and private lighting. Responsibility for maintenance of these improvements usually rests with the landowner.

BUILDING COSTS

Building costs result when buildings are acquired in one of three ways: (1) they are purchased already constructed, with the land; (2) they are built by an independent contractor; or (3) they are constructed with internal resources. Each method of acquisition presents different accounting issues.

Basket Purchase. In a basket purchase, one lump sum is paid for more than one item—for example, land and building purchased together. For such basket purchases, also called *lump-sum purchases,* the relative-market-value method is used to assign the total purchase cost in the same proportion that each component's individual market value bears to the total market value of all items purchased. Exhibit 12–1 illustrates this method of assigning the purchase cost. The method has intuitive appeal in that it relies on the fair market value of the individual assets purchased to assign or allocate the total purchase cost.

Independent Contracts. Construction of a building by an independent contractor requires the capitalization of the contract price plus the cost of any subsequent changes. Architectural and legal fees normally are included as part of the building cost. Theoretically, all costs associated with the completion of the contract should be capitalized.

Self-Constructed Assets. Self-constructed assets are generally recorded in the same manner as the acquisition of any other long-term asset. Capitalization of the cost of direct materials and direct labor used in the construction process is clear. However, the cost of related overhead and interest is not so clear. These two issues are the most intriguing and distinguishing accounting features of self-constructed assets.

Capitalization of Overhead. There are three schools of thought on this issue:

1. Charge the asset with its fair share of the manufacturing fixed overhead in the same manner as that allocated to inventory.

EXHIBIT 12–1
Relative-Market-Value Method Used with Basket Purchase

Assume that a $1 million purchase includes the following:

1. A parcel of real estate composed of 10 acres of land.
2. A general-purpose warehouse containing 100,000 square feet of storage space.
3. A new parking lot.
4. Three acres of concrete open-air storage.

The following facts are available:

1. Unimproved land in this area sells for $20,000 per acre.
2. Warehouse purchase costs for assets of similar-type construction and condition are $10 per square foot.
3. Estimated construction cost for the parking lot is $100,000.
4. The estimated fair market value of the concrete storage area is $100,000 per acre.

The total fair market (relative sales) value of the separate components is determined as follows:

Land ($20,000 per acre × 10)	$ 200,000
Building ($10 × 100,000 sq. ft.)	1,000,000
Parking lot	100,000
Storage ($100,000 × 3)	300,000
Total	$1,600,000

The assignment of costs to each of the separate components based upon its relative sales (market) value follows:

Land ($200,000/$1,600,000) × $1,000,000	$ 125,000
Building ($1,000,000/$1,600,000) × $1,000,000	625,000
Parking lot ($100,000/$1,600,000) × $1,000,000	62,500
Storage ($300,000/$1,600,000) × $1,000,000	187,500
Total	$1,000,000

2. Charge the asset only with the identifiable incremental fixed overhead.
3. Allocate no overhead charges to the project.

At present there is no standard that deals specifically with this issue. However, *Accounting Research Monograph 1* offers the following thought:

> In the absence of compelling evidence to the contrary, overhead costs considered to have "discernible future benefits" for the purposes of determining the cost of inventory should be presumed to have "future discernible benefits" for purposes of determining the cost of a self-constructed asset.

This implies agreement with the first position that applicable overhead should be charged to the cost of construction.

Capitalization of Interest. Historically, interest incurred on self-constructed assets was capitalized only in the utility industries. The reason for inclusion of interest by utilities is that their billable rates are a function of a return on assets employed, thus providing the motivation to capitalize all possible expenditures. Other industries generally seek immediate tax relief by expensing the interest in the period incurred. The position taken by the FASB in SFAS Nos. 34 and 42 requires capitalization of interest and follows the general rule of capitalization of all material costs at acquisition.

To capitalize interest, three conditions must exist:

1. Construction expenditures must be made.
2. Interest must be incurred.
3. Activities to prepare the asset for use must be ongoing.

The overriding requirement, however, is that expenditures must have been made. Two items are concerned with the capitalization of interest—the duration of the capitalization period and the amount to be capitalized.

Interest is capitalized during the ongoing construction period. However, no interest is to be capitalized until an expenditure has been made, and then only until the project is substantially completed and put to its intended use. If for some reason the construction process is interrupted for a substantial period, the interest during the period of interruption must be expensed and not capitalized. Temporary interruptions due to inclement weather or short work stoppages over labor disputes do not preclude capitalization of interest.

The amount of interest to be capitalized is the lesser of the actual interest or the avoidable interest for the period. The avoidable interest is the amount directly attributable to the construction project during the period of active ongoing construction. The interest rate used to determine the avoidable interest should be the actual interest rate charged for those loans obtained specifically for the project, and excess amounts at a weighted average rate on previously existing long-term debt.

The interest rate on the specifically borrowed funds is applied to an amount called the **average accumulated expenditures.** The payments actually made for the project are weighted by the portion of the year and summed to find the average accumulated expenditures. For example, if payments of $100,000 were made on April 1 and July 1, the average accumulated expenditures would be determined as follows:

4/1 payment $100,000 × 9/12	=	$ 75,000
7/1 payment 100,000 × 6/12	=	50,000
Average accumulated expenditures	=	$125,000

This is the amount on which interest should be capitalized for the year. If a construction loan in the amount of $125,000 or greater had been taken to finance the construction, the interest rate on the construction loan would be applied to the $125,000 of average accumulated expenditures to determine the avoidable interest. If the construction loan was less than $125,000—say, only $80,000 at a rate of 12%—then 12% would be applied to $80,000 of the accumulated expenditures, and the weighted average rate of the previously outstanding long-term debt would be applied to the remaining $45,000.

The avoidable interest must then be compared to the actual interest because the amount of interest capitalized during a period must not exceed the actual amount of interest incurred during that period. Exhibits 12–2 through

12–6 provide an example of interest capitalization on a self-constructed asset. Exhibit 12–2 contains the data for the project. Exhibit 12–3 shows the calculations for the amount of avoidable interest in 1997, and Exhibit 12–4 the journal entries for that year. Exhibit 12–5 shows the interest calculations for 1998, and Exhibit 12–6 the journal entries for that year. Note that the interest capitalized

EXHIBIT 12–2
Capitalization of Interest on Self-Constructed Assets: Data

Assume that the Bandy Body Shop is engaged in construction of a plant. Construction started June 1, 1997. Bandy halted the project because of legal problems from January 1, 1998, until March 1, 1998, at which time construction was resumed. The project was completed October 31, 1998, and payments were made to the contractor as follows:

June 1, 1997	$ 200,000
August 1, 1997	300,000
October 31, 1997	400,000
April 1, 1998	500,000
August 1, 1998	400,000
October 31, 1998	200,000
Total	$2,000,000

Bandy borrowed $1,000,000 for five years at 12% interest on May 1, 1997, specifically for the building project. No other funds were borrowed to complete the project. However, Bandy had a long-term note outstanding for $1,000,000 at 9% and 12% bonds (sold at par) outstanding in the amount of $2,000,000 during the construction of the building.

EXHIBIT 12–3
Capitalization of Interest on Self-Constructed Assets: 1997 Activity

Average Accumulated Expenditures

EXPENDITURE DATE	EXPENDITURE AMOUNT		PORTION OF CAPITALIZATION PERIOD		AVERAGE ACCUMULATED EXPENDITURES
June 1, 1997	$200,000	×	7/12	=	$116,667
August 1, 1997	300,000	×	5/12	=	125,000
October 31, 1997	400,000	×	2/12	=	66,667
Total	$900,000			=	$308,334

Avoidable Interest in 1997

Interest rate = 12% on $1,000,000 of funds borrowed specifically for the project.

Avoidable Interest ($308,334 × .12)	= $ 37,000
Actual Interest:	
Construction loan (1,000,000 × 12% × 8/12)	= $ 80,000
Long-term note (1,000,000 × 9%)	= 90,000
Long-term bonds (2,000,000 × 12%)	= 240,000
Total actual interest	= $410,000
Avoidable interest (capitalized)	= (37,000)
Interest expensed in 1997	= $373,000

Exhibit 12–4
Capitalization of Interest on Self-Constructed Assets: 1997 Journal Entries

6/1	Building	200,000	
	Cash		200,000
8/1	Building	300,000	
	Cash		300,000
10/31	Building	400,000	
	Cash		400,000
12/31	Interest Expense	373,000	
	Building	37,000	
	Interest Payable		410,000

The interest expense of $373,000 and the capitalized interest of $37,000 are calculated in Exhibit 12–3.

Exhibit 12–5
Capitalization of Interest on Self-Constructed Assets: 1998 Activity

Assume no construction activity from January 1, 1998, to March 1, 1998, and project is completed on October 31, 1998. Thus, the active ongoing construction period is eight months, from March 1 through October 31, of 1998. Interest must be capitalized for this 8-month period.

Average Accumulated Expenditures

Expenditure Date	Expenditure Amount		Capitalization Period[a]		Average Accumulated Expenditures
1/1/98	$ 937,000[b]	×	8/12	=	$ 624,667
4/1/98	500,000	×	7/12	=	291,667
8/1/98	400,000	×	3/12	=	100,000
10/31/98	200,000	×	0/12	=	0
Total	$2,037,000				$1,016,334

[a]The capitalization period does not include downtime of two months because no progress toward completion was made.
[b]$937,000 = $900,000 + $37,000 from 1997.

Avoidable Interest in 1998

$1,016,334	Total accumulated expenditures	
1,000,000	Construction loan amount of 12%	= $120,000
16,334	at weighted-average rate of 11%[a]	= 1,797
	Total avoidable interest	$121,797

[a]Determination of weighted-average rate.

$1,000,000 × 9% =	$ 90,000	(9% long-term note payable)
2,000,000 × 12% =	240,000	(12% bond payable)
$3,000,000	$330,000	Interest per year

$330,000/$3,000,000 = 11% Weighted-Average Rate

Actual Interest:		
1,000,000 × 12% =	$120,000	
1,000,000 × 9% =	90,000	
2,000,000 × 12% =	240,000	
Total actual interest		$ 450,000
Avoidable interest (capitalized)		(121,797)
Interest expense for 1998		$ 328,203

EXHIBIT 12–6
Capitalization of Interest on Self-Constructed Assets: Journal Entries for 1998

4/1/98	Building	500,000	
	Cash		500,000
8/1/98	Building	400,000	
	Cash		400,000
10/31/98	Building	200,000	
	Cash		200,000
12/31/98[a]	Building	121,797	
	Interest Expense		121,797
	To reduce the interest expense for the portion of interest capitalized.		
12/31/98[a]	Interest Expense	450,000	
	Interest Payable		450,000

[a]These two entries could have been made in one single entry at the end of 1998 in the same manner as at the end of 1997. The adjusting entry at the end of 1998 then would be:

Interest Expense	328,203	
Building	121,797	
Interest Payable		450,000

in the project is charged to expense over the useful life of the asset as depreciation. This differs from the normal recognition of interest expense, which is over the term of the debt.

If the total cost of a self-constructed asset exceeds the fair market value (FMV) of the asset, the asset must be written down to the FMV. The resultant loss is charged to the period in which the construction is completed. The rationale for immediate recognition of the loss is that the excess cost *does not* and *will not* benefit any future operating periods.

ACQUISITIONS INVOLVING CREDIT

If an asset is purchased with some amount of credit, at what value should the asset be recorded? Financing arrangements that specify the interest rate and the purchase price pose no unusual problems. There are, however, two other financing arrangements that are not as straightforward: lease arrangements and noninterest-bearing notes. Leases are discussed at length in Chapter 15.

Noninterest-bearing notes receivable were discussed in Chapter 8, and noninterest-bearing notes payable are the other side of the same transaction. The underlying economic reality of a noninterest-bearing note is that the interest is included in the face amount of the note. The face amount of the note is equal to the purchase price of the asset minus any cash down payment plus the interest.

When the purchase price is known, an effective interest rate must be determined such that the present value of the future payments (face amount of the note) equals the purchase price. When the purchase price is not known, it must be determined as the present value of the cash payments based upon some imputed interest rate.

To illustrate: Assume a truck with a FMV of $10,000 is purchased and the seller accepts a noninterest-bearing, long-term note for $15,209 due at the end of three years. Clearly, the purchase price of the asset is $10,000, and the balance of the note represents interest. The entry to record the purchase is

Truck	10,000	
Discount on Notes Payable	5,209	
Notes Payable		15,209

CONCEPT Valuation of asset at cost.

LOGIC Since the FMV of the asset is $10,000, this represents the cost of the asset. The difference between the FMV and the face amount of the note represents interest that will accrue over the life of the note. The discount amount must be allocated (amortized) using an effective rate for which $10,000 is the present value of the future $15,209. Effective-interest-rate allocation was first illustrated in Chapter 5.

The account Discount on Notes Payable is a contra account to the Notes Payable account reported on the balance sheet. The discount is amortized over the life of the note using the effective-interest-rate method. The amortization table and journal entries to record the amortization and subsequent payment of the note appear in Exhibits 12–7 and 12–8.

EXHIBIT 12–7
Noninterest-Bearing Notes: Calculation of Interest Rate and Amortization Table

Assumptions

1. Truck FMV = $10,000.
2. Note payable with face amount of $15,209, 3 years, no interest rate stated, issued January 1, Year A, due December 31, Year C.

To determine the annual interest charged in this transaction, divide the note amount by the fair market value (cash purchase price) of the asset. This is the time-value-of-money factor used to find the future value of a single amount. Thus $15,209/$10,000 = 1.5209. This factor is found in Appendix A, Table A–1, using three periods to find 15%. The entry to record the purchase was illustrated in the text and follows.

Truck	10,000	
Discount on Notes Payable	5,209	
Notes Payable		15,209

Amortization Table for Discount

	Note Amount	Discount	Carrying Value	Effective Interest of 15%	Discount After Amortization
Year A	$15,209	$5,209	$10,000	$1,500	$3,709
Year B	15,209	3,709	11,500	1,725	1,984
Year C	15,209	1,984	13,225	1,984	0

EXHIBIT 12–8
Noninterest-Bearing Notes: Journal Entries to Amortize Discount and Pay Note

Year A	Interest Expense	1,500	
	Discount on Notes Payable		1,500
Year B	Interest Expense	1,725	
	Discount on Notes Payable		1,725
Year C	Interest Expense	1,984	
	Discount on Notes Payable		1,984
Year C	Notes Payable	15,209	
	Cash		15,209

NONMONETARY ASSET EXCHANGES

Explain the conceptual and accounting differences between dissimilar and similar assets for nonmonetary asset exchanges.

Nonmonetary-asset exchanges are exchanges of one productive asset for another. The assets exchanged may be dissimilar or similar. A dissimilar asset exchange might involve a crane and computer, while a similar asset exchange might involve two parcels of land. Nonmonetary exchange transactions are assumed to be *arm's-length transactions,* meaning they involve an exchange of goods of equal fair market values. That is, the total value given up will be equivalent to the total value received.

Accounting for nonmonetary asset exchanges depends on whether the assets are similar or dissimilar, a gain or loss is involved, and whether any cash is involved in the transaction. Exhibit 12–9 presents a summary of the different types of nonmonetary exchanges.

The basis of these exchanges is the negotiated exchange value or fair market value (FMV). The FMV is determined by the value of the asset surrendered or the value of the asset received, whichever is more clearly determinable. For example, if machine A is traded for machine B, the basis of the exchange would be the FMV of whichever machine is more certain. If machine A has an established cash market value of $4,500, then $4,500 would be recognized as the basis of exchange. If the market value of A is unknown, but machine B has a clearly established market value of $3,800, then $3,800 is the basis of the exchange.

The gain or loss on the transaction is the difference between the book value (BV) and the FMV of the old asset surrendered. If the FMV of the old asset is unknown, the gain or loss is the difference between the BV of the assets given up and the FMV of the assets received. If neither the FMV of the old asset nor the FMV of the new asset is known, the basis of the new asset is the BV of the old asset.

A series of examples follows to illustrate these concepts.

DISSIMILAR-ASSET EXCHANGES

Both gains and losses are recognized on exchanges involving assets that are dissimilar. Recognition of gains on dissimilar-asset exchanges is appropriate because the earnings process in which the old asset was utilized has been completed. The realization of the economic benefits of the old asset has been completed. The assumption is that the asset given up could have been sold for cash and the proceeds used to acquire the dissimilar asset. If the old asset indeed had been sold for cash greater than its BV, a gain would have been recognized.

EXHIBIT 12–9
Nonmonetary Asset Exchanges

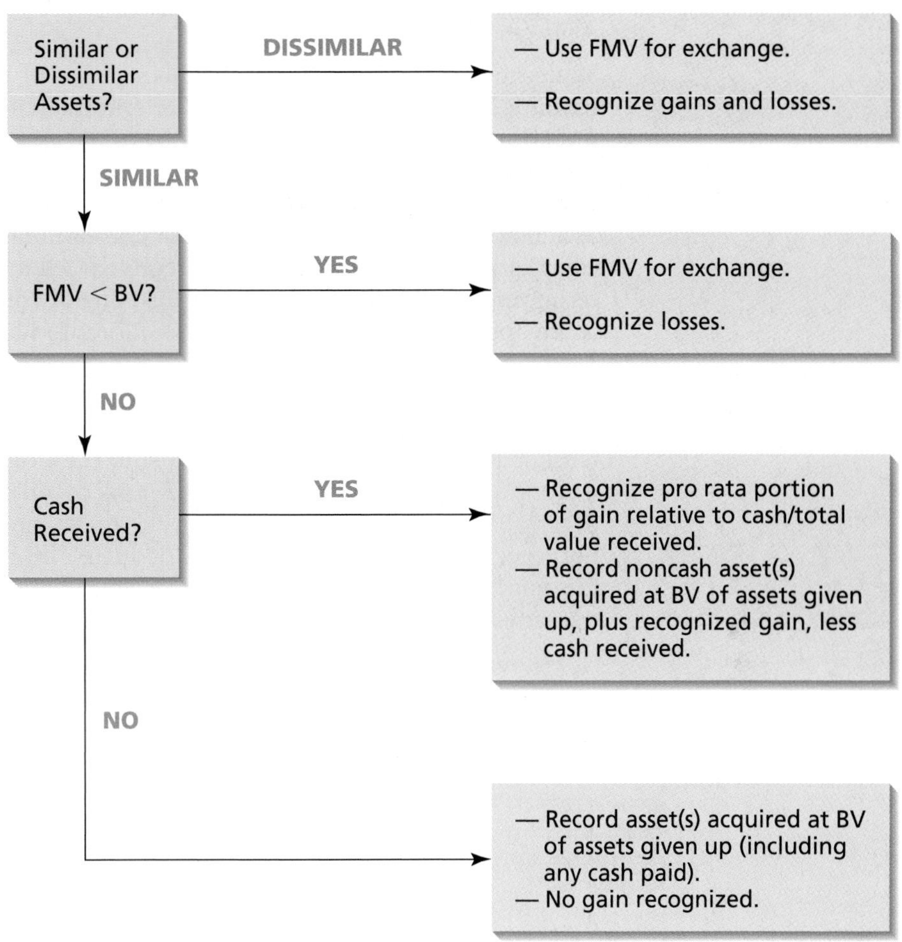

To illustrate a dissimilar-asset exchange, assume that an asset had an original cost of $10,000, accumulated depreciation of $6,000, and a FMV of $5,000. Rather than sell the asset for cash, a dissimilar asset with a FMV of $5,000 is accepted in exchange. The journal entry to record the exchange would be

Asset (New)	5,000	
Accumulated Depreciation (Old)	6,000	
Asset (Old)		10,000
Gain on Exchange		1,000

CONCEPT Recognition of gains and losses at completion of earnings process.

LOGIC A dissimilar-asset exchange presumes that the earnings process has been completed; thus, recognition of a gain or loss on the disposal is appropriate. The receipt of a dissimilar asset with a FMV greater than the BV of the old asset is evidence that cash could have been received for the same value; thus, a gain has occurred.

SIMILAR-ASSET EXCHANGES

Similar assets need not be identical but rather of the same general type and used for the same general purpose. For example, exchanging a Chevrolet truck for a Ford truck with the same load-bearing capacity would be viewed as an exchange of similar assets. Recognition of a gain on the exchange depends on whether the earnings process has been completed. The receipt of cash as well as another similar asset is evidence that the earnings process has been partially completed to the extent of the cash received. All losses on such exchanges are recognized immediately, following the general concept of recognizing losses when apparent. A series of examples follows to illustrate these concepts.

Similar-Asset Exchange with No Cash. Assume that the BB Company exchanges a similar asset with JA Company, and the FMV of both assets is determined to be $5,000. The original cost of the asset surrendered was $10,000, and the accumulated depreciation is $6,000, or a BV of $4,000. BB has a gain of $1,000 ($5,000 FMV − $4,000 BV) on the exchange that must be deferred and not recognized. The deferred gain is deducted from the FMV of the new asset to provide the basis for recording the new asset. The basis of the new asset is the same amount as the BV of the old asset surrendered.

Accumulated Depreciation	6,000	
Asset (new) ($5,000 − $1,000)	4,000	
Asset (old)		10,000

CONCEPT Deferral of gain recognition until completion of the earnings process.

LOGIC The earnings process in which the old asset was used has not been completed, since there was an exchange of like assets. The process in which the old asset was utilized continues with the new asset. The gain will be recognized over the life of the new asset during the earnings process through reduced depreciation expense charges. The basis of the new asset is $4,000 instead of $5,000. Therefore, the depreciation charges will be correspondingly less each period. This effectively spreads the gain over the life of the new asset and reduces the periodic depreciation charge against income.

Now assume that the FMV of the assets exchanged is $3,000. BB would have a loss of $1,000 ($4,000 BV − $3,000 FMV) and would recognize it immediately.

Accumulated Depreciation (old)	6,000	
Asset (new at FMV)	3,000	
Loss on the Exchange	1,000	
Asset (old)		10,000

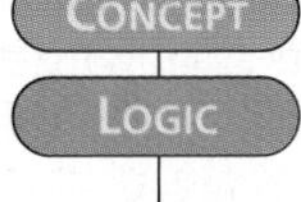

CONCEPT Recognition of loss.

LOGIC When the FMV of the asset surrendered (or as measured by the FMV of the asset received) is less than the BV of the asset surrendered, a loss should be recognized. The new asset is recorded at FMV.

Similar-Asset Exchange with Cash Given. Assume that BB gives $1,000 cash plus an old asset costing $10,000, with accumulated depreciation of $6,000 for a similar asset with a FMV of $3,500. BB has a loss of $1,500 determined as follows:

BV given up	$4,000
Cash given up	1,000
Total given up	$5,000
FMV of new asset received	3,500
Loss on exchange	$1,500

Since the FMV of the old asset is unknown, the basis of the exchange is the FMV of the new asset, $3,500. BB gives up $5,000 in cash and BV, recording this transaction as follows:

Accumulated Depreciation (old)	6,000	
Asset (new)	3,500	
Loss on the Exchange (3,500 − 5,000)	1,500	
Asset (old)		10,000
Cash		1,000

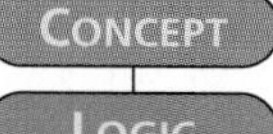

CONCEPT

All losses recognized when apparent.

LOGIC

When the BV of the asset surrendered plus the cash given is greater than the FMV of the asset received, a loss results and should be recognized at the time of the exchange. The new asset is recorded at its FMV.

Now suppose that the total of the cash and the BV of the asset surrendered ($1,000 cash plus $4,000 BV of old asset) is less than the FMV of the asset received. Assume that the FMV of the asset received is $5,500, and a gain of $500 results ($5,500 FMV − $5,000 cash and BV). The gain must be deferred and reduces the carrying value of the new asset. The new asset is recorded at FMV less the deferred gain.

Accumulated Depreciation (old)	6,000	
Asset (new) ($5,500 − $500)	5,000	
Asset (old)		10,000
Cash		1,000

CONCEPT

Deferral of gain recognition on the exchange of similar assets.

LOGIC

The earnings process has not been completed, since there was an exchange of similar assets. The gain ($500) will be recognized over the life of the new asset through reduced depreciation expense charges. The basis of the new asset is $5,000 instead of $5,500. Therefore, the depreciation expense will be less each period.

Similar-Asset Exchange with Cash Received. Again assume that BB exchanges similar assets with JA and that BB's asset has a FMV of $4,000 with a BV of $4,000. The asset received has a FMV of $3,000, and BB also receives $1,000 in cash. The basis of the exchange is $4,000, and BB has no gain or loss to recognize because the BV of the old asset as well as its FMV was $4,000. BB's journal entry to record the exchange is

Cash	1,000	
Asset (new at FMV)	3,000	
Accumulated Depreciation (old)	6,000	
Asset (old)		10,000

CONCEPT Asset valuation at acquisition.

LOGIC Assets are recorded at cost at acquisition. Cost is measured in this instance as FMV, since no gain or loss is recognized on the exchange. There is no gain or loss because the value received is equal to the value surrendered.

Now assume that the asset received by BB has a known FMV of $4,000, and BB also receives cash of $2,000. The basis of the exchange is now $6,000, and BB has a gain of $2,000. The gain is the difference between the BV of the old asset and its FMV. The FMV in this case must be $6,000, since BB received an asset with a FMV of $4,000 and cash of $2,000. The part of the gain recognized is determined by the ratio of the cash received to the total value received.

$$\frac{\text{Cash Received}}{\text{Cash + FMV of Asset Received}} \times \text{Gain} = \text{Gain Recognized}$$

$$\frac{\$2{,}000}{\$2{,}000 + \$4{,}000} \times \$2{,}000 = \$667 \text{ Gain Recognized}$$

The unrecognized portion of the gain ($2,000 − $667 = $1,333) is deferred and reduces the carrying value of the new asset. BB would record the exchange as follows:

Cash	2,000	
Asset (new) ($4,000 − $1,333)	2,667	
Accumulated Depreciation	6,000	
Asset (old)		10,000
Gain on the Exchange		667

The fact that a substantial amount of cash is included along with a similar asset creates a package significantly different from the one surrendered. One could argue that the earnings process was substantially complete, given the

CONCEPT — Recognition of gain on the exchange of similar assets when cash is received.

LOGIC — Gains on the exchange of similar assets are recognized in proportion to the cash received to the total value received. The reasoning behind this approach is that the earnings process is only partially completed, i.e., to the extent of the cash received in relation to the total value received. The $2,000 gain is partially realized ($667) and the remaining portion ($1,333) is deferred (subtracted from the FMV of the new asset). Thus, the new asset is recorded at $2,667 ($4,000 − $1,333), and the deferred gain will be recognized over the life of the new asset through reduced depreciation charges.

magnitude of the cash received in relation to the total value of the transaction.[1] However, at the present time, APB Opinion No. 29 indicates that only a proportionate part of the gain may be recognized.

ASSETS ACQUIRED BY OTHER MEANS

Account for assets obtained through exchanges for stock or by donation.

EXCHANGES OF STOCK FOR ASSETS

Sometimes corporations issue stock as payment for assets rather than cash. Valuation of assets obtained in this manner follows the same guidelines as earlier described. The basis of the new asset is the FMV of the stock given up or the FMV of the asset received, whichever is more clearly determinable. For example, assume that LD Corporation issues 10,000 shares of $5 par stock for a parcel of land and a building advertised at $100,000. The land is appraised for $20,000 and the building for $75,000. The stock is from a closely held corporation, and there has been no sale of stock for three years. LD would record this transaction, as follows:

Land	20,000	
Building	75,000	
Common Stock (10,000 × $5)		50,000
Paid-In Capital in Excess of Par		45,000

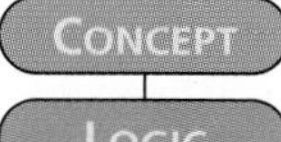

CONCEPT — Valuation of assets at acquisition at cost.

LOGIC — Assets are recorded at acquisition at cost. In this instance, cost is measured as the FMV of the item surrendered or the item received, whichever is more clearly determinable.

Only arbitrarily determined par values were given for the stock surrendered, whereas appraised values are available for the assets received. The advertised price is frequently only the starting point for negotiating a price and is normally more than the agreed-upon price in real estate transactions.

[1]The Emerging Issues Task Force reached a consensus in Issue Number 86–29 about this particular instance. The guideline suggested by the task force was that if the cash equaled or exceeded 25% of the total fair value received, then all the potential gain on a nonmonetary transaction should be recognized. This is a recommendation that may or may not receive consideration by the FASB.

Now assume that the stock is actively traded with the last trade at $8 per share, and all other conditions remain the same. The basis of the exchange is now the stock value ($80,000), because it is more clearly determinable. The separate appraisal values would, however, be used to apportion the total cost to the land and building similar to the basket purchase discussed earlier in the chapter. The entry would be

Land	16,842*	
Building	63,158	
Common Stock (5 × $10,000)		50,000
Paid-In Capital in Excess of Par		30,000

*($20,000/$95,000) × 80,000 = $16,482
($75,000/$95,000) × 80,000 = $63,158

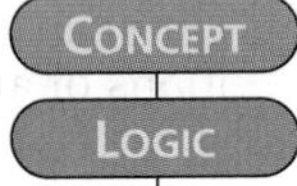

Valuation of assets at acquisition.

Assets are recorded at cost. Cost is measured as the FMV of the item surrendered or the item received, whichever is more clearly determinable. The stock price is the most reliable because of the recent transactions establishing the price. Stock-market prices are usually determined by many independent transactions and should be more reliable than appraisals in establishing FMVs. The appraisal values are used to apportion the cost to the land and building.

DONATIONS AND GIFTS

In general, the same measurement method outlined in the previous section is used to assign values to assets that are donated to an entity. Many cities and counties entice industries to locate in their political subdivisions by donating property, creating employment opportunities for their citizens, and enhancing the economic climate.

To illustrate, assume that Huntsville donates land to Mercedes-Benz as part of an economic assistance package to entice Mercedes-Benz to locate in Huntsville. Mercedes-Benz has received an economic benefit, an asset that has future economic worth. The question is, at what value should the land be recorded? The best that can usually be done in these cases is to use appraisal values with a corresponding credit entry to the account, Donated Capital. Any additional costs incurred with such transfers are normally incidental in nature and of such small magnitude that they are expensed in the period incurred. Items such as attorney's fees, deed-transfer cost, and so on, usually are not material and, as a practical matter, are expensed.

Some would argue that the receipt of such donations should be recognized as income or a gain during the period of receipt.[2] A reasonable case can be

[2]SFAS No. 116, "Accounting for Contributions Received and Contributions Made," addresses donations and requires that unrestricted donations be reported as revenue during the period of receipt. However, the standard specifically excludes donations by government units to business enterprises. Paragraph 4 states, in part, "[the requirement] does not apply to tax exemptions, tax incentives, or tax abatements, or to transfers of assets from governmental units to business enterprises."

made to treat the transaction as a nonreciprocal transfer—one in which the first party receives a benefit without making any sacrifice to the second party—and thus recognize an extraordinary gain. Such transactions normally meet both tests of being unusual and infrequent under the criteria of APB Opinion No. 30, discussed in Chapter 6. However, gains are not usually recorded at the time of asset acquisition, but rather at the time of disposition, signaling that the earnings process has been completed. Others argue that a memorandum entry is all that is necessary until the asset is sold. However, it seems a better case can be made to record the asset at FMV (appraisal value) and amortize the cost (for assets other than land) over the useful productive life of the asset following the realization and matching concepts.

COST INCURRED AFTER ACQUISITION

Account for costs incurred after the initial acquisition of assets.

Expenditures incurred after the initial acquisition costs and the asset is placed into operation are either revenue expenditures or capital expenditures. Revenue expenditures occur as part of the normal operations of an enterprise and benefit the current period only. They are expensed in the period incurred. Capital expenditures, however, benefit the operations for more than one period and are capitalized. *Capitalized,* you will recall, means that the expenditure is debited to an asset account because the expenditure is expected to provide benefit in future periods as well as the current period. The accounting issue is to determine if these costs provide benefit to more than one operating period.

Costs for repairs and maintenance, additions, improvements, replacements, rearrangements, and reinstallations are examples of expenditures that take place after acquisition. In general, any cost incurred that extends the productive life of the asset, increases productivity, or enhances the quality of the services delivered is capitalized. These attributes are associated with providing additional service potential that should increase future net cash inflows to the entity.

While these conceptual guidelines seem straightforward, judgment, materiality, and expediency sometimes modify them in practice. For example, a wastepaper basket has a useful life of more than one year but is usually expensed. The amount is not material, and the cost of recording the item and allocating the cost through depreciation charges over its useful life exceeds the benefit that would be derived from capitalizing its cost. Many entities have established policies regarding minimum dollar amounts to be spent before expenditures are capitalized.

ADDITIONS

Entities frequently expand existing facilities to increase productive capacity with the expectation of increased future net cash inflows. Expenditures for additions should be capitalized and the cost allocated over the expected useful life of the addition. If the addition is an integral part of an old asset, such as an additional floor of a building, the expenditure is added to the old asset account and the new balance allocated over the remaining useful life of the old building. However, if the life of the addition has a shorter life expectancy than the original asset, then a separate asset account is established, and the cost is allocated over the life of the addition.

IMPROVEMENTS AND REPLACEMENTS

Improvements are distinguished from replacements by the impact on the old asset. An expenditure enhancing the life, the productivity, or the quality of the service rendered by an asset is classified as an improvement. An expenditure necessitated by normal wear and tear but providing no enhancement of life, productivity, or quality is a replacement. Replacements differ from normal repairs in that they involve replacing a major part of equipment. Normal repairs do not include major parts, nor do they enhance future service potential the way improvements do. Both improvements and replacements are capitalized, while normal repairs are expensed. Three methods are used to account for improvements and replacements:

1. Reduce the Accumulated Depreciation account associated with the asset.
2. Establish a new asset account.
3. Increase the old asset account.

Reduction of Accumulated Depreciation. Reduction of the Accumulated Depreciation account is appropriate when the expenditure extends the useful life of the old asset. The expenditure may not enhance the quality or quantity provided by the asset, but the life is prolonged. Reduction of the Accumulated Depreciation account originated in the railroad industry. As new railroad cars were purchased to replace the old cars, the Accumulated Depreciation account was reduced, thus recapturing some of the depreciation. This automatically raised the carrying value of the assets by an amount equal to the purchase price of the newly acquired cars.

Establish New Asset Account. Many assets consist of major components that have predictably different useful lives. A separate asset account can be established for each major component. From a theoretical standpoint, this is the best way to capitalize depreciable assets. Practical problems often preclude the use of this method, however, because both the original cost and subsequent depreciation charges associated with the asset must be known. For example, a diesel engine has a life expectancy shorter than that of the truck chassis. An internal revenue tax case was won by a controller in the trucking industry using separate lives of these major components. His records verified that the diesel engines required major repairs approximately every 250,000 miles, while trucks averaged about 125,000 miles per year. As a result, he depreciated the engines over a two-year period and the chassis over a ten-year period.

Major components of buildings can be handled in this manner if the components can be separately identified. The main structure of the building has a different life from the roof, the heating and cooling system, or the elevator. If the original acquisition costs and subsequent depreciation charges of the separate components can be determined, each component can be treated as a separate asset for valuation and allocation purposes. However, components are usually not identified and accounted for separately. Thus, expenditures for major component replacements are usually accounted for either by reducing accumulated depreciation or by increasing the old asset account.

Increase Old Asset Account. The expenditure amount is capitalized in the old asset account if a component cost cannot be identified and if the expenditure does not necessarily increase the asset life. If the asset life is increased, the Accumulated Depreciation account is reduced. The net effect is the same: the book value of the asset is increased.

REARRANGEMENTS AND REINSTALLATIONS

Remodeling in a factory by rearranging the machinery to achieve a more efficient work flow could be a major expenditure. These costs should be treated as an asset expenditure (capitalized) and allocated over the expected life of the rearrangement. The expenditures are incurred under the assumption that the operations will be more efficient during future operating periods and provide future benefits. Thus, the expenditure qualifies as an asset.

If the original installation cost and the contra account of Accumulated Depreciation are known or can be determined, then the expenditure should be treated as a replacement. Frequently, though, the original cost and accumulated depreciation are not known, and a new account must be established to record the event.

DISPOSITION OF PLANT ASSETS

Record the final disposition of property, plant, and equipment assets.

SALE

The sale of a plant asset signals the need to remove the asset from the books along with the corresponding accumulated depreciation. Recognition of a gain or loss on the disposition of these assets is appropriate, since the earnings process has been completed. For example, if a piece of machinery with an original cost of $20,000 and a current book value of $10,000 is sold for $11,000, a $1,000 gain would be recognized. Depreciation must be brought up to date in a manner consistent with the company's policy before the gain or loss is determined.

INVOLUNTARY CONVERSIONS

Involuntary conversions occur through acts and/or events not under the control of the entity. For example, a condemnation of a rented building by the local government is an involuntary conversion. States exercising the right of eminent domain for road construction is another example of involuntary conversion. The difference between the amount received, if any, and the book value of the asset is treated as a gain or a loss. A gain or loss is recognized even if the proceeds are reinvested in a similar asset because they are considered monetary exchanges for nonmonetary assets. The gain or loss is reflected in the proper section of the income statement—either the operating section, disposal-of-a-segment section, or the extraordinary-items section—depending on the circumstances.

ABANDONMENTS

Sometimes an asset is still operable but inefficient. Additional expenditures cannot be cost-justified, and there is no viable market for the asset. Any carrying value is written down to zero, and a loss is recognized. Any cost associated with the removal or storage of the items is charged against current revenues. If there is a residual or scrap value amount, an asset account such as Scrap Inventory or Abandoned-Asset Inventory is established.

FINANCIAL ANALYSIS

DISCLOSURE

The accounting policies of an entity regarding nonmonetary assets must be adequately disclosed in its financial statements. *Disclosure* includes the basis of accounting for assets, the depreciation methods, and the nature of any transactions resulting in gains and losses. Separately, SFAS No. 34 requires footnote disclosure for interest incurred and the amount capitalized during interest capitalization periods for self-constructed assets. SFAS No. 34 also requires separate disclosure of the amount of interest expense applicable to noncapitalization periods of self-constructed assets.

IMPACT ON FINANCIAL STATEMENTS

Transactions that involve property, plant, and equipment ultimately affect all the statements. The initial acquisition is reported as an investment activity in the statement of cash flows (SCF) in the year of acquisition, and it is reported on the balance sheet as long as the asset is held. As the asset is amortized (with the exception of land) over its useful life, the depreciation is charged against income, reducing net income from operations.

Some acquisitions are partially self-financed and partially financed through borrowing. The portion financed through borrowing appears in the financing section of the SCF as a cash inflow, with the remainder of the asset's cost footnoted. The asset partially financed must also be reported as a cash outflow in the investing section of the SCF in the amount of the cash outflow. Even material noncash transactions involving acquisitions of property, plant, and equipment must be shown in a special section of the SCF, as outlined in Chapter 7.

Self-constructed assets frequently are reported in both the investing and financing sections of the SCF. For example, using the information contained in Exhibit 12–2, the $1,000,000 borrowed specifically for the building project would appear as a cash inflow in the financing section of the SCF for the year 1997. As the costs are capitalized, they appear in the investing section as a cash outflow in the SCF. Cash outflows of $937,000 would be reported in the investing section of the SCF for the year 1997, and $1,221,797 would be reported there for the year 1998. Capitalized interest on self-constructed assets is reported as part of the aggregate cash outflow for assets acquired in this manner.

SOLVENCY ANALYSIS

6 Interpret the fixed-asset-utilization and the return-on-assets ratios.

Long-term assets are used for analysis of the *solvency* of the enterprise, that is, its debt-paying ability. Measures of solvency include the fixed-asset utilization ratio and the rate of return on assets. The **rate of return on assets (ROA)** is derived from the return-on-investment (ROI) ratio introduced in Chapter 6.

The **fixed-asset-utilization ratio** is the ratio of sales to fixed assets and measures the utilization of property, plant, and equipment. This ratio is frequently called the **fixed-asset-turnover ratio.** It is determined by the following formula:

$$\text{Fixed-Asset-Utilization Ratio or Asset-Turnover Ratio} = \frac{\text{Sales}}{\text{Average Fixed Assets}}$$

For example, assume the following:

Sales	$1,000,000
Beginning fixed assets	400,000
Ending fixed assets	600,000

The fixed-asset turnover is two times ($1,000,000/$500,000). Comparison with industry averages provides an indication of the efficient use of productive assets relative to other companies in the industry. If the ratio is appreciably lower than the industry norm, future requests by production for additional fixed assets should be reviewed critically by upper management.

The asset-turnover ratio should be used with caution because of the historical-cost valuation used under current GAAP. Many firms acquire their productive assets over a long period of time, and the original costs remaining, as shown in the financial statements, do not reflect current market values. This makes interfirm comparisons especially difficult because asset purchases occur over different time periods for each firm. The basis of the ratio is a stable monetary unit, but the monetary unit has not demonstrated historical stability.

Return-on-investment (ROI) was introduced in Chapter 6 as a ratio that measures profitability. A derivation of ROI can be used to measure managerial efficiency in the utilization of assets. This derivation is called rate of return on assets (ROA) because it compares profit to the assets employed (investment) in the revenue-generation process. Calculation of ROA is similar to that for ROI; ROA equals the asset-turnover ratio multiplied by the sales-profit margin. The **asset-turnover ratio** is found by dividing the sales for the period by average total assets, and the **sales-profit margin** is found by dividing net income by net sales. Exhibit 12–10 provides an illustration of the computations necessary.

While ROA is a frequently used measure of managerial performance in the utilization of assets, it does require some cautions. Because average total assets are used in the denominator, the values assigned to the "Property, Plant & Equipment (PPE)" section of the balance sheet are based on historical costs adjusted for depreciation charges. As the PPE assets get older, the book values become smaller, thus providing a higher rate of return for an older company than for a new company with new assets and the same level of sales. Even with reduced net income, this ratio can provide the illusion of a steady return or perhaps even increasing returns.

In fact, companies that employ this ratio as part of their reward structure may be rewarding behavior that is detrimental to the firm in the long term. Managers soon learn the positive effect on ROA of not purchasing additional long-lived assets. Even if these expenditures are necessary for long-term survival of the firm, there may be short-run benefits to the manager that encourage him or her to postpone these expenditures.

EVALUATION AND DISCUSSION

IMPAIRMENT OF LONG-LIVED ASSETS

The discussion in this chapter presumes that the carrying values of the property, plant, and equipment are based on the historical cost of those assets. The point was made that reported book values on the balance sheet may not represent faithfully the underlying economic reality of the value of the assets. However,

EXHIBIT 12–10
Financial Analysis: Asset Turnover, Sales-Profit Margin, and Return on Investment

Assume the following data for the Tully Company:

	1997	1998	1999
Assets	$1,000,000	$1,500,000	$1,850,000
Liabilities	300,000	500,000	600,000
Equity	700,000	1,000,000	1,250,000
Net Sales		2,250,000	3,350,000
Net Income		135,000	167,500
Asset Turnover		1.80	2.00
Sales-Profit Margin		0.06	0.05
Return on Investment		0.108	0.10

The ratios are calculated as follows for the 1998 year:

Asset Turnover = Net Sales/Average Total Assets
= $2,250,000/[($1,000,000 + 1,500,000)/2]
= $2,250,000/$1,250,000
= 1.8

Sales-Profit Margin = Net Income/Net Sales
= $135,000/$2,250,000
= .06

Return on Investment = Net Income/Average Total Assets
= $135,000/[($1,000,000 + 1,500,000)/2]
= $135,000/$1,250,000
= 0.108

or

Return on Investment = Asset Turnover × Sales-Profit Margin
= 1.8 × .06
= 0.108

the use of historical cost is justified on the basis of its objectivity and, to some extent, conservatism.

The FASB in SFAS No. 121 requires a modification to the use of historical cost as the basis for measurement in certain instances.[3] In situations where long-lived assets have become "impaired" to a significant degree, SFAS No. 121 requires the write-down of the asset book value to fair value. Fair value is measured in terms of market value. If an active market exists for similar assets, that market value should be used to establish fair value. If an active market does not exist, fair value would be estimated as the discounted present value of estimated future cash flows. SFAS No. 121 does not suggest the write-up of asset value in

[3]"Accounting for the Impairment of Long-Lived Assets and for Long-Lived Assets to Be Disposed Of," FASB No. 121, March 1995.

cases where fair value exceeds book value. It is concerned only with impairment and write-downs.

Indications of an impairment would include the adverse effect of new technology on an old asset, a significant change in the manner of use of the asset, a significant adverse change in the business climate, significant cost overruns on construction projects, or forecasts of continuing losses associated with an asset. The standard indicates that if any of these conditions exists with respect to an asset, an investigation should be undertaken to determine if impairment exists.

ETHICS IN PRACTICE

Earnings Not Always What They Seem

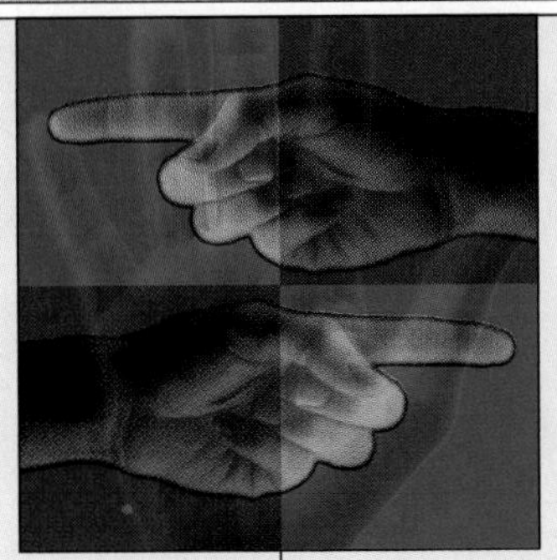

. . . "Thanks to a new accounting standard—SFAS No. 121—which ***PepsiCo*** and some others implemented at the end of last year and is mandatory in 1996, a wave of new write offs is on the way.... The purpose of this rule is to set standards for when the value of ongoing but "impaired assets" should be written down.

The Financial Accounting Standards Board designed the rule to enhance the conservatism of balance sheets, but in so doing, it will further subvert the integrity of earnings. Even Dennis Beresford, FASB's chairman, concedes the new rule "will make it more difficult to understand the quality of earnings."

This trade-off is unfortunate, because while the FASB is *balance-sheet* driven, investors are mostly, and most often properly, concerned with *earnings*. The fact that PepsiCo's book value is $9.28 a share is virtually irrelevant to the stock price, now $62.75.

PepsiCo's restaurants *as a group* were worth more than their book value. But because PepsiCo chose to evaluate them on a restaurant-by-restaurant basis, it created a half-billion charge. Another restauranteur, PepsiCo concedes, might group its stores by region and get a lower charge.

PepsiCo also had wide latitude in estimating the future cash flows of its impaired restaurants and the discount rate for figuring the present value of those cash flows. . . . PepsiCo wasn't required to disclose how it arrived at the final figure, and didn't. . . . Thus, impaired assets are written off once; good ones are sold quarter by quarter, benefiting earnings, just as lowered depreciation creates an ongoing benefit.

Source: Roger Lowenstein, "Intrinsic Value," *The Wall Street Journal*, February 15, 1996, p. C1.

The determination of whether to record an impairment rests on the difference between the book value of the asset and the estimated *undiscounted* future cash flows resulting from the use and ultimate disposition of the asset. If the sum of the undiscounted future cash flows is less than the book (or carrying) value of the asset, an impairment is deemed to exist. Measurement of the amount of impairment, however, is at fair value, as explained earlier. However, if the sum of undiscounted future cash flows is equal to or greater than the book value, then the assets are assumed to be unimpaired.

The accounting requirements under SFAS No. 121 are similar to accounting for inventories using the lower-of-cost-or-market rule. Write-downs are prescribed for losses in value, but there are no write-ups for increases in value.

The use of fair value is similar to the requirements of SFAS No. 115 for investment securities if an active market exists for valuation of the asset. In the absence of an active market, the discounted present value of future cash flows is used to determine value.

The level of aggregation of assets or asset groups will significantly effect the amount to be recognized, which is illustrated by the accompanying excerpt about PepsiCo's implementation of SFAS No. 121. The effect can be to reduce the total carrying value of long-lived assets if looked at separately. If different aggregation levels had been used, little or no impairment would have been recognized. Exhibit 12–11 provides different possible scenarios of the evaluation process for recognizing impairment of assets.

EXHIBIT 12–11
Impairment of Long-Lived Assets Determination and Valuation

Assume that the Carl Co. has the following long-lived assets all of which have a remaining life of 15 years and the company uses a discount rate of 10%:

	BOOK VALUE	MARKET VALUE	ANNUAL INCOME STREAM
Asset A	$100,000	$120,000	$10,000
Asset B	100,000	unknown	6,000
Asset C	100,000	90,000	12,000
Asset D	100,000	unknown	12,000
Total	$400,000		

Analysis:

- Assume that the assets are evaluated individually.
- Asset A is not impaired. The current market value is known and exceeds the current carrying value.
- Asset B is impaired. While the market value is unknown, the sum of the undiscounted future net cash flows is less than the carrying value of the asset (6,000 × 15 = 90,000). The present value of the future cash flows discounted at 10% is $45,637 (7.6061 × 6,000 = 45,637). The asset would be written-down $54,363.
- Asset C is not impaired. While the current market value is known and is less than the carrying value, the sum of the future undiscounted cash flows is higher than the carrying value. The higher carrying value, indicating a possible impairment, is a function of the depreciation used and a case could be made to review the depreciation policy but no impairment would be recognized.
- Asset D is not impaired. While the market value is unknown, the sum of the future net cash flows exceeds the carrying value (12,000 × 15 = 180,000). Even though the present value of the future cash is only $91,273 (7.6061 × 12,000 + 91,273) no impairment under SFAS No. 121 is deemed to have taken place.
- The total carrying value of the assets would become $345,637.
- Now assume that the assets are analyzed as a group. No impairment is recognized. Assets (A and C) with a known market value of $210,000 are greater than the book value of $200,000. Assets without a known market value (B and D) have future cash flows totaling $270,000 [(6,000 + 12,000) × 15 = 270,000] which exceeds the carrying value of $200,000.

END-OF-CHAPTER REVIEW

SUMMARY

1. **Calculate the cost basis of a productive asset acquired through a monetary exchange.** Material expenditures for items with productive lives longer than one year or operating cycle are capitalized. All costs associated with the acquisition and preparation of the asset for its intended use should be included in establishing its original basis. The asset basis then is allocated (expensed) over its useful life.

   The most frequent method of acquisition of land, buildings, and equipment is by monetary exchange. The financing arrangements can be cash only, some combination of cash and credit, or credit through such instruments as leases, mortgages, or notes. The notes may be either interest-bearing or so-called noninterest-bearing.

   In some instances the assets are acquired through self-construction. Self-constructed assets have two unique accounting issues: (1) the treatment of overhead cost and (2) the treatment of interest charges that result from the construction project. Little guidance is provided for accounting for overhead costs associated with self-constructed assets. However, specific rules exist governing the amount of interest that may be capitalized for self-constructed assets.

2. **Explain the conceptual and accounting differences between dissimilar and similar assets for nonmonetary asset exchanges.** Accounting for nonmonetary exchanges of dissimilar assets is based on the assumption that the earnings process in which the old assets were engaged has been completed. Therefore, gains and losses on these exchanges are fully recognized. However, accounting for exchanges of similar assets is based on the assumption that the earnings process in which the old assets were engaged has not been completed. Therefore, all losses are recognized but gains are deferred unless cash is received in the exchange. If cash is received, part of the gain is recognized in the proportion of the cash received to the total value received. The unrecognized portion of the gain reduces the basis of the new asset.

3. **Account for assets obtained through exchanges for stock or by donation.** Assets acquired through exchanges for stock or by donation are valued at the fair market value (FMV) of the asset received or the FMV surrendered, whichever is the most determinable. If actively traded stock is used to acquire assets, the FMV of the stock would be used to determine the value of the asset. If the stock was not actively traded and the FMV is unknown, or if the assets were donated, the appraisal values of the assets would be used to establish the initial book value.

4. **Account for costs incurred after the initial acquisition of assets.** Costs incurred after acquisition of assets that are material in nature are capitalized and treated as additions, improvements, or replacements, depending on the circumstances. Determination of whether the life of the asset has been extended or if the service or quality of the asset output has been improved, or both, dictates the accounting required. Rearrangement and reinstallation costs are normally capitalized and amortized over the new lives.

5. **Record the final disposition of property, plant, and equipment assets.** Gains and losses are recognized at the time of the final disposition of producing assets. The method of disposal may be by sale, involuntary conversion, or abandonment. Depreciation charges must be brought up to date before the determination of any gain or loss, and the gain or loss is the difference between the FMV received (if any) and book value of the asset.

6. **Interpret the fixed-asset-utilization and the return-on-assets ratios.** The fixed-asset-utilization ratio (or fixed-asset-turnover ratio) is used to evaluate the effective employment of the producing assets. It compares sales with the average fixed assets employed. The ROA ratio is a combination of the asset-turnover ratio and the sales-margin ratio. ROA evaluates the profit, or return on investment, in these assets. Both of these ratios should be compared with industry standards. If they fall below industry norms, it could be an indication that the entity is not an efficient user of these resources or that the firm has newer than average assets.

KEY TERMS

asset-turnover ratio *659*
avoidable interest *643*
basket purchase *641*
capital expenditures *655*
capitalized *639*
fixed-asset-utilization ratio *658*
improvements *656*
involuntary conversions *657*
nonreciprocal transfer *655*
productive or capital assets *638*
rate of return on assets (ROA) *658*
relative-market-value method *641*
replacements *656*
revenue expenditures *655*

ASSIGNMENT MATERIAL

CASES

C12–1 Acquisition Costs—Report Preparation

The Webb Company is a major construction company that has building projects all over the world. It has a staff that continually evaluates sites for profitable construction projects. The annual cost of maintaining this staff averages $600,000 per year. The company follows the practice of buying options on building sites that meet certain criteria.

Required: Prepare a report that explains how the costs associated with the site evaluations should be handled and how the purchase-option costs should be treated. Should successful options be treated differently than those that are allowed to expire?

C12–2 Depreciation—Discussion Case

Regarding depreciation, distinguished Professor Robert Sterling of the University of Utah highlights this excerpt from the AICPA Committee on Terminology:

> The term [depreciation] . . . does not attempt to determine the sum allocated to an accounting period solely by relation to occurrences within the period which affect either the length of life or the monetary value of the property. Definitions are unacceptable which imply that depreciation for the year is a measurement, expressed in monetary terms, of the physical deterioration within the year, or of the decline in monetary value within the year, or, indeed, of anything that actually occurs within the year.[4]

[4]Committee on Terminology, "Accounting Terminology Bulletins, Number 1, Review and Resume," *Accounting Research and Terminology Bulletins* (New York: 1969), p. 24.

He then states,

> Let me repeat: *Definitions* are unacceptable which imply that *depreciation* . . . is a measurement . . . of the physical deterioration . . . or the decline of monetary value . . . , or, indeed, of anything that actually occurs within the year.[5]

Required:

A. How, then, should one interpret depreciation expense recorded on an income statement?

B. How, then, should one interpret the book value of depreciable assets as recorded on the balance sheet?

C12–3 Depreciation and Asset Revaluation—Group Discussion Case

The use of historical cost as a basis for reporting fixed assets is frequently criticized. This chapter notes how companies in some countries revalue assets to current values or to reflect inflation. Suppose that GAAP did permit the use of current market values for reporting fixed assets.

Required:

A. How could current values for fixed assets be determined?

B. What ethical and auditing concerns might the use of current values present?

C. If current market values are used for reporting fixed assets, how would depreciation (if any) be determined for a period?

D. Could a company have "negative" depreciation in a period? Explain.

E. If values for fixed assets significantly increased resulting in substantial appreciation, how would you recommend reporting this appreciation?

C12–4 Donated Assets

Lintel Corporation has been enticed by the Tempe Arizona Chamber of Commerce to locate its new production facility on land owned by the city of Tempe. The land has been owned by Tempe for decades, and there have been no recent sales of similar acreage in that area. Tempe agrees as part of the package to donate the land (40 acres) and to bring sewer and water lines to the property, which will cost Tempe taxpayers $1,000,000. Lintel also will benefit from a 10-year tax exemption on any of the property or equipment located on this site.

Tempe, however, will hold in escrow 100,000 shares of Lintel common stock for 10 years. Lintel stock is currently selling at $50 per share. In the event that Lintel decides to sell or abandon the property prior to the end of the 10-year period, the city of Tempe will sell the stock and keep the proceeds.

Required: What are the accounting issues in this case? What course of action would you recommend in determining the accounting entries on the books of Lintel? What is your rationale for these entries?

[5] R. Sterling, "Toward a Science of Accounting," *Financial Analysts Journal*, September–October 1975, p. 33.

C12–5 Financial Analysis and Decision Making

Use some financial database of corporations (such as the database diskette accompanying this text) and the financial data from the balance sheets and income statements for JAK Inc. shown here to answer the following:

Required: Calculate both the fixed-asset-utilization ratio and the ROI ratio for the 1997 year. Choose two different industries for the most recent year available and calculate the average ratios for the industries chosen. How do the ratios you determined above compare with industry norms? Do you think that the management of the JAK Inc. is doing a good job based upon the information that you have discovered? Would you invest in JAK? Why or why not? What comparability problems might affect your analysis? How could you resolve these problems?

JAK INC.
Balance Sheet
December 31, 1996

Assets			
Current assets:			
Cash		$ 42,000	
Trading securities		150,000	
Accounts receivable		250,000	
Inventories		225,000	
Prepaid items		8,000	
Total current assets			$ 675,000
Noncurrent assets:			
Investments:			
Land		$225,000	
Investment in subsidiary		100,000	325,000
Property, plant, & equipment:			
Land		$150,000	
Plant & equipment	$700,000		
Less: Allowance for depreciation	100,000	600,000	750,000
Total assets			$1,750,000
Liabilities			
Current liabilities:			
Accounts payable		$600,000	
Accrued taxes		25,000	$ 625,000
Long-term debt			200,000
Total liabilities			825,000
Stockholders' Equity			
Paid-in capital		$500,000	
Retained earnings		425,000	925,000
Total liabilities and stockholders' equity			$1,750,000

JAK INC.
Balance Sheet
December 31, 1997

Assets			
Current assets:			
Cash		$300,000	
Trading securities		200,000	
Accounts receivable		450,000	
Inventories		275,000	
Prepaid items		6,000	
Total current assets			$1,231,000
Noncurrent Assets:			
Investments:			
Land		$225,000	
Investment in subsidiary		100,000	325,000
Property, plant, and equipment:			
Land		$150,000	
Plant & equipment	$700,000		
Less: Allowance for depreciation	150,000	550,000	700,000
Total assets			$2,256,000
Liabilities			
Current liabilities:			
Accounts payable		$800,000	
Accrued taxes		30,000	$ 830,000
Long-term debt			200,000
Total liabilities			$1,030,000
Stockholders' Equity			
Paid-in capital		$500,000	
Retained earnings		726,000	1,226,000
Total liabilities and stockholders' equity			$2,256,000

JAK INC.
Income Statement
For the Year Ended December 31, 1997

Sales	$1,500,000
Less: Sales returns & allowances	(30,000)
Net sales	$1,470,000
Cost of goods sold	(750,000)
Gross profit	$ 720,000
Selling & administrative expenses	(360,000)
Net income before taxes	$ 360,000
Income taxes	(90,000)
Net income after taxes	$ 270,000

C12–6 Ethical Issues—Group Report

Darnoc Notlih is the principal stockholder of Notlih International Hotels. Notlih Hotels are among the most prestigious hotels in the world. Many of the hotels are situated on extremely valuable real estate that was acquired many years ago. The book values of the fixed assets are significantly below the current market values of those assets. The market price of the stock was about $30 per share when Darnoc Notlih announced that he planned to liquidate his hotel chain. The market price of the stock jumped to over $90 per share after his announcement to liquidate the holdings. This increase was clearly the market's assessment of the current value of the long-term assets held by the firm.

After the market price increase in the shares of stock, Notlih personally (not the company) sold 100,000 shares over a 10-day period in order to not depress the market price of the stock. After the sale, he announced that he had changed his plans to liquidate the holdings.

What are the ethical issues involved here? Does the accounting profession have any responsibility to address this issue? Did Notlih act in an unethical manner in this situation? Evaluate Notlih's actions using the ethical framework model presented in Chapter 1.

QUESTIONS

Q12–1 What is meant by the term *productive assets*? What types of assets are included as productive assets? How do they differ from other long-lived assets?

Q12–2 What are the major characteristics of property, plant, and equipment?

Q12–3 What acquisition costs should be included as part of an asset account?

Q12–4 What is the major weakness of the reported values of long-term assets on the balance sheet? Why is this a weakness?

Q12–5 What are the two accounting questions that must be resolved in any transaction that involves the utilization of property by an entity?

Q12–6 Indicate which items should or should not be included as part of the cost of land, and explain why.

1. Attorney's fees as part of the closing costs of a real estate transaction.
2. Filing fees associated with the property.
3. The salary of the officer responsible for the acquisition.
4. The prorated property taxes included in the closing costs.
5. Interest on the money borrowed to obtain the property.
6. The mortgage assumed.
7. Special assessment for the construction of sewer lines to the property.
8. Present value of the monthly sewer-tax payments.
9. Cost of landscaping the property.
10. Pro rata share of retainer fees paid to an attorney.

Q12–7 Indicate which items should or should not be included as part of the cost of plant assets, and explain why.

1. Attorney's fees as part of the closing costs of the real estate transaction.
2. Filing fees associated with the property.
3. The salary of the officer responsible for the acquisition.
4. Interest on the money borrowed to obtain the property.
5. Architect's fees.

6. Excavation costs.
7. Interest on the money borrowed to construct the plant.
8. Present value of the monthly payments on the debt at acquisition date.
9. Fringe-benefit cost of company employees constructing the building.
10. Replacement of the roof.

Q12–8 Indicate which items should or should not be included as part of the cost of equipment, and explain why.

1. Cash plus the present value of the monthly loan payments assumed to acquire the asset.
2. Insurance and transportation costs to bring the asset to the site.
3. Cost of the concrete base needed for the equipment.
4. Costs of production runs needed to get the machine operating properly.
5. Spoilage and defective units associated with the production runs.
6. Costs of repairing a hole that was made in the wall in order to get the equipment in the building.
7. Present value of future replacement costs of major components.
8. Costs of repairs and maintenance.

Q12–9 What is the relative-market-value method, and when is it used?

Q12–10 What are the two major accounting issues involved in self-constructed assets? How do these issues affect the income statement and balance sheet?

Q12–11 Why is the amount of interest that is capitalized for self-constructed assets limited by the amount of actual interest incurred?

Q12–12 What is the weighted-average rate of interest, and how does it relate to the average accumulated expenditures?

Q12–13 What are the general guidelines used in exchanges of similar assets?

Q12–14 When is it appropriate to recognize a gain on the exchange of similar assets? What is the amount of gain that may be recognized? How is the gain reflected on the statement of cash flows?

Q12–15 Why are the general guidelines used in exchanges of dissimilar assets different from those applicable to similar assets?

Q12–16 How are values assigned to assets obtained by the issuance of stock?

Q12–17 At what value are donated assets recorded? How are donated assets reflected on the statement of cash flows?

Q12–18 What are the general guidelines for costs incurred on assets subsequent to acquisition? Where are these costs found on the statement of cash flows?

Q12–19 What is the conceptual difference between an addition and a replacement? between a replacement and an improvement? What are the accounting requirements for additions, replacements, and improvements?

Q12–20 What is the difference between an involuntary conversion and an abandonment? How do the accounting requirements differ?

Q12–21 How is the ROA ratio computed? What information does it convey to the user?

Q12–22 How is the fixed-asset-utilization ratio computed? What information does it provide to the user? Identify at least one problem associated with the use of this ratio.

EXERCISES

E12–1 Capital and Revenue Expenditures

Ace Hardware's current parking area is too small to accommodate its customers. Ace acquires a large lot next to the current lot, which is to be developed for expanded parking. The following transactions result:

1. The lot with a small building on it was purchased for $14,000.
2. The building was razed at a cost of $1,000.
3. The lot was leveled and a drainage system installed for $2,000.
4. An asphalt surface cost $8,000.
5. The asphalt contractor repaired the old lot for $1,000.
6. A lighting system was installed at a cost of $3,000.
7. A new section of fence was added at a cost of $4,500.
8. Signs were placed on the fence indicating that the parking was reserved for Ace customers only. The signs cost $150.
9. The old section of fence was painted for $300.
10. The parking lines cost $500.

Required:

A. Classify each of the expenditures above as either a capital expenditure or a revenue expenditure.
B. Indicate how these transactions affect the statement of cash flows.

E12–2 Capital Expenditures

Use the data from E12–1 to answer the following:

Required:

A. Indicate the accounts to which the expenditures should be charged and the account totals.
B. Since all of the expenditures in E12–1 are related to the parking area, why would Ace Hardware want to spend the time to allocate each expenditure to the proper account? Wouldn't it be better to just lump all of these amounts in one Parking Area account? Explain your answer.

E12–3 Noninterest-Bearing Note

Hungry Harry's Pizza Parlor acquired a delivery vehicle by agreeing to pay $2,500 down and $2,400 per year for the next three years. The cash sales price was $8,000.

Required:

A. What is the entry to record this transaction?
B. What is the implicit rate of interest to the nearest percent?
C. How would the transaction be reflected on the statement of cash flows?

E12–4 Noninterest-Bearing Note

Jane's Jewelry acquired a safe by agreeing to pay $4,000 down and $2,600 per year for the next three years. The cash sales price was $9,800.

Required:

A. What is the entry to record this transaction?
B. What is the implicit rate of interest to the nearest percent?
C. How would the transaction be reflected on the statement of cash flows?

E12–5 Dissimilar-Asset Exchange

Land on the books of Company A at $20,000 (appraisal value was $25,000) is exchanged for a computer that has a book value (BV) on Company B's books of $30,000 (cost was $35,000).

Required:

A. Prepare the journal entries for both companies.
B. How would this transaction be reflected on a statement of cash flows for Company A?

E12–6 Dissimilar-Asset Exchange

Land on the books of Company G at $40,000 (appraisal value was $50,000) is exchanged for a computer that has a BV on Company F's books of $60,000 (cost was $70,000).

Required:

A. Prepare the journal entries for both companies.
B. How would this transaction be reflected on a statement of cash flows for Company G?

E12–7 Financial Analysis

Pertinent data for the Jones Company are shown.

	1997	1998	1999
Current assets	$ 800,000	$1,135,000	$1,835,000
Fixed assets	800,000	900,000	1,000,000
Liabilities	480,000	660,000	900,000
Equity	1,120,000	1,375,000	1,935,000
Net sales		2,250,000	3,350,000
Net income		255,000	560,000

Required:

A. Calculate the following for 1998 and 1999:
 1. Fixed-asset-turnover ratio
 2. Sales-profit margin
 3. Return on investment

B. Would you invest in this company? Why or why not?

E12–8 Financial Analysis

Pertinent data for the Smiley Company are shown.

	1997	1998	1999
Current assets	$ 900,000	$1,035,000	$1,735,000
Fixed assets	900,000	800,000	1,200,000
Liabilities	580,000	560,000	1,100,000
Equity	1,220,000	1,275,000	1,835,000
Net sales		2,000,000	3,000,000
Net income		200,000	500,000

Required:

A. Calculate the following for 1998 and 1999:
   1. Fixed-asset-turnover ratio
   2. Sales-profit margin
   3. Return on investment

B. Would you invest in this company? Why or why not?

E12–9 Similar-Asset Exchange

Land on Company C's books at $18,000 is exchanged for land on Company D's books at $14,000. The fair market value (FMV) of each is $15,000.

Required: Prepare the journal entries for both companies. Can Company D recognize the gain on exchange? Why or why not?

E12–10 Similar-Asset Exchange

Land on Company J's books at $36,000 is exchanged for land on Company K's books at $28,000. The FMV of each is $40,000.

Required: Prepare the journal entries for both companies. Can Company K recognize the gain on exchange? Why or why not?

E12–11 "Cash Boot" Exchanges

Company E traded in a truck that had a book value of $2,000 (cost was $10,000; FMV is $2,200), along with "cash boot" of $10,000 to a dealer for a new truck that had a sticker price of $12,500. ("Boot" refers to cash received or paid in the asset exchange.)

Required: Prepare the journal entry for Company E.

E12–12 Cash Boot Exchanges

Company B traded in a forklift that had a book value of $21,000 (cost was $30,000; FMV is $25,000) and received cash of $10,000 and an older forklift with a FMV of $15,000.

Required:

A. Prepare the journal entry for Company B to record the trade.

B. Assuming that Company B uses the indirect method for the operating section of the statement of cash flows, how would this transaction be reflected on B's statement of cash flows?

E12–13 Cash Boot Exchanges

Furniture that cost Company R $22,000 (book value is $12,000; FMV is $8,000) was traded to Company S for furniture with a book value of $10,000 (cost was $20,000). Company R had to pay Company S a cash boot of $6,000.

Required: Prepare the journal entries for both companies.

E12–14 Donated Assets

Chicago agreed to donate water-frontage property to Under Water Repair (UWR) Inc. if the company would locate its business in that city. The land was recently appraised for $800,000. Property values have been increasing at 5% per year. Assume that UWR accepts the offer. What journal entry should UWR make under current GAAP?

E12–15 Stock for Assets

Sherton Hotels agrees to give 20,000 shares of its $10 par common stock for acreage located on Maui Beach. The tax base of the property is $1,000,000, and the property was recently appraised at $1,500,000.

Required:

A. What is the value assigned to the property by Sherton?

B. Assume that the market value per share of Sherton is $80 and the stock is traded actively, with 1,000,000 shares outstanding. What journal entry would Sherton make in this case?

E12–16 Postacquisition Expenditures

The Hardware Wholesale Company recorded the following transactions.

1. The oil line was severed by the phone company installing a new phone line. The repair cost was $680.
2. The outside of the brick building was sandblasted and painted at a total cost of $15,000.
3. New display equipment was acquired and installed for $3,000. The removal of the old display cost $1,000.
4. The interior of the whole building was painted at a cost of $12,000.
5. The roof was replaced for $35,000.

Required: Prepare the journal entries for each item (assume cash was paid in each case). Be explicit in using account titles; that is, indicate if the debit is to an old asset, new asset, accumulated depreciation, or expense account.

E12–17 Retirement of Fixed Assets

Weir Company uses straight-line depreciation for its property, plant, and equipment, which, stated at cost, consisted of the following:

	12/31/92	12/31/91
Land	$ 25,000	$ 25,000
Buildings	195,000	195,000
Machinery and equipment	695,000	650,000
	$915,000	$870,000
Less: Accumulated depreciation	400,000	370,000
	$515,000	$500,000

Weir's depreciation expense for 1992 and 1991 was $55,000 and $50,000, respectively. What amount was debited to Accumulated Depreciation during 1992 because of property, plant, and equipment retirements? [AICPA Adapted, Practice I, MC No. 23, November 1993]

E12–18 Classifying Costs Related to Fixed Assets

During 1992, Sloan Inc. began a project to construct new corporate headquarters. Sloan purchased land with an existing building for $750,000. The land was valued at $700,000 and the building at $50,000. Sloan planned to demolish the building and construct a new office building on the site. Items A through I represent various expenditures by Sloan for this project.

Required: For each expenditure in the "Item" list shown here, select the appropriate accounting treatment from the following list:

- Classify as land and do not depreciate.
- Classify as building and depreciate.
- Expense.

Item:

A. Architect's fee of $100,000.
B. Purchase of land for $700,000.
C. Interest of $147,000 on construction financing incurred after completion of construction.
D. Interest of $186,000 on construction financing paid during construction.
E. Purchase of building for $50,000.
F. Payment of $18,500 in delinquent real estate taxes assumed by Sloan on purchase.
G. Liability insurance premium of $12,000 during the construction period.
H. Cost of $65,000 for razing existing building.
I. Moving costs of $136,000.

[AICPA Adapted, Practice I, No. 4a, November 1993]

E12–19 Cash Flow Statements

Alberg Company sold a fixed asset on June 30, 1997, for $200,000. The asset was originally purchased for $500,000 on July 1, 1992. It has been depreciated using the straight-line method, with no salvage value, and an estimated 10-year life. Depreciation for 1997 has not been recorded as of the date the asset was sold.

Required:

A. Prepare the journal entry to record the sale.
B. Illustrate how the impact of the transaction would be depicted in a statement of cash flows using the indirect method.

PROBLEMS

P12–1 Asset Acquisitions

The following are independent transactions.

1. A lot was purchased for $10,000 cash down and a noninterest-bearing promissory note for $20,000 due in two years. The company's borrowing rate is 10%.
2. A total of $45,000 was paid for three town lots for a building site. Each lot contained a small house. These houses were sold for $3,000 each and moved by the purchaser. The lots were bulldozed and leveled at a total cost of $1,500.
3. Machinery was purchased with a list price of $20,000. A 10% preferred-customer discount was received and cash paid for the remainder. Freight and insurance charges were $400. A hole had to be made in the wall of the building where it was installed. The demolition and subsequent repair was done by company employees at a cost of $3,000. A special foundation costing $2,000 was also constructed. The cost of calibrating the equipment was an additional $2,500. Assume all these costs were paid.

Required: Prepare the journal entries.

P12–2 Lump-Sum (or Basket) Purchases

Figaro Inc., an Italian importer, decided to produce its own food products and made the following acquisitions:

1. A total of $1,500,000 was paid for property containing a 140,000-square-foot building on 30 acres of land. Contiguous land recently sold for $20,000 per acre. The FMV of the building is estimated at $1,200,000. Renovation costs of $200,000 are required to bring the building up to present building codes.
2. A total of $40,000 was paid for five used delivery trucks from U-Haul-It. The expected average remaining life of the trucks is five years, and the average current age is three years. Two of the trucks are one year old and two are three years' old.
3. Used processing equipment was purchased from A&P, located on the West Coast, for $300,000. The transportation and insurance cost an additional $20,000. The FMV for two vats was $100,000 each, and the estimated useful life of each was 10 years. It cost $4,000 to put both in operating order. The FMVs of the blender, washer, and canner, respectively, were $50,000, $50,000, and $100,000. The set-up costs were $2,000, $3,000 and $5,000, respectively. Each had an estimated useful life of five years.

Required:

A. Identify the separate accounts that are needed and the current balance of each after consideration of these transactions.
B. Why is it usually necessary to allocate purchase prices across assets rather than just leaving the total purchase price in one account?
C. How would the FMV of the building in (**A**) be determined?

P12–3 Credit Acquisitions

Pitino Enterprises entered into the following credit contracts in the acquisition of producing assets.

1. A car was purchased with $4,000 down and a 10%, 2-year, interest-bearing note payable with a face amount of $8,000 for the balance.
2. A truck with a cash price of $20,000 was purchased with $5,000 down and a 2-year, noninterest-bearing note for $18,816.

Required:

A. Provide the initial valuations and the loan interest rates of these assets.
B. Prepare the journal entries to record the acquisition.

P12–4 Credit Acquisitions

Minardi Inc. entered into the following credit contracts in the acquisition of producing assets.

1. A truck was purchased with $8,000 down and a 10%, 2-year, interest-bearing note payable with a face amount of $30,000 for the balance.
2. A crane with a cash price of $30,000 was purchased with $10,000 down and a two-year, noninterest-bearing note for $26,452.

Required:

A. Provide the initial valuations and the loan interest rates of these assets.
B. Prepare the journal entries to record the acquisition.

P12–5 Self-Constructed Asset

Madden and Madden (M&M) entered into a $1,500,000 construction contract with All Purpose Construction (APC). M&M agrees to pay APC partial payments at various stages of the construction. The payment schedule to APC was as follows: $300,000 at the beginning of the contract on July 1, 1997, and $300,000 every three months until the completion date of July 1, 1998. There were no delays in the construction, and the plant was delivered on time.

The funds for the project were obtained from Fourth National Bank. A $1,500,000, 10-year note at 10% was signed by M&M on July 1, 1997. Interest is payable each December 31 and June 30. M&M's annual reporting period is December 31 each year.

Required: Provide all of M&M's journal entries for the life of the construction contract relevant to the contract.

P12–6 Self-Constructed Asset

Clark Industries decided to construct its own asset and hired Capital Construction for most of the work. Construction began on September 1, 1997, and was completed on February 1, 1998. There were no delays.

Funds for the project were borrowed on July 1, 1997, from the Left Bank of Mississippi. The amount borrowed was $1,000,000 at 14% interest, with the principal to be repaid at the end of two years. Interest was payable annually on June 30.

Clark had three other long-term notes outstanding during the entire period of construction:

- $1,000,000, 10%, 10-year note, due in 1999.
- $2,000,000, 12%, 5-year note, due in 1999.
- $1,000,000, 14%, 8-year note, due in 2000.

The interest on these notes is payable annually on December 31.

Clark is on a calendar-year basis, and the payments made to Capital were as follows:

Sep. 1, 1997	$300,000
Oct. 1, 1997	200,000
Nov. 1, 1997	200,000
Dec. 1, 1997	200,000
Jan. 1, 1998	400,000
Feb. 1, 1998	400,000

Required:

A. Provide all of Clark's journal entries relevant to the contract.

B. What amounts will appear on the financial statements related to this construction at the end of 1997? 1998?

P12–7 Similar-Asset Exchange

Jenkins Inc. had the following transactions during 1997:

1. Traded an old truck (FMV $6,000, BV $4,000; original cost $10,000) for a different truck from Helms (BV $6,000; original cost $12,000).
2. Same as no. 1, but also paid a $2,000 cash boot to Helms.

Required: Provide all of the entries for both parties to the transactions.

P12–8 Similar-Asset Exchange

Wilson Co. had the following transactions during 1997:

1. Traded an old truck (FMV $12,000, BV $8,000; original cost $20,000) for a different truck from Faye (BV $12,000; original cost $24,000).
2. Assume the same data as in (1) but that a $4,000 cash boot was also paid to Faye.

Required: Provide all of the entries for both parties to the transactions.

P12–9 Dissimilar-Asset Exchange

Swap, Trade and Sell Inc. had the following business transactions:

1. Traded a drill press machine (BV $2,000; FMV $3,000) and $500 cash for a cabinet (FMV $3,500).
2. Traded an antique firearm (BV $4,000) for a car (FMV $5,000) to be used in the business.
3. Traded a bookshelf (BV $2,000; FMV $3,000) and clock (BV $2,500; FMV $3,000) for a pickup truck (list price $6,500) to be used in the business.
4. Traded an old pickup truck (BV $2,000; cost $12,000), for an old trenching machine. The fair market values are unknown.

Required: Provide all the entries for Swap, Trade and Sell Inc.

P12–10 Asset Exchange

Emory Delivery entered into the following transactions:

1. Traded one auto (BV $2,000; FMV $5,000) for another (BV $2,000; FMV $4,000), plus received cash of $1,000.
2. Traded one auto (BV $2,000; FMV $3,000) for another (BV $2,000; FMV $4,000), plus paid cash of $1,000.

Required: Provide all the entries for Emory Delivery.

P12–11 Asset Exchange

Gatton Delivery entered into the following transactions:

1. Traded one auto (BV $3,000; FMV $9,000) for another (BV $3,000; FMV $7,000), plus received cash of $2,000.
2. Traded one auto (BV $4,000; FMV $6,000) for another (BV $4,000; FMV $8,000), plus paid cash of $2,000.

Required: Provide all the entries for Gatton Delivery.

P12–12 Assets Acquired by Other Means

Gems Inc. entered into the following asset acquisitions:

1. Gems gave 10,000 shares of its $10 par common stock for the mineral rights of 100,000 acres of land owned by Azco. Gems also gave Azco 100,000 shares of $10 par common stock for a 100-year lease of the land. Gems has 5,000,000 shares of its common stock outstanding. The stock is traded daily and was selling at $12 per share on the contract date.
2. Nevada City (NC) agreed to donate 10 acres of land located in the city industrial area to Gems. Property in the area recently sold for $10,000 per acre. Gems plans to construct a $1,000,000 plant on the donated site to be completed before the end of the first year.

Required: Provide the journal entries on the books of Gems.

P12–13 Cost After Acquisition

During 1997, Alpo Inc. expanded the operations in Georgetown. The following transactions took place.

1. Two additional floors were added to an existing structure. This project took nine months to complete at a cost of $800,000. Payments were made to Arnold Construction Company during construction in the following manner:

7/1/96	$200,000 (the beginning of the project)
9/30/96	200,000
12/31/96	200,000
3/31/97	200,000 (the completion of the project)

   Alpo had two long-term notes outstanding during the entire construction period for $500,000 each, with interest rates of 7% and 9%, respectively. Interest is payable annually on these notes on December 31.
2. A food-processing mill was completely overhauled and new components added to increase the productivity to twice its previous level at a cost of $65,000. The mill's book value before the overhaul was $20,000.
3. The old bagging machine was given its annual overhaul at a cost of $5,000, which included $4,000 cash and $1,000 of supplies.
4. Additional machinery was transferred from existing plants at a cost of $45,000. This included transportation, installation, and setup cost. Supplies of $3,000 were used.
5. An on-site piece of equipment (conveyor) had all of its belts changed at a cost of $4,000. The new belts were purchased for cash.

Required:

A. Prepare all the journal entries for the transactions.
B. What impact would each of these items have on the statement of cash flows?

P12–14 Basket Purchase

Jane Johnson is employed by the Atal Corporation as an accountant with responsibility for the property accounts. Atal has recently purchased property from Wesex Corporation. The purchase price was $1,000,000.

The property is composed of 10 acres of land on which there is a building containing 100,000 square feet of space. The property also contains a parking lot, a private driveway, and three acres of open concrete storage.

Johnson determines the following: Land in that area recently sold for $20,000 per acre. The parking lot is brand new and cost $100,000 to construct. The current replacement cost of the open air storage is $100,000 per acre, and construction costs for a similar building currently approximate $25 per square foot.

Required: What costs should be assigned to each of these components? What rationale is used in making these allocations? Are there any alternate approaches that could be used?

P12–15 Overhead Allocation to Self-Constructed Asset

Johnson Inc. wants to begin building its own machinery for use in its production process in an effort to save money. The company knows that it must track all direct costs of constructing each machine it builds. In addition to direct materials and labor, overhead allocation must also be considered.

The president of Johnson Inc. has reviewed the proposed cost allocation of overhead to the machines. She has decided that if the company allocates overhead to construction of the machines, the machines will appear to cost too much to build. (This is an important issue to her because it was her suggestion that Johnson Inc. could save money by building its own machines, and she wants the decision to turn out to be correct.)

Required:

A. The president thinks that allocation of overhead to construction projects is optional. Is she correct? Explain.

B. How does the decision to allocate or not allocate overhead affect the cost of the machines that Johnson Inc. will build?

C. How will this accounting decision affect Johnson Inc.? Be specific.

P12–16 Self-Construction—Interest Capitalized

Johnson Inc. constructs machines it uses in its production process. Each machine takes about six months to complete. The average cost of a machine is about $400,000, which is borrowed at the beginning of construction of each machine. Interest incurred during construction of the machines is material to Johnson Inc. One machine is built each year. Data for 1997 related to this construction is as follows:

Average accumulated expenditures in 1997	$380,000
Borrowing rate on construction loan	6%
Actual interest paid on construction loan	$6,000
Months of construction in 1997	5

Required:

A. How much interest should Johnson Inc. capitalize as machinery for this project in 1997?

B. Which accounting principles and/or conventions are consistent with interest capitalization?

C. The president of Johnson Inc. believes that construction projects underway have no effect on the 1997 income statement of the company because construction costs are all capitalized. Is she correct? Explain.

P12–17 Financial Analysis

Johnson Inc. is interested in buying another company, Barnes Company. Johnson has the financial data shown here available on Barnes. As a preliminary explanation for any unusual findings in its financial data, Barnes has explained to Johnson that it substantially changed its operations in 1997 by downsizing and changing its product mix in an effort to become more profitable.

	1997	1998	1999
Total Assets	$3,000,000	$600,000	$450,000
Fixed Assets	150,000	250,000	350,000
Net Sales	400,000	400,000	400,000
Net Income	60,000	80,000	30,000

Required:

A. Using the financial information provided, compute the following ratios for 1998 and 1999 for Barnes Company:
   1. Fixed-assets-turnover
   2. Sales-profit-margin
   3. Asset-turnover
   4. Return-on-assets

B. Do your calculations support the claims of Barnes Company regarding downsizing and increased profitability? Explain.

C. What additional information is essential before you can adequately evaluate the ratios computed in (A)? Be specific.

D. Do you advise Johnson to invest in Barnes given your computations in (A)? Explain.

E. Does your decision in (C) change if Barnes is a manufacturer of heavy machinery? Does it change if Barnes is a clothing retailer? Explain each answer.

P12–18 Impairment of Long-lived Assets

Becker Corp. has a policy of reviewing long-lived assets on annual basis. The following information pertains to all long-lived assets which have remaining lives of 10 years:

	BOOK VALUE	MARKET VALUE	ANNUAL NET CASH FLOWS
Asset A	$200,000	$180,000	$22,000
Asset B	200,000	unknown	19,000
Asset C	200,000	220,000	22,000
Asset D	200,000	unknown	21,000

The discount rate used by Becker is 10%.

Required: Determine under each of the conditions below the amount of impairment if any.

A. Assets are evaluated separately.

B. Assets are evaluated as a group.

RESEARCH ACTIVITIES

R12–1 GAAP Research—Changing Prices, Report Preparation

SFAS No. 33 was an effort by the FASB to provide supplemental information regarding changing prices.

Required: Prepare a report based on SFAS No. 33 that addresses the following:

A. Distinguish between monetary and nonmonetary assets.

B. Does holding fixed assets result in purchasing-power gains or losses? Explain.

C. What were disclosure requirements for fixed assets?

D. What is the current status of the requirements of SFAS No. 33?

R12–2 GAAP Research—Natural Resources

Gonzalez Products purchased 100 acres of timberland for $10,000 per acre. The appraised value of the land without the timber was $2,000 per acre. During 1997, lumber was cut from 20 acres of the land. The cost to cut down the trees for lumber was $30,000. In addition, the company spent $10,000 to plant new trees on the 20 acres.

Required: Determine the proper accounting treatment for the

A. Purchase of the timberland
B. Cutting down of trees on the 20 acres
C. Costs incurred to plant new trees

R12–3 Motorola and Financial Research

Compare ***Motorola's*** annual report in the appendix with the annual report of a competitor.

Required: Determine the fixed-asset utilization and fixed-asset-turnover ratios for each company. How do they compare? Also find a trade publication that publishes key average ratios and compare the two firms these norms.

R12–4 South-Western Homepage Research

Access the homepage for this text at *www.swcollege.com/hartman.html.*

Required: Go to the Intermediate Homepage and see what is posted for Chapter 12.

R12–5 Case Involving Financial Research, GAAP Research, Audit Guide Research, Report Preparation

Note: This case revolves around identification of procedures used by airlines to account for major overhauls to airframes, engines, and components. The case requires students (1) to perform library research using textbooks, financial statements, and industry audit guides; (2) to describe procedures used by the airline industry to account for major overhauls; and (3) to respond to an intrusive requirement by a government agency in a professional and ethical manner. This could be used as a group project.

Your employer, Wing Air Technology (a fictitious company), provides aircraft maintenance and support services for large commercial air cargo and passenger aviation companies. Since its inception, the company's headquarters and operations have been located inside four maintenance hangers at a centrally located airport within the boundaries of Central City. The company's services include airframe and engine inspection and maintenance, aircraft modification, and airframe, engine, and avionics (aircraft communication and flight instrumentation) repair. Approximately 50 percent of the company's 1996 revenue arose from the performance of two types of extensive overhauls, which are the subject of this case.

Within the commercial aviation industry, scheduled maintenance and inspection procedures are closely regulated by the Federal Aviation Administration (FAA). The FAA requires that certain inspection and maintenance procedures be performed on a regular basis. These checks, in increasing order of complexity, are referred to as A, B, C, and D checks. A and B checks are typically performed while the aircraft is parked at the airport gate, while C and D checks require much more downtime and are performed inside maintenance hangers. C checks are performed every 5,000 to 7,000 flight hours and typically require over a week of downtime. D checks, which involve extensive inspection and testing of the airframe, operating parts, engines, and avionics, are performed every four to five years and may require as much as 60 days downtime. Although airlines and cargo carriers generally perform these procedures using their own personnel, the carriers turn to Wing Air and a number of other vendors to perform these procedures on an as-needed, competitive-bid basis when scheduling or other conflicts arise. In 1996, C checks accounted for 38 percent and D checks accounted for 15 percent of Wing Air's total revenue of $4,252,000.

Early in 1997, Wing Air's controller (your direct superior) received a letter from the administrator of Central City's sales-tax division regarding the company's sales tax exemption for revenues generated by C and D checks. Previously, Wing Air received an exemption for such revenue on the basis that major overhauls to airplanes were capitalized by the plane's owners; hence the overhauls generated "revenue-producing capital equipment" that was specifically exempted from city sales tax. The administrator's letter reads in part:

> We have conducted extensive research to identify the capitalization policy followed by airlines in regard to major overhauls. Our investigation included reviewing financial statements of airlines as well as the airline industry audit guide issued by the American Institute of Certified Public Accountants. The results of this research indicate there are a variety of accounting methods followed by airlines in regard to major overhauls, including directly expensing these costs. Accordingly, the city will no longer provide a blanket sales tax exemption for these repairs, and will hereafter require evidence that an air carrier actually capitalizes the cost of the overhaul before the city will grant a sales tax exemption for the specific transaction.

After consulting with the company president and the financial vice-president, the controller calls you into her office. After reading you the letter from the sales-tax administrator, the controller outlines a number of concerns and a course of action for you to follow in addressing the concerns. Your notes of the meeting include the following:

- Pres. mad! VP-F also mad!
- Customers won't want to provide details on how they account for repairs. Proprietary info.
- Customers won't pay additional 4% in sales tax. Wing Air will lose customers to competitors, or cut price we charge customers for repairs. Already-low margin business.
- Pres. wants to move operation to TX where bus. climate more favorable.
- Getting evidence on each transaction is unreasonable.
- For sales tax reasons, Wing Air always asks customers whether the costs are capitalized, and customers always say yes.
- GAAP says if expenditure enhances operating capacity or increases the useful life, capitalize.
- Capitalization makes financial statements look better; why would a company expense?

Required: After discussing the issue at length, the controller provides you with the following work assignment:

A. Investigate authoritative accounting literature to determine alternative accounting procedures to account for overhauls, and the accounting procedures supported by GAAP for C checks and D checks.

B. To the extent possible, document the actual accounting policies followed by carriers in this regard.

C. Prepare a response to the sales-tax administrator, and draft a letter containing the response. The letter should emphasize the concerns of your superiors and also address the issues raised by the sales-tax administrator.

13

Intangible Assets

Learning Objectives

After studying this chapter, you should be able to:

1. Apply the recognition and measurement criteria associated with intangible assets.
2. Prepare the accounting requirements for research and development costs and software development costs.
3. Discuss the nature of and apply the accounting requirements for goodwill-related costs.
4. Interpret the limitations of current practices related to intangible assets.
5. Estimate the economic value of corporate goodwill.
6. Account for insurance costs.

RJR Nabisco's Use of Accounting Technique Dealing with Goodwill Is Getting a Hard Look

With the tobacco-stock slump already haunting ***RJR Nabisco*** Holdings' plan to sell $1.5 billion of new shares tied to its Nabisco food business, some people on Wall Street are taking a harder look at an unusual accounting feature of the deal.

The offering's success depends greatly on the little-noticed accounting technique, which makes Nabisco's earnings appear larger—93 percent larger, to be exact.

What RJR is doing is presenting Nabisco's annual earnings without the burden of $206 million of 1992 "goodwill," leaving this earnings-depressing item with the parent company instead. Goodwill is a noncash accounting entry piled up on the books of companies such as RJR whenever they make acquisitions at prices above the book value of the companies acquired.

And there's goodwill aplenty at RJR Nabisco. A group led by ***Kohlberg Kravis Roberts*** paid a premium of $21.7 billion *over* book value when it spent $25 billion in 1989 to acquire the food and tobacco colossus in history's largest takeover.

Under accounting rules, the premium over book value, or goodwill, must be amortized (thus reducing RJR's earnings). . . . [M]any investors use reported earnings, penalizing companies with heaps of goodwill.

RJR is eager to focus attention on the value of its food business with the offering. Why? Because food stocks trade at about 16 times this year's expected earnings, while tobacco stocks trade at a multiple of only 8. Because the stock market will pay twice as much for food earnings as for tobacco, it makes sense for RJR to put as much of its profits as possible in the food company. . . . The rationale of RJR . . . is that both General Motors Corporation and USX Corporation, which created similar stocks tied to specific subsidiaries, did things the same way . . . but the field of special stock is so new that the rules aren't well established.

Source: Randall Smith, "RJR Nabisco's Use of Accounting Technique Dealing with Goodwill Is Getting a Hard Look," *The Wall Street Journal,* April 8, 1993.

As discussed in prior chapters, an asset is a resource from which a firm expects to derive future economic benefits. All *necessary* costs incurred to acquire an asset should be capitalized and charged to future periods of benefit . . . *if* there are likely to be significant future benefits. Otherwise, acquisition costs should be expensed as incurred. Determining which incremental costs are "necessary" and which costs will yield predictable future benefits is often difficult, even when dealing with tangible assets (such as shopping malls or specialty equipment).

These judgments may be even more difficult when dealing with intangible assets (such as research and development costs, franchise rights, and goodwill). Further, as the excerpted article testifies, the amounts involved may be very large, and the method of charging off (expensing) costs over time may be a point of contention. In the RJR Nabisco article, the issue was not only when and how much to charge off against income, but also whether the charges are to be made solely against the income of the parent firm (RJR Nabisco Holdings, Inc.) or also against the income of the acquired subsidiary (Nabisco). Investors' financial analyses may be significantly affected by the accounting methods adopted; thus, the accountant may be held liable if the financial statements are later deemed misleading. The accountant must fully understand the issues involved and be prepared to defend the judgments made.

Unlike tangible assets, intangible assets lack physical substance. This factor tends to make judgments such as those just discussed especially difficult. The lack of physical substance may cause an intangible asset to have fewer alternative uses and thus have a more indeterminate future value. For example, many physical assets, such as equipment or automobiles, have several alternative uses. Future benefits are more predictably anticipated for these assets than for intangible ones, such as computer software costs, which usually have a single purpose. If such intangibles do not meet their primary purpose, future benefits evaporate, since no alternative uses exist. Also, the lack of physical substance makes it harder to separate intangible assets from the other assets of a firm. Goodwill, for example, cannot be severed easily from other assets of the firm and sold. So, for this reason, too, intangible assets have limited or no alternative uses, making their economic life (period of benefit) more difficult to estimate.

ACCOUNTING FOR ACQUISITIONS OF INTANGIBLES

Apply the recognition and measurement criteria associated with intangible assets.

The complexities surrounding intangible assets would be less worrisome if intangible assets were relatively equal in amount, if they were consistent in type and method of accounting across firms and industries, or if they were not material. However, this is not the case. In some cases they are the most important assets of a firm. For both the user and provider of corporate financial information, a sound understanding of principles of accounting for intangibles is critical. In the sections that follow we will focus on several major categories of intangible assets. We will consider which costs should be expensed as incurred and which costs should be capitalized and allocated (expensed) over future periods of benefit. We will also consider the reasons for current accounting standards regarding intangibles and how a thorough understanding of accounting for intangibles can aid in sound financial statement analysis. Our discussions begin with research and development (R&D) costs.

RESEARCH AND DEVELOPMENT COSTS

Prepare the accounting requirements for research and development costs and software development costs.

Borrowing from definitions developed by the National Science Foundation, SFAS No. 2 defined **research and development (R&D)** as follows:[1]

> **Research** is a planned search or critical investigation aimed at the discovery of new knowledge with the hope that such knowledge will be useful in developing a new product or service or a new process or technique or in bringing about a significant improvement to an existing product or process.
>
> **Development** is the translation of research findings or other knowledge into a plan or design for a new product or process or for a significant improvement to an existing product or process whether intended for use or sale.

[1]SFAS No. 2, "Accounting for Research and Development Costs," FASB, 1974, par. 8.

Prior to the adoption of SFAS No. 2, R&D costs were accounted for in various fashions. Some firms charged all R&D costs to expense when incurred, and other firms capitalized all costs. Some firms capitalized certain costs and expensed others depending on whether selected conditions were met. For example, a firm might capitalize costs if the determination was made that a specific R&D project was successful and would lead to a commercially viable product. Capitalized costs were subsequently allocated (amortized) over future periods of benefit. With the adoption of SFAS No. 2, the FASB sought to achieve a greater degree of comparability across enterprises. The motivation for a standard on R&D costs was the increased importance of R&D in American industry.

APB Statement No. 4 (not Opinion No. 4) delineated three pervasive operational principles for determining when to recognize costs as expenses under the general "matching concept." The three principles were

1. Associative cause and effect.
2. Systematic and rational allocation.
3. Immediate recognition.

A salesperson's commission for a sale made is an example of a direct association of cause and effect, or expense and revenue. Many accounting costs, however, cannot be so directly (objectively) related to specific revenues. Costs incurred with *assumed* future benefits are frequently capitalized in practice and subsequently amortized or depreciated in a systematic and rational fashion.[2] *Amortization* is the appropriate terminology with intangible assets, whereas *depreciation* is the appropriate terminology used with tangibles.

APB Statement No. 4 observes that the third alternative, the immediate-recognition alternative, is appropriate when "costs incurred during the period provide *no discernible future benefits*" or "allocating costs . . . is considered to *serve no useful purpose*."[3] In SFAS No. 2, the FASB directs that all R&D costs must be expensed immediately. The FASB expressed the belief that an allocation of R&D costs to several years "would serve no useful purpose."[4] In addition, the arbitrary allocation to one year rather than multiple years of R&D costs is required by the FASB because (1) the FASB is not convinced that R&D costs satisfy the characteristics of an asset, and (2) the FASB is not convinced that future benefits, if they exist, are demonstrable and measurable. (Assets, recall, are defined as probable future economic benefits obtained or controlled by a particular entity as a result of past transactions or events.) That is, the board believes that any allocation pattern of R&D costs over future years would be excessively arbitrary because a definitive method of determining to which years R&D costs provide benefit (in the form of increased revenues) cannot be established. The FASB wanted to improve comparability across firms in the way in which similar events are reported. The requirement that all R&D costs be allocated to the year incurred is meant to provide that consistency in treatment.

[2]When consistently applied, systematic and rational allocation procedures serve to mitigate the dangers of income manipulation. Also, and very importantly, net income and other financial figures and ratios developing from the existing accrual-based accounting system *do* exhibit significant predictive ability with respect to future cash flows and other user relevant events, such as bankruptcy.

[3]"Basic Concepts and Accounting Principles Underlying Financial Statements of Business Enterprises," *Accounting Principles Board Statement No. 4*, 1970, par. 156–160.

[4]"Accounting for Research & Development Costs," *SFAS No. 2*, Financial Accounting Standards Board, 1974, par. 41.

Many commentators in the accounting literature, however, take exception to the conclusions of the FASB and its requirement for immediate expensing of all R&D costs. The point has been repeatedly and strongly made that the board's statements appear inconsistent with the views of business leaders, who expend nearly $50 billion annually on R&D in the United States. Certainly, these leaders of business expect to reap future economic benefits. However, the accounting problem is mainly a measurement problem; few businesspeople (including members of the FASB) believe there are no benefits that accrue from R&D. The method selected by the board, immediate recognition, nonetheless, is just as arbitrary as the method rejected, deferred recognition.

In summary, current U.S. standards require all R&D expenditures to be expensed as incurred. The purpose of this highly restrictive ruling is to increase the comparability or consistency with which similar costs are accounted for by different firms. It is questionable whether this end has been achieved by this standard. This is the case for several reasons. First, this requirement is not common in many other countries that are major trading partners of the United States. Most western economies do not require that R&D costs be expensed immediately. Of the major accounting systems, only the United States, Germany, and Mexico require immediate expensing of R&D expenditures. Accordingly, financial statement analyses of international corporations must be conducted with this in mind. If R&D costs of a U.S. firm were capitalized instead of expensed (as is the case with most non-U.S. companies), net income for the period would be increased, and the asset base would also be increased. Hence, profitability analyses would be affected by the difference in income and assets caused by expensing versus capitalization of R&D costs.

Second, the treatment of R&D costs, under current standards, varies depending upon whether the costs are incurred internally (in successful efforts leading to a patent) or acquired through the external purchase of a patent secured by another firm. See Exhibit 13–1. Where internal R&D efforts do allow a firm to achieve a multiyear strategic advantage, users must recognize that U.S. corporations usually will not include this economic resource among its assets. When successful research is conducted by others, that research may lead to the procurement of a patent. The patent may then be purchased by a U.S. corporation, which would record the full cost of the patent on the corporate financial statements. Further, nonpatented benefits of research might make their way onto a corporation's financial statements as "goodwill" through the purchase of one firm by another firm.

Another type of exception may develop in instances of contracted R&D. See the In Practice feature "Motorola and the Iridium Venture."

The FASB has conceded (and this is important to understanding financial statements in general, and not only with respect to R&D) that

> "[Not] all of the economic resources of an enterprise are recognized as assets for financial accounting purposes. . . . The criterion of *measurability* would require that a resource not be recognized as an asset for accounting purposes unless at the time it is acquired or developed its future economic benefits can be *identified and objectively measured*."[5]

[5]Ibid., pars. 43 and 44.

EXHIBIT 13–1
Research and Development Costs

A. Internally Conducted R&D

Alpha Industries incurred the following research and development costs in 1997:

Materials and supplies	$ 50,000
Salaries of research staff	360,000
Depreciation on research facility	140,000

During 1997, eleven research projects were undertaken. Two projects developed patentable products; additional legal and patent fees were $35,000 for each product. Nine projects did not lead to economically feasible products, and related research was discontinued.

1997 journal entries were as follows:

Research and Development Expense	550,000	
Inventories of Materials and Supplies		50,000
Cash and/or Salaries Payable		360,000
Accumulated Depreciation		140,000
To expense all R&D incurred during 1997.		

CONCEPT: Matching of period revenues and expenses.

LOGIC: Immediate expensing of R&D costs is required by the FASB because the Board believes that firms are unable to measure and relate R&D costs to specific years of identifiable future benefits. Thus, all benefits are assumed to be realized in the year of expenditure.

Patents	70,000	
Cash		70,000
To capitalize costs of patents; costs to be amortized over future years of benefit.		

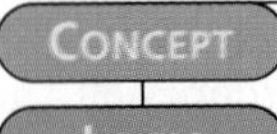

CONCEPT: Matching of period revenues and expenses.

LOGIC: Costs to secure patents are assumed to be related to those products and processes with high likelihood of benefits expected in future years. Thus, necessary costs to achieve those legal benefits are deferred to those years of benefits when the capitalized costs are amortized.

B. Externally Contracted R&D

Alpha Industries contracted with Clarion Laboratories for R&D services related to eleven projects in 1997. The fee Alpha agreed to pay was $600,000. Alpha, in return,

(continued)

EXHIBIT 13–1
(Continued)

received all rights to research results. That is, Alpha bore all risks (costs) and retained all rights (benefits). As a result of Clarion's research efforts, two projects developed patentable products for Alpha; additional legal and patent fees were $35,000 for each product. Nine projects did not lead to economically feasible products, and related research was discontinued.

1997 journal entries for Alpha were as follows:

Research & Development Expense	600,000	
Cash		600,000

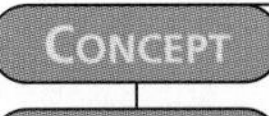

Matching of period revenues and expenses.

LOGIC

Immediate expensing of R&D costs is required by the FASB. The board believes that firms are unable to measure and relate R&D costs to specific years of identifiable future benefits. Thus, all benefits are assumed to be realized in the year of expenditure. Since Alpha is the bearer of all risks and beneficiary of all rewards that may accrue from the R&D expenditures, these costs represent R&D costs for Alpha.

Patents	70,000	
Cash		70,000

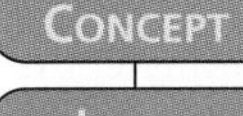

Matching of period revenues and expenses.

LOGIC

Costs to secure patents are assumed to be related to those products and processes with a high likelihood of benefits expected in future years. Thus, necessary costs to achieve those legal benefits are deferred to those years of benefits when the capitalized costs are amortized.

C. Acquisition of Externally Developed Patents

During 1997, Alpha Industries purchased two patents from Eta Enterprises for $670,000. Eta Enterprises had conducted noncontracted research on eleven projects during 1997, two of which resulted in products that Eta patented. That is, Eta incurred all risks of success or failure during the research stage. Specific costs incurred by Eta during 1997 were as follows:

Materials and supplies	$ 50,000
Salaries of research staff	360,000
Depreciation on research facility	140,000
Patent fees	70,000

Eta sold the two patented products to Alpha at a price to allow full recovery of all R&D costs plus a profit margin of $50,000.

(continued)

EXHIBIT 13–1
(Concluded)

1997 journal entries by Alpha Industries were as follows:

Patents	670,000	
Cash		670,000
To record costs of acquired patents; costs to be amortized over future years of benefit.		

CONCEPT Matching of period revenues and expenses.

LOGIC Patents purchased from other parties are capitalized at acquisition cost. This includes previously incurred patent registration costs as well as the prior research and development costs. Capitalization of these costs is considered appropriate in this instance because a high likelihood of future benefits exists, or the patent would not have been purchased.

IN PRACTICE—GENERAL

Motorola and the Iridium Venture

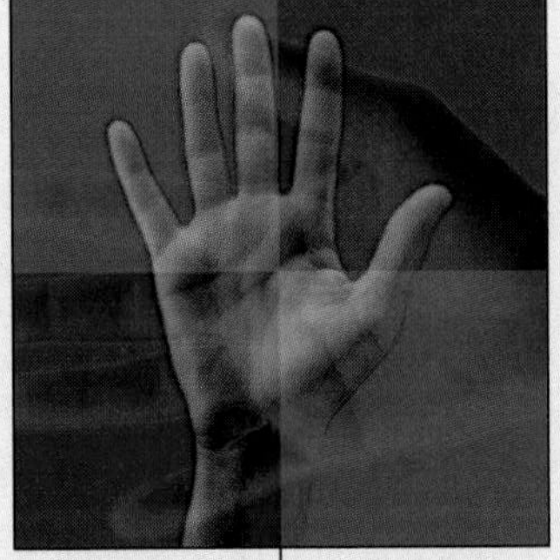

In the early 1990s, ***Motorola*** initiated the Iridium system and joint venture—a worldwide, satellite-based, wireless communication network. The system promised to revolutionize worldwide communication in the commercial, rural, and mobile areas by providing universal portable service. The satellite network was to be comprised of 66 satellites placed in low earth orbit.

Motorola initially owned approximately 35 percent of the joint venture when ***Iridium, Inc.***, was incorporated. Plans existed to secure additional new joint-venture partners worldwide and reduce Motorola's interest to about 15 percent. Motorola signed a $6 billion-plus contract with Iridium, Inc., to manufacture and deliver an operational system and to maintain the system for its first five years of operation. Significant R&D costs were anticipated and indeed occurred during the development and establishment of the system. But no R&D expense appeared on Motorola's income statements during these years. Why not?

The answer is because Motorola was not to be the direct recipient of indeterminate future benefits from the R&D efforts. Instead, Iridium, Inc., was. Motorola had a determinable future benefit; it was providing a *contracted* R&D service. For Motorola, then, the R&D costs were capitalizable contract costs. As such, they were capitalized when incurred and subsequently subject to expensing (as costs of contracted services) only when related contract revenues were recognized, as per the matching concept.

Thus, in this case, another exception exists with respect to the accounting treatment of R&D costs. These costs are recognized as such only when incurred by the firm potentially benefiting from their indeterminate future value (Iridium, Inc.). A corporate enterprise conducting research under contract for others' benefit should capitalize these costs as incurred and expense those costs later according to principles of revenue and expense matching.

Thus, SFAS No. 2 directs that all R&D costs should be expensed as incurred. Of course, this issue applies to more items than just R&D costs. A major limitation of the present accounting system in the United States is that a number of assets are not formally recognized in the accounts or statements. See the In

Practice feature "The Twilight Zone." Advocates of the current system, however, correctly point out that more flexible regulation of asset recognition would also provide greater opportunities for abuse.

IN PRACTICE—GENERAL

The Twilight Zone

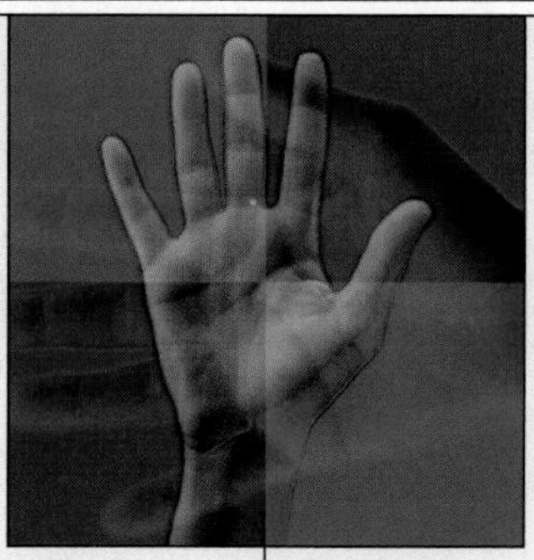

"I mean, you have assets, lots of assets, but they're intangible—between your ears, on this little diskette, in that patent filing. The whole point is to build a virtual corporation; you'll contract out the manufacturing, warehousing, distribution. You don't need brick and mortar, and you don't want it. But banks don't know the difference between assets and a hole in the ground.

A memory stirs—a smirking, familiar voice: Welcome to that corner of the Information Age that is known as . . . The Twilight Zone.

Some real-life version of this fable occurs every day: managers, owners, and business investors struggle to make sense of a business whose true assets aren't on the books. A report prepared by Arthur Andersen for 11 large British companies states: 'In successful companies, the value of such assets is growing as a proportion of total shareholder value.' Indeed: Margaret Blair, a Brooklings Institution economist, has calculated the relationship between tangible assets (property, plant, and equipment) and total market value for U.S. manufacturing and mining companies in the Compustat data-base. In 1982, she found, hard assets accounted for 62 percent of the companies' market value; ten years later they made up only 38 percent. And these were industrials."

Source: Fortune, October 2, 1995.

QUALIFYING COSTS

While the FASB wanted to provide relatively general definitions of R&D, the board also recognized the need to provide better guidelines to preparers of financial statements. Otherwise, the goal of improving the comparability of financial statements would not be achieved. Accordingly, SFAS No. 2 provides the following "examples of activities that typically would be included in research and development."[6]

1. Laboratory research aimed at discovery of new knowledge.
2. Searching for applications of new research findings or other knowledge.
3. Conceptual formulation and design of possible product or process alternatives.
4. Testing as a part of the search for or evaluation of product or process alternatives.
5. Modification of the formulation or design of a product or process.
6. Design, construction, and testing of production prototypes and models.
7. Design of tools, jigs, molds, and dies involving new technology.
8. Design, construction, and operation of a pilot plant that is not of a scale economically feasible to the enterprise for commercial production.

[6]Ibid., par. 9.

9. Engineering activity required to advance the design of a product to the point where it meets specific functional and economic requirements and is ready for manufacture.

If classified as an R&D activity, all costs incurred pursuant to that activity should be expensed. These costs include:[7]

1. Materials, whether taken from normal inventory or acquired specifically for the research.
2. Labor, including salaries, wages, and other related costs (such as health insurance and retirement benefits, etc.) of personnel directly engaged in R&D activities.
3. Overhead, including a reasonable allocation of indirect costs (general and administrative costs not clearly related should not be included).
4. Contract services, including the cost of research and development services performed by other firms under contract on behalf of the enterprise.
5. Intangibles purchased from others, i.e., intangibles purchased from others for a particular R&D project and that have no alternative uses (even in other R&D projects).
6. Equipment and facilities that are constructed or acquired for a particular R&D project and have no alternative future uses (in other R&D projects or otherwise).

If equipment or facilities are constructed or acquired for general R&D activities (not limited to one project), or if equipment or facilities have alternative future uses, the equipment or facilities should be capitalized as tangible assets. When depreciated, the charge (debit) would nonetheless be to R&D expense, not depreciation expense.

NON-R&D COSTS

In contrast to these *pre-commercial* production-type (R&D) costs, the board also defined several *commercial-stage* activities typically not considered as R&D. They include:[8]

1. Engineering follow-through in an early phase of commercial production.
2. Quality control during commercial production, including routine testing of products.
3. Troubleshooting in connection with breakdowns during commercial production.
4. Routine, ongoing efforts to refine, enrich, or otherwise improve upon the qualities of an existing product.
5. Adaptation of an existing capability to a particular requirement or customer's need as part of a continuing commercial activity.
6. Seasonal or other periodic design changes to existing products.
7. Routine design of tools, jigs, molds, and dies.

[7]Ibid., par. 11.
[8]Ibid., par. 10.

8. Activity, including design and construction engineering, related to the construction, relocation, rearrangement, or startup of facilities or equipment other than (a) pilot plants and (b) facilities or equipment whose sole use is for a particular R&D project.
9. Legal work in connection with patent application or litigation and the sale or licensing of patents.

Costs incurred in activities not considered R&D either should be expensed or capitalized. The treatment depends on whether the costs produce future economic benefits that can be separately identified and objectively measured.

Thus, in summary, three treatments of expenditures exist. The first is for costs that qualify as research and development. These costs must be expensed as incurred. The second and third treatments are for costs that do not qualify as research and development. Non-R&D costs that have no separately identifiable and objectively measurable future economic benefits must be expensed as incurred. However, non-R&D costs with separately identifiable and objectively measurable future benefits would appropriately require capitalization of costs.

SOFTWARE DEVELOPMENT

With the rapid and extensive worldwide application of computer-based technologies, the FASB in 1985 issued SFAS No. 86: "Accounting for the Costs of Computer Software to Be Sold, Leased, or Otherwise Marketed." The standard was made necessary by the vague language of SFAS No. 2, "Accounting for Research and Development Costs," and was issued at the explicit request of the SEC and the AICPA. The purpose of the standard was to clarify which software-related costs were to be considered R&D and which were to be treated otherwise. The FASB opined that "all costs incurred to establish the *technological feasibility* of a computer software product to be sold, leased, or marketed are research and development costs" and as such must be "charged to expense as incurred."[9]

Technological feasibility is established when the enterprise has completed *all* planning, designing, coding, and testing activities conducted pursuant to meeting design specifications. See the In Practice feature "Software Games." After establishing technological feasibility, all costs of producing *product masters,* including additional coding and testing costs, should be capitalized. When the product is ready for general release to the public, capitalization of product master costs stops. Additional costs are then considered to be maintenance and customer support and, as such, should be expensed as incurred. The costs of manufacturing copies from masters are considered production costs, and are treated as inventory costs.

Annual amortization of capitalized software costs is the greater of (1) straight-line amortization over the estimated useful life or (2) capitalized costs multiplied by the ratio of current gross revenues to total current plus anticipated future gross revenues. The following equations illustrate this.

[9]"Accounting for the Costs of Computer Software to Be Sold, Leased, or Otherwise Marketed," SFAS No. 86, Financial Accounting Standards Board, 1985, par. 3.

IN PRACTICE—GENERAL

Software "Games"

Five years ago it took ***Sierra*** only six months and an average of $600,000 to develop a game; now it takes at least a year and $1 million to $2 million. All that spending has taken its toll. In the first quarter of fiscal 1993, despite a nearly 50 percent jump in revenues, the company lost $74,000 from operations.

More bad news: The operating earnings are really much worse because of some aggressive accounting Williams [owner] has encouraged. Here's how. Three years ago Sierra expensed all its software development costs. But by the end of fiscal 1992 the company was capitalizing 80 percent of its $12 million research and development budget. Had it expensed the costs instead of capitalizing them, the company would have netted just $565,000 pretax income last year, versus the reported $5.4 million.

"Sierra is raping the accounting rules," charges ***Crowell, Weedon & Co.*** analyst Seth Feinstein. "Accounting rules tell us we have to capitalize," retorts Sierra's executive vice president.

Not exactly, says Richard Reck, partner in charge of software practice at ***KPMG Peat Marwick***. Reck agrees that the rules call for companies to capitalize development costs when they are sure the product has reached technological feasibility. But they have a lot of leeway in picking that point. . . . Most software companies capitalize around 20 percent of R&D costs. Competitors ***Broderbund Software*** and San Mateo, California-based ***Electronic Arts*** capitalize no more than 10 percent of their R&D costs.

Broderbund, for example, considers that products haven't reached technological feasibility until its staff can play the games on the screen. By contrast, Sierra starts capitalizing its costs as soon as it sees a five-page memo that gives an idea of what the game is about, who the writer is, and what the art is likely to look like.

Source: Roula Khalaf, "Accounting Adventure," *Forbes,* September 28, 1992.

Select greater of:

$$\text{Amortization Expense} = \frac{\text{Capitalized Cost}}{\text{Estimated Useful Life}}$$

$$\text{Amortization Expense} = \frac{\text{Current-Year Revenues}}{\text{Current Plus Anticipated Future Gross Revenue}} \times \text{Capitalized Cost}$$

SFAS No. 86 does not address accounting for costs incurred in developing software for internal use. Accordingly, these costs may be capitalized and amortized over the period of assumed future benefit.

NATURAL RESOURCE DEVELOPMENT

While analogies are commonly drawn between R&D activities, software development activities, and activities common to extractive industries such as prospecting, drilling, and so forth, SFAS No. 2 does not require the immediate expensing of these latter oil exploration items. Rather, SFAS No. 25 allows capitalization of exploratory costs under two methods: successful efforts and full costing. As with R&D costs, two major matters of controversy addressed by the FASB were what costs are considered necessary and what costs, if any, lead to future economic benefits that can be identified and objectively measured.

Under **successful-efforts accounting**, only costs incurred pursuant to successful exploration (exploration climaxing in discovery of commercially exploitable resources) can be capitalized. For example, if $250,000 is expended in drilling each of ten oil wells ($2,500,000 in total), and only one oil well develops significant oil reserves, then, successful-efforts advocates argue, only $250,000 in costs may be capitalized. The other $2,250,000 (the cost of drilling the nine unsuccessful wells) would be expensed under the logic that those costs were unnecessary costs and/or did not lead to future benefits.

On the other hand, the **full-costing method** allows capitalization of all $2,500,000 of exploration costs. These costs subsequently are expensed in future years of benefit (those years when the discovered resources are extracted and sold). Thus, while the FASB does not regard R&D expenditures, even on projects determined to be successful, as leading to future benefits that are identifiable and objectively measurable, current standards do allow capitalization of exploration costs, even when specific efforts fail to lead to discovery. (For example, the costs of sinking "dry holes" would be capitalized under the full-costing method.) Thus, once again, it is questionable whether the FASB has been successful in achieving its proposed goal of consistency in accounting for similar costs across firms. Whether the underlying conditions in these two instances are sufficiently different to warrant these distinct treatments may be argued. It is important to note, however, that initially, in an effort to be consistent with the R&D standard, the FASB assumed a position permitting only the successful-efforts method in SFAS No. 19 ("Financial Accounting and Reporting by Oil and Gas Producing Companies"). Political opposition and the intervention of Congress and the SEC required the FASB to amend its position in SFAS No. 25 ("Suspension of Certain Accounting Requirements for Oil and Gas Producing Companies"). The FASB has chosen not to revisit accounting for R&D costs or software development costs but to accept any inconsistency that has developed.

In practice, most exploration costs are capitalized under the full-costing method. However, a cost capitalization ceiling has been imposed by the SEC, in "Regulation S–X, Rule 4–10." Specifically, a quarterly test of asset impairment is required. If the present value of future net revenues (discounted at 10% and based on current prices and costs) from production or proved oil and gas reserves plus the cost of properties not being amortized exceeds the unamortized capitalized costs (adjusted for deferred taxes) an impairment is deemed to exist, and an asset write-down is required. In addition, once an impairment is recorded, costs cannot be reinstated for a subsequent recovery (i.e., increased estimates of future net revenues based on rebounding oil prices.) This creates yet another financial statement distortion, argue Adams, Bach, Bickett, Carroll, Gallun, and Kuiper in a 1994 *Journal of Accountancy* article (April 1994).

> "When the ceiling-test rules result in values that do not reflect permanent impairment or the fair value of the underlying assets, the financial statements are distorted. Permanent write-downs based on current full-cost rules could be misinterpreted by financial statement users because they usually do not approximate fair market values and may not reflect permanent declines in value."

PATENTS

A patent is an exclusive, legal right (granted by the U.S. Patent Office) to use, manufacture, or sell a product or process. The legal life of a patent is 17 years. A patent's economic life, however, may be much shorter, depending on the pace of technological advancement in an industry. As with other *identifiable* intangibles, all necessary costs incurred to achieve the benefits of a patent are capitalizable *if* future economic benefits are identifiable and objectively measurable. Because SFAS No. 2 requires the immediate expensing of all R&D costs, irrespective of whether they lead to a patented product or process, R&D costs cannot be considered necessary costs of a patent, *if the R&D costs are internally expended*. Those costs considered necessary frequently are restricted to U.S. Patent Office application fees and attorney costs. Typically, these costs are nominal.

Material patent book values most frequently arise from the purchase of an existing patent from another firm. All costs of acquisition, which may be considerable, are capitalizable in this event. Thus, an apparent inconsistency develops over the capitalized values of purchased patents versus patents obtained on the basis of internal R&D activities. The inconsistency occurs because a firm selling a patent will most certainly seek a price allowing recovery of all R&D costs incurred.

In analyzing financial statements, therefore, it is important to consider the underlying economic value of a firm's patents and not rely on book values. Patent book values will deviate from current economic values not only because of prior cost allocations (amortization) but also because R&D costs cannot be capitalized for patents obtained based on internally conducted R&D.

Whether internally developed or purchased, patents are frequently the basis of litigation. If a firm unsuccessfully litigates and fails to obtain relief from alleged competitor patent infringements, all costs of the litigation should be expensed. In addition, it is incumbent on the firm to reevaluate whether a significant and permanent erosion in the value of the asset (patent) has occurred. If there is a significant decline in expected future economic benefits, a partial or complete write-down of the patent asset is appropriate.

On the other hand, if litigation is successful in stopping future infringement by competitors, these legal costs may be capitalized. Capitalization of successful defense of a patent is based on the theory that such costs are *necessary* costs to make the patent useful (that is, necessary to secure the benefits of the patent).

GOODWILL

Discuss the nature of and apply the accounting requirements for goodwill-related costs.

Another poorly understood intangible asset that is potentially very important for many firms is goodwill. The confusion surrounding this intangible seems to develop from two sources: (1) misunderstanding of what goodwill is and (2) confusion between an economic valuation of goodwill and the valuation required by GAAP. Let us start with an understanding of the concept itself.

Goodwill is an intangible asset that cannot be separately identified and valued. Instead, it potentially consists of a number of elements (favorable firm characteristics) that allow a firm to earn greater returns than would be possible in the absence of these goodwill elements. "Accounting Research Study (ARS) No. 10," issued in 1968, observed that conceptually, goodwill included such characteristics as:

1. Superior enterprise management, or the marked weakness in management (or other competitive factor) of a major competitor.
2. A superior, and yet secret, manufacturing process.
3. Superior labor relations.
4. Superior creditor relations.
5. Superior employee-training programs.
6. Superior community relations (image).
7. Superior advertising department and brand image.
8. Strategic location.
9. Discovery of natural resources.
10. Favorable tax condition and/or government regulations.
11. Favorable strategic association with other firms.

GAAP Valuation of Goodwill. GAAP requires that costs related to the following matters be expensed as incurred:

1. Community improvement.
2. Employee or creditor relations.
3. Forging strategic relationships with other firms.
4. Promoting a favorable tax or regulatory condition for the firm.
5. Promoting other goodwill-related advantages.

Again, as with R&D and software development costs, the measurability criterion is the focal issue. That is, the costs of a resource cannot be recognized as an asset for accounting purposes unless at the time it is acquired or developed, its future economic benefits can be separately identified and objectively measured.

Current GAAP holds that this is not the case with regard to goodwill-related expenditures, except in one instance. That one exception occurs when all three of the following conditions are met: (1) a business combination (corporate merger) takes place, (2) the combination is accounted for using the *purchase method*,[10] and (3) the "purchase" cost exceeds the aggregate market-adjusted book values of the identifiable assets of the "purchased" firm.

100 Percent Purchase of Stock. To illustrate, assume that Harper Conglomerated Enterprises acquires a controlling interest in Markmen Industries by cash acquisition of 100 percent of Markmen's outstanding voting stock for $100,000,000. Relevant data regarding Markmen's net assets (assets minus liabilities) are provided in Exhibit 13–2.

On Harper's books, and on Harper's financial statements, the account called Investment in Markmen Common Stock is recorded and reported *at cost*, $100,000,000. However, it is typical for a corporation that has control over another to issue additional *consolidated financial statements*. Consolidated financial statements combine and adjust the book values of Harper and Markmen so as to provide a perspective of the aggregate *economic* (rather than *legal*) unit. On consolidating working papers, leading to consolidated financial statements, the investment account (Investment in Markmen Common Stock) is eliminated by

[10]The alternative to the purchase method is the pooling method. The distinction between the two and requirements of each are found in Accounting Principles Board Opinion No. 16, "Accounting for Business Combinations," 1970.

IN PRACTICE—GENERAL

What's in a Name?

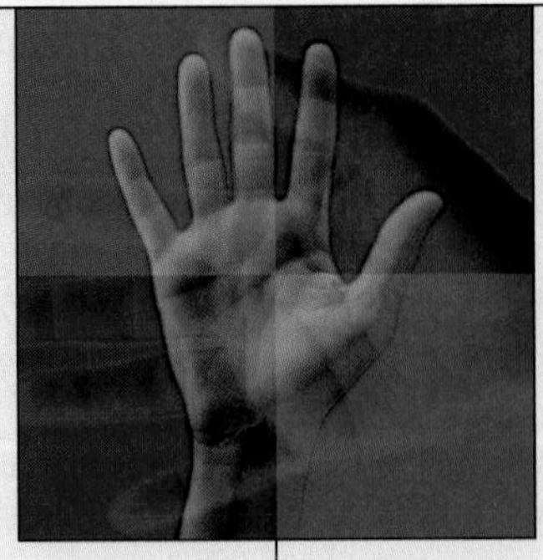

Marlboro is the best-known brand on the face of the earth. But how much is it worth?

About $31 billion, twice its annual revenue, says *Financial World*. The magazine, in an article appearing today, takes on one of the toughest tasks in business: putting dollar values on brand names.

Conventional accounting doesn't have an accepted way to value the trade names companies back with millions in marketing money. *Financial World* used its own complex formula to pin down brand's market value.

"It's an absurd fiction to say it's impossible to value them," says *Financial World* Editor Goeffrey Smith. "It's not fair to these branded-good companies. You're talking about their most valuable assets by far."

Financial World estimates how much the U.S.'s major consumer brands would be worth in cash.

BRAND	COMPANY	VALUE (BILLIONS)	REVENUES (BILLIONS)
1. Marlboro	*Philip Morris*	$31.2	$15.4
2. Coca-Cola soft drinks	*Coca-Cola*	24.4	8.4
3. Budweiser beer	*Anheuser-Busch*	10.2	6.2
4. Pepsi-Cola soft drinks	*PepsiCo*	9.6	5.5
5. Nescafé instant coffee	*Nestlé*	8.5	4.3
6. Kellogg cereals	*Kellogg*	8.4	4.7
7. Winston cigarettes	*RJR Nabisco*	6.1	3.6
8. Pampers diapers	*Procter & Gamble*	6.1	4.0
9. Camel cigarettes	*RJR Nabisco*	4.4	2.3
10. Campbell soups	*Campbell Soup*	3.9	2.4
11. Nestlé sweets	*Nestlé*	3.7	6.0
12. Hennessy cognac	*LVMH*	3.0	.9
13. Heineken beer	*Heineken*	2.7	3.5
14. Johnnie Walker red scotch	*Guinness*	2.6	1.5
15. Louis Vuitton baggage	*LVMH*	2.6	.9
16. Hershey sweets	*Hershey*	2.3	2.6
17. Guinness beer	*Guinness*	2.3	1.8
18. Barbie dolls, accessories	*Mattel*	2.2	.8
19. Kraft cheese	*Philip Morris*	2.2	2.8
20. Smirnoff vodka	*Grand Metropolitan*	2.2	1.0

Source: "What's in a Name?" *USA Today*, August 12, 1992, Sec. B. p. 1.

EXHIBIT 13–2
GAAP Valuation of Goodwill Markmen Industries Data

ACCOUNT	BOOK VALUE	FAIR MARKET VALUE	DIFFERENCE
Cash	$ 3,000,000	$ 3,000,000	$ 0
Accounts receivable	10,000,000	9,000,000	(1,000,000)
Inventory	40,000,000	42,000,000	2,000,000
Plant and equipment	80,000,000	86,000,000	6,000,000
Liabilities	(43,000,000)	(43,000,000)	0
Total	$ 90,000,000	$ 97,000,000	

a $100,000,000 credit and replaced by the specific undervalued (overvalued) Markmen asset accounts, which total $90,000,000. The remaining $10,000,000 is allocated as follows:

Accounts receivable	$(1,000,000)	Credit
Inventory	2,000,000	Debit
Plant and equipment	6,000,000	Debit
Goodwill	3,000,000	Debit

That is, the specific assets are adjusted to reflect market value, and any remaining amount is classified as goodwill. Thus, goodwill of $3,000,000 will be reported on the consolidated balance sheet and is the excess cost over the fair market value of the net assets acquired. The journal entry on the books of Harper to record the purchase of 100% of Markmen would be as follows:

Investment in Markmen	100,000,000	
Cash		100,000,000
To record the investment at cost at time of purchase.		

One entry on the consolidating working paper might be as follows. (This entry, however, is *not* made on either company's books.)

Cash	3,000,000	
Accounts Receivable	9,000,000	
Inventory	42,000,000	
Plant and Equipment	86,000,000	
Goodwill	3,000,000	
Liabilities		43,000,000
Investment in Markmen		100,000,000

Asset valuation at acquisition.

Assets are recorded at the cost of acquisition, which in this case is their fair market value. The excess acquisition cost over the fair market value of the net assets acquired is recorded in the asset account Goodwill.

PURCHASE OF LESS THAN 100 PERCENT INTEREST

Assume now that Harper Conglomerated Enterprises acquires 80 percent of Markmen's outstanding common stock for $80,000,000 cash. Data regarding Markmen's book and fair market values are provided in Exhibit 13–2. An 80 percent interest in the fair market value of the net assets of Markmen would amount to $77,600,000 (80% × $97,000,000). Harper would record the net assets at FMV of $77,600,000. The excess cost over fair market value of $2,400,000 ($80,000,000 − $77,600,000) would be recorded as goodwill. The journal entry on Harper's books would be as follows:

Investment in Markmen	80,000,000	
Cash		80,000,000

One entry on the year-end working papers made to produce consolidated financial statements might be:

Cash ($3,000,000 × 80%)	2,400,000	
Accounts Receivable ($9,000,000 × 80%)	7,200,000	
Inventory ($42,000,000 × 80%)	33,600,000	
Plant and Equipment ($86,000,000 × 80%)	68,800,000	
Goodwill	2,400,000	
Liabilities ($43,000,000 × 80%)		34,400,000
Investment in Markmen		80,000,000
The consolidating entry to record 80 percent of assets and liabilities of Markmen purchased.		

CONCEPT Asset valuation at acquisition cost.

LOGIC Assets are valued at their cost of acquisition, which in this case is their fair market value. The goodwill is valued at the difference between the price paid ($80 million) and the fair market value of the net assets purchased ($77.6 million).

Exhibit 13–3 provides an analysis of the source of the goodwill. Harper is willing to pay the extra amount for goodwill because Markmen possesses some advantage that Harper perceives will lead to excess earnings, or earnings greater than would be normal in the industry. Measurement and valuation of these excess earnings are discussed and illustrated in the first appendix to this chapter, "Economic Valuation of Goodwill."

EXHIBIT 13–3 GAAP Valuation of Goodwill: Adjustments to Tangible Assets

The book values of Markmen's identifiable net assets total $90,000,000, and the fair market values total $97,000,000. An 80% interest in the book value of these assets would be $72,000,000 ($90 million × 80%). However, Harper pays $80,000,000 for an 80% interest. An excess purchase price of $8,000,000 occurs because either or both of the following conditions exist. First, the identified assets are undervalued. Second, other nonidentified assets (goodwill) exist. In this instance, both conditions exist. First, Markmen's net assets are understated by $7,000,000; *Harper's interest in these understated assets is $5,600,000,* as detailed here in the adjustments to tangible assets.

ACCOUNT	BOOK VALUE	FAIR MARKET VALUE	DIFFERENCE	× 80% = ADJUSTMENT
Cash	$ 3,000,000	$ 3,000,000	$ 0	$ 0
Accounts receivable	10,000,000	9,000,000	(1,000,000)	(800,000)
Inventory	40,000,000	42,000,000	2,000,000	1,600,000
Plant and equipment	80,000,000	86,000,000	6,000,000	4,800,000
Liabilities	(43,000,000)	(43,000,000)	0	0
Total	$ 90,000,000	$ 97,000,000		$5,600,000

This leaves $2,400,000 in excess cost over the fair market value of the net assets acquired ($8,000,000 – $5,600,000). This $2,400,000 is reported on the consolidated balance sheet as goodwill.

As with all intangibles, capitalized costs should be expensed (called *amortization*) over the future period of benefit. To reduce "unnecessary" variation in practice, GAAP requires all capitalized costs of intangibles to be amortized over a period not exceeding 40 years.

In summary, the only circumstances under which goodwill appears on U.S. corporate financial statements arise solely from the purchase of another enterprise in which the purchase price exceeds the book value of the purchased firm.[11] However, accounting standards for goodwill differ internationally. The In Practice feature "International Accounting for Goodwill" points out some of the effects of these differences in standards for U.S.-based firms.

IN PRACTICE—GENERAL

International Accounting for Goodwill

U.S. accounting rules require the expensing of goodwill against earnings, whereas other major economic powers can charge the entire goodwill to stockholders' equity—not affecting earnings per share—or even ignore it entirely. Consider a simple example. Company A (acquirer) makes $1 million a year. Company B (target) makes $1 million a year. If Company A is an American company and paid for goodwill, then 1 plus 1 does not equal 2—earnings of the combined company will be less than $2 million because of goodwill amortization. There is also a reduction in return on investment (ROI) and return on equity (ROE). Such would not usually be the case if the acquirer were a U.K., German, Dutch, or Japanese company.

A recent acquisition was that of ***Pillsbury*** by ***Grand Met***, a British company. If an American company had acquired Pillsbury at the price Grand Met paid, it would have had an annual charge against earnings of about $50 million a year for 40 years (the calculated goodwill of $2 billion divided by 40). Because Grand Met is a British company, it could charge the entire goodwill to stockholders' equity—never to be seen again. In another recent acquisition, ***Unilever***, a Dutch company, paid $3.1 billion for ***Cheeseborough-Pond's***. Goodwill was $2.4 billion. If an American company had been the acquirer, it would have a $60 million charge to earnings for each of the next 40 years. Speculation in the financial community is that one of the reasons American companies did not top the foreign bidders is that none could afford the high goodwill charge.

Voluntary International Accounting Standards

"Starting next year, new international accounting rules will force foreign companies to deduct from profits the value of goodwill, as is required of U.S. companies here. Currently, many foreign companies deduct goodwill from equity or net worth. The new rules have been set by the International Accounting Standards Committee, a worldwide group of national accounting bodies. The standards it sets are mandatory *only for countries that accept them*, including Switzerland and Italy, although numerous individual companies worldwide accept the rules voluntarily."

Source: Joseph C. Corry, "Accounting Aspects of Takeovers," *Management Accounting*, September 1990, pp. 47–48; Lee Berton and Greg Steinmetz, *The Wall Street Journal*, July 1, 1994.

[11]We noted earlier that three conditions are necessary for goodwill to appear on financial statements. They were (1) a business combination (corporate merger) takes place, (2) the combination is accounted for using the *purchase method*, and (3) the "purchase" cost exceeds the relevant fair value of the "purchased" firm's net assets. It is important to note that had the merger been recorded as a "pooling of interests" rather than a "purchase" (both GAAP-acceptable methods), *no* goodwill would have been reported nor are any tangible asset book values adjusted. As both methods are common in practice, the intelligent user of financial data must be mindful of the differing effects on standard ratio analyses.

It was noted earlier that typically, when one corporation has control over another, consolidated financial statements are issued in addition to the acquiring firm's statements. The subsidiary firm may also issue its own separate statements, and as noted in the excerpted article introducing this chapter, the subsidiary corporation also may subsequently issue new stock. The subsequent issue of new stock by the acquired corporation has given rise to a new controversy in the field. The controversy is whether any amortization of goodwill should be reported on the subsidiary's (nonconsolidated) financial statements. Current standards are unclear as to whether the goodwill should or should not be "pushed down" to the subsidiary whose acquisition gave rise to the goodwill or whether the goodwill amortization should be reported only on the parent (acquiring) firm's statements and the consolidated statements.

Professional skepticism continues to surround large goodwill write-offs taken by some firms in the name of asset impairment. Large-scale write-offs of goodwill by some but not other firms creates an additional example of inconsistent accounting practices that frustrate users of financial statements. See the In Practice feature "When Is Bad News Good News?"

IN PRACTICE—GENERAL

When Is Bad News Good News?

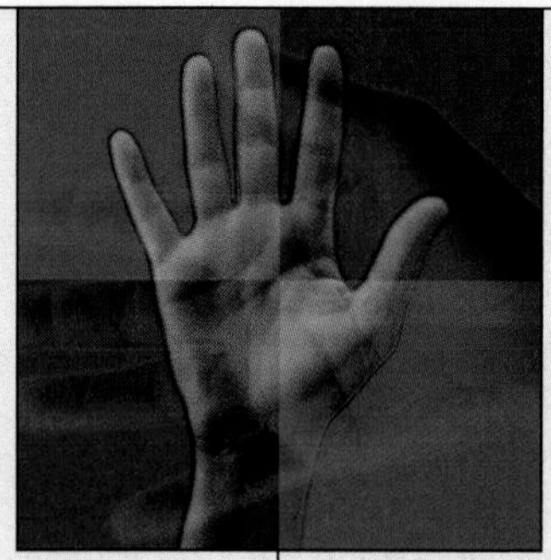

How did ***Supermarkets General*** get away with its write-off of $600 million in goodwill in 1992? By finding a loophole. Seems the language governing all this is murky. The accounting rule actually says that goodwill should be reevaluated more or less continually and reduced if need be. Certainly, a company that decided to sell or wind down a business it had previously acquired could get rid of the associated goodwill. The rule also gives a break to companies that suffer losses over several years and expect only lackluster results in the future. They, too, can write off part or all of the goodwill on their books....

Supermarkets General told the Securities and Exchange Commission ... that its total operating income for the next 35 years, the duration of the remaining goodwill, would not reach $600 million, the amount of the goodwill remaining.

A dire forecast, you might say for a company about to tap the public markets. But you can be sure Supermarkets General peddled a different story to investors ... in March, Supermarkets General announced a restructuring.... The restructuring gave a whole new look to the company's past and future. The company told investors to look at income after the effects of the restructuring. Instead of flat sales and net losses it reported last year, Supermarkets General said now that ***Pathmark's*** (Supermarkets General Corp.'s brand name line of grocery stores) net income was $42 million.

"Supermarkets General essentially told the SEC to ignore the restructuring in calculating goodwill impairment but told investors to feel good about it," says ***Lehman Brothers*** accounting expert Robert Willens.... Before the write-off, the goodwill amortization costs were $17 million per year. The write-off eliminated the charge, enhancing aftertax income by that amount. Figure at 11 times earnings the change adds about $200 million to Pathmark's valuation. Pretty neat. Take a $600 million bookkeeping hit and increase the company's market value by $200 million.

Source: Amy Feldman, "Goodwill Games," *Forbes,* September 13, 1993.

Badwill. Accounting recognition (treatment) of badwill occurs in selected rare instances where (1) the adjusted book value of the "purchased" interest exceeds the costs of acquisition, (2) the difference cannot be attributed to overvalued identifiable assets, and (3) the adjusted book values of non-fair-value-based assets are insufficient to absorb the negative residual. In these instances, assets are first adjusted as illustrated in Exhibit 13–3. However, a negative residual will develop. Again referring to Exhibit 13–3, this would be the case if the purchase price of the 80% interest was $76,000,000 rather than $80,000,000 (as initially posed in the example.) In this revised example, a difference between cost and initial book value would be $4,000,000. Following fair value adjustments (see Exhibit 13–3) that increase or adjust book values by $5,600,000, a negative residual of $1,600,000 would develop. This negative residual next would be proportionally written off against non-fair-value-measured assets (i.e., long-term assets other than investments in marketable securities) to arrive at adjusted book values. If sufficient asset book values exist to absorb this negative residual (as they clearly do in Exhibit 13–3 where assets exceed $100,000,000 and the negative residual is only $1,600,000), no badwill remains. If assets, however, had been inadequate to absorb the negative residual (such as in some professional service firms or firms that mostly rent facilities and equipment), those non-fair-value-measured assets would be reduced to a book value of zero and the remaining residual would be reported on financial statements as "Excess of Book Value Over Cost."

OTHER INTANGIBLE ASSETS

The significance of any intangible asset or category of intangible assets will depend in large measure on the industry itself. The intangible assets discussed thus far may affect a great number of firms. Other intangible assets may affect a lesser number of firms and are therefore discussed here in less detail. However, the relatively brief discussion does not suggest that these assets are less important than others; to some firms, they are of utmost consequence. See the In Practice feature "Allocating Promotional Costs" for a discussion of how accounting treatment of advertising/promotional costs can be centrally important to public perceptions of success in a service industry.

Copyrights. For authors of literary, musical, artistic, and similar creative works, copyrights grant certain exclusive rights under the law. Examples include the exclusive right to perform or record a work and/or exclusive rights to reprint and sell copies of a work. Copyrights in the United States are granted for the author's life plus 50 years. Copyrights may be sold or otherwise contractually assigned. Similar to a patent, copyright costs related to application and attorney fees may be capitalized. In addition, as a separately identifiable intangible, developmental costs also may be capitalized. As with all intangibles, any capitalized costs must be amortized over the estimated useful life, but not over a period exceeding 40 years, as specified in APB Opinion No. 17.

Trademarks and Trade Names. Firms that register their trademarks (and trade names) with the U.S. Patent Office receive legal right to the exclusive use of these identifying symbols (names) for renewable periods of 20 years. All costs

IN PRACTICE—GENERAL

Allocating Promotional Costs

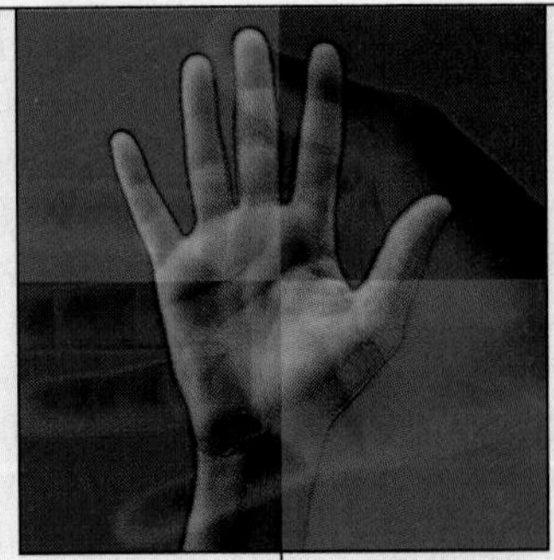

America Online's biggest expenditure is the cost of attracting subscribers, who each pay $9.95 a month for limited access to the electronic data system. America Online sends out millions of pieces of mail solicitations and works deals with computer manufacturers to give away free trial subscriptions with every computer sold. This is expensive promotion. For fiscal 1994, subscriber acquisition costs amounted to $37 million—over $40 per new subscriber. With subscribers paying an average $15.50 a month, including extra on-line time, it costs about three months in revenue to buy a new subscriber.

Basic accounting question: Is that $37 million subscriber acquisition figure an expense against income? Or is it an investment undertaken to create an asset?

Here are the numbers: In America Online's report for fiscal 1994, revenues were $104 million, and total costs and expenses $96 million. But that cost figure included only $23 million in subscriber acquisition expenses and other marketing expenses. These were costs incurred the year before. The costs for fiscal 1994, $37 million, were entirely capitalized, and were amortized for up to 18 months after they were incurred. Had the $37 million been expensed as incurred, America Online would have lost around $6 million before taxes. But by capitalizing and amortizing, the company was able to report net income of $6.2 million.

Source: Gary Samuels, "What Profits," *Forbes*, October 24, 1994.

incurred to purchase a trademark from another firm should be capitalized. If internally developed, all costs directly related to the development, registration, and legal defense of a trademark (trade name) should be capitalized. (Internal developmental costs typically are capitalizable if the intangible is a separately identifiable asset with measurable future economic benefit.) The period of amortization should be the lesser of the economic useful life or 40 years.

Organizational Costs. Those costs incurred and directly related to the organization of a business are known as organizational costs. They may include accounting and clerical costs, legal costs and application filing fees, promotional costs, and costs of initial directors' meetings and similar items. These initial costs are believed to provide benefits over a number of future years of firm operations. Accordingly, organizational costs should be capitalized and subsequently expensed (amortized) over future periods of benefit. Given that the period of benefit is highly subjective, if not largely indeterminate, organizational costs typically are written off over a relatively short period; usually significantly less than the 40-year maximum period allowed for intangibles. Organizational costs are not to include deficits from the early years of a firm's operations.

Franchise and License Costs. A franchise is a contractual agreement wherein the franchisor grants the franchisee the right to perform certain services, to sell certain products, and/or to otherwise use certain trademarks (trade names) within a limited geographic area. The rights typically are granted for only a designated period of time and may be renewed under certain conditions. To secure these rights, the franchisee often will be charged a significant initial fee as well as continuing annual charges. In return for these initial costs, the franchisor also may provide a variety of legal, promotional, and management-training services. Initial franchise costs should be capitalized and subsequently amortized over the period of expected future benefit.

Similar to a franchising arrangement, a government unit may grant exclusive rights (*license*) to use public properties or to provide a designated service within its jurisdiction. Examples are exclusive cable television license rights and exclusive license to provide mass transit (bus) services. In return for these rights, the private enterprise may be charged a significant initial fee as well as continuing annual charges. Periodic or annual payments should be recorded as expenses as incurred. However, as with initial franchise costs, initial license costs should be capitalized and subsequently amortized over the period of benefit but not over a period exceeding 40 years.

POSTACQUISITION ACCOUNTING FOR INTANGIBLES

In conformity with the matching concept, all capitalized costs related to the acquisition of intangible assets should be expensed over their productive lives. When the costs of intangibles must be expensed over their lives, the method used should be systematic and rational. Further, unless a firm can "demonstrate [that] another systematic method is more appropriate," APB No. 17 requires that the straight-line method of equal annual charges be used (unless otherwise directed by specific subsequent SFAS, such as in the case of computer software costs). Amortization Expense is debited, and either the intangible asset or a contra account (Accumulated Amortization) is credited.

The process is somewhat complicated by the fact that the useful life of an intangible may be very hard to determine, as is also the likelihood and amount of any residual value. Accordingly, to somewhat constrain excessively lengthy amortization periods, APB No. 17 directs a maximum 40-year period for intangibles acquired after 1970. Also toward this end of establishing a shorter amortization period, APB No. 17 directs that the following factors be considered in the estimated life of an intangible:[12]

1. Initial legal, regulatory, and/or contractual life.
2. Legal, regulatory, and/or contractual provisions for renewal.
3. Effects of technological or demand obsolescence.
4. Related life expectancies of critical individuals or groups of individuals.
5. Anticipated competitive responses that may mitigate competitive advantages.
6. Composite nature of asset (the intangible is made up of several assets of varying life expectancies).
7. Inability to reasonably project a specific pattern of benefits.

While the annual provision for amortization is an allocation procedure and not a valuation procedure, it is still necessary that one be alert to any permanent decline in the economic value of an intangible. Such impairment is more likely with intangible assets than tangible assets, given the uncertainty surrounding their future benefits, as discussed earlier. If during a current period there does

[12]APB Opinion No. 17, par. 27.

occur a permanent impairment in the value of an intangible asset, such that the present value of its remaining future benefits is less than book value, an asset write-down and a charge against income will be necessary. Footnote disclosure also is required.[13]

When an intangible asset is sold or otherwise disposed of, any remaining book value must be removed from the accounts (the principal asset account and any contra accounts). In interpreting a gain or loss that results from a sale or exchange transaction, one must recall that the size of any gain or loss relates not only to current economic events but also to the degree to which amounts were arbitrarily, albeit systematically, expensed (or not expensed) in prior periods.

Discussion and Evaluation

Interpret the limitations of current practices related to intangible assets.

The intangible assets of a firm may be vitally important to the future profitability of the firm. Accordingly, a clear picture of the value of a firm's intangibles is highly pertinent to an evaluation of a firm's past performance and future prospects. In the area of intangibles, authoritative rule-making bodies in the United States (the Accounting Principles Board and the Financial Accounting Standards Board) have confronted some difficult choices. Should the variety of ways for which intangibles are accounted be limited for the sake of enhanced interfirm domestic comparability? Should this be done by adoption of a set of arguably arbitrary, if not inconsistent, rules? And would such a practice place American industry at an international disadvantage or advantage?

The orientation of recent standards on intangibles might be portrayed as relatively defensive or conservative compared to prior U.S. practices and current international practices. Current U.S. GAAP shows a marked reticence to overstate intangible assets, even at a cost of probable understatement in many instances. As discussed before, the costs of internally conducted research and development, internally conducted software development costs, and internally developed goodwill, under current GAAP, must be written off to expense as incurred. This is not the case universally outside the United States. Furthermore, where costs are capitalized, those costs must be charged against income (amortized) over a period not exceeding 40 years, even if the economic value of the intangible is maintained.

The members of the FASB have confronted many difficult decisions with respect to accounting and reporting requirements. Their objective is always to provide relevant and reliable information for decision making. It is critical that both the preparer and user of accounting information consciously consider the effects of current standards on financial statements. Many financial ratios are influenced by standards that markedly lower net income and the balance sheet asset position. Both the numerator and denominator in return-on-assets calculations, for example, are affected. Internationally, U.S. firms that write off intangible assets will report less income, a smaller asset base, and a reduced equity position. As discussed in the first case in the end-of-chapter materials (C13–1), significantly reduced debt-to-equity ratios also are likely.

Not all firms are alike. Some firms have few especially valuable intangibles, while others have many. Current GAAP, in general, does not allow one to easily distinguish between the two conditions.

[13]Ibid., par. 31.

APPENDIX: ECONOMIC VALUATION OF GOODWILL

Estimate the economic value of corporate goodwill.

Two methods are commonly used to establish an initial estimate of the relative value of goodwill to an enterprise. The first is the residual-valuation approach, and the second is the capitalization-of-excess-earnings approach.

The residual-valuation method starts with a measure of the average continuing earnings of a firm. This is an average of recent years' earnings adjusted for unusual or nonrecurring items. That is, unusual gains are subtracted and unusual losses are added back. For example, assume the following data relate to recent experiences of AJAX Enterprises:

	NET INCOME	EXTRAORDINARY (GAINS) LOSSES	ACCOUNTING CHANGES	ADJUSTED INCOME
1993	$600,000	$ (40,000)		$ 560,000
1994	700,000		$60,000*	760,000
1995	750,000	110,000		860,000
1996	820,000			820,000
Total				$3,000,000
Average				$750,000

*This change in accounting practice reduced income in 1994.

Next, the residual-valuation approach requires an assumption of a normal return on assets in the industry in which the enterprise operates. For AJAX, assume a return of 12%. From these data, a value is inferred for aggregate net assets by dividing the average recurring earnings figure by the typical industry rate-of-return figure ($750,000/12% = $6,250,000). The logic here is that a return of 12% is typical, and the enterprise is representative within its industry—that is, earning 12% on its assets. Consequently, the firm must have an asset value of $6,250,000, because a 12% return on $6,250,000 is consistent with average income figures of $750,000.

Having determined the aggregate value of the firm's net assets (assets minus liabilities), the residual-valuation method directs that this aggregate figure ($6,250,000) be compared to the current net *economic* value (the fair market value, not the book value) of *identifiable* assets and liabilities. The difference between the aggregate inferred economic value of net assets and the economic value of identifiable net assets (that is, the *residual,* hence the name) is assumed to be the *economic value of nonidentifiable assets, or goodwill.* Thus, in the AJAX example, if the fair market value of identifiable net assets is $5,500,000, the value of goodwill would be set at $750,000 ($6,250,000 − $5,500,000).

A related approach to calculating an economic value for goodwill is the capitalization-of-excess-earnings method. This method uses much the same data as does the residual-valuation approach. The steps involved in the capitalization-of-excess-earnings method are as follows:

1. Calculate an expected (normal) return on the fair market value of identifiable net assets. For AJAX,

   $5,500,000 of Net Assets × 12% = $660,000

2. Calculate the amount by which the firm's average earnings exceed an expected normal return. For AJAX,

   $750,000 − $660,000 = $90,000

These excess returns presumably are made possible by the existence of goodwill factors. The final step in deriving an *economic* value for goodwill is to calculate a present value for the future excess income stream of $90,000.

The period over which these future excess incomes are assumed likely to continue and the appropriate discount rate are important evaluations, yet also very subjective. It might be argued that true excess economic income is likely to be short-lived and of a higher risk than returns on tangible assets; this would argue for a short discount period and a higher than normal discount rate.

Irrespective of the calculation, however, the figures at which one arrives are not the figures one will find reported on the firm's balance sheet. These figures may be used as reference points in the negotiation process between buyer and seller. The sales price results from the negotiations. The residual-valuation approach and the capitalization-of-excess-earnings methods are presented for two purposes. First, they are presented for purposes of strengthening the understanding of the basic concept of goodwill. Second, they provide a vehicle by which financial statement users can approach an estimate of goodwill, if goodwill is deemed to be a potentially important asset for firms under scrutiny. The balance sheet figure will not provide a current value for goodwill. See the text for valuation of goodwill under GAAP.

APPENDIX: COSTS OF INSURANCE

Account for insurance costs.

To protect valuable assets, corporations, as well as individuals, frequently take out insurance contracts. The rights obtained under these contracts are themselves intangible assets.

When insurance prepayments are for a short period of time, the asset is a current asset. When insurance prepayments are for multiyear coverage, the asset is a long-term intangible asset. If a casualty loss on insured assets occurs (due to fire, flood, wind damage, etc.), the amount of insurance recovery will depend on conditions of the contract and relevant state law. Generally, the insured will recover the lowest of the following three amounts:

1. Face value of the policy
2. Economic loss
3. Coinsurance limit

The coinsurance limit (CL) is calculated as follows:

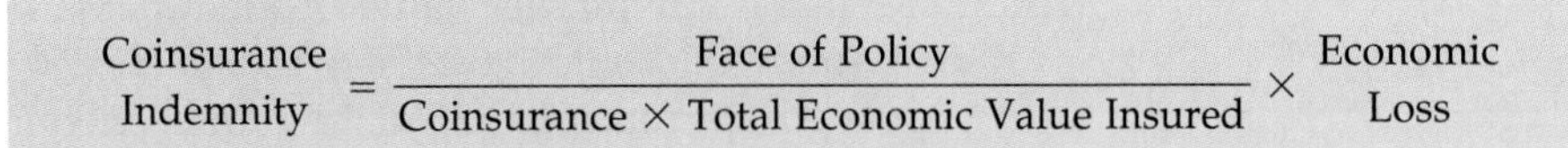

$$\text{Coinsurance Indemnity} = \frac{\text{Face of Policy}}{\text{Coinsurance} \times \text{Total Economic Value Insured}} \times \text{Economic Loss}$$

If multiple insurance policies are in force on the damaged or destroyed property, the coinsurance indemnity formula for each policy is calculated according to the following modified formula:

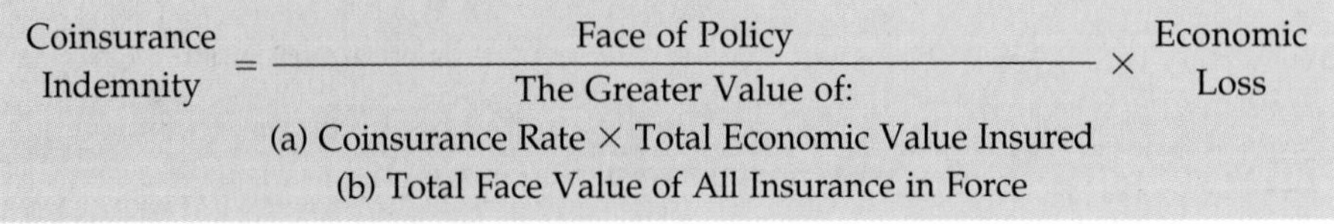

$$\text{Coinsurance Indemnity} = \frac{\text{Face of Policy}}{\begin{array}{c}\text{The Greater Value of:}\\ \text{(a) Coinsurance Rate} \times \text{Total Economic Value Insured}\\ \text{(b) Total Face Value of All Insurance in Force}\end{array}} \times \text{Economic Loss}$$

To illustrate, assume the following for Ward Corporation:

1. Assets damaged: Book value of $170,000 and economic value of $200,000.
2. Economic loss (50% destruction): $100,000.
3. Insurance policies: One with face value of $80,000 and coinsurance of 80%; another with face value of $40,000 and coinsurance of 40%.

Recovery will be as follows:

	POLICY 1	POLICY 2
Face value	$ 80,000	$ 40,000
Economic loss	100,000	100,000
Indemnity	**50,000**	**33,333**

Computation of the indemnity is as follows:

$$\text{Policy 1: Indemnity} = \frac{\$80{,}000}{\text{Greater of}} \times \$100{,}000$$

(a) 80% × $200,000
(b) $120,000

$$\text{Policy 2: Indemnity} = \frac{\$40{,}000}{\text{Greater of}} \times \$100{,}000$$

(a) 40% × $200,000
(b) $120,000

Accounting for a casualty loss and insurance recoveries is usually done through a Casualty Loss account. Typically, this account is:

1. Debited for all assets lost (or portions of assets lost) at book value.
2. Credited for all insurance recoveries (cash or insurance receivable).
3. Closed (balance) to Income Summary and Retained Earnings.

Depending on the insurance contract, remaining prepaid insurance also may be refunded.

END-OF-CHAPTER REVIEW

SUMMARY

1. **Apply the recognition and measurement criteria associated with intangible assets.** General guidance for accounting for intangibles was provided in APB No. 17, "Intangible Assets," issued in 1970. It was there directed that

> A company should record as assets the costs of intangible assets acquired from other enterprises or individuals. Costs of developing, maintaining, or restoring intangible assets that are *not specifically identifiable, have indeterminate*

lives, or are inherent in a continuing business and related to a business as a whole—such as goodwill—shall be expensed from income when incurred.[14]

2. **Prepare the accounting requirements for research and development costs and software development costs.** SFAS No. 2 defines and provides examples of costs that are to be considered research and development. SFAS No. 86 provides similarly for software development costs. These standards state that research and development and software development costs exhibit indeterminate future lives and accordingly direct that such costs must be expensed as incurred.
3. **Discuss the nature of and accounting requirements for goodwill-related costs.** ARS No. 10 observed that goodwill was not a separately identifiable asset but rather consisted of a number of favorable firm characteristics. APB No. 17 reiterated that costs of developing and maintaining firm goodwill are inherent to a continuing business and related to a business as a whole. Accordingly, internally developed or maintained goodwill is neither severable nor salable. As such, costs incurred internally to develop or maintain goodwill must be expensed as incurred.

   Goodwill may be reported only in selected instances when externally acquired —i.e., selected instances in which one corporate enterprise "purchases" another existing corporate enterprise for an amount in excess of the aggregate market-adjusted book values of identifiable corporate assets.
4. **Interpret the limitations of current practices related to intangible assets.** Current U.S. GAAP exhibits a reticence to overstating intangible assets, even at a cost of understatement. Rule-making bodies have confronted difficult decisions with respect to accounting reporting requirements. The objective is consistently to provide relevant and reliable information for decision making. Valuation of intangible assets will have a definite impact on financial ratios because of the effects on net income and net asset valuation.
5. **Estimate the economic value of corporate goodwill.** Appendix 13A illustrates two means of estimating corporate *economic* goodwill: the residual-value and capitalization-of-excess-earnings methods. While estimates derived using these methods may serve decision-making purposes, they are unacceptable for financial accounting reporting purposes. Goodwill is defined very precisely by GAAP for calculation. However, the resulting numbers may not represent the value of goodwill.
6. **Account for insurance costs.** Appendix 13B illustrates the significance of coinsurance limitations in corporate recovery of casualty losses. Generally, the insured will recover the lowest of the following three elements:
   1. Face value of the insurance policy.
   2. Economic value of the loss.
   3. Coinsurance formula provision.

KEY TERMS

amortization *688*
badwill *705*
capitalization-of-excess-earnings method *709*
copyrights *705*
development *687*
franchise *706*
full-costing method *697*
goodwill (conceptually) *698*
goodwill (operationally) *698*
organizational costs *706*
patent *698*

[14]Ibid., par. 24.

ASSIGNMENT MATERIAL

CASES

C13–1 International Versus U.S. Treatment of Goodwill—Report Preparation
Two articles appearing in *Forbes* magazine ("Britain's Goodwill Games," October 2, 1989, pp. 65–66 and "The Unlevel Accounting Field," November 28, 1988, p. 170) relate to varying international standards for calculating, reporting, and amortizing goodwill. After reading the articles, prepare a report to answer the following questions.

1. Under what conditions can a U.S. firm report goodwill (or elements thereof) among its assets in published financial statements? Are these standards similar in other major western nations?
2. Discuss U.S. standards for expensing goodwill once it is reported. Also discuss foreign practices regarding amortization of goodwill and other intangible assets.
3. What effects do U.S. versus foreign nations' accounting treatments have on such fundamental performance measures as net income and the debt-to-equity ratio?
4. How significant are the effects of the differences in treatments—that is, are the figures likely to be material?
5. Discuss the issue of whether a nation's accounting standards for reporting financial information are likely to influence the economic decisions of its corporate management.

C13–2 International Versus U.S. Treatment of R&D—Report Preparation
Current U.S. reporting standards regarding research and development (R&D) require the immediate expensing of those costs. Corporations of other nations who compete in international capital (money) markets frequently are allowed to capitalize R&D expenditures. Prepare a report discussing the relative disadvantage at which these disparate practices may place U.S. corporations in their bid for international investment dollars.

Also discuss whether the requirement that corporations immediately expense all R&D has likely deleterious effects on the amount of R&D effort forthcoming by U.S. firms. In other words, does this requirement hurt the competitiveness of U.S. industry? In setting accounting standards, should the FASB take such issues into consideration? If so, why? What are the objectives of corporate financial reporting, and how does immediate write-off of R&D best serve those objectives?

QUESTIONS

Q13–1 Discuss and provide examples of the three bases upon which costs are matched with revenues (i.e., the associative cause-and-effect basis, the systematic-and-rational-allocation basis, the immediate-write-off basis). Which of these methods is (are) arbitrary in nature? How do artificial allocations of costs interfere with or enhance sound economic analyses of business conditions and financial performance and evaluations of future cash-flow-generation potential?

Q13–2 What is the "measurement criterion," and how is it significant to the valuation of intangibles?

Q13–3 Define "research" and "development," and give examples of each.

Q13–4 How should R&D costs be accounted for under SFAS No. 2, and what was the basis of the FASB's ruling in this instance?

Q13–5 Discuss similarities and differences between the economics of R&D efforts and oil-exploration efforts. Also discuss the similarities and differences in accounting for R&D costs and oil-exploration costs.

Q13–6 Discuss similarities and differences between the economics of R&D efforts and software development efforts. Also discuss similarities and differences in accounting for each.

Q13–7 Computer software development costs incurred prior to establishing 'technological feasibility" must be expensed as incurred. What is meant by "technological feasibility'? How does the technological-feasibility criterion apply to software development costs incurred to produce software exclusively for internal use—that is, software not for sale or lease to other corporations or individuals?

Q13–8 Current GAAP explicitly directs how capitalized computer software costs are to be amortized. Discuss allowable procedures.

Q13–9 Discuss what costs may appropriately be included in organizational costs of a corporation and capitalized. Do operating losses (or deficits) incurred in early stages of development qualify for capitalization? Why or why not?

Q13–10 How is the amortization of intangibles reported in the statement of cash flows?

Q13–11 In 1993 the U.S. Congress passed a tax law that allowed goodwill amortization to be deducted from income when calculating income subject to corporate income tax. The amortization period specified is 15 years. What impact, if any, will this change in tax law have on accounting practices for goodwill amortization?

EXERCISES

E13–1 General Intangibles

Wrexell Inc. began operations in 1998 and has a product line called FreshLike. The following debits to intangible asset accounts were made on the books of Wrexell Inc. during 1998:

1. Promotional costs related to the grand opening of the business on January 10, 1998, of $84,000.
2. Research and development costs of $43,000 incurred from February 1 to June 12 of 1998 on Project 12, which resulted in a commercially viable product.
3. Attorneys' fees of $21,000 incurred on July 6 related to the purchase by Wrexell of a patent on the product that resulted from Project 12.
4. Operating losses incurred during Wrexell's first year of operations of $37,000.
5. Costs of $11,000 during August of 1998 resulting from a successful defense of a patent.
6. Promotional costs of $19,000 incurred to enhance the FreshLike brand image.

Required:

A. Describe the proper accounting treatment of each of the above entries.
B. If these are the only entries to intangible accounts during 1998, what should the balance in the intangible asset accounts be before amortization?

E13–2 Organizational Costs

Fancy Pants Industries began operations in 1998, incurring the following costs during the first year of operations:

Attorneys' fees related to state incorporation	$29,000
Annual state licensing fees	12,000
Costs of initial stock offerings	17,000
Organizational meetings of incorporators and board of directors:	
Transportation	16,000
Accommodations	10,900
Annual board of directors' stipend	45,000
Operational losses in 1998	84,000

Required:

A. Compute the amount of organizational costs.

B. Record each of the transactions in general journal format as appropriate.

*E13–3 Calculation of Economic Goodwill: Residual Method

Fugiwara & Frost, Inc., are considering the acquisition of a major interest in Kobayashi Industries. The current fair value of the identifiable net assets of Kobayashi is estimated to be $10,000,000. Kobayashi's income in recent years has been stable, running about $1,800,000 annually.

Required: Estimate goodwill under each of the following conditions, using the residual-valuation method.

A. A normal rate of return on total assets in the industry is 14%.

B. A normal rate of return on total assets in the industry is 10%.

*E13–4 Calculation of Economic Goodwill: Capitalization-of-Excess-Earnings Method

Smithe & Frawley, Inc., are considering the acquisition of a major interest in Chadwick Industries. The current fair value of the identifiable net assets of Chadwick is estimated to be $10,000,000. Chadwick's income in recent years has been stable, running about $1,800,000 annually.

Required: Estimate goodwill under each of the following conditions, using the capitalization-of-excess-earnings method.

A. A normal rate of return in the industry on tangible assets is 16%. Goodwill is valued at the net present value of a 10-year annuity of excess earnings, discounted at 20%.

B. A normal rate of return in the industry on tangible assets is 14%. Goodwill is valued at the net present value of excess earnings, discounted at 25%, assuming a 30-year stream of excess earnings.

*Refers to material in chapter appendix.

*E13–5 Calculation of Economic Goodwill: Residual Method

Embassy Services Inc. is considering the purchase of NUTOWN Corporation but is unsure as to the amount of goodwill that exists. In recent years, NUTOWN has reported the following income figures:

YEAR	NET INCOME	EXTRAORDINARY ITEMS	ACCOUNTING CHANGES
1997	$250,000		$(90,000)
1998	295,000		
1999	220,000	$(70,000)	
2000	300,000		
2001	317,000		

In 1999 an extraordinary loss occurred relating to an early extinguishment of debt. In 1997 inventory accounting methods were changed, effecting a $90,000 charge against income.

Required:

A. Estimate goodwill using the residual method and assuming the fair value of NUTOWN's net assets is $800,000. Capitalize average recurring (normal) income at 14% for perpetuity.

B. Estimate goodwill using the residual method and assuming the fair value of NUTOWN's net assets is $1,000,000. Capitalize average recurring (normal) income at 25% for 10 years.

E13–6 Research and Development

Mercer Scientific Laboratories provides contract R&D development services for major corporations. During the current year, Mercer signed a $350,000 contract with SXC Corporation to conduct some laboratory experiments and provide a report of findings for this project in 18 months. The contract provides for payment by SXC of $150,000 during the current year and the remainder at completion. During the current year, Mercer incurred the following costs:

Equipment purchased for use on several projects over the next five years	$34,000
Allocation to current SXC project	2,000
Equipment purchased exclusively for the SXC project	65,000
Salaries for employees directly engaged on SXC project	83,000
Benefits costs (health insurance and pensions) accruing to employees directly engaged on SXC project	8,200

Required: Record the above transactions in general journal form on the books of both Mercer and SXC Corporation for the current year.

E13–7 Software Development

During 1998, Computer Jockeys Inc. (CJI) spent $3,000,000 developing its new EZ-Records software package. All these costs were incurred prior to establishing technological feasibility on June 30. Another $500,000 was expended in producing master copies necessary to the manufacture of the software. Still another $400,000 was expended in additional coding and testing in late 1998. CJI expects to be able to market the new EZ-Records software for at least 60 months. Estimated total revenues are projected at $8,000,000 on 80,000 units. In 1999, the first year of sales, 24,000 copies of the software were sold for $2,400,000, and 30,000 copies were produced at the following costs:

Direct material	$300,000
Direct labor	400,000
Depreciation on manufacturing equipment	100,000
Amortization	?
Other overhead	100,000

Required:

A. Prepare journal entries for 1998 and 1999, including the amortization and cost-of-goods-sold entries for 1999.

B. At what amount should computer software costs appear on the 1999 balance sheet?

E13–8 Software Development

Coleman & Wainfleet incurred $680,000 in software development costs in 1998. These costs included all necessary costs of planning, designing, coding, and testing the software preparatory to worldwide adoption and implementation, which took place in January of 1999. Coleman & Wainfleet developed its own software for internal use due to the lack of availability of an appropriate product in the commercial market. The firm expects the newly developed software to meet its worldwide needs for eight years.

Required: Prepare appropriate journal entries for the above for 1998 and 1999.

E13–9 GAAP Goodwill

On December 31, 1999, Hawthorne Industries acquired control of the Hammel & Robbi (H&R) Company in a cash purchase of voting common stock. At that time, the book and fair values of H&R's net assets were as follows:

ACCOUNT	BOOK VALUE	FAIR VALUE
Cash	$ 100,000	$ 100,000
Marketable securities	90,000	90,000
Accounts receivable	60,000	60,000
Inventory	200,000	300,000
Other current assets	40,000	20,000
Plant and equipment	900,000	1,100,000
Accounts payable	(140,000)	(140,000)
Notes/bonds payable	(400,000)	(300,000)
	$ 850,000	$1,230,000

Required:

A. Determine the value of goodwill reported on the consolidated balance sheet for 1999 and 2000, assuming Hawthorne purchased 100 percent of H&R for $1,400,000. Also assume amortization over 10 years.

B. Determine the value of goodwill reported on the consolidated balance sheet for 1999 and 2000, assuming Hawthorne purchased 70 percent of H&R for $1,000,000. Also assume amortization over the maximum period.

E13–10 Measurability Criterion

For each of the following costs, indicate whether the "asset" meets the measurability criterion and whether the costs should be capitalized by writing YES or NO in the appropriate place on the table.

ITEM	IDENTIFIABLE AND MEASURABLE FUTURE BENEFITS	CAPITALIZED
1. Purchase cost of patent from another firm.	________	________
2. Internal R&D costs leading to patent.	________	________
3. Costs of artistic efforts leading to copyright.	________	________
4. Five-year prepaid insurance premium.	________	________
5. Purchase cost of trade name from another firm.	________	________
6. Charges by advertising agency to develop copyrighted logo.	________	________
7. Purchase cost of five-year, fast-food franchise.	________	________
8. Cost of marketing analyses leading to new trademark.	________	________

E13–11 Patents

Ace Exercise Equipment Co. acquired a patent in exchange for land and $18,000 cash. At the time of the exchange, the land had a book value of $42,000 and a fair market value (FMV) of $54,000. The patent had a legal life of 12 years and an estimated useful life of 6 years.

Required:

A. Prepare the journal entries to record the purchase of the patent.
B. Prepare the journal entries to record the amortization for the first full year.

E13–12 Research and Development

Western Research acquired three machines at a cost of $50,000 each. Each machine has a useful life of five years, with no residual value. Machine A is a specialty laser machine to be used in a particular research project and has no alternative use. Machine B is a machine that is capable of doing a variety of X-ray tasks and can be used in a number of projects. Machine C has uses beyond research, and Western anticipates that it will be used in research projects about 20 percent of the time. Assume straight-line cost allocation and that Western follows the practice of taking a full year's allocation expense in the year of acquisition.

Required:

A. Calculate the capitalized cost of intangible assets related to these machine purchases.
B. Calculate the R&D expense reported on the income statement for the year.

E13–13 Goodwill

Jones purchased 80 percent of the net assets of Smith for $800,000. At the time of purchase, the book value of the assets was $800,000 and liabilities were $200,000.

Required: Determine goodwill at acquisition using the following assumptions:

A. At the acquisition date, the FMV of the assets was equal to $800,000 and liabilities $200,000.
B. At the acquisition date, the FMV of the assets was equal to $900,000 and liabilities $200,000.
C. At the acquisition date, the FMV of the assets was equal to $1,000,000 and liabilities $200,000.

E13–14 Patents

On January 1, 1998, Pancer and Damon Inc. purchased a patent from James Barbeck, agreeing to pay Barbeck $20,000 each January 1 for five years beginning January 1, 1999. Pancer and Damon also agreed to pay Barbeck, on January 1 of each year, 10 percent of the gross profits earned on sales of the patented product made in the preceding year, for a period of ten years. Estimated gross profits were as follows:

1998–2002	$300,000 annually
After 2002	200,000 annually

Required:

A. Record the purchase of the patent in 1998. Be sure to note any assumptions made about interest rates or guarantees of future revenues by the patent buyer.
B. Record any year-end 1998 adjustment entries appropriate to this set of conditions, assuming gross profits were as expected.

E13–15 Trademarks

J. Floman Enterprises purchased a trademark from ClarkCo on January 1, 1998, for $172,000. An independent consultant for Floman estimated the trademark's remaining useful life at 50 years. The unamortized cost of the trademark on ClarkCo's books was $50,000. It was Floman's desire to amortize the trademark over the longest period allowable. How much should be amortized for the year 1999?

E13–16 Trademarks

On January 1, 1998, Sanders Corporation bought a trademark for $400,000. The trademark was estimated to have a remaining useful life of 10 years. In January 2000, Sanders paid $50,000 for legal fees in a successful defense of the trademark. Trademark amortization, using the straight-line method, for 2002 should be what amount?

E13–17 Patents

On January 1, 2005, Terrence Toy Company purchased a patent from Springdale Industries for $300,000. Terrence estimated a 15-year life and began to straight-line depreciate the patent. During 2010 Terrence incurred costs of $40,000 in an unsuccessful legal suit to defend the patent against alleged competitor infringement. What patent-related charges against income are appropriate in 2010?

E13–18 Research and Development

Wormwood & Company incurred the following costs in 2000:

Design of tools, jigs, molds, and dies involving new technology	$100,000
Modification of the formulation of a process	70,000
Troubleshooting with respect to breakdowns during commercial production	40,000
Adaptation of an existing capability to a particular customer's need as part of a continuing commercial activity	85,000

In its 2000 income statement, how much R&D expense should Wormwood report?

E13–19 R&D Expense

During 1998, Polchinski Enterprises incurred the following costs:

Testing in search of process alternatives	$100,000
Routine design of tools, jigs, molds, and dies	95,000
Modification of the formulation of a process	67,000
R&D services performed by Ward Corporation for Polchinski Enterprises	119,000

In its 1998 income statement, how much R&D expense should Polchinski report?

E13–20 R&D Expense

Friye Corporation incurred R&D costs in 1998 as follows:

Equipment acquired for use in various research and development projects (five-year life)	$324,000
Materials used	39,000
Direct personnel costs	67,000
Allocated central administration personnel costs	21,000

The total R&D costs to be charged against income in 1998 should be what amount?

E13–21 R&D Expense

Huff & Company incurred the following costs in 2000:

Engineering follow-through in an early phase of commercial production	$ 19,000
Design, construction, and testing of preproduction prototypes and models	137,000
Periodic design changes to existing products	94,000
Equipment acquired for exclusive use on R&D Project A-14, completed November 1, 2000	190,000

Determine total R&D expense for 2000.

E13–22 Goodwill

On July 1, 1999, Gerard Corporation purchased goodwill of $200,000 when it acquired the net assets of Hendrix Inc. During 1999, Gerard incurred additional costs of developing goodwill by training Gerard employees ($50,000) and hiring additional public relations employees ($25,000 search costs). Determine, before amortization of goodwill, Gerard's December 31 goodwill balance.

E13–23 Developmental Costs

Food products firms engage in activities to improve their products. One example of such an "improvement," which turned out to be a relative failed attempt, was the development of the "new Coke" (as opposed to "Coke Classic"). This product was the result of substantial consumer research and formula testing that indicated that many people preferred a sweeter taste than that of the old ***Coca-Cola*** product. Another example of such "improvement" in product is the production of a version of a product with a "new and improved taste," for example, some microwave products. In this case, the change is due to continuing efforts to make the product more palatable as well as convenient. Should these two types of expenditures be treated differently for purposes of financial reporting? Why or why not?

E13–24 Patent Entries

Jenex Corporation purchases a patent for a drug on January 1, 2005, for $50,000. It has an expected useful life of 10 years. The firm uses straight-line amortization for patents, recorded annually on December 31 of each year. A competitor discovers a drug that is as effective as Jenex's product and has fewer side effects. This competitor launches its new drug on January 1, 2007. Jenex estimates that this competing drug will replace its product in the marketplace by the end of the year. Make the required entries for Jenex for 2005–2008 for this product.

E13–25 Representative Financial Statements

Required: Use the opening vignette to this chapter along with your own knowledge of accounting to answer the following:

A. Describe the two alternative treatments of goodwill mentioned in the article, and describe what difference the two treatments would make to the parent company and the food products group in terms of their financial statements.

B. Given your knowledge of the purpose of financial reporting and the information in the article, can you decide which of the two alternatives is most appropriate? Why or why not?

E13–26 Alternative Uses

The text describes "lack of alternative uses" for intangibles as one reason why it is more difficult to determine a future value for them than for tangible assets. Construct an argument (using specific examples) for tangible assets also being very difficult to value due to lack of alternative uses.

PROBLEMS

P13–1 Software Development Costs

Katsworth Corporation is in the business of developing and distributing computer software for the personal and small-business market. Jason Katsworth, founder and CEO, is very attentive to maintaining the high-quality reputation of the Katsworth brand label. Accordingly, extensive developmental lab and field testing precede introduction of any Katsworth product. The following costs were incurred in 2005 prior to establishing technological feasibility:

Wages of programmers engaged in research	$350,000
Fringe benefits of research programmers	70,000
Supplies and materials used in research	60,000
Utility costs at research facility	30,000
Depreciation of research facility (which has alternative uses)	100,000
Central administrative personnel costs (allocated to research activities)	50,000

Costs incurred after establishing technological feasibility but before commercial production were as follows for that year:

Wages of programmers, coders, etc.	$120,000
Personnel fringe benefits	70,000
Supplies and materials used in testing	60,000
Depreciation of general-purpose equipment (which has alternative uses)	40,000
Central administrative personnel costs (allocated to preproduction efforts)	50,000

Other costs for the same year were as follows:

Amortization of capitalized software costs (current and prior years)	$ 67,000
Costs of software produced (100,000 units)	320,000
Selling and unallocated administrative costs	94,000

Revenues from sale of 80,000 units at $12 apiece totaled $960,000 for 2005.

Required: Prepare an income statement for Katsworth for 2005. Ignore income tax.

P13–2 Trademarks, Patents

Laura Enterprises lists two major intangible assets on its 2004 balance sheet (the WOW clothes trademark and the patented No-Crinckle fabric-conditioning process). Both intangibles were purchased at 2004 year-end from Wong-On-Wing Enterprises. The trademark was expected to have an indefinite economic life. It was decided to amortize its $100,000 cost over 10 years. The patent was expected to yield equal benefits over the next 10 years also; its cost was $75,000.

Required:

A. Make appropriate general journal entries to record amortization in 2005.

B. At the beginning of 2007, after taking two full years' amortization, it is determined that the remaining economic life of the patent is only five years. Make any appropriate 2007 patent-related entries.

C. At the end of 2008, Laura Enterprises decides to discontinue the use of the WOW brand name because of very poor market performance. Make any appropriate 2008 trademark-related entries.

P13–3 Franchise Costs

On January 1, 2006, Marsha Whitman signed a franchise agreement with King Tire Corporation providing Whitman with exclusive distribution rights for King products in the Baton Rouge, Louisiana, area. The agreement required Whitman to pay an initial franchise fee of $60,000 and annual royalty payments based on sales. In return, King promised to provide services that included national promotion of King products, continuing market analysis, and product-line updating in response to new competitive products. The franchise period was for 12 years, with a renewal option for a second 12 years. The initial nonrefundable fee of $60,000 was to be paid in three installments of $20,000 each, payable each January 1, beginning January 1, 2006. The appropriate market rate of interest for loans such as these was 10%.

Required:

A. Make the appropriate general journal entry to record the franchise agreement and initial payment of $20,000.

B. Make any and all appropriate year-end adjusting entries for 2006.

*P13–4 Coinsurance

During 2005, Lambers Lumber Company suffered a major fire loss at one of its yards. On January 1, the inventory on hand had a book value of $390,000; this figure also was approximately the replacement cost. During the year, additional wholesale purchases of lumber at the yard amounted to $900,000. Lambers' accounting records report sales for that period before the fire of $1,000,000. Lambers' gross profit percentage in recent years has consistently been 40%. Only $100,000 in inventory survived the fire. The company had insured its inventory with two insurance firms. The first policy has a face value of $500,000 and a coinsurance clause of 80 percent. The second policy has a face value of $300,000 and a coinsurance requirement of 70 percent.

Required:

A. Determine the amount of insurance recovery from each policy.

B. Make the appropriate general journal entries to record the inventory loss and insurance recovery. That is, open up a Casualty Loss account, and establish appropriate receivable accounts from the insurance carriers.

P13–5 Research and Development

During 2000, LaRue & Company made several expenditures related to the ongoing research efforts of the firm. They were as follows:

1. LaRue purchased a building site in suburban Dallas for $600,000. LaRue planned to build an office-type building on the site for purposes of providing laboratory space for the firm's expanding research interests. Need for the expansion was expected within the decade.
2. LaRue also purchased a building adjacent to the above building site. This building was acquired to provide immediately available research laboratory space. It was estimated that the building would be used for general research purposes for the next 40 years. The cost was $1,400,000.
3. In 2000 LaRue also built a project-specific research facility in the Arizona desert approximately 70 miles from Phoenix. The cost was $290,000. The expected useful physical life of the building is 20 years. The research project (Project A–218), however, is expected to take only four years. There are no alternative uses for the facility after completion of Project A–218.

*Relates to material in chapter appendix.

4. Equipment to be used in the research labs was acquired at a cost of $440,000, of which $100,000 was for equipment specially designed for individual research projects. Another $250,000 of the equipment will be used over several years on many research projects, and the remaining equipment is made up of general manufacturing equipment that can be used in research activities and/or later converted to other uses.
5. In a 50–50 joint venture with Carson Laboratories, LaRue invested $800,000 in a pilot plant built to test the commercial viability of a new chemical-refining process. While some production will be sold to commercial customers, the facility is not large enough to be commercially viable currently, nor easily convertible into a full-production-stage operation later.
6. At a cost of $400,000 in R&D, LaRue developed a new fuel additive that it subsequently patented. LaRue then sold the patent for $750,000, only later realizing the full commercial importance of the patent and thus reacquiring it at a cost of $1,000,000.
7. Litigation was pursued related to several LaRue patents. Total litigation costs amounted to $370,000, of which $200,000 related to cases ending in favorable resolution, and $100,000 to cases ending in unfavorable resolution. The remaining cases are still in litigation.

Required: Discuss the accounting treatment of each of the preceding activities.

P13–6 Ratio Analysis

Kline Enterprises operates a chain of corporate-owned, fast food-retail stores. The corporate financial statement of December 31, 1998, reveals the following:

(IN THOUSANDS OF DOLLARS)	
Cash	$ 24,000
Receivables	26,000
Inventories	160,000
Properties	130,000
Prepaid expenses	6,000
Property, plant and equipment (net)	600,000
Total assets	$946,000
Accounts payable	$ 90,000
Due to banks	56,000
Long-term debt	400,000
Contributed capital	200,000
Retained earnings	200,000
Total liabilities and equity	$946,000

Required:

A. Assuming net income for 1998 was $100,000,000, calculate the following:
   1. Return on assets.*
   2. Return on equity.*

*While it is preferable to use averages for the denominators for these ratios, simple current year values may be used for this problem.

3. Debt ratio.
4. Long-term debt-to-equity ratio.

B. Over the years, Kline has expended significant funds ($100,000,000) for purposes of (1) intense consumer analyses, leading to acquisition of optimal retail locations; (2) thorough market analyses of changing consumer tastes, leading to introduction of highly successful new products; (3) an effective national quality-control program; and (4) national media advertising to establish a positive consumer image. These costs have produced significant commercial goodwill, estimated at $200,000,000. Continuing annual expenditures for R&D are $12,000,000. Ignore income tax. If past and current costs had been recorded as goodwill on the firm's books rather than being written off as expenses, an asset account balance of $80,000,000 would remain. How would this have changed the above ratios? Assume amortization of goodwill over the maximum allowable period.

P13–7 Consolidation

Spencer Amalgamated Enterprises acquired a controlling interest in Carmen Industries by cash acquisition of 60% of Carmen's outstanding common stock for $90,000,000. Relevant data regarding Carmen's book values of identifiable net assets are provided here. Since these book values total $90,000,000, Spencer's share of identifiable Carmen assets is only $54,000,000 ($90,000,000 × 60%). Spencer nonetheless paid $90,000,000. Thus, $36,000,000 in purchase price (cost) remains unexplained. Logic suggests that Spencer paid $36,000,000 more than a 60% share of Carmen's book value because either or both of the following conditions exist: first, the identified assets are undervalued; second, other nonidentified assets (goodwill) exist. In this instance, both conditions may exist. A review of current market values reveals that Carmen's net assets are understated, as shown.

ACCOUNT	BOOK VALUE	CURRENT VALUE	DIFFERENCE
Cash	$ 3,000,000	$ 3,000,000	$ 0
Accounts receivable	10,000,000	11,000,000	1,000,000
Inventory	40,000,000	38,000,000	(2,000,000)
Plant and equipment	80,000,000	90,000,000	10,000,000
Liabilities	(43,000,000)	(40,000,000)	3,000,000
Total	$ 90,000,000	$102,000,000	

Required: Determine the value of goodwill and the amounts reported for other asset and liability accounts in Spencer's consolidated financial statements.

P13–8 Economic Goodwill: Residual Method

PS&M is considering the acquisition of a major interest in Fluffy Friends Manufacturing. The current fair market value of the identifiable assets of Fluffy Friends is estimated to be $2,000,000. Fluffy Friend's income in recent years has been stable at about $350,000 annually.

Required: Determine goodwill under each of the following conditions, using the residual-value method.

A. A normal rate of return on total assets in the industry is 12%.
B. A normal rate of return on total assets in the industry is 10%.

P13–9 Economic Goodwill: Capitalization of Excess Earnings Method

Three Star, Inc., is considering the acquisition of a major interest in Galaxy Industries. The current fair value of the identifiable net assets of Galaxy is estimated to be $1,000,000. Galaxy's income in recent years has been stable, running about $200,000 annually.

Required: Determine goodwill under each of the following conditions, using the capitalization-of-excess-earnings method.

A. A normal rate of return in the industry on tangible assets is 12%. Goodwill is valued at the net present value of a 10-year annuity of excess earnings, discounted at 20%.
B. A normal rate of return in the industry on tangible assets is 16%. Goodwill is valued at the net present value of excess earnings, discounted at 24%, assuming a perpetual stream of excess earnings.

P13–10 GAAP Goodwill

On December 31, 1998, Boxer Industries acquired control of Mesa Company in a cash purchase of voting common stock. At that time, the book and market values of Mesa's net assets were as follows:

ACCOUNT	BOOK VALUE	CURRENT VALUE
Cash	$ 80,000	$ 80,000
Short-term securities	50,000	52,000
Accounts receivable	75,000	75,000
Inventory	90,000	110,000
Other current assets	32,000	38,000
Plant and equipment	300,000	610,000
Accounts payable	(54,000)	(54,000)
Notes payable	(98,000)	(98,000)
Total	$475,000	$813,000

Assume the firm amortizes goodwill over the maximum allowable period.

Required:

A. Determine the value of goodwill reported on the consolidated balance sheet for 1998 and 1999, assuming Boxer purchased 100 percent of Mesa for $920,000.
B. Determine the value of goodwill reported on the consolidated balance sheet for 1998 and 1999, assuming Boxer purchased 75 percent of Mesa for $625,000.

P13–11 GAAP Goodwill

On December 31, 1998, Pearlman Corporation purchased 80% of the voting common stock of Vasquez Industries in an acquisition treated as a "purchase." Pearlman paid $1,000,000 for its 80% investment. Other relevant December 31, 1998, data for Vasquez are presented at the top of the following page.

Required:

A. Determine the amount of goodwill (badwill), if any, and determine the values at which the above accounts will be reported on the consolidated balance sheet at December 31, 1998.
B. What subsequent disposition is made of goodwill (badwill)? Does it increase or decrease income? If amortized, what is the appropriate period and method?
C. How would your answers change if Pearlman paid $600,000 for the 80% interest?

ACCOUNT	BOOK VALUE	CURRENT VALUE
Cash	$ 130,000	$ 130,000
Trading securities	90,000	90,000
Accounts receivable	400,000	360,000
Inventory	300,000	200,000
Other current assets	100,000	50,000
Plant and equipment	100,000	140,000
Investments in held-to-maturity securities	100,000	100,000
	$1,220,000	$1,070,000
Accounts payable	(100,000)	(100,000)
Bonds payable	(200,000)	(100,000)
Net assets	$ 920,000	$ 870,000

P13–12 Coinsurance

During 1999, Hammett Company suffered a major fire loss at one of its retail outlets. On January 1, the inventory on hand had a book value of $500,000; this figure also was approximately the replacement cost. During the year, additional wholesale purchases of inventory at the fire-damaged store amounted to $1,000,000. Hammett's accounting records report sales for that period before the fire of $1,000,000. Hammett's gross profit percentage in recent years has consistently been 70%. Only $100,000 in inventory survived the fire.

Hammett Company had insured the inventory with two insurance firms. The first policy has a face value of $750,000 and a coinsurance clause of 80 percent. The second policy has a face value of $300,000 and a coinsurance requirement of 50 percent.

Required:

A. Determine the amount of insurance recovery from each policy.

B. Make the appropriate general journal entries to record the inventory loss and insurance recovery. That is, open up a Casualty Loss account and establish appropriate receivable accounts from the insurance carriers.

P13–13 General Intangibles

Visbane Properties built a retail plaza in suburban Los Angeles. The plaza was scheduled to open on January 1, 2005. However, in the fall of 2004, wildfires swept through the area in which the plaza was built and through much of the surrounding area. The plaza suffered significant damage, and reconstruction delayed the opening of the plaza until January 1, 2006. The costs of reconstruction were 80 percent insured. Items not insured included interest costs on continuing debt on the plaza, promotional costs to announce the opening of the plaza, and costs to secure tenants. Promotional costs to reannounce the opening of the plaza were necessary, given the protracted delay. Also, significant new costs were necessary (that were not insured) to obtain new tenants; 50 percent of those tenants who initially signed one-year leases, to begin January 1, 2005, canceled their leases after the fires. The other 50 percent signed new 12-month leases on the same terms as the 2005 canceled leases.

	2005 COSTS	2006 COSTS
Interest on plaza debt	$100,000	$100,000
Opening promotional costs	75,000	75,000
Costs related to securing tenants	70,000	35,000

Required: Explain the appropriate treatment of the various costs incurred in 2005 and 2006. Which costs, if any, are intangibles?

P13–14 Trademarks

In 2006, Trefill Inc. applied for a trademark for its newly designed company logo. The design costs were $70,000, and the legal fees associated with the application were $20,000. Trefill amortizes trademarks over the maximum period allowed. On July 1, 2007, Trefill incurred an additional $35,000 in legal fees related to defense of this trademark. Assume the trademark was used for a full year in 2006. Note any effect that amortization recorded monthly rather than at year-end would have on your response.

Required:

A. Determine the amount of these costs that should be expensed in 2006 and 2007. Assume Trefill was successful in its defense of its trademark in 2007.

B. Determine the amount of these costs that should be expensed in 2006 and 2007. Assume Trefill was unsuccessful in its defense of its trademark in 2007 and that a large discount chain obtained permission to continue use of a very similar logo.

P13–15 Computer Software

SFAS No. 86 provides two ways to compute the annual amortization for capitalized software: (1) straight-line amortization over the estimated useful life or (2) capitalized costs multiplied by the ratio of current gross revenues produced by the product to total current plus anticipated future gross revenues. The larger of these two is to be used.

The product to be amortized is computer software purchased for $10,000 with an expected useful life of ten years. Consider two alternative expected gross revenue streams:

YEAR	ALTERNATIVE 1	ALTERNATIVE 2
1	$10,000	$ 4,000
2	9,000	4,000
3	8,000	4,000
4	7,000	4,000
5	1,000	4,000
6	1,000	4,000
7	1,000	4,000
8	1,000	4,000
9	1,000	4,000
10	1,000	4,000
Total	$40,000	$40,000

Required:

A. Compute the proper amortization for each expected gross revenue stream.

B. What purpose is served by this restriction?

P13–16 Research and Development Costs

The text states that R&D costs should be expensed and that non-R&D costs should be capitalized if they are expected to produce economic benefits that can be separately identified and objectively measured and expensed otherwise. Given this, respond to the following.

Required:

A. Royale Corporation has been a customer of Metals, Inc., for years. Each year, Royale purchases a slightly different souvenir item to use for promotional purposes. Metals, Inc., has to adapt some of their usual production processes in order to produce these items. How should the costs of these adaptations be treated?

B. A cereal manufacturer modifies its production processes each year to follow the tastes of children for differently shaped cereals. How should the costs of these modifications be treated?

C. A manufacturing firm currently sending all products through several departments (mixing, forming, and packaging) has decided to move to cellular manufacturing where each product line has its own set of mixing, forming, and packaging equipment that is exclusively devoted to making that particular product line. This is expected to facilitate the identification of costs with products and to allow the firm to better price their products in the market. Two sets of costs are associated with this change. One is the design of the new plant layout. The second is the actual moving of equipment, changing of partitions, installing of extra structural support where needed, and the addition of electrical lines where needed. How should these two sets of costs be treated?

P13–17 Oil Exploration Costs

While analogies between R&D activities, software development activities, and activities common to extractive industries such as prospecting, drilling, and so forth, are commonly drawn, SFAS No. 2 does not require the immediate expensing of these latter oil exploration items. Rather, SFAS No. 25 allows capitalization of exploratory costs under two methods: successful efforts and full costing. As with R&D costs, two major matters of controversy addressed by the FASB were what costs are considered necessary and what costs, if any, lead to future economic benefits that can be identified and objectively measured.

Under successful-efforts accounting, only costs incurred pursuant to successful exploration (explorations climaxing in discovery of commercially exploitable resources) can be capitalized. For example, if $250,000 is expended in drilling each of 10 oil wells ($2,500,000 in total), only one of which discovers significant oil reserves, then, successful-efforts advocates argue, only $250,000 in costs may be capitalized. The other $2,250,000 (the cost of drilling the nine unsuccessful wells) would be expensed under the logic that those costs were unnecessary and/or did not lead to future benefits.

On the other hand, the full-costing method allows capitalization of all $2,500,000 of exploration costs. These costs subsequently are expensed in future years of benefit (those years when the discovered resources are extracted and sold). Thus, although the board does not regard R&D expenditures, even on projects determined to be successful, as leading to future benefits that are identifiable and objectively measurable, it does allow capitalization of exploration costs, even when specific efforts fail to lead to discovery. Whether the underlying conditions in these two instances are sufficiently different to warrant these distinct treatments may be argued. Initially, in an effort to be consistent with the R&D standard, the FASB assumed a position permitting only the successful-efforts method in SFAS No. 10. Political opposition and the intervention of Congress and the SEC required the FASB to amend its position in SFAS No. 25.

Required:

A. Describe the two alternatives permitted under GAAP for accounting for the costs of oil and gas exploration.
B. Which of the two is more conservative? more realistic? Why?
C. The above discussion states that FASB "does not regard R&D expenditures, even on projects determined to be successful, as leading to future benefits that are identifiable and objectively measurable. But it does allow capitalization of exploration costs, even when specific efforts fail to lead to discovery." What public policy might be served by allowing oil exploration companies this exception to the usual rules?

P13–18 Capitalizing R&D Expenditures

The In Practice insert entitled "Motorola and the Iridium Venture" shows how one firm has managed to show R&D costs on its books even though the R&D was (more or less) internally generated. Use the information in this insert and the information in the chapter on the U.S. and foreign requirements for the accounting treatment of R&D to answer the following:

A. How do the accounting requirements for R&D expenses vary across nations?
B. What difference does this variation make to U.S. firms?
C. Does it seem likely that multinationals, particularly cross-listed ones (ones listed on U.S. stock exchanges and on foreign ones), will be especially pressured to follow Motorola's lead in finding ways to capitalize R&D expenditures? Why or why not?

RESEARCH ACTIVITIES

R13–1 Badwill (Negative Goodwill)

On December 31, 1997, Broky & Toye Corporation purchased 80 percent of the voting common stock of Dangle Industries in an acquisition treated as a "purchase." Broky and Toye paid $400,000 for its 80 percent investment. Other relevant December 31, 1997, data follow:

ACCOUNT	BOOK VALUE	CURRENT VALUE
Cash	$ 130,000	$ 130,000
Marketable securities	90,000	90,000
Accounts receivable	400,000	360,000
Inventory	300,000	200,000
Other current assets	100,000	50,000
Plant and equipment	100,000	140,000
Long-term investments in available-for-sale securities	100,000	100,000
	$1,220,000	$1,070,000
Accounts payable	100,000	100,000
Bonds payable	200,000	100,000
Net assets	$ 920,000	$ 870,000

Required:

A. Determine the amount of badwill, if any, and determine the values at which the different accounts will be reported on the consolidated balance sheet at December 31, 1997.

B. What subsequent disposition is made of badwill (or the Excess of Book Value Over Cost)? Is badwill amortized? Does it increase or decrease income? If amortized, what is the appropriate period and method?

C. How would your answers change if Broky and Toye paid $550,000 for the 80 percent interest?

14

Long-Term Liabilities

Learning Objectives

After studying this chapter, you should be able to:

1. Demonstrate the impact of financial leverage on profitability and solvency.
2. Demonstrate how bond premiums and discounts are related to the interest rate stated on the face of the bond.
3. Amortize premiums and discounts using the effective-interest and straight-line methods.
4. Account for bonds issued between interest dates.
5. Account for early redemptions of debt, and explain the rationale for treating gains and losses as extraordinary.
6. Understand the accounting issues associated with convertible bonds and bonds issued with detachable warrants.
7. Differentiate between long-term notes and bonds.

Big Banks' Goal: Higher Ratings

In 1993 the ***Chase Manhattan Corporation*** presented its 34,000 employees with a four-page pamphlet detailing the bank's mission for the turn of the century: to be world-class, balanced, financially strong, and big. Amid those broad goals, however, there was one strikingly concrete objective: By 1995, Chase wanted to raise its credit rating to the pristine double-A. At that time it was triple-B, the level just above junk bonds.

Chase was not alone in this ambitious goal. After waves of bad loans, starting with the developing-country debt crises in the mid-1980s to the real estate collapse of the 1990s, America's largest banks are trying to recover their financial strength. And like Chase, several other large banks publicly have set goals for raising their credit ratings.

When it merged with ***Manufacturers' Hanover Corporation*** in 1991, for example, the ***Chemical Banking Corporation*** said it wanted to raise its rating from triple-B to double-A by 1994. At ***Citicorp's*** annual meeting in April 1992, John S. Reed, the chairman, said that the bank also wanted to be rated double-A by 1995. Now Citicorp is rated triple-B by some rating agencies and single-A by others. . . . There are pragmatic reasons for these goals: higher rated companies borrow money at lower interest rates.

Source: Saul Hansell, *The New York Times*, June 8, 1993, Sec. C. p. 1.

FINANCIAL ANALYSIS

Demonstrate the impact of financial leverage on profitability and solvency.

The mix of debt and equity as sources of funding reflects management's philosophy, style, and penchant for risk taking. Debt as a source of financing introduces more risk to the business than financing obtained through equity sources. The risk is greater because debt financing requires periodic outflows of resources in the form of interest payments and principal repayments. Equity financing, on the other hand, does not require periodic payments of any sort, nor does it require the repayment of principal amounts. The credit rating of a business is a reflection of the perceived risk to creditors. One element of this perceived risk is the amount of debt financing used by the enterprise.

The relative mix of debt and equity financing in an enterprise is referred to as the degree of **financial leverage** employed in the business. A high degree of financial leverage means that the entity has a relatively high proportion of debt funds in its capital structure, and therefore more risk. Conversely, a low degree of financial leverage implies that the entity finances a large proportion of its assets with equity funds and employs only small amounts of debt funding, meaning there is less risk.

In most industries, however, the use of some financial leverage is considered to be beneficial. Interest payments are tax-deductible, but dividends paid to shareholders are not. In fact, dividends paid to shareholders are taxed twice, first as income to the corporation and then as income to the shareholder. Because interest is a tax-deductible expense to the corporation, a portion of the interest cost is borne by the government. Additionally, no voting rights are given up when using debt financing; thus, the existing ownership does not dilute its ownership position.

Offsetting these benefits are two major disadvantages: (1) the interest must be paid periodically according to the debt contract, and (2) the principal must be repaid when it is due. If the interest payments are not made on a timely basis, the company is considered in default, and the debt holders can demand immediate repayment of the entire amount of the debt. This could force the company into bankruptcy proceedings.

Besides the interest payments, the principal must be repaid on schedule. Debt is only temporary financing compared to permanent equity financing. Even long-term bond issues eventually must be repaid. Of course, in many instances long-term debt seems to be similar to equity financing as the entity refinances the maturing debt and replaces it with new long-term debt. The use of financial leverage can affect a company's performance in terms of profitability and in terms of risk, as we will discuss in the next section.

PROFITABILITY

To understand how financial leverage affects profitability, consider the following example. Three companies (A, B, and C) are the same in all respects except in the sources of financing. Information from the condensed balance sheets for the three firms follows:

	A	B	C
Total assets	$100,000,000	$100,000,000	$100,000,000
Total debt (12%)	75,000,000	50,000,000	25,000,000
Total equity	25,000,000	50,000,000	75,000,000

Assume that the par value of the capital stock is $10 per share for each company, there is no preferred stock, and each company has $5 million of retained earnings. The number of shares outstanding for each company is

Retained earnings	5,000,000	5,000,000	5,000,000
Common equity	20,000,000	45,000,000	70,000,000
(divide by $10 par equals number of shares)	2,000,000	4,500,000	7,000,000

Also assume for each firm that the interest rate on the debt is 12%, the income tax rate is 40%, and earnings before interest and taxes (EBIT) amount to $10,000,000. The net income for each firm is calculated as follows:

	A	B	C
EBIT	$10,000,000	$10,000,000	$10,000,000
Interest (12% × debt)	9,000,000	6,000,000	3,000,000
EBT	$ 1,000,000	$ 4,000,000	$ 7,000,000
Tax (40%)	400,000	1,600,000	2,800,000
Net Income	$ 600,000	$ 2,400,000	$ 4,200,000

One measure of profitability is earnings per share (EPS) on the common stock:

EPS	600/2,000	2,400/4,500	4,200/7,000
	$ .30	$ .53	$ .60

A second measure of profitability is return on equity, the net income divided by common equity.

Return on equity	600/25,000	2,400/50,000	4,200/75,000
	2.4%	4.8%	5.6%

Based on these measures of profitability, financial leverage does not appear to be advantageous. Clearly, A has not performed as well as B or C. However, if income increases, the results change considerably. Suppose that income before interest and tax increases the following year to $15 million, a 50 percent increase in profit before interest and tax. The following results are obtained:

	A	B	C
EBIT	$15,000,000	$15,000,000	$15,000,000
Interest	9,000,000	6,000,000	3,000,000
EBT	$ 6,000,000	$ 9,000,000	$12,000,000
Tax (40%)	2,400,000	3,600,000	4,800,000
Net income	$ 3,600,000	$ 5,400,000	$ 7,200,000
EPS	$1.80	$1.20	$1.03
Return on equity	3,600,000 / 25,600,000	5,400,000 / 52,400,000	7,200,000 / 79,200,000
	14.06%	10.3%	9.09%

EPS for A has increased by six times, from $.30 to $1.80, based on a 50 percent increase in EBIT. These results illustrate the positive effects of financial leverage. Of course, if earnings were decreasing, the results would go in the opposite direction just as dramatically.

SOLVENCY

Solvency is a measure of risk inherent in a business. Introduced in Chapter 3 was one measure of solvency, the *debt ratio,* which is the portion of assets financed by the total debt. Related to the debt ratio is another measure of solvency, the **debt-to-equity ratio**, which is the total debt divided by the total equity. In our example involving companies A, B, and C, the debt-to-equity ratios are

A = 75,000,000/25,000,000 = 3
B = 50,000,000/50,000,000 = 1
C = 25,000,000/75,000,000 = 0.333

A second measure of solvency and risk is the **times-interest-earned ratio**, calculated by dividing the earnings before interest and taxes (EBIT) by the interest expense. In our example, using the first assumption of earnings of $10 million, the results would be

A = 10,000,000/9,000,000 = 1.1 times
B = 10,000,000/6,000,000 = 1.67 times
C = 10,000,000/3,000,000 = 3.33 times

These ratios should be compared with the industry averages to obtain an indication of the relative amount of risk inherent in the company. Industries that have stable revenues, such as public utilities, generally can use a greater degree of financial leverage than industries with wide fluctuations in revenues. A more stable revenue base allows better planning of cash flows for interest payments.

With this understanding of the impact of financial leverage on profitability and risk analysis, we can better appreciate the way debt financing affects a business. Long-term debt is debt that is not due within the normal operating cycle or one year, whichever is longer. Different kinds of long-term debt financing are available to a corporation, including leases, bonds, and long-term notes. Leases are discussed in Chapter 15, and we examine bonds and long-term notes in this chapter. The discussion of bonds payable includes bonds issued at par, at a discount or premium, between interest-payment dates, and finally, settlement or retirement of the bonds.

BONDS PAYABLE

A bond payable is a long-term promissory note that contains an issue date, a maturity date, a par value, a stated interest rate, and a schedule of interest payment dates. The *par value* is the principal, the amount stated on the face of the debt instrument that must be paid at maturity, and usually is stated as $1,000 or $100 per bond.[1] The bond *indenture* contains the details of the agreement, such as any specific assets pledged as security, the repayment schedule, any restrictive covenants prohibiting additional borrowing, sale of assets or dividend payments, or stipulations that particular financial ratios meet certain standards. The bond indenture also identifies the trustee for the bondholders. The trustee's duty is to ensure that the company carries out its obligations to the bondholders as specified in the indenture.

Typically there are certain costs that are incurred with issuing bonds. Bond issue costs are all costs directly associated with issuing and selling a bond issue. Such costs include attorney fees, broker fees, and so forth. If the amounts are material, they should be capitalized and amortized over the life of the bond issue. Bond issue costs that are immaterial are expensed in the period of issue or more frequently offset against the proceeds of the bond issue.

TYPES AND FEATURES OF BONDS PAYABLE

The stated interest rate of a bond (also called the *coupon rate*) is usually a function of the prevailing market interest rate at the time of issue for the risk category and maturity of the bond. In most bond issues, as the term of the bond increases, the interest rate also increases because of the heightened perceived risk of nonrepayment of the face value. If the market interest rate happens to be especially low, a longer maturity date may be affixed. In 1993, for example, ***Walt Disney*** issued bonds with 100-year maturities because the interest rates were very low at the time of issue.

The method of retirement or repayment is specified in the bond indenture. Serial bonds have portions of the bond issue mature at different dates. For example, a series of bonds issued in 1997 might have portions mature in the

[1]We will assume that each bond has a $1,000 denomination in the examples of this chapter.

years 2002, 2003, 2004, and so forth.[2] A **sinking fund** is a retirement method in which periodic payments are made to the trustee. The amounts paid, depending on the indenture agreement, may be invested until the maturity dates or used to purchase the company's outstanding bonds on the open market.

Most bonds are **callable bonds**, meaning the company can retire them at a designated price above par (referred to as a *call premium*) before maturity. For example, a call price of 102 means that the issuer must pay 102% of the face value of the bond if called before maturity.

Some bonds are **convertible bonds**, meaning they can be exchanged for a fixed number of common stock shares. Convertible bonds typically can be issued at an interest rate lower than the current market rate because the lender has the option to convert the bonds to common stock. The attractiveness of the conversion feature is illustrated in the excerpt presented in the In Practice feature "Convertible Bonds."

IN PRACTICE—GENERAL

Convertible Bonds

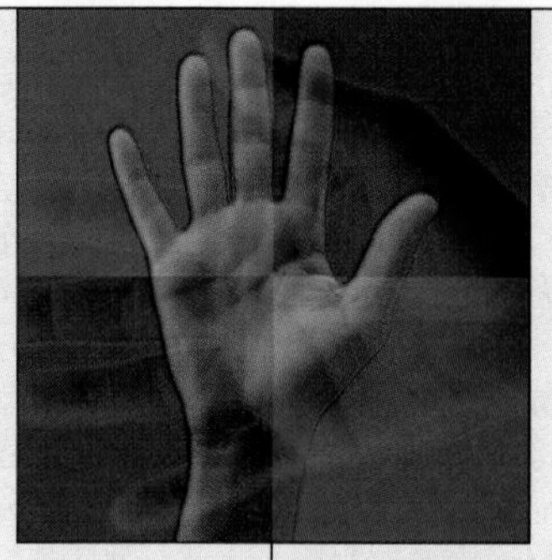

Edgy investors who want a piece of the big bull market but worry that it could soon end are taking a new look at an old but little used alternative: convertible bonds. Convertibles, issued by a growing number of companies, are corporate bonds that can be exchanged at any time for a fixed number of shares of common stock. As hybrids, they act like both stock and bonds. When the company's stock rises, its convertibles go up almost as much, since they can be "converted" into the higher-priced shares of stock. If the stock drops, a convertible's fixed yield still delivers a steady, predictable stream of income like any bond.

The appeal is that convertibles typically offer about two-thirds of the profit potential of stocks with only half the risk because their relatively high fixed yields come to the rescue when a stock craters.

Source: Steven D. Kaye, "It's a Bond! It's a Stock!" *U.S. News & World Report,* March 2, 1992, p. 68.

Companies may improve the credit ratings of their bonds by pledging specific assets as collateral. A **mortgage bond** is backed by specifically identified assets, while **debenture bonds** are backed only with the general creditworthiness of the issuing company. In cases of bankruptcy, debenture bondholders have the same status as other unsecured lenders.

Interest is the cost to the borrower for the use of borrowed funds. Interest rates change over time as a result of investor expectations with regard to inflation, risk, and general economic and environmental conditions. In recent years, the environment of business has expanded because of the increase in foreign trade as well as an increase in foreign investors providing funds for bond issues. The increasing globalization of business can be seen in the excerpt from *The Wall Street Journal* depicting the impact of the turmoil in Russia on bond prices. Foreign markets are affecting interest rates on an increasing scale.

The interest rate is stated as an annual rate. If the length of time is less than one year, the interest rate should be adjusted for the different time period. The

[2]Serial bonds are discussed in the chapter appendix.

IN PRACTICE—INTERNATIONAL

Impact of Soviet Tensions on Bond Prices

New York—Bond prices rose as increased tensions in the Soviet Union prompted nervous investors to buy bonds.

Trading was again hectic, with the prices rising after reports that tanks were moving toward the Russian Parliament, raising the possibility of military conflict. In times of political uncertainty, investors often cash out of other investments and buy Treasury, which are considered the safest securities in the world. The move is called a "flight to quality."

But when no major confrontations occurred, prices fell back somewhat.

Source: Constance Mitchell and Sharon R. King, "Credit Markets: Bonds Prices Rise as Increasing Soviet Tensions Push Investors to Seek Safety of U.S. Treasuries," *The Wall Street Journal,* August 21, 1991; Sec. C, p. 17.

adjustment for the time period results in the *effective interest rate.* The effective interest rate, or **annual percentage rate (APR),** also referred to as *yield,* or *market interest rate,* is found by dividing the amount of interest charged by the amount invested (loaned) adjusted for the length of time of the investment.[3]

BOND VALUES ILLUSTRATED

2 Demonstrate how bond premiums and discounts are related to the interest rate stated on the face of the bond.

Exhibits 14–1 and 14–2 illustrate the calculations required to determine the *issue price* of bonds, which is stated as a percentage of the par value. For example, bonds issued at 100% of par would be issued for $1,000 each. Bonds issued at 92 would be issued for $920 each. In Exhibit 14–1, the bonds are issued at 100% of par value, but in Exhibit 14–2, they are issued at a discount. Bonds, like most liabilities, are valued on the transaction date at the present value of the future cash outlays or the monetary equivalent necessary to settle the debt. The present

EXHIBIT 14–1
Bonds Issued at Par

On January 1, 1997, the Johnstown Corporation issued $10,000 of debenture bonds. Each bond has a face value of $1,000 with a stated rate of interest of 8% to be paid every six months on June 30 and December 31. The bonds all mature on January 1, 2007.

There are two cash flows associated with these bonds: (1) the face amount, a single sum of $10,000, and (2) the interest, an annuity of $400 for 20 periods. If the bonds are sold to yield 8%, each of the cash flows is discounted at 4% for 20 periods as follows:

PV of maturity value	= $10,000 × .4564	=	$ 4,564
PV of annuity	= $400 × 13.5903	=	5,436
Total issue price	=		$10,000

[3]For example, assume that $100 is borrowed for one year, and $110 is paid to satisfy the debt. The effective rate of interest is 10% ($10 interest divided by $100 of principal). Now assume that the same $100 is borrowed for eight months rather than a year, and $110 is paid to satisfy the loan agreement. The effective annual interest rate is now 15% [($10/$100)/(8/12)]. A time adjustment is necessary in this case because the borrower had the use of the money for less than one year, in fact, only 8/12 of a year. Therefore, dividing $10 by $100 results in only 8/12 of the interest rate.

value is based on an effective interest rate at the date of issue, which may or may not be the stated interest rate of the bond.

Accounting for bonds issued at face value is straightforward. For example, to record the issue of bonds in Exhibit 14–1, the journal entry is

1997			
Jan. 1	Cash	10,000	
	Bonds Payable		10,000

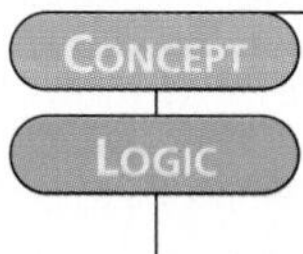

Valuation of a liability.

The liability is recorded at the face value of the bonds, which equals the present value of the future cash outlays required to settle the debt.

Since the effective annual interest rate for this example is 8%, the effective semiannual rate is 4% (.08/2). The journal entry to record the interest payment at each interest payment date is

Interest Expense	400*	
Cash		400

**$10,000 × (.08/2)*

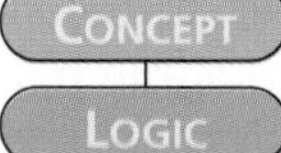

Recognition and measurement of expense.

Interest represents the cost of using the funds for a period of time. This is treated as a financing expense and is recognized (charged to expense) during the period in which the benefits were derived. The benefits, in this case, are the use of the funds from the bond issue.

Discounts and Premiums on Bonds. Discounts and premiums result from issuance of bonds at less than (discount) or greater than (premium) the par value.

Bonds Issued at a Discount. As explained in Chapter 9, bonds selling at prices above or below the face value reflect a price adjustment necessary to equate the stated rate of interest on the issued bond with the market rate of interest (or yield) for bonds of that risk level. The market rate of interest is referred to as the effective rate of interest. Exhibit 14–2 illustrates how the price of a bond is determined if the stated rate of the bond is less than the market rate (or yield) desired by investors. Such a bond would sell at a discount, or a price below the face value of the bond by an amount necessary to provide the desired yield to the investor. The discount amount represents an adjustment to the stated interest rate on the bond, which is lower than the prevailing market rate. The net issue price is at the prevailing market rate. In an active market, bond prices may change on a daily basis as a result of changes in environmental factors and the composite market's assessment of the risk inherent in those changes. Market

EXHIBIT 14–2
Bonds Issued at a Discount

Assume that the bonds in Exhibit 14–1 are issued to yield 10%. Again, the purchase price includes two components: (1) the present value (PV) of the maturity value discounted at 5% for 20 periods and (2) the PV of an ordinary annuity of $400 discounted at 5% for 20 periods. Appendix A contains an explanation of PV calculations.

(1) PV of maturity value = $10,000 × .3769 =	$ 3,769
(2) PV of annuity = $400 × 12.4622 =	4,985
Total issue price =	$ 8,754
Face amount of bond	10,000
Discount	$ 1,246

Amortization Table: Effective-Interest Method

DATE	(1) BEGINNING BOOK VALUE	(2) CASH PAID	(3) INTEREST EXPENSE	(4) DISCOUNT AMORTIZED	(5) ENDING BOOK VALUE
01/01/97	$8,754				$ 8,754
06/30/97	8,754	$ 400	$ 438	38	8,792
12/31/97	8,792	400	440	40	8,832
06/30/98	8,832	400	442	42	8,873
12/31/98	8,873	400	444	44	8,916
06/30/99	8,916	400	446	46	8,962
12/31/99	8,962	400	448	48	9,010
06/30/00	9,010	400	451	51	9,061
12/31/00	9,061	400	453	53	9,114
06/30/01	9,114	400	456	56	9,170
12/31/01	9,170	400	458	58	9,228
06/30/02	9,228	400	461	61	9,290
12/31/02	9,290	400	464	64	9,354
06/30/03	9,354	400	468	68	9,422
12/31/03	9,422	400	471	71	9,493
06/30/04	9,493	400	475	75	9,568
12/31/04	9,568	400	478	78	9,646
06/30/05	9,646	400	482	82	9,728
12/31/05	9,728	400	486	86	9,815
06/30/06	9,815	400	491	91	9,905
12/31/06	$9,905	400	495	95	$10,000
Totals		$8,000	$9,246*	$1,246	

(2) = 10,000 × 8% × 6/12
(3) = (1) × 10% × 6/12
(4) = (2) − (3)
(5) = (1) + (4)

Cash interest paid =	$ 8,000	
Principal =	10,000	
Total paid =	$18,000	$1,246
Amount borrowed =	8,754	discount
*Total interest expense =	$ 9,246	

*Table contains rounding differences

interest rates change in response to economic conditions, inflationary expectations, conflicts between nations, and a host of other environmental factors.

In Exhibit 14–2, the issue price of the bonds is $8,754. The discount ($1,246) is recorded in a contra account, Discount on Bonds Payable, which offsets the bond liability in the balance sheet. The liability account and the contra account are considered to be an integral part of the same transaction and, therefore, under current GAAP, are reported together on the balance sheet. In essence, $8,754 is borrowed, but $10,000 as well as periodic interest must be paid to satisfy the debt. The $1,246 discount is additional interest required for the higher effective interest rate. The discount is allocated (or amortized) over the life of the bonds, and it effectively increases the interest expense recognized each period.

The initial entry to record the issuance of the bonds in Exhibit 14–2 is

1997			
Jan. 1	Cash	8,754	
	Discount on Bonds Payable	1,246	
	Bonds Payable		10,000

CONCEPT Valuation of liabilities.

LOGIC Bond liabilities are valued at the present value of the future obligations necessary to settle the debt. At the time of issue, the contra account (Discount on Bonds Payable) is used to adjust the bond liability to the amount of cash received. The contra account is allocated to expense over the life of the bond, and it is amortized to zero by the maturity date of the obligation. The two accounts together (Bonds Payable less Discount on Bonds Payable) represent the book value of the obligation at any point in time and provide the basis for determining subsequent interest expense.

The interest expense each period includes an amortized portion of the discount (or premium). Two methods of amortizing discounts and premiums on bonds are the effective-interest method and the straight-line method. These were first introduced in Chapter 5.

Amortize premiums and discounts using the effective-interest and straight-line methods.

The **effective-interest method** derives its name from the manner in which the amount of discount or premium amortized is determined. The amortized discount or premium is the difference between the effective interest expense charged to income for the period and the actual cash paid for the use of the funds. In effect, the amortized amount is a plug figure for the difference between the cash paid and the effective interest recognized. Exhibit 14–2 contains the amortization table for the bonds based on the effective-interest method.

Because the bonds in Exhibit 14–2 were sold to investors desiring a 10% return on their investment, the effective interest rate (or yield) is 10% on the unpaid balance. At the date of sale, $8,754 was received for bonds that will subsequently be retired at $10,000, the contract amount. The effective interest expense is $438 ($8,754 × .10 × 1/2) for the first half-year, and $400 is the contractual amount of interest ($10,000 × .08 × 1/2). The difference, $38, is the amount of discount amortized. The journal entries for the first two interest payments are

1997			
June 30	Interest Expense	438*	
	Cash		400
	Discount on Bonds Payable		38
	*\$8,754 × .10 × 1/2) = \$438		
Dec. 31	Interest Expense	440*	
	Cash		400
	Discount on Bonds Payable		40
	*\$8,792 × .10 × 1/2 = \$440 (rounded)		

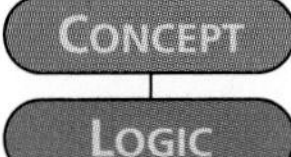

CONCEPT Expense recognition and valuation of a liability.

LOGIC Interest is the cost of using borrowed funds. The amount of the expense recognized is based on the book value (carrying value) of the debt. The book value of the debt is the amount that would settle the debt at any point in time if there were no change in the interest rates after the bonds were issued. Thus, liabilities are valued at the present value of the assets required to satisfy the debt.

From the preceding entry and from examining Exhibit 14–2, note that the bond liability (the net book value) increases as the discount is amortized. As the bond discount is reduced, the book value increases and interest expense is increased. At the maturity date, the book value of the bond liability and the face amount required to be paid are the same, \$10,000.

Straight-line amortization is allowed under current GAAP *only if the amounts are not materially different* from the amounts obtained in the effective-interest method. The straight-line method amortizes or allocates to each period an equal amount of any discount (premium). For the bonds issued in Exhibit 14–2 with a discount of \$1,246, the straight-line amortization of the discount is \$62.30 per interest payment (\$1,246/20). The entry at each interest payment date would be

June 30 and Dec. 31	Interest Expense (\$400 + \$62)	462	
	Discount on Bonds Payable		62*
	Cash		400
	Rounded to nearest dollar.		

In the straight-line amortization method, the amount of interest expense charged to each period is the same (\$462), but the interest rate decreases as the book value increases. This is just the opposite of the effective-interest method, in which the rate is a constant 5% of the book value, and therefore the amount recognized as expense increases as the book value increases. Exhibit 14–3 compares the two amortization methods.

Bonds Issued at a Premium. Bonds issued at an amount greater than the face amount are issued at a **premium**. The extra cash received over the par value essentially reduces the stated interest rate on the bond to the prevailing market interest rate. Premiums on bonds payable are amortized (reduced) in the same manner as discounts. The difference between the cash paid and the effective interest expense recognized represents the amount of premium amortized. By the maturity date, the book value of the bond is equal to the face amount that must be paid. Exhibit 14–4 illustrates the calculation of the issue price for bonds issued at a premium and an amortization table for the premium when ten-year bonds with an 8% stated rate paid semiannually are issued to yield 6% interest. The entries to issue the bonds and for the first two interest-payment dates appear on p. 746. These journal entries use the data in Exhibit 14–4.

EXHIBIT 14–3
Interest-per-Period Comparison between Effective and Straight-Line Methods

	Effective Method			Straight-Line Method		
Date	Interest Expense	Net Book Value	Percent Interest	Interest Expense	Book Value	Percent Interest
01/01/97		$ 8,754.00			$ 8,754.00	
06/30/97	$ 437.70	8,791.70	5.00%	$ 462.30	8,816.30	5.28%
12/31/97	439.59	8,831.29	5.00	462.30	8,878.60	5.24
06/30/98	441.56	8,872.85	5.00	462.30	8,940.90	5.21
12/31/98	443.64	8,916.49	5.00	462.30	9,003.20	5.17
06/30/99	445.82	8,962.32	5.00	462.30	9,065.50	5.13
12/31/99	448.12	9,010.43	5.00	462.30	9,127.80	5.10
06/30/00	450.52	9,060.95	5.00	462.30	9,190.10	5.06
12/31/00	453.05	9,114.00	5.00	462.30	9,252.40	5.03
06/30/01	455.70	9,169.70	5.00	462.30	9,314.70	5.00
12/31/01	458.49	9,228.19	5.00	462.30	9,377.00	4.96
06/30/02	461.41	9,289.60	5.00	462.30	9,439.30	4.93
12/31/02	464.48	9,354.08	5.00	462.30	9,501.60	4.90
06/30/03	467.70	9,421.78	5.00	462.30	9,563.90	4.87
12/31/03	471.09	9,492.87	5.00	462.30	9,626.20	4.83
06/30/04	474.64	9,567.51	5.00	462.30	9,688.50	4.80
12/31/04	478.38	9,645.89	5.00	462.30	9,750.80	4.77
06/30/05	482.29	9,728.18	5.00	462.30	9,813.10	4.74
12/31/05	486.41	9,814.59	5.00	462.30	9,875.40	4.71
06/30/06	490.73	9,905.32	5.00	462.30	9,937.70	4.68
12/31/06	495.27	$10,000.00	5.00	462.30	$10,000.00	4.65
Totals	$9,247.00*			$9,246.00*		

*Rounding difference.
Note: Interest expense percentages are based on the previous book value balances.

EXHIBIT 14–4
Bonds Issued at a Premium

Assume that $10,000 par value bonds with an 8% stated rate of interest are issued to yield 6% interest. The bonds pay interest semiannually on June 30 and December 31, and are 10-year bonds. The purchase price includes two components: (1) The present value (PV) of the maturity value discounted at 3% for 20 periods, and (2) the PV of an ordinary annuity of $400 for 20 periods discounted at 3%.

PV of maturity value = $10,000 × .5537 =	$ 5,537
PV of annuity = $400 × 14.8775 =	5,951
Total issue price	$11,488
Face amount of bond	10,000
Premium	$ 1,488

Amortization Table: Effective-Interest Method

DATE	(1) BEGINNING BOOK VALUE	(2) CASH PAID	(3) INTEREST EXPENSE	(4) PREMIUM AMORTIZED	(5) ENDING BOOK VALUE
01/01/97					$11,488
06/30/97	$11,488	$ 400	$ 345	$ 55	11,433
12/31/97	11,433	400	343	57	11,376
06/30/98	11,376	400	341	59	11,317
12/31/98	11,317	400	340	60	11,256
06/30/99	11,256	400	338	62	11,194
12/31/99	11,194	400	336	64	11,130
06/30/00	11,130	400	334	66	11,064
12/31/00	11,064	400	332	68	10,996
06/30/01	10,996	400	330	70	10,926
12/31/01	10,926	400	328	72	10,854
06/30/02	10,854	400	326	74	10,780
12/31/02	10,780	400	323	77	10,703
06/30/03	10,703	400	321	79	10,624
12/31/03	10,624	400	319	81	10,543
06/30/04	10,543	400	316	84	10,458
12/31/04	10,458	400	314	86	10,372
06/30/05	10,372	400	311	89	10,283
12/31/05	10,283	400	308	92	10,191
06/30/06	10,191	400	306	94	10,097
12/31/06	10,097	400	303	97	$10,000
Totals		$8,000	$6,512*	$1,488	

(2) = 10,000 × 8% × 6/12
(3) = (1) × 6% × 6/12
(4) = (2) − (3)
(5) = (1) + (4)

Cash interest paid =	$ 8,000	
Principal =	10,000	
Total paid =	$18,000	$1,488 premium
Amount borrowed =	11,488	
*Interest expense =	$ 6,512	

*Table contains rounding differences.

1997			
Jan. 1	Cash	11,488	
	Bonds Payable		10,000
	Premium on Bonds Payable		1,488
June 30	Interest Expense	345*	
	Premium on Bonds Payable	55	
	Cash		400
	**$11,488 × .06/2 = $345*		
Dec. 31	Interest Expense	343*	
	Premium on Bonds Payable	57	
	Cash		400
	**[(11,488 − 55) × .06/2] = $343*		

BONDS ISSUED OR SOLD BETWEEN INTEREST DATES

4 Account for bonds issued between interest dates.

Frequently, bonds initially are issued between interest payment dates or are sold by subsequent bondholders between interest dates. Because the bond contains a contractual obligation for the issuing institution to make fixed-sum payments at definite intervals, the sales amount includes interest accrued up to the date of sale. Therefore, the cash proceeds consist of two amounts: (1) the bond price and (2) the accrued interest from the last interest payment date to the sale date.

Bonds Issued at Par. For example, assume that the bonds in Exhibit 14–1 are sold at par on April 1, 1997, instead of January 1. The buyer of the $10,000 of bonds will receive $400 interest on June 30, 1997, because the bonds were dated January 1. However, the buyer is entitled only to three months' interest, the holding period of the investment. The seller receives the $10,000 par value plus accrued interest for three months ($10,000 × 8% × 3/12 = $200). The journal entry to issue these bonds at April 1, 1997, and the subsequent interest payment at June 30, 1997, follow:

1997			
Apr. 1	Cash	10,200	
	Interest Expense*		200
	Bonds Payable		10,000
	**Or Interest Payable*		
June 30	Interest Expense*	400	
	Cash		400
	**If Interest Payable had been charged at 4/1/97, then it would be debited now for $200, and interest expense debited for $200.*		

The buyer is charged for the $200 accrued interest because the buyer will receive $400 cash interest on the interest payment date.

Bonds Issued at Other Than Par. If bonds are issued between interest payment dates at other than par, the present values of the future cash flows are somewhat more complex. To find the issue price, the present value of the future cash flows at the issue date must be calculated as follows.

First, the present value of the principal plus the present value of the interest payments at the next interest payment date (in this case, June 30, 1997) is calculated.

Next, this amount is discounted back to the issue date. To illustrate, assume that the bonds in Exhibit 14–2 are issued on April 1, 1997, to yield 10%. The proceeds received would be $8,772 rounded, plus accrued interest of $200 from January 1 to April 1, 1997. The $8,772 is calculated as follows:

1. The present value (PV) of the future cash flows on June 30, 1997, must be found.

PV of $10,000 @ 5%, 19 periods	$10,000	×	.3957 =	$3,957
PVAD of $400 @ 5%, 20 periods	$ 400	×	13.0853 =	5,234
Total PV at 6/30/95			=	$9,191

2. This total of $9,191 must now be discounted for three months at 5% (which is equivalent to being discounted for one period at 2.5%) to obtain the present value at April 1, 1997:

PV of $9,191 @ 2.5% for 1 period = $9,191 × .9756 = $8,967

3. The $8,967 represents the present value of all future cash flows including the $200 of accrued interest. Therefore, the present value of the interest must be deducted:

PV of 200 @ 2.5% for 1 period = $200 × .9756 = $195

Therefore, the amount attributable to the bond issue is

$8,967 − $195 = $8,772

The entry to record this transaction is

1997			
Apr. 1	Cash	8,972*	
	Discount on Bonds Payable	1,228**	
	Interest Payable [or Interest Expense]		200
	Bonds Payable		10,000

**$8,772 + $200 = $8,972*
***$10,000 − $8,772 = $1,228*

The entry at the interest payment date amortizes the discount for one-half of an interest period. In this case, we have already computed the present value as of June 30, 1997, to be $9,191. The difference between $9,191 and $8,972 is the effective interest for three months. The journal entry at the interest payment date would be:

Interest Expense	219	
Interest Payable	200	
Discount on Bonds Payable (plug)		19
Cash		400

Note that the carrying value of the bond on June 30, 1997, becomes $8,791 ($8,772 + $19). The $1 difference from the table value results from rounding. The normal practice is to correct these differences on the last interest payment date.

The issue price of bonds sold between interest payment dates at a premium or discount also can be estimated (or approximated) using a straight-line interpolation procedure. We can illustrate using the same information from Exhibit 14–2 and the previous example. If the bonds are issued on April 1, 1997, three months would have elapsed from January 1, 1997, the date stated on the face of the bond. On April 1, 1997, the carrying value (or book value) of the bonds would be 3/6 of the way between the carrying value at January 1, 1997 ($8,754) and the carrying value at June 30, 1997 ($8,792), or $8,773.

If the bonds had been issued on March 1, 1997, the fractional difference would be four months divided by six months or two-thirds, since that is the fractional time left until the next interest payment date, and that fraction would be used to determine the effective interest of $292 (4/6 × $438).

EXTINGUISHMENT OF DEBT

Obligations arising from bonds payable can be extinguished by (1) retirement at maturity, (2) open-market acquisition of the bonds, (3) exercise of a call provision in the bond indenture, or (4) conversion to equity securities.

BONDS RETIRED AT MATURITY

When the bondholder receives cash for remitting the bond to the company's agent, the liability (Bonds Payable) is removed from the company's books, and cash is reduced by the amount paid. However, if the bonds are redeemed for an asset other than cash, a gain or loss on the redemption may occur. If the fair market value (FMV) of the asset exchanged is materially different from the book value (BV), recognition of a gain or loss on that asset is necessary.

Assume that bonds maturing with a face value of $10,000 are exchanged for land having a FMV of $10,000 and a BV of $5,000 on the issuing company's books. A $5,000 gain for the difference between the FMV and the BV of the land is recognized. Since the FMV of the land and the maturity value of the bonds are both $10,000, no further gain or loss is recognized. The journal entry follows:

Bonds Payable	10,000	
Land		5,000
Gain on Exchange		5,000

OPEN-MARKET ACQUISITIONS

Account for early redemptions of debt, and explain the rationale for treating gains and losses as extraordinary.

Bonds Payable can be retired by purchase on the open market. The price paid for these bonds may be more or less than the current book value of the bonds, and as a result, an extraordinary gain or loss must be recognized (see Chapter 6). Treatment of these gains and losses as extraordinary was mandated by the FASB in SFAS No. 4 because acquisition of outstanding bonds is interpreted as occurring not in the normal course of business, and any gain or loss is shown separately on the income statement.[4] Accounting for bonds presumes the bonds will be held to maturity, and the premium or discount is amortized over the life of the bond. Repurchase of the bonds is an abrupt departure from the assumptions being used as the basis for the accounting over the life of the bond.

Treatment of the gain as extraordinary is a position taken by the FASB in recognition of the realities existent in the bond market. Many companies take advantage of decreases in interest rates if they have sufficient cash or they can refinance the debt in a timely fashion. These events happen so often that the tests of "unusual and infrequent" are not relevant. However, gains or losses from bond reacquisitions do not seem to be proper inclusions in operating income, either. The "extraordinary" classification of these transactions forces the resultant gain or loss to be highlighted on the income statement.

For example, assume that the bonds issued in Exhibit 14–4 were reacquired on the open market at 110 ($11,000) on June 30, 1999. The book value of the bonds after recognition of the interest payment and bond premium amortization on June 30, 1999, is $11,194 (see Exhibit 14–4). The net book value is $194 more than the reacquisition price. Stated differently, the acquisition price of $11,000 is $194 less than the book value ($11,194) of the bonds. The difference between the book value and the acquisition price must be recognized as an extraordinary gain. The journal entries follow:

1999			
June 30	Interest Expense	338	
	Premium on Bonds Payable	62	
	Cash		400
	Bonds Payable	10,000	
	Premium on Bonds Payable	1,194	
	Cash		11,000
	Extraordinary Gain from Bond Retirement		194

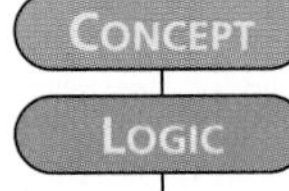

Proper accounting and reporting of extraordinary items.

Gains or losses on the reacquisition of debt are defined as being outside the normal course of business by the FASB and therefore are classified as extraordinary.

During the 1980s, many mergers and acquisitions were financed by so-called *junk bonds*. These were high-risk bonds with very high interest rates. The proceeds

[4]SFAS No. 4, FASB, Appendix A, par. 15.

were used to acquire other businesses. Then, the assets of the acquired businesses were frequently sold piecemeal to retire the junk bonds. In some cases, defaults on the interest payments occurred, causing a precipitous drop in the bond price. The issuer then could purchase the bonds at drastically reduced prices, creating what appeared to be gains on the transactions. This sometimes created questions of ethical operations, as illustrated in the article in the Ethics in Practice feature.

ETHICS IN PRACTICE

Michael Milken's Junk Bonds

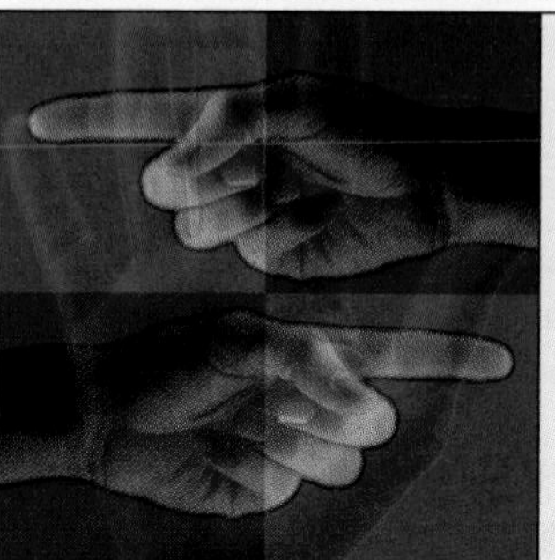

But . . . it came to be said of him that he had been more sinned against than sinning; and that, but for jealousy of the old stagers in the mercantile world, he would have done very wonderful things."

Those words dispatch the great crooked financier Augustus Melmotte whose rise and fall is the focus of Trollope's 1814 novel, *The Way We Live Now*. The same is being said about the greatest real crooked financier of our own day, Michael Milken: that he was a brilliant innovator done in by the envy of lesser mortals and older money. . . .

One of Mike's most ardent defenders in the past, newspaper magnate Ralph Ingersoll II, has turned oddly silent. When Milken was indicted last year, Ingersoll praised him as a hero on "Nightline" and said the prosecution was "as revolting as . . . the McCarthy hearings." Ingersoll and others signed a newspaper ad headlined, "Mike Milken, We believe in you: Mike cares about people. . . . Mike has always performed according to the highest standards of professionalism, honesty, integrity and ethical conduct. . . ."

"Mike" helped Ingersoll to raise $500 million in junk bonds (or, if you prefer, "high-yield, fixed-return securities'), which he used to buy up newspaper companies, often at startlingly high prices. Now the revenues from the newspapers don't begin to cover interest payments, and Ingersoll is sleazily offering to buy back his debts for as little as twenty-eight cents on the dollar. William Farley, another former loudmouth about Michael Milken, has defaulted on $1.5 million of bonds he used to overpay for companies.

Source: Michael Kinsey, "Sour Milken," *The New Republic*, May 21, 1990, p. 4.

BONDS CALLED AND RETIRED

Assume that the bonds sold in Exhibit 14–4 have a call provision stating that the issuing company may call them at 104 any time after December 31, 2001. Further assume that the company exercises this call provision on January 1, 2002. The amortization schedule in Exhibit 14–4 indicates that the book value of the bonds at December 31, 2001, is $10,854. Since the call price is $10,400 ($10,000 × 1.04), the company has an extraordinary gain of $454. This is similar to the retirement of bonds through open-market acquisition.

BONDS RETIRED THROUGH CONVERSION TO EQUITY SECURITIES

Bonds issued with conversion privileges have been the subject of considerable debate. These bonds give rise to some unique problems, both when issued and when the conversion right is exercised.

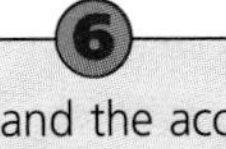

Understand the accounting issues associated with convertible bonds and bonds issued with detachable warrants.

As previously mentioned, the effective interest rate on convertible debt security issues is lower than that on similar bonds without the conversion feature. There are two views regarding the issue of convertible debt securities. One is that the proceeds from the initial issue should be treated entirely as debt. The other view is that the conversion privilege has economic value and should be accounted for separately and treated as equity. Proponents of the second view argue that bonds with the same stated rate of interest and comparable risk, in the absence of any conversion feature, have different market values.

Opponents of allocating value to the conversion features point out that convertible bonds require the bondholder to surrender the bonds in exchange for stock. The debt and conversion right are inseparable in the instrument, and as a consequence, the selling price is inseparable. APB Opinion No. 14 supports the debt argument, stating that "no portion of the proceeds from the issuance of the types of convertible debt securities . . . should be accounted for as attributable to the conversion feature." The APB goes on to state, in the same paragraph, that the APB places "greater weight on the inseparability of the debt and conversion option . . . and less weight on practical difficulties."[5]

Arguments also have been made that the purchaser of convertible bonds is acquiring both a debt security and the right to convert the debt into equity when acquiring convertible bonds. Also, if the bonds are issued with detachable warrants, both debt and equity are reflected in the accounts from the proceeds of the bond issue (discussed in a later section). The argument against separate recognition is that the instrument does not provide for separability of these rights.

However, should the inseparability issue preclude the proper recognition of the underlying economic event in the accounts of the issuing entity? For example, suppose that two different entities issue debt securities at the same stated rate of interest and are viewed as being of comparable risk in the market place. Company A issues $1,000,000 of debt securities at par with a stated rate of interest of 12%. Company B issues the same amount of debt at the same stated rate of interest. However, B's debt is convertible into common stock, and so B receives a premium of $134,210 over the face amount, making the effective interest rate 8%. In this case the market value of the conversion privilege appears to be $134,210.

Exhibit 14–5 contains the basic information concerning the call option and conversion privilege of a bond issue. It will be used to illustrate current GAAP. Assume that the company announces on October 1, 2001, that it intends to exercise its call option on all bonds outstanding on January 1, 2002. It is common for companies to announce calls and induce conversions of convertible securities on or about an interest-payment date. Because of this announcement, assume that all bondholders exercise the conversion privilege on December 31, 2001. There are two methods of valuing the securities exchanged for the debt: the book value method and the market value method. In the **book value method**, the equity securities issued are recorded at the carrying value (book value) of the debt on the books of the debtor. In the **market value method**, the equity securities issued are recorded at current market value and a gain or loss is recognized for any difference from the book value of the debt.

[5]APB Opinion No. 14, par. 12.

EXHIBIT 14–5
Bonds Issued at a Premium Containing Conversion Privileges

As illustrated in Exhibit 14–4, these $10,000 par value 10-year bonds with an 8% stated rate of interest are issued on January 1, 1997 to yield 6%. The bonds pay interest semiannually on June 30 and December 31, and they contain a call provision of 104 exercisable after December 31, 2001. The bonds also contain a conversion privilege of 40 shares of the company's $10 par common stock for each $1,000 face value of bonds held. At the time that the bonds were sold, January 1, 1997, the fair market value of the common stock was $20. The company has performed well, and the prices of its stocks and bonds have continuously risen as a result. The year-end prices for the last five years for the company's common stock and bonds are as follows:

	STOCK PRICES	BOND PRICES
12/31/97	23	110 3/8
12/31/98	27	115 11/32
12/31/99	31	128 1/4
12/31/00	36	150 1/16
12/31/01	41	164

To record the conversion under either method, several journal entries are required. The first entry is the same for both methods and records the interest payment and amortization of the premium:

2001			
Dec. 31	Interest Expense ($10,926 × .06 × 1/2)	328*	
	Premium on Bonds Payable ($400 − $328)	72	
	Cash		400
	*Rounded; $10,926 is book value @ 6/30/01 from Exhibit 14–4.		

In the book value method, the second entry records the exchange of the bonds for equity securities. The book value of the debt is converted into equity and the reclassification shown as follows:

2001			
Dec. 31	Bonds Payable	10,000	
	Premium on Bonds Payable	854	
	Common Stock—$10 Par (40 × 10 × $10)		4,000
	Paid-In Capital in Excess of Par		6,854*
	\$10,854 − $4,000		

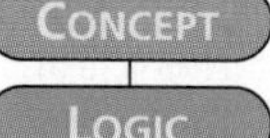

Valuation of equity securities.

In an exchange of equity securities for debt securities, the book value method is followed per APB Opinion No. 14 if the equity securities are valued at the book value of the debt securities retired. This is treated as an even exchange of securities used to finance the operations of the business. Since it is considered an even exchange of financing securities, recognition of gain and/or loss is not appropriate.

To illustrate the market value method, let us assume that at the time of the exchange the market value of the equity securities exchanged is $16,400. Assuming the same information as used in the book value method example, we see that a loss of $5,546 would be recognized, as shown in the following entry:

2001			
Dec. 31	Bonds Payable	10,000	
	Premium on Bonds Payable	854	
	Loss on Redemption	5,546*	
	Common Stock—$10 Par ($400 × 10)		4,000
	Paid-In Capital in Excess of Par		12,400**

**$16,400 FMV − $10,000 − $854 = $5,546*
***16,400 − $4,000 = $12,400*

CONCEPT The proper classification of existing obligations and equity.

LOGIC The debt associated with the convertible bonds no longer exists, and shares of stock have been issued. The fair market value of the stock was $16,400, resulting in a loss to be recognized. The loss is the difference between the fair market value of the stock and the book value of the bonds.

The book value method is the most commonly used method in these conversions for the following reasons:

1. No new assets flow to the entity as a result of the conversion.
2. The gain or loss recognized as a result of the market value method is an opportunity gain or loss that historically has not been recognized.
3. The conversion does not represent the culmination of an earnings process and is simply a transfer from a potential stockholder into a shareholder.
4. Use of the book value method avoids recognition of a loss on conversion.

INDUCED CONVERSIONS

In the preceding example, the company forced conversion by calling the bonds when the fair value of the stock exceeded the call price of the bonds. Conversions are considered to be **induced conversions** when something of value in addition to the initial contract terms is offered to entice the conversion. Cash, more favorable conversion ratios, and warrants are frequently offered for a limited time to induce conversion. These "sweeteners" must, according to SFAS No. 84, be treated as an expense, which is determined by the fair market value of the sweetener (additional gain) to the bondholder.

For example, assume that there was no call provision as outlined in Exhibit 14–5, and the company wanted to reduce its debt-to-equity ratio before issuing additional debt. The existing debt could be reduced by inducing conversion of the outstanding convertible bonds to equity securities. To encourage conversion, assume the company offers for a limited time a conversion ratio of 44 shares (instead of 40 shares) of common stock for each $1,000 of convertible bonds held on December 31, 2001. Based upon the market value of the stock on that date, the sweetener is about 10% in excess of the existing value of the bonds. Each bondholder would receive $1,804 (44 shares at $41 per share) in fair market value of stocks for a bond worth $1,640. The expense to the company is $164, based on the market value of the increased number of shares (4 shares × $41) for each bond converted, or a total of $1,640 for all 10 bonds. Note that the gain to the bondholder and the expense to the company are the same only when the market value of the bond is equal to the conversion ratio times the market value of the stock. In Exhibit 14–5, an efficient market was assumed, and the bond price on or near the exercise date should be close to the common-stock equivalent valuation since it is to the advantage of the bondholder to exercise the conversion.

To record the induced conversion, the following journal entry is made:

2001			
Dec. 31	Bonds Payable	10,000	
	Premium on Bonds Payable	854	
	Bond Conversion Expense	1,640*	
	Common Stock—$10 Par (44 × 10 × 10)		4,400
	Paid-In Capital in Excess of Par		8,094

**[(44 − 40) × $41 × 10] = 1,640*

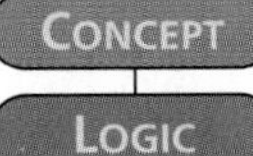

Valuation of equity securities.

In an exchange of equity securities for debt securities, the book value of the debt securities provides the basis of the exchange. The fair market value (FMV) of any additional shares required to induce conversion is treated as an expense of the transaction. Thus, the stock is issued at FMV, with the par value credited to common stock, and the difference between FMV and par credited to Paid-In Capital in Excess of Par.

BONDS AND EQUITY RIGHTS SOLD AT THE SAME TIME

Bonds are frequently sold with detachable **stock warrants**, which give the holders of the warrants the right to purchase stock at a fixed price for a limited period of time. In such cases, both bonds and equity are sold, because the warrants are detachable and the bonds need not be surrendered to obtain the equity. APB Opinion No. 14 requires recognition of the equity portion from the proceeds received. The relative-market-value method is used to allocate the proceeds to the two components. If only one security has a known market value, that known value is assigned to the security, and the remainder of the proceeds is assigned to the other security.

To illustrate a situation where only the bonds have a market value, and not the warrants, assume that the Lark Company issues 100, $1,000, 8%, 10-year bonds for $103,000 on January 1, 1997, with interest payable semiannually. Each $1,000 bond contains 10 warrants. The warrants must be exercised on or before December 31, 1997. Two warrants and $30 will obtain one share of Lark's $10 par common stock. The same bonds, without any warrants, immediately after issuance sold at par. The entry to record the entire issue, $100,000 of bonds, is

1997			
Jan. 1	Cash	103,000	
	Bonds Payable		100,000
	Paid-In Capital—Stock Warrants		3,000*

**$103,000 − $100,000*

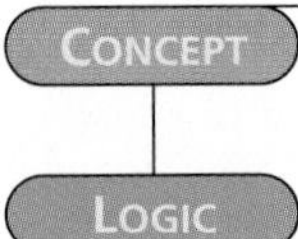

Liability valuation and proper account classification for financial statement presentation.

The market value of the bonds immediately after issuance were selling at par ($1,000). The liability is equal to $100,000, and the remainder of the funds received represents the value of the stock warrants, an equity account.

If all of the stock warrants are exercised on December 31, 1997, the journal entry is

1997			
Dec. 31	Cash (500 × 30)	15,000*	
	Paid-In Capital—Stock Warrants	3,000	
	Common Stock—$10 Par (500 × 10)		5,000
	Paid-In Capital in Excess of Par		13,000

**100 bonds × 10 warrants)/2 = 500 shares*

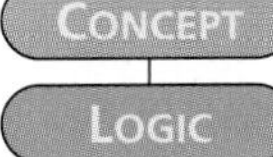

Valuation of equity securities.

Stock is valued at the fair market value of the assets received or the market price of the stock issued, whichever is more clearly determinable. The assets received were two cash payments; $3,000 when the warrants were purchased and $15,000 when the warrants were exercised. The current market price is not relevant because a contract price was established when the warrants were issued. If all or part of the warrants are allowed to expire, the remaining amount paid for the warrants stays in paid-in capital.

IN-SUBSTANCE DEFEASANCE OF DEBT

Defeasance of debt means that the entity is released from any legal liability. **In-substance defeasance of debt** occurs when an entity places sufficient risk-free assets in an irrevocable trust for the sole purpose of servicing and extinguishing the debt. The entity is not released from legal liability but has, "in substance," extinguished the debt.

In-substance defeasance can occur if a firm has sufficient resources and wishes to retire a debt but is precluded from doing so because of covenants in a bond indenture, or simply because the investor does not wish to sell prior to maturity. In such cases, the firm may set up an irrevocable trust to service the debt. Exhibit 14–6 contains an illustration of an in-substance defeasance opportunity.

EXHIBIT 14–6
In-Substance Defeasance

Assume that five years ago, $10,000 of 10-year, 8% semiannual interest-paying bonds were issued at par. The same bonds are selling today to yield an effective rate of 12%. Further assume that an equal face amount of 8% U.S. government bonds that mature in five years were purchased at 92 9/32, thus yielding approximately 10%. The U.S. government bonds were placed in an irrevocable trust for the sole purpose of servicing the 10-year, 8% bonds. By this process an in-substance defeasance transaction was created, because the trust assets are sufficient to meet the bond's interest and principal obligations as they come due.

Investment in U.S. Government Bonds	9,228	
Cash		9,288
Bonds Payable	10,000	
Investment in U.S. Government Bonds		9,228
Extraordinary Gain—Bond Extinguishment		772

LONG-TERM NOTES PAYABLE

Differentiate between long-term notes and bonds.

Long-term notes payable also are used as a source of capital. The accounting and conceptual issues for long-term notes are essentially the same as those for bonds. However, the following differences exist:

1. Notes normally are issued for a shorter period than bonds.
2. Notes may or may not have annual interest payments.
3. Notes frequently are placed with a single lender.
4. Notes, while negotiable, are not normally traded on the open market (with the exception of U.S. Treasury notes).
5. Notes normally are used to raise smaller amounts of capital than bond issues.
6. Small companies sometimes find it easier and more efficient to obtain long-term loans through the issuance of notes than bonds.

NOTES ISSUED FOR CASH

Normally the interest rate is set by the lender and agreed to by the borrower before the note is issued. Therefore, the face amount and the present value of a note equal the cash received. Some lenders, however, provide funds through the use of so-called **noninterest-bearing notes**. Despite their name, these loans are in fact interest-bearing if the proceeds received are less than the face amount of the note. Conceptually, this type of debt is the same as bonds issued at a discount. Accounting for noninterest-bearing notes payable was discussed in Chapter 11 and is not repeated here.

NOTES IN PARTIAL CASH TRANSACTIONS

Notes payable can be issued for other consideration in addition to the cash received. The other consideration can be tangible or intangible assets. Exchanges for tangible assets other than cash are discussed in the next section. Of concern here is the recognition of rights received in lieu of cash assets and the proper valuation of the liability. Assume that Smith Company needs cash. In lieu of paying interest in cash, Smith agrees to provide favorable purchase terms, up to the amount of the loan, for the life of the loan to the lender. Clearly, the borrower, through such an agreement, is paying for the use of the money through foregone profits from the sales. The foregone profits, unearned revenue, are assumed to be equal to the discount based upon the incremental borrowing rate. Exhibit 14–7 contains the details of the agreement, the determination of the interest expense, and the journal entries for the transaction.

NOTES IN NONCASH TRANSACTIONS

Notes payable are often given in exchange for noncash assets. In such instances the amount of the debt is determined by the fair market value of the assets received less the fair market value of any assets surrendered. Assume that B&B acquires land and a building with fair market values of $20,000 for the land and $75,000 for the building. In return for these assets, B&B gives a down payment

EXHIBIT 14–7
Notes Issued with Other Rights

The Jones Corporation agrees to lend Smith Inc., a supplier, $400,000 for a period of two years. Smith signs a two-year noninterest-bearing $400,000 promissory note payable to Jones. The note includes an agreement to provide Jones, over the 2-year period, up to $400,000 of purchases at reduced prices. Smith's incremental borrowing rate is 12%.

The present value of the debt is determined using a discount rate of 12%, Smith's incremental rate. The present value of the note is subtracted from the face amount to determine the discount.

(1) PV of Note = $400,000 × .7972 = $318,880
(2) Discount = Face Value of Note − PV of Note
Discount = $400,000 − $318,880
= $81,120

The interest expense and amortization of the discount are determined by using the effective-interest method.

(3) Interest Expense = Book Value × Interest Rate
Interest Expense = ($400,000 − $81,120) × .12
Interest Expense = $38,266

The delayed revenue should be recognized when the discounted sales are made to the lender. Assume that $300,000 of purchases were made by Jones during 1995, which is 75 percent of the allowed discounted purchases.

$$(4)\ \text{Sales Recognized} = \text{Unearned Revenue} \times \frac{\text{Current Discounted Purchases}}{\text{Total Allowed}}$$

$$= \$81{,}120 \times \frac{\$300{,}000}{\$400{,}000}$$

$$= \$60{,}840$$

(*continued*)

EXHIBIT 14–7
(Concluded)

Smith's Books

1997			
Jan. 1	Cash	400,000	
	Discount on Note Payable	81,120	
	Note Payable		400,000
	Unearned Revenue		81,120
Dec. 31	Interest Expense	38,266*	
	Discount on Note Payable		38,266
	*($400,000 − $81,120) × .12		
	Unearned Revenue	60,840*	
	Sales		60,840
	*$81,120 × $300,000/$400,000		

CONCEPT

Proper recognition and classification of expenses and revenues for reporting purposes—Notes payable are valued at present value; revenues are recognized when earned; expenses are matched against the revenues generated.

LOGIC

The face amount of the note equals the present value of the debt. The interest rate, while unstated, is assumed equal to the firm's incremental borrowing rate. Since purchase discounts are given for the use of the borrowed funds in lieu of interest payments, the discounted interest is used to determine the present value of the future revenues surrendered for interest payments.

of a 1976, XJ6 Jaguar that has a fair market value of $10,000, and a three-year, 8% promissory note for the remaining $85,000, with interest payable annually. The Jaguar has a book value of $15,000. B&B's entry to record this transaction is as follows:

Land	20,000	
Building	75,000	
Loss on the Exchange*	5,000	
Note Payable		85,000
Jaguar		15,000
*$10,000 − 15,000		

CONCEPT

Valuation of a liability.

LOGIC

Notes payable are valued at the present value of the future cash payments necessary to satisfy the obligation. The interest rate is stated and agreed to by both parties in a normal transaction. Therefore, the face value of the note is assumed equal to its present value.

IMPUTING INTEREST

Interest must be *imputed* whenever the face amount of the note is substantially different from the fair market value of the assets received. This situation frequently occurs when noninterest-bearing notes payable are given in exchange for the assets received. For example, assume that the three-year note in the preceding illustration does not state an interest rate, and the amount of the note is $107,080. To value the note at its present value, the interest rate that is implicit in the terms of the contract must be determined.

One method of finding the interest rate is to find the ratio of the face amount of the note to the present value of the liability. The fair market value of the assets received less the fair market value of the assets given represents the present value of the liability, that is, $85,000. Dividing this amount into the face amount of the note ($107,080/$85,000), yields a factor of 1.2597. Since this is the ratio of the future amount to the present amount, Table A–1 in Appendix A can be used by scanning across row 3. The factor appears in the 8% column, which is the implicit rate of the contract.

Another method that provides the same implicit interest rate is to find the ratio of the present value of the liability to the face amount of the note (85,000/107,080).[6] Table A–2, "Present Value of 1," is used to find the 8% interest rate that is implicit in the contract if this approach is used.

The journal entry to record this transaction is

Land	20,000	
Building	75,000	
Loss on the Exchange	5,000	
Discount on Note Payable	22,080*	
Note Payable		107,080*
Jaguar		15,000

**$107,080 − $22,080 = $85,000, the PV of the debt*

Valuation of assets and liabilities.

LOGIC

Notes payable are valued at their present value and assets are valued at fair market. The fair market values of the assets are known; therefore, the present value of the liability cannot be equal to the face amount of the note. In such cases the unstated but implied interest rate must be imputed. This implicit rate is used to determine the amount of the discount on the note. The book value of the note is then equal to the present value of the debt.

APPENDIX: TROUBLED DEBT RESTRUCTURING

There are times when the obligation of a loan cannot be met by the debtor. In this event, the debtor defaults on the obligation, and the creditor is faced with unpleasant choices: (1) the creditor may agree to settle the claim immediately for less than the original debt, or (2) the debtor and creditor may agree to continue the debt with a modification of the original terms of the loan agreement. The

[6]This is just the inverse of the first method.

creditor might choose the first option if the creditor believes that early settlement will provide more benefit than protracted legal proceedings or trying to make an arrangement involving a modification of the terms of the original agreement.

IMMEDIATE SETTLEMENT AT LESS THAN FACE VALUE

As an illustration, assume that the note in Exhibit 14–7 for $400,000 matures, and Smith Inc. has insufficient cash to pay the note. Jones Corporation agrees to accept $350,000 in cash and a parcel of land with a fair market value of $40,000 in full settlement of the claim. The book value of the land is $30,000. Smith Inc., the debtor, recognizes two gains of $10,000 each: $10,000 for the increase in the value of the property since acquisition ($40,000 − $30,000) and $10,000 as an extraordinary gain in settling the claim for less than the full amount ($400,000 − $390,000).

The entry for Smith to record the settlement is

1999			
Dec. 31	Note Payable	400,000	
	Gain on Sale of Land		10,000
	Extraordinary Gain—Extinguishment of Debt		10,000
	Land		30,000
	Cash		350,000

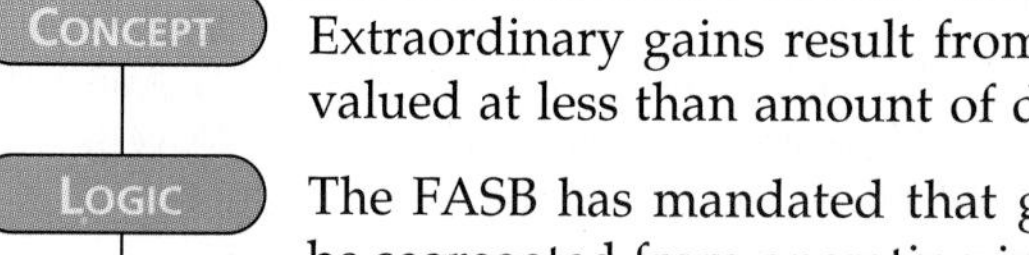

CONCEPT Extraordinary gains result from extinguishment of debt with assets valued at less than amount of debt.

LOGIC The FASB has mandated that gains from these transactions should be segregated from operating income and reported as extraordinary.

Note that a gain is also recognized on the exchange of the property, since its current market value is higher than the carrying value on the company's books. The assumption is that the asset could have been sold for cash and the funds used to reduce the debt. The creditor, however, preferred to receive the property.

The creditor, Jones, records a bad debts expense for the difference between the fair value received and the face value of the asset. The entry for Jones is

Cash	350,000	
Land	40,000	
Bad Debts Expense*	10,000	
Note Receivable		400,000

*Or Allowance for Bad Debts

MODIFICATION OF TERMS

In a troubled debt restructure with a modification of the original terms of the loan agreement, the provisions of SFAS No. 15 still apply to the debtor. Following the prescriptions of SFAS No. 15, debtors recognize extraordinary gains for the difference between the settlement amount and the amount owed.

On the creditor's side of the same transaction, SFAS No. 114 applies for financial statements for fiscal years beginning after December 15, 1994. For the creditor, SFAS Nos. 5 and 15 were amended and superseded by SFAS No. 114 with one exception: loans that were restructured with a modification of terms prior to the effective date of SFAS No. 114. For loans restructured prior to the effective date, "a creditor may continue to account for the loan in accordance with the provisions of Statement 15 prior to its amendment by this Statement.[7]

The FASB recognized that SFAS No. 114 introduced an inconsistency between creditors' and debtors' accounting for troubled debt restructuring with modification of terms. However, the FASB elected to issue SFAS No. 114 without addressing the debtors' side so as not to delay its issuance.

The inconsistency arises from the manner in which the gains are reported by the debtor compared to the manner in which losses are reported by the creditor in the same transaction. On the debtor's books, the gains follow the prescriptions of SFAS Nos. 5 and 15, and are reported as extraordinary gains. On the creditor's books, however, losses resulting from impairment recognition are reported as adjustments to bad debts expense instead of extraordinary items. For the creditor, subsequent changes in expected present values of future cash flows are recognized either as interest income (if attributable to the passage of time), or as bad debts expense (if attributable to changes in the amount or timing of the future cash flows).

Lenders at times will agree to modification of terms rather than foreclosing or taking legal action on debt that is due. The debtor recognizes a gain if the future cash flows of the assets surrendered is less than the book value of the debt before restructuring. However, if the future cash flows or equivalents are equal to or greater than the book value of the debt after restructuring, a new rate of interest[8] is assumed to be associated with the debt, even if it is unstated.

To illustrate, assume that the previous note by Smith to Jones for $400,000 is restructured at maturity and a new note is given to Jones instead of paying the debt. The new note is a noninterest-bearing note for $432,640 due in two years. If the future cash flows are equal to or greater than the book value of the debt prior to restructuring, no gain is recognized by the debtor. The entry to record this transaction is

1999			
Dec. 31	Note Payable to Jones—Old	400,000	
	Discount on Note Payable to Jones—New	32,640	
	Note Payable to Jones—New		432,640

CONCEPT No gain to debtor results from extinguishment of debt by restructuring in which future cash flows are equal to or greater than book value of debt prior to restructuring.

LOGIC SFAS No. 15, paragraph 16, does not require the reporting of gains or losses on troubled debt restructuring if future cash flows exceed the carrying value of the debt prior to restructuring.

[7]SFAS No. 114, "Accounting by Creditors for Impairment of a Loan," FASB, May 1993, par. 27.
[8]The creditor uses the effective rate of interest determined at the original issue date (SFAS No. 114).

SFAS No. 15 explains that the restructuring "affects primarily the effective interest rate and results in no loss as long as the effective rate does not fall below zero.[9] Therefore, using backhanded logic, if there is no loss to the creditor, then it follows that there is no gain to the debtor. The new effective interest rate is the same effective rate resulting from the restructuring (which is the rate that the debtor is still required to use), not the original effective rate at issuance. Jones, the creditor, must follow the prescriptions of SFAS No. 114 for this transaction. SFAS No. 114 requires that the creditor use the effective rate of interest from the original issue date to determine the value of the note. For this note, the effective rate of interest at the original issue date was 12%; therefore, the present value of the new note is computed at 12% for two years ($432,640 × .7972 = $344,900). The discount is the difference between the face value and the present value ($432,640 − $344,900 = $87,740). The journal entry for Jones is

Notes Receivable—New	432,640	
Bad Debts—Expense*	55,100	
Notes Receivable—Old		400,000
Discount on Notes Receivable—New		87,740

**Or Allowance for Bad Debts*

Given the recent position of the board in SFAS No. 114 (which specifically excluded the debtor), requiring the creditor to use the original effective interest rate determined at the time of the original loan, it will be interesting to see the board's position when (if?) a new pronouncement is made on this issue for the debtor side of this type of transaction.

APPENDIX: SERIAL BONDS

Bond issues in which portions of the issue mature at different dates are known as *serial bonds*. Investors may prefer different maturity dates for their investment, and the debtor has a schedule for retirement of the debt. The simplest way to view serial bonds is to think of them as separate issues by maturity date and treat each maturing portion as a separate issue. At the issue date, the bonds are recorded in the same manner as other bonds. A premium or discount is recognized for any difference between the proceeds and the face amount of the bonds.

Exhibit 14–8 contains the information relative to a serial-bond issue. The original entry is the same as any bond issue. If the bonds sell at more or less than par, a premium or discount is recorded for the difference. The amortization of the premium or discount is discussed in the next section.

AMORTIZATION OF SERIAL-BOND ISSUES

There are three generally recognized methods of amortization: straight-line, bonds-outstanding, and effective-interest.

Straight-Line Method. The straight-line method can be used only if the difference between the effective-interest method and the straight-line method is not material. Exhibit 14–9 contains an illustration of the straight-line method of amortization for the serial bonds issued in Exhibit 14–8.

[9]SFAS No. 15, par. 148.

EXHIBIT 14–8
Serial-Bond Computations

Assume that Lexington Inc. issues $300,000 of 8% bonds on January 1, 1997, with $100,000 maturing at the end of each successive year. The first $100,000 matures on December 31, 1997. In most bond issues, the longer the maturity date is from the issue date, the greater the required interest rate because of the increase in the perceived risk of nonpayment.

The amounts received for each maturity portion with the effective rate of interest for each follow:

MATURITY DATE	STATED FACE AMOUNT	STATED RATE OF INTEREST	EFFECTIVE RATE OF INTEREST	PROCEEDS RECEIVED	DISCOUNT
12/31/97	$100,000	8%	8%	$100,000	$ 0
12/31/98	100,000	8%	10%	96,524 (1)	3,476
12/31/99	100,000	8%	12%	90,394 (2)	9,606
Totals	$300,000			$286,918	$13,082

(1) 100,000 × .8264 = $82,640	PV of $100,000 discounted at 10% for two years
8,000 × 1.7355 = 13,884	PV of an $8,000 annuity discount at 10% for two years
Proceeds = $96,524	

(2) 100,000 × .7118 = $71,180	PV of $100,000 discounted at 12% for three years
8,000 × 2.4018 = 19,214	PV of an $8,000 annuity discount at 12% for three years
Proceeds = $90,394	

Journal entry to record issue:

1997			
Jan. 1	Cash	286,918	
	Discount on Bonds Payable	13,082	
	Bonds Payable		300,000

The straight-line method assumes that the premium or discount is known for bonds sold by each maturity date. Frequently the sales transactions are handled by brokers, so the total net premium or discount is all that is known. In such cases an average straight-line method would be used. The total discount of $13,082 would be amortized over three years, resulting in $4,361 per year.

Bonds-Outstanding Method. Exhibit 14–10 illustrates the **bonds-outstanding method** and includes the subsequent entries assuming that each portion of the bond issue is paid at maturity. The amortization amount each year is a percentage of the total premium or discount. The percentage used is the ratio of the total bonds outstanding in that year divided by the cumulative total bonds outstanding during the entire life of the bond issue. In the example in Exhibit 14–10, the total bonds outstanding in each year are:

1997	300,000
1998	200,000
1999	100,000

EXHIBIT 14–9
Serial-Bond Discount Amortized with Straight-Line Method

MATURITY DATE	FACE AMOUNT	DISCOUNT	YEARS TO MATURITY	STRAIGHT-LINE AMORTIZATION (DISCOUNT DIVIDED BY YEARS)
12/31/97	$100,000	$ 0	1	$ 0
12/31/98	100,000	3,476	2	1,738
12/31/99	100,000	9,606	3	3,202
Totals	$300,000	$13,082		$4,940

		Debit	Credit
1997			
Dec. 31	Interest Expense	28,940	
	Discount on Bonds Payable ($1,738 + $3,202)		4,940
	Cash ($300,000 × .08)		24,000
	Bonds Payable	100,000	
	Cash		100,000
1998			
Dec. 31	Interest Expense	20,940	
	Discount on Bonds Payable		4,940
	Cash ($200,000 × .08)		16,000
	Bonds Payable	100,000	
	Cash		100,000
1999			
Dec. 31	Interest Expense	11,202	
	Discount on Bonds Payable		3,202
	Cash ($100,000 × .08)		8,000
	Bonds Payable	100,000	
	Cash		100,000

The cumulative total is $600,000 and is the denominator for the ratio each year.

In this method, because the earliest years have the greatest weights, those years receive a greater amount of amortization. In this example, the bonds that mature first were sold at par and had zero discount, and yet they increase the relative portion of discount recognized the first year.

Effective-Interest Method. The effective-interest method is illustrated in Exhibit 14–11. This illustration assumes that the average rate of interest is 10.57%. This blended rate is a weighted average of interest for all bonds in the issue.[10]

REDEMPTION BEFORE MATURITY

If serial bonds are redeemed prior to the maturity date, the amortization and interest are brought up to date for the redeemed bonds. Any difference between

[10]The effective rate of 10.57% is found by discounting the cash flows from the bond issue. The present value of the future cash flows is $286,918, the issue price. Therefore,

$$\begin{aligned} \$286{,}918 &= (\text{PV } 100{,}000 \text{ @ } x\%, \text{1st } n + 8{,}000 \text{ @ } x\%, 1n) + \\ &\quad (\text{PV } 100{,}000 \text{ @ } x\%, \text{2nd } n + 8{,}000 \text{ @ } x\%, 2n) + \\ &\quad (\text{PV } 100{,}000 \text{ @ } x\%, \text{3rd } n + 8{,}000 \text{ @ } x\%, 3n) \\ x\% &= 10.57\% \end{aligned}$$

EXHIBIT 14–10
Serial-Bond Discount Amortized with Bonds-Outstanding Method

MATURITY DATE	FACE AMOUNT	DISCOUNT	TOTAL BONDS OUTSTANDING DURING YEAR	RATIO OF BONDS OUTSTANDING DURING YEAR TO TOTAL	YEARLY FRACTION OF TOTAL DISCOUNT AMORTIZED
12/31/97	$100,000	$ 0	$300,000	(300/600 × $13,082)	$ 6,541
12/31/98	100,000	3,476	200,000	(200/600 × $13,082)	4,361
12/31/99	100,000	9,606	100,000	(100/600 × $13,082)	2,180
Totals	$300,000	$13,082	$600,000		$13,082

1997			
Dec. 31	Interest Expense	30,541	
	Discount on Bonds Payable		6,541
	Cash ($300,000 × .08)		24,000
	Bonds Payable	100,000	
	Cash		100,000
1998			
Dec. 31	Interest Expense	20,361	
	Discount on Bonds Payable		4,361
	Cash ($200,000 × .08)		16,000
	Bonds Payable	100,000	
	Cash		100,000
1999			
Dec. 31	Interest Expense	10,180	
	Discount on Bonds Payable		2,180
	Cash ($100,000 × .08)		8,000
	Bonds Payable	100,000	
	Cash		100,000

the current book value and the price paid to redeem the bonds is treated as an extraordinary gain or loss. The method used to accrue the interest for the redeemed bonds is a function of the method being used to amortize the discount (premium). The straight-line method is identical to the illustration in Exhibit 14–9, so we will turn to the other two methods.

Bonds-Outstanding Method. The amount of unamortized discount (premium) associated with a bond that is amortized by the bonds outstanding method can be determined by the following formula:

$$\frac{\text{Number of Years Remaining to Maturity} \times \text{Par Value of Redeemed Bonds} \times \text{Total Discount (Premium)}}{\text{Total Cumulative Value of Outstanding Bonds}}$$

The total cumulative value refers to the bonds outstanding at the end of each year. In this example, prior to the serial retirements, there are $300,000 at

EXHIBIT 14–11
Serial-Bond Discount Amortized with Average-Effective-Interest Method

DATE	INTEREST EXPENSE AT 10.57% OF PREVIOUS BOOK VALUE	CASH PAID FOR INTEREST	DISCOUNT AMORTIZED	CASH PAID FOR BOND RETIREMENT	BOOK VALUE OF BONDS
01/01/97					$286,918
12/31/97	30,327	$24,000	$ 6,327	$100,000	193,245
12/31/98	20,426	16,000	4,426	100,000	97,671
12/31/99	10,329	8,000	2,329*	100,000	0
Totals		$48,000	$13,082	$300,000	

*Plug

1997			
Dec. 31	Interest Expense	30,327*	
	Discount on Bonds Payable		6,327
	Cash		24,000
	**$286,918 × 10.57% = $30,327)*		
	Bonds Payable	100,000	
	Cash		100,000
1998			
Dec. 31	Interest Expense	20,426*	
	Discount on Bonds Payable		4,426
	Cash		16,000
	**$193,245 × 10.57% = $20,426*		
	Bonds Payable	100,000	
	Cash		100,000
1999			
Dec. 31	Interest Expense	10,329*	
	Discount on Bonds Payable		2,329
	Cash		8,000
	**$97,671 × 10.57% = $10,329* (Note that $10,329 includes a $5 rounding difference.)		
	Bonds Payable	100,000	
	Cash		100,000

December 31, 1997, $200,000 at December 31, 1998, and $100,000 at December 31, 1999. This represents a cumulative total of $600,000. Suppose that $50,000 of bonds that mature on December 31, 1999, are acquired for $51,000 on January 1, 1998. This is two years prior to maturity, and $2,180 of unamortized discount associated with the redeemed bonds should be written off:

$$\frac{2 \times \$50{,}000 \times \$13{,}082}{\$600{,}000}$$

Each year $1,090 (50/600 of the total discount of $13,082) is amortized for the $50,000 of bonds redeemed. For the two remaining years $2,180 is unamortized. The entry to record the redemption in this case is:

1998			
Jan. 1	Bonds Payable	50,000	
	Extraordinary Loss on Bond Redemption	3,180	
	Discount on Bonds Payable		2,180
	Cash		51,000

Effective-Interest Method. Under the effective-interest method, the average interest rate is used to determine the present value of the bonds that are redeemed. The difference between the PV of the bonds and par is the unamortized discount. In our example, the average rate is 10.57%.

PV of $50,000 discounted at 10.57% for two years = 50,000 × .8179 =	$40,895
PV of a $4,000 annuity discounted at 10.57% for two years = 4,000 × 1.7224 =	6,890
Total PV	$47,785

The extraordinary loss is $3,215 ($51,000 − $47,785), and the discount to be written off is $2,215 ($50,000 − $47,785). The journal entry follows:

1998			
Jan. 1	Bonds Payable	50,000	
	Extraordinary Loss on Bond Redemption	3,215	
	Discount on Bonds Payable		2,215
	Cash		51,000

APPENDIX: CASH FLOWS

Long-term bonds payable affect cash flows at the date of issue, throughout the period the bonds are outstanding, and at the time the bonds are retired. The affects of bonds on the statement of cash flows are summarized below:

I. Bonds Sold for Cash
   A. At Issuance, a financing activity for cash inflow equal to sales price of bonds.
   B. Bond Issue Costs—Cash outflows from investing activity if Unamortized Bond Issue Costs debited
      1. Ongoing: Cash Flow from Operations:
         a. Direct Method: No amortization of issue costs
         b. Indirect Method: Adjust net income (add back bond issue costs amortized).

II. Periodic Interest Payments:
   A. Cash Outflow from operations:
      1. Cash Paid for Interest:
         a. Direct Method: Interest Expense plus Premium (minus discount) amortized, plus decrease (minus increase) in Interest Payable
         b. Indirect Method: Adjust net income:
            —Add discount (subtract premium) amortized
            —Add increase (subtract decrease) in Interest Payable

III. Extinguishment of Debt-Retirement at Maturity:
   —Financing Activity: Outflow Equal to Par Value

IV. Early Extinguishment: Repurchases, Calls, Redemptions:
   A. Bring debt to book value as an operating item
   B. Financing Activity: Outflow for purchase, call, or redemption price
   C. Cash Flow from Operations:
      1. Direct Method: Ignore extraordinary gain/loss*
      2. Indirect Method: Adjust net income
         —Add total extraordinary loss (subtract gain)*

V. Conversion of Debt
   A. Book Value Method: Noncash financing activity for the book value of the debt on the date of conversion.
   B. Market Value Method: Noncash financing activity for the book value of the debt on the date of conversion.
   C. Cash Flow from Operations: Gain/loss for the difference between book value of debt and FMV of the stock.
      1. Direct Method: Ignore gain/loss
      2. Indirect Method: Adjust net income
         —Add total loss (subtract gain).

*Extraordinary gains and losses are shown Net of the Tax Effect. The adjustment is for the total gain/loss before tax effects. However, the tax effect must be considered in both the direct and indirect methods when computing cash paid for income taxes.
Source: Used with permission of Mary A. Flanigan.

END-OF-CHAPTER REVIEW

SUMMARY

1. **Demonstrate the impact of financial leverage on profitability and solvency.** Financial leverage is the relative mix of debt and equity funds in the capital structure. Firms with large amounts of debt show dramatic increases in profitability as earnings increase, and decreases when earnings decrease. The amount of risk is directly related to the degree of financial leverage. Firms with stable revenues can use a higher degree of financial leverage than firms with widely fluctuating revenues.

2. **Demonstrate how bond premiums and discounts are related to the interest rate stated on the face of the bond.** Bonds may sell at more or less than the face amount of the instrument. These premiums or discounts are adjustments to the stated rate of interest and reflect the market's assessment of the risk associated with a bond issue.

3. **Amortize premiums and discounts using the effective-interest and straight-line methods.** Both premiums and discounts are amortized to reflect the proper amount of interest expense for the period. The amount of amortization is a function of the method used. The amount amortized under the effective-interest method is the difference between the cash interest paid and the effective interest charged to income per interest period. The effective-interest amortization method is required unless the difference between the two methods is not material.
4. **Account for bonds issued between interest dates.** Accounting for bonds sold or reacquired at other than interest dates requires that interest be accrued up to the transaction date. Any discount or premium also must be amortized for the fractional period of time elapsed.
5. **Account for early redemption of debt, and explain the rationale for treating gains and losses as extraordinary.** Reacquisitions of bonds for less or more than the book value results in an extraordinary gain or loss because the FASB has deemed it proper. The FASB rationale is that these gains and losses do not belong in operating income. This treatment also reduces a potential income manipulation opportunity for management in which losses could be reported as extraordinary and gains as ordinary if left to their discretion.
6. **Understand the accounting issues associated with convertible bonds and bonds issued with detachable warrants.** Some bonds have equity rights. They are either convertible into common stock, or detachable warrants are issued with the bond entitling the holder to acquire common stock at a fixed price for a limited time. Upon conversion of convertible bonds into equity securities, the book-value method or the market value method is used for recording the transfer. When bonds are sold with detachable warrants, the relative market value method is used to allocate the proceeds to the debt and warrants.
7. **Differentiate between long-term notes and bonds.** Notes payable have most of the same accounting requirements as bonds but are simpler. So called noninterest-bearing notes issued for more than the proceeds received contain hidden interest. An imputed interest rate is determined and is used to amortize the discount in the same fashion that the effective-interest method is used for bonds.

KEY TERMS

average rate of interest *764*
bond payable *737*
bond issue costs *737*
*bonds-outstanding method *763*
book value method *751*
callable bonds *738*
convertible bonds *738*
debenture bonds *738*
debt-to-equity ratio *736*
defeasance of debt *755*
discount (on bonds) *740*
effective-interest method *742*
financial leverage *734*
induced conversions *753*
interest *738*
in-substance defeasance of debt *755*
long-term debt *737*
market value method *751*
mortgage bond *738*
noninterest-bearing notes *756*
premium *744*
restrictive covenants *737*
*serial bonds *737*
sinking fund *738*
solvency *736*
stated interest rate *737*
stock warrants *754*
straight-line amortization *743*
times-interest-earned ratio *736*

*Refers to material in chapter appendix.

ASSIGNMENT MATERIAL

CASES

C14–1 Comparative Analysis Class Presentation—Group Assignment
According to GAAP, bond-issue costs should be deferred and amortized over the life of the bond issue. However, such deferred costs do not meet the definition of an asset as presented in the concepts statements. Assume that the concepts statements are GAAP and that the bond-issue costs should be netted against the proceeds of the bond issue.

Required: Develop an illustration showing that if the bond-issue costs are amortized using the same method as the premium or discount, the effect on net income is the same.

C14–2 Decision Analysis—Communication
Your company needs cash for planned capital expansion. The company has been very profitable in the past. Based upon the best estimates available from independent sources, the planned expansion should cost $15 million and take two years to complete. The expansion should pay for itself in the next five years, after which a 15% net return on the invested capital for the next 15 years is expected. An investment banker has agreed to underwrite a $16 million bond issue for $1 million cost in which interest is paid annually. The bonds would have a 20-year life at an anticipated 8% interest rate. As an alternative, your bank has agreed to provide a long-term loan of up to $15 million at 10% interest paid annually. The maturity date of the note would be seven years. As controller of the corporation, you have been asked to provide a recommendation.

Required: Prepare a report containing your recommendation with supporting reasons.

C14–3 Decision Analysis—Financing Strategy
Your firm is considering alternative sources of capital for planned expansion. At the present time, the company does not have any long-term debt and is trying to decide whether to borrow the money on a long-term basis or to raise the funds through equity securities. An abbreviated balance sheet is as follows:

BALANCE SHEET
December 31, 1997

Current assets	$ 100,000	
Noncurrent assets	3,000,000	
Total assets		$3,100,000
Current liabilities		$ 46,000
Common stock		
($5 par 100,000 shares issued)	$ 500,000	
Paid-in capital in excess of par	500,000	
Retained earnings	2,054,000	
Total stockholders' equity		3,054,000
Total liabilities and stockholders' equity		$3,100,000

The funds required for the expansion amount to $2,000,000. The president currently owns 60 percent of the stock and wants to maintain control of the firm. The president, however, does not want to invest more than an additional $400,000 in the firm but does want to expand operations. The current market price of the stock is $50 per share. The company is currently earning approximately 12% on the invested capital, and the anticipated cost of borrowed funds is 10%. You estimate that the new investment will return 15% before interest charges.

Required: After analyzing this information, what do you recommend as a financing strategy to meet the objective and yet also meet the ownership constraint?

C14–4 Decision Analysis—Alternative Evaluation

Oldnew Inc. has a long-term debt of $500,000 due currently and does not have the resources to pay the debt in cash. The lender suggests two alternatives to extinguish the obligation. The first is to issue 20,000 shares of common stock to the lender. The second is to cancel the old note in consideration of a new note for $600,000 due in two years. An abbreviated balance sheet follows:

BALANCE SHEET
December 31, 1997

Assets	
Current assets	$ 400,000
Noncurrent assets	4,000,000
Total assets	$4,400,000
Liabilities	
Current liabilities	$ 150,000
Long-term debt ($500,000 due currently)	1,500,000
	$1,650,000
Stockholders' Equity	
Common stock ($5 par 100,000 shares issued)	$ 500,000
Paid-in capital in excess of par	500,000
Retained earnings	1,750,000
Total stockholders' equity	$2,750,000
Total liabilities and stockholders' equity	$4,400,000

Oldnew Inc.'s other long-term debt of $1,000,000 is due in two years. Oldnew would like to renew that note with the lender for another 3-year term.

Required: Prepare a balance sheet for Oldnew under both conditions, and make a recommendation as to which alternative would enhance the likelihood that the $1,000,000 note would be extended.

QUESTIONS

Q14–1 How is financial leverage related to profitability?

Q14–2 How is financial leverage related to risk?

Q14–3 How would restrictive covenants on bonds affect management strategy and options?

Q14–4 Explain the difference between a debenture and a mortgage bond.

Q14–5 What is a callable bond?

Q14–6 Why would bonds be called prior to maturity?

Q14–7 What determines the market value of any bond issue?

Q14–8 How are premiums and discounts related to the stated or coupon rate of interest?

Q14–9 If bonds are sold between interest dates, what happens to the interest on the bonds?

Q14–10 Suppose that bond-issue costs are material; suggest some alternative ways to account for them.

Q14–11 Why is the effective-interest method of amortizing bond premiums (discounts) preferred to the straight-line method?

Q14–12 What are four ways that bond debt can be extinguished?

Q14–13 Why does early extinguishment of long-term debt result in an extraordinary gain or loss?

Q14–14 What are convertible bonds? What are the accounting requirements at issue? At conversion?

Q14–15 What are warrants? What are the accounting requirements for bonds issued with detachable warrants?

Q14–16 Explain why companies may want to induce conversions of convertible bonds.

Q14–17 What is defeasance of debt? What is in-substance defeasance?

Q14–18 Explain what is meant by so-called noninterest-bearing, long-term notes.

Q14–19 What does imputed interest mean in relation to notes?

***Q14–20** What adjustment to net income is needed for bond interest expense in order to determine cash flow from operations?

Q14–21 What is a zero coupon bond? How is a zero coupon bond similar to a non-interest-bearing note?

***Q14–22** If the future cash flows exceed the book value of debt prior to restructuring, how is the restructuring accounted for, and why?

***Q14–23** What is the purpose of issuing serial bonds?

EXERCISES

E14–1 Bond-Price Determination

Assume the following:

1. A 5-year, 8%, $20,000 bond paying interest semiannually is sold to yield 10% interest.
2. A 5-year, 8%, $20,000 bond paying interest semiannually is sold to yield 6% interest.

Required:

A. Determine the selling price for each condition.

B. Why would a company sell an 8% bond to yield 10%, a higher rate of interest?

*Refers to material in chapter appendix.

E14–2 Bond-Price Determination

Assume the following:

1. A 5-year, 10%, $20,000 bond paying interest semiannually is sold to yield 8% interest.
2. A 5-year, 10%, $20,000 bond paying interest semiannually is sold to yield 12% interest.

Required:

A. Determine the selling price for each condition.
B. Why would an investor invest in 10% bonds that are priced to yield 8%, a lower interest rate?

E14–3 Bonds Sold at Premium on Interest Date

Jones Company sold to Smith Company $40,000 of 5-year, 10% bonds at 103⅛.The interest is paid semiannually on June 30 and December 31. The bonds are dated January 1, 1997—the date of the sale.

Required: Prepare journal entries for the first complete year, assuming straight-line method of amortization is used.

E14–4 Bonds Sold at Premium on Interest Date

Jones Company sold to Smith Company $40,000 of 5-year, 8% bonds for a price of $42,100. The interest is paid semiannually on March 1 and September 1. The bonds are dated March 1, 1997—the date of the sale. Assume that the bonds were issued to yield 7%.

Required:

A. Prepare journal entries for first complete year, assuming the straight-line method of amortization is used.
B. Prepare journal entries for first complete year, assuming effective-interest method of amortization is used.
C. Why would an investor pay more than face value (a premium) to invest in a bond?

E14–5 Bonds Sold at Premium between Interest Dates

Jones Company sold to Smith Company $40,000 of 5-year, 10% bonds for $43,246 plus accrued interest. The interest is paid semiannually on June 30 and December 31. The bonds are dated January 1, 1997. The date of the sale is March 1, 1997. Assume that the bonds are issued to yield 8%.

Required: Prepare journal entries for 1997, assuming effective-interest method of amortization is used.

E14–6 Bonds Sold at Premium between Interest Dates

Jones Company sold to Smith Company $40,000 of 5-year, 8% bonds at 105 plus accrued interest. The interest is paid semiannually on March 1 and September 1. The bonds are dated March 1, 1997. The date of the sale is June 1, 1997.

Required: Prepare journal entries for 1997, assuming straight-line method of amortization is used.

E14–7 Bonds Sold at Discount on Interest Date

Jones Company sold to Smith Company $40,000 of 5-year, 10% bonds at 97⅛. The interest is paid semiannually on June 30 and December 31. The bonds are dated January 1, 1997—the date of the sale.

Required:

A. Prepare journal entries for 1997, assuming straight-line method of amortization is used.

B. Why would a bond issuer choose to issue bonds below their face value (a discount)?

E14–8 Bonds Sold at Discount on Interest Date

Jones Company sold to Smith Company $40,000 of 5-year, 8% bonds for $36,911. The interest is paid semiannually on March 1 and September 1. The bonds are dated March 1, 1997—the date of the sale.

Required:

A. Calculate the effective rate of interest.

B. Prepare journal entries for 1997, assuming effective-interest method of amortization is used.

E14–9 Bonds Sold at Discount between Interest Dates

Jones Company issued to Smith Company $40,000 of 5-year, 10% bonds at 92.64% of par plus accrued interest. The interest is paid semiannually on June 30 and December 31. The bonds are dated January 1, 1997. The date of the sale is March 1, 1997. Assume the bonds were issued to yield 12%.

Required: Prepare journal entries for 1997, assuming effective-interest method of amortization is used.

E14–10 Bonds Sold at Discount between Interest Dates

Jones Company sold to Smith Company $40,000 of 5-year, 8% bonds at 98¼ plus accrued interest. The interest is paid semiannually on March 1 and September 1. The bonds are dated March 1, 1997. The date of the sale is June 1, 1997.

Required: Prepare journal entries for 1997, assuming straight-line method of amortization is used.

*E14–11 Troubled Debt Restructuring

Renfroe Inc. has a long-term 10% note payable due on March 1, 1997 for $20,000 (including interest of $2,000) but does not have sufficient cash to pay the note. Hammer, the lender, agrees to accept $10,000 in cash plus land that has a current market value of $10,000 and is carried on Renfroe's books at $5,000.

Required: Prepare journal entries for both parties.

*E14–12 Troubled Debt Restructuring

Parton Inc. has a long-term 10% note payable due on June 1, 1997 for $50,000 (including interest of $5,000) but does not have sufficient cash to pay the note. Dolly, the lender, agrees to accept $10,000 in cash plus equipment that has a current market value of $40,000 and is carried on Parton's books at $35,000.

Required: Prepare journal entries for both parties.

*Refers to material in chapter appendix.

E14–13 Convertible Bonds

Henry Company issued $1,000,000 of 12%, 10-year convertible bonds for $1,080,000 on January 1, 1997. The conversion ratio is 40 shares of $10 par common stock for each $1,000 of bonds. The interest is paid annually on December 31. Henry Company uses the straight-line method of amortization for premiums and discounts. On November 1, 1999, Henry Company offered a sweetener of two extra shares for each $1,000 of bonds to bondholders that convert by December 31, 1999. The market price of the stock during the sweetener period hovered around $30 per share. Half of the outstanding bonds were converted during this period.

Required:

A. Prepare journal entries to record the conversions, assuming all conversions occurred on December 31, 1999. Use the book value method.

B. Why did Henry Company issue convertible bonds in the first place?

C. Why would the "sweetened" offer convince an investor to convert his or her bonds into stock?

E14–14 Convertible Bonds

Keller Company issued $500,000 of 10%, 10-year convertible bonds for $540,000 on January 1, 1997. The conversion ratio is 40 shares of $10 par common stock for each $1,000 of bonds. The interest is paid annually on December 31. Keller Company uses the straight-line method of amortization for premiums and discounts. On November 1, 1999, Keller Company offered a sweetener of two extra shares for each $1,000 of bonds to bondholders that convert by December 31, 1999. The market price of the stock during the sweetener period hovered around $35 per share. Half of the outstanding bonds were converted during this period.

Required:

A. Prepare journal entries to record the conversions, assuming all conversions occurred on December 31, 1999. Use the book value method.

B. Why did Keller Company issue convertible bonds in the first place?

C. Why would the "sweetened" offer convince an investor to convert his or her bonds into stock?

E14–15 Bond Redemptions

At December 31, 1997, Title Inc. called and redeemed its outstanding bonds. After recording and paying interest, Title Inc. had outstanding bonds in the amount of $500,000, with an unamortized discount of $10,000. The company then called these bonds and redeemed them at 99.

Required: Record the bond redemption.

E14–16 Bond Redemptions

At December 31, 1997, Ashley Company had outstanding 5% bonds in the amount of $300,000, maturing December 31, 2002, with an unamortized discount of $10,000. Interest is paid annually every December 31, and the bonds were issued to yield 6%. On May 1, 1998, the bonds are retired at 96 plus accrued interest.

Required:

A. Record the bond retirement.

B. Regarding these bonds, identify what should be reported on the income statement and statement of cash flows (indirect method) for 1998.

*E14–17 Statement of Cash Flows

Kansas Warehousing, Inc., had the following entries related to its bonds during 1997.

3/1/97	Cash	10,200,000	
	Bonds Payable		10,000,000
	Bond Premium		200,000
	To record bond issuance.		
9/1/97	Interest Expense	459,000	
	Bond Premium	41,000	
	Cash		500,000
	To record semiannual interest payment.		
12/31/97	Interest Expense	305,000	
	Bond Premium	28,333	
	Interest Payable		333,333

Required: Identify how bond-related activities would be reported on a 1997 statement of cash flows for both the direct and indirect methods.

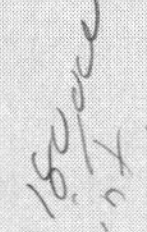

E14–18 Zero Coupon Bonds

On December 31, 1997, Financial Corporation issued $3,000,000 in 20-year, zero coupon bonds maturing December 31, 2017. The bonds were issued to yield 6%.

Required: Prepare journal entries for the bond issuance, interest for three years, and the retirement of the bonds on December 31, 2017.

E14–19 Zero Coupon Bonds

On January 31, 1997, Basic Corporation issued $2,000,000 in 10-year, zero coupon bonds maturing January 31, 2007. The bonds were issued to yield 10%.

Required: Prepare journal entries for the bond issuance, interest for three years, and the retirement of the bonds on January 31, 2007.

PROBLEMS

P14–1 Effective Rate of Interest—Bonds Sold at Premium

Carson Inc. issued $100,000 of 10% bonds paying interest semiannually on June 30 and December 31. The bonds mature five years from the issue date of January 1, 1997. Carson received $108,115 as proceeds from the bond issue.

Required:

A. Determine the effective rate of interest incurred from the bond-issue debt.
B. Prepare an amortization table for the life of the issue.
C. Prepare all the journal entries required for 1997.
D. What effect does the amortization of the premium have on the statement of cash flows for both the direct and indirect methods?

P14–2 Effective Rate of Interest—Bonds Sold at Premium

Freeborn Inc. issued $200,000 of 6% bonds paying interest semiannually on April 1 and October 1. The bonds mature five years from the issue date of April 1, 1997. Freeborn received $217,956 as proceeds from the bond issue. Assume a calendar-year basis.

*Refers to material in chapter appendix.

Required:

A. Determine the effective rate of interest on the bond issue.
B. Prepare an amortization table for the life of the issue.
C. Prepare the journal entries for 1997.

P14–3 Effective Rate of Interest—Bonds Sold at Discount

Jason Company issued $100,000 of 10% bonds paying interest semiannually on June 30 and December 31. The bonds mature five years from the issue date of January 1, 1997. Jason received $92,640 as proceeds from the bond issue. Jason Inc.'s year-end is December 31.

Required:

A. Determine the effective rate of interest for the bond issue.
B. Prepare an amortization table for the life of the issue.
C. Prepare all journal entries required for 1997 related to the bond issue.
D. If the prevailing market rate of interest for similar investments suddenly changed to 9.8% on May 1, 1997, what effect would this change have on 1997 interest expense for these bonds?

P14–4 Effective Rate of Interest—Bonds Sold at Discount

Lincoln Inc. issued $200,000 of 5-year, 6% bonds paying interest semiannually on March 1 and September 1 on March 1, 1997. Lincoln received $183,785 as proceeds from the bond issue. Lincoln's reporting year ends on December 31.

Required:

A. Determine the effective rate of interest on the bond issue.
B. Prepare an amortization table for the life of the issue.
C. Prepare the journal entries for 1997.
D. If the prevailing market rate of interest for similar investments suddenly changed to 6.2% on May 1, 1997, what effect would this change have on 1997 interest expense for these bonds?

P14–5 Convertible Callable Bonds

Phillippi Inc. issued $500,000 of convertible, 10%, 10-year bonds on January 1, 1997. The bonds pay semiannual interest on June 30 and December 31. The selling price of the bonds provided a yield of 8% effective interest. The bonds are callable at 102 two years after the issue date. The conversion ratio is 30 shares of $5 par common for each $1,000 of bonds.

On November 1, 1998, Phillippi indicated that the call privilege would be exercised for all outstanding bonds after December 31, 1998. As a consequence, all of the bonds were converted effective December 31, 1998, when the current market price of the stock was $35.

Required: Prepare all of the entries for the life of the bond issue using

A. The book value method for conversion.
B. The market value method for conversion.

P14–6 Convertible Callable Bonds

Sigma Inc. issued $500,000 of convertible, 8%, 10-year bonds on January 1, 1997. The bonds were sold to yield 10% effective interest and pay interest each June 30 and December 31. Two years after the issue date, the bonds are callable at 102. The conversion ratio is 40 shares of $5 par common for each $1,000 of bonds.

On November 1, 1998, Sigma indicated that the call privilege would be exercised for all outstanding bonds after December 31, 1998. As a consequence, all the bonds were converted effective December 31, 1998, when the current market price of the stock was $30.

Required:

A. Prepare all of the entries for the life of the bond issue using (1) the book value method and (2) the market value method.

B. What is the difference to an investor between a bond with a conversion feature and a bond with a call feature?

*P14–7 Troubled Debt Restructuring

The Tube Company has an outstanding debt of $300,000 to Hathaway Inc. The maturity date of the 10% interest-bearing note is December 31, 1997. Prior to 1997, Tube Company has always paid the annual interest when due on December 31. However, the company has experienced a severe net cash outflow for the last several months and is unable to meet the terms of the debt at December 31, 1997.

Required: For each of the following scenarios prepare the journal entries for Tube Company necessary to record the new agreement and the additional journal entries over the life of any new agreement.

A. Hathaway agrees to forgive the interest for the current year and accepts a $330,000, 16% note due in two years with interest payable every December 31.

B. Hathaway agrees to accept $200,000 in cash and a building valued at $80,000 as full payment of the debt. The book value of the building at the time of the agreement is $40,000.

C. Hathaway agrees to accept $50,000 in cash and 10,000 shares of Phillippi's $5 par value stock. The stock's current market value at the time is unknown.

D. Hathaway agrees to accept $50,000 in cash and 10,000 shares of Phillippi's $5 par value stock. The stock's current market value at the time is $30.

E. Assume the same data as in (**D**) except that the current market value of the stock is $24 per share.

P14–8 Detachable Warrants

Baird Corporation issued 2,000, $1,000, 10-year, 10% bonds paying interest semiannually on March 31 and September 30 of each year. The bonds were dated and issued March 31, 1997, for $2,283,830.

Each $1,000 bond has two detachable warrants. The warrants provide that one share of Baird Corporation's $10 par common stock can be acquired with one warrant and $20 within one year of the issue date. Baird's common stock was selling at $23 on March 31, 1997. The bonds are callable at 103 after September 30, 1999.

Required: Provide the journal entries necessary for the life of the bond issue using the following assumptions:

A. The bonds were sold to yield 8%.

B. All warrants were exercised on February 28, 1998.

C. All bonds were called on October 1, 1999.

P14–9 Detachable Warrants

Ray Corporation issued 1,000, $1,000, 10-year, 10% bonds paying interest semiannually on March 31 and September 30 of each year. The bonds were dated and issued March 31, 1997, for $1,139,915.

Each $1,000 bond has two detachable warrants. The warrants provide that one share of Ray Corporation's $10 par common stock can be acquired with one warrant and $15 within one year of the issue date. Ray's common stock was selling at $17 on March 31, 1997. The bonds are callable at 103 after September 30, 1999.

Required: Provide the journal entries necessary for the life of the bond issue using the following assumptions:

A. The bonds were sold to yield 8%.
B. All warrants were exercised on February 28, 1998.
C. All bonds were called on October 1, 1999.

P14–10 Notes With Other Rights

Jordon Corporation agrees to lend to Siler Inc., a supplier, $200,000 for a period of two years. Siler signs a 2-year, noninterest-bearing note payable to Jordon dated January 1, 1997. The note contains a provision to provide Jordon, over the 2-year period, up to $200,000 of purchases at reduced prices. Siler's incremental borrowing rate is 12%.

Required: Provide Siler's journal entries for 1997. Assume that Jordon purchases $100,000 from Siler in 1997.

P14–11 Notes With Other Rights

James Corporation agrees to lend to Sam Inc., a supplier, $300,000 for a period of two years. Sam signs a 2-year, noninterest- bearing note payable to James dated January 1, 1997. The note contains a provision to provide James, over the 2-year period, up to $300,000 of purchases at reduced prices. Sam's incremental borrowing rate is 14%.

Required: Provide Sam's journal entries for 1997. Assume that James purchases $150,000 from Sam in 1997.

P14–12 Financial Analysis and Business Reasoning

Becker Construction needs $1 million in cash to expand its business. Becker is considering both debt and equity issuances, and is trying to determine which of these choices is best for the future of the company. You have been hired to help. Financial data from Becker and industry data are provided as follows:

1997 earnings before interest and taxes	$400,000
Interest rate on debt	7%
Income tax rate	40%
Total debt	$1,000,000
Total equity	$800,000
Industry return on equity	25%
Industry debt-to-equity ratio	2
1996 industry average net income	$200,000

Required:

A. What are the advantages of stock issuance over debt issuance?
B. Compute net income for 1997 under both stock- and debt-issuance scenarios.
C. Compute return on equity and debt-to-equity ratios for 1997 under both scenarios.
D. Compare your answers in (**B**) and (**C**) to industry statistics, and advise the management of Becker Construction as to the better alternative for raising the $1 million cash it needs. Explain your answer.

P14–13 Supporting Contentions That Are Easily Made, Hard to Prove

Dwyer Inc. wants to raise $1 million so that it can add a product line to its business. Current financial data for the company are shown here. Dwyer estimates that it can increase earnings before interest and taxes (EBIT) by $400,000 per year, starting the first year after the new product is added, and so it is anxious to raise the $1 million.

Dwyer has gone to the bank to ask for a loan of the $1 million at 6% interest. The bank turned down the request, stating that Dwyer's ability to repay the loan is uncertain at this time. The banker specifically pointed to the times-interest-earned ratio as a weakness.

You are the Controller of Dwyer Inc., and you think that the bank has improperly computed the financial ratios used in its decision because it did not consider future sales from the new product.

	1997	1998
Total liabilities	$ 900,000	$1,200,000
Total equity	600,000	700,000
Net sales	1,500,000	1,800,000
EBIT	300,000	750,000
Interest expense	150,000	300,000
Income tax rate	40%	40%

Required:

A. Compute the debt-to-equity and times-interest-earned ratios for 1997 and 1998.

B. Compute the debt-to-equity and times-interest-earned ratios for 1999 using the assumptions of management about profits from the new products and assuming no other changes from 1998 data.

C. Compare (**A**) with (**B**). If management's predictions about the future of the new product are accurate, do you think the loan should be granted? Explain.

D. What information could Dwyer Inc. gather to prove to the bank that its predictions about the new product's sales are valid? Be specific.

P14–14 Ratios, Industry Comparisons, Industry Bias

Companies in certain industries are less likely to attract new stockholders for new stock issuances because of the nature of the industry. In other industries, it may be difficult to attract debt financing. When such biases are removed from decision making, financial ratios take on more importance than they otherwise might. In this problem, you will attempt to make a decision without specific knowledge of the kinds of industries. Financial ratios for two companies in different industries are presented.

	A	A's INDUSTRY	B	B's INDUSTRY
Net Sales	$2 million		$2 million	
EBIT	$500,000		$200,000	
Interest Expense	50,000		50,000	
Income Taxes	180,000		60,000	
Net Income	270,000		90,000	
Sales Profit Margin	0.135	0.15	0.045	0.03
Return on Investment	0.20	0.10	0.02	0.02
Earnings per Share	0.27	0.35	0.09	0.07
Debt-to-Equity	2.50	1.80	1.50	1.00
Times Interest Earned	6.50	5.00	2.00	1.75

Note: All data are for the same year.

Required:

A. In which company are you more likely to invest in stock? In which company would you prefer to invest in debt? Explain.

B. What information other than that given here would be helpful in making your decision? How important is it for you to know which industries you are dealing with in (**A**)? Why?

P14–15 Comprehensive Bond Problem

On December 1, 1997, the Cone Company issued its 8%, 10-year, $2,000,000 face value bonds to yield 6%. Interest is payable on November 1 and May 1. On July 1, 2000, Cone reacquired the bonds at 98 plus accrued interest. Cone appropriately uses the effective interest method for the amortization of bond discounts or premiums. Round all calculations to the nearest dollar amount.

Required:

A. Prepare an amortization schedule through November 1, 2000. (*Hint:* Even though the bond was issued December 1, 1997, begin the amortization table with the present value as of November 1, 1997. Also, carry it through November 1, 2000, even though the bonds were retired in July.)

B. Determine the cash proceeds for the bond when issued on December 1, 1997.

C. Prepare journal entries for the following dates:

1. December 1, 1997
2. December 31, 1997 (year-end)
3. May 1, 1998
4. November 1, 1998
5. December 31, 1998 (year-end)
6. July 1, 2000

D. Determine interest expense as shown on the income statement for 1998.

E. Show balance sheet presentation related to the bonds as of December 31, 1998.

F. Show presentation related to the bonds for a cash flow statement, using the indirect method for the year 1998.

P14–16 Effective-Interest versus Straight-Line Amortization

On May 1, 1997, $200,000 of 10-year bonds paying $9,000 interest every May 1 and November 1 were issued by Not GAAP, Inc., for $187,540. The T-accounts shown here reflect postings for 1997's bond-related transactions as recorded by Al Wrong, Not GAAP's bookkeeper, who knew how to use only straight-line amortization. As the company's new accountant, you are aware that the effective-interest method is required by GAAP. Wrong tells you that the bonds were issued to yield either 8% or 10%, but he can't remember which.

DATE	CASH	BONDS PAYABLE	DISCOUNT	INTEREST PAYABLE	INTEREST EXPENSE
5/1/97	$187,540 Dr.	$200,000 Cr.	$12,460 Dr.		
11/1/97	9,000 Cr.		623 Cr.		$9,623 Dr.
12/31/97			208 Cr.	$3,000 Cr.	3,208 Dr.

Required:

A. What is the appropriate effective interest rate for this bond? Why do you think so?

B. Using the effective-interest method, complete the bond amortization schedule through May 1, 1999.
C. Based on this amortization schedule, reconstruct the journal entries for November 1 and December 31, 1997.
D. What will be 1997's interest expense for the bonds? Show computations to determine this amount.

DATE	INTEREST	CASH PAID	DISCOUNT AMORTIZATION	UNAMORTIZED DISCOUNT	CARRYING VALUE
5/1/97					
11/1/97					
5/1/98					
11/1/98					
5/1/99					

RESEARCH ACTIVITIES

R14–1 Issue Price of Bonds Class Presentation

Examine the alternative for calculating the issue price of a bond as illustrated in the article "Calculating the Present Value of a Bond: An Alternative Approach" by A. Spurrell in *Issues in Accounting Education* (Spring, 1990), pp. 120–122. Then, select two exercises or problems from this chapter that require determination of the issue price of bonds—one for a premium and another for a discount. Use the alternative method to determine the issue price for the bonds in the two selected exercises or problems.

R14–2 Financial Research—Debt Ratios

Examine any database with which you are familiar, including your DISCLOSURE database, to determine the following.

A. What are the three companies with the highest debt ratios?
B. In your opinion, is the solvency of these three companies in jeopardy? Explain.
C. Are the three companies from the same industry? For these companies, are there industry considerations which might lend themselves to relatively higher proportions of debt than for other industries?
D. Which industry has the highest average debt ratio? What characteristics of the industry contribute to this high average?

R14–3 Financial Research—Debt Ratios

Examine any database with which you are familiar, including your DISCLOSURE database, to determine the following.

A. What are the three companies with the lowest debt ratios?
B. In your opinion, could these companies be more efficient if more resources were financed using debt? Explain.
C. Are the three companies from the same industry? For these companies, are there industry considerations which might lend themselves to relatively lower proportions of debt than for other industries?
D. Which industry has the lowest average debt ratio? What characteristics of the industry contribute to this low average?

R14–4 Financial Research—Debt Covenants

Find an annual report for a corporation that identifies debt covenants in the footnotes accompanying the financial statements. Prepare a report that summarizes these debt covenants. In the report, estimate how much additional debt the company could sustain and still not violate the provisions of the existing debt covenants.

R14–5 Financial Analysis—Motorola

Examine the footnote pertaining to debt in ***Motorola***'s annual report in Appendix C.

A. The company lists $13 million as current maturities on December 31, 1995. What long-term debt is included with these current maturities?

B. The note indicates conversion of some zero coupon notes during 1995. Did Motorola use the market value or book value method for the conversion? What sources in the annual report suggest which method Motorola would have used? Prepare a journal entry for the conversion of this debt.

C. Focus on the zero coupon notes due 2013 that were issued in 1993.

1. What is the book value of these notes on December 31, 1995?
2. What would cause the difference between this ending book value and the original amount received?
3. Estimate the portion of 1995's interest expense that would be attributable to these zero coupon notes.

D. Estimate 1996's interest for both the 2009 and 2013 zero coupon notes.

R14–6 Financial Research—Disclosure

Examine the DISCLOSURE database for this assignment.

A. Look at ***Microsoft***'s long-term liabilities. Is the company's strategy regarding financing of resources typical of many businesses?

B. Determine companies with relatively high proportions of long-term debt compared to equity.

R14–7 Internet Research

Use one of the search engines on the World Wide Web keying in key words or phrases found in this chapter such as bonds payable. Print out several items that you found such as bond prospectuses of domestic and foreign bond issues and any other information that you found relevant to this chapter.

15

Accounting for Leases

Learning Objectives

After studying this chapter, you should be able to:

1. Differentiate between capital leases and operating leases.
2. Determine if a lease qualifies as a capital lease for both the lessee and the lessor.
3. Distinguish between a direct-financing lease and a sales-type lease, and demonstrate the accounting treatment for both the lessee and the lessor.
4. Illustrate the accounting differences for residual values and bargain purchase options in lease contracts.
5. Explain the basic concepts involved in sale-leasebacks, real estate leases, and leveraged leases.
6. Analyze the impact that capital leases have on certain key financial ratios.

A lease is a contract between a lessor, the owner of the property involved, and a lessee, the person or entity wishing to use that property in exchange for a certain number of cash payments. Leases have become an increasingly important means of financing the productive resources needed to compete in today's business environment. Leases have also become an important marketing tool in many industries, especially the automotive industry. The accompanying excerpt illustrates this point.

> *"Auto Makers Sing the Praises of Leasing"*
>
> Detroit—Auto makers have just the answer for those that say they can't afford a new car: Borrow it.
>
> Marketers from ***Mercedes-Benz*** to ***General Motors Corp.'s*** Chevrolet division are promoting heavily subsidized lease deals as the latest solution to a fundamental and growing problem: New car prices are higher than most consumers can afford, particularly now that finance companies are discouraging long-term loans.
>
> Indeed, many manufacturers are offering better deals to lease than to buy. Chrysler will lease a $20,078 Dodge Grand Caravan LE for 36 months for $379 a month, after a $2,008 down payment. To finance the same $18,070 balance with a 5-year purchase contract would cost $402 per month. After 36 months, the person who leased would have saved a total of $809 on monthly payments.
>
> The person who buys the Caravan will own it after 60 payments totalling $24,120. But the person who leases could buy the van for $8,634 after $13,663 in payments. The van would then have cost $22,297, or $1,873 less than with a 5-year loan. But the real advantage would be to the customer who wanted to trade for a new van within three years. Leasing may be the only way to do that without losing money.

Source: Joseph B. White, "Automakers Sing the Praise of Leasing," *The Wall Street Journal*, April 10, 1991, Sec. B, p. 1.

ADVANTAGES AND DISADVANTAGES OF LEASING

Some advantages to leasing economic resources rather than purchasing them outright or financing them by other means include:

1. Leases provide a more flexible means of financing.
2. Significant initial cash outlays are avoided.
3. The risk of technological obsolescence is reduced by cancellation or substitution provisions of the lease.
4. Direct disclosure of financing means is avoided in the financial statements.

Disadvantages also may be associated with leasing rather than purchasing assets. The two major disadvantages are

1. Total costs frequently are higher.
2. Occasionally, use restrictions apply to leased assets.

The length of the lease and the fixed nature of the payments can be either an advantage or a disadvantage, depending upon future economic conditions. The In Practice features illustrate the advantages and disadvantages of leasing.

IN PRACTICE—GENERAL

Long-Term Leases

[In 1950] Hugo Herschend signed a 99-year lease on a cave near Branson, Mo. He figured Marvel Cave, with its vaulted ceiling and crystalline stalactites, would make a nice little family business.

A branch manager for ***Electrolux*** in Evanston, Ill., Herschend kept his job in order to keep cash rolling in, but sent his wife, Mary, south to manage the cave; sons Peter and Jack helped during the summer vacations.

Hugo joined them four years later after suffering a heart attack. When he died, in 1955, the $5,000-a-year lease was his only valuable asset. It turned out to be quite a legacy. Today Pete Herschend, and brother Jack, 59, run ***Silver Dollar City Inc.***, a small conglomerate of four theme parks—including Dolly Parton's Dollywood—a 4,000-seat music theater and, of course, Marvel Cave. Last year the privately held firm took in $93 million in revenues.

Source: Lisa Gubernick, "A Curb on the Ego," *Forbes*, September 14, 1992.

IN PRACTICE—GENERAL

Long-Term Real Estate Leases

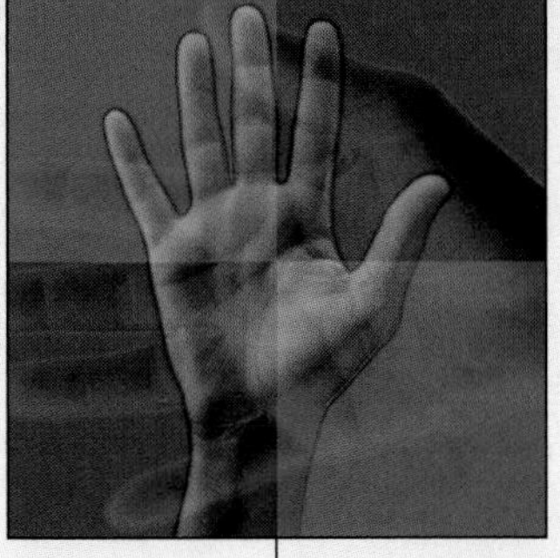

Long-term leases for office space, vestiges of the 1980s, are haunting law firms struggling for survival in the tougher competitive environment of the 1990s.

Real estate costs weighed heavily on the balance sheets of many industries during the economic downturn, and law firms were no exception. Indeed, many of the 30-odd firms that have disbanded in the last five years had real estate problems in addition to other woes, according to Howard Mudrick, a consultant with ***Hildebrandt Inc.*** Coming at a time when business for law firms is slow and professional liability problems are on the rise, the real estate bind sometimes proves to be the last straw.

"Real estate is destiny," says Jonathan A. Lindsey, a legal consultant with ***Major, Wilson and Africa*** in New York. "The lease is often overlooked, but it's an important part of a firm's economic health."

Source: Arthur S. Hays, "Laws-Legal Beat: Long-Term Deals for Office Space Are a Heavy-Duty Weight on Law Firms," *The Wall Street Journal*, June 26, 1992, Sec. B, p. 11.

CONCEPTUAL CONSIDERATIONS

Standard setters have struggled for a long time with accounting for leases. A lengthy list of standards is testimony to the importance that leasing plays in today's economy.[1]

[1]The following standards currently apply:

1. SFAS No. 13, Accounting for Leases (the basic standard dealing with leases) (November 1976)
2. SFAS No. 27, Classification of Renewals or Extensions of Existing Sales-Type or Direct Financing Leases (May 1979)
3. SFAS No. 28, Accounting for Sales With Leasebacks (May 1979)
4. SFAS No. 29, Determining Contingent Rentals (June 1979)
5. SFAS No. 91, Accounting for Nonrefundable Fees and Costs Associated with Originating or Acquiring Loans and Initial Direct Costs of Leases (December 1986)
6. SFAS No. 98, Accounting for Leases: Sale-Leaseback Transactions Involving Real Estate, Sales-Type Leases of Real Estate, Definition of Lease Term, Initial Direct Costs of Direct Financing Leases (May 1988)

As the standards have changed, new leasing arrangements have emerged in response, thereby necessitating further changes in the standards. The contentious issue is the *representational faithfulness* of the accounting treatments frequently favored by corporate managements. A fundamental question is whether lease contracts should be reported as long-term assets and liabilities or disclosed only in financial statement footnotes. For the lessor, the accounting question is whether the asset under contract is in substance sold (and thus removed from the balance sheet). These basic questions center on the issue of ownership.

Our discussion of leases and the accounting requirements of various lease arrangements will follow the flowchart presented in Exhibit 15–1. Basic lease terminology is presented in Exhibit 15–2.

QUESTION OF OWNERSHIP

Differentiate between capital leases and operating leases.

The first question posed in Exhibit 15–1 is one of asset ownership. Does a particular lease contract result in a transfer of ownership? The answer to this question is crucial in determining the appropriate accounting treatment. If the lease provisions are deemed to result in a substantive transfer of the risks and rights of ownership, the lease is treated as a **capital lease**. If it is deemed that a substantive transfer of the risks and rights of ownership does not occur, the lease is treated as an **operating lease**. Four criteria are used to determine if a substantive transfer of the risk and rights of ownership has occurred. In Exhibit 15–1, these are referred to as the *four-condition test*. If none of these criteria is met, the lease is treated as an operating lease by both the lessee and the lessor because none of the rights and risks of ownership have transferred. However, if any one or more of these conditions are met, the lease is treated as a capital lease by the lessee. The criteria, as stated in SFAS No. 13, are

1. Ownership actually transfers to the lessee by the end of the lease argument.
2. A **bargain purchase option (BPO)** is contained in the lease. This allows the lessee to purchase the leased property at a price expected to be lower than fair market value on a date before or at expiration of the lease.
3. The life of the lease is equal to or greater than 75 percent of the remaining economic life of the leased asset. (This provision does not apply, however, when the beginning of the lease is within the last 25 percent of the economic life of the leased property.)
4. The present value of the *minimum lease payments* (discussed shortly), net of some costs, over the life of the lease is equal to or greater than 90 percent of the fair value of the property at the inception of the lease. (This condition does not apply when the beginning of the lease is within the last 25 percent of the economic life of the leased property.)

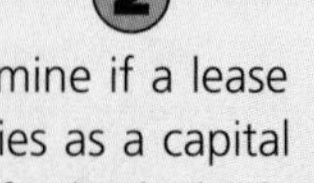

Determine if a lease qualifies as a capital lease for both the lessee and the lessor.

If any one of the four conditions is met, the lessor must then determine if the following two additional tests are met.

1. Collection of the minimum lease payment is reasonably assured.
2. No important uncertainties are attached to any future unreimbursable cost associated with the lease.

EXHIBIT 15–1 Flowchart for Lease Arrangements

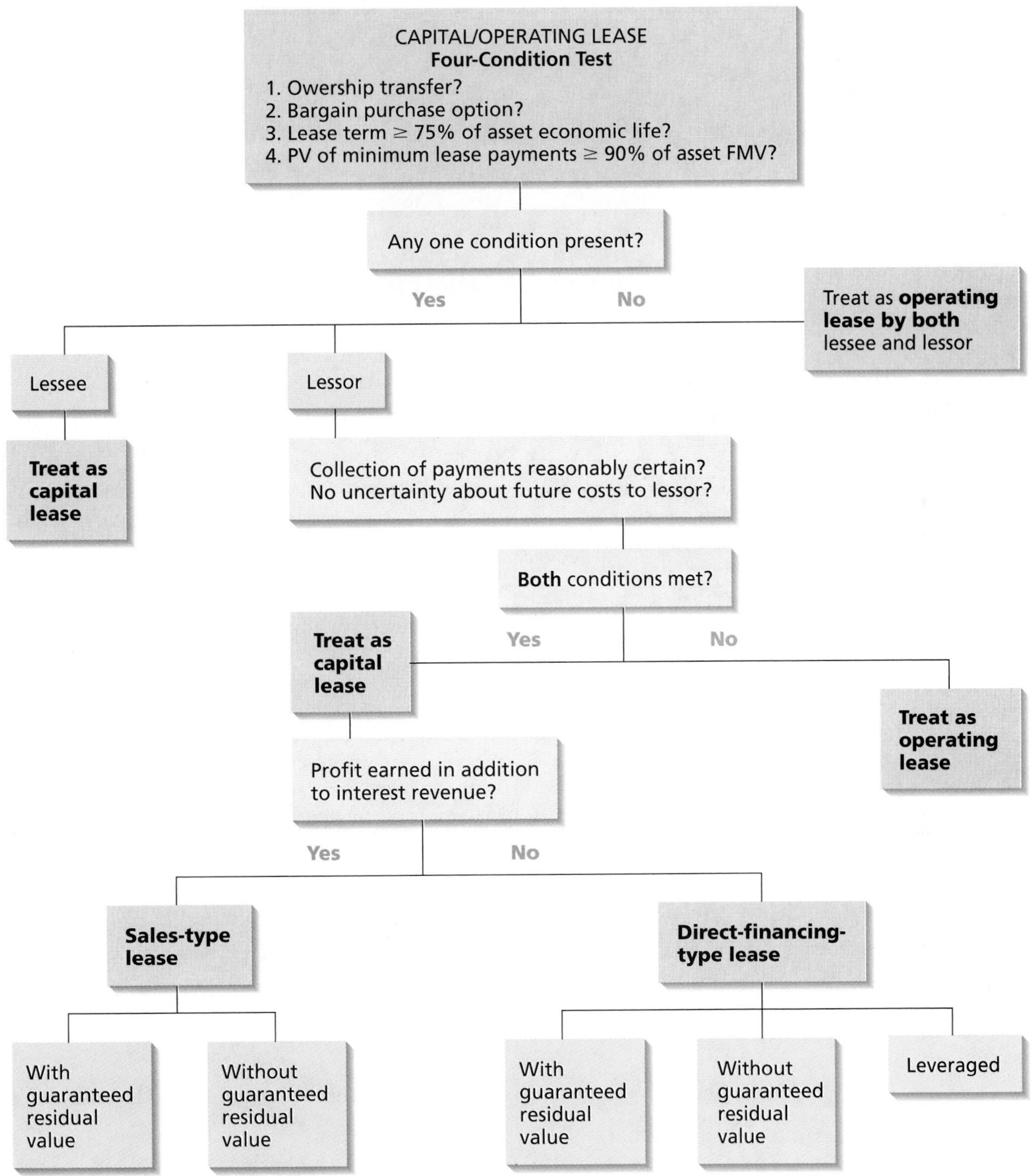

If both these additional conditions also are met, the lease is treated as a capital lease by the lessor. Virtually all risks and benefits of asset ownership are deemed to have been transferred to the lessee. If either or both additional tests are not met, the lease is treated as an operating lease by the lessor.

IN FOCUS

Kenneth W. Mai
VP—Finance and Treasurer
BA, Accounting and Management, Thomas More College
Information Leasing Corporation

"Every transaction has three sources of risk. Our job is to evaluate and balance these risks."

How important is leasing to corporate America? Important enough to spawn an entire industry to facilitate it: third party leasing. Firms like ***Information Leasing*** allow companies that need new computers, phone systems, and other equipment to lease rather than purchase even if the equipment vendor does not offer its own lease program. And in cases where the supplier does offer leasing, third party lessors may provide lease options that are less expensive or more flexible.

CPA Ken Mai manages all financial, operational, and administrative functions at Information Leasing. But as the company's financial expert, he is often involved in the sales process as well. "Before we can proceed with a lease, we need to look at the creditworthiness of the lessee," says Mai. "We review their financial statements to make sure they will be able to handle the added cash flow for the term of the lease."

When the lease is signed, the four-condition test is applied, and the lease is booked as an operating or capital lease, according to SFAS No. 13. From there, most of the process is automated by the company's lease management system, which generates monthly billing and appropriate accounting entries. While much of the process for a new lease is automated, the unique circumstances of mid-term changes require significant attention. Changes such as adding equipment, replacing equipment, or extending or restructuring the lease all require careful recalculation.

Mai emphasizes the importance of the time value of money concept to the leasing business. "Essentially every transaction we are involved in revolves around the time value of money. Our ability to make a profit relies on executing those deals where the net present value is clearly positive," Mai says. And while leasing can produce considerable profits, it is far from risk-free. Mai describes every transaction as having three sources of risk: (1) credit risk, (Can the lessee make its payments?), (2) residual risk (Can we recoup the residual value of the equipment at lease-end?), and (3) interest rate risk (Will our cost of funds rise during the course of the lease to a level where our cash flow is negative?). "Our job is to evaluate and balance these risks. For instance, if a company has exceptionally strong credit, we may assume a somewhat higher level of risk on residual value," asserts Mai.

Mai points to his Big Six experience prior to his current position as an important learning period. He also emphasizes the importance of understanding fundamental accounting principles. "Almost everything that happens in business can be described and understood in terms of accounting," he says. "It's easy to lose track of the big picture because there is so much detail to learn, but it's important to understand the fundamentals. Once you comprehend what the accounting pronouncements are really trying to accomplish, it's easier to apply what you know to a variety of new situations and industries."

The minimum lease payments (MLP) for the lessee referred to in Criterion No. 4 include

1. Minimum rental payments.
2. Guaranteed residual value (GRV), if such a provision exists, guaranteeing that the fair market value of the property returned to the lessor upon termination of the lease shall be a specified amount or more.
3. Bargain purchase option, if one exists.
4. Penalty for failure to renew or extend the lease.

EXHIBIT 15–2 Lease Terminology

LEASE	A contract between the *lessor* (owner of the property) and a *lessee* that provides the lessee the right to use the property for the term of the lease in return for a minimum number of specified cash amounts.
LESSEE	The person or entity using the asset being leased.
LESSOR	The person or entity who owns the asset being leased.
MINIMUM LEASE PAYMENTS (MLP)	The minimum payments by the lessee to the lessor necessary under the terms of the lease. Besides rental payments, the MLP also includes any payments for a bargain purchase option, a provision for guaranteed residual value, or a penalty payment for failure to extend or renew the contract.
BARGAIN PURCHASE OPTION (BPO)	A contractual stipulation that allows the lessee to purchase the leased property at a specified price significantly less than its anticipated fair market value at the option date (a date at or prior to expiration of the lease). A bargain purchase price option is set low to assure exercise.
GUARANTEED RESIDUAL VALUE (GRV)	A provision that provides that the fair market value (FMV) of the property returned to the lessor at the termination of the lease shall be equal to or greater than a specified amount. This provision is placed in the contract to minimize abuse to the property. The lessee is liable for the difference if the leased property upon return does not have a FMV at least equal to the GRV.
OPERATING LEASES	Leases that do not meet any of the tests of ownership per SFAS No. 13 for classification as a capital lease. The assets are treated as rented assets by both lessee and lessor.
CAPITAL LEASES	Leases that meet at least one of the tests per SFAS No. 13 for classification as a capital lease for the lessee, and meet both additional tests for classification on the part of the lessor. The assets leased are treated as a purchase by the lessee and a sale by the lessor.
SALES-TYPE LEASE	A capital lease in which the lessor earns a profit as well as interest revenue on the transaction.
PROFIT EARNED ON SALES-TYPE LEASE	The difference between the fair market value and the book value of the leased asset at the inception of the lease.
DIRECT-FINANCING-TYPE LEASE	A capital lease in which the lessor earns interest revenue only.
LEVERAGED LEASE	A capital lease in which the lessor finances the leased asset through an outside third party.

The lease receivable for the lessor includes

1. Minimum lease payment.
2. Any **unguaranteed residual value (URV)** provision, the opposite of GRV.

ACCOUNTING FOR OPERATING LEASES

The accounting treatment of an operating lease by the lessee is straightforward. Operating leases are period charges that are expensed in the period in which the benefits of the asset leased are received. This achieves a proper matching of benefit and expense. The amount of the expense is determined by the lease agreement, which specifies the rental payments for the use of the asset for given periods.

Reporting leases as operating leases rather than as capital leases has a potential material impact on the financial statements of the lessee. An operating lease is not reflected as a liability on the balance sheet. By keeping a large liability off the balance sheet, a company improves its debt-to-equity ratio. Furthermore, the leased asset is not reported on the asset side of the balance sheet, either. Profitability measures such as return on assets are thus improved because the asset base is smaller.

These features of operating leases are attractive enough to entice some financial officers to have leases written in such a fashion as to qualify as an operating lease while keeping many of the parameters of a capital lease. The practice is known as *off-balance-sheet financing* since neither the asset under the control of the lessee nor the corresponding claims against future revenues as a liability appears on the balance sheet of the lessee. An example of an operating lease is contained in the In Practice feature "Operating Leases."

Accounting for an operating lease by the lessor is also straightforward. Since the lessor owns the asset and merely rents it to the lessee, the lessor records rental revenue in the period that it is earned. The asset remains on the balance sheet of the lessor, and it is depreciated over its useful life similar to any other revenue-producing asset.

IN PRACTICE—GENERAL

Operating Leases

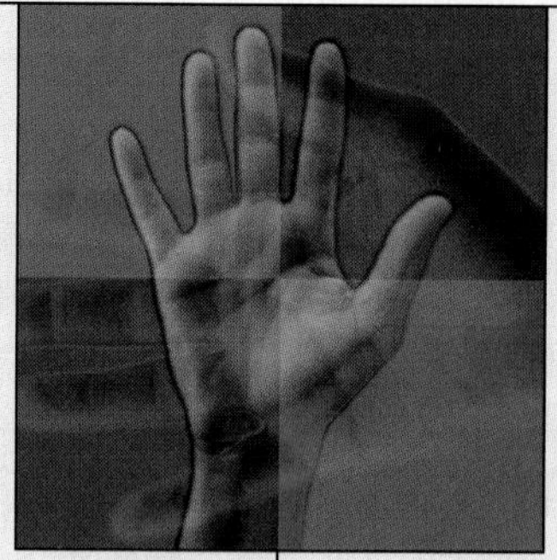

Hong Kong—***Hong Kong Dragon Airlines*** plans to seek board permission next week to take as many as 10 ***Airbus Industries*** twin jets on operating leases from ***International Lease Finance Corp.***, people familiar with the agreement said.

Dragonair, a regional carrier 35 percent owned by ***Cathay Pacific Airways*** and that airline's parent, ***Swire Pacific Ltd.***, was pursued for months by both Airbus and ***Boeing Co.*** to buy new planes. But the carrier reportedly chose to lease instead because there are excess planes on the world market, many of them in the hands of big leasing firms which are offering favorable terms. Operating leases, as opposed to capital . . . leases, are like rentals, with the lease liability kept off the airlines' balance sheet.

Source: "International: Dragonair Will Seek Clearance from Board to Lease Airbus Jets," *The Wall Street Journal,* December 4, 1991, Sec. A, p. 12.

ACCOUNTING FOR CAPITAL LEASES BY THE LESSEE

If any one of the four tests of constructive ownership transfer is met, the lease transaction must be treated as a capital lease by the lessee. Instead of treating the asset as a rented item, the lessee must treat it as an asset purchased and financed by debt. An asset account is established (debited), equal to the present value of the minimum lease payments, not to exceed the fair market value of the leased asset. The asset cost is then allocated over the period benefited, either the life of the lease or the economic life of the asset, whichever is appropriate. At the same time, a liability is established for future obligations to make minimum lease payments (MLP). The amount of the liability is also equal to the present value of the MLP.

Exhibit 15–3 illustrates the calculations necessary to determine the lease payments of an example company. The lessee (Henry Hungry) capitalizes the fair market value of the asset (which is equal to the present value of the minimum lease payments), and treats the lease obligation as an interest-bearing note. Exhibit 15–4 shows the amortization table for the lease. The entries on the lessee's books are:

1997			
Jan. 1	Leased Equipment	27,215	
	Lease Liability—Lease One		27,215
	Lease Liability—Lease One	8,000	
	Cash		8,000

CONCEPT Asset and liability valuation.

LOGIC Assets are recorded at fair market value at the date of acquisition. Liabilities are valued at the present value of future resources surrendered to settle the debt. In theory, the cash purchase price of the asset leased was $27,215, which could have been borrowed independently of the lease. If cash had been borrowed for the asset purchase, the net effect would be to have a liability equal to the value of the asset purchased at the date of acquisition.

EXHIBIT 15–3
Determining Lease Payments

Assume that Henry Hungry wishes to lease equipment that has a fair market value of $27,215. Hungry enters into a 4-year leasing agreement with Lease One Company on January 1, 1997. The initial payment is due at the inception of the lease, and the equipment reverts to the lessor at the end of the lease. Lease One desires a 12% return on the money invested in the property to be leased to Hungry.

The initial lease payment made at the beginning of the lease term and annual payments thereafter are determined as follows:

$$\text{FMV of Asset} = \left[\begin{array}{l}\text{Present Value of Annuity due} \\ \text{@ 12\% for 4 years}\end{array}\right] \times \text{Payment}$$

$$\$27{,}215 = 3.4018 \times \text{Payment}$$

$$\$27{,}215/3.4018 = \text{Payment}$$

$$\underline{\underline{\$8{,}000}} = \text{Payment}$$

DEPRECIATION OF LEASED PROPERTY

The cost of the asset, the leased property, is allocated by the lessee over the economic life of the asset or the life of the lease, whichever is appropriate. If the property is returned to the lessor at the end of the lease, the lease life is applicable, and the asset is assumed to have zero residual value to the lessee. If the lease contains a bargain purchase option (Criterion 2) or if the title will transfer to the lessee at a future date (Criterion 1), then the extended economic life is used and a residual value should be assigned to the asset.

LEASE PAYMENTS AND INTEREST AMORTIZATION

Exhibit 15–4 contains an amortization table illustrating the interest revenue/expense for each period and the amortization of the debt. The journal entries required by the lessee over the life of the lease follow:

12/31/97	Interest Expense	2,306	
	Interest Payable		2,306
	Depreciation Expense—Leased Equipment	6,804*	
	Accumulated Depreciation—Leased Equipment		6,804
	$27,215/4 years = $6,804 rounded		
1/1/98	Interest Payable	2,306*	
	Lease Liability—Lease One	5,694	
	Cash		8,000
	*Assumes accruals are not reversed.		
	•		
	•		
	•		
12/31/99	Interest Expense	857	
	Interest Payable		857
	Depreciation Expense—Leased Equipment	6,804	
	Accumulated Depreciation—Leased Equipment		6,804
1/1/00	Interest Payable	857*	
	Lease Liability—Lease One	7,143	
	Cash		8,000
	*Assumes accruals are not reversed.		
12/31/00	Depreciation Expense—Leased Equipment	6,804	
	Accumulated Depreciation—Leased Equipment		6,804
	Accumulated Depreciation—Leased Equipment	27,215	
	Leased Equipment		27,215

CONCEPT Representational faithfulness.

LOGIC The underlying substance of a capital-lease transaction is that the lessee is borrowing from the lessor to obtain a capital asset. Thus, to represent the transaction faithfully, it is treated as a purchase, recognizing both the asset and the liability created by the acquisition.

Note that the last entry on the part of the lessee signals the end of the lease. The asset is returned to the lessor and taken off the books of the lessee.

EXHIBIT 15–4
Lease-Amortization Table
January 1, 1997

DATE	(A) BEGINNING BALANCE	(B) LEASE PAYMENT	(C) INTEREST 12%	(D) REDUCTION OF PRINCIPAL (AMORTIZATION)	(E) ENDING BALANCE
1/1/97	$27,215	$ 8,000	$ 0	$ 8,000	$19,215
1/1/98	19,215	8,000	2,306	5,694	13,521
1/1/99	13,521	8,000	1,622	6,378	7,143
1/1/00	7,143	8,000	857	7,143	0
Totals		$32,000	$4,785	$27,215	

(A) Beginning balance of $27,215 is present value of lease in Exhibit 15–3.
(B) Lease payment of $8,000 in Exhibit 15–3.
(C) = (A) × 12%
(D) = (B) − (C)
(E) = (A) − (D)

INTEREST RATE FOR LEASE

The interest rate used to determine both the liability and the initial carrying value of the leased asset *by the lessee* should be the same rate used by the lessor if it is known, or if it can be determined from the conditions of the contract. This would be the **implicit interest rate**. If the rate is unknown and not determinable, the **incremental borrowing rate** of the lessee is used.

The incremental borrowing rate of the lessee is the rate of interest that would have to be paid by the lessee to obtain a loan to purchase the asset. The lessee uses the incremental borrowing rate to determine the present value of the minimum lease payments (MLP). The leased asset and lease obligation are recorded at this amount unless the fair market value (FMV) is lower. If the FMV is lower, the implicit rate, the rate that will equate the present value of the MLP to the FMV of the asset is used to calculate the present value of the MLP.

For example, assume the incremental borrowing rate of Henry Hungry in Exhibit 15–3 is 10%. The present value of the MLP discounted at 10% is 3.4869 × $8,000 = $27,895, which is greater than the FMV of the asset ($27,215). Therefore, the leased asset should be recorded at its FMV. The fact that the lessee chose to finance the asset through a lease agreement instead of a cash purchase should not influence the recorded value. Consequently, an implicit interest rate needs to be determined.

An implicit rate of interest is the rate needed to equate the present value of the MLP to the FMV of the asset at the beginning of the lease. In Exhibit 15–3, the implicit rate of interest is derived in the following manner:

$$\begin{aligned}\text{FMV @ inception of lease} &= \text{PV of MLP}\\ \$27{,}215 &= \text{PV of Annuity Due @ ?\% for 4 payments of } \$8{,}000\\ \$27{,}215 &= (\text{PV of Annuity Due @ ?\%, } 4n) \times \$8{,}000\\ \frac{\$27{,}215}{\$8{,}000} &= (\text{PV of Annuity Due @ ?\%, } 4n)\\ 3.4019 &= \text{Annuity Factor for 4 periods}\end{aligned}$$

From Appendix A, Table A-6, the rate is 12%.

ACCOUNTING FOR CAPITAL LEASES BY LESSOR

Distinguish between a direct-financing lease and a sales-type lease, and demonstrate the accounting treatment for both the lessee and the lessor.

Capital leases for the lessor are first classified as either **direct-financing-type leases** or as **sales-type leases.** Direct-financing-type leases are those in which the lessor derives revenue exclusively from the interest earned on the lease. In a sales-type lease, the lessor derives profit from two sources—the interest revenue on the lease and the difference between the cost and fair market value of the asset at the date of effective sale (that is, the inception or beginning of the capital lease).

DIRECT-FINANCING-TYPE LEASES

Exhibit 15–3 provided an illustration of the calculation of the lease payment amounts. Recall that this example was used to illustrate the accounting necessary for a lessee with a capital lease. Now we examine the lessor's side of the same lease transaction.

As stated previously, the FMV of the asset leased is $27,215, and the four lease payments are each $8,000, with the first payment made at the beginning of the lease and the others annually thereafter. In a departure from normal accounting methods, the lessor records the lease receivable at the gross amount of MLP, or $32,000 (4 × $8,000). The difference between the gross receivable and the present value of the lease payments ($27,215) is unearned interest revenue ($4,785). This transaction is similar to a noninterest-bearing note transaction. The initial entries on the books of the lessor are

1/1/97	Lease Receivable—Hungry	32,000*	
	Equipment		27,215
	Unearned Interest Revenue		4,785
	**$8,000 × 4 = $32,000*		
	Cash	8,000	
	Lease Receivable—Hungry		8,000

CONCEPT: Sale of an asset at book value—representational faithfulness.

LOGIC: The underlying economic substance of this transaction is the sale of an asset. Because the sale occurs at its book value, no gain or loss recognition is warranted. A new asset (Lease Receivable) replaces the equipment on the balance sheet. The account, Unearned Interest Revenue, is reported on the balance sheet contra to the Lease Receivable account. This account is amortized by periodic recognition of interest income on the lease contract.[2]

[2]While the authors believe separate reporting of the gross receivable offset by unearned interest revenue provides important cash flow information, many companies elect to report the net receivable on their balance sheet even though they maintain accounts for the gross receivable and unearned revenue.

Recall that Exhibit 15–4 contains an amortization table for the interest revenue/expense of each period and the amortization of the debt. At fiscal year-end, the lessor recognizes interest revenue for the period between the lease inception and the year-end date. The journal entries required by the lessor at fiscal year-end and over the life of the lease follow:

12/31/97	Unearned Interest Revenue	2,306	
	Interest Revenue		2,306
1/1/98	Cash	8,000	
	Lease Receivable		8,000
	•		
	•		
	•		
12/31/99	Unearned Interest Revenue	857	
	Interest Revenue		857
1/1/00	Cash	8,000	
	Lease Receivable—Hungry		8,000

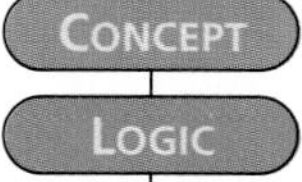

Revenue recognition.

Revenue is recognized when earned or realized. Interest is earned on the lease receivable and recognized periodically using the effective-interest method at 12% over the life of the lease.

In this example of a direct-financing lease, the lessor earns interest on the financing provided. There is no other revenue earned, because the book value (BV) and the FMV of the lease are the same at the inception of the lease. If, at the end of the lease period, the FMV of the returned asset is significant, the lessor would record the receipt of the asset at its FMV and recognize a gain on the transaction for the FMV amount.

SALES-TYPE LEASES

Sales-type leases are capital leases used by dealers and manufacturers. A sales lease is distinguished from a direct-financing lease in that the FMV of the asset exceeds the BV of the asset at the time of the lease inception. Because the transaction is in substance a sale of the asset, the lessor recognizes a profit for the difference between the BV and the FMV (that is, the selling price) and records unearned interest income at the inception of the lease. The accounting treatment is different only for the lessor and then only for the initial entry.

Assume the same information as shown in Exhibit 15–3 for the direct-financing lease except that the BV of the equipment is $24,000 and the FMV is $27,215. The lessor recognizes gross profit at the time of the inception of the lease by recording a sale in the amount of the present value of the lease payments ($27,215) and by charging the BV of the equipment ($24,000) to cost of goods sold. The journal entries on the lessor's books at the inception of the lease to record the lease and receipt of the first payment are

1/1/97	Cost of Goods Sold	24,000	
	Lease Receivable—Hungry	32,000	
	Equipment Inventory		24,000
	Sales		27,215
	Unearned Interest Income		4,785*
	*$32,000 − $27,215 = $4,785		
	Cash	8,000	
	Lease Receivable—Hungry		8,000

CONCEPT Recognition of gross profit on sale of an asset.

LOGIC The underlying economic substance of the transaction is the sale of an asset. Because the asset was sold for an amount greater than the book value, recognition of a profit is proper. The amount of the gross profit is the difference between the fair market value and the book value of the asset sold.

The other journal entries for the lessor are the same as in the previous example for the direct-financing lease. The present value of the MLP ($27,215) reflects the FMV (and selling price) of the asset at the inception of the lease. The difference between the sales price and the BV ($24,000) is gross profit, and the unearned interest revenue ($4,785) is the difference between the total of the lease payments ($32,000) and the present value of the lease payments ($27,215).

The first entry shown earlier could be made in two entries instead:

1/1/97	Lease Receivable—Hungry	32,000	
	Sales		27,215
	Unearned Interest Revenue		4,785
	Cost of Goods Sold	24,000	
	Equipment Inventory		24,000

The net effect of the two entries is the same as the previous entry. The difference between the sales and cost of goods sold represents the gross profit on the transaction.

RESIDUAL VALUES

The residual value of a leased asset is the expected economic value or FMV of the asset at the termination of the lease. The lease contract may contain a provision guaranteeing that the residual value of the asset will be equal to or exceed a certain amount at the end of the lease. As explained earlier, this is referred to as a guaranteed residual value (GRV). If the contract does not contain such

Illustrate the accounting differences for residual values and bargain purchase options in lease contracts.

a provision, the residual value is an unguaranteed residual value (URV). GRV clauses are for the benefit of the lessor, and they are included in lease contracts in an attempt to minimize abuse of the asset. The lessee is responsible for the difference between the FMV and the GRV at the completion of the lease if the FMV is lower than the GRV.

Residual values must be considered by the lessor when establishing the terms of the lease. If the residual value is guaranteed, it is included by the lessee in the calculations determining the MLP to the lessor. This is illustrated in Exhibit 15–5. The GRV of $3,000 is included in the calculations to determine the annual payment amount.

Exhibit 15–6 presents an amortization schedule for the GRV lease in Exhibit 15–5. The beginning balance in the schedule ($29,121) includes the present value of the payments ($27,215) plus the present value of the residual value ($1,906). Also note that the ending balance in the schedule is the residual value of $3,000.

Exhibit 15–7 presents an amortization schedule for the lessee for the same lease with an *unguaranteed* residual value (URV). The beginning balance in this schedule includes only the present value of the payments ($27,215), and not the residual value, because it is not guaranteed. The ending balance in this schedule is therefore zero instead of $3,000.

The information from Exhibits 15–5 through 15–7 will now be used to illustrate the journal entries required for the lessor and the lessee in the following sections.

EXHIBIT 15–5
Leases with Guaranteed Residual Value

Assumptions

1.	Asset FMV at lease inception	$29,121
2.	Asset BV at lease inception	$24,000
3.	Term of lease	4 years
4.	First payment due:	1/1/97
5.	Residual value at end of lease	$3,000
6.	Discount rate	12%

The initial lease payment and annual payments thereafter are determined as follows:

$$\text{FMV of Asset} = [(\text{PV Annuity Due @ } 12\%, 4n) \times \text{Payment}] + [(\text{PV of Single Sum @ } 12\%, 4n) \times \text{Residual Value}]$$

$$\$29{,}121 = (3.4018 \times \text{Payment}) + (.6355 \times \$3{,}000)$$

$$\$29{,}121 = (3.4018 \times \text{Payment}) + 1{,}906$$

$$\$29{,}121 - \$1{,}906 = 3.4018 \times \text{Payment}$$

$$\$27{,}215 = 3.4018 \times \text{Payment}$$

$$\$27{,}215/3.4018 = \text{Payment}$$

$$\underline{\underline{\$8{,}000}} = \text{Payment}$$

EXHIBIT 15–6
Lease-Amortization Table

Lessee: Guaranteed Residual Value

Lessor: Guaranteed or Unguaranteed Residual Value

DATE	(A) BEGINNING BALANCE	(B) LEASE PAYMENT	(C) INTEREST 12%	(D) REDUCTION OF PRINCIPAL (AMORTIZATION)	(E) ENDING BALANCE
1/1/97	$29,121	$ 8,000		$ 8,000	$21,121
1/1/98	21,121	8,000	$2,535	5,465	15,656
1/1/99	15,656	8,000	1,879	6,121	9,535
1/1/00	9,535	8,000	1,144	6,856	2,679
12/31/00	2,679		321		3,000
Totals		$32,000	$5,879	$26,442	

(A) = (PV 8,000 Annuity Due @ 12%, 4*n*) + (PV 3,000 Single Sum @ 12%, 4*n*)
= $29,121
(C) = (A) × 12%
(D) = (B) − (C)
(E) = (A) − (D)

EXHIBIT 15–7
Lease-Amortization Table

Lessee: Unguaranteed Residual Value

DATE	(A) BEGINNING BALANCE	(B) LEASE PAYMENT	(C) INTEREST 12%	(D) REDUCTION OF PRINCIPAL (AMORTIZATION)	(E) ENDING BALANCE
1/1/97	$27,215	$ 8,000		$ 8,000	$19,215
1/1/98	19,215	8,000	$2,306	5,694	13,521
1/1/99	13,521	8,000	1,623	6,377	7,143
1/1/00	7,143	8,000	857	7,143	0
12/31/00					
Totals		$32,000	$4,786	$27,215*	

(A) PV 8,000 Annuity Due @ 12%, 4*n* = $27,215
(C) = (A) × 12%
(D) = (B) − (C)
(E) = (A) − (D)

*Differences due to rounding.

LESSOR BOOKS

Exhibit 15–8 illustrates the journal entries required on the books of the lessor for guaranteed and unguaranteed residual values. The journal entry for the lessor at the inception of the lease depends on whether the lease is a direct-financing or sales type. In the direct-financing lease, the equipment is credited for the FMV ($29,121), which is equal to the assumed BV. The difference between the FMV and the gross receivable ($35,000) represents unearned interest that will be recognized over the lease term.

EXHIBIT 15–8 Residual Values: Lessor Books

Assumptions:

1.	Asset FMV at lease inception	$29,121
2.	Asset BV at capital lease inception	$24,000
3.	Asset BV at financing lease inception	$29,121
4.	Residual value, end of lease	$ 3,000
5.	Four annual payments @ $8,000 each	$32,000
6.	FMV at end of lease	$ 2,500
7.	Discount rate	12%
8.	Amortization tables in Exhibit 15–6 and 15–7 used	

		Direct-Financing Type				Sales Type			
		Guaranteed		Unguaranteed		Guaranteed		Unguaranteed	
1/1/97	Cost of Goods Sold	0		0		24,000		22,094[a]	
	Lease Receivable	35,000		35,000		35,000		35,000	
	Unearned Interest Rev.		5,879		5,879		5,879		5,879
	Equipment Inventory		29,121		29,121		24,000		24,000
	Sales		0		0		29,121		27,215[b]
	Cash	8,000		8,000		8,000		8,000	
	Lease Receivable		8,000		8,000		8,000		8,000
12/31/97	Unearned Interest Rev.	2,535		2,535		2,535		2,535	
	Interest Revenue		2,535		2,535		2,535		2,535
	•								
	•								
	•								
1/1/00	Cash	8,000		8,000		8,000		8,000	
	Lease Receivable		8,000		8,000		8,000		8,000
12/31/00	Unearned Interest Rev.	321		321		321		321	
	Interest Revenue		321		321		321		321
	Used Equipment Inv.	2,500		2,500		2,500		2,500	
	Loss	0		500		0		500	
	Cash	500		0		500		0	
	Lease Receivable		3,000		3,000		3,000		3,000

[a]$22,094 = $24,000 − $1,906[c]
[b]$27,215 = $29,121 − $1,906
[c]1,906 = PV of residual value at lease inception (see Exhibit 15–5)

The assumed BV in the sales-type lease is $24,000. Thus, the difference between the BV and the present value (PV) of the lease payments ($29,121) represents gross profit on the transaction that is properly recognized at the lease inception. However, these amounts depend on whether the residual value is guaranteed or not guaranteed.

If the residual is unguaranteed, the PV of the residual amount ($1,906) must be deducted from both the BV amount and the PV of the lease payments in determining the amount of gross profit. The lessor must reduce both the cost of goods sold and the sales amounts by the PV of the residual. The following table illustrates calculations of these amounts at the inception of the lease.

	GUARANTEED	UNGUARANTEED
Gross amount of lease payments	$35,000	$35,000
PV of lease payments	29,121	29,121
Unearned interest revenue	$ 5,879	$ 5,879
Sales (PV of lease payments)	$29,121	$29,121
Less: PV of residual	0	(1,906)
Sales recorded	$29,121	$27,215
Cost of goods sold (BV)	$24,000	$24,000
Less: PV of residual	0	(1,906)
Cost of goods sold recorded	$24,000	$22,094

The journal entries to record the lease would be

	Guaranteed Dr.	Guaranteed Cr.	Unguaranteed Dr.	Unguaranteed Cr.
Lease Receivable	35,000		35,000	
Cost of Goods Sold	24,000		22,094	
Unearned Interest Revenue		5,879		5,879
Equipment Inventory		24,000		24,000
Sales		29,121		27,215

At the termination of the lease at December 31, 2000, the lessor must record a $500 loss when the equipment is returned if the residual value is unguaranteed. If the residual is guaranteed, the lessor receives cash of $500, the difference between the FMV and guaranteed amount, and no gain or loss is recorded.

LESSEE BOOKS

The journal entries for the lessee are presented in Exhibit 15–9. If the residual value is guaranteed, the lessee includes the PV of the residual in the MLP calculation. If the residual is not guaranteed, it is not included in the MLP calculation. The depreciable basis of the leased asset excludes the residual value.

At the termination of the lease, if the FMV is less than the guaranteed residual, the lessee records a loss and pays the difference to the lessor. If the residual is not guaranteed, the lessee simply returns the asset to the lessor.

BARGAIN PURCHASE OPTIONS

Leases containing bargain purchase options (BPOs) receive similar treatment as those containing GRV provisions. The determination of the lease payments and the PV of the MLP include all payments prior to the date of the BPO plus the option payment amount. Recall that the BPO is expected to be exercised since the price is set substantially below the anticipated FMV at the option date. Exhibit 15–10 describes the lease and illustrates the computations used to determine

EXHIBIT 15–9
Residual Values: Lessee Books

Assumptions:

1. Asset FMV at lease inception = $29,121
2. Asset BV at lease inception = $24,000
3. Four annual payments at $8,000 = $32,000
4. Guaranteed residual value at end = $3,000
5. Assumed FMV at end of lease = $2,500
6. Discount rate used = 12%
7. Amortization tables in Exhibits 15–6 and 15–7 used.

		Direct-Financing and Sales Type			
		Guaranteed		Unguaranteed	
1/1/97	Leased Equipment	29,121		27,215	
	Lease Liability		29,121		27,215
	Lease Liability	8,000		8,000	
	Cash		8,000		8,000
12/31/97	Interest Expense	2,535		2,306	
	Interest Payable		2,535		2,306
	Depreciation Expense	6,530		6,804	
	A/D—Leased Equipment [(29,121 − 3,000)/4] and (27,215/4)		6,530		6,804
1/1/98	Lease Liability	5,465		5,694	
	Interest Payable	2,535		2,306	
	Cash		8,000		8,000
12/31/98	Interest Expense	1,879		1,623	
	Interest Payable		1,879		1,623
	Depreciation Expense	6,530		6,804	
	A/D—Leased Equipment		6,530		6,804
1/1/99	Lease Liability	6,121		6,377	
	Interest Payable	1,879		1,623	
	Cash		8,000		8,000
12/31/99	Interest Expense	1,144		857	
	Interest Payable		1,144		857
	Depreciation Expense	6,530		6,804	
	A/D—Leased Equipment		6,530		6,804
1/1/00	Lease Liability	6,856		7,143	
	Interest Payable	1,144		857	
	Cash		8,000		8,000
12/31/00	Interest Expense	321			
	Interest Payable		321		
	Depreciation Expense	6,531		6,803	
	A/D—Leased Equipment		6,531		6,803
	A/D—Leased Equipment	26,121		27,215	
	Loss	500		0	
	Interest Payable	321		0	
	Lease Liability	2,679		0	
	Leased Equipment		29,121		27,215
	Cash		500		0

the PV of the MLP. The lease conditions include a BPO at the end of the third year for $8,000, and the FMV of the asset leased is $29,121. Exhibit 15–11 shows the amortization table.

The journal entries for both the lessor and the lessee are illustrated in Exhibits 15–12 and Exhibit 15–13. The lease receivable is recorded on the books of the lessor at the actual amounts to be received under the conditions of the lease [($8,709 × 3) + $8,000]. The lease liability and the leased asset are recorded on the books of the lessee at the PV of the MLP including the BPO. The depreciation expense assumes an economic life of four years and zero salvage value. The interest amounts are found in Exhibit 15–11.

EXHIBIT 15–10
Leases with Bargain Purchase Options: Determining Payment Amounts

Assume that Henry Hungry leases equipment from Lease One that has a 4-year economic life and a fair market value (FMV) of $29,121. The lease contains a bargain purchase option (BPO) for $8,000 at the end of the third year. Lease One desires a 12% return on the money invested in the leased property. The initial lease payment and annual payments thereafter are determined as follows:

FMV of Asset = [(PV of Annuity Due, 12%, 3*n*) × Payment] + [(PV of Single Sum @ 12%, 3*n*) × BPO]

$29,121 = [(2.6901 × Payment) + (.7118 × $8,000)]

$29,121 = (2.6901 × Payment) + 5,694

$29,121 − $5,694 = 2.6901 × Payment

$23,427/2.6901 = Payment

$8,709 = Payment

EXHIBIT 15–11
Leases with Bargain Purchase Options: Amortization Table

DATE	(A) BEGINNING BALANCE	(B) LEASE PAYMENT	(C) INTEREST 12%	(D) REDUCTION OF PRINCIPAL (AMORTIZATION)	(E) ENDING BALANCE
1/1/97	$29,121	$ 8,709		$ 8,709	$20,412
1/1/98	20,412	8,709	$2,449	6,260	14,152
1/1/99	14,152	8,709	1,698	7,011	7,141
12/31/99	7,141	8,000	859*	7,141	0
Totals		$34,127	$5,006	$29,121	

(A) = FMV of Asset = PV of Future Payments
(B) = Payment (from Exhibit 15–10)
(C) = (A) × 12%
(D) = (A) − (C)
(E) = (A) − (D)

*Rounding difference (8,000 − 7,141 or 5,006 − 2,449 − 1,698)

EXHIBIT 15–12
Leases with Bargain Purchase Options: Journal Entries for Lessor Books

Date	Account	Debit	Credit
1/1/97	Leases Receivable—Hungry	34,127	
	Equipment		29,121
	Unearned Interest Revenue		5,006
1/1/97	Cash	8,709	
	Lease Receivable—Hungry		8,709
12/31/97	Unearned Interest Revenue	2,449	
	Interest Income		2,449
1/1/98	Cash	8,709	
	Lease Receivable—Hungry		8,709
12/31/98	Unearned Interest Revenue	1,698	
	Interest Income		1,698
1/1/99	Cash	8,709	
	Lease Receivable		8,709
12/31/99	Unearned Interest Revenue	859	
	Interest Income		859
12/31/99	Cash	8,000	
	Lease Receivable		8,000

EXHIBIT 15–13
Leases with Bargain Purchase Options: Journal Entries for Lessee Books

Date	Account	Debit	Credit
1/1/97	Leased Equipment	29,121	
	Lease Liability—Lease One		29,121
1/1/97	Lease Liability—Lease One	8,709	
	Cash		8,709
12/31/97	Depreciation Expense	7,280	
	Accumulated Depreciation— Leased Equipment ($29,121/4)		7,280
12/31/97	Interest Expense	2,449	
	Interest Payable		2,449
1/1/98	Lease Liability	6,260	
	Interest Payable	2,449	
	Cash		8,709
12/31/98	Depreciation Expense	7,280	
	Accumulated Depreciation— Leased Equipment		7,280
12/31/98	Interest Expense	1,698	
	Interest Payable		1,698

(continued)

EXHIBIT 15–13
(Concluded)

Date	Account	Debit	Credit
1/1/99	Lease Liability	7,011	
	Interest Payable	1,698	
	Cash		8,709
12/31/99	Depreciation Expense	7,280	
	Accumulated Depreciation—Leased Equipment		7,280
12/31/99	Interest Expense	859	
	Interest Payable		859
12/31/99	Lease Liability	7,141	
	Interest Payable	859	
	Cash		8,000
12/31/99	Equipment	29,121	
	Accumulated Depreciation—Leased Equipment	21,840	
	Leased Equipment		29,121
	Accumulated Depreciation—Equipment		21,840
	To reclassify accounts		

The amortization table assumes that the BPO is exercised. The lessee, on the BPO date, reclassifies the asset from a leased asset to equipment, indicating that legal title has changed. Also, the contra account for the leased asset is closed, and a new contra account called Accumulated Depreciation—Equipment is opened.

SALE-LEASEBACKS

Explain the basic concepts involved in sale-leasebacks, real estate leases, and leveraged leases.

In a sale-leaseback, the owner (seller-lessee) sells the property and simultaneously leases it back from the purchaser (lessor). Even if these are two separate but connected transactions, the economic substance of these transactions is that of a single financing arrangement. SFAS No. 14 generally requires that a sale-leaseback be treated as a single financing transaction with any profit on the sale deferred and amortized over the life of the lease. The gain is treated as a contra asset if the lease is a capital lease, or it is treated as a deferred credit (a liability account) if the lease is an operating lease. A loss, however, should be recognized immediately (up to an amount equal to the difference between the BV and FMV).

If the transaction is a sale and partial leaseback, the gain is deferred and amortized as before, but with two exceptions. If only a *minor portion* of the property is leased back (defined as less than 10 percent of the FMV of the total property), the transactions are treated as separate sales and lease transactions and any gain (or loss) is recognized in that period.

If the portion leased is greater than a "minor portion," and the gain is greater than the recorded amount of the leased property, the excess of the gain over the recorded amount of the lease is recognized as income of that period. The remainder of the gain is deferred and amortized over the life of the lease.

Sale-leaseback transactions provide a source of financing to the seller/lessee. Cash realized from the sale of an asset can be used for other operations

IN PRACTICE—GENERAL

Summagraphics' Sale-Leaseback

Summagraphics Corp. (NASDAQ:SUGR) announced Tuesday that it will conclude a sale and leaseback of its Austin, Texas, production facility. The property was purchased by two real estate investment trusts managed by ***W.P. Carey & Co. Inc.***, an investment banking firm specializing in lease financing. Net proceeds in excess of $6 million were generated from this transaction.

Summagraphics will realize a small gain on the sale of the property which will be amortized over the 18-year life of the lease and therefore not have a material impact on net income in the fourth quarter just concluded.

William J. Lifka, president, CEO, and chairman, stated, "The sale/leaseback enables us to redeploy assets from real estate investments to a myriad of opportunities consistent with our long-term strategic objectives of product portfolio expansion via product licensing, acquisition, technology partnerships, and/or joint ventures."

Source: Fran Barsky, "Summagraphics Concludes $6 Million Sales/Leaseback of Texas Facility," *Business Wire*, June 9, 1992, Sec. 1, p. 1.

of the business. The In Practice feature on ***Summagraphics*** is an example of a sale-leaseback.

The seller/lessee has the use of an asset that was specifically constructed to meet the needs of the enterprise. The buyer/lessor on the other hand has a long-term "collateralized" investment providing a desired rate of return—a "win" situation for both parties to the contract. The data and the amortization table for a sale-leaseback are presented in Exhibit 15–14.

The journal entries on the books of the seller/lessee for the first year of the sale-leaseback are illustrated in Exhibit 15–15. In Entry 1, the seller/lessee records the sale of the property. The gain on the sale is the difference between the sales price and the BV, and it is recorded as a deferred gain. The Deferred Gain account appears as a contra account to the Leased Property account on the balance sheet. Thus, the carrying value (BV) of the leased asset is the same as the BV prior to the sale-leaseback transaction. The gain on the sale (recorded as the deferred gain of $589,722) is recognized over the life of the lease by reducing the depreciation expense charge. This is shown in Entry 5.

Entry 2 records the leased asset at its FMV ($6,089,722) and the corresponding lease liability. Entry 3 reflects the lease payment.

At December 31, Entry 4 records depreciation based on the FMV of the leased asset, which includes the deferred gain. The final entry (6) records the interest expense on the lease per the amortization table in Exhibit 15–14.

Exhibit 15–16 illustrates the journal entries for the buyer/lessor. These are similar to sales-type capital leases.

REAL ESTATE LEASES

Real estate leases involve property such as land, buildings (or portions of buildings), and equipment that has been included in the contract (as in the case of Summagraphics, described in the earlier In Practice feature, where the entire plant was leased back).

EXHIBIT 15–14
Sale-Leaseback: Data and Amortization Table

Data

Assume the actual sales price of a building in a sale-leaseback transaction is $6,089,722 and the book value is $5,500,000. The buyer/lessor requires a 12% return on investment. If 18 annual lease payments are required, each payment would be $750,000, starting at the beginning of the lease (assume January 1, 1997).

Amortization Table

DATE	(A) BEGINNING BALANCE	(B) LEASE PAYMENT	(C) INTEREST 12%	(D) REDUCTION OF PRINCIPAL (AMORTIZATION)	(E) ENDING BALANCE
1/1/97	$6,089,722	$ 750,000	$ 0	$ 750,000	$5,339,722
1/1/98	5,339,722	750,000	640,767	109,233	5,230,489
1/1/99	5,230,489	750,000	627,659	122,341	5,108,147
1/1/00	5,108,147	750,000	612,978	137,022	4,971,125
1/1/01	4,971,125	750,000	596,535	153,465	4,817,660
1/1/02	4,817,660	750,000	578,119	171,881	4,645,779
1/1/03	4,645,779	750,000	557,493	192,507	4,453,273
1/1/04	4,453,273	750,000	534,393	215,607	4,237,666
1/1/05	4,237,666	750,000	508,520	241,480	3,996,186
1/1/06	3,996,186	750,000	479,542	270,458	3,725,728
1/1/07	3,725,728	750,000	447,087	302,913	3,422,815
1/1/08	3,422,815	750,000	410,738	339,262	3,083,553
1/1/09	3,083,553	750,000	370,026	379,974	2,703,579
1/1/10	2,703,579	750,000	324,429	425,571	2,278,008
1/1/11	2,278,008	750,000	273,361	476,639	1,801,369
1/1/12	1,801,369	750,000	216,164	533,836	1,267,533
1/1/13	1,267,553	750,000	152,104	597,896	669,637
1/1/14	669,637	750,000	80,363	669,637	0
Totals*		$13,500,000	$7,410,278	$6,089,722	

(A) = Cash sales price
(B) = Lease payment amount to provide a 12% return over 18 periods.
(C) = (A) × 12%
(D) = (B) − (C)
(E) = (A) − (D)

*Totals may have slight rounding differences.

REAL ESTATE LEASES INVOLVING LAND ONLY

To determine if a real estate lease involving land only is a capital lease, only the first two criteria must be applied. That is, if such a lease contains a provision for either a transfer of title at the end of the lease or a BPO, then the lease is treated as a capital lease. If neither of these tests is met, the lease is an operating lease, and the lease payments are treated as expenses in the periods paid.

EXHIBIT 15–15
Sale-Leaseback: Journal Entries for Seller/Lessee

1/1/97	(1)	Cash	6,089,722	
		Property		5,500,000
		Deferred Gain on Sale		589,722
	(2)	Leased Property	6,089,722	
		Lease Liability		6,089,722
	(3)	Lease Liability	750,000	
		Cash		750,000
12/31/97	(4)	Depreciation Expense	338,318*	
		Accumulated Depreciation— Leased Property		338,318
		*$6,089,722/18 = $338,318		
	(5)	Deferred Gain on Sale	32,762*	
		Depreciation Expense		32,762
		*$589,722/18 = $32,762)		
	(6)	Interest Expense	640,767*	
		Accrued Interest Payable		640,767
		*($6,089,722 − $750,000) × .12 = $640,767		

EXHIBIT 15–16
Sale-Leaseback: Journal Entries for Buyer/Lessor

1/1/97	Property	6,089,722	
	Cash		6,089,722
	Lease Receivable	13,500,000	
	Property		6,089,722
	Unearned Interest Revenue		7,410,278
	*$18 × $750,000 = $13,500,000		
	Cash	750,000	
	Lease Receivable		750,000
12/31/97	Unearned Interest Revenue	640,767	
	Interest Income		640,767

The lessor also treats the lease as a capital lease if the collectability and uncertainty tests are met and if the lease meets one of the first two criteria for all leases. The lessor replaces the land account with a receivable equal to the PV of the MLP and recognizes any gain or loss. If either the collectability or uncertainty test fails, then the lease is treated as an operating lease by the lessor.

REAL ESTATE LEASES INVOLVING BOTH LAND AND BUILDINGS

If leases involving both land and buildings contain either a title transfer or a BPO, they must be accounted for by the lessee as a capital lease. This is consistent with the purchase of an asset. The land and building are accounted for separately based upon their relative FMVs at the date of the lease. This is necessary because the building is depreciable property and the land is not. The building is depreciated over its economic life, since the lessee is the ultimate owner of the property based upon the lease provisions.

SFAS No. 14 sets a 25 percent materiality criterion for the land portion of real estate leases in which there is no title transfer or BPO. The land portion is presumed to be immaterial if the FMV of the land is less than 25 percent of the aggregate FMV of the assets leased.

If the land portion is deemed immaterial, then all four capital-lease criteria become operational again. If the lease term is for 75 percent or more of the estimated economic life of the building, or if the PV of the MLP is equal to or greater than 90% of the FMV of the leased property, the lease is treated as a capital lease. The depreciable property is amortized over the term of the lease since there is no presumed transfer of ownership.

If the land portion is material, the capital-lease criteria should be applied separately to the land and building portions of the lease. If there is no transfer of ownership (that is, Criteria 1 and 2 are not met, but either 3 or 4 is), the land portion is treated as an operating lease and the applicable rents charged against periodic income. The building portion that meets any of the four tests is capitalized. The PV of the MLP that apply to the building is the initial carrying value of the leased building.

LEASES INVOLVING REAL ESTATE AND EQUIPMENT

Occasionally, a lease may involve real estate and equipment. In this situation, the equipment portion of the lease should be considered separately and subjected to the capitalization criteria. If any of the four capitalization tests is met, the equipment portion is capitalized independently of any other leased assets. If none of the criteria is met, the equipment portion is treated as an operating lease.

LEVERAGED LEASES

Leveraged leases are direct-financing lease agreements (sales-type leases do not qualify) in which the assets leased by the lessor are substantially financed by a third party. While SFAS No. 13 does not define "substantial," the general interpretation is 50 percent or more of lease value. In essence, the lessor borrows from a third party to acquire the asset being leased. Thus, the third party receives principal and interest payments from the lessor; the lessor receives lease payments from the lessee, and the lessee obtains use of the asset. Leveraged leases are characterized by certain tax benefits to the lessor, such as retention of any investment tax credits, accelerated depreciation, and interest deductions.

At the inception of a leveraged lease, the lessor establishes the following accounts:

1. A receivable equal to the gross rental payments to be received less the total principal and interest to be paid to the third-party creditor.
2. A receivable for any investment tax credit associated with the property.
3. An estimate of the residual value recorded as an asset.

4. An account to record the lessor's equity in the property leased.
5. An unearned and deferred income account equal to the estimated pretax revenue to be earned plus any investment tax credit.

The technical details for the subsequent entries for these types of leases on the part of the lessor are complex and beyond the scope of this text. The entries for the lessee are similar to previously illustrated entries for direct-financing leases.

FINANCIAL ANALYSIS

Analyze the impact that capital leases have on certain key financial ratios.

The main type of classification of leases is capital- versus operating-lease treatment for both the lessor and the lessee. In general, the lessor tends to prefer capital-lease treatment for classification purposes, and the lessee tends to prefer operating-lease treatment. The lessor's preference for capital-lease treatment is most pronounced if the lessor wishes to report the lease as a sales-type lease. Recall that in a sales-type lease, gross profit on the sale is recognized at the lease inception. The lessee's preference for operating-lease treatment is usually based on a desire to exclude the liability from the balance sheet. Exclusion of the liability from the balance sheet has a favorable impact on solvency ratios of the lessee. Understanding these preferences and motivations of the lessor and lessee assists in understanding the effects of lease contracts on the financial statements.

LESSOR FINANCIAL STATEMENTS

Recall that the distinction between a capital and operating lease is whether or not the sale of an asset is deemed to have been made. An asset sale is accomplished when the lessor trades one asset (building, equipment, and so forth) for another asset (lease receivable). If the lessor is a dealer and the sale includes profit, and if all the conditions are met, the lessor also recognizes profit at the inception of the lease. In an operating lease, the profit recognition occurs over the life of the lease as the lease payments are received.

Consider the impact on the financial statements of the lessor of the same lease classified as a capital lease and treated as a direct-financing type rather than a sales-type, compared with treatment as an operating lease at the lease inception (see Exhibit 15–17). To clearly isolate the effects of alternative lease treatment, ignore residual values and BPOs and use the illustration from Exhibit 15–3.

In the sales-type lease, net assets increase by the same amount as the gross profit recognized at the inception of the lease. However, the net change for the direct-financing lease is zero because the net increase in assets ($27,215) is offset by the reduction of the equipment balance ($27,215). For an operating lease, there is no recognized change at all on the financial statements at the inception of the lease.

In subsequent periods, as the lease payments are received, the lease-receivable amount of the capital lease is reduced, and the unearned interest is recognized as earned. For operating leases, the lease payments are recognized as rental revenue and partially offset by depreciation expense on the asset. Thus, over the life of the lease, the differences in the methods occur because of differences in the timing of recognition.

EXHIBIT 15–17
Effects of Lease Treatments on Financial Statements

HENRY HUNGRY
Balance Sheet

	CAPITAL LEASE		
	DIRECT-FINANCING-TYPE	SALES-TYPE	OPERATING LEASE
Balance Sheet:			
Assets			
Lease receivable	$ 32,000	$ 32,000	$0
Unearned interest	(4,785)	(4,785)	0
Net receivable	$ 27,215	$ 27,215	
Equipment	(27,215)	(24,000)	0
Net asset effect	$ 0	$ 3,215	0
Income Statement:			
Sales	0	$ 27,215	0
Cost of goods sold	0	24,000	0
Gross profit	0	$ 3,215	0

LESSEE FINANCIAL STATEMENTS

Using the same illustration for the lessee, we can see that the main distinction is capital- versus operating-lease classification. If the lessee is able to treat the lease as operating, both the asset and the liability obligation are excluded from the balance sheet. However, in a capital lease, both are included on the balance sheet. Thus, solvency ratios for the lessee can be improved if the lease is treated as operating.

LEASES AND STATEMENT OF CASH FLOWS

The effects of leases on the statement of cash flows depend on classification of the lease as operating versus capital and on whether the capital lease is treated as a direct-financing or sales type. Further, BPOs and residual values will also affect cash flows at the termination of the lease.

Lessor. In general, a direct-financing lease for the lessor is a significant noncash investing/financing activity at the lease inception. Cash inflows at lease inception (annuity due) are investing activities. A sales-type lease for the lessor at lease inception is also a significant noncash investing/financing activity at inception. Cash inflows at inception are investing activities, and cash flows from operations are affected by the amount of gross profit recognized. Periodic lease payments for either method affect cash flows from investing activities (for the reduction of net lease receivable) and cash flows from operating activities (for interest revenue recognized). The effects of lease treatments on cash flows for the lessor are presented in Exhibit 15–18.

EXHIBIT 15–18
Statement of Cash Flows: Lessor

I. Inception of the Lease: Treatment is determined by the type of lease:
   A. Direct-Financing Lease:
      1. Noncash Investing/Financing Activity: Report the amount of the initial entry to Net Lease Receivable/Inventory (or other account where asset was carried) as a significant noncash activity.
      2. Investing Activities: Outflow for cost of asset if purchased in same period to accomplish the lease.
      3. Investing Activities: If the lease is an annuity due, include inflow equal to the payment received at the inception of the lease.
   B. Sales-Type Lease*
      1. Noncash Investing/Sales Activity: For the amount of the initial entry to Net Lease Receivable.
      2. Investing Activities: Inflow if the lease is an annuity received at the inception of the lease.
      3. Cash Flow from Operations:
         Inventory/COGS adjustment included in the normal computation for cash paid for inventory.
            Direct Method: Subtract lease sales from revenue.
            Indirect Method: Adjust Net Income by subtracting lease sales.

II. Periodic Lease Payments:
   A. Investing Activities: Each period includes an inflow in the amount of the reduction in Net Lease Receivable.
   B. Cash Flow from Operations: Lease Interest Revenue would be computed as part of the overall interest revenue:
      1. Direct Method: Interest Revenue plus the decrease (minus the increase) in Interest Receivable.
      2. Indirect Method: Adjust Net Income by adding decrease (minus increase) to Interest Receivable.

III. Conclusion of Lease: Treatment is determined by the terms of the lease:
   A. Bargain Purchase Option
         Investing Activity: Inflow for amount of BPO.
   B. Guaranteed (GRV) or Unguaranteed (URV) Residual Value: Compare GRV or URV—the book value (BV) of Lease Receivable—to fair market value (FMV) of asset returned.
      1. If FMV = BV: Noncash investing activity.
      2. If FMV > BV: Noncash investing activity to the extent of FMV. Operations:
            Direct Method: Ignore gain (FMV − BV).
            Indirect Method: Subtract gain from net income.
      3. If BV > FMV: Noncash investing activity to the extent of FMV.
            GRV: Cash inflow investing for cash received for difference between GRV and FMV.
            URV: Operations.
               Direct Method: Ignore loss (URV − FMV).
               Indirect Method: Adjust Net Income by adding back loss (URV − FMV).

*Depending on the terms of the lease, an alternative method for sales-type leases would be to include reduction in Net Lease Receivable as Cash inflows from Operations.

Source: Used with permission of Mary A. Flanigan.

Lessee. In general, the lessee reports the initial lease transaction as a significant noncash investing/financing transaction. If the first payment is due immediately, it is reported as a financing activity. The periodic lease payments are treated as financing activities for the amount of the reduction of the lease obligation. The portion of payment that is interest is reported as cash flow from operations. Exhibit 15–19 summarizes the effects of leases on the statement of cash flows.

DISCLOSURES REQUIRED FOR LEASES

Because these transactions can be very complex, very detailed disclosures are required for both the lessor and the lessee. The amount of detail required in the disclosures is necessary to provide users with relevant and reliable financial information for decision making.

All parties to lease agreements must provide a general description of the lease agreement in their financial statements. Other financial-statement disclosure requirements vary for the lessor and the lessee and by the nature of the lease (operating or capital). The disclosures are specific reporting requirements in addition to the general requirement to provide a description of the conditions of the lease. The reporting requirements for leases are presented in Exhibit 15–20.

EXHIBIT 15–19
Statement of Cash Flows: Lessee

1. Inception of the Lease:
   A. Noncash Investing/Financing Transaction: Report the amount of the initial entry to Lease Obligation/Leased Asset as a significant noncash activity.
   B. Financing Activities: If the lease is an annuity due, include an outflow equal to the payment made at the inception of the lease.
2. Periodic Lease Payments:
   A. Financing Activities: Each period includes an outflow in the amount of the reduction in lease Obligation.
   B. Cash Flow from Operations: Lease Interest Paid would be computed as part of the overall interest paid:
      1. Direct method: Interest Expense plus the decrease (minus the increase) in Interest Payable.
      2. Indirect Method: Adjust Net Income by adding increase (minus decrease) to Interest Payable.
3. Conclusion of Lease: Treatment is determined by the terms of the lease.
   A. Bargain Purchase Option
      Financing Activity: Outflow for amount of BPO.
   B. Guaranteed Residual Value: Noncash financing activity to the extent of the book value of the asset.
      Investing Activity: Outflow to the extent of any cash payment needed to satisfy the guaranteed value.
   C. Unguaranteed Residual Value: If the asset was not depreciated to zero, a loss will be recognized on the income statement for any book value of the asset on the last day of the lease.
      Direct Method: Ignore the loss.
      Indirect Method: Add the loss back to Net Income.

Source: Used with permission of Mary A. Flanigan.

EXHIBIT 15–20
Lease-Reporting Requirements

Lessor—Operating Leases

1. The cost of the property (by major category) less any related accumulated depreciation.
2. Minimum rentals receivable on noncancellable leases in the aggregate and for each of the next five years.
3. The total of contingent rentals included in income for each period that an income statement is presented.

Lessee—Capital Leases

1. The gross amount of the assets recorded (by major classes and aggregate).
2. Minimum remaining payments required in aggregate and for the next five years (reduced by executory costs).*
3. Total contingent rentals incurred for each period that an income statement is shown.
4. The total of minimum sublease rentals receivable under noncancellable leases.

Lessee—Operating Leases

1. For leases in excess of one year:
   a. The minimum remaining payments required in the aggregate and for each of the next five years.
   b. The total minimum rentals to be received under subleases under noncancellable leases.
2. For all leases: Rental expenses for each period that an income statement is shown, with separate disclosure of contingent rentals, subleases, and minimum rentals.

*Executory costs include taxes, maintenance, and insurance, which are costs of ownership. If the lease contract requires the lessee to pay the lessor (rather than a third party), and the costs are included as part of the periodic rental payments, they should be deducted in determining the present value of minimum lease payments.

END-OF-CHAPTER REVIEW

SUMMARY

1. **Differentiate between capital leases and operating leases.** Two major categories of leases are operating leases and capital leases. Operating leases assume that ownership remains with the lessor; hence, it is treated strictly as a rental agreement. Capital leases, on the other hand, presume a transfer of ownership to the lessee. Thus, the lessee records the asset and the lease liability on the balance sheet. The details of the lease contract are disclosed in the notes to the financial statements.

2. **Determine if a lease qualifies as a capital lease for both the lessee and the lessor.** A lease is a capital lease to the lessee if it contains any one of the following four criteria: (1) transfer of ownership, (2) a bargain purchase option, (3) the lease term is for 75 percent or more of the economic life of the asset, or (4) the present value of the resources surrendered are equal to or greater than 90 percent of the fair market value of the asset leased at lease date. A lease is a capital lease for the lessor if it meets one of these four criteria plus both of two additional tests: (1) no uncertainties

exist concerning collection of the lease payments, and (2) no uncertainties are associated with future expenses to be incurred by the lessor.

3. **Distinguish between a direct-financing lease and a sales-type lease, and demonstrate the accounting treatment for both the lessee and the lessor.** A direct-financing lease is a capital lease in which the fair market value of the leased asset is equal to the book value at the time of lease inception. No profit is recognized by the lessor. A sales-type lease is a capital lease in which the fair market value of the leased asset is greater than the book value at the date of inception. The lessor recognizes a profit in the amount of the difference.

4. **Illustrate the accounting differences for residual values and bargain purchase options in lease contracts.** Residual values and bargain purchase options are very similar in that both represent a final payment at the end of the lease. The lessor records the lease receivable for the gross amount of the minimum liability payments and recognizes unearned interest revenue for the difference between the receivable and the fair market value of the asset surrendered. In a sales-type lease, a gain is also recognized for the difference between the cost of the asset and its fair market value. The accounting treatment for the lessee is the same for both direct-financing and sales-type leases. The leased asset is recorded at the same amount as the liability, which is the present value of the minimum lease payments. Both parties to capital leases recognize accrued interest revenue/expenses at the end of each accounting period, and the lessee makes an entry to record depreciation expense.

5. **Explain the basic concepts involved in sale-leasebacks, real estate leases, and leveraged leases.** In a sale-leaseback transaction, the seller/lessee sells the property to the buyer/lessor. This financing agreement provides capital for the seller/lessee while the same assets are utilized as before. The buyer/lessor in turn is provided the desired rate of return on long-term investments.

   If the land portion of a real estate lease is less than 25 percent of the FMV of the aggregated assets, the lease is considered to be for the building only, and the 75 percent and 90 percent criteria are applied to the building to determine if the lease is a capital lease. In those cases in which the land is considered to be a material part of the agreement, the lease agreement is split into component parts by using the relative FMV of the two components to determine the amounts assigned to the land and the other assets in the lease agreement.

6. **Analyze the impact that capital leases have on certain key financial ratios.** Capital leases have a favorable impact on the relevant ratios of the lessor and an unfavorable impact on the lessee's ratios. The lessee profitability, solvency, and turnover ratios are negatively affected by capital leases because the lessee is required to record the asset and the liability on the balance sheet.

KEY TERMS

bargain purchase option (BPO) *788*
capital lease *788*
direct-financing-type lease *796*
guaranteed residual value (GRV) *790*
incremental borrowing rate *795*
implicit interest rate *795*
lease *786*
lessee *786*
lessor *786*
leveraged lease *810*
minimum lease payments (MLP) *790*
operating leases *788*
sale-leaseback *806*
sales-type lease *797*
unguaranteed residual value (URV) *791*

ASSIGNMENT MATERIAL

CASES

C15–1 Determination of Interest Rate—Class Presentation

Reread the excerpt "Auto Makers Sing the Praises of Leasing" at the beginning of the chapter and determine the interest rate used for the lease. Also find the interest rate assuming the van was purchased and financed for five years. Is leasing really a better deal as indicated in the article? If so, why would anyone purchase?

C15–2 Sale-Leaseback Proposal—Team Project

You have designed and constructed a physical plant to suit your basic production needs on land that cost $500,000. The physical plant cost $4,500,000 to build, and you have exhausted your credit line and need working capital. Your accountant suggests that you enter into a sale-leaseback agreement. An appraiser indicates that the fair market value of the property is $6,500,000. Meanwhile, your accountant has located a potential investor that desires a long-term investment at no less than a 12% return. Prepare a sale-leaseback proposal for the investor for a 30-year period.

C15–3 International with Exchange Rate Decision

Your company is considering expanding into France. An ideal location is available just south of Paris, and the owner is willing to lease the land for 30 years with the right of renewal. As an alternative, the owner will construct a facility that you design and then lease the land and facility to you under the same time conditions. In either case, the owner desires to be paid in French francs rather than U.S. dollars. The current exchange rate is six francs to one U.S. dollar.

If only the land is leased, the cost is 1,200,000 francs per year, adjusted every five years for inflation, but not to exceed 25 percent. The estimated cost of construction is $3,000,000 in U.S. currency and will take one year to complete. The French owner agrees to lease both the land and facility to you for 2,200,960 francs with the same inflation provisions.

Assume that your current cost of capital is 12%. Is the interest rate on the proposed lease less? If so, which lease agreement would you choose and why? Are there other risks involved in this arrangement?

C15–4 Real Estate Lease

The University of Kentucky through a wholly owned subsidiary is leasing land at $675 per acre per year on 30-year leases in an area designated as a technological research center. The lease agreements contain an escalation clause allowing increases at the end of every five years in the lease payments equal to 25 percent of the increase in the consumer price index. Several companies have already signed such leases and are constructing facilities on the leased land. Assume that your company enters into such a lease and constructs a facility that costs $150,000 for a parking area, $2,100,000 for the office complex, and $300,000 for landscaping. How should you account for the lease agreement and the property constructed? Does the escalation clause create any unique accounting problems at the beginning of the lease?

C15–5 Financial Analysis

Pertinent data for the Jones Company are shown at the top of the following page.

	1997	1998	1999
Assets	$1,600,000	$2,035,000	$2,835,000
Liabilities	400,000	660,000	900,000
Equity	1,200,000	1,375,000	1,935,000

	1997	1998	1999
Net sales		$2,250,000	$3,350,000
Cost of goods sold		1,695,000	2,480,000
Other expenses		300,000	400,000
Interest expense		60,000	108,000
Interest income—Leases		200,000	326,000
Income taxes		55,000	86,000
Sales from leases		1,400,000	2,280,000
Cost of sales—Leases		1,050,000	1,710,000

Required: Using the pertinent ratios discussed in previous chapters, provide an opinion about the company's progress from 1998 to 1999. What is your overall evaluation of the Jones Company? Support your observations with data from the ratio analysis.

C15–6 Comprehensive Case—Research and Report

Note: The procedures used in this case are based in part on "Operating leases: Impact of constructive capitalization," by Eugene Imhoff, Robert Lipe, and David Wright, *Accounting Horizons 5,* March 1991: pp. 51–63.

Late in 1994 your mother, who is retired, comes to you for investment advice. She has been dabbling in investments for the past year or so and has some knowledge regarding accounting, including a basic understanding of the income statement and balance sheet. A basic finance course at a community college has familiarized her with the debt-to-equity ratio and other common balance sheet ratios. She also thinks she understands the balance sheet categories of assets, liabilities, and shareholders' equity.

Recently she has become enthused about investing in airlines and is considering two different carriers, ***Delta*** and ***Southwest***. The companies are indeed different. Delta is one of the "Big 3" commercial airlines in the United States, with a vast network of domestic and overseas routes. The company prides itself on providing a high level of customer service. On the other hand, Southwest is a much smaller carrier with no international routes. The company focuses on short-haul routes in the western United States and provides a "no frills" level of service to its customers: There are no seat assignments given before departure, and bags of peanuts take the place of meals.

Your mother has obtained the most recent annual report for both airlines, and she wants you to look over the financial statements and tell her about any "red flags" that you run across.

After working through the financial statements, your big concern turns out to be buried in the notes. Specifically, you notice that both companies have a large amount of future payments under noncancellable operating leases.

Required: Using the balance sheet, footnote, and additional information provided here, write a two- to three-page report to your mom detailing the effects of the operating-lease commitments on the outlook of the companies. You don't have to recommend for or against buying one company or another; simply explain to the extent possible the effect of lease accounting on the picture of the companies provided by the financial statements. To do an effective job, it will probably be necessary to explain the following for any lessee:

A. The difference between capital and operating leases.
B. The different accounting procedures used to account for each type of lease.
C. The comparative impact of capital and operating leases on the financial statements.

It will also be necessary to explain the following for Delta and Southwest:

D. How the companies' balance sheets would change if the operating-lease commitments were capitalized (see the additional information).
E. The effect of such capitalization on common balance sheet ratios such as debt-to-equity.

Hints on Estimating Effect of Capitalizing Operating-Lease Commitments: Exhibits 15–21 through 15–24 provide the relevant financial statement data and footnote disclosures for both Delta and Southwest.

EXHIBIT 15–21 Comparative Balance Sheets

	DELTA AIR LINES, INC. CONSOLIDATED BALANCE SHEET (IN THOUSANDS OF DOLLARS)		SOUTHWEST AIRLINES CO. CONSOLIDATED BALANCE SHEET (IN THOUSANDS OF DOLLARS)	
	JUNE 30, 1993	JUNE 30, 1992	DECEMBER 31, 1992	DECEMBER 31, 1991
Assets:				
Current assets	$ 2,821,920	$ 1,698,444	$ 506,086	$ 340,001
Plant & equipment (net)	7,140,745	7,093,312	1,784,292	1,494,194
Other assets	1,908,358	1,369,818	2,599	3,096
Total assets	$11,871,023	$10,161,574	$2,292,977	$1,837,291
Liabilities and equity:				
Current liabilities	$ 2,972,831	$ 3,542,814	$ 368,360	$ 254,869
Long-term debt	3,619,473	2,723,135	699,123	617,016
Other long-term liabilities	2,186,929	590,815	—	—
Deferred credits	1,096,364	1,339,754	371,241	336,885
Total liabilities	$ 9,875,597	$ 8,196,518	$1,438,724	$1,208,770
Equity in employee stock ownership plan	$ 82,321	$ 70,988	—	—
Preferred stock	23	—	—	—
Common stock	163,351	163,262	92,473	42,438
Additional paid-in capital	2,011,879	885,680	155,938	81,987
Retained earnings	35,907	1,176,796	605,928	507,259
Unrealized loss on noncurrent marketable equity securities	(855)	(11,739)	(86)	(3,163)
Treasury stock at cost	(297,200)	(319,931)		
Total shareholders' equity	1,913,105	1,894,068	854,253	628,521
Total liabilities & equity	$11,871,023	$10,161,574	$2,292,977	$1,837,291

EXHIBIT 15–22
Southwest's Lease Footnote

SOUTHWEST AIRLINES CO.
Notes to Consolidated Financial Statements
6. LEASES Total rental expense for operating leases charged to operations in 1992, 1991, and 1990 was $115,335,000, $2,546,000, and $55,726,000, respectively. The majority of the Company's terminal operations' space, as well as 54 aircraft, were under operating leases. The amounts applicable to capital leases included in property and equipment were (in thousands):

	1992	1991
Flight equipment	$230,140	$197,607
Less accumulated amortization	59,569	46,599
	$170,571	$151,008

Future minimum lease payments under capital leases and noncancellable operating leases with initial or remaining terms in excess of one year at December 31, 1992, were (in thousands):

	CAPITAL LEASES	OPERATING LEASES
1993	$ 25,813	$ 113,661
1994	25,808	113,766
1995	25,802	104,525
1996	28,855	95,741
1997	26,843	88,614
After 1997	244,870	983,343
Total minimum lease payments	$377,991	$1,499,650
Less amount representing interest	166,942	
Present value of minimum lease payments	$211,049	
Less current portion	7,522	
Long-term portion	$203,527	

From your study of the chapter on leases, you know that the footnote disclosure required for leases is similar to that for bonds. The company must disclose minimum cash flows to which it is committed under noncancellable operating leases in each of the next five years, and in total for years following the fifth year. In other words, the footnotes provide a rough guide regarding the amount and timing of cash outflows for the leases. Determining the present value of these cash outflows would provide an estimate of the additional balance sheet liability the company would face if the operating-lease commitments were capitalized.

There are, however, assumptions that have to be made. First, in a capital lease, lessees discount future cash flows using either the implicit or incremental rate, and neither are disclosed in the financial statements. However, interest rates on long-term debt are

EXHIBIT 15–23
Delta's Lease Footnote

DELTA AIR LINES, INC.
Notes to Consolidated Financial Statements

4. LEASE OBLIGATIONS The Company leases certain aircraft, airport terminal and maintenance facilities, ticket offices, and other property and equipment under agreements with terms of more than one year. Rent expense is generally recorded on a straight-line basis over the lease term.

Amounts charged to rental expense for operating leases were $1.08 billion in fiscal 1993; $997.3 million in fiscal 1992; and $668.8 million in fiscal 1991.

At June 30, 1993, the Company's minimum rental commitments under capital leases and noncancellable operating leases with initial or remaining terms of more than one year were as follows:

	CAPITAL LEASES	OPERATING LEASES
1994	$ 20,565	$ 904,637
1995	18,323	916,243
1996	18,274	940,614
1997	17,530	940,070
1998	14,873	923,527
After 1998	57,970	13,202,192
Total minimum lease payments	$147,535	$17,827,283
Less: Amounts representing interest	38,029	
Present value of future minimum capital-lease payments	$109,506	
Less: Current obligations under capital leases	12,307	

EXHIBIT 15–24
Additional Information

	DELTA	SOUTHWEST
Average interest rate on unsecured long-term debt	10.0	9.0
Ratio of lease liability to lease asset*	.84	.85

*Assumes that 30% of the original lease has expired, the leases have an average 15-year lease life, and the interest rate is equal to the average interest rate on unsecured debt as provided above.

disclosed in a footnote, and it is generally safe to assume that interest rates implicit in operating leases are not dramatically different from interest rates for other obligations. To arrive at a conservative estimate, using a low rate such as the prime rate will provide the highest estimate of the future liability faced by the company. On the other hand, choosing the highest rate faced by the company on its debt will provide a low estimate of the liability posed by operating leases. The case material provides an average interest rate for the two companies' long-term debt.

A second problem is that the footnotes don't indicate exactly when the cash flows occur. For the first five years, assuming that the payment occurs in a single lump sum either at the beginning, middle, or end of the year will provide you with reasonable estimates. A greater challenge is to determine the present value of the payments occurring after five years, which are summed together in a single number. The most conservative assumption (providing the largest liability) would be that the entire amount was due on the first day of the sixth year. More reasonable estimates can be made by determining the average amount to be paid during the first five years and assuming that amount will continue in Year 6 and beyond. For example, if the summed total of cash outflows for Year 6 and beyond is $1,000 and the average payment during Years 1 through 5 is $100, then it may be reasonable to assume that the $1,000 payments are spread evenly over the 10-year period ($1,000/$100) from Years 6 through 16. Still another way to arrive at an estimate is to consider the average life of aircraft and aircraft leases. Information relating to these lives may be contained in the footnotes.

Once a liability has been estimated for the operating leases, the next challenge is to determine the corresponding asset balance. Remember that when leases are capitalized, the asset and liability go on the books at the same amount on the date of signing. However, after that time, the asset is reduced (usually straight-line) through depreciation, but the liability is reduced using the interest method. During the first years under the interest method, the bulk of payments represents interest expense, not reduction of principal; later payments reverse this trend. What this implies is that the book value of the liability will be greater than the book value of the underlying assets. By comparing asset and liability book values using different time assumptions, a ratio of the assets to the liabilities can be computed at different points in time. For this case, reasonable ratios are provided in the additional information.

Once you have estimates of the unrecorded liability and asset, you can use the balance sheet equality to arrive at an estimate of the impact of capitalization on equity. This represents the cumulative impact on net income if the operating lease commitments had been capitalized from their inception.

Remember that the overall goal of this exercise is not to arrive at an exact estimate of the liability faced by the company if operating-lease commitments were placed on the balance sheet but to arrive at a reasonable estimate of that number. By carefully considering each assumption and its impact on your overall estimate, you will be able to arrive at values that provide reasonable estimates.

QUESTIONS

Q15–1 What are the advantages of leasing productive assets as opposed to outright purchases?

Q15–2 What are the disadvantages of long-term leases?

Q15–3 What is the conceptual difference between an operating lease and a capital lease?

Q15–4 What are the lessee's criteria for determining if a lease is a capital lease?

Q15–5 What are the criteria for determining if a lease is a capital lease for the lessor?

Q15–6 How is the value of a capital lease for the lessor established?

Q15–7 Why might the amount shown by the lessor as a receivable be different than the amount shown by the lessee as a liability? Could they be the same?

Q15–8 Explain the following terms:

a. Minimum lease payments.
b. Bargain purchase option.
c. Guaranteed residual value.

Q15–9 Why is there a difference in accounting for a direct-financing lease and a sales-type lease by the lessor but not by the lessee?

Q15–10 How do lease terms affect the depreciable life and base of a leased asset?

Q15–11 What interest rate does the lessee use?

Q15–12 Define the following:

a. Incremental borrowing rate.

b. Implicit rate of interest.

Q15–13 How do guaranteed residual value (GRV) and bargain purchase option (BPO) clauses affect the initial recorded value for the lessee?

Q15–14 Explain what a sale-leaseback is, and name some of its advantages for both parties.

Q15–15 What is the effect of leasing back a minor portion of property sold? Define "minor" as it is used here.

Q15–16 What is the accounting treatment for gains on a sale-leaseback transaction? What if the portion leased back is considered to be minor?

Q15–17 What is the accounting treatment for real estate leases involving both land and buildings? To what does the 25 percent rule refer in leases of this nature?

Q15–18 Explain the accounting treatment of leases that involve real estate and equipment.

Q15–19 What is a leveraged lease?

Q15–20 What are the reporting requirements for the lessor for both capital leases and operating leases?

Q15–21 What are the reporting requirements for the lessee for both capital leases and operating leases?

Q15–22 Compare the effects of a capital lease to those of an operating lease on the debt-to-equity ratio of a lessor.

Q15–23 How are lease payments by the lessee reflected in the statement of cash flows for operating leases? for capital leases?

Q15–24 How are lease payments received by the lessor reflected in the statement of cash flows for operating leases? for capital leases?

EXERCISES

E15–1 Interest Rate

On January 1, 1997, Save A Buck, a general leasing corporation, acquired an asset for $40,000 with a rental life of 10 years. Save A Buck desires a 12% return on its investment. On January 1, 1997, the asset is rented by Madden Inc. for a 10-year period with the first payment made on January 1, 1997. Save A Buck uses straight-line depreciation with zero salvage.

Required: Determine the annual rental fees that Save A Buck should charge for the use of the asset. Provide the entries for the first two years for Save A Buck.

E15–2 Interest Rate

On January 1, 1997, Rentall, a general leasing corporation, acquired an asset for $50,000 with a rental life of 5 years. Rentall desires a 20% return on its investment. On January 1, 1997, the asset is rented by Frugal Inc. for a 5-year period with the first payment made on January 1, 1997. Frugal uses straight-line depreciation with zero salvage.

Required: Determine the annual rental fees that Rentall should charge for the use of the asset. Provide the entries for the first two years for Rentall.

E15–3 Direct-Financing Lease

On January 1, 1997, Sea Corporation (lessor) and Beach Boy (lessee) sign an 8-year lease contract for equipment that has an economic life of 10 years. The first payment was made on January 1, 1997, for $6,000 and annually thereafter for seven more payments. The present value (PV) of the minimum lease payments (MLP) is $35,200, discounted at 10%, which was the purchase price to Sea Corporation.

Required: Determine the interest income/expense for the first two years.

E15–4 Direct-Financing Lease

On January 1, 1997, Sun Corporation (lessor) and Farm Boy (lessee) sign a 4-year lease contract for equipment that has an economic life of 5 years. The first payment was made on January 1, 1997, for $10,000 and annually thereafter for three more payments. The present value (PV) of the minimum lease payments (MLP) is $34,018, discounted at 12%, which was the purchase price to Sun Corporation.

Required: Determine the interest income/expense for the first two years.

E15–5 Sales-Type Lease

On January 1, 1997, an 8-year lease agreement is signed by Sea Corporation (lessor) and Beach Boy (lessee) for equipment that has an economic life of 10 years. The lease terms provide an initial payment of $6,000 at January 1, 1997, and annually thereafter for seven more payments. The PV of the MLP is $35,200, discounted at 10%, which is equal to the FMV of the asset. The purchase price to Sea Corporation was $30,000.

Required: Determine the income to be reported by Sea Corporation for the first two years.

E15–6 Sales-Type Lease

On January 1, 1997, a 4-year lease agreement is signed by Bee Corporation (lessor) and Cee Co. (lessee) for equipment that has an economic life of 5 years. The lease terms provide an initial payment of $12,500 at January 1, 1997, and annually thereafter for three more payments. The PV of the MLP is $42,522, discounted at 12%, which is equal to the FMV of the asset. The purchase price to Cee Co. was $35,000.

Required: Determine the income to be reported by Cee Co. for the first two years.

E15–7 Lease Determination

On January 1, 1997, Sea Corporation (lessor) and Beach Boy (lessee) agree to an 8-year lease for equipment that has an economic life of 15 years. The first payment was made on January 1, 1997, for $6,000. Thereafter, seven more annual payments are due. The purchase price to Sea Corporation was $30,000. Beach Boy uses straight-line depreciation and assumes zero salvage value. Assume a 10% interest rate.

Required:

A. Is this a capital or operating lease? How do you know?
B. Prepare the journal entries for both parties for the first two years.

E15–8 Lease Determination

On January 1, 1997, John Corp. (lessor) and Steven (lessee) agree to a 5-year lease for equipment that has an economic life of 6 years. The first payment was made on January 1, 1997, for $10,000. Thereafter, four more annual payments are due. The purchase price to John Corp. was $35,000. Steven uses straight-line depreciation and assumes zero salvage value. Assume a 15% interest rate.

Required:

A. Is this a capital or operating lease? How do you know?
B. Prepare the journal entries for both parties for the first two years.

E15–9 Bargain Purchase Option

Key provisions of a lease starting January 1, 1997, between High Company (Lessor) and Low Corporation are outlined below:

FMV of property	$60,000
Term of lease	3 years
BPO at end of Year 3	$5,000
Beginning-of-the-year annual lease payments	$20,981
Interest rate used by lessor	12%
Economic life of property	6 years

Required:

A. Prepare a lease amortization table usable by both parties.
B. Prepare the journal entries for the third year of the lease for the lessee.

E15–10 Implicit Interest Rate

Able Office Equipment sells and leases equipment. The cash selling price of the equipment that Baker desires is $48,000. Able agrees to lease the equipment for 10 years, with $7,585 paid at the first of each year. Title passes to Baker with the last payment.

Required: Determine the interest rate used by Able.

E15–11 Implicit Interest Rate

Frank's Rental sells and leases equipment. The cash selling price of the equipment that Sinclair desires is $39,137. Frank agrees to lease the equipment for 5 years, with $10,000 paid at the first of each year. Title passes to Sinclair with the last payment.

Required: Determine the interest rate used by Frank's Rental.

E15–12 Guaranteed Residual Value

Tenover agrees to lease an auto to Ajax for three years. Lease payments of $6,365 are made at the beginning of each year, and the lessor's interest rate of 12% is known. Ajax agrees to return the auto with an FMV of $5,000. The estimated economic life of the auto is four years.

Required:

A. Provide the journal entries for both parties for the last year of the lease, assuming that the FMV of the auto exceeds $5,000 at the end of the lease.
B. Provide the journal entries for both parties for the last year of the lease, assuming that the FMV of the auto is $4,500 at the end of the lease.

E15–13 Unguaranteed Residual Value—Lessor

On January 1, 1997, Fields (lessor) entered into a sales-type lease agreement with Rhodes. The key terms of the lease are as follows:

Cost of property	$48,000
FMV of property	$60,000
Term of lease	5 years
URV	$5,000
Beginning-of-the-year annual lease payments	$13,644
Interest rate used by lessor	10%
Economic life of property	6 years

Required:

A. Prepare a lease-amortization table for Fields, the lessor.
B. Prepare the journal entries for the first and last years by Fields.

E15–14 Unguaranteed Residual Value—Lessee

Use the information in E15–13 to prepare the journal entries for Rhodes, the lessee, at January 1, 1997, 1998, 1999, and 2001, and also December 31, 2001.

E15–15 Unguaranteed Residual Value

Assume the following:

Cost of property	$80,000
FMV of property at lease inception	$85,000
Term of lease	4 years
URV	$3,000
Interest rate of lessor	12%
Economic life of property	4 years

Payments are due at January 1 of each year, starting January 1, 1997.

Required:

A. Determine the annual payment.
B. Prepare lease amortization tables for both parties to the lease.
C. Prepare the journal entries for both parties for the first and the last years.

E15–16 Sale-Leaseback

On July 1, 1997, Miller sold equipment costing $200,000 to Hanks for its FMV of $250,000 and immediately leased it back for 10 years. The estimated economic life of the equipment is 30 years. The lease payments are $39,506, providing a 12% return. The lease contract does not provide for a transfer of title nor a bargain purchase option. Assume straight-line depreciation with zero salvage value and that the lease payments begin immediately.

Required: Prepare the journal entries for both parties for the first year.

E15–17 Sale-Leaseback

On July 1, 1997, Payne sold equipment costing $300,000 to Floyd for its FMV of $500,000 and immediately leased it back for 5 years. The estimated economic life of the equipment is 8 years. The lease payments are $129,700, providing a 15% return. The lease contract does not provide for a transfer of title nor a bargain purchase option. Assume straight-line depreciation with zero salvage value and that the lease payments begin immediately.

Required: Prepare the journal entries for both parties for the first year.

E15–18 Financial Analysis

Refer to the basic information in C15–5.

Required:

A. Calculate the profitability ratios 1998 and 1999.
B. Calculate the leverage ratios for 1998 and 1999.

E15–19 Capital Lease—Cash Flows

On December 29, 1997, a lease agreement was signed by Stark (lessor) and Reality (lessee). The details of the agreement are as follows:

Cost of equipment	$54,710
FMV of equipment	$54,710
Lease life	3 years
Equipment life	4 years
Annual lease payments	$20,000
Date of first payment	12/29/97
Interest rate	10%

Required: Ignore any interest accrual for the two days at the end of 1997. Assume that both firms report on a calendar-year basis. Prepare the pertinent sections of the balance sheet and the statement of cash flows for (1) the lessee and (2) the lessor for 1997 and 1998.

PROBLEMS

P15–1 Capital Leases

On January 1, 1997, a lease agreement was signed by Ace Leasing (lessor) and Z Corporation (lessee). The details of the agreement are

Cost of equipment	$40,000
FMV	$40,000
Lease life	4 years
Equipment life	5 years
Annual lease payments	$11,471
Date of first payment	1/1/97

Required:

A. Determine the interest rate of the lessor.
B. Provide the entries for both the lessee and the lessor for the first two years of the lease.

P15–2 Operating Lease

Assume the lease in P15–1 was for a 3-year term and qualified as an operating lease instead of a capital lease.

Required: Prepare the journal entries for both the lessee and the lessor for the first two years of the lease as an operating lease under the assumptions you made in (**A**).

P15–3 Capital Leases

On January 1, 1997, a lease agreement was signed by One Leasing (lessor) and EZ Corporation (lessee). The details of the agreement are

Cost of equipment	$60,000
FMV	$60,000
Lease life	3 years
Equipment life	4 years
Annual lease payments	$22,670
Date of first payment	1/1/97

Required:

A. Determine the interest rate of the lessor.

B. Provide the entries for both the lessee and the lessor for the first two years of the lease.

P15–4 Operating Lease

Assume the lease in P15–3 was for a 2-year term and qualified as an operating lease instead of a capital lease.

Required: Prepare the journal entries for both the lessee and the lessor for the first two years of the lease as an operating lease under the assumptions you made in (**A**).

P15–5 Bargain Purchase Option

A lease agreement dated January 1, 1997, between Black (lessor) and Blue (lessee) contains a BPO at the end of the second year. Blue uses straight-line depreciation and assumes zero salvage value. Pertinent data for the lease follow:

Cost and FMV of equipment	$22,397
Economic life of leased asset	5 years
Date of first payment	1/1/97
BPO	$4,000
Desired interest rate	10%

Required:

A. Determine the amount of the lease payment.

B. Prepare the journal entries for both the lessee and the lessor for the two years of the lease.

P15–6 Bargain Purchase Option

A lease agreement dated January 1, 1997, between Klein (lessor) and Parker (lessee) contains a BPO at the end of the second year. Parker uses straight-line depreciation and assumes zero salvage value. Pertinent data for the lease follow:

Cost and FMV of equipment	$30,687
Economic life of leased asset	5 years
Date of first payment	1/1/97
BPO	$10,000
Desired interest rate	12%

Required:

A. Determine the amount of the lease payment.

B. Prepare the journal entries for both the lessee and the lessor for the two years of the lease.

P15–7 Sales-Type Lease With BPO

Assume the same information as in P15–5 except as follows:

Cost of equipment	$18,320
FMV of equipment	$21,720
Depreciation method	Sum-of-years'-digits
Economic life of leased asset	5 years
Lease payments	$10,000
Date of first payment	1/1/97
BPO	$4,000

Required:

A. Determine the interest rate of the lessor.

B. Prepare the journal entries for both the lessee and the lessor for the first two years of the lease.

P15–8 Sales-Type Lease With BPO

Assume the same information as in P15–6 except as follows:

Cost of equipment	$27,689
FMV of equipment	$30,689
Depreciation method	Double-Declining Balance
Economic life of leased asset	5 years
Lease payments	$12,000
Date of first payment	1/1/97
BPO	$10,000

Required:

A. Determine the interest rate of the lessor.

B. Prepare the journal entries for both the lessee and the lessor for the first two years of the lease.

P15–9 Guaranteed Residual Value

A 3-year lease agreement dated July 1, 1997, between Frakes (lessor) and Wilson (lessee) contains a GRV clause. Both use straight-line depreciation and assume zero salvage value, and their fiscal year-end is December 31. Pertinent data to the lease are as follows:

Cost and FMV of equipment	$30,460
Economic life of leased asset	4 years
Lease payments	$10,000
Date of first payment	7/1/97
GRV	$5,000
FMV at end of lease period	$5,000

Required:

A. Determine the interest rate of the lessor.

B. Prepare the entries for both the lessee and the lessor for the three years of the lease.

P15–10 Guaranteed Residual Value

A 3-year lease agreement dated July 1, 1997, between Smart (lessor) and Payne (lessee) contains a GRV clause. Both use straight-line depreciation and assume zero salvage value, and their fiscal year-end is December 31. Pertinent data to the lease are as follows:

Cost and FMV of equipment	$59,089
Economic life of leased asset	4 years
Lease payments	$20,000
Date of first payment	7/1/97
GRV	$10,000
FMV at end of lease period	$9,000

Required:

A. Determine the interest rate of the lessor.

B. Prepare the entries for both the lessee and the lessor for the three years of the lease.

P15–11 Sales-Type Lease With Unguaranteed Value

A 3-year lease agreement dated January 1, 1997, between Swinger (lessor) and Benson (lessee) was signed. Both use straight-line depreciation and assume zero salvage value. Pertinent data to the lease are as follows:

Cost of equipment	$19,500
FMV of equipment	$25,080
Economic life of leased asset	4 years
Lease payments	$8,000
Date of first payment	1/1/97
URV	$5,000
Interest rate of lessor	12%
FMV at end of lease term	$5,000

Required: Prepare the journal entries for both the lessee and the lessor for the three years of the lease.

P15–12 Sales-Type Lease With Unguaranteed Value

A 3-year lease agreement dated January 1, 1997, between Batman (lessor) and Wilson (lessee) was signed. Both use straight-line depreciation and assume zero salvage value. Pertinent data to the lease are as follows:

Cost of equipment	$40,000
FMV of equipment	$45,100
Economic life of leased asset	4 years
Lease payments	$15,000
Date of first payment	1/1/97
URV	$8,000
Interest rate of lessor	14%
FMV at end of lease term	$7,000

Required: Prepare the journal entries for both the lessee and the lessor for the three years of the lease.

P15–13 Sale-Leaseback

On January 1, 1997, Sinnomore Inc. entered into a sale-leaseback transaction with Heaven Hills Inc. The sale by Sinnomore included land acquired the previous year at a cost of $200,000 and a building that cost $400,000 to construct during the year. Other pertinent data to the transaction are as follows:

Sales price	$750,000
Economic life of building	25 years
Lease payments	$99,332
Lease life	20 years
Date of first payment	1/01/97
Interest rate of lessor	14%
BPO at end of lease	$1
FMV of building at lease inception	$500,000

There is no uncertainty as to the collection of lease payments, and no unforeseen costs are associated with the lease.

Required:

A. Prepare an amortization table through the year 2002.
B. Prepare journal entries for both parties for the first two years.
C. Indicate the balance sheet amounts and accounts at the end of the first year for both parties.

P15–14 Sale-Leaseback

On January 1, 1997, Lincoln Inc. entered into a sale-leaseback transaction with Davis Inc. The sale by Lincoln included land acquired the previous year at a cost of $350,000 and a building that cost $700,000 to construct during the year. Other pertinent data to the transaction are as follows:

Sales price	$1,500,000
Economic life of building	25 years
Lease payments	$179,300
Lease life	20 years
Date of first payment	1/1/97
Interest rate of lessor	12%
BPO at end of lease	$1
FMV of building at lease inception	$1,200,000

There is no uncertainty as to the collection of lease payments, and no unforeseen costs are associated with the lease.

Required:

A. Prepare an amortization table through the year 2002.
B. Prepare journal entries for both parties for the first two years.
C. Indicate the balance sheet amounts and accounts at the end of the first year for both parties.

P15–15 Sales-Type Lease—Determination of Implicit Rate of Lessor and Comparison With Incremental Borrowing Rate

Freddi M. and Fast Foods entered into a 5-year lease for equipment dated January 1, 1997. Both parties assume zero salvage on equipment and use straight-line depreciation. Data pertinent to the transaction are as follows:

Cost to Freddi	$80,000
Sales price and FMV	$100,000
Economic life of equipment	10 years
Lease payments	$22,790
Date of first payment	1/1/97
Marginal borrowing rate of lessee	11%
Interest rate of lessor	Unknown
BPO at end of lease	$8,000

There is no uncertainty as to the collection of lease payments, and there are no unforeseen costs associated with the lease.

Required:

A. Determine the interest rate used.
B. Prepare an amortization table through the year 2002.
C. Prepare journal entries for both parties for the first two years.
D. Indicate the balance sheet amounts and accounts at the end of the first year for both parties.

P15–16 Sales-Type Lease—Determination of Implicit Rate of Lessor and Comparison With Incremental Borrowing Rate

Hanks and Quick Foods entered into a 5-year lease for equipment dated January 1, 1997. Both parties assume zero salvage on equipment and use straight-line depreciation. Data pertinent to the transaction are as follows:

Cost to Hanks	$75,000
Sales price and FMV	$86,420
Economic life of equipment	10 years
Lease payments	$20,000
Date of first payment	1/1/97
Marginal borrowing rate of lessee	10%
Interest rate of lessor	Unknown
BPO at end of lease	$10,000

There is no uncertainty as to the collection of lease payments, and there are no unforeseen costs associated with the lease.

Required:

A. Determine the interest rate used.
B. Prepare an amortization table through the year 2002.
C. Prepare journal entries for both parties for the first two years.
D. Indicate the balance sheet amounts and accounts at the end of the first year for both parties.

P15–17 Capital Lease—Cash Flows

On July 1, 1997, a lease agreement was signed by Black (lessor) and Hawk (lessee). The details of the agreement are as follows:

Cost of equipment	$69,736
FMV of equipment	$69,736
Lease life	4 years
Equipment life	5 years
Annual lease payments	$20,000
Date of first payment	7/01/97
Interest rate	10%

Required: Assume that both firms report on a calendar-year basis. Also assume that title transfers to Hawk at the end of Year 4 and that the equipment is estimated to have a $1,000 residual value at the end of its productive life. Straight-line depreciation is used. Prepare the pertinent sections of the balance sheet and the statement of cash flows for 1997 and 1998 for (1) the lessee and (2) the lessor.

RESEARCH ACTIVITIES

R15–1 Financial Analysis—Motorola

Examine the financial statements of ***Motorola*** in Appendix C of the text. Answer the following:

A. How does Motorola primarily account for its leases?
B. Is any lease activity reported as a separate item for any of Motorola's financial statements?
C. Do any of Motorola's lease obligations affect its debt ratio?
D. What amount of lease payments were made by Motorola in 1993 and 1994?
E. As of 12/31/95, what is the total amount of future minimum lease payments for which Motorola is obligated? Are these liabilities?
F. Using a 10% rate, estimate the present value of Motorola's future lease payment obligations. State any assumptions you make in estimating this present value.
G. How would Motorola's debt ratio change if the present value estimated above was "effectively capitalized" adding both to total assets and to total debt? Would you consider this a material change?
H. What simplifying assumption must be made to add this present value to assets as well as debt?

R15–2 Financial Research

Select one industry from the a database with which you are familiar or the one that accompanies this text to examine for lease activity.

Required:

A. Prepare a summary table of the companies in the industry that report:
  1. The number of companies that report the following as *lessors:*
    a. Operating lease contracts
    b. Capital lease contracts (both sales-type and direct-finance-type)

2. The number of companies that report the following as *lessees:*
   a. Operating lease contracts
   b. Capital lease contracts
3. The total dollar amounts for each company in 1 and 2 above.

B. Prepare a brief analysis summarizing leasing activity in general for the industry.

R15–3 Financial Research—Capital Leases (Report Preparation)

Examine recent annual reports for ***Shoney's Inc.*** and ***Wal-Mart Stores, Inc.*** Prepare an analysis summarizing the extent to which these companies utilize capital leases and the impact of these leases on their profitability and solvency.

R15–4 Constructive Capitalization of Operating Leases (Report Preparation)

Study and prepare a report summarizing the article entitled "Operating Leases: Impact of Constructive Capitalization," by E. Imhoff, R. Lipe, and D. Wright in *Accounting Horizons,* March 1991, pp. 51–63.

R15–5 Internet Search

Use a search engine on the Internet keying words such as leasing, capital leases, and leases, for example. Print out any material that you think is relevant to this chapter.

PART 4

INTEGRATIVE CASES

INTEGRATIVE PRACTICE PROBLEM

The following represents the financial position of Test Company Inc. at the end of 1996.

TEST COMPANY INC.
Balance Sheet
December 31, 1996

Cash		$ 100,000
Accounts Receivable	$300,000	
Less Allowance for Bad Debt	6,000	294,000
Inventory		400,000
Equipment	$800,000	
Less Accumulated Depreciation	200,000	600,000
		$1,394,000
Accounts Payable		$ 200,000
Common Stock		700,000
Retained Earnings		494,000
		$1,394,000

The following events occurred in 1997. These are organized into operating activities, acquisitions, and dispositions.

OPERATING ACTIVITIES

A. The following summarize operating activities for 1997. Prepare journal entries for each.
   1. Sales for the year totaled $5,000,000. All were credit sales with terms 2/10, n/30; the company uses the gross method to record sales.
   2. Cash collected for credit sales totaled $4,750,000. Further, there were discounts totaling $50,000 for customers paying within the discount period.
   3. Specific accounts with a total balance of $4,000 were deemed uncollectible and written off.
   4. Credit purchases of inventory totaled $2,000,000. There were no discounts available from vendors.
   5. Payments to vendors for credit purchases totaled $1,700,000.

B. Related to selling and purchasing activity, prepare adjusting entries required on December 31, 1997, for the following.
   1. Two percent (2%) of accounts receivable are expected to become uncollectible in the future.
   2. The company uses LIFO for its only inventory item. The reported inventory of $400,000 depicted on December 31, 1996, consisted of two layers: 1,900 units costing $100 each and 2,000 units costing $105 each. The $2,000,000 purchases of inventory in 1997 consisted of the these two purchases, in order of occurrence: 10,000 units costing $120 each and 6,400 units costing $125 each. At the end of 1997, 5,000 units remained as ending inventory. (Hint: Before preparing the adjusting entry, you must first determine the amount to report for inventory on December 31, 1997.)

ACQUISITIONS

On January 2, 1997, the company purchased machinery by paying $30,000 down and signing a note to pay $300,000 in three years on January 2, 2000. The effective interest rate for the note is 6%. The machinery is estimated to have a five-year life and no salvage value. The company uses straight-line depreciation.

A. Rounding to the nearest $1,000, determine the present value of the note and the purchase price of the equipment.
B. Complete the following amortization schedule for the note. Round amounts to the nearest dollar.

DATE	INTEREST	UNAMORTIZED DISCOUNT	CARRYING VALUE
1/2/97			
12/31/97			
12/31/98			
12/31/99			

C. Journalize the acquisition on January 2, 1997, and the adjusting entries on December 31, 1997, to accrue interest and to record depreciation.

DISPOSITIONS

On March 30, 1997, the company sold all of its equipment listed on the December 31, 1996, balance sheet for an agreed upon price of $500,000. The buyer paid $100,700 down and signed a two-year, 8% note with Test Company for the remainder. To satisfy the note, the buyer must make four equal semiannual loan payments each September 30 and March 30. Test Company's straight-line depreciation for the equipment was based upon a ten-year life and no salvage value.

A. Rounding to the nearest $1,000, determine the amount of each semiannual loan payment.
B. Determine the gain or loss (if any) on the sale.
C. Complete the following amortization schedule for the note. Round amounts to the nearest dollar.

DATE	INTEREST	PAYMENT	PRINCIPAL REDUCTION	BALANCE
3/30/97				
9/30/97				
3/30/98				
9/30/98				
3/30/99				

D. Prepare entries required for Test Company on March 30, September 30, and December 31, 1997.

FINANCIAL STATEMENTS

Based solely upon the December 31, 1996, balance sheet and the events described in this problem, prepare a 1997 income statement, a December 31, 1997, balance sheet, and a 1997 statement of cash flows for Test Company Inc.

INTRODUCTION

Apparently, some public accountants don't understand the need for making independent decisions on the financial statements of their clients. In a recent article, Walter Schuetze, then Chief Accountant of the Securities and Exchange Commission, provides some interesting examples encountered by the SEC in which he alleges that public accountants didn't display the necessary "independent mind set" when evaluating accounting positions proposed by clients.

In making the case for independence in the public accounting profession, Mr. Schuetze quotes from John L. Carey's book *Professional Ethics of Public Accountants:*

> The basic differentiation between privately employed accountants and professional practitioners is in their responsibilities, moral or legal, to the corporation or the public, and in the extent to which their relationship may tend to influence their judgment. In the last analysis, therefore, it is his independence which is the certified public accountant's economic excuse for existence. (New York: American Institute of Accountants, 1946)

Following are two of the real-world examples provided by Mr. Schuetze in which external auditors supported questionable client accounting positions. After reading each case, determine whether the positions adopted by the clients were defensible or not.

CASE 1: DEFERRED MAINTENANCE COSTS: CURRENT OR LONG-TERM?

Passenger airline companies incur large costs to maintain and repair airframes and engines of their aircraft. While many large, slow-growth airline companies expense these costs based on their materiality and recurring nature, smaller companies may properly capitalize such costs and amortize them over their expected future benefit period.

The internal accountants for one SEC registrant which capitalized these costs proposed that the classification for these capitalized costs be divided between current and long-term assets: The deferred costs would be classified as long-term, except for the portion of the total cost amortized in the next period. (This accounting parallels the treatment of long-term serial debt that is not expected to be refinanced or eliminated through use of a sinking fund: The portion due in the next period is classified as a current liability as of the most recent balance sheet date.) According to Mr. Schuetze's article, this accounting treatment was supported by the engagement partner as well as partners in the national office of the airline company's public accounting firm.

REQUIRED

Place yourself in the position of the outside auditor for the airline company in the previous paragraph. Your client is considering two ways to account for major airframe maintenance expenditures: Dividing such expenditures between current and long-term in the manner discussed, or classifying all such expenditures as long-term deferred charges in the tangible asset portion of the balance sheet.

1. How do the two procedures differ in terms of their impact on your client's financial statement ratios?
2. What incentives does your client have for preferring one method over the other? Which method do you think would be preferred by your client?
3. Which method is the correct way to account for these expenditures? Assuming that the method preferred by your client and the correct method are different, what reasoning would you use to convince your client to account for the expenditures properly?

CASE 2: ACCOUNTING FOR SUBLEASE PAYMENTS IN THE FORM OF BARTER CREDITS

Mr. Schuetze's article described a second situation involving sublease payments for the use of a building. In this instance, X Company entered into a long-term noncancellable lease to lease building space at

$35 per square foot. The company appropriately accounted for the lease as an operating lease.

Two years after signing the lease, the market rate for comparable rental space in the same city is $20 per square foot, owing to oversupply in the commercial real estate market. At that time, X Company subleases the building to a third party. However, the sublessee does not make cash rental payments to X Company, but it instead provides X Company with barter credits which may be exchanged for advertising and product discounts from a number of vendors.

X Company, with the support of partners in the national office of its auditor, values the barter credits at an amount equal to a rental rate of $35 per square foot.

REQUIRED

1. If the sublessee made cash payments rather than issuing barter credits, how much would the payments be per square foot? What alternative valuations could be assigned to the barter credits on X Company's income statement?
2. If the sublessee made cash payments of $20 per square foot, how would X Company account for the sublease payments on its financial statements? How would X Company account for the barter credits valued at $35 per square foot? Which valuation do you think X Company prefers? Why?
3. How should X Company account for the barter credits? Why?

REPORTING CONTINGENCIES: HOW DOW CORNING DISCLOSED LOSSES RELATED TO SILICONE GEL BREAST IMPLANTS

The objective of this case is threefold. First, it provides a timely, real-world illustration of how large litigation contingencies affect *both sides* of the balance sheet. Second, the example has sufficient descriptive material in the note to allow students to relate much of the footnote disclosure with information contained in the balance sheet. Finally, the case compels students to consider basic issues related to discounting; the application of these issues extends beyond litigation contingencies.

BACKGROUND

Dow Corning Corporation is a joint venture owned equally by Dow Chemical Company and Corning, Incorporation. Until 1992, Dow Corning was the largest manufacturer of silicone gel breast implants, although less than 1% of its sales derived from implants.

In January 1992, Dow Corning suspended manufacture and sale of the implants at the request of the Food and Drug Administration, which was reviewing the safety and effectiveness of the devices. Significantly, Dow Corning had recently received a $7.3 million adverse judgment related to a suit brought by a California woman whose implants ruptured. Her attorney stated that "the verdict sends a message to Dow Corning that it cannot sacrifice the health and safety of women to enhance its balance sheet."

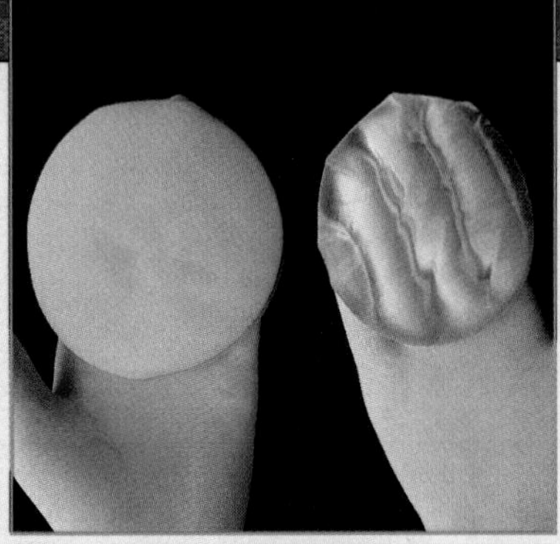

"SILICONE GEL BREAST IMPLANTS"

Following these two events, a significant number of lawsuits were filed against Dow Corning alleging that silicone gel implants caused a number of ailments, including joint swelling, autoimmune disorders, and chronic fatigue. The accompanying graph illustrates the drama-tic increase in lawsuits brought by individuals against Dow Corning after 1991.

EXHIBIT 1
Growth in Dow-Corning Breast Implant Lititgation, 1991-1994

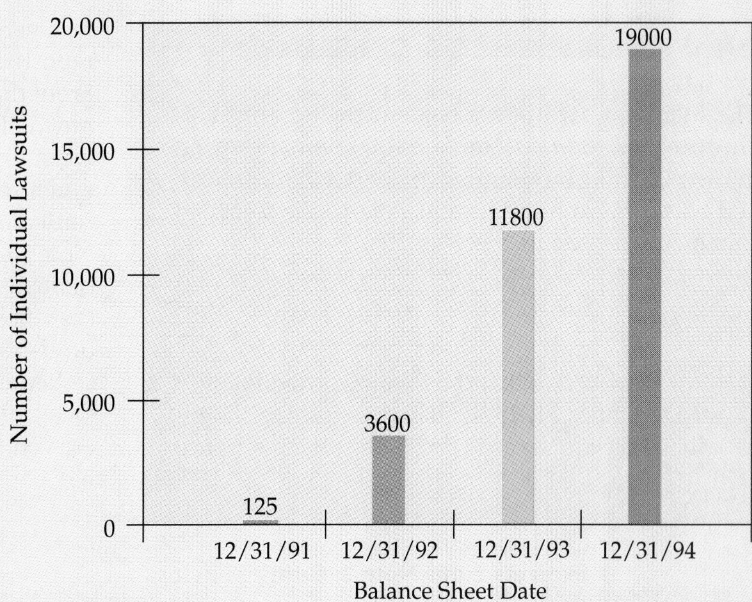

Because of the large number of cases brought against Dow Corning (and other manufacturers), many of the cases were consolidated for purposes of reaching a settlement. By early 1994, it appeared that such a settlement had been reached with a major portion of the plaintiffs. However, some plaintiffs exercised their right to "opt out" of the settlement agreement. Accordingly, there were two types of liability faced by Dow Corning: One related to negotiated payments under the settlement agreement, and the other related to potential liabilities to "opt out" plaintiffs.

Dow Corning's obligation under the proposed settlement agreement required it to contribute more than $2 billion over a 30-year period to cover present and future claims. Payments were to be made according to the following schedule:

	(IN MILLIONS OF $)
1994	$ 42.50
1995	275.00
1997	275.00
1998	275.00
1999 through 2011	51.17 per year
2012 through 2019	38.38 per year
2020 through 2026	25.57 per year

In 1994, the company also placed $275 million into an escrow account pending the final approval and signing of the agreement.

Balance Sheet Accounts Related to Litigation:

	1994	1993
Current Assets:		
Anticipated implant insurance receivable	157.5	
Other current assets—Implant deposit	275.0	
Other Assets:		
Anticipated implant insurance receivable	943.6	663.7
Current Liabilities:		
Implant reserve	475.4	158.7
Other Long-Term Liabilities:		
Implant reserve	1,286.9	1,100.0

Dow Corning's 1994 Disclosure

The following two boxes contain the account balances related to breast implant litigation appearing in Dow Corning's December 31, 1994, balance sheet, and excerpts from the second note to the financial statements related to contingencies.

Required

1. Note 2 indicates that the total recorded liability at December 31, 1994 related to implant litigation and claims was $1,762.3; the total insurance receivable was $1,101.1 How are these amounts reported on the balance sheet?
2. From the information provided, determine how much of the total liability of $1762.3 million relates to the settlement agreement, and how much relates to potential claims outside of the settlement agreement.
3. Note 2 states that the liability related to the settlement agreement is $1,158.7 when the future cash flows are discounted at a 7% rate; on an undiscounted basis the liability related to the settlement agreement is given as $1,976.2. Determine how the undiscounted liability was arrived at.

Excerpts from Note 2: Contingencies:

. . . The Company (Dow-Corning) has made efforts in the past to reflect anticipated financial consequences to the Company of the breast implant situation. During 1991 and 1992, the Company recorded $25.0 and $69.0, respectively, of pretax costs related to breast implant matters. In 1993 the Company recorded a pretax charge of $640.0. This charge included the Company's best estimate of its potential liability for breast implant litigation based on settlement negotiations, and also included provisions for legal, administrative, and research costs related to breast implants, for a total of $1.24 billion, less anticipated insurance recoveries of $600.0. As discussed below, the Company recorded the liability attributable to the Settlement Agreement and the related insurance receivable on a present value basis. . . .

As a result of the provisions described above, as of December 31, 1994 the Company's financial statements reflect a total liability of $1,762.3 and a total anticipated implant insurance receivable of $1,101.1. Of these amounts, a liability of $603.6 and an anticipated implant insurance receivable of $398.3 have been recorded to reflect costs and insurance recoveries, respectively, relevant to breast implant liabilities not covered by the Settlement Agreement; these amounts are recorded on an undiscounted basis. Because the amount and timing of the liability attributable to the Settlement Agreement is reliably determinable, the Company recorded this liability and the related anticipated implant insurance receivable on a present-value basis using a discount rate of 7.0% over a period of more than 30 years. This rate approximated the interest rate on monetary assets that are risk free and that have maturities corresponding with the scheduled cash payments. The Settlement Agreement liability recorded in the financial statements at December 31, 1994 is $1,158.7; this amount is $1,976.2 on an undiscounted basis. The Settlement Agreement anticipated implant insurance receivable recorded in the financial statements at December 31, 1994 is $702.8; this amount is $1,156.2 on an undiscounted basis.

4. Why do you think Dow Corning reported amounts related to the settlement agreement on a discounted basis, but amounts outside on the settlement agreement on an undiscounted basis? Do you think Dow Corning's discounting treatment for different liabilities is appropriate? Why or why not?

5. Note that Dow Corning discounted both the liability and the receivable related to the settlement agreement using an essentially risk-free rate of 7%. Is it appropriate to discount both items using the same rate?

PART 5

DISCLOSURE AND REPORTING

16

Postemployment Benefits

Learning Objectives

After studying this chapter, you should be able to:

1. Differentiate between defined-contribution and defined-benefit plans.
2. Understand the theoretically correct pension-related journal entries for defined-benefit plans and understand the practical compromises of SFAS No. 87.
3. Measure and account for actuarial gains and losses.
4. Apply the disclosure requirements of SFAS No. 87.
5. Explain the general accounting requirements for other postretirement benefits.

Pension Benefits at Risk

As more giant companies fall on hard times, retirees may face a wave of broken promises. The government, through the PBGC [Pension Benefit Guarantee Corporation], backstops the pensions of 41 million Americans . . . But often pensions promised by employers aren't fully covered [by the companies or] by the agency. . . .

Many employers, if they're low on funds, take the path of least resistance" to worker demands for improved wages or benefits, says Howard Weizmann, vice president for benefits consulting at ***Aetna Life Insurance Co.*** Since more generous pension benefits are costs that aren't incurred for years . . . some companies would rather promise bigger pension benefits than face the immediate costs of higher wages. . . .

As employers struggle to make ends meet, it's relatively easy to give short shrift to pension plans. The money isn't paid out until workers retire, and then only in monthly increments over decades. Funding can be postponed until a hoped-for sunnier day [which may never come!]

Source: Albert Karr, "Risk to Retirees Rises as Firms Fail to Fund Pensions They Offer," *The Wall Street Journal,* February 4, 1993, pp. A1, A12.

As the accompanying excerpt suggests, it is easier to promise to pay benefits tomorrow than it is to actually pay benefits today. Likewise, corporations would prefer to record expenses tomorrow rather than record expenses today. Recording expenses later (among other things) increases current income reports, which are frequently the basis of management-incentive compensation plans. Recognizing liabilities later rather than sooner is similarly popular among corporate executives as (among other things) it preserves favorable debt-to-equity ratios. It should not be surprising that historically pension and postretirement health-benefit costs were not expensed nor liabilities recognized until cash distributions were made in years after retirement. Thus, a cash-basis system was followed.

However, the U.S. accounting system is essentially an accrual-based system, and the cash-basis treatment of postretirement benefits created an inconsistency in practice. As the numbers involved became larger, pressure for change became greater. Consistent with the matching principle, current standards require that all the costs of labor (including postretirement benefits) must be recognized as expenses in the periods of benefit (when the labor services are provided by employees, not after retirement). While this concept is simple, application of the concept for postretirement labor costs can be complex. These costs, which may be paid in the distant future, are hard to estimate, and the amounts are frequently subject to changing labor contracts as well as changing environmental conditions. In addition, the complexity of the current pension standard is caused in part by the CPA firms themselves and their corporate clients, who continue to prefer to *not recognize selected events today* but would rather recognize them tomorrow. On this point, Walter Schuetze, former ***KPMG Peat Marwick*** partner and Chief Accountant of the SEC observes,

> Some of the FASB's recent and not-so-recent statements are far too complicated. FASB Statement No. 96 (Income Taxes), Statement No. 87 (Pensions) and Statement No. 13 (Leases) are examples of mind-numbing complexity. Those

> statements are so complicated that ordinary people cannot understand and apply them. . . . How did we get here? How did accounting standards get so complex? Some of the responsibility lies with the Securities and Exchange Commission. Over the years, the SEC has layered complexity on top of complexity. . . . Some of the complexity arises because transactions are complex. However, by far most of the recent complexity arises because preparers of financial statements and their CPA firms have asked for it. Pension accounting is complicated because most preparers, and their CPA firms, are unwilling to see [*current*] changes in market values of plan assets and settlement values of plan liabilities entered [*currently*] into earnings . . . Spread those changes, they say. A large part of FASB Statement No. 87 is devoted to smoothing the hills and valleys of change.[1]

Thus, reliable analysis of financial statements requires a thorough understanding of complex accounting standards. The prudent individual will need to know what to look for and where to look. For most firms, postemployment and postretirement labor costs constitute a highly significant portion of labor costs on the income statement and a major cash outflow. For example, ***Goldman Sachs & Company*** estimates annual ongoing postretirement health expenses are equal to 5% of net income for ***General Electric***, 15% to 18% for ***W. R. Grace***, and 20% for ***Monsanto***.[2] In addition, future labor cost commitments represent significant liabilities to many firms. For example, even at the beginning of the current decade, the pension cost commitments of ***General Motors*** and ***IBM*** exceeded $15 billion each; ***Ford*** reported figures in excess of $8 billion, and ***Bethlehem Steel*** checked in at about $4.5 billion. Of course, measurement issues abound. Still, the correct interpretation of many commonly used financial ratios (such as the return-on-assets ratio, the debt-to-equity ratio, and the gross margin) depends to a great extent on a thorough understanding of the accounting treatment of postemployment and postretirement labor costs.

POSTEMPLOYMENT BENEFITS

The term **postemployment benefits** refers to promises made by many companies to terminated or laid-off employees. These benefits may include continuations of salary or benefits (such as insurance), severance pay, unemployment pay, job training, or employment counseling. In recent years, because of widespread corporate downsizing, more and more employees need such benefits. They provide an economic safety net to laid-off workers. Postemployment benefits may originate in union contracts, or they may be offered by firms as incentives for workers to quit prior to retirement.

Accounting for these postemployment benefits may follow SFAS No. 43, "Accounting for Compensated Absences," or SFAS No. 5, "Accounting for Contingencies." Both of these topics have been covered elsewhere in this text. Essentially, SFAS No. 43 requires that a liability be recorded if (1) postemployment benefits *vest*, or accumulate (vesting will be discussed later in this chapter), (2) the obligation is attributable to services already rendered, (3) payment is probable, and (4) the amount can be reasonably estimated. The costs must be expensed in the periods benefiting from the labor services giving rise to the obligations. If these conditions do not exist, accounting is in accordance with SFAS No. 5.

[1]W. Schuetze, "Keep It Simple," *Accounting Horizons*, June 1991, pp. 113–117.

[2]Goldman, Sachs & Company, "Strategy Brief, FAS No. 106: The Deadline Approaches," (1992).

POSTRETIREMENT BENEFITS

Two types of postretirement benefits exist: (1) pension plans and (2) postretirement benefits other than pensions, including life insurance and health-care benefits. Approximately 85 percent of private employers provide pension plans for employees, contributing, on average, an amount nearly equaling 7 percent of payroll. Private and public pension plans (excluding social security) hold nearly $1.5 trillion in assets. Postretirement benefits are a form of deferred compensation. The advantages to the employee of deferred earnings are largely tax-related. In employee-sponsored pension plans, employees can (1) avoid current taxes on earnings and (2) avoid current taxes on savings growth—that is, pension plans grow tax-free until retirement, at which time the earnings and accumulated interest are taxed at lower marginal rates (than if they had not been deferred).

Approximately 40 percent of workers in private firms with 100 employees or more also have health insurance plans that will continue coverage after early retirement. More than 30 percent have plans that will continue coverage after normal retirement. The median retiree health obligation for companies having such plans is estimated at $46 million, or 6% of the market value of the companies.

The advantages to employees of pre- and postretirement health-care programs rest, in part, with risk avoidance. The last two decades have witnessed rapid growth in medical costs. Now a single illness can wipe out a family's savings and put people hopelessly in debt. Employer-funded health-care programs provide insurance against current catastrophic illness and a hedge against future medical-cost escalations. The same programs, however, place corporations at greater risk. Accordingly, many corporations are trying to renegotiate downward their commitments as the twenty-first century approaches.

This chapter discusses in detail pension benefits. Postretirement health insurance benefits and other postretirement benefits are also addressed, but in less detail.

PENSION PLANS

Differentiate between defined-contribution and defined-benefit plans.

In the United States there are essentially two types of pension plans: defined-contribution plans and defined-benefit plans. In defined-contribution plans the employer fulfills all obligations to the employee by making periodic payments to an independent third party who administers a trust fund. (Alternatively, in some instances, defined-contribution plans may be self-directed.) The ultimate benefit to be received by the employee is not defined in this type of arrangement; only the contribution to the fund by the employer is defined. Retirement income benefits depend on the administration of the pension trust fund and the quality of the investments. The investment risk of the defined contribution plan, thus, is borne by the employee, not the employer. The amount of the periodic required contribution (or *defined contribution*) is most often determined by negotiated contract. The contribution may be set as a fixed amount, a fixed percentage of the employee's salary or wages, a negotiated percentage of employer's net income, or some other combination.

In contrast, in a defined-benefit plan the ultimate benefit to be received by the employee is defined in the plan and is the ultimate responsibility of the employer. Annual contributions made by the employer to the pension plan are undefined. Only ultimate benefits (obligations) are defined. The amount that the employer contributes annually to the pension plan will depend on actuarial estimates of the future obligations, fund earnings projections, federal law, and the cash position of the firm.

Thus, defined contribution plans leave undefined the specific benefits that employees will receive, while defined-benefit plans leave undefined specific annual contributions to the pension plan by the firm.

DEFINED-CONTRIBUTION PLANS

Accounting for labor costs under defined-contribution pension plans is relatively straightforward. SFAS No. 87 directs that contributions to the pension plan must be expensed as incurred. For example, assume Fred Michaels serves on the faculty of accounting at State College. During 1997 Michaels earned $48,000. In addition, he is covered by State College's defined-contribution plan, which requires the college to contribute the equivalent of 7 percent of his pay to North America Retirement and Annuity Association. Assuming monthly contributions, the appropriate monthly entry would be to debit pension expense and credit cash for $280 ($48,000/12 × 7%). Having made the defined contribution, the employer's obligation is fulfilled and no further entries are required by the employer.

DEFINED-BENEFIT PLANS

Accounting for defined-benefit plans is quite different from accounting for defined-contribution plans and is best illustrated by the use of an extended example. Assume Karen Bloom is an employee of Kent Corporation. She is 40 years of age and has worked for Kent Corporation for five years. Bloom earns $25,000 per year and is covered by a defined-benefit pension plan that her union negotiated with Kent Corporation. Under the terms of the agreement, she will be entitled at retirement to an annual income determined according to the following formula:

$$\frac{\text{Annual Defined}}{\text{Pension Benefit}} = \frac{\text{Number of Years}}{\text{of Service}} \times 2\% \times \frac{\text{Average Salary}}{\text{Last 5 Years' Service}}$$

Thus, at retirement at age 65, she will have worked for Kent for 30 years (65 − 40 + 5) and will have earned retirement benefits equivalent to 60 percent of her average salary calculated for the last five years of her employment. (Such agreements are typical of defined-benefit plans.)

Note that Bloom has already earned five years' credit, and each additional year of service adds to her pension benefits. To estimate the specific amount of the benefit claims requires an estimate to be made of the average salary for her last five years of service. Few of us would envision working for an employer for an additional 25 years without any further pay raises, and presumably the employer anticipated giving future pay raises when negotiating the benefits formula.

For purposes of this example, we estimate that the average salary for the last five years of employment will be $75,000. Accordingly, if Bloom retires at age 65 with 30 years' service credit, she will be entitled to annual pension benefits of $45,000 (30 years × 2% × $75,000). To date, she has earned five years' credit, or annual pension benefits of $7,500 (5 years × 2% × $75,000). For each additional year of service, Bloom will earn one more year's credit, or annual benefits increments of $1,500 (1 year × 2% × $75,000).

IN FOCUS

Michael Hackman
Insurance and Investment Broker
Hackman Financial Group
BS, Business, Miami University

"The pension commitment can be a big burden."

Employers can choose among a variety of postemployment benefit plans. And while many employers would prefer to offer comprehensive pension and medical plans to attract the best employees, such programs are often very expensive and may even jeopardize a firm's long-term financial health, according to Mike Hackman, owner of ***Hackman Financial Group.***

Hackman handles the insurance and investment needs of small to mid-sized firms and individual investors and helps them understand their options regarding benefits. More and more, Hackman says, companies—especially smaller firms—are turning to the 401-k plan as opposed to the traditional pension plan where the employer is the sole contributor to the employee's retirement benefits. 401-k plans are profit-sharing plans that allow employees to contribute to their own retirement accounts in addition to any contributions that the employer may make.

"Defined-contribution and defined-benefit plans, while they use different methods to determine the dollar amount, are both fixed commitments for the employer," Hackman describes. "The firm needs to pay in a fixed amount to the pension plan, regardless of the financial results of the company. When the company's doing well, it's no problem, but if profits are down or the company wants to make a big investment in R&D or build a new plant, the pension commitment can be a big burden."

These problems are most acute for smaller firms with less predictable results. A smaller firm is more likely to institute a 401-k plan because of its flexibility. When company results are weak, the employer may make reduced payments to the plan, or none at all. "A nice feature of a 401-k plan is that even if the employer lacks the resources to fund the plan, the employee can contribute to his or her own account and, in many cases, direct how it is invested," says Hackman. "It puts the employee in control of his or her own retirement planning."

The administrative costs of a 401-k plan are also lower for most firms. A defined-benefit plan, for instance, requires an annual actuarial calculation to determine the plan's projected benefit obligation. This is a complex net present value calculation based on the age, length of service, and projected future salary of *every* employee. The pension plan administrator is paid to make this calculation; the cost is borne by the employer.

The same general concerns that affect the selection of pension plans—flexibility and cost—prevent most small firms from offering medical benefits for their retired employees. "A small company generally doesn't have a large enough employee population to support the insurance costs for retirees. If you only have a hundred employees, just one or two seriously ill retirees could make your insurance premiums unaffordable," Hackman says.

EMPLOYER'S PENSION ACCOUNTING

From Kent Corporation's perspective, one question to be addressed is, what is the current cost of future benefits for reporting purposes? SFAS No. 87 requires that the estimate of future benefits be discounted at rates that "reflect the rates at which the pension benefits could be effectively settled." This means that employers should use rates equivalent to rates implicit in the current prices of annuity contracts that could be used to pay off (to effect settlement of) the obligation. It is important to note that this is a genuine alternative that many firms have: to purchase an annuity contract in the name of the employee from an insurance company. As an alternative interest measure, an employer may use a rate equivalent to the current rate of return on high-quality fixed-income investments.[3] The exact discount rate to be used is not explicitly identified in SFAS No. 87, and yet proper determination of this rate is critical, as illustrated in the In Practice feature "The Importance of Interest Rate Assumptions."

IN PRACTICE—GENERAL

The Importance of Interest Rates Assumptions

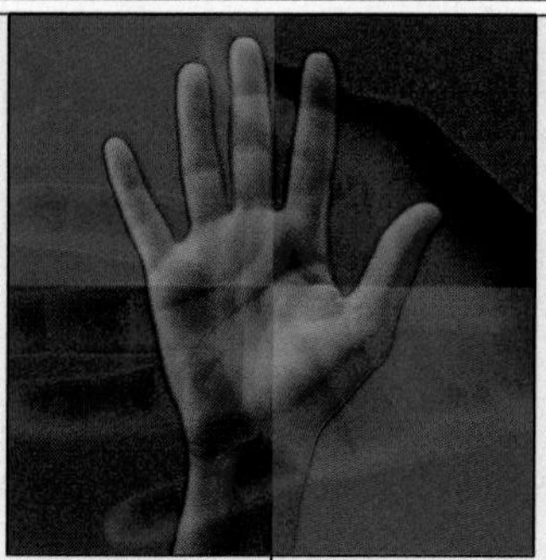

For millions of people counting on company pensions to see them through the golden years of retirement, the news last week from the ***Pension Benefit Corporation*** was chilling . . . The government agency, which insures private pension plans, said the already serious problem of underfunding in many corporate plans grew a lot worse last year.

[T]he real root of the current underfunding problem . . . [is] the sharp drop in interest rates during the past few years. Different interest-rate assumptions can radically change the "present value" of companies' future pension costs. The lower the interest rate, the more money a company must set aside today in order to cover a given pension liability tomorrow. . . .

By the same token, when interest rates change, actuaries have to change the amount of money that must be earmarked to offset companies' future pension liabilities. And because pension liabilities tend to be quite long-term, they quickly inflate as interest rates fall.

As a rule of thumb, "for every one-percentage-point decline in interest rates, you can expect a 20 percent increase in liabilities," figures Ann O'Connell, national defined-benefit business leader for the accounting firm ***Coopers & Lybrand***.

Source: Ellen Schultz, "Underfunded Pension Plan? Don't Panic," *The Wall Street Journal,* March 25, 1993, pp. C1, C21.

The fact that "for every one-percentage-point decline in interest rates, you can expect a 20 percent increase in liabilities" (as the excerpted article quotes a defined-benefit expert), is certainly a sobering comment on the critical nature of interest rate estimates. It also helps explain the reluctance of many corporations to revise their assumptions when rates do fall. Some companies find it advantageous to use higher rates. The use of inappropriately higher rates, however, can mislead the public and can result in a risk of underfunding the pension plan, as discussed in the In Practice feature on such underfunding.

To continue our example of Karen Bloom, assume a discount rate of 10% and a life expectancy of eight years beyond retirement. That is, she is expected to receive pension benefits for eight years. For each year of service, then, Bloom earns the right to receive $1,500 annually for eight years, until her death. For simplicity of calculation, assume these benefits will be paid annually, at year-end. (In reality, of course, benefits are paid monthly.) Exhibit 16–1 illustrates how the present value of eight annual pension payments might be calculated as of the beginning of Bloom's sixth year of employment (that is, after five years of employment).

[3]FASB, Statement of Financial Accounting Standards No. 87, "Employers' Accounting for Pensions," December 1985, par. 44.

EXHIBIT 16–1
Present Value of Expected Future Payments

Current point in time: January 1, Year 6
Scheduled retirement date: January 1, Year 31
(assumes 25 years' additional employment)
Expected date of death: January 1, Year 39
(assumes 8 years of life after retirement)

	30 YEARS
Annual benefit ($75,000 × 2% × 30 years)	$ 45,000
× Annuity factor (8 years, 10%)	× 5.335
Future value (1/1/31)	$240,075
× Present-value factor (25 years, 10%)	× 0.0923
Present value (1/1/6)	$ 22,159

FUNDAMENTAL PENSION-ACCOUNTING CONCEPTS

Service Costs. During Year 5, Bloom earned one year's benefits. The present value of the best estimate of those benefits is $739, calculated as follows:

Service Cost:

	1 YEAR
Annual benefit ($75,000 × 2% × 1 Year)	$ 1,500
× Annuity factor (8 years, 10%)	× 5.335
Future value (1/1/31)	$ 8,002
× Present-value factor (25 years, 10%)	× 0.0923
Present value (1/1/6)	$ 739

SFAS No. 87 terms this calculation service cost, the actuarial present value of benefits attributed by the plan's benefit formula to services rendered by employees during the current period.

Projected Benefit Obligation. As of the beginning of Year 6, the present value of all benefits earned by Bloom for services rendered *during the past five years* is known as the pension plan's projected benefit obligation (PBO), and in this instance, amounts to $3,693, calculated as follows:

Projected Benefit Obligations:

	5 YEARS
Annual benefit ($75,000 × 2% × 5 Years)	$ 7,500
× Annuity factor (8 years, 10%)	× 5.335
Future value (1/1/31)	$ 40,012
× Present-value factor (25 years, 10%)	× 0.0923
Present value (1/1/6)	$ 3,693

That is, "the projected benefit obligation as of a particular date is the actuarial present value of all benefits attributed by the plan's benefit formula to employee service rendered *prior to that date* (5 years, in this case)"[4] and based on future compensation levels.

We must pay particular attention to the relationship between service costs and projected benefit obligations. Under the simplest conditions, projected benefit obligations for all employees change annually because of three factors: current service costs, interest costs, and current benefits paid. The relationship between service cost and projected benefit obligations is as follows:

Projected Benefit Obligations, Beginning of Year
\+ Current Service Costs
\+ Interest Costs
− Current Benefits Paid
= Projected Benefit Obligations, End of Year

Projected benefit obligations are fundamentally the accumulation of all the individual years' service costs. As each year passes, one additional year's service cost obligation is added to the prior year's projected benefit obligation to determine the current year's projected benfit obligation. Since service costs and projected benefit obligations are expressed in present-value form, however, other adjustments also must be made.

Specifically, as each year passes, the employee retirement date becomes one year closer. Accordingly, accumulated service costs (projected benefit obligations) are discounted by one less year than in the preceding year's calculations. This process is the same as the effective-interest method for other debt; that is, it adds (accrues) interest on the prior year's ending balance.

One other shared characteristic of service costs and projected benefit obligations is that both are measured based on *future* compensation levels. Although estimates of future compensation levels are inexact, they are the best measures available of the value of payments actually expected to be made. They are ideally the best currently available information upon which current economic decisions are being made by the firm, its employees, and their union.

ALTERNATIVE PENSION-ACCOUNTING CONCEPTS

While many accountants, including the current members of the FASB, favor the use of future compensation levels (as just illustrated), this view is not universally shared, nor is it the basis upon which prior pension-related GAAP was based. Alternative measures of pension obligations might be calculated relying only on current and past compensation levels. **Accumulated benefit obligation** is the term reserved for this alternative measurement of pension obligation. That is, the accumulated benefit obligation is the actuarial present value of benefits attributed by the pension benefit formula to employee service rendered prior to that date and based on *current and past compensation levels.* In our continuing example, accumulated benefit obligations based on a $25,000 average compensation level *actually earned* by Karen Bloom *over the last five years* (Years 1 through 5, not Years 25 through 30) was only $1,231 (whereas the projected benefit obligation for the past 5 years was $3,693).

[4]Ibid., par. 17.

Accumulated Benefit Obligations After Five Years of Service:

	5 YEARS
Annual benefit ($25,000 × 2% × 5 years)	$ 2,500
× Annuity factor (8 years, 10%)	× 5.335
Future value (1/1/31)	$ 13.337
× Present-value factor (25 years, 10%)	× 0.0923
Present value (1/1/16)	$ 1,231

In most instances, of course, calculations based on current and past compensation levels provide significantly lower obligations than calculations based on projections of future compensation levels. The controversy over which approach to follow is considerable. The use of current and past compensation levels rather than estimated future compensation levels leads to the reporting of smaller liability and expense figures. One argument offered in support of measurements based on current and past compensation levels is that they provide better information on what the employer's current obligation would be if the plan were discontinued.

Actually, though, if a plan is discontinued or the employee terminated, the best measure of employer obligation is the *vested benefit obligation.* **Vesting** means that an employee becomes eligible to receive benefits at retirement regardless of whether or not the employee continues working for the employer. Benefits are said to be vested when the employee has met certain specified requirements, such as continuous service for five years. Vesting is a key element in all pension plans.

A major impact of the Employee Retirement Income Security Act of 1974 (ERISA) was much earlier vesting of employee pension rights than previously had been the case. Still a negotiable provision in an employment contract within the guidelines of ERISA, vesting commonly occurs either immediately or after five years of employment.

Arguments are also offered against measurements based on estimated future compensation levels because of the uncertainty of those projections. Some argue that "the uncertainties inherent in predicting future interest rates and salary levels are sufficiently great that available measures of the projected benefit obligation fail to achieve the level of reliability needed for recognition in financial statements."[5] The prevailing view of the FASB is that the principles of (1) relevancy and (2) consistency with the going-concern assumption necessitate selection of measures based on projected compensation levels. The FASB does not believe that figures based upon the employer's current obligation if the plan were discontinued are appropriate for most firms because this eventuality is not likely.

> The Board concluded that, in the absence of evidence to the contrary, accounting should be based on a going-concern assumption that, as applied to pensions, assumes that the plan will continue in operation and the benefits defined in the plan will be provided. Under that assumption, the employer's probable future sacrifice is not limited to either termination liability or amounts already vested. The Board

[5]Ibid., par. 100.

believes, nonetheless that the actuarial measurement of the obligation encompasses the probability that some employees will terminate and forfeit nonvested benefits.[6]

SFAS No. 87 was adopted in 1985, based on a simple majority vote. Four members of the board supported adoption of the standard; three members dissented. Obviously, the matter was contentious, and it remains so. As of January 1, 1991, a "super majority" (five to two, or greater) is now required for adoption of new Statements of Financial Accounting Standards (or recision of old standards.)

PENSION-FUNDING PRACTICES

While the FASB may set standards regulating how financial transactions are reported, it does not dictate the transactions in which a firm must engage. However, it is within the authority of the U.S. Congress to regulate how and when pension plans are funded. Congress did so in 1974 as a result of many pension plan abuses and irregularities. The Employee Retirement Income Security Act of 1974 (ERISA) was a massive piece of legislation that established federal regulation of U.S. pension plans. It is beyond the scope of this book to go into all the provisions of that law, but we should note that it specifies minimum funding standards. Management and its financial counsel determine annual pension plan funding, not the FASB. Also, it is important to observe that the *expensing* of pension costs and the *funding* of those obligations are two distinct and unrelated matters, much as is the recording of depreciation expense on a building and repayment of the debt incurred pursuant to its purchase. Both the amounts funded and expensed, however, are critically affected by interest rate assumptions made by the corporation.

PENSION-RELATED ENTRIES

Understand the theoretically correct pension-related journal entries for defined-benefit plans and understand the practical compromises of SFAS No. 87.

In applying accrual accounting to pensions, SFAS No. 87 retained three fundamental aspects of past pension accounting: (1) netting pension-related expenses and revenues, (2) netting pension-related assets and liabilities, and (3) delaying recognition of certain events. While these three features have shaped financial reporting for pensions for many years, they have also led to much confusion. In fact, the board explicitly acknowledges that these provisions of pension accounting are "not widely understood."[7] Further, while SFAS No. 87 continues these practices, the board observed that they conflict with accounting principles applied elsewhere. Accordingly, we first present more theoretically fundamental pension-related entries. Then we make comparisons to the following generic entry required annually by SFAS No. 87 (where **Cash** is credited in the amount of funds deposited with the pension trustee, **Pension Cost** is the amount of expense debited per a formula including six elements and **Prepaid/Accrued Pension Cost** is the asset or liability account "plugged" for any remaining debit or credit required to balance the entry. Thus, the GAAP entry is:

Pension Cost (expense)	xxxx	
Cash		xxxx
Prepaid/Accrued Pension Cost		xxxx

[6]Ibid., par. 149.
[7]Ibid., par. 84.

PENSION ACCOUNTING, THEORETICAL (AND DISAGGREGATED)

Continuing the Karen Bloom example introduced previously, the following section focuses on the entries of Bloom's employer, Kent Corporation, for Year 6. Assume that the pension plan was first adopted at the end of Year 5, with all employees, including Karen Bloom, receiving credit for services rendered prior to plan adoption. The cost of extending retroactive credit is termed prior-service cost—the actuarial present value of benefits attributed by the plan's benefit formula to services rendered by the employee during periods preceding adoption of the plan, but service for which benefit is granted. The prior-service cost for Karen Bloom amounts to $3,693—the present value of five years' cumulative credit (equal to the projected benefit obligations at the beginning of Year 6).

These costs are incurred (retroactive credit for prior service granted) with the expectation that the employer will realize economic benefits in future periods. Thus, by definition, these costs are assets. The expected future benefits are assumed to be greater employee productivity due to relatively more positive employer-employee relations and morale. Therefore, consistent with the matching principle, the costs of the asset must be allocated (expensed) over the period of benefit.[8] SFAS No. 87 also provides an alternative approach that is substantially the same but easier to compute—see the first appendix to this chapter (p. 880).

The journal entries to record the pension-related costs (and their subsequent amortization) for Karen Bloom's prior service using the theoretically correct accounting procedures are as follows:

ENTRY ONE

Date	Account	Debit	Credit
Year 6			
Jan. 1	Prior-Service Costs (Asset)	3,693*	
	Projected Benefit Obligation (Liability)		3,693
	**$3,693 from Exhibit 16–1.*		

CONCEPT Valuation of assets and liabilities.

LOGIC Assets are recorded at the net present value of expected future benefits; liabilities are recorded at the net present value of future commitments. The firm has agreed to provide certain contractually defined postemployment benefits. As with all long-term liabilities, these commitments should be reflected at their net present value. In return for these incurred costs, the firm expects to receive benefits in the form of greater employee productivity due to enhanced morale, motivation, and so forth.

ENTRY TWO

Date	Account	Debit	Credit
Years 6–30			
Dec. 31	Amortization Expense ($3,693/25)	148	
	Prior-Service Costs		148

[8]SFAS No. 87, par. 25, specifies that "prior-service costs shall be amortized by assigning an equal amount to each future period of service of each employee" active at the date of the plan initiation.

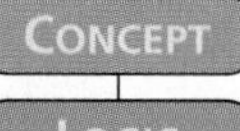

Matching—recognition of expense in period of benefit.

LOGIC The cost of the asset is charged off over the assumed 25-year life of the asset; the asset value is reduced and the expired portion is expensed.

The prior-service cost in Entry One was recorded as an asset because Kent expects future benefits. This asset is charged off (amortized) on a straight-line basis over the asset life of 25 years. Entry two is similar to any straight-line depreciation or amortization entry where the asset life is 25 years (the remaining number of service periods before Karen Bloom retires).

For purposes of this example, further assume that Kent funds $2,000 of the prior-service cost immediately, on January 1, Year 6 (intending to fund the remainder at a later date). **Funding** refers to the process of transferring assets, most frequently cash, to an independent third party who serves as a trustee for the pension plan assets received. The journal entry to fund the initial $2,000 would be

ENTRY THREE

Year 6			
Jan. 1	Pension Plan Assets	2,000	
	Cash		2,000

Asset valuation at acquisition.

LOGIC Asset valuation at acquisition is at cost. The Cash account is reduced for the amount of the check written to the pension plan trustee. Investments purchased with the provided funds are recorded at cost in the Pension Plan Assets account.

During the course of the year, at least four other events typically occur that require journal entries related to the Kent Corporation pension plan. The first two relate to the changing values of the pension liability, called Projected Benefits Obligation. First, Bloom provides one more year of service to the company. For that year of service, in addition to monthly salary, she earns additional pension rights, and Kent Corporation incurs additional "service costs." The theoretically appropriate entry to record these costs as expenses of the current period and to increase the liability to be paid later would be as follows:

ENTRY FOUR

Year 6			
Dec. 31	Compensation Expense	812	
	Projected Benefit Obligation		812
	($1,500 × 5.335 × 0.1015)		
	(5.335 = PV Annuity Factor @ 10%, 8 yrs.)		
	(0.1015 = PV Single Sum @ 10%, 24 yrs.)		

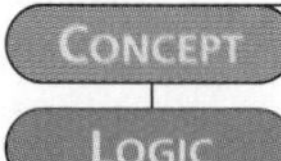

Matching—liability recognition.

Proper matching of expenses and revenues requires recognition of expense in the year in which benefit is derived. Recognition of liabilities is at the time they are incurred. The costs of labor should be recognized in those years when the benefits of labor are received—that is, during the productive life of the employee, not during retirement, when labor services are no longer being rendered to the firm. Labor costs include costs paid currently and costs paid in the future for current services. Labor costs include wages and benefits. The liability should be recognized because an event giving rise to the obligation requiring future economic sacrifice has occurred, and those costs can be estimated with acceptable accuracy.

Service costs for Year 6 are calculated in the same fashion as were the service (1 year) costs, illustrated above. The only difference is that Year 6 is one year closer to the retirement date, and accordingly, the future value of $8,002 needs to be further discounted at 10% for only 24 years, not 25 years. The specific calculations for Year 6 are as follows:

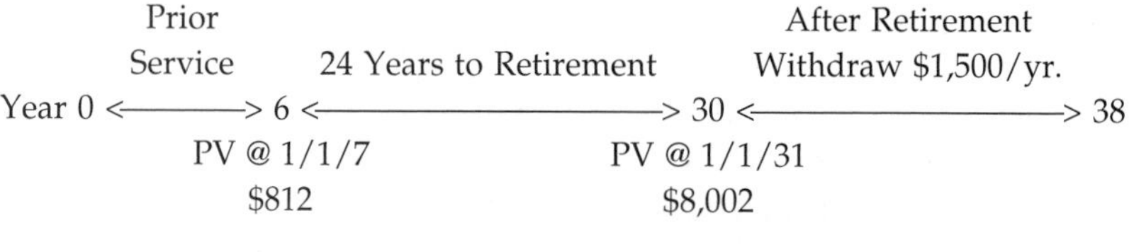

Service Cost (for Year 6)

Annual annuity benefit (Years 31–38)	$ 1,500
× Present value of annuity (8 yrs., 10%)	× 5.3350
Fund requirement (at 1/1/31)	$ 8,002
× Present-value factor (24 yrs., 10%)	× 0.1015
Service cost for Year 6 (PV at end of Year 6)	$ 812

This means that because Bloom worked one additional year, she has earned an additional $1,500 of retirement benefits in each of her retirement years (i.e., Years 31 through 38). To fund those benefits, Kent has a current service-cost requirement of $812. Note that Year 6 service-costs computations are similar to the effective-interest method. They are simply 10 percent greater than the Year 5 service costs (that is, Year 5 service costs of $739 multiplied by 110% equals $812, allowing for rounding).

The second item that must be accounted for in Year 6 is the interest expense accrued on the January 1, Year 6 Projected Benefit Obligation liability balance. Since the Projected Benefit Obligation is measured at its net present value, interest must be accrued as time expires and the retirement date approaches. Using the effective-interest method, the theoretically appropriate entry in this instance would be:

ENTRY FIVE

Year 6			
Dec. 31	Interest Expense	369*	
	Projected Benefit Obligation		369
	*\$3,693 × 10%		

CONCEPT Matching—recognition of expenses in period of benefit.

LOGIC By not currently paying existing obligations, the firm retains the use of those funds for other current purposes. The uses to which those retained funds are put presumably benefit the current period. The matching concept requires, therefore, that the cost of the use of funds (interest) be accrued currently. Interest expense, by nature, is a function of time.

The amount of the interest expense is simply the beginning-of-the-year balance (in this case \$3,693) multiplied by the appropriate interest rate (in this case 10%).

The other two events that require recognition in the accounting books during Year 6 relate to pension plan assets. First, the value of pension plan assets is likely to change. Hopefully, these assets have appreciated in value. For purposes of this example, assume that the initially funded pension plan assets of \$2,000 (see entry three) yield an 8% return. The theoretically correct entry would be as follows:

ENTRY SIX

Year 6			
Dec. 31	Pension Plan Assets	160*	
	Investment Income		160
	*\$2,000 × 8%		

CONCEPT Revenue recognition.

LOGIC Interest income earned on investments in debt securities is recognized as accrued. Dividend income earned on investments in equity securities is recognized when dividends are declared. Investments in trading securities are marked to market, and the appreciation in value is recorded as income.

Finally, it is customary for the employer to provide some annual funding of future obligations. Assume that Kent chooses to fund service costs currently and records the following entry:

ENTRY SEVEN

Year 6			
Dec. 31	Pension Plan Assets	812*	
	Cash		812
	*\$1,500 × 5.335 × 0.1015		

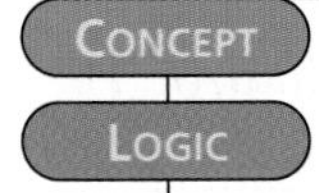

CONCEPT: Asset valuation at cost.

LOGIC: The Cash account is reduced for the amount of the check written to the pension plan trustee. Investments purchased with the provided funds are recorded at cost in the Pension Plan Assets account.

PENSION ACCOUNTING, SFAS NO. 87

Operational Compromises. While the preceding series of entries are correct from a theoretical standpoint, they differ from the requirements of SFAS No. 87 in selected ways. As noted before, the discrepancy between theory and practice results from the continuation of three past pension accounting practices. Those are (1) reporting pension-related revenues and expenses *net,* as *pension costs,* (2) reporting pension-related assets and liabilities *net,* that is, offsetting assets and liabilities, as *prepaid/(unfunded) accrued pension costs* and (3) delaying recognition of certain events from the present year to future years (primarily, prior-service costs arising from pension plan initiation or amendment).

Exhibit 16–2 illustrates the four entries that have an income statement effect, that is, are related to pension revenue or expense. SFAS No. 87 requires these to be netted (combined).

EXHIBIT 16–2
Theoretic Journal Entries for Pension-Related Costs

Entry Two			
Year 6			
Dec. 31	Amortization Expense	148	
	Prior-Service Cost		148
Entry Four			
Year 6			
Dec. 31	Compensation Expense	812	
	Projected Benefit Obligation		812
Entry Five			
Year 6			
Dec. 31	Interest Expense	369	
	Projected Benefit Obligation		369
Entry Six			
Year 6			
Dec. 31	Pension Plan Assets	160	
	Investment Income		160

Specifically, entries two, four, and five recognize pension-related expenses, and entry six recognizes pension-related revenue. Continuing prior practices, the FASB required that these four revenues and expenses should be netted and reported under one designation—Pension Costs (usually a net expense). (See Exhibit 16–3 for reconcilation of all entries with SFAS No. 87.)

Pension costs, thus, per SFAS No. 87 are comprised of several elements. Specifically, periodic pension costs equal amortization of prior-service costs (entry two), plus current-period service costs (entry four), plus interest costs incurred on projected benefit obligations (entry five), minus investment income on plan assets (entry six). These are summarized as follows and also appear in Exhibit 16–3:

ENTRY	DESCRIPTION	AMOUNT
Two	Amortization of prior-service cost	$ 148
Four	Compensation expense for current year	812
Five	Interest expense on prior-service cost	369
Six	Investment income on pension plan assets	(160)
	Net amount of pension cost (expense)	$1,169

The net amount of pension cost ($1,169) *per SFAS No. 87 is recorded in a single entry,* not four entries, as will be soon illustrated.

SFAS No. 87 also requires that pension-related asset and liability accounts be offset. If the *credits* recorded to pension assets and liabilities in entries two through seven (see Exhibit 16–2) exceed the debits, a net liability emerges. If the *debits* recorded in these entries exceed the credits, a net asset is recorded. Irrespective of whether a net debit or net credit occurs, the appropriate account to be used for the net figure is the same account: **Prepaid/Accrued Pension Costs**. For financial reporting purposes, if this account exhibits a year-end credit balance, accrued pension costs will be reported among liabilities on the balance sheet; if a debit balance results, prepaid pension costs will be reported among the assets on the balance sheet.

In our example, debits occur to assets and liabilities (excluding cash) in entries three, six, and seven; credits occur to assets and liabilities (excluding cash) in entries two, four, and five. In aggregate, there is a net debit of $1,643 that will end up in the Prepaid/Accrued Pension Costs account. See Exhibit 16–2 and column 2 of Exhibit 16–3.

In contrast to the theoretic entries, SFAS No. 87 employs only two entries to arrive at the same net debit of $1,643. The first entry is made at the beginning of the year, because $2,000 was funded at the beginning of the year.

REVISED ENTRY ONE

Year 6			
Jan. 1	Prepaid/Accrued Pension Cost	2,000	
	Cash		2,000

The second entry is made at year-end because this is the typical point at which accounting accruals are made. (In subsequent years, only one entry will be required: the year-end entry. The initial funding at the time of plan adoption only occurs in the first year.)

REVISED ENTRY TWO

Year 6			
Dec. 31	Pension Cost	1,169*	
	Cash (funding equal to service cost)		812
	Prepaid/Accrued Pension Cost		357
	*$1,169 = $148 + $812 + $369 − $160		

Exhibit 16–3 illustrates the reconciliation of the two SFAS No. 87 entries with the seven *theoretic* journal entries. Exhibit 16–3 also reflects the final compromise retained by SFAS No. 87: the delayed recognition (or nonrecording) of entry one.

Two entries thus result in place of six entries, with entry one being omitted.

The accrued pension cost of $357 represents a **liability** for the difference between the **pension cost** (which is the net expense for the period: $1,169) and the current funding of that cost ($812).

Exhibit 16–3 reconciles *theoretic* entries two through seven with the two *revised* (or SFAS No. 87) entries. Both sets of entries produce the same set of year-end account balances, with one exception. That exception is *theoretic* entry one. SFAS No. 87 does not record this event. Note the financial statement effect of omitting entry one. It excludes from the financial statements both assets (prior-service costs) and liabilities (projected benefit obligation) of $3,693. This ommission affects such critical ratios as Return on Total Assets and Debt to Equity.

The FASB's decision to continue the practice of netting (offsetting) pension-related assets and liabilities and netting (offsetting) pension-related expenses and revenues also is significant as it relates to the usability of accounting information. The board explicitly acknowledged this, observing that one of the factors that made pension information difficult to understand was that past practice and terminology combined elements that are different in substance into net amounts

EXHIBIT 16–3
Reconciliation of SFAS No. 87 with Disaggregated Theoretic Entries

Original Theoretic Entries:

	ACCOUNTS				
	PENSION EXPENSE OR REVENUES	PENSION ASSETS OR LIABILITIES	PRIOR-SERVICE COSTS (ASSET)	PROJECTED BENEFIT OBLIGATION (LIABILITY)	CASH
Entry One			$3,693	$3,693	
Entry Two	$ 148	$ (148)			
Entry Three		2,000			$2,000
Entry Four	812	(812)			
Entry Five	369	(369)			
Entry Six	(160)	160			
Entry Seven		812			812
Balance	$1,169	$1,643	$3,693	$3,693	$2,812

()s = credit

(continued)

Exhibit 16–3
(Concluded)

Explanation of Entries:

Entry One: New Pension Plan is adopted; and credit is given to employees for past service. A liability is recorded at the net present value of future pension commitments made. An asset is recorded in an amount equal to liability relying on the logic that the business receives value in exchange for its pension commitments made.

Entry Two: The cost of the asset acquired in Entry One is amortized over a 25-year life; the remaining service life of the employee.

Entry Three: The firm uses cash to purchase pension plan assets (typically investments).

Entry Four: In return for labor services, employee earns additional pension rights. Firm incurs expense (cost of labor charged to current period) and liability (for payment of future pension benefits).

Entry Five: Interest Expense is accrued on pension liability: expense increases, liability increases.

Entry Six: Investments in Pension Plan Assets generate income (i.e., interest and dividends on stocks and bonds.)

Entry Seven: The firm uses cash to purchase pension plan assets.

SFAS No. 87 Revised Entries:

	Accounts		
	Pension Cost	Prepaid/ Accrued Pension Costs	Cash
Entry One		$2,000	$2,000
Entry Two	$1,169	(357)	812
Balance	$1,169	$1,643	$2,812

Explanation of Entries:

Entry One: Firm uses $2,000 of cash to purchase pension plan assets. Balance sheet account Prepaid/Accrued Pension Cost used.

Entry Two: Single entry is used to *net* the following:

- Past Service Costs (unrecorded *assets*) are amortized over 25-year life, *expense* debited in net income statement account (Pension Cost) and credit established in net balance sheet account (Prepaid/Accrued Pension Costs): $148.
- Employee provides labor services; one cost thereof is wages expense. Another is pension *expense* (service cost) recorded as debit in net income statement account (Pension Cost). Because payment is deferred until after retirement, the *liability* is increased by crediting net balance sheet account (Prepaid/Accrued Pension Cost): $812.
- Interest *expense* is recorded (debit net income statement account, Pension Cost); because payment is deferred *liability* increases (credit net balance sheet account, Prepaid/Accrued Pension Cost): $369.
- Pension Plan Assets earn investment *revenue* (credit net income statement account, Pension Cost) and *assets* are written up (debit net balance sheet account, Prepaid/Accrued Pension Cost): $160.

(assets with liabilities and revenues and gains with expenses and losses)."[9] See the In Practice feature, " 'Netting' Overfunding Credits and Operating Expenses," for an example of how investment income on pension plan assets can distort perceptions of ongoing operating expenses (costs of labor) and corporate operating (as opposed to investment) performance.

IN PRACTICE—GENERAL

"Netting" Overfunding Credits and Operating Expenses

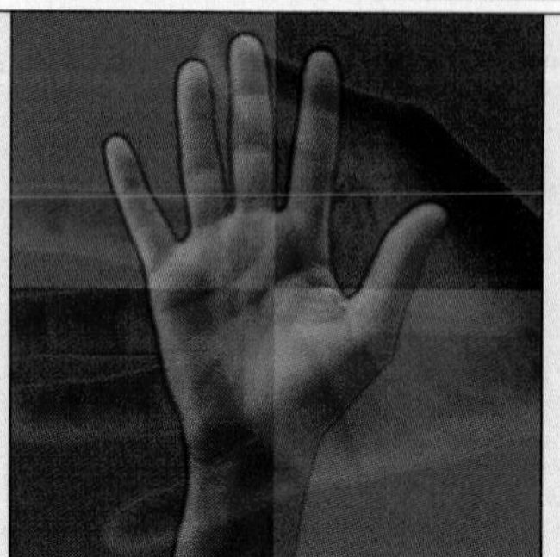

In a year when ***Stone & Webster*** earned less than $2 million, the invisible pension fund credit manufactured more income than any item on the income statement except core engineering. Since 1987, when Stone & Webster started tapping this source, the income statement has buried $101 million of pension credits as reductions in operating expenses. Without them, $152 million in reported net income boils down to less than $87 million, net of federal income taxes...

Citing detailed notes to financial statements and entries for prepaid pension costs on cash flow statements, CFO William Egan insists that the pension reporting issue makes much ado about nothing. "We did everything on the level," Egan declares. Additional references to an overfunded pension appear on the balance sheet and in the discussion and analysis of financial condition ... Indeed, the pension credits seem to show up nearly everywhere except on the income statement, where they would have the most meaning.

Source: S.L. Mintz, "True Lies: How GAAP Conceals the Real Story at Stone & Webster," *CFO,* September 1994, pp. 49–51.

ACCOUNTING FOR PRIOR-SERVICE COSTS

The board also was aware that its decision against requiring prior-service costs to be recognized as an asset and a liability as incurred (original entry one) could impede reliable financial statement analyses. In fact, the board conceded the point, observing, "The Board believes that it would be conceptually appropriate and preferable [emphasis added] to recognize a net pension liability or asset measured as the difference between the projected benefit obligation and plan assets."[10]

Although the board agreed in SFAS No. 87 to retain, from past practice, the basic features of (1) reporting revenues and expenses net, (2) reporting liabilities and assets net, and (3) delaying recognition of prior-service costs, the Board did require full disclosure of the components of periodic pension cost (expense) and projected benefit obligation in the financial footnotes. In the end, the board acknowledged, "This Statement results in excluding the most current and relevant information from the employer's statement of financial position... and to do otherwise ... would be too great a change from present practice to be adopted at the present time."[11]

[9]FASB, Statement of Financial Accounting Standards No. 87, "Employers Accounting for Pensions," December 1985, par. 106; parenthetical additions are those of the board.
[10]Ibid., par. 107.
[11]Ibid., pars. 104, 107.

OTHER PRIOR-SERVICE COSTS/CHANGES IN PLAN BENEFITS

In the earlier illustration for Karen Bloom, pension expense included amortization of prior-service costs. Those prior-service costs were of a single origin, those incurred by granting retroactive credit for services provided before the pension plan was adopted. Prior-service costs also may include changes in projected benefit obligations because of amendments to the pension-benefits formula. To illustrate, in the earlier example, Karen Bloom was assumed to earn pension benefits according to the following formula:

Annual Defined Pension Benefit	=	Number of Years' Service	×	2% Average Salary for Last 5 Years' Service

At the end of six years' service, the projected benefit obligation was $4,874, based on annual benefits at retirement of $9,000 (six years' service × 2% × $75,000). Assume now, at the beginning of Year 7, a new union contract is negotiated in which the formula is revised as follows:

Annual Defined Pension Benefit	=	Number of Years' Service	×	3% Average Salary for Last 5 Years' Service

Such a renegotiated formula would increase projected benefit obligations by 50 percent. SFAS No. 87 requires that these additional costs, although related to credit given for prior years of employee service, must be allocated to future years of employment. The rationale of the FASB is that the costs of plan amendments are similar to the costs of granting retroactive service credit at plan initiation; that is, plan amendment is "invariably made with a view *to benefiting the employer's operations in future periods* rather than the past or only in the year of change. The Board believes economic value exists, the cost of acquiring the benefit can be determined, and that amortization of the cost over future periods is consistent with accounting practice in other areas."[12] A requirement to recognize a liability and an asset currently was not adopted; this is consistent with the treatment of other prior-service costs discussed earlier in the chapter.

Ideally, the board believes, amortization of prior-service costs should recognize the cost of each individual's added benefits over that individual's remaining service period. In practice, the board concedes, the precision of such a computation on an individual basis might not warrant the additional costs likely to be incurred beyond simpler amortization methods. The first appendix to this chapter (see page 880) illustrates a more practical expedient method still acceptable to the board.

ACCOUNTING FOR GAINS AND LOSSES

In preceding sections of this chapter four elements of pension cost have been described. This section focuses on two additional elements: deferral of current-period gain or loss and amortization of unrecognized net gain or loss. These

[12]Ibid., par. 159.

Measure and account for actuarial gains and losses.

gains and losses are sometimes called *actuarial gains and losses*. They arise from (1) changes in the fair value of plan assets and (2) changes in projected benefit obligations. These gain and loss items are related to the return on plan assets item. A recap of pension-expense components (i.e., pension cost) follows:

Previously Discussed Items:

1. Current-period service cost.
2. Plus interest (on projected benefit obligations).
3. Plus amortization of prior-service costs.
4. Minus return on plan assets (actual).

New Items:

5. Plus (or minus) deferral of net period gain/(loss).
6. Plus (or minus) amortization of net loss/(gain).

Actuarial gains and losses relate to differences between actual returns and expected returns. In calculating the expected return on plan assets, SFAS No. 87 requires that an *expected* long-term rate of return on plan assets should be multiplied by a market-related value of plan assets. In paragraph 81, the board defines "market-related value of plan assets" as either (1) current fair value or (2) a calculated value that recognizes changes in fair value in a systematic and rational manner over not more than five years.

Calculated market-related values thus can be calculated in a variety of ways; the second appendix to this chapter (p. 881) illustrates two. The expected-returns figure is relevant because the difference between actual returns and expected returns must be recognition-delayed. That is, while item four in the preceding list requires the subtraction of actual returns, item five requires deferral of net period gains. In combination, then, items four and five require periodic pension costs to be reduced by the expected return on plan assets, not the actual return.

> The calculation of this item is complex and not intuitive. Gains and losses result from changes in either the PBO [projected benefit obligation] or MVA [market value of assets]. These changes occur because either actual experience is different from the expected or the actuary revises assumptions about the future. FASB No. 87 does not require immediate recognition of the changes. The FASB did not want companies to be subject to market volatility in calculating pension cost . . . the net effect of adding the deferred gain or subtracting the deferred loss is that *the expected return and not the actual return is used in calculating the current period pension cost* [emphasis added].[13]

Item six allows for reversal of these deferrals over time. To illustrate, assume that service costs are $100,000 and interest on the projected benefit obligation is $20,000. Also assume amortization of prior-service costs is $10,000. If actual return on plan assets is $30,000, whereas expected return was $25,000, pension cost (i.e., annual expense) would be calculated as follows:

[13]F. A. Bayer and N. Wilner, "Accounting for Pensions Under FASB 87: A Case Study," *The Practical Accountant*, June 1990, p. 44.

Service cost		$100,000
Interest on projected benefit obligation		+ 20,000
Amortization of prior-service cost		+ 10,000
Actual return on plan assets	−$30,000	
Deferral of net gain	+ 5,000	
Expected return on plan assets		− 25,000
		$105,000

The addition of the $5,000 net gain, which is deferred, cancels out $5,000 of the $30,000 actual return, which had been subtracted, thereby reducing current pension expense by the expected return of $25,000.

Once deferred, the net gain of $5,000 can be reversed in two fashions. First, deferred gains (losses) might offset other past or future deferred losses (gains). Second, if the resulting net gains or losses aggregated over time become large (material), explicit amortization is required. These methods of offset and amortization are described in detail in a later section, but before illustrating this portion of the standard, we must understand why the FASB chose not to require recognition of gains and losses currently.

A number of respondents to the Exposure Draft preceding SFAS No. 87 voiced concern about the volatility of both plan asset measures and measures of projected benefit obligations. The general philosophy of the board, however, is that reporting volatility per se is not undesirable. "If a financial measure purports to represent a phenomenon that is volatile, the measure must show that."[14] Still, specifically regarding projected benefit obligations, the board recognized the fragile and imprecise nature of projections of future interest rates, compensation levels, length of employee service, mortality, retirement ages, and other pertinent actuarial data. To the extent that these matters may contribute to the appearance of greater volatility than in fact exists, the FASB chose to allow deferral of gains and losses rather than require immediate recognition. The FASB also noted, however, that it believed "both the extent of the volatility reduction and the mechanism adopted to effect it are essentially practical issues without conceptual basis."[15]

MEASURING ACTUARIAL GAINS AND LOSSES

In the preparation of SFAS No. 87, the board had to contend with two major matters. First was the issue of how to determine a market-related value for plan assets. Second, a mechanism had to be devised to amortize gains and losses that had been deferred. Regarding the first matter, as mentioned earlier, the board defined "market-related asset value" as either (1) current fair value or (2) a calculated value that "recognizes changes in fair value in a systematic and rational manner over not more than five years." Reporting entities may select either approach but should be consistent in their application. The second appendix to this chapter (see page 881) illustrates methods of generating figures that meet the criteria of the calculated value. In the following example fair values will be used.

[14]SFAS No. 87, par. 174.
[15]SFAS No. 87, par. 177.

The board also needed to develop a mechanism to amortize deferred gains and losses. Part of the rationale for deferral of gains and losses was the expectation that, over time, many would offset. Accordingly, under this logic/approach, amortization occurs only for net gains or losses that have built up over time to such a substantial amount that they are not expected to offset in the relatively near future.

A simple example is provided here to illustrate how gains and losses are calculated. Following this example, we will illustrate how to amortize gains and losses. Assume that the beginning-of-the-year fair value of plan assets is $100,000, and the expected long-term rate of return is 10%, or $10,000. An actual return of $55,000 is calculated as follows:

Fair value of plan assets, January 1 of Year 1	$100,000
+ Contributions made in Year 1	40,000
− Benefits paid in Year 1	(30,000)
Value of plan if no gain or loss	$110,000
− Fair value of plan assets, December 31 of Year 1	(165,000)
= Actual return on plan assets	$ (55,000)

The **actual return on plan assets** is the necessary reconciling figure between the beginning- and end-of-year fair values and known current contributions to the plan and benefit payments. The difference between actual returns of $55,000 and expected returns of $10,000 is a gain of $45,000.

Actual returns	$55,000
Expected returns	(10,000)
Gain	$45,000

AMORTIZING GAINS AND LOSSES

This gain of $45,000 is combined with the unamortized net balance of all preceding years' gains and losses. The result is the **cumulative unrecognized net gain or loss**. Any amount in excess of 10 percent of the greater of (1) projected benefit obligations or (2) the value of plan assets requires amortization *in the following year*. This is termed the **corridor method**, as amortization is calculated only on amounts outside the 10% corridor.

For example assume the year-end market value of (plan) assets (MVA) is $165,000, and the year-end value of projected benefit obligations (PBO) is $300,000. Also assume that the net gains experienced in prior years that remain unamortized amount to $40,000. The $45,000 current gain is combined with the $40,000 net gain surviving from prior years for a net cumulative gain of $85,000. The $85,000 exceeds 10 percent of the greater of $300,000 (PBO) or $165,000 (MVA). This excess of $55,000 ($85,000 − $30,000) must be amortized over the average remaining service lives (assume 10 years.) Next year's **pension cost** (expense) thus would be calculated as follows:

Current-period service cost	$ xxxx
+ Interest (on projected benefit obligations)	xxxx
+ Amortization of prior-service costs	xxxx
− Return on plan assets (actual)	(xxxx)
+ Deferral of net period gain (or less loss)	(xxxx)
− Amortization of net gain	(5,500)
Net periodic pension cost (expense)	$ xxxx

UNAMORTIZED NET GAIN	P.B.O.	PLAN ASSETS	CORRIDOR	EXCESS	AMORTIZATION
$85,000	$300,000	$165,000	$30,000	$55,000	$5,500

Each year amortization is calculated only on amounts outside the corridor. However, each year the corridor itself is likely to change, and thus, one year's amortization probably will not equal the next year's amortization.

PROVISION FOR MINIMUM LIABILITY

SFAS No. 87 clearly is the product of compromise, and compromise solutions often beget unforeseen complications. In this instance one foreseen complication relates to the possibility that the described approaches might fail to record any pension liabilities or lead to the reporting of pension liabilities that were perceived as too low *in certain circumstances.* Accordingly, the FASB made provision for recognition of a **minimum liability** in those circumstances.

The general subject of what was the most appropriate measure of pension liabilities was the most controversial issue faced by the FASB. While most provisions of the standard are based on calculations related to projected benefit obligation (PBO), the section relating to the minimum-liability provision is based on the concept of accumulated benefit obligation (ABO). Recall that accumulated benefit obligation is the actuarial present value of benefits attributed by the pension-benefit formula to employee service rendered prior to that date. Further, the benefits are based on *current and past compensation levels.* The FASB determined that if the fair market value of the pension assets was less than the accumulated benefit obligation at year-end, a liability in the amount of that "underfunding" must be established. The liability must take into account any existing asset or liability account (that is, Prepaid/Accrued Pension Cost).

To illustrate, assume the fair value of plan assets at year-end is $500,000, but the accumulated benefit obligation is $700,000. Financial statements must then report a pension liability of not less than $200,000. If a Prepaid/Accrued Pension Cost credit balance already exists in excess of $200,000, no additional entry is required.

On the other hand, if a debit balance exists in the Prepaid/Acrrued Pension Cost account, or the credit balance is less than $200,000, then an entry to record an additional liability to establish a net $200,000 credit balance is required. The offsetting debit is made to an intangible asset called *Intangible Pension Assets,* up to the amount of unrecognized prior-service costs. Any further charges are made to an equity account called *Excess of Additional Pension Liability Over Unrecognized Prior-Service Costs.*

Assuming that an existing Prepaid/Accrued Pension Cost account exists in the amount of $100,000, pension liabilities will require an additional credit of $300,000 in our ongoing example to (1) negate the $100,000 debit balance in the Prepaid/Accrued Pension Cost account and (2) to establish the $200,000 desired credit balance. If unrecognized prior-service costs amount to only $90,000, a prepaid asset will be debited for $90,000, and the remaining debit made to an equity account as follows:

Excess of Additional Pension Liability		
Over Unrecognized Prior-Service Cost	210,000	
Intangible Pension Assets	90,000	
Prepaid/Accrued Pension Cost		300,000

The Prepaid Pension Cost and (unfunded) Accrued Pension Cost accounts are one and the same. It is this account (Prepaid/(unfunded) Accrued Pension Cost) that is credited for any necessary additional liability per minimum liability provisions. Specifically, SFAS No. 87, par. 35, says,

> A liability (unfunded accrued pension cost) is recognized if net periodic pension cost recognized pursuant to this Statement exceeds the amounts the employer has contributed to the plan. An asset (prepaid pension cost) is recognized if net periodic pension cost is less than amounts the employers has contributed to the plan.

Thus, the Prepaid/Accrued Pension Cost account is a plug figure in the routine SFAS No. 87 year-end pension accrual entry. The entry will take the following form *if* the period's expense (called pension cost by SFAS No. 87) exceeds the current contribution made by the firm to the pension plan. From Exhibit 16–3 a typical year-end entry would be:

Pension Cost	1,169	
Cash		812
Prepaid/Accrued Pension Cost		357

Alternatively, if the current contribution (say $2,000) exceeded the periodic pension expense, the following entry would be made:

Pension Cost	1,169	
Prepaid/Accrued Pension Cost	831	
Cash		2,000

If an additional liability must be recognized under the minimum liability provisions of SFAS No. 87, the Prepaid/Accrued Pension Cost account will be credited additionally, as illustrated above. When financial statements are prepared, if the balance residing in this "net" account is a debit, the account is listing among the firm's assets; if a credit balance prevails, the account is listed among the liabilities.

If at the end of next year, the additional liability is no longer needed, the entry will be reversed.

Under- and Overfunded Pension Plans

Discussions regarding the funding status of a firm's pension plan in the popular press may be confusing . . . in large part because a firm's financial statements and standards of the FASB are confusing on the point. However, even if we agree on the projected benefit obligation (PBO) as the appropriate comparative benchmark against which to compare plan assets, the confusion may persist. The question of whether a firm's pension plan is over- or underfunded, depends on the assumed discount (interest) rate. These rates vary greatly across firms and what rate is the "right" rate is a perennially contentious matter. Earlier in this chapter it was noted that a one percent decline in the assumed discount rate would boost liabilities by about 20 percent. Accordingly, analyses of funding status as well as analyses of financial statements in general turn in substantive fashion on careful consideration of this variable. See the In Practice feature "Challenging Pension Plan Profits and Rate Assumptions."

In Practice—General

Challenging Pension Plan Profits and Rate Assumptions

Even some of the healthiest penion plans may soon look a little pale. The Securities and Exchange Commission is lobbing what amounts to a grenade into the books of many large companies, by effectively challenging whether corporate pension plans are as fat and happy as they seem.

As a result, a number of companies that are happily sitting with more assets than they need to meet their pension obligations will lose this cherished "overfunded" status this year, falling into the underfunded realm.

And the corporate fallout will be big.

Some companies will be forced to start making cash contributions to their pension funds once again. Some will show lower earnings. And some will be disclosing the tab they face for pension obligations on their balance sheets for the first time.

Technically, the SEC is stepping up the pressure by making a stricter application of existing pension accounting standards . . . The agency is concerned that many companies have been minimizing their obligations to retirees by using a higher assumed interest rate to calculate today's pension liability. To better reflect today's lower rate climate, the SEC is urging companies to reduce this "discount rate" to about 7%, roughly the current yield on long-term, high-grade corporate bonds.

According to a ***Goldman, Sachs & Co.*** study, 307 companies out of 366 surveyed assume a discount rate of 8% or more to calculate pension obligations. These companies will show a higher pension liability if they assume a 7% rate.

Source: L. Jereski, "SEC is Challenging Funding for Plans," *The Wall Street Journal,* November 17, 1993, p. C22.

If firms use unrealistically high interest rates, balance sheet liabilities will be understated. This leads to the reporting of artificially low debt-to-equity ratios, implying less risk for the firm than is the case. Likewise, if the PBO is understated, interest on PBO (a component of annual pension cost [expense]) is understated, and thus income is overstated. Inflated income figures will affect a host of performance ratios.

Further complicating analyses, during a period of falling interest rates (as described above), the prices of stocks and bonds in which Pension Plan assets are invested can be relied on to increase. By their very nature, bond prices increase when interest rates fall. This then gives rise to pension plan gains. While firms may choose *not* to reduce discount rates assumptions on the liability side of the equation; they can be counted on to recognize gains on the assets, which can be substantial. Thus, the best of both worlds may be sought: avoid expense and liability increases but recognize revenue and asset increases. See the In Practice feature "Corporate Perfomance Measures and Pension Plan Gains." Great vigilance is required of the financial statement user to avoid falling prey to these accounting practices.

IN PRACTICE—GENERAL

Corporate Performance Measures and Pension Plan Gains

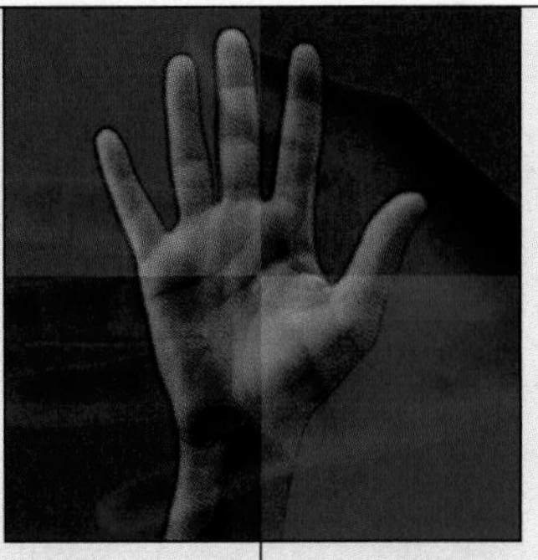

As the stock and bond markets surge, so does the value of corporate pension plan assets. The ***Pension Benefit Guaranty Corp.*** estimates that 75 percent of all defined benefit corporate pension plans are now fully funded. (*Or, are reported as such, given understated liabilities and currently priced pension plan assets.*) Companies are now using these surpluses to boost reported earnings. In the real world, these pension plan credits are adding a lot of fat to corporate bottom lines, as shown in the table below.

Jack Ciesielski, president of accounting research firm ***R. G. Associates*** and publisher of the *Analyst's Accounting Observer*, notes that at Cincinnati Milacron last year, aftertax pension credits represented over 30 percent of net income from continuing operations.

COMPANY	ADJUSTED EPS	ESTIMATED AFTERTAX PENSION CREDIT	AFTERTAX CREDIT AS % OF EPS	ASSUMED RETURN RATE
Teledyne	$0.56	$0.45	80.4%	6.0%
USX-US Steel Group	−5.08	2.73	53.7	11.0
Monarch Machine Tool	−0.45	0.24	53.3	8.5
Cincinnati Milacron	0.58	0.18	31.0	9.5
WestVaco	2.06	0.38	18.4	11.5

Source: Norm Alster, "Dark Lining to a Silver Cloud," *Forbes*, November 8, 1993, p. 137.

REQUIRED DISCLOSURES SFAS No. 87

In formulating SFAS No. 87, the board made several concessions to past practice, most notably concessions relating to the netting of expenses and revenues, the netting of assets and liabilities, and the delayed recognition of projected benefit obligation and changes therein. Because of these concessions, much of the most

Apply the disclosure requirements of SFAS No. 87.

current and relevant information regarding the pension plan is excluded from the employer's financial statements. Accordingly, while noting that "footnote disclosure is not an adequate substitute for recognition" the board provided for greatly enhanced footnote disclosure of pension commitments and elements of periodic pension cost. Exhibit 16–4 provides the disclosure requirements of SFAS No. 87.

EXHIBIT 16–4
Disclosure Requirements of SFAS No. 87

Specifically, the standard requires that an employer sponsoring a defined-benefit pension plan must disclose the following:

A. *A descipriton of the plan,* including employee groups covered, type of benefit formula, funding policy, types of assets held, significant nonbenefit liabilities, if any, and the nature and effect of significant matters affecting comparability of information for all periods presented.
B. *Components of periodic pension expense,* including the amount of net periodic pension cost for the period and the following elements:
   1. Service cost component.
   2. Interest cost component.
   3. Actual return on assets for the period.
   4. Net total of other components.
C. *A reconciling schedule* reconciling the funded status of the plan with amounts reported in the employer's statement of financial position, showing separately
   1. Fair value of plan assets.
   2. Projected benefit obligation, accumulated benefit obligation, and vested obligation.
   3. Amount of unrecognized prior-service costs.
   4. Amount of unrecognized net gain or loss.
   5. Amount of any remaining unrecognized net obligation or net asset existing at the date of initial application of the statement.
   6. Amount of any additional liability.
D. *Critical plan assumptions,* including the weighted average assumed discount rate; the rate of compensation increase, if applicable, used to measure the projected benefit obligation; and the weighted average expected long-term rate of return on plan assets.
E. *Other information* related to
   1. Amounts and types of any securities of the employer and related parties included in plan assets.
   2. Approximate amount of annual benefits of employees and retirees covered by annuity contracts issued by the employer and related parties.
   3. Amortization methods used.

Potentially, the most confusing of these disclosure requirements relates to the reconciliation schedule (requirement C in the exhibit). The purpose of the schedule is to provide additional information not explicitly available from a review of the financial statements, and to illustrate how they relate. Frequently the schedule will take a form similar to the following:

RECONCILIATION OF FUNDED STATUS	
Projected benefit obligation	$(100,000)
Plan assets at fair value	70,000
Funded status	$ (30,000)
Unrecognized net obligation at plan initiation	40,000
Unrecognized prior-service costs	50,000
Unrecognized net (gain) or loss	(20,000)
(Accrued)/prepaid pension cost	$ 40,000

For simplicity, in this illustration it was assumed there was no additional liability recorded relating to the minimum-liability provision of the standard. Also, accumulated and vested obligations are not typically disclosed in this schedule. To facilitate a clear understanding of how this schedule reconciles funded status with the net balance sheet account of Accrued/Prepaid Pension Cost, recall the general nature of the periodic pension cost entry:

Pension Cost (Expense)	xxxx	
Cash		xxxx
Accrued Pension Costs		xxxx

In essence, the reconciliation schedule reconciles simultaneously (1) projected benefit obligation (PBO) with pension expense and (2) plan assets with cash payments into the plan, as it is the debits to pension cost (expense) and credits to cash that determine the balance in the Accrued/Prepaid Pension Cost account. The PBO is given delayed-recognition status under SFAS No. 87; that is, not all obligations are recognized immediately. Therefore, the difference between the total PBO and the portion recognized is that portion unrecognized—or in the reconciliation schedule just shown, unrecognized net obligation at plan initiation and unrecognized prior-service costs.

Reduced to its fundamentals, the difference between the fund's asset balance and cash contributions relates to gains and losses on plan assets—or in the reconciliation schedule—unrecognized net gain or loss. (Recall that expected returns on plan assets are an element of pension expense and thus included in either cash contributed or accrued/prepaid pension cost, the balance sheet amount to which the reconciliation is made.)

OTHER POSTRETIREMENT BENEFITS

Explain the general accounting requirements for other postretirement benefits.

In addition to pension benefits, retirees may receive other postretirement benefits, including, but not limited to, postretirement health care, life insurance, and other welfare benefits such as tuition assistance, day care, legal services, and housing subsidies. Of these, the postemployment health-care benefit is the most frequently received and the most financially significant. According to a Bureau of Labor Statistics survey, approximately one-half of medium and large U.S. companies provide employees (and dependents) with free or highly subsidized health benefits upon retirement.

The granting of postretirement health-care benefits began quietly during World War II. With wages frozen by the federal government, labor extracted pension, health, and other fringe benefits in place of wage concessions. These initial benefits were modest. Later, coverages were extended in amount and scope. These benefits were generally looked upon as gratuities and were subject to the granting corporation's unilateral decision to amend or cancel them. Accordingly, expenses were recognized on a *pay-as-you-go* (cash) basis. Costs for these plans for many years were relatively small. Recently, however, skyrocketing health-care costs, early retirement programs and increased longevity have combined to cause dramatic escalation of employer costs for retiree health plans. At the turn of the decade of the 1990s, even on a pay-as-you-go basis, employee health benefits for many firms were measured in the hundreds of millions of dollars. For example, ***AT&T***'s payout exceeds \$300 million, and ***DuPont***'s payout is over \$400 million—relatively typical charges for many large U.S. firms.[16] See the In Practice feature "SFAS No. 106 and the Growing Cost of Health Insurance."

IN PRACTICE—GENERAL

SFAS No. 106 and the Growing Cost of Health Care

The costs of health-care plans have been growing at staggering rates over the last decade. Seldom have these costs appeared on the face of financial statements, however. SFAS No. 106 changes all that. Employers now have two unappetizing choices. Unrecorded past costs may be charged off immediately or amortized over the next 20 years. Either alternative can devastate corporate profits.

Some examples of estimates of unrecorded past costs include (from company reports):

COMPANY	ESTIMATE
General Motors	\$16–\$24 Billion
Hewlett-Packard	\$544 Million
McDonnell Douglas	\$700 Million
Navistar	\$2.5 Billion

Legal and practical considerations also have changed, making postemployment health benefits fairly fixed obligations. Of 467 letters received in response to the exposure draft preceding adoption of SFAS No. 106 ("Employers' Accounting for Postretirement Benefits Other than Pensions"), only 14 disputed that a liability existed. Moreover, as a legal matter, the ability of employers to cancel or amend benefits may remain somewhat uncertain in selected jurisdictions because of different precedents established in various federal court circuits in interpreting the language of contracts and the intention of relevant parties. Issues of *ethics* may also be involved as suggested in the In Practice feature "The Changing Landscape of Postretirement Benefits."

[16]C. Loomis, "The Killer Cost Stalking Business," *Fortune,* February 27, 1989, p. 62.

In 1984, as a temporary measure, pending promulgation of final guidelines the FASB in SFAS No. 81 ("Disclosure of Pension Health Care and Life Insurance Benefits") required employers to

1. Disclose material annual cash outflows for retiree health benefits.
2. Describe the benefits provided.
3. Describe the employee groups covered.
4. Describe the accounting and funding policies.

In 1990 the FASB issued SFAS No. 106 with the following four objectives stated:

1. To enhance the relevance and representational faithfulness of the employer's reported results of operations (income statement) by recognizing net periodic postretirement benefit cost.
2. To enhance the relevance and representational faithfulness of the employer's statement of financial position (balance sheet) by including a measure of the obligation to provided postretirement benefits.
3. To enhance the ability of users to understand the employer's financial statements by requiring disclosure of selected additional relevant information.
4. To improve the understandability and comparability of employers with similar plans by requiring the same method to measure their accumulated postretirement benefit obligations and related periodic costs.

Thus, with the promulgation of SFAS No. 106, the FASB explicitly took the position that retiree health benefits were a form of deferred compensation and not a gratuity. Accordingly, the FASB imposed the requirement, for the first time, that accrual accounting methods be applied—in particular, accrued expense was to replace the pay-as-you-go cost on the income statement, and an estimate of the accrued liability was mandated to be disclosed in the financial statement footnotes. It should be emphasized that SFAS No. 106 did not create expenses or liabilities for businesses; it does force them to recognize already existing liabilities. SFAS No. 106 was required for fiscal years beginning after December 15, 1992.

The economic consequences of this particular rule has, in some cases, been particularly harsh for both employees and the employer entity. Some companies have dropped health insurance benefits for retirees while others are requiring retirees to pay a larger portion of the insurance premium. While this is partially in response to rising health-care costs, it is also widely attributed to the requirement that these costs be recognized currently instead of at the time that they are actually incurred. The impact on the reported earnings of some corporations has been huge. For example, ***General Motors*** reported a $16 billion charge against earnings in the first quarter of 1993 for past services only. There will also be an increased annual accrual for health-care costs. Retiree accrual costs for many firms run three to six times higher than retiree pay-as-you-go costs.

ACCOUNTING FOR POSTRETIREMENT HEALTH BENEFITS

For the most part, the method of accounting for retiree health benefits promulgated in SFAS No. 106 parallels the current method of accounting for pensions.

IN PRACTICE—GENERAL

The Changing Landscape of Postretirement Benefits

Small and midsize businesses are cutting retiree health benefits much more aggressively than large companies . . . Many large companies made their big cuts in medical benefits to retirees a few years ago. A change in accounting rules then required companies to set up a reserve for such benefits, resulting in higher payroll costs. . . .

The share of companies with 500–999 employees offering medical benefits to at least some retirees plunged to 35 percent last year from 50 percent in 1993. . . . In contrast, 61 percent of employers with more than 1,000 employees offer retiree medical benefits. . . . Companies (also) are finding other ways besides eliminating retiree programs to trim health-care costs. . . . Business use of so-called indemnity plans, in which employees generally use doctors of their own choice and seek reimbursement from their employer, dropped to 46 percent last year from 57% in 1993. Such plans have been replaced by managed-care plans, such as health maintenance organizations (HMOs), in which insurance companies negotiate deep discounts for medical care from physicians and hospitals.

Source: S. Mehta, "Many Small Companies Drop Retiree Health Benefits," *The Wall Street Journal,* August 22, 1995, p. B2.

IN PRACTICE—GENERAL

Cutting Pension Plans

Is ***Allstate***'s war with its agents reaching a cease fire? . . . Recently a federal judge in Jacksonville ruled that Allstate had illegally altered the pension plan of its 13,500 agents. Specifically, in 1989, the company froze all retirement benefits and then reduced the benefits of its higher-paid agents . . . by 20 percent, retroactively, without bothering to send the agents proper notices, as required by federal law. Moreover, Allstate's agents were not properly informed that their retirement age had been changed from 63 to 65, which also had the effect of lowering benefits.

Allstate was spun off by ***Sears, Roebuck and Co.*** this summer. Ironically, the agents' pension plan had long supplemented the Sears profit-sharing program, which was built (and heavily guarded) by the famous General Robert Wood. . . . He once warned his top executives: "The future of thousands of people lies in profit sharing, and if you don't run this company right and [you] destroy their values, you've committed a crime."

Source: Richard Behar, "Allstate Slapped for Pension Ploy," October 30, 1995, p. 20.

The following components are included in annual postretirement benefit costs by an employer sponsoring a defined postretirement plan:

1. Service cost
2. Interest cost
3. Amortization of prior-service cost
4. Actual return on plan assets

5. Gain or loss on plan assets and amortization of unrecognized gain or loss
6. Amortization of unrecognized transition obligation

Except for items 1 and 6, these items are calculated in a fashion similar to pension costs. While item 6 relates to specific and distinct transitional treatments, item 1 relates to a substantive continuing difference.

Service costs are defined in SFAS No. 106 as the actuarial present value of benefits attributed to services rendered by employees during the period. While employees earn health benefits through services rendered, as with pension benefits, health-benefit formulas are of a different character from the pension-benefit formulas discussed earlier in this chapter. Under plans where health benefits increase with the length of service, those increased benefits typically take the form of declining required employee insurance contributions or changes in deductibles of coinsurance provisions.

The **accumulated postretirement benefit obligation** is the actuarial present value of all future benefits attributed to an employee's service rendered to that date. Prior to the date on which an employee attains full eligibility for all available benefits, accumulated postretirement benefit obligation is a portion of *expected* postretirement benefit obligation (the actuarial present value of all future benefits attributed to an employee's service, assuming continued employ). That is, *accumulated benefits* are those benefits earned to date; *expected benefits* are those benefits expected to be paid, under reasonable assumptions of continuity. SFAS No. 106 requires that expected postretirement benefit obligation be attributed to periods extending from (1) the date of hire or (2) a later date, if the benefit formula only grants credit for service from a later date to (3) the date of full eligibility. Unlike many pension formulas, full health-benefit eligibility may be achieved before retirement, such as in cases where full eligibility is granted to employees who render 30 years or more of service or who render at least 10 years service and attain age 55. Because the obligation to provide benefits arises as employees render the services necessary to earn the benefits, the board believes that the cost of providing the benefits should be recognized over the service period. The expense recognition method is the same as that used with pensions (that is, a benefits/years-of-service approach).

LIABILITY MEASUREMENT

The liability for retiree health benefits is measured using actuarial assumptions regarding the discount rate and the amount and timing of future benefit payments. These assumptions rest in turn on assumptions about per capita claims cost by age, health-care cost trends, the medicare reimbursement rate, employee turnover, retirement age, mortality, and the number of covered dependents. The discount rate must reflect rates of return on high-quality, fixed-income investments. The trend rate of health-care costs should reflect such factors as health-care inflation, changes in health-care utilization, and technological advances. The assumed rate of medicare reimbursement should be consistent with current law.

All of this leads to very *imprecise* measures! The excerpted *Fortune* magazine article speculates about the future of medical care and cost, and the implications for business, in the In Practice feature "Health Care Estimates Versus Guestimates."

Still, it is the FASB's position that the new data are better than what came before, which was nearly nothing. Prior to implementation of SFAS No. 106 it

IN PRACTICE—GENERAL

Health Care Estimates Versus Guestimates

Imagine a recent Fortune 500 retiree named Fred, a prince of an employee over the years, but right now a corporate horror. Fred, 60, is covered by his company's health plan and has a life expectancy of 78; that's 18 years of health benefits. Young at heart, Fred has a new, 30-year-old wife who can be expected to live to 80. She also comes under the company's health plan. So, gulp, does Fred Jr., 1 year old, whose coverage extends through the year he reaches 21. Add it up: 88 years of health benefits to be bestowed on a family that will be performing no work whatsoever for the company.

Estimating these obligations will be only slightly easier than making the sun rise in the west and set in the east. Take the example of Mrs. Fred. The company responsible for her must, in effect, estimate what her medical costs will be over 50 years, taking into account price inflation (what will a hip replacement cost?), the frequency with which she may use medical services (one hip or two?), and the impact of technology (will they be using gold by then for hips?). And what to make of Medicare, the primary provider for those over 65, with business picking up the extras? Lately Medicare, by extending catastrophic coverage to citizens over 65, has assumed billions in costs formerly borne by business. But will this munificence last—through the next year, much less for 49 more?

Source: C. Loomis, "The Killer Cost Stalking Business," *Fortune,* February 27, 1989, pp. 58–68.

was estimated that annual accrued expenses would run three to six times higher than retiree pay-as-you-go costs, and the accumulated postretirement benefit about 30 times higher than the pay-as-you-go cost. Experiences have been consistent with intial estimates.

INTERPRETING SFAS NO. 87 AND SFAS NO. 106 DATA

As with pension data, the usability of the new data should be expected to improve with time. The FASB explicitly noted in both SFAS No. 87 and No. 106 that current guidance regarding both accounting for pensions and other postemployment benefits can be expected to continue to evolve. The user must be aware of the relative imprecision of the data provided and the critical nature of the underlying assumptions. On the other hand, to ignore the massive pension and health-care commitments to which many firms have committed themselves would be folly. A principal objective of financial reporting is to provide the user with information about future cash flows and the uncertainty surrounding them. To the extent that recent pronouncements regarding pensions and other postemployment benefits do so, it is essential for the serious student of accounting to become familiar with these standards. This chapter has attempted to provide a framework to assist in that study. The impact of these FASB standards on net income measurement is frequently very material.

The usefulness of the information may be compromised by netting of expenses and revenues and netting of assets and liabilities. Netting of expenses may cloud such measures as *times interest earned,* a ratio frequently used to measure a firm's ability to pay its interest obligations. Likewise, the netting of assets and liabilities will potentially impede financial statement analysis. The ratios most affected in this area would be the debt-to-equity ratio and the return-on-assets ratio.

APPENDIX: ALTERNATIVE PROCEDURE FOR AMORTIZING PRIOR-SERVICE COSTS

Conceptually, amortization of prior-service cost should recognize the cost of each individual's added benefits over that individual's remaining service life. As such, the individual method would result in a declining amortization charge for the cost of a particular plan amendment. This is the case because some of the employees can be expected to retire each year, and the greatest amount of retroactive benefit will be to those nearest retirement. The method illustrated below is consistent with a declining-charge approach. This method has been noted by the board as acceptable in meeting the objectives of SFAS No. 87. Note that each expected "future service year" is assigned an equal share of prior-service cost (i.e., the projected benefit obligation increment affected by plan amendment). The portion of prior-service cost to be recognized in any individual year is the *service year's equivalent* rendered in that year. In the example that follows, assume the following:

Date of amendment	January 1, Year 10
Number of employees:	100*
Rate of retirement:	10% per year
Prior-service cost	$200,000

AMORTIZATION SCHEDULE

EMPLOYEES' IDENTIFICATION NUMBER	SERVICE YEARS										TOTAL
	10	11	12	13	14	15	16	17	18	19	
1–10	10										10
11–20	10	10									20
21–30	10	10	10								30
31–40	10	10	10	10							40
41–50	10	10	10	10	10						50
51–60	10	10	10	10	10	10					60
61–70	10	10	10	10	10	10	10				70
71–80	10	10	10	10	10	10	10	10			80
81–90	10	10	10	10	10	10	10	10	10		90
91–100	10	10	10	10	10	10	10	10	10	10	100
	100	90	80	70	60	50	40	30	20	10	550

Annual Fraction:

$\frac{100}{550}$ $\frac{90}{550}$ $\frac{80}{550}$ $\frac{70}{550}$ $\frac{60}{550}$ $\frac{50}{550}$ $\frac{40}{550}$ $\frac{30}{550}$ $\frac{20}{550}$ $\frac{10}{550}$

Annual Amortization = $200,000 × Annual Fraction
For Example: Year 14 = $200,000 × 60/550 = $21,818

*Designates employees who are expected to receive benefit. Others may be employed at the time of amendment but are expected to be terminated without benefits due.

APPENDIX: ALTERNATIVE PROCEDURE FOR CALCULATING A MARKET-RELATED VALUE FOR PLAN ASSETS

In determining the expected return on plan assets, either of two approaches may be used. The first, illustrated in the chapter, uses *fair value*. The other alternative is to use a *calculated market-related value*, which may be computed in a variety of ways. The first approach illustrated below adds 20% of each of the five prior years' gains or losses. SFAS No. 87 itself illustrates this procedure, noting, "The only objective of the market-related calculation is to reduce the volatility of net pension cost" (SFAS No. 87, Appendix B). Using the same example as presented in the chapter, the following calculation of market-related asset values might be made for Year X1:

Market-related value of assets, 1/1/X1	$100,000
+ Contributions made in year	40,000
− Benefits paid in year	(30,000)
+ *Expected* return on plan assets	10,000
+ 20% of the last five years' gains	17,000*
= Market-related value of assets, 12/31/X1	$137,000

*20% × (current year's gain of $45,000 + net gain of prior four years of $40,000).

This year's expected return was 10% (the expected long-run rate of return) multiplied by the beginning-of-the-year, market-related value of $100,000. Next year's expected return will be 10% (the expected long-run rate of return) multiplied by $137,000, this year's ending and next year's beginning market-related value.

Another alternative method to calculating a market-related value would be to simply take an average of the last five years' fair values.

END-OF-CHAPTER REVIEW

SUMMARY

1. **Differentiate between defined-contribution and defined-benefit plans.** Two types of pension plans were discussed in this chapter, defined-contribution plans and defined-benefit plans. The latter assures the future retiree of specific benefits. Market risks are borne by the employer. Under defined-contribution plans the employer fulfills its obligation by making annual payments to a plan trustee. The employee bears the risk of market performance of plan investments. Accounting for a defined-contribution plan is relatively simple: expenses are recorded for the required annual contribution to the plan. Accounting for a defined-benefits plan is relatively more complex, requiring actuarial estimates of future obligations.
2. **Understand the theoretically correct pension-related journal entries for defined-benefit plans, and understand the practical compromises of SFAS No. 87.** Inconsistent with prevailing practice elsewhere, SFAS No. 87 permits pension-related revenues and expenses to be netted, pension-related assets and liabilities to be similarly offset, and recognition of prior-service cost commitment to be deferred.

3. **Measure and account for actuarial gains and losses.** Actuarial gains and losses arise from changes in (1) the fair value of plan assets, and (2) the projected benefit obligation. The changes in projected benefit obligation arise from changes in actuarial assumptions and from experience. Cumulative unrecognized net gain or loss refers to the current year's gain or loss combined with the unamortized balance of all preceding years' gains and losses. Any amount of cumulative unrecognized gain or loss in excess of 10 percent of the greater of projected benefit obligation or the value of the plan assets must be amortized in the following year.
4. **Apply the disclosure requirements of SFAS No. 87.** Given the myriad of reporting compromises institutionalized by SFAS No. 87, the board found it necessary to require extensive footnote disclosures in addition to financial information embedded in the statements themselves. It is incumbent on the serious reader to carefully examine the pension footnotes.
5. **Explain the general accounting requirements for other postretirement benefits.** Other postretirement benefits typically include health care, life insurance, tuition assistance, day care, legal services, and housing subsidies. SFAS No. 106 requires that the costs of these benefits be recognized and accrued on a current basis. The accounting required is very similar to pension accounting. The main difference is found in the computation of service costs. For health insurance in particular, the future service cost estimate will change as the deductible, copayment, and amount of required employee contribution change over time.

KEY TERMS

accrued pension costs *862*
accumulated benefit obligation *853*
accumulated postretirement benefit obligation *878*
actual return on plan assets *868*
corridor method *868*
cumulative unrecognized net gain/loss *868*
defined benefit plan *848*
defined contribution plan *848*
funding *857*
gain/loss *865*
minimum liability *869*
pension costs (expense) *861*
postemployment benefits *847*
postretirement benefits *848*
prepaid/accrued pension costs *861*
prior-service cost *856*
projected benefit obligation (PBO) *852*
service costs *852*
vesting *854*

ASSIGNMENT MATERIAL

CASES

C16–1 Overfunded Plan Replaced—Ethical Dimensions

Because of higher than expected interest rates in preceding years, Prudow Inc. in 1997 found itself with an "overfunded" defined-benefit pension plan. Returns on pension plan assets had exceeded prior projections (i.e., the market value of pension plan assets, $40,000,000, exceeded the accumulated benefit obligation, $30,000,000). Prudow was experiencing financial distress as a result of four successive years of net losses. Accordingly, Prudow terminated the pension plan and replaced it with a new pension plan. The "excess" funds of $10,000,000 were withdrawn and used to finance the purchase of new, more technologically competitive equipment.

Required:

A. Do you believe pension plans are "overfunded" when pension plan assets exceed accumulated benefit obligations?

B. Discuss to whom these funds belong.

C. Discuss ethical dimensions of this issue and the need or lack thereof for greater government regulation than currently exists. What stakeholders are there, and how might they be affected by different policies?

D. If the funds had been withdrawn and used for other purposes, such as investment in highly speculative junk bonds, new business ventures, or foreign operations, would your views as to the ethics of funds withdrawal be different? Why or why not?

16–2 Assumptions Underlying Plan

In a study released in 1993, it was reported that approximately 25% of pension funds surveyed were projecting investment returns for their plan assets in excess of 8.75%. For 17%, the projections exceeded an 11% return. In the preceding year, Standard & Poors 500 stocks yielded a return of only about 7%, and 30-year bonds were paying 6.8%. Thus, many firms were apparently not basing their estimates of pension plan returns on reality.

Most of these firms had not changed their investment strategies although a subset had by switching to more risky investments that might produce rates of return more consistent with their actuarial assumptions.

Required: Discuss what might motivate such a significant percentage of firms to resist adjusting pension plan actuarial assumptions downward.

16–3 Reduction of Benefits—Ethical Considerations

In recent years, many pensioners have received letters from their former employers altering health-care benefits provided. These changes have nearly universally reduced benefits or set ceilings for the employer. In some instances, the retiree's copayments or deductibles have been increased. In other instances, the firm has informed retirees that if total postretirement health-care costs exceed existing levels, the retirees' portions of these costs will be increased in the subsequent year.

Arguably, these actions are legal because of the fine print customarily included in health-care plans that notes the right of the employer to change these provisions at will. Numerous lawsuits, nonetheless, have been brought contesting the validity of these clauses. Consider the following information from C. Loomis, "The Killer Cost Stalking Business," *Fortune*, February 27, 1989, p. 63.

At issue is a matter of "social consciousness," argues Ballas Salisbury, president of the ***Employee Benefit Research Institute***. Those not yet retired, Salisbury says, have time to adjust to changes in coverage: "They have time to work longer, time to save." They also have leverage, including the ability to strike or take another job. But, says Salisbury, "Someone who is 78 and already has bad health problems does not have the option of finding new savings to pay health insurance premiums he never thought he would have to pay."

With an adjustment for age, Salisbury could almost have been talking about Charles Fletcher, 59, a retired distribution manager of ***American Forest Products*** (AFP), a California company taken private in 1981 by ***Kohlberg Kravis Roberts*** (KKR) and that firm's most notable financial disaster. In 1983, as AFP cut back operations, Fletcher received $22,500 in severance pay and round-tripped $13,000 of it to AFP in exchange, so he thought, for lifetime health insurance for himself and his wife. Then, in early 1988, he learned he had leukemia.

Three months later KKR sold AFP to ***Georgia Pacific***. AFP's retirees, including Fletcher, received notice from AFP that their health insurance would be terminated, but that they would each be paid $25,000 as compensation. Says Fletcher: "Most are older and come under Medicare, so they accepted. But for me, after taxes, that wouldn't cover one stay in the hospital." So he bitterly refused the $25,000 and is suing AFP and KKR. A lawyer for those companies says a clause in Fletcher's health plan permits the cancellation.

Required:

A. Discuss some of the impediments to making reliable projections of postretirement health-care benefits.

B. Discuss the ethics of the various behaviors discussed here. Is greater government regulation of postretirement health plans necessary?

QUESTIONS

Q16–1 Which of the following ratios is (are) influenced by alternate approaches to pension accounting, and how?

1. Return-on-investment (net income/owners' equity).
2. Debt-to-equity.
3. Current ratio (current assets/current liabilities).

Q16–2 In what ways does SFAS No. 87 facilitate evaluation of financial flexibility?

Q16–3 Distinguish between a defined-contribution pension plan and a defined-benefit pension plan.

Q16–4 Provide an example of a defined-benefit pension formula.

Q16–5 SFAS No. 87 requires that estimates of earned future employee pension benefits be discounted to obtain current-period equivalents. What discount rate does SFAS No. 87 direct to be used when discounting future benefits?

Q16–6 Distinguish between projected benefit obligation and accumulated benefit obligation.

Q16–7 In developing SFAS No. 87, the FASB retained three fundamental aspects of past pension accounting that are highly controversial—delayed recognition of certain events, reporting net costs, and offsetting assets and liabilities. Discuss the pros and cons of these three conventions of past and current practice.

Q16–8 Enumerate and discuss the six elements of current-period pension costs.

Q16–9 Explain what is meant by "underfunded PBO."

Q16–10 Discuss how pension accounting relies on accounting and actuarial assumptions and estimates.

EXERCISES

E16–1 Defined Contributions

Roland C. Clarke Enterprises makes annual contributions to Provident Insurance Annuity Association on behalf of its employees under a defined-contribution pension agreement with its employees. In 2003 Clarke Enterprises made payments of $47,000 to Provident in fulfillment of the pension agreement for employee pension rights earned in 2003.

Required: Prepare the appropriate journal entry.

E16–2 Defined Contributions

Chi Ho makes annual contributions to Metropolis Insurance Annuity Association on behalf of her employees under a defined-contribution pension agreement requiring contributions equivalent to 7% of gross payroll. Gross payroll in 2005 was $1,000,000. Ho Enterprises operates on a calendar-year basis. Contributions to pensions plans are made February 1 of each year for the preceding year.

Required: Prepare the appropriate journal entries for 2005 and 2006 relative to the 2005 payroll.

E16–3 Projected Benefit Obligation

As of January 1, 2006, the projected benefit obligation of Romistar Corporation to its employees was determined to be $563,000. Estimated future benefits had been discounted at an 8% rate in arriving at this figure. During 2006, service costs amounted to $72,000, and employee pension benefits in the amount of $31,000 were disbursed at year-end.

Required: Determine the projected benefit obligation at 2006 year-end.

E16–4 Annual Pension Expense

Dan O'Dell, chief accountant for McGill Corporation, is currently reviewing pension information provided to him by his staff pursuant to the recording of the firm's annual pension expense. His staff reports that current-period service cost amounts to $97,000. Projected benefit obligation at the beginning of the year was $530,000, and there were no changes in any assumptions used in arriving at that figure (including the 10% discount rate).

Last year, prior-service costs were amortized in the amount of $28,000, and a comparable figure appears appropriate this period. While plan assets of $400,000 (fair value at the beginning of the current year) were expected to provide a return of 11%, the current actual experience was a return on investment of $48,000. The calculated current amortization of past actuarial gains amounts to $4,000.

Required: Determine this period's net pension expense.

E16–5 Projected Benefit Obligation

As of January 1, 2005, the projected benefit obligation of Harvey Corporation to its employees was determined to be $840,000. Estimated future benefits had been discounted at a 12% rate in arriving at this figure. During 2005, service costs amounted to $80,000, and no employee pension benefits were disbursed.

Required: Determine the projected benefit obligation at 2005 year-end.

E16–6 Annual Pension Expense

William Bell, controller for Protechnique Corporation, is reviewing pension information provided by his staff relevant to recording the firm's annual pension expense. The information indicates that current-period service costs amount to $165,000. Projected benefit obligation at the beginning of the year was $1,100,000, and there were no changes in any assumptions used to arrive at that figure (including the 9% discount rate). Accumulated benefit obligation was $675,000. Prior-service costs amount to $480,000 and are to be amortized over 12 years.

While plan assets of $800,000 (fair market value at the beginning of the year) were expected to provide a return of 10%, the actual current experience was a return on investment of $96,000. Net unamortized gains and losses from prior periods amount to a net gain of $210,000. Gains and losses are amortized over 20 years.

Required: Determine this period's net pension expense.

E16–7 Expected Return on Plan Assets

On January 1, 2003, the market-related value of Ashley Enterprises' pension plan assets was $100,000. Additional contributions to plan assets made during the year were $40,000, and distributions (benefits paid) were $25,000. Actual returns on investment of $17,000 exceeded the $10,000 (10%) expected return. Ten percent is the long-term expected rate of return; however, over the last five years (including the current year), net gain has been $26,000.

Required: If one follows the approach illustrated in Appendix B of SFAS No. 87, what is the market-related value of pension plan assets on December 31, 2003, and what is the expected return for 2004? (See the second appendix to this chapter, on page 881.)

E16–8 Minimum Pension Liability

For each case, prepare any necessary entry to provide for a minimum pension liability.

	CASE 1	CASE 2	CASE 3
Fair value of plan assets	$400,000	$400,000	$400,000
Projected benefit obligation	600,000	700,000	800,000
Accumulated benefit obligation	500,000	550,000	600,000
Prepaid pension costs (Dr.)	40,000		
Accrued pension costs (Cr.)		100,000	120,000
Unrecognized prior-service costs	150,000	70,000	40,000

E16–9 Reconciliation Disclosures

SFAS No. 87 requires that a schedule be provided among footnote disclosures to reconcile the funded status of a firm's pension plan with amounts reported in the employer's statement of financial position. Given the information provided here, provide such a reconciling schedule for each case.

	CASE 1	CASE 2	CASE 3
Fair value of plan assets	$400,000	$600,000	$400,000
Projected benefit obligation	600,000	700,000	800,000
Accumulated benefit obligation	300,000	500,000	500,000
Prepaid pension costs	50,000		
Accrued pension costs		10,000	100,000
Unrecognized net loss or (gain)	20,000	20,000	(20,000)
Unrecognized prior-service costs	170,000	60,000	260,000
Unrecognized net obligation at plan initiation	60,000	10,000	60,000

E16–10 Minimum Pension Liability

For each case, prepare any necessary entry to provide for a minimum pension liability. The figures provided are year-end numbers.

	CASE 1	CASE 2	CASE 3
Fair value of plan assets	$370,000	$800,000	$600,000
Projected benefit obligation	500,000	920,000	860,000
Accumulated benefit obligation	450,000	650,000	800,000
Prepaid pension costs (Dr.)	20,000		
Accrued pension costs (Cr.)		110,000	150,000
Unrecognized prior-service costs	80,000	100,000	60,000

E16–11 Reconciliation Disclosures

SFAS No. 87 requires that a schedule be provided among footnote disclosures to reconcile the funded status of a firm's pension plan with amounts reported in the employer's statement of financial position. Given the information provided here, provide such a reconciling schedule for each case.

	CASE 1	CASE 2	CASE 3
Fair value of plan assets	$400,000	$600,000	$400,000
Projected benefit obligation	600,000	700,000	800,000
Accumulated benefit obligation	300,000	500,000	500,000
Prepaid pension costs	120,000		
Accrued pension costs		30,000	40,000
Unrecognized net loss or (gain)	90,000	20,000	(20,000)
Unrecognized prior-service costs	170,000	20,000	200,000
Unrecognized net obligation at plan initiation	60,000	30,000	180,000

E16–12 Projected Benefit Obligation

Sam Miller will receive an annual pension of $35,000 for 10 years when he retires. The first payment will occur on January 1, 2010.

Required:

A. Using an interest rate of 9%, how much must be in the pension fund on January 1, 2010, to provide for Sam's retirement?

B. If funds were to be isolated for this purpose now (January 1, 2006), what amount would need to be placed with the pension plan trustee?

E16–13 Projected Benefit Obligation

Merle Joseph will receive an annual pension in the amount of $50,000 for 14 years when he retires. The first payment will occur on January 1, 2020.

Required:

A. Using an interest rate of 10%, how much must be in the pension fund on January 1, 2020, to provide for Merle's retirement?

B. If funds were to be isolated for this purpose currently (January 1, 2005), what amount would need to be placed with the pension plan trustee?

E16–14 Corridor Method

The following information relates to the Frank E. Smithe & Company's noncontributory, defined-benefit pension plan:

	JAN. 1 PBO	JAN. 1 PLAN ASSETS	GAIN OR (LOSS)
2000	$5,000,000	$4,800,000	$ 300,000
2001	5,500,000	5,600,000	(1,200,000)
2002	6,000,000	5,900,000	(400,000)
2003	7,000,000	6,900,000	700,000

The cumulative unrecognized gain or loss on plan assets (from prior years) as of January 1, 2000, was a net gain of $600,000. The average remaining service life per employee in each year may be assumed to be 10 years.

Required: Using the corridor approach, for each year, compute (1) the cumulative unrecognized gain or loss and (2) the annual amortization.

E16–15 Corridor Method

The following information relates to the Little Genevieve Company's noncontributory, defined-benefit pension plan:

	JAN. 1 PBO	JAN. 1 PLAN ASSETS	GAIN OR (LOSS)
2003	$8,000,000	$7,800,000	$ 200,000
2004	8,300,000	7,000,000	(600,000)
2005	7,000,000	6,900,000	1,200,000
2006	7,000,000	6,900,000	700,000

The cumulative unrecognized net gain on plan assets (from prior years) as of January 1, 2003, was $900,000. The average remaining service life per employee in each year may be assumed to be 10 years.

Required: Using the corridor approach, for each year, compute (1) the cumulative unrecognized gain or loss and (2) the annual amortization.

E16–16 Defined Contibution/Defined Benefit Plans

Discuss the advantages and disadvantages of a defined-contribution plan versus a defined-benefit plan from the point-of-view of the employer.

E16–17 Pension Obligation

Joe Williams has been an employee of Trevor Corporation for the last four years. Trevor has a defined-contribution pension plan that vests after five years of employment. Joe is a good employee, and Trevor is a stable, well-established company.

A. What pension obligation is Trevor *required* to recognize for Joe?

B. What pension obligation *should* Trevor recognize for Joe given the purpose of financial statements? (Take the point-of-view of an auditor.)

E16–18 Pension Costs

Elizabeth has worked for Duofold Inc. for six years. The firm has just established a defined-benefit plan for employees that provides a pension benefit equal to years of service times 3% times average salary during the last five years of employment. The pension benefits vest after five years of service and allow benefits for years of service prior to the establishment of the plan. Elizabeth's current salary is $35,000 per year, and her average earnings over the past five years were $30,000. The firm expects her to work for another 20 years before retirement. What is the accumulated benefit obligation for Elizabeth? Assume a discount rate of 10% and a life expectancy of 10 years after retirement and benefits paid at the end of each year.

E16–19 Pension Costs

Ralph Weston has worked for Inverness Corporation for 5 years. The firm has just established a pension plan that recognizes prior service for benefit purposes. Ralph's current salary is $40,000, and his average pay over the last five years was $30,000. Assume a discount rate of 10%, and that Ralph will work for another 10 years with an average salary during the last five years of $50,000. The firm established a defined-benefit plan with benefits equal to 2.5% of the average pay over the last five years of employment times the years of service for the individual. Assume benefits are paid at the end of each year.

A. What is the accumulated benefit obligation (ABO) for Ralph if he is expected to live 15 years after retirement?
B. What is the ABO for Ralph if he is expected to live five years after retirement?
C. How does the firm choose between alternative life expectancies?

E16–20 Pension Rules

Consider a defined-benefit pension plan from the point-of-view of a covered employee. What aspects of the pension plan should be of concern to the employee?

PROBLEMS

P16–1 Projected and Accumulated Benefit Obligations

Helen Maxwell began working for Medical Products Corporation on January 1, 1995, at 35 years of age. At that time Medical Products was a small company and had no formal pension plan. On January 1, 2003, Medical Products instituted a new, formal, noncontributory, defined-benefits plan that provided for annual employee retirement benefits calculated according to the following formula:

$$\text{Annual benefit} = (\text{Years of service} \times 2.5\% \times \text{Highest Year's Pay})$$

Full credit for years of service prior to the establishment of the pension plan was granted.

Helen's annual salary was $12,000 when she began working for Medical Products and has gradually increased to $30,000 in 2003. It is expected to reach $60,000 in 2025 when she plans to retire. A normal life expectancy following retirement is 12 years.

Required: If the appropriate discount rate is 10%, determine the projected benefit obligation and accumulated benefit obligation on January 1, 2003, for Helen. For simplicity of calculation, assume retirement benefits are paid annually at the beginning of each retirement year.

P16–2 Changes to Projected and Accumulated Benefit Obligations

Using the information provided in P16–1, calculate 2003 pension service costs related to the continued employment of Helen during 2003. Assume that prior estimates of salary levels and discount rates remain the same. Also determine the projected and accumulated benefit obligations to Helen as of January 1, 2004.

P16–3 Pension Entries Disaggregated

During 2003, Gerard Corporation hired a new accountant, Will Sharply. Will acknowledged a lack of experience with regard to pension accounting, but set about the task as best he could. During the year, Sharply made the following entries.

Jan. 1	Prior-Service Costs (Asset)	50,000	
	Projected Benefit Obligation (Liability)		50,000
	To record increase in PBO due to amendment of pension-benefits formula.		
Jan. 1	Pension Plan Assets	30,000	
	Cash		30,000
	To record cash disbursed to pension plan trustee.		
Dec. 31	Amortization of PSC (Expense)	10,000	
	Prior-Service Costs		10,000
	To amortize PSC equally to each future period of employee service.		
Dec. 31	Compensation Expense	24,000	
	Projected Benefit Obligation		24,000
	To record annual service costs.		
Dec. 31	Interest Expense	20,000	
	Projected Benefit Obligation		20,000
	To record increase in PBO as employees' retirements become one year nearer.		
Dec. 31	Pension Plan Assets	28,000	
	Investment Income		28,000
Dec. 31	Pension Plan Assets	26,000	
	Cash		26,000
	To record cash disbursed to pension plan trustee.		

Required: Prepare the journal entries required by SFAS No. 87 given the above.

*P16–4 Prior-Service Cost Amortization

On January 1, 1993, Brian Collier & Company calculated projected benefit obligations (PBO) to employees to be $100,000. As a result of a renegotiated defined-benefits formula, PBO will increase by 50 percent. Collier has ten employees. Two employees are expected to retire in each of the next five years.

Required: Using the method illustrated in the first appendix to this chapter (page 880), provide an amortization schedule for the next five years.

P16–5 Amortization of Gains and Losses

On January 1, 2003, the fair value of the pension plan assets of Roger Stevens & Company amounted to $400,000 (PBO was $530,000). The expected long-term rate of return on plan assets is 11%. During 2003, actual returns on plan assets amounted to $50,000, or $6,000 greater than expected (since the expected return was $400,000 × 11% = $44,000, $50,000 represents a $6,000 gain).

Contributions to the plan made in 2003 amounted to $40,000, and $50,000 in employee benefits were paid. The net balance of preceding years' gains and losses amount to a net $65,000 gain. PBO at year-end amounted to $590,000.

Required: Determine the amount of gain amortization to be included in calculating next year's pension expense. The gain should be amortized over the remaining service lives of the employees (assume 10 years in this case).

P16–6 Prior-Service Cost Amortization

On January 1, 2005, Sandy Layman Company calculated PBO to employees to be $400,000. As a result of a renegotiated defined-benefits formula, PBO will increase by 25 percent. Layman has 90 employees. Fifteen employees are expected to retire at the end of each of the next six years.

Required: Using the method illustrated in the first appendix to this chapter, provide an amortization schedule for prior service costs for the next six years.

P16–7 Amortization of Gains and Losses

On January 1, 2005, the fair value of the pension plan assets of Ann Hough & Company amounted to $600,000 (PBO was $500,000 using a discount rate of 10% and ABO was $400,000). The expected long-term rate of return on plan assets is 12%. During 2005 actual returns on plan assets amounted to $90,000, or $18,000 greater than expected (i.e., an $18,000 gain). Contributions to the plan made in 2005 at year-end amounted to $100,000, and $150,000 in employee benefits were paid (assume at year end). The net balance of preceding years' gains and losses (1/1/05) amount to a net $165,000 gain. Service costs for 2005 were $80,000.

Required:

A. Determine PBO at year-end.

B. Determine the amount of gain amortization to be included in calculating pension expense for 2005 and 2006. The gain should be amortized over the remaining service lives of the employees (assume 10 years in this case for both 2005 and 2006).

P16–8 Projected and Accumulated Benefit Obligations

Carl Knoblett started working for KENCO Enterprises on January 1, 1984, when he was 35 years of age. KENCO did not have a pension plan at that time. On January 1, 2004, KENCO established a noncontributory, defined-benefits pension plan, which provided benefits calculated as follows:

$$\text{Annual Benefit} = (\text{Years of Service} \times 3\% \times \text{Highest Year's Pay})$$

Knoblett was granted full credit for his 20 years of prior service. Knoblett's current salary is $30,000. It is projected to reach $40,000 by retirement on January 1, 2014. A normal life expectancy after retirement is estimated to be 12 years. For simplicity, assume retirement benefits are paid on January 1, commencing on January 1, 2014.

Required: Determine PBO and ABO on January 1, 2004. Assume a discount rate of 10%.

P16–9 Changes to Projected and Accumulated Benefit Obligations

Using the information in P16–8, calculate 1994 pension service costs related to the continued employment of Carl Knoblett during 2004. Also determine PBO and ABO as of January 1, 2005.

P16–10 GAAP Pension Expense

Beltramini Corporation introduced a noncontributory, defined-benefit pension plan on January 1, 2001. Information available for 2002 is shown.

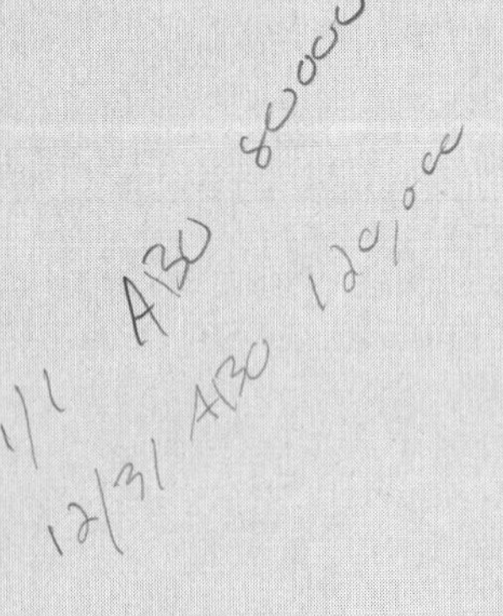

Projected benefit obligation, 1/1/02	$100,000
Service cost, 2002	40,000
Interest costs (at 10%)	10,000
Amortization of prior-service costs ($70,000/20 years = $3,500)	3,500
Pension benefits paid	12,000
Employer pension contributions, 2002	60,000
Plan assets, 1/1/02	50,000
Actual return on plan assets, 2002	15,000
Expected return on plan assets, 2002	4,000
Actual return on plan assets, 2001	16,000
Expected return on plan assets, 2001	1,000
Plan assets, 12/31/02	113,000

Required:

A. Compute net periodic pension expense for 2002 assuming that gains on plan assets are amortized over ten years.

B. Provide an entry to record the 2002 pension expense and pension funding.

C. Provide an entry to record the 2002 pension expense and pension funding if the 2002 funding was $50,000.

P16–11 Minimum Liabilities

FastTec Corporation maintains a noncontributory, defined-benefits pension plan for its employees. The firm applies minimum pension liability provisions of SFAS No. 87.

A. For each of the following years, calculate the additional minimum liability, if any, and provide requisite entries. All figures are in thousands of dollars.

	2005	2006	2007
Prepaid pension costs	$1,000	$ 400	
Accrued pension costs			$ 600
Projected benefit obligation	8,500	9,000	9,800
Accumulated benefit obligation	6,000	6,300	7,000
Pension plan assets (fair value)	4,200	6,500	6,900
Unrecognized prior-service cost	1,200	800	400

B. If you were an employee of FastTec, would you feel that your pension was becoming more secure over time or less secure (with respect to the above information only)? Why? Discuss the changes from 2005 to 2006 and the changes from 2006 to 2007 separately.

P16–12 Pension Entries Disaggregated

During 2004, Herman Wand Corporation hired a new accountant, Dorothy Haxel. Haxel had little experience with pension accounting. During the year, she made the following entries:

Date	Account	Debit	Credit
Jan. 1	Prior-Service Costs (Asset)	100,000	
	Projected Benefit Obligation (Liability)		100,000
	To record increase in PBO due to amendment of pension-benefits formula.		
Jan. 1	Pension Plan Assets	60,000	
	Cash		60,000
	To record cash disbursed to pension plan trustee.		
Dec. 31	Amortization of PSC (Expense)	30,000	
	Prior-Service Costs		30,000
	To amortize PSC equally to each future period of employee service.		
Dec. 31	Compensation Expense	75,000	
	Projected Benefit Obligation		75,000
	To record annual service costs.		
Dec. 31	Interest Expense	20,000	
	Projected Benefit Obligation		20,000
	To record increase in PBO as employees' retirements become one year closer.		
Dec. 31	Pension Plan Assets	33,000	
	Investment Income		33,000
Dec. 31	Pension Plan Assets	75,000	
	Cash		75,000
	To record cash disbursed to pension plan trustee.		

Required: Prepare the journal entries required by SFAS No. 87 given the above.

P16–13 Pension Expense

On January 1, 1994, Raymond Dietrich Enterprises initiated a noncontributory, defined-benefit pension plan for firm employees. Relevant information is provided here respecting years 2003 and 2004 (unrecognized prior-service costs and gains and losses are amortizable straight-line over 20 years):

	2003	2004
Projected benefit obligation, January 1	$5,000	$ (c)
Pension-plan assets, fair value, January 1	5,000	(d)
Service costs	1,150	1,200
Unrecognized prior-service costs	1,000	(e)
Interest costs (10% settlement rate)	(a)	(f)
Actual return on plan assets	400	600
Expected return on plan assets (7%)	350	(g)
Contribution to plan	150	200
Benefits paid	200	210
Cumulative Prior Losses, January 1	600	?
Net pension expense (costs)	(b)	(h)

Required: Fill in the missing amounts.

P16–14 Pension Entries

On January 1, 2003, J&R Manufacturing Company instituted a noncontributory, defined-benefits pension plan for its employees. On this date, the firm's actuary determined that prior-service costs amounted to $400,000 and that service costs for each of the next five years would be $120,000. The actual and the expected return on plan assets was 7% per annum. Future benefits are discounted using a 9% rate to determine service costs and projected benefit obligations.

J&R plans to fund service costs annually, and to fund prior-service costs over the next eight years, in equal amounts. The average remaining service lives for employees receiving pension benefits for services rendered prior to adoption of the pension plan is 16 years.

Over the next five years, employee benefits will be paid in the following amounts: $20,000 in 2003, $26,000 in 2004, $30,000 in 2005, $29,000 in 2006, and $32,000 in 2007.

Required: Make all necessary pension-related entries for the Years 2003–2005. Compute return on plan assets as if benefits are paid at the end of each year. Show the calculations required to obtain these entries. Assume plan assets earn returns as expected.

P16–15 Pension Expense

On January 1, 1994, Diane Galvez & Company initiated a noncontributory, defined-benefit pension plan. Selected information is provided here. Unrecognized prior-service costs and cumulative gains and losses are amortized on a straight-line basis over 20 years.

	2004	2005
Projected benefit obligation, January 1	$8,000	$ (c)
Pension plan assets, fair value, January 1	8,000	(d)
Service costs	800	900
Unrecognized prior-service costs	800	(e)
Interest costs (8%)	(a)	(f)
Actual return on plan assets	1,000	3,000
Expected return on plan assets	640	(g)
Contributions to plan at year-end	100	100
Benefits paid	50	50
Cumulative prior gains, Janauary 1	1,200	(h)
Net pension expense	(b)	(i)

Recall that amortization of gains in 2004 depends on status as of December 31, 2003.

Required: Complete the missing data.

P16–16 Minimum Liabilities

T. Jed Corporation established a noncontributory, defined-benefits pension plan for its employees in 1990. On January 1, 2000, Jed began applying minimum pension liability provisions of SFAS No. 87. For each of the following years, calculate the additional minimum liability, if any, and provide requisite entries. All figures are in thousands.

	2000	2001	2002
Prepaid pension costs	$ 700	$ 400	
Accrued pension costs			$ 900
Projected benefit obligation	7,500	8,000	8,300
Accumulated benefit obligation	4,000	5,000	5,300
Pension plan assets (fair value)	4,300	4,100	5,400
Unrecognized prior-service cost	900	400	100

P16–17 Accuracy of Reporting

What opportunities does a firm have to manipulate (i.e., to depart from their true "best guess" of what to report) the reporting of pension obligations under current regulations? Whose concurrence is needed for such manipulations?

P16–18 Pension Expense and Pension Funding

The text notes that the expensing of pension costs and the funding of pension costs are two distinct and unrelated matters. Should they be? Consider the viewpoints of investors, employees, and firm managers. Also consider a public policy perspective (societal viewpoint).

P16–19 Management Behavior

What effects on the behavior of management could be expected to result from the change in reporting requirements for postretirement benefits from pay-as-you-go to an accrual basis? Why? Is this a desirable change? Why or why not?

P16–20 Pension Entries Under Alternative Assumptions

On January 1, 2002, Mays Corporation began a noncontributory, defined-benefits pension plan for its employees. On this date, the firm's actuary calculated prior-service costs of $600,000. The firm's actuary also estimated that service costs would be $100,000 for 2002 and rise by 7% per year thereafter. Future benefits are discounted using a 10% rate to determine service costs and projected benefit obligations.

The firm plans to fund service costs annually. The average remaining service lives for employees receiving pension benefits for services rendered prior to adoption of the pension plan is 15 years.

Over the next five years, the firm expects to pay employee benefits of $30,000 in 2002, $33,000 in 2003, $35,000 in 2004, $39,000 in 2005, and $42,000 in 2006.

Required: Make all necessary pension-related entries for the Years 2002–2004 under the two following alternative assumptions. Show the calculations required to obtain these entries (i.e., show how you obtain year-end PBO and the annual pension expense).

A. Pension plan assets are estimated to earn 8% per year, and prior-service costs are funded over 10 years, in equal amounts each year.

B. Pension plan assets are estimated to earn 12% per year, and prior-service costs are funded over 15 years, in equal amounts each year.

P16–21 Estimation of Pension Expense

On January 1, 2003, Spirex Corporation initiated a noncontributory, defined-benefits pension plan for its employees. On this date, the firm placed funds of $50,000 in the hands of pension plan trustees to begin funding the prior-service costs. Total prior-service costs were estimated to be $360,000. The firm plans to fund service costs annually. The estimated remaining average service life for employees receiving pension benefits for services rendered prior to the adoption of the pension plan is 15 years. The prior-service costs will be charged to operations over 15 years. Spirex expects to pay pension benefits of $8,000 during 2003. Service cost for 2003 is estimated to be $80,000. The firm's chief financial officer, responsible for recommending the proper pension costs to recognize to top management, has before him the following two alternatives (representing "worst" and "best" case estimates) for estimating 2003 pension costs prepared by his staff:

1. Fund the remaining PSC over 10 years, discount future benefits using a 12% rate to determine service costs and projected benefit obligations, and assume that plan assets will earn a 7% return.
2. Fund the remaining PSC over 15 years, discount future benefits using an 8% rate to determine service costs and projected benefit obligations, and assume that plan assets will earn an 11% return.

Required: Ignore any requirements for minimum funding while working this problem.

A. Calculate 12/31/03 PBO and 2003 pension expense and dollar funding under each alternative.

B. Discuss the factors that should be considered in choosing between the alternatives.

C. Which of the factors discussed in **(2)** above must the firm consider (that is, which are they forced to use in computing/funding pension expenses)? Is this reasonable from a public policy perspective?

D. Is there anything in the information provided in this problem that indicates whether top management is (relatively) conservative or not in its approach to pension obligations? The term "conservative" is meant to indicate a desire to be sure that these obligations will definitely be paid in the future.

RESEARCH ACTIVITIES

R16–1 Motorola—Financial Analysis

The information to answer this question can be found in the SEC's Edgar database. The address for this database is *http://www.sec.gov/edgarhp.htm*

Select Search the Edgar Database and then select Search the Edgar Archives. Using the keyword ***Motorola*** will display the documents on file with the SEC for Motorola. Included among these are proxy statements which, beginning in 1995, inlcude the detailed financial information that used to be included in the company's annual report. The proxy statement for 1995 is denoted as follows:

Def 14 A (filed 3/19/1996)

Selecting this document will allow you to page down to find footnote 5, which concerns the firm's pension and other postretirement benefits.

Required:

A. What is the status of the company's pension plans? Do plan assets exceed plan obligations or vice versa? Does Motorola have to report a liability for pensions? If so, by what amount on December 31, 1995?

B. What is the status of the company's other postretirement benefit obligations? Are these fully funded? Does Motorola have to report a liability for postretirement benefits? If so, by what amount on December 31, 1995?

C. What are the total reported liabilities, if any, on December 31, 1995 for both pension and other postretirement benefits? Where are these liabilities reported, if at all, on Motorola's balance sheet?

D. What are the total expenses for 1995 related to both pension and other postretirement benefits? Where are these expenses reported on Motorola's income statement?

R16–2 GAAP Research—Postemployment Benefits

How are postemployment benefits different from postretirement benefits? Examine FASB statements after SFAS No. 106 concerning postretirement benefits to determine if accounting for postemployment benefits has been specifically addressed. Summarize any requirements you find.

R16–3 Financial Research

Examine a recent annual report for some well-known corporation. Based upon this report, prepare a report that summarizes the status and magnitude of the company's pension and other postretirement benefits. Include PBO, ABO, fair market value of plan assets, interest rate used, and over/under funding. One source for annual report information is the World Wide Web. Some firms have individual home pages with annual report information. Some addresses to try include: *http://www.ibm.com* and *http://www.ford.com*

One way to find corporate home page addresses is to use *http://www.hoovers.com*

This home page lists (among other things) a group of firms that pay to have corporate information available to investors (go to the Corporate Web register). These listings provide access to corporate home pages. You will have to search to find ones that include financial statement footnote information: some home pages (for example, ***Anheuser Busch***) are mostly advertising.

Another possible source is filings with the SEC available at: *http://www.sec.gov*

At this location one can find information on how to use the site, and 10–K and 10–Q reports for firms traded on U.S. exchanges. A sequence of selections that works is:

- EDGAR Database of Corporate Information
- Search the EDGAR Database
- Search the EDGAR Archives
- Enter the search keywords

When entering the keywords try firm names, such as Ford or Motorola or ***Rockwell***. The SEC uses the letters ARS (Annual Report to Shareholders) to denote an annual report in their database.

R16–4 Financial Research

Examine the database that accompanies this text or any database with which you are familiar for the following.

A. Determine the number of firms (and the proportion of these to the total number of firms) who report a separate classification in their balance sheets as liabilities for pension or other postretirement benefits. What is the average reported liability for these firms? On average, what is the percentage of the reported liability to total liabilities?

B. Now select a sample of five firms who did not report a separate classification in their balance sheet. What is the average liability for pension and other postretirement benefits of these sample firms and what percentage is the liability to their total liabilities? Are these significantly different from those in (**A**) above?

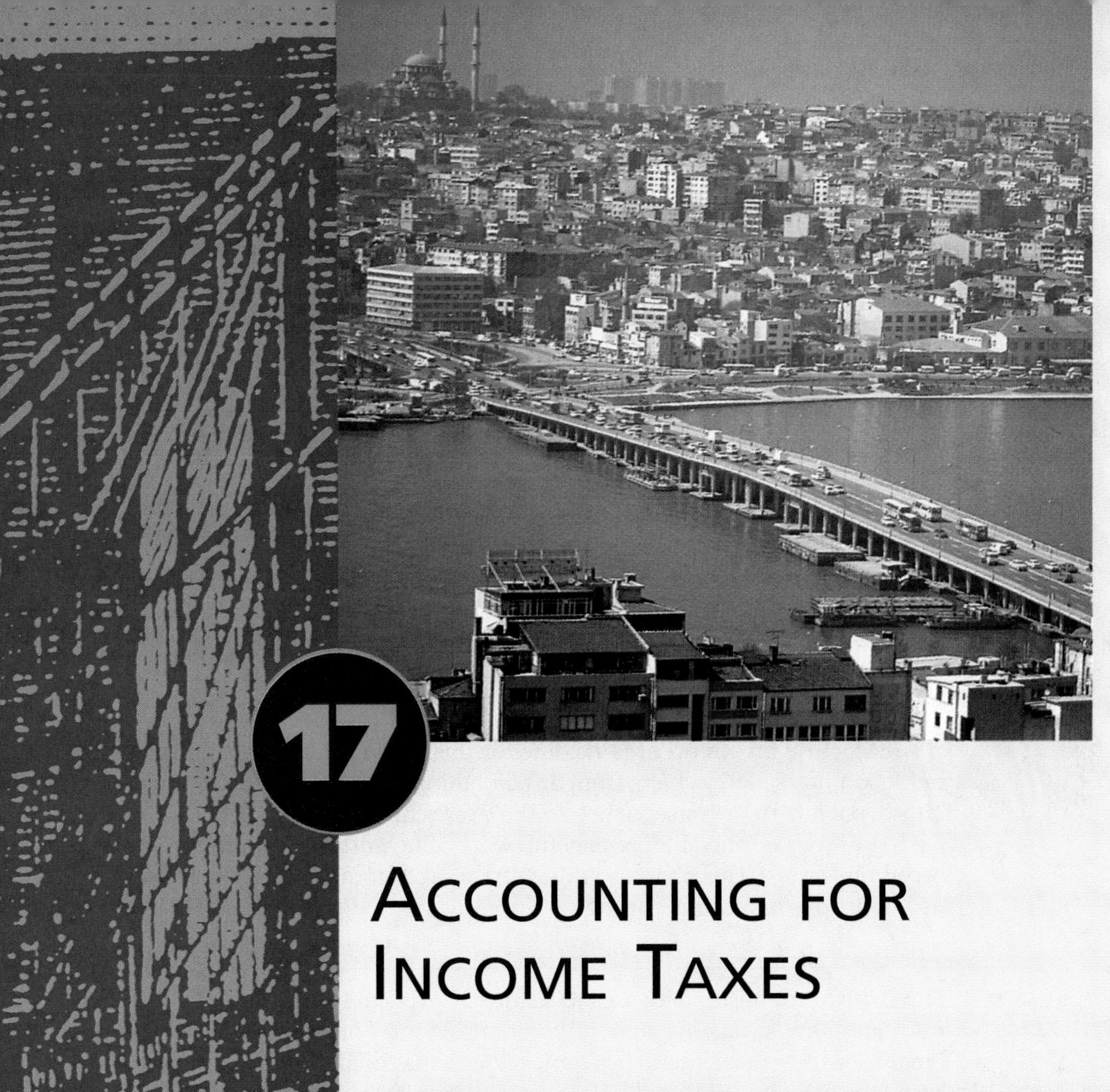

17

Accounting for Income Taxes

Learning Objectives

After studying this chapter, you should be able to:

1. Contrast the objectives of income tax determination with the objectives of financial reporting.
2. Apply the liability approach to determine (a) temporary differences and carryforwards, (b) deferred income tax assets and liabilities, and (c) income tax expense.
3. Interpret the major issues central to the historical development of accounting for income taxes.
4. Analyze the financial reporting of income tax information disclosed in notes to financial statements.
5. Interpret the impact income tax accounting principles can have on analyzing a company's financial position and results of operations.

Throughout this text, the economic consequences of financial reporting practices are emphasized. Consider the following impact from adopting a new pronouncement for income taxes that ***IBM*** (*www.ibm.com* or *www.swcollege.com/hartman.html*) reported in its 1992 annual report.

> *Deferred Tax Assets for IBM*
>
> In 1992, the company implemented Statement of Financial Accounting Standards (SFAS) 109, "Accounting for Income Taxes." This statement superseded the previous accounting standard for income taxes, SFAS 96, which the company adopted in 1988. Under SFAS 109, the company recognizes deferred tax assets if it is more likely than not that a benefit will be realized.
>
> The cumulative effect of this accounting change, which resulted in recognizing previously unrecognized tax benefits for years prior to January 1, 1992, increased net earnings for 1992 by $1,900 million, or $3.33 per share.

IBM's $1.9 billion boost to income for this accounting change resulted in a reduction of its 1992 *net loss* from $6.865 billion to $4.965 billion, a substantial improvement. As a consequence of the new standard, anticipated but previously unreported income tax benefits were allowed to be reported as part of corporate assets. This chapter is devoted to accounting for income taxes and its impact on financial reporting.

NATURE OF INCOME TAXES

Contrast the objectives of income tax determination with the objectives of financial reporting.

SFAC No. 6 identifies expenses as actual or expected cash outflows resulting from an entity's ongoing major operations. Actual or expected payments for **income taxes**—domestic or foreign, federal (national), state, and local taxes based on income—fit this description. The specific rules and regulations governing the calculation of income taxes to be paid encompass (1) revenue items to be included in the determination of **taxable income** (the amount on a tax return on which current year's income tax is computed), (2) expense items permitted to be deducted in the determination of taxable income, (3) the rates to be applied to taxable income, and (4) tax credits permitted as direct reductions to the income tax liability.

Most corporations pay income taxes to several tax jurisdictions, including the U.S. federal government and various state governments, as well as foreign governments. Generally, separate accounting records must be maintained for each jurisdiction. Most of the examples in this chapter pertain to a single jurisdiction, the U.S. federal government. However, the principles illustrated apply to all jurisdictions.

Besides providing an important source of revenue for government operations, income tax laws are an important instrument of economic and fiscal policy. For example, one of the oldest and most frequently used provisions involves the amount of depreciation deduction permitted for income tax purposes. Special rules for the calculation of depreciation for tax purposes appeared as early as 1946, and special rules are still in effect. Accelerated-depreciation methods encourage investment in capital equipment and thereby stimulate economic activity.

Calculation of earnings for financial reporting and for income tax assessment thus have different goals. Earnings for financial reporting are based upon accrual accounting concepts in accordance with GAAP in an attempt to meet the main objective of the conceptual framework—that of providing information to assist users in financial decision making. Taxable income is determined in accordance with enacted laws and regulations for purposes of assessing income tax from reporting entities and to influence economic and fiscal policy. Since the goals differ, the rules to follow in determining earnings (GAAP for financial reporting and tax laws for income taxes) frequently differ. Therefore, financial statement pretax accounting income (earnings) frequently differs from taxable income for a given period.

To illustrate, Exhibit 17–1 on the next page provides three scenarios comparing pretax accounting income to taxable income. In Case A, pretax accounting income and taxable income are identical. Under this scenario, revenues and expenses recognized for financial reporting each period are the same as revenues and expense deductions included on the company's income tax return each period. Thus, income tax expense each period is the income tax currently payable based upon that period's income tax return. **Income tax expense** is frequently called the **provision for income taxes**, with **income tax currently payable (refundable)** labeled the **current provision for income taxes**.

In Case B of Exhibit 17–1, pretax accounting income in 1997 is $50,000 greater than taxable income. In this example, the $50,000 difference is a **temporary difference** because the difference reverses the next year in 1998 when pretax accounting income is less than taxable income by $50,000. Such a temporary difference can occur for (1) amounts recognized as part of revenue for financial reporting prior to the period when the amounts are taxable or (2) amounts deducted as expenses in a tax return prior to the period in which the amounts are recognized as expenses for financial reporting.

Note that cumulative pretax accounting income of $600,000 for the two years is the same as the combined taxable income for both years, so the income tax expense for the two-year period is the $180,000 in income taxes payable for the two years, which is identical to Case A. However, in 1997, $50,000 in earnings is not taxable until the 1998 tax year, so the taxes currently payable are $45,000 (30% of $150,000 taxable income). Income taxes of $15,000 for the $50,000 difference are not payable until the earnings are part of the 1998 tax return. Still, the $15,000 ultimately becomes payable and should be considered expense for financial reporting in 1997 (the period for which the $50,000 earnings are recognized), not in 1998 (the period in which the $50,000 is taxable and the $15,000 actually becomes payable). Thus, Case B of Exhibit 17–1 includes the $15,000 as part of income tax expense in 1997 and excludes it from income tax expense in 1998.

Increases to income tax expenses when taxes for temporary differences are included as part of income tax expense are frequently labeled **deferred tax expenses**[1] (or the deferred provision for income taxes). In 1997 for Case B, payment of the $15,000 is deferred until the $50,000 is part of taxable income. Reductions for income tax expenses when taxes for temporary differences are

[1]For convenience, the profession frequently drops the word income when referring to income taxes. Thus, deferred tax expenses and benefits refer to deferred *income* tax expenses and benefits, even though other forms of taxes could conceptually be deferred as well. Similarly, deferred tax liabilities and assets refer to deferred *income* tax liabilities and assets.

EXHIBIT 17–1 Example Comparisons of Pretax Accounting Income and Taxable Income

For each of the following cases, assume a 30% income tax rate. Thus, the taxes currently payable are 30 percent of taxable income. In Cases B and C, taxes currently payable are adjusted by 30 percent of temporary differences in order to determine income tax expense.

Case A: Pretax accounting income (earnings) *equal to* taxable income

	1997	1998	TOTAL
Pretax accounting income and taxable income	$200,000	$400,000	$600,000
Taxes currently payable and income tax expense	$60,000	$120,000	$180,000

Case B: Pretax accounting income (earnings) *initially greater than* taxable income

	1997		1998	TOTAL
Pretax accounting income	$200,000		$400,000	$600,000
Taxable income	150,000		450,000	600,000
Temporary difference	$ 50,000		$ (50,000)	$ 0
Taxes currently payable	$ 45,000		$135,000	$180,000
Plus: Amount payable in subsequent period for earnings this period (Deferred tax expense)	15,000	Less: Amount currently payable for earnings previously recognized (deferred tax benefit)	(15,000)	0
Income tax expense	$ 60,000		$120,000	$180,000

Case C: Pretax accounting income (earnings) *initially less than* taxable income

	1997		1998	TOTAL
Pretax accounting income	$200,000		$400,000	$600,000
Taxable income	250,000		350,000	600,000
Temporary difference	$ (50,000)		$ 50,000	$ 0
Taxes currently payable	$ 75,000		$105,000	$180,000
Less: Amount payable for earnings to be recognized in a subsequent period (deferred tax benefit)	(15,000)	Plus: Amount previously paid for earnings recognized this period (deferred tax expense)	15,000	0
Income tax expense	$ 60,000		$120,000	$180,000

excluded from income tax expenses are labeled **deferred tax benefits**. In 1998 for Case B, deferred tax benefits reduce income tax expenses for the $15,000 payment deferred back in 1997.

In Case C of Exhibit 17–1, pretax accounting income in 1997 is $50,000 less than taxable income. Again, the $50,000 difference is a temporary difference because the difference reverses the next year in 1998 when pretax accounting income is greater than taxable income by $50,000. Such a temporary difference can occur for (1) amounts included as part of taxable revenue prior to the period when the amounts are recognized as revenue for financial reporting or (2) amounts included as expenses for financial reporting prior to the period in which the amounts are deducted as expenses in a tax return.

Like the two previous cases, cumulative pretax accounting income of $600,000 for the two years is the same as the combined taxable income for both years, so the income tax expense for the two-year period is the $180,000 in income taxes payable for the two years. However, in 1997, $50,000 is taxable that is not a part of accounting earnings until 1998, so the taxes currently payable of $75,000 (30% of $250,000 taxable income) includes $15,000 that should not be part of income tax expenses until the $50,000 difference is recognized as earnings in 1998. Thus, Case C of Exhibit 17–1 excludes the $15,000 from income tax expense in 1997 and includes it as part of income tax expense in 1998.

This chapter next presents the current requirements of SFAS No. 109, which requires a liability approach regarding financial reporting for income taxes. The liability approach provides a background of the concepts related to reporting for income taxes. This background then allows discussion of other income tax accounting issues central to the evolution of GAAP.

LIABILITY APPROACH

Apply the liability approach to determine (a) temporary differences and carryforwards, (b) deferred income tax assets and liabilities, and (c) income tax expense.

The conceptual basis of the liability method is that **deferred income tax liabilities** represent future amounts expected to become payable as a result of current or past financial statement earnings. That is, these liabilities represent expected future income tax increases because of earnings already recognized in the financial statements.

For example, suppose a corporation recognizes $50,000 of revenue in 1997 in accordance with GAAP, but this revenue is not taxable until the 1998 income tax year. As depicted in Case B of Exhibit 17–1, the $50,000 temporary difference is eventually considered revenue both for financial reporting (in 1997) and for income taxes (in 1998). At a 30% tax rate, the company has to eventually pay $15,000 in income taxes for this revenue when included in the 1998 income tax return. Thus, a deferred tax liability occurs when the $15,000 is included as part of income tax expense in 1997.

CONCEPT Matching and liability recognition.

LOGIC In accordance with the matching principle, expected future tax increases are accrued as expense and recognized as liabilities in the period in which the earnings are recognized for financial reporting rather than in the future period when the taxes actually become payable.

Therefore, deferred tax liabilities occur when some portion of a period's earnings is not included in that period's taxable income but instead is expected to become a part of future taxable income.

In a similar manner, **deferred tax assets** represent amounts expected to reduce future income taxes payable, thus providing future economic benefits. Deferred tax assets occur when some portion of a period's taxable income is *not* recognized in that period's financial statement earnings but is instead expected to be recognized as earnings in the future. Consequently, taxes paid for this portion of taxable income are *prepaid expenses* that become *expenses* when matched with earnings recognized in the future.

For example, suppose a corporation with a 30% marginal income tax rate includes, in accordance with income tax regulations, $50,000 of revenue in its 1997 tax return that, in accordance with GAAP, will be recognized in 1998. As depicted in Case C of Exhibit 17–1, the company would pay $15,000 in taxes for this temporary difference prior to expensing this amount, and a deferred tax asset (that is, a prepaid expense) results when the $15,000 is excluded from income tax expense in 1997.

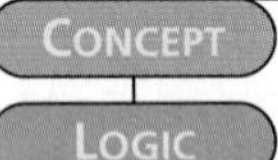

Matching and asset recognition.

In accordance with the matching principle, income tax expense should be matched to the period when the associated revenue is recognized. Payments for income taxes expected to be expensed in a subsequent period are prepaid expenses to be recognized as assets for financial reporting.

Deferred tax assets also occur when current or past *taxable losses* are expected to reduce future income taxes payable by offsetting future taxable income. Such taxable losses are called *net operating loss (NOL) carryforwards*. Similarly, *tax credit carryforwards* are unused tax credits to be applied to reduce future income taxes payable and result in deferred tax assets. Carryforwards and tax credits are discussed later in this chapter.

Both deferred tax liabilities and deferred tax assets are the focus of the liability approach (method) currently required for financial reporting. The method is so named because deferred tax liabilities have been more prevalent than deferred tax assets. Exhibit 17–2 summarizes the application of the liability approach.

The **liability method** first focuses on determination of the appropriate balance sheet amounts for deferred taxes at the beginning of the year and at the end of the year. Then, deferred tax increases to (reductions of) income tax expenses result from the differences between the balance sheet deferred taxes at the beginning of the year and at the end of the year.

In 1997 of Case B in Exhibit 17–1, for example, the ending deferred tax liability is $15,000 and the beginning deferred tax liability is $0. The increase in the liability for 1997 corresponds to the $15,000 increase to deferred tax expense for 1997. Then, in 1998, the ending deferred tax liability of $0, coupled with the beginning deferred tax liability of $15,000, results in a decrease to the liability and an associated reduction of income tax expenses for 1998.

Similarly, Case C of Exhibit 17–1 illustrates for 1997 an ending deferred tax asset of $15,000 and beginning deferred tax asset of $0. The increase to the deferred tax asset corresponds with an associated reduction of $15,000 in income tax expenses for 1997. Then, in 1998, the ending deferred tax asset of $0, coupled with the 1998 beginning balance of $15,000, results in a decrease to the deferred tax asset and associated increase to income tax expenses for 1998.

EXHIBIT 17–2
Liability Approach to Deferred Taxes

Implementation of the liability approach follows a very basic computational model:

A. Calculate income taxes payable on current year's taxable income.
B. Calculate the year-end deferred tax balance sheet amounts.
C. Compute the change for the year in deferred tax balance sheet amounts to determine deferred tax increases to (reductions of) income tax expense.
D. Combine income tax currently payable **(A)** with deferred tax increases to (reductions of) income tax expense **(C)** to compute total income tax expense.

A simple example of this approach follows:

A. Calculation of income tax currently payable:		
Book income before income taxes	$ 3,990	
Plus: Nondeductible expense—premiums on officer's life insurance	10	
Less: Temporary difference—excess of tax depreciation over book depreciation	(500)	
Taxable Income	$ 3,500	
Effective tax rate	40%	
Income tax currently payable		$1,400
Deferred tax calculation:		
Book-basis net fixed assets	$10,000	
Tax-basis net fixed assets	8,000	
Cumulative temporary differences	$ 2,000	
Effective tax rate	40%	
B. Ending balance of balance sheet deferred tax liability	$ 800	
Beginning balance of balance sheet deferred tax liability	600	
C. Deferred tax increase to tax expense		$ 200
D. Combine taxes currently payable with deferred tax increase to determine total income tax expense		$1,600

To conform with the general principles of the liability method and to provide more specific guidance regarding the computational matters involved in computing income tax expense, SFAS No. 109 describes a procedure for the annual computation of deferred tax liabilities and assets. We first quote this procedure, then the following sections illustrate the approach through a series of exhibits (17–3 through 17–9).

Deferred taxes shall be determined separately for each tax-paying component . . . in each tax jurisdiction. That determination includes the following steps:

- Identify (1) the types and amounts of existing temporary differences and (2) the nature and amount of each type of operating loss and tax credit carryforward and the remaining length of the carryforward period.

- Measure the total deferred tax liability for taxable temporary differences using the applicable tax rate.
- Measure the total deferred tax asset for deductible temporary differences and operating loss carryforwards using the applicable tax rate.
- Measure deferred tax assets for each type of tax credit carryforward.
- Reduce deferred tax assets by a valuation allowance if, based on the weight of available evidence, it is more likely than not (a likelihood of more than 50 percent) that some portion or all of the deferred tax asset will not be realized. The valuation allowance should be sufficient to reduce the deferred tax asset to the amount that is more likely than not to be realized.[2]

TEMPORARY DIFFERENCES

A temporary difference is the difference between the tax basis of an asset or liability and its reported balance sheet amount, where such difference will result in a taxable or deductible amount in future years. *Taxable temporary differences* result in taxable amounts in future years when the related asset is recovered or liability is settled. Taxable differences thus cause deferred tax liabilities. Case B of Exhibit 17–1 provides an example of a taxable difference. Similarly, *deductible temporary differences* result in deductible amounts in future years, when the related asset is recovered or liability is settled. Deductible differences thus cause deferred tax assets, subject to a valuation allowance (discussed later). Case C of Exhibit 17–1 provides an example of a deductible difference.

Exhibit 17–3 illustrates various types of temporary differences and the balance sheet deferred tax items resulting from them. Note that many of the common temporary differences are classified as revenue- or expense-type differences. These differences also result in related balance sheet differences. The balance sheet differences provide the basis for determining deferred tax assets and liabilities. Then, changes to deferred tax assets and liabilities result in deferred tax expenses or benefits for purposes of determining income tax expenses for a period.

Taxable Differences. Exhibit 17–4 provides an example of the first temporary difference noted in Exhibit 17–3: a revenue that is taxable after being recognized in income for financial reporting. As illustrated, the $10,000 of uncollected sales that is not taxable in 1997 is a taxable difference. The $10,000 results in a deferred tax liability of $4,000 for the income taxes expected to become payable in the future period when the $10,000 is collected. Since the $10,000 is already a part of financial revenue in 1997, the expected $4,000 in taxes matches to this revenue as an increase to income tax expense (i.e., a deferred tax expense) for 1997. Thus, an increase to the deferred tax liability (a credit) is accompanied by an increase to income tax expense (a debit).

[2]FASB, *Statement of Financial Accounting Standards No. 109,* "Accounting for Income Taxes," 1992, par. 17.

EXHIBIT 17–3 Categories of Temporary Differences

CATEGORY	EXAMPLE	TYPE OF TEMPORARY DIFFERENCE	RESULTING BALANCE SHEET DEFERRED TAX
Taxable Income versus Financial Statement Income			
Revenue/Expense Differences			
• Revenue or gains taxable after being reported in income for financial reporting	Gross profit on installment sales is recognized in income in the financial statements when the sale occurs but is taxed on the installment method when the proceeds are received.	Taxable	Liability
• Expense or losses deductible for tax purposes before being reported in income for financial reporting	Accelerated Cost Recovery System (ACRS) depreciation is used for tax purposes and straight-line depreciation is used in financial statements.	Taxable	Liability
• Revenue or gains taxable before being reported in income for financial reporting	Advance rental income is taxable when collected, but the revenue is recognized in income for financial reporting purposes over the rental period.	Deductible	Asset
• Expense or losses deductible for tax purposes after being reported in income for financial reporting	Provision for product warranty is expensed in financial statements when product is sold but deductible for tax purposes later when claims are paid.	Deductible	Asset
Other Causes of Temporary Differences			
Basis Differences			
• Reduction of tax basis of depreciable assets because of tax credits	The 1982 Tax Act allowed the choice of (1) the full ACRS deduction and reduced Investment Tax Credit (ITC) or (2) reduced ACRS deduction and full ITC.	Taxable	Liability
• An increase in tax basis of assets because of indexing where local currency is the functional currency	Tax law may require adjustment of the tax basis for effects or inflation.	Deductible	Asset
• Business combinations accounted for by the purchase method	There may be differences arising between assigned values and the tax bases of assets acquired and liabilities assumed in a purchase business combination.	Taxable or Deductible	Liability or Asset

Source: Adapted from "Accounting for Income Taxes An Analysis of FASB Statement No. 109," Deloitte & Touche, 1992, p. 14.

EXHIBIT 17–4 Example Company: 1997 Deferred Income Tax Liability

For 1997, Example Company reports net income before income taxes of $100,000. Included in determining this net income are uncollected installment sales (i.e., accounts receivable) of $10,000. The company's installment sales are taxable when cash is collected so the uncollected installment sales would not be a part of 1997 taxable income. Example company's effective tax rate for 1997 is 40%. The company had *no* deferred taxes at the beginning of 1997.

Income Tax Currently Payable:

Reported net income before income taxes	$100,000
Uncollected installment sales not taxable for 1997	(10,000)
1997 taxable income	90,000
Effective tax rate	0.40
Income tax currently payable	$ 36,000

Deferred Tax:

TEMPORARY DIFFERENCE OR CARRYFORWARD	BALANCE SHEET AMOUNTS			TAXABLE DIFFERENCE: DEFERRED TAX LIABILITY	DEDUCTIBLE DIFFERENCE: DEFERRED TAX ASSET
	BOOK	TAX	DIFFERENCE		
Accounts receivable	$10,000	$0	$10,000	$10,000	
Effective tax rate				0.40	
Deferred tax balance at year-end				$ 4,000	
Deferred tax balance at beginning of year				0	
Deferred tax increase (reduction) to income tax expense				$ 4,000	

Income Tax Expense:

Income tax currently payable	$36,000
Deferred tax increase to expense	4,000
Income tax expense	$40,000

The journal entry to record income taxes for 1997 would be[3]:

12/31/97	Income Tax Expense	40,000	
	Deferred Tax Liability		4,000
	Income Taxes Payable		36,000

Exhibit 17–5 illustrates the next year, when the $10,000 difference reverses and another difference occurs. As indicated, the related balance sheet account associated with uncollected sales revenue is Accounts Receivable. The taxable difference at the end of 1998 is $6,000, resulting in a deferred tax liability of

[3]This entry assumes there were no prepayments for income taxes during the year. In actuality, corporations typically make periodic income tax payments quarterly. Any year-end adjusting entry would have to consider prior entries during the year.

EXHIBIT 17–5 Example Company: 1998 Deferred Income Tax Liability

For 1998, Example Company reports net income before income taxes of $120,000. Included in determining this net income are uncollected installment sales (i.e., accounts receivable) of $6,000. The company's installment sales are taxable when cash is collected so the uncollected installment sales would not be a part of 1998 taxable income. However, $10,000 cash collected in 1998 for 1997 installment sales are a part of 1998 taxable income. The company's effective tax rate for 1998 is 40%.

Income Tax Currently Payable:

Reported net income before income taxes	$120,000
Cash collected for 1997 credit sales	10,000
Uncollected installment sales not taxable for 1998	(6,000)
1998 taxable income	$124,000
Effective tax rate	0.40
Income tax currently payable	$ 49,600

Deferred Tax:

TEMPORARY DIFFERENCE OR CARRYFORWARD	BALANCE SHEET AMOUNTS BOOK	TAX	DIFFERENCE	TAXABLE DIFFERENCE: DEFERRED TAX LIABILITY	DEDUCTIBLE DIFFERENCE: DEFERRED TAX ASSET
Accounts receivable	$6,000	$0	$6,000	$ 6,000	
Effective tax rate				0.40	
Deferred tax balance at year-end				$ 2,400	
Deferred tax balance at beginning of year				4,000	
Deferred tax increase (reduction) to income tax expense				$(1,600)	

Income Tax Expense:

Income tax currently payable	$49,600
Deferred tax reduction of expense	(1,600)
Income tax expense	$48,000

$2,400. Since the deferred tax liability at the beginning of 1998 was $4,000, a reduction of the liability by $1,600 is necessary. The income statement effects of deferred taxes result from changes in deferred tax assets and liabilities. Here, a reduction of the liability (a debit) correspondingly reduces the related income tax expense (i.e., a deferred tax benefit) below that resulting from the taxes currently payable.

An entry to record income taxes for 1998 would be:

12/31/98	Income Tax Expense	48,000	
	Deferred Tax Liability	1,600	
	Income Taxes Payable		49,600

The current income taxes payable for 1998 of $49,600 includes $4,000 in income taxes expensed in 1997 for the $10,000 temporary difference, which is "reversed" and included in 1998 taxable income. The $4,000 in taxes is thus not expensed in 1998 but instead will be a payment of the deferred tax liability. Further, the income taxes payable in 1998 of $49,600 does not include $2,400 in taxes for the $6,000 temporary difference for year-end uncollected sales that is expected to be taxable in the future. By itself, the $6,000 temporary difference would cause an increase to 1998 deferred income tax expense of $2,400. Thus, the total income tax expense for the period is the $49,600 payable, less the $4,000 already expensed in 1997, plus the $2,400 additional expenses for expected future taxes payable. Combining the $4,000 and the $2,400 results in a net reduction of $1,600 from the payable amount, yielding an income tax expense of $48,000.

In this example, notice that the income tax expense is 40% (the tax rate) of reported income before income taxes ($120,000 × 0.40 = $48,000). This relationship to pretax accounting income holds *if* (1) there are no changes to the effective tax rates and (2) all differences between taxable income and pretax accounting income are revenue/expense temporary differences as identified in Exhibit 17–3 (for example, there are no permanent differences or carryforwards). We discuss these limiting conditions throughout the remainder of the chapter.

TAX RATES TO BE APPLIED

While the accounting objective for the calculation of deferred tax liabilities and assets is to measure the future tax consequences of events, a simplifying provision mandates use of only enacted tax laws and rates. Future changes not yet enacted into law cannot be anticipated.

A change in an enacted tax rate is reflected in the financial statements of the year of enactment. This is accomplished by applying the new rate to cumulative temporary differences based on their expected reversal dates and the effective dates of the newly enacted rates. Exhibit 17–6 illustrates.

The exhibit assumes the same facts as Exhibit 17–5, except that the effective tax rate changed in 1998 to 30%. Accordingly, the deferred tax liability at the end of 1998 for the $6,000 taxable difference is $1,800. Since the beginning balance for the deferred tax liability was $4,000, the reduction to the liability and to income tax expense for 1998 is $2,200.

An interpretation of the expense is that $3,000 of the $37,200 currently payable is attributable to taxes payable (at the new rate) for the $10,000 temporary difference that reversed. This $3,000 was already expensed in 1997 and should not be expensed again. Also attributable to this $10,000 temporary difference is another $1,000 of expected taxes previously expensed when the tax rate was 40%, an amount that will not be paid since the rate dropped to 30%. Rather than retroactively reducing previous expenses and restating financial statements, SFAS No. 109 requires prospective treatment as a change in estimate (see Chapter 6). So the $1,000 reduces income tax expense for the current period, not previous periods. Finally, the $37,200 currently payable does not include $1,800 in taxes for the $6,000 temporary difference for year-end uncollected sales. Any year-end uncollected sales are expected to be taxable in the future and should increase 1998 income tax expense.

EXHIBIT 17–6 Example Company: 1998 Deferred Income Tax Liability with Changes to Effective Tax Rate

For 1998, Example Company reports net income before income taxes of $120,000. Included in determining this net income are uncollected installment sales (i.e., accounts receivable) of $6,000. The company's installment sales are taxable when cash is collected so the uncollected installment sales would not be a part of 1998 taxable income. However, $10,000 cash collected in 1998 for 1997 installment sales are a part of 1998 taxable income. The company's effective tax rate changed in 1998 to 30% from the 1997 rate of 40%.

Income Tax Currently Payable:

Reported net income before income taxes	$120,000
Cash collected for 1997 credit sales	10,000
Uncollected installment sales not taxable for 1998	(6,000)
1998 taxable income	$124,000
Effective tax rate	0.30
Income tax currently payable	$ 37,200

Deferred Tax:

TEMPORARY DIFFERENCE OR CARRYFORWARD	BALANCE SHEET AMOUNTS			TAXABLE DIFFERENCE: DEFERRED TAX LIABILITY	DEDUCTIBLE DIFFERENCE: DEFERRED TAX ASSET
	BOOK	TAX	DIFFERENCE		
Accounts receivable	$6,000	$0	$6,000	$ 6,000	
Effective tax rate				0.30	
Deferred tax balance at year-end				$ 1,800	
Deferred tax balance at beginning of year				4,000	
Deferred tax increase (reduction) to income tax expense				$(2,200)	

Income Tax Expense:

Income tax currently payable	$37,200
Deferred tax reduction of expense	(2,200)
Income tax expense	$35,000

The income tax expense for the period is therefore the $37,200 payable, less the $3,000 of this amount that was already expensed in 1997, less the $1,000 previously expensed that will not be paid, plus the $1,800 additional expenses for expected future taxes payable. The result is a net reduction of $2,200 from the payable to obtain an income tax expense of $35,000.

Notice that the income tax expense is *not* 30% of reported net income before income taxes ($120,000 × 0.30 = $36,000, not $35,000). That is, the effective tax rate is 29.2% ($35,000/$120,000). Supplemental footnote disclosures include a schedule reconciling income taxes at the federal statutory income tax rate and the actual, effective tax rate (for example, see the section on disclosures under the heading of "Financial Reporting" later in this chapter).

When different income tax rates become effective immediately, as illustrated in Exhibit 17–6, no special scheduling calculations are necessary. However, if the enacted rate will take effect in the future, the tax effect of temporary differences reversing during the period before enactment should be computed at the old rate, and the tax effect of temporary differences reversing after the effective date should be computed based on the new effective tax rates.

Whenever changes in deferred taxes resulting from changes in laws or rates exist, the effects are included in income tax expense related to continuing operations and not reported as an extraordinary item. Disclosure of tax rate changes is also required.

PERMANENT DIFFERENCES

Certain revenue or expense items either are exempted from taxation or are not deductible in computing taxable income. For example, interest from investments in state and municipal bonds is not subject to federal income taxes. The interest is therefore never included as part of federal taxable income but still is revenue recognized as part of financial statement earnings. When accounting income is reconciled with taxable income, nontaxable interest is subtracted from accounting income.

Similarly, some financial statement expenses are never deductible in determining taxable income. An example was illustrated in Exhibit 17–2—the premium for life insurance policies for corporate officials. In reconciling accounting income with taxable income, nondeductible expenses are added back to accounting income.

These types of differences between income for financial reporting and taxable income do not result in future settlement or recovery of taxes and are not temporary differences. Earlier accounting literature referred to these as **permanent differences**. SFAS No. 109 excludes them from the definition of temporary differences and gives no other explicit recognition to them. However, as illustrated in Exhibit 17–2, consideration of these differences is necessary to reconcile pretax financial statement earnings with taxable income.

CLASSIFICATION OF BALANCE SHEET ASSETS AND LIABILITIES

In classified balance sheets, the deferred tax amounts are classified as current or noncurrent based on how the related asset or liability that gave rise to the deferred tax amount is classified. A deferred tax asset or liability without such a relationship to an asset or liability is classified according to when the temporary difference is expected to reverse.

Exhibit 17–7 illustrates this concept. In addition to the uncollected sales depicted in earlier exhibits, Exhibit 17–7 presents the second type of temporary difference described in Exhibit 17–3: an expense deductible for tax purposes before reducing income for financial reporting. The additional depreciation reported on the tax return results in lower taxable income and thus lower income taxes currently payable. The reduced income taxes are expected to become payable in the future, when the difference reverses as depreciation for tax purposes falls below book depreciation, resulting in higher future taxable income. Thus, the temporary difference for depreciation is a taxable difference resulting in a deferred tax liability.

EXHIBIT 17–7 Example Company: Classification of Deferred Income Taxes

For 1997, Example Company reports net income before income taxes of $100,000. Included in determining this net income are uncollected installment sales (i.e., accounts receivable) of $10,000. The company's installment sales are taxable when cash is collected so the uncollected installment sales would not be a part of 1997 taxable income.

The company uses straight-line depreciation for financial reporting and accelerated depreciation for income taxes. For 1997, the deduction for depreciation expense on the tax return is $20,000 higher than the straight-line depreciation expense on the income statement. The reported balance sheet basis for net fixed assets at year end was $175,000 and $115,000, respectively, for financial reporting (book) and tax reporting. The company began 1997 with a $40,000 difference in net book value and a noncurrent deferred tax liability of $16,000.

Example company's effective tax rate for 1997 is 40%.

Income Tax Currently Payable:

Reported net income before income taxes	$100,000
Uncollected installment sales not taxable for 1997	(10,000)
Additional depreciation on tax return	(20,000)
1997 taxable income	$ 70,000
Effective tax rate	0.40
Income tax currently payable	$ 28,000

Deferred Tax:

Temporary Difference or Carryforward	Balance Sheet Amounts: Book	Tax	Difference	Taxable Difference: Deferred Tax Liability: Current	Noncurrent	Deductible Difference: Deferred Tax Asset: Current	Noncurrent
Accounts receivable	$ 10,000	$ 0	$10,000	$10,000			
Fixed assets (net)	175,000	115,000	60,000		$60,000		
Totals				$10,000	$60,000		
Effective tax rate				0.40	0.40		
Deferred tax balance at year-end				$ 4,000	$24,000		
Deferred tax balance at beginning of year				0	16,000		
Deferred tax increase (reduction) to income tax expense				$ 4,000	$ 8,000		

Income Tax Expense:

Income tax currently payable	$28,000
Deferred tax increase [current]	4,000
Deferred tax increase [noncurrent]	8,000
Income tax expense	$40,000

Since accounts receivable is a current asset on the balance sheet, the $4,000 deferred tax liability related to uncollected sales is a current liability. However, the $24,000 deferred tax liability related to depreciation differences is noncurrent, since fixed assets are noncurrent.

DEFERRED TAX ASSETS

Items resulting in deferred tax assets include

1. Deductible temporary differences.
2. Net operating loss carryforwards.
3. Tax credit carryforwards.

SFAS No. 109 permits recognition of deferred tax assets, subject to a valuation allowance if it is "more likely than not" that some portion of the deferred tax asset will not be realized. In the following sections, the three items resulting in deferred tax assets and the valuation allowance are discussed.

Deductible Differences. Exhibit 17–8 illustrates a deductible temporary difference. This difference is the third type of temporary difference described in Exhibit 17–3: revenue that is taxable before being recognized for financial reporting. Rent collected in advance represents unearned revenue; however, the rent is taxable income in the period collected. Thus, income taxes paid for this taxable income are not expensed in the period the rent is collected. Instead, the taxes paid are reported as a deferred tax asset (that is, prepaid expense) and are expensed when the revenue is recognized for financial reporting. Since unearned rental income is classified as a current liability, the $6,000 deferred tax asset is also classified as current.

Exhibit 17–9 illustrates a more complex determination of deferred taxes. This exhibit combines the previous three temporary differences for 1997 depicted in earlier exhibits as well as adding some other complexities. One addition is the fourth type of temporary difference shown in Exhibit 17–3: expenses deductible for tax purposes after being reported in income for financial reporting. Note from Exhibit 17–9 that the product warranty accrual results in a current deferred tax asset.

Exhibit 17–9 is also used to develop other issues related to deferred taxes, beginning with net operating loss carryforwards, our next subject.

Loss Carrybacks and Carryforwards. Whenever deductible expenses exceed taxable revenues, a tax loss, labeled a **net operating loss (NOL)**, occurs. In the United States, corporations generally can utilize this loss to recover taxes paid in the three years prior to the loss year (a *carryback*), or to reduce future net taxable income over the ensuing 15 years (a *carryforward*). A carryback results in a receivable from the government and the benefit is recognized currently. Carrybacks must begin with the earliest taxable year possible and progress forward.

For example, suppose NotSoLucky Corporation has a net operating loss for 1997 of $50,000. This loss can be used to obtain a tax refund of income taxes paid on taxable income for 1994, 1995, and 1996. If taxable income was $20,000 for each of these three years, then the full amount of the loss can be used as a carryback, since the total taxable income in the prior three years exceeds the net operating loss. For a tax rate of 30%, the amount of the refund is $15,000. An entry for this carryback is:

12/31/97	Income Tax Refund Receivable	15,000	
	Income Tax Benefit from NOL Carryback		15,000

EXHIBIT 17–8 Example Company: Deferred Income Tax Assets

For 1997, Example Company reports net income before income taxes of $100,000. Excluded from determining this net income is unearned rent income of $15,000 collected in advance. As a cash-basis taxpayer, this cash collected for future rent service is included as part of 1997 taxable income. Example company's effective tax rate for 1997 is 40%.

Income Tax Currently Payable:

Reported net income before income taxes	$100,000
Rent collected in advance and taxable for 1997	15,000
1997 taxable income	$115,000
Effective tax rate	0.40
Income tax currently payable	$ 46,000

Deferred Tax:

TEMPORARY DIFFERENCE OR CARRYFORWARD	BALANCE SHEET AMOUNTS			TAXABLE DIFFERENCE: DEFERRED TAX LIABILITY		DEDUCTIBLE DIFFERENCE: DEFERRED TAX ASSET	
	BOOK	TAX	DIFFERENCE	CURRENT	NONCURRENT	CURRENT	NONCURRENT
Unearned rental income	$15,000	$0	$15,000			$15,000	
Effective tax rate						0.40	
Deferred tax balance at year-end						$ 6,000	
Deferred tax balance at beginning of year						0	
Deferred tax increase (reduction) to income tax expense						$ (6,000)[a]	

Income Tax Expense:

Income tax currently payable	$46,000
Deferred tax reduction of expense	(6,000)
Income tax expense	$40,000

[a]Increases to deferred tax assets result in deferred tax reductions of income tax expense.

The tax benefit offsets the operating loss. If the pretax loss for financial reporting was the same as the taxable loss (that is, there were no temporary or permanent differences), the company would report a net loss for 1997 of $35,000—the pretax loss of $50,000 offset by the tax benefit of $15,000. Note that prior periods' income tax expenses and net income are not restated; the impact of the tax refund is treated prospectively as a change in estimate.

Suppose that NotSoLucky's taxable income was only $10,000 for each of the prior three years. Then, the carryback for the $50,000 net operating loss could only be $30,000; for a 30% tax rate, the income tax refund would be $9,000. The remaining NOL of $20,000 can be carried forward to reduce income taxes on future taxable income. Assuming a 30% rate, there is a potential tax benefit to

EXHIBIT 17–9 Example Company: Deferred Tax Calculation for the Year Ended December 31, 1997

Assume the temporary differences in Exhibits 17–7 and 17–8 for accounts receivable, fixed assets, and unearned rental income exist. Also assume a temporary difference for product warranties which had resulted in a beginning-of-year deferred tax asset of $2,834. Further, the company has a NOL carryforward at year-end of $50,000, a valuation allowance of 50% for the tax effect of the carryforward, and a beginning-of-year deferred tax asset of $14,166 for NOL Carryforwards.

Deferred Tax:

Temporary Difference or Carryforward	Balance Sheet Amounts			Taxable Difference: Deferred Tax Liability		Deductible Difference: Deferred Tax Asset	
	Book	Tax	Difference	Current	Noncurrent	Current	Noncurrent
Assets:							
Accounts receivable	$ 10,000	$ 0	$10,000	$10,000			
Fixed assets (net)	175,000	115,000	60,000		$60,000		
Liabilities:							
Unearned rental income	15,000	0	15,000			$15,000	
Product warranty accrual	12,000	2,000	10,000			10,000	
Other Items:							
Tax loss carryforward							$50,000
Totals				$10,000	$60,000	$25,000	$50,000
Effective tax rate				0.40	0.40	0.40	0.40
Preliminary deferred tax balance				$ 4,000	$24,000	$10,000	$20,000
Less valuation reserve						(3,333)	(6,667)[a]
Deferred tax balance at year-end				$ 4,000	$24,000	$ 6,667	$13,333
Deferred tax balance at beginning of year				0	16,000	2,834	14,166
Deferred tax increase (reduction) to income tax expense				$ 4,000	$ 8,000	$ (3,833)	$ 833
Net increase to income tax expense					$9,000		

Balance Sheet Reporting:

Current deferred tax asset	$ 6,667
Current deferred tax liability	(4,000)
Net current deferred tax asset	$ 2,667
Noncurrent deferred tax asset	$ 13,333
Noncurrent deferred tax liability	(24,000)
Net noncurrent deferred tax liability	$(10,667)

[a]Valuation Allowance of $10,000 is allocated ratably between current (1/3) and noncurrent (2/3) deferred tax assets.

reduce future income taxes by $6,000. However, this benefit will be realized only if the company has sufficient taxable income in the future.

Realization of the benefit of a carryforward, then, is uncertain. SFAS No. 109 permits recognition of deferred tax assets for NOL carryforwards, subject to a valuation allowance for portions of deferred tax assets that "more than likely" will not be realized. Valuation allowances are discussed later in this chapter.

Assume NotsoLucky expects sufficient future taxable income, so a valuation allowance is not necessary. The anticipated $6,000 reduction of future income taxes is a deferred tax asset. The company's total tax benefit related to the $50,000 taxable loss is still $15,000, consisting of $9,000 in taxes refundable and $6,000 in future reductions. Thus, the net loss for 1997 is still $35,000—the pretax loss of $50,000 offset by the $15,000 tax benefit. An entry for this situation is:

12/31/97	Income Tax Refund Receivable	9,000	
	Deferred Tax Asset	6,000	
	Income Tax Benefit from		
	NOL Carryback and Carryforward		15,000

A NOL carryforward of $50,000 is shown as part of the determination of deferred tax in Exhibit 17–9. This carryforward represents tax losses for current or prior periods. At a 40% rate, the carryforward can reduce future taxes by $20,000, which potentially is recognized as a deferred tax asset, subject to the need for a valuation allowance.

Notice that any deferred tax asset resulting from a NOL carryforward is not related to an existing balance sheet account. The deferred tax asset would thus be classified as current or noncurrent based on when the benefit is expected to be realized.

Tax Credit Carryforwards. A tax credit is a direct reduction to an entity's income tax liability for some specific, qualifying reason. For example, an energy tax credit permits a taxpayer to directly reduce income taxes for qualified expenditures related to measures to save energy. Tax credit carryforwards occur when an entity is entitled to tax credits that directly reduce income taxes due, but because taxes due are less than the credit, some portion of the credit is unused and thus carried forward. For example, suppose that in the previous section, NotSoLucky had a $50,000 tax loss and was also entitled to a $5,000 tax credit. Since there is a tax loss, no income taxes are due and NotSoLucky is unable to use the credit to reduce its taxes. If NotSoLucky is entitled to use the $5,000 to reduce future taxes, a potential deferred tax asset results.

A net tax loss is not required to incur a tax credit carryforward. If NotSoLucky had taxable income of $10,000 rather than the tax loss, a 30% tax rate would cause preliminary taxes of $3,000. The $5,000 tax credit eliminates any taxes currently due, and a tax credit carryforward of $2,000 remains. Like NOL carryforwards, recognition of tax credit carryforwards as deferred tax assets may be subject to a valuation allowance.

Valuation Allowances. After the total amount of deferred tax assets is calculated, management must assess the potential realizability of these assets. In so doing, management applies a "more likely than not" criterion to assess whether there is a greater than 50 percent chance that some portion or all of the deferred tax asset will not be realized. If so, management must reduce deferred tax assets by a valuation allowance sufficient to bring the net deferred tax asset recognized on the balance sheet to an amount that is "more likely than not" to be realized.

Obviously, in accounting for income taxes, as in many other areas of accounting, substantial professional and management judgment must be applied. This highly judgmental area of accounting for income taxes is one that has been the subject of speculation on management's tendency to utilize such allowances to "manage" earnings. The Ethics in Practice feature deals with this subject. Clearly, this is an important area where professional accountants and management must exercise their responsibilities with care and judgment. SFAS No. 109 provides instructions and guidelines to assist management in making these judgments.

ETHICS IN PRACTICE

Hidden Reserves and Management Judgment

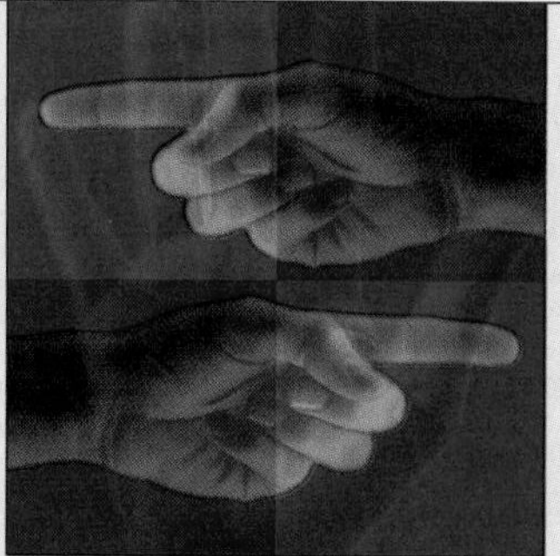

A new accounting rule makes financial statements difficult to compare—and gives management a new way to massage earnings.

Hidden reserves, which allow managements to smooth out reported earnings, are making a quiet comeback. Their vehicle: the Financial Accounting Standards Board's new Statement 109, which tells companies how to account for tax credits. Some companies have already adopted the new rule, but most will adopt it by the first quarter of 1993.

Suppose that as the result of a big restructuring, a company generates a $1 billion loss. For tax purposes, losses can be carried forward for 15 years. Assuming the company makes money after the restructuring and pays taxes at the full corporate income tax rate of 34%, that $1 billion loss could save the company $340 million.

The accounting question is: When and how should the company account for that potential tax savings?

According to the FASB's Statement 109, managements must peer into the future. If management believes it is "more likely than not" that the company will generate enough earnings in the future to warrant the use of the credits, then the company must book the value of the tax credit as income immediately, and label the earnings infusion as a one-time accounting change.

What if management isn't so sure about future earnings? Then Statement 109 tells the company to set the tax credit aside in a reserve. This reserve can be dipped into in future years at management's discretion—and thus could be used to offset earnings disappointments.

Companies looking to set up tax credit reserves won't encounter much resistance from their auditors. That's because Statement 109 gives managements a great deal of latitude as to the outlook for future earnings. "The 'more likely than not' provision is perhaps the most judgmental clause in accounting," says ***Ernst & Young*** partner Norman Strauss.

Source: R. Khalaf, "Read Those Footnotes!" *Forbes,* February 15, 1993.

The general rule of classifying deferred tax items in accordance with the asset or liability to which they are related is not applied to valuation allowances. Regardless of the classification of the asset or liability giving rise to a deferred tax asset, the valuation allowance is allocated on a *pro rata basis* to the current and noncurrent portions of the deferred tax assets.

Assume, for example, that management expects to realize only half of the $20,000 potential deferred tax asset associated with the NOL carryforward illustrated in Exhibit 17–9. Thus, a valuation allowance of $10,000 is appropriate. This allowance is allocated to both current and noncurrent deferred tax assets, even though the valuation allowance is attributable to the noncurrent asset for the carryforward. So one-third (that is, $10,000 of a total $30,000 potential asset shown in the exhibit) of the allowance reduces current deferred tax assets by $3,333 to $6,667, and two-thirds ($20,000 of a total $30,000) reduces noncurrent deferred tax assets by $6,667 to $13,333.

The need for an allowance should be determined on a "gross" basis for deferred tax assets, regardless of whether deferred tax liabilities exceed the amount of deferred tax assets. SFAS No. 109 further states,

> [F]uture realization of the tax benefit of an existing deductible temporary difference or carryforward ultimately depends on the existence of sufficient taxable income of the appropriate character (for example, ordinary income or capital gain) within the carryback, carryforward period available under the tax law.[4]

Similar to other financial statement amounts determined based on management's estimates, the valuation allowance sometimes changes as a result of a change in judgment about the realizability of a deferred tax asset. Such changes are shown as a component of income tax expense from continuing operations, not as an extraordinary item.

NETTING DEFERRED TAX ASSETS AND LIABILITIES

Deferred tax assets and liabilities may be offset and reported "net." For example, from the deferred tax balances determined from Exhibit 17–9, current assets of $6,667 are offset by current liabilities of $4,000; so a net current deferred tax asset of $2,667 is reported. Similarly, noncurrent assets of $13,333 and noncurrent liabilities of $24,000 result in reporting a net noncurrent deferred tax liability of $10,667.

However, netting is permitted only within a tax-paying component of an entity and within a specific tax jurisdiction. The reported amounts in Exhibit 17–10 assume one entity and one jurisdiction. A deferred tax asset arising from a deductible difference for state income tax purposes may not be offset against deferred tax liabilities arising from federal income tax items. In the following example, no "netting" would be permitted, and each total would be separately presented.

	DEFERRED TAX LIABILITIES		DEFERRED TAX ASSETS	
	CURRENT	NONCURRENT	CURRENT	NONCURRENT
U.S. federal income taxes	$ —	$20,000	$5,000	$ —
State income taxes:				
Subsidiary A	1,500			
Subsidiary B				2,500
Foreign income taxes		1,000		
Totals	$1,500	$21,000	$5,000	$2,500

[4]*SFAS No. 109*, par. 21.

With this background regarding the liability method of accounting for income tax, some of the major tax accounting issues central to the evolution of current practice are discussed next.

As tax regulations developed and became more complex, accounting for income taxes became more difficult in the face of a broadening divergence between financial statement pretax income and taxable income. A summary of historical developments related to accounting for income taxes is presented in Exhibit 17–10. A discussion of major conceptual issues follows.

EXHIBIT 17–10 Time Line of Major Tax Accounting Developments

ARB No. 23	ARB No. 44	ARB No. 44 (REVISED)	APB No. 11	SFAS No. 96	SFAS No. 109
1944	1954	1958	1967	1987	1992

Major Features

1944	ARB No. 23	**"Accounting for income taxes"** introduced the broad concept of timing differences, and concluded that income taxes are an expense properly allocable to income included in the income statement for the year.
1954	ARB No. 44	**"Accounting for income taxes"** responded to the Internal Revenue Code of 1954 allowing general use of accelerated depreciation methods by sanctioning recording of deferred taxes when timing differences reverse in relatively few years in the future. It also permitted nonrecognition where differences were for a longer term.
1958	ARB No. 44 (revised)	**"Declining-balance depreciation"** was the first authoritative pronouncement requiring recording of deferred taxes for all timing differences (comprehensive allocation). When the differences reverse over a long or indefinite period, ARB 44 permitted the "net-of-tax" approach of showing the effect on taxes as an adjustment of the related balance sheet account (similar to a valuation allowance or contra account) instead of using a deferred tax account.
1967	APB No. 11	**"Accounting for income taxes"** required recognition of deferred taxes for tax effects of all transactions in a period, mandated the deferred method (not net-of-tax), dealt with recognition of loss carrybacks (recognize benefit in loss period) and carryforwards (usually delay recognition until realized), and required certain tax-related disclosures in the notes to financial statements.
1987	SFAS No. 96	**"Accounting for income taxes"** responded to both the FASB conceptual framework and criticisms of existing practice by shifting to a balance sheet instead of an income statement approach and mandated the "liability method", focusing on the accrual of a liability for the future tax return consequences of temporary differences based on when and how they are expected to affect the tax return. Retained comprehensive allocation; and defined strict, complex rules for the recognition of the benefit of carryforwards and differences deductible in the future (Deferred tax assets).
1992	SFAS No. 109	**"Accounting for income taxes"** responded to the overly restrictive criteria for the recognition of deferred tax assets and the complex calculations required by SFAS No. 96. Retained the liability approach, permitted the recognition of deferred tax assets for all deductible temporary differences and operating loss and tax credit carryforwards, but required such assets to be reduced by a valuation allowance when realization is not assured.

MAJOR TAX ACCOUNTING ISSUES

Interpret the major issues central to the historical development of accounting for income taxes.

DEFERRED METHOD VERSUS LIABILITY METHOD

The deferred method was promulgated by APB No. 11 and used in practice for many years. It measured the income statement tax effects of *timing differences* using tax rates and laws in effect when the timing differences originated. The ultimate income taxes actually paid (or saved) when these differences reversed were not considered by the deferred method. Timing differences were basically the revenue/expense type of temporary differences shown in Exhibit 17–3.

Implementation of this method essentially determined income tax expense based on what income taxes would be if the timing differences did not exist. The difference between this expense and the current taxes based on actual taxable income was the effect of the timing differences and the change to deferred taxes on the balance sheet. The method is therefore said to be *income statement oriented.* The resulting balance sheet amounts were repositories of the effects of these timing differences which, over time, bore little relationship to assets or liabilities consistent with SFAC No. 6.

In contrast, the liability method (first mandated by SFAS No. 96) is *balance sheet oriented.* The liability method attempts to accrue a liability (or asset) for the tax that will be assessed (recovered) on temporary differences at the time they reverse. The deferred tax increase to (reduction of) income tax expense for a period is based upon changes to these deferred tax liabilities (assets) and is more inclusive than solely representing the impact of timing differences. The FASB (both in SFAS No. 96 and No. 109) concluded that the liability approach was most consistent with the conceptual framework.

COMPREHENSIVE VERSUS PARTIAL ALLOCATION

Comprehensive allocation means that financial statement recognition must be given for all temporary differences between financial statement income and taxable income. Before 1967, various alternatives for selective recognition of the financial impact of timing differences were acceptable. Some professionals still contend that partial allocation is preferable to comprehensive allocation. Under partial allocation, a company would not recognize deferred income taxes for certain temporary differences characterized by two possible conditions: (1) very long or "indefinite" periods over which certain types of temporary differences would reverse, or (2) originating differences in subsequent years are expected to offset reversing differences from prior years, resulting in a cancellation of the effect on net income. For example, deferred taxes for excess depreciation deductions would not be recognized because of the long periods prior to reversal. Also, the excess depreciation on newly purchased assets would offset the reversals from the depreciation of older assets.

All authoritative accounting pronouncements from APB No. 11 through SFAS No. 109 require comprehensive allocation. Proponents of comprehensive allocation argue that assets and liabilities should be based on current or past transactions. Therefore, consistent with historical-cost concepts, the offsetting of anticipated or estimated future tax implications should not enter into the determination of current-year, financial statement income.

NET-OF-TAX PRESENTATION

Net-of-tax presentation of income tax amounts in the financial statements deducts the deferred tax amount from the account to which it is related, similar to a valuation allowance or contra account. For example, assume a company has book and tax balance sheet amounts as follows:

	BALANCE SHEET AMOUNTS			RESULTING DEFERRED TAX ASSET
	BOOK	TAX	DIFFERENCE	@ 40%
Deferred rental income	$15,000	—	$15,000	$ 6,000
Product-warranty accrual	12,000	2,000	10,000	4,000
				$10,000

To present its financial statements on a net-of-tax basis, the company would report the following liabilities on its balance sheet:

Deferred rental income	$9,000
Accrued product warranty	8,000

This presentation nets the deferred tax asset from the balance of the related liability:

Deferred rental income: $15,000 − $6,000 = $9,000
Accrued product warranty: $12,000 − $4,000 = $8,000

With the net-of-tax approach, fixed assets would be reported at cost less accumulated depreciation less the deferred tax liability associated with excess depreciation deductions.

APB No. 11 did not permit the net-of-tax approach, and required one or more deferred tax liability or asset accounts to be used to show the effects of deferred taxes. In contrast, APB No. 16 on Business Combinations required acquired assets in a purchase business combination to be recorded net of tax. SFAS Nos. 96 and 109 reversed the position of APB No. 16 and required acquired assets and assumed liabilities to be recorded at fair value and a deferred tax liability or asset to be recorded for any temporary differences. Current standards, then, do *not* permit the net-of-tax approach.

DISCOUNTING

Arguments over the appropriateness of including present-value adjustments in the measurement of assets and liabilities are not new, particularly for the "long-term" items that are typical with deferred taxes. APB No. 11 continued the prohibition of discounting deferred tax amounts set forth as part of APB No. 10 (Omnibus Opinion, 1966). This position has been continued because in both SFAS Nos. 96 and 109, the FASB declined to consider the complex issues discounting would bring to accounting for income taxes. Yet, discounting is required for such complex issues as leases and postretirement benefits. Why it is not considered for deferred income taxes is an unexplained anomaly.

RECOGNITION OF DEFERRED TAX DEBITS

Because of the uncertainty associated with potential benefits of deferred tax assets, accountants have struggled with the appropriate criteria to permit recognition in financial statements. APB No. 11 permitted recognition of deferred tax debits in the calculation of deferred taxes when using the "income" approach and subject to a "reasonable likelihood of realization" standard. However, recognition of NOL carryforwards was permitted only when "realization was assured beyond a reasonable doubt," a very tough standard. SFAS No. 96 applied strict rules for scheduling temporary difference reversals and complex recognition criteria for deferred tax assets. SFAS No. 109 removed much of the complex scheduling, and permitted the recognition of deferred tax assets, subject to a valuation allowance, if it was "more likely than not" that some portion of the deferred tax asset would not be realized—a less onerous but more judgmental approach.

EXCEPTION TO LIABILITY RECOGNITION

Complexities arise not only from tax regulations but from some corporate organizational structures. A particularly thorny area has been whether and when to provide income tax expense on the undistributed earnings of subsidiaries and corporate joint ventures. Up to and including SFAS No. 96, companies with "permanent" investments did not have to provide deferred income taxes on such earnings. SFAS No. 109 judged that the concept of "indefinite reversal," which supported this approach, was inconsistent with the liability method, and

IN PRACTICE—INTERNATIONAL

Income Taxes in Other Countries

For income taxes, substantially different accounting principles and reporting requirements apply in other countries. A sense of a few such differences and their impact is clear from the following:

Taxation systems are one of the most influential reasons for how and why accounting standards are established. In many countries, these systems influence financial reporting. In Japan, for example, all expenses and write-downs of assets for tax purposes must be recorded for accounting purposes. Tax regulations also affect U.S. reporting. The use of last-in, first-out (LIFO) inventory valuation started with tax regulations passed in the 1950s. In many countries, depreciation lives recognized for tax purposes are accepted for financial reporting purposes as well. . . .

In the United Kingdom, the liability method is used for some timing differences, but only to the extent it is likely a tax liability or asset will materialize—generally within the following five years. In Germany, there are relatively few timing differences because many accounting methods required for taxes are required for financial reporting also. In Japan, deferred taxes are not recognized at all.

Source: N. Anderson, "The Globalization GAAP," *Management Accounting,* August 1993.

the standard eliminated most such exceptions. However, because of the complexities of determining the amount of liability to recognize, exceptions to providing deferred income taxes on undistributed earnings from *foreign* subsidiaries and *foreign* corporate joint ventures were retained where the earnings are invested indefinitely. Whenever this occurs, disclosure of the circumstances is required.

FINANCIAL REPORTING

This section discusses other reporting and disclosure requirements to help users understand the current and future cash flow impact of taxes on the reporting entity.

Analyze the financial reporting of income tax information disclosed in notes to financial statements.

INCOME STATEMENT PRESENTATION

Accounting principles generally require that income statement items be classified in four general categories: continuing operations, discontinued operations, extraordinary items, and changes in accounting principles. Total income tax expense (current and deferred) is allocated among these categories.

The amount of tax allocated to continuing operations includes routine tax effects arising from current-year operations plus the effects of (1) changes in circumstances that cause a change in judgment about the realizability of deferred tax assets, (2) changes in tax laws and rates, and (3) changes in the tax status of the entity, such as a change from a partnership (nontaxable) to a corporation (taxable). Tax expense from continuing operations also includes the effects (benefit) of NOL carrybacks and carryforwards, irrespective of whether they originated from discontinued operations or were realized by carryback to years in which taxable income arose from a discontinued operation. The tax impact of items other than continuing operations are allocated based on their individual effects on tax expense. Recall, for example, that discontinued operations, extraordinary items, and cumulative effects of accounting changes are reported net of their respective income tax effects.

DISCLOSURES—NOTES TO FINANCIAL STATEMENTS

Current practice mandates that management provide a number of supplemental explanations and presentations regarding income taxes. The purpose of these disclosures is to provide better understanding of the tax position of the company, its strategies and exposures, and to permit users to more readily make judgments about the future impact of income taxes on a company's operations and cash flows.

Disclosures related to the balance sheet include:

- The total amount and changes in any deferred tax valuation allowance.
- The types of temporary differences and carryforwards that give rise to a significant portion of deferred tax assets or liabilities. Public companies must also disclose the amounts of such components and any uncertainties regarding the realization of deferred tax assets.
- Where exceptions permit no provision for deferred taxes, a description of the types and amounts of temporary differences for which a deferred tax has not been recognized and the types of events that would cause them to become taxable.

Disclosures related to the income statement include:

- The significant components of income tax expense attributable to continuing operations (for example, current and deferred tax expense, any tax credits, benefits or operating loss carryforwards, effects of changes in laws or rates, changes in beginning-of-year deferred tax asset valuation reserves resulting from changes in circumstances). Public companies must also disclose the foreign and domestic components of pretax income and tax expense.
- The amounts of tax expense allocated to separate items other than continuing operations.
- The nature of significant differences between the amount of reported income tax expense from continuing operations and the amount of income tax expense that would result from applying domestic federal income tax rates to pretax income from continuing operations (for example, state income tax, nontaxable income or nondeductible expenses, and tax credits). Public companies must also present either the dollar or percentage amount of such differences.
- The nature and effect of any items affecting comparability of information for all periods presented in the financial statements.
- The amounts and expiration dates of operating loss and tax credit carryforwards for tax purposes.

Exhibit 17–11 provides an illustration of disclosure. The subsequent In Practice feature also gives an example of the large number of items causing deferred tax balances for ***IBM***.

EXHIBIT 17–11
Example Company: Note to Financial Statements

Note X—Income Taxes

Deferred income taxes have been provided for the tax effects of temporary differences between the carrying amounts of assets and liabilities for financial reporting purposes and the amounts for income tax purposes. Components of the Company's deferred tax liabilities and assets as of December 31, 1997, are as follows:

Deferred tax liabilities:	
Installment sale deferred revenues	$ 4,000
Accelerated depreciation	24,000
Total deferred tax liabilities	$ 28,000
Deferred tax assets:	
Deferred rental income	$ 6,000
Product warranty accrual	4,000
Tax-loss carryforward	20,000
Total deferred tax assets	$ 30,000
Valuation allowance	(10,000)
Net deferred tax assets	$ 20,000
Net deferred tax liabilities	$ 8,000

(continued)

EXHIBIT 17–11
(Concluded)

The components of the provision for income taxes attributable to continuing operations are as follows:

Current:	
Federal	$10,000
Foreign	1,500
State	$1,000
Total current	$12,500
Deferred:	
Federal	$ 8,100
State	900
Total deferred	$ 9,000
	$21,500

The components of the provision (benefit) for deferred income taxes are as follows:

Installment sale	$ 4,000
Accelerated depreciation	8,000
Rental income	(6,000)
Product warranty	—
Increase in valuation allowance	3,000
	$ 9,000

The reconciliation of income taxes computed at U.S. statutory rates to income tax expense is:

	AMOUNT	PERCENT
Tax at U.S. statutory rates	$20,000	36.0%
State income taxes, net of federal tax benefit	1,900	3.3
Higher effective tax rates in other countries	600	1.0
General business credits	(4,820)	(8.3)
Increase in deferred tax asset valuation allowance	3,000	5.2
Other—net	120	.2
	$21,500	37.4%

At December 31, 1997, the company had net operating loss (NOL) carryforwards of $50,000 which expire in Years 2001 through 2005. For financial reporting purposes a valuation allowance of $10,000 at December 31, 1997, has been provided to reduce the net deferred tax asset to the amount management believes will be realized. During 1997, this allowance was increased by $3,000, reflecting management's more conservative estimate of the potential for realization of the NOL benefits associated with its real estate subsidiary.

Undistributed earnings of the Company's foreign subsidiaries totaled approximately $100,000 at December 31, 1997. No provision for income taxes related to these earnings has been made because it is management's intention to maintain these investments indefinitely. If such earnings were distributed to the parent company, the Company would be subject to U.S. income taxes, which may be reduced by any unused NOL carryforwards available at that time. Due to the complexities and uncertainties impacting the calculation, it is not practical to determine the amount of unrecognized deferred taxes.

IN PRACTICE—GENERAL

Deferred Income Taxes for IBM

In the notes to consolidated financial statements of International Business Machines Corporation and Subsidiary Companies, the significant components of deferred tax assets and liabilities included on the balance sheet were as follows:

(DOLLARS IN MILLIONS)	AT DECEMBER 31 1995	1994*
Deferred Tax Assets		
Retiree medical benefits	$ 2,632	$ 2,500
Restructuring charges	2,003	2,446
Capitalized research and development	1,772	2,057
Foreign tax credits	1,183	1,380
Alternative minimum tax credits	859	738
Inventory	674	633
Doubtful accounts	517	453
General business credits	452	452
Equity alliances	407	445
Employee benefits	405	363
Intracompany sales and services	325	357
Foreign tax-loss carryforwards	303	469
State and local tax-loss carryforwards	236	370
Warranty	233	163
Software income deferred	205	199
Depreciation	172	249
Retirement benefits	101	127
U.S. federal tax-loss carryforwards	—	230
Other	2,800	2,564
Gross deferred tax assets	$15,279	$16,195
Less: Valuation allowance	(3,868)	(4,551)
Total deferred tax assets	$11,411	$11,644
Deferred Tax Liabilities		
Sales-type leases	$ 2,898	$ 2,862
Retirement benefits	1,919	1,061
Depreciation	1,787	1,653
Software costs deferred	967	1,283
Other	1,320	823
Gross deferred tax liabilities	$ 8,891	$ 7,682

*Reclassified to conform to 1995 presentation.

INCOME TAXES AND FINANCIAL ANALYSIS

Interpret the impact income tax accounting principles can have on analyzing a company's financial position and results of operations.

Assessing future income tax–related cash flows with any degree of reliability is a challenge to the owners and management of companies. They must critically and carefully consider the makeup, volatility, and trends of items that influence both balance sheet and income statement tax amounts in order to assess future tax-related cash flows with any degree of reliability. To illustrate, the following sections examine tax notes contained in the financial statements of publicly reporting companies.

TAX-EXEMPT INCOME

The **statutory rate reconciliation** computes a tax amount at statutory rates applied to pretax income from continuing operations and shows the major items that reconcile this amount to the actual tax expense the entity has recorded. This reconciliation presents some of the most important information regarding a company's tax structure, strategies, and so forth. Exhibit 17–12 illustrates this for several years for ***Hibernia Corporation,*** a publicly reporting bank holding company.

This schedule shows a relatively stable and growing earnings picture where tax expense based on federal statutory rates is increasing over the eleven-year period. Note, however, that Hibernia's shareholders received the full benefit of pretax earnings in the earliest two years presented (1984 and 1985). As a result of tax-exempt interest, virtually no income tax expense was incurred.

EXHIBIT 17–12 Statutory Rate Reconciliation

HIBERNIA CORPORATION

The reconciliation of the federal statutory income tax rate to the company's effective rate is as follows:

	YEAR ENDED DECEMBER 31							
	1995		1994		1985*		1984*	
(DOLLARS IN THOUSANDS)	AMOUNT	RATE	AMOUNT	RATE	AMOUNT	RATE	AMOUNT	RATE
Tax expense based on federal statutory rate	$46,645	35.0%	$35,202	35.0%	$11,160	46.0%	$7,683	46.0%
Tax-exempt interest	(3,356)	(2.5)	(3,244)	(3.2)	(10,339)	(42.8)	(8,864)	(53.1)
State income tax, net of federal benefit	2,411	1.8	2,151	2.1	—	—	—	—
Goodwill**	1,088	0.8	6,706	6.7	309	1.3	—	—
Change in deferred tax valuation reserve	(36,551)	(27.4)	(36,586)	(36.4)	—	—	—	—
Other	(824)	(0.6)	1,329	1.3	(1,130)	(4.5)	513	3.1
Income tax expense	$ 9,413	7.1%	$ 5,558	5.5%	$ —	0	$ (668)	(4.0)

*Reclassified by the authors to conform to 1995 presentation.
**The goodwill in this example are permanent differences for goodwill amortized for financial reporting that is not permitted as deductions for income tax purposes. This amortization would be for goodwill purchased prior to the December 31, 1994. As illustrated in the text, amortization of goodwill purchased after December 31, 1994, may now be deducted using a fifteen-year useful life.

However, tax-exempt interest is affected heavily by the municipal bond market and interest rate fluctuations, as well as by management's discretion in changing its asset mix between tax-exempt and taxable sources of income. Prevailing interest rates were much lower a decade later in 1994 and 1995. Thus, while tax-exempt interest in 1994 and 1995 also reduced the tax expense of the company, the reductions were not as substantial as in the earlier two years depicted.

Hibernia's rate for income tax expenses in 1994 of 5.5% and in 1995 of 7.1% were still substantially lower than its 35% federal statutory rate. The primary reason for the lower rates were for changes to its deferred tax valuation reserve, which is discussed next.

VALUATION ALLOWANCES AND CARRYFORWARDS

The "more likely than not" criterion is the guideline for recording valuation allowances against deferred tax assets. That is, the deferred tax asset valuation allowance is the amount needed to reduce deferred tax assets to amounts that are more likely than not to be realized. Changes to a company's valuation allowance affects its reported net deferred tax assets, so related income tax expenses are also affected. As illustrated in Exhibit 17–12, Hibernia substantially reduced its income tax expenses in 1994 and 1995 through changes to its valuation allowance. To reduce expenses, these changes had to be reductions to the allowance which, other things being equal, would cause net deferred tax assets to increase. Increases to net deferred tax assets are associated with deferred tax benefits or reductions to expense. Through its valuation allowance, Hibernia is delaying recognition of the benefits of potential deferred tax assets, possibly until the benefits are actually realized. This strategy is similar to that described for ***Ceridian***, as opposed to ***Unisys***, in the In Practice feature on valuation allowances.

In Exhibit 17–13, ***Avondale Industries***, a marine repair and shipbuilding contractor, reports substantial amounts of deferred tax assets for operating loss carryforwards, as well as smaller amounts for tax credit carryforwards. Like Hibernia, potential deferred tax assets are offset by a valuation allowance which was substantially reduced in 1995. The note at the bottom of the exhibit describes a reduction of approximately $19 million, $6 million of which reduced goodwill,[5] with the remaining $13 million reducing income tax expense (i.e., the provision/benefit for income taxes). Note that the $13 million reduction for deferred benefits reduced income tax expense to such an extent that a $4.4 million benefit was recognized, thus increasing income from continuing operations to over $28 million.

The exhibit labels the $13 million deferred benefit as "attributable to the realization of net operation loss carryforwards." A valuation allowance must have been associated with the tax benefits for these loss carryforwards, so that net deferred tax assets for the carryforwards were not previously recognized. Had there been no associated valuation allowance so that deferred tax assets were previously recognized, the reduction to income tax expense would have occurred in earlier years, not in 1995. Thus, the $13 million reduction for the deferred tax benefit associated with the loss carryforwards results from changing the valuation allowance to permit recognition of related deferred tax assets.

[5]The reduction to goodwill is related to federal income taxes of business combinations which are beyond the scope of this text.

IN PRACTICE—GENERAL

Valuation Allowances

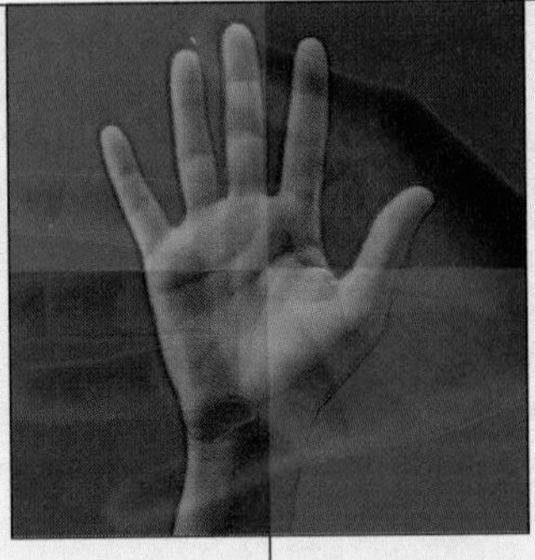

Statement No. 109 certainly won't make it easy to compare companies' financial statements. Consider how computer systems maker ***Unisys*** (1992 revenues, $8.4 billion) and information services provider ***Ceridian*** (estimated 1992 revenues, $825 million) are following the new rule.

As a result of its 1991 restructuring, Unisys is sitting on tax-loss carryforwards that could save it up to $500 million (about $3 a share) in taxes. Unisys management believes the earnings outlook is reasonably bright; therefore, Unisys will book most of its tax credit as income up front. The company recently said it will record a one-time gain of between $325 million and $425 million in its quarter ending Mar. 31. The remainder of the credit will most likely go into a reserve and could be taken into income slowly, over the next several years.

Now look at Ceridian, which is the successor company to the money-losing computer systems maker ***Control Data***. Last year Ceridian spun off its unprofitable operations, leaving it with a profitable core business in information services—and tax credits worth over $450 million, about $10.60 a share. Ceridian will book its $450 million tax credit as a reserve, and take a fresh look at the reserve after several profitable years.

Result: Unisys' reported net income will get a big, nonrecurring infusion this year. Ceridian's after-tax earnings will get nothing this year but could instead enjoy a steady stream of infusions in the future—assuming, of course, Ceridian makes money.

Companies to Watch

COMPANY	NET OPERATING LOSS CARRYFORWARD* (DOLLARS IN MILLIONS)
Armco	$1,031
Black & Decker	596
Data General	490
Michigan National Corp.	215
Occidental Petroleum	990
Penn Central	940
PHM Corp.	638
Southland Corp.	916
Temple-Inland	598
Wang Laboratories	1,800

*For financial reporting. Numbers as of most recent fiscal year available.

Source: R. Khalaf, "Read Those Footnotes!" *Forbes*, February 15, 1993.

Clearly, policy regarding valuation allowances is a major area where the exercise of judgment determines the amount of deferred tax assets and related benefit that an entity reflects in its financial statements. Financial statement users do not have access to the detailed analyses and thought processes applied by management in regard to valuation allowances provided against deferred tax assets. However, at least the tax notes to audited financial statements provide a scorecard. Users can track the amount of valuation allowance provided, along with the net change during the year. More importantly, any adjustments to a valuation allowance because of a change in circumstances that affects the predicted realizability of the related tax asset must be disclosed. These items taken together provide the user with information on management's philosophy about providing such allowances and its accuracy in estimating allowance amounts.

EXHIBIT 17–13 Effects of NOL Carryforwards and Valuation Allowances

AVONDALE INDUSTRIES, INC.

Excerpted from Income Statement:

(DOLLARS IN THOUSANDS)	1993	YEARS ENDED DECEMBER 31, 1994	1995
Income (loss) from continuing operations before income taxes	$(5,233)	$13,375	$23,780
Income taxes (Note 7)	—	300	(4,400)
Income (loss) from continuing operations	(5,233)	13,075	28,180

Excerpted from Note 7:

The company has provided for federal income taxes as follows:

(DOLLARS IN THOUSANDS)	1993	1994	1995
Current provision	$ —	$ 600	$ 1,500
Deferred provision (benefit)	—	(300)	7,100
Deferred benefit attributable to the realization of net operating loss carryforwards	—	—	(13,000)
Provision (benefit) for income taxes	$ —	$ 300	$ (4,400)

(DOLLARS IN THOUSANDS)	1994	1995
Deferred tax liabilities:		
Differences between book and tax basis of property, plant and equipment	$27,018	$26,266
Other	1,511	759
Total	$28,529	$27,025
Deferred tax assets:		
Reserves not currently deductible	$ 6,020	$ 5,174
Long-term contracts	5,252	18,557
Other temporary differences	3,598	4,263
Operating loss carryforwards	47,600	24,334
Tax credit carryforwards	5,800	7,200
	$68,270	$59,528
Valuation allowance	(28,641)	(9,703)
Total	$39,629	$49,825
Net deferred tax assets	$11,100	$22,800

During 1995, the deferred tax valuation allowance decreased approximately $19.0 million as a result of the company's current year operating results and a reevaluation of its expectations of the likelihood of future operating income related to its existing backlog. Approximately $6.0 million of this decrease in the valuation allowance was recorded as a reduction in goodwill in accordance with SFAS No. 109, which requires that the realization of tax benefits first be attributed to any acquired tax assets. In the event that additional tax benefits are realized in future periods, all such benefits will be recorded as a reduction of income tax expense.

DEPRECIATION

Capital-intensive corporations like Avondale (Exhibit 17–13) frequently take advantage of accelerated depreciation to reduce their tax burden. At the end of 1995, Avondale reports deferred tax liabilities of over $26 million for tax depreciation (based upon accelerated depreciation) in excess of amounts recorded for financial reporting (which is typically based upon straight-line depreciation). The company, then, has deferred paying $26 million in income taxes that it would have had to pay had it used straight-line depreciation for tax purposes. Even though these amounts have been previously recognized as deferred tax expense increasing income tax expenses (or reducing to the benefit for income taxes), payment is deferred. Thus, tax policies taking advantage of accelerated depreciation can significantly improve the cash flow of a company.

DOMESTIC VERSUS FOREIGN INCOME TAXES

Income taxes to foreign tax jurisdictions can differ substantially from taxes to domestic jurisdictions. The following In Practice feature illustrates domestic and foreign earnings and income taxes with excerpts from ***Motorola***'s 1995 annual report. Motorola's average foreign income tax rate is approximately 20% each year (e.g., $386/$1,875 = 20.6%). This rate is substantially less than the marginal U.S. federal income tax rate of 35%. To the extent that Motorola can invest earnings from other nations abroad and exclude these earnings from U.S. federal taxation, the company will incur a smaller income tax burden in other nations. Such a favorable income tax rate may partially explain why a growing percentage of Motorola's earnings have been from other nations.

The U.S. component of income taxes for Motorola ($400 million in 1995) is very high compared to the U.S. component of earnings before taxes ($907 million in 1995). Had the U.S. component of taxes been based solely on the U.S. component of earnings, the tax rates would have been approximately 44% ($400/$907), 64% ($728/$1,140), and 55% ($197/$360) for 1995, 1994, and 1993, respectively. Since these rates are substantially higher than statutory rates, some of the U.S. component of taxes is likely based upon estimation of some portion of earnings from other nations as well as the U.S. portion of earnings. Thus, Motorola is probably not excluding all earnings from other nations from U.S. federal income taxes. Yet, the note in the In Practice feature illustrates that there is still a substantial amount of cumulative, undistributed earnings that have been excluded with no provision for U.S. income tax ($3.5 billion at the end of 1995).

In sum, it is probably fair to say that financial analysts sometimes focus on pretax income as a measure of the performance of management over time. In so doing, they avoid dealing with the complexities and volatility of bottom-line earnings that result from the provision of income taxes for financial statement purposes. However, income taxes clearly make a difference to a number of constituents, including management, employees, owners, and potential owners. Through knowledgeable and careful analysis of all of the income tax–related information provided in financial statements, users of those statements will be able to ascertain the impact of income taxes on prior years and consequently assess their potential impact on future operations and cash flows.

IN PRACTICE—INTERNATIONAL

Domestic Versus Foreign Income Tax Rates

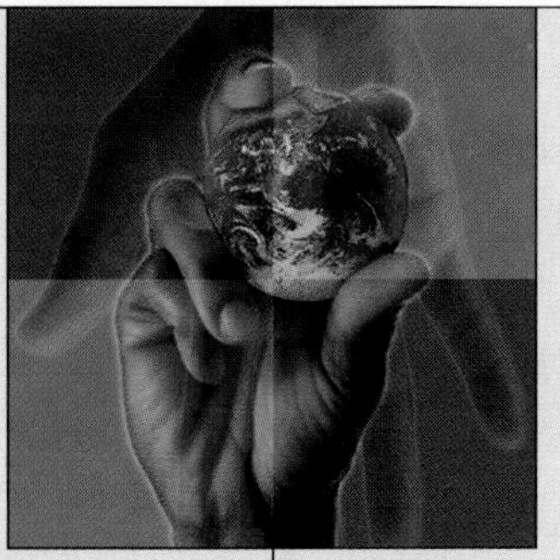

Excerpted from Motorola's 1995 annual report:

> Except for certain earnings that Motorola, Inc., intends to reinvest indefinitely, provisions have been made for the cumulative estimated U.S. federal income tax liabilities applicable to undistributed earnings of affiliates and associated companies. Undistributed earnings for which no U.S. income tax has been provided aggregated $3.5 billion and $2.9 billion at December 31, 1995 and 1994, respectively. Should these earnings be distributed, foreign tax credits would reduce the additional U.S. income tax which would be pay-able. In cases where taxes are provided on such undistributed earnings, those taxes have been included in U.S. income taxes.

MOTOROLA, INC. AND CONSOLIDATED SUBSIDIARIES
(Dollars in millions, except as noted)

Components of Earnings Before Income Taxes

	1995	1994	1993
United States	$ 907	$1,140	$ 360
Other nations	1,875	1,297	1,165
Total	$2,782	$2,437	$1,525

Components of Income Taxes Provided on Earnings

	1995	1994	1993
Current:			
United States	$ 400	$ 728	$ 197
Other nations	386	254	234
State income taxes (U.S.)	50	72	22
	$ 836	$1,054	$ 453
Deferred	165	(177)	50
Income taxes	$1,001	$ 877	$ 503

END-OF-CHAPTER REVIEW

SUMMARY

1. **Contrast the objectives of income tax determination with the objectives of financial reporting.** In the United States and in many other countries, income taxes are important business expenses because they significantly reduce earnings. Unlike most business expenses, income taxes are not incurred to provide a product or service, but instead they are calculated and assessed based on the profits of a business. Because different objectives are being pursued by taxing authorities and by authoritative

bodies responsible for the formulation of GAAP, differences exist between taxable income and pretax income for general financial statements purposes. Given that circumstance, accountants must deal with the question of whether and how to reflect, in general-purpose financial statements, the tax impact (deferred taxes) of items causing such differences.

2. **Apply the liability approach to determine (a) temporary differences and carryforwards, (b) deferred income tax assets and liabilities, and (c) income tax expense.** Consistent with the conceptual framework's emphasis on financial statements providing information to permit users to predict future cash flows, and in accord with the definition of assets and liabilities as probable future economic benefits obtained or sacrificed, the FASB has promulgated use of the liability method through SFAS No. 109. The objective of the liability method is to accrue balance sheet deferred income tax amounts that represent future amounts that will become payable to (deferred tax liabilities) or receivable from (deferred tax assets) the taxing authorities. Companies apply current (enacted) tax rates to (1) temporary differences between the amounts at which assets and liabilities are reported in financial statements and in tax returns and (2) NOL and tax credit carryforwards.

   Income tax expense for the year is computed by combining the amount of income taxes calculated on the current year's taxable income, with changes to deferred income tax balance sheet amounts. Consideration must be given to the realizability of deferred tax assets resulting from this process. If needed, a valuation allowance is provided against deferred tax assets to reduce them to an amount that is "more likely than not" to be realized.

3. **Interpret the major issues central to the historical development of accounting for income taxes.** Several key issues have been central to the development of accounting for income taxes. One involves the choice of method between the currently prescribed liability method—a balance sheet oriented approach—and the previously required deferred method—an income statement oriented approach. Another involves the requirement for comprehensive tax allocation rather than partial allocation. Currently, deferred tax assets and liabilities are reported independently from the associated balance sheet accounts for temporary differences. A contrasting, but currently disallowed, approach is to report the associated balance sheet accounts net of tax. Still other controversies concern discounting deferred tax balances, use of a valuation allowance for deferred tax assets, and exceptions to liability recognition.

4. **Analyze the financial reporting of income tax information disclosed in notes to financial statements.** To enhance the financial statement user's ability to understand the tax position of a company and to better make predictions about the future cash flows resulting from its tax position, a number of disclosures of tax information are required. These include a description of accounting policies, details regarding temporary differences and carryforwards and their effects, disclosures regarding a company's effective income tax rate compared to the statutory rate, information on certain changes in the valuation allowance, and discussion of temporary differences for which deferred tax liabilities have not been provided.

5. **Interpret the impact income tax accounting principles can have on analyzing a company's financial position and results of operations.** Through analysis of financial statement amounts resulting from the application of the liability method and the information provided in the notes to financial statements, users are able to assess the impact of income taxes on a company's operations and cash flows. Some key items to examine include the effects of carryforwards, permanent differences like tax-exempt income, and foreign income taxes.

KEY TERMS

comprehensive allocation *921*
current provision for income taxes *901*
deferred income tax liability *903*
deferred method *921*
deferred tax asset *903*
deferred tax asset valuation allowance *929*
deferred tax benefits *902*
deferred tax expenses *901*
income tax currently payable (refundable) *901*
income tax expense *901*
income taxes *900*
liability method *904*
net operating loss (NOL) *914*
net-of-tax presentation *922*
partial allocation *921*
permanent difference *912*
provision for income taxes *901*
statutory rate reconciliation *928*
tax credit *917*
taxable income *900*
temporary difference *901*

ASSIGNMENT MATERIAL

CASES

C17–1 Discussion Case—Comprehensive versus Partial Allocation

Imagine that a company's receivables for installment sales increase by 5 percent each year. What would happen to the balance for deferred tax liabilities associated with these receivables? Are these liabilities ever paid? Discuss the rationale for recognition of these liabilities (and the associated increase to income tax expense) based upon comprehensive tax allocation versus partial tax allocation.

C17–2 Discussion Case—Deferred versus Liability Method

Examine the impact of the tax rate change illustrated in Exhibit 17–6. How would the income tax expense, deferred tax liability at year-end, and change to deferred taxes for the year differ if the deferred tax method was applied rather than the liability method? How would the methods differ if the $10,000 difference in 1997 had not reversed in 1998, leaving receivables of $16,000 instead of $6,000? Which is more consistent with SFAC No. 6?

Now consider the alternative methods for estimating bad debts using either a percentage of credit sales or a percentage of accounts receivable. Draw parallels between the emphasis toward the income statement or the balance sheet for these alternative methods and for the deferred tax method versus the liability method for income tax accounting.

C17–3 Discussion Case—Deferred Tax Liability and Adjustment

Many analysts make adjustments to reported financial statement amounts when evaluating a company's solvency. One such adjustment excludes reported deferred tax liabilities from the numerator of debt ratios. The rationale is that such reported liabilities are not, in the analyst's opinion, truly debt that will result in future cash outflows. What is your opinion of this adjustment? If deferred tax liabilities are not recognized as liabilities, what should also be adjusted (other than total debt) to properly exclude them?

C17–4 Discussion Case—Deferred Taxes at IBM

The In Practice excerpt in the chapter from IBM's 1995 annual report indicates that deferred tax assets were $11,411 and $11,644 million as of December 31, 1995 and 1994, respectively. Similarly, deferred tax liabilities for the same respective dates are $8,891 and $7,682 million. The company's balance sheet for the same dates reflect respective current liabilities for taxes of $2,634 and $1,771 million and respective long-term deferred income tax liabilities of $1,807 and $1,881 million. These are the only items directly related to income taxes on the balance sheet. Can the amounts on the balance sheet be reconciled with the significant deferred tax assets and liabilities reported in the footnotes? Based upon this extremely limited information, how would you explain any apparent discrepancies?

C17–5 Deferred Taxes and Depreciation

Assume that after an initial $150,000 for capital purchases in the first year, Winwood Corporation's capital purchases increase by 5% each year. Assume straight-line depreciation using a three-year life for financial reporting, and accelerated depreciation for tax purposes using 50%, 30%, and 20% for each succeeding year (these are not the real rates for MACRS depreciation, but they will highlight the purpose of this case). Finally, assume a tax rate of 30%. Following is an incomplete table for comparing depreciation and calculating deferred taxes.

		For Financial Reporting		For Income Taxes		
Year	Capital Purchases	Depreciation	Book Value	Depreciation	Book Value	Deferred Tax Liability
1	$150,000	$ 50,000	$100,000	$75,000	$75,000	$7,500
2	$157,500	$102,500	$155,000			

Required:

A. Create a spreadsheet to complete the preceding table for ten years. Depreciation and book value for each year is the total for all capital assets, not just the annual purchase.

B. What happens to the deferred tax liability over time? Is it ever "paid"?

C. Based upon this scenario, what arguments favor comprehensive tax allocation? partial tax allocation? Which approach regarding deferred taxes do you favor and why?

D. How would you incorporate present-value concepts regarding the deferred tax liability? Should discounting and the time value of money be a factor?

QUESTIONS

Q17–1 How do the objectives of determining taxable income differ from the objectives of financial reporting?

Q17–2 Describe in your own words an interpretation of a deferred tax liability and the events that would cause its recognition.

Q17–3 Describe in your own words an interpretation of a deferred tax asset and the events that would cause its recognition.

Q17–4 Chapter 2 distinguishes between accruals and deferrals. Are deferred tax assets and liabilities accruals or deferrals? Explain.

Q17–5 Distinguish between temporary and permanent differences.

Q17–6 Valuation adjustments may be necessary for deferred tax assets. Yet, valuation adjustments are *not* applied for deferred tax liabilities. What aspects of the conceptual framework would justify such an adjustment for assets but not for liabilities?

Q17–7 Explain how the effects of changes in tax rates and changes to valuation adjustments are treated like changes in estimates rather than prior-period adjustments or cumulative effects of accounting changes.

Q17–8 How would deferred taxes be reported (if at all) in the statement of cash flows?

Q17–9 Substantial increases to long-term liabilities for bonds payable, notes payable, or mortgages payable are frequently the result of cash inflows reported as part of financing operations in the statement of cash flows. Are increases to long-term deferred tax liabilities also a source of cash? Are such increases reported as part of financing operations in the statement of cash flows? Explain.

Q17–10 A company has a deferred tax liability for temporary differences due to depreciation of an asset. The asset has only one more year of depreciation left, so the temporary difference will reverse next year. How should the deferred tax liability be classified on the balance sheet?

Q17–11 Is it permitted to apply present-value concepts to discount deferred tax assets and liabilities? How would you do it if it were?

Q17–12 Based upon the concepts presented in this chapter, what effect do you think the use of the equity method for investments would have upon accounting for income taxes?

Q17–13 Distinguish between comprehensive and partial income tax allocation.

Q17–14 Distinguish net-of-tax presentations for deferred taxes from the current reporting requirements.

Q17–15 How are the undistributed earnings from foreign subsidiaries treated in accounting for income taxes? Do they result in deferred income tax liabilities? Should income taxes paid to the foreign governments for taxable income in those countries be included in reporting income tax expense for a period?

Q17–16 Briefly describe the income tax disclosure required for statutory rate reconciliation.

EXERCISES

E17–1 Income Tax Entries

Refer to Exhibits 17–6 through 17–8.

Required:

A. Assume the company maintains only a single account for deferred income taxes. Further assume that prepayments for income taxes have not been made. Prepare the income tax journal entry for each exhibit.

B. Assume the company maintains separate accounts for current and noncurrent deferred tax assets and liabilities. Further assume that prepayments for income taxes have not been made. Prepare the income tax journal entry for each exhibit.

E17–2 Deferred Tax Liabilities

Regional Inc. has taxable income for 1997 of $300,000, with an income tax rate of 30%. Its only temporary difference results in a year-end deferred tax liability of $25,000. This liability at the beginning of 1997 was $20,000.

Required: For 1997 determine income taxes currently payable, the deferred tax increase (reduction) to expense, and the income tax expense.

E17–3 Deferred Tax Liabilities

Regina Inc. has taxable income for 1997 of $3,500,000, with an income tax rate of 30%. Its only temporary difference results in a year-end deferred tax liability of $400,000. This liability at the beginning of 1997 was $500,000.

Required: For 1997 determine income taxes currently payable, the deferred tax increase (reduction) to expense, and the income tax expense.

E17–4 Deferred Tax Assets

Reginald Inc. has taxable income for 1997 of $200,000, with an income tax rate of 34%. Its only temporary difference results in a year-end deferred tax asset of $40,000 with no associated valuation allowance. This asset at the beginning of 1997 was $20,000.

Required: For 1997 determine income taxes currently payable, the deferred tax increase (reduction) to expense, and the income tax expense.

E17–5 Deferred Tax Assets

Nationwide Inc. has taxable income for 1997 of $55,000,000, with an income tax rate of 30%. Its only temporary difference results in a year-end deferred tax asset of $550,000 with no associated valuation allowance. This asset at the beginning of 1997 was $900,000.

Required: For 1997 determine income taxes currently payable, the deferred tax increase (reduction) to expense, and the income tax expense.

E17–6 Taxable Differences

Register Corporation has taxable income for 1997 of $3,300,000, with an income tax rate of 30%. The company has a year-end taxable difference of $900,000. At the beginning of 1997, the company had a deferred tax liability of $150,000.

Required: For 1997 determine income taxes currently payable, the deferred tax increase (reduction) to expense, and the income tax expense.

E17–7 Taxable Differences

National Register Corporation has pretax accounting income for 1997 of $1,200,000, with an income tax rate of 30%. The company has a year-end taxable difference of $700,000. This taxable difference increased $300,000 for the year 1997. The 1997 beginning deferred tax balance was also based upon a 30% rate.

Required: For 1997 determine taxable income, income taxes currently payable, the deferred tax increase (reduction) to expense, and the income tax expense.

E17–8 Deductible Differences

NatReg Inc. has taxable income for 1997 of $500,000, with an income tax rate of 34%. The company has a year-end deductible difference of $200,000. Only half of any deferred tax assets is expected to be realized. At the beginning of 1997, NatReg had deferred tax assets of $30,000 offset by a valuation allowance of $15,000.

Required: For 1997 determine income taxes currently payable, the deferred tax increase (reduction) to expense, and the income tax expense.

E17–9 Deductible Differences

Reggie Corp. has pretax accounting income for 1997 of $5,000,000, with an income tax rate of 34%. The company has a year-end deductible difference of $800,000. At the beginning of 1997, this deductible difference was $300,000 with deferred tax assets also based on a 34% tax rate. A valuation allowance is not deemed necessary.

Required: For 1997 determine taxable income, income taxes currently payable, the deferred tax increase (reduction) to expense, and the income tax expense.

E17–10 Taxable Differences

Randall Corporation has taxable income for 1997 of $60,000,000, with an income tax rate of 30%. The company has a year-end taxable difference of $12,000,000. At the beginning of 1997, the company had a deferred tax liability of $5,000,000.

Required: For 1997 determine income taxes currently payable, the deferred tax increase (reduction) to expense, and the income tax expense.

E17–11 Deductible Differences

Nathinger Inc. has taxable income for 1997 of $25,000,000, with an income tax rate of 34%. The company has a year-end deductible difference of $5,000,000. Only sixty percent of any deferred tax assets is expected to be realized. At the beginning of 1997, Nathinger had net deferred tax assets (after deducting a valuation allowance) of $2,000,000.

Required: For 1997 determine income taxes currently payable, the deferred tax increase (reduction) to expense, and the income tax expense.

E17–12 Intangible Assets

Grandice Corporation purchased another business on July 1, 1997, resulting in goodwill of $3,000,000. For financial reporting, the company elects to amortize goodwill over the maximum allowable period, 40 years. For federal income tax purposes, intangibles are amortized using a 15-year life.

Required: Assume pretax accounting income every year of $5,000,000 and an income tax rate of 30%. Prepare the adjusting entries for income taxes for 1997, 1998, and 2013 (the 17th year).

E17–13 Computing Deferred Taxes

Signal Corporation reported the following taxable and pretax accounting income:

	1997	1998	1999
Taxable income	$300,000	$400,000	$500,000
Pretax accounting income	340,000	410,000	450,000

All differences are attributable to the same type of temporary difference, and the company began 1997 without any deferred tax accounts. The tax rate for each year is 30%. If applicable, a valuation allowance is unnecessary.

Required:

A. For each year, determine the current taxes payable, the year-end deferred tax balance, indicating whether it is an asset or liability, the change to deferred taxes for the year, and the income tax expense.

B. Prepare an adjusting entry for income taxes for each year.

E17–14 Computing Deferred Taxes

Sign Post Corporation reported the following taxable and pretax accounting income:

	1997	1998	1999
Taxable income	$800,000	$700,000	$800,000
Pretax accounting income	700,000	650,000	950,000

All differences are attributable to the same type of temporary difference, and the company began 1997 without any deferred tax accounts. The tax rate for each year is 30%. If applicable, a valuation allowance is unecessary.

Required:

A. For each year, determine the current taxes payable, the year-end deferred tax balance, indicating whether it is an asset or liability, the change to deferred taxes for the year, and the income tax expense.

B. Prepare an adjusting entry for income taxes for each year.

E17–15 Permanent and Temporary Differences

Presented are condensed income statements of Tiggle Corporation for the last four years:

	1997	1998	1999	2000
Revenues	$600,000	$640,000	$720,000	$900,000
Expenses	(400,000)	(500,000)	(600,000)	(700,000)
Pretax accounting income	$200,000	$140,000	$120,000	$200,000

Expenses include premiums on life insurance for officers of $10,000 each year. These premiums are not allowable deductions for income tax purposes. At the beginning of 1997, Tiggle purchased new machinery at a cost of $280,000. The company uses straight-line depreciation for financial statement purposes and the sum-of-the-years'-digits method for tax purposes. The machinery has a useful life of four years, with no salvage value. There are no other differences between taxable income and pretax accounting income. The tax rate is 35%.

Required: For each year, determine

A. Taxable income.

B. Taxes currently payable.

C. Year-end deferred tax balance (indicate whether it is an asset or liability).

D. Deferred tax increase (reduction) to income tax expense.

E. Income tax expense.

E17–16 Permanent and Temporary Differences

Presented are condensed income statements of Toggle Corporation for the last four years:

	1997	1998	1999	2000
Revenues	$600,000	$640,000	$720,000	$900,000
Expenses	(420,000)	(480,000)	(580,000)	(740,000)
Pretax accounting income	$180,000	$160,000	$140,000	$160,000

Revenues include nontaxable interest received on municipals bonds of $40,000 each year. On September 1, 1997, Toggle rented part of its office space for three years with yearly rental of $150,000 collectible in advance each year. This amount was collected on September 1 of each year of the rental period. The company properly reported unearned rent revenue on its balance sheets at the end of 1997, 1998, and 1999. However, the company reports taxable income for this revenue in the year collected. There are no other differences between taxable income and pretax accounting income, and if applicable, a valuation allowance is unnecessary. The tax rate is 30%.

Required: For each year, determine

A. Taxable income.
B. Taxes currently payable.
C. Year-end deferred tax balance (indicate whether it is an asset or liability).
D. Deferred tax increase (reduction) to income tax expense.
E. Income tax expense.

E17–17 Net Operating Losses

Ann Marie Company reported the following earnings (loss) before income taxes for its first three years of operations:

1997	1998	1999
$30,000	$(120,000)	$70,000

For these three years, the tax rate was 34%, and there were no temporary differences. The company elects to carry back whenever possible. Sufficient evidence exists to suggest that the company will be profitable over the next several years.

Required: For each year, determine

A. Taxable income (loss).
B. Taxes currently payable (refundable).
C. Year-end deferred tax balance (indicate whether it is an asset or liability).
D. Deferred tax increase (reduction) to income tax expense (benefit).
E. Income tax expense (benefit).
F. Net income (loss).

E17–18 Net Operating Losses

MaryAnne Company reported the following earnings (loss) before income taxes for its first three years of operations:

1997	1998	1999
$50,000	$(150,000)	$20,000

For these three years, the tax rate was 30% and there were no temporary differences. The company elects to carry back whenever possible. Based upon available evidence, the company estimated that a valuation allowance for 50% of any NOL carryforwards is required.

Required: For each year, determine

A. Taxable income (loss).
B. Taxes currently (payable) refundable.
C. Year-end deferred tax balance (indicate whether it is an asset or liability).
D. Deferred tax increase (reduction) to income tax expense (benefit).
E. Income tax expense (benefit).
F. Net income (loss).

E17–19 Tax Credit Carryforwards

Agassi Corporation had taxable income in 1997 of $50,000 and is entitled to a tax credit of $20,000. The tax rate is 35%. Evidence indicates that the company is likely to have substantial taxable income over the next few years. There are no temporary differences.

Required: Determine the taxes currently payable, any year-end deferred tax asset, the deferred tax increase (reduction), and income tax expense (benefit).

E17–20 Tax Credit Carryforwards

Sampras Corporation had taxable income in 1997 of $200,000 and is entitled to a tax credit of $100,000. The tax rate is 30%. Evidence indicates that the company is likely to have substantial taxable income over the next few years. There are no temporary differences.

Required: Determine the taxes currently payable, any year-end deferred tax asset, the deferred tax increase (reduction), and income tax expense (benefit).

E17–21 Classification of Valuation Allowance

Adele Company has preliminary current and noncurrent deferred tax assets of $20,000 and $80,000, respectively. All of the current assets are expected to be realized, but only three-fourths of the noncurrent assets are expected to be realized.

Required: Determine the amount of the valuation allowance and the reported amounts for both current and noncurrent deferred tax assets.

E17–22 Classification of Valuation Allowance

Bandele Company has preliminary current and noncurrent deferred tax assets of $120,000 and $80,000, respectively. All of the current assets are expected to be realized, but only one-half of the noncurrent assets are expected to be realized.

Required: Determine the amount of the valuation allowance and the reported amounts for both current and noncurrent deferred tax assets.

E17–23 Accounting Changes

Imagine that in the year 2010, Switchover company changed from the previously accepted method of accounting for deferred income taxes to the method prescribed by a recent accounting pronouncement. Under the new method, deferred income tax liabilities for estimated future income taxes payable are higher than the previous method. Had the company been using the new method all along, it would have reported higher income tax expenses in previous years. A comparison of the company's liabilities under the previous and current methods follows:

DEFERRED TAX LIABILITY	PREVIOUS METHOD	CURRENT METHOD
1/1/10	$35,000	$50,000
12/31/10	45,000	75,000

Taxable income for 2010 is $100,000, and the tax rate is 35%.

Required:

A. Indicate how the accounting change would be reported.

B. Determine the income taxes currently payable, the deferred tax increase (reduction) to income tax expense, and the income tax expense for 2010.

E17–24 Deferred Taxes and Cash Flows

The following selected information is from Jinder Corporation's 1997 annual report.

BALANCE SHEET

	12/31/97	12/31/96
Current liabilities:		
Income taxes payable	$350,000	$500,000
Long-term liabilities:		
Deferred income taxes	600,000	550,000

INCOME STATEMENT

	1997	1996
Income from continuing operations before income taxes	$999,000	$888,000
Provision for income taxes	(299,000)	(288,000)
Income from continuing operations	$700,000	$600,000
Loss from discontinued operations (net of income tax reductions of $30,000 and $20,000, respectively)	(100,000)	(90,000)
Net income	$600,000	$510,000

Required:

A. Determine the cash paid for income taxes in 1997.

B. Demonstrate how income taxes would be reported on a statement of cash flows using the indirect method.

E17–25 Deferred Taxes and Trading Securities

Investiture Company first purchased trading securities in 1997. The respective cost and fair value of its portfolio of trading securities on December 31, 1997, were $200,000 and $250,000. The respective cost and fair value on December 31, 1998 were $300,000 and $330,000. The income tax rate is 30%.

Required: For each year and year-end, determine amounts, if any, of deferred tax expense (benefit) and deferred tax assets (liabilities) to report in the company's financial statements.

E17–26 Deferred Taxes and Trading Securities

Windfall Company first purchased trading securities in 1997. The respective cost and fair value of its portfolio of trading securities on December 31, 1997, were $200,000 and $180,000. The respective cost and fair value on December 31, 1998 were $300,000 and $310,000. The income tax rate is 30%.

Required: For each year and year-end, determine amounts, if any, of deferred tax expense (benefit) and deferred tax assets (liabilities) to report in the company's financial statements.

PROBLEMS

P17–1 Income Tax Entries

Most businesses make periodic estimated payments for income taxes. Harold's Shops, Inc., made estimated quarterly income tax payments of $100,000 each on the 15th of April, June, and September of 1997, and on January 15, 1998. The books for 1997 are completed on February 15, 1998, with final adjusting entries prepared. Income tax expense for 1997 was $500,000, and deferred tax liabilities increased during 1997 by $120,000. Any remaining income taxes due for 1997 were paid when the corporate income tax return was filed on April 15, 1998.

Required: The chapter did not explicitly address estimated payments. Use logic and your understanding of the conceptual framework to complete this problem.

A. Prepare all necessary journal entries.

B. Prepare all entries assuming the $120,000 was a reduction rather than increase to deferred tax liabilities.

P17–2 Multiple Temporary Differences

Unicard Corporation's tax returns disclosed the following:

YEAR	TAXABLE INCOME
1997	$10,000,000
1998	15,000,000
1999	14,000,000
2000	20,000,000

Additional Information:

1. Trade accounts receivable at the end of the years 1996 through 2000 were $8,000,000, $9,000,000, $11,000,000, $7,000,000, and $5,000,000, respectively. These are taxable when collected.
2. Unicard signed a five-year operating lease on July 1, 1997. In complying with the lease, the company made annual lease payments of $4,000,000 every July 1. Payments are deductible on tax returns in the year paid.
3. Equipment costing $25,000,000 was purchased in the beginning of 1997. The company uses straight-line depreciation, with a five-year useful life and no salvage value on the financial statements. It uses accelerated depreciation for five-year property on its tax return. The appropriate percentages (rounded to the nearest percent to simplify the problem) of cost for each successive year are 20%, 32%, 19%, and 12%. (Note: A half-year convention is applied for depreciation on tax returns in the year of acquisition. So even though accelerated depreciation is used, 20% rather than 40% is used for the first year.)
4. The tax rate for each year is 30%.

Required:

A. Determine deferred tax balances for each year-end.
B. Determine income tax expense for each year.
C. Assume the tax rate changed in 1999 to 35%, effective with the 1999 tax year. Repeat (A) and (B).

P17–3 Multiple Temporary Differences

Multicard Corporation's tax returns disclosed the following:

YEAR	TAXABLE INCOME
1997	$12,000,000
1998	14,000,000
1999	15,000,000

Additional Information:

1. On July 1, 1997, the company purchased a copyright for $6,000,000. For financial reporting, the copyright is amortized over three years. For tax purposes, the useful life for intangibles is 15 years. For both financial reporting and tax purposes, half-year amortization was taken in 1997.
2. Equipment costing $12,000,000 was purchased in the beginning of 1997. The company uses straight-line depreciation, with a five-year useful life and no salvage value on the financial statements. It uses accelerated depreciation for three-year property on its tax return. Assume the appropriate percentages of cost for each successive year are 30%, 40%, and 15%. (NOTE: These are not precisely the percentages, but they appropriately illustrate the use of percentages for income tax depreciation.)
3. The tax rate for each year is 30%.

Required:

A. Determine deferred tax balances for each year-end.
B. Determine income tax expense for each year.
C. Assume the tax rate changed in 1999 to 35%, effective with the 1999 tax year. Repeat (A) and (B) for 1999 only.

P17–4 Computing Deferred Taxes

An incomplete table for computing deferred taxes for 1997 is shown. The temporary differences in this table result from

1. Payment in advance for an insurance policy. At year-end, there are two more years left on the policy. Payments are deductible from taxable income when paid.
2. Straight-line depreciation for financial reporting and accelerated depreciation for income tax purposes.
3. Regarding investments, use of the equity method for financial reporting increases the investment for undistributed earnings of investee. Earnings are taxable, however, when dividends are received (assume they are taxable in full for this problem).
4. Advances are for prepayments by customers for special orders that will be complete and shipped next year. These are taxable in the year payments are received.

   The company expects to recognize all of the benefits for current deferred tax assets but establishes a valuation allowance for 25% of all noncurrent deferred tax assets.

Required: Complete the deferred-tax table.

TEMPORARY DIFFERENCE OR CARRYFORWARD	BALANCE SHEET AMOUNTS: BOOK	TAX	DIFFERENCE	TAXABLE DIFFERENCE: DEFERRED TAX LIABILITY: CURRENT	NONCURRENT	DEDUCTIBLE DIFFERENCE: DEFERRED TAX ASSET: CURRENT	NONCURRENT
Assets:							
1. Prepaid insurance	$150,000	$ 0					
2. Fixed assets (net)	500,000	300,000					
3. Investments	200,000	50,000					
Liabilities:							
4. Advances from customers	140,000	0					
Other Items:							
Tax loss carryforward							$60,000
Totals							
Effective tax rate (34%)				0.34	0.34	0.34	0.34
Preliminary deferred tax balance							
Less valuation reserve							
Deferred tax balance at year-end							
Deferred tax balance at beginning of year				$ 0	$50,000	$ 0	$20,000
Deferred tax increase (reduction) to income tax expense							
Net increase (reduction) to income tax expense							

Balance Sheet Reporting

Current deferred tax asset	
Current deferred tax liability	
Net Current Deferred Tax Asset (Liability)	
Noncurrent deferred tax asset	
Noncurrent deferred tax liability	
Net Noncurrent Deferred Tax Asset (Liability)	

P17–5 Computing Deferred Taxes

An incomplete table for computing deferred taxes for 1997 is shown. For financial reporting, purchases add to inventory available when purchased rather than when paid. For tax purposes, payments made for inventory add to inventory available. Since ending inventory is the same for both financial reporting and tax purposes, the expense and deduction for cost of goods sold differ by the difference between purchases and payments for purchases. This is reflected as a temporary difference related to accounts payable. Sufficient evidence exists that a valuation allowance for deferred tax assets is not required.

Required: Complete the deferred-tax table.

TEMPORARY DIFFERENCE OR CARRYFORWARD	BALANCE SHEET AMOUNTS BOOK	TAX	DIFFERENCE	TAXABLE DIFFERENCE: DEFERRED TAX LIABILITY CURRENT	NONCURRENT	DEDUCTIBLE DIFFERENCE: DEFERRED TAX ASSET CURRENT	NONCURRENT
Assets:							
1. Accounts receivable	$300,000	$ 0					
2. Fixed assets (net)	900,000	700,000					
Liabilities:							
3. Accounts payable	400,000	0					
Other Items:							
Tax loss carryforward							$20,000
Totals							
Effective tax rate (30%)				0.30	0.30	0.30	0.30
Deferred tax balance at year-end							
Deferred tax balance at beginning of year				$120,000	$100,000	$70,000	$10,000
Deferred tax increase (reduction) to income tax expense							
Net increase (reduction) to income tax expense							

Balance Sheet Reporting

Current deferred tax asset	______
Current deferred tax liability	______
Net Current Deferred Tax Asset (Liability)	______
Noncurrent deferred tax asset	______
Noncurrent deferred tax liability	______
Net Noncurrent Deferred Tax Asset (Liability)	______

P17–6 Net Operating Losses

Alexander Company has the following earnings (loss) before income taxes over the last eight years.

1994	$ 45,000
1995	20,000
1996	10,000
1997	(30,000)
1998	(140,000)
1999	20,000
2000	40,000
2001	80,000

For each year, the tax rate was 34%, and there were no temporary differences. The company elects to carry back whenever possible. Sufficient evidence exists to suggest that the company will remain profitable from the year 2002 and beyond.

Required: For each year from 1997 through 2001, determine

A. Taxable income (loss).

B. Taxes currently payable (refundable).

C. NOL carryforward.
D. Year-end deferred tax balance (indicate whether it is an asset or liability).
E. Deferred tax increase (reduction) to income tax expense (benefit).
F. Income tax expense (benefit).
G. Net income (loss).

P17–7 NOL Loss Carryforwards

Assume the same facts as in P17–6 except that the tax rate changed in 2000, effective with the year 2000, to 30%.

Required: For each year, from 1997 through 2001, determine

A. Taxable income (loss).
B. Taxes currently payable (refundable).
C. NOL carryforward.
D. Year-end deferred tax balance (indicate whether it is an asset or liability).
E. Deferred tax increase (reduction) to income tax expense (benefit).
F. Income tax expense (benefit).
G. Net income (loss).

P17–8 Valuation Allowances

Assume the same facts as in P17–6, but not in P17–7, except for the following: Up to and including the end of 1999, significant uncertainties existed regarding the realization of any deferred tax assets. Management therefore estimated that only one-third of any such potential assets would be realized. However, by the end of 2000, sufficient evidence existed regarding the company's future profitability and realization of deferred tax assets such that a valuation allowance was no longer necessary.

Required: For each year, from 1997 through 2001, determine

A. Taxable income (loss).
B. Taxes currently payable (refundable).
C. NOL carryforward.
D. Potential year-end deferred tax asset, valuation allowance, and net deferred tax asset balance.
E. Deferred tax increase (reduction) to income tax expense (benefit).
F. Income tax expense (benefit).
G. Net income (loss).

P17–9 Investments and Income Taxes

U.S. corporations are *not* required to pay federal income taxes on most of the dividends received from investments in other U.S. corporations. This dividend exclusion attempts to minimize double taxation and is a permanent difference between financial and tax reporting. Assume here that 85% of such dividends are nontaxable.

Dimitri Corporation received $120,000 from Jones Corporation for dividends declared and paid in 1997. Both are U.S. corporations. Dimitri owns less than 20% of the outstanding stock of Jones, and there was no change in the market value of Jones stock for the year. Dimitri's pretax accounting income was $700,000 (including income from the investment), and the applicable income tax rate is 30%. Accounting for the investment is the only difference between Dimitri's financial and tax reporting.

Required:

A. Prepare the entry for Dimitri's 1997 income taxes assuming no prepayments.

B. Assume the $120,000 in dividends were from Dimitri's 40% investment in Jones. Net income for Jones in 1997 was $500,000. Dimitri's pretax accounting income was still $700,000. Prepare Dimitri's income tax adjusting entry. Show schedules to support your computations.

P17–10 Deferred Taxes and Pensions

Clear Sky Company has the following information related to its pension plan, effective January 1, 1997:

Projected benefit obligation	$6,000,000
Accumulated benefit obligation	4,000,000
Market value of plan assets	5,000,000
Unamortized prior service costs	300,000
Accrued pension costs (a liability)	150,000
Deferred tax asset	45,000

The effective interest rate for benefit obligations, expected return on plan assets, and actual return on plan assets is 10%. Prior service costs originally totaled $500,000 and are being amortized over 20 years. For 1997, service costs were $700,000, and Clear Sky contributed $755,000 to the pension fund.

The deferred tax asset is based on a $150,000 deductible difference. The difference resulted because deductions for pensions on the tax return are on a cash basis for employer cash payments to the pension fund. For tax purposes, then, prepaid/accrued pension costs are $0. (Note: These facts are not based on actual tax laws, but pretend they are.) Clear Sky expects to realize all benefits from deferred tax assets, so a valuation allowance is unnecessary.

For financial reporting, pretax accounting income for 1997 was $3,000,000. The appropriate income tax rate for all years is 30%.

Required:

A. Determine the following related to the pension plan:
   1. Pension expense for 1997
   2. Projected benefit obligation (12/31/97)—Assume $0 benefit payments to retirees.
   3. Accrued pension costs (12/31/97)

B. Determine the following related to Deferred income taxes for 1997:
   1. Taxable income
   2. Income taxes currently payable
   3. Year-end deductible difference
   4. Year-end deferred tax asset
   5. Deferred tax increase (reduction) to income tax expense
   6. Income tax expense

P17–11 Permanent and Temporary Differences

At the end of 1996, Revolving Door Company had a deferred tax liability of $64,000 based upon a taxable difference of $200,000 at a 32% income tax rate. This difference resulted from depreciation on fixed assets which cost $1,000,000. For financial reporting, accumulated depreciation for these assets was $200,000 based upon a 10-year useful life and no salvage value. For income tax purposes, the company had deducted a total of

$400,000 for depreciation on these assets based upon applicable accelerated depreciation percentages.

Revolving Door Company had pretax accounting income of $5,000,000 and $8,000,000 for 1997 and 1998, respectively. Included in the determination of this income was the depreciation on the above fixed assets and nontaxable interest revenue from municipal bonds of $50,000 each year.

For depreciation on the income tax returns, respective depreciation percentages are 15% and 8% for 1997 and 1998. These percentages are applied to the cost of the assets to determine depreciation deductions each year. Effective for 1997 and subsequent years, the enacted income tax rate changed to 30%.

Required: For both 1997 and 1998, determine

A. Taxable income
B. Income taxes currently payable
C. Year-end deferred tax liability
D. Deferred tax increase (reduction) to income tax expense
E. Income Tax Expense

P17–12 Income Taxes (CPA Adapted, Practice I, MC#27, November 1992)
For the year ended December 31, 1997, Mont Company's books showed income of $600,000 before provision for income tax expense. To compute taxable income for federal income tax purposes, the following items should be noted:

Income from tax-exempt municipal bonds	$ 60,000
Depreciation deducted for tax purposes in excess of depreciation recorded on the books	120,000
Nontaxable proceeds received from life insurance on death of officer	100,000
Estimated tax payments	0
Enacted corporate tax rate	30%

Required: Determine

A. Taxable income for 1997.
B. Current federal income tax liability on December 31, 1997.
C. Changes in 1997 to deferred tax assets and liabilities.
D. Income tax expense for 1997.

P17–13 Long-Term Liabilities (CPA Adapted, Practice I, No. 5, May 1992)
The following is the "long-term liabilities" section of Tempo Company's December 31, 1996, balance sheet:

Long-Term Liabilities:		
Note payable—bank; 15 principal payments of $5,000, plus 10% interest due annually on September 30	$75,000	
Less current portion	5,000	$ 70,000
Capital lease obligation—16 payments of $9,000 due annually on January 1	$76,600	
Less current portion	1,340	$ 75,260
Deferred income tax liability		15,750
Total long-term liabilities		$161,010

Additional Information:

1. Tempo's incremental borrowing rate on the date of the lease was 11%, and the lessor's implicit rate, which was known by Tempo, was 10%.
2. The only difference between Tempo's taxable income and pretax accounting income is depreciation on a machine acquired on January 1, 1996, for $250,000. The machine's estimated useful life is five years, with no salvage value. Depreciation is computed using the straight-line method for financial reporting purposes and the MACRS method for tax purposes. Depreciation expense for tax and financial reporting purposes for 1997 is $80,000 and $50,000, respectively.
3. For the year ended December 31, 1997, Tempo's income before income taxes was $430,000. The enacted federal income tax rate is 30%.
4. On July 1, 1997, Tempo received proceeds of $459,725 from a $500,000 bond issuance. The bonds mature in 30 years, and interest of 11% is payable each January 1 and July 1. The bonds were issued at a price to yield the investors 12%. For both financial and income tax reporting, Tempo uses the effective-interest method to amortize the bond discount.

Required:

A. Prepare a schedule showing Tempo's income before income taxes, current income tax expense, deferred income tax expense, and net income. Show supporting calculations for current and deferred income tax amounts.

B. Prepare a schedule showing the calculation of Tempo's interest expense for the year ended December 31, 1997.

C. Prepare the "long-term liabilities" section of Tempo's December 31, 1997, balance sheet. Show supporting calculations.

P17–14 Deferred Income Taxes

Enter the following information in the template and follow the instructions found there.

For 1997, North-South Company reports book net income before income tax expense of $500,000. Considered in arriving at this number were straight-line depreciation expense of $12,000 (sum-of-years'-digits depreciation of $16,000 was recognized for tax purposes), installment sales revenue of $20,000 ($5,000 of which was collected and recognized for tax purposes), and $10,000 in rental income collected in advance and earned in 1997 ($50,000 in rental income was collected in advance in 1997, including the $10,000, all of which was recognized for tax purposes).

The depreciation expense difference results from a depreciable item of equipment purchased on January 1, 1996, at a cost of $60,000, with an estimated useful life of five years and no estimated salvage value. It is being depreciated on a straight-line basis for book purposes and a sum-of-years'-digits basis for tax purposes. Thus, the reported balance sheet basis for net fixed assets at December 31, 1996 (last year), was $48,000 for financial reporting (book) purposes and $40,000 for tax reporting purposes, an $8,000 difference in net book value. Because the effective tax rate is 40%, a deferred tax liability of $3,200 existed at the beginning of this year. (Recommendation: Verify these numbers!)

This is the first year installment sales have been made. The Installment Receivables total of $15,000 on the books is classified as a current asset because it is expected to be collected in total next year. This is also the first year rent has been collected in advance. The $40,000 in Unearned Rent Revenue at the end of 1997 is classified as follows: $30,000 as a current liability because it will be earned in 1998; $10,000 as a noncurrent liability because it will be earned in 1999. Management has decided that no valuation allowance for deferred tax assets will be necessary at the end of 1997.

Required: Determine the following for North-South Company:

A. The book and tax bases, and resulting differences, at December 31, 1997, for each of the above items.
B. Taxable differences, and whether they will result in current or noncurrent deferred tax liabilities as of the same date.
C. Deductible differences, and whether they will result in current or noncurrent deferred tax assets as of the same date.
D. Income tax currently payable.
E. Deferred tax account balances, and classifications, at December 31, 1997.
F. Income tax expense for 1997.

RESEARCH ACTIVITIES

R17–1 Financial Analysis—Income Tax Disclosures

Examine a recent annual report for some well-known corporation. Based upon your examination, prepare an analysis of the impact of income taxes on the company's financial position and operations. Use as a guide the analysis for the companies at the end of this chapter.

R17–2 Financial Analysis—Domestic Versus Foreign Income Taxes

Examine a recent annual report for some well-known international corporation. Based upon your examination, prepare an analysis comparing domestic and foreign components of earnings and income taxes.

R17–3 GAAP Research—Interim Reporting

Prepare a memorandum to a client that outlines the reporting requirements for income taxes on quarterly (interim) reports. Start your research by examining SFAS No. 109.

R17–4 GAAP Research—Valuation Adjustments

Based upon the contents of SFAS No. 109, prepare a memorandum to a client that summarizes the types of positive and negative evidence to consider when making a judgment regarding the necessity of a valuation adjustment for deferred tax assets.

R17–5 Financial Analysis—Motorola

Examine Motorola's Annual Report provided in Appendix C.

Required: Reconcile the income tax related elements of Motorola's balance sheet with the significant deferred tax assets (liabilities) reported in the company's notes accompanying the financial statements. What amount is reported as a December 31, 1995, liability for deferred income taxes? Can you identify the significant components of this liability in the footnote?

R17–6 Financial Research—Deferred Tax Liabilities

Examine a computerized database such as the one that accompanies this text, and find the firms who report a separate classification for deferred income taxes in the liability section of their balance sheets. What proportion are these number of firms to the total number of firms in the database? What is the average amount of the reported deferred income tax liability for these firms?

R17–7 Financial Research—Accounting Changes

Examine a computerized database such as the one that accompanies this text, and find the firms who reported a *gain* (i.e., an increase to earnings) for a cumulative effect of an accounting change for either 1992 or 1993. For which of these companies is the gain due to the adoption of SFAS No. 109, "Accounting for Income Taxes"?

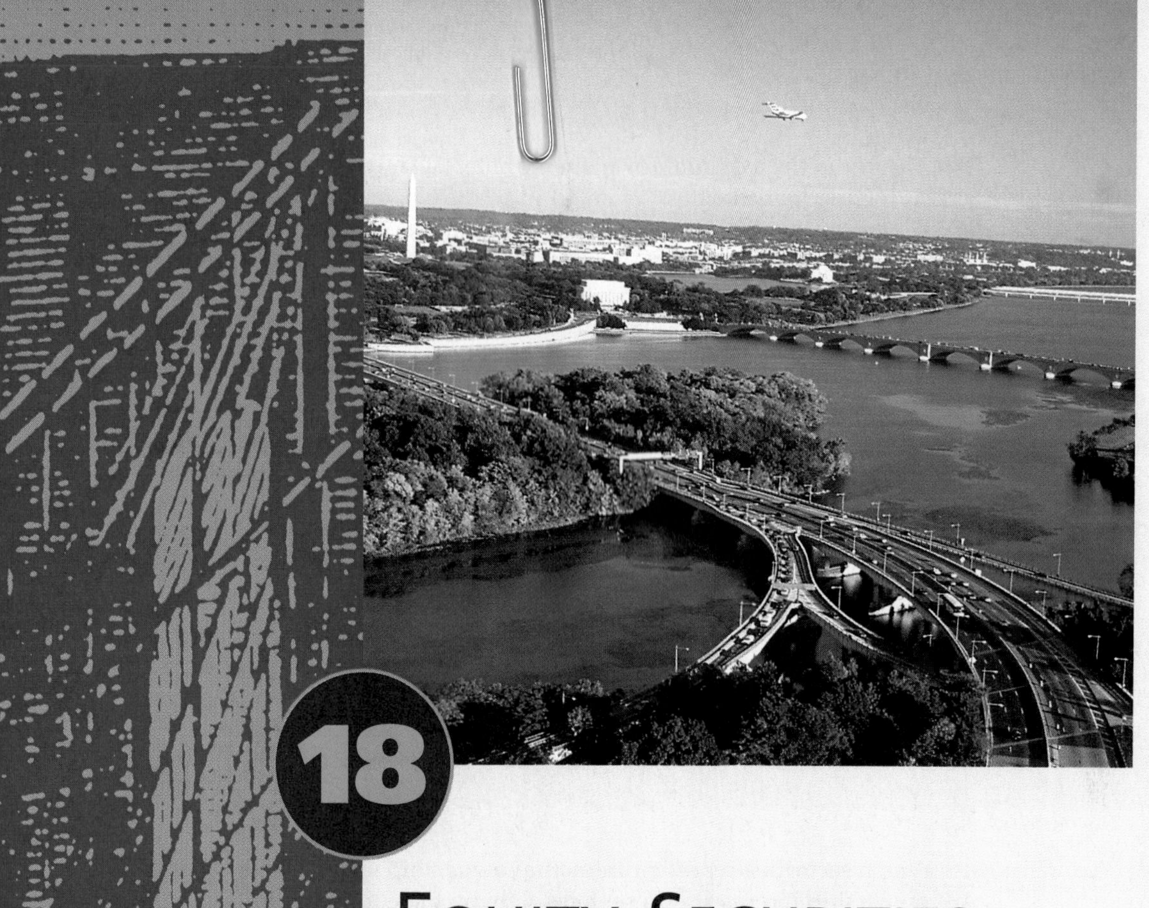

18

Equity Securities

Learning Objectives

After studying this chapter, you should be able to:

1. Record the issuance of capital stock.
2. Interpret the features of different types of preferred stock.
3. Evaluate and record transactions for other equity securities and adjustments, such as those for options, warrants, and stock subscriptions.
4. Interpret supplemental disclosures related to equity.
5. Prepare and analyze key profitability and solvency ratios that use equity information.

Equity is the residual (or owners') interest in enterprise assets after deducting its liabilities. As noted in SFAC No. 6, equity is a basic component of financial statements. Understanding the complexities involved with ownership interests (equity) of financial instruments issued by corporations is a nontrivial exercise.

Debt or Equity?

An article appearing in *Forbes* "laments the parade of new financial instruments Wall Street brings out. Many of these behave like both common stock and debt. 'The distinction between debt and equity has become so muddied that the accounting rules seem more arbitrary than ever,' says Wayne Kolins, national director of accounting and auditing for ***Seidman & Seidman.***" A more detailed discussion of complex financial instruments is presented in the FASB's Discussion Memorandum entitled "Distinguishing between Liability and Equity Instruments with Characteristics of Both" (1990).

Source: R. Greene, "What, and Whose, Bottom Line?" *Forbes,* Oct. 7, 1988, p. 101.

Which securities represent the actual ownership interests of a corporation? Are ownership interests represented solely by the equity interests of common shareholders? Should the interests of shareholders of preferred stock be included as owners' equity? Should the interests of those who hold options granting the right to obtain common stock be included as ownership interests? What about the potential common stock ownership interests of debt holders with conversion rights?

This chapter discusses various types of corporate equity securities. Recall that Chapter 3 first introduced the corporate form of business and the reporting of shareholders' equity. In this chapter, we expand on this introduction and begin with accounting for the issuance of capital stock. Retained earnings and distributions to shareholders are discussed in the next chapter.

STOCK ISSUANCE

Record the issuance of capital stock.

Exhibit 18–1 provides several examples of the issuance of capital stock. Part A of the exhibit demonstrates the traditional approach, using a separate classification (that is, account) for the par value or stated value of the stock. Additional Paid-In Capital frequently is shown simply as Paid-In Capital; other account names used include Capital in Excess of Par, Premium on Common Stock, and Capital Surplus (to imply a "surplus" contributed in excess of a legal capital amount). The profession does not recommend the latter two because they inappropriately imply "extra" value.

Part B of Exhibit 18–1 illustrates the use of a single equity account (Common Stock) to record the entire proceeds of a stock issue. Companies whose capital stock is designated as no-par, meaning it has no designated stated or legal value, would record their stock issuance in this manner. Many companies whose stock has a par or stated value also elect to use this method of reporting instead of splitting the proceeds between the par or stated value and additional paid-in

EXHIBIT 18–1
Issuance of Capital Stock

A. **Classification for Par or Stated Value:**
Issued 100,000 shares of $1 par (or stated) value common stock for $25 per share

Cash	2,500,000	
Common Stock		100,000
Additional Paid-In Capital		2,400,000

B. **No Classification for Par or Stated Value:**
For a company with no-par stock without a stated value, or for a company which has par or stated value stock but merely *elects* not to report a separate classification for it.

Issued 100,000 shares of common stock for $25 per share

Cash	2,500,000	
Common Stock		2,500,000

C. **Stock Issued for Other Than Cash:**
Generally, value the transaction at the market value of the assets or services rendered in conjunction with the issuance or at the market value of the stock issued, whichever is more clearly determinable.

1. Issued 500 shares of $0.50 par value common stock for land appraised at $4,000—using a classification for par

Land	4,000	
Common Stock		250
Additional Paid-In Capital		3,750

2. Issued 300 shares of $10 par common stock for legal services when the market value of the stock was $30 per share—electing no classification for par

Expense for Legal Services	9,000	
Common Stock		9,000

D. **Preferred Stock:**
Typically, maintain a separate preferred stock account (as distinguished from common stock); like common stock, classification by par or stated value (when one exists) is traditional but optional.

Issued 20,000 shares of $100 par preferred stock for $200 per share

Cash	4,000,000	
Preferred Stock		2,000,000
Additional Paid-In Capital		2,000,000

capital amounts.[1] For example, ***Walt Disney Company*** (*www.disney.com*) reports a single amount totaling $1,226.3 million in its September 30, 1995, balance sheet as equity for its 575.4 million shares issued of $0.025 par common stock.[2]

[1]This statement presumes the companies' state laws permit such reporting practice.
[2]To view Walt Disney's reported shareholders' equity, see Exhibit 3–6 in Chapter 3.

IN PRACTICE—INTERNATIONAL

Privatization

Many Eastern European and former Soviet countries have undertaken a process coined as privatization. Essentially, government-owned operations become private enterprises. Accordingly, these enterprises issue capital stock to become established, and stock markets within these countries develop for trading securities. Frequently, citizens are given vouchers which can be used to "buy" stock in privatized companies. Further, capital from outside investors is generally encouraged.

For example, the following excerpt addresses investment opportunities in Russia:

Over 4,000 large and medium companies have been privatized over the past year; virtually all of them need capital and Western technology. Some 400 stocks are now quoted on Russia's 70 or so stock exchanges. . . .

Investor beware: Russia is the ultimate in emerging markets. The stock markets are totally unregulated. Companies publish virtually no financial statements. Equities trading is unregulated, and it's hard to get reliable price quotes. . . . And once you have bought the shares, it is a struggle even to get your name down in the shareholders' register.

Source: P. Klebnikov, "Go East, Young Man," *Forbes,* December 20, 1993, pp. 102–106.

The subdivision of this equity into common stock of $14.4 million (i.e., 575.4 million shares × $0.025 par value) and paid-in capital of $1,211.9 million is disclosed in the company's footnotes.

Part C of Exhibit 18–1 illustrates the issuance of stock for nonmonetary assets or services. As with any other nonmonetary exchange, the general principle is to record the transaction at the fair market value of the asset or service exchanged. The fair market value is based on stock market prices, appraisal values, dealer list prices, or other currently available information. Thus, either the fair value of the assets received or the market value of the stock issued, whichever is more clearly determinable, provides the basis for valuation.

ISSUE COSTS

Corporations generally contract with service agencies called *underwriters* to perform administrative functions of selling or issuing stock to investors. A percentage of the proceeds from issuing stock is normally retained as a fee by the underwriters. Other typical costs associated with a stock issue include legal fees, registration fees with the SEC, and printing costs. Most companies elect to deduct all issue costs from the proceeds of the stock issuance and report the net proceeds as contributed capital.

Alternatively, companies may record contributed capital as the total price of the stock issued. Any issue costs that are not material would be expensed in the period the stock is issued. Issue costs that are material may be capitalized as an intangible asset, and allocated to expense (that is, amortized) over some estimated useful life. Conceptually, transactions limited to equity interest represent changes to contributed capital, not increases or decreases to earnings. So the preference of the authors is to treat issue costs as reductions to contributed capital (that is, recording net proceeds).

PREFERRED STOCK

2 Interpret the features of different types of preferred stock.

Another type (or class) of capital stock is called **preferred stock.** As its name implies, preferred stock possesses "preferential" rights relative to common stock. There are many different types of preferential rights, but these typically relate to dividend distributions and resource distributions in the event of liquidation. Preferred shareholders usually have no voting rights, however, in the management of the corporation. Different types of preferred stock are described in this section, and the various types of distributional preferences are discussed in the next chapter.

IN PRACTICE—GENERAL

Preferred Stock

The following is an excerpt from *Management Accounting* concerning preferred stock:

> The 1980s witnessed two major changes in the market for preferred stock. First, a number of new types have been introduced since 1982, including a variety of adjustable-rate, variable-rate, and auction-rate preferred stock—accounting for approximately 20% of all new issues.
>
> Second, there has been a major shift in industry participation among firms issuing preferred stock. Industrials accounted for 60% and financials for 30% of all preferred-stock issues during the period from 1981 through 1987. This stands in sharp contrast to earlier periods in which the utility industry dominated this market.

Primarily, the "new types" of preferred stock allow the rate that determines dividend amounts to be periodically adjusted to reflect changes in other economic interest rates. This varying rate is consistent with many of today's long-term debt agreements where interest rates are periodically adjusted.

Based upon executives' survey responses, the article also notes that "the most common use of preferred stock was to facilitate merger activity." For example, when acquiring a subsidiary, the acquiring company can issue its preferred stock instead of common as part of the purchase price to shareholders of the subsidiary company. Presumably, the recipients of the preferred stock receive a less risky investment than do recipients of common stock. The acquiring company does not incur substantial debt for the acquisition, nor are its existing shareholders' interests diluted.

Source: A. L. Houston and C. O. Houston, "The Changing Use of Preferred Stock," *Management Accounting,* December 1991, pp. 47 and 49.

Preferred stock combines some of the features of debt and common stock. Like debt, its dividend preference practically assures a relatively fixed return, and preferred shareholders have priority over common shareholders upon liquidation. However, interest on debt is an expense reducing income and is deductible for income tax purposes, while dividends on preferred stock do not reduce income and are not deductible for income taxes. Further, like common stock, the equity of preferred shareholders is a residual interest subordinate to debt.

Most corporations use a separate account for each class of stock. Thus, as depicted in part D of Exhibit 18–1, a preferred stock account is traditionally credited for its par value (assuming one exists) when preferred stock is issued. Like common stock, a corporation may elect to distinguish or not to distinguish between par (or stated) value and additional paid-in capital. Further, when classifying by par value, companies may maintain separate additional paid-in capital accounts for various classes of stock and other sources of capital, or they may report only a single additional paid-in capital amount, thereby blurring any distinction between additional paid-in capital from different sources. For example, ***Harcourt General*** (see Exhibit 18–2) has three classes of stock but reports one paid-in capital amount for all three classes combined.

Many corporations have more than one class of preferred stock, with different classes having different types of preferences. As an extreme example, the stock quotes in *The Wall Street Journal* list separately the prices of nine different classes of preferred stock for the ***Georgia Power Company***.[3] A few corporations

EXHIBIT 18–2 Shareholders' Equity with Different Classes of Stock

HARCOURT GENERAL, INC. & SUBSIDIARIES

October 31	1995	1994
Shareholders' Equity (In Thousands)		
Preferred stock		
Series A cumulative convertible—$1 par value		
Issued and outstanding—1,210 and 1,453 shares	$ 1,210	$ 1,453
Common stocks		
Class B stock—$1 par value		
Issued and outstanding—20,802 and 21,444 shares	20,802	21,444
Common stock—$1 par value		
Issued and outstanding—51,897 and 56,443 shares	51,897	56,443
Paid-in capital	727,285	726,505
Cumulative translation adjustments	(5,166)	(4,710)
Retained earnings	145,085	246,220
Total shareholders' equity	$941,113	$1,047,355

Consolidated Statement of Shareholders' Equity (one year only)

(in thousands)	COMMON STOCK	SERIES A STOCK	PAID-IN CAPITAL	CUMULATIVE TRANSLATION ADJUSTMENTS	RETAINED EARNINGS
Balance at October 31, 1994	$77,887	$1,453	$726,505	$(4,710)	$ 246,220
Net earnings	—	—	—	—	165,883
Cash dividends paid	—	—	—	—	(47,730)
Conversion of series A stock	243	(243)	—	—	—
Repurchase of common stock	(5,539)	—	—	—	(219,288)
Translation adjustments	—	—	—	(456)	—
Other equity transactions, net	108	—	780	—	—
Balance at October 31, 1995	$72,699	$1,210	$727,285	$(5,166)	$ 145,085

(continued)

[3] *The Wall Street Journal*, February 9, 1994, p. C4.

EXHIBIT 18–2 (Concluded)

From Footnote 7: Shareholders' Equity

SERIES A Cumulative Convertible Stock. Each share of Series A stock is convertible into 1.1 shares of common stock and is entitled to a quarterly dividend equal to the quarterly dividend on each share of common stock multiplied by 1.1, plus $.0075. Each share of Series A stock is entitled to a liquidation preference of $5.00 plus any accrued but unpaid dividends. Liquidation proceeds remaining after the satisfaction of such preference and the payment of $4.55 per share of common stock would be distributed ratably to the holders of common stock and Series A stock. There were 10,000,000 authorized shares of Series A stock at October 31, 1995.

Class B Stock and Common Stock. The Class B stock is not transferable except to family members and related entities, but is convertible at any time on a share-for-share basis into common stock. The holders of Class B Stock are entitled to cash dividends which are 10% lower per share than the cash dividends paid on each share of common stock. The Class B stock and the common stock are each entitled to vote separately as a class on charter amendments, mergers, consolidations and certain extraordinary transactions which are required to be approved by shareholders under Delaware law. Under certain circumstances, the holders of Class B stock have the right to cast 10 votes per share for the election of directors. There were 40,000,000 and 100,000,000 shares of Class B stock and common stock authorized for issuance at October 31, 1995, respectively.

In April 1995, the company completed a "Dutch Auction" tender offer and repurchased approximately 5.4 million shares of the company's common stock at $40.50 per share. In May 1995, the company's board of directors authorized the purchase of an additional 2.5 million shares of common stock in the open market. From October 31, 1995 through November 30, 1995, the company repurchased approximately 1.1 million shares at an average price of approximately $39.40 per share.

even have two or more classes of common stock. For example, ***Harcourt General*** (Exhibit 18–2) has preferred stock and two classes of common stock. Among other distinctions, its Class B stock is not transferable except to family members and related entities, while its common stock is traded publicly.

CONVERTIBLE PREFERRED STOCK

Some preferred stock has a conversion feature that allows the shares to be exchanged for (converted to) shares of common stock. Various **convertible preferred stock** differs for such features as (1) the time period after which conversion is possible, (2) the number of shares of common to be issued when each share of preferred is converted, and (3) any cash payments required for conversion. The conversion feature is designed to make the preferred stock more attractive to potential investors by allowing them to participate in future market price increases of the common stock. Because the conversion feature is perceived to have some potential value, companies usually are able to obtain a higher price when issuing convertible stock or can make the dividend preference rate lower than if the stock were not convertible.

However, even though the conversion features allow the issuing corporation to receive a higher price or assign a lower dividend rate to the preferred stock, no value is assigned to the conversion right at the issue date. The entire proceeds of the stock issue are assigned to the preferred stock account. If preferred stock eventually is converted to common stock, then the accounts for the preferred stock are reduced (that is, debited), and common stock accounts are increased (that is, credited). For example, Exhibit 18–3 illustrates the conversion of 25 percent of a hypothetical company's convertible preferred stock. The transaction does not change the total shareholder's equity. One form of equity financing (or source of capital) is merely exchanged for another form of equity financing. To illustrate, Exhibit 18–2 portrays one year of ***Harcourt General's*** three-year consolidated statement of shareholders' equity. Notice that the company converted some of its Series A convertible preferred stock.

EXHIBIT 18–3
Convertible Preferred Stock and Its Conversion to Common Stock

GRIFFIN COMPANY
Shareholders' Equity
December 31, 1997

Before Conversion:

Convertible preferred; $100 par; 8,000 shares issued and outstanding	$ 800,000
Paid-in capital—preferred	200,000
Common stock; $1 par; 100,000 shares issued and outstanding	100,000
Paid-in capital—common	700,000
Retained earnings	2,200,000
	$4,000,000

Conversion of 2,000 Shares (25%) of Preferred Stock into 2,000 Shares of Common Stock on December 31, 1997:

12/31/97	Convertible Preferred	200,000	
	Paid-In Capital—Preferred	50,000	
	Common Stock		2,000
	Paid-In Capital—Common		248,000

GRIFFIN COMPANY
Shareholders' Equity
December 31, 1997

After Conversion:

Convertible preferred; $100 par; 6,000 shares issued and outstanding	$ 600,000
Paid-in capital—preferred	150,000
Common stock; $1 par; 102,000 shares issued and outstanding	102,000
Paid-in capital—common	948,000
Retained earnings	2,200,000
	$4,000,000

Recall from Chapter 14 that conversion of convertible bonds may be recorded using either the book value or market value methods. Although less prevalent, the market value method permits recognition of gains or losses on conversions from debt to equity, while the book value method does not.

Recognition of gains or losses is not appropriate, however, for transactions occurring exclusively between owners and limited to equity interests. So only the book value method is permitted for conversion of convertible preferred stock. Unless additional cash or other valuable consideration is received by the corporation at the time of exchange, the corporation receives *no* further equity. Thus, total contributed capital remains unchanged—gains or losses are not recognized from such conversion.

If any cash or other consideration is received as part of a conversion, contributed capital increases by the amount received. That is, common stock accounts increase by the book value of the preferred stock converted and the consideration received.

CALLABLE AND REDEEMABLE PREFERRED STOCK

Callable preferred stock contains a provision whereby the corporation may "call" the stock to retire it, usually at some prespecified price and possibly after some prespecified date. When the stock is called, preferred shareholders are required to turn the stock in, or "redeem" it, for consideration. The corporation has the option of calling the stock or not.

Redeemable preferred stock contains a provision whereby preferred stock *must be redeemed* by shareholders and retired by the corporation by some prespecified date at some prespecified price. In some cases, shareholders may be entitled to redeem their shares anytime prior to the prespecified date.

As stated earlier, preferred stock combines characteristics of both debt and equity. With a mandatory maturity date, or redemption date, redeemable preferred stock is so similar to debt that the SEC *prohibits* its balance sheet presentation in the same section with common stockholders' equity. Redeemable preferred stock is one of many of today's complex, hybrid financing agreements which have characteristics of both debt and equity instruments.[4]

CONCEPT Liabilities versus equity.

LOGIC Concepts Statement No. 6 (SFAC No. 6) distinguishes between liabilities and equity on the basis of whether an instrument obligates the issuer to transfer its assets (or to use its assets in providing services) to the holder. A liability embodies such an obligation, while an equity instrument does not.[5]

[4]The FASB periodically wrestles with distinguishing between these hybrid financial instruments regarding their classification as liabilities or equities, or some combination of both. See its discussion memorandum, "Distinguishing between Liability and Equity Instruments with Characteristics of Both," FASB, 1990.

[5]FASB Exposure Draft, "Accounting for Stock-based Compensation," June 30, 1993, par. 164.

The required maturity would seem to make redeemable preferred stock, in substance, a liability. Yet the accounting profession and the SEC are currently at odds with respect to the classification of redeemable preferred stock. Separate balance sheet classification of redeemable preferred stock is not required by GAAP. However, the SEC does require separate reporting. Faced with SEC reporting demands, some companies therefore classify preferred stock separately from common stockholders' equity. For example, Exhibit 18–4 depicts the liabilities and stockholders' equity for ***Sprint Corporation*** (*www.sprint.com*). Note that (1) redeemable preferred stock is not in a stockholders' equity classification,

EXHIBIT 18–4 Reporting Redeemable Preferred Stock

PARTIAL CONSOLIDATED BALANCE SHEETS
Sprint Corporation

	AS OF DECEMBER 31,	
(DOLLARS IN MILLIONS)	1995	1994
Liabilities and Shareholders' Equity		
Current liabilities		
Current maturities of long-term debt	$ 280.4	$ 332.4
Short-term borrowings	2,144.0	—
Accounts payable	938.9	927.8
Accrued interconnection costs	617.7	527.6
Accrued taxes	235.5	237.9
Other	925.6	817.4
Total current liabilities	$ 5,142.1	$ 2,843.1
Long-term debt	3,253.0	4,604.8
Deferred credits and other liabilities		
Deferred income taxes and investment tax credits	843.4	1,197.5
Postretirement and other benefit obligations	889.3	845.9
Other	393.0	494.3
	$ 2,125.7	$ 2,537.7
Redeemable Preferred Stock	32.5	37.1
Common stock and other shareholders' equity		
Common stock, par value $2.50 per share, authorized 500.0 million shares, issued 349.2 million (348.6 million in 1994), and outstanding 349.2 million (348.3 million in 1994)	$ 872.9	$ 871.4
Capital in excess of par or stated value	960.0	942.9
Retained earnings	2,766.5	2,730.9
Other	43.2	(20.4)
	4,642.6	4,524.8
	$15,195.9	$14,547.5

(continued)

EXHIBIT 18–4 (Concluded)

From Footnote 7: Redeemable Preferred Stock

Sprint has 20 million authorized shares and subsidiaries have approximately 5 million authorized shares of preferred stock, including nonredeemable preferred stock. The redeemable preferred stock outstanding, as of December 31, is as follows (in millions):

	1995	**1994**
Third series—stated value $100 per share, shares—184,000 in 1995 and 196,000 in 1994, nonparticipating, nonvoting, cumulative 7.75% annual dividend rate	$18.4	$19.6
Fifth series—stated value $100,000 per share, shares—95 in 1995 and 1994, voting, cumulative 6% annual dividend rate	9.5	9.5
Subsidiaries—stated value ranging from $10 to $100 per share, shares—110,675 in 1995 and 364,345 in 1994, annual dividend rates ranging from 4.7% to 5.0%	4.6	8.0
Total redeemable preferred stock	$32.5	$37.1

Sprint's third series preferred stock was called in January 1996. In March 1996, 24,000 shares will be redeemed at a price of $100.00 per share and the remaining shares will be redeemed at a price of $101.77 per share. Sprint's fifth series preferred stock must be redeemed in full in 2003.

(2) no subtotal is provided for total liabilities, leaving any distinction for the redeemable preferred stock as debt or equity to the reader, and (3) a separate classification is used for *common* stockholders' equity. Even some companies whose preferred stock is not redeemable elect to report common stockholders' equity rather than classifying preferred stock in a shareholders' equity section of their balance sheets.

OTHER EQUITY SOURCES AND ADJUSTMENTS

3

Evaluate and record transactions for other equity securities and adjustments, such as those for options, warrants, and stock subscriptions.

The stockholders' equity section of the balance sheet frequently contains accounts for items other than the traditional preferred stock, common stock, paid-in capital, and retained earnings. In this section, we discuss the following:

1. Valuation adjustments
2. Stock-based compensation
3. Stock warrants
4. Stock subscriptions

VALUATION ADJUSTMENTS

Current standards require valuation adjustments to equity for such things as unrealized holding gains or losses for available-for-sale investment securities and temporary exchange rate fluctuations when translating accounts maintained using foreign currencies.

IN PRACTICE—INTERNATIONAL

Equity Reserves

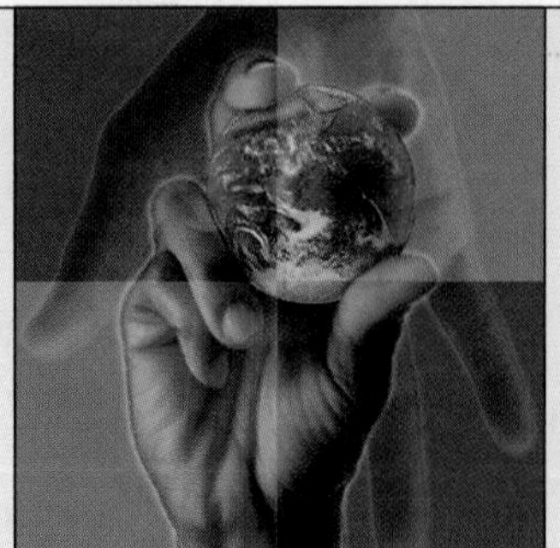

Most countries in the European Community (EC) establish reserves as part of shareholders' equity. Two of these are revaluation reserves and statutory reserves, as discussed in the following excerpt from the *Journal of Accountancy*.

> France, Greece, Portugal, and Spain use a countrywide revaluation approach—all companies are required by the government to revalue [assets] to current cost at the same time. The government normally specifies an indexing system or provides other write-up guidelines. Companies essentially have no choice but to revalue. When a countrywide approach is used, the revaluation occurs once every few years. Most other EC countries allow companies to revalue assets periodically at their own discretion. . . . Only Germany and Luxembourg prohibit write-ups and instead stick with historical cost. . . . [T]he key account for U.S. CPAs to watch for is the revaluation reserve account, which must be disclosed and is found in the equity section of the balance sheet. . . .
>
> Several countries have statutory reserves. Denmark, for example, requires 10% of profit to be allocated to a reserve account. This account accumulates until it is 10% of share capital. Statutory reserves protect creditors in that some portion of profits must be permanently retained as assets.

Source: L. Sundby and B. Schweiger, "EC, EZ?" *Journal of Accountancy*, March 1992, pp. 72–73.

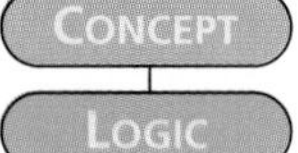

Valuation adjustments versus gains or losses.

The rationale is that these particular adjustments represent temporary changes to asset values and equity rather than permanent gains or losses for purposes of income determination.

Transamerica Finance Corporation reports both types of adjustments in Exhibit 18–5. Discussion of the classification and adjustments for investment securities is found in Chapter 9. Regarding foreign currency, financial records are typically maintained in the currency of the host country. For example, the assets and operating activity of a U.S. corporation's operations in France are recorded in francs. To prepare financial reports, accounts from global operations must be combined into a single currency. In the process, translation differences between accounting periods arise due to fluctuations in exchange rates. Details related to foreign currency translations are generally among the topics in Advanced Accounting.

STOCK-BASED COMPENSATION

Performance incentives increasing employee stock ownership are quite popular. In the following sections, we address the following types of stock-based compensation: (1) employee stock options, (2) stock appreciation rights (SARs), and (3) employee stock ownership plans (ESOPs).

EXHIBIT 18–5 Valuation Adjustments to Shareholders' Equity

TRANSAMERICA FINANCE CORPORATION AND SUBSIDIARIES
(Amounts in thousands, except for share data)

	December 31,	
	1995	**1994**
Stockholders' equity:		
Preferred stock—authorized, 250,000 shares without par value; none issued		
Common stock—authorized, 2,500,000 shares of $10 par value; issued and outstanding, 1,464,285 shares	$ 14,643	$ 14,643
Additional paid-in capital	1,594,637	1,455,717
Retained earnings	103,480	124,347
Net unrealized gain (loss) from investments marked to fair value	**6,624**	**(3,272)**
Foreign currency translation adjustments	**(4,870)**	**(9,094)**
Total stockholders' equity	$1,714,514	$1,582,341

Excerpts From Note A—Significant Accounting Policies

Foreign Currency Translation—The net assets and operations of foreign subsidiaries included in the consolidated financial statements are attributable to Canadian and European operations. The accounts of these subsidiaries have been converted at rates of exchange in effect at year-end as to balance sheet accounts and at average rates for the year as to operations. The effect of changes in exchange rates in translating foreign subsidiaries' financial statements is accumulated in a separate component of stockholders' equity.

New Accounting Standards—In 1994, the Company adopted the Financial Accounting Standards Board's new standard on accounting for certain investments in debt and equity securities. Beginning in 1994 with the adoption of this standard, all of the Company's investments in debt securities have been classified as available for sale and reported at fair value. The effect of this adjustment, net of federal income taxes, is recorded in a separate component of stockholders' equity. There is no effect on the income statement. Prior to 1994, investments in debt securities were carried at amortized cost.

Stock Options. **Stock options** are rights granted to purchase shares of stock at a preestablished exercise price extending over some exercise period. Key executives in large corporations typically receive both salary and stock options as compensation for their services. Continuing controversy regards both the size of compensation to top executives (see the Ethics In Practice feature on the next page) and the amount of compensation, if any, that should be expensed for employee stock options.

There are currently two acceptable methods of accounting for employee stock options. In 1995, the FASB issued SFAS No. 123 establishing a **fair-value-based method** of accounting for stock based compensation plans. The statement *encourages* companies to use this fair value method for recognizing compensation expenses but also *permits* recognition using an **intrinsic-value-based**

ETHICS IN PRACTICE

Compensation to Top Executives

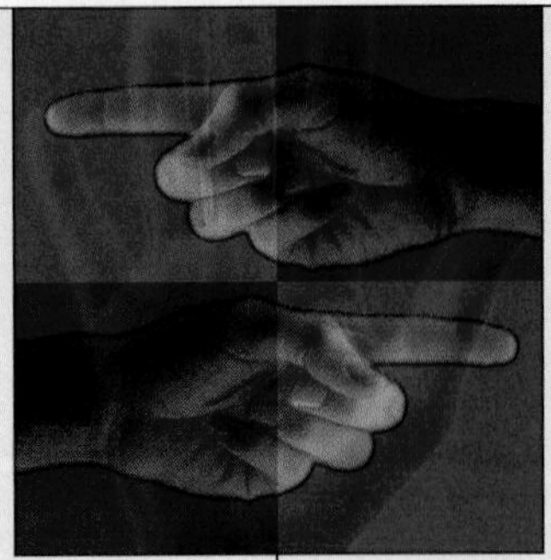

Recent public controversy concerns top executive compensation, particularly that of corporate chief executive officers (CEOs). Executives have a stewardship function to protect and manage resources provided by creditors and owners. From both an ethical and economic standpoint, concern arises regarding the amount of compensation to top management and whether it is exorbitant and thus detrimental to the interests of shareholders. In many instances, a large portion of this compensation is in some form of stock compensation (i.e., exercising stock options or SARs). In 1993, for example, "CEOs of Fortune 100 companies derived 29% of their total pay from options . . . Executives of some startup companies draw as much as 80% of their pay from options."

The vast majority of employee stock option plans by U.S. companies are limited to top executives. The size of such awards can be staggering.

In 1992, "**Walt Disney Co.** Chairman Michael D. Eisner and President Frank G. Wells exercised options to buy a total of about 6.6 million Disney shares, then immediately sold nearly 5.1 million of them for a combined indicated pretax profit exceeding $187 million."

In 1990, the CEO of ***Time Warner*** (*www.time.com*) received $78.1 million (of which $57.2 million was through stock compensation) while the company reported a loss for the year of $227 million.

Sources: C. Harlan, "Accounting Proposal Stirs Unusual Uproar in Executive Suites," *The Wall Street Journal*, March 7, 1994, p. A1; J. Mathews, "Stock Options Rule Fight Escalates," *The Washington Post*, September 1, 1994, p. B11; "What 800 Companies Paid Their Bosses," *Forbes*, May 27, 1991, pp. 236–289.

method established by APB No. 25. The decision to recommend rather than require recognition based on fair value came after tremendous public pressure and impending Congressional intervention surrounding the statement's exposure draft which had proposed to require the fair value method. The In Practice feature "SFAS No. 123—Controversy and Compromise" highlights the FASB's compromise.

Recognizing Compensation. A key distinction between the intrinsic value method and the fair value method is in the determination of the amount of compensation to be recognized for stock-based compensation plans. Essentially, under the intrinsic value method in APB No. 25, compensation is the excess of the market price over the option price for the shares of stock as of the *measurement date*.[6] The measurement date is the date that both (1) the option price for obtaining shares and (2) the number of shares that each employee is eligible to obtain are known. Frequently, the measurement date is the *grant* date (the date when employees are awarded options).

Under the intrinsic value method, many employee stock option plans result in zero compensation since the exercise price typically equals or exceeds the market price on the grant date. The proceeds received when the options are

[6]APB No. 25 categorizes employee stock options as compensatory plans (those with compensation to expense) and noncompensatory plans (those without a compensation element). With the fair value-based method, essentially all employee stock options would have a compensation element, so the categorization becomes irrelevant.

IN PRACTICE—GENERAL

SFAS No. 123—Controversy and Compromise

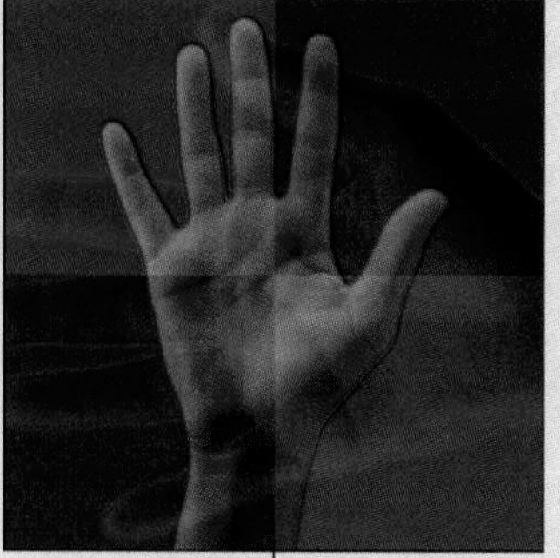

. . . "Bowing to pressure from business and Congress, the Financial Accounting Standards Board dropped a two-year-old proposal that would have forced companies to deduct the cost of employee stock options from earnings. [They voted instead] to require that companies simply disclose in footnotes to financial statements the impact of such options on net profit and per share earnings. The FASB also voted to encourage companies to voluntarily deduct the cost of options from earnings, though few are expected to do so.

In a written commentary, FASB Chairman Dennis Beresford states

'While Statement No. 123 is different from what the FASB had envisioned, it's a significant step toward more consistent measurement and more informative disclosure. Companies will be reporting the information about the cost of stock compensation that investors and creditors said they need. A defined measure of compensation cost must be calculated by all employers for all options and other stock-based compensation. And while companies will still be permitted to keep the compensation cost out of their income statements for most fixed options, accounting recognition is established as preferable.

Yes, we did less than we had wanted to do. But it's a lot more than nothing.'"

Sources: L. Berton and J. Lublin, "FASB Softens Plan On Deducting Costs Of Stock Options," *The Wall Street Journal,* December 15, 1995, p. A2; D. Beresford, "What Did We Learn from the Stock Compensation Project?" *Accounting Horizons,* June 1996, pp. 125–126.

exercised and stock issued is treated like other stock issuances, as depicted in Exhibit 18–1.

Under the fair value method, compensation is the estimated fair value of the options on the grant date. This estimated value is determined using an option-pricing model that considers such things as expected stock volatility, expected dividend yields, and risk-free interest rates.[7] Essentially all stock options have value, so virtually all employee stock options will have a compensation cost.

Exhibit 18–6 illustrates the two different treatments. Under the intrinsic value method, a compensation element results when the exercise price for stock is less than its market price at the measurement date. The presumption is that a company is providing value to employees for their service; this value is the amount employees may save by purchasing stock at the lower exercise price instead of the higher market price. In the exhibit, a total compensation of $100,000 is expensed equally over a two-year service period and is recognized as contributed capital from employee service (that is, Paid-In Capital—Stock Options).[8]

[7]SFAS No. 123 provides some guidance for applying acceptable pricing models. In this text, we assume values resulting from these models and do not address the details for computing these values. This approach is similar to accepting actuarially determined amounts for postretirement benefits.

[8]Stock Options Exercisable is another title used instead of Paid-In Capital—Stock Options. Note that funds are not really paid in when employees are granted options. The contributed capital they "pay" is their service from employment.

An alternative bookkeeping approach is to record Paid-In Capital—Stock Options at the grant date for the total compensation and then offset this by a contra account entitled Deferred Compensation. Then, when compensation expense is recognized, the contra account is reduced.

EXHIBIT 18–6 Employee Stock Option Plans—Intrinsic Value vs. Fair Value Methods

On November 30, 1996, Hoffman Corporation voted to grant a total of 50,000 nonqualified employee stock options on January 1, 1997. Each option permits the purchase of one share of $1 par common stock anytime after December 31, 1998, until December 31, 2001, for an exercise price of $20. The market price of the common stock on January 1, 1997, was $22. Based upon an options pricing model, the options had a fair value of $5 each on the grant date. The compensation to employees for the options has an assumed service period of two years from the grant date to the vesting date of December 31, 1998. During 1999, when the market price of the common stock was $26 per share, 75 percent of the options were exercised; 37,500 shares (50,000 × 0.75) were issued for $750,000 (37,500 shares × $20 exercise price). The remaining 25 percent were never exercised and expired. The appropriate income tax rate is 34%.

	Intrinsic Value (APB No. 25)		Fair Value (SFAS No. 123)	
Total compensation:	50,000 shares × ($22 − $20) = $100,000		50,000 shares × $5 = $250,000	
Annual Compensation:	$100,000/2 years = $50,000		$250,000/2 years = $125,000	
Entries:				
12/31/97 and 12/31/98				
Compensation Expense	50,000		125,000	
Paid-In Capital—Stock Options		50,000		125,000
Deferred Tax Asset	17,000		42,500	
Income Tax Expense*		17,000		42,500
	($50,000 × 0.34 = $17,000)		*($125,000 × 0.34 = $42,500)*	
During 1999 (Exercise)				
Cash	750,000		750,000	
Paid-In Capital—Stock Options	75,000		187,500	
Common Stock		37,500		37,500
Additional Paid-In Capital		787,500		900,000
	($100,000 × 0.75 = $75,000)		*($250,000 × 0.75 = $187,500)*	
Note: (Total Tax Deduction = 37,500 shares × [26 − 20] = $225,000; Reduction of Taxes = $225,000 × 0.34 = $76,500)				
Income Tax Payable	76,500		76,500	
Deferred Tax Asset		25,500		63,750
Paid-In Capital—Stock Options		51,000		12,750
	($17,000 × 2 yrs. × 0.75 = $25,500)		*($42,500 × 2 yrs. × 0.75 = $63,750)*	
12/31/01 (Expiration)				
Paid-In Capital—Stock Options	25,000		62,500	
Additional Paid-In Capital		25,000		62,500
	($100,000 × 0.25 = $25,000)		*($250,000 × 0.25 = $62,500)*	
Paid-In Capital—Stock Options	8,500		12,750	
Income Tax Expense	—		8,500	
Deferred Tax Asset		8,500		21,250
	($17,000 × 2 yrs. × 0.25 = $8,500)		*($42,500 × 2 yrs. × 0.25 = $21,250)*	

*The income tax entries illustrate the changes to income tax expense and income tax payable assuming a separate entry to income tax expense and income tax payable for other revenue and expense items. Further, we assume realization of the deferred tax benefits, so do not recognize a valuation allowance for the deferred tax asset.

Under the fair value method, the compensation is more than the difference between market price and exercise price at the grant date. This is partly because the market price may be even higher when options are exercised and stock issued, so employees may benefit more as the stock price increases. Exhibit 18–6 assumes that a pricing model estimates the fair value of each option at the grant date as $5, resulting in total compensation of $250,000. This compensation cost is expensed equally over a two-year service period and is recognized as contributed capital from employee service (that is, Paid-In Capital—Stock Options).

Both approaches allocate compensation cost to service periods.[9] When options are awarded for past service, the cost is allocated to the period of the award. Alternatively, as illustrated in Exhibit 18–6, the cost may be allocated to future service periods. Frequently, the service period covers the time from when options are awarded to when they vest.

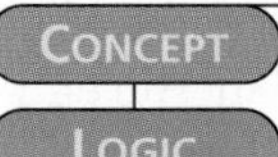

Matching.

When employees receive benefit from an employer for services rendered, the cost to the employer for providing the benefit is allocated to expense in the period(s) when the service is provided by the employee rather than the period in which the benefit is received by the employee.

As the previous In Practice Features suggests, continuation of the intrinsic value method is expected by most companies, so these companies will generally not recognize compensation expense for their stock options. However, SFAS No. 123 requires disclosure based on fair value. Companies using the intrinsic value method must also provide footnote disclosure of pro forma net income and earnings per share based upon the fair value method.

Deferred Taxes. The income tax status of stock option plans depends upon a distinction between qualified and nonqualified plans as specified by IRS regulations. For a **qualified stock option plan** (also called an *incentive plan*), the exercise price must not be less than the market price of the stock at the measurement date. In this type of plan, there is no deductible compensation by the employer. Thus, the tax basis of qualified plans for contributed capital from employee service is zero. Any differences between financial reporting and income tax reporting are permanent differences. So, there are no resultant deferred taxes.

The advantage of a qualified plan to eligible employees is that they are not required to recognize income and pay income taxes on any excess of market value over option price when they exercise their options. Employees' profit recognition and related income taxes are deferred until disposition of the stock itself.

[9]For simplicity, we allocate to compensation expense in this chapter. Some compensation costs may be allocated to production (i.e., work-in-process) rather than to an expense for the period.

For a **nonqualified stock option plan**, corporations are permitted a compensation-expense deduction for amounts that employees are required to recognize as taxable income for stock options. Usually, the recognition occurs when employees exercise their options and equals the excess of the stock's market price at exercise over the exercise price paid by employees.[10] Since the employer is ultimately permitted a deduction for stock options, a deductible temporary difference arises when compensation expense for financial reporting precedes the deduction. The deductible difference results in a deferred tax asset. The tax basis for contributed capital from employee service is zero until the deduction is allowed. Therefore, as illustrated in Exhibit 18–6 for 1997 and 1998, increases to deferred tax assets result in reductions to income tax expense as compensation expense is recognized each period.

Exercise of Stock Options. As Exhibit 18–6 portrays for both approaches, the total amount recorded as contributed capital when options are exercised and stock is issued includes both the cash proceeds and the employee-service element. Since the options are part of a nonqualified plan, the employer is permitted an income tax deduction when the options are exercised. The deduction reduces taxes currently payable as benefits related to deferred tax assets are realized. SFAS No. 123 specifies that, for any stock-based compensation plan, any tax benefit for actual compensation deductions in excess of recognized deductions (i.e., recognized compensation expenses) are considered additional contributed capital rather than reductions to expense. Therefore, Exhibit 18–6 shows respective increases of $51,000 and $12,750 to paid-in capital for the intinsic value and fair value methods. Note that, even though the tax liability is reduced by the allowable deduction, income tax expense is unchanged.

In the event that actual deductions allowed are less than recognized deductions expenses, the decrease to income tax payable will be less than the related deferred tax asset so not all expected benefits are realized. Unrealized benefits reduce equity recorded for any previous excesses (i.e. paid-in capital), if any; otherwise, they are allocated to income tax expense.

Expiration of Stock Options. Even when options expire without exercise, the amount of the recorded employee-service element is not revised. It remains as a source of contributed capital, although it is typically reclassified as shown in Exhibit 18–6. Further, unrealized benefits from deferred tax assets reduce equity recorded for any previous excesses (i.e. paid-in capital), if any; otherwise, they are allocated to income tax expense. For example, paid-in capital in the exhibit is reduced for the full $8,500 balance in deferred tax assets for the intrinsic value method, since $51,000 was previously recorded for excesses when options were exercised in 1999. For the fair value method, the remaining balance in deferred tax assets is $21,250, but paid-in capital can only be reduced by $12,750 based upon the previous amount recorded in 1999 when options were exercised. So, the difference of $8,500 is charged to income tax expense.

[10]If nonqualified stock options have a readily ascertainable fair market value when issued, employees must recognize taxable income when the options are received. Currently, most employee stock options are not deemed to have such a readily indentifiable market value, so income is not recognized until the options are exercised.

Adjustments to Option-Pricing Model. Employee stock options typically can only be used by employees, so they cannot be traded. There is usually a vesting period over which employees must remain employed to keep from forfeiting the options. Further, the exercise period is generally lengthy, frequently 10 years. Option-pricing models were developed, not for employee stock options, but for marketable options that can be traded and are generally of much shorter duration, frequently a few months.

The fair value method requires adjustments to these pricing models to reflect characteristics of employee stock options. Total compensation is determined by considering either estimated forfeitures or unvested options that are not forfeited. Further, the expected life of the options (time until expected exercise) rather than the full term (maximum life) is used to determine fair value. Subsequent changes to these estimated adjustments are often required to reflect changing conditions; these changes are treated as changes in estimates.

For example, Exhibit 18–6 determines total compensation on the fair value of all 50,000 stock options. This determination is based either upon unvested options not forfeited (i.e., all of them) or assumes estimated forfeitures are zero (i.e., all eligible employees will become entitled to the options at the end of the vesting period because all eligible employees are expected to remain employed through 1998). Imagine that an executive entitled to 20% of the options unexpectedly resigns during 1998 and forfeits the options. Thus, only 40,000 options vest instead of the anticipated 50,000; total compensation based upon the fair value of $5 estimated by the option-pricing model becomes $200,000, not $250,000. The compensation expense for 1998 would be only $75,000, since $125,000 of the now $200,000 total compensation was previously expensed. The expense and related deferred tax entries would be recorded as follows:

12/31/98	Compensation Expense	75,000	
	Paid-In Capital—Stock Options		75,000
	To record expense for 1998 and adjust for change in estimate.		
12/31/98	Deferred Tax Asset	25,500	
	Income Tax Expense		25,500
	To record deferred tax effect of compensation expense.		

Note that no adjustments are made for changes in the market price of the stock. The estimated value of each option is determined at the date the options are awarded and not generally adjusted for changing market conditions. The rationale is that conditions in effect at the time options are awarded provide the basis for compensation agreed to by the employer and its employees.

Fixed versus Performance Stock Options. The example provided in Exhibit 18–6 illustrates a **fixed stock option plan**. The number of options and exercise price are fixed at the date options are awarded, so the measurement date is the grant date. Alternatively, **performance stock option plans** specify additional requirements that must be met for options to vest. For example, suppose a stock option plan awarded 10,000 options plus an additional 10,000 if the employer earns a certain market share by the vesting date. The measurement date for the intrinsic value method becomes the future vesting date rather than the grant date. Thus, under the provisions of APB No. 25, most performance plans result in recognized compensation, since the market price of stock typically rises and exceeds the exercise price by the vesting date.

Generally, a fixed option has more value than an otherwise equivalent performance option. Yet, under the intrinsic value method, most fixed options result in no recognized compensation, since the exercise price generally equals or exceeds the stock's market price on the grant date. Most performance options, on the other hand, do have recognized compensation. The fair value method eliminates this apparent anomaly. It directs that the value of both fixed and performance options be estimated at the grant date and that both result in recognized compensation. As with adjustments for forfeitures and expected exercise dates, adjustments would be frequently required as estimated results of performance conditions change.

Measurement Controversy. The measurement of the compensation element is extremely controversial. Some argue that the actual compensation to employees is the excess of the market value of the stock over the exercise price, not at the measurement date, but at the actual exercise date when employees purchase the stock. Thus, the compensation element should be recorded at this ultimate value of the options. More conservatively, one might calculate the compensation as the excess when the options vest and first become exercisable.

Another, less popular argument is that there is no real cost to the company for providing employee stock options. As options are exercised, the company merely issues stock in return for some value received (that is, the option price). This argument suggests that contributed capital should be recorded solely for the amount equal to the proceeds received when this stock is issued upon exercise of the options. Thus, there would be no compensation element. In other words, any costs of providing employee stock options are opportunity costs, which are generally not recognized as expenses.

SFAS No. 123 endorses the concept of fair value when plans are awarded to employees, which is consistent with the general notion of recording transactions for the market value of the exchange. The concept would be implemented by "proven" option-pricing models. The FASB argues that options have value, that this value is compensation to employees, and that the value is reasonably estimable. They therefore encourage recognition based on fair value. Opponents to the fair value method focus on what they see as the inappropriateness of option-pricing models and on the potential detrimental economic impact of the new requirements. The In Practice feature "Fair Value and Economic Consequences" further highlights the controversy.

Stock Appreciation Rights (SARs). Exercise of stock options requires that employees have access either to their own or to borrowed funds. **Stock appreciation rights (SARs)** were developed to eliminate this cash requisite. SARs grant eligible employees compensation based on the difference between the market price of the stock at a prespecified date and a base price. As the stock appreciates in value, the ultimate compensation increases in amount. However, no actual funds are required of employees to exercise their rights because the employees are not required to actually purchase stock. The stock price movement is simply used as the vehicle to measure the amount of the compensation for the employee.

IN PRACTICE—GENERAL

Fair Value and Economic Consequences

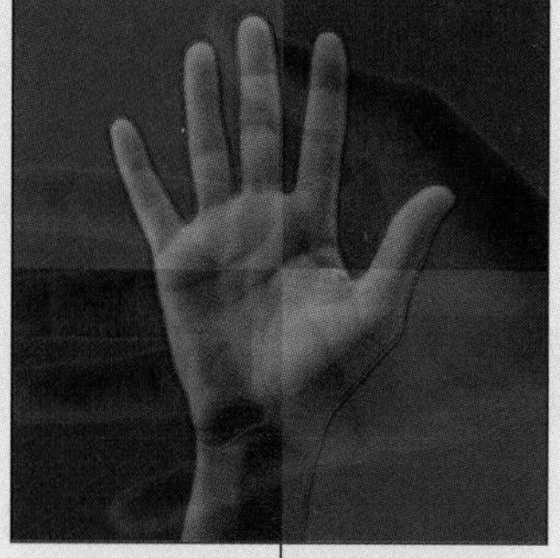

Throughout the text, we discuss the notion that accounting practices and changes have economic consequences. Accounting for stock options is a prime example. Opponents to the fair value method argue either against the validity of the option-pricing model for determining fair value or against perceived economic consequences of using fair value.

One critic argues,

> The option-pricing models FASB plans on requiring are for traded options that are typically traded. Options granted by companies do not trade, and they usually have a longer life. "Why introduce an extremely subjective measure into financial statements?" asks Norman Strauss, a partner at ***Ernst & Young*** (*www.ey.com*).

The FASB contends that the uncertainties in measurement are no more significant than those inherent for measurements of many other estimates currently recognized for financial reporting (e.g., loan loss reserves, valuation allowances for deferred tax assets, and postretirement benefits).

The following were suggested as potential economic consequences when FASB proposed to require recognition.

> The ruling will severely impact new companies. Many startups depend heavily on stock options to attract top-rate people. . . . Startups are the source of most of our innovation and new jobs. Between 1982 and 1986 the U.S. economy created 18.7 million additional jobs. Fourteen million came from new companies.

If the rule had already been in effect, it would have reduced ***Lotus's*** (*www.lotus.com*) per-share profits in 1992 by 49.6 percent and ***Software Publishing's*** per-share net last year by 40.9 percent.

Sources: R. Khalaf, "If It Ain't Broke . . . ," *Forbes,* April 12, 1993, p. 100; FASB Exposure Draft; "FASB's Folly," *Forbes,* January 31, 1994, p. 26; L. Berton, "New Payroll Rule May Eat Into 1997 Profits," *The Wall Street Journal,* June 3, 1993, p. C1.

Depending upon the agreement, the compensation itself may be in cash or in stock. If stock is the required form of compensation, SARs are treated as a form of performance-based compensation with contributed capital credited for the estimated compensation. If the compensation is most likely to be in cash, or if the employee can elect either cash or stock, a liability is credited instead of equity.

Measurement of the compensation is complex because the measurement date that determines the total cash or shares to be awarded is the future compensation date, yet the period of service to expense this compensation generally precedes this date. Thus, compensation is estimated using existing market values, and adjustments are made as these market values change prior to the compensation date. This process is illustrated in Exhibit 18–7.

Note from the exhibit that in order to accrue expenses for the service element in the years 1994, 1995, and 1996, the compensation must be estimated using existing market prices at the time. As the market price changes, adjustments for changes in estimates are required (see 1996 and 1997). Also notice that the amount of appreciation (the compensation) is based upon the agreed 10,000 shares of stock, but that management does not actually receive these shares. Instead, management receives either the $70,000 appreciation in cash or its equivalent in shares of stock (approximately 1,892 shares).

EXHIBIT 18–7
Stock Appreciation Rights (SARs)

Data: On January 1, 1994,, management is granted stock appreciation rights (SARS) based upon 10,000 shares of common stock using the then current market price of $30 per share as the base price. The rights are to be awarded on December 31, 1997 either in cash or shares of common stock using the market price at that date. These rights are for employee service during January 1, 1994 (the grant date) to December 31, 1997 (the compensation and measurement date).

Date	Description		Debit	Credit
1/1/94	No Entry			
12/31/94	Market price of stock: $36			
	Total estimated compensation: 10,000 × (36 − 30) = $60,000			
	Expense for 1994: $60,000/4 years = $15,000			
	Entry:			
	Compensation Expense		15,000	
	Liability for SARs			15,000
12/31/95	Market price of stock: $36 (same as last year)			
	Entry:			
	Compensation Expense		15,000	
	Liability for SARs			15,000
	(Liability balance = $30,000)			
12/31/96	Market price of stock: $40			
	Total estimated compensation: 10,000 × ($40 − $30) =	$100,000		
	Less: Total accrued expenses to date:	30,000		
	Remaining estimated compensation:	$ 70,000		
	Expense for 1996: $70,000/2 more years = $35,000			
	Entry:			
	Compensation expense		35,000	
	Liability for SARs			35,000
	(Liability balance = $65,000)			
12/31/97	Market price of stock: $37			
	Total actual compensation: 10,000 × ($37 − $30) =	$70,000		
	Less: Total accrued expenses to date:	65,000		
	Remaining compensation for 1997:	$ 5,000		
	Entry:			
	Compensation Expense		$5,000	
	Liability for SARs			$5,000
	(Liability balance = $70,000)			
12/31/97	Assuming cash is awarded:			
	Entry:			
	Liability for SARs		70,000	
	Cash			70,000
	Assuming stock is awarded:			
	Approx. 1,892 shares of stock issued to management based upon $70,000 in SARs using a $37 price.			
	Entry:			
	Liability for SARs		70,000	
	Common Stock ($1 par)			1,892
	Paid-In Capital			68,108

Like stock options, employers may be permitted income tax deductions for compensation from these type of plans. When permitted, deductible temporary differences result in deferred tax assets. This occurs as financial compensation expense is recognized prior to the actual tax deductions that usually await the ultimate awarding of the cash or stock.

These type of compensation plans are based upon stock prices. Stock prices can be volatile and do not necessarily correlate closely with employee performance. Other incentive plans base compensation upon corporate performance measures such as growth in sales, return on assets, return on shareholders' equity, and growth in earnings per share. The bonuses discussed in Chapter 11 are an example of compensation base on performance measures.

Employee Stock Ownership Plans (ESOPs). An **employee stock ownership plan (ESOP)** is a special type of retirement plan called a qualified defined-contribution plan. These plans offer certain advantages both to employers and employees. Basically, a trustee for an ESOP purchases and holds shares of stock in which employees have an ownership interest. Subject to certain requirements, corporations are allowed income tax deductions for dividends paid by the corporation to the holder of the stock in the ESOP. Stock contributions by the corporate employer to these plans are also a form of compensation to be recognized as contributed capital by the corporation.

STOCK WARRANTS

Like stock options, **stock warrants** provide the right to purchase shares of stock for a specified price. Warrants have a market value because the exercise price is usually effective for a period of time, and the price of the stock is expected to increase above the exercise price. Generally, any proceeds received for warrants are a form of contributed capital (accounts would be Paid-In Capital—Stock Warrants or Stock Warrants Exercisable). As the warrants are exercised and stock is issued, contributed capital is increased by the proceeds received from exercising the warrants. If warrants expire, all proceeds from the original sale of the warrants remain contributed capital but are reclassified as Paid-In Capital or Stock Warrants—Lapsed.

A special problem arises when stock warrants are issued in combination with other securities (such as bonds)—that of deciding the portion of the total proceeds to attribute to the warrants. Current standards direct different accounting treatments depending on whether or not a warrant is a severable security that can be traded separately. If severable, it is called a **detachable stock warrant**, and some of the proceeds are attributed to the warrant. The portion of the proceeds attributed to detachable warrants is determined based on relative market values for the warrants and the other securities. This procedure was discussed in Chapter 14 for bonds issued with warrants. For **nondetachable warrants**, none of the proceeds are attributed separately to the warrant since they are not viewed as a separate security.

STOCK SUBSCRIPTIONS

Corporations may offer investors the opportunity to contract (or subscribe) to purchase shares of stock within a certain time frame at a specified price. In return, investors are required to make periodic payments or installments toward this purchase. A parallel to these **stock subscriptions** are credit sales to customers, where customers must make periodic installment payments to pay for their purchase. A key distinction, however, is that credit customers usually obtain their purchases at the time of sale. Here, the shares of stock either are not issued until after the investors have made all their payments or are issued proportionately with payments.

When stock is subscribed, a receivable is established for the remaining payments, and contributed capital is recognized at the full price subscribed. Since the stock is not issued, an equity account indicating stock subscribed is typically recognized rather than increasing the stock account itself. Further, subscriptions receivable are considered either a contra-equity account or an asset. The SEC requires the former since the amounts receivable have yet to be contributed as equity. For example, assume that investors subscribe to 2,000 shares of $1 par common stock at a price of $25 per share with an initial payment of $10 per share and the remainder to be paid within one year. The journal entry is

Cash	20,000	
Subscriptions Receivable	30,000	
Common Stock—Subscribed (par)		2,000
Additional Paid-In Capital		48,000

If the company does not have a separate classification for par, Common Stock—Subscribed could be credited for the full $50,000.

As subscription payments are received, the Subscriptions Receivable account is reduced. After all the payments have been received and stock is issued, the Common Stock—Subscribed account is eliminated, and the Common Stock account is increased for the amount that had been in the subscribed account. If subscribers default on the payments, and the stock is not issued, any proceeds not returned to subscribers remain contributed capital.[11]

SUPPLEMENTAL DISCLOSURES

Interpret supplemental disclosures related to equity.

In the notes accompanying the financial statements, corporations are required to disclose pertinent information concerning each class of capital stock and other potential equity sources of capital such as stock options, warrants, subscriptions, and convertible securities. For example, Exhibit 18–2 describes ***Harcourt General's*** three classes of stock, and Exhibit 18–4 describes ***Sprint's*** redeemable preferred stock.

SFAS No. 123 specifies several disclosures related to stock-based employee compensation. Part of the disclosures detail options granted during the period by providing, as of the grant date, the fair value of these options and the relation of their exercise prices to stock market prices. Further, companies must provide a schedule reconciling changes throughout the reporting periods. Such a schedule lists options available at the beginning of the period, additional options issued, options exercised for which stock was issued, and options expiring thus indicating options available at the end of the period. An example is provided in Exhibit 18–8.

[11]Defaults for stock subscriptions can be handled in a myriad of ways. Some of these include full return of subscription payments, partial return of payments, partial issuance of stock equivalent to payments, and full forfeiture of payments by subscribers. Details regarding defaults should be a part of the subscription contract and may be governed by state laws.

EXHIBIT 18–8 Disclosure of Stock-Based Compensation Plans

The following is an excerpt from ***Neiman Markus Group's*** Notes to Consolidated Financial Statements (August 3, 1996).

Common Stock Incentive Plan. The Company has established a common stock incentive plan allowing for the granting of stock options, stock appreciation rights (SARs) and stock-based awards to its employees. The aggregate number of shares of common stock that may be issued pursuant to the plan is 1.3 million shares. At August 3, 1996, there were 179,060 shares of common stock available for grant under the plan.

Options outstanding at August 3, 1996, were granted at prices (not less than 100% of the fair market value on the date of the grant) varying from $11.63 to $19.27 per share and expire between 1996 and 2005. There were 93 employees with options outstanding at August 3, 1996. The weighted average exercise price for all outstanding shares at August 3, 1996, was $14.41.

The Company has allowed SAR treatment in connection with the exercise of certain options. Optionees allowed SAR treatment surrender an exercisable option in exchange for an amount of cash equal to the excess of the market price of the common stock at the time of surrender over the option exercise price.

Option activity was as follows:

	YEARS ENDED		
	JULY 30, 1994	JULY 29, 1995	AUGUST 3, 1996
Options outstanding—beginning of year	684,136	666,348	784,864
Granted	214,100	228,050	128,600
SAR surrenders	(43,715)	(13,470)	(202,192)
Exercised	(10,401)	(1,644)	(2,900)
Canceled	(177,772)	(94,420)	(55,295)
Options outstanding—end of year	666,348	784,864	653,077
Exercisable options—end of year	294,800	356,064	239,247

FINANCIAL ANALYSIS

Prepare and analyze key profitability and solvency ratios that use equity information.

PROFITABILITY

Profitability typically is measured by comparing earnings to the investment or resources available for generating those earnings. For example, Chapter 6 illustrates that *return on total assets* provides a measure of how well a company utilizes all of its resources. When the investment utilized is considered as the owners' equity, two popular measures for efficiency of owners' resource usage are *earnings per share* (EPS) and *return on (stockholders') equity* (ROE). Both are frequently used by management when stating corporate goals. For example, in its 1989 annual report, ***Walt Disney Company*** states the following as financial objectives:

> The Walt Disney Company's economic goal is to maximize stockholders' value by consistently meeting the following objectives.
>
> - Increase earnings per share (EPS) at 20% annually over any five-year period.
> - Maintain high capital productivity with 20% return on equity (ROE) through profitable reinvestment of cash flows.[12]

[12]Annual report of The Walt Disney Company and Subsidiaries, 1989.

These same measures (EPS and ROE) frequently are used to determine profit-based compensation and bonuses.

Earnings Per Share. Recall that, for limited situations, earnings per share is simply net income divided by the outstanding shares of common stock. The limiting conditions are that

1. The company has no common stock transactions during the period so that the same number of shares of common stock were outstanding throughout the entire period.
2. The company has no preferred stock.[13]
3. The company has no other financial securities or contingencies that could result in the issuance of additional shares of common stock.

Each of these conditions will be discussed briefly.

Condition 1. Earnings are determined for some period of time, such as a year or a quarter. Yet, a differing number of shares of common stock may be outstanding during this period of time. For example, assume that Kemp Inc. began 1997 with 15,000 common shares outstanding and no preferred stock, and that on October 1, 1997, an additional 10,000 shares of common were issued.

If Kemp Inc. has 1997 earnings of $70,000, how should EPS be determined? During the period that Kemp was earning the $70,000, the company had 15,000 shares outstanding for three-quarters of the year and 25,000 shares outstanding for the other quarter. Should EPS for 1997 be $4.67 ($70,000/15,000 shares)? Should it be $2.80 ($70,000/25,000 shares)? Since the $70,000 was earned throughout 1997, some average number of shares outstanding more clearly reflects the EPS concept of incremental residual equity from periodic earnings.

Thus, GAAP requires that a weighted average number of common shares outstanding be used in computing EPS. The 15,000 shares that were outstanding throughout the entire year should be weighted in their entirety (or by 12/12 in terms of months outstanding). The 10,000 shares outstanding for only 1/4 of the year should be weighted by 25% (or by 3/12 in terms of months outstanding). The **weighted average shares outstanding**, then, are

DATE		ACTUAL SHARES		WEIGHT		WEIGHTED SHARES
1/1/97	Beginning shares	15,000	×	12/12	=	$15,000
10/1/97	Stock issued	10,000	×	3/12	=	2,500
						$17,500

In this simple example, EPS is $4 ($70,000/17,500).

Condition 2. The equity interest of common shareholders is a residual interest in the resources of a corporation. Thus, if EPS is to represent the incremental equity interest from earnings for a share of common stock, equity interests with priority claims on an enterprise's resources must be excluded. These priority

[13]Or, if the company has preferred stock, it is noncumulative and no dividends have been declared. The classification of preferred stock as cumulative or noncumulative is addressed in Chapter 19.

interests are those of creditors and preferred shareholders. Creditors' interests in a corporation's earnings are recognized as periodic interest expense, which is already subtracted from revenues in determining net income. However, since preferred dividends are not considered an expense, they are not subtracted from revenues to determine net income. Therefore, in determining EPS, preferred dividends must be subtracted from net income to determine common shareholders' residual equity interest in earnings.[14]

Condition 3. A simple capital structure results when a company has no financial securities or contingencies that could result in the issuance of additional shares of common stock. For companies with simple capital structures,

$$\text{Basic EPS} = \frac{\text{Net Income} - \text{Preferred Dividends}}{\text{Weighted Average Shares of Common Stock}}$$

However, if a corporation has convertible bonds, convertible preferred stock, stock warrants and options, or certain other contingent issuance agreements, that corporation has a complex capital structure. Here the potentially dilutive effect (that is, the potential reduction of EPS) of the possible issuance of additional common shares must be considered. SFAS No. 128 standard requires the determination of two EPS amounts for complex capital structures: (1) **basic EPS** as illustrated above and (2) diluted EPS, which considers potentially dilutive effects if additional common shares were issued. Purportedly, basic EPS provides an historical view of performance, while diluted EPS provides a prospective or future orientation of performance. The determination of diluted EPS is fairly complex and is addressed in Appendix B of this text.

Return on Equity. Basically, return on equity (ROE) is net income expressed as a percentage of shareholders' equity. ***Walt Disney,*** for example, reported in its management discussion a return on equity of 26% for the year ended September 30, 1989. A minor complication arises because net income is determined for a period of time, and shareholders' equity typically changes during this span of time. Whenever possible, average shareholders' equity should be used to calculate the return. Because net income may include some uncommon or nonrecurring items, as listed in Chapter 6, some analysts prefer to determine ROE using income from continuing operations rather than net income.

The ownership interests of *common* shareholders are the true residual interests in an enterprise. Therefore, an alternative measure of efficiency of resource usage is a return on *common* shareholders' equity rather than on *total* shareholders' equity.

Book Value Versus Market Value of Equity. Stockholders' equity is frequently referred to as the enterprise's net assets, net worth, or *book value.* Financial reports often provide *book value per share,* which is, essentially, common shareholders' equity divided by the common shares outstanding.

[14]Dividends on cumulative preferred stock must be subtracted each year whether declared or not. Dividends on noncumulative preferred stock are subtracted only when declared. Chapter 19 distinguishes cumulative preferred stock from noncumulative preferred stock.

IN PRACTICE—GENERAL

Book Value per Share

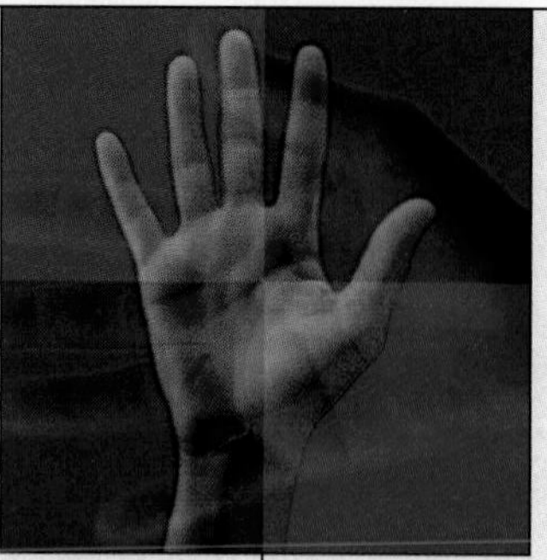

The following observations concerning a company's book value (shareholders' equity) were recently reported in *The Wall Street Journal:*

> For value investors, who favor beaten-down stocks that are cheap compared with corporate assets, book value used to provide an easy way to find bargains. All you had to do was compare a company's stock price with its book value on a per share basis, which can be calculated using the balance sheet in a company's annual report. Value investors would often be drawn to companies whose shares were trading near or below book value.
>
> These days, however, few stocks are at such depressed levels. According to the ***Leuthold Group***, a Minneapolis research firm, the companies in the Standard & Poor's 500-stock index are trading at an astounding 3.1 times book value. . . .
>
> [M]any companies have seen their book values shrink sharply because of share repurchases, write-offs caused by corporate restructurings, and the adoption of a new accounting rule that requires the setup of a reserve to cover retiree health benefits. Many money managers believe these items sometimes artificially depress a company's book value.
>
> Last year, for instance, ***General Motors'*** *(www.gm.com)* book value shrank to $8.47 a share, from $42.89, in large part because of new accounting rules regarding retiree benefits.

Source: J. Clements, "Book Value Is More Rarely Required Reading Now," *Wall Street Journal,* September 10, 1993, p. C1.

The book value per share is seldom equal to the market value of a share of stock. Further, the contributed capital of a corporation is the investment received when shares were first issued. Many current shareholders in a corporation may have purchased their shares in a secondary market, investing amounts far different than the original contributed capital received by the corporation.

Thus, while the ROE may provide some index of a company's profitability, investors should be more interested in a return on their own investment, or a return on the market value of equity. The latter is measured as the percentage of net income to the total market value of all shares of stock outstanding. The inverse of this relationship is a price-earnings relationship. Many market analysts utilize a **price-earnings (P/E) ratio** (market price of a share of common stock divided by its EPS) in their analysis. Finally, in terms of market performance for a given period, return can be perceived as the ratio of dividends plus (less) market appreciation (decline) to the beginning market value for the period.

SOLVENCY

The capital structure of a corporation provides an indication of its solvency. As stated previously, a **debt-to-equity ratio** portrays the proportion of an enterprise's debt to its owners' equity and is frequently used in financial analysis. Many lending institutions set an upper limit on the debt-to-equity ratios of borrowers as part of the debt covenants in their lending agreements.

END-OF-CHAPTER REVIEW

SUMMARY

The ownership interest of an enterprise is an important basic element of financial accounting. This chapter focuses upon corporate equity securities, and the introduction to the chapter raises several questions regarding which interests to report as equity.

1. **Record the issuance of capital stock.** The chapter discusses stock issuance for cash and other consideration, and for both par and no-par stock.
2. **Interpret the features of different types of preferred stock.** Various types of preferred stock include convertible preferred stock, callable preferred stock, and redeemable preferred stock. The various classes of stock are typically reported as part of shareholders' equity. Some firms, however, elect to report preferred stock separately after liabilities thus reporting a separate *common* shareholders' equity.
3. **Evaluate and record transactions for other equity securities and adjustments, such as those for options, warrants, and stock subscriptions.** In the chapter, we describe the conditions for which various other types of equity securities, such as options and warrants, are also included as part of shareholders' equity. We also note that *no* portion of the proceeds from issuing either convertible debt or convertible preferred stock is allocated to the conversion right. Thus, potential ownership interests of creditors holding convertible debt are *not* included as shareholders' equity.
4. **Interpret supplemental disclosures related to equity.** Detailed information concerning equity securities, including the existence of any conversion rights, must be disclosed supplementally as an integral part of financial statements.
5. **Prepare and analyze key profitability and solvency ratios that use equity information.** Shareholders' equity is important for examining operating efficiency contributing to firm profitability and solvency. Two popular indicators of profitability are earnings per share and return on equity. A debt-to-equity ratio provides an indication of a firm's solvency.

KEY TERMS

ASSIGNMENT MATERIAL

CASES

C18–1 Discussion—Preferred Stock

Why do you think companies authorize and issue preferred stock compared to common stock? compared to debt? Alternatively, why do you think investors purchase preferred stock as opposed to bonds or common stock?

C18–2 Discussion—Book Value

A company's book value is rarely equal to its market value. What are some factors that cause them to differ?

C18–3 Judgment and Decision—Employee Compensation

Consider the following three types of employee compensation:

1. Employers occasionally make advances to employees or prepay some of their forthcoming salary.
2. A "signing bonus" is paid to an athlete when he or she first contracts with a professional team.
3. For future service periods, employers often provide stock options to key employees with an exercise price below the market price of the stock at the measurement date.

Required:

A. What characteristics make each of the preceding types of compensation a form of deferred-compensation expense?
B. How do you think each of these three types should be reported in the employer's financial statements?
C. How are the first two forms of deferred-compensation expense treated differently from deferred-compensation expense for employee stock options? Should they be treated differently?

C18–4 Economic Consequences and Ethics—Stock-Based Compensation

Consider the criticisms of expense recognition using the fair value-based method that are located in the In Practice feature "Fair Value and Economic Consequences:"

Required:

A. In your opinion, does recognition of stock-based compensation using the fair value method have detrimental economic consequences? Consider the consequences from the perspectives of employees, creditors, shareholders, and the overall economy.
B. What are some ethical issues regarding employee stock options?
C. In what ways do the criticisms regarding economic consequences of the standard for stock-based compensation parallel those regarding standards for postemployment benefits?

C18–5 Judgment and Analysis—Stock Options

On December 31, 1997, Ball & Chain, Inc., issued to key employees a total of 100,000 stock options. Each option grants the right to purchase a share of common stock for an exercise price of $25. The market price of the stock on that date was $30. An appropriate option-pricing model estimates the value of each option as $7; and all options are expected to vest. The options were granted for the excellent employee service during 1997. The company's marginal income tax rate is 30%.

Before recognizing any compensation expense for 1997 associated with the stock options, net income for the year is $11,000,000. Further, shareholders' equity on December 31, 1997, exclusive of the stock options, is:

Common stock ($5 par)	$ 30,000,000
Paid-in capital	30,000,000
Retained earnings	100,000,000
	$160,000,000

Required:

A. First, based on intrinsic value and then on fair value, determine how net income for 1997 and shareholders' equity at December 31, 1997, would change in order to account for the options.

B. In your opinion, what is the cost to the corporation for issuing these options?

C. On July 1, 1998, all of the options are exercised, with stock thus issued for $25 per share. The market price of the stock on this date was $35 per share. What benefit do you think the employees received for these options? What do you think is the real cost to the corporation for issuing these options?

D. Now imagine that instead of the stock options, the employees were granted the right to purchase 100,000 units of Ball & Chain's product—tire chains—for $25 each when the selling price was $30, and that in 1998, when the company raised the price to $35, the employees were still allowed to purchase them for $25. How do these events and accounting for them differ from those with the stock options?

E. Finally, suppose the $25 rights to purchase the tire chains were granted to a preferred customer as part of a purchase commitment rather than to employees. Would the accounting for the purchase commitment be different than for the employee offer?

C18–6 The Purpose of Financial Reporting

Consider the following citations from recent professional literature and discuss the purpose of financial reporting. Should accounting standards be used for achieving some purpose? Should economic consequences be considered when setting accounting standards?

> Accounting standards seek to measure and report faithfully the economic events and transactions that have taken place. That objective applies equally to events and transactions that are favorable to the business and those that are unfavorable. Accounting standards are not and should not be designed to obscure or distort reality. If the reality is that stock options have value and are intended to motivate employees and to compensate them for their services, accounting should reflect that reality.
>
> In the United States, accounting standards are not designed to color the numbers, rosy or otherwise. Resource providers need good financial information to determine whether an entrepreneurial business is deserving of capital. It seems to me that to argue against an accounting standard because it might provide information that will discourage investment in any particular company or industry is to argue in favor of perpetrating a fraud on the capital provider. [P. Pacter, "FASB's Stock Option Proposal: Correcting a Serious Flaw, *The CPA Journal*, March, 1994, p. 60.]

> If I had to succinctly describe the purpose of corporate financial reporting, I would say accounting means telling it like it is, without bias or intent to encourage any particular mode of behavior by the use of the information . . . I think it is fair to say that none of us [FASB Board Members] believes that corporate financial reporting should purposefully try to influence behavior toward achieving some perceived social, economic, or public policy goal. To the contrary, we see an important part of our mission as providing unbiased information that can be used by the Congress and others who are responsible for establishing and pursuing national, social, and economic goals. [D. Beresford, "What Did We Learn from the Stock Compensation Project," *Accounting Horizons*, June, 1996, p. 129.]

C18–7 Profitability Analysis

Partially completed financial information for three different manufacturing companies in the same industry follow:

	BATON ROUGE	FRESNO	LEXINGTON
Net income for 1997	$ 500,000	$ 750,000	$ 1,000,000
As of 12/31/97:			
Total liabilities	$2,500,000	$1,250,000	$ 5,000,000
Shareholders' equity:			
Common stock, $10 par	$ 250,000	$ 500,000	$ 1,000,000
Paid-in capital	2,750,000	2,500,000	2,000,000
Retained earnings	2,000,000	2,000,000	2,000,000
	$5,000,000	$5,000,000	$ 5,000,000
Total liabilities and shareholders' equity	$7,500,000	$6,250,000	$10,000,000
Earnings per share	?	?	?
Return on shareholders' equity	?	?	?
Return on total assets	?	?	?

Required:

A. Complete the table for earnings per share and the returns on both shareholders' equity and total assets. Because of the limited information provided, use the ending balances for shareholders' equity and total assets when calculating the returns.

B. For each of the three profitability measures you just calculated, what is the ranking of the three companies from best performance to worst?

C. With respect to profitability, which company would you favor and why? Was this choice an obvious one?

D. What dangers are there to making these comparisons for only a single, isolated year?

C18–8 Discussion—Cost Comparison

Lars Inc. is considering offering its employees stock options as additional compensation. Forty employees would be eligible for the options, and a total of 2,000 options would be granted for the current year. The board of directors of Lars Inc. has met to discuss this plan.

A board member has proposed that the company offer stock appreciation rights (SARs) rather than options under the assumption that SARs are always cheaper for the company than options. He states that 2,000 SARs would cost less to grant than 2,000 options.

Required:

A. Is the board member's statement about the relative costs of options and SARs true? Explain.

B. What information is needed to determine which type of compensation scheme is best in this case?

QUESTIONS

Q18–1 According to the conceptual framework, what is owners' equity?

Q18–2 What are the two primary means by which ownership equity interests in an enterprise increase?

Q18–3 Describe different types of equity securities that might be considered part of owners' equity.

Q18–4 What are issue costs? What alternatives does a company issuing stock have for recording issue costs? Which of these alternatives do you prefer? Why?

Q18–5 Explain the difference between the book-value and market-value methods for conversion of convertible securities. Which method is required for convertible preferred stock?

Q18–6 What is the rationale for not recognizing gains when convertible preferred stock is converted to common stock?

Q18–7 Describe the difference between callable preferred stock and redeemable preferred stock.

Q18–8 Examine the note in Exhibit 18–4 regarding Sprint's redeemable stock. What are the characteristics of this security that resemble debt? What characteristics resemble equity?

Q18–9 Some companies are electing to report *common* shareholders' equity, classifying preferred stock before this, just after liabilities. Why are they selecting this reporting framework, and what is your opinion of this practice?

Q18–10 Under APB Opinion No. 25, what two factors determine the measurement date for stock options and stock appreciation rights?

Q18–11 Why is the measurement date for the intrinsic value method typically the grant date for stock options, but not for stock appreciation rights?

Q18–12 Under the intrinsic value method, companies do not recognize additional compensation for most fixed employee stock options. Why?

Q18–13 Why are nonqualified employee stock option plans advantageous to employers compared to qualified plans? Why, then, would employers offer qualified plans rather than nonqualified plans?

Q18–14 Identify the primary differences between the intrinsic value and the fair value methods for employee stock options.

Q18–15 Describe the difference between options that are forfeited and options than expire.

Q18–16 When are stock appreciation rights recognized as additional capital rather than liabilities?

Q18–17 What is an ESOP?

Q18–18 When warrants are issued with other securities like bonds, what condition must exist to recognize part of the proceeds as contributed capital attributed to the warrants?

Q18–19 What are stock subscriptions?

Q18–20 How are stock subscriptions similar to installment sales?

Q18–21 How are subscriptions receivable reported?

Q18–22 Why is contributed capital recognized for the full contracted price of stock subscriptions, even though only part of this price is received as down payment for the stock subscribed?

Q18–23 Under what limited set of conditions is EPS appropriately calculated by dividing net income by the number of common shares outstanding at the end of the period?

Q18–24 A weighted-average-shares-outstanding is used to determine EPS; average shareholders' equity is preferred in determining a return on equity (ROE); yet an average is *not used* when determining a debt-to-equity ratio. Explain the rationale for using an average for the first two ratios but not for the latter.

Q18–25 Generally, the concept of return on investment provides an indication of the efficiency of resource usage. Differentiate whose resources are the primary focus of a return on total assets compared to a return on owner's equity.

Q18–26 Refer to the discussion in the chapter located in the In Practice feature regarding statutory reserves for companies in the European Community. How would the "reserved" earnings as described be classified in the United States?

EXERCISES

E18–1 Stock Issuance

On October 31, 1997, L. Denburg Corporation issued 6,000 shares of $5 par common stock, receiving $15 per share.

Required: Journalize the transaction using a classification for par.

E18–2 Stock Issuance for Land

On February 10, 1997, Den Elberg, Inc., issued 20,000 shares of $1 par common stock in exchange for land appraised at $45,000. The stock is not actively traded on an exchange, but a prior issuance of shares eight months ago was for $2 per share.

Required: Journalize the transaction electing *not* to use a separate classification for par.

E18–3 Stock Issuance for Equipment

On April 15, 1997, Elden Burgers & Company acquired used specialized restaurant equipment by issuing 15,000 shares of no par common stock. New equipment would have cost $300,000. According to the stock exchange, the stock had a market price of $17 per share.

Required: Journalize the transaction.

E18–4 Preferred Stock Issuance

On July 1, 1997, Eldenberry & Associates obtained controlling interest in Garo Winery, Inc., by acquiring 51 percent of Garo's 100,000 outstanding shares of common stock. The shares were acquired by issuing both an 8%, 10-year, $500,000 note and 30,000 shares of Eldenberry's preferred stock. This is the first issuance of preferred stock for Eldenberry.

Required:

A. Using the $40 per share listed market price on that date for Garo's stock, journalize the transaction.

B. Do you think this market value represents an appropriate reflection of the value for the acquisition?

E18–5 Preferred Stock Conversion

On November 1, 1997, 20,000 shares of Up&Coming Inc.'s convertible, no-par preferred stock were converted into 20,000 shares of $1 par common stock. The preferred stock was originally issued two years ago for $50 per share. The market prices on the conversion date for the preferred and common stock were $60 and $65 per share, respectively.

Required: Using a classification for the par of the common stock, journalize the conversion.

E18–6 Lump Sum Stock Issuance

Occasionally, a company may issue two different classes of stock for a single lump sum. When such an event occurs, the amount of the total attributable to each class of stock must be determined.

Required: Prepare entries for each of the following two independent events.

A. **Proportional Allocation** (market value of both classes known). A company issues 1,000 shares of no-par preferred stock and 2,000 shares of $1 par common stock for a total price $81,000 when the market value for the stocks are determined to be $50 and $20 per respective share.

B. **Residual Allocation** (market value of one class known). A company issues 1,000 shares of no-par preferred stock and 2,000 shares of $1 par common stock for a total price $81,000 when the market value for the common stock is determined to be $20 per share but the market value of preferred stock is indeterminable.

E18–7 Preferred-Stock Conversion

Refer to Exhibit 18–3 concerning the conversion of convertible preferred stock.

Required:

A. Redo the exhibit assuming that Griffin Company only uses a single Paid-In Capital account for all capital in excess of par.

B. Assume that Griffin's convertible preferred stock has a conversion price of $20 per share. Redo the journal entry for the conversion of the 2,000 shares upon the receipt of this conversion price by Griffin.

E18–8 Bond Conversion (CPA Adapted, Part I, MC#37, November 1993)

On July 1, 1997, after recording interest and amortization, York Company converted $1,000,000 of its 12% convertible bonds into 50,000 shares of $1 par value common stock. On the conversion date the carrying amount of the bonds was $1,300,000, the market value of the bonds was $1,400,000, and York's common stock was publicly trading at $30 per share.

Required: Using the book value method, determine what amount of additional paid-in capital York should record as a result of the conversion.

E18–9 Issue Costs

Regal, Inc., recently issued 250,000 shares of $1 par common stock for a price of $20 per share. However, the underwriters retain 2% for service fees. In addition to underwriter fees, Regal incurred other issue costs totaling $40,000. This $40,000 was paid prior to the stock issuance and debited to an account called Prepaid Issue Costs.

Required:

A. Journalize the issuance of the stock assuming that Regal recognizes contributed capital for the net proceeds from issuance.
B. Journalize the issuance of the stock assuming that Regal recognizes contributed capital for the full price of the shares issued and immediately expenses all issue costs.
C. Journalize the issuance of the stock assuming that Regal recognizes contributed capital for the full price of the shares issued and records the issue costs as organization costs to be amortized over five years. Also prepare an entry for one full year's amortization.
D. How would stockholders' equity differ for these three different methods?
E. Which of the methods in (**A**) through (**C**) would you recommend and why?

E18–10 Stock Options

On January 1, 1997, Gracious Corporation granted 100,000 stock options for common stock with an exercise price equal to the stock price of $35. The options are for employee service from the grant date until the options vest on December 31, 2000. An options pricing model estimates a fair value for each option of $8 and all options are expected to vest. The company's marginal income tax rate is 30%.

Required:

A. Use the intrinsic value method to prepare any necessary entries for December 31, 1997.
B. Use the fair value method to prepare any necessary entries for December 31, 1997.
C. During 1999, 10,000 options are forfeited. Using fair value, prepare any necessary entries for December 31, 1999.

E18–11 Stock Options

On January 1, 1997, Hugh Grant Corporation granted 100,000 stock options for common stock with an exercise price of $25. The stock price on the grant date was $28. The options are for employee service from the grant date until the options vest on December 31, 1999. An options-pricing model estimates a fair value for each option of $9, and 10 percent of the options are expected to be forfeited although none were forfeited in 1997. The company's marginal income tax rate is 30%.

Required:

A. Use the intrinsic value method to prepare any necessary entries for December 31, 1997.
B. Use the fair value method and consider actual unforfeited options (rather than expected forfeitures) to prepare any necessary entries for December 31, 1997.

C. Use the fair value method and consider expected forfeitures (rather than actual unforfeited options) to prepare any necessary entries for December 31, 1997.

E18–12 Exercise of Stock Options

As of January 1, 1997, Rock Solid Company had deferred tax assets of $34,000 and additional paid-in capital for stock options of $100,000, both related to 20,000 employee stock options. The vesting and service periods for these options has already passed. On May 1, 1997, all of the options are exercised for $40 each when the company's no par common stock has a market price of $50 per share. Assume an income tax rate of 34%.

Required:

A. Prepare entries for the exercise of the options and related income tax effects.

B. Redo Part A assuming the market price per share on the exercise date was $43 instead of $50.

E18–13 Exercise and Expiration of Stock Options

As of January 1, 1997, Solid Rock Company had deferred tax assets of $68,000 and additional paid-in capital for stock options of $200,000, both related to 50,000 employee stock options. The vesting and service periods for these options has already passed. On October 1, 1997, 25,000 options were exercised for $40 each when the company's $1 par common stock had a market price of $44 per share. The remaining 25,000 options expired on December 31, 1997. Assume an income tax rate of 34%.

Required:

A. Prepare entries on October 1, 1997 for the exercise of the options and related income tax effects.

B. Prepare entries on December 31, 1997 for the expiration of the options and related income tax effects.

E18–14 Stock Appreciation Rights

On January 1, 1997, Carriage Corporation granted its CEO stock appreciation rights (SARs) based upon appreciation of 100,000 shares of common stock above its then current market price of $33 per share. The SARs are for the CEO's service for 1997 and 1998 and are to be awarded in cash on December 31, 1998. The market prices of the stock at the end of 1997 and 1998 were $40 and $45, respectively.

Required: Prepare the entries for December 31, 1997 and 1998.

E18–15 Stock Appreciation Rights

As of January 1, 1997, Star Company had a liability for stock appreciation rights of $20,000 which resulted from compensation recognized in 1996. The SARs are for appreciation of 40,000 shares over a base price of $30 per share and are to be awarded on December 31, 1998. On December 31, 1997, the price of the stock was $33 per share.

Required: Determine compensation expense for 1997.

E18–16 Stock Appreciation Rights and Deferred Taxes

Refer to Exhibit 18–7 in the text. Assume that the compensation is deductible for income tax purposes and that the company's marginal income tax rate is 30%.

Required: Prepare entries for the income tax effects each year.

E18–17 Weighted Average Shares

Johnson Inc. began 1997 with 500,000 common shares outstanding, and issued another 80,000 shares on October 1, 1997.

Required: What is the weighted average number of shares outstanding for 1997?

E18–18 Weighted Average Shares

Kenney Inc. began 1997 with 3,000,000 common shares outstanding, issued 200,000 shares on April 1, 1997, and another 500,000 on July 1, 1997.

Required: What is the weighted average number of shares outstanding for 1997?

E18–19 Basic EPS

On January 1, 1997, Leslie Company had outstanding 45,000 shares of $5 par value common stock. During 1997, the company declared and paid $6,000 in dividends on preferred stock. It also issued 3,000 common shares on May 1, 1997. Net income for the year was $100,000.

Required: Determine basic earnings per share.

E18–20 Basic EPS

On January 1, 1997, Lester Company had outstanding 50,000 shares of $5 par value common stock. During 1997, the company declared and paid $10,000 in dividends on preferred stock. It also issued 20,000 common shares on July 1, 1997. Net income for the year was $100,000.

Required: Determine basic earnings per share.

E18–21 Return on Equity—Walt Disney

Walt Disney Company reported net income and return on equity for 1989 as $703.3 million and 26%, respectively. Shareholders' equity at the beginning and end of 1989 was $3,044.0 and $2,359.3 million, respectively.

Required: Calculate the return on equity three ways, using beginning, average, and ending shareholders' equity. Which did Disney use?

E18–22 Return on Equity—Harcourt General

Harcourt General's (see Exhibit 18–2) net income for the year ended October 31, 1995, was $165,883,000.

Required: Using average shareholders' equity, determine its return on equity for the year.

E18–23 Equity Transactions—Harcourt General

In Exhibit 18–2, ***Harcourt General's*** statement of shareholders' equity depicts the conversion of series A stock and the repurchase (and retirement) of common stock.

Required: Prepare journal entries for these transactions. Do you find anything unusual about the repurchase and retirement of the common stock?

E18–24 Equity Transactions—Sprint Corporation

The footnote in Exhibit 18–4 indicates provisions for calling ***Sprint's*** third series preferred stock.

Required: Prepare two journal entries for the redemption of the third series stock—one for the 24,000 shares redeemed in March 1996 and another for the remaining shares. What assumption must you make for the second entry?

PROBLEMS

P18–1 Issue Price of Stock

For this problem, refer to the exhibits in the chapter.

Required:

A. Referring to Exhibit 18–4, determine the average price per share for ***Sprint's*** issuance of common stock.
B. Referring to Exhibit 18–3, determine the average issue price of Griffin's preferred stock and its common stock (1) before the conversion and (2) after the conversion. Was there any change? If so, how would you interpret such changes?
C. What complicates a similar determination of the average issue price for the different classes of stock for ***Harcourt General*** (Exhibit 18–2)?

P18–2 Equity Transactions

Shareholders' equity for Ghi Ghi, Inc., on January 1, 1997, was:

Common stock, $1 par	$ 500,000
Paid-in capital	6,500,000
Retained earnings	2,000,000
	$9,000,000

The following equity events occurred throughout 1997:

1. On March 1, 30,000 shares of common stock were issued for $25 per share.
2. On April 1, 20,000 shares of $50 par convertible preferred stock were issued for par.
3. On July 1, 6,000 shares of the convertible preferred stock were converted to common stock. Each preferred share is convertible into two shares of common stock without any additional considerations required for the conversion. The market values of preferred stock and the common stock on the conversion dates were $56 and $28, respectively.
4. On December 31, the company paid $72,000 in dividends to preferred shareholders.
5. Net income for 1997 was $1,000,000.

Required:

A. Prepare journal entries for each transaction and the entry to close income summary.
B. Prepare the shareholders' equity section of the balance sheet on December 31, 1997.
C. Describe how the equity transactions would be reported in a statement of cash flows for 1997.
D. Ignoring the potential conversion feature of the remaining preferred stock, determine basic earnings per share for 1997.

P18–3 Equity Transactions

Shareholders' equity for HoHo, Inc., on January 1, 1997, was

Common stock, $10 par	$ 50,000,000
Paid-in capital	20,000,000
Retained earnings	230,000,000
	$300,000,000

The following equity events occurred throughout 1997:

1. On January 2, the company issued 20,000 options granting key employees the right to obtain for each option one share of common stock at an exercise price of $30 per share. The market value of the common stock on this date was $40 per share. Options may be exercised during the two-year period of January 1, 1999, through December 31, 2000. The options are to reward employees for expected future service during the years 1997 and 1998. The company elects to use the provisions of APB No. 25.
2. On July 1, the company awarded to top management stock appreciation rights (SARs) based upon 10,000 shares of common stock at the then current market price of $37 per share. The rights are for service from this date until the SARs are awarded in the form of common stock on June 30, 2001.
3. On December 31, the market price of the stock was $44 per share.
4. Net income for 1997 was $15,000,000. There were no dividends declared or paid in 1997. The income tax rate is 30%, and compensation for both the options and SARs are deductible differences.

Required:

A. Prepare the necessary journal entries to reflect these events, including the closing entry for income summary.
B. Prepare the shareholders' equity section of the balance sheet on December 31, 1997.
C. Describe how the equity events would be reported in a statement of cash flows for 1997.

P18–4 Book Value of Equity

For this problem, refer to the exhibits in the chapter.

Required:

A. Determine the book value per common share for each period reported of
   1. Griffin Company after the conversion (Exhibit 18–3).
   2. *Sprint Corporation* (Exhibit 18–4).
B. What assumptions would you have to make to determine the book value per common share for ***Harcourt General*** in Exhibit 18–2?
C. Determine the percentage change for ***Sprint***.

P18–5 Stock Options

The following repeats the facts presented in case C18–5. On December 31, 1997, Ball & Chain, Inc., issued to key employees a total of 100,000 stock options. Each option grants the right to purchase a share of common stock for an exercise price of $25. The market price of the stock on that date was $30. An appropriate option-pricing model estimates the value of each option as $7, and all options are expected to vest. The options were granted for the excellent employee service during 1997. The company's marginal income tax rate is 30%.

Before recognizing any compensation expense for 1997 associated with the stock options, net income for the year is $11,000,000. Further, shareholders' equity on December 31, 1997, exclusive of the stock options, is:

Common stock ($5 par)	$ 30,000,000
Paid-in capital	30,000,000
Retained earnings	100,000,000
	$160,000,000

Required:

A. Using the intrinsic value method, prepare the stockholders' equity section of the balance sheet for December 31, 1997.

B. Using the fair value method, prepare the stockholders' equity section of the balance sheet for December 31, 1997.

P18–6 Stock Options (Intrinsic Value vs Fair Value)

Refer to Exhibit 18–6 for Hoffman Corporation's stock option plan. Assume that on January 1, 1997, Hoffman had 800,000 shares of its common stock issued and outstanding, for an average issue price of $20 per share, and that retained earnings were $40 million.

Required:

A. Prepare the shareholders' equity section of the balance sheet as of January 1, 1997.

B. Assume that net income in 1997 was $800,000 before considering expenses and deferred taxes related to the stock options. Determine net income, first assuming the intrinsic value method and then assuming the fair value method.

C. There were no dividends nor stock issued during 1997. Prepare the shareholders' equity for December 31, 1997, first assuming the intrinsic value method and then assuming the fair value method.

D. Summarize the impact of using the fair value method rather than the intrinsic value method. Would adoption of the fair value method have economic consequences?

P18–7 Stock Options—Intrinsic Value Method

On January 1, 1997, Pararex Company granted 80,000 stock options to upper management, with each option allowing the purchase of one share of Pararex's $1 par common stock anytime during the period of January 1, 1999, through December 31, 2003, for an exercise price of $10. The options are for employee service for 1997 and 1998. The company's marginal tax rate is 34%. On December 30, 2002, the employees exercised all of their options. Following are market prices for Pararex' common stock:

1/1/97	$12 per share
12/31/97	$13 per share
1/1/98	$14 per share
12/31/98	$15 per share
1/1/99	$14 per share
12/30/2002	$20 per share

Required: Using the requirements for the intrinsic value method,

A. Determine the total compensation, if any, for the options that Pararex would recognize.

B. Prepare entries for the annual compensation expense, if any, and for related deferred income taxes for both 1997 and 1998.

C. Prepare the necessary entries when the options are exercised on December 30, 2002.

D. How would your answers change if the market price for the stock on January 1, 1995, was $9 per share?

P18–8 Stock Options—Fair Value Method

Examine the details for Pararex's employee stock options described in the previous problem. On January 1, 1997, the estimated fair value of each option based on an approved option-pricing model is $5.

Required: Using the requirements for the fair value method,

A. Prepare the entries, including those for deferred taxes, for December 31 of 1997 and 1998.
B. Assume that the company expects total forfeitures due to employee turnover of 5 percent. Considering these expected forfeitures, prepare the entries, including those for deferred taxes, for December 31 of 1997 and 1998.
C. Assume that all eligible employees unexpectedly remained employed so all options vested, but that the company had considered expected forfeitures in determining compensation expense on December 31, 1997 (Part B above). Prepare the entries for December 31, 1998, considering this change in estimate for forfeitures.
D. Assuming that all options vested, prepare the entries when the employees exercised their options.

P18–9 Stock Options—Comparison of Fair Value and Intrinsic Value Methods
On July 1, 1997, Quest Corporation awarded 200,000 common stock options to upper management. The exercise price per option to obtain a share of common stock is $40, and options may be exercised any time after they vest on July 1, 2001, until July 1, 2008. The market price per share of Quest's common stock on July 1, 1997, was also $40 and the par value was $10. The estimated fair value of each option on the grant date is $6. Expected forfeitures are 10%. The compensation period is assumed from the grant date to the vesting date. The company's marginal tax rate is 34%. Assume a calendar year.

Required:

A. Use the requirements of the intrinsic value method to prepare any necessary entries related to the options for July 1, 1997, through July 1, 2001.
B. Use the requirements of the fair value method and consider expected forfeitures to prepare any necessary entries related to the options for July 1, 1997, through July 1, 2001.
C. No options were forfeited in 1997, but 4 percent were forfeited in 1998, and another 6 percent of the original total were forfeited in 1999. Use the requirements of the fair value method and consider options not forfeited to prepare any necessary entries related to the options for July 1, 1997, through July 1, 2001.

P18–10 Stock Appreciation Rights
On January 1, 1997, WeCARE Corporation granted its CEO stock appreciation rights (SARs) based upon appreciation of 300,000 shares of common stock above its then current market price. The SARs are for the CEOs service for 1997, 1998, and 1999. The SARs are to be awarded on December 31, 1999. Following are market prices for WeCARE's common stock:

1/1/97	$20 per share
12/31/97	$23 per share
1/1/98	$23 per share
12/31/98	$25 per share
12/31/99	$28 per share

Required:

A. Determine the total compensation, if any, for the SARs that WeCARE would recognize.

B. Determine the annual compensation expense, if any, for the SARs for 1997, 1998, and 1999.

C. How would your answers to (B) change if the market price for the stock on December 31, 1999, is $20 per share?

D. If you were an employee of WeCARE Corporation, would you rather receive stock appreciation rights or stock options as added compensation? Why?

P18–11 Report Preparation—SARs Versus Stock Options

The labor union of Bruce Company is negotiating for compensation for the next three-year contract period of 1999–2001. The union has received management's proposal for additional compensation in the form of a stock option plan. Management is offering the 50 employees of Bruce Company 100 options each. The exercise period for the options is 2002–2003; the current market value of the stock is $65, and the exercise price of each option is $65.

The labor union has made a counteroffer to the proposed stock option plan. The union thinks most of its members would prefer stock appreciation rights over stock options because the employees cannot afford to buy shares of stock. Further, the union points to the fact that the price of Bruce Company stock has risen an average of one dollar per share for each of the past 10 months. The union has proposed that, rather than stock options, the 50 employees receive 100 SARs each payable at the end of 2001. The union thinks that management will accept its proposal because linking compensation to the stock prices will encourage employees to work harder.

Management has asked you to determine whether the management or the union proposal is best for management. You have found the following information relevant:

Stock price at negotiation date (12/1/98)	$65
Stock price at 1/1/98	$54
Estimated option price	$15
Assumed service period for stock options	3 years

Required:

A. Determine the estimated total compensation for Bruce Company as of 12/1/98 under each proposal.

B. Assuming stock prices continue to rise $1 per month, estimate the total compensation by the end of the contract period (2001) for each proposal.

C. Prepare a report for management explaining why Bruce would be better off with SARs or with stock options.

P18–12 Profitability Analysis

Jeff Jones is president of Morris Company. Jones has been called to a special meeting of the board of directors because one board member feels that the company's profitability is decreasing. Jones has asked you to help with financial analysis that refutes the concerns of the board.

Specifically, Jones is concerned about how to explain the decreasing rate of increase in net income for the past two years. You have gathered the financial information shown here. Jones thinks that ratio analysis will help prove his point and has asked for certain computations as follows:

	1997	1998
Net sales	$1,400,000	$1,960,000
Net income	500,000	530,000
Total liabilities	3,400,000	4,200,000
Total equity	1,800,000	2,100,000

Required: Assume that at the end of 1996, total equity was $1,600,000 and total assets were $5,000,000.

A. Compute the sales profit margin, return on equity and return on assets ratios for 1997 and 1998.

B. Is the company more profitable than is shown by the trend in net income alone? Explain.

P18–13 Financing Alternatives

Quandry Corporation needs to raise $800,000 to purchase fixed assets. The company currently has $4,200,000 in total assets and $3,000,000 in shareholders' equity that consists of 500,000 outstanding shares of $1 par common stock. The company estimates future annual after-tax income of $1,000,000 before any expenses related to financing the fixed assets. Depreciation is included when estimating this income. Management is considering three possible financing alternatives for raising the $800,000:

1. Long-term debt with interest of 7%. The marginal income tax rate is 34%.
2. Issuing $50 par preferred stock that would require dividends of $2.50 per share. The company estimates an issue price of $80 per share, so it would have to issue 10,000 shares.
3. Issuing 16,000 shares of $1 par common stock at an estimated issue price of $50 per share.

Required:

A. For each financing alternative, assuming occurrence at the beginning of the year, determine
   1. Net income
   2. EPS
   3. Debt ratio
   4. Return on total assets (add the full $800,000 to assets, ignoring depreciation since it would be the same for each alternative)
   5. Return on shareholders' equity
   6. Return on common shareholders' equity

B. Which financing alternative would you select and why?

C. How would the above financial measures and your selection change if the common stock could be issued for only $20 per share, requiring the issuance of 40,000 shares?

D. When considering the issuance of common stock, how would estimated dividends on the stock issued alter your analysis?

P18–14 Comprehensive Problem: Income Statement, Deferred Taxes, Shareholders' Equity (CPA Adapted Problem, Part I, No. 5, November 1992)

The following condensed trial balance of Powell Corporation, a publicly owned company, has been adjusted except for income tax expense:

POWELL CORPORATION
Condensed Trial Balance
June 30, 1997

	DEBIT	CREDIT
Total assets	$25,080,000	
Total liabilities		$ 9,900,000
5% cumulative preferred stock		2,000,000
Common stock		10,000,000
Retained earnings		2,900,000
Machine sales		750,000
Service revenues		250,000
Interest revenues		10,000
Gain on sale of factory		250,000
Cost of sales—machines	425,000	
Cost of services	100,000	
Administrative expenses	300,000	
Research & development expenses	110,000	
Interest expense	5,000	
Loss from asset disposal	40,000	
	$26,060,000	$26,060,000

Other information and financial data for the year-ended June 30, 1997, follows:

1. The weighted average number of common shares outstanding during the period was 200,000.
2. On May 1, 1997, Powell's directors paid dividends totaling $100,000 to preferred stockholders.
3. During 1997 one of Powell's foreign factories was expropriated by the foreign government, and Powell received a $900,000 payment from the foreign government in settlement. The carrying value of the plant was $650,000 for both financial reporting and income tax purposes. Any gains or losses on disposal of the plant are taxable. Powell has never disposed of a factory.
4. Administrative expenses include a $5,000 premium payment for a $1,000,000 life insurance policy on Powell's president, of which the corporation is the beneficiary. These premiums are not tax-deductible.
5. Powell depreciates its assets using the straight-line method for financial reporting purposes and an accelerated method for tax purposes. Tax depreciation for the year ended June 30, 1997, exceeded book depreciation by $15,000. The company began the year with a deferred tax liability for temporary differences related to fixed assets. There were no other temporary differences.
6. Powell's enacted tax rate for the current and future years is 30%.

Required:

A. Using the single-step format, prepare Powell's income statement for the year ended June 30, 1997. Be sure to report EPS in the income statement.

B. Prepare a schedule reconciling Powell's financial statement net income to taxable income for the year ended June 30, 1997.

C. Prepare the June 30, 1997, adjusting entry for income taxes assuming Powell has not made any prepayments.

D. Prepare a condensed balance sheet for Powell as of June 30, 1997, with details only for shareholders' equity.

P18–15 Book Value of Common Stock

As input to this problem, refer to any of the stockholders' equity sections previously used in the exercises or problems in this chapter or elsewhere in the text, financial statements provided in class, or the following summarized stockholders' equity section for Equity, Inc.

	December 31 of	
	This Year	Last Year
Preferred stock (1,000 shares, 8%, $100 par; 1,000 shares issued)	$100,000	$100,000
Common stock (10,000 shares, $10 par; 8,000 shares issued)	80,000	80,000
Additional paid-in capital, common	40,000	40,000
Total contributed capital	$220,000	$220,000
Retained earnings	195,000	170,000
Treasury stock—Cost		
1,000 shares, common	(11,000)	
1,500 shares, common		(18,000)
Total stockholders' equity	$404,000	$372,000

Note: Dividends in the amount of $8,000 were in arrears on the preferred stock at December 31 of last year. There are no dividends in arrears on preferred stock at the end of this year.

Required:

A. Enter the preceding information in the template and follow the instructions found there. Determine the following for each company examined:
1. Common stock book value per share for each year reported.
2. The percentage change in book value per share from last year to this year.

B. If you used actual companies as your input for this template, compare the book value per share numbers to reported market value per share numbers at year end for the companies. What information can you get from this comparison?

C. In general, how can book value per share be used for analysis purposes?

P18–16 Stock Appreciation Rights

Assume that at the beginning of Year 1, X Corporation granted a total of 10,000 SARs to certain employees. The SARs are exercisable beginning on January 1 of Year 6. Compensation is based on the difference between the market price of the stock and a price of $7 per SAR. Ending market prices were as follows:

Year 1	$10
Year 2	11
Year 3	8
Year 4	5
Year 5	9

Required:

A. Enter the preceding information in the template and follow the instructions found there. Make the entries for Years 1–5 on the books of X related to the SARs. Assume expected exercise of the SARs will be for cash rather than stock.

B. Explain the credit in the entry at the end of Year 3.

C. Assume instead that the market price at the end of Year 3 is $6. Make the new journal entry required at the end of Year 3, and explain the amount of the credit.

D. In general, what is the rationale for making these computations? How are measurement difficulties still evident in the ongoing debate about recognizing stock option compensation?

E. If you were an employee under this SAR plan, what perspective might you take to company performance—"short-run" (up to five years) or "long-run" (sixth year and beyond), and why?

RESEARCH ACTIVITIES

R18–1 Market Values

Examine past issues of *The Wall Street Journal* to determine the market prices of ***Sprint*** at the close of each report date in Exhibit 18–4. Then, using the results from the problem concerning book values (P18–4), determine the ratio of book value to market value for each report date. Do you detect any patterns concerning this ratio?

R18–2 Cost of Equity

Locate and study these two short articles: "Special Report—What Does Equity Financing Really Cost," *Business Week*, November 7, 1988, pp. 146–147; and K. L. Fisher, "Portfolio Strategy—Three Easy Steps," *Forbes*, October 30, 1989, p. 253. What is a conceptual interpretation of the cost of equity? How would you explain the concept of leverage? Are the two articles in harmony with one another? Finally, based upon the two articles together, express your opinion concerning the choice of increasing resources by using either debt or equity as the source of capital.

R18–3 GAAP Search and Analysis—Stock Issued in Absence of Market Values

The chapter discusses the issuance of stock in exchange for noncash assets or services. Some high-tech, development-stage companies issue stock for things like patent rights. In many of these cases, there is no determinable market value either for the stock or for the assets or skills exchanged for the stock. Determine what is required to account for stock issued in the absence of market values.

R18–4 GAAP Search and Analysis—Dissenting Views of FASB Board Members

Examine the text of SFAS No. 123, "Accounting for Stock Based Compensation." As one possible source, the standard was reprinted in the *Journal of Accountancy*, January 1996, pp. 99–105. From your examination, determine the vote on whether to adopt the standard. If there were any board members with dissenting opinions, summarize the major issues to which they took exception.

R18–5 Option Pricing Model

Use the article "FASB No. 123: Putting Together the Pieces" by J. Mountain in the *Journal of Accountancy*, January 1996, pp. 73–78, to prepare a report on using the Black-Scholes option pricing model to determine the fair value of stock options.

R18–6 Stock Options—Contrasting Views

Prepare a report that summarizes the views expressed in the following three citations:

1. H. Wolk, and J. Rozycki, "Stock Options Are Not an Expense," *Financial Executive*, July/August 1994, pp. 12–15.
2. M. Bohan, "Who Says the FASB Isn't Listening?", *Financial Executive*, November/December 1994, pp. 11–12.
3. P. Pacter, "FASB's Stock Option Accounting Proposal: Correcting a Serious Flaw," *The CPA Journal*, March 1994, pp. 60–61.

R18–7 Financial Analysis—Redeemable Preferred Stock

Examine subsequent annual reports of ***Sprint Corporation*** to determine the status of the redeemable preferred stock reported December 31, 1995 (see Exhibit 18–4). Has the company issued more? Has any been retired?

R18–8 Financial Analysis—Motorola

Examine ***Motorola's*** annual report in the appendix.

Required:

A. How does the company's book value per share compare with its market value per share?
B. Does the company have any preferred stock?
C. Does the company have any outstanding employee stock options? Which accounting standard regarding employee stock options applies to Motorola's 1995 annual report? Did Motorola recognize any expense in 1995 for employee stock options? Why or why not?

R18–9 Financial Research

Examine an electronic database, such as the one that accompanies this text, for the following.

Required:

A. How many companies have shares of preferred stock outstanding? What proportion are these companies to the total number of companies in the database?
B. Identify companies that have redeemable preferred stock outstanding. For each company, specify the percentage that the redeemable preferred stock is to total assets.

R18–10 Financial Research—Internet and Stockmaster

Use your Web browser to find Stockmaster's homepage through *http://www.swcollege.com/hartman.html*. The Stockmaster Web site lists recent stock prices.

Required:

A. Determine the latest market prices for the common stock of ***Sprint*** and ***Motorola.*** For each stock, indicate the price, date, time, and market change.

B. Examine the graph provided by Stockmaster for each of the two companies in (**A**). Provide a brief statement about each company's market price during the last three months.

C. How do the recent market prices in (**A**) compare to the companies' market prices as of the balance sheet dates reported in this chapter (see R18–1 and R18–8)?

R18–11 Financial Research—Internet and Edgar

Use EDGAR to obtain the most recent 10K report of ***Walt Disney.***

Required: Use the information is this 10K to prepare a report concerning executive compensation at Walt Disney. In the report, be sure to present information on stock-based compensation to executives.

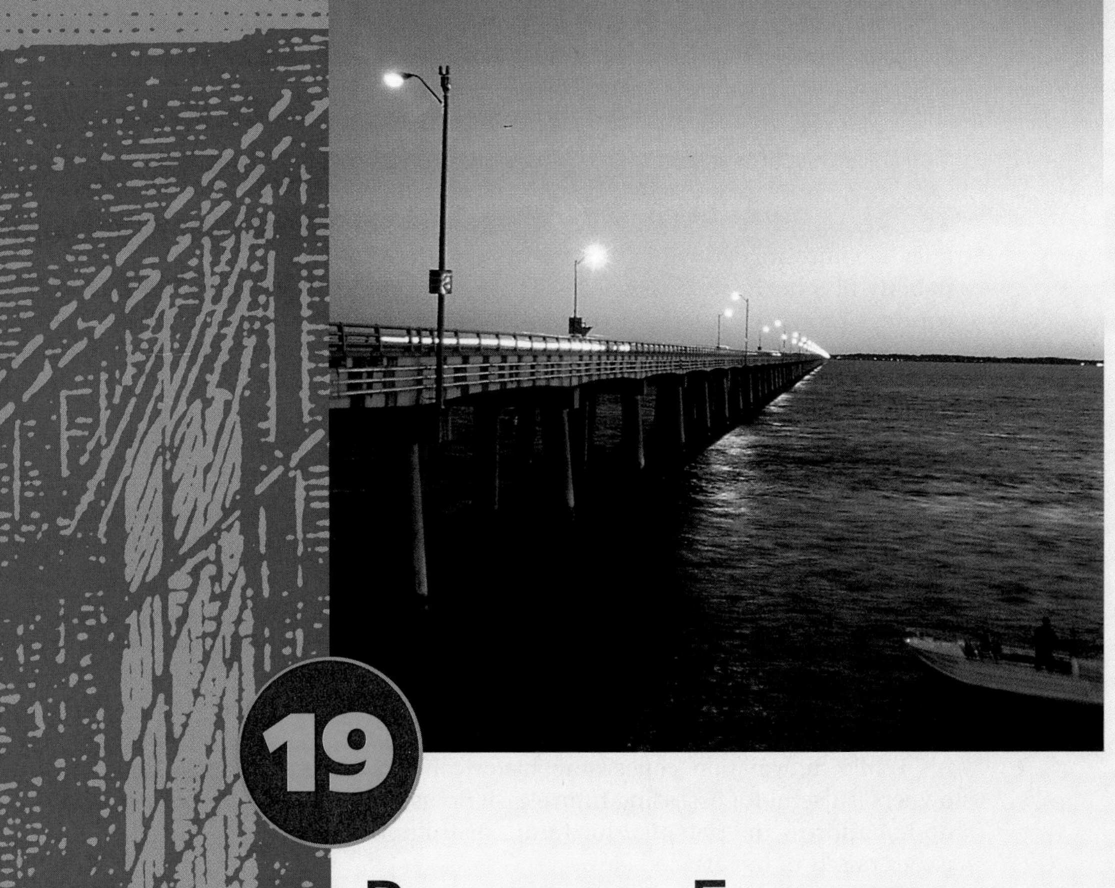

19

Retained Earnings and Distributions to Shareholders

Learning Objectives

After studying this chapter, you should be able to:

1. Record the declaration and distribution of dividends.
2. Determine amounts distributable as dividends for various types of preferred stock.
3. Distinguish between accounting for stock dividends and stock splits.
4. Evaluate and record treasury stock transactions.
5. Explain the significance and limitations of appropriated retained earnings.
6. Evaluate and record quasi-reorganizations.
7. Interpret the significance and limitations of current standards for reporting retained earnings and distributions to owners.

As the name implies, *retained earnings* represent owners' equity resulting from an enterprise's current and prior periods' undistributed earnings. According to SFAC No. 6, "Equity is a residual interest—what remains after liabilities are deducted from assets—and depends significantly on the profitability of a business enterprise."[1] That is, as profitability increases, retained earnings grows, increasing owners' residual interests in enterprise assets.

SFAC No. 6 further states,

> A business enterprise may distribute assets resulting from income to its owners, but distributions to owners are discretionary, depending on the volition of owners or their representatives after considering the need of the enterprise and restrictions imposed by law, regulation, or agreement. An enterprise is generally not obligated to transfer assets to owners except in the event of the enterprise's liquidation.[2]

Obviously, "assets resulting from income" that are distributed to owners reduce the owners' residual interest in enterprise assets and thus reduce retained earnings. Such corporate distributions are called *dividends*. Other types of distributions (such as treasury stock repurchases) also may reduce owners' equity, but without affecting retained earnings.

While information concerning historical or prospective distributions to owners is useful for assessing future cash flows, traditional reporting practices do not address the potential for future distributions to owners. Consider the issues raised in the article below.

This decade has also seen massive distributions of assets to shareholders. This chapter addresses retained earnings and distributions to owners. After a brief review of reporting retained earnings, several types of ownership distributions are discussed, including leveraged buyouts, debt-financed dividends,

The Stockholders' Equity Section: Form without Substance

The takeover fever of the 1980s produced hundreds of leveraged buyouts, debt-financed dividend distributions, and treasury stock repurchases involving massive distributions of corporate assets to stockholders. In many of these restructurings, distributions to stockholders exceeded the net book value of the corporations's assets and were possible only because corporate managers and creditors relied on the fair values (i.e., the current appraised values) of the assets to maintain a positive net worth. These distributions would not have been possible under traditional state legal capital requirements which restricted distributions to earned and contributed capital in excess of the par value of the corporation's outstanding stock. Indeed, the resulting effect of many of the debt-financed restructurings on corporate stockholders' equity sections has been to produce deficit balances not only in retained earnings, but also in total stockholders' equity. This phenomenon leads us to question the relevance of current stockholders' equity disclosures, which focus attention on the source of capital but ignore the capacity of the corporation for making distributions to stockholders.

Source: M. L. Roberts, W. D. Samson, and M. T. Dugan, "The Stockholders' Equity Section: Form Without Substance," *Accounting Horizons*, December 1990, p. 35.

[1]SFAC No. 6, par. 54.
[2]Ibid., par. 54.

and treasury stock repurchases. Then, qualifications to retained earnings for appropriations and quasi-reorganizations are presented. Finally, the impact of retained earnings and distributions upon financial analysis is analyzed, along with the limitations cited in the article.

RETAINED EARNINGS

Earlier chapters noted that corporations traditionally report shareholders' equity by source—contributed capital and retained earnings. However, this traditional reporting is not required. Exhibit 19–1, for example, portrays ***Union Pacific's*** liabilities and stockholders' equity in which common shareholders' equity is reported as a single amount, without the traditional source classifications. Those traditional classifications and changes to them are, however, reported in a separate statement of changes in shareholders' equity, as shown in Exhibit 19–2.

The primary elements for the changes to retained earnings within an accounting period are

	Beginning Retained Earnings
+(−)	Prior-Period Adjustments[3]
+(−)	Net Income (loss) for Period
−	Dividends Declared within Period
	Ending Retained Earnings

EXHIBIT 19–1
Shareholders' Equity: Not Reported by Source of Capital

UNION PACIFIC CORPORATION AND SUBSIDIARY COMPANIES
Liabilities and Stockholders' Equity

MILLIONS OF DOLLARS	1995	1994
Current Liabilities:		
Accounts payable	$ 145	$ 132
Accrued wages and vacation	284	217
Income and other taxes	178	134
Dividends and interest	203	191
Accrued casualty costs	192	163
Debt due within one year	132	427
Other current liabilities	765	736
Total	$ 1,899	$ 2,000
Other Liabilities and Stockholders' Equity:		
Debt due after one year	$ 6,232	$ 4,052
Deferred income taxes	3,498	2,398
Retiree benefits obligation	588	535
Other long-term liabilities	649	427
Minority interest in consolidated subsidiary	216	—
Common stockholders' equity	6,364	5,131
Total liabilities and stockholders' equity	$19,446	$14,543

[3]Recall that prior-period adjustments are used for correction of errors and certain accounting changes. See Chapter 6 for details.

EXHIBIT 19–2
Example of Statement of Changes in Shareholders' Equity

UNION PACIFIC CORPORATION AND SUBSIDIARY COMPANIES
Statement of Changes in Common Stockholders' Equity

DOLLARS IN MILLIONS	1995	1994	1993
Common Stock:			
Common Stock, $2.50 par value (authorized 500,000,000 shares)			
Balance at beginning of year (231,837,976 issued shares in 1995; 230,788,175 in 1994; 229,774,547 in 1993)	$ 580	$ 577	$ 574
Conversions,exercises of stock options and other (479,034 shares in in 1995; 1,049,801 in 1994; 1,013,628 in 1993)	1	3	3
Balance at end of year (232,317,010 issued shares in 1995; 231,837,976 in 1994; 230,788,175 in 1993)	$ 581	$ 580	$ 577
Paid-In Surplus:			
Balance at beginning of year	$1,428	$1,383	$1,339
Issuance of resources' no par common stock	638	—	—
Conversions, exercises of stock options and other	45	45	44
Balance at end of year	$2,111	$1,428	$1,383
Retained Earnings:			
Balance at beginning of year	$4,734	$4,529	$4,338
Net income	946	546	530
Total	$5,680	$5,075	$4,868
Cash dividends declared	(353)	(341)	(315)
Exchangeable note conversion	—	—	(24)
Balance at end of year	$5,327	$4,734	$4,529
Treasury Stock:			
Balance at end of year, at cost (26,737,806 shares in 1995; 25,900,775 in 1994; 25,626,946 in 1993)	(1,655)	(1,611)	(1,604)
Total common stockholders' equity	$6,364	$5,131	$4,885

Occasionally these changes may be reported in a separate financial statement called a *statement of retained earnings*. Some companies elect to report a combined statement of income and retained earnings. Most companies today, however, report the statement of changes in stockholders' equity, which includes the changes to retained earnings. Notice in Exhibit 19–2, for example, how Union Pacific depicts its changes to retained earnings.

DISTRIBUTIONS TO OWNERS

Record the declaration and distribution of dividends.

According to SFAC No. 6,

> Equity sets limits, often legal limits, on distributions by an enterprise to its owners, whether in the form of cash dividends or other distributions of assets. Owners' and others' expectations about distributions to owners may affect the market prices of an enterprise's equity securities, thereby indirectly affecting owners' compensation for providing equity or risk capital to the enterprise. Thus, the essential characteristics of equity center on the conditions for transferring enterprise assets to owners. Equity—an excess of assets over liabilities—is a necessary but not sufficient condition; distributions to owners are at the discretion and volition of the owners or their representatives after satisfying restrictions imposed by law, regulations, or agreements with other entities.[4]

In the following sections, two primary forms of corporate ownership distributions are discussed: *dividends,* which result in distributions to all shareholders and *treasury stock repurchases,* which result in distributions only to those shareholders whose stock is repurchased.

IN PRACTICE—GENERAL

Announcements of Dividends and Repurchase Plans

Corporations typically make public their plans to increase dividends or to repurchase treasury shares. Here are two examples.

Chrysler Corp. (*www.chrysler.com*) boosted its quarterly dividend by 10 cents to 60 cents a share—a 20% increase . . . It was Chrysler's fifth dividend increase in two years . . . In addition, Chrysler has undertaken to buy back $2 billion of its common shares.

Ford Motor Co.'s (*www.ford.com*) board voted to raise the company's quarterly dividend 13%—the fourth increase in seven quarters...Ford also said that its holding company for the financial units—***Ford Holdings Inc.***—will move ahead with plans to buy back $2 billion of preferred stock.

Sources: A. Hernandez, "Chrysler Boosts Quarter Payout 20% to 60 Cents," *The Wall Street Journal,* December 8, 1995, p. A4, and O. Suris, "Ford Votes to Lift Payout, Mulls Sale of Finance Units," *The Wall Street Journal,* October 13, 1995, p. A3.

DIVIDENDS

Although dividend distributions to corporate shareholders are generally discretionary, many corporations try to maintain distinct dividend policies or trends. Further, different investors can have different perspectives concerning the importance of dividends. One investor, interested primarily in periodic income enhancement, may prefer a company that has historically maintained a steady growth in dividends. Another investor, less interested in periodic income enhancement and primarily interested in long-term asset appreciation, may prefer

[4]SFAC No. 6, par. 61.

a company that reinvests most of its earnings and provides relatively small dividend distributions. For either investor, dividend information is important for assessing the cash flows of an enterprise.

Three dates are of importance to corporate dividends: (1) the declaration date, (2) the date of record, and (3) the distribution date. The **dividend declaration date** is the date that a company declares that it will distribute a dividend. Once declared, the corporation is obligated to ultimately make the distribution, so a liability is recognized. The shareholders on the **dividend date of record** receive the dividend, and the actual dividend payment or asset transfer occurs on the **dividend distribution date**. Between the date of record and the distribution date, publicly held stock is listed on exchanges as *ex-dividend,* meaning without the impending dividend.

To illustrate, assume that on June 30, 1997, the board of directors declares a $50,000 dividend to be paid on August 1, 1997, to the common shareholders of record on July 15, 1997. The appropriate entries would be

6/30/97	(Declaration Date)		
	Dividends (or Retained Earnings)	50,000	
	Dividends Payable		50,000
7/15/97	(Date of Record)		
	(No entry required)		
8/1/97	(Distribution Date)		
	Dividends Payable	50,000	
	Cash		50,000

Companies frequently use a Dividends account to monitor such distributions over an accounting period. If used, this account must be closed to retained earnings as part of the closing process. Alternatively, as indicted in the journal entry for June 30, 1997, a company may choose to reduce retained earnings directly when recording a dividend and thus have no Dividends account to close.

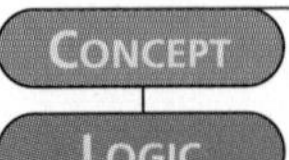

CONCEPT Return on investment.

LOGIC Dividends are generally considered a distribution of assets generated by corporate earnings and thus represent a return to shareholders for the capital contributed or invested when stock was issued. This return *on* investment results in a reduction of retained earnings. This type of distribution is distinguished from a return *of* investment in which capital contributed when stock was issued is returned to shareholders. Returns of invested capital are considered **liquidating dividends** and result in a reduction of contributed capital rather than retained earnings. State corporate laws frequently restrict these types of distributions.

As illustrated, a liability for a dividend distribution is incurred when a dividend is declared; that is, the corporation becomes obligated to pay the dividend once declared. For expediency, if the time between the dividend

ETHICS IN PRACTICE

Debt-Financed Dividends

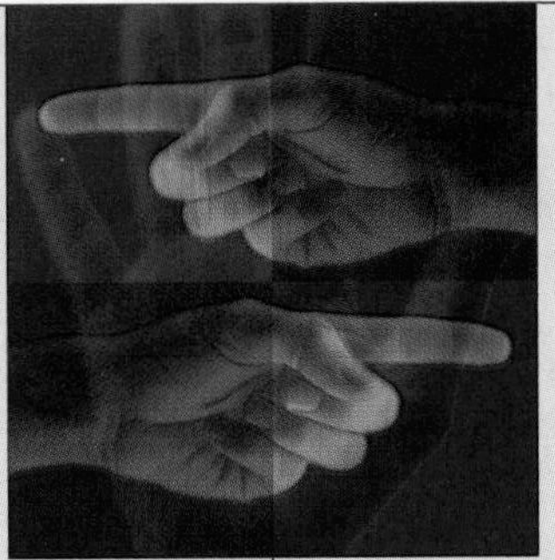

Some corporations borrow funds in order to make dividend distributions to shareholders. The relative size of such debt can be enormous. For example, in 1988 as part of a "recapitalization plan," ***Shoney's, Inc.***, distributed $20 per share for a total dividend of approximately $728 million; $16 per share was paid in cash and a $4 per share, 12% debt was issued to the shareholders as **Scrip dividends**. The cash distribution was financed by $585 million of debt. Although the plan was approved by shareholders, the economic soundness of such a decision can surely be questioned. Ethically, one can't help but wonder if this type of transaction isn't a case of "borrowing from Peter to pay Paul." Were the shareholders selfishly promoting their own self-interests to the detriment of the interests of other corporate stakeholders such as employees and creditors?

Sources: Shoney's, Inc. 1998 annual report.

declaration and distribution is relatively short, recording the liability might be forgone, with the dividend first recorded on the distribution date. For example, even though the dividend illustrated here is declared on June 30, 1997, the first entry related to this dividend might be deferred until distribution on August 1, 1997, as follows:

8/1/97	Dividends (or Retained Earnings)	50,000	
	Cash		50,000

To simplify many examples in this text, we frequently use such an expediency. However, this approach is not appropriate when the end of an accounting period occurs between the declaration and distribution of a dividend. That is, if financial statements for the company in our example were prepared as of June 30, 1997, the liability for dividends payable should be recognized.

PREFERRED STOCK

> **2** Determine amounts distributable as dividends for various types of preferred stock.

Shareholders of preferred stock generally have priority claims over common-stock shareholders with respect to dividend distributions. That is, corporations must satisfy dividend rights for preferred shareholders before dividends can be distributed to common shareholders. The amount of any preferred dividend rights depends upon the type of dividend preference associated with the stock, which in turn depends upon whether the stock is (1) cumulative or noncumulative, (2) participating or nonparticipating, or (3) fixed or variable.

A company is generally not obligated to distribute dividends in a given period, but with **cumulative preferred stock**, dividends for undistributed periods accumulate and become **dividends in arrears**. Dividends in arrears have not been declared and, therefore, are not considered liabilities. However, dividends in arrears are disclosed in annual reports. In a period of dividend distribution, both the current period's preferred dividends and dividends in arrears take precedence over common-stock dividend distributions. With **noncumulative preferred stock**, only the current period's preferred dividend portion is awarded; dividends in arrears are nonexistent.

Participating preferred stock entitles preferred shareholders to "participate," or receive extra dividends over and above a set preference. With **nonparticipating preferred stock**, only the set preferences are distributed to preferred shareholders. All extra dividends distributed then go to common shareholders.

Exhibit 19–3 illustrates preferred-stock dividends. In the first example, the preferred stock is noncumulative and nonparticipating, so the dividends to preferred shareholders are only the current year's preference of $105,000 (7% of par value). All remaining dividends are distributed to common shareholders. If the board of directors had declared only a $100,000 dividend, all of it would be distributable to preferred shareholders, since it is less than the stated preferred preference. For some preferred stock the preference is stated as an amount per share (for example, $3.50 per share) rather than a percentage of par.

EXHIBIT 19–3
Preferred Dividends

Listed below is the stockholders' equity for Kelly, Inc., as of December 31, 1997. A $750,000 dividend is declared at the end of 1997; no other dividends were declared in 1997 nor in the previous two years.

Stockholders' Equity as of December 31, 1997:

7% preferred stock, $50 par, 30,000 shares issued and outstanding	$ 1,500,000
Common stock, $2 par, 150,000 shares issued and outstanding	3,000,000
Paid-in capital	4,000,000
	$ 8,500,000
Retained earnings	8,000,000
	$16,500,000

A. Dividend Distributions for *Noncumulative, Nonparticipating* Preferred Stock:

Preferred stock:	
Current annual preference (7% of $1,500,000)	$105,000
Common stock:	
Remaining amount declared	645,000
Total Dividend	$750,000

B. Dividend Distributions for *Cumulative, Nonparticipating* Preferred Stock:

Preferred stock:	
In arrears (2 years @ 7% of $1,500,000)	$210,000
Current annual preference	105,000
	$315,000
Common stock:	
Remaining amount declared	435,000
Total Dividend	$750,000

(continued)

EXHIBIT 19–3
(Concluded)

C. Dividend Distributions for *Cumulative, Fully Participating* Preferred Stock:

Preferred stock:	
In arrears	$210,000
Current annual preference	105,000
Participating amount	75,000*
	$390,000
Common stock:	
Preference equivalent (7% of $3,000,000)	$210,000
Participating amount	150,000*
	$360,000
Total Dividend	$750,000

*We illustrate participation based upon each stock's proportion or pro rata share of par value ($1,500,000 and $3,000,000 totaling $4,500,000). The participating amounts are determined as follows:

Total dividend		$750,000
Less: Arrears	$210,000	
Current preference	105,000	
Common preference equivalent	210,000	525,000
Total participating amount		$225,000
Allocation of total participating amount (based upon proportion of par value):		
Preferred (1,500,000/4,500,000 or 1/3)		$ 75,000
Common (3,000,000/4,500,000 or 2/3)		150,000
		$225,000

In the second example in Exhibit 19–3, the preferred stock is cumulative but nonparticipating. All dividends in arrears are thus a part of the preferred dividend rights and also must be distributed to preferred shareholders. Amounts exceeding the preferred rights are distributable to common shareholders. Had the declared dividend been only $300,000, the entire amount would be distributable to preferred shareholders, since it is less than the preferred rights of $315,000; the undistributed $15,000 would become dividends in arrears for future distributions.

In the last example in Exhibit 19–3, the preferred stock is both cumulative and fully participating. First, the preferred rights for dividends in arrears and the current-year preference must be satisfied. Then, common shareholders must be allocated a pro rata amount equivalent to the current-year preference (i.e., 7% of par value). This is frequently called a "like" dividend. This example is based upon par value. Depending upon the participating agreement, the equivalent and pro rata amount also might be based on contributed capital. After allocating these amounts, $225,000 remains from the total dividend as the participating amount. Because the preferred stock is fully participating, preferred shareholders and common shareholders share the $225,000 proportionately, based on the par value (one-third and two-thirds, respectively). Depending upon the participating agreement, the proportions might also be based upon respective proportions of contributed capital instead.

Preferred stock also might be partially (rather than fully) participating. For example, suppose the stock in the last example in Exhibit 19–3 is partially participating up to 10% rather than fully participating. The participating amount for preferred stock would than be an additional 3% (that is, 10% − 7%) of par value, or $45,000. Thus, preferred shareholders would receive $210,000 + $105,000 + $45,000 = $360,000, and common shareholders would receive $750,000 − $360,000 = $390,000.

These examples are applicable to traditional preferred stock with a *fixed-dividend* preference. Some of the more recent types of preferred stock are known as **adjustable (variable) preferred stock**, and have provisions whereby the preferred dividend rate is adjusted, or variable, primarily in accordance with changes in selected national interest rates. The procedures outlined in Exhibit 19–3 would be the same for *variable-dividend* preferred stock, except that the periodic preferences (either for current dividends or those in arrears) would be determined using the appropriate rate in effect for the appropriate period.

IN PRACTICE—GENERAL

Fixed-Dividend Preferred Stock

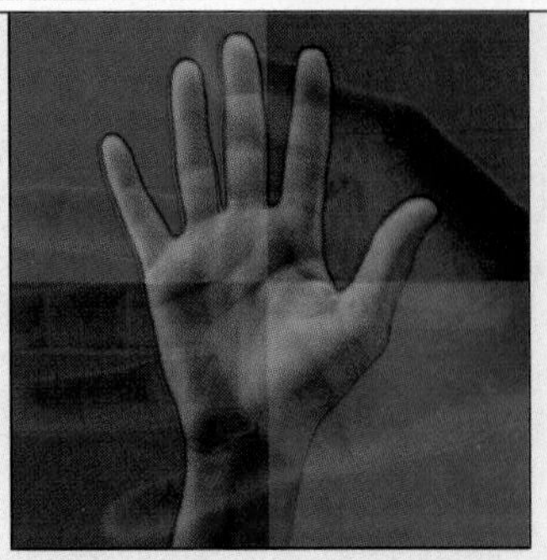

For current business practices, perpetual, fixed-dividend, preferred stock is infrequently issued. A study of 892 issues of preferred stock over the period 1981 to 1987 revealed only 19 issues that were perpetual, fixed-dividend preferred. The majority, though fixed-dividend, were either convertible or redeemable preferred, and a growing number were newer types where the dividend preference can vary. Previously issued perpetual, fixed-dividend, preferred stock, however, still remains outstanding for many corporations.

Source: A. L. Houston and C. O. Houston, "The Changing Use of Preferred Stock," *Management Accounting,* December 1991, pp. 47–48.

STOCK DIVIDENDS AND STOCK SPLITS

Distinguish between accounting for stock dividends and stock splits.

Additional shares of common stock distributed to existing common shareholders are either stock dividends or stock splits. Typically, **stock dividends** refer to relatively small proportionate distributions (25% or less of existing shares). **Stock splits** refer to relatively large proportionate distributions (***Walt Disney,*** [*www.disney.com*] for example, had a four-for-one, or 400%, split in 1992). Accounting Research Bulletin (ARB) No. 43 describes a stock dividend as "prompted mainly by a desire to give the recipient shareholders some ostensibly separate evidence of a part of their respective interests in accumulated corporate earnings without distribution of cash or other property."[5] It goes on to describe a stock split as "prompted mainly by a desire to increase the number of outstanding shares for the purpose of effecting a reduction in their unit market price and, thereby, of obtaining wider distribution and improved marketability of the shares."[6]

[5]ARB No. 43, Chap. 7, Sec. B, par. 1.
[6]Ibid., par. 2.

A presumption which guides current practice regarding stock dividends and stock splits is that a relatively small increase in outstanding corporate shares has little, if any, affect upon market price per share, but a large increase significantly affects market price per share. This presumption, however, is not supported by market-based research. Such research findings suggest that even small changes to corporate shares outstanding have market effects. Regardless of the validity of such a presumption, we examine current practice for three somewhat different types of distributions:

1. "Typical" (or small) stock dividends.
2. Stock splits.
3. Stock splits in the form of stock dividends.

First, however, note that *with either stock dividends or stock splits, corporate assets, liabilities, and residual interests (that is, equity) are unchanged.* In other words, "there is no distribution, division, or severance of corporate assets."[7] Although existing shareholders may receive additional shares of stock, their proportionate interest or percentage ownership in the corporation is unchanged. In essence, they receive no further rights to the net assets of the corporation. Thus, "there is nothing resulting therefrom that the shareholder can realize without parting with some of his proportionate interest in the corporation."[8]

Stock dividends typically are not distributed for treasury stock. Stock splits, on the other hand, will usually apply to treasury stock, and change the cost per share.

Typical (Small) Stock Dividends. Exhibit 19–4 illustrates a typical stock dividend. Accounting for stock dividends is often referred to as capitalization of earnings since retained earnings are reduced while contributed capital is increased by the fair (market) value of the stock issued. ARB No. 43 recommends this accounting treatment for relatively small issues of less than 20% to 25% of the previously outstanding shares of stock; the SEC prescribes this treatment for stock dividends of less than 25% of previously issued shares.

ARB No. 43 justifies this accounting treatment as follows:

> As has been previously stated, a stock dividend does not, in fact, give rise to any change whatsoever in either the corporation's assets or its respective shareholders' proportionate interests therein. However, it cannot fail to be recognized that, merely as a consequence of the expressed purpose of the transaction and its characterization as a **dividend** in related notices to shareholders and the public at large, many recipients of stock dividends look upon them as distributions of corporate earnings and usually in an amount equivalent to the fair value of the additional shares received. Furthermore, it is to be presumed that such views of recipients are materially strengthened in those instances, which are by far the most numerous, where the issuances are so small in comparison with the shares previously outstanding that they do not have any apparent effect upon the share market price and, consequently, the market value of the shares previously held remains substantially unchanged.

[7]Ibid., par. 6.
[8]Ibid.

EXHIBIT 19–4
Stock Dividends

Before Stock Dividend:

Gracious Corp. Shareholders' Equity (12/31/97):

Common Stock, $1 par; 2,000,000 shares authorized; 1,000,000 issued and outstanding	$ 1,000,000
Paid-in capital	54,000,000
Retained earnings	44,000,000
	$99,000,000

Stock Dividend:
A 10% stock dividend is issued on December 31, 1997, when the market value of the stock was $50 per share. Since 1,000,000 shares were outstanding prior to the stock dividend, an additional 100,000 shares (10%) are issued as a result of this stock dividend.

Entry:

12/31/97	Retained Earnings (100,000 × $50)	5,000,000	
	Common Stock (100,000 × $1)		100,000
	Paid-In Capital		4,900,000

After Stock Dividend:

Gracious Corp. Shareholders' Equity (12/31/97):

Common stock, $1 par; 2,000,000 shares authorized; 1,100,000 issued and outstanding	$ 1,100,000
Paid-in capital	58,900,000
Retained earnings	39,000,000
	$99,000,000

> The committee therefore believes that where these circumstances exist the corporation should in the public interest account for the transaction by transferring from earned surplus [i.e., retained earnings] to the category of permanent capitalization (represented by the capital stock and capital surplus [i.e., paid-in capital] accounts) an amount equal to the fair value of the additional shares issued. Unless this is done, the amount of earnings which the shareholder may believe to have been distributed to him will be left, except to the extent otherwise dictated by legal requirements, in earned surplus subject to possible further stock issuances or cash distributions [bracketed text added].[9]

Notice in Exhibit 19–4 that total shareholders' equity is unchanged. A 1% owner of the corporation would have possessed 10,000 shares before the stock dividend and, after receiving the additional 1,000 shares, would possess 11,000 of 1,100,000 shares (still 1%). There is no change in this owner's residual interest in the net assets of the company.

[9] Ibid., par. 10.

For expediency in this example, we record the stock dividend when the stock is issued. Had the stock dividend been declared but unissued as of the report date, retained earnings should still be reduced, with common stock distributable reported as part of shareholders' equity, not as a liability. Recall that cash dividends declared but unissued represent a liability.

Stock Splits. When a company records share distributions as a stock split, the characteristics for each share of stock are changed proportionately, but *the dollar amounts for all equity accounts are unaffected.* For example, a two-for-one stock split doubles the number of shares authorized, issued, and outstanding and reduces the par or stated value per share in half. ***Walt Disney's*** common stock changed from $0.10 par with 300 million shares authorized to $0.025 par with 1.2 billion shares authorized, but the reported dollar amounts for equity were unchanged. Adequate disclosure is required for stock splits, but no entry is needed to record a split, since contributed capital accounts, retained earnings, and total shareholders' equity are all unchanged.

IN PRACTICE—INTERNATIONAL

Stock Splits

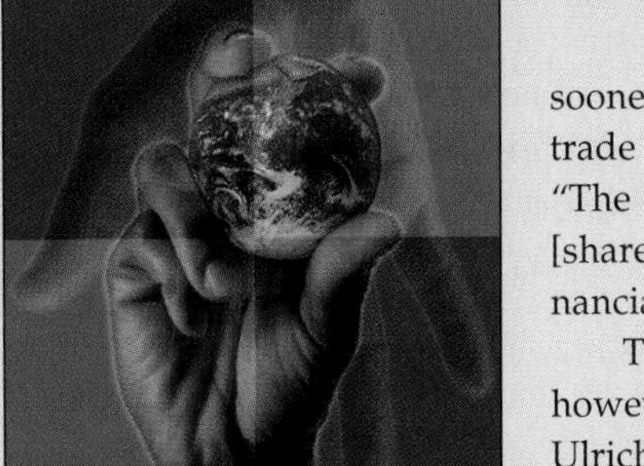

The name of the game in Switzerland is share splitting. . . .

[Several] announced plans to split stock are the result of a revised Swiss Company Law that will go into effect July 1. The new legislation lowers the minimum legal par value of shares to 10 Swiss francs ($6.57) from 100 francs, making it possible for companies to easily split their stock. . . .

Looking at the weight of some Swiss shares, the surprise is that splits haven't become regular practice sooner. ***Nestlé*** (*www.nestle.com*) shares trade at more than 9,000 francs. . . . "The small investor buys one Nestlé [share] today, if that," says Zurich financial writer Werner Leibacher.

The main targets of Swiss splits, however, are non-Swiss investors. Says Ulrich Grete, executive vice president of Union Bank of Switzerland: "By international standards, our shares are highly priced. Given the growing interest shown by foreign investors, the need to move into line with international trends cannot be underestimated."

Source: M. Studer, "Swiss Companies Move to Lighten Prices on Stocks as Law Brings Wave of Splits," *The Wall Street Journal*, March 9, 1992, p. B4D.

Many professionals feel that publicly traded stocks with per share market prices within a certain range are more marketable. When per share prices for a given company's stock rise well above this range, stock splits accomplish a per share price reduction, although total market value for all shares outstanding are relatively unchanged. For example, ***JC Penney Company*** (*www.jcpenney.com*) had a two-for-one split in 1993. Its price per share closed the day before the split at $86⅛; its price per share the next morning opened at $43 (the market does not report increments of 1/16). Thus, the primary reason for stock splits is to reduce the market value per share, presumably in an effort to make the stock more marketable. That is, individual shares are made more affordable to investors.

True stock splits actually replace previously existing shares. Rather than meeting any regulatory requirements for replacing shares and changing the number of authorized shares and par value of common stock, many companies issue stock splits in the form of stock dividends.

Stock Splits in Form of Stock Dividends. When the number of shares issued to existing shareholders is relatively large (more than 25% of prior outstanding shares), reducing retained earnings by the fair value of the stock issued, as is the practice for small stock dividends, is inappropriate. Current requirements are not clear with respect to midrange stock distributions (greater than 25% but less than 100%). Accordingly, practice varies when these occur. Some companies treat such distributions as stock splits and restate their par or stated values and number of shares. However, the most prevalent practice is not to restate par values and number of shares.[10] When not restated, current practice typically uses the following terminology as recommended in ARB No. 43: "stock splits in the form of stock dividends." This terminology is even possible for distributions greater than 100% when restatement does not occur. To illustrate use of this terminology, the following is excerpted from the footnotes in the 1992 annual report of ***One Valley Bancorp*** of West Virginia.

> (from Note P) On April 22, 1992, One Valley's Board of Directors authorized a three-for-two stock split of common shares effected in the form of a 50% stock dividend to shareholders of record on May 1, 1992. On January 20, 1993, One Valley's Board of Directors authorized a six-for-five stock split of common shares effected in the form of a 20% stock dividend to shareholders of record on February 1, 1993. Average shares outstanding and per share amounts included in the consolidated financial statements and notes have been adjusted for these stock splits. The six-for-five split has been given retroactive effect in the December 31, 1992, consolidated balance sheet.

When authorized shares and par value are not revised as prescribed above for "true" stock splits, common-stock accounts that are maintained at par or stated value must be increased for the par or stated value of the shares issued. GAAP, however, is silent regarding what account to decrease, so decreasing either retained earnings or paid-in capital is acceptable. A recent study of midrange stock distributions noted that over 75% of its sample of 388 distributions did *not* reduce retained earnings. Most companies treated the distribution as a transfer from paid-in capital to common stock at par or stated value.[11]

Retroactive Adjustments. The preceding footnote of One Valley Bancorp also illustrates that additional shares of stock issued for both traditional stock splits and stock splits in the form of stock dividends are typically reported retroactively. That is, share quantities are adjusted as if the shares were outstanding for all periods reported. The presumption is that since there is no real change to equity and only the per share basis for each share changes, all share amounts should be reported on the same new per share basis. Thus, in its 1992 annual

[10]L. Zucca, and D. Kirch, "A Gap in GAAP: Accounting for Midrange Stock Distributions," *Accounting Horizons*, June 1996, pp. 100–112.
[11]Ibid.

report, One Valley reduced retained earnings and increased common stock for the par value of the shares issued for both the three-for-two split in 1992, and for the six-for-five split still to occur in 1993. Further, the share quantities were reported as if both splits already had occurred.

Exhibit 19–5 highlights the retroactive treatment for the two-for-one split by JC Penney, which also was reported in the form of a stock dividend. For the calendar-year 1992, the adjustment to retained earnings and common stock was $59 million, even though the split generating additional shares occurred in May 1993. Further, the share quantities reported in the 1992 annual report for the 1990 year are twice those reported in the 1990 annual report. Thus, previous periods' share quantities also were retroactively adjusted. Reported dollars amounts were unchanged.

EXHIBIT 19–5 Stock Splits Recorded in the Form of a Stock Dividend Retroactive Treatment

JC PENNEY COMPANY

From the 1992 Annual Report:

Common stock. The quarterly common dividend was 33 cents per share in 1992, 1991, and 1990, or an indicated annual rate of $1.32 per share in each year. Common dividends declared were $309 million in 1992, $308 million in 1991, and $311 million in 1990. On March 10, 1993, the Board of Directors increased the quarterly common dividend to 36 cents per share, or an indicated annual rate of $1.44 per share. The Board of Directors also declared on March 10, 1993, a two-for-one stock split in the form of a stock dividend payable May 1, 1993, to stockholders of record on April 12, 1993. The stock split has been reflected on the Company's consolidated balance sheet as a reduction of reinvested earnings of $59 million and as an addition to common stock of the same amount, reflecting 50 cents per share for the outstanding shares at January 30, 1993.

CHANGES IN OUTSTANDING COMMON STOCK	SHARES (IN THOUSANDS) 1992	1991	1990	AMOUNTS (IN MILLIONS) 1992	1991	1990
Balance at beginning of year	233,302	233,122	240,694	$857	$850	$865
Two-for-one stock split	—	—	—	59	—	—
Common stock issued	1,476	180	358	39	7	12
Common stock purchased and retired	—	—	(7,930)	—	—	(27)
Balance at end of year	234,778	233,302	233,122	$955	$857	$850

From the 1990 Annual Report:

CHANGES IN OUTSTANDING COMMON STOCK	SHARES (IN THOUSANDS) 1990	1989	1988	AMOUNTS (IN MILLIONS) 1990	1989	1988
Balance at beginning of year	120,347	122,830	138,388	$865	$862	$960
Common stock issued	179	572	377	12	24	11
Common stock purchased and retired	(3,965)	(3,055)	(15,935)	(27)	(21)	(109)
Balance at end of year	116,561	120,347	122,830	$850	$865	$862

TREASURY STOCK

Evaluate and record treasury stock transactions.

Corporate shares of stock repurchased and held by the corporation itself are called **treasury stock**. A company might elect to buy back its own stock for a number of reasons, including: (1) having shares available for the future exercise of stock options, (2) trying to boost stock prices, and (3) attempting to block potential takeovers.

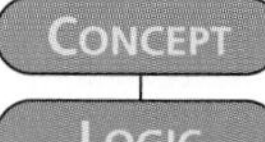

CONCEPT: Distribution of capital.

LOGIC: The repurchase of treasury stock distributes capital to selective shareholders (those whose shares are purchased) and thus reduces the capital contributed from outstanding shares of capital stock.

The purchase of treasury stock is recorded as a reduction of equity, yet the purchase of another company's stock is recorded as an investment. When possessing treasury stock, a corporation does *not* have rights like outstanding shareholders. The corporation has no voting rights for the shares it holds in treasury; dividends (cash or stock) are not distributed by the corporation to itself for such shares; the corporation has no preemptive rights when new shares are issued; and the corporation has no residual interest in itself upon liquidation. Thus, *treasury stock is not an asset but rather a reduction of shareholders' equity.*

When stock held in treasury is subsequently reissued, the proceeds represent capital contributed by the shareholders. Consequently, contributed capital is increased by the full amount of the reissuance regardless of the relationship of the reissue price to the previous repurchase price of the stock. In other words, *gains or losses are not recognized when treasury stock is reissued for more or less than the price for which it was repurchased.* While the purchase of treasury stock at a relatively low price with subsequent reissuance at a higher price might represent wise economic decision making (and the opposite action less wise), such transactions are considered by the profession as capital transactions, with fluctuations in the amount of capital contributed by outstanding shareholders, and not as investment transactions resulting in gains or losses.

Conceptually, treasury stock is viewed as a reduction of contributed capital. However, direct reductions to capital stock accounts are restricted to retirement (or liquidation) of outstanding stock. Operationally, then, a Treasury Stock account is used to record shares repurchased but not retired. Such an account is reported as a contra-equity account reducing shareholders' equity.

Exhibit 19–6 illustrates the two acceptable alternatives for recording treasury stock transactions: the cost method and the par value method. These alternatives are purely a matter of form; total shareholders' equity is the same using either method.

Cost Method. Under the **cost method**, a Treasury Stock account is recorded for the full cost to repurchase the stock. The entire reduction to shareholders' equity is recorded in this account. When the stock is reissued, the Treasury Stock account is reduced by the cost of the shares reissued (the cost per share originally recorded in the account). Any difference between the proceeds from reissuance and the cost either increases or decreases paid-in capital. For in-

EXHIBIT 19–6 Treasury Stock

STOCKHOLDERS' EQUITY OF HARRISON, INC.

Prior to treasury stock transactions:	Common stock, $1 par, 200,000 shares issued and outstanding	$ 200,000
Pro rata or average issue price per share =	Paid-in capital	4,800,000
($200,000 + $4,800,000)/200,00 share = $25	Retained earnings	4,444,444
	Total stockholders' equity	$9,444,444

TREASURY STOCK TRANSACTIONS	COST METHOD			PAR VALUE METHOD		
1. Acquire 15,000 shares of common stock for $30 per share (15,000 × $30 = $450,000)	Treasury Stock	450,000		Treasury Stock	15,000	
	Cash		450,000	Paid-In Capital	360,000[a]	
				Retained Earnings	75,000	
				Cash		450,000
2. Reissue 9,000 shares for $33 per share (9,000 × $33 = $297,000)	Cash	297,000		Cash	297,000	
	Treasury Stock		270,000[b]	Treasury Stock		9,000
	Paid-In Capital		27,000	Paid-In Capital		288,000
3. Reissue 4,000 shares $20 per share (4,000 × $20 = $80,000)	Cash	80,000		Cash	80,000	
	Paid-In Capital	40,000[c]		Treasury Stock		4,000
	Treasury Stock		120,000[b]	Paid-In Capital		76,000
4. Retire remaining 2,000 shares	Common Stock	2,000		Common Stock	2,000	
	Paid-In Capital	48,000[d]		Treasury Stock		2,000
	Retained Earnings	10,000				
	Treasury Stock		60,000[b]			

[a]Reduce contributed capital up to pro rata or average issue price per share; paid-in capital is [15,000 shares × ($25 − $1 par in treasury)] = $360,000.
[b]For reissues and retirement, reduce treasury stock by acquisition cost, $30 per share.
[c]Reduce paid-in capital by no more than its credit balance; otherwise reduce retained earnings.
[d]Reduce contributed capital up to pro rata or average issue price per share; paid-in capital is [2,000 shares × ($25 − $1 par in common)] = $48,000.

creases, some companies elect to use a separate account for Paid-In Capital from Treasury Stock in order to distinguish it from original Paid-In Capital.

If treasury stock is retired, contributed capital must be reduced for the retired shares. Thus, common stock and paid-in capital are reduced in total by the pro rata or average issue price per share ($25 per share in the exhibit—$1 par in common stock and $24 in paid-in capital). Treasury stock must be reduced by its cost; retained earnings then is adjusted for any difference between the cost and the average issue price.

Par Value Method. Under the par value method, the Treasury Stock account is recorded only for the par value of the stock reacquired. Paid-in capital is reduced for the cost of treasury stock above par up to the pro rata or average amount per share at the original issue ($24 in the exhibit). If the cost of the treasury stock exceeds this average amount of original issue price, further reductions are made to retained earnings. Under the par value method, the purchase of treasury stock is, in substance, treated much like a retirement of the

ETHICS IN PRACTICE

Treasury Stock

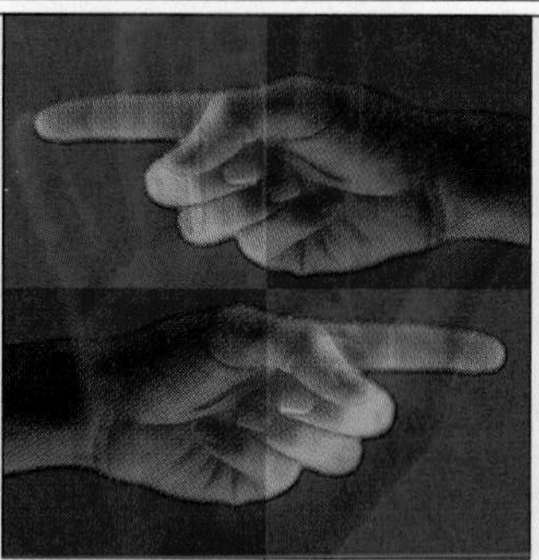

Repurchase plans soared in 1994 and 1995, according to *The Wall Street Journal*. By October, 1995, repurchase announcements for 1995 had reached $72.5 billion, more than the $60 billion of 1994. During the earlier part of the 1990's, such announcements had not passed $40 billion. Sometimes, these plans are accomplished by debt financing—witness ***Hershey's*** recent $500 million debt-financed stock repurchase. On other occasions, repurchase plans supplant the alternative of reducing debt.

Many professionals question the ethical and economic soundness of massive repurchase plans. An argument for such plans is an effort to boost share prices:

> A popular, though expensive, way to bolster the [stock] price is to repurchase shares on the open market—thus reducing the supply and, by spreading profits over fewer shares, enabling per-share earnings to increase faster than total net income.
>
> A lot is riding on such decisions. If many companies carry out big buybacks, the reduction in shares outstanding could buoy stock prices in the short run. But it could prove costly in the long run if, as some companies say, they thereby lose their painfully acquired competitive edge in world markets.

If history is a lesson, consider companies in the late 1980's and early 1990's who subsequently issued shares for less than they had earlier repurchased them.

> In May 1990, ***Westinghouse Electric Corp.***'s (*www.westinghouse.com*) management believed its stock was so undervalued by the market that it launched a big stock-purchase program. By the time the buy-back was halted last February [1991], Westinghouse had bought back 5.3 million of its common shares for $172 million, or an average of $32.42 each.
>
> But then, plagued by problems with its financial services unit, Westinghouse did an about-face. Needing to boost the equity base of the over-leveraged unit, Pittsburgh-based Westinghouse sold 21.5 million new shares of common in May [1991]. This time, the shares fetched only $26.50 each.
>
> Westinghouse isn't the only company that has bought back its stock at high prices and then turned around and issued shares at lower prices . . . ***Tenneco Inc.*** (*www.tenneco.com*) and ***Marriott Corp.***, (*www.marriott.com*) for example, announced they would issue securities at depressed prices only months after completing stock buy-backs. Now ***Chrysler Corp.***, (*www.chrysler.com*) too, is considering issuing new stock. Between 1984 and March 1990, Chrysler spent $1.85 billion buying back 87.7 million of its shares—at an average of $21.13 each. That is well above Friday's closing price of $14.625.

Sources: F. Bleakley, "Management Problem: Reinvest High Profits or Please Institutions?" *The Wall Street Journal*, October 16, 1995, pp. A1, A8, and L. P. Cohen, "Why Companies Buy Their Stock High, Then Sell Low," *The Wall Street Journal*, July 15, 1991, p. C1.

shares purchased, except common stock cannot be reduced until actual retirement. Thus, treasury stock is recorded for the par value rather than reducing common stock.

When treasury stock is subsequently reissued, the issuance is recorded much like a new issuance except the Treasury Stock account is credited for par rather than the Common Stock account. When treasury stock is retired, common stock is reduced by the par value of the shares retired with the associated amount in treasury stock removed.

General Observations. Exhibit 19–7 illustrates reporting treasury stock using each of these methods. Under the cost method, which is by far the most prevalent in practice, companies typically report the reduction to equity as the last element of shareholders' equity. Note that, while equity is reduced, this reporting practice fails to clearly designate the cost of treasury stock as a reduction to contributed capital. The cost method's prevalent usage is probably because it is easier to use when the stock is not retired.

EXHIBIT 19–7
Reporting Treasury Stock

THE WALT DISNEY COMPANY AND SUBSIDIARIES

Cost Method:

(DOLLARS IN MILLIONS) SEPTEMBER 30	1995	1994
Shareholders' equity		
Preferred stock, $0.10 par value		
Authorized—100.0 million shares		
Issued—none		
Common stock, $.025 par value		
Authorized—1.2 billion shares		
Issued—575.4 and 567.0 million shares	$1,226.3	$ 945.3
Retained earnings	6,990.4	5,790.3
Cumulative translation and other adjustments	37.3	59.1
	8,254.0	6,794.7
Less: Treasury stock, at cost—51.0 million shares and 42.9 million shares	(1,603.2)	(1,286.4)
	$6,650.8	$5,508.3

DYNAMICS RESEARCH CORPORATION

Par Value Method:

(DOLLARS IN THOUSANDS, EXCEPT PER SHARE DATA) DECEMBER 30	1995	1994	1993
Shareholders' investment			
Preferred stock, par value, $.10 per share, 5,000,000 shares authorized, none issued			
Common stock, par value, $.10 per share:			
Authorized—15,000,000 shares			
Issued—6,618,880 shares in 1995, 6,571,495 shares in 1994 and 6,028,155 shares in 1993	$ 662	$ 657	$ 603
Less: Treasury stock—996,108 shares in 1995, 940,047 shares in 1994 and 927,357 shares in 1993, at par value	(100)	(94)	(93)
Capital in excess of par value	9,219	9,284	6,977
Retained earnings	23,425	22,866	24,950
Total shareholders' investment	$33,206	$32,713	$32,437

Under the par value method, the reduction for the par value of treasury stock typically is reported with the associated capital stock account. It may also be netted with the associated capital stock account to report the net outstanding stock. This practice is more consistent with the concept that treasury stock reduces contributed capital.

The resources used by corporations to buy back their own shares can be substantial. Notice in Exhibit 19–7, for example, that Walt Disney paid more in total to repurchase the treasury shares than it received when all of its stock was issued. While paying a reported $1,603.2 million for 57.0 million shares, the company received only $1,226.3 million when 575.4 million shares were issued. Such large investments of capital for repurchase plans were common in the 1980s and early 1990s.

In a financial transaction known as a leveraged buyout (LBO), borrowed funds are used to purchase the stock. This financial maneuver is often instigated by management in an attempt to "take over" the company. In some LBOs, the price paid is substantially more than the market value of the stock. The motivation of management to employ this type of strategy usually is an attempt to block a takeover attempt by an outside group. After an LBO, the company essentially becomes a privately held company.

QUALIFICATIONS TO RETAINED EARNINGS

Previous sections of this chapter and the prior chapter illustrate events that can result in adjustments to retained earnings besides the traditional changes for net income (loss) and dividends. For example, retained earnings can be adjusted for certain treasury stock transactions and for deferred tax effects related to exercise or expiration of employee stock options. Stock dividends transfer amounts from retained earnings to common stock accounts. These type of events cloud the distinction of equity into its two traditional parts: contributed capital and retained earnings. That is, for many companies, the balances for capital stock and additional paid-in capital no longer represent amounts received when the stock was issued, and the balance in retained earnings no longer represents cumulative undistributed earnings. In this section, we look at two other, although seldom used, qualifications to retained earnings: appropriated retained earnings and quasi-reorganizations.

APPROPRIATED RETAINED EARNINGS

5

Explain the significance and limitations of appropriated retained earnings.

Some companies subdivide their retained earnings into appropriated and unappropriated accounts (see Exhibit 19–8 for an example). Conceptually, resources provided by the earnings process of an enterprise are available for distribution to shareholders as dividends (at the option of the board of directors). To communicate that some resources must be retained to fulfill contractual commitments, to provide for plant expansion, or to indicate other important purposes, boards of directors may direct an appropriation of retained earnings.

The existence of an Appropriated Retained Earnings account, however, does *not* signal that resources (particularly, cash resources) are available for the purposes of the appropriation. Equity accounts (retained earnings included) indicate *sources* of capital or financing for resources; they do not represent the resources themselves. Assets represent the various resources of an enterprise. Thus, appropriated retained earnings do not identify specific resources or assets. To illustrate, note that just because it reports appropriated retained earnings,

EXHIBIT 19–8
Reporting Appropriated Retained Earnings

UNIVERSAL DYNAMICS, INC.
Stockholders' Equity

JULY 31	1992	1991
Common stock, $.01 par value. 2,532,000 shares authorized, issued 1,754,161 and 1,757,907 at July 31, 1992 and 1991 respectively.	$ 17,542	$ 17,580
Capital in excess of par value	414,931	419,175
Retained earnings—appropriated (Note 8)	150,000	150,000
Retained earnings—unappropriated	3,956,318	3,559,144
Total stockholders' equity	$4,538,791	$4,145,899

From Note 8—Contingencies and Commitments. As of January 1, 1988, the Company had purchased product liability insurance on currently manufactured products. The Company has appropriated $150,000 of retained earnings as a reserve for future claims on previously manufactured products. At the present time, no additional claims have been asserted.

Universal Dynamics (Exhibit 19–8) does not necessarily have $150,000 cash set aside specifically for future product-liability claims.

Today, few companies actually report appropriated retained earnings in their balance sheets. Instead, restrictions are more often found as disclosures in the footnotes.

QUASI-REORGANIZATIONS

6 Evaluate and record quasi-reorganizations.

When accumulated net losses exceed prior accumulated undistributed net income, a corporation reports a deficit (that is, a debit) balance for retained earnings. Reporting such a deficit from prior performance may negatively affect prospects for future performance even in situations where a company would otherwise be profitable. Depending upon state corporate laws, a deficit in retained earnings also could prohibit distributions of dividends in future profitable years. A deficit in retained earnings may also hinder prospects for obtaining future funds from debt financing or equity securities issues.

Rather than liquidating or incurring the costs of formal business reorganization through bankruptcy proceedings, some states permit corporations to restructure their equity using a **quasi-reorganization**.

CONCEPT: Going concern.

LOGIC: The general philosophy behind a quasi-reorganization is to permit an entity still considered a going concern to report a "fresh start" by (1) recognizing that the past has negatively affected—that is, reduced—remaining contributed capital and (2) by starting over with subsequent retained earnings based upon future profitability after this fresh start, irrespective of previous performance.

ARB No. 43 permits two different procedures for quasi-reorganizations:

1. A **deficit reclassification**, in which contributed capital is simply reduced to remove the deficit in retained earnings.
2. An **accounting reorganization**, in which relevant assets and liabilities are restated to fair value, with an adjusted retained-earnings deficit charged to contributed capital.

The SEC, however, requires restatement of corporate assets and liabilities for any type of reorganization.[12] Thus, SEC-registered companies can only use accounting reorganizations.

The accounting procedures necessary for an accounting reorganization involve (1) restating relevant assets and liabilities to fair value, with a corresponding adjustment to retained earnings; and (2) charging contributed capital for the adjusted retained-earnings deficit, leaving retained earnings with a balance of zero. In restating assets to fair value, individual assets may be written either up or down in value depending upon the relation of fair value to book value. Again, the SEC is more restrictive in that it generally does not allow an overall increase in net assets resulting from restatement.[13] Thus, companies falling under the SEC's domain can write up individual assets (or write down liabilities) only to offset other asset write-downs (or liability write-ups).

When contributed capital is charged for the retained-earnings deficit, additional paid-in capital is reduced first, but not by more than its balance. Any additional charges are made directly to common stock, which can result in a need to restate either par value or the number of shares outstanding.

In conjunction with a quasi-reorganization, the company must meet several requirements:

1. Notification and approval of the shareholders.
2. A zero balance for retained earnings as of the date selected for the quasi-reorganization.
3. Reporting, for 10 years, the date of the quasi-reorganization when reporting retained earnings in subsequent financial statements, as well as reporting the amount of the deficit removed for three years (see Exhibit 19–9 for an example).
4. Adopting any new accounting standards whose implementation date is forthcoming.

The In Practice feature notes that quasi-reorganizations are rarely used in practice. Formally reorganized companies emerging from bankruptcy also may use the procedures described here for accounting reorganizations. When doing so, even these formally reorganized companies often refer to the restatement of assets and liabilities as following a quasi-reorganization.

[12]SEC, SAB No. 78, *Quasi-Reorganization*, 1998.
[13]Ibid.

IN PRACTICE—GENERAL

Quasi-Reorganization

In an article examining the frequency and usefulness of quasi-reorganizations, Professors Davis and Largay state, "It is our conclusion that the quasi-reorganization concept has little theoretical validity, and we urge the Financial Accounting Standards Board to delete it from GAAP." They further note that the use of quasi-reorganizations is rare. In a survey of the National Automated Accounting Research System (NAARS) maintained by the AICPA, which contains annual reports for thousands of companies each year, they found only 164 quasi- reorganizations from 1964 to 1992 with enough information to analyze. Of these 164, only 22 occurred after 1988 since the SEC began requiring accounting reorganizations. Most were "concentrated between 1979 and 1988, when corporate restructurings were more common."

Source: M. Davis, and J. Largay, "Quasi Reorganization: Fresh or False Start," *Journal of Accountancy*, July 1995, pp. 79–82.

EXHIBIT 19–9
Reporting Quasi-Reorganizations

Retained Earnings, as of the date of a quasi-reorganization, becomes zero after the deficit is removed (see the December 31, 1991, reported amount below). Subsequent reporting requires notification for a ten-year period of the date of this quasi-reorganization as well as notification for a three-year period of the amount of the deficit removed. The example below for Magma Copper Company illustrates.

MAGMA COPPER COMPANY
Stockholders' Equity

(DOLLARS IN THOUSANDS) DECEMBER 31	1992	1991
Series B cumulative, convertible preferred stock . . .*	—	9
Class A common stock—$.01 par value . . .*	—	42
Class B common stock—$.01 par value . . .*	—	259
Common Stock—$.01 par value . . .*	455	—
Capital in excess of par value	425,369	409,905
Retained earnings, (deficit of $15,469,000 eliminated in quasi-reorganization at December 31, 1991)	**42,671**	—
Unearned stock grant compensation	(3,121)	(2,504)
Dividend payable in common stock	—	1,366
Total stockholders' equity	$465,374	$409,077

*For simplicity, the descriptions related to shares for the various classes of stock are not presented here.

(*continued*)

EXHIBIT 19–9
(Concluded)

From Note B—Restructuring and Quasi-Reorganization. . . . the company implemented, as of December 31, 1991, the following adjustments: . . . (3) Implementation of a "quasi-reorganization," in which certain assets and liabilities were restated and the accumulated deficit of [approximately] $15 million remaining after these adjustments was reclassified to capital in excess of par value. [bracketed text added]

FINANCIAL ANALYSIS

Interpret the significance and limitations of current standards for reporting retained earnings and distributions to owners.

Changes to retained earnings and other equity accounts affect several key financial measures. For example, increases to retained earnings for periodic income lower the debt-to-equity ratio, generally considered an improvement. Distributions to owners in the form of dividends or purchases of stock result in decreases to assets and equity. Distributions in this manner have the effect of increasing returns on total assets, increasing returns on equity, and increasing debt-to-equity ratios. Additionally, payments for dividends or treasury stock repurchases reduce working capital and the current ratio. Before declaring dividends or repurchasing treasury stock, firms must make sure that they do not violate provisions regarding current ratios and debt ratios in existing debt covenants. The financial measures described here are unaffected by retained earnings appropriations or by stock dividends and stock splits since total equity is unchanged by these events.

Recall from the previous chapter that dividends for preferred stock must be subtracted from net income to determine earnings per share (EPS). Exhibit 19–10 illustrates how treasury stock transactions, stock dividends, and stock splits affect the weighted average shares outstanding, which are used to determine EPS. Consistent with reporting practice noted earlier in this chapter, shares outstanding prior to stock dividends and stock splits are retroactively restated.

The FASB has noted that earnings and thus EPS provide an indication of prospective cash flows to investors. However, because all earnings generally are not distributed as dividends, EPS does not portray current cash flows to investors. Dividends are the current cash flows to shareholders. Therefore, analysts frequently examine a corporation's **dividend payout ratio**—the ratio of dividends per share to EPS for a period. Companies with higher dividend payout ratios distribute assets equivalent to a larger percentage of their income as dividends. Companies with lower ratios distribute less, retaining a larger percentage of earnings for such things as internal growth.

From an economic perspective, a firm should distribute all funds to shareholders that the firm cannot reinvest at a rate greater than the shareholder could earn in an alternative investment. This dividend policy would be consistent with the efficient allocation of resources in the economy as a whole. Higher dividend payout ratios would be expected for older, more matured industries, and lower ratios in newer, emerging and growth industries.

LIMITATIONS

These last two chapters discussed the major components of shareholders' equity or corporate "book value." Some analysts compare corporate book values to market values, yet note the following:

> Money managers are closing the book on book value.

EXHIBIT 19–10
Weighted Average Shares Outstanding

Treasury Stock Transactions:

During 1997, Scotty, Inc., (1) began the year with 120,000 shares outstanding, (2) issued 30,000 shares on April 1, (3) purchased treasury stock of 9,000 shares on September 1, and (4) reissued 2,400 shares of the treasury stock on November 1. Notice below that the number of shares for each transaction is weighted by the fraction of the period remaining at the time of the transaction.*

DATE	TRANSACTIONS	SHARES	×	WEIGHT	=	WEIGHTED SHARES
1/1/97	Beginning shares	120,000	×	12/12	=	120,000
4/1/97	Issuance	30,000	×	9/12	=	22,500
9/1/97	Treasury purchase	(9,000)	×	4/12	=	(3,000)
11/1/97	Treasury reissue	2,400	×	2/12	=	400
	Weighted average shares outsanding					139,900

Stock Dividends and Stock Splits:

Weighted shares before a stock dividend or split are restated to reflect the associated shares from the dividend or split. Suppose that Scotty, Inc., as described in the last example also distributed a ten percent stock dividend on October 1, 1997. The restatement of the stock transactions prior to the stock dividend are shown below; each of these is multiplied by 1.10 (or 110%—the original shares [100%] plus the stock dividend [10%]). If Scotty instead had a two-for-one split, prior weighted transactions would be restated by a factor of 2.00, or 200%.

DATE	TRANSACTIONS	SHARES	×	WEIGHT	=	WEIGHTED SHARES
1/1/97	Beginning shares	120,000	×	12/12 × 1.10	=	132,000
4/1/97	Issuance	30,000	×	9/12 × 1.10	=	24,750
9/1/97	Treasury purchase	(9,000)	×	4/12 × 1.10	=	(3,300)
10/1/97	10% stock dividend—restate above					—
11/1/97	Treasury reissue	2,400	×	2/12	=	400
	Weighted average shares outstanding					153,850

*There are numerous alternative ways to determine weighted average shares outstanding. As shown below, another popular technique weights total shares outstanding by the fraction of the period that total was outstanding. To minimize rounding problems, shares are also frequently weighted by the numerator only, summed, and then this sum is divided by the denominator.

Weighted Average Shares for Scotty, Inc.:

DATES	OUTSTANDING SHARES	×	WEIGHT	=	WEIGHTED SHARES
1/1/95–3/31/95	120,000	×	3/12	=	30,000
4/1/95–8/31/95	150,000	×	5/12	=	62,500
9/1/95–10/31/95	141,000	×	2/12	=	23,500
11/1/95–12/31/95	143,400	×	2/12	=	23,900
					139,900

> Bargain-hunting investors used to pay a lot of attention to book value, namely a company's assets minus its liabilities. But now even die-hard fans concede that this measure of a company's worth has lost much of its meaning because of new accounting rules, share buy-backs and write-offs. . . .
>
> Unfortunately, book value is more than simply the sum of equity raised and earnings retained.[14]

Several types of transactions and events erode the simple concept of shareholders' equity and reporting equity by source—contributed capital and retained earnings. Additional equity accounts such as Stock Options Outstanding and Valuation Adjustments for Foreign Currency Translations complicate reporting equity. Changes to retained earnings and capital accounts for prior-period adjustments, quasi-reorganizations, stock dividends, stock splits, and treasury stock transactions further cloud the distinctions between contributed capital and retained earnings.

Consider that corporate distributions to owners are generally permitted as long as the corporation remains solvent; and one critical condition of solvency is that assets exceed liabilities. *However, in some states, the excess of assets over liabilities is based upon appraised fair values and not reported book values.* In some instances, corporations have distributed vast resources to owners, financing the distributions through debt: "the resulting effect of the debt-financed restructurings on corporate stockholders' equity sections has been to produce deficit balances not only in retained earnings, but also in total stockholders' equity."[15]

Exhibit 19–11, for example, presents the shareholders' equity from the 1988 annual report of Shoney's, Inc. As part of a restructuring plan during 1988, Shoney's borrowed $728 million to distribute dividends to shareholders.[16] As a result, shareholders' equity fell from a positive $301 million to a deficit of $379 million.

EXHIBIT 19–11
Shoney's, Inc.

SHAREHOLDERS' EQUITY (DEFICIT)

(DOLLAR AMOUNTS IN MILLIONS)	10/30/88	10/25/87
Common stock, $1 par value: authorized 100,000,000 shares; issued 36,720,683 in 1988 and 36,502,909 in 1987	$ 36,720	$ 36,502
Additional paid-in capital	280	29,799
Retained earnings (deficit)	(411,770)	239,081
	(374,769)	305,382
Less: Treasury shares, at cost (200,000 shares)	(4,439)	(4,439)
Total shareholders' equity (deficit)	$(379,209)	$300,943

[14]J. Clements, "Book Value Is More Rarely Required Reading Now," *The Wall Street Journal*, September 10, 1993, p. C1.
[15]M. L. Roberts, W. D. Samson, and M. T. Dugan, "The Stockholders' Equity Section: Form Without Substance," *Accounting Horizons*, December 1990, p. 35.
[16]As shown in the In Practice feature on debt-financed dividends earlier in this chapter, part of the $728 million debt was for funds from creditors ($585 million) and part was debt issued through scrip dividends to shareholders ($4 per share).

Certainly, creditors would not have lent the funds if they had considered Shoney's insolvent or as having negative net worth. That is, state corporate laws and Shoney's creditors relied on fair values to assess Shoney's net assets or equity. Thus, book value should be used as a measure of financial condition only with some degree of caution and care.

END-OF-CHAPTER REVIEW

SUMMARY

1. **Record the declaration and distribution of dividends.** Corporations are not obligated to pay dividends to their shareholders. However, many corporations elect through dividend distributions to provide shareholders with a relatively steady return on their investment. Generally, an obligation to pay dividends occurs once they are declared; thus, a liability is incurred until the dividends are distributed.
2. **Determine amounts distributable as dividends for various types of preferred stock.** As stated, corporations are not obligated to pay dividends. However, they must pay dividends to any preferred-stock shareholders prior to (or concurrent with) dividends paid to common-stock shareholders. Preferred stock varies with respect to these designated dividends depending upon whether it is cumulative or noncumulative, participating or nonparticipating, and carries a fixed or variable dividend preference rate.
3. **Distinguish between accounting for stock dividends and stock splits.** Stock dividends are relatively small (less than 25%) distributions of shares to existing shareholders. The market price of the stock is used to capitalize retained earnings under the presumption that the market price of the stock is relatively unaffected by the small proportion of additional shares outstanding. Thus, retained earnings is reduced and contributed capital increased by the market price.

   In a stock split, the market price per share usually decreases proportionately to the split ratio. For true stock splits, the per share par value is reduced proportionately, but the total equity amount (the total par in the Common Stock account) is unchanged. For stock splits in the form of stock dividends (greater than 25%), the par value per share is not changed, so common stock is increased by the par, or legal, capital per share issued, and either paid-in capital or retained earnings is reduced.

   Even though shareholders receive additional shares in a stock dividend or stock split, the proportional interest of each shareholder is unchanged. Corporate assets and liabilities also are unchanged, and thus total shareholders' equity remains the same. Stock dividends and stock splits require retroactive restatement of the number of shares authorized, issued, and outstanding, even when issuance of the stock is declared for a future date.
4. **Evaluate and record treasury stock transactions.** Two acceptable methods for recording treasury stock are the cost method and the par value method. The cost method, more frequently used in practice, records the full cost of stock repurchase in the Treasury Stock account. The par value method records only the par value of the shares repurchased in the Treasury Stock account. Differences between the cost of the treasury shares and average recorded values of those shares are charged to paid-in capital and, possibly, retained earnings. Total shareholders' equity is identical for the two methods.

   Subsequent reissuance of treasury stock increases contributed capital. Differences between the cost and resale of treasury stock are *not* considered gains or losses but rather adjustments to contributed capital.

5. **Explain the significance and limitations of appropriated retained earnings.** A corporation may choose to earmark some of its retained earnings by creating an equity classification for appropriated retained earnings. This signals that portions of retained earnings are reserved for some designated purpose like future plant expansion or debt retirement and are not available for dividends. Appropriated retained earnings, however, do not signal that specific resources are available for the purpose of the appropriation. Further, whether appropriated or not, corporations usually maintain significant amounts of retained earnings and do not distribute assets for all of their earnings. Thus, corporations infrequently use appropriated retained earnings in today's reporting environment.
6. **Evaluate and record quasi-reorganizations.** Corporations with deficits in retained earnings, upon approval of the shareholders, can get a "fresh start" through a quasi-reorganization. Upon reorganization, contributed capital is reduced in order to eliminate the retained-earnings deficit. Subsequent retained earnings (or deficit), then, represent undistributed earnings (or losses), since the reorganization. Deficit classifications and accounting reorganizations are two alternative methods for quasi-reorganizations. In an accounting reorganization, the most prevalent type, assets and liabilities are restated to fair values as part of the process. The SEC requires such restatement.
7. **Interpret the significance and limitations of current standards for reporting retained earnings and distributions to owners.** It is important to assess the impact of equity transactions on profitability, liquidity, and solvency. Increases to retained earnings as a result of periodic income and decreases to equity as a result of distributions to shareholders affect several key financial measures, such as earnings per share, returns on assets or equity, and debt-to-equity ratios.

KEY TERMS

accounting reorganization *1024*
adjustable (variable) preferred stock *1012*
appropriation of retained earnings *1022*
capitalization of earnings *1013*
cost method *1018*
cumulative preferred stock *1009*
deficit reclassification *1024*
dividend date of record *1008*
dividend declaration date *1008*
dividend distribution date *1008*
dividend payout ratio *1026*
dividends in arrears *1009*
leveraged buyout (LBO) *1022*
liquidating dividend *1008*
noncumulative preferred stock *1009*
nonparticipating preferred stock *1010*
participating preferred stock *1010*
par value method *1019*
quasi-reorganization *1023*
scrip dividend *1009*
stock dividend *1012*
stock split *1012*
treasury stock *1018*

ASSIGNMENT MATERIAL

CASES

C19–1 Oral Report—Dividend Policies

Upstart Corporation has been in business for five years as of December 31, 1997. Establishing a sound financial capital structure was a key objective for the company. Thus, it has elected to reinvest all of its earnings into the operations of the business and has not yet distributed any dividends to shareholders. In a meeting of the board of directors, the CEO suggests examination of the no dividend policy, and states,

> In these first few years, it made good business sense to hold onto our earnings in an effort to become established. Now that we are an established and viable concern, however, it's time to reward our shareholders. Everyone knows that dividends are generally paid from retained earnings. In looking at our year-end balance sheet, I see that we now have ample retained earnings to pay dividends and provide our owners with a return on their investments. I therefore propose that we distribute half of our retained earnings as dividends, keeping the remainder to support our continually growing operations.

The 1997 year-end balance sheet referred to by the CEO is

Assets		**Liabilities**	
Cash	$ 1,111	Accounts payable	$ 25,000
Accounts receivable (net)	10,000		
		Shareholders' Equity	
Inventory	500,000	Capital stock	300,000
Fixed assets (net)	600,000	Retained earnings	1,786,111
	$1,111,111		$1,111,111

Assume that you are the chief financial officer of this company, and also a member of the board of directors. The CEO's proposal catches you off-guard in that the CEO has not discussed this with you in advance. One of the outside directors asks for your opinion.

Required: Respond to the CEO's proposal in the board meeting.

C19–2 Written Memo—Appropriated Retained Earnings

The controller for a small corporation is in an executive conference with the other officers of the corporation. The conference was called by the company president who is currently speaking:

> I am concerned about our ability to pay off the sizable note payable that comes due next year. To ensure that we won't have any trouble, let's have our board of directors appropriate retained earnings for this debt. We would still have ample unappropriated retained earnings to continue faithfully paying dividends to our shareholders.

At this point, the meeting is interrupted by the president's secretary, causing the president to adjourn the meeting. The controller is not a member of the board of directors, but knows that the next board meeting is scheduled for the following day.

Required: Prepare a memo for the company president responding to her proposal.

C19–3 Discussion—Dividends in the Statement of Cash Flows

Distributions to shareholders as dividends are reported as part of financing activities in the statement of cash flows. Distributions to creditors as interest are reported as part of operating activities.

Required:

A. What do you think is the rationale for these two reporting practices?

B. Do you think there is any inconsistency with respect to these two alternative classifications? Why or why not?

C19–4 Written Memo—Preferred-Stock Dividends

As part of your audit, you discover that your client has not declared any dividends for the year, the first such year in which dividends have not been awarded to shareholders. This company has outstanding cumulative preferred stock, and omission of the dividend has resulted in dividends in arrears of $2,000,000. Because dividends in arrears must be paid before any dividends can be paid to common shareholders, the company reduced retained earnings and recognized a liability for dividends payable.

Required: Prepare a memo for your client discussing the appropriateness of this treatment of dividends in arrears.

C19–5 Judgment—Distributions to Owners

Alicia Fernandez is the proprietor of a small business. She invested $25,000 to begin operations two years ago. To help the business grow during the course of the two years, Fernandez retained all resources in the business and made no withdrawals. The company has reported modest profits of $2,000 and $4,000 in the first and second year, respectively. Therefore, Fernandez' capital in the business is $31,000 at the end of the second year.

Even though most proprietorships maintain only a single capital account, Fernandez elected to subdivide her equity into a Contributed Capital account of $25,000 and Retained Earnings of $6,000. Now, at the beginning of the third year, confident that the business can support itself financially without additional investment, Fernandez decides to reward herself and withdraw $5,000 from the business.

Required:

A. What capital account should Fernandez reduce when she withdraws the $5,000? Is the withdrawal a return *of* her investment or is it a return *on* her investment and why?

B. How would your answer change (if at all) if the initial $25,000 investment was from shareholders when capital stock was issued to establish a corporation and the $5,000 was a dividend? Why?

C. Do you consider the distinctions of distributions to owners (i.e., withdrawals and dividends) as either reductions to contributed capital or reductions to retained earnings an important one? Why?

C19–6 Judgment—Contingent Securities and Stock Dividends or Stock Splits

Considering the following scenarios, discuss the economics related to contingent securities (those which provide the opportunity to obtain shares of common stock) when a common stock dividend or split occurs. What happens to the equity interests (rights, claims, or whatever you want to call them) for holders of contingent securities?

- **Scenario A:** If you hold convertible preferred stock with the right to convert each share to one share of common stock, do you have a 1 to 1.10 conversion right after a 10% common stock dividend? If you don't, aren't your equity interests diluted?
- **Scenario B:** As a more extreme example, imagine that you held convertible preferred stock in Disney with a right to convert each share to one share of its $0.10 par common stock prior to their 4- for-1 split in the early 1990's (assuming of course

that Disney had such preferred stock). After the split, could you convert each preferred share to 4 shares of $0.025 par common stock? If not, haven't your equity interests been diluted?

- **Scenario C:** Such consideration is not limited to convertible preferred and convertible bonds, but is applicable for all contingent securities (options, warrants, SARs, etc.). Imagine that you have employee stock options with an exercise price of $40 and the stock splits 2-for-1. After the split, can you get 2 shares for $20 each when you exercise an option or will one share still cost $40?

QUESTIONS

Q19–1 What transactions or events result in changes to retained earnings?

Q19–2 Are dividend distributions to shareholders required by state corporate laws? Explain.

Q19–3 Identify the three important dates related to dividend distributions. Explain what happens on each date.

Q19–4 Distinguish returns *of* capital from returns *on* capital. Which of these types of returns would dividends generally be considered? Explain.

Q19–5 What are the primary types of dividend preferences for preferred stock? Explain each type.

Q19–6 What are dividends in arrears?

Q19–7 It is generally acknowledged that receipt of a stock dividend by shareholders does not increase their residual interests in a corporation. Why, then, might shareholders consider that they have received value when receiving shares from a stock dividend? Do you think that value has been received by shareholders for such a distribution?

Q19–8 Why do corporations elect to "split" their stock?

Q19–9 What is the rationale behind the use of market value for recording stock dividends but not for recording stock splits?

Q19–10 Why is stock purchased and held in treasury not a corporate asset?

Q19–11 Identify and differentiate between the two accepted methods of accounting for treasury stock.

Q19–12 Explain how cash dividends, stock dividends, stock splits, and treasury stock transactions would be reported in the statement of cash flows.

Q19–13 What is meant by retroactive restatement for stock dividends and stock splits?

Q19–14 How is the pro rata or average issue price per share determined for use with treasury stock transactions? How does its use differ for the cost method versus the par value method?

Q19–15 Explain why reported shareholders' equity does not necessarily set limits on the amounts that may be distributed to shareholders.

Q19–16 SFAC No. 6 states that equity is a necessary but not sufficient condition for shareholder distributions. What is meant by the phrase "necessary but not sufficient"?

Q19–17 Preferred dividends generally must be subtracted from net income to determine EPS. For each independent situation that follows, use logic and your understanding of the different types of preferred stock to describe what amounts would be subtracted from net income for 1997. (For each event, assume that the others listed never occurred.)

A. A company has cumulative preferred stock, but it did not declare or pay dividends in 1997.

B. A company has cumulative preferred stock, and in 1997 it declared and paid dividends that included two years of dividends in arrears.

C. A company has noncumulative preferred stock, but it did not declare or pay dividends in 1997.

D. A company has noncumulative preferred stock, and it declared and paid dividends in 1997.

Q19–18 What impact does a stock split have on retained earnings? What if the stock split is in the form of a stock dividend?

Q19–19 Explain the purpose of appropriated retained earnings.

Q19–20 Explain how a corporation gets a "fresh start" through a quasi-reorganization.

Q19–21 Differentiate between a deficit reclassification and an accounting reorganization. Which is required by the SEC?

Q19–22 Does a quasi-reorganization ensure a company's future profitability? Explain.

Q19–23 What are the requirements for reporting retained earnings after a quasi-reorganization?

Q19–24 In what ways can key financial ratios like earnings per share, returns on equity, and debt ratios be manipulated by treasury stock transactions? Would such manipulation constitute appropriate reasons for such transactions?

EXERCISES

E19–1 Preferred Stock—Dividends in Arrears

Fielder Company has two classes of preferred stock outstanding: Class A is a 6% cumulative, $10 par preferred stock with 500,000 shares outstanding and contributed capital of $15,000,000. Class B is noncumulative, no-par preferred stock with a specified dividend preference of $1.50 per share. There are 250,000 shares outstanding and contributed capital of $25,000,000. Dividends for 1995 and 1996 are in arrears. Both classes of stock are nonparticipating.

Required: Determine the amount of dividends that must be paid to preferred shareholders if dividends are declared in 1997.

E19–2 Preferred Stock—Dividends

EndZone, Inc., has the following shareholders' equity:

Preferred stock—$20 par, 8% cumulative (100,000 shares outstanding)	$ 2,000,000
Common stock—$.10 par (5,000,000 shares outstanding)	15,000,000
Retained earnings	43,000,000
	$60,000,000

A $1,700,000 dividend is declared on September 30, 1997, to be distributed on October 31, 1997, to shareholders of record on October 15, 1997.

Required:

A. Assume that there are no dividends in arrears and the preferred stock is nonparticipating. Prepare the entries related to the dividend, and indicate amounts to be distributed to preferred and to common shareholders.

B. Assume that dividends are in arrears for one year and the preferred stock is nonparticipating. Determine the amounts to be distributed to preferred and to common shareholders.

C. Assume that there are no dividends in arrears and that the preferred stock is fully participating based upon contributed capital. Determine the amounts to be distributed to preferred and common shareholders.

D. Assume that there are no dividends in arrears and that the preferred stock is fully participating based upon par values. Determine the amounts to be distributed to preferred and common shareholders.

E19–3 Preferred Stock—Dividends

End Run, Inc., has the following shareholders' equity:

Preferred stock—$50 par, 6% cumulative	
(1,000,000 shares outstanding)	$ 50,000,000
Common stock—$1 par	
(50,000,000 shares outstanding)	150,000,000
Retained earnings	300,000,000
	$500,000,000

A $10,000,000 dividend is declared on October 30, 1997, to be distributed on December 15, 1997, to shareholders of record on November 15, 1997.

Required:

A. Assume that there are no dividends in arrears and the preferred stock is nonparticipating. Determine amounts to be distributed to preferred and to common shareholders.

B. Assume that dividends are in arrears for one year and the preferred stock is nonparticipating. Determine the amounts to be distributed to preferred and to common shareholders.

C. Assume that there are no dividends in arrears and that the preferred stock is fully participating based upon contributed capital. Determine the amounts to be distributed to preferred and common shareholders.

D. Assume that there are no dividends in arrears and that the preferred stock is fully participating based upon par values. Determine the amounts to be distributed to preferred and common shareholders.

E19–4 Stock Dividends—Journal Entries

On December 15, 1997, Peggy & Francis, Inc., declared a 10% common stock dividend to be distributed on March 1, 1998, to shareholders of record on January 31, 1998. On the date of declaration, the company had 1,500,000 shares of $1 par common stock outstanding, with total contributed capital of $30,000,000. Peggy & Francis had no other equity transactions during the relevant periods. Listed below are per share market prices of the stock on various dates of interest:

12/15/97	$20
12/31/97	18
1/31/98	25
3/1/98	21

Required:

A. Prepare the entries required (if any) for 12/15/97, 12/31/97, 1/31/98, and 3/1/98.
B. Why would Peggy and Francis issue stock rather than cash dividends?

E19–5 Stock Dividends and Stock Splits

Just before a 6% stock dividend, Francis & Francis Company had outstanding 4,000,000 shares of $1.50 par common stock. The market value of the company's stock on the dividend date was $35 per share.

Required:

A. Prepare the entry (if any) to record the stock dividend.
B. Assume that, instead of the stock dividend, the company split three-to-one. Prepare the entry (if any) to record the split.
C. Assume the stock split in part B was recorded in the form of a stock dividend. Prepare the required entry (if any).
D. Determine the difference (if any) in total shareholders' equity for these three events.
E. What is the difference in effects on the investor when the investor receives a stock dividend as compared to a stock split?

E19–6 Stock Splits

Refer to Exhibit 19–4 in the chapter to do the following exercise.

Required:

A. Assume that a two-for-one split occurred on December 31, 1997, instead of the depicted 10% stock dividend. Prepare the shareholders' equity section after the split.
B. Assume that a three-for-two split in the form of a 50% stock dividend occurred on December 31, 1997. Prepare the shareholders' equity section after this split.
C. What is the difference on the financial statement of the issuing company between giving a stock dividend and a stock split?

E19–7 Treasury Stock—Cost Method

On June 30, 1996, McGowan Corporation purchased 300,000 shares of its own $1 par common stock for $25 per share. It reissued half of these shares on June 30, 1997, for $28 per share and then the other half on June 30, 1998, for $24 per share.

Required:

A. Use the cost method to prepare journal entries to record these three treasury stock transactions.
B. Why would a company want to repurchase its own stock? Give at least two reasons.

E19–8 Treasury Stock—Cost Method and Par Value Method

Refer to Exhibit 19–6 in the chapter, illustrating the two alternative treasury stock methods.

Required:

A. Based solely on the treasury stock transactions depicted in the exhibit, prepare the stockholders' equity section for each method after each transaction.
B. What is the difference, if any, for total stockholders' equity between the two methods?

E19–9 Treasury Stock

Shareholders' Equity for Curly, Moe & Larry, Inc., on January 1, 1997, was

Common stock—$1 par	$ 1,000,000
Paid-in capital	4,000,000
Retained earnings	5,000,000
	$10,000,000

During 1997, the company acquired 50,000 of its own shares of stock on April 1 for $15 each; sold 10,000 of these shares for $18 per share on July 1; sold another 25,000 shares for $13 per share on November 1; and retired the remaining 15,000 shares on December 31 when the market price per share was $12.

Required:

A. Prepare journal entries to record the treasury stock transactions using the cost method.

B. Prepare journal entries to record the treasury stock transactions using the par value method.

E19–10 Treasury Stock

Shareholders' Equity for Stooges, Inc., on January 1, 1997, was

Common stock—$1 par	$ 20,000,000
Paid-in capital	60,000,000
Retained Earnings	20,000,000
	$100,000,000

During 1997, the company acquired 150,000 of its own shares of stock on May 1 for $25 each; sold 100,000 of these shares for $28 per share on August 1; sold another 25,000 shares for $23 per share on December 1; and retired the remaining 25,000 shares on December 31 when the market price per share was $22.

Required:

A. Prepare journal entries to record the treasury stock transactions using the cost method.

B. Prepare journal entries to record the treasury stock transactions using the par value method.

E19–11 Treasury Stock Eliminated

In its 1991 annual report, ***Gerber Products Company and Subsidiaries*** reported the selected equity accounts shown at the top of the following page.

Required:

A. Notice that Gerber eliminated its treasury stock between March 31, 1990, and March 31, 1991. The company either reissued these shares or retired them. Which do you think occurred and why?

B. Based upon your answer to (**A**), prepare a journal entry to eliminate the treasury stock.

MARCH 31	(DOLLARS IN THOUSANDS) 1991	1990
Common stock—par $2.50 a share (authorized 200,000,000 shares; issued 37,392,560 shares in 1991 and 41,653,722 shares in 1990)	$ 93,481	$104,134
Paid-in capital	5,382	6,390
Retained earnings	322,121	377,768
.		
.		
Cost of common stock in treasury (deduct 3,956,768 shares in 1990)		(113,728)

E19–12 Stock Splits and Treasury Stock

Shareholders' equity for Small Rock, Inc., on December 31, 1996, was

Common stock—$1 par (authorized 500,000 shares, issued 250,000 shares)	$ 250,000
Paid-in capital	1,150,000
Retained earnings	3,000,000
	$4,400,000
Less: Treasury stock—at cost (25,000 shares)	(1,000,000)
	$3,400,000

The company had a four-for-one stock split on May 1, 1997, and reissued 30,000 shares of treasury stock for $15 per share on November 1, 1997. Net income for 1997 was $250,000.

Required: Prepare entries required for the equity transactions, then prepare the stockholders' equity section of a balance sheet for December 31, 1997.

E19–13 Quasi-Reorganization—Retained Earnings

Prior to a quasi-reorganization at the end of 1995, Schultz Company had a deficit in retained earnings of $5,000,000. The company did not restate assets and liabilities as part of the quasi-reorganization. Schultz experienced a $350,000 net loss in 1996. Then, in 1997, the company had net income of $2,500,000 and declared a $500,000 dividend.

Required: Indicate how retained earnings would be reported on a balance sheet in a 1997 annual report that includes comparative statements from 1995 and 1996.

E19–14 Quasi-Reorganization

Jeopardized Company had the following just prior to an accounting reorganization:

Jeopardized Corp. shareholders' equity (12/31/97):	
Common stock, $10 par, 200,000 shares issued and outstanding	$ 2,000,000
Paid-in capital	40,000,000
Retained earnings (deficit)	(12,000,000)
	$30,000,000

In order to restate assets and liabilities to estimated fair values, the company must increase inventory by $100,000 and decrease net plant assets by $250,000.

Required: Prepare the necessary entries for an accounting reorganization and then prepare the resultant shareholders' equity section of a balance sheet.

E19–15 Quasi-Reorganization

The shareholders' equity of Martinez Products Corp. below indicates a deficit in retained earnings:

Common stock—$1 par (2,000,000 shares outstanding)	$2,000,000
Paid-in capital	6,500,000
Retained earnings (deficit)	(1,000,000)
	$7,500,000

In preparation for a quasi-reorganization, the company determines that the fair value of certain plant assets is $150,000 lower than existing book value and that the fair value of land held is $50,000 greater than book value.

Required:

A. Prepare the necessary entries to accomplish a deficit reclassification and then recast the shareholders' equity above.

B. Prepare the necessary entries to accomplish an accounting reorganization and then recast the shareholders' equity above.

C. Assume the Paid-In Capital account above was only $800,000 not $6,500,000. Prepare the necessary entries to accomplish an accounting reorganization and then determine what changes would be necessary to par or shares outstanding.

D. Accounting rules normally require the use of historical cost amounts on the balance sheet. Do the rules for quasi-reorganizations conflict with this general rule? Are there any other instances you can think of in accounting when historical cost amounts do not provide the basis of accounting? Be specific.

E19–16 Earnings per Share

At December 31, 1997 and 1996, Sharon Corporation had 3,000,000 shares of common stock and 300,000 shares of 5%, $100 par value cumulative preferred stock outstanding. No dividends were declared on either the preferred or common stock in 1997 or 1996. Net income for 1997 was $15,000,000.

Required: Determine EPS for 1997.

E19–17 Weighted Average Shares

On January 1, 1997, Klein Corporation had 200,000 outstanding common shares. During 1997, it had a two-for-one stock split on July 1 and issued an additional 45,000 shares on September 1.

Required: Determine Klein's weighted average shares outstanding for 1997.

E19–18 Weighted Average Shares

On January 1, 1997, Stein Corporation had 20,000,000 outstanding common shares. During 1997, the company issued another 300,000 shares on May 1, had a 5% stock dividend on July 1, and issued an additional 400,000 shares on October 1.

Required: Determine Stein's weighted average shares outstanding for 1997.

E19–19 Earnings per Share

Martinez Corporation has 1997 net income of $220,000. The company began the year with 200,000 outstanding common shares, and it issued a 10% common stock dividend on March 1, 1997. Martinez also paid $55,000 in yearly dividends on its nonconvertible preferred stock.

Required: Assuming an income tax rate of 25%, determine the company's earnings per share.

PROBLEMS

P19–1 Dividends

Baker Supplies Inc. has not declared or paid any dividends this year or in the past two years. Shareholders' equity for Baker Supplies Inc. just prior to dividends is

Preferred stock—$10 par, 5% (100,000 shares outstanding)	$ 1,000,000
Common stock—$1 par (500,000 shares outstanding)	500,000
Paid-in capital	8,500,000
Retained earnings	32,000,000
	$42,000,000

Required:

A. If the preferred stock is noncumulative and nonparticipating, and the company declares a $45,000 dividend, what total and per share amounts would be distributed to each class of stock?
B. If the preferred stock is noncumulative and nonparticipating, and the company declares a $450,000 dividend, what total and per share amounts would be distributed to each class of stock?
C. If the preferred stock is cumulative and nonparticipating, and the company declares a $450,000 dividend, what total and per share amounts would be distributed to each class of stock?
D. If the preferred stock is cumulative and fully participating based upon pro rata proportions of par, and the company declares a $450,000 dividend, what total and per share amounts would be distributed to each class of stock?
E. Assume that the preferred stock is cumulative and fully participating based upon pro rata proportions of contributed capital. Further assume that paid-in capital was all from issuing common stock. If the company declares a $1,000,000 dividend, what total and per share amounts would be distributed to each class of stock?
F. Assume that the preferred stock is cumulative and fully participating. The participating provision dictates first a common stock equivalency based on par and then participation based upon pro rata proportions of contributed capital. Further assume that $3,000,000 of the paid-in capital was from issuing preferred stock. If the company declares a $1,000,000 dividend, what total and per share amounts would be distributed to each class of stock?
G. Assume that the preferred stock is cumulative and partially participating up to 10% based on par values. If the company declares a $1,000,000 dividend, what total and per share amounts would be distributed to each class of stock?

H. Assume that the preferred stock is cumulative and partially participating up to 10% based upon par values. If the company declares a $230,000 dividend, what total and per share amounts would be distributed to each class of stock?

P19–2 Equity Transactions

The T-accounts below are incomplete. They partially reflect the following transactions that occurred during 1997 that relate to Sloppy, Inc.'s stockholders' equity:

3/1/97	Issued an additional 5,000 shares.
5/1/97	Repurchased 4,000 shares.
7/1/97	Sold 1,000 shares of the stock purchased 5/1/97.
9/1/97	Issued a 10% stock dividend when the market value of the stock was $55 per share.

The account balances as of January 1, 1997, are also shown in the T-accounts. The company uses the cost method for treasury stock. Net income for the year was $330,000.

CASH

	Debit	Credit
Bal.	500,000	
3/1	300,000	
5/1		200,000
7/1	70,000	
9/1		

COMMON STOCK

	Debit	Credit
Bal.		200,000
3/1		100,000
5/1		
7/1		
9/1		

PAID-IN CAPITAL

	Debit	Credit
Bal.		300,000
3/1		
5/1		
7/1		
9/1		42,000

TREASURY STOCK

	Debit	Credit
Bal.	0	
3/1		
5/1		
7/1		50,000
9/1		

RETAINED EARNINGS

	Debit	Credit
Bal.		300,000
3/1		
5/1		
7/1		
9/1		

Required:

A. Create the journal entries for the transactions.

B. Complete the T-accounts and include ending balances.

C. Prepare the stockholders' equity section of a balance sheet for December 31, 1997.

P19–3 Equity Transactions, Journal Entries, Stockholders' Equity Section

The following represents the stockholders' equity of Columbian Coffee Inc. as of December 31, 1996.

Preferred stock—$30 par, 8% noncumulative (authorized 15,000 shares, issued ????? shares)		$ 300,000
Common stock—$20 par (authorized 40,000 shares, issued ????? shares)		600,000
Additional paid-in capital:		
Preferred	$100,000	
Common	300,000	400,000
Retained earnings		500,000
Total stockholders' equity		$1,800,000

The following equity events occurred during 1997:

Feb.	1	Issued 4,000 shares of common for $30 per share.
Mar.	1	Declared a cash dividend to be distributed on June 30 to shareholders of record on May 31. The dividend included the preferred preference and a $1 per share dividend for common shareholders.
June	5	Reacquired 1,200 of its common shares for $32 each.
June	30	Paid the dividend.
Aug.	1	Reissued 700 of its treasury shares for $35 each.

Required:

A. Determine the number of shares issued and the average issue price per share for both common and preferred stock as of December 31, 1996.

B. Journalize the transactions in 1997. Use the cost method for treasury stock.

C. Net income for 1997 was $75,000. Prepare the stockholders' equity section of a balance sheet for Columbian as of December 31, 1997.

P19–4 Equity Transactions, Journal Entries

Shareholders' equity for Rafael & Rachel Corporation on January 1, 1997 was

Common stock—$1 par	$ 5,000,000
Paid-in capital	65,000,000
Paid-in capital—stock options	500,000
Retained earnings	90,000,000
Treasury stock (200,000 shares at cost)	(4,000,000)
	$156,500,000

The primary reason for the company's repurchase of treasury stock was to have shares available for the exercise of stock options and for stock dividends. Outstanding were 100,000 fixed options, which were valued at $5 each at the grant date.

Required: Prepare journal entries for each of the following independent events. (For each event, assume that the others listed never occurred.)

A. The company reissued 5,000 shares of treasury stock when employees exercised their stock options for a $22 per share exercise price. The market price of the stock on the exercise date was $27 per share.

B. Repeat (**A**), but assume the exercise price per share was $12 when the market price was $22 per share.

C. The company declared and issued a 2% stock dividend when the market price per share was $25. Treasury stock was reissued for the dividend.

P19–5 Equity Transactions

Here is the shareholders' equity for TryTone Corporation, as of December 31, 1996:

Cumulative, nonparticipating, 6% Preferred Stock, par $20	$ 20,000,000
Paid-in capital—preferred	10,000,000
Common stock, par $1	5,000,000
Paid-in capital—common	110,000,000
Retained earnings	555,000,000
	$700,000,000

The following events related to equity occurred in 1997:

1. On January 1, key executives were awarded 500,000 stock options granting the rights to acquire one share of common stock per option for an exercise price of $50. The options may be exercised anytime after December 31, 1998 and are awarded for employee service during 1997 and 1998. The market price of common stock on January 1, 1997 was $40, and based upon an options pricing model, the fair value of each option is $5. All options are expected to vest. The company elects to use the fair value method of accounting for employee stock options as specified in SFAS No. 123. The income tax rate is 30%.
2. On March 1, the board of directors declared a $6,000,000 cash dividend to be paid on April 15, 1997 to shareholders of record on March 31, 1997. The dividend was properly paid on March 31, 1997. The last dividend was one for $5,000,000 in 1995.
3. On June 30, the board of directors declared and issued a 5% common stock dividend. The market price of the stock on that date was $42 per share.
4. On September 1, the company acquired 300,000 shares of its common stock for a market price of $35 per share. The cost method is used for treasury stock.
5. On November 1, the company reissued 120,000 shares of treasury stock for the market price of $41 per share.
6. Net income for 1997 was $12,000,000.

Required:

A. Prepare journal entries for the above events, including any necessary adjusting and closing entries on December 31, 1997. For the cash dividend, show the total and per share amounts distributed for preferred stock and for common stock.

B. Prepare the shareholders' equity section of the balance sheet as of December 31, 1997.

C. For the stock options, determine the total compensation if the company had elected to use the intrinsic value method as prescribed by APB No. 25.

D. Assume the company used the par value method rather than the cost method for treasury stock. Redo (**A**) for those entries that would be different.

P19–6 Substance over Form?

In 1997 Allison Corporation purchased 5,000,000 shares of its own common stock on April 15 for $20 per share. Later that year, on October 1, Allison issued these shares for $30 per share.

Required:

A. Journalize the two treasury stock transactions using the cost method.

B. Assume that instead of Allison's own stock, the above shares purchased were those of Bradford, Inc. Journalize the two stock transactions assuming the shares are treated as trading securities.

C. Assume that instead of shares of stock, Allison purchased and then sold 5,000,000 inventory items. Journalize these two transactions.

D. Do you think the economic substance of these three scenarios is sufficiently different to warrant such diverse accounting treatment? Explain.

E. Do you agree with the assessment that treasury stock is not an investment to be classified as an asset? Explain.

P19–7 Equity Transactions

Shareholders' equity for Jolly Folly, Inc., on January 1, 1997, was

Preferred stock—$50 par, 6% cumulative (100,000 shares outstanding)	$ 5,000,000
Common stock—$2 par (1,000,000 shares outstanding)	2,000,000
Paid-in capital	10,000,000
Retained earnings	53,000,000
	$70,000,000

The following equity events occurred throughout 1997:

1. On March 1, 30,000 shares of common stock were acquired as treasury stock for $20 per share.
2. On June 30, the board of directors declared a dividend for both the preferred shareholders' preference and $2 per share for common shareholders; the dividend was distributed on August 15 to shareholders of record on July 31. There were no dividends in arrears.
3. On September 30, the company reissued 10,000 shares of treasury stock for $18 per share.
4. On December 30, the company declared a 10% common stock dividend to be distributed on January 31, 1998, to shareholders of record on January 15, 1998. The market price per share was $21 on 12/30/97, $22 on 1/15/98, and $23 on 1/31/98.
5. Net income for 1997 was $11,000,000.

Required:

A. Using the cost method for treasury stock, prepare journal entries for each transaction.

B. Prepare the shareholders' equity section of the balance sheet on December 31, 1997.

C. Demonstrate how the impact of each of the four equity transactions would be reported on a statement of cash flows.

D. Determine earnings per share for 1997.

P19–8 Par Value Method for Treasury Stock

Refer to the information in P19–7.

Required:

A. Using the par value method for treasury stock, prepare journal entries for each transaction.

B. Prepare the shareholders' equity section of the balance sheet on December 31, 1997.

P19–9 Equity Transactions

Shareholders' equity for Gala, Inc., on January 1, 1997, was

Common stock—$1 par	$ 1,000,000
Paid-in capital	6,500,000
Retained earnings	12,500,000
	$20,000,000

The following equity events occurred throughout 1997:

1. On May 1, the company acquired 40,000 shares of common stock as treasury stock for $25 per share.
2. On August 1, 12,000 shares of treasury were sold for $30 per share.
3. On September 30, the company split its stock in a two-for-one split. The market value per share closed before the split at $32 per share and opened after the split at $16 per share.
4. On November 1, the company reissued 16,000 shares of treasury stock for $14 per share.
5. On December 31, the company paid dividends of $1 per share.
6. Net income for 1997 was $1,000,000.

Required:

A. Using the cost method for treasury stock, prepare journal entries for each transaction.
B. Prepare the shareholders' equity section of the balance sheet on December 31, 1997.
C. Demonstrate how the impact of each of the five equity transactions would be reported on a statement of cash flows.
D. Determine earnings per share for 1997.
E. Identify any differences to the above if the company had used the par value method for treasury stock.

P19–10 Comprehensive Problem—Shareholders' Equity (Adapted CPA Exam Question, Practice I, No. 4, November 1993)

Trask Corporation, a public company whose shares are traded in the over-the-counter market, had the following stockholders' equity account balances at December 31, 1996:

Common stock	$ 7,875,000
Additional paid-in capital	15,750,000
Retained earnings	16,445,000
Treasury common stock	750,000

Transactions during 1997, and other information relating to the stockholders' equity accounts were as follows:

1. Trask had 4,000,000 authorized shares of $5 par value common stock; 1,575,000 shares were issued, of which 75,000 were held in treasury.
2. On January 21, 1997, Trask issued 50,000 shares of $100 par value, 6% cumulative preferred stock in exchange for all of Rover Company's assets and liabilities. On that date, the net carrying amount of Rover's assets and liabilities was $5,000,000. The carrying amounts of Rover's assets and liabilities equaled their fair values. On January 22, 1997, Rover distributed the Trask shares to its stockholders in complete liquidation and dissolution of Rover. Trask had 150,000 authorized shares of preferred stock.

3. On February 17, 1997, Trask formally retired 25,000 of its 75,000 treasury common stock shares. The shares were originally issued at $15 per share and had been acquired on September 25, 1996, for $10 per share. Trask uses the cost method to account for treasury stock.
4. On January 2, 1995, Trask granted qualified stock options to employees to purchase 200,000 shares of the company's common stock at $12 per share, which was also the market price on that date. The options are exercisable within a three-year period, beginning January 2, 1997. On June 1, 1997, employees exercised 150,000 options when the market value of the stock was $25 per share. Trask issued new shares to settle the transaction.
5. On October 27, 1997, Trask declared a two-for-one stock split on its common stock and reduced the per share par value accordingly. Trask stockholders of record on August 2, 1997, received one additional share of Trask common stock for each share of Trask common stock held. The number of shares and cost of treasury stock were adjusted for the split.
6. On December 12, 1997, Trask declared the yearly cash dividend on preferred stock, payable on January 11, 1998, to stockholders of record on December 31, 1997.
7. On January 16, 1998, before the accounting records were closed for 1997, Trask became aware that depreciation expense was understated by $350,000 for the year ended December 31, 1996. The after-tax effect on 1996 net income was $245,000. The appropriate correcting entry was recorded on the same day.
8. Net income for 1997 was $2,400,000.

Required: Showing all supporting calculations in good form,

A. Prepare Trask's statement of changes in stockholders' equity for the year-ended December 31, 1997. Assume that Trask prepares only single-period financial statements for 1997.
B. Prepare the stockholders' equity section of Trask's balance sheet at December 31, 1997.
C. Compute the book value per share of common stock at December 31, 1997.

P19–11 Comprehensive Shareholders' Equity (Adapted CPA Exam Question, Practice I, No. 5, November 1991)

Mart Inc. is a public company whose shares are traded in the over-the-counter market. At December 31, 1996, Mart had 6,000,000 authorized shares of $5 par value common stock, of which 2,000,000 shares were issued and outstanding. The stockholders' equity accounts at December 31, 1996, had the following balances:

Common stock	$10,000,000
Additional paid-in capital	7,500,000
Retained earnings	3,250,000

Transactions during 1997 and other information relating to the stockholders' equity accounts were as follows:

1. On January 5, 1997, Mart issued at $54 per share, 100,000 shares of $50 par value, 9% cumulative, convertible preferred stock. Each share of preferred stock is convertible, at the option of the holder, into two shares of common stock. Mart had 250,000 authorized shares of preferred stock. The preferred stock has a liquidation value of $55 per share.

2. On February 1, 1997, Mart reacquired 20,000 shares of its common stock for $16 per share. Mart uses the cost method to account for treasury stock.
3. On March 15, 1997, Mart paid $200,000 for 10,000 shares of common stock of Lew, Inc., a public company whose stock is traded on a national stock exchange. This stock was classified as available-for-sale and had a fair market value of $15 per share on December 31, 1997.
4. On April 30, 1997, Mart had completed an additional public offering of 500,000 shares of its $5 par value common stock. The stock was sold to the public at $12 per share, net of offering costs.
5. On June 17, 1997, Mart declared a cash dividend of $1 per share of common stock, payable on July 10, 1997 to stockholders of record on July 1, 1997.
6. On November 6, 1997, Mart sold 10,000 shares of treasury stock for $21 per share.
7. On December 7, 1997, Mart declared the yearly cash dividend on preferred stock, payable on January 7, 1998 to stockholders of record on December 31, 1997.
8. On January 17, 1998, before the books were closed for 1997, Mart became aware that the ending inventories at December 31, 1996, were overstated by $200,000. The after-tax effect on 1996 net income was $140,000. The appropriate correction entry was recorded the same day.
9. After correction of the beginning inventories, net income for 1997 was $2,250,000.

Required: Showing all supporting calculations in good form,

A. Prepare a statement of changes in stockholders' equity for the year-ended December 31, 1997. Assume that only single-period financial statements for 1997 are presented.
B. Prepare the stockholders' equity section of Mart's balance sheet at December 31, 1997.
C. Compute the book value per share of common stock at December 31, 1997.

P19–12 Quasi-Reorganization

Laura Inc. finds itself in an unusual situation. The company has an accumulated deficit in its Retained Earnings account of $2,000,000 and wants to undergo quasi-reorganization. However, because it must follow SEC rules, it must first restate its assets and liabilities.

The problem is that all of its assets have market values at least as high as their original cost, while the market value of liabilities initially recorded at $5,000,000 is now $4,000,000 due to interest rate changes.

Required:

A. What entry(ies) should Laura Inc. make for this quasi-reorganization?
B. Why is it necessary to limit asset and liability restatement in most quasi-reorganizations?

P19–13 Accounting Reorganization

GB Company has experienced severe operating losses in recent years that have resulted in a retained earnings deficit of $3,500,000 at the end of the current year, August 31, 1998. The deficit is causing GB problems in securing new bank loans needed for expansion. The company has decided to undertake an accounting reorganization to eliminate the deficit as of September 1, 1998. It has common stock of $2,000,000 and paid-in capital of $4,000,000 at the time of the reorganization. In preparation for an accounting reorganization, GB has gathered the following information:

	HISTORICAL COST	CURRENT MARKET VALUE
Land	$1,000,000	$1,400,000
Inventory	2,500,000	1,800,000
Liabilities	4,000,000	4,700,000

Required:

A. Prepare the journal entries for the accounting reorganization.

B. "Accounting reorganizations are simply bookkeeping changes designed to make financial statements look better. They have no basis in actual transactions, and therefore should not be allowed." Do you agree? Why or why not?

C. GB Company has bond covenants that require certain specified levels of debt-to-equity and return on equity each year. Will the accounting reorganization enable GB to meet the terms of these covenants? If it fails to meet these covenants, what should GB do? Be specific.

P19–14 Footnote Preparation

Consider the reorganization of GB Company in P19–13.

Required:

A. Write the required footnote disclosures for GB Company at the end of the year in which the reorganization took place.

B. If you saw the footnote you just wrote in the financial statements of a company you were considering investing in, would your investment decision be negative because of the reorganization? Why or why not?

P19–15 Growth in Earnings per Share and Dividend Policies

Growth in EPS is an explicitly stated goal of many corporate managers. Imagine two practically identical companies (Company A and Company B) with identical growth in EPS but with different dividend policies. Assume each company begins with equity per common share of $50, has EPS of $4 in the first year, and thereafter has EPS growth of 10% of the previous year's EPS. However, Company A consistently follows the policy of distributing 25% of its earnings as dividends, and Company B consistently distributes 50% of its earnings. A partially completed analysis of Company A is shown, depicting growth in EPS, equity per share, return on equity, and dividends per share.

ANALYSIS OF COMPANY A

YEAR	BEGINNING EQUITY PER SHARE	EPS (10% GROWTH)	RETURN ON EQUITY	DIVIDENDS PER SHARE (25% OF EPS)	ENDING EQUITY PER SHARE
1	$50.00	$4.00	0.08	$1.00	$53.00
2	53.00	4.40			
3					
4					
5					

Required:

A. For a five-year period, complete the table for Company A, and then prepare a similar one for Company B.

B. How do the two companies compare in relation to EPS?
C. How do the two companies compare in relation to return on equity?
D. How can you explain the difference between these two comparisons?
E. Based upon this analysis, what dangers are there to using EPS growth to gauge company performance?
F. The equity per share is essentially book value per share. How do fluctuating market prices impact this analysis, if at all?

P19–16 Stock Dividends and Stock Splits

Assume the following balance sheet information for Alpha Company:

Common stock shares outstanding—$2 par	$300,000
Contributed capital in excess of par	200,000
Retained earnings	750,000

In addition, assume the following two independent cases: (1) Alpha declares and distributes a 10% stock dividend when the market value for the stock is $20, and (2) Alpha announces a three-for-one stock split.

Required:

A. Enter the preceding information in the template and follow the instructions found there. What method will be used to account for each of these two situations and why?
B. Make the entry on the books of Alpha to account for (1) the stock dividend and (2) the stock split.
C. What effect does a stock dividend have on shareholders' equity? Why is this so?
D. Assume instead that a 40% stock dividend was declared. Use the par value method to account for this dividend, and make the journal entry on the books of Alpha to account for it.
E. What are some reasons why a company would have a stock dividend or stock split (as opposed to a cash dividend)?

P19–17 Cash Dividends

During 1997, Williams Corporation declared dividends of $200,000. William has 35,000 shares of $10 par, 8% preferred stock outstanding. The preferred stock is cumulative and participating up to an additional 15%. Dividends are in arrears for 1995 and 1996. There are 120,000 shares of $2 par common stock.

Required:

A. Enter the preceding information in the template and follow the instructions found there. What is the total amount of dividends distributed to each group? What are the dividends per share figures?
B. How was the amount of "current year's dividend" to common stockholders' determined?
C. Recalculate the preferred-stock participation rate. At what rate will the preferred stock actually participate?
D. What entries are required on the books of Williams when the dividends are declared?
E. Let the preferred stock be noncumulative and nonparticipating. Repeat (**D**).

F. What effect (increase or decrease) would each of the following independent situations have on the total amount of dividends allocated to preferred stockholders above? Explain each answer briefly. (*Note:* Reset the template to the initial inputs—see (A) above—prior to *each* of the following modifications.)
   1. Total dividends paid was $50,000.
   2. The preferred stock was noncumulative.
   3. The par value of the common stock was $5.

P19–18 Treasury Stock Transactions

Assume the following balance sheet information for Acme Company on January 1, 1997:

1. Common stock—$5 par (20,000 shares authorized, 18,000 shares outstanding, and zero treasury shares).
2. Paid-in capital in excess of par is $25,000.
3. Retained earnings are $50,000.

Assume that on January 1, 1997, Acme repurchases 2,000 shares of its own stock for $25 per share.

Required:

A. Enter the preceding information in the template and follow the instructions found there. Make the entries on Acme's books to account for the repurchase under both the cost and par value methods.
B. Assume now that on January 1, 1998, Acme reissued 1,000 of the treasury shares for $30 per share. Make the entries under both the par and cost methods to account for the reissuance.
C. Assume instead that the treasury shares reissued on January 1, 1998, were sold for $20 per share. Make the entries under both the par and cost methods to account for the reissuance.
D. The nature of treasury stock transactions is viewed differently under each of the two methods. Briefly explain the conceptual difference between the cost and par value methods. Briefly explain why, following a treasury stock transaction, there is no difference in total stockholders' equity regardless of the method used.

RESEARCH ACTIVITIES

R19–1 Report Preparation—Dividend Policies

Examine some reference material, like *Value Line* or *Moody's Investment Service*, that provides financial information for the various companies. Prepare a brief report that describes the manner in which dividend information is provided by the service and how this information might be used in financial analysis.

R19–2 Report Preparation—Stock Splits

Locate and study the article entitled "Anatomy of a Stock Split" by E. F. McGough in *Management Accounting*, September 1993, pp. 58–61. Prepare a report that summarizes the issues raised in the article.

R19–3 Report Preparation—Midrange Stock Distributions

Locate and study the article entitled "A Gap in GAAP: Accounting for Midrange Stock Distributions" by L. Zucca and D. Kirch in *Accounting Horizons*, June 1996, pp. 100–112. Prepare a report that summarizes the issues raised in the article.

R19–4 GAAP Research—Property Dividends

During a recessionary period, Rashad Corporation is experiencing a downturn in sales and a temporary cash shortage. During a brainstorming session, management is concerned with two areas.

1. The cash shortage threatens the continuation of the company policy for steady growth in dividends.
2. Sales of a particular inventory item have seriously declined, and there is some uncertainty as to whether the company will be able to sell all of it. At best, it is expected to take a considerable amount of time to sell.

Someone suggests, "Let's kill two birds with one stone. Instead of giving our shareholders a cash dividend this year, why don't we send them this inventory as a property dividend."

Another states, "You know, I'm pretty sure noncash equity transactions are recorded at fair value. We can record the property dividend based on a reasonable sales price. This would reduce retained earnings by more than the book value of the inventory so we would have a gain to increase our earnings."

Required:

A. Examine existing pronouncements to determine the proper treatment of the proposed property dividend.

B. Are there any ethical issues to consider regarding the proposal?

R19–5 Financial Research—Reverse Stock Splits

Determine what is meant by a reverse stock split. Find an example of a company that had a reverse split, and briefly describe its impact and the general rationale for such an event.

R19–6 Financial Analysis—Motorola

Examine ***Motorola's*** annual report in the appendix.

Required:

A. If you own 200 shares of stock in the company, what activity related to these shares could you expect from Motorola in 1996?

B. For each year reported, determine the dividend payout ratio and the proportion of dividends to average market price for Motorola. (For the average market price, use the low price for the first quarter and the high price for the fourth quarter—this may be somewhat of an oversimplification, but should suffice for this problem.) Would you say that Motorola is a company with a history of high dividend returns to investors?

R19–7 Financial Research—Shoney's

Exhibit 19–11 illustrates the deficit in shareholders' equity that resulted from ***Shoney's*** large debt-financed dividend distribution in 1988. From an annual report at least five years later, determine if Shoney's still has a deficit in shareholders' equity? How much has retained earnings and shareholders' equity changed during this period?

R19–8 Financial Research—Treasury Stock

Examine an electronic database, such as the one that accompanies this text, for the following.

Required: What proportion of companies in the database have treasury stock reported? For a sample of ten companies with treasury stock, identify the proportion of treasury stock to total contributed capital.

20

The Gap in GAAP

Learning Objectives

After studying this chapter, you should be able to:

1. Relate the significance of representational faithfulness to alternative accounting methods.
2. Explain the relationship between GAAP, financial reporting, and underlying economic reality.
3. Explain the economic consequences of financial reporting and disclosure.
4. Understand the political nature of the standard-setting process.
5. Understand the role of U.S. accounting standards in the international business arena.

Investors Will Fish for Footnotes In "Abbreviated" Annual Reports

There are investors for whom the sight of an annual report is like a still-wrapped present on Christmas morning—replete with the promise of unknown treasure and hours of pleasurable diversion. Now, the Securities and Exchange Commission wants to ruin the fun.

With little fanfare, the agency has asked for comment on a proposal to permit corporations to omit numerous (and often juicy) footnotes from their annual reports. . . .

Under the SEC proposal, a company could distribute an "abbreviated" report, devoid of many now-required footnotes. Companies would still have to file all footnotes with the SEC, and they would have to provide them to investors brazen enough to ask.

. . . An SEC questionnaire for small investors lists the footnotes that would still be included in the abbreviated report and coyly asks respondents to name any others they can think of that they would miss. Good luck, folks. (More than 25 types of notes would be omitted.)

What's driving the SEC proposal is the fear, shared by accountants who have lobbied for the change, that readers of financial statements are suffering from overload.

Many companies' activities are quite complex, however, and will remain so even if their reports are purged of 'confusing' details.

Source: Roger Lowenstein, *The Wall Street Journal,* September 14, 1995, p. C1.

The excerpt from *The Wall Street Journal* above indicates that the SEC is considering reducing the disclosure provided in annual reports. Reduction of information available to users is contrary to the objectives and purposes of the accounting profession. Business is complex. To understand and evaluate the workings of large businesses, users need a great deal of information. As pointed out in the first chapter of the text, an objective of financial reporting identified in the conceptual framework is to provide information *useful* for decision making.

This final chapter begins by observing several instances in which the usefulness of accounting information may be compromised by GAAP procedures. For example, the accounting policies used by ***IBM*** during the 1980s and early in the 1990s illustrate that while the technical requirements of GAAP were met by IBM, the accounting choices made by management masked serious business problems faced by the company. In the second section of this chapter, the different financial statement effects of various accounting standards are discussed. Further, the importance of a thorough understanding of disclosure requirements is emphasized. In the third section of the chapter, the process of formulating accounting standards and the attendant political pressures are discussed. Finally, in the last section, the internationalization of accounting standards, and its importance to the future of business and accounting are addressed.

"FUZZY" GAAP AND ACCOUNTING ALTERNATIVES

Relate the significance of representational faithfulness to alternative accounting methods.

In the beginning of this text, we pointed out that the conceptual framework and the writing and adoption of accounting and reporting standards is an ongoing project for the FASB. Instances in which use of acceptable accounting methods results in an inaccurate portrayal of the economic realities of underlying events present a continuous challenge to the FASB.

Accounting policy choice is made by management. Issues such as the timing of revenue recognition, the choice between cost capitalization versus expensing, the treatment of loss contingencies, and the choice of amortization policies for goodwill are just a few examples of how managerial decisions can have profound effects on financial statements.

IBM is an interesting case study of a firm that changed accounting practices and methods. For many years known as the company with the bluest of blue-chip stocks, ***IBM*** reported large losses in 1991 through 1993. Examination of its accounting policies indicates that the problems may have begun in the early 1980s, when some notable changes were made. The following excerpt from an article appearing in *The Wall Street Journal* in 1993 chronicles the events at IBM.

IBM's Change in Accounting Policy

To all outward appearances, ***IBM*** ran into trouble with startling speed.

Even its harshest critics have been stunned by its nearly $5 billion of losses last year, its first layoffs in half a century, and an unprecedented purge of top executives. Its stock has lost more than $70 billion in market value since it peaked in 1987. . . .

Now, considerable evidence suggests that IBM may have helped delay its day of reckoning with some surprisingly aggressive accounting moves. The moves didn't violate any laws or cause the company's fundamental business problems. Some, though not all, of the moves were fully disclosed to the public.

But some finance experts say that just as IBM's business started to sour, its accounting became markedly less conservative. "Since the mid-1980s, IBM has been borrowing from the future to bolster today's profits," says Thornton O'Glove, a frequently critical San Francisco accounting expert and former publisher of the *Quality of Earnings* newsletter. . . .

Although IBM doesn't dispute any of the facts about the accounting changes, it takes strong issue with the conclusion by some experts that it was stretching to make its numbers look better, while pushing possible bad news into the future.

Source: Michael W. Miller and Lee Burton, "Softer Numbers As IBM's Woes Grew, Its Accounting Tactics Got Less Conservative," *The Wall Street Journal,* April 7, 1993, pp. A1, 6.

Throughout this text, attention has been directed to many areas where arbitrary accounting policy choice exists. Corporate management may choose among alternatives as long as adequate disclosure is made. It is hoped that management will choose those alternatives that represent the economic substance of the underlying events. That is, the resultant corporate financial statements should exhibit the characteristics of representational faithfulness and neutrality.

IBM's changes in accounting policies shifted from positions that were fundamentally sound representations of events to positions that were very aggressive representations. An overview of those changes follows:

- IBM's former chief outside auditor, ***Price Waterhouse's*** Donald Chandler, wrote IBM a blistering 20-point memo in November 1988 suggesting that the company was reporting revenue that it might never get. For example, he criticized IBM for booking revenue when its products were shipped to dealers who could return them, and sometimes even to its own warehouses—a far more aggressive approach than many companies take.

- For more than 10 years, IBM has quietly turned to ***Merrill Lynch & Co.*** and others to execute a rare financial maneuver that propped up the results of IBM's big leasing business. The maneuver allowed IBM to book immediately all the revenue from a long-term computer lease—even though the actual dollars would flow in only over the life of the lease. That didn't break any accounting rules, but some accountants term it an end-run that most blue-chip companies would avoid. Chandler called the revenue booster "troubling indeed" and urged IBM to take "immediate action" to use the maneuver less—advice that IBM ignored. . . .

- Footnotes in IBM's annual reports disclose that, in 1984 it adopted more liberal accounting for its huge investments in equipment and for its retirement plan. The changes—a bit like removing a car's shock absorbers—enabled IBM to push the cost of its investments into the future. While similar to moves at many other companies, they may have increased IBM's profits more than many investors realize. Although IBM disclosed details of the changes, it never said how much they lifted earnings, and still refuses to do so.[1]

Each of these issues is discussed later in this chapter. Also we must emphasize that none of the items mentioned in the quoted material were in violation of accounting standards. Further, they were disclosed in the footnotes of the financial statements.

Yet certain questions persist. Were these representations of events adequate and faithful to the underlying economic realities? Were analysts simply not skeptical enough to carefully read the available notes? It is difficult to speculate on the reasons.

A similar example of accounting policy choice is found at another "blue chip" company, ***General Electric.*** According to a November, 1994 article, management at GE chooses among accounting alternatives to assure a smooth and steady earnings growth.

In the following sections, several examples of "fuzzy GAAP" are presented, using some of IBM and GE's accounting policies as illustrations as well as accounting policies from other companies.

[1]Michael W. Miller and Lee Burton, "Softer Numbers: As IBM's Woes Grew, Its Accounting Tactics Got Less Conservative," *The Wall Street Journal*, April 7, 1993, p. A1.

Managing Profits—How General Electric Damps Fluctuations in its Annual Earnings

The debacle at ***Kidder, Peabody & Co.*** might ruin the year for most companies.

But the roughly $750 million in losses and after-tax charges that ***General Electric Company*** will incur this year before finally unloading Kidder will barely dent GE's smooth, consistent earnings growth. Despite those losses, some analysts believe, GE may be able to match or top last year's profit of $5.18 billion.

In the past decade, GE's earnings have risen every year, although net income fell in 1991 and 1993 because of accounting changes related to postretirement benefits. The gains, ranging between 1.7% and 17%, have been fairly steady—especially for a company in a lot of cyclical businesses. As a result, GE almost seems able to override the business cycle.

How does GE do it? One undeniable explanation is the fundamental growth of its eight industrial businesses and 24 financial-services units. . . .

But another way is "earnings management," the orchestrated timing of gains and losses to smooth out bumps and, especially, avoid a decline. . . .

To smooth out fluctuations, GE frequently offsets one-time gains from big asset sales with restructuring charges; that keeps earnings from rising so high that they can't be topped the following year. GE also times sales of some equity stakes and even acquisitions to produce profit gains when needed.

Source: Randall Smith, Steven Lipin and Amal Kumar Naj, "*Managing Profits,* How General Electric Damps Fluctuations In Its Annual Earnings," *The Wall Street Journal*, November 3, 1994, pp. A1, 11.

REVENUE RECOGNITION

Recall that **revenue recognition** dictates that realization of revenue (inflow of an asset) must occur before recognition (recording) in financial statements. But exactly when revenue should be recognized is often debatable. Arguably, ***IBM*** may have taken advantage of this flexibility in accounting standards and pressured its employees to accelerate revenue recognition.

IBM's Story Continued: When Is a Sale a Sale?

As competition in the computer market heated up over the past decade, ***IBM's*** sales force dreamed up new gimmicks . . . And at IBM's Armonk, N.Y., headquarters, accountants struggled to keep up with all the twists and turns of its sales deals. Their basic question: How much money should be recorded as revenue in IBM's financial reports? . . .

[A] former IBM accounting manager said he and his colleagues were under pressure to make more liberal interpretations of IBM's sales policies. "It amazed me to see how aggressive IBM became to help bolster a revenue stream that was slowing down significantly," he said. . . .

> Donald Chandler, Price Waterhouse auditor, detailed the practices that upset him and his team of accountants. Chandler's fundamental complaint: that IBM was rushing to record revenue on its books as soon as it shipped a product, even for sales with escape hatches that could reduce the revenue IBM ultimately received.
>
> For example, Chandler wrote, IBM's computer shipments to dealers "are recorded as sales at time of shipment" even though the dealers have the right to return the computers. . . . IBM was recording revenue when it shipped products merely to its own warehouses. . . .
>
> IBM concedes that it sometimes books revenue when it ships a product to its own warehouses—for "temporary in-transit storage" enroute to a customer. But it says it does so only when "installation at the customer" is "expected within 30 days." . . .
>
> Chandler also found "very troubling" IBM's handling of "price protection"—its term for assuring customers that if it later cut prices, they would owe only the reduced price. He said IBM was booking full revenue as soon as it shipped its products despite "ample evidence" that it would later cut prices and thus receive less money. IBM says Chandler wasn't giving it enough credit for "revenue adjust-ments," which was "based on historical experience and was applied to all revenue."
>
> *Source:* Michael W. Miller and Lee Burton, "Softer Numbers As IBM's Woes Grew, Its Accounting Tactics Got Less Conservative," *The Wall Street Journal,* April 7, 1993, pp. A1, 6.

IBM is not the only company that accelerates revenue recognition to an early point in the value-added process (as discussed in Chapter 4). Recall the example of ***Topps Sports Card Company*** in the chapter on receivables (Chapter 8). There too, revenue recognition occurred at the time of card shipment, even though the dealers had the right to return any unsold cards. The article cited in Chapter 8 suggested that Topps would incur a significant loss in future periods because of returned cards. In fact, this did occur in the fourth quarter, ending February 27, 1993, when Topps reported a quarterly loss of $21.4 million compared with a year-earlier profit of $12.7 million.[2]

At General Electric, similar results were achieved by simply changing the assumed rate of return on its pension funds:

> One financial calculation that helped smooth earnings at GE a few years ago was an increase in the assumed rate of future investment returns on pension funds. In 1991, a weak year at many companies, GE raised its return-rate assumption a full percentage point, to 9.5% from the 8.5% in effect for five years. That change, by reducing GE's pension costs, helped lift what it terms the profits on its pension fund to $696 million in 1991 from $380 million in 1990, a pretax swing of $316 million. How much did GE's overall profit rise in 1991? Just $132 million after tax.[3]

Revenue Recognition on Executory Contracts. In a policy similar to that of IBM, ***Enron Corporation*** accelerates revenue recognition on long-term executory contracts. **Executory contracts** are contracts that will be fulfilled in future

[2]*The Wall Street Journal,* March 31, 1993.
[3]GE, *The Wall Street Journal,* November 3, 1994, p. A1.

periods; they are long-term purchase commitments and agreements to sell natural gas. As of 1993, Enron Corporation was the third largest independent power producer in the world. It also sold or transported 20% of the nation's gas supply. In 1992 Enron's earnings amounted to $306 million, $2.58 per share, an increase of 20% over 1991. The stock price increased by 30% in March of 1993. How did Enron achieve these results? The following excerpt explains how.

Enron's Mark-to-Market Accounting Policy

Enron chairman Kenneth Lay . . . and his protégé, Enron Gas Services Group's Jeffrey Skilling, have adopted some very aggressive accounting practices. In 1991 Enron became the first and only nonfinancial public company to adopt mark-to-market accounting principles. For Enron, this means it books the discounted present value of future profits from fixed-price gas contracts as soon as the contracts are signed. . . .

Suppose Enron has two, five-year contracts, one to sell a certain amount of gas to a utility, another to buy the same amount of gas from a producer. Netting one against the other yields a gross profit to Enron of $2.2 million. Enron then deducts shipping costs and reserves for unforeseen costs. That leaves profits of $930,000 over the life of the contracts, or $729,000 at present value after discounting at 8.7%.

This is presumably what an outside buyer would pay for that pair of contracts. So as soon as the contracts are signed, Enron takes all $729,000 into profits immediately. . . . Enron Gas Services' Skilling says roughly half of the company's $122 million profit last year came from marking contracts to market in this manner.

Source: "Hidden Risks," *Forbes,* May 24, 1993, pp. 54–55.

Note that Enron is not violating GAAP. However, its practice of recognizing revenue from totally executory contracts is contrary to *traditional* accounting methods. Traditionally, these revenues would be recognized and taken into profit over the lifetime of the contract. So what is wrong with what Enron is doing? Technically, nothing is wrong. It could be argued that nothing is wrong as long as it is highly likely that the contracts will be executed without significant modification of their terms. Conceptually, however, the issue reduces to one of revenue recognition, that is: when is the revenue "earned"? If modifications in contractual terms occur, or if some of the parties fail (or are unable) to perform in the future, Enron could incur substantial future "unexpected" losses.

Perhaps even more interesting to note is the similarity between these practices and the acceleration of revenue by ***IBM*** discussed earlier. Like IBM, Enron is recognizing revenue in current periods that many firms would ordinarily recognize in future periods. To sustain earnings growth, Enron must sign increasingly larger numbers of contracts each year. Investors have become aware of Enron's accounting policies, and have penalized the company's stock price.

The morning after panicky investors drove Enron's stock down 2⅞ amid rumors of huge trading losses on natural gas, Enron Corporation Chairman Kenneth Lay reassured them in a conference call the rumors were unfounded.

While the stock promptly bounced back 2⅜, the incident highlighted Enron's huge but obscure trading operation, Enron Capital & Trade Resources, which accounted for 26% of Enron's income before interest and taxes in the third quarter.

At any given moment, Enron executives say the trading unit, which also manages contracts for Enron's core natural gas operations, has open agreements to buy and sell gas with a total value of $12 billion. While they insist that their maximum exposure to trading losses is never more than $25 million, some analysts are nervous. . . .

Enron executives say the potential for volatility introduced by the trading operation is misunderstood. "We're much stricter than Wall Street thinks," says Edmund Segner, an executive vice president. . . .

In many ways, the market jitters are natural. It was only two years ago this month that the U.S. trading arm of the German conglomerate ***Metallgesellschaft*** took a $1 billion hit for losses in energy derivatives.

Enron is starting to understand the stock market's sensitivity to such factors. . . .

Five years ago, fast-growing Enron's stock traded at a premium to competitors as a multiple of its earnings. Today that premium is gone.

Source: Peter Fritsch, "Size of Enron's Big Trading Operation Worries Some Analysts; Firm Says It's Misunderstood" *The Wall Street Journal*, December 29, 1995, p. C2.

Lease Contracts—Revenue Recognition. Another area in which revenue recognition becomes somewhat confusing and troubling is lease accounting. Accounting rules for leases are complex, and it is not clear that accounting theory and current standards are in alignment. Accordingly, recognition of revenues from lease contracts has the potential to be problematic (or misleading). ***IBM*** also used an aggressive accounting policy with respect to its lease revenues, with the effect of accelerating the timing of revenue recognition, as described in the following excerpt.

IBM's Leasing Game

In 1982 IBM asked Merrill Lynch to perform a rare, inventive piece of financial surgery that directly affected its profits, though few shareholders or analysts ever heard of it. Experts say that in the arcane area of lease financing, IBM exploited accounting rules in a troubling way.

When companies lease out equipment, they can account for it as an "operating" or a "sales-type" lease. An operating lease is conservative; revenues go on the books as they actually flow in each year. A sales-type lease is more liberal; all the revenue that will ever come in is recorded in the first year.

To restrain revenue hungry companies, the FASB has extensive rules . . . about sales-type leases. IBM's accountants zeroed in on a formula in paragraph 7D: Add up all the lease payments, plus the value of the computer when the lease expires. If the total is 90% of the computer's value today, the lease can be considered a sales-type one.

> In the hotly competitive market, IBM was offering terms that didn't add up to the 90% mark. Merrill's solution: It sold IBM "7D insurance" guaranteeing a certain value of the computer at the end of the lease—enough to push IBM over 90%. . . .
>
> Some accounting experts call 7D insurance a surprising tactic for a conservative company. . . .
>
> The experts also note great danger in recording a lease's entire revenue up front: What if it never materializes? That has become increasingly likely in the computer industry, where the breakneck pace of change has customers constantly switching to ever-cheaper machines.
>
> *Source:* Michael W. Miller and Lee Burton, "Softer Numbers as IBM's Woes Grew, Its Accounting Tactics Got Less Conservative," *The Wall Street Journal,* April 7, 1993, pp. A1, 6.

In these transactions, IBM restructured the leases to meet the technical requirements needed to report them as sales-type leases. Thus, the leases met the requirements of GAAP. However, reporting the leases as sales-type leases may not portray the economic substance of these transactions or accurately reflect the risks of noncollectibility or significant uncertainties. Arguably, results lacked representational faithfulness. And clearly, IBM was aggressive in revenue recognition. IBM was able to accelerate its revenues in the near term, but at the expense of the long term.

Lease Contracts—Liability Recognition. On the other side of the lease transaction, some large companies avoid recognition of the lease liability by structuring the lease as an operating lease instead of a capital lease. The excerpt from *U.S. News and World Report* raises some disturbing questions about these types of transactions.

Avoiding Recognition of Lease Liability

> Say you decide to rent instead of buy a house. But when you file your federal tax return, you claim to own the residence and blithely take a mortgage-interest deduction. That seems outrageous.
>
> Yet to some extent, that's what many of America's biggest corporations are doing. . . . [C]ompanies are increasingly reluctant to add huge slugs of debt to balance sheets. So instead of borrowing to pay for new factories and other major capital expenditures, they are telling lenders to structure the financings as leases. . . . The leasing arrangements also may leave investors in the dark about how much a company owes.
>
> Some really big leases: Enron, the country's largest natural-gas company, is leasing a $600 million plant in Louisiana. ***Phillips Petroleum*** and ***Marathon Oil*** are leasing two new liquified natural gas tankers together worth nearly $400 million. ***Texaco*** has taken out a $500 million lease on a chemical plant being built in Texas.
>
> *Source:* "A New Balance-Sheet Act," *U.S. News and World Report,* May 31, 1993, p. 79.

The economic substance of these transactions appears to be that of a purchase and resultant ownership of long-term assets. If these transactions had been reported as capital leases, they would have been reported as assets and liabilities on the balance sheet. However, by structuring the leases as operating leases, large amounts of debt were omitted from the balance sheet. This treatment is not technically wrong, but it may fail the test of representational faithfulness. Certainly, omission of long-term obligations from the liability section of the balance sheet poses added risk to users of financial statements. The comment from the *U.S. News and World Report* follows:

> Investors need to be on the lookout for these mega-leases. A leasing arrangement that lets a company avoid listing a huge obligation on the liability side of its balance sheet allows the company to paint an artificially rosy portrait of its financial health. "These deals are being driven by chief financial officers who are trying to protect their debt-to-equity ratios," . . .
>
> Synthetic leases also can artificially pump up reported earnings. That's because with an off-balance-sheet lease, a company doesn't need to deduct depreciation costs (even though exactly that deduction is taken to lower a company's tax bill). Analysts at the corporate credit rating firms aren't fooled. They count such off-balance-sheet items as "debt equivalents." In the case of Enron, total debt equivalents, including such leases and various other liabilities, come to between $1 billion and $1.5 billion, says John Bilardello of ***Standard & Poor's*** debt rating group. That's beyond the $2.5 billion of long-term debt Enron reported on its balance sheet as of the end of 1992.
>
> At minimum, it seems, there's a case for better disclosure to shareholders. Though leases are mentioned in a footnote to a company's annual report, the descriptions are so condensed they are virtually impossible to fathom. The real issue here is that companies should not be permitted to use synthetic financial transactions to cosmetically enhance their balance sheets and bottom line.[4]

LOSS CONTINGENCIES

The underlying basis of accounting policy with regard to revenue recognition is portrayal of economic events in a representationally faithful fashion. This means a good-faith effort is made to accurately illustrate events without intentional bias or selective reporting. In the same fashion, accurate portrayal of events and economic conditions is the underlying motivation in accounting for **loss contingencies**—the future outflow of resources that will occur if certain conditions or events occur (or fail to occur). The circumstances surrounding loss contingencies dictate the accounting treatment. GAAP requires recognition of a loss and recording a liability if the loss is judged probable and the amount can be reasonably estimated. When these two conditions exist, it is inappropriate to bias accounting representations by suggesting that liabilities do not exist.

Judgment is required in the determination of the probability of the loss and the estimated amount. In the mid 1990's, many companies engaged in "downsizing" and reductions of personnel and divisions to focus on core businesses. As part of this process, "restructuring charges" frequently were seen on the income statement. Restructuring charges usually encompassed such items as

[4]"A New Balance-Sheet Act," *U.S. News and World Report*, May 31, 1993, p. 79.

early retirement or severance pay packages, relocation costs, lease agreement penalty payments, and a host of other costs associated with closing a portion of a business. These were losses that were charged against income, anticipating the large write-offs that were to occur in the future.

Some companies used "restructuring charges" to manage income. The following excerpt from the article on General Electric illustrates how GE used restructuring charges to offset large one-time gains in other parts of their business in an effort to maintain a steady earnings growth pattern.

> The clearest way GE manages earnings is through restructuring charges. When GE sells a business at a profit or takes an unusual gain, it generally takes an offsetting restructuring charge of roughly equal size. In six of the years since 1983, GE has taken charges totaling $3.95 billion. . . .
>
> Last year, when GE booked a $1.43 billion pretax gain on the sale of its aerospace business, for example, it took a $1.101 billion charge to cover costs of "closing and downsizing and streamlining of certain production, service and administrative facilities world-wide." After tax, the gain and the charge matched up exactly at $678 million.
>
> And that 1993 charge, by anticipating some specific 1994 expenses such as "asset write-offs, lease termination and severance benefits," is helping GE report better profits this year. Without the 1993 charge, some of those expenses could have reduced this year's net income. Because some of the expenses eventually would have to be paid anyway, First Boston's Sankey says, this reporting strategy allows GE to "transmute" one-time gains into future operating income.
>
> Dammerman, the finance chief, says that whenever GE anticipates a gain on an asset sale or a tax or accounting change, its executives "sit down with our businesses and say, "What are some strategic decisions that you would make to make the business better going forward?" He says GE's use of such changes is one way it pursues both short-term and long-term goals; without such gains, he adds, some of the spending wouldn't have been planned or would have been timed differently.
>
> . . . accounting rule-makers, under prodding by the Securities and Exchange Commission, are expected to sharply limit such big one-time write-offs. The new rules would force companies to spread such charges over future years or take them when the relevant expenses are actually paid rather than when planned.[5]

THE BIG BATH

In some cases, companies may record several large losses all in the same year. In Chapter 1, we referred to this as the "Big Bath" phenomenon—taking all the charges at once and cleaning up the financial statements. Often this action has a positive impact on the stock price because investors feel that the entity is well positioned for future growth. This was exactly the case with ***Tenneco*** in 1992 and 1993, described in the In Practice feature.

[5]Randall Smith, Steven Lipin, and Amal Kumar Naj, "*Managing Profits,* How General Electric Damps Fluctuations In its Annual Earnings," *The Wall Street Journal*, November 3, 1994, pp. A1,11.

IN PRACTICE—GENERAL

Tenneco's "Big Bath"

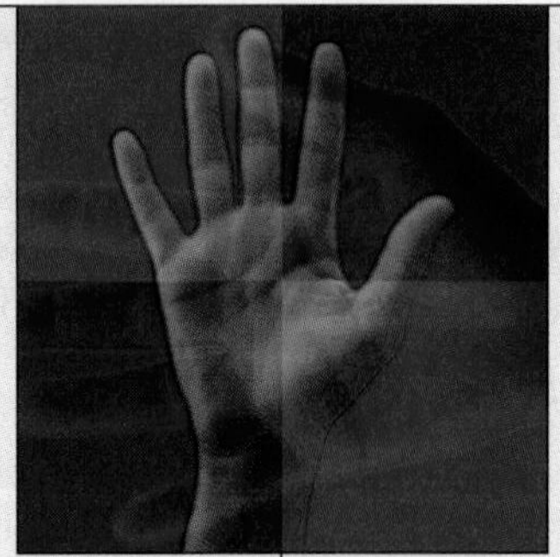

Tenneco Inc. said it would take an aftertax charge of $843 million to further restructure its unprofitable *Case Corporation* agricultural and construction equipment unit.

Additionally, Michael Walsh, the chairman and chief executive officer who was recruited in September 1991 to turn Tenneco around, speeded up his strategy to strengthen its balance sheet. He said Tenneco will record retroactively both the restructuring costs and the after-tax $699 million in accounting charges previously scheduled for 1993.

Thus, Tenneco restated results for the fourth quarter and full year 1992, posting net losses for periods previously reported as profitable. Walsh insisted that the bad news for the bottom line is only temporary, . . .

Walsh asserted that putting the charges behind Tenneco helps position the company for a strong 1993. . . .

Standard & Poor's said Tenneco's plan for Case "is expected to improve operating profits and pretax cash flow by up to $200 million annually."

Source: The Wall Street Journal, March 23, 1993.

The charges for restructuring taken by Tenneco presumably represent probable losses of amounts that could be reasonably estimated, and they resulted in the write-down in carrying value of assets of the J. I. Case subsidiary. In the judgment of management, the assets had lost value, and thus the loss was recorded. Does the reduced carrying and book value now represent the underlying economic value of those assets?

The objective of GAAP is to portray as accurately as possible the underlying economic reality of the events, and the accounting requirements for loss contingencies are straightforward. But, clearly, as the Tenneco example shows, the amount and timing of the write-down is dependent on the judgment of management.

GAAP, Financial Reporting, and Economic Reality

Explain the relationship between GAAP, financial reporting, and underlying economic reality.

The conceptual framework states that the purpose of accounting data is to provide information useful for economic decision making. An implicit assumption is that useful information reflects economic reality; therefore, the decision maker has relevant and reliable information on which to base decisions. Unfortunately, there are still instances in which accounting standards mandate practices that result in information that does not reflect the underlying economic reality. Two examples are discussed here (1) the use of the historical cost principle for valuation and reporting of long-term assets, and (2) the accounting treatment of research and development costs.

Historical Cost Principle

Assets, in general, are stated at **historical cost** (the original cost at the time of acquisition) because this valuation method possesses the qualitative characteristic of reliability. Historical cost is both objective and verifiable. However, the question can be posed as to whether historical cost is relevant. Reporting long-

IN FOCUS

Karl Schieneman
Associate
Marcus & Shapira, LLP
BBA, University of Massachusetts
MSIA, Carnegie Mellon University
JD, University of Pittsburgh

"Auditors everywhere were reminded that if something looks weird, keep asking questions."

What happens when the gap is not in GAAP but in ethics and audit procedures? Who's responsible when financial statements are inaccurate? Who checks the numbers? Who checks the checkers? Who pays the price when major misstatements cause investors to lose money? All of these questions and many others were raised in the rather incredible case of ***Phar-Mor Inc.***, a fast-growing company that was funded largely on the basis of falsified financial statements.

While the whole story would far exceed the space available here, one important problem involved inaccurate inventory figures. Inventory was critically important to Phar-Mor, a discount drug store chain. Phar-Mor's inventory system relied on an estimated cost complement to value inventory (refer to Chapter 10 for discussion of retail inventory methods). Beginning in 1989, when physical inventory counts revealed inventory shortfalls, Phar-Mor's accounting staff, under the direction of President Mickey Monus, made fraudulent journal entries instead of showing shrinking gross margins. As a result, the inventory value shown on the balance sheet consistently exceeded the inventory actually held by Phar-Mor and counted in physical inventories.

By 1991, the inventory shown on the company's balance sheet was overstated by approximately $150 million. Making matters much worse, these figures were being used to attract capital for the company. Impressed by Phar-Mor's numbers, investors that included ***Debartolo, Sears, Westinghouse,*** and ***Corporate Partners*** pumped hundreds of millions into the operation to fund the opening of new stores. Phar-Mor grew from a handful of locations in 1983 to more than 300 in 1992.

How could this happen? What about audits? The accounting world learned several serious lessons as the scheme was unraveled. Karl Schieneman, an attorney with an accounting background, was one of hundreds of legal, business, and regulatory experts called upon to determine what Phar-Mor had done and how its practice had gone undetected for so long.

"The numbers Phar-Mor used in raising capital from investors included this vastly overvalued inventory," says Schieneman. "Investors thought they were buying stock in, or lending money to, a company that had assets much greater than was actually true. The company was really experiencing large losses, but they weren't recorded." Certain Phar-Mor executives were responsible for falsifying records, but as legal investigations and proceedings began, ***Coopers and Lybrand,*** the Big Six firm that audited Phar-Mor's financial statements, became a prime target of scrutiny. "I was involved in the analysis of how Coopers and Lybrand had conducted its audits. In short, the jury held that Coopers failed to look in adequate detail at Phar-Mor's records and its procedures for producing them."

There was no happy ending to this tale. Phar-Mor went into bankruptcy, Monus and CFO Patrick Finn went to jail, thousands of Phar-Mor employees lost their jobs, and Coopers and Lybrand was held liable for conducting a reckless audit. "This case opened a lot of eyes. For investors, it again proved the idea "If it looks too good to be true, it probably is," Schieneman says. "And auditors everywhere were reminded that if something looks weird, keep asking questions. As the 'independent auditor,' you should not buy into unverified management explanations because *you* may end up responsible for actions taken based on your audit opinions."

term assets at historical cost may not represent current economic reality and in fact may be misleading to users of financial statement data.

Many entities possess assets acquired in earlier years carried on their books at the original acquisition costs. For example, many paper companies own timberland acquired in the early 1900s and carry this land at its acquisition cost. Is this a relevant disclosure to readers of the paper company's financial statements? Does it significantly understate assets? Even if assets are understated, is there harm done?

Potential harm arises in that the comparability of accounting information might be distorted. Economic theory dictates that resources flow to the most efficient users, but if the measures of efficiency are distorted, the flow process is altered. One measure of efficiency of resource use is return on investment (ROI). If the ROI in the paper industry is overstated, comparison with alternative investment opportunities may be distorted.

RESEARCH AND DEVELOPMENT (R&D) COSTS

Research and development (R&D) costs are those outflows of resources incurred to obtain valuable products or processes that potentially have some future benefit. The accounting treatment of R&D costs is also criticized by some as not representative of economic reality. SFAS No. 2, in an attempt to bring uniformity and comparability to accounting for R&D expenditures, requires that such costs be expensed when incurred. Prior to adoption of SFAS No. 2, the accounting standard setters were criticized because of the lack of uniformity. Although the standard was adopted, criticism continues, but now on the basis that the standard ignores the future benefits of these expenditures.

For example, as we saw in Chapter 13, the capitalized cost of internally developed patents includes basically only the legal fees incurred to register the patent and the costs to successfully defend them. The entire expenditure incurred in the development of the patented product or process is expensed when incurred. Some would argue that the most valuable asset an entity possesses is its research capability and the results derived therefrom. The economic effect of expensing R&D is similar to recording land at historical cost—understatement of asset values. Understatement of patent value provides a return on assets that is artificially inflated. For example, drug firms have relatively high return-on-asset ratios compared to other manufacturing companies, and command relatively high price-earning multiples in the stock markets.

Or consider the impact that research has on technology companies. In the mid 1980s, ***Motorola*** invested more in R&D than it made in profit. This investment began to pay for itself in the early 1990s as Motorola became one of the leaders in computer chip design and manufacturing. The industry leader, ***Intel,*** spent billions of dollars on R&D in the mid to late 1980s, and by the early 1990s was the dominant force in computer chip manufacturing. These huge investments in R&D were all expensed instead of capitalized; yet, clearly, future value did exist.

As emphasized again and again, the objective of financial reporting is to portray the **economic realities of the underlying events and transactions**. The FASB continues to try to achieve this objective, recognizing that there is also a cost or, economic consequence, associated with accurate portrayal of the underlying circumstances. In some instances the consequences are positive, and in others negative. The objective of the accounting data is to provide a neutral representation of the economic events.

FINANCIAL REPORTING: DISCLOSURE AND ECONOMIC CONSEQUENCES

Explain the economic consequences of financial reporting and disclosure.

The objective of financial reporting is to provide information useful for economic decision making. As a part of the financial statements, the disclosures found in the footnotes must be evaluated on this basis. That is, what are the economic consequences of footnote disclosure?

A footnote can have economic consequences if it makes a difference in users' decisions. In some instances cited earlier in this chapter, investors and other users of financial statements apparently did not read or understand the disclosures provided. In other instances, where they did, disclosures have made significant differences.

In the IBM example, proper disclosure was made of all changes in accounting policies, but those apparently went unheeded. Possibly the readers did not understand the footnotes, or perhaps the footnotes did not contain sufficient detail to portray the changing conditions. Or maybe the readers simply chose to ignore the information presented in the footnotes.

Taking Off Shock Absorbers— The Investors' Neglect of the IBM Footnotes

In hindsight, 1984 was almost precisely when the computer industry dynamics began to turn against IBM. The personal computer boom was just starting to erode the role of IBM's mighty mainframes in office work. IBM's return on equity hit a peak of 26.5% that year—before plunging to 9.6% by 1989 and disappearing amid losses in 1991 and 1992.

Footnotes in IBM's 1984 annual report show that it began overhauling its accounting tactics to spread the costs of factories and other investments far into the future, instead of recording them in the short term. IBM also reduced the estimated cost of its retirement plans, which then would take a smaller chunk out of each year's earnings. The accounting changes themselves were standard practice at many companies and hardly a secret; IBM's annual report disclosed them.

But in hindsight, IBM's critics say the changes were more evidence that IBM was imprudently shifting away from its traditional conservatism. Confident that mainframe computers would again yield enormous profits, IBM chose to defer more costs into the future, the critics suggest.

Source: Michael W. Miller and Lee Burton, "Softer Numbers As IBM's Woes Grew, Its Accounting Tactics Got Less Conservative," *The Wall Street Journal*, April 7, 1993, pp. A1, 6.

The economic consequences of not paying attention to those disclosures were significant for IBM shareholders. In other instances, financial reporting standards also have had significant economic consequences. For example, some critics claim that SFAS No. 106 has contributed greatly to the reduction or elimination of health-care benefits for some retirees and for some current employees. While this standard does not change the cash flow of companies, it has caused companies to recognize the existence and amount of the future liability.

The response at many companies has been to reduce benefits. Health-care benefits to be paid to retirees have been reduced in amount and breadth of coverage. In addition, the retirees are being required to contribute a greater portion of the total cost of the benefits.

At smaller companies, employees are experiencing the same effects as at larger firms. In fact, health-care coverage at small and mid-size firms is being reduced to a greater extent than at the larger firms. The primary motivation for these actions by employer firms is the necessity to contain rising health-care costs. By requiring current measurement and reporting of these future costs for retirees, SFAS No. 106 has caused employers to take note of the amount of the future liability.

Reduction or elimination of health-care benefits arguably is a negative economic consequence. It is unclear, however, whether this results from the change in accounting standards, rising health-care costs, or some combination of the two. It is probably fair to say that SFAS No. 106 helped management to understand the absolute need to control these future costs. Management then must decide the best course of action to take. The accounting data itself is neutral, and does not cause the economic effect.

A different kind of example of the economic consequences of financial reporting and disclosure can be seen in the 1993 experience of ***RJR Nabisco*** featured next. RJR had planned to sell shares in Nabisco to the public. However, after disclosure of the accounting treatment of goodwill and bonds payable, the stock sale was canceled.

RJR Nabisco's Accounting Technique for Goodwill

With the tobacco-stock slump already haunting RJR Nabisco Holdings' plan to sell $1.5 billion of new shares tied to its Nabisco food business, some investors are taking a harder look at an unusual accounting feature of the deal.

The offering's success depends greatly on the little-noticed accounting technique, which makes Nabisco's earnings appear bigger—93% larger, to be exact.

What RJR is doing is presenting Nabisco's annual earnings without the burden of $206 million of 1992 "goodwill," leaving this earnings-depressing item with the parent company instead. Goodwill is a non-cash accounting entry piled up on the books of companies such as RJR whenever they make acquisitions at prices above the book value of the companies acquired.

And there's goodwill aplenty at RJR Nabisco. A group led by Kohlberg Kravis Roberts paid a premium of $21.7 billion over book value when it spent $25 billion in 1989 to acquire the food and tobacco colossus in history's largest takeover.

Under accounting rules, the premium over book value, or goodwill, must be amortized (thus reducing RJR's earnings) annually over decades. So, RJR Nabisco Holdings, which returned to public ownership in 1990, has been cutting its pretax earnings by $607 million annually to amortize its goodwill; about one-third of that is Nabisco's share.

Because goodwill charges are noncash, many investors disregard them in valuing stocks, using a multiple of cash flow instead. But many investors use reported earnings, penalizing companies with heaps of goodwill.

RJR is eager to focus attention on the value of its food business with the offering. Why? Because food stocks trade at about 16 times this year's expected earnings, while tobacco stocks trade at a multiple of only 8. Because the stock market will pay twice as much for food earnings as for tobacco, it makes sense for RJR to put as much of its profits as possible in the food company, whose stock price will benefit more. . . .

The impact on Nabisco's reported earnings is huge, according to the preliminary prospectus for the planned food-stock offering. Keeping all the goodwill with the parent increases Nabisco's 1992 after-tax profit to $345 million from $179 million, and to 93 cents from 48 cents a share.

At a meeting with analysts in late March, Nabisco executives indicated the food company could generate 1993 earnings of as much as $1.30 a share. That earnings level might justify the proposed selling price of $17 to $19 a share for the new Nabisco shares, analysts say. But subtracting 45 cents for goodwill makes it more of a stretch.

RJR also favored the food business, which accounted for 42% of the parent company's 1992 sales, by assigning it only $2.5 billion in debt, 18% of the parent company's total.

Source: "RJR Nabisco's Use of Accounting Technique Dealing with Goodwill Is Studied by Investors," *The Wall Street Journal,* April 8, 1993.

Nabisco's proposed treatment of goodwill and the debt did not violate accounting standards. On the other hand, whether this treatment fairly represented the underlying facts in a neutral manner might be questioned. After disclosure of these facts was publicized, investor interest was reduced enough to force cancellation of the planned sale. In this particular case, the disclosure did provide relevant and useful information for decision making by potential investors.

Another interesting treatment of Goodwill occurred with the acquisition of ***RCA*** by General Electric.

The RCA Acquisition

One of GE's most intriguing moves to boost its net income was in its accounting for its $6.4 billion acquisition of RCA Corporation in 1986. Anytime an acquisition is made for a price exceeding the book value of the business, the premium over book value must be recorded on the buyer's books.

In the case of RCA, one former GE executive recalls that GE allocated a disproportionate amount of this so-called goodwill to ***NBC,*** increasing the TV network's book value while reducing that of other RCA assets. GE's own annual reports appear to substantiate his recollection. In 1987, the year after the acquisition, GE raised NBC's book value to $3.8 billion from $3.4 billion. The higher book value for NBC and the resulting lower value for other RCA assets raised GE's profits on sales of RCA's non-NBC assets.

Source: Randall Smith, Steven Lipin and Amal Kumar Naj, "*Managing Profits,* How General Electric Damps Fluctuations in its Annual Earnings," *The Wall Street Journal,* November 3, 1994, pp. A1, 11.

In this instance, GE was able to increase profits derived from the future sale of non-NBC assets by reducing the value assigned to those assets. Instead it assigned a higher value to the NBC assets. Assignment of goodwill to the various businesses acquired is in fact at the discretion of management. In the case of GE, management did not violate GAAP. Whether it reflected the underlying economic reality is speculative.

Over the years, the **economic consequences of accounting standards** have been difficult to predict. When the FASB proposes a new standard, those entities adversely affected by it lobby very strongly against adoption and predict dire consequences. Frequently, however, after the standard is adopted, the net impact is very positive for investors and other users. Standard setting is, as has been mentioned frequently in this text, a very politicized process. We must keep in mind, however, that it was designed that way to ensure that all users and preparers of accounting data would have input to the process. The political nature of the standard-setting process will be examined next.

THE POLITICAL NATURE OF STANDARD SETTING

Understand the political nature of the standard-setting process.

The political nature of the standard-setting process can be seen in the circumstances surrounding two recent standards adopted by the FASB. SFAS No. 115 requires certain debt securities to be valued at current market prices. The other was a proposal that would have required the value of stock options granted to officers to be deducted from profits of the company. Both actions by the FASB were very controversial and strongly opposed by the industries affected and by some accounting firms as well. The opposition was strong enough that some questioned the very survival and influence of the FASB. The exposure draft on Stock Options in particular met with a great deal of opposition from all sides.

FASB Exposure Draft on Stock Options

New York—The Financial Accounting Standards Board, in a closely watched decision, moved to force businesses to deduct the value of employee stock options from their earnings.

But in a concession to critics in business and the accounting industry, the board delayed implementing its proposal until 1997 financial statements, at the earliest.

The six-to-one vote came amid a torrent of opposition from business groups, institutional investors, compensation consultants, and the six major accounting firms. But the action was supported by some shareholder groups and lawmakers who consider stock option packages for top executives to be excessive. . . .

The FASB, the accounting profession's chief rulemaking body, bowed to industry critics by delaying the earnings charge beyond the usual one-to-two-year consideration period. In the interim, the board proposed that companies disclose options' value by adding a footnote to their 1994 financial statements at the earliest. . . .

Stock options, perhaps the most popular form of executive pay, currently are the only major type of compensation that isn't deducted from reported profits. Dennis Beresford, FASB chairman, said that companies "could be giving away what they shouldn't" because "they don't have to account for the value of options."

Source: "FASB Moves to Make Firms Deduct Options," *The Wall Street Journal,* April 8, 1993.

An article appearing in the April 12, 1993, issue of *Forbes* was also highly critical of this proposed standard.

More on the FASB Exposure Draft

America Online Inc. is a $27 million (1992 sales) Vienna, Va.-based maker of interactive networks founded in 1985 with $10 million in venture capital. Like many startups, the company relied heavily on stock options to attract good people. "We paid less cash, we didn't provide a pension plan or a 401(k)," says Chief Executive James Kinsey, who gives options to all employees, including secretaries.

But under the accounting change being considered by the Financial Accounting Standards Board, new businesses will get less help from the use of options. The accounting rulemakers say they want to start making stock option grants an expense on the profit and loss statement. That would have cut American Online's 1992 earnings of 40 cents a share by at least 25% and might have aborted the company's 1992 initial public offering.

Is this the way to encourage new businesses and new jobs?

Silicon Graphics Inc. is another fast-growing technology company, with an estimated $1 billion in sales this year. According to ***Robertson, Stephens & Co.,*** a San Francisco investment bank, the company's earnings would drop by nearly 40% this year if it were forced to record the value of options as an expense.

Senator Carl Levin (D-Mich.) has introduced legislation that would require companies to deduct the value of options from their earnings. Levin must imagine he is punishing big companies that give handsome rewards to their top executives. But the FASB move will hit across the board and throttle down the growth of promising small businesses. . . .

"Who is it that FASB is protecting?" asks Sarah Reslik, executive director of the Council of Institutional Investors, which represents over 85 pension funds. "Every major constituency that has an interest in this agrees there's no need for a change in accounting."

The whole thing is silly. When an employee exercises an option, the exercise dilutes the per-share value of other shareholders. So why count the same cost twice?

Source: "If It Ain't Broke . . . ," *Forbes,* April 12, 1993.

On the other hand, some have a more balanced view, more supportive of the FASB. Supporters suggest that similar to adoption of the pension and post-retirement benefit standards, critics are overstating the negative consequences. The supporters further suggest that the likely outcome is that financial statements will be more meaningful when the standard becomes effective.

In spite of the political pressures, the FASB indicates that it will continue to press for passage of controversial standards. In general, the accounting standards are higher and disclosure requirements greater in the United States than in other parts of the world. These high standards form the basis for the very active securities markets trading today. In the last section of this chapter and book, we discuss the growing internationalization of business and the necessity for U.S. accounting standards to be in harmony with international accounting standards.

THE FUTURE: INTERNATIONALIZATION OF ACCOUNTING STANDARDS

Understand the role of U.S. accounting standards in the international business arena.

International accounting standards are developed and set by the International Accounting Standards Committee (IASC). The international standards are not presently accepted in the United States as the SEC does not permit offerings of securities prepared under international accounting standards. Stocks of foreign companies that do not prepare their financial statements in accordance with U.S. GAAP are precluded from listing on U.S. stock exchanges as well. The reason is that U.S. GAAP requires much more disclosure and stricter standards than some of the international standards.

In March of 1993, ***Daimler-Benz,*** the maker of Mercedes-Benz automobiles, applied for listing on the New York Stock Exchange (see the In Practice feature). Daimler-Benz wanted to be listed on the exchange to avail itself of additional sources of capital. To be considered, several changes had to be made in its financial statements and the notes to those financial statements. The changes provided disclosure of "hidden assets," a common practice of German companies.

IN PRACTICE—GENERAL

Daimler-Benz of Germany and the New York Stock Exchange

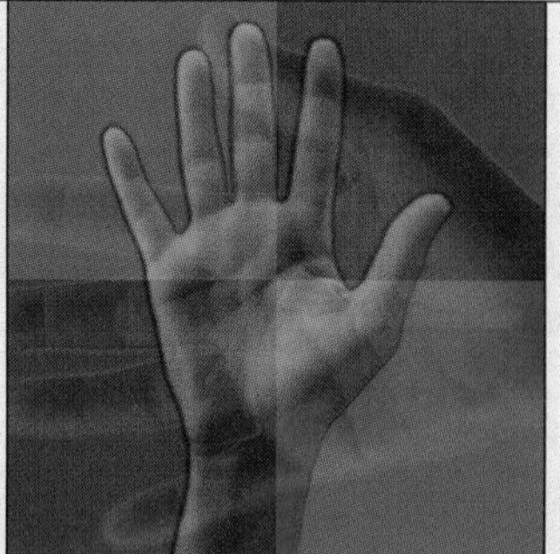

Bonn—Daimler-Benz AG, Germany's biggest industrial group, said it will declare four billion marks ($2.45 billion) in hidden reserves as an extraordinary profit on its 1992 balance sheet. It is making the disclosure as part of an effort to become the first German company to list its shares on the New York Stock Exchange.

The group, which includes luxury car maker Mercedes-Benz AG, has long sought entry to the U.S. stock market but was blocked by differences with U.S. regulators over accounting procedures. U.S. regulators say German companies generally provide too little transparency in their accounts. . . .

The company wouldn't elaborate but said the accord with the SEC would include the disclosure of hidden assets. The four-billion-mark figure, officials say, emerged as a result of applying uniform valuation methods throughout the company.

"This is money that we've had in the back room," said a spokeswoman, "but it will be visible now."

German companies are notorious for squirreling away cash that never appears on their balance sheets. This is a main complaint foreign investors have about German corporate accounting procedures.

Source: "Daimler-Benz Discloses Hidden Reserves of $2.45 Billion, Seeks Big Board Listing," *The Wall Street Journal,* March 25, 1993.

The listing of Daimler-Benz is seen as an icebreaker role for foreign companies wishing to have access to U.S. capital markets. Many professionals in public accounting believe that the trend toward globalization and harmonization of accounting standards will accelerate in the near future. The **internationalization of accounting standards** is accelerating today because the business environment is becoming increasingly global.

END-OF-CHAPTER REVIEW

SUMMARY

1, 2, 3. **Understand the relationships between GAAP, representational faithfulness, and economic consequences of financial reporting and disclosure.** The accounting standards and disclosure requirements in the United States today are far from perfect. The objectives of the conceptual framework have not been met in all instances. Accounting alternatives currently exist that allow entities to report results that may not represent their true financial health, direction, and business conditions. However, a wealth of information is provided in the statements and the accompanying footnotes. Careful reading and examination of the statements and other financial information of a company should provide the user with enough information to make intelligent decisions.

As a final note on the travails of IBM, on July 28, 1993, the company reported a loss of $8.04 billion for the second quarter of 1993. The loss reflected a $6 billion pretax charge for work-force reductions, a $2.9 billion pretax charge to shrink capacity and office space, and losses stemming from revenue declines. The aggressive accounting policies followed by IBM in the 1980s certainly did not reflect the severity of future problems. It was not until the mid to late 1990s that IBM appears to have recovered and is again reporting profits.

4. **Understand the political nature of the standard-setting process.** Accounting standards are not promulgated in a void. The process is highly politicized, and the economic consequences of proposed rules are debated thoroughly. In some cases, the economic consequences are negative, having a social cost, at least in the short term. On balance, it seems that there is an overall positive impact of accounting rules in that they do succeed in providing the information necessary to ensure an active trading securities market.

5. **Understand the role of U.S. accounting standards in the international business arena.** In the future, standard setters will have to consider the globalization of business. Accounting standards may need to be compromised in some areas to accommodate the international community because the United States must participate in the international business arena.

KEY TERMS

Economic consequences of accounting standards *1070*
Economic reality of underlying events and transactions *1066*
Executory contracts *1058*
"Fuzzy" GAAP *1056*
Historical cost *1064*
Internationalization of accounting standards *1073*
Loss contingency *1062*
Research and development (R&D) costs *1066*
Revenue recognition *1057*

ASSIGNMENT MATERIAL

CASES

C20–1 IBM Accounting Policies (Report Preparation and/or Discussion)

Part of the discussion in this chapter focused on the problems IBM encountered because of the aggressive accounting policies it adopted in the 1980s. Adoption of these policies accelerated revenue recognition and deferred some cost and expense recognition. The net result of these policy choices was to increase profitability during the 1980s.

Required:

A. The apparent purpose of adoption of the specific accounting policies was to maintain and increase profitability in the short run. Is maximization of short-run profitability an acceptable management objective? Why or why not?

B. How are management objectives related to investor expectations?

C. If IBM did not violate GAAP, and disclosed all its accounting policies in the notes to the financial statements, is criticism of its policies justified?

C20–2 The "Big Bath" and Social Consequences of Downsizing

In 1993, IBM hired a new CEO, Lewis Gerstner, to restore profitability to the company. Gerstner reduced the work force by thousands of employees at a cost in the billions of dollars. He also sold or abandoned manufacturing plants, offices, and equipment at a cost of billions more. These downsizing costs were treated as one-time charges.

Required:

A. What is the motivation for any company to take the "Big Bath"?

B. Are there social consequences of downsizing like IBM did? Discuss the pros and cons.

C20–3 Ethical Considerations of Accounting Changes

Mary Hopkins has recently assumed a new position, chief financial officer (CFO) of Systems Logic Software. Systems has been marginally profitable over the years. Hopkins is one of a team of new managers brought in to improve profitability. After a thorough review of all operations and accounting policies and procedures, she makes the following recommendations to the CEO:

1. Change from LIFO to FIFO inventory accounting.
2. Change from MACRS depreciation over a 10-year period for certain assets to straight-line depreciation over 20 years.
3. Change the assumed discount rate of the pension plan from 6% to 8%.
4. Drop company sponsorship of retiree health benefits.
5. Treat all program lease arrangements as sales-type leases instead of operating leases.
6. Sell the company headquarters building and lease it back in a long-term, operating-lease arrangement.

Required:

A. Discuss Hopkins' motivation for these changes.

B. Is GAAP violated by any of these changes?

C. Do you agree with these changes? Why or why not?

C20–4 Revenue Recognition

When a new customer joins Affiliated ATM Services, Inc.'s ATM network, an entrance fee of $5,000 is due and payable on the day the contract is signed. When should this fee be recognized as revenue in the financial statements?

C20–5 Revenue and Bad Debts Expense Recognition

Affiliated ATM Services, Inc., entered into a contract with Los Angeles County, California, to provide authorization services for the Office for Aid to Dependent Families. Each person eligible for aid was required to dial into the computer and answer a set of questions each week in order to maintain eligibility. Approximately 1.5 million transactions were authorized each month via this process. Affiliated ATM Services, Inc., billed the county a transaction fee based on the number of transactions processed each month plus any other incidental expenses incurred, with a small markup.

The program proved to be very popular. The transaction fees for the first year and one-half exceeded the county's budget for the program for the first two years it was in operation. Prior to the contract's expiration (it was a two-year contract, expiring on December 31, 1990), Los Angeles County expressed a desire to continue the program if Affiliated ATM was willing to negotiate the pricing. Affiliated agreed to adjust its pricing to meet the county's budget constraints as long as the program continued to be profitable to ATM. Contract negotiations began in the third year and were not completed until eight months into the third year.

During the new contract negotiations, it was thought that the current pricing structure would remain in place, with a cap equal to the county's total dollars budgeted to the program for all of Year 3. The total dollars budgeted to the program by Los Angeles County for Year 3 was $3 million. Affiliated continued to bill the county the full transaction cost for each month during the negotiation period (which consistently exceeded $250,000 per month at an increasing rate), knowing that the $3 million cap would be exceeded during the year.

Required: How would you account for the revenue from this contract? Suppose your supervisor tells you to record the difference between the actual bill and the allotted $250,000 per month as a debit to bad-debt expense and a credit to the allowance for doubtful accounts. Does this reflect the economic reality of the situation? Is it representationally faithful?

C20–6 Ethical Considerations of Revenue and Expense Recognition

Affiliated ATM Services, Inc., entered into a contract with First Dallas National Bank in which it agreed to perform ATM transaction-processing and data-processing services for the next three years. The contract is for a flat fee per month, provided First Dallas National Bank does not exceed its current processing volume. If the processing volume is less in any given month than the volumes established in the first month of the contract, then a credit is established that will carry forward to be netted against any overages in the future. Any unused credits established during the first year should be used during the first year or they are lost. The credits are wiped clean and start reaccumulating after the end of each year.

Upper management at Affiliated ATM Services, Inc., has just learned that First Dallas National Bank intends to use up its accumulated credits by installing 50 new automatic teller machines in its various branches in the last quarter of the year. Affiliated ATM Services is furious about this new development and is looking for ways to prevent First

Dallas National from using this loophole. Installing the ATMs would cause Affiliated ATM Services, Inc., to incur several huge expenses for which there would be no offsetting revenue stream.

The accountant who prepares the First Dallas National Bank's monthly invoice has been very meticulous and followed the contract specifications very closely. The invoice is formatted and prepared exactly the same way it is demonstrated in the appendices to the contract.

Upper management has come up with a brainstorm that will prevent First Dallas National Bank from using the accumulated credits. They have decided to interpret the contract in such a way that the credits from the ATM transaction processing may be used only on ATM transaction processing, and the credits from data processing may be used only on data-processing transaction volumes. The two systems are separate, and the credits established by each should remain separate and not be added to or netted against each other.

This is not the method illustrated in the appendices to the contract. However, upper management feels the wording in the actual contract should take precedence over the illustrations in the appendices. Therefore, upper management has asked you, the accountant, to recalculate the invoices for the past months using this new method.

Required:

A. What should you do if you feel the original invoices were correct and upper management is wrong?

B. Should an allowance account be established to record the unused credits at the end of each period?

C. Should the expenses associated with installing the ATMs for First Dallas National Bank be accrued just in case Affiliated loses its argument?

C20–7 Integrative, Ethical Considerations

The condensed balance sheet (In Thousands of Dollars) of S&S Corporation follows:

Assets:		
Cash	$ 1,000	
Investments in trading securities	500	
Accounts receivable (net)	2,000	
Inventories (LIFO)	4,500	
Total current assets		$ 8,000
Investments in debt securities, held-to-maturity	$ 3,000	
Property, plant & equipment (net)	19,000	
Total property, plant & equipment		22,000
Total assets		$30,000
Liabilities:		
Current	$12,000	
Long-term	15,000	
Total liabilities		$27,000
Equity:		
Capital stock	$ 4,000	
Deficit	(1,000)	
Total equity		3,000
Total liabilities & equity		$30,000

Sally Swift, president and CEO, is contemplating a serious problem: S&S is in violation of the bond indenture, which states that S&S must maintain a current ratio in excess of 2:1, or the entire amount of bonds can be called at the option of the holder. Swift has asked James Starr, the CFO, for his recommendations and received the following:

1. Reclassify the investment in debt securities, held-to-maturity, as short-term trading securities since they could be easily liquidated.
2. Reclassify $4,000 of current liabilities as long-term liabilities since they could be refinanced with long-term debt (if a lender could be found).
3. Restate inventory at its FIFO cost of $9,500.

Required:

A. Recast the balance sheet to reflect these actions.
B. Discuss the propriety of these actions.

C20–8 Integrative, Ethical Considerations

Sandy Stryker was hired in 1998 as the CEO of Fashion Favorites, a discount retail chain. The company had been losing money for several years, and she was brought in to restore profitability.

During her first year on the job, Stryker reduced the work force by 40%, sold all the store buildings and entered into long-term lease agreements to rent them, consolidated several stores, and instituted easier credit terms to stimulate sales. The net effect of these moves was to reduce the total assets, reduce expenses, and increase sales. At the end of 1998, Fashion Favorites reported large losses because of these write-offs, but Stryker was confident that the company was well positioned for the next several years.

During 1999, operating results were not what was expected, and it appeared that Fashion would barely break even. Stryker had assured the board of directors that 1999 would be very profitable, and thus has decided to do the following:

1. Delay purchases of new inventory, thus using up LIFO layers of lower-cost merchandise.
2. Reduce the estimated bad-debt expense percentage from 4% of credit sales to ½% of credit sales.
3. Certain merchandise has been shipped on consignment to another retailer. Stryker directs that these shipments be recorded as sales.

Required:

A. Discuss the short-run propriety of each of these actions.
B. What are some long-run consequences of these actions?

C20–9 Revenue and Cost-of-Goods-Sold Expense Recognition

Affiliated ATM Services, Inc., sells its services for ATM transaction processing to financial institutions. Once a customer signs a contract, it takes approximately 90 days to make that customer's ATM operational. During the implementation period, Affiliated ATM Services, Inc., incurs several expenses on behalf of it customers. These expenses are accumulated in a balance sheet account until the customer's ATM is live and the customer receives the first bill. There is no mark-up on the first bill, and the expenses are credited to the balance sheet account that they were originally debited to when the invoice was recorded in the financial statements.

Required:

A. Does this practice follow GAAP?

B. Does it reflect the economic reality of the transaction?

QUESTIONS

Q20–1 Define the qualitative characteristic of representational faithfulness.

Q20–2 Define the accounting convention of conservatism.

Q20–3 Is there any relationship between representational faithfulness and conservatism? Explain.

Q20–4 Discuss the relationship between alternative accounting methods and representational faithfulness.

Q20–5 Discuss the interrelationships between GAAP, alternative accounting methods, conservatism, and representational faithfulness.

Q20–6 Provide an example in which GAAP is followed but does not represent the underlying economic transaction.

Q20–7 On what basis can Topps Card Company and IBM defend their accounting policies with respect to receivables?

Q20–8 Enron Corporation is the first and only nonfinancial company to use mark-to-market accounting. Explain how this method is applied by Enron. What do you suppose the motivation of Enron management is for adoption of this policy?

Q20–9 Describe the similarities in the accounting policies of Enron, IBM, and Topps.

Q20–10 Should the FASB be concerned about the possibility of unfavorable economic consequences resulting from adoption of a standard? Why or why not?

Q20–11 What is the role of the qualitative characteristic of neutrality in financial reporting and disclosure?

Q20–12 SFAS No. 106 has been blamed for erosion of retiree health-care benefits. Do you agree? Why or why not?

Q20–13 Why was there concern over the treatment of goodwill by RJR Nabisco in the aborted stock offering?

Q20–14 Should accounting standards reflect political compromises?

Q20–15 Why are there relatively few foreign companies listed on U.S. stock exchanges?

Q20–16 What benefits could be gained by foreign firms from listing on U.S. stock exchanges?

Q20–17 Is it important to have a single set of accounting standards worldwide? Why or why not?

Q20–18 Have the objectives of the conceptual framework been achieved by the FASB?

Q20–19 Why are property, plant, and equipment ordinarily carried on the books at historical cost? Is there anything wrong with using historical cost as the basis for valuation of long-term assets?

Q20–20 What does U.S. GAAP prescribe as accounting treatment for research and development expense? Does this differ from international standards? If so, in what way?

EXERCISES

E20–1 Financial Analysis

The condensed balance sheet and income statement for the NNA Company for the current year appear on the following page:

BALANCE SHEET

(IN THOUSANDS OF DOLLARS)		
Assets:		
Cash	$ 1,000	
Investment in trading securities	500	
Accounts receivable (net)	2,000	
Inventories (FIFO-LCM)	4,500	
Total current assets		$ 8,000
Investments in debt securities, held-to-maturity	$ 3,000	
Property, plant & equipment (net)	19,000	
Total property, plant & equipment		22,000
Total assets		$30,000
Liabilities:		
Current	$12,000	
Long-term	15,000	
Total liabilities		$27,000
Equity:		
Capital stock	$ 4,000	
Deficit	(1,000)	
Total equity		3,000
Total liabilities and equity		$30,000

INCOME STATEMENT

(IN THOUSANDS OF DOLLARS)	
Sales and other revenues	$22,000
Cost of goods sold	16,000
Gross profit	$ 6,000
Operating expenses	5,500
Net income	$ 500

Required:

A. Evaluate the liquidity of NNA.
B. Evaluate the solvency position of NNA.
C. Evaluate the profitability of NNA for the year.

E20–2 Financial Statement Errors—Integrative

RTS Corporation discovered that several errors have been made in the preparation of prior years' financial statements. The errors include the following:

1. Three years ago, depreciation expenses for equipment were inadvertently omitted.
2. Two years ago, the inventory value was overstated because some damaged merchandise was counted as regular merchandise.
3. Five years ago, a catastrophic loss resulting from a major flood was reported as an extraordinary loss in the financial statements. While the amount of the loss was material, it did not meet the criteria necessary to be reported as an extraordinary item.
4. Last year, equipment for the research laboratory was purchased at a cost of $5,000,000. The cost was expensed as research and development expense.
5. Five years ago, RTS received 100 acres of land from the city as a plant site in exchange for $1. The land had a fair market value of $10 million. RTS did not record the transaction.
6. Bonds payable with a par value of $1 million were issued last year at a discount. RTS recorded the sale of the bonds as if they had been issued at par for cash.

Required: What are the effects of these items on the financial statements of RTS?

E20–3 Effects of Alternative Accounting Methods

Redstick discloses the following significant accounting policies in the notes to its financial statements:

1. Inventories are based on LIFO.
2. MACRS depreciation is used for tax purposes and straight-line financial reporting purposes.
3. Sales are recorded at the time the products are shipped. All products can be returned for full refunds for up to six months if the customer is dissatisfied. Redstick provides an allowance for potential sales returns of 10% of total sales. The last two years, returns have been 15% of total sales.
4. All lease contracts for assets acquired are treated as operating-lease commitments.
5. The discount rate used in determining the pension expense was changed in the current year from 5% to 12%. This change was made at the suggestion of the actuary, who indicated a 12% return would be easy to achieve on the assets in the fund.

Required:

A. What alternative accounting policies might have been used in each situation?
B. Indicate the effects on the financial statements of the accounting policies used compared to the alternative policies that could have been used.

E20–4 Adjusting and Correcting Entries

At December 31, 1995, you are reviewing the transactions of IMA Corporation and find the following material items.

1. BNK has filed a lawsuit against IMA for patent infringement in the amount of $5,000,000. IMA attorneys have advised you that a loss in the amount of $2,000,000 is probable.
2. In 1989 depreciation on a piece of machinery was incorrectly recorded as $11,000. The correct amount should have been $1,000.
3. In 1992 a customer of IMA declared bankruptcy, and IMA properly wrote off the customer's account in the amount of $15,000. You discover a letter received from the customer on December 22, 1995, indicating the customer's intent to pay the debt within the next three months.

4. In September of 1995, $35,000 (at cost) of merchandise was shipped on consignment to Rex Corporation. The transaction was recorded as a sale ($50,000) at the time of shipment. As of December 31, 1995, $7,500 has been received from Rex, representing the proceeds of the sales of $8,000 of merchandise less a commission withheld of $500.

Required: Prepare the adjusting and/or correcting entries for each situation.

E20–5 Correction of Errors

The annual audit of the financial statements and the accounting records of Sally's Supermarket, Inc., reveals that the accountant has violated some accounting conventions, assumptions, and constraints. The following transactions were involved:

1. Ordinary repairs to the refrigeration units were recorded as follows:

Equipment	8,000	
Cash		8,000

2. The expected useful life of the freezer meat cases was reduced from 25 years to 15 years. This resulted in additional depreciation expense in the current year of $22,000 above what had been recorded in previous years. The $22,000 was recorded as a debit to Retained Earnings.
3. Dry goods purchased for resale were recorded as a debit to Purchases for the invoice price of $10,000. The Accounts Payable account was credited for the same amount. Terms were 2/10, n/30. Eight days later, when the account was paid, Accounts Payable was debited and Cash was credited for $9,800.
4. The supermarket sustained extensive structural damage in the amount of $450,000, caused by a tornado. The insurance recovery was only $150,000. The entire amount of the loss ($450,000) was recorded and reported as an extraordinary loss on the income statement, and the cash recovery from the insurance company was recorded as follows:

Cash	150,000	
Income from Insurance		150,000

5. Accounts receivable of $30,000 was reported on the balance sheet; included in this amount was a loan of $10,000 to the manager's son. The loan will mature in three years.
6. A new delivery van was purchased for $28,500. The entire amount was debited to Automobile Expense on the income statement.

Required: For each transaction, give the entry that should have been made, and indicate what the appropriate reporting should have been. In addition, identify the inappropriate treatment and the accounting assumptions, conventions, and constraints violated.

E20–6 Correction of Errors

The following transactions contain information related to Physical Therapy Inc. For each transaction, determine what accounting convention or assumption was violated, if any, and explain the nature of the violation. Also, for each transaction, indicate how it should have been recorded.

1. The company purchased a state-of-the-art exercise machine that had a list price of $248,000. The machine was paid for by issuing 10,000 shares of common stock. The par value was $8 per share and the current market value was $22 per share. The transaction was recorded as follows:

Equipment, Exercise Machine	248,000	
Common Stock		80,000
Gain on Purchase		168,000

2. One of the physical therapists, Wood, bought a new BMW for her husband. The vehicle was strictly for his personal use, but the therapist told the bookkeeper to charge the car to her expense account. The following entry was made:

Travel and Entertainment—Wood	51,000	
Cash		51,000

3. The business collected $35,000 in January 19B for services rendered in December 19A. No entry was made in the year 19A, and the books have been closed.
4. The company is being sued for $1,250,000 by a patient who claims she cannot lift heavy objects due to therapy malpractice. The company attorney believes the patient has no grounds for a lawsuit and has advised them not to worry. Being conservative, the bookkeeper made the following entry:

Loss from Lawsuit—Back Patient	1,250,000	
Liability for Lawsuit		1,250,000

5. The company owns a storage building that is located in a flood zone near the Red River. In April of 19A, severe flooding caused extensive damage. The company carries flood insurance because the area floods on a regular basis. Unfortunately, the insurance expired in March of 19A and the company did not renew its policy. The cost to repair the building was $8,500. The following entry was made:

Retained Earnings—Flood Loss	8,500	
Cash		8,500

E20–7 Cash versus Accrual

The following summarized data were taken from the balance sheet and income statement of Lea's Companies at the end of December 19A. Lea's fiscal year-end is based on the calendar year.

Sales (cash)	$675,000
Sales (on account)	15,000
Purchases (cash only)	245,000
Purchases (on credit)	54,000
Accounts receivable:	
Balance on 1/1/19A	8,700
Balance on 12/31/19A	11,000
Accounts payable:	
Balance on 1/1/19A	18,000
Balance on 12/31/19A	22,500

Inventory:	
Beginning 1/1/19A	$123,000
Ending 12/31/19A	140,000
Operating expenses (cash paid)	190,000
Prepaid expenses at 12/31/19A (none at 1/1/19A)	11,000
Wages payable at 12/31/19A (none at 1/1/19A)	6,000
Depreciation expense for year	28,000

Required:

A. Without reference to the specific numbers given, discuss accrual versus cash-basis accounting and explain the conceptual basis for each.

B. Which method is in conformity with GAAP? Explain.

C. Using the data presented, compute the accrual and cash-basis income for the year ending December 31, 19A.

E20–8 Comprehensive Financial Ratios

Required:

A. Refer to the Motorola annual report reproduced in Appendix C: Calculate as many of the following ratios (in **B**) as possible. *Note:* you may have to calculate some of the values as they may not be given to you directly. Don't forget the footnotes as a source of information! [*Important:* If a needed data item is not provided somewhere in the financial statements, including the notes, enter $0 in the ratio. If, however, the data item is available and happens to be equal to $0, enter a very small amount in the ratio (i.e., $1). This will not materially affect the value of your ratios.]

B. Classify each of the ratios listed as liquidity, activity/turnover, leverage, or profitability. Then, describe what the ratio measures and/or how the ratio might be helpful to management.

1. Current ratio
2. Inventory turnover
3. Total assets turnover
4. Total liabilities/total assets
5. Times interest earned
6. Profit margin
7. Net operating margin
8. Return on total assets
9. Dividend payout ratio

PROBLEMS

P20–1 Revenue Recognition

Part of the discussion in this chapter was related to Enron Corporation's mark-to-market policy for the gas contracts of their subsidiary Enron Gas Services. With regard to these contracts, answer the following questions.

A. What is the meaning of the term "executory contracts"?

B. Briefly describe Enron's mark-to-market policy for its gas contracts.

C. What is the conceptual issue raised by this practice? Why might this be a problem in the future?

P20–2 Memo Preparation—Loss Contingencies

Loss contingencies were discussed in Chapter 11 as well as in this chapter. Prepare a short memo that describes the proper accounting for loss contingencies.

P20–3 Research and Development

Research and development costs are outflows of resources to obtain (hopefully) some future benefits. Current GAAP requires that R&D expenditures be expensed in the period incurred. Critics of the FASB argue that this policy ignores future benefits of these expenditures and therefore does not represent economic reality.

Required:

A. Contrast the capitalized cost of patents acquired externally with the capitalized cost of patents developed internally.

B. An example of an industry that has large expenditures for research and development is the drug industry. The drug industry has also been heavily criticized for generating excessive profits on individual drugs. Explain the relationship between past R&D expenditures and excessive profits generated on an individual drug.

P20–4 Economic Consequences of Accounting Standards

Some observers have stated that SFAS No. 106, "Accounting for Postretirement Benefits," has caused reduction or elimination of health care benefits for some retirees and for some current employees. If true, this appears to be an extremely negative consequence of an accounting standard.

Required: How would you respond to these comments?

P20–5 Economic Consequences of Disclosure

One of the chapter excerpts described the accounting technique for Goodwill by RJR Nabisco in its proposed spinoff of the food business from tobacco. After the details of the proposed offering were made public, and analysts had an opportunity to study it, the offering was canceled.

Required:

A. Briefly describe how the goodwill was to be accounted for in the offering.

B. Briefly describe the effect on projected earnings of the goodwill treatment.

P20–6 Goodwill and General Electric

Part of the discussion of this chapter concerned the treatment of the excess purchase price over the fair market value paid by GE in the acquisition of RCA.

Required: Prepare a short report that succinctly describes

A. the allocation of the excess purchase price by GE.

B. the impact on future profitability to GE.

RESEARCH ACTIVITIES

R20–1 Research—R&D Expenditures

In your database of companies (or from other sources), locate two examples of companies in which R&D expenditures are equal to or greater than 50 percent of reported earnings. Insofar as the data permit, do a trend analysis of earnings per share, return on equity, and return on assets for up to ten years.

R20–2 Research and Report Preparation—Undervalued Assets

In your database of companies (or from other sources), find one example of a company that has undervalued assets.

Required:

A. Explain how you selected that company (in other words, why do you think the assets are undervalued).

B. Prepare a profitability analysis for the company comparing its return on investment, using the published numbers, with numbers that you think would be more representative. Explain how you determined the more representative numbers.

R20–3 Research—The "Big Bath"

In your database of companies (or from other sources), find three examples of companies that incurred large one-time charges for restructuring or downsizing or any other reason. Trace the profitability of the companies before and after the write-offs, and compare the profitability trend with the price trend of the stock.

R20–4 Research—Leasing Arrangements

In your database of companies (or from other sources), find two examples of companies for each of the following lease arrangements:

1. Liability—Capital-lease arrangement
2. Liability—Operating-lease arrangement

Required: Calculate the following ratios for each of the companies for the same two-year period:

A. Debt-to-equity

B. Return on assets

C. Return on equity

R20–5 Internet Activity

Visit the ***IBM*** homepage. Prepare a short report about any financial data available relative to the assumed rate of return on its pension investments, the trend of total revenues over the last five years, and reported operating income over the last five years.

R20–6 Internet Activity

Visit the SEC EDGAR database. Calculate the return on total assets for ***Merck*** (a drug company), ***International Paper,*** and ***WalMart*** for the last three years.

R20–7 Internet Activity

Visit the homepage for this text at *www.swcollege.com/hartman.html* to see if there is anything posted for Chapter 20.

PART 5

Integrative Cases

Restructuring Charges and Accounting Changes

In this case, students evaluate the income and cash implications of *GTE*'s recent restructuring charges and accounting changes.

Your friend Mark has had a hot tip from a broker about telecommunications stocks and is ready to make a substantial investment in GTE stock.

"Mark, don't you think you should look at the financials before deciding to buy?"

"What for? That's my broker's job. I don't understand most of that stuff, anyway. All I know is that cell phones are big, and GTE is big in cellular. You're the business major; you worry about the bean counting."

"Mark, that's the problem. I have worried about the bean counting. I've looked at the statements, and the picture isn't so rosy. With about five minutes of work I can tell you that GTE, your "hot pick," lost $780 million a couple of years ago and had a $1.8 billion charge to earnings last year. And that stuff's on the first page!"

For the first time in the discussion, Mark hesitates.

"Seriously? A charge over a billion dollars? That's a lot of cash."

"Well, it might be a lot of cash and it might not be any cash. Give me a couple of hours and let me find out, OK? The company won't go anywhere while I look this information over."

The Company

Mark is right about one thing: GTE *is* big in cellular. At the end of 1994 it had the second largest cellular business in the United States. Additionally, the company owns the largest non-*Bell* telecommunications system in the United States. The company has been shedding noncore businesses (including a 20 percent stake in ***US Sprint*** and its electrical products group in 1992), and serves about 17 million access lines in 28 states.

GTE

Effect of Restructuring Charges and Accounting Changes on the Financial Statements

GTE's 1994 balance sheet, income statement, and selected notes are provided in the exhibits accompanying this case. Use the statements and notes to draft a response to Mark regarding the financial health of GTE as exhibited by the financial statements, focusing on the impact of accounting changes. Use the following questions to guide your response. To help gauge your audience, assume that Mark is a college graduate with no background in business.

Using the financial statements and notes, consider the following questions. (Notes 2 and 4 are most relevant, but others may be used.)

- In 1993, the income statement shows a $1.84 billion charge for "restructuring costs." What were the major components of the charge? Why was the charge taken in 1993 rather than in future periods as the restructuring is completed?
- Note 3 indicates that in 1994, "expenditures of $343 million were made in connection with the implementation of the reengineering plan." How did the company account for these expenditures?
- What income statement charge was primarily responsible for the $780 million loss in 1992? Using note 5, determine the components of this charge.
- SFAS No. 109 related to income taxes did not have to be adopted until 1993, but GTE chose to adopt in 1992, thereby incurring an additional $100 million charge in that year. Considering this, why would the company choose to adopt the pronouncement in 1992 rather than 1993?
- Finally, reconsider your friend Mark's initial question: Did the company lose a lot of cash in 1993 and 1992? Is the company as healthy at the end of 1994 as it was at the beginning of 1992? Why or why not?

Exhibit 1
GTE's Balance Sheet

GTE Corporation and Subsidiaries
Consolidated Balance Sheets
December 31

	1994	1993
Total current assets	$ 5,634	$ 5,948
Tangible assets (net)	29,328	28,720
Total investments and other assets	7,538	6,907
Total assets	$42,500	$41,575
Total current liabilities (includes $436 and $540 of accrued restructuring costs in 1994 and 1993, respectively)	$ 8,221	$ 7,933
Long-term debt	12,163	13,019
Reserves and deferred credits:		
Deferred income taxes	3,522	3,128
Employee benefit obligations	4,651	4,667
Restructuring costs and other	1,729	1,973
Total reserves and deferred credits:	$ 9,902	$ 9,768
Minority interests in equity of subsidiaries	1,622	1,106
Mandatorily redeemable preferred stock	109	156

(continued)

EXHIBIT 1
(Concluded)

	1994	1993
Shareholders' equity:		
Preferred stock	10	111
Common stock	48	48
Additional paid-in capital	7,627	7,309
Retained earnings	3,422	2,769
ESOP obligation	(624)	(644)
Total stockholders' equity	$10,483	$ 9,593
Total liabilities and stockholders' equity	$42,500	$41,575

EXHIBIT 2 GTE's Income Statement

GTE CORPORATION AND SUBSIDIARIES
Consolidated Statements of Income
For Years Ending December 31

(DOLLARS IN MILLIONS)	1994	1993	1992
Total revenues and sales	$19,994	$19,748	$19,984
Costs and expenses:			
Telephone operations	11,667	11,765	11,828
Telecommunications products and services	3,431	3,578	3,940
Restructuring costs	—	1,840	—
Total costs and expenses	$15,098	$17,183	$15,768
Operating income	$ 4,846	$ 2,565	$ 4,216
Other deductions:			
Interest expense (net)	1,059	1,197	1,332
Other (net)	(196)	(190)	130
Total other deductions	$ 863	$ 1,007	$ 1,462
Income before income taxes	$ 3,983	$ 1,558	$ 2,754
Income tax provision	1,532	568	967
Income from continuing operations	$ 2,451	$ 990	$ 1,787
Discontinued operations	—	—	(48)
Extraordinary charge	—	(90)	(52)

(continued)

EXHIBIT 2 (Concluded)

(DOLLARS IN MILLIONS)	1994	1993	1992
Cumulative effect of accounting changes	—	—	(2,441)
Net income (loss)	$ 2,451	$ 900	$ (754)
Preferred stock dividends	10	18	26
Net income applicable to common stock	$ 2,441	$ 882	$ (780)
Earnings (loss) per common share:			
Continuing operations	$ 2.55	$ 1.03	$ 1.95
Discontinued operations	—	—	(.05)
Extraordinary charge	—	(.10)	(.06)
Cumulative effect of accounting changes	—	—	(2.70)
Consolidated net income	$ 2.55	$ .93	(.86)
Average common shares outstanding	958 million	945 million	905 million

EXHIBIT 3 GTE's Statement of Cash Flows

GTE CORPORATION AND SUBSIDIARIES
Consolidated Statements of Cash Flows
For Years Ending December 31

	1994	1993	1992
Cash flows from operations:			
Income from continuing operations	$ 2,451	$ 990	$ 1,787
Adjustments to reconcile income to net cash from operations:			
Depreciation and amortization	3,432	3,419	3,289
Restructuring costs	—	1,840	—
Deferred income taxes	248	(864)	37
Change in current assets and current liabilities, excluding the effects of acquisitions and dispositions	(1,029)	(13)	(268)
Other—net	(362)	(95)	(13)
Net cash from operations	$ 4,740	$ 5,277	$ 4,832
Cash flows from investing:			
Capital expenditures	$(4,192)	$(3,893)	$(3,909)
Acquisitions and investments	(244)	(46)	(84)
Proceeds from sales of assets	1,163	2,267	662
Other—net	4	(66)	55
Net cash used in investing	$(3,269)	$(1,738)	$(3,276)

(continued)

EXHIBIT 3 (Concluded)

	1994	1993	1992
Cash flows from financing:			
GTE common stock issued	$ 422	$ 383	$ 1,513
Long-term debt and preferred securities issued	2,345	2,325	590
Long-term debt and preferred securities retired	(2,481)	(4,836)	(2,002)
Dividends to shareholders of parent	(1,806)	(1,744)	(1,572)
Increase (decrease) in short-term obligations, excluding current maturities	25	304	(254)
Other—net	25	(3)	6
Net cash used in financing	$(1,470)	$(3,571)	$(1,719)
Increase (decrease) in cash and temporary cash investments	1	(32)	(163)
Cash and temporary cash investments:			
Beginning of year	322	354	517
End of year	$ 323	$ 322	$ 354

GTE Corporation and Subsidiaries Selected Notes to Consolidated Financial Statements

Note 3. Restructuring Costs

Results for 1993 include one-time restructuring costs of $1.8 billion, which reduced net income by $1.2 billion, or $1.22 per share.

These restructuring costs included $1.4 billion at telephone operations primarily to implement its reengineering plan. This plan is intended to redesign and streamline processes in order to improve customer responsiveness and product quality, reduce the time necessary to introduce new products and services and further reduce costs. The reengineering plan included $680 million to upgrade or replace existing customer service and administrative systems and enhance network software, $410 million for employee separation benefits associated with workforce reductions and $210 million primarily for the consolidation of facilities and operations and other related costs.

Implementation of the reengineering plan began during 1994 and is expected to be completed by the end of 1996. Reductions of approximately 17,000 telephone operations employees are expected during that time.

During 1994, 67 customer contact, network operations and operator service centers were closed and employee reductions of nearly 3,000 occurred. During the year, expenditures of $343 million were made in connection with the implementation of the reengineering plan. These expenditures were primarily associated with the closure and relocation of the various centers described above, separation benefits from employee reductions and incremental expenditures to redesign and streamline processes. The level of reengineering activities and related expenditures are expected to accelerate in 1995.

The 1993 restructuring charge also included a $400 million reduction in the carrying value of satellite communication assets of *GTE* Spacenet ("Spacenet") and certain other assets to estimated net realizable value. This action primarily reflected the development of alternative transmission methods through technological advances and increased competition. During 1994, GTE sold Spacenet at a price that approximated its book value.

During 1993, telephone operations offered various voluntary separation programs to its domestic workforce. These programs resulted in a pre-tax charge of $74 million which reduced net income by $46 million, or $.05 per share.

Note 5. Accounting Changes

In 1992, GTE adopted Statements of Financial Accounting Standards No. 106, "Employers' Accounting for Postretirement Benefits Other Than Pensions" ("SFAS No. 106") and No. 109, "Accounting for Income Taxes" ("SFAS No. 109").

SFAS No. 106 requires the expected cost of postretirement health care and life insurance benefits to be recognized during the years that employees render service. GTE adopted SFAS No. 106 on the immediate recognition basis effective January 1, 1992, and recorded a one-time, noncash charge of $2.3 billion (net of deferred tax benefits of $1.4 billion), or $2.59 per share, to give effect to past service costs. Pursuant to SFAS No. 71, a regulatory asset was not recorded due to GTE's assessment of the long-term competitive environment and the uncertainties surrounding the timing and extent of recovery.

SFAS No. 109 changed the method by which companies account for income taxes. Among other things, the statement requires that deferred tax balances be adjusted to reflect new tax rates when they are enacted into law. The cumulative prior years' effect of this change reduced net income by $100 million, or $.11 per share, in 1992.

Note 10. Employee Benefit Plans: Retirement Plans

Most subsidiaries have trusteed, noncontributory, defined benefit pension plans covering substantially all employees. The benefits to be paid under these plans are generally based on years of credited service and average final earnings. GTE's funding policy, subject to the minimum funding requirements of employee benefit and tax laws, is to contribute such amounts as are determined on an actuarial basis to provide the plans with assets sufficient to meet the benefit obligations of the plans. The assets of the plans consist primarily of corporate equities, government securities and corporate debt securities.

The components of the net pension credit for 1994–1992 were as follows (in millions of dollars):

	1994	1993	1992
Benefits earned during the year	$ 269	$ 295	$ 288
Interest cost on projected benefit obligations	542	584	602
Return on plan assets:			
Actual	(29)	(2,073)	(732)
Deferred	(971)	1,110	(201)
Other—net	(168)	(174)	(197)
Net pension credit	$(357)	$ (258)	$(240)

The expected long-term rate of return on plan assets was 8.5% for 1994 and 8.25% for 1993 and 1992.

The funded status of the plans and the prepaid pension costs at December 31, 1994 and 1993, were as follows (in millions of dollars):

	1994	1993
Plan assets at fair value	$11,950	$12,840
Projected benefit obligations	6,724	7,391
Excess of assets over projected obligations	$ 5,226	$ 5,449
Unrecognized net transition asset	(644)	(778)
Unrecognized net gain	(2,270)	(2,797)
Prepaid pension costs	$ 2,312	$ 1,874

The projected benefit obligations at December 31, 1994 and 1993, include accumulated benefit obligations of $5.1 billion and $5.5 billion and vested benefit obligations of $4.5 billion and $4.9 billion, respectively.

Assumptions used to develop the projected benefit obligations at December 31, 1994 and 1993, were as follows:

	1994	1993
Discount rate	8.25%	7.50%
Rate of compensation increase	5.50%	5.25%

Postretirement Benefits Other Than Pensions

Substantially all of GTE's employees are covered under postretirement health-care and life insurance benefit plans. In addition, many retirees outside the United States are covered by government sponsored and administered programs. The health care benefits paid under the GTE plans are generally based on comprehensive hospital, medical and surgical benefit provisions. GTE funds amounts for postretirement benefits as deemed appropriate from time to time.

The postretirement benefit cost for 1994–1992 included the following components (in millions of dollars):

	1994	1993	1992
Benefits earned during the year	$ 57	$ 96	$ 97
Interest on accumulated postretirement benefit obligations	259	290	293
Actual return on plan assets	6	(6)	(4)
Amortization of prior service benefits	(54)	(4)	—
Other—net	(14)	2	—
Postretirement benefit cost	$254	$378	$386

The following table sets forth the plans' funded status and the accrued obligations as of December 31, 1994 and 1993 (in millions of dollars):

	1994	1993
Accumulated postretirement benefit obligations attributable to:		
Retirees	$2,731	$2,723
Fully eligible active plan participants	234	231
Other active plan participants	912	1,106
Total accumulated postretirement benefit obligations	$3,877	$4,060
Fair value of plan assets	244	181
Excess of accumulated obligations over plan assets	$3,633	$3,879
Unrecognized prior service benefits	656	710
Unrecognized net loss	(99)	(345)
Accrued postretirement benefit obligations	$4,190	$4,244

The assumed discount rates used to measure the accumulated postretirement benefit obligations were 8.25% at December 31, 1994, and 7.5% at December 31, 1993. The assumed health care cost trend rates in 1994 and 1993 were 12% and 13% for pre-65 participants and 9% and 9.5% for post-65 retirees, each rate declining on a graduated basis to an ultimate rate in the year 2004 of 6%. A one percentage point increase in the assumed health-care cost trend rates for each future year would have increased 1994 costs by $33 million and the accumulated postretirement benefit obligations as of December 31, 1994, by $343 million.

During 1993, GTE made certain changes to its postretirement health care and life insurance benefits for nonunion employees retiring on or after January 1, 1995. These changes include, among others, newly established limits to GTE's annual contribution to postretirement medical costs and a revised cost-sharing schedule based on a retiree's years of service. The net effect of these changes reduced the accumulated postretirement benefit obligations at December 31, 1993, by $710 million. The resulting unrecognized prior service benefits are being amortized over the average remaining service lives of the employees.

Note 14. Income Taxes

Income from continuing operations before income taxes is as follows (in millions of dollars):

	1994	1993	1992
Domestic	$3,475	$1,002	$2,300
Foreign	508	556	454
	$3,983	$1,558	$2,754

The income tax provision (benefit) is as follows (in millions of dollars):

	1994	1993	1992
Current:			
Federal	$ 927	$1,088	$655
Foreign	192	183	171
State and local	165	161	104
	$1,284	$1,432	$930
Deferred:			
Federal	$ 269	$ (682)	$105
Foreign	(1)	2	1
State and local	56	(100)	35
	$ 324	$ (780)	$141
Amortization of deferred investment tax credits—net	(76)	(84)	(104)
Total	$1,532	$ 568	$967

The amortization of deferred investment tax credits—net, relates to the amortization of investment tax credits previously deferred by GTE's regulated telephone subsidiaries.

The components of the deferred income tax provision (benefit) are as follows (in millions of dollars):

	1994	1993	1992
Depreciation and amortization	$ (88)	$ 32	$ 125
Employee benefit obligations	(3)	(80)	(114)
Restructuring costs	299	(667)	—
Prepaid pension costs	144	111	75
Other—net	(28)	(176)	55
	$324	$(780)	$ 141

A reconciliation between taxes computed by applying the statutory federal income tax rate to pre-tax income and income taxes provided in the consolidated statements of income is as follows (in millions of dollars):

	1994	1993	1992
Amounts computed at statutory rates	$1,394	$545	$936
State and local income taxes, net of federal tax benefits	144	40	91
Depreciation of telephone plant construction costs previously deducted for tax purposes—net	42	48	46
Minority interests and preferred stock dividends of subsidiaries	39	40	40
Amortization of investment tax credits—net	(76)	(84)	(104)
Rate differentials applied to reversing temporary differences	(34)	(30)	(35)
Other differences—net	23	9	(7)
Total provision	$1,532	$568	$967

The tax effects of temporary differences that give rise to the current deferred income tax benefits and deferred income tax liabilities at December 31, 1994 and 1993, are as follows (in millions of dollars):

	1994	1993
Depreciation and amortization	$ 4,165	$ 4,180
Employee benefit obligations	(1,853)	(1,850)
Restructuring costs	(368)	(667)
Prepaid pension costs	783	639
Investment tax credits	226	321
Other—net	248	241
Total	$ 3,201	$ 2,864

Note 15. Supplemental Cash Flow Disclosures

The changes in current assets and current liabilities, excluding the effects of acquisitions and dispositions, and the cash paid for interest and income taxes are as follows (in millions of dollars):

	1994	1993	1992
(Increase) decrease from current assets:			
Receivables—net	$ (554)	$ (706)	$ (231)
Other current assets	(4)	168	69
Increase (decrease) from current liabilities:			
Accrued taxes and interest	(209)	465	(41)
Other current liabilities	(262)	60	(65)
Net cash used	$(1,029)	$(13)	$(268)
Cash paid during the year for:			
Interest	$ 1,084	$1,373	$1,477
Income taxes	1,598	880	1,016

Using Postretirement and Deferred Tax Footnotes

The previous case focused on the effect of accounting changes and restructuring announcements on GTE Corporation's 1994 balance sheet and income statement. The accounting changes reflected in the 1994 financials include adoption of both *Statement of Financial Accounting Standards No. 106—Employers' Accounting for Postretirement Benefits Other than Pensions* (SFAS No. 106) and *Statement of Financial Accounting Standards No. 109—Accounting for Income Taxes* (SFAS No. 109). This case requires using the 1994 GTE financial statements and notes to answer the following questions regarding postretirement benefits and deferred taxes. Remember: For some questions, there is no definitive answer. The purpose is to arrive at a reasoned response based upon knowledge of appropriate accounting procedures discussed in the fourth section of the textbook.

Employee Benefit Plans—Note 10

Pensions

GTE

1. What type of pension plans are provided by the company and its subsidiaries? Provide an example of a benefit formula similar to that used by GTE to calculate pension benefits for a retiree. How would you explain this benefit formula to an individual who has no familiarity with technical aspects of pension plans?
2. What is the pension funding policy of the company?
3. The pension footnote indicates that GTE's pension plan *increased* income in each year from 1992 through 1994. What are some reasonable circumstances under which the pension provision would *increase* earnings, rather than be a charge against earnings?
4. **(Challenging)** The pension credit increased each year from 1992 through 1994. What are the probable reasons for the increase? Are your conjectures supported in note 10 or other notes?

5. Is GTE's pension plan overfunded or underfunded at the end of 1994? What amount(s) should be shown on the balance sheet related to the pension plan at the end of 1994? In what balance sheet summary account is the prepaid pension cost probably included?
6. **(Challenging)** How much did the company contribute to the plan in 1994? How much was distributed to retirees?

Postretirement Benefits Other Than Pensions

7. What are the principal nonpension benefits provided retirees by GTE?
8. Did the company adopt SFAS No. 106 with a one-time charge to earnings, or amortize the transition obligation over twenty years?
9. In the disclosure of the APBO, what is the distinction between "retirees," "fully eligible active plan participants," and "other active plan participants?" How do these three groups differ in regard to accounting for and paying out postretirement benefits?
10. **(Challenging)** In 1993, GTE established limits on its annual contribution to postretirement medical costs and began to base contributions on a retiree's years of service with the company. The changes reduced the accumulated postretirement obligation at December 31, 1993, by about $710 million. What effect, if any, will these changes have on future earnings of the company?
11. What is the primary reason for the reduction in the accumulated postretirement benefit obligation from $4,060 to $3,877 million at December 31, 1993 and 1994, respectively?
12. After considering the status of both pension and other postretirement obligations, would you anticipate that the pension overfunding will continue to increase? Explain.

Income Taxes—Note 14

13. At the end of 1994, what is the combined net statutory federal, state, and local income tax *rate*?
14. What was the provision for income taxes shown on the income statement in 1994? How was the provision divided between current and deferred amounts?
15. Using information in Note 14, what percentage of GE's income came from foreign sources in 1994?
16. **(Challenging)** Using information in the footnotes and on the face of the financial statements, reconstruct GTE's entry to record the provision for taxes at the end of 1994.

Reconciling Foreign Earnings and Equity with U.S. GAAP: The Case of British Steel

Introduction

Many companies headquartered in foreign countries list their stocks and bonds on U.S. exchanges or the NASDAQ. Foreign companies desire to list their securities in the United States for many reasons, but the depth and liquidity of the U.S. market, combined with the effective oversight of the SEC in maintaining integrity and fairness, are certainly in the forefront. In 1996, 808 companies headquartered in 47 countries reported to the SEC. The percentage of reporting foreign issuers by geographic region is provided in Exhibit 1.

Since 1982, the Securities and Exchange Commission (SEC) has required foreign companies desiring to be listed on U.S. stock exchanges or the NASDAQ to either issue financial statements in accordance with U.S. GAAP or provide a reconciliation of any material differences between the foreign registrants' financial statements and statements prepared in accordance with U.S. GAAP. This disclosure, filed on form 20-F, provides insight into differences between U.S. and foreign GAAP.

EXHIBIT 1
Percentage of Reporting Foreign Issuers by Region (as of June 30, 1996)

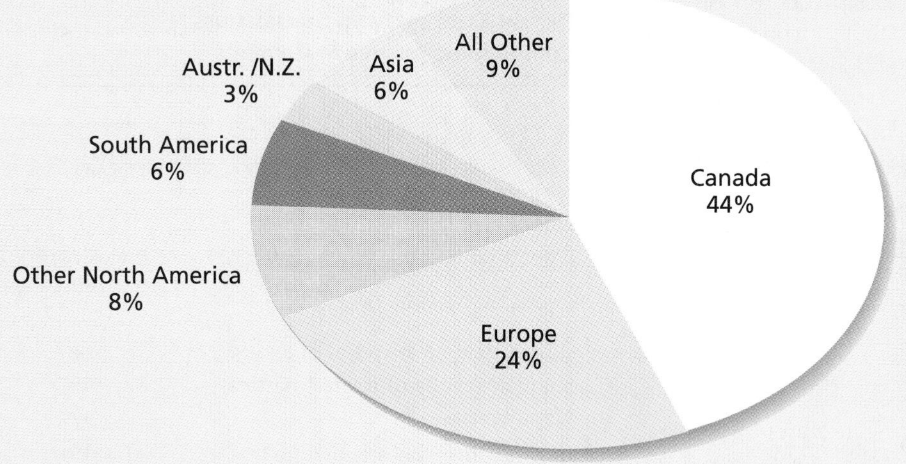

BRITISH STEEL'S 20-F DISCLOSURES

BRITISH STEEL

British Steel plc has listed its shares, in the form of American Depositary Receipts (ADRs) (or American Depositary Shares), on the New York Stock Exchange for a number of years. (ADRs allow foreign companies to list on U.S. exchanges without actually issuing stock denominated in dollars.) To do so, British Steel files a form 20-F each year with the SEC; among other items, the filing contains British Steel's U.K. financial statements and the reconciliation of income and equity from U.K. GAAP to U.S. GAAP. Exhibit 2 contains British Steel's 1995 income statement and statement of changes in shareholders' equity prepared in accordance with U.K. GAAP.

British Steel's 20-F also contains a reconciliation of the U.K. financial statements with U.S. GAAP. In British Steel's case, the reconciliation is contained in note 30, which is provided in Exhibit 2.

Required

1. Some commentators have argued that foreign companies wishing to list their stock in the United States should not have to reconcile their financial statements with U.S. GAAP. What are the pros and cons of requiring such a reconciliation?
2. In 1995, British Steel had operating income, based on U.K. GAAP, of £468 million (about $758 million at then current exchange rates). What is British Steel's operating income (in pounds) based on U.S. GAAP? What items cause a difference in U.K. and U.S. operating income?
3. Shareholders' equity at April 1, 1995 under U.K. and U.S. GAAP is £4,087 million and £4,112 million, respectively. The difference is caused by differences in accounting for five items. For each item, (1) explain the differences in the U.K. and U.S. accounting procedure; (2) indicate the size of the adjustment in reconciling from U.K. to U.S. GAAP caused by the item; and (3) explain why the item is added to or deducted from U.K. shareholders' equity in reconciling to U.S. shareholders' equity (that is, explain the direction of the adjustment from U.K. to U.S. GAAP).

EXHIBIT 2 British Steel's Income Statement and Statement of Changes in Shareholders' Equity (from British Steel's 1992 20-F filing)

BRITISH STEEL PLC AND SUBSIDIARIES
Consolidated Income Statements

	YEAR ENDED		
	APRIL 3, 1993	APRIL 2, 1994	APRIL 1, 1995
Sales (in millions)	£4,303	£4,191	£4,784
Operating costs	(4,416)	(4,075)	(4,338)
Operating income (loss)	£ (113)	£ 116	£ 446
(Loss)/gain on disposal of assets	—	0	4
Share of results of related parties	(19)	(19)	135
Net interest	(17)	(17)	(7)
Income/(loss) before income tax	£ (149)	£ 80	£ 578
Income tax (expense)/credit	19	(10)	(107)
Minority interests	—	(1)	(3)
Net income/(loss)	£ (130)	£ 69	£ 468

BRITISH STEEL PLC AND SUBSIDIARIES
Consolidated Statements of Changes in Shareholders' Equity

	SHARE CAPITAL AND PREMIUM	STATUTORY RESERVE	RETAINED EARNINGS	TOTAL
At April 3, 1993	£1,000	£2,338	£382	£3,720
Net income	—	—	69	69
Goodwill	—	—	(1)	(1)
Exchange translation difference	—	—	6	6
Dividend	—	—	(40)	(40)
At April 2, 1994	£1,000	£2,338	£416	£3,754
Net income	—	—	468	468
Goodwill	—	—	5	5
Exchange translation difference	—	—	(8)	(8)
New shares issued	20	—	—	20
Dividend	—	—	(152)	(152)
At April 1, 1995	£1,020	£2,338	£729	£4,087

EXHIBIT 3 Selected Notes from British Steel's 1992 20-F Filing

(30) Differences Between United Kingdom and United States/Canadian Generally Accepted Accounting Principles

The financial statements are prepared in accordance with generally accepted accounting principles (GAAP) applicable in the UK which differ in certain significant respects from those applicable in the United States and Canada. These differences and the adjustments necessary to restate net (loss)/income and shareholders' equity in accordance with US and Canadian GAAP are shown in the tables set out below:

(i) Goodwill—U.K. GAAP allows the write-off of goodwill arising on acquisition direct to retained earnings in the period of acquisition. Negative goodwill is similarly credited direct to shareholders' equity. This is not in accordance with the United States and Canadian practice of amortizing acquired goodwill over periods of up to 40 years and applying negative goodwill as a reduction to the net book value of any fixed assets acquired. For the purpose of compliance with United States and Canadian GAAP, goodwill arising on acquisitions prior to March 31, 1990 has been amortized over a period of 5 years. Goodwill arising on acquisitions since that date is being amortized over a period of 20 years. Negative goodwill has been treated as a reduction in fixed asset values. The Company periodically assesses the recoverability of unamortized goodwill based on anticipated future earnings.

(ii) Capitalization of interest costs relating to the construction of property, plant and equipment—U.K. GAAP does not require the capitalization of interest costs incurred in connection with the financing of expenditures for the construction of property, plant and equipment. Such costs are required to be capitalized under U.S. GAAP and may be capitalized under Canadian GAAP. For the purpose of compliance with U.S. and Canadian GAAP, the amount of interest that would have been capitalized on construction costs incurred on major capital projects has been determined and depreciated over the lives of the related assets.

(iii) Pensions—U.K. GAAP requires the expected cost of providing pension benefits to be expensed so as to spread the cost over the expected average remaining service lives of employees (see Note 20). Under U.S. and Canadian GAAP the annual pension cost comprises the estimated cost of benefits accruing in the period plus/(less) an adjustment where the scheme is in deficit/(surplus) at the time the standard was adopted. The charge is further adjusted to reflect the cost of benefit improvements and any surpluses/deficits which emerge as a result of the actuarial assumptions made not being borne out in practice. For U.S. purposes, only those surpluses/deficits falling outside a 10% fluctuation "corridor" are being recognized. Under Canadian GAAP, total surpluses/deficits are being recognized.

Under Canadian GAAP, the pension cost for the year ended April 1, 1995 would have been £36 million (1993/94: £28 million; 1992/93: £32 million) lower than under US GAAP and shareholders' equity at April 1, 1995 would have been £153 million (1994: £117 million; 1993: £89 million) higher than under U.S. GAAP. The effects of these differences have been shown in parenthesis where relevant.

(iv) Deferred taxation—Under U.K. GAAP, provision is made for deferred income tax only when it is expected that a liability will become payable in the foreseeable future and at the expected future rates of tax. Advance corporation tax is set off against actual or deferred tax liabilities to the maximum allowable amount and any surplus is written off. U.S. GAAP requires full provision for deferred tax to be made on the basis of enacted tax rates at the year-end. Canadian GAAP requires full provision for deferred tax to be made on the basis of tax rates in effect at the time the timing differences originate. As a result of the increased deferred tax liability under U.S. and Canadian GAAP no advance corporation tax is written off.

(v) Proposed dividend—Under U.K. GAAP, dividends are provided for in the financial statements for the fiscal year when they are recommended by the Board of Directors. Under U.S. and Canadian GAAP, dividends are only recorded as a liability in the period in which they are declared by the Board of Directors. For the purpose of compliance with U.S. and Canadian GAAP, the final dividend declared at the Annual General Meeting on July 26, 1995 and payable on August 14, 1995 has been added back to shareholders' equity.

(*continued*)

EXHIBIT 3 (Continued)

(vi) Statement No. 121 of the U.S. Financial Accounting Standards Board "Accounting for the Impairment of Long-Lived Assets and for Long-Lived Assets to Be Disposed Of" was issued in March 1995 and will not be effective for British Steel until the year ended March 30, 1996. SFAS No. 121 requires that assets to be held and used be reviewed for impairment whenever events or changes in circumstances indicate that the carrying amount of the asset in question may not be recoverable. Assets to be disposed of, with certain exceptions, would be reported as the lower of cost or fair value less the cost to sell the asset. British Steel has not yet fully determined the effect on its balance sheet and results of operations although it is not expected to be significant.

Effect on net (loss)/income of differences between U.K. and U.S. and Canadian generally accepted accounting principles.

	YEAR ENDED		
	APRIL 3, 1993	APRIL 2, 1994 (IN MILLIONS, EXCEPT PER SHARE AMOUNTS)	APRIL 1, 1995
(Loss)/profit attributable to shareholders U.K. GAAP	£ (130)	£ 69	£ 468
Adjustments:			
Amortization of goodwill (i)	(21)	(19)	(13)
Interest costs capitalized (ii)	28	12	9
Depreciation of capitalized interest (ii)	(5)	(7)	(7)
Pension costs (iii)	17	(6)	1
Related parties' pension costs (iii)	—	(4)	(1)
Deferred taxation (iv)	22	(22)	(106)
Related parties' deferred taxation (iv)	—	10	(9)
Net (loss)/income before cumulative effect of change in accounting U.S. GAAP	£ (89)	£ 33	£ 342
Cumulative effect of change in accounting from April 4, 1993:			
Related parties	—	(21)	—
Deferred taxation	—	20	—
Net (loss)/income in accordance with:			
U.S. GAAP	£ (89)	£ 32	£ 342
Net (loss)/income in accordance with U.S. GAAP:			
Per ordinary share	£(0.04)	£0.02	£0.17

(a) The results and shareholders' equity of related parties were restated in accordance with U.S. and Canadian GAAP for the first time in 1993/1994, prior to deriving the Group's share. The cumulative effect of this change in accounting from April 4, 1993 is recorded under U.S. GAAP as an adjustment to current year's net income, and under Canadian GAAP as an adjustment to opening shareholders' equity.

(b) British Steel adopted U.S. Statement of Financial Accounting Standards No. 109 "Accounting for Income Taxes" from April 4, 1993 (previously applied APB 11), which requires full provision for deferred taxation on the basis of enacted tax rates at the year-end. The release of £20 million under U.S. GAAP in 1993/1994 relates wholly to changes in income tax rates in prior years. No release arises under Canadian GAAP which requires full provision for deferred taxation on the basis of tax rates in effect at the time the timing differences originate.

(continued)

EXHIBIT 3 (Concluded)

Cumulative effect on shareholders' equity of differences between UK and US and Canadian generally accepted accounting principles:

	YEAR ENDED		
	APRIL 3, 1993	APRIL 2, 1994 (IN MILLIONS, EXCEPT PER SHARE AMOUNTS)	APRIL 1, 1995
Shareholders' equity in accordance with U.K. GAAP	£3,720	£3,754	£4,087
Adjustments:			
Goodwill (i)	237	237	235
Interest costs capitalized (net of depreciation) (ii)	99	104	106
Pension costs (iii)	(25)	(31)	(38)
Related parties' pension costs (iii)	—	(4)	—
Deferred taxation (iv)	(231)	(233)	(365)
Related parties' deferred taxation (iv)	—	(29)	(25)
Proposed dividend (v)	20	30	112
Shareholders' equity in accordance with:			
U.S. GAAP	£3,820	£3,828	£4,112

ACCOUNTING FOR STOCK COMPENSATION AWARDS: DISCLOSURE UNDER SFAS No. 123

INTRODUCTION

Following many years of deliberation, the FASB issued in 1995 *Statement of Financial Accounting Standards No. 123—Accounting for Stock-Based Compensation*. As indicated in the text, the statement:

- Recommends, but does not require, that companies change how they account for stock-based compensation to reflect the fair value of such options at the grant date, rather than at a portion of their fair value, as under APB Opinion 25.
- Allows companies that do not wish to change how they account for stock-based compensation to maintain their current accounting (APB Opinion 25) for stock options, but requires them to provide pro forma disclosure of earnings and earnings per share to reflect the fair value of stock compensation awards.
- Requires all companies to provide expanded disclosure about their stock compensation plans.

The issuance followed two years of controversy regarding the Statement's exposure draft, which *required* all companies to use fair value in accounting for their options.

As indicated in the text, compensation expense for options granted under APB Opinion 25 is measured as the difference between the option price and the market price on the measurement date (typically, the date of grant). This measure of value is the *intrinsic value* of the option. The recommended accounting procedure in *SFAS No. 123* measures compensation expense using total market value, which is the sum of the intrinsic value and an additional component called time value. Time value incorporates both the effect of discounting future prices back to the present and any expected increase due to variation in the price of the stock. The total value measured by the exposure draft is *always* greater than the intrinsic value measured under APB Opinion 25, resulting in higher compensation expense being recognized during the service period.

Largely because of this additional compensation expense, opposition to the issuance of the exposure draft—that required use of fair value accounting—was vehement. The chairman of the National Venture Capital Association stated that the exposure draft, "represents a knife through the heart of what we are all about [in Silicon Valley]." *Intel* Chairman Gordon Moore urged Intel option holders to write their Congressional representatives expressing opposition to the proposed standard, and stated in a letter to the FASB, "We believe that these proposed accounting changes will do enormous damage to the entrepreneurial culture of vital high-growth industries in the United States." San Jose Congresswoman Anna Eshoo, submitted an advisory resolution in the House of Representatives calling on the FASB to retain current accounting procedures for options, and stated that the exposure draft posed "a threat to economic recovery and entrepreneurship in the United States."

Phelps Dodge Corporation

Phelps Dodge Corporation consists of *Phelps Dodge Mining,* which is one of the world's largest producers of copper, and *Phelps Dodge Industries,* which produces carbon black, wheels and rims, and wire and cable. In 1995, the mining segment accounted for about 60 percent of total sales and 80 percent of total operating income.

PHELPS DODGE

Case Requirements

Phelps Dodge chose to adopt SFAS No. 123 in 1995, one year prior to mandatory adoption. Exhibit 1 contains the 1995 financial statement note related to stock option plans prepared in conformity with SFAS No. 123. After studying the exhibit, answer the following questions concerning Phelps Dodge's stock option plans.

1. The note states that "the Corporation applies APB Opinion 25 and related interpretations in accounting for its stock option plans, and, accordingly, does not recognize compensation cost." Specify precisely why the company is not obligated to recognize any compensation expense in its income statement per the requirements of APB Opinion 25.
2. According to the note, the company granted 953,838 options during 1995. How much total compensation is represented by the fair value of these options?
3. The note indicates the assumptions used to value the options using the Black-Scholes option-pricing model. How would an increase in each of the following affect the estimated fair value of an option using this model?
   a. the expected dividend yield.
   b. the expected stock price volatility.
   c. the risk-free interest rate.
   d. the term (expected life) of the options.
4. The note indicates that the recommended accounting of SFAS No. 123 would have had a minimal effect on Phelps Dodge's 1995 net income and earnings per share, reducing these amounts by $5,000,000 and $.05, respectively. What are the pros and cons of following the FASB's recommended accounting procedures for Phelps Dodge?
5. As noted in question 4, the recommended accounting under SFAS No. 123 would have had a minor impact on Phelps Dodge's income. What type of companies would be more significantly affected by the recommended accounting?

Exhibit 1 Please Supply Exhibit Title

Note 14. Stock Option Plans; Restricted Stock

Executives and other key employees have been granted options to purchase common shares under stock option plans adopted in 1979, 1987 and 1993. In each case, the option price equals the fair market value of the common shares on the day of the grant and an option's maximum term is ten years. Options granted vest ratably over a three-year period. The options include limited stock appreciation rights under which an optionee has the right, in the event common shares are purchased pursuant to a third party tender offer or in the event a merger or similar transaction in which the Corporation shall not survive as a publicly held corporation is approved by the Corporation's shareholders, to relinquish the option and to receive from the Corporation an amount per share equal to the excess of the price payable for a common share in such offer or transaction over the option price per share.

The Corporation has elected early adoption of Statement of Financial Accounting Standards (SFAS) No. 123, "Accounting for Stock-Based Compensation," issued in October 1995. In accordance with the provisions of SFAS No. 123, the Corporation applies APB Opinion 25 and related Interpretations in accounting for its stock option plans and, accordingly, does not recognize compensation cost. If the Corporation had elected to recognize compensation cost based on the fair value of the options granted at grant date as prescribed by SFAS No. 123, net income and earnings per share would have been reduced to the pro forma amounts indicated in the table below (in millions except per share amounts):

	1995	1994	1993
Net income—as reported	$746.6	$271.0	$187.9
Net income—pro forma	741.6	266.8	184.7
Earnings per share—as reported	10.65	3.81	2.66
Earnings per share—pro forma	10.60	3.76	2.62

The fair value of each option grant is estimated on the date of grant using the Black-Scholes option-pricing model with the following assumptions:

Expected dividend yield	3.34%
Expected stock price volatility	22.10%
Risk-free interest rate	6.00%
Expected life of options	3 years

The weighted-average fair value of options granted during 1995 is $11.04 per share.

The 1993 plan provides (and the 1987 plan provided) for "reload" option grants to executives and other key employees. If an optionee exercises an option under the 1993 or 1987 plan with already-owned shares of the Corporation, the optionee receives a reload option that restores the option opportunity on a number of common shares equal to the number of shares used to exercise the original option. A reload option has the same terms as the original option except that it has an exercise price per share equal to the fair market value of a common share on the date the reload option is granted and is exercisable six months after the date of grant.

The 1993 plan provides (and the 1987 plan provided) for the issuance to executives and other key employees, without any payment by them, of common shares subject to certain restrictions (restricted stock). The 1993 plan limits the award of restricted stock to 1,000,000 shares.

(continued)

EXHIBIT 1 (Concluded)

Under a stock option plan adopted in 1989, options to purchase common shares have been granted to directors who have not been employees of the Corporation or its subsidiaries for one year or are not eligible to participate in any plan of the Corporation or its subsidiaries entitling participants to acquire stock, stock options or stock appreciation rights.

At December 31, 1995, options for 627,187 shares, 38,643 shares and 826,272 shares were exercisable under the 1987 plan, the 1989 plan and the 1993 plan, respectively, at average prices of $43.46, $39.82 and $52.70 per share. In addition, 225,925 shares of restricted stock issued under the 1993 plan were outstanding at December 31, 1995. Also at December 31, 1995, 2,650,259 shares were available for option grants (including 761,258 shares as restricted stock awards) under the 1993 plan (plus an additional 600,999 shares that may be issued as reload options) and 92,403 shares were available for option grants under the 1989 plan. These amounts are subject to future adjustment. No further options may be granted under the 1987 plan.

Changes during 1993, 1994 and 1995 in options outstanding for the combined plans were as follows:

	SHARES	AVERAGE OPTION PRICE PER SHARE
Outstanding at December 31, 1992	1,975,850	$36.78
Granted	831,896	45.11
Exercised	(377,203)	28.03
Expired or terminated	(50,982)	41.37
Outstanding at December 31, 1993	2,379,561	40.88
Granted	961,087	58.35
Exercised	(479,660)	37.32
Expired or terminated	(28,802)	44.34
Outstanding at December 31, 1994	2,832,186	47.38
Granted	953,838	66.37
Exercised	(635,881)	38.19
Expired or terminated	(110,345)	51.03
Outstanding at December 31, 1995*	3,039,798	55.13

*Exercise prices for options outstanding at December 31, 1995, range from a minimum of approximately $27 per share to a maximum of approximately $68 per share. The average remaining maximum term of options outstanding is approximately 8 years.

A

Time Value of Money

Learning Objectives

After studying this appendix, you should be able to:

1. Differentiate between simple and compound interest.
2. Distinguish a single sum from an annuity.
3. Differentiate between an ordinary annuity and an annuity due.
4. Solve representative problems based on the time value of money.

Recognition and measurement of assets and liabilities in the financial statements can be based on different valuation methods. The fifth measurement basis identified in SFAC No. 5, is the present (or discounted) value of future cash flows. Present and future values are applications of time value for measurement purposes. Accounting measurement includes a number of instances in which time value is an important component of costs and/or revenues.

Some of the applications of time value are listed below.

1. Long-term investments in bonds and long-term notes receivable and payable use time-value techniques to determine the implicit rates of interest for cost or revenue-recognition.
2. Determination of the issue price of bonds payable in which the amount received is greater or less than the face amount of the bonds is based on time-value techniques.
3. Capital leases are recorded at the present value of the future cash flows of the lease payments.
4. Pension fund liabilities are determined by a combination of actuarial and present-value techniques. Accounting for pension expenses requires an understanding of these concepts.
5. Capital asset investment choices are frequently evaluated using present-value concepts.
6. Sinking fund amounts necessary for future needs are determined through the use of time-value concepts.

Many of the concepts discussed in this appendix affect our daily lives as well. The alternative methods available for auto financing, home mortgages, college-expense savings plans, and retirement plans are examples of the time value of money in everyday living.

Compound-interest, annuities, future-value and present-value concepts have applicability in many courses of study other than accounting—namely, finance, marketing, management, banking, and insurance. Knowledge of these concepts for personal financial and investment decisions is essential to financial well-being.

THE TIME VALUE OF MONEY AND THE NATURE OF INTEREST

1 Differentiate between simple and compound interest.

Interest is the charge for the use of money for a specified period of time. Interest is the basis of the time value of money. The amount of interest is calculated as follows:

$$I = P \times r \times n$$

where

I = amount of interest.
P = principal amount borrowed.
r = interest rate charged on the debt.
n = number of periods or time.

Because money earns interest, there is value in accelerating the receipt (or delaying the payment) of money. The initial amount loaned or borrowed is referred to as the *principal*. The *interest rate* is expressed as a percent and may be referred to as the *coupon rate, face rate,* or *stated rate.* Interest rates are normally stated as an annual rate and, therefore, frequently must be adjusted for time. Time is the duration of the loan expressed in days, months, or years. The interest charges can be either simple or compound.

Simple interest means that interest accrues on the principal only. For example, assume that $1,000 is borrowed at 10% simple interest for three years. The amount owed on the settlement date, including interest, is $1,300 as shown below:

$$A = P + (P \times r \times n)$$

Where

A = amount owed.
P = principal.
r = interest rate.
n = time periods.

Therefore,

$$\begin{aligned}\text{Amount Owed} &= \$1{,}000 + (\$1{,}000 \times .10 \times 3)\\ &= \$300 + \$1{,}000\\ &= \$1{,}300\end{aligned}$$

While simple interest is used in certain situations, *compound interest,* which accrues interest not only on the principal but also on unpaid interest charges, is more common. Assume a three-year, 10% loan for $1,000. Using the same symbols as previously defined, this can be expressed as

$$A = P \times (1 + r)^n$$

Substituting the corresponding values yields

$$\begin{aligned}A &= \$1{,}000 \times (1. + .1)^3\\ &= \$1{,}000 \times (1.1)^3\\ &= \$1{,}000 \times (1.331)\\ &= \$1{,}331\end{aligned}$$

Under the compound-interest method, $31 more is earned. The extra $31 results from earning interest on the accrued interest.

YEAR	
1	$1,000 × 1.10 = $1,100
2	1,100 × 1.10 = 1,210
3	1,210 × 1.10 = 1,331

SINGLE SUMS

Distinguish a single sum from an annuity.

FUTURE AMOUNT OF SINGLE SUM

The future amount of a single sum, is the value that the principal will attain after accruing compound interest for a designated time period. To illustrate, assume a 10% interest rate compounded for three years. The future-value factor would be 1.1 (1 + .1) at the end of the first year, 1.21 $(1 + .1)^2$ at the end of the second year, and 1.331 $(1 + .1)^3$ at the end of the third year. Table A–1, **The Future Amount of 1,** provides factors for various interest rates for different periods of time that can be used to determine the future amount of a single sum. For example, $500 at 8% interest is equal to $629.85 ($500 × 1.2597) at the end of three years. If the interest rate were 10% rather than 8%, the amount would be $665.50 ($500 × 1.3310).

If more than one compounding period is in one year, the above formula $[A = P(1 + r)^n]$ holds, but the values for the variables must be adjusted by the number of compounding periods. Suppose that in the previous example of $500 at 8% for three years, the interest rate had been compounded *semiannually* (twice per year) instead of annually. The interest rate would be divided by 2, and the compounding periods multiplied by 2. Thus, $500 at 8% annual interest compounded semiannually is equivalent to six compounding periods at 4%, or $632.65 ($500 × 1.2653). If the interest rate had been compounded quarterly, the number of compounding periods would become 12 and the interest per period, 2%, resulting in the amount of $641.10 ($500 × 1.2682). The factor (1.2682) is found at the intersection of the twelfth row and the 2% column in Table A–1.

PRESENT VALUE OF A SINGLE SUM

A **present value** is the current monetary equivalent of a future monetary amount discounted at a given rate of interest. It is the monetary amount expressed in today's dollars necessary to satisfy a future debt. Another way of expressing this concept is to determine the amount that would have to be invested at the beginning of a period at a given rate of interest to grow to a given amount at the end of the nth period.

Table A–2, **Present Value of 1,** contains factors for finding the present value of a single sum and is the reciprocal of Table A–1. The general formula for the present value (PV) of 1 is

$$PV = 1/(1 + r)^n$$

To illustrate, assume that at the age of 29 you will receive $100,000 if you have earned a degree in accounting. Your current age is 19, and you would like to know the value today of the $100,000 if the discount rate is 10%. The formula can be used to express the present value as follows:

$$PV = \$100{,}000 \times [1/(1 + .1)^{10}]$$
$$PV = \$100{,}000 \times [1/(2.5936)]$$
$$PV = \$100{,}000 \times (.3855645)$$
$$PV = \$38{,}556$$

Alternatively, the present value could be found by using the factor for these conditions in Table A–2 (0.3855) multiplied by $100,000 to obtain $38,550. (The difference is due to rounding the Table values to only four decimal places.) The present-value amount of $38,550 means that if $38,550 were invested today, and earned 10% interest compounded annually for 10 periods, it would be equal to $100,000 at the end of the tenth period.

The **discount rate** is a combination of prevailing interest rate, future expectations of interest rates, and the degree to which the recipient wishes to have immediate cash. If the recipient needs to have cash immediately, a 12% discount rate might be offered to a potential investor to induce immediate payment. The amount received would then be $32,200 ($100,000 × 0.3220).

DETERMINING OTHER VALUES FOR SINGLE SUM PROBLEMS

Finding the Number of Periods. If all the values except one in a problem situation are known, the missing value can be found through algebraic manipulation of the formulas. As an example, how long will it take $30,000 invested at 10% per annum to grow to $100,000? The problem can be expressed as follows:

$$\$100{,}000 = \$30{,}000 \times (1 + .1)^n$$
$$3.3333 = (1.1)^n$$

In Table A–1, the factor, 3.3333 for 10% interest is between periods 12 and 13 meaning that it would take between 12 and 13 periods for the amount to grow to $100,000.

Finding the Rate of Interest. Consider a case in which we wish to find the rate of interest necessary for an investment of $25,000 compounded annually to grow to $100,000 at the end of ten years. Using the formula for the future value of an amount and substituting the known values, the following is obtained:

$$\$100{,}000 = \$25{,}000 \times (1 + r)^{10}$$
$$\$100{,}000/\$25{,}000 = (1 + r)^{10}$$
$$4.000 = (1 + r)^{10}$$

The interest rate is found by examining Table A–1. First find the row for the number of compounding periods, in this case, n = 10. Next scan across the row, looking at each column amount to find the factor nearest in amount to 4.0000. The factor at 14% is 3.7072 and at 15% is 4.0456 which is closer to 4.000. Therefore, the necessary interest rate would be slightly less than 15%.

Finding the Principal Amount. Suppose that you wish to establish a fund for your newborn child to attend college at the age of 18. The amount needed at that time is estimated to be $100,000. If 8% can be earned on the investment, the problem can be expressed as:

$$\$100{,}000 = P \times (1 + .08)^{18}$$
$$100{,}000 = P \times (3.9960)$$
$$25{,}025 = P$$

This same college-fund problem could also be stated as a present-value problem, and a factor could be obtained from Table A–2 directly. Using Table A–2, the present value of $100,000 discounted at 8% for 18 periods is $100,000 × 0.2502 = $25,020. The difference is due to rounding.

ANNUITIES

Differentiate between an ordinary annuity and an annuity due.

Annuities are fixed payments or receipts (cash flows) over a period of time, a series of cash flows. Annuities are classified as either ordinary or due, depending on whether the cash flow occurs at the beginning or end of the period. A future-value annuity is classified as *ordinary* if the final cash flow occurs at the end of the last period. If the final cash flow occurs at the beginning of the last period, the future-value annuity is classified as an *annuity due.*

A present-value annuity is classified as *ordinary* if the first cash flow occurs at the end of the first period. If the first cash flow occurs at the beginning of the first period, the present-value annuity is considered as an **annuity due.** Note the timing of cash flows for the situation of three $100 annuity payments in the sketch in Exhibit A–1 illustrating the difference between an ordinary annuity and an annuity due.

The difference between an ordinary annuity and an annuity due is the timing of the cash flow. The first cash flow in an annuity due occurs immediately, while the first cash flow in an ordinary annuity occurs at end of the first period.

FUTURE VALUE OF ORDINARY ANNUITY

An ordinary annuity contains one more cash flow than the number of interest-earning periods because the cash flows occur at the end of the interest-earning period. To illustrate, assume that $100 is invested at the end of each period at 10% compound interest for three periods. This results in three deposits of $100 and two interest-earning periods. To find the future value of this investment, the future value of each separate deposit could be found and summed as follows:

1st deposit:	$100 × (1 + .10) × (1 + .10)	= $121
2nd deposit:	100 × (1 + .10)	= 110
3rd deposit:	100 × 1	= 100
Total future value		= $331

A more efficient process would be to use the following formula:

$$\begin{aligned} FVOA &= [(1 + r)^n - 1]/r \\ &= [(1 + .1)^3 - 1]/.1 \\ &= 3.310 \end{aligned}$$

EXHIBIT A–1
Ordinary Annuity Versus Annuity Due

Time Period	0		1		2		3
Ordinary Annuity			$100	*i*	$100	*i*	$100
Annuity Due	$100	*i*	$100	*i*	$100	*i*	

i = interest-earning periods

The factor, 3.310, multiplied by the ordinary annuity of $100 equals $331. Table A–3 contains factors for the future values of ordinary annuities of $1 for various rates and years.

FUTURE VALUE OF ANNUITY DUE

The number of cash flows and interest-earning periods are the same for the future value of an annuity due. In the preceding example, with deposits made at the beginning of the period (starting immediately) rather than at the end of the first period, an additional interest-earning period occurs for each deposit. Table A–4 contains factors for the future value of an annuity due. The use of the table is the same as the other tables previously described. Thus, the future value of an annuity due of $100 at 10% for three periods would be $364.10 (3.641 × $100).

PRESENT VALUE OF ORDINARY ANNUITY

The present value of fixed payments or receipts (cash flows) at the end of each period for a number of periods is the present value of an ordinary annuity. To illustrate, assume a $100 cash flow occurs at the end of each period for three periods. To find the present value of this stream of cash flows at a discount rate of 10 percent, use the factor 2.4869 from Table A–5 ($100 × 2.4869 = $248.69). Thus, the present value of $100 received at the end of each of the next three periods discounted at an interest rate of 10% is equal to $248.69. Alternatively, we can also say that an investment of $248.69 made today, and earning 10% interest compounded annually, would allow withdrawals of $100 at the end of each period for the next three periods. After the last withdrawal, the investment fund would be zero.

PRESENT VALUE OF ANNUITY DUE

The present value of fixed payments or receipts (cash flows) at the beginning of each period for a number of periods is the present value of an annuity due. To illustrate, assume a $100 cash flow occurs for three periods starting immediately. Because the cash flow begins immediately, this is an annuity due. To find the present value of an annuity due of $100 discounted at 10% for three periods, use Table A–6. The factor from Table A–6 is 2.7355, so the present value of this stream of cash flows is $273.55 ($100 × 2.7355 = $273.55). This amount ($273.55) is slightly greater than the present value of an ordinary annuity above ($248.69) because the cash flows occur at the beginning of the period instead of at the end. Thus, one extra interest-earning period exists. Alternatively, we can also say that an existing fund of $273.55 allows an investor to withdraw $100 at the beginning of each period for three periods, starting immediately, and deplete the fund completely with the last withdrawal.

DEFERRED ANNUITIES

A **deferred annuity** is an annuity that is delayed for two or more periods before the cash flows begin. For example, an ordinary annuity of four cash flows of $100 deferred three years is illustrated in Exhibit A–2.

EXHIBIT A–2
Ordinary Deferred Annuity

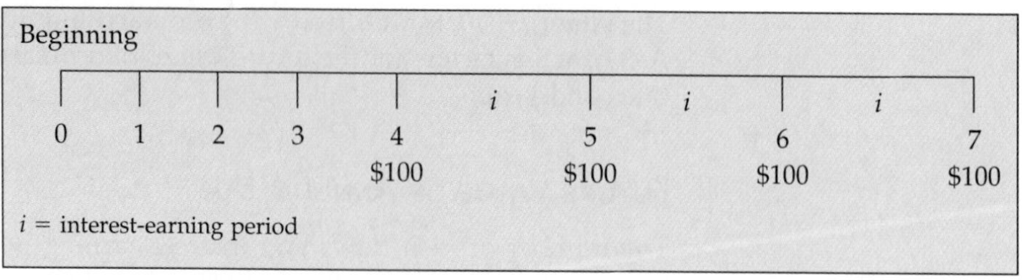

Note that the first cash flow occurs at the end of the fourth interest period, which is also the beginning of the fifth interest period. If we say the cash flows occur at the beginning of the fifth interest period, then these cash flows represent an annuity deferred four periods. There are four cash flows and three interest-earning periods in this example.

Future Value of Deferred Annuity. If the interest rate were 10% compounded annually in Exhibit A–2, the future amount of the deferred annuity is determined by using Table A–3 to find the factor 4.6410, the factor for 10% and four cash flows. A $100 ordinary annuity compounded for four periods at 10% is worth $464.10 at the end of period 7. Because no cash flows occur in the first three periods, no interest is earned during the first three periods. The graph in Exhibit A–3 illustrates this concept.

EXHIBIT A–3
Future Value of Deferred Annuity

	0	1	2	3	4	5	6	7
CF period 4					$100	$110	$121	$133.10
CF period 5						100	110	121.00
CF period 6							100	110.00
Cf period 7								100.00
								$464.10

CF = Cash Flow

Present Value of Deferred Annuity. To find the present value of the deferred annuity illustrated in Exhibit A–2 requires two calculations:

1. Find the present value of an ordinary annuity at 10% for four periods using Table A–5.

$$\$100 \times 3.1699 = \$316.99$$

2. The single sum ($316.99) is then discounted at 10% for three periods. The present-value factor for a single sum discounted for three periods at 10%, found in Table A–2, is .7513, as shown:[1]

$$\$316.99 \times .7513 = \$238.15$$

[1]We could have multiplied the two factors together and then multiplied the result by the annuity amount of $100 and obtained the same answer (3.1698 × .7513 × 100 = 238.15).

Another method to attain the same result would be to find the difference between the factor for seven periods (4.8684) and the factor for three periods (2.4869) for the present value of an annuity of 1. The difference (2.3815) is then multiplied by the annuity amount as illustrated:

n/r	= 10%
7	= 4.8684
3	= 2.4869
	2.3815 × $100 = $238.15

EXAMPLE PROBLEMS

Solve representative problems based on the time value of money.

Following are four examples of the application of these concepts.

EXAMPLE ONE—AUTOMOBILE PROBLEM

Jane Johnson has decided to purchase a Chevrolet Camaro with a list price of $17,800 excluding tax and title. Johnson has three alternatives to evaluate:

1. Pay a cash price of $16,500.
2. Finance the Camaro with a cash down payment of $4,000, and 30 monthly payments of $500 each at the end of each month.
3. Lease the car. The lease terms call for an initial down payment of $2,000 and 30 monthly payments of $400 each at the end of each month. If she wants to buy the car at the end of the lease, she could make a lump-sum payment in the amount of $5,000 at the end of the 30-month period.

For simplicity, assume that the current rate of interest is 12%. What should Johnson do?

Solution: This should be evaluated as a present value problem. We must find the present value (PV) of each of the three alternatives.

1.	PV of $16,500 cash now	= $16,500
2.	PV of $4,000 (4,000 × 1.00)	= $ 4,000.00
	PV of $500 ordinary annuity, (@1%, 30n), 500 × 25.8077*	= 12,903.85
	Total PV of purchase	= $16,903.85

*Because the payments are monthly payments, the interest rate of 12% is divided by 12, or 1% per month. The factor, 25.8077, is the factor for 30n @ 1%.

3.	PV of lease	
	PV of $2,000 (2,000 × 1.00)	= $ 2,000.00
	PV of $400 ordinary annuity, (@1%, 30n) 400 × 25.8077	= 10,323.08
	PV of single sum (@1%, 30th n) 5,000 × .7419	= 3,709.50
	Total PV of lease	= $16,032.58

Because the present value of the lease is the smallest, Johnson should choose the lease financing for the new Camaro.

EXAMPLE TWO—RETIREMENT PROBLEM

Sean Meares is a self-employed consultant. Meares expects to work 20 more years and then retire. She estimates that she will need $50,000 per year in retirement funds for 15 years, and will begin making those withdrawals one year after the last deposit to the fund. She wants to make 20 annual savings deposits to the retirement fund, starting at the end of the current year. She will earn an average of 8% on the fund throughout the entire time. Determine the amount of each deposit required assuming the first deposit will be made at the end of the current year.

Solution: This problem requires a two-step solution: first, find the present value of the withdrawals of $50,000 each, the present value of an ordinary annuity (PVOA) of 15n at 8%. Table A–5 is used.

PV of Withdrawals = 50,000 × 8.5595 = $427,975

This amount ($427,975) is required to be in the retirement fund after the last deposit is made to support the future withdrawals that will begin one year later. Therefore, $427,975 is the future value of an ordinary annuity (FVOA) of an unknown deposit for 20n at 8%. Table A–3 is used.

FVOA = Deposit × Factor for 20n, 8%
$427,975 = Deposit × 45.7620
Deposit = $427,975/45.7620
Deposit = $9,352.19

EXAMPLE THREE—BOND INVESTMENT PROBLEM

Fidelity Investments recently purchased bonds with a face value of $10,000,000. The bonds will mature at the end of 15 years, and carry a stated interest rate of 7%. The current market rate of interest for bonds of this risk and maturity is 10%. Assume the bonds pay interest annually at the end of the period.

Required:

A. What was the purchase price of the bonds for Fidelity?
B. If the market rate of interest was 6% instead of 10%, what would be the purchase price?

Both (**A**) and (**B**) require the same analysis. We must find the present value of two cash flows from the bonds: the face value (a single sum), and the interest payments (an ordinary annuity). Both cash flows are discounted at the market rate of interest. Table A–2 is used to find the present value of the principal, and Table A–5 to find the present value of the interest receipts. For the purchase price at 10% interest,

A. PV of Principal = PV of $10,000,000 discounted @ 10%, 15n
= $10,000,000 × .2394
= $ 2,394,000

PV of Interest = PVOA of 700,000 discounted @ 10%, 15n
= $700,000 × 7.6061
= $5,324,270

Total Paid = \$2,394,000 + \$5,324,270
= \$7,718,270

For the purchase price at 6% interest,

B. PV of Principal = PV of \$10,000,000 discounted @ 6%, 15n
= \$10,000,000 × .4173
= \$ 4,173,000

PV of Interest = PVOA \$700,000 discounted @ 6%, 15n
= \$700,000 × 9.7122
= 6,798,540

Total Paid = \$ 4,173,000 + \$6,798,540
= \$10,971,540

EXAMPLE FOUR—BOND ISSUE PROBLEM

Summit Technology issued bonds with a par value of \$100,000 on July 1. The bonds will mature at the end of 20 years, and carry a stated rate of 8% to be paid annually on June 30 (end of the period). The current market rate of interest for bonds of this risk and maturity is 12%.

Required:

A. Calculate the proceeds of the bond issue realized by Summit.
B. If the market rate of interest were 6%, what would be the proceeds?

Both (**A**) and (**B**) require the same analysis. The present value of the par value at maturity (a single sum), and the present value of the interest payments (an ordinary annuity), must be calculated. Both cash flows are discounted at the market rate of interest.

For the proceeds at 12% interest,

A. PV of Principal = PV of \$100,000 @ 12%, 20n
= \$100,000 × .1037 (from Table A–2)
= \$10,370

PV of Interest = PVOA of 8,000 @ 12%, 20n
= \$8,000 × 7.4694 (from Table A–5)
= \$59,755

Total Proceeds = \$10,370 + \$59,755
= \$70,125

For the proceeds at 6% interest,

B. PV of Principal = PV of \$100,000 @ 6%, 20n
= \$100,000 × .3118 (from Table A–2)
= \$31,180

PV of Interest = PVOA of \$8,000 @ 6%, 20n
= \$8,000 × 11.4699 (from Table A–5)
= \$91,759

Total Proceeds = \$31,180 + \$91,759
= \$122,939

TABLE A–1 Future Amount of 1: A = (1 + r)

N/R	1%	2%	3%	4%	5%	6%	7%	8%	9%	10%	N/R
1	1.0100	1.0200	1.0300	1.0400	1.0500	1.0600	1.0700	1.0800	1.0900	1.1000	1
2	1.0201	1.0404	1.0609	1.0816	1.1025	1.1236	1.1449	1.1664	1.1881	1.2100	2
3	1.0303	1.0612	1.0927	1.1249	1.1576	1.1910	1.2250	1.2597	1.2950	1.3310	3
4	1.0406	1.0824	1.1255	1.1699	1.2155	1.2625	1.3108	1.3605	1.4116	1.4641	4
5	1.0510	1.1041	1.1593	1.2167	1.2763	1.3382	1.4026	1.4693	1.5386	1.6105	5
6	1.0615	1.1262	1.1941	1.2653	1.3401	1.4185	1.5007	1.5869	1.6771	1.7716	6
7	1.0721	1.1487	1.2299	1.3159	1.4071	1.5036	1.6058	1.7138	1.8280	1.9487	7
8	1.0829	1.1717	1.2668	1.3686	1.4775	1.5938	1.7182	1.8509	1.9926	2.1436	8
9	1.0937	1.1951	1.3048	1.4233	1.5513	1.6895	1.8385	1.9990	2.1719	2.3579	9
10	1.1046	1.2190	1.3439	1.4802	1.6289	1.7908	1.9672	2.1589	2.3674	2.5937	10
11	1.1157	1.2434	1.3842	1.5395	1.7103	1.8983	2.1049	2.3316	2.5804	2.8531	11
12	1.1268	1.2682	1.4258	1.6010	1.7959	2.0122	2.2522	2.5182	2.8127	3.1384	12
13	1.1381	1.2936	1.4685	1.6651	1.8856	2.1329	2.4098	2.7196	3.0658	3.4523	13
14	1.1495	1.3195	1.5126	1.7317	1.9799	2.2609	2.5785	2.9372	3.3417	3.7975	14
15	1.1610	1.3459	1.5580	1.8009	2.0789	2.3966	2.7590	3.1722	3.6425	4.1772	15
16	1.1726	1.3728	1.6047	1.8730	2.1829	2.5404	2.9522	3.4259	3.9703	4.5950	16
17	1.1843	1.4002	1.6528	1.9479	2.2920	2.6928	3.1588	3.7000	4.3276	5.0545	17
18	1.1961	1.4282	1.7024	2.0258	2.4066	2.8543	3.3799	3.9960	4.7171	5.5599	18
19	1.2081	1.4568	1.7535	2.1068	2.5270	3.0256	3.6165	4.3157	5.1417	6.1159	19
20	1.2202	1.4859	1.8061	2.1911	2.6533	3.2071	3.8697	4.6610	5.6044	6.7275	20
21	1.2324	1.5157	1.8603	2.2788	2.7860	3.3996	4.1406	5.0338	6.1088	7.4002	21
22	1.2447	1.5460	1.9161	2.3699	2.9253	3.6035	4.4304	5.4365	6.6586	8.1403	22
23	1.2572	1.5769	1.9736	2.4647	3.0715	3.8197	4.7405	5.8715	7.2579	8.9543	23
24	1.2697	1.6084	2.0328	2.5633	3.2251	4.0489	5.0724	6.3412	7.9111	9.8497	24
25	1.2824	1.6406	2.0938	2.6658	3.3864	4.2919	5.4274	6.8485	8.6231	10.8347	25
26	1.2953	1.6734	2.1566	2.7725	3.5557	4.5494	5.8074	7.3964	9.3992	11.9182	26
27	1.3082	1.7069	2.2213	2.8834	3.7335	4.8223	6.2139	7.9881	10.2451	13.1100	27
28	1.3213	1.7410	2.2879	2.9987	3.9201	5.1117	6.6488	8.6271	11.1671	14.4210	28
29	1.3345	1.7758	2.3566	3.1187	4.1161	5.4184	7.1143	9.3173	12.1722	15.8631	29
30	1.3478	1.8114	2.4273	3.2434	4.3219	5.7435	7.6123	10.0627	13.2677	17.4494	30
31	1.3613	1.8476	2.5001	3.3731	4.5380	6.0881	8.1451	10.8677	14.4618	19.1943	31
32	1.3749	1.8845	2.5751	3.5081	4.7649	6.4534	8.7153	11.7371	15.7633	21.1138	32
33	1.3887	1.9222	2.6523	3.6484	5.0032	6.8406	9.3253	12.6760	17.1820	23.2252	33
34	1.4026	1.9607	2.7319	3.7943	5.2533	7.2510	9.9781	13.6901	18.7284	25.5477	34
35	1.4166	1.9999	2.8139	3.9461	5.5160	7.6861	10.6766	14.7853	20.4140	28.1024	35
36	1.4308	2.0399	2.8983	4.1039	5.7918	8.1473	11.4239	15.9682	22.2512	30.9127	36
37	1.4451	2.0807	2.9852	4.2681	6.0814	8.6361	12.2236	17.2456	24.2538	34.0039	37
38	1.4595	2.1223	3.0748	4.4388	6.3855	9.1543	13.0793	18.6253	26.4367	37.4043	38
39	1.4741	2.1647	3.1670	4.6164	6.7048	9.7035	13.9948	20.1153	28.8160	41.1448	39
40	1.4889	2.2080	3.2620	4.8010	7.0400	10.2857	14.9745	21.7245	31.4094	45.2593	40

N/R	11%	12%	13%	14%	15%	16%	20%	22%	24%	25%	N/R
1	1.1100	1.1200	1.1300	1.1400	1.1500	1.1600	1.2000	1.2200	1.2400	1.2500	1
2	1.2321	1.2544	1.2769	1.2996	1.3225	1.3456	1.4400	1.4884	1.5376	1.5625	2
3	1.3676	1.4049	1.4429	1.4815	1.5209	1.5609	1.7280	1.8158	1.9066	1.9531	3
4	1.5181	1.5735	1.6305	1.6890	1.7490	1.8106	2.0736	2.2153	2.3642	2.4414	4
5	1.6851	1.7623	1.8424	1.9254	2.0114	2.1003	2.4883	2.7027	2.9316	3.0518	5
6	1.8704	1.9738	2.0820	2.1950	2.3131	2.4364	2.9860	3.2973	3.6352	3.8147	6
7	2.0762	2.2107	2.3526	2.5023	2.6600	2.8262	3.5832	4.0227	4.5077	4.7684	7
8	2.3045	2.4760	2.6584	2.8526	3.0590	3.2784	4.2998	4.9077	5.5895	5.9605	8
9	2.5580	2.7731	3.0040	3.2519	3.5179	3.8030	5.1598	5.9874	6.9310	7.4506	9
10	2.8394	3.1058	3.3946	3.7072	4.0456	4.4114	6.1917	7.3046	8.5944	9.3132	10
11	3.1518	3.4785	3.8359	4.2262	4.6524	5.1173	7.4301	8.9117	10.6571	11.6415	11
12	3.4985	3.8960	4.3345	4.8179	5.3503	5.9360	8.9161	10.8722	13.2148	14.5519	12
13	3.8833	4.3635	4.8980	5.4924	6.1528	6.8858	10.6993	13.2641	16.3863	18.1899	13
14	4.3104	4.8871	5.5348	6.2613	7.0757	7.9875	12.8392	16.1822	20.3191	22.7374	14
15	4.7846	5.4736	6.2543	7.1379	8.1371	9.2655	15.4070	19.7423	25.1956	28.4217	15
16	5.3109	6.1304	7.0673	8.1372	9.3576	10.7480	18.4884	24.0856	31.2426	35.5271	16
17	5.8951	6.8660	7.9861	9.2765	10.7613	12.4677	22.1861	29.3844	38.7408	44.4089	17
18	6.5436	7.6900	9.0243	10.5752	12.3755	14.4625	26.6233	35.8490	48.0386	55.5112	18
19	7.2633	8.6128	10.1974	12.0557	14.2318	16.7765	31.9480	43.7358	59.5679	69.3889	19
20	8.0623	9.6463	11.5231	13.7435	16.3665	19.4608	38.3376	53.3576	73.8641	86.7362	20
21	8.9492	10.8038	13.0211	15.6676	18.8215	22.5745	46.0051	65.0963	91.5915	108.4202	21
22	9.9336	12.1003	14.7138	17.8610	21.6447	26.1864	55.2061	79.4175	113.5735	135.5253	22
23	11.0263	13.5523	16.6266	20.3616	24.8915	30.3762	66.2474	96.8894	140.8312	169.4066	23
24	12.2392	15.1786	18.7881	23.2122	28.6252	35.2364	79.4968	118.2050	174.6306	211.7582	24
25	13.5855	17.0001	21.2305	26.4619	32.9190	40.8742	95.3962	144.2101	216.5420	264.6978	25
26	15.0799	19.0401	23.9905	30.1666	37.8568	47.4141	114.4755	175.9364	268.5121	330.8722	26
27	16.7386	21.3249	27.1093	34.3899	43.5353	55.0004	137.3706	214.6424	332.9550	413.5903	27
28	18.5799	23.8839	30.6335	39.2045	50.0656	63.8004	164.8447	261.8637	412.8642	516.9879	28
29	20.6237	26.7499	34.6158	44.6931	57.5755	74.0085	197.8136	319.4737	511.9516	646.2349	29
30	22.8923	29.9599	39.1159	50.9502	66.2118	85.8499	237.3763	389.7579	634.8199	807.7936	30
31	25.4104	33.5551	44.2010	58.0832	76.1435	99.5859	284.8516	475.5046	787.1767	1009.7420	31
32	28.2056	37.5817	49.9471	66.2148	87.5651	115.5196	341.8219	580.1156	976.0991	1262.1774	32
33	31.3082	42.0915	56.4402	75.4849	100.6998	134.0027	410.1863	707.7411	1210.3629	1577.7218	33
34	34.7521	47.1425	63.7774	86.0528	115.8048	155.4432	492.2235	863.4441	1500.8500	1972.1523	34
35	38.5749	52.7996	72.0685	98.1002	133.1755	180.3141	590.6682	1053.4018	1861.0540	2465.1903	35
36	42.8181	59.1356	81.4374	111.8342	153.1519	209.1643	708.8019	1285.1502	2307.7070	3081.4879	36
37	47.5281	66.2318	92.0243	127.4910	176.1246	242.6306	850.5622	1567.8833	2861.5567	3851.8599	37
38	52.7562	74.1797	103.9874	145.3397	202.5433	281.4515	1020.6747	1912.8176	3548.3303	4814.8249	38
39	58.5593	83.0812	117.5058	165.6873	232.9248	326.4838	1224.8096	2333.6375	4399.9295	6018.5311	39
40	65.0009	93.0510	132.7816	188.8835	267.8635	378.7212	1469.7716	2847.0378	5455.9126	7523.1638	40

TABLE A–2 Present Value of 1: $PV = 1/[(1 + r)^n]$

N/R	1%	2%	3%	4%	5%	6%	7%	8%	9%	10%	N/R
1	0.9901	0.9804	0.9709	0.9615	0.9524	0.9434	0.9346	0.9259	0.9174	0.9091	1
2	0.9803	0.9612	0.9426	0.9246	0.9070	0.8900	0.8734	0.8573	0.8417	0.8264	2
3	0.9706	0.9423	0.9151	0.8890	0.8638	0.8396	0.8163	0.7938	0.7722	0.7513	3
4	0.9610	0.9238	0.8885	0.8548	0.8227	0.7921	0.7629	0.7350	0.7084	0.6830	4
5	0.9515	0.9057	0.8626	0.8219	0.7835	0.7473	0.7130	0.6806	0.6499	0.6209	5
6	0.9420	0.8880	0.8375	0.7903	0.7462	0.7050	0.6663	0.6302	0.5963	0.5645	6
7	0.9327	0.8706	0.8131	0.7599	0.7107	0.6651	0.6227	0.5835	0.5470	0.5132	7
8	0.9235	0.8535	0.7894	0.7307	0.6768	0.6274	0.5820	0.5403	0.5019	0.4665	8
9	0.9143	0.8368	0.7664	0.7026	0.6446	0.5919	0.5439	0.5002	0.4604	0.4241	9
10	0.9053	0.8203	0.7441	0.6756	0.6139	0.5584	0.5083	0.4632	0.4224	0.3855	10
11	0.8963	0.8043	0.7224	0.6496	0.5847	0.5268	0.4751	0.4289	0.3875	0.3505	11
12	0.8874	0.7885	0.7014	0.6246	0.5568	0.4970	0.4440	0.3971	0.3555	0.3186	12
13	0.8787	0.7730	0.6810	0.6006	0.5303	0.4688	0.4150	0.3677	0.3262	0.2897	13
14	0.8700	0.7579	0.6611	0.5775	0.5051	0.4423	0.3878	0.3405	0.2992	0.2633	14
15	0.8613	0.7430	0.6419	0.5553	0.4810	0.4173	0.3624	0.3152	0.2745	0.2394	15
16	0.8528	0.7284	0.6232	0.5339	0.4581	0.3936	0.3387	0.2919	0.2519	0.2176	16
17	0.8444	0.7142	0.6050	0.5134	0.4363	0.3714	0.3166	0.2703	0.2311	0.1978	17
18	0.8360	0.7002	0.5874	0.4936	0.4155	0.3503	0.2959	0.2502	0.2120	0.1799	18
19	0.8277	0.6864	0.5703	0.4746	0.3957	0.3305	0.2765	0.2317	0.1945	0.1635	19
20	0.8195	0.6730	0.5537	0.4564	0.3769	0.3118	0.2584	0.2145	0.1784	0.1486	20
21	0.8114	0.6598	0.5375	0.4388	0.3589	0.2942	0.2415	0.1987	0.1637	0.1351	21
22	0.8034	0.6468	0.5219	0.4220	0.3418	0.2775	0.2257	0.1839	0.1502	0.1228	22
23	0.7954	0.6342	0.5067	0.4057	0.3256	0.2618	0.2109	0.1703	0.1378	0.1117	23
24	0.7876	0.6217	0.4919	0.3901	0.3101	0.2470	0.1971	0.1577	0.1264	0.1015	24
25	0.7798	0.6095	0.4776	0.3751	0.2953	0.2330	0.1842	0.1460	0.1160	0.0923	25
26	0.7720	0.5976	0.4637	0.3607	0.2812	0.2198	0.1722	0.1352	0.1064	0.0839	26
27	0.7644	0.5859	0.4502	0.3468	0.2678	0.2074	0.1609	0.1252	0.0976	0.0763	27
28	0.7568	0.5744	0.4371	0.3335	0.2551	0.1956	0.1504	0.1159	0.0895	0.0693	28
29	0.7493	0.5631	0.4243	0.3207	0.2429	0.1846	0.1406	0.1073	0.0822	0.0630	29
30	0.7419	0.5521	0.4120	0.3083	0.2314	0.1741	0.1314	0.0994	0.0754	0.0573	30
31	0.7346	0.5412	0.4000	0.2965	0.2204	0.1643	0.1228	0.0920	0.0691	0.0521	31
32	0.7273	0.5306	0.3883	0.2851	0.2099	0.1550	0.1147	0.0852	0.0634	0.0474	32
33	0.7201	0.5202	0.3770	0.2741	0.1999	0.1462	0.1072	0.0789	0.0582	0.0431	33
34	0.7130	0.5100	0.3660	0.2636	0.1904	0.1379	0.1002	0.0730	0.0534	0.0391	34
35	0.7059	0.5000	0.3554	0.2534	0.1813	0.1301	0.0937	0.0676	0.0490	0.0356	35
36	0.6989	0.4902	0.3450	0.2437	0.1727	0.1227	0.0875	0.0626	0.0449	0.0323	36
37	0.6920	0.4806	0.3350	0.2343	0.1644	0.1158	0.0818	0.0580	0.0412	0.0294	37
38	0.6852	0.4712	0.3252	0.2253	0.1566	0.1092	0.0765	0.0537	0.0378	0.0267	38
39	0.6784	0.4619	0.3158	0.2166	0.1491	0.1031	0.0715	0.0497	0.0347	0.0243	39
40	0.6717	0.4529	0.3066	0.2083	0.1420	0.0972	0.0668	0.0460	0.0318	0.0221	40

N/R	11%	12%	13%	14%	15%	16%	20%	22%	24%	25%	N/R
1	0.9009	0.8929	0.8850	0.8772	0.8696	0.8621	0.8333	0.8197	0.8065	0.8000	1
2	0.8116	0.7972	0.7831	0.7695	0.7561	0.7432	0.6944	0.6504	0.6504	0.6400	2
3	0.7312	0.7118	0.6931	0.6750	0.6575	0.6407	0.5787	0.5245	0.5245	0.5120	3
4	0.6587	0.6355	0.6133	0.5921	0.5718	0.5523	0.4823	0.4230	0.4230	0.4096	4
5	0.5935	0.5674	0.5428	0.5194	0.4972	0.4761	0.4019	0.3411	0.3411	0.3277	5
6	0.5346	0.5066	0.4803	0.4556	0.4323	0.4104	0.3349	0.2751	0.2751	0.2621	6
7	0.4817	0.4523	0.4251	0.3996	0.3759	0.3538	0.2791	0.2218	0.2218	0.2097	7
8	0.4339	0.4039	0.3762	0.3506	0.3269	0.3050	0.2326	0.1789	0.1789	0.1678	8
9	0.3909	0.3606	0.3329	0.3075	0.2843	0.2630	0.1938	0.1443	0.1443	0.1342	9
10	0.3522	0.3220	0.2946	0.2697	0.2472	0.2267	0.1615	0.1164	0.1164	0.1074	10
11	0.3173	0.2875	0.2607	0.2366	0.2149	0.1954	0.1346	0.0938	0.0938	0.0859	11
12	0.2858	0.2567	0.2307	0.2076	0.1869	0.1685	0.1122	0.0757	0.0757	0.0687	12
13	0.2575	0.2292	0.2042	0.1821	0.1625	0.1452	0.0935	0.0610	0.0610	0.0550	13
14	0.2320	0.2046	0.1807	0.1597	0.1413	0.1252	0.0779	0.0492	0.0492	0.0440	14
15	0.2090	0.1827	0.1599	0.1401	0.1229	0.1079	0.0649	0.0397	0.0397	0.0352	15
16	0.1883	0.1631	0.1415	0.1229	0.1069	0.0930	0.0541	0.0320	0.0320	0.0281	16
17	0.1696	0.1456	0.1252	0.1078	0.0929	0.0802	0.0451	0.0258	0.0258	0.0225	17
18	0.1528	0.1300	0.1108	0.0946	0.0808	0.0691	0.0376	0.0208	0.0208	0.0180	18
19	0.1377	0.1161	0.0981	0.0829	0.0703	0.0596	0.0313	0.0168	0.0168	0.0144	19
20	0.1240	0.1037	0.0868	0.0728	0.0611	0.0514	0.0261	0.0135	0.0135	0.0115	20
21	0.1117	0.0926	0.0768	0.0638	0.0531	0.0443	0.0217	0.0109	0.0109	0.0092	21
22	0.1007	0.0826	0.0680	0.0560	0.0462	0.0382	0.0181	0.0088	0.0088	0.0074	22
23	0.0907	0.0738	0.0601	0.0491	0.0402	0.0329	0.0151	0.0071	0.0071	0.0059	23
24	0.0817	0.0659	0.0532	0.0431	0.0349	0.0284	0.0126	0.0057	0.0057	0.0047	24
25	0.0736	0.0588	0.0471	0.0378	0.0304	0.0245	0.0105	0.0046	0.0046	0.0038	25
26	0.0663	0.0525	0.0417	0.0331	0.0264	0.0211	0.0087	0.0037	0.0037	0.0030	26
27	0.0597	0.0469	0.0369	0.0291	0.0230	0.0182	0.0073	0.0030	0.0030	0.0024	27
28	0.0538	0.0419	0.0326	0.0255	0.0200	0.0157	0.0061	0.0024	0.0024	0.0019	28
29	0.0485	0.0374	0.0289	0.0224	0.0174	0.0135	0.0051	0.0020	0.0020	0.0015	29
30	0.0437	0.0334	0.0256	0.0196	0.0151	0.0116	0.0042	0.0016	0.0016	0.0012	30
31	0.0394	0.0298	0.0226	0.0172	0.0131	0.0100	0.0035	0.0013	0.0013	0.0010	31
32	0.0355	0.0266	0.0200	0.0151	0.0114	0.0087	0.0029	0.0010	0.0010	0.0008	32
33	0.0319	0.0238	0.0177	0.0132	0.0099	0.0075	0.0024	0.0008	0.0008	0.0006	33
34	0.0288	0.0212	0.0157	0.0116	0.0086	0.0064	0.0020	0.0007	0.0007	0.0005	34
35	0.0259	0.0189	0.0139	0.0102	0.0075	0.0055	0.0017	0.0005	0.0005	0.0004	35
36	0.0234	0.0169	0.0123	0.0089	0.0065	0.0048	0.0014	0.0004	0.0004	0.0003	36
37	0.0210	0.0151	0.0109	0.0078	0.0057	0.0041	0.0012	0.0003	0.0003	0.0003	37
38	0.0190	0.0135	0.0096	0.0069	0.0049	0.0036	0.0010	0.0003	0.0003	0.0002	38
39	0.0171	0.0120	0.0085	0.0060	0.0043	0.0031	0.0008	0.0002	0.0002	0.0002	39
40	0.0154	0.0107	0.0075	0.0053	0.0037	0.0026	0.0007	0.0002	0.0002	0.0001	40

TABLE A–3 Future Amount of an Ordinary Annuity of 1: FVOA = $[(1 + r)^n - 1]/r$

N/R	1%	2%	3%	4%	5%	6%	7%	8%	9%	10%	N/R
1	1.0000	1.0000	1.0000	1.0000	1.0000	1.0000	1.0000	1.0000	1.0000	1.0000	1
2	2.0100	2.0200	2.0300	2.0400	2.0500	2.0600	2.0700	2.0800	2.0900	2.1000	2
3	3.0301	3.0604	3.0909	3.1216	3.1525	3.1836	3.2149	3.2464	3.2781	3.3100	3
4	4.0604	4.1216	4.1836	4.2465	4.3101	4.3746	4.4399	4.5061	4.5731	4.6410	4
5	5.1010	5.2040	5.3091	5.4163	5.5256	5.6371	5.7507	5.8666	5.9847	6.1051	5
6	6.1520	6.3081	6.4684	6.6330	6.8019	6.9753	7.1533	7.3359	7.5233	7.7156	6
7	7.2135	7.4343	7.6625	7.8983	8.1420	8.3938	8.6540	8.9228	9.2004	9.4872	7
8	8.2857	8.5830	8.8923	9.2142	9.5491	9.8975	10.2598	10.6366	11.0285	11.4359	8
9	9.3685	9.7546	10.1591	10.5828	11.0266	11.4913	11.9780	12.4876	13.0210	13.5795	9
10	10.4622	10.9497	11.4639	12.0061	12.5779	13.1808	13.8164	14.4866	15.1929	15.9374	10
11	11.5668	12.1687	12.8078	13.4864	14.2068	14.9716	15.7836	16.6455	17.5603	18.5312	11
12	12.6825	13.4121	14.1920	15.0258	15.9171	16.8699	17.8885	18.9771	20.1407	21.3843	12
13	13.8093	14.6803	15.6178	16.6268	17.7130	18.8821	20.1406	21.4953	22.9534	24.5227	13
14	14.9474	15.9739	17.0863	18.2919	19.5986	21.0151	22.5505	24.2149	26.0192	27.9750	14
15	16.0969	17.2934	18.5989	20.0236	21.5786	23.2760	25.1290	27.1521	29.3609	31.7725	15
16	17.2579	18.6393	20.1569	21.8245	23.6575	25.6725	27.8881	30.3243	33.0034	35.9497	16
17	18.4304	20.0121	21.7616	23.6975	25.8404	28.2129	30.8402	33.7502	36.9737	40.5447	17
18	19.6147	21.4123	23.4144	25.6454	28.1324	30.9057	33.9990	37.4502	41.3013	45.5992	18
19	20.8109	22.8406	25.1169	27.6712	30.5390	33.7600	37.3790	41.4463	46.0185	51.1591	19
20	22.0190	24.2974	26.8704	29.7781	33.0660	36.7856	40.9955	45.7620	51.1601	57.2750	20
21	23.2392	25.7833	28.6765	31.9692	35.7193	39.9927	44.8652	50.4229	56.7645	64.0025	21
22	24.4716	27.2990	30.5368	34.2480	38.5052	43.3923	49.0057	55.4568	62.8733	71.4027	22
23	25.7163	28.8450	32.4529	36.6179	41.4305	46.9958	53.4361	60.8933	69.5319	79.5430	23
24	26.9735	30.4219	34.4265	39.0826	44.5020	50.8156	58.1767	66.7648	76.7898	88.4973	24
25	28.2432	32.0303	36.4593	41.6459	47.7271	54.8645	63.2490	73.1059	84.7009	98.3471	25
26	29.5256	33.6709	38.5530	44.3117	51.1135	59.1564	68.6765	79.9544	93.3240	109.1818	26
27	30.8209	35.3443	40.7096	47.0842	54.6691	63.7058	74.4838	87.3508	102.7231	121.0999	27
28	32.1291	37.0512	42.9309	49.9676	58.4026	68.5281	80.6977	95.3388	112.9682	134.2099	28
29	33.4504	38.7922	45.2189	52.9663	62.3227	73.6398	87.3465	103.9659	124.1354	148.6309	29
30	34.7849	40.5681	47.5754	56.0849	66.4388	79.0582	94.4608	113.2832	136.3075	164.4940	30
31	36.1327	42.3794	50.0027	59.3283	70.7608	84.8017	102.0730	123.3459	149.5752	181.9434	31
32	37.4941	44.2270	52.5028	62.7015	75.2988	90.8898	110.2182	134.2135	164.0370	201.1378	32
33	38.8690	46.1116	55.0778	66.2095	80.0638	97.3432	118.9334	145.9506	179.8003	222.2515	33
34	40.2577	48.0338	57.7302	69.8579	85.0670	104.1838	128.2588	158.6267	196.9823	245.4767	34
35	41.6603	49.9945	60.4621	73.6522	90.3203	111.4348	138.2369	172.3168	215.7108	271.0244	35
36	43.0769	51.9944	63.2759	77.5983	95.8363	119.1209	148.9135	187.1021	236.1247	299.1268	36
37	44.5076	54.0343	66.1742	81.7022	101.6281	127.2681	160.3374	203.0703	258.3759	330.0395	37
38	45.9527	56.1149	69.1594	85.9703	107.7095	135.9042	172.5610	220.3159	282.6298	364.0434	38
39	47.4123	58.2372	72.2342	90.4091	114.0950	145.0585	185.6403	238.9412	309.0665	401.4478	39
40	48.8864	60.4020	75.4013	95.0255	120.7998	154.7620	199.6351	259.0565	337.8824	442.5926	40

N/R	11%	12%	13%	14%	15%	16%	20%	22%	24%	25%	N/R
1	1.0000	1.0000	1.0000	1.0000	1.0000	1.0000	1.0000	1.0000	1.0000	1.0000	1
2	2.1100	2.1200	2.1300	2.1400	2.1500	2.1600	2.2000	2.2200	2.2400	2.2500	2
3	3.3421	3.3744	3.4069	3.4396	3.4725	3.5056	3.6400	3.7084	3.7776	3.8125	3
4	4.7097	4.7793	4.8498	4.9211	4.9934	5.0665	5.3680	5.5242	5.6842	5.7656	4
5	6.2278	6.3528	6.4803	6.6101	6.7424	6.8771	7.4416	7.7396	8.0484	8.2070	5
6	7.9129	8.1152	8.3227	8.5355	8.7537	8.9775	9.9299	10.4423	10.9801	11.2588	6
7	9.7833	10.0890	10.4047	10.7305	11.0668	11.4139	12.9159	13.7396	14.6153	15.0735	7
8	11.8594	12.2997	12.7573	13.2328	13.7268	14.2401	16.4991	17.7623	19.1229	19.8419	8
9	14.1640	14.7757	15.4157	16.0853	16.7858	17.5185	20.7989	22.6700	24.7125	25.8023	9
10	16.7220	17.5487	18.4197	19.3373	20.3037	21.3215	25.9587	28.6574	31.6434	33.2529	10
11	19.5614	20.6546	21.8143	23.0445	24.3493	25.7329	32.1504	35.9620	40.2379	42.5661	11
12	22.7132	24.1331	25.6502	27.2707	29.0017	30.8502	39.5805	44.8737	50.8950	54.2077	12
13	26.2116	28.0291	29.9847	32.0887	34.3519	36.7862	48.4966	55.7459	64.1097	68.7596	13
14	30.0949	32.3926	34.8827	37.5811	40.5047	43.6720	59.1959	69.0100	80.4961	86.9495	14
15	34.4054	37.2797	40.4175	43.8424	47.5804	51.6595	72.0351	85.1922	100.8151	109.6868	15
16	39.1899	42.7533	46.6717	50.9804	55.7175	60.9250	87.4421	104.9345	126.0108	138.1085	16
17	44.5008	48.8837	53.7391	59.1176	65.0751	71.6730	105.9306	129.0201	157.2534	173.6357	17
18	50.3959	55.7497	61.7251	68.3941	75.8364	84.1407	128.1167	158.4045	195.9942	218.0446	18
19	56.9395	63.4397	70.7494	78.9692	88.2118	98.6032	154.7400	194.2535	244.0328	273.5558	19
20	64.2028	72.0524	80.9468	91.0249	102.4436	115.3797	186.6880	237.9893	303.6006	342.9447	20
21	72.2651	81.6987	92.4699	104.7684	118.8101	134.8405	225.0256	291.3469	377.4648	429.6809	21
22	81.2143	92.5026	105.4910	120.4360	137.6316	157.4150	271.0307	356.4432	469.0563	538.1011	22
23	91.1479	104.6029	120.2048	138.2970	159.2764	183.6014	326.2369	435.8607	582.6298	673.6264	23
24	102.1742	118.1552	136.8315	158.6586	184.1678	213.9776	392.4842	532.7501	723.4610	843.0329	24
25	114.4133	133.3339	155.6196	181.8708	212.7930	249.2140	471.9811	650.9551	898.0916	1054.7912	25
26	127.9988	150.3339	176.8501	208.3327	245.7120	290.0883	567.3773	795.1653	1114.6336	1319.4890	26
27	143.0786	169.3740	200.8406	238.4993	283.5688	337.5024	681.8528	971.1016	1383.1457	1650.3612	27
28	159.8173	190.6989	227.9499	272.8892	327.1041	392.5028	819.2233	1185.7440	1716.1007	2063.9515	28
29	178.3972	214.5828	258.5834	312.0937	377.1697	456.3032	984.0680	1447.6077	2128.9648	2580.9394	29
30	199.0209	241.3327	293.1992	356.7868	434.7451	530.3117	1181.8816	1767.0813	2640.9164	3227.1743	30
31	221.9132	271.2926	332.3151	407.7370	500.9569	616.1616	1419.2579	2156.8392	3275.7363	4034.9678	31
32	247.3236	304.8477	376.5161	465.8202	577.1005	715.7475	1704.1095	2632.3439	4062.9130	5044.7098	32
33	275.5292	342.4294	426.4632	532.0350	664.6655	831.2671	2045.9314	3212.4595	5039.0122	6306.8872	33
34	306.8374	384.5210	482.9034	607.5199	765.3654	965.2698	2456.1176	3920.2006	6249.3751	7884.6091	34
35	341.5896	431.6635	546.6808	693.5727	881.1702	1120.7130	2948.3411	4783.6447	7750.2251	9856.7613	35
36	380.1644	484.4631	618.7493	791.6729	1014.3457	1301.0270	3539.0094	5837.0466	9611.2791	12321.9516	36
37	422.9825	543.5987	700.1867	903.5071	1167.4975	1510.1914	4247.8112	7122.1968	11918.9861	15403.4396	37
38	470.5106	609.8305	792.2110	1030.9981	1343.6222	1752.8220	5098.3735	8690.0801	14780.5428	19255.2994	38
39	523.2667	684.0102	896.1984	1176.3378	1546.1655	2034.2735	6119.0482	10602.8978	18328.8731	24070.1243	39
40	581.8261	767.0914	1013.7042	1342.0251	1779.0903	2360.7572	7343.8578	12936.5353	22728.8026	30088.6554	40

TABLE A–4 Future Amount of an Annuity Due of 1: FVAD = $[(1 + r)^n - 1]/r \times (1 + r)$

N/R	1%	2%	3%	4%	5%	6%	7%	8%	9%	10%	N/R
1	1.0100	1.0200	1.0300	1.0400	1.0500	1.0600	1.0700	1.0800	1.0900	1.1000	1
2	2.0301	2.0604	2.0909	2.1216	2.1525	2.1836	2.2149	2.2464	2.2781	2.3100	2
3	3.0604	3.1216	3.1836	3.2465	3.3101	3.3746	3.4399	3.5061	3.5731	3.6410	3
4	4.1010	4.2040	4.3091	4.4163	4.5256	4.6371	4.7507	4.8666	4.9847	5.1051	4
5	5.1520	5.3081	5.4684	5.6330	5.8019	5.9753	6.1533	6.3359	6.5233	6.7156	5
6	6.2135	6.4343	6.6625	6.8983	7.1420	7.3938	7.6540	7.9228	8.2004	8.4872	6
7	7.2857	7.5830	7.8923	8.2142	8.5491	8.8975	9.2598	9.6366	10.0285	10.4359	7
8	8.3685	8.7546	9.1591	9.5828	10.0266	10.4913	10.9780	11.4876	12.0210	12.5795	8
9	9.4622	9.9497	10.4639	11.0061	11.5779	12.1808	12.8164	13.4866	14.1929	14.9374	9
10	10.5668	11.1687	11.8078	12.4864	13.2068	13.9716	14.7836	15.6455	16.5603	17.5312	10
11	11.6825	12.4121	13.1920	14.0258	14.9171	15.8699	16.8885	17.9771	19.1407	20.3843	11
12	12.8093	13.6803	14.6178	15.6268	16.7130	17.8821	19.1406	20.4953	21.9534	23.5227	12
13	13.9474	14.9739	16.0863	17.2919	18.5986	20.0151	21.5505	23.2149	25.0192	26.9750	13
14	15.0969	16.2934	17.5989	19.0236	20.5786	22.2760	24.1290	26.1521	28.3609	30.7725	14
15	16.2579	17.6393	19.1569	20.8245	22.6575	24.6725	26.8881	29.3243	32.0034	34.9497	15
16	17.4304	19.0121	20.7616	22.6975	24.8404	27.2129	29.8402	32.7502	35.9737	39.5447	16
17	18.6147	20.4123	22.4144	24.6454	27.1324	29.9057	32.9990	36.4502	40.3013	44.5992	17
18	19.8109	21.8406	24.1169	26.6712	29.5390	32.7600	36.3790	40.4463	45.0185	50.1591	18
19	21.0190	23.2974	25.8704	28.7781	32.0660	35.7856	39.9955	44.7620	50.1601	56.2750	19
20	22.2392	24.7833	27.6765	30.9692	34.7193	38.9927	43.8652	49.4229	55.7645	63.0025	20
21	23.4716	26.2990	29.5368	33.2480	37.5052	42.3923	48.0057	54.4568	61.8733	70.4027	21
22	24.7163	27.8450	31.4529	35.6179	40.4305	45.9958	52.4361	59.8933	68.5319	78.5430	22
23	25.9735	29.4219	33.4265	38.0826	43.5020	49.8156	57.1767	65.7648	75.7898	87.4973	23
24	27.2432	31.0303	35.4593	40.6459	46.7271	53.8645	62.2490	72.1059	83.7009	97.3471	24
25	28.5256	32.6709	37.5530	43.3117	50.1135	58.1564	67.6765	78.9544	92.3240	108.1818	25
26	29.8209	34.3443	39.7096	46.0842	53.6691	62.7058	73.4838	86.3508	101.7231	120.0999	26
27	31.1291	36.0512	41.9309	48.9676	57.4026	67.5281	79.6977	94.3388	111.9682	133.2099	27
28	32.4504	37.7922	44.2189	51.9663	61.3227	72.6398	86.3465	102.9659	123.1354	147.6309	28
29	33.7849	39.5681	46.5754	55.0849	65.4388	78.0582	93.4608	112.2832	135.3075	163.4940	29
30	35.1327	41.3794	49.0027	58.3283	69.7608	83.8017	101.0730	122.3459	148.5752	180.9434	30
31	36.4941	43.2270	51.5028	61.7015	74.2988	89.8898	109.2182	133.2135	163.0370	200.1378	31
32	37.8690	45.1116	54.0778	65.2095	79.0638	96.3432	117.9334	144.9506	178.8003	221.2515	32
33	39.2577	47.0338	56.7302	68.8579	84.0670	103.1838	127.2588	157.6267	195.9823	244.4767	33
34	40.6603	48.9945	59.4621	72.6522	89.3203	110.4348	137.2369	171.3168	214.7108	270.0244	34
35	42.0769	50.9944	62.2759	76.5983	94.8363	118.1209	147.9135	186.1021	235.1247	298.1268	35
36	43.5076	53.0343	65.1742	80.7022	100.6281	126.2681	159.3374	202.0703	257.3759	329.0395	36
37	44.9527	55.1149	68.1594	84.9703	106.7095	134.9042	171.5610	219.3159	281.6298	363.0434	37
38	46.4123	57.2372	71.2342	89.4091	113.0950	144.0585	184.6403	237.9412	308.0665	400.4478	38
39	47.8864	59.4020	74.4013	94.0255	119.7998	153.7620	198.6351	258.0565	336.8824	441.5926	39
40	49.3752	61.6100	77.6633	98.8265	126.8398	164.0477	213.6096	279.7810	368.2919	486.8518	40

N/R	11%	12%	13%	14%	15%	16%	20%	22%	24%	25%	N/R
1	1.1100	1.1200	1.1300	1.1400	1.1500	1.1600	1.2000	1.2200	1.2400	1.2500	1
2	2.3421	2.3744	2.4069	2.4396	2.4725	2.5056	2.6400	2.7084	2.7776	2.8125	2
3	3.7097	3.7793	3.8498	3.9211	3.9934	4.0665	4.3680	4.5242	4.6842	4.7656	3
4	5.2278	5.3528	5.4803	5.6101	5.7424	5.8771	6.4416	6.7396	7.0484	7.2070	4
5	6.9129	7.1152	7.3227	7.5355	7.7537	7.9775	8.9299	9.4423	9.9801	10.2588	5
6	8.7833	9.0890	9.4047	9.7305	10.0668	10.4139	11.9159	12.7396	13.6153	14.0735	6
7	10.8594	11.2997	11.7573	12.2328	12.7268	13.2401	15.4991	16.7623	18.1229	18.8419	7
8	13.1640	13.7757	14.4157	15.0853	15.7858	16.5185	19.7989	21.6700	23.7125	24.8023	8
9	15.7220	16.5487	17.4197	18.3373	19.3037	20.3215	24.9587	27.6574	30.6434	32.2529	9
10	18.5614	19.6546	20.8143	22.0445	23.3493	24.7329	31.1504	34.9620	39.2379	41.5661	10
11	21.7132	23.1331	24.6502	26.2707	28.0017	29.8502	38.5805	43.8737	49.8950	53.2077	11
12	25.2116	27.0291	28.9847	31.0887	33.3519	35.7862	47.4966	54.7459	63.1097	67.7596	12
13	29.0949	31.3926	33.8827	36.5811	39.5047	42.6720	58.1959	68.0100	79.4961	85.9495	13
14	33.4054	36.2797	39.4175	42.8424	46.5804	50.6595	71.0351	84.1922	99.8151	108.6868	14
15	38.1899	41.7533	45.6717	49.9804	54.7175	59.9250	86.4421	103.9345	125.0108	137.1085	15
16	43.5008	47.8837	52.7391	58.1176	64.0751	70.6730	104.9306	128.0201	156.2534	172.6357	16
17	49.3959	54.7497	60.7251	67.3941	74.8364	83.1407	127.1167	157.4045	194.9942	217.0446	17
18	55.9395	62.4397	69.7494	77.9692	87.2118	97.6032	153.7400	193.2535	243.0328	272.5558	18
19	63.2028	71.0524	79.9468	90.0249	101.4436	114.3797	185.6880	236.9893	302.6006	341.9447	19
20	71.2651	80.6987	91.4699	103.7684	117.8101	133.8405	224.0256	290.3469	376.4648	428.6809	20
21	80.2143	91.5026	104.4910	119.4360	136.6316	156.4150	270.0307	355.4432	468.0563	537.1011	21
22	90.1479	103.6029	119.2048	137.2970	158.2764	182.6014	325.2369	434.8607	581.6298	672.6264	22
23	101.1742	117.1552	135.8315	157.6586	183.1678	212.9776	391.4842	531.7501	722.4610	842.0329	23
24	113.4133	132.3339	154.6196	180.8708	211.7930	248.2140	470.9811	649.9551	897.0916	1053.7912	24
25	126.9988	149.3339	175.8501	207.3327	244.7120	289.0883	566.3773	794.1653	1113.6336	1318.4890	25
26	142.0786	168.3740	199.8406	237.4993	282.5688	336.5024	680.8528	970.1016	1382.1457	1649.3612	26
27	158.8173	189.6989	226.9499	271.8892	326.1041	391.5028	818.2233	1184.7440	1715.1007	2062.9515	27
28	177.3972	213.5828	257.5834	311.0937	376.1697	455.3032	983.0680	1446.6077	2127.9648	2579.9394	28
29	198.0209	240.3327	292.1992	355.7868	433.7451	529.3117	1180.8816	1766.0813	2639.9164	3226.1743	29
30	220.9132	270.2926	331.3151	406.7370	499.9569	615.1616	1418.2579	2155.8392	3274.7363	4033.9678	30
31	246.3236	303.8477	375.5161	464.8202	576.1005	714.7475	1703.1095	2631.3439	4061.9130	5043.7098	31
32	274.5292	341.4294	425.4632	531.0350	663.6655	830.2671	2044.9314	3211.4595	5038.0122	6305.8872	32
33	305.8374	383.5210	481.9034	606.5199	764.3654	964.2698	2455.1176	3919.2006	6248.3751	7883.6091	33
34	340.5896	430.6635	545.6808	692.5727	880.1702	1119.7130	2947.3411	4782.6447	7749.2251	9855.7613	34
35	379.1644	483.4631	617.7493	790.6729	1013.3457	1300.0270	3538.0094	5836.0466	9610.2791	12320.9516	35
36	421.9825	542.5987	699.1867	902.5071	1166.4975	1509.1914	4246.8112	7121.1968	11917.9861	15402.4396	36
37	469.5106	608.8305	791.2110	1029.9981	1342.6222	1751.8220	5097.3735	8689.0801	14779.5428	19254.2994	37
38	522.2667	683.0102	895.1984	1175.3378	1545.1655	2033.2735	6118.0482	10601.8978	18327.8731	24069.1243	38
39	580.8261	766.0914	1012.7042	1341.0251	1778.0903	2359.7572	7342.8578	12935.5353	22727.8026	30087.6554	39
40	645.8269	859.1424	1145.4858	1529.9086	2045.9539	2738.4784	8812.6294	15782.5730	28183.7152	37610.8192	40

TABLE A–5 Present Value of an Ordinary Annuity of 1: PVOA = $[1 - (1/(1 + r)^n)]/r$

N/R	1%	2%	3%	4%	5%	6%	7%	8%	9%	10%	N/R
1	0.9901	0.9804	0.9709	0.9615	0.9524	0.9434	0.9346	0.9259	0.9174	0.9091	1
2	1.9704	1.9416	1.9135	1.8861	1.8594	1.8334	1.8080	1.7833	1.7591	1.7355	2
3	2.9410	2.8839	2.8286	2.7751	2.7232	2.6730	2.6243	2.5771	2.5313	2.4869	3
4	3.9020	3.8077	3.7171	3.6299	3.5460	3.4651	3.3872	3.3121	3.2397	3.1699	4
5	4.8534	4.7135	4.5797	4.4518	4.3295	4.2124	4.1002	3.9927	3.8897	3.7908	5
6	5.7955	5.6014	5.4172	5.2421	5.0757	4.9173	4.7665	4.6229	4.4859	4.3553	6
7	6.7282	6.4720	6.2303	6.0021	5.7864	5.5824	5.3893	5.2064	5.0330	4.8684	7
8	7.6517	7.3255	7.0197	6.7327	6.4632	6.2098	5.9713	5.7466	5.5348	5.3349	8
9	8.5660	8.1622	7.7861	7.4353	7.1078	6.8017	6.5152	6.2469	5.9952	5.7590	9
10	9.4713	8.9826	8.5302	8.1109	7.7217	7.3601	7.0236	6.7101	6.4177	6.1446	10
11	10.3676	9.7868	9.2526	8.7605	8.3064	7.8869	7.4987	7.1390	6.8052	6.4951	11
12	11.2551	10.5753	9.9540	9.3851	8.8633	8.3838	7.9427	7.5361	7.1607	6.8137	12
13	12.1337	11.3484	10.6350	9.9856	9.3936	8.8527	8.3577	7.9038	7.4869	7.1034	13
14	13.0037	12.1062	11.2961	10.5631	9.8986	9.2950	8.7455	8.2442	7.7862	7.3667	14
15	13.8651	12.8493	11.9379	11.1184	10.3797	9.7122	9.1079	8.5595	8.0607	7.6061	15
16	14.7179	13.5777	12.5611	11.6523	10.8378	10.1059	9.4466	8.8514	8.3126	7.8237	16
17	15.5623	14.2919	13.1661	12.1657	11.2741	10.4773	9.7632	9.1216	8.5436	8.0216	17
18	16.3983	14.9920	13.7535	12.6593	11.6896	10.8276	10.0591	9.3719	8.7556	8.2014	18
19	17.2260	15.6785	14.3238	13.1339	12.0853	11.1581	10.3356	9.6036	8.9501	8.3649	19
20	18.0456	16.3514	14.8775	13.5903	12.4622	11.4699	10.5940	9.8181	9.1285	8.5136	20
21	18.8570	17.0112	15.4150	14.0292	12.8212	11.7641	10.8355	10.0168	9.2922	8.6487	21
22	19.6604	17.6580	15.9369	14.4511	13.1630	12.0416	11.0612	10.2007	9.4424	8.7715	22
23	20.4558	18.2922	16.4436	14.8568	13.4886	12.3034	11.2722	10.3711	9.5802	8.8832	23
24	21.2434	18.9139	16.9355	15.2470	13.7986	12.5504	11.4693	10.5288	9.7066	8.9847	24
25	22.0232	19.5235	17.4131	15.6221	14.0939	12.7834	11.6536	10.6748	9.8226	9.0770	25
26	22.7952	20.1210	17.8768	15.9828	14.3752	13.0032	11.8258	10.8100	9.9290	9.1609	26
27	23.5596	20.7069	18.3270	16.3296	14.6430	13.2105	11.9867	10.9352	10.0266	9.2372	27
28	24.3164	21.2813	18.7641	16.6631	14.8981	13.4062	12.1371	11.0511	10.1161	9.3066	28
29	25.0658	21.8444	19.1885	16.9837	15.1411	13.5907	12.2777	11.1584	10.1983	9.3696	29
30	25.8077	22.3965	19.6004	17.2920	15.3725	13.7648	12.4090	11.2578	10.2737	9.4269	30
31	26.5423	22.9377	20.0004	17.5885	15.5928	13.9291	12.5318	11.3498	10.3428	9.4790	31
32	27.2696	23.4683	20.3888	17.8736	15.8027	14.0840	12.6466	11.4350	10.4062	9.5264	32
33	27.9897	23.9886	20.7658	18.1476	16.0025	14.2302	12.7538	11.5139	10.4644	9.5694	33
34	28.7027	24.4986	21.1318	18.4112	16.1929	14.3681	12.8540	11.5869	10.5178	9.6086	34
35	29.4086	24.9986	21.4872	18.6646	16.3742	14.4982	12.9477	11.6546	10.5668	9.6442	35
36	30.1075	25.4888	21.8323	18.9083	16.5469	14.6210	13.0352	11.7172	10.6118	9.6765	36
37	30.7995	25.9695	22.1672	19.1426	16.7113	14.7368	13.1170	11.7752	10.6530	9.7059	37
38	31.4847	26.4406	22.4925	19.3679	16.8679	14.8460	13.1935	11.8289	10.6908	9.7327	38
39	32.1630	26.9026	22.8082	19.5845	17.0170	14.9491	13.2649	11.8786	10.7255	9.7570	39
40	32.8347	27.3555	23.1148	19.7928	17.1591	15.0463	13.3317	11.9246	10.7574	9.7791	40

N/R	11%	12%	13%	14%	15%	16%	20%	22%	24%	25%	N/R
1	0.9009	0.8929	0.8850	0.8772	0.8696	0.8621	0.8333	0.8197	0.8065	0.8000	1
2	1.7125	1.6901	1.6681	1.6467	1.6257	1.6052	1.5278	1.4915	1.4568	1.4400	2
3	2.4437	2.4018	2.3612	2.3216	2.2832	2.2459	2.1065	2.0422	1.9813	1.9520	3
4	3.1024	3.0373	2.9745	2.9137	2.8550	2.7982	2.5887	2.4936	2.4043	2.3616	4
5	3.6959	3.6048	3.5172	3.4331	3.3522	3.2743	2.9906	2.8636	2.7454	2.6893	5
6	4.2305	4.1114	3.9975	3.8887	3.7845	3.6847	3.3255	3.1669	3.0205	2.9514	6
7	4.7122	4.5638	4.4226	4.2883	4.1604	4.0386	3.6046	3.4155	3.2423	3.1611	7
8	5.1461	4.9676	4.7988	4.6389	4.4873	4.3436	3.8372	3.6193	3.4212	3.3289	8
9	5.5370	5.3282	5.1317	4.9464	4.7716	4.6065	4.0310	3.7863	3.5655	3.4631	9
10	5.8892	5.6502	5.4262	5.2161	5.0188	4.8332	4.1925	3.9232	3.6819	3.5705	10
11	6.2065	5.9377	5.6869	5.4527	5.2337	5.0286	4.3271	4.0354	3.7757	3.6564	11
12	6.4924	6.1944	5.9176	5.6603	5.4206	5.1971	4.4392	4.1274	3.8514	3.7251	12
13	6.7499	6.4235	6.1218	5.8424	5.5831	5.3423	4.5327	4.2028	3.9124	3.7801	13
14	6.9819	6.6282	6.3025	6.0021	5.7245	5.4675	4.6106	4.2646	3.9616	3.8241	14
15	7.1909	6.8109	6.4624	6.1422	5.8474	5.5755	4.6755	4.3152	4.0013	3.8593	15
16	7.3792	6.9740	6.6039	6.2651	5.9542	5.6685	4.7296	4.3567	4.0333	3.8874	16
17	7.5488	7.1196	6.7291	6.3729	6.0472	5.7487	4.7746	4.3908	4.0591	3.9099	17
18	7.7016	7.2497	6.8399	6.4674	6.1280	5.8178	4.8122	4.4187	4.0799	3.9279	18
19	7.8393	7.3658	6.9380	6.5504	6.1982	5.8775	4.8435	4.4415	4.0967	3.9424	19
20	7.9633	7.4694	7.0248	6.6231	6.2593	5.9288	4.8696	4.4603	4.1103	3.9539	20
21	8.0751	7.5620	7.1016	6.6870	6.3125	5.9731	4.8913	4.4756	4.1212	3.9631	21
22	8.1757	7.6446	7.1695	6.7429	6.3587	6.0113	4.9094	4.4882	4.1300	3.9705	22
23	8.2664	7.7184	7.2297	6.7921	6.3988	6.0442	4.9245	4.4985	4.1371	3.9764	23
24	8.3481	7.7843	7.2829	6.8351	6.4338	6.0726	4.9371	4.5070	4.1428	3.9811	24
25	8.4217	7.8431	7.3300	6.8729	6.4641	6.0971	4.9476	4.5139	4.1474	3.9849	25
26	8.4881	7.8957	7.3717	6.9061	6.4906	6.1182	4.9563	4.5196	4.1511	3.9879	26
27	8.5478	7.9426	7.4086	6.9352	6.5135	6.1364	4.9636	4.5243	4.1542	3.9903	27
28	8.6016	7.9844	7.4412	6.9607	6.5335	6.1520	4.9697	4.5281	4.1566	3.9923	28
29	8.6501	8.0218	7.4701	6.9830	6.5509	6.1656	4.9747	4.5312	4.1585	3.9938	29
30	8.6938	8.0552	7.4957	7.0027	6.5660	6.1772	4.9789	4.5338	4.1601	3.9950	30
31	8.7331	8.0850	7.5183	7.0199	6.5791	6.1872	4.9824	4.5359	4.1614	3.9960	31
32	8.7686	8.1116	7.5383	7.0350	6.5905	6.1959	4.9854	4.5376	4.1624	3.9968	32
33	8.8005	8.1354	7.5560	7.0482	6.6005	6.2034	4.9878	4.5390	4.1632	3.9975	33
34	8.8293	8.1566	7.5717	7.0599	6.6091	6.2098	4.9898	4.5402	4.1639	3.9980	34
35	8.8552	8.1755	7.5856	7.0700	6.6166	6.2153	4.9915	4.5411	4.1644	3.9984	35
36	8.8786	8.1924	7.5979	7.0790	6.6231	6.2201	4.9929	4.5419	4.1649	3.9987	36
37	8.8996	8.2075	7.6087	7.0868	6.6288	6.2242	4.9941	4.5426	4.1652	3.9990	37
38	8.9186	8.2210	7.6183	7.0937	6.6338	6.2278	4.9951	4.5431	4.1655	3.9992	38
39	8.9357	8.2330	7.6268	7.0997	6.6380	6.2309	4.9959	4.5435	4.1657	3.9993	39
40	8.9511	8.2438	7.6344	7.1050	6.6418	6.2335	4.9966	4.5439	4.1659	3.9995	40

TABLE A–6 Present Value of an Annuity Due of 1: $PVAD = 1 + \{1 - [1/(1 + r)^{n-1}]\}/r$

N/R	1%	2%	3%	4%	5%	6%	7%	8%	9%	10%	N/R
1	1.0000	1.0000	1.0000	1.0000	1.0000	1.0000	1.0000	1.0000	1.0000	1.0000	1
2	1.9901	1.9804	1.9709	1.9615	1.9524	1.9434	1.9346	1.9259	1.9174	1.9091	2
3	2.9704	2.9416	2.9135	2.8861	2.8594	2.8334	2.8080	2.7833	2.7591	2.7355	3
4	3.9410	3.8839	3.8286	3.7751	3.7232	3.6730	3.6243	3.5771	3.5313	3.4869	4
5	4.9020	4.8077	4.7171	4.6299	4.5460	4.4651	4.3872	4.3121	4.2397	4.1699	5
6	5.8534	5.7135	5.5797	5.4518	5.3295	5.2124	5.1002	4.9927	4.8897	4.7908	6
7	6.7955	6.6014	6.4172	6.2421	6.0757	5.9173	5.7665	5.6229	5.4859	5.3553	7
8	7.7282	7.4720	7.2303	7.0021	6.7864	6.5824	6.3893	6.2064	6.0330	5.8684	8
9	8.6517	8.3255	8.0197	7.7327	7.4632	7.2098	6.9713	6.7466	6.5348	6.3349	9
10	9.5660	9.1622	8.7861	8.4353	8.1078	7.8017	7.5152	7.2469	6.9952	6.7590	10
11	10.4713	9.9826	9.5302	9.1109	8.7217	8.3601	8.0236	7.7101	7.4177	7.1446	11
12	11.3676	10.7868	10.2526	9.7605	9.3064	8.8869	8.4987	8.1390	7.8052	7.4951	12
13	12.2551	11.5753	10.9540	10.3851	9.8633	9.3838	8.9427	8.5361	8.1607	7.8137	13
14	13.1337	12.3484	11.6350	10.9856	10.3936	9.8527	9.3577	8.9038	8.4869	8.1034	14
15	14.0037	13.1062	12.2961	11.5631	10.8986	10.2950	9.7455	9.2442	8.7862	8.3667	15
16	14.8651	13.8493	12.9379	12.1184	11.3797	10.7122	10.1079	9.5595	9.0607	8.6061	16
17	15.7179	14.5777	13.5611	12.6523	11.8378	11.1059	10.4466	9.8514	9.3126	8.8237	17
18	16.5623	15.2919	14.1661	13.1657	12.2741	11.4773	10.7632	10.1216	9.5436	9.0216	18
19	17.3983	15.9920	14.7535	13.6593	12.6896	11.8276	11.0591	10.3719	9.7556	9.2014	19
20	18.2260	16.6785	15.3238	14.1339	13.0853	12.1581	11.3356	10.6036	9.9501	9.3649	20
21	19.0456	17.3514	15.8775	14.5903	13.4622	12.4699	11.5940	10.8181	10.1285	9.5136	21
22	19.8570	18.0112	16.4150	15.0292	13.8212	12.7641	11.8355	11.0168	10.2922	9.6487	22
23	20.6604	18.6580	16.9369	15.4511	14.1630	13.0416	12.0612	11.2007	10.4424	9.7715	23
24	21.4558	19.2922	17.4436	15.8568	14.4886	13.3034	12.2722	11.3711	10.5802	9.8832	24
25	22.2434	19.9139	17.9355	16.2470	14.7986	13.5504	12.4693	11.5288	10.7066	9.9847	25
26	23.0232	20.5235	18.4131	16.6221	15.0939	13.7834	12.6536	11.6748	10.8226	10.0770	26
27	23.7952	21.1210	18.8768	16.9828	15.3752	14.0032	12.8258	11.8100	10.9290	10.1609	27
28	24.5596	21.7069	19.3270	17.3296	15.6430	14.2105	12.9867	11.9352	11.0266	10.2372	28
29	25.3164	22.2813	19.7641	17.6631	15.8981	14.4062	13.1371	12.0511	11.1161	10.3066	29
30	26.0658	22.8444	20.1885	17.9837	16.1411	14.5907	13.2777	12.1584	11.1983	10.3696	30
31	26.8077	23.3965	20.6004	18.2920	16.3725	14.7648	13.4090	12.2578	11.2737	10.4269	31
32	27.5423	23.9377	21.0004	18.5885	16.5928	14.9291	13.5318	12.3498	11.3428	10.4790	32
33	28.2696	24.4683	21.3888	18.8736	16.8027	15.0840	13.6466	12.4350	11.4062	10.5264	33
34	28.9897	24.9886	21.7658	19.1476	17.0025	15.2302	13.7538	12.5139	11.4644	10.5694	34
35	29.7027	25.4986	22.1318	19.4112	17.1929	15.3681	13.8540	12.5869	11.5178	10.6086	35
36	30.4086	25.9986	22.4872	19.6646	17.3742	15.4982	13.9477	12.6546	11.5668	10.6442	36
37	31.1075	26.4888	22.8323	19.9083	17.5469	15.6210	14.0352	12.7172	11.6118	10.6765	37
38	31.7995	26.9695	23.1672	20.1426	17.7113	15.7368	14.1170	12.7752	11.6530	10.7059	38
39	32.4847	27.4406	23.4925	20.3679	17.8679	15.8460	14.1935	12.8289	11.6908	10.7327	39
40	33.1630	27.9026	23.8082	20.5845	18.0170	15.9491	14.2649	12.8786	11.7255	10.7570	40

N/R	11%	12%	13%	14%	15%	16%	20%	22%	24%	25%	N/R
1	1.0000	1.0000	1.0000	1.0000	1.0000	1.0000	1.0000	1.0000	1.0000	1.0000	1
2	1.9009	1.8929	1.8850	1.8772	1.8696	1.8621	1.8333	1.8197	1.8065	1.8000	2
3	2.7125	2.6901	2.6681	2.6467	2.6257	2.6052	2.5278	2.4915	2.4568	2.4400	3
4	3.4437	3.4018	3.3612	3.3216	3.2832	3.2459	3.1065	3.0422	2.9813	2.9520	4
5	4.1024	4.0373	3.9745	3.9137	3.8550	3.7982	3.5887	3.4936	3.4043	3.3616	5
6	4.6959	4.6048	4.5172	4.4331	4.3522	4.2743	3.9906	3.8636	3.7454	3.6893	6
7	5.2305	5.1114	4.9975	4.8887	4.7845	4.6847	4.3255	4.1669	4.0205	3.9514	7
8	5.7122	5.5638	5.4226	5.2883	5.1604	5.0386	4.6046	4.4155	4.2423	4.1611	8
9	6.1461	5.9676	5.7988	5.6389	5.4873	5.3436	4.8372	4.6193	4.4212	4.3289	9
10	6.5370	6.3282	6.1317	5.9464	5.7716	5.6065	5.0310	4.7863	4.5655	4.4631	10
11	6.8892	6.6502	6.4262	6.2161	6.0188	5.8332	5.1925	4.9232	4.6819	4.5705	11
12	7.2065	6.9377	6.6869	6.4527	6.2337	6.0286	5.3271	5.0354	4.7757	4.6564	12
13	7.4924	7.1944	6.9176	6.6603	6.4206	6.1971	5.4392	5.1274	4.8514	4.7251	13
14	7.7499	7.4235	7.1218	6.8424	6.5831	6.3423	5.5327	5.2028	4.9124	4.7801	14
15	7.9819	7.6282	7.3025	7.0021	6.7245	6.4675	5.6106	5.2646	4.9616	4.8241	15
16	8.1909	7.8109	7.4624	7.1422	6.8474	6.5755	5.6755	5.3152	5.0013	4.8593	16
17	8.3792	7.9740	7.6039	7.2651	6.9542	6.6685	5.7296	5.3567	5.0333	4.8874	17
18	8.5488	8.1196	7.7291	7.3729	7.0472	6.7487	5.7746	5.3908	5.0591	4.9099	18
19	8.7016	8.2497	7.8399	7.4674	7.1280	6.8178	5.8122	5.4187	5.0799	4.9279	19
20	8.8393	8.3658	7.9380	7.5504	7.1982	6.8775	5.8435	5.4415	5.0967	4.9424	20
21	8.9633	8.4694	8.0248	7.6231	7.2593	6.9288	5.8696	5.4603	5.1103	4.9539	21
22	9.0751	8.5620	8.1016	7.6870	7.3125	6.9731	5.8913	5.4756	5.1212	4.9631	22
23	9.1757	8.6446	8.1695	7.7429	7.3587	7.0113	5.9094	5.4882	5.1300	4.9705	23
24	9.2664	8.7184	8.2297	7.7921	7.3988	7.0442	5.9245	5.4985	5.1371	4.9764	24
25	9.3481	8.7843	8.2829	7.8351	7.4338	7.0726	5.9371	5.5070	5.1428	4.9811	25
26	9.4217	8.8431	8.3300	7.8729	7.4641	7.0971	5.9476	5.5139	5.1474	4.9849	26
27	9.4881	8.8957	8.3717	7.9061	7.4906	7.1182	5.9563	5.5196	5.1511	4.9879	27
28	9.5478	8.9426	8.4086	7.9352	7.5135	7.1364	5.9636	5.5243	5.1542	4.9903	28
29	9.6016	8.9844	8.4412	7.9607	7.5335	7.1520	5.9697	5.5281	5.1566	4.9923	29
30	9.6501	9.0218	8.4701	7.9830	7.5509	7.1656	5.9747	5.5312	5.1585	4.9938	30
31	9.6938	9.0552	8.4957	8.0027	7.5660	7.1772	5.9789	5.5338	5.1601	4.9950	31
32	9.7331	9.0850	8.5183	8.0199	7.5791	7.1872	5.9824	5.5359	5.1614	4.9960	32
33	9.7686	9.1116	8.5383	8.0350	7.5905	7.1959	5.9854	5.5376	5.1624	4.9968	33
34	9.8005	9.1354	8.5560	8.0482	7.6005	7.2034	5.9878	5.5390	5.1632	4.9975	34
35	9.8293	9.1566	8.5717	8.0599	7.6091	7.2098	5.9898	5.5402	5.1639	4.9980	35
36	9.8552	9.1755	8.5856	8.0700	7.6166	7.2153	5.9915	5.5411	5.1644	4.9984	36
37	9.8786	9.1924	8.5979	8.0790	7.6231	7.2201	5.9929	5.5419	5.1649	4.9987	37
38	9.8996	9.2075	8.6087	8.0868	7.6288	7.2242	5.9941	5.5426	5.1652	4.9990	38
39	9.9186	9.2210	8.6183	8.0937	7.6338	7.2278	5.9951	5.5431	5.1655	4.9992	39
40	9.9357	9.2330	8.6268	8.0997	7.6380	7.2309	5.9959	5.5435	5.1657	4.9993	40

ASSIGNMENT MATERIAL

CASES

CA–1 Report Preparation—Insuring the Basketball Coach

A very successful basketball coach has been able to achieve success without incurring sanctions from the NCAA. The coach has already won two national championships in his eight years at the University. Additionally, his teams have appeared in the final four six times. The alumni have proposed a scheme to help keep the coach at the current school. If he remains in his present position ten more years without being sanctioned by the NCAA, he will receive $1,000,000 cash.

1. Nine individual alumni have agreed to participate in the plan and want to know how much will be required to contribute today to pay their proportionate share.
2. Three of the nine want to participate but because of cash flow problems need to know if there are any alternatives available.

Required: Prepare a report to the alumni outlining the requirements for their participation. Include in the report any assumptions made in calculating the amounts, and provide several alternative donation schedules that the alumni may examine.

CA–2 Report Preparation—Retirement Problem

A self-employed accountant doing mainly tax practice and write-up work wishes to retire at the age of 57. The accountant's present age is 27. The current rate of inflation indicates that $100,000 per year will be necessary to live in the life-style desired. Family history suggests that he is likely to attain an age of 87.

Required:

A. Determine the amount of money necessary to be accumulated by age 57, along with the assumptions used in the determination.

B. Prepare a report in which several alternative plans suggest different levels of funding and retirement benefits. Indicate the assumptions made for the different plans.

CA–3 Financing a New Auto Acquisition

You need a new automobile in your line of work, and you are comparing two alternative means of financing the acquisition. The first alternative is to borrow from your company credit union. The credit union will lend the full purchase price, $15,000, less a $1,000 down payment. The loan would be repaid over the next 36 months at $445.20 per month with the last payment being $445.05.

Before the loan can be approved, your down payment must be available, but you have $1,200 in the bank at the present time. The other alternative is to lease the car from an automobile agency over a five-year period. The lease will require equal monthly payments of $294 with the last payment $296. At the end of the lease, you will be able to purchase the car for $1,000 or return it to the dealership.

Required:

A. What is the rate of interest for each alternative?

B. Which alternative would you choose, and why?

QUESTIONS

QA–1 What is meant by the time value of money?

QA–2 What types of problems require the use of the time-value concepts for solution?

QA–3 Identify the components that are necessary in determining the time value of money.

QA–4 What is the difference between simple and compound interest?

QA–5 What is the effective interest rate?

QA–6 What is the effective interest rate in each of the following:

- **a.** A loan of $100 for which you pay $110 is repaid at the end of one year?
- **b.** A note payable due in one year in the amount of $100 that has been discounted by the lender at 10%?
- **c.** A note payable due in nine months in the amount of $110 for which $100 was received?

QA–7 Why would interest rates change from one period to the next?

QA–8 The following values are taken from the tables in the exhibits in this chapter. In each case the number of periods and the interest rate are the same. Identify the appropriate Table for each, and explain what the table values mean.

- **a.** 2.5937
- **b.** 15.9374
- **c.** 0.3855
- **d.** 6.1446
- **e.** 6.7590
- **f.** 17.5312

QA–9 What is the interest rate and the number of periods used to compound interest in each of the following:

- **a.** $100 invested at 12% for four years compounded annually.
- **b.** $100 invested at 12% for four years compounded semiannually.
- **c.** $100 invested at 12% for four years compounded quarterly.
- **d.** $100 invested at 12% for four years compounded monthly.

QA–10 What is the difference between the present value of 1 and the future value of 1? How are they related?

QA–11 The present value of 1 due at the end of 10 years at 16% interest is .2267. What is the future value of 1 for the same conditions?

QA–12 What is an annuity? What is the difference between an annuity due and an ordinary annuity?

QA–13 John has determined that he needs $100,000 at the end of 20 years. He believes that he can obtain an average rate of return on his investments of 8%. How much must he invest at the end of each of the 20 years to obtain that amount?

QA–14 A woman recently won $10,000,000 in the Kentucky lottery to be paid in 20 equal annual amounts with the first payment received immediately. If she would accept a 10% discount rate, what would be the present value of the lottery payments?

EXERCISES

EA–1 Simple and Compound Interest

Assume a loan in the amount of $10,000 with a 12% stated interest rate. The total amount of principal and interest is to be repaid in one lump sum at the end of two years. What is the total amount paid under the following assumptions?

- **A.** Simple interest is used.
- **B.** Interest is compounded annually.
- **C.** Interest is compounded semiannually.

EA–2 Effective Interest

Use the information contained in EA–1 and determine the effective annual interest rate under each condition.

EA–3 Future Values

Assume that you invest $5,000 immediately and another $5,000 at the end of 5 years. Calculate the amount at the end of five years under the following conditions:

A. Interest is 8% compounded annually for 5 years.
B. Interest is 8% compounded quarterly for five years.

EA–4 Present Values

Suppose you win a $1,000,000 lottery to be paid in 20 equal installments, with the first installment paid immediately. Determine the present value of the winnings assuming the following discount rates:

A. 10% discount rate.
B. 8% discount rate.
C. 12% discount rate.

EA–5 Unknown Investment Periods

Johnson needs $40,000 to be available sometime in the future. Determine the number of periods it will take to accumulate $40,000 assuming the following investment annuities: (Assume ordinary annuity.)

A. $5,184 is invested at 10%.
B. $2,108 is invested at 8%.
C. $1,249 is invested at 25%.

EA–6 Unknown Interest Rates

Determine the interest rate needed to provide $1,000,000. (Assume an annuity due.)

A. $75,719 invested annually for ten years and interest compounded annually.
B. $132,705 invested annually for five years and interest compounded annually.

EA–7 Future Value of Ordinary Annuity

Determine the future value of the following investments made at the end of the year.

A. $2,000 semiannual deposits at 10% per annum compounded semiannually for 4 years.
B. $4,000 annual deposits at 12% per annum compounded annually for 4 years.
C. $1,000 quarterly deposits at 8% per annum compounded quarterly for 4 years.

EA–8 Future Values of Annuity Due

Determine the future value of the following investments made at the beginning of each year.

A. $2,000 semiannual deposits at 10% per annum compounded semiannually for four years.
B. $4,000 annual deposits at 12% per annum compounded annually for four years.
C. $1,000 quarterly deposits at 8% per annum compounded quarterly for four years.

EA–9 Determining Annuity Payments

Determine the periodic payments necessary at the end of each period to settle (pay in full) the following loans (Assume ordinary annuity.)

A. $10,000 at 8% interest compounded annually with annual payments over 10 years.
B. $10,000 at 8% interest compounded semiannually with semiannual payments over 10 years.

EA–10 Determining Annuity Payments

Determine the periodic payments necessary at the beginning of each period to settle (pay in full) the following loans. (Assume annuity due.)

A. $10,000 at 8% interest compounded annually with annual payments over 10 years.
B. $10,000 at 8% interest compounded semiannually with semiannual payments over 10 years.

EA–11 Determining Ordinary Annuity

Calculate the end-of-period investments necessary for the following:

A. $400,000 retirement fund at the end of 2 years with monthly payments invested at 12% per annum.
B. $1,200 at the end of 2 years with quarterly payments invested at 20% per annum.
C. $1,200,000 building fund at the end of 5 years invested at 16% per annum with semiannual payments.

EA–12 Determining Annuity Due

Find the periodic investment necessary for the following: (Assume beginning-of-period deposits.)

A. $400,000 retirement fund at the end of 2 years with monthly payments invested at 12% per annum.
B. $1,200 at the end of 2 years with quarterly payments invested at 20% per annum.
C. $1,200,000 building fund at the end of 5 years invested at 16% per annum with semiannual payments.

EA–13 Present Value of Ordinary Annuity

Determine the original price of the following items. (Assume ordinary annuity.)

A. $47.07 monthly payments for two years with 12% per annum interest compounded monthly.
B. $4,492.56 quarterly payments for five years at 16% interest per annum compounded quarterly.

EA–14 Present Values of Annuity Due

Determine the original price of the following items. The periodic payment plan requires the first payment made at the beginning of the period as a down payment.

A. $93.21 monthly payments for two years with 12% per annum interest compounded monthly.
B. $1,475.04 quarterly payments for five years at 16% interest compounded quarterly.

EA–15 Bond Investment

United Companies purchased $100,000 par value bonds of Shaw Industries on July 1, 1997. The bonds mature on June 30, 2007, and pay interest on June 30 and December

effective I.R. yield

31 at an annual rate of 10%. The current market rate of interest is 8%. What was the purchase price of the bonds for United Companies?

EA–16 Bond Issue

Intel Corp. issues $10 million face value bonds on January 1, 1997. The bonds are 20-year bonds and pay interest annually on December 31 at the rate of 12%.

Required: Calculate the proceeds of the issue if the current market rate of interest is

A. 10%
B. 12%
C. 14%

PROBLEMS

PA–1 Future Values

Assume $200,000 of surplus cash is invested for five years at 12% per annum interest. Calculate the fund balance assuming interest on the investment is compounded:

A. Annually.
B. Semiannually.

PA–2 Future Values

You have recommended that your company invest $200,000 of surplus cash for a duration of two years at 12% per annum interest.

Required: Prepare a schedule indicating the fund balance at the end of each year assuming interest on the investment is compounded:

A. Annually.
B. Semiannually.
C. Prepare the journal entries at the end of each year for parts A and B.

PA–3 Present Values

Ajax Company needs $500,000 for plant expansion at the beginning of 2001. Assume that Ajax can obtain a 12% return. Determine the amount that needs to be invested now (the beginning of 1997) under the following conditions.

A. Interest is compounded annually.
B. Interest is compounded semiannually.

PA–4 Present Values

Becker Company estimates that it will require $800,000 for replacement of machinery two years from this date. Becker currently can obtain a 10% return on invested funds. Determine the amount that needs to be invested now under the following conditions.

A. Interest is compounded annually.
B. Interest is compounded semiannually.

PA–5 Finding Unknown Variables

Determine the unknown variable for each of the following cases:

A. You invest $20,000 in a trust fund for your one-year-old child to attend college. If an average yield of 10% is expected, what will be the balance when your child is 18 years old?

B. Your company wants to have a $2,000,000 retirement fund balance at the end of 30 years. You estimate an average rate of return of 8% over the 30-year period. What amount should be invested today?

C. Your company wants to have a $2,000,000 retirement fund and will invest $199,665 at the end of this year and each year thereafter. At 8%, how many years will it take to reach the stated goal?

D. Assume the same facts as in (C), but the first deposit is at the beginning of the year.

PA–6 Finding Unknown Variables

Determine the unknown variable for each of the following scenarios.

A. You invest $20,000 in a trust fund for your one-year-old child to attend college. The balance is estimated to be $185,530 when your child is 18 years old. What is the estimated annually compounded interest?

B. Your company wants to have a $2,000,000 retirement fund balance. If it invests $222,612 at the end of each year at 10%, how many years will it take to reach the stated goal?

C. Assume the same basic information as in part B, except the first deposit is at the beginning of the year.

PA–7 Present Value of a Single Sum and an Annuity

The chief financial officer is accumulating information for a bond issue. The market rate of return demanded in the relevant risk class is 10%. The bond issue will be $1,000,000, with a life of 10 years and interest paid semiannually.

Required:

A. If at the date of issue, the market interest rate is 12%, how much will be received for the entire bond issue?

B. If at the date of issue the market rate is only 8%, how much will be received for the entire issue?

PA–8 Sinking Fund Requirements

Refer to the bonds issued in PA–7. Assume that a sinking fund is established to retire the bonds at the end of the 10 years by making annual deposits to the fund.

Required: Determine the annual deposits necessary at the end of each period under the following assumptions:

A. An average rate of return of 8% compounded annually can be earned during the life of the bonds.

B. An average rate of return of 10% compounded annually can be earned during the life of the bonds.

C. The deposits will earn 8% compounded annually for the first 5 years and 10% compounded annually thereafter.

PA–9 Present-Value Asset Purchase

Assume ordinary annuities. The estimated net cash inflows from investing in an asset with an estimated life of eight years appear below. Ignore income tax considerations, and assume all cash flows occur at the end of the year.

YEAR	NET CASH INFLOW	YEAR	NET CASH INFLOW
1	$20,000	5	$30,000
2	$20,000	6	$30,000
3	$20,000	7	$40,000
4	$30,000	8	$25,000

Required: Calculate the maximum amount that would be paid for the asset under the following assumptions:

A. An 8% return is required.
B. A 12% return is required.

PA–10 Finding Interest Rates

Today is your lucky day! You receive notice that you have inherited $75,000 and will receive the cash via special messenger tomorrow. After the usual dreaming of fast cars and vacations, you decide the best course of action would be to invest the entire sum until after graduation, 4 years from now. The following alternative investments are available.

1. 10% compounded annually.
2. 8% compounded semiannually.
3. 8% compounded quarterly.

Required:

A. What is the effective rate of interest in each case?
B. Assume that you invest $25,000 in each, what would be the annual rate of return?
C. If the money is invested for four years at 8% compounded quarterly, what amount will be available at the end of four years?

PA–11 Lease-Purchase

An asset may be purchased for $100,000 or leased for five years. The lease terms require a payment of $22,292 per year, with the first payment made immediately. The residual value of the asset after five years is $10,000, and the lease agreement allows the purchase of the asset at that price. If the asset is purchased, a down payment of $10,000 is required with the balance financed at 10% for five years.

Required: Determine whether the asset should be leased or purchased in each of the following cases:

A. The objective is to minimize annual cash outflows.
B. The objective is to minimize interest costs.

PA–12 Retirement

Jane Jackson will be 21 tomorrow. Jackson wants to retire at the age of 51 and expects to live until 71.

Required: For each of the following situations, calculate the annual deposits required by Jackson to fund her retirement needs.

A. She wants to have $60,000 a year available at the beginning of the year for each year of retirement. She expects to earn an average rate of 8% over the entire time, and plans to make deposits to the fund at the beginning of each period, starting on her birthday (tomorrow).

B. Assume the same facts as in part A but interest is expected to be 12%.

PA–13 Retirement Proceeds

John Dorr will retire on August 1 of this year, after 33 years with RMT Corp. Dorr started working for RMT at the age of 17 before finishing high school. Based on current mortality tables, his average life expectancy is 78 years of age. Dorr has spoken with the employee-benefits officer, Sharon Payne, who has given him the following options for his retirement monies:

A. A lump-sum payment in the amount of $400,000. However, no other payments would be forthcoming.

B. A yearly amount of $40,000, guaranteed for 20 years and beginning one year after retirement, with no other payments after the final payment. If Dorr dies before 20 years, the payments will revert to his estate.

C. A yearly amount of $30,000, guaranteed for the rest of his life and beginning one year after retirement. The payments will end at his death.

Required: Evaluate each of the retirement options, assuming that the current rate of interest is 10%. Which is more desirable?

B

Earnings per Share for Complex Capital Structures

Learning Objectives

After studying this appendix, you should be able to:

1. Calculate diluted earnings per share for corporations with convertible securities in its capital structure.
2. Calculate diluted earnings per share for corporations with options and warrants in its capital structure.
3. Calculate diluted earnings per share for corporations with contingent issue agreements.
4. Calculate diluted earnings per share for corporations with multiple potential diluters.
5. Demonstrate the effect of dilutive securities on earnings per share, net income, return on assets, and return on shareholders' equity.

Earnings per share (EPS) for simple capital structures is discussed in the main body of this text. A **simple capital structure** is one in which no financial securities or contingencies exist that could result in the issuance of additional shares of common stock. Exhibit B–1 provides an example of basic EPS for firms with simple capital structures.

EXHIBIT B–1
Basic EPS

Scotty, Inc., reports 1997 net earnings of $400,000. The company has 60,000 shares of $5 par, 7% cumulative preferred stock outstanding for the entire reporting period. The dividend preference for this stock is $21,000 (60,000 shares × $5 par × 0.07). During 1997, Scotty (1) began the year with 120,000 common shares outstanding, (2) issued 30,000 shares on April 1, and (3) purchased treasury stock of 9,000 shares on September 1. As shown below, weighted average common shares outstanding for the year were 139,500 shares. Thus, basic EPS is:

$$\text{Basic EPS} = \frac{\underset{\$400{,}000}{\text{Net Income}} - \underset{\$21{,}000}{\text{Preferred Dividends}}}{139{,}500 \text{ Weighted Average Shares}} = \$2.72$$

DATE	TRANSACTIONS	SHARES	×	WEIGHT	=	WEIGHTED SHARES
1/1/97	Beginning shares	120,000	×	12/12	=	120,000
4/1/97	Issuance	30,000	×	9/12	=	22,500
9/1/97	Treasury purchase	(9,000)	×	4/12	=	(3,000)
						139,500

IN PRACTICE—GENERAL

The Usefulness of EPS

Dr. John W. Coughlan states that "it is EPS and the related price/earnings ratio —not income, not assets, not equity, and not any other accounting magnitudes— that are the most widely reported numbers in the investment services. . ."

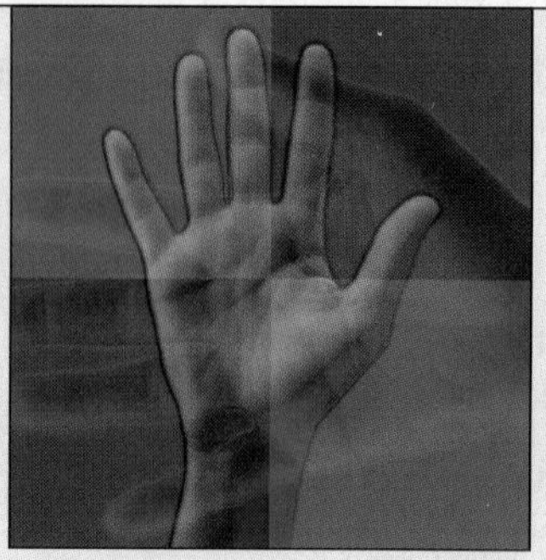

"Yet, [t]he preparation of earnings per share (EPS) disclosures for public companies with complex capital structures is much more complicated than dividing income by outstanding common shares. Much of this complexity results from the efforts of standard setters to make EPS disclosures reflect the effects of potentially dilutive securities. A critical evaluation of current EPS disclosures suggests that they are of questionable usefulness."

Sources: J. W. Coughlan, "Fully Diluted Arithmetic," *Management Accounting,* October 1991, p. 45; R. D. Mautz, Jr., and T. J. Hogan, "Earnings per Share Reporting: Time for an Overhaul?" *Accounting Horizons,* September 1989, p. 21.

Basic EPS is also the starting point for reporting EPS for firms with complex capital structures.[1] A **complex capital structure** results when a corporation has convertible bonds, convertible preferred stock, stock warrants and options, or certain other contingent issuance agreements. For firms with complex capital structures, the potentially dilutive effect (i.e., the potential reduction of EPS) of the issuance of additional common shares must be considered.

COMPLEX CAPITAL STRUCTURES

DILUTED EPS

Whenever a corporation has securities or contingencies that could result in the issuance of additional shares of common stock, dilution or reduced residual equity interests per common share is a possibility. Basic EPS does not reflect the impact of possible dilution. Therefore, the recent SFAS No. 128 requires that firms with complex capital structures consider the impact of such potential dilution and also report **diluted EPS** on a *pro forma* (that is, as if shares were issued) basis as well as **basic EPS**, which is determined on a historical basis. Diluted EPS considers all securities and contingencies that would reduce EPS if the contingent shares of common stock had been issued.

Each security or contingent issuance is deemed as either potentially dilutive or antidilutive. It is considered potentially **dilutive** if treating the contingent common shares *as if* they were issued reduces EPS for continuing operations. If potentially dilutive, it is considered for diluted EPS. When it is **antidilutive** (that is, not potentially dilutive), it is *not* used to calculate diluted EPS.

Exhibit B–2 summarizes the procedures for reporting EPS. Use this exhibit as a guide to help clarify the following presentation. The guidelines for determining potential dilution depend upon the nature of the security or contingency. Essentially, there are three main types: (1) convertible securities (such as convertible preferred stock and convertible bonds), (2) common stock options and warrants, and (3) contingent stock-issuance agreements. The existence of each is potentially dilutive if its inclusion in an EPS calculation would result in a number less than basic EPS.

CONVERTIBLE SECURITIES

Calculate diluted earnings per share for corporations with convertible securities in its capital structure.

Convertible preferred stock and convertible bonds are securities that may be exchanged or converted into common stock.[2]

Convertible Preferred Stock. The determination of whether convertible securities are dilutive is based upon a "what if" scenario in which these securities are assumed converted into common stock and are no longer preferred stock. The assumed conversion recognizes that the securities could actually be converted in the following year and that EPS figures are used primarily for projective purposes. The assumed conversion presumably assists such projections. This **"if converted" method** examines the impact on EPS of the hypothetical common shares of stock.

[1]The term simple EPS, historical EPS or base EPS are also used for basic EPS.

[2]Accounting for convertible preferred stock and its conversion is discussed in Chapter 18, and accounting for convertible bonds is covered in Chapter 14. The focus in this appendix is not on the accounting procedures for these securities but on their impact on diluted EPS.

EXHIBIT B–2 Summary of EPS Calculations

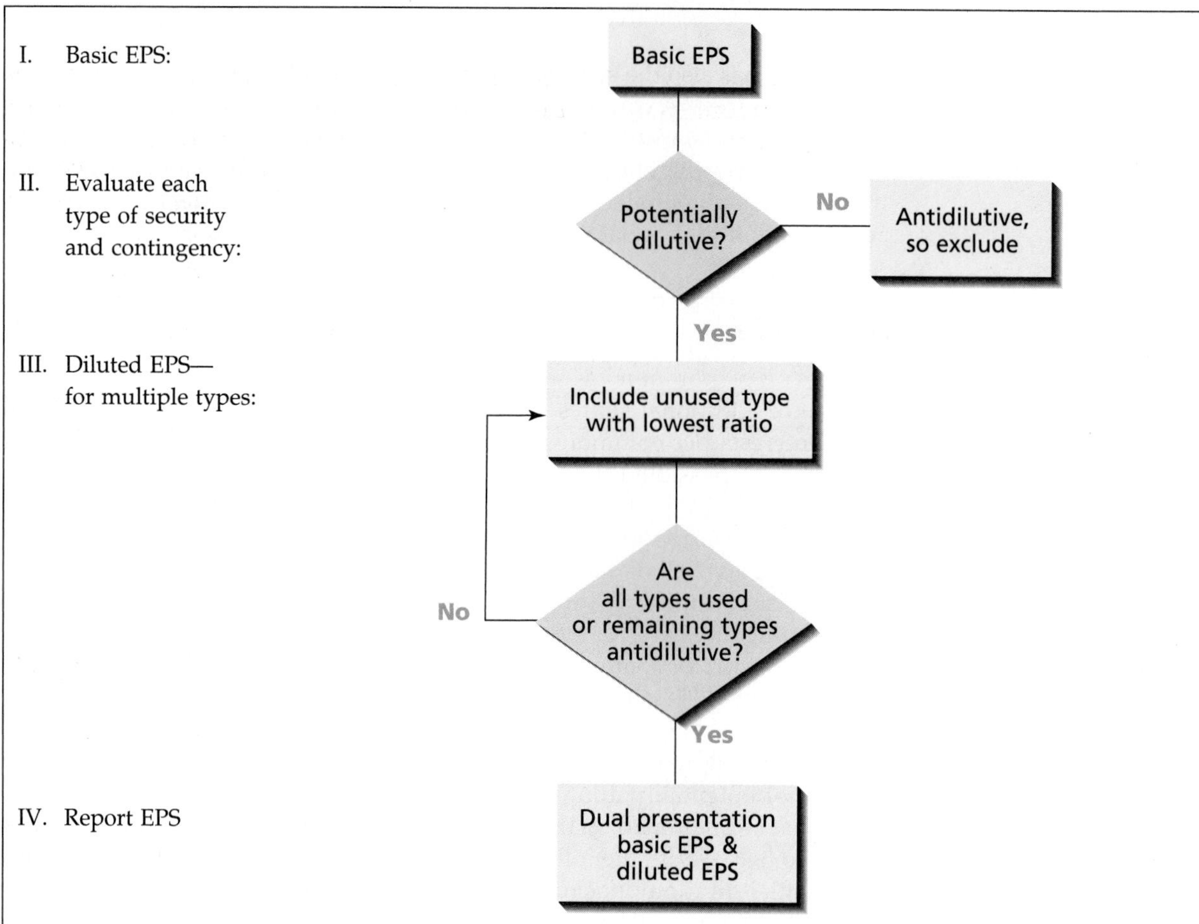

I. Determine basic EPS. Subtract preferred dividends from net income and divide by weighted average common shares.

II. Based upon the chart below, determine which securities and contingencies are potentially dilutive.

TYPE	POTENTIALLY DILUTIVE?	NUMERATOR EFFECT	DENOMINATOR EFFECT
Convertible securities	If converted method: Ratio < basic EPS	Preferred dividends or after-tax bond interest expense	Number of possible shares of common
Options and warrants	Treasury stock method: Average market price > exercise price	-0-	Incremental shares based upon average market price
Other contingent issuance agreements	If stock issuance would reduce EPS: Ratio < basic EPS	Any unmet earnings contingency	Number of contingent common shares

III. Determine diluted EPS. For multiple types of potential diluters, begin including the type with the lowest positive ratio of the numerator and denominator effects. Then, iteratively add types with the next lowest ratio, continuing until all types are used or all unused types become antidilutive.

IV. Report dual presentation of basic and diluted EPS.

For example, assume that each share of the 60,000 shares of preferred stock for Scotty, Inc., in Exhibit B–1 is convertible into two shares of common stock. If converted at the beginning of the year, the hypothetical 120,000 shares of common stock would have been outstanding rather than the actual 60,000 convertible preferred shares.[3] Further, since there would be no preferred stock outstanding, there would be no preferred dividend preference of $21,000. This dividend preference was already subtracted, however, when determining basic EPS.

To adjust basic EPS for the potential impact of convertible securities, we must consider both a numerator and denominator effect. For the convertible preferred of Scotty, Inc., the numerator effect is the presumed elimination of $21,000 in preferred dividends, and the denominator effect is the 120,000 additional weighted shares of common. As a convenient benchmark, if the ratio of the numerator effect to the denominator effect ($21,000/120,000 shares = 0.175) is less than basic EPS ($2.72), then it is potentially dilutive. If the ratio equals or exceeds basic EPS, the security is antidilutive and may be disregarded in determining EPS.

Exhibit B–3 summarizes the example for Scotty, Inc., with convertible preferred stock. Since the security is potentially dilutive (0.175 < 2.72), its impact would be used to determine diluted EPS of $1.54.

EXHIBIT B–3
Diluted EPS with Convertible Preferred Stock

Assume the same facts as described in Exhibit B–1. Also assume that each share of the 60,000 shares of preferred stock for Scotty, Inc., is convertible into two shares of common stock.

$$\text{Basic EPS} = \frac{\overbrace{\$400{,}000 - \$21{,}000}^{\$379{,}000}}{139{,}500 \text{ shares}} = \$2.72$$

Numerator effect = $21,000 preferred dividends

Denominator effect = 60,000 preferred shares × 2
= 120,000 potential common shares

TYPE	NUMERATOR EFFECT	DENOMINATOR EFFECT	RATIO
Convertible preferred	$21,000	120,000 shares	0.175

$$\text{Diluted EPS} = \frac{\$379{,}000 + \$21{,}000}{139{,}500 + 120{,}000} = \$1.54$$

[3]Consistent with the weighted average common shares concept, the hypothetical shares are weighted by the length of time they could have been outstanding during the reporting period. Since Scotty's convertible preferred was outstanding for the entire year, the potential common shares are weighted in their entirety. If the preferred shares had been just issued October 1, 1997, then the hypothetical common shares would be weighted by 3/12. Also, for actual conversions to common stock within a reporting period, refer to Curtis L. DeBerg's article "Earnings per Share and the Actual Conversion of Convertible Securities," *Journal of Accounting Education*, Spring 1990, pp. 137–151.

Convertible Bonds. Convertible bonds potentially affect EPS in a manner similar to convertible preferred stock. If convertible bonds are converted to common stock and no longer held as bonds (i.e., debt), the issuing corporation will not have the interest expense associated with the debt. However, if the company does not have this interest expense, it will have higher pretax earnings and thus larger income tax expense. Therefore, the *numerator effect* in computing EPS is not the full interest expense of the bonds, but the net after-tax interest expense (that is, the expense reduced by the potential extra taxes). Recall from Chapter 14 that interest expense must consider amortization of any discount or premium, so the expense is not necessarily the cash interest paid for the year. The *denominator effect* is the number of shares of common that would be issued if the bonds were converted.

To illustrate, assume that Scotty's preferred stock is not convertible, but the company has convertible bonds and that the conversion of these bonds would result in the issuance of 25,000 shares of common stock (denominator effect). Suppose also that Scotty's 1997 income statement reports $70,000 as interest expense for these bonds and that Scotty has a 30% marginal income tax rate. The after-tax rate then is 70% (100% − 30%), and the numerator effect for these bonds is the net after-tax interest expense of $49,000 ($70,000 × 0.70).

Since the ratio of these effects ($49,000/25,000 shares = 1.96) is less than basic EPS ($2.72), the convertible bonds are potentially dilutive, and the inclusion of their effect, as shown in Exhibit B–4, reduces diluted EPS to $2.60.

Calculate diluted earnings per share for corporations with options and warrants in its capital structure.

OPTIONS AND WARRANTS

Common stock options and **common stock warrants** grant the holder the right to purchase shares of stock for a guaranteed exercise price during a defined period of time. A principal difference between convertible securities and options or warrants is that the opportunity to obtain common stock is the

EXHIBIT B–4
Diluted EPS with Convertible Bonds

Assume the same facts as described in Exhibit B–1. Also assume the company has $875,000 in 8% convertible bonds issued for par. Conversion of these bonds would result in the issuance of 25,000 shares of common stock. Scotty's 1997 income statement reports $70,000 as interest expense for these bonds, and Scotty has a 30% marginal income tax rate.

$$\text{Basic EPS} = \frac{\$379{,}000}{139{,}500 \text{ shares}} = \$2.72$$

Numerator effect = $70,000 × (1.00 − 0.30) = $49,000

Denominator effect = 25,000 potential common shares

TYPE	NUMERATOR EFFECT	DENOMINATOR EFFECT	RATIO
Convertible bonds	$49,000	25,000 shares	1.96

$$\text{Diluted EPS} = \frac{\$379{,}000 + \$49{,}000}{139{,}500 + 25{,}000} = \$2.60$$

sole economic value of options or warrants. The opportunity to obtain common stock through conversion is only part of the economic value of convertible securities; the preferred stock or debt itself also has value. Further, the exercise of options or warrants requires investors to pay an exercise price to the issuing company in order to obtain common stock.

As a general guideline, options or warrants are considered potentially dilutive if it is reasonable to expect them to be exercised (that is, used to purchase common shares). According to current reporting standards, this reasonable expectation occurs when the exercise price is below the average market price for a share of common stock.

On a pro forma basis, if options or warrants are exercised and additional shares of common stock are issued, what would be the impact upon EPS? The potential exercise of options or warrants generally does not affect earnings; that is, there is typically no *numerator* effect. However, additional shares of common stock would be issued, so there is a *denominator* effect.

Based upon the guidelines for convertible securities, the denominator effect would seem to be the number of common shares that would be issued if options or warrants were exercised. However, remember that diluted EPS is a pro forma number for projective purposes (and thus not based entirely upon actual historical events). Pro forma, or "what if," analysis may consider not only the additional shares that would be issued if options or warrants are exercised but also what might be done with the funds raised when exercised.

Current standards take this extra pro forma step and require that a **treasury stock method** be applied to options and warrants. This controversial method assumes that funds raised from the exercise of options or warrants (that is, exercise price times quantity exercised) would be used to acquire treasury stock. Thus, the denominator effect is *not* the total number of shares that would be issued through exercise, but instead, it is the incremental shares issued—the excess of the number of shares issued compared to the number of shares repurchased with the proceeds.

Exhibit B–5 illustrates the method. Assume that a company has issued 12,000 warrants, each granting the bearer the right to purchase a share of common stock for $45 (the exercise price). Assume also that the average market price for the stock is $50 per share.[4] Since the market price exceeds the exercise price, the warrants are potentially dilutive. If all 12,000 warrants are exercised and 12,000 shares of stock issued, the company will receive $540,000 (see "Assumed proceeds" portion of Exhibit B–5). At the average market price of $50, this $540,000 could be used to repurchase 10,800 shares as treasury stock. Thus, the denominator effect is the 1,200 incremental shares (12,000 − 10,800).

An efficient way to determine the number of incremental shares is to multiply the number of shares that would be issued by the percentage of the market price in excess of the exercise price. For our example here, the 12,000 shares that would be issued is multiplied by the 10% by which the market price exceeds the exercise price:

$$\frac{\$50 - \$45}{\$50} = 10\%$$

[4]The use of an average market price for the full reporting period obviously presumes that the option to exercise existed for the full period. If not, an average market price for the partial period of the exercise option would be appropriate, and incremental shares would be weighted by this partial period.

EXHIBIT B–5
Diluted EPS with Options or Warrants

Assume the same facts as described in Exhibit B–1. Also assume the company has issued 12,000 warrants with each granting the bearer the right to purchase a share of common stock for $45 (i.e., the exercise price). The average market price for the stock is $50.

$$\text{Basic EPS} = \frac{\$379{,}000}{139{,}500 \text{ shares}} = \$2.72$$

Assumed proceeds if warrants exercised	12,000 shares × $45	= $540,000
Treasury shares repurchased	$540,000/$50	= 10,800 shares
Incremental shares	12,000 − 10,800	= 1,200 shares

TYPE	NUMERATOR EFFECT	DENOMINATOR EFFECT	RATIO
Warrants	-0-	1,200 shares	-0-

$$\text{Diluted EPS} = \frac{\$379{,}000 + 0}{139{,}500 + 1{,}200} = \$2.69$$

The result is 1,200 incremental shares. Note that market price, not exercise price, is used in the denominator.

If an investor were to exercise warrants when the exercise price exceeded the market price (an unlikely event), more treasury shares could be purchased than were issued from the exercise of the warrants. This would decrease shares in the EPS calculation, and thus increase EPS. Therefore, this scenario is anti-dilutive, and the warrant's effect would not be used to calculate diluted EPS.

Employee Stock Options. The treasury stock method also applies to stock-based compensation, such as employee stock options and stock appreciation rights. However, the assumed proceeds include not only the amounts expected if options were exercised, but also the amount of unamortized compensation cost (i.e., those costs attributable to future service and not recognized as expense). Also included are tax benefits, if any, that would be credited to paid-in capital if options were exercised (i.e., benefits for excess of actual compensation deduction allowed in excess of previously recognized compensation). The increased assumed proceeds would increase the treasury shares assumed purchased, which in turn would reduce the incremental shares used to calculate EPS. Chapter 18 discusses stock-based compensation in detail.

3
Calculate diluted earnings per share for corporations with contingent issue agreements.

CONTINGENT ISSUANCE AGREEMENTS

Corporations may have contingent common stock issuance agreements other than convertible securities, options, and warrants. For example, the terms of a merger might include an agreement to issue additional shares when earnings meet or exceed a certain level.

Contingent issuance agreements are potentially dilutive and are considered in calculating diluted EPS if the issuance of common stock would reduce EPS below basic EPS. When an agreement stipulates that a conditional level of earnings must be met, then at least this level of earnings must be assumed in calculating EPS.

For example, imagine that Scotty, Inc., had agreed to issue an additional 10,000 shares when annual earnings first reached $500,000. Since the actual earnings this period were $400,000, assuming attainment of $500,000 would result in a numerator effect of an additional $100,000. With the denominator effect of 10,000 shares potentially issued, the ratio is $100,000/10,000 shares = $10. This is an example of potential antidilution because the $10 ratio exceeds Scotty's basic EPS of $2.72, and this agreement would not be used in calculating EPS. If, however, the agreement was potentially dilutive, it would be considered just like other potential diluters.

MULTIPLE POTENTIAL DILUTERS

4

Calculate diluted earnings per share for corporations with multiple potential diluters.

When a corporation has more than one type of potentially dilutive security or contingent issuance agreement, each must be considered. Diluted EPS must be determined using the combination of securities and contingencies that results in the most conservative, or lowest, EPS amount. A security may appear dilutive when first compared to basic EPS and yet be antidilutive after the impact of other, more dilutive types of securities and contingencies are considered.

To illustrate, assume now that Scotty, Inc. has *all* three types of potential diluters illustrated earlier in Exhibits B–3 through B–5. The potential impact of these are now included together in Exhibit B–6. To determine diluted EPS, we must find the combination that yields the lowest amount.

One approach is to begin including the impact of the type with the lowest positive ratio and then successively adding the type with next lowest ratio, continuing until any remaining types become antidilutive.[5] In Exhibit B–6, we

EXHIBIT B–6
Diluted EPS with Multiple Types of Potential Diluters

Assume the same facts as described in Exhibit B–1. Also assume the company has all three types of potential diluters illustrated in Exhibits B–3 through B–5.

$$\text{Basic EPS} = \frac{\$379{,}000}{139{,}500 \text{ shares}} = \$2.72$$

TYPE	NUMERATOR EFFECT	DENOMINATOR EFFECT	RATIO	USE?
Convertible preferred	$21,000	120,000	0.175	Yes
Convertible bonds	$49,000	25,000	1.96	No
Warrants	0	1,200	0	Yes

(continued)

[5] S. Davidson and R. L. Weil, "A Shortcut in Computing Earnings Per Share," *The Journal of Accountancy*, December 1975, pp. 45–47.

EXHIBIT B–6
(Concluded)

Sequence of Inclusion in Diluted EPS:

1. Use the warrants (ratio = 0):

$$\text{Diluted EPS} = \frac{\$379{,}000 + 0}{139{,}500 + 1{,}200} = \$2.69$$

2. Use the convertible preferred stock (ratio = 0.175)

$$\text{Diluted EPS} = \frac{\$379{,}000 + 0 + \$21{,}000}{139{,}500 + 1{,}200 + 120{,}000} = \$1.53$$

3. Do **not** use the convertible bonds, as they are now antidilutive (ratio = $1.96)

Amounts to Report:

Basic EPS = $2.72
Diluted EPS = $1.53

begin with the stock warrants since their ratio is zero. Inclusion of the warrants lowers diluted EPS to $2.69. The next lowest ratio is for the convertible preferred stock. As shown, diluted EPS becomes $1.53.

At this point, the convertible bonds become antidilutive for diluted EPS, because the associated ratio of 1.96 is larger than diluted EPS of $1.53 as calculated to date. Thus, it is **not** used to calculate diluted EPS. Notice that a column was added in Exhibit B–6 to indicate whether each type of potential diluter was used (or not) in the diluted EPS calculation.

FINANCIAL ANALYSIS AND EARNINGS PER SHARE

Demonstrate the effect of dilutive securities on earnings per share, net income, return on assets, and return on shareholders' equity.

Earnings per share (EPS) is certainly one indicator of a company's current and prospective profitability. Despite controversy surrounding reporting requirements for complex capital structures, EPS remains a viable yardstick of performance used by many financial analysts. EPS figures are reported in such venerable advisory services as *Value Line* and *Moody's Investment Service.* Further, growth in EPS is an explicit goal of many corporate managers. EPS frequently is used in calculating two other financial indicators: a price-earnings ratio (P/E) and a dividend payout ratio. The P/E ratio is discussed in Chapter 18 and the dividend payout in Chapter 19.

The quality of any analysis based upon EPS is dependent upon the quality of EPS. Therefore, we next address criticisms of EPS reporting requirements.

CONTROVERSY ABOUT EPS

Naturally, all criticisms levied toward earnings as reported in accordance with GAAP are also applicable to EPS. We discuss interpretational issues related to earnings throughout the text, so they are not elaborated on here.

One controversy directly related to EPS focuses upon the use of the treasury stock method for options and warrants. The treasury stock method assumes that proceeds from exercise of options or warrants would be used to reacquire a company's own stock. Yet,

> Reacquisition by a company of its own stock, however, may not be possible, likely, or the best use of the proceeds from exercise. The opinion [APB No. 15] itself states that the treatment it prescribes isn't based on the assumption that the funds provided by exercise would actually be used in this manner.[6]

Using the treasury stock method softens the potential dilution of EPS because only an incremental number of shares rather than all shares assumed exercised are used.[7] Further, options and warrants are excluded from EPS calculations (that is, are considered antidilutive) when current market prices are less than the exercise price. But future, not current, market prices determine whether options or warrants are ultimately exercised.[8]

Thus, diluted EPS does not really reflect maximum potential dilution. Therefore, it does not reflect what it purports to measure—which cannot help but cast doubt on its usefulness.

SIMPLIFICATION AND IMPROVEMENT

The recent standard for EPS issued by the FASB, SFAS No. 128, greatly simplified the determination of EPS for firms with complex capital structures. Previously, GAAP required determination of two prospective EPS amounts: one called primary EPS, which purportedly represented a "more likely" scenario, and another called fully diluted EPS, which purportedly represented a "worst case" scenario. If these amounts were materially different from basic EPS, they were reported; otherwise, basic EPS was reported. Since the new standard was not issued until 1997, annual reports or 10ks prior to December 15, 1997, will likely report EPS based on the prior requirements.

IN PRACTICE—INTERNATIONAL

Joint Project by FASB and IASC

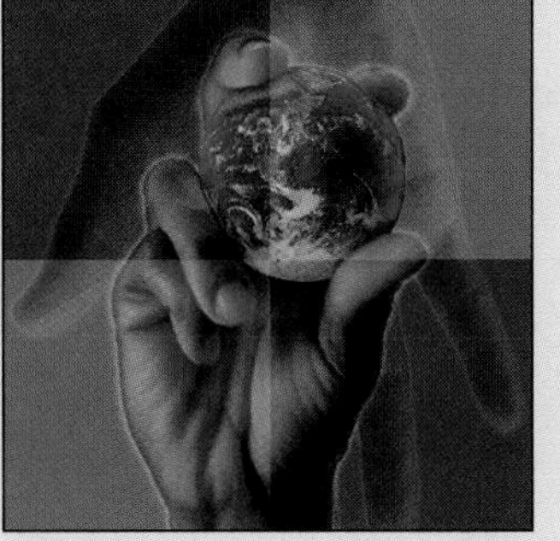

Both the FASB and the IASC are tackling the issue of earnings per share. For the FASB, the objective is to simplify the calculations and enhance international comparability. For financial information users, the result should be easier-to-understand performance data for enterprises of various nations.

The joint EPS project is part of the FASB's plan to become more active in international accounting matters.

Source: D. M. Blasch, J. Kelliher, and W. J. Read, "The FASB and the IASC Redeliberate EPS," *Journal of Accountancy,* February 1996, p. 43.

[6]L. W. Dudley, "A Critical Look at EPS," *Journal of Accountancy,* August 1985, p. 107.

[7]R. D. Mautz, Jr., and T. J. Hogan, "Earnings per Share Reporting: Time for an Overhaul?" *Accounting Horizons,* September 1989, p. 24.

[8]Dudley, p. 108.

After considerable controversy mainly focusing upon primary EPS concerning (1) arbitrary rules for determining which securities to include as part of primary EPS, (2) whether it truly resulted in a "more likely" scenario, and (3) the usefulness of primary EPS, the recent standard dropped it from reporting requirements. Except for some very minor differences, diluted EPS as currently required is the same as the previously required fully diluted EPS. Most professionals agree that the current requirement to report basic EPS, which provides a historical viewpoint, and also diluted EPS, which provides a more prospective viewpoint, not only simplifies, but improves current EPS reporting. Others, however, would argue for a more complete overhaul of EPS reporting requirements.

Footnote disclosure is another area of improved reporting required by the new standard. Among other things, the standard requires disclosure of a reconciliation between basic EPS and diluted EPS for both numerator and denominator effects. Thus, readers of financial statements can determine the impact of various convertible and contingent securities themselves.

END-OF-APPENDIX REVIEW

SUMMARY

Earnings per share, currently required of publicly held corporations, are popular financial performance indicators. When potential dilution due to convertible securities, options, warrants, and other contingent issuance agreements exists, firms with complex capital structures must display the dual presentation of basic EPS and diluted EPS. Although recently simplified, the guidelines for determining EPS are still fairly complex and procedural. These guidelines presume that EPS is primarily used for prospective purposes. However, whether the complex procedures improve EPS as a useful piece of information for prospective purposes is controversial.

KEY TERMS

antidilutive *B–3*
basic EPS *B–3*
common stock options *B–6*
common stock warrants *B–6*
complex capital structure *B–3*
diluted EPS *B–3*
dilutive *B–3*
"if converted" method *B–3*
simple capital structure *B–2*
treasury stock method *B–7*

ASSIGNMENT MATERIAL

CASES

CB–1 Discussion Case

Valley Oak Company began 1997 with 100,000 shares of common stock issued and outstanding. Throughout 1997, the company also had convertible bonds which may be converted into 100,000 shares of common stock. On December 31, 1997, Valley Oak completed a new public offering and issued another 100,000 shares of common stock. For 1997, the company's after-tax interest expense on the bonds was $40,000 and net income was $260,000.

Required:

A. Determine basic EPS and diluted EPS for 1997.

B. Imagine that the convertible bonds were converted to common stock on January 1, 1998, and that Valley Oak's revenues and expenses other than interest in 1998 were identical to 1997 (i.e., net income without the interest was $300,000). Determine basic EPS and diluted EPS for 1998.

C. When computing diluted EPS for 1997, discuss how the weighting of the shares already issued on December 31, 1997 compares to the weighting of shares not really issued but presumed issued for the convertible bonds. Do you agree with the weightings? Would you suggest any alternative weightings?

QUESTIONS

QB–1 Under what limited set of conditions is EPS appropriately calculated by dividing net income by the number of common shares outstanding at the end of the period?

QB–2 How are the numerator and denominator effects for convertible preferred stock determined?

QB–3 How is the numerator effect determined for convertible bonds issued at a discount or premium?

QB–4 For options and warrants, what pro forma assumptions are made to apply the treasury-stock method? How do these assumptions differ from the "if converted" method for convertible securities?

QB–5 Why are options or warrants considered antidilutive when their exercise price exceeds the market price of common stock?

QB–6 With multiple potential diluters, one might try to calculate diluted EPS considering all potential diluters together. Thus all numerator effects would be summed as would all denominator effects, and these two totals then used in the EPS calculation. This approach often yields a correct amount. What dangers are there to using a total approach like this rather than the iterative approach recommended in this chapter?

QB–7 What are criticisms regarding the usefulness of EPS?

QB–8 Do you think the recent changes for reporting EPS improves its usefulness? Why or why not?

EXERCISES

EB–1 Weighted Average Shares

Kessler, Inc., began 1997 with 900,000 common shares outstanding, and issued another 216,000 shares on August 1, 1997.

Required: What is the weighted-average number of shares outstanding for 1997?

EB–2 Weighted Average Shares

On January 1, 1997, Lola Corporation had 400,000 outstanding common shares. During 1997 it had a two-for-one stock split on July 1 and issued an additional 60,000 shares on October 1.

Required: Determine Lola's weighted-average shares outstanding for 1997.

EB–3 Basic EPS

On January 1, 1997, Maigh Daigh Company had outstanding 180,000 shares of $5 par value common stock and 60,000 shares of 5% cumulative, nonconvertible, $10 par value, preferred stock. During 1997 the company declared and paid $120,000 in total dividends; there were no preferred dividends in arrears. It also issued 6,000 common shares on July 1, 1997. Net income for the year was $396,000.

Required: Determine earnings per share.

EB–4 Basic EPS

Natalie Corporation has 1997 net income of $420,000. The company began the year with 300,000 outstanding common shares, and it issued a 10% common stock dividend on March 1, 1997. Natalie also paid $30,000 in yearly dividends on its nonconvertible preferred stock.

Required: What are Natalie's earnings per share?

EB–5 Convertible Preferred

Throughout 1997 Nash & Company had outstanding 100,000 shares of $5 par common stock and 15,000 shares of 8% convertible, $15 par, preferred stock. The preferred shares were issued for $20 per share, and each share of preferred is convertible into one share of common. Net income for 1997 was $433,000.

Required: Determine basic and diluted EPS.

EB–6 Convertible Preferred

Throughout 1997, Marsh Corp. had outstanding 60,000 shares of $1 par common stock and 20,000 shares of 5% convertible, $10 par, preferred stock. The preferred shares were issued for $12 per share, and each share of preferred is convertible into one share of common. Net income for 1997 was $250,000.

Required: Determine basic and diluted EPS.

EB–7 Convertible Preferred

The following summarizes Oscar Awards, Inc., contributed capital as of December 31, 1997:

9% Convertible preferred stock—$20 par (50,000 shares issued and outstanding)	$1,000,000
Additional paid-in capital, preferred	200,000
Common stock—$10 par (300,000 shares issued and outstanding)	3,000,000
Additional paid-in capital, common	1,200,000
Total contributed capital	$5,400,000

Oscar's net income for 1997 was $1,890,000. There were no stock transactions during 1997, but the company has paid dividends every year. Each share of preferred stock is convertible into two shares of common stock.

Required: Determine basic and diluted EPS.

EB–8 Convertible Bonds

During 1997, Palo Alto Company had 25,000 common shares outstanding as well as $500,000 in 6% convertible bonds issued for par. Each $1,000 bond is convertible into five shares of common stock. Net income for 1997 was $500,000, and the income tax rate is 30%.

Required: Determine basic and diluted EPS. (*Note:* Interest expense on bonds issued for par is merely the stated percentage of the stated value.)

EB–9 Convertible Bonds

During 1997, Palace Company had 1,000,000 common shares outstanding as well as $5,000,000 in 6% convertible bonds issued to yield 4%. Each $1,000 bond is convertible into two shares of common stock. Net income and interest expense for 1997 were $22,804,000 and $280,000, respectively. The income tax rate is 30%.

Required: Determine basic and diluted EPS.

EB–10 Convertible Bonds

On July 1, 1990, Quality Construction issued $2,000,000 in convertible bonds. These bonds were issued to yield 9% and are convertible into 10,000 shares of common stock. For the current year, 1997, Quality has interest expense for these bonds totaling $190,000. Net income for 1997 is $1,200,000, and there is a marginal income tax rate of 30%. Throughout 1997, the company had 120,000 shares of common stock outstanding.

Required:

A. Are the bonds potentially dilutive? Why or why not?
B. What amount(s) should Quality report as EPS for 1997?

EB–11 Options

Throughout 1997, Reliance, Inc., had outstanding 180,000 common stock options with an exercise price of $25. The market price of the common stock averaged $30 for 1997, and at the end of 1997, the price was $40.

Required: For these options, what incremental number of shares would be used to calculate diluted EPS?

EB–12 Options

Throughout 1997, Relativity, Inc., had outstanding 1,200,000 common stock options with an exercise price of $35. The market price of the common stock averaged $50 for 1997, and at the end of 1997, the price was $45.

Required: For these options, what incremental number of shares would be used to calculate diluted EPS?

EB–13 Warrants

During 1997, Sunrise Company had outstanding 100,000 shares of 6%, $20 par non-convertible, cumulative, preferred stock, 450,000 shares of $10 par common stock, and 75,000 common stock warrants with an exercise price of $15. Net income for 1997 was $870,000. The average market price of the common stock for 1997 was $20.

Required:

A. What EPS amount(s) should Sunrise report for 1997?
B. Would your answer change if the exercise price of the warrants was $25? If so, how?

EB–14 Warrants

During 1997, Sundown Company had outstanding 5,000,000 shares of $10 par common stock, and 500,000 common stock warrants with an exercise price of $44. Net income for 1997 was $12,00,000. The average market price of the common stock for 1997 was $50.

Required: Determine basic and diluted EPS.

EB–15 Employee Stock Options

Throughout 1997, New Relics, Inc., had outstanding 2,000,000 employee stock options with an exercise price of $30. The market price of the common stock averaged $40. Compensation cost attributed to employee service beyond 1997 and not yet recognized as expense totaled $6,000,000. No additional tax benefits are expected to be credited to paid-in capital.

Required: For these options, what incremental number of shares would be used to calculate diluted EPS?

EB–16 Employee Stock Options

Throughout 1997, Old Relics, Inc., had outstanding 1,000,000 employee stock options with an exercise price of $48. The market price of the common stock averaged $50 for 1997. Compensation cost attributed to employee service beyond 1997 and not yet recognized as expense totaled $400,000. Additional tax benefits of $200,000 are expected to be credited to paid-in capital.

Required: For these options, what incremental number of shares would be used to calculate diluted EPS?

EB–17 Contingent Issuance Agreements

Two years ago, Oregon Supply Company purchased the Beaver Lumber Company. As part of the purchase, Beaver shareholders exchanged their 600,000 shares of Beaver Lumber common stock for 300,000 shares of Oregon Supply common stock. Further, Oregon Supply contracted to issue an additional 45,000 shares (15% more) at the end of five years. For the current year, 1997, Oregon supply had 1,000,000 common shares outstanding and had $19,500,000 in net income.

Required: Determine basic and diluted EPS.

EB–18 Contingent Issuance Agreements

At the end of 1997, the board of directors of Free Spirit Company voted to issue a 10% stock dividend on February 1, 1998. For the current year, 1997, the company had 1,000,000 common shares outstanding and had $5,500,000 in net income.

Required: Determine basic and diluted EPS.

EB–19 Stock Dividends and Convertible Preferred

Throughout 1997, Peach Corp. had outstanding 50,000 shares of 5% convertible, $10 par, preferred stock. Preferred dividends are declared and paid every year. Each share of preferred is convertible into one share of common. The company began 1997 with 200,000 shares of $1 par common stock and issued a 10% stock dividend on July 1, 1997. Net income for 1997 was $550,000.

Required: Determine basic and diluted EPS.

PROBLEMS

PB–1 Convertible Securities (AICPA Adapted, November 1985—Practice I, MC#54&55)

Information relating to the capital structure of Parke Corporation is as follows:

	DECEMBER 31	
	1996	1997
Outstanding shares of:		
Common stock	90,000	90,000
Preferred stock, convertible into 30,000 shares of common	30,000	30,000
10% Convertible bonds, convertible into 20,000 shares of common	$1,000,000	$1,000,000

During 1997, Parke paid $45,000 dividends on the preferred stock. Parke's net income for 1997 was $980,000 and the income tax rate was 40%.

Required: Determine basic and diluted EPS for 1997.

PB–2 Multiple Potential Diluters

Regalia, Inc., has, in addition to its common stock, two classes of convertible preferred stock (Class A and Class B), convertible bonds, and options granting issuance of common stock. Basic EPS and a table for the effect of the potential diluters are presented.

$$\text{Basic EPS} = \frac{\overset{\text{Net Income}}{\$600{,}000} - \overset{\text{Dividends Preferred Class A}}{\$20{,}000} - \overset{\text{Preferred Class B}}{\$30{,}000}}{110{,}000 \text{ weighted ave. shares}} = \frac{\$550{,}000}{110{,}000} = \$5.00$$

TYPE	NUMERATOR EFFECT	DENOMINATOR EFFECT	RATIO	USE?
Options	$ 0	8,000	0	?
10% Conv. Bonds	60,000	20,000	3.00	?
9% Conv. Pref. A	20,000	4,200	4.76	?
11% Conv. Pref. B	30,000	15,000	2.00	?

Required: Complete the Use? column of the table and determine diluted EPS.

PB–3 Multiple Potential Diluters

Sabrina, Inc., has, in addition to its common stock, convertible preferred stock, two types of convertible bonds, and warrants granting issuance of common stock. Basic EPS and a table for the effect of the potential diluters are presented.

$$\text{Basic EPS} = \frac{\overset{\text{Net Income}}{\$2{,}000{,}000} - \overset{\text{Preferred Dividends}}{\$400{,}000}}{200{,}000 \text{ weighted ave. shares}} = \frac{\$1{,}600{,}000}{200{,}000} = \$8.00$$

TYPE	NUMERATOR EFFECT	DENOMINATOR EFFECT	RATIO	USE?
Warrants	$ 0	10,000	0	?
10% Conv. Bonds	600,000	100,000	6.00	?
9% Conv. Bonds	200,000	40,000	5.00	?
11% Conv. Pref.	400,000	100,000	4.00	?

Required: Complete the Use? column of the table and determine diluted EPS.

PB–4 Comprehensive EPS Problem

Here is the shareholders' equity for Tundra Corporation, as of December 31, 1996:

Cumulative, nonparticipating, convertible 6% preferred stock, par $20	$ 20,000,000
Paid-in capital—preferred	10,000,000
Common stock, par $1	5,000,000
Paid-in capital—common	110,000,000
Retained earnings	555,000,000
	$700,000,000

The following events related to equity occurred in 1997:

1. On January 1, key executives were awarded 500,000 stock options granting the rights to acquire one share of common stock per option for an exercise price of $50. Compensation was for prior service, so by December 31, 1997, there is no unrecognized compensation nor any expected credits to paid-in capital for tax benefits.
2. On March 1, the board of directors declared a $6,000,000 cash dividend to be paid on April 15, 1997 to shareholders of record on March 31, 1997. The dividend was properly paid on March 31, 1997. The last dividend was one for $5,000,000 in 1995.
3. On September 1, the company acquired 300,000 shares of its common stock for a market price of $35 per share. The cost method is used for treasury stock.
4. On November 1, the company reissued 120,000 shares of treasury stock for the market price of $41 per share.
6. Net income for 1997 was $12,000,000.

Additional Information: Each share of preferred stock is convertible into one share of common stock. The market price for common stock on January 1, 1997, was $40, the average market price during 1997 was $42, and the market price on December 31, 1997, was $55.

Required: Determine amounts to report for EPS. In your answer, be sure to show the following:

A. Weighted-average shares of common stock outstanding
B. Basic EPS
C. A table depicting the numerator effect, denominator effect, and ratio for both the options and the convertible preferred stock
D. Diluted EPS

PB–5 Multiple Potential Diluters

A partial balance sheet for Smith & Smythe, Inc., as of 12/31/97 follows:

Liabilities		
Notes payable (10%)	$ 100,000	
8% Convertible bonds	500,000	$ 600,000
Shareholders' Equity		
8% Cumulative, convertible preferred (par $100)	$ 600,000	
Paid-in capital—preferred	200,000	
Common stock, par $10	800,000	
Paid-in capital—common	900,000	
Retained earnings	700,000	
	$3,200,000	
Less: Treasury stock—common (8,000 shares @ $25 cost)	(200,000)	3,000,000
		$3,600,000

Notes:

1. The convertible bonds were issued at par on 1/1/90 and are convertible into 10,000 shares of common stock.
2. The only common stock transaction was the purchase of the treasury shares on 4/1/97.
3. All preferred stock was issued in 1992 for the same price and is convertible into four shares of common for each share of preferred.
4. Options grant the purchase of 10,000 shares of common at $25 per share.
5. Common stock: Average market price is $30.
6. Assume an applicable income tax rate of 40%.
7. Net income for the year was $233,000.

Required:

A. Calculate basic EPS.
B. Prepare a table of potentially dilutive securities that is similar to that shown above for PB–2.
C. Determine diluted EPS.

PB–6 Earnings per Share CPA Exam Questions

1. **Practice I, MC#57, November 1988.** On January 1, 1987, Apex Company, whose stock is publicly traded, had 100,000 shares of common stock issued and outstanding. On April 1, 1987, Apex issued a 10% stock dividend. The number of shares to be used in the computation of earnings per share for 1987 is
   a. 100,000
   b. 105,000
   c. 107,500
   d. 110,000
2. **Practice II, MC#17, November 1986.** At December 31, 1985 and 1984, Gow Corporation had 100,000 shares of common stock and 10,000 shares of 5%, $100 par value, cumulative, preferred stock outstanding. No dividends were declared

on either the preferred or common stock in 1985 or 1984. Net income for 1985 was $1,000,000. For 1985, earnings per common share amounted to

a. $10.00
b. $ 9.50
c. $ 9.00
d. $ 5.00

3. **Theory, MC#25, May 1989 (modified).** Antidilutive stock options would generally be used in the calculation of

	BASIC EPS	DILUTED EPS
a.	Yes	Yes
b.	Yes	No
c.	No	No
d.	No	Yes

4. **Theory, MC#29, November 1988.** EPS data should be reported on the face of the income statement for

	INCOME BEFORE EXTRAORDINARY ITEMS	CUMULATIVE EFFECT OF A CHANGE IN ACCOUNTING PRINCIPLE
a.	Yes	Yes
b.	Yes	No
c.	No	No
d.	No	Yes

RESEARCH ACTIVITIES

RB–1 Reporting EPS

Use the SEC's EDGAR or some other resource to obtain a recent annual report (or 10K) for some company with a complex capital structure. From this report, determine if the reported EPS amounts were determined by the new FASB standard or are still reported based upon prior standards. How can you tell? If the report is based on the new standard, illustrate the reconciliation between basic and diluted EPS.

RB–2 EPS Criticisms

From the article "Fully Diluted Arithmetic" by J. Coughlan in *Management Accounting*, October 1991, pp. 45–49, prepare a report which summarizes Professor Coughlan's criticisms of EPS. Be sure to include a numerical example to highlight the main criticism in the article. The criticisms in the article were based upon prior accounting standards. Do the criticisms still apply to the requirements based upon the recent EPS standard?

RB–3 Financial Research

Examine a computerized database, such as the database that accompanies this text, to determine what proportion of firms in the database report complex capital structures.

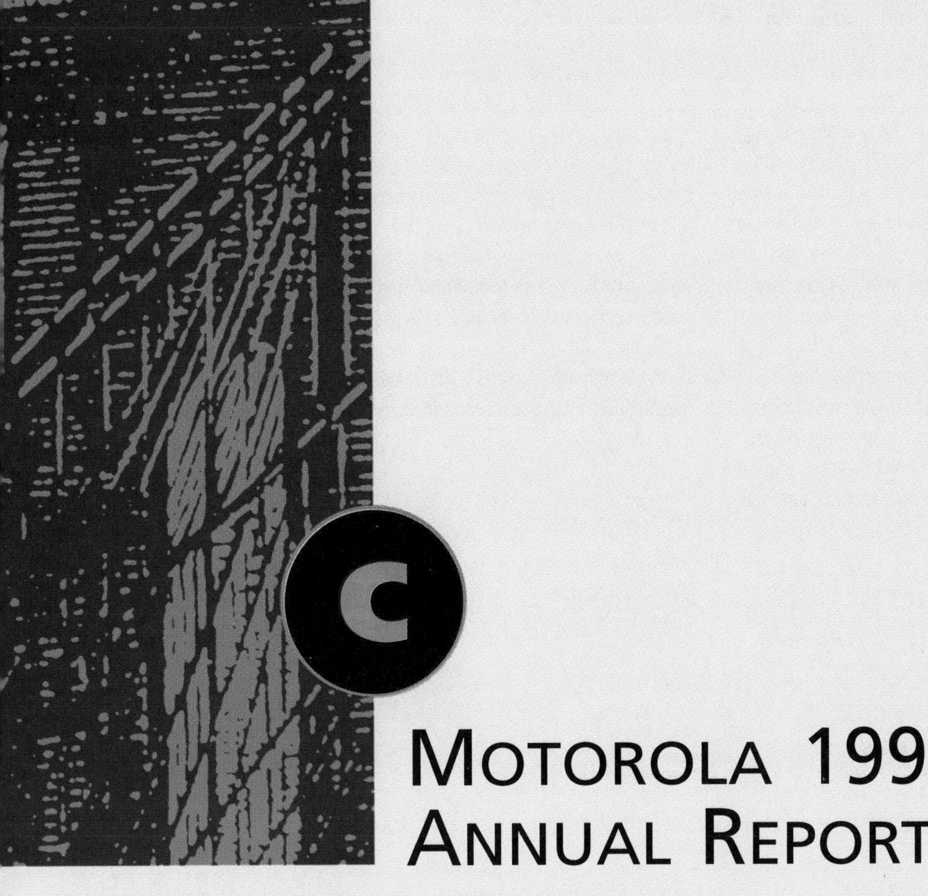

MOTOROLA 1995 ANNUAL REPORT

FINANCIAL HIGHLIGHTS

(In millions, except as noted)	*Motorola, Inc. and Consolidated Subsidiaries*	
Years ended December 31	**1995**	1994
Net sales	**$27,037**	$22,245
Earnings before income taxes	**2,782**	2,437
% to sales	**10.3%**	11.0%
Net earnings	**1,781**	1,560
% to sales	**6.6%**	7.0%
Primary net earnings per common and common equivalent share (in dollars)	**2.93**	2.66
Fully diluted net earnings per common and common equivalent share (in dollars)	**2.93**	2.65
Research and development expenditures	**2,197**	1,860
Fixed asset expenditures	**4,225**	3,322
Working capital	**2,717**	3,008
Current ratio	**1.35**	1.51
Return on average invested capital[1]	**14.7%**	17.5%
% of net debt to net debt plus equity[2]	**19.8%**	12.1%
Book value per common share (in dollars)	**18.68**	15.47
Year-end employment (in thousands)	**142**	132

[1] *Average invested capital is defined as stockholders' equity plus long and short-term debt less short-term investments (includes short-term investments categorized as cash equivalents).*
[2] *Includes short-term investments categorized as cash equivalents.*

Motorola, Inc. and Consolidated Subsidiaries

Management is responsible for the preparation, integrity and objectivity of the consolidated financial statements and other financial information presented in this report. The accompanying condensed consolidated financial statements were prepared in accordance with generally accepted accounting principles, applying certain estimates and judgments as required.

Motorola's internal controls are designed to provide reasonable assurance as to the integrity and reliability of the financial statements and to adequately safeguard, verify and maintain accountability of assets. Such controls are based on established written policies and procedures, are implemented by trained, skilled personnel with an appropriate segregation of duties and are monitored through a comprehensive internal audit program. These policies and procedures prescribe that the Company and all its employees are to maintain the highest ethical standards and that its business practices throughout the world are to be conducted in a manner which is above reproach.

KPMG Peat Marwick LLP, independent auditors, are retained to audit Motorola's financial statements. Their accompanying report is based on audits conducted in accordance with generally accepted auditing standards, which includes the consideration of the Company's internal controls to establish a basis for reliance thereon in determining the nature, timing and extent of audit tests to be applied.

The Board of Directors exercises its responsibility for these financial statements through its Audit Committee, which consists entirely of independent non-management Board members. The Audit Committee meets periodically with the independent auditors and with the Company's internal auditors, both privately and with management present, to review accounting, auditing, internal controls and financial reporting matters.

Gary L. Tooker
Vice Chairman and
Chief Executive Officer

Carl F. Koenemann
Executive Vice President
and Chief Financial Officer

INDEPENDENT AUDITORS' REPORT

The Board of Directors and Stockholders of Motorola, Inc.:

We have audited, in accordance with generally accepted auditing standards, the consolidated balance sheets of Motorola, Inc. and consolidated subsidiaries as of December 31, 1995 and 1994, and the related statements of consolidated earnings, stockholders' equity, and cash flows for each of the years in the three-year period ended December 31, 1995, appearing in the appendix to the proxy statement for the 1996 Annual Meeting of Shareholders of the Corporation (not presented herein); and in our report dated January 9, 1996, except for Note 6, which is as of February 16, 1996, also appearing in that proxy statement appendix, we expressed an unqualified opinion on those consolidated financial statements. In our opinion, the information set forth in the accompanying condensed consolidated financial statements is fairly presented, in all material respects, in relation to the consolidated financial statements from which it has been derived.

KPMG Peat Marwick LLP

KPMG Peat Marwick LLP
Chicago, Illinois

February 16, 1996

STATEMENTS OF CONSOLIDATED EARNINGS

(In millions, except per share amounts)	*Motorola, Inc. and Consolidated Subsidiaries*		
Years ended December 31	**1995**	1994	1993
Net sales	**$27,037**	$22,245	$16,963
Costs and expenses			
Manufacturing and other costs of sales	**17,545**	13,760	10,351
Selling, general and administrative expenses	**4,642**	4,381	3,776
Depreciation expense	**1,919**	1,525	1,170
Interest expense, net	**149**	142	141
Total costs and expenses	**24,255**	19,808	15,438
Earnings before income taxes	**2,782**	2,437	1,525
Income taxes provided on earnings	**1,001**	877	503
Net earnings	**$ 1,781**	$ 1,560	$ 1,022
Fully diluted net earnings per common and common equivalent share[1,2]	**$ 2.93**	$ 2.65	$ 1.78
Fully diluted average common and common equivalent shares outstanding[1,2]	**609.8**	592.7	583.7

[1] *Primary earnings per common and common equivalent share were the same as fully diluted for all years shown, except in 1994 when they were one cent higher than fully diluted. Average primary common and common equivalent shares outstanding for 1995, 1994 and 1993 were 609.7, 591.7 and 582.6, respectively (which includes the dilutive effects of the convertible zero coupon notes and the outstanding stock options).*

[2] *Includes adjustments for the 1994 two-for-one stock split effected in the form of a 100 percent stock dividend.*

STATEMENTS OF CONSOLIDATED STOCKHOLDERS' EQUITY

(In millions, except per share amounts)	Common Stock and Additional Paid-in Capital[1]			Retained Earnings		
Years ended December 31	**1995**	1994	1993	**1995**	1994	1993
Balances at January 1	**$3,179**	$1,875	$1,510	**$5,917**	$4,534	$3,634
Net earnings	–	–	–	**1,781**	1,560	1,022
Conversion of zero coupon notes	**23**	251	216	–	–	–
Stock issuance[2]	–	973	–	–	–	–
Unrealized net gain (loss) on certain investments	**328**	(8)	–	–	–	–
Stock options exercised and other	**57**	88	149	–	–	–
Dividends declared ($.40 per share in 1995, $.31 in 1994 and $.22 in 1993)	–	–	–	**(237)**	(177)	(122)
Balances at December 31	**$3,587**	$3,179	$1,875	**$7,461**	$5,917	$4,534

[1] *1994 Stock Split: An amount equal to the par value of the additional shares issued has been transferred from additional paid-in capital to common stock due to the two-for-one stock split effected in the form of a 100 percent stock dividend. All references to shares outstanding, dividends and per share amounts during 1994 and 1993 have been adjusted on a retroactive basis.*

[2] *During November 1994, the Company completed a public equity offering of 17.1 million shares of common stock.*

See accompanying condensed notes to consolidated financial statements.

(In millions, except per share amounts)	Motorola, Inc. and Consolidated Subsidiaries	
December 31	**1995**	1994
Assets		
Current assets		
Cash and cash equivalents	**$ 725**	$ 741
Short-term investments	**350**	318
Accounts receivable, less allowance for doubtful accounts (1995, $123; 1994, $118)	**4,081**	3,421
Inventories	**3,528**	2,670
Future income tax benefits	**1,222**	928
Other current assets	**604**	847
Total current assets	**10,510**	8,925
Property, plant and equipment, less accumulated depreciation (1995, $8,110; 1994, $6,657)	**9,356**	7,073
Other assets	**2,935**	1,538
Total assets	**$22,801**	$17,536
Liabilities and Stockholders' Equity		
Current liabilities		
Notes payable and current portion of long-term debt	**$ 1,605**	$ 916
Accounts payable	**2,018**	1,678
Accrued liabilities	**4,170**	3,323
Total current liabilities	**7,793**	5,917
Long-term debt	**1,949**	1,127
Deferred income taxes	**968**	509
Other liabilities	**1,043**	887
Stockholders' equity		
Common stock, $3 par value Authorized shares: 1995 and 1994, 1,400 Issued and outstanding shares: 1995, 591.4; 1994, 588.0	**1,774**	1,764
Preferred stock, $100 par value issuable in series Authorized shares: 0.5 (none issued)	**–**	–
Additional paid-in capital	**1,813**	1,415
Retained earnings	**7,461**	5,917
Total stockholders' equity	**11,048**	9,096
Total liabilities and stockholders' equity	**$22,801**	$17,536

See accompanying condensed notes to consolidated financial statements.

(In millions)		*Motorola, Inc. and Consolidated Subsidiaries*	
Years ended December 31	**1995**	1994	1993
Operating			
Net earnings	**$ 1,781**	$ 1,560	$ 1,022
Add (deduct) non-cash items			
Depreciation	**1,919**	1,525	1,170
Deferred income taxes	**(55)**	(177)	50
Amortization of debt discount and issue costs	**12**	22	26
Gain on disposition of investments in affiliated companies	**(111)**	(9)	(9)
Change in assets and liabilities, net of effects of acquisitions and dispositions			
Accounts receivable, net	**(653)**	(945)	(439)
Inventories	**(856)**	(806)	(539)
Other current assets	**(100)**	(328)	(44)
Accounts payable and accrued liabilities	**1,172**	1,134	927
Other assets	**30**	595	(95)
Other liabilities	**148**	(19)	245
Net cash provided by operations	**3,287**	2,552	2,314
Investing			
Acquisitions and advances to affiliated companies	**(563)**	(894)	(408)
Dispositions of investments in affiliated companies	**252**	23	67
Payments for property, plant and equipment	**(4,225)**	(3,320)	(2,187)
Other changes to property, plant and equipment, net	**(11)**	183	126
(Increase) decrease in short-term investments	**(32)**	40	(105)
Net cash used for investing activities	**(4,579)**	(3,968)	(2,507)
Financing			
Net increase (decrease) in commercial paper and short-term borrowings less than 90 days	**686**	517	(38)
Proceeds from issuance of debt	**851**	32	521
Repayment of debt	**(74)**	(190)	(74)
Issuance of common stock	**49**	1,061	113
Payment of dividends	**(236)**	(149)	(120)
Net cash provided by financing activities	**1,276**	1,271	402
Net increase (decrease) in cash and cash equivalents	**$ (16)**	$ (145)	$ 209
Cash and cash equivalents, beginning of year	**$ 741**	$ 886	$ 677
Cash and cash equivalents, end of year	**$ 725**	$ 741	$ 886

Supplemental Cash Flow Information

(In millions)		*Motorola, Inc. and Consolidated Subsidiaries*	
Years ended December 31	**1995**	1994	1993
Non-Cash Activities			
Conversion of zero coupon notes	**$ 23**	$251	$216
Unrealized net gain (loss) on certain investments	**$336**	$ (8)	–
Issuance of common stock for investment acquisition	**$ –**	$ –	$ 36

See accompanying condensed notes to consolidated financial statements.

1. Summary of Significant Accounting Policies

Consolidation: The consolidated financial statements include the accounts of the Company and those majority-owned subsidiaries where the Company has control. All significant intercompany accounts and transactions are eliminated in consolidation.

Cash Equivalents: The Company considers all highly liquid investments purchased with an original maturity of three months or less to be cash equivalents.

Marketable Securities: Effective January 1, 1994, the Company adopted Statement of Financial Accounting Standards (SFAS) No. 115, "Accounting for Certain Investments in Debt and Equity Securities." SFAS No. 115 requires that the carrying value of certain investments be adjusted to their fair value. As of December 31, 1995, the Company recorded an increase to stockholders' equity, other assets and deferred taxes of $328 million, $543 million and $215 million, respectively, primarily due to the fair value recognition of the Nextel investment which was completed during July of 1995. As of December 31, 1994, the effects of SFAS No. 115 were immaterial.

Revenue Recognition: The Company uses the percentage-of-completion method to recognize revenues and costs associated with most long-term contracts. For contracts involving certain technologies, revenues and profits or parts thereof, are deferred until technological feasibility is established and customer acceptance is obtained. For other product sales, revenue is recognized at the time of shipment, and reserves are established for price protection and cooperative marketing programs with distributors.

Inventories: Inventories are valued at the lower-of-average cost (which approximates computation on a first-in, first-out basis) or market (i.e., net realizable value or replacement cost), less progress payments on certain long- term contracts.

Property, Plant and Equipment: Property, plant and equipment are stated at cost less accumulated depreciation. Depreciation is recorded principally using the declining-balance method, based on the estimated useful lives of the assets (buildings and building equipment, 5–50 years; machinery and equipment, 2–12 years).

Foreign Currency Translation: The Company's European and Japanese operations use the respective local currencies, instead of the U.S. dollar, as the functional currency. For all other operations, the Company uses the U.S. dollar as the functional currency. The effects of translating the financial position and results of operations of local functional currency operations are included in stockholders' equity. The effects of foreign currency transactions are included in the statement of earnings.

The Company uses financial instruments to hedge, and therefore attempt to reduce, its overall exposure to the effects of currency fluctuations on cash flows of foreign operations and investments in foreign countries. The Company's strategy is to offset the gains or losses of the financial instruments against losses or gains on the underlying operational cash flows or investments based on the operating business units' assessment of risk. Gains and losses on hedges of existing assets or liabilities are marked to market on a monthly basis. Other gains or losses on financial instruments that do not qualify as hedges are recognized immediately as income or expense. Gains and losses on financial instruments which hedge firm future commitments are deferred until such time as the underlying transactions are recognized or immediately when the transaction is no longer expected to occur. The Company does not speculate in these financial instruments for profit on the exchange rate price fluctuation alone. The Company does not trade in currencies for which there are no underlying exposures, nor enter into trades for any currency to intentionally increase the underlying exposure.

Many of the Company's non-functional currency receivables and payables denominated in major currencies which can be traded on open markets are hedged. Some of the Company's exposure is to currencies which are not traded on open markets, such as those in Latin America and China, and these are addressed, to the extent reasonably possible, through managing net asset positions, product pricing, and other means, such as component sourcing. Currently, the Company primarily hedges firm commitments. The Company expects that there could be hedges of anticipated transactions in the future.

Stock Options: The Company has evaluated the effects of the recent accounting pronouncement, SFAS No. 123, "Accounting for Stock-Based Compensation," which will be effective for the Company's fiscal year-end 1996. Based on an initial evaluation, the effects are not expected to have a material effect on the Company's consolidated financial position, liquidity or results of operations.

Disclosure of Certain Significant Risks and Uncertainties: The preparation of financial statements in conformity with generally accepted accounting principles requires management to make certain estimates and assumptions that affect the reported amounts of assets and liabilities and disclosure of contingent assets and liabilities at the date of financial statements and the reported amounts of revenues and expenses during the reporting period. Actual results could differ from those estimates. The Company's periodic filings with the Securities and Exchange Commission include, where applicable, disclosures of estimates, assumptions, uncertainties and concentrations in products, sources of supply and markets which could affect the financial statements and future operations of the Company.

Reclassifications: Certain amounts in prior years' financial statements and related notes have been reclassified to conform to the 1995 presentation.

2. Income Taxes

Components of Earnings Before Income Taxes

	1995	1994	1993
United States	**$ 907**	$1,140	$ 360
Other nations	**1,875**	1,297	1,165
Total	**$2,782**	$2,437	$1,525

Components of Income Taxes Provided on Earnings

	1995	1994	1993
Current:			
United States	**$ 400**	$ 728	$197
Other nations	**386**	254	234
State income taxes (U.S.)	**50**	72	22
	836	1,054	453
Deferred	**165**	(177)	50
Income taxes	**$1,001**	$ 877	$503

Income tax payments were $947 million in 1995, $962 million in 1994 and $286 million in 1993.

Except for certain earnings that Motorola, Inc. intends to reinvest indefinitely, provisions have been made for the cumulative estimated U.S. federal income tax liabilities applicable to undistributed earnings of affiliates and associated companies. Undistributed earnings for which no U.S. income tax has been provided aggregated $3.5 billion and $2.9 billion at December 31, 1995 and 1994, respectively. Should these earnings be distributed, foreign tax credits would reduce the additional U.S. income tax which would be payable. In cases where taxes are provided on such undistributed earnings, those taxes have been included in U.S. income taxes.

At December 31, 1995, certain non-U.S. subsidiaries had loss carryforwards for income tax reporting purposes of $18.7 million, with expiration dates starting in 1996.

Differences Between Income Tax Expense Computed at the U.S. Federal Statutory Tax Rate of 35% for 1995, 1994 and 1993 and Income Taxes Provided on Earnings

	1995	1994	1993
Income tax expense at statutory rate	**$ 974**	$853	$534
Taxes on non-U.S. earnings	**47**	13	(21)
State income taxes	**30**	46	14
Foreign sales corporation	**(45)**	(46)	(29)
Tax credits	**(8)**	(6)	(4)
Other	**3**	17	9
Income taxes	**$1,001**	$877	$503

Significant Deferred Tax Assets (Liabilities)

December 31	**1995**	1994
Depreciation	**$(197)**	$(135)
Deferred taxes on non-U.S. earnings	**(382)**	(165)
Inventory reserves	**345**	255
Employee benefits	**286**	248
Capitalized items	**89**	91
Other deferred income taxes	**113**	125
Net deferred tax asset	**$ 254**	$ 419

Gross deferred tax assets were $1,753 million and $1,320 million at December 31, 1995 and 1994, respectively. Gross deferred tax liabilities were $1,499 million and $901 million at December 31, 1995 and 1994, respectively.

The deferred tax assets are considered realizable considering past income and estimates of future income. These include, but are not limited to, carrybacks, earnings trends and tax planning strategies.

The Internal Revenue Service (IRS) has examined the federal income tax returns for Motorola, Inc. through 1987 and has settled the respective returns through 1985. The IRS has completed its field audit of the years 1986 and 1987. In connection with these audits, the IRS has proposed adjustments to the Company's income and tax credits for those years which would result in additional tax. The Company disagrees with most of the proposed adjustments and is contesting them. In the opinion of the Company's management, the final disposition of these matters, and proposed adjustments from other tax authorities, will not have a material adverse effect on the consolidated financial position, liquidity or results of operations of the Company.

3. Debt and Credit Facilities

Long-Term Debt

December 31	**1995**	1994
7.5% debentures due 2025	**$ 397**	$ —
6.5% debentures due 2025 (redeemable at the holders' option in 2005)	**397**	—
7.6% notes due 2007	**300**	300
6.5% debentures due 2008	**199**	199
Zero coupon notes due 2009	**34**	55
Zero coupon notes due 2013	**325**	316
6.75% industrial revenue bonds due 2014	**20**	20
8.4% debentures due 2031 (redeemable at the holders' option in 2001)	**200**	200
Other long-term debt	**90**	48
	1,962	1,138
Less current maturities	**13**	11
Long-term debt	**$1,949**	$1,127

Short-Term Debt

December 31	**1995**	1994
Notes to banks	**$ 212**	$147
Commercial paper	**1,375**	745
Other short-term debt	**5**	13
	1,592	905
Add current maturities	**13**	11
Notes payable and current portion of long-term debt	**$1,605**	$916

Weighted-Average Interest Rates on Short-Term Borrowings

	1995	1994
Commercial paper	5.9%	4.6%
Other short-term debt	6.8%	7.5%

As of December 31, 1995, the outstanding zero coupon notes due 2009, referred to as Liquid Yield Option™ Notes (LYONs™), had a face value at maturity of $76 million. The 2009 LYONs were priced at a 6% yield to maturity and are now convertible into 18.268 shares of Motorola common stock for each $1,000 note. During 1995, various holders of the 2009 LYONs exercised conversion rights for approximately 54,000 notes ($54 million face value; $23 million net carrying value).

At December 31, 1995, the LYONs due 2013 had a face value of approximately $480 million at maturity. The 2013 LYONs were priced to yield 2.25% to maturity and are convertible into 11.178 shares of Motorola common stock for each $1,000 note.

Both LYONs issues are subordinated to all existing and future senior indebtedness of the Company, rank on a parity with each other, and may be put back to the Company by the holders on specific dates prior to the stated maturities.

During December 1995, the Company's universal shelf registration totaling $1.0 billion of debt and equity securities was declared effective by the Securities and Exchange Commission. As of December 31, 1995, no securities had been issued under this universal shelf statement.

Lyons Is a Trademark of Merrill Lynch & Co., Inc.

In 1994, the Company's universal shelf registration statement for $800 million of debt and equity securities was declared effective by the Securities and Exchange Commission. As of December 31, 1995, the Company had issued under this universal shelf registration $400 million in aggregate principal amount of 7.5% debentures due May 2025 and an additional $400 million in aggregate principal amount of 6.5% debentures due September 2025 (which may be put back to the Company in 2005 at 100% of the principal amount, plus accrued interest).

Aggregate requirements for long-term debt maturities, in millions, during the next five years are as follows: 1996, $13; 1997, $23; 1998, $21; 1999, $23; 2000, $5.

During 1995, the Company and its finance subsidiary increased its one- and five-year revolving domestic credit agreements with a group of banks from $1.5 billion to $2.0 billion. These revolving domestic credit agreements contain various conditions, covenants and representations. At December 31, 1995, the Company's total domestic and foreign credit facilities aggregated $3.5 billion, of which $299 million were used and the remaining $3.2 billion were not drawn, but were available to back up outstanding commercial paper which totaled $1,375 million at December 31, 1995.

Outstanding letters of credit aggregated approximately $285 million and $426 million at December 31, 1995 and 1994, respectively.

4. Other Financial Data

Income Statement and Balance Sheet Information

Income Statement Information

	1995	1994	1993
Research and development	**$2,197**	$1,860	$1,521
Maintenance and repairs	**343**	276	267
Foreign currency losses	**4**	25	18
Interest expense, net:			
Interest expense	**213**	192	182
Interest income	**(64)**	(50)	(41)
Interest expense, net	**$ 149**	$ 142	$ 141

The Company's cash payments for interest expense were $193 million in 1995, $209 million in 1994 and $126 million in 1993.

Balance Sheet Information

December 31	**1995**	1994
Inventories:		
Finished goods	**$ 1,026**	$ 699
W.I.P. and production materials	2,502	1,971
Total	**$ 3,528**	$ 2,670
Property, plant and equipment:		
Land	**$ 201**	$ 169
Buildings	**4,754**	3,504
Machinery	**12,511**	10,057
	$17,466	$13,730
Less: Accumulated depreciation	**8,110**	6,657
Total	**$ 9,356**	$ 7,073
Other assets:		
Investments in nonconsolidated subsidiaries	**$ 1,438**	$ 739
Fair value adjustment of qualified SFAS No. 115 investments	**543**	(13)
Other	**954**	812
Total	**$ 2,935**	$ 1,538
Accrued liabilities:		
Compensation	**$ 682**	$ 613
Deferred revenue	**287**	219
Accrued warranties	**309**	283
Taxes other than income	**162**	162
Income taxes payable	**125**	76
Contribution to employees' profit-sharing funds	**194**	176
Dividends payable	**59**	59
Other	**2,352**	1,735
Total	**$ 4,170**	$ 3,323

Derivative Financial Instruments

As of December 31, 1995 and 1994, the Company had net outstanding foreign exchange contracts totaling $1.2 billion for both years. Most of the hedge contracts, which are over-the-counter instruments, mature within three months with the longest maturity extending out twenty-seven months. Management believes that these forward contracts should not subject the Company to undue risk due to foreign exchange movements because gains and losses on these contracts should offset losses and gains on the assets, liabilities and transactions being hedged. At December 31, 1995, deferred gains totaled $1.5 million and deferred losses totaled $0.5 million. At December 31, 1994, deferred gains totaled $1.2 million and deferred losses totaled $0.2 million. The following schedule shows the five largest net foreign exchange hedge positions as of December 31, 1995:

Foreign Exchange Net Hedge Positions at December 31

In Millions of U.S. Dollars

Buy (Sell)	**1995**	1994
Japanese Yen	**$(373)**	$(578)
British Pound Sterling	**(226)**	(227)
Spanish Peseta	**(98)**	(30)
Singapore Dollar	**83**	2
German Deutsche Mark	**(45)**	(162)

The Company is exposed to credit-related losses if counterparties to financial instruments fail to perform their obligations. However, it does not expect any counterparties, which presently have high credit ratings, to fail to meet their obligations.

The Company's finance subsidiary had at December 31, 1995, $25 million of an outstanding floating to fixed interest rate commercial paper swap, which will mature in November 1996. Amounts receivable and payable under swap agreements and gains and losses realized on swaps are recognized as yield adjustments over the life of the related debt which were immaterial during 1995.

Fair Value of Financial Instruments

The Company's financial instruments include accounts receivable, short-term investments, long-term receivables, accounts payable, notes payable, long-term debt, foreign currency contracts and other financing commitments. The fair values of such financial instruments have been determined based on quoted market prices and market interest rates, as of December 31, 1995.

At December 31, 1995, the fair value of the convertible zero coupon notes due 2009 and 2013 were $79 million and $368 million compared to the carrying values of $34 million and $325 million, respectively. The convertible zero coupon notes due 2009 are callable by the Company at the carrying value at any time and the convertible zero coupon notes due 2013 will be callable by the Company commencing September 1998. The fair values of all other financial instruments were not materially different than their carrying (or contract) values.

Finance Subsidiary

The Company's finance subsidiary purchases customer obligations under long-term contracts from the Company at net carrying value.

The finance subsidiary's interest revenue is included in the Company's consolidated net sales. Interest expense totaled $15 million in 1995 and 1994, and $12 million in 1993 and is included in manufacturing and other costs of sales. In addition, long-term finance receivables of $290 million in 1995 and $257 million in 1994 are included in other assets.

Financial Data of Consolidated Finance Subsidiary

	1995	1994	1993
Total revenue	**$ 34**	$ 40	$ 37
Net earnings	**11**	16	16
Total assets	**369**	339	361
Total liabilities	**(304)**	(285)	(298)
Stockholder's investments and advances	**$ 65**	$ 54	$ 63

Leases

The Company owns most of its major facilities, but does lease certain office, factory and warehouse space, land, and data processing and other equipment under principally noncancelable operating leases. Rental expense, net of sublease income, was $222 million in 1995, $185 million in 1994 and $152 million in 1993. At December 31, 1995, future minimum lease obligations, net of minimum sublease rentals, for the next five years and beyond are as follows: 1996, $148; 1997, $103; 1998, $77; 1999, $59; 2000, $45; beyond, $135.

5. Employee Benefit and Incentive Plans

Pension Benefits

The Company's noncontributory pension plan covers most U.S. employees after one year of service. The benefit formula is dependent upon employee earnings and years of service. The Company's policy is to fund the accrued pension cost or the amount allowable based on the full funding limitations of the Internal Revenue Code, if less. The Company has a noncontributory supplemental retirement benefit plan for its elected officers. The plan contains provisions for funding the participants' expected retirement benefits when the participants meet the minimum age and years of service requirements.

Certain non-U.S. subsidiaries have varying types of retirement plans providing benefits for substantially all of their employees. Amounts charged to earnings for all non-U.S. plans were $82 million in 1995, $68 million in 1994 and $41 million in 1993.

The Company uses a three-year, market-related asset value method of amortizing asset-related gains and losses. Net transition amounts and prior service costs are being amortized over periods ranging from 10 to 15 years.

Benefits under all U.S. pension plans are valued based upon the projected unit credit cost method. The assumptions used to develop the projected benefit obligations for the plans for 1995 and 1994 were as follows:

	1995	1994
Discount rate for obligations	**7.75%**	8.50%
Future compensation increase rate	**4.50%**	5.50%
Investment return assumption (regular)	**9.00%**	9.00%
Investment return assumption elected officers)	**6.50%**	7.75%

Accounting literature requires discount rates to be established based on prevailing market rates for high-quality fixed-income instruments that, if the pension benefit obligation was settled at the measurement date, would provide the necessary future cash flows to pay the benefit obligation when due. The Company has decreased the discount rate in determining the pension obligation from 8.50% to 7.75% to comply with these guidelines. As of December 31, 1995, the investment portfolio was predominantly equity investments, which have historically realized annual returns at or significantly above the assumed investment return rate. The Company believes that discount rate fluctuations are short-term in nature and should not adversely affect the Company's long-term obligation.

Components of Net U.S. Pension Expense for the Regular Pension Plan

	1995	1994	1993
Service costs	**$ 126**	$ 119	$ 92
Interest cost on projected obligation	**107**	83	67
Actual return on plan assets	**(334)**	7	(80)
Net amortization and deferral	**213**	(113)	(11)
Net pension expense	**$ 112**	$ 96	$ 68

The net U.S. pension expense for the elected officers' supplemental retirement benefit plan was $31 million in 1995, $27 million in 1994 and $19 million in 1993. The net U.S. pension expense for the Motorola Supplemental Pension Plan was $2 million in 1995.

U.S. Funded Pension Plans

December 31	1995		1994	
	Regular	**Elected Officers and Other**[1]	Regular	Elected Officers and Other[1]
Actuarial present value of:				
Vested benefit obligation	**$(1,110)**	**$ (55)**	$ (831)	$(40)
Accumulated benefit obligation	**(1,193)**	**(96)**	(904)	(76)
Projected benefit obligation for service rendered to date	**(1,585)**	**(113)**	(1,239)	(96)
Plan assets at fair value, primarily bonds, stocks and cash equivalents	**1,537**	**74**	1,090	56
Plan assets less than the projected benefit obligation	**(48)**	**(39)**	(149)	(40)
Unrecognized net loss	**41**	**26**	127	28
Unrecognized prior service cost	**1**	**32**	1	33
Unrecognized net transition (asset) liability	**(35)**	**6**	(46)	7
Adjustment required to recognize minimum liability	**—**	**(47)**	—	(47)
Pension liability recognized in balance sheet	**$ (41)**	**$ (22)**	$ (67)	$(19)

[1]*Includes the Motorola supplemental pension plan which became effective January 1, 1994. The Plan was established and will be maintained by Motorola, Inc. for the purpose of providing supplemental benefits in excess of the limitation imposed by the Internal Revenue Code on defined benefit plans for certain of its employees (excluding elected officers) who participate in the Motorola, Inc., pension plan.*

Postretirement Health Care Benefits

In addition to providing pension benefits, the Company provides certain health-care benefits to its retired employees. The majority of its domestic employees may become eligible for these benefits if they reach normal retirement age while working for the Company. The Company's policy is to fund the maximum amount allowable based on funding limitations of the Internal Revenue Code.

The assumptions used to develop the accumulated postretirement benefit obligation for the retiree health-care plan for 1995 and 1994 were as follows:

	1995	1994
Discount rate for obligations	**7.75%**	8.50%
Investment return assumption	**9.00%**	9.00%

Net retiree health-care expenses recognized in 1995 were $29 million, $26 million in 1994 and $23 million in 1993.

U.S. Funded Retiree Health Care Plan

December 31	**1995**	1994
Actuarial present value of accumulated postretirement benefit obligation	**$(342)**	$(281)
Plan assets at fair value, primarily listed stocks, bonds and cash equivalents	**121**	64
Unrecognized prior service cost	**2**	2
Unrecognized net loss	**66**	47
Retiree health care liability recognized in balance sheet	**$(153)**	$(168)

The health-care trend rate used to determine the pre-age 65 accumulated postretirement benefit obligation was 8.78% for 1995, decreasing to 6% by the year 2000 and beyond. A flat 5% rate per year is used for the post-age 65 obligation. Increasing the health care trend rate by one percentage point would increase the accumulated postretirement benefit obligation by $42 million as of December 31, 1995 and would increase the 1995 net retiree health care expense by $5 million. There are no significant postretirement health care benefit plans outside of the United States.

Other Benefits

Profit Sharing Plans: The Company and certain subsidiaries have profit-sharing plans, principally contributory, in which all eligible employees participate. The Company makes contributions to profit-sharing funds in the United States and other nations, which are generally based upon percentages of pretax earnings, as defined, from those operations. Company contributions to all profit-sharing plans totaled $194 million, $176 million and $107 million in 1995, 1994 and 1993, respectively.

Motorola Executive Incentive Plan: The Company may provide up to 7% of its annual consolidated pretax earnings, as defined in the Motorola Executive Incentive Plan, for the payment of cash incentive awards to key employees. During 1995, $137 million was provided for incentive awards, as compared to $129 million and $78 million in 1994 and 1993, respectively.

Long-Range Incentive Plan: The Company maintains a long-range incentive plan (LRIPL) to reward participating elected officers for the Company's achieving outstanding long-range performance, based on four preestablished performance objectives measured over four year cycles. These objectives are benchmarked and evaluated against companies with industries similar to Motorola, and to Motorola's internal objectives. The maximum amount to be awarded to an individual participant under this plan during any cycle can not exceed the lesser of $5 million or 200 percent of each participants' respective base salary. Payouts under the LRIPL will occur subsequent to 1997 at which time the current long range incentive program (LRIPR) will terminate. During 1995, $51 million was provided for the long-range incentive awards and $13 million was disbursed to qualifying participants. In 1994, when the LRIPL was approved and adopted, $12 million was provided and no disbursements were made.

Rona Incentive Program: The RONA (Return On Net Assets employed) incentive program is available to eligible employees who are not participating in the Motorola Executive Incentive Plan. RONA awards are earned and paid semiannually to participants and depend, first, on the Company and, in most cases, the major business unit for which the participant works, exceeding a minimum RONA percentage (as determined by the Company) during the six-month period and, second, the extent to which such minimum percentage was exceeded. During 1995, $234 million was provided for RONA awards, as compared to $269 million and $205 million in 1994 and 1993, respectively.

Stock Options: Under the Company's employee stock option plans, shares of common stock have been made available for grant to key employees. The exercise price of each option granted is 100% of market value on the date of the grant.

Options exercised during 1995 were at per share prices ranging from $7.79 to $57.69. Options outstanding at December 31, 1995 were at per share prices ranging from $8.83 to $79.31. There are approximately 11,400 total current stock option holders. All 1994 and 1993 share amounts and prices have been adjusted to reflect the 1994 two-for-one stock split.

Shares Subject to Options

(In Thousands, Except Employee Data)	**1995**	1994	1993
Options outstanding at January 1	**24,104**	22,906	26,018
Additional options granted	**4,931**	3,972	3,530
Options exercised	**(2,535)**	(2,654)	(6,326)
Options terminated, cancelled or expired	**(115)**	(120)	(316)
Options outstanding at December 31	**26,385**	24,104	22,906
Shares reserved for future option grants	**8,786**	13,602	17,454
Total shares reserved	**35,171**	37,706	40,360
Total options exercisable	**21,455**	20,137	19,376
Approximate number of employees granted options	**10,000**	7,300	5,100 F-23

6. Commitments and Contingencies

Financial: In July 1995, the Company completed the sale of its 800 megahertz specialized mobile radio businesses, systems and licenses in the continental United States to Nextel Communications, Inc. for approximately 59 million shares of Nextel stock. The transaction was accounted for as an exchange of production assets with no gain realized in the statement of consolidated earnings. Nextel agreed to purchase, subject to specified conditions, substantial quantities of equipment from Motorola over a five-year period which began in 1994 for use on its specialized mobile radio systems. Motorola has agreed to provide up to $685 million of secured vendor financing for such equipment and related services to Nextel and certain of its subsidiaries, subject to certain lending conditions. As of December 31, 1995, Nextel had drawn $225 million of such financing commitment. Nextel will require financing in addition to Motorola's vendor financing to complete its currently planned networks and acquisitions. Nextel's failure to obtain additional financing or to meet the conditions for any financing could adversely affect future sales and orders of the Company's iDEN—Registered Trademark—equipment. There can be no assurance that such additional financing will be obtained or such conditions met.

The Company further advanced its strategic investment in the IRIDIUM—Registered Trademark—global communications system. At December 31, 1995, the Company's equity investment in and commitments to make equity investments in Iridium, Inc. was approximately $400 million; additionally, it has committed, subject to action by the Iridium, Inc. Board of Directors, to additional equity investments totaling approximately $60 million. In February 1996, the Company committed to purchase approximately $160 million of securities to be issued by Iridium, Inc., during 1996. Iridium, Inc., will require additional funding and, quite possibly, other financial support from various sources in order to complete the global communications system, which is expected to take place over the next three years. There can be no assurance that Motorola or any other person will provide such funding or financial support. Motorola is the largest investor in Iridium, Inc. and a failure of Iridium, Inc. to obtain additional funding or financial support would materially adversely affect Motorola's investment in Iridium, Inc. and in ancillary products. The Company's investment in Iridium, Inc. is included in the consolidated balance sheet category "Other Assets."

The Company has executed three contracts with Iridium, Inc. for the construction and operation of the global communications system, providing for approximately $6.5 billion in payments by Iridium, Inc., over a ten-year period which began in 1993. The Company has in turn entered into significant subcontracts for portions of the system, for which it will generally remain obligated even if Iridium, Inc. is unable to satisfy the terms of the contracts with the Company, including funding. Separately, the Company is making significant investments to produce ancillary products for the system, such as subscriber units. The Federal Communications Commission (FCC) has issued a license to a Motorola subsidiary to construct, operate and launch the IRIDIUM system. However, other authorizations are still required for the IRIDIUM system to begin commercial service in the U.S. and in other countries in which service will be provided. Except as noted above, the Company had no significant concentrations of credit risk as of December 31, 1995.

The Company has entered into arrangements with nonconsolidated affiliates whereby the Company may increase, for an amount up to approximately $250 million, its percentage interest in these affiliates at the option of each respective affiliate or Motorola at various dates which are not to extend beyond June 1997.

Other off-balance-sheet commitments to extend or guarantee financing and recourse obligations under receivable sales arrangements which represent firm obligations at December 31, 1995 and 1994, aggregated approximately $173 million and $273 million, respectively. Commitments to extend or guarantee financing include commitments for customer financing and for the financing of nonconsolidated affiliates. Customer financing commitments require the customer to meet certain conditions established in the financing arrangements. Commitments represent the maximum amounts available under these arrangements and may not be completely utilized.

Environmental and Legal: Under the Comprehensive Environmental Response Compensation and Liability Act of 1980, as amended (CERCLA, or Superfund), the Company has been designated as a potentially responsible party by the United States Environmental Protection Agency with respect to certain waste sites with which the Company may have had direct or indirect involvement. Such designations are made regardless of the extent of the Company's involvement. These claims are in various stages of administrative or judicial proceedings. They include demands for recovery of past governmental costs and for future investigations or remedial actions. In many cases, the dollar amounts of the claims have not been specified, and have been asserted against a number of other entities for the same cost recovery or other relief as was asserted against the Company. The Company accrues costs associated with environmental matters when they become probable and reasonably estimable, which totaled $86 million and $70 million as of December 31, 1995 and 1994, respectively. The amount of such charges to earnings was $24 million, $20 million and $36 million in 1995, 1994 and 1993, respectively. However, due to their uncertain nature, the amounts accrued could differ, perhaps significantly, from the actual costs that will be incurred. These amounts assume no substantial recovery of costs from any insurer. The remedial efforts include environmental cleanup costs and communication programs. These liabilities represent only the Company's share of any possible costs incurred in environmental cleanup sites, since in most cases, potentially responsible parties other than the Company may exist.

The Company is a defendant in various suits, including environmental and product-related suits, and is subject to various claims which arise in the normal course of business. In the opinion of management, the ultimate disposition of these matters will not have a material adverse effect on the consolidated financial position, liquidity or results of operations of the Company.

IRIDIUM—Registered Trademark—is a Registered Trademark and Service Mark of IRIDIUM, Inc.

7. Information by Industry Segment and Geographic Region

The Company operates predominantly in the wireless communication, semiconductor technology and advanced electronic industries. Operations involve the design, manufacture and sale of a diversified line of products, which include, but are not limited to, cellular phones and systems; semiconductors, including discrete semiconductors and integrated circuits; two-way radios, pagers, data communication, personal communications equipment and systems; automotive, defense and space electronic products; and computer equipment. As of December 31, 1995, manufacturing and distribution operations in any one foreign country did not account for more than 10% of consolidated net sales or total assets.

Sales and operating profits by geographical area are measured by the locale of the revenue-producing operations. Operating profits (revenues less operating expenses) exclude general corporate expenses, net interest and income taxes. Intersegment and intergeographic transfers are accounted for on an arm's length pricing basis.

Identifiable assets (excluding intersegment receivables) are the Company's assets that are identified with classes of similar products or operations in each geographic area. Corporate assets primarily include cash, marketable securities, equity investments and the administrative headquarters of the Company.

In 1995, no single customer or group under common control represented 10% or more of the Company's sales. The equity in net assets of non-U.S. subsidiaries amounted to $5.5 billion at December 31, 1995 and $4.2 billion at December 31, 1994.

Information for 1994 and 1993 has been reclassified to reflect the realignment of various business units. Messaging, Information and Media Products segment includes the Paging Products and Wireless Data groups (formerly reported as part of the Communications segment) and the Information Systems Group (formerly reported as part of the Other Products segment). Land Mobile Products (formerly reported as part of the Communications segment) is a separate reportable segment. The Government and Space Technology Group is reported as part of the Other Products segment.

Industry Segment Information

	Net Sales			Operating Profit					
Years Ended December 31	**1995**	1994	1993	**1995**		1994		1993	
General systems products	**$10,660**	$ 8,613	$ 5,236	**$1,266**	**11.9%**	$1,214	14.1%	$ 718	13.7%
Semiconductor products	**8,539**	6,936	5,707	**1,218**	**14.3%**	996	14.4%	801	14.0%
Messaging, information and media product	**3,681**	2,981	2,574	**310**	**8.4%**	282	9.5%	219	8.5%
Land mobile products	**3,598**	3,399	2,882	**324**	**9.0%**	311	9.1%	150	5.2%
Other products	**3,346**	2,660	2,009	**131**	**3.9%**	97	3.6%	63	3.1%
Adjustments and eliminations	**(2,787)**	(2,344)	(1,445)	**(48)**	—	(29)	—	(11)	—
Industry segment totals	**$27,037**	$22,245	$16,963	**$3,201**	**11.8%**	2,871	12.9%	1,940	11.4%
General corporate expenses				**(270)**		(292)		(274)	
Interest expense, net				**(149)**		(142)		(141)	
Earnings before income taxes				**$2,782**	**10.3%**	$2,437	11.0%	$1,525	9.0%

(In millions, except as noted) *Motorola, Inc. and Consolidated Subsidiaries*

	Assets			Fixed Asset Expenditures			Depreciation Expense		
Year Ended December 31	**1995**	1994	1993	**1995**	1994	1993	**1995**	1994	1993
General systems products	**$ 6,181**	$ 4,740	$ 3,223	**$ 762**	$ 621	$ 453	**$ 450**	$ 327	$ 227
Semiconductor products	**7,938**	5,886	4,507	**2,530**	1,640	1,120	**909**	683	529
Messaging, information and media products	**2,527**	2,087	985	**357**	270	237	**204**	167	72
Land mobile products	**2,097**	2,232	2,673	**169**	217	141	**155**	142	225
Other products	**1,839**	1,470	805	**285**	320	136	**154**	143	63
Adjustments and eliminations	**(224)**	(72)	(24)	**—**	—	—	**—**	—	—
Industry segment totals	**20,358**	16,343	12,169	**4,103**	3,068	2,087	**1,872**	1,462	1,116
General corporate	**2,443**	1,193	1,329	**122**	254	100	**47**	63	54
Consolidated totals	**$22,801**	$17,536	$13,498	**$4,225**	$3,322	$2,187	**$1,919**	$1,525	$1,170

Geographic Area Information[1]

	Net Sales			Operating Profit					
Years Ended December 31	**1995**	1994	1993	**1995**		1994		1993	
United States	**$19,187**	$16,297	$12,924	**$1,681**	**8.8%**	$1,932	11.9%	$ 970	7.5%
Other nations	**16,954**	12,758	10,066	**1,901**	**11.2%**	1,292	10.1%	1,164	11.6%
Adjustments and eliminations	**(9,104)**	(6,810)	(6,027)	**(381)**	**—**	(353)	—	(194)	—
Geographic totals	**$27,037**	$22,245	$16,963	**3,201**	**11.8%**	2,871	12.9%	1,940	11.4%
General corporate expenses				**(270)**		(292)		(274)	
Interest expense, net				**(149)**		(142)		(141)	
Earnings before income taxes				**$2,782**	10.3%	$2,437	11.0%	$1,525	9.0%

	Assets		
December 31	**1995**	1994	1993
United States	**$12,552**	$10,750	$ 7,731
Other nations	**8,260**	5,943	4,674
Adjustments and eliminations	**(454)**	(350)	(236)
Geographic totals	**20,358**	16,343	12,169
General corporate assets	**2,443**	1,193	1,329
Consolidated totals	**$22,801**	$17,536	$13,498

[1]*As measured by the locale of the revenue-producing operations.*
1994 and 1993 have been reclassified to reflect the realignment of various business units.

8. Stockholder Rights Plan

Each outstanding share of common stock carries with it one-quarter of a preferred share purchase right. Each right becomes exercisable for $150 (subject to adjustment) for one-thousandth share of junior participating preferred stock, if a person or group acquires 20% or more of the outstanding common stock or announces an offer for 30% or more of the outstanding common stock. If a person or group acquires 20% or more of the outstanding common stock and in certain other circumstances, each right (except, in some cases, those held by an acquiror) becomes exercisable for common stock (or that of the acquiror) with a market value of twice the exercise price. In some cases, the Board of Directors may exchange rights for shares of common stock (or the equivalent) and may suspend the rights' exercisability. The rights have no voting power, expire in November 1998, and may be redeemed for $.05 per right prior to a public announcement that 20% or more of the outstanding common stock has been accumulated by a person or group.

Five-Year Financial Summary

(In Millions, Except per Share Amounts and Other Data) Motorola, Inc. and Consolidated Subsidiaries

Years Ended December 31		**1995**	1994	1993	1992	1991
Operating Results	Net sales	**$27,037**	$22,245	$16,963	$13,303	$11,341
	Manufacturing and other costs of sales	**$17,545**	$13,760	$10,351	$ 8,395	$ 7,134
	Selling, general and administrative expenses	**4,642**	4,381	3,776	2,951	2,579
	Depreciation expense	**1,919**	1,525	1,170	1,000	886
	Interest expense, net	**149**	142	141	157	129
	Total costs and expenses	**$24,255**	19,808	15,438	12,503	10,728
	Earnings before income taxes and cumulative effect of change in accounting principle	**$ 2,782**	$ 2,437	$ 1,525	$ 800	$ 613
	Income taxes provided on earnings	**(1,001)**	(877)	(503)	(224)	(159)

(continued)

(In millions, except as noted) *Motorola, Inc. and Consolidated Subsidiaries*

(In Millions, Except per Share Amounts and Other Data) Motorola, Inc. and Consolidated Subsidiaries

Years Ended December 31		**1995**	1994	1993	1992	1991
Operating Results	Net earnings before cumulative effect of change in accounting principle	**$ 1,781**	$ 1,560	$ 1,022	$ 576	$ 454
	Net earnings	**$ 1,781**	$ 1,560	$ 1,022	$ 453	$ 454
	Net earnings before cumulative effect of change in accounting principle as a percent of sales	**6.6%**	7.0%	6.0%	4.3%	4.0%
	Net earnings as a percent of sales	**6.6%**	7.0%	6.0%	3.4%	4.0%
Per Share Data[1,2] (In Dollars)	Fully diluted					
	Net earnings before cumulative effect of change in accounting principle	**$2.93**	$2.65	$1.78	$1.05	$0.84
	Cumulative effect of change in accounting principle	—	—	—	(0.22)	—
	Net earnings	**$2.93**	$2.65	$1.78	$0.83	$0.84
	Average common and common equivalent shares outstanding	**609.8**	592.7	583.7	567.1	558.5
	Dividends declared	**$ 0.400**	$ 0.310	$ 0.220	$ 0.198	$ 0.190
Balance Sheet	Total assets	**$22,801**	$17,536	$13,498	$10,629	$ 9,375
	Working capital	**2,717**	3,008	2,324	1,883	1,424
	Long-term debt	**1,949**	1,127	1,360	1,258	954
	Total debt	**3,554**	2,043	1,915	1,695	1,806
	Total stockholders' equity	**$11,048**	$ 9,096	$ 6,409	$ 5,144	$ 4,630
Other Data	Current ratio	**1.35**	1.51	1.53	1.56	1.46
	Return-on-average invested capital before cumulative effect of change in accounting principle	**14.7%**	17.5%	15.3%	9.4%	7.8%
	Return-on-average invested capital	**14.7%**	17.5%	15.3%	7.5%	7.8%
	Return-on-average stockholders' equity before cumulative effect of change in accounting principle	**17.7%**	21.0%	17.8%	11.7%	10.2%
	Return-on-average stockholders' equity	**17.7%**	21.0%	17.8%	9.4%	10.2%
	Fixed asset expenditures	**$ 4,225**	$ 3,322	$ 2,187	$ 1,442	$ 1,387
	Percent to sales	**15.6%**	14.9%	12.9%	10.8%	12.2%
	Research and development expenditures	**$ 2,197**	$ 1,860	$ 1,521	$ 1,306	$ 1,133
	Percent to sales	**8.1%**	8.4%	9.0%	9.8%	10.0%
	Year-end employment (in thousands)	**142**	132	120	107	102

[1]All earnings per share, dividends and outstanding shares data have been restated to reflect the 1994 and 1992 two-for-one stock splits.
[2]Primary earnings per common and common equivalent share were the same as fully diluted for all years shown except in 1994 and 1991 when primary earnings per share were one cent higher than fully diluted. Average primary common and common equivalent shares outstanding for 1995, 1994, 1993, 1992 and 1991 were 609.7, 591.7, 582.6, 565.6 and 555.6, respectively.

Quarterly and Other Financial Data

(In Millions, Except Per Share Amounts; Unaudited) Motorola, Inc. and Consolidated Subsidiaries

		1995				1994			
Quarterly		1st	2nd	3rd	4th	1st	2nd	3rd	4th
Operating Results	Net sales	**$6,011**	**$6,877**	**$6,851**	**$7,298**	$4,693	$5,439	$5,660	$6,453
	Gross profit	**2,133**	**2,483**	**2,463**	**2,413**	1,785	2,060	2,121	2,519
	Net earnings	**372**	**481**	**496**	**432**	298	367	380	515
	Net earnings as a percent of sales	**6.2%**	**7.0%**	**7.2%**	**5.9%**	6.4%	6.7%	6.7%	8.0%
Per Share Data (In Dollars)	Primary net earnings per common and common equivalent share	**$0.61**	**$0.80**	**$0.81**	**$0.72**	$0.51	$0.63	$0.65	$0.87
	Fully diluted net earnings per common and common equivalent share	**0.61**	**0.79**	**0.81**	**0.72**	0.51	0.63	0.65	0.86
	Dividends declared	**0.100**	**0.100**	**0.100**	**0.100**	0.070	0.070	0.070	0.100
	Dividends paid	**0.100**	**0.100**	**0.100**	**0.100**	0.055	0.070	0.070	0.070
	Stock prices								
	High	**$64.75**	**$67.88**	**$82.50**	**$77.38**	$54.83	$54.00	$55.75	$61.13
	Low	**53.00**	**51.50**	**66.75**	**56.00**	43.25	42.13	43.38	49.00

The number of stockholders of record of Motorola common stock on January 31, 1996 was 60,983.

A

Accelerated depreciation (cost allocation) methods. Methods of cost allocation that charge progressively decreasing amounts of depreciation over the useful life of the asset.

Accounting changes. A change in an accounting principle or a change in an accounting estimate.

Accounting equation. Assets equal liabilities plus shareholders' equity (A = L + E).

Accounting Principles Board (APB). Successor to CAP; issued 31 opinions between 1959 and 1973.

Accounting reorganization. A method of quasi-reorganization that first restates assets and liabilities to fair values (with net write-ups prohibited by the SEC) and then removes the retained earnings deficit.

Accounts receivable. Credit extended to customers for sale of goods or services.

Accounts receivable assigned. Accounts receivable used as collateral in a borrowing transaction.

Accrual-based income. The residual after matching period losses and expenses with period revenues and gains.

Accrual-basis method of accounting for warranty costs. Recognition of warranty costs as expense in the period in which the product is sold, regardless of when the costs are actually incurred.

Accrual. A condition that requires recognition of a revenue or an expense prior to the related cash transaction.

Accrued pension costs. Liability for the difference between the pension expense for the period and the cash deposited in the pension-plan asset account during the period.

Accumulated postretirement benefit obligation. The actuarial present value of all future benefits attributed to an employee's service rendered to that date.

Actual return on plan assets. Fair value of plan assets at beginning of year plus current-year contributions, less benefits paid during year, minus fair value of assets at end of year.

Additional markup. The amount added to the original sales price.

Adequacy ratios. Cash flow ratios that measure the adequacy of COCF to provide for permanent and seasonal working capital, net fixed assets, payment of interest and debt principal, and payment of dividends. Also called *risk ratios.*

Adjustable (variable) preferred stock. A type of preferred stock whose preference rate is adjusted, or variable, primarily in accordance with changes in selected national interest rates.

Adjusted trial balance. A report prepared after posting adjusting entries that lists the balances of all the general ledger accounts of an enterprise.

Adjusting entries. The process to recognize significant but unrecorded relationships among financial elements of an enterprise at the end of an accounting period.

Allowance for bad debts. A contra asset account used to reflect the net realizable value of accounts receivable.

Amortization. The systematic and rational allocation of the capitalized cost of an intangible asset over the period of economic benefit; Allocation of bond premium or discount to revenue or expense in a systematic manner over the life of an asset.

Antidilutive. A condition whereby a security or contingency that could result in additional shares of common stock would fail to decrease EPS if considered in the EPS determination.

Appropriated retained earnings. A classification of a portion of retained earnings to communicate restrictions from owner distributions; does not identify specific resources that are restricted.

Articulated statement. Any statement of results (including the statement of cash flows) that can be calculated using information contained in the other three GAAP-required statements.

Articulation. The link between the income statement and balance sheet whereby net income increases (net loss decreases) the reported equity.

Asset. A probable future economic benefit obtained or controlled by a particular entity as a result of a past transaction or event.

Asset management ratios. Accounts receivable turnover and average collection period, used to assess managerial performance regarding credit policies.

Asset-turnover ratio. The ratio obtained by dividing net sales by average total assets. A measure of the efficiency with which assets are used.

Available-for-sale securities. Debt and equity securities that management declares are not for trading purposes or realization of profit on short-term changes in price.

Average costing method. An inventory valuation system based on weighted average cost of purchases.

Average rate of interest. The weighted-average effective rate of interest for all bonds sold in a given bond issue.

Avoidable interest. The interest attributable to the construction project.

B

Badwill. The excess of the aggregate market-adjusted book values of a firm's identifiable net assets over the purchase price (cost) incurred by an acquiring firm, and reported as Deferred Excess Fair Value Over Cost under purchase accounting methods.

Balance sheet. The financial statement reporting the assets, liabilities, and owners' equity of an enterprise at a given point in time.

Bank reconciliation. Process of finding the correct balance in the cash account by bringing the bank balance and book balance into agreement.

Bargain purchase option (BPO). A clause that allows the lessee to purchase the leased property at a specified price significantly less than its anticipated fair market value at the option date prior to or at expiration of the lease. The bargain purchase price option is normally set low enough to ensure exercise.

Base year. Year in which LIFO is adopted.

Basic EPS. Historical earnings per share determined without considering the potentially dilutive effects of contingent issuance agreements.

Basket purchase. A purchase of more than one asset for a single sum, also referred to as a *lump-sum purchase.*

Bond payable. A financial debt instrument indicating the amount due at maturity at a stated rate of interest payable at specified time periods.

Bond-issue costs. All costs directly associated with issuing and selling a bond issue.

Bonds-outstanding method. A method of amortizing the premium or discount on the total issue of serial bonds. The amount amortized per year is the ratio of the amount of outstanding bonds in a year to the cumulative total of the bonds outstanding for the life at issuance date.

Book value. The net recorded value for an enterprise or an element of an enterprise; the book value of an enterprise itself is the residual owners' equity or net assets; the book value for a fixed asset is the original cost less the accumulated depreciation.

Book-value method. Equity securities issued are recorded at the carrying value (book value) of the debt on the books of the debtor.

C

Callable bonds. Bonds that can be recalled at the option of the issuing company after a stated date at a stated percent of face value.

Callable preferred stock. Preferred stock that the issuing corporation may, but is not required to, retire. That is, shareholders may be required to surrender or redeem shares in exchange for consideration.

Capital assets. *See* productive or capital assets.

Capital expenditures. Expenditures that benefit more than one operating cycle or calendar year.

Capital leases. Leases that meet at least one of the tests per SFAS No. 13 for inclusion as a capital lease. The assets leased are treated as a purchase by the lessee and a sale by the lessor.

Capitalization of earnings. A term used for accounting techniques that reduce retained earnings and increase contributed capital; frequently performed in association with stock dividends.

Capitalization-of-excess-earnings method. A method of estimating corporate goodwill in which the excess of a firm's average projected income over an expected normal return on investment is discounted to produce a net present value figure.

Capitalized. Treating an expenditure as an asset.

Cash. Currency, coins, and checking and savings accounts.

Cash equivalents. Extremely short-term temporary investments purchased (with excess cash) within ninety days of maturity.

Cash-basis income. The change in the cash balance from the beginning of the period to the end of the period as a result of operations.

Cash-basis method of accounting for warranty cost. Recognition of warranty costs as expense in the period in which the costs are incurred.

Ceiling. A parameter in determination of market value. The selling price less the estimated cost of completion and disposal. Also called net realizable value.

Change in accounting estimate. Change in an amount determined by judgment, such as service life of an asset.

Change in accounting principle. Change from one acceptable accounting method to another acceptable accounting method.

Classified balance sheet. Presentation of accounts is in categories of assets and liabilities.

Closing entries. The final journal entries of an accounting period that transfer the balances of all nominal accounts to equity, leaving only balance sheet accounts with nonzero balances.

Committee on Accounting Procedures (CAP). First private body to write accounting standards; issued 51 accounting research bulletins.

Common stock equivalents. A convertible security or contingency that may dilute EPS and is used in calculation of both primary and Diluted EPS.

Common stock options. Grant the holder the right to purchase shares of stock for a guaranteed exercise price during a defined period of time. (See also common stock warrants).

Common stock warrants. Grant the holder the right to purchase shares of stock for a guaranteed exercise price during a defined period of time. Warrants may trade separately in the market, and have a value independent of the stock.

Common stock. Subdivision of shareholders' equity denoting an ownership interest.

Common-size financial statements. Account balances presented as percentages; balance sheet accounts as percentage of total assets; income statement balances as percentages of net sales.

Comparative financial statements. Financial statements prepared for multiple years.

Completed-contract method. Revenue recognition method in which all revenue is recognized at the end of the contract.

Complex capital structure. The designation for a corporation with financial securities or contingencies that could result in the issuance of common stock.

Composite depreciation method. An expedient method of effectively applying straight-line depreciation to a group (pool) of dissimilar assets, to which items are continually being added or deleted.

Comprehensive allocation. Tax effects are recognized in financial statements for all differences between financial statement income and taxable income.

Consignee. Holder of merchandise for sale belonging to another party.

Consignor. Owner of merchandise held by another party for sale.

Consistency. Use or application of the same accounting principles or methods to the same events over a span of time.

Consolidated financial statements. Elements of financial statements of two or more entities combined because of ownership control.

Contingent liability. Liability whose existence depends on one or more future events.

Contra account. An account used to adjust the valuation or reduce the reported amount (book value) for some primary element of financial accounting.

Contributed capital. Equity interest from investments into a business by its owners; in a corporation, investments are made by stockholders.

Convertible bonds. Bonds that are convertible into a fixed number of shares of equity securities at the option of the bondholder.

Convertible preferred stock. Preferred stock that may be exchanged for (converted to) common stock.

Copyright. An exclusive, legal right of authors, musicians, and artists to reprint and sell copies of their works. Granted in the United States for a period equal to the author's life plus 50 years.

Corridor method. Amortization of amounts of accumulated gains or losses in excess of 10% of the greater of projected benefit obligations or the value of plan assets.

Cost allocation. The process of assigning costs incurred to either assets produced or periods in which produced assets are consumed, generating net revenues. Assignments may be made based on clear cause-and-effect relationships or, alternatively, via systematic and rational application of arbitrary procedures.

Cost method. The accounting method that records a Treasury Stock account for the full cost of repurchased shares.

Cost/benefit concept. In accounting, the concept that the additional benefits received from recording, summarizing, and reporting an item or event must exceed the costs incurred in the process.

Coupons. A cash discount offered to consumer upon purchase of manufacturer's product.

Credit. Record on the right side of a journal entry or ledger account.

Critical event. That operational event or activity that determines (subject to minor variation) the profitability of the undertaking.

Cumulative preferred stock. Preferred stock with a dividend provision requiring dividends in arrears to take precedence over common stock dividends.

Cumulative unrecognized net gain/loss. The current year's gain or loss combined with the unamortized net balance of all preceding years' gains and losses.

Current approach (treatment). Method for treating most changes in accounting principles. Under this method, the cumulative effect over prior years of using an alternative generally accepted accounting principle is reflected in the income statement of the year of change as an increase or decrease to current net income. Figures appearing in republished prior financial statements are not altered from those originally appearing in published statements.

Current assets. Those assets expected to be converted to cash within one year or operating cycle.

Current cost. The amount of cash, or its equivalent, that would have to be paid if the same or an equivalent asset were acquired currently. Traditionally spoken of as an *entry value* or *replacement cost.*

Current liability. A liability whose settlement is required within one year or operating cycle and whose settlement must be from existing current assets or creation of new current liabilities.

Current operating cash flows. Cash made available from normal operations; cash inflows from sales revenues less cash outflows for all necessary costs to produce revenues.

Current provision for income taxes. The income taxes currently payable based upon a given period's income tax returns.

Current ratio. Current assets divided by current liabilities.

D

Debenture bonds. Unsecured bonds.

Debit. Record on the left side of a journal entry or ledger account.

Debt ratio. Total liabilities divided by total assets.

Debt-to-equity ratio. Total debt divided by total shareholders' equity.

Decelerated depreciation (cost allocation) methods. Methods of cost allocation that charge progressively increasing amounts of depreciation over the useful life of an asset.

Declining-balance methods. A family of accelerated depreciation (amortization) methods. Usually restricted to a rate not greater than 200% of straight-line (as in the double-declining-balance method).

Defeasance of debt. The guarantee and payment of debt by another source so that legal liability is transferred.

Deferral. A condition whereby some cash transaction occurs prior to recognition of the related revenue or expense.

Deferred income tax liability. The deferred tax consequences attributable to taxable temporary differences.

Deferred method. A method of accounting for deferred income taxes that measures the income statement tax effects of timing differences using tax rates and laws in effect when the timing differences originate.

Deferred tax asset. The deferred tax consequences attributable to deductible temporary differences and carryforwards.

Deferred tax asset valuation allowance. The amount needed to reduce a deferred tax asset to an amount that is more likely than not to be realized.

Deferred tax benefit. A reduction for income tax expense for a period as a result of decreases to deferred tax liabilities or increases to deferred tax assets.

Deferred tax expense. An increase to income tax expense for a period as a result of increases to deferred tax liabilities or decreases to deferred tax assets.

Deficit reclassification. A method of quasi-reorganization that simply removes the retained earnings deficit without restating assets and liabilities.

Defined benefit plan. The retirement benefits are defined by the plan, but the employer's contribution to periodic payments is dependent on actuarial estimates of future obligations.

Defined contribution plan. The contribution by the employer to periodic payments is defined by the plan, but retirement benefits depend on management of plan assets and thus are not defined.

Depletion. Allocated costs of natural resources.

Depreciation. Allocated costs of long-lived tangible assets.

Derivative financial instrument. A financial instrument that is based on an underlying financial instrument or contract, a hedge against financial risk stemming from changes in fair values, cash flows, or foreign exchange exposures.

Detachable stock warrants. Warrants issued with other securities such as bonds or preferred stock but severable from the associated securities, thus being negotiable instruments.

Determinable current liabilities. Liabilities that may be precisely measured and are definite in amount. Examples include accounts and notes payable, advances and deposits received, accrued liabilities, dividends payable, collections for third parties, revenues received in advance, compensated absences, current maturities of long-term debt, and obligations expected to be refinanced under certain conditions.

Development. Translation of research findings or other knowledge into a plan or design for a new product or process; it may also be used to make a significant improvement to an existing product or process whether intended for use or sale.

Diluted EPS. An alternative EPS amount required for corporations with complex capital structures; it considers dilutive effects of potential additional shares of common stock (see Appendix B).

Dilutive. A condition whereby a security or contingency that could result in additional shares of common stock would decrease EPS if considered in the EPS determination.

Direct cash flow method. One of two acceptable methods (formats) for the statement of cash flows. Within the direct format, the "Cash Flows from Operating Activities" section is essentially a cash-basis income statement. This is the method preferred by the FASB.

Direct cost. A cost traceable to an object, product, or process.

Direct write-off method. Charging bad debts expenses against accounts receivable directly; not considered consistent with GAAP.

Direct-financing-type lease. A capital lease in which the lessor earns only interest revenue on the transaction.

Discontinued operations. Disposal of a segment of the business by sale or abandonment.

Discount. The difference between the purchase price and the par value; the purchase price is less than the par value.

Discount (on bonds). The excess of the par value of bonds over the lower issue price.

Dividend date of record. The effective date to determine which entities are to receive dividends as shareholders.

Dividend declaration date. The date on which dividends are declared by a corporation's board of directors.

Dividend distribution date. The date on which dividends that have been declared are paid or distributed to shareholders of record.

Dividend payout ratio. The proportion of dividends per share to earnings per share for capital stock.

Dividends in arrears. Dividend preferences for a period that are not declared or distributed to shareholders of cumulative preferred stock; these accumulate and must be satisfied prior to (or concurrently with) dividends to common shareholders.

Dollar-value LIFO. An inventory valuation method in which the LIFO layers consist of dollars instead of quantities.

Double-entry accounting. The system for recording equal debits and credits for every transaction.

E

Earned. Revenues are earned when the entity has *substantially* completed what it must do to be entitled to the benefits represented by the revenues.

Earnings per share. Net income minus preferred dividends divided by average number of common shares outstanding.

Economic consequences of accounting standards. The macroeconomic impact of the adoption of a particular accounting rule.

Economic entity. A separate unit for reporting financial information.

Economic income. The maximum amount of value that a person can consume during a period and still be as well off at the end as at the beginning.

Economic reality of underlying events and transactions. The actual financial situation resulting from an event or transaction.

Effective interest. Interest revenue recognized on the book value of the asset at a constant rate (effective rate) over the life of the asset.

Effective-interest method. A method of amortizing the premium or discount by using the difference between the interest expense (determined by the effective rate of interest) and the cash interest paid (determined by the stated rate of interest). The most common method of decelerated cost allocation.

Efficient-markets hypothesis (EMH). The belief that stock prices continuously reflect all available and relevant information.

Emerging Issues Task Force (EITF). Identifies emerging issues for which a diversity of practices is likely to evolve.

Employee stock ownership plans (ESOPs). A retirement plan for which a trustee manages employees' interests in shares of an employer's stock.

Equity method. Accounting method required for those investments in which 20 percent to 50 percent of voting stock is owned.

Executory contracts. Contracts or agreements that will be satisfied in future periods.

Expenses. Outflows, or other "using up," of assets or incurrences of liabilities (or a combination of both) from delivering or producing goods, rendering services, or carrying out other activities that constitute the entity's ongoing major or central operations.

Extraordinary item. An event that is unusual in nature and infrequent in occurrence, taking into consideration the environment in which the enterprise operates.

F

Face value (of liability). Total amount to be paid to settle the obligation.

Factoring receivables. Sale of receivables to a third party.

Fair value. The market value as determined by trading prices on a stock exchange registered with the SEC or traded over the counter and registered with the NASD.

Fair-value-based method. The recommended method to determine employee stock-based compensation using estimated fair value of options.

Feedback value. Confirmation or correction of earlier expectations of past or present events.

Financial Accounting Foundation (FAF). Group established to fund activities of the FASB; appoints members of the FASB and the Financial Accounting Standards Advisory Committee (FASAC).

Financial Accounting Standards Advisory Committee (FASAC). Assists the FASB on policy and technical issues and choosing task force members.

Financial Accounting Standards Board (FASB). Establishes financial accounting and reporting standards.

Financial leverage. The relative mix of debt and equity financing in an enterprise.

Financing activities. All cash transactions involving noncurrent liabilities and equities.

First-in, first-out (FIFO). An inventory valuation system that expenses oldest cost and records latest cost as inventory value.

Fixed stock option plans. Employee stock option plans specifying a fixed number of options and a fixed exercise price.

Fixed-asset-utilization ratio. The ratio of sales to average fixed assets. This ratio measures the efficiency with which fixed assets are employed. It is also called the *fixed-asset-turnover ratio.*

Floor. Net realizable value less the normal profit.

Franchise. A contractual agreement wherein the franchisor grants the franchisee the right to perform certain services, to sell certain products, and/or to otherwise use certain trademarks (trade names) within a limited geographic area.

Free on board (F.O.B.) destination. Indication that title passes to the buyer at the destination.

Free on board (F.O.B.) shipping point. Indication that title passes to the buyer at the shipping point.

Full-costing method. One of two acceptable methods of accounting for costs associated with exploration for natural resources. This method allows all costs incurred in exploring for oil or gas deposits to be capitalized and amortized over the future periods benefiting from any found commercially exploitable deposits. These costs include costs incurred in specifically unsuccessful efforts as well as successful searches conducted during the period.

Funding. The process of transferring assets, most frequently cash, to an independent third party who serves as a trustee for the pension plan assets received.

Fuzzy GAAP. The term used in this chapter to denote instances in which the use of one acceptable accounting method over another results in an inaccurate portrayal of the economic realities of the underlying transaction.

G

Gain contingency. Possible future gain that ultimately will be resolved when one or more future events occur or fail to occur.

Gain/loss. The difference between actual return and expected return on plan assets.

Generally accepted accounting principles. Comprehensive set of standards that prescribe the preparation of financial statements.

Goods in transit. Merchandise being shipped from seller to buyer.

Goodwill. The difference between the fair market value of the proportion of assets purchased and the purchase price. A long-lived, intangible asset representing the excess earning capacity of an entity.

Goodwill (conceptually). An intangible asset that cannot be separately identified and valued. Goodwill consists of a number of elements (favorable firm characteristics) that allow a firm to earn greater returns than would be possible in their absence.

Goodwill (operationally). The excess of the purchase price (cost) incurred by an acquiring firm over the fair market value of a firm's net identifiable assets, and reported as goodwill under purchase accounting methods.

Gross method. Recording credit sales or credit purchases at the full price, without consideration of any cash discount terms.

Gross-profit method. An inventory estimation method based on markup and cost percentages.

Group depreciation method. An expedient method of effectively applying straight-line depreciation to a group (pool) of similar assets, to which items are continually being added or deleted.

Guaranteed residual value (GRV). A provision that provides that the fair market value of the property returned to the lessor upon termination of the lease shall be equal to or greater than a specified amount. The lessee is liable for the difference if the leased property upon return does not have a fair market value at least equal to the GRV.

H

Held-to-maturity securities. Debt securities that the entity has the positive intent and ability to hold to maturity.

Historical cost. The amount of cash, or its equivalent, paid to acquire an asset, adjusted after acquisition for depreciation, depletion, or amortization. For liabilities, the historical cost is the proceeds received when the obligation was incurred, adjusted for amortization or other allocations.

Horizontal analysis. Percentage of change within an account from a base year to the current year.

I

If converted method. The method used for convertible securities to determine Diluted EPS assuming the securities are converted into common stock.

Impairment. Probable loss in value that is other than temporary.

Implicit interest rate. The determined rate of interest used to discount the minimum lease payment (MLP) so that the present value of the MLP is equal to the fair market value of the asset leased.

Improvements. Expenditures that enhance the life, the productivity, or the quality of service rendered by a capital asset.

In-substance defeasance of debt. Arrangements for debt to be serviced and retired from an irrevocable trust fund.

Income. The degree to which an entity is "better off" as a result of operations.

Income statement. One of four required financial statements. This accrual-based accounting statement provides information about inflows and outflows of resources (i.e., revenues and expenses) for a stated period of time.

Income tax currently payable (refundable). The amount of income taxes paid or payable (or refundable) for a year, as determined by applying the provisions of the tax laws to taxable income (or loss) for that year.

Income tax expense. The combination of income taxes currently payable and the deferred income tax increase (reduction) to expense for the year.

Income taxes. Foreign, federal (national), state, and local taxes based on income.

Incremental borrowing rate. The rate of interest that would have to be paid by the lessee to obtain a loan to purchase the asset.

Indirect cash flow method. One of two acceptable methods (formats) for the statement of cash flows. The "Cash Flows from Operating Activities" section under this method begins with accrual net income, which is adjusted for noncash revenue and expense accruals. This is the older of the two acceptable methods and the most common method used in current practice.

Indirect cost. Cost not traceable to an object or process.

Induced conversions. Conversion of bonds into equity securities because of actions taken by the debtor to make conversion more attractive.

Industry practices. Accounting practices peculiar to a particular industry and different from GAAP, but allowed because of the nature of the industry.

Insolvent. Unable to meet long- and short-term obligations.

Installment sale. The seller retains title to merchandise until all payments are received.

Intangible assets. Resources with expected but uncertain future benefits, and lacking a physical substance.

Interest. The amount paid for the use of money.

Internationalization of accounting standards. The process of bringing standardization and harmony to the various accounting systems used around the world.

Intraperiod tax allocation. The process of associating income taxes with related items in an income statement.

Intrinsic-value-based method. The method where compensation for employee stock options is the excess of the stock market price over the exercise price at the measurement date.

Inventory. Merchandise held for resale in the normal course of business operations.

Investing activities. All cash transactions involving noncurrent assets.

Involuntary conversions. Assets surrendered or converted through acts and/or events not under control of the entity.

J

Joint costs. Costs that relate to multiple products or periods.

Journal. The accounting vehicle for recording the transactions of an enterprise. Sometimes called *books of original entry.*

L

Last-in, first-out (LIFO). An inventory valuation system that expenses most recent costs and records oldest cost as inventory value. *See also* LIFO-layer liquidation.

Lease. A contract between a lessor (owner of the property) and a lessee that provides the lessee the right to use the property for the term of the lease in return for a minimum number of specified cash payments.

Ledger. The accounting vehicle for recording activity for the various accounts of an enterprise. Sometimes called *books of final entry.*

Legal capital. Minimum equity based on state corporate laws; frequently the total par value or stated value of the common stock.

Lessee. The person or entity who is using the asset being leased.

Lessor. The person or entity who owns the asset being leased.

Leveraged buyout (LBO). A series of transactions where funds are borrowed to purchase, or buy out, shares of stock from a shareholder or group of shareholders.

Leveraged lease. A capital lease in which the lessor finances the leased asset through an outside third party.

Liability. A probable future sacrifice of economic benefits arising from present obligations of a particular entity to transfer assets or provide services to other entities in the future as a result of past transactions or events.

Liability method. Method of accounting for deferred income taxes, the objective of which is to accrue a liability (or asset) for the tax that will be assessed (recovered) on temporary differences when they reverse.

LIFO-layer liquidation. Elimination of a LIFO layer of inventory.

Liquidating dividend. Distributions to owners as a return of capital, reducing contributed capital rather than retained earnings; typically restricted to stock retirements.

Liquidity. Current debt-paying ability.

Liquidity ratios. Current ratio and acid-test ratio, or quick ratio. Used to assess short-term, debt-paying ability.

Long-term debt. Debt that is not due within the normal operating cycle or one year, whichever is longer.

Long-term liabilities. Future sacrifices of economic benefits occurring subsequent to the next accounting period.

Loss contingency. A future outflow of resources that will occur if certain conditions or events occur (or fail to occur). Loss contingencies should be recognized in the financial statements if the likelihood of the loss occurring is probable and if the amount of the loss can be reasonably estimated.

Lower of cost or market (LCM). Consideration of market value when reporting inventory. The recognition of loss of utility of inventory during period.

M

Maintenance of capital. A concept of maintenance of capital (or recovery of cost) is a prerequisite separating a return on capital from a return of capital. Only revenue inflows in excess of amounts to maintain the preexisting status contribute to a change in equity and income.

Markdown. The amount subtracted from original selling price.

Markdown cancellation. Cancellation of part or all of the markdown.

Market value. The amount of cash, or its equivalent, that could be obtained by selling an asset in an orderly liquidation, or the amount of cash or its equivalent necessary to retire an obligation currently. Traditionally spoken of as an *exit value.*

Market-value method. Equity securities issued in bond conversion are recorded at current market value and a gain or loss recognized for any difference from the book value of the debt.

Markup. Normal profit, or the original sales price less cost.

Markup cancellation. Cancellation of all or part of the additional markup.

Matching concept. The accounting concept ruling when expenses are recognized. The matching concept directs that expenses should be recognized in the same period (or periods) in which the benefits are recognized that are derived from those costs.

Materiality. "The magnitude of [an omission or misstatement of accounting information that, in light of surrounding circumstances, makes it] probable that the judgment of a reasonable person relying [on the information] would have been changed or influenced by the inclusion or correction of the item." (SFAC No. 2); For corporations with complex capital structures, primary and Diluted EPS are reported when either of these pro forma amounts is at least 3% less than Basic EPS. The threshold value for recognition in the financial statements.

Measurability. The characteristic of an item that makes it quantifiable in monetary terms.

Measurement. The amount at which an item is reported in the financial statements.

Measurement date. Date of commitment to a formal plan to dispose of a segment of a business.

Minimum lease payments (MLP). Minimum payments by the lessee to the lessor necessary under the terms of the lease.

Minimum liability. Accumulated benefit obligation at year-end less fair value of pension assets considering any prepaid or accrued pension costs.

Mortgage bond. A bond backed by using specifically identified assets as collateral.

Multi-step income statement. Disaggregates revenues and gains, expenses and losses into several different categories in order to obtain income from continuing operations.

N

Net markdown. Total markdowns less the markdown cancellations.

Net markup. Additional markups less markup cancellations.

Net method. Recording credit or credit purchases sales at the sales price less the discount.

Net operating loss (NOL). The excess of deductible expenses and exemptions over taxable revenues. Under U.S. law an NOL may be carried back to recover previously paid taxes or forward to reduce future income tax payments.

Net profit margin. The amount of operating profit derived from each dollar of revenue.

Net realizable value. The amount of cash, or its equivalent, that is expected to be received upon disposition of an asset in the normal course of business less any direct costs of disposition.

Net-of-tax presentation. Deducts the deferred tax amount from the account to which it is related, similar to a valuation account (allowance for bad debts) or contra account.

Neutrality. Accounting information is free from bias, does not try to influence one economic interest as opposed to another.

Nominal (or temporary) accounts. Accounts to be closed at the end of an accounting period.

Non-interest-bearing notes. Notes that do not state an interest rate but contain implicit interest in the face amount of the note.

Noncumulative preferred stock. A type of preferred stock in which only the current periods' dividend portion is awarded when dividends are declared; dividends in arrears are nonexistent.

Noncurrent assets. Resources whose benefits will be realized over more than one year or operating cycle.

Noncurrent liabilities. Obligations whose settlement extends beyond one year or operating cycle.

Nondetachable stock warrants. Warrants issued with other securities such as bonds or preferred stock and not severable from the associated securities; thus, they may not be separately traded.

Nonparticipating preferred stock. A type of preferred stock that allows only the specified dividend preference to be awarded to its shareholders, without any additional participating amounts.

Nonqualified stock option plans. Stock option plans that permit employer tax deductions for compensation when employees exercise options, and employees report taxable income.

Nonreciprocal transfer. A transfer in which one party receives a benefit without any sacrifice to the other party.

Nonsufficient funds (NSF) check. A check that the bank will not clear because there are insufficient funds in the maker's account.

Note receivable discounted. Note receivable that has been sold to a third party, either with or without recourse.

Notional amount. The underlying basis amount for a derivative financial instrument.

O

Operating activities. All cash transactions not classified as financing or investing activities.

Operating cycle. The length of time required for the manufacture and sale of a product and collection of the proceeds of the sale.

Operating leases. Leases that do not meet any of the tests of ownership per SFAS No. 13 for inclusion as a capital lease. The assets are treated as rented assets by both lessee and lessor.

Opportunity cost. Profit forgone by choosing one alternative over another.

Organizational costs. Costs incurred and directly related to the organization of a business; may include, but are not restricted to, accounting and clerical costs, legal costs and application fees, promotional costs, and costs of initial directors' meetings.

P

Par value. Value designated by the board of directors for stock.

Par value method. The accounting method that records a Treasury Stock account only for the par value of repurchased shares, with remaining costs reducing contributed capital accounts.

Partial allocation. Nonrecognition of tax effects for (1) differences with "indefinite" reversals or (2) originating differences offset by similar reversing differences.

Participating preferred stock. A type of preferred stock that permits its shareholders to receive not only a preferred amount over common shareholders but also a participating amount for extra dividends declared; some may be only partially participating—that is, participating only up to some limit.

Patent. An exclusive, legal right (granted by the U.S. Patent Office) to use, manufacture, or sell a product or process. Its legal life is 17 years.

Pension costs (expense). Amortization of prior-service costs plus current-period service costs, plus interest costs incurred on projected benefit obligations, minus investment return on plan assets (net of deferrals and amortizations).

Percentage-of-completion method. Revenue recognition method in which revenue is recognized in proportion to costs incurred compared to total estimated costs.

Percentage-of-receivables method. Outstanding receivables are categorized by age and a percentage of each age group is determined to find the balance needed in the allowance account.

Percentage-of-sales method. Estimating bad debts based on a percentage of the credit sales for the period.

Performance ratios. Cash flow ratios that measure the efficiency of resource use and/or the impact of arbitrary accrual practices on counterpart income performance ratios. Also called *efficiency ratios.*

Performance stock option plans. Employee stock options specifying performance criteria for determining either the number of vested options or the exercise price for options.

Period cost. Cost related to time and therefore expensed in current period.

Periodic inventory system. A method of recording inventory purchases in an account called Purchases. The Purchases account is added to beginning inventory to obtain goods available for sale. Cost of goods sold then is found by subtracting the ending inventory from the goods available for sale.

Periodicity. The practice of relating to periods of time the benefits and costs of operations not necessarily both started and completed in that same period (usually year or quarter-year).

Permanent (or real) accounts. Accounts that are not closed at the end of an accounting period; balance sheet accounts.

Permanent difference. Revenue or expense included for financial reporting that is not permitted for tax purposes, or vice versa; that is, a difference that never reverses.

Permanent working capital. A firm's permanent investment in net operating assets.

Perpetual inventory system. A method of recording purchases in the Inventory account, reducing it for cost of goods sold and thus maintaining a current Inventory account balance.

Petty cash. A fund of currency on hand for small expenditures.

Post-closing trial balance. A report prepared after posting closing entries that lists the balances of all the general ledger accounts of an enterprise to prove the equality of debits and credits.

Postemployment benefits. Promises made by many companies to terminated or laid-off employees, including severance pay, job training, and counseling.

Posting. The process of transferring transaction information from journals to ledgers.

Postretirement benefits. Includes pension plans and life insurance and health-care benefits; a form of deferred compensation.

Predictive value. Quality of accounting information that assists in assessing outcomes of future events.

Preemptive stock right. The right of an existing shareholder to purchase additional shares from a new issue in proportion to current holdings.

Preferred stock. Class of stock with preference rights to dividends and in liquidation.

Premium. An inducement in the form of a special offer made by a manufacturer to increase sales. The amount received in excess of the par value of the bond, effectively reducing the interest expense.

Prepaid expenses. Amounts paid in advance that will be used up and allocated to expense in a subsequent period.

Prepaid/accrued pension costs. Pension assets in excess of pension liabilities or vice versa.

Present value of future cash flows. The discounted value of expected future cash inflows arising from disposition of an asset in the normal course of business less the discounted value of expected cash outflows necessary to effect the disposition.

Price index. A ratio reflecting current-year prices compared to base-year prices.

Price-earnings (P/E) ratio. The market price of a share of common stock divided by its EPS.

Prior-period adjustment. Correction of a non-self-correcting error made in a prior period.

Prior-service cost. The actuarial present value of benefits attributed by the plan's benefit formula to services rendered by the employee prior to adoption or amendment of the plan.

Product cost. Cost related to product, inventoried during current period, and expensed in future.

Productive or capital assets. Assets that are long-term tangible assets used in the process of manufacturing goods and delivering services. Sometimes also titled as *property, plant, and equipment,* or *fixed assets, long-term assets.*

Profitability analysis. Assessment of the underlying operating process and trends of a business.

Projected benefit obligation (PBO). The actuarial present value of all benefits attributed by the plan's benefit formula to employee service rendered prior to the date and based on future compensation levels.

Property, plant, and equipment. Productive assets of a firm, sometimes referred to as fixed assets.

Prospective method (treatment). Method for treating changes in accounting estimates. The method does not change previously published income statements, balance sheets, or statements of retained earnings. Remaining unexpensed costs are expensed over the current and future periods as part of continuing operations.

Provision for income taxes. Income tax expense (benefit) for a given period

Purchase commitment. A noncancellable, long-term contract to buy merchandise at a specified price in the future.

Q

Qualified stock option plans. Stock option plans that do not permit employer deductions for compensation and employees do not report taxable income; also called *incentive plans.*

Quasi-reorganization. An accounting technique to remove a deficit in retained earnings by reducing contributed capital; intended to provide companies with optimistic future prospects with a "fresh start."

R

Rate of return on assets (ROA). The ratio of net income divided by average total assets.

Readily convertible. Assets that have (1) interchangeable units and (2) quoted prices available in an active market that can readily absorb the quantity held by an entity without significantly affecting the price.

Realizable. When related assets received or held are readily convertible to known amounts of cash or claims to cash.

Realized. When products (goods or services), merchandise, or other assets are exchanged for cash or claims to cash.

Recognition. Inclusion of an item in the financial statements. The process of formally recording or incorporating an information item into the financial accounts of an entity.

Recourse. Determination of ultimate responsibility for payment of receivable. *With recourse* means that seller of a receivable has contingent liability; *without recourse* means that the seller of a receivable has no contingent liability.

Redeemable preferred stock. Preferred stock that the issuing company must redeem, usually by some prespecified date.

Relative-market-value method. The assignment of costs to individual assets on the basis of their individual relative market values divided by the total market value for lump-sum (basket) purchases.

Relevance. Characteristic indicating that accounting information has the capacity to make a difference in a decision. That capacity of an information item to influence the decisions of investors, creditors, or other financial statement users through its feedback value, predictive value, or both.

Reliability. The characteristic indicating that accounting information is correct. The objectivity and verifiability of an information item. Information about a change in an asset or liability that is too uncertain (unreliable) cannot be recognized.

Replacement depreciation method. An expedient method of effectively applying straight-line depreciation to a pool of assets that are systematically replaced on a regular schedule.

Replacements. Expenditures made for an asset because of normal wear and tear that do not increase the productivity or the quality of an asset. Replacements differ from normal repairs in that they involve replacing a major part of equipment.

Representational faithfulness. Characteristic indicating that accounting information portrays the underlying economic event.

Research and development (R&D) costs. Those outflows of resources incurred to obtain valuable products or processes that potentially have some future benefit.

Research and development (R&D). *See* Development; Research.

Research. A planned search or critical investigation aimed at the discovery of new knowledge with the hope that such knowledge will be useful in developing a new product or service or a new process or technique or in bringing about a significant improvement in an existing product or process.

Residual allocation. Remaining nondepreciated (amortized) costs charged against income in the year of sale, trade, or abandonment of an asset.

Residual-valuation method. A method of estimating corporate goodwill in which the aggregate value of the firm's net identifiable assets (assets minus liabilities) is subtracted from an aggregate inferred economic value for the firm.

Restrictive covenants. Restrictive financial promises made by the debtor in the debt instrument: i.e., minimum (maximum) financial ratios will be maintained.

Retail inventory methods. An inventory valuation method used by retailers based on retail value of merchandise.

Retained earnings. Undistributed cumulative earnings of a business (income ñ losses ñ dividends).

Retirement depreciation method. An expedient method of effectively applying straight-line depreciation to a pool of assets that are systematically retired and replaced on a regular schedule.

Retroactive approach (treatment). Method for treating selected, unusual changes in accounting principles and prior-period adjustments. Changes are made to previously published income statements, balance sheets, and statements of retained earnings. If an entry is required, retained earnings and selected other asset and liability accounts will be affected. No adjustment is made to current-period income for cumulative prior-period effects of change or prior-period adjustments.

Return of capital. That portion of revenues needed to replenish assets consumed in generating the revenues; equivalent to expenses.

Return on capital. That portion of revenues remaining after providing a return of investment.

Return on equity (ROE). Net income divided by average owners' equity.

Revenue expenditures. Expenditures made in the normal course of business, from which the benefits are derived in one year or operating cycle.

Revenue recognition. The accounting principle stating that realization of revenue (inflow of an asset) must occur before recognition (recording) in financial statements.

Revenues. Inflows and other enhancements of assets of an entity or settlement of its liabilities (or a combination of both) from delivering or producing goods, rendering services, or other activities that constitute the entity's ongoing major or central operations.

Reversing entries. Journal entries that at the beginning of a new period reverse certain adjusting entries made in the prior period in order to facilitate the recording of a future event or condition.

Risk analysis. Assessment of potential impediments to trend progression of operations.

S

Sale-leaseback. The seller/lessee sells the asset to the buyer/lessor and immediately leases the asset back.

Sales with right of return. The buyer has the right to return the merchandise within a specified period after the sale.

Sales-type lease. A capital lease in which the lessor earns a profit as well as interest revenue on the transaction.

Scrip dividend. A debt agreement issued to shareholders as a form of dividend; future asset distributions generally include interest on the debt to shareholders.

Seasonal working capital. A firm's temporary investments in incremental net operating assets required to meet seasonal (higher than normal) sales demands.

Serial bonds. A bond issue in which fixed portions mature at different specified dates.

Service costs. The actuarial present value of benefits attributed by the plan's benefit formula to services rendered by employees during the current period.

Simple capital structure. The designation for a corporation without financial securities or contingencies that could result in the issuance of common stock.

Single-step income statement. Combines revenues and gains in one category and expense and losses in a second category in order to derive income from continuing operations.

Sinking fund. A retirement method for debt in which periodic payments are made to a fund that builds to the amount of the debt.

Solvency. Ability to meet long- and short-term obligations; the measure of risk inherent in a business

Special-reporting items. Discontinued operations, extraordinary items, and accounting changes.

Specific-identification method. The exact matching of unit cost and unit flow.

Stated interest rate (or coupon rate). The rate of interest stated on the face of the financial instrument which is used to determine the cash paid on the interest date.

Stated value. Value designated by board of directors for stock when the stock has no par value.

Statement of cash flows. The financial statement reporting the cash activity for a period related to operating, investing, and financing activities.

Statement of changes in owners' (or shareholders') equity. The financial statement reporting the activity pertaining to owners' equity accounts for a period and articulating the income statement with the balance sheet.

Statement of retained earnings. Statement that provides a reconciliation of beginning and ending balances in retained earnings.

Statutory rate reconciliation. Disclosure, in percentages and/or dollars, of the amount of income tax calculated based on current statutory rates applied to pretax accounting income and the major items that reconcile that amount to the actual income tax expense the entity has reported.

Stock appreciation rights (SARs). Employee rights to receive compensation for the appreciation in market value of the employer's capital stock.

Stock dividend. A distribution of additional shares of stock, usually a relatively small percentage of outstanding shares, to existing shareholders.

Stock options. Rights to acquire a specified number of shares of capital stock for a guaranteed exercise price.

Stock rights. The rights to purchase newly issued stock.

Stock split. A large distribution of additional shares to existing shareholders that changes proportionately the stock's par value, shares issued and outstanding, and market price per share.

Stock subscriptions. Pledges to purchase shares of capital stock for some subscription price.

Stock warrants. Negotiable security interests that give the holder the right to acquire equity securities at a fixed price by surrendering a stated number of warrants.

Stockholders' (or shareholders') equity. The residual owners' interest of a corporation usually consisting of contributed capital and retained earnings.

Straight-line amortization method. The premium or discount is divided by the number of periods from issuance to maturity to obtain the amortization for a period.

Straight-line depreciation (cost allocation) method. A method of cost allocation that charges equal amounts of depreciation to each year of an asset's useful life.

Subsequent event. Transaction either settled or originating during period between closing date of financial statements and issue date for statements.

Successful-efforts accounting method. One of two acceptable methods of accounting for costs associated with the exploration for natural resources. This method allows capitalization of only those exploration costs associated with successful discoveries of viable commercial deposits. These costs subsequently are amortized over the future periods benefiting from these discoveries. Costs associated with unsuccessful searches are expensed as incurred.

Sum-of-the-years'-digits method. One of several accelerated depreciation (amortization) methods.

T

Tax credit. A direct reduction to an entity's income tax liability for some specific, qualifying reason.

Taxable income. The excess of taxable revenues over tax-deductible expenses and exemptions for the year as defined by the government taxing authority.

Technological feasibility. That stage in the development of computer software when all planning, designing, coding, and testing activities conducted pursuant to meeting design specification have been achieved.

Temporary difference. A difference between the tax basis of an asset or liability and its reported amount in the financial statements that will result in taxable or deductible amounts in future years, when the reported amount of the asset or liability is recovered or settled.

Timeliness. Information is available at the time it can affect the decision.

Times-interest-earned ratio. Earnings before interest and income taxes divided by interest.

Trademarks. Exclusive legal rights granted by the U.S. Patent Office for use of identifying symbols for renewable periods of 20 years.

Trading securities. Debt and equity securities bought and held principally for the purpose of realization of profit on short-term changes in price.

Treasury stock. Previously issued stock of a corporation that has been repurchased and is held by the corporation.

Treasury stock method. The method used for options and warrants to determine Diluted EPS assuming the proceeds from hypothetical exercise of options or warrants are used to purchase treasury stock.

Trial balance. A listing of each ledger account and its balance with totals for debits and credits.

U

Unadjusted trial balance. A report prepared prior to adjusting entries that lists the balances of all the general ledger accounts of an enterprise in order to prove the equality of the debits and credits.

Understandability. Quality of accounting information that enables users to perceive its significance.

Unguaranteed residual value (URV). The fair market value of the property at the termination of the lease is not specified.

Units-of-production depreciation methods. Method of depreciation (or depletion) that charges equal portions of asset costs to units produced (or natural resources extracted.)

V

Valuation adjustment. A contra account that reduces the carrying value (or book value) of a particular account —for example, Accumulated Depreciation.

Verifiability. A consensus among measures to arrive at same result.

Vertical analysis. Account balances presented as percentages of a total. Same as common-size financial statements.

Vested benefits. Those benefits that have already been earned by the employees and do not require any future employment.

W

Warranty. A promise by a manufacturer (or seller) of a product to ensure the quality or performance of the product for a specified period of time.

Weighted average shares outstanding. The sum of shares of stock weighted by the period of time they were outstanding during a period; for common stock, this weighted average is used to compute EPS.

Work sheet. An optimal tool to assist in compiling adjusting entries and preparing financial statements.

Working capital. Current assets minus current liabilities.

Y

Yield. Present value of all future cash flows of a security, discounted at the current market rate of interest.

Subject Index

A

B

C

D

E

F

J

M

N

P

S

T

U

V

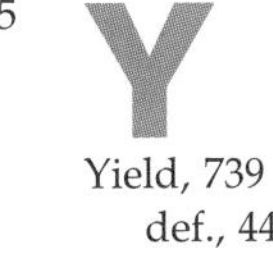

Company Index

A

B

C

D

E

F

G

T

U

V

W

X

Y

Z

Photo Credits

Credit for internal text photos is given to the following:

© *North Wind Picture Archives*
for all part openers (pages 1, 143, 385, 635, and 843).

© *1996 Jeff Greenberg*
for all chapter openers, as detailed below:
Chapter 1 (page 3): London Bridge reconstructed in desert at Lake Havasu City, AZ, in 1971
Chapter 2 (page 45): Coral World walkway to underwater observatory/Nassau, Bahamas
Chapter 3 (page 93): Brooklyn Bridge over East River connects Brooklyn to Manhattan, NYC
Chapter 4 (page 145): Greater New Orleans Bridge over Mississippi River, Natchez Riverboat
Chapter 5 (page 201): Bow Bridge/Central Park, NYC: c.1862 over The Lake
Chapter 6 (page 251): Natural Bridge/VA: 90′ span, 125′ high, Thomas Jefferson paid 20 shillings to own
Chapter 7 (page 315): Central Avenue Bridge over Mississippi River, Minneapolis
Chapter 8 (page 387): MacArthur Causeway, Biscayne Bay, Miami Beach
Chapter 9 (page 443): George Washington Bridge over Hudson River, NY–NJ
Chapter 10 (page 511): Old Order Brethrens near covered bridge, Manheim, PA
Chapter 11 (page 575): St. Petersburg, Russia—footbridge over Griboedov Canal
Chapter 12 (page 637): Manhattan Bridge over East River connects Brooklyn to Manhattan, NYC
Chapter 13 (page 685): Royal Gorge Bridge, 1,053′ over Arkansas River, highest bridge in world
Chapter 14 (page 733): Golden Gate Bridge, San Francisco Bay
Chapter 15 (page 785): Train track along James River, Richmond, VA
Chapter 16 (page 845): Old Bahia Honda Bridge, Florida Keys
Chapter 17 (page 899): Ataturk Bridge over Golden Horn, Istanbul, Turkey
Chapter 18 (page 953): Theodore Roosevelt Memorial Bridge, Potomac River, Washington, D.C.
Chapter 19 (page 1003): Chesapeake Bay Bridge Tunnel, 17 miles long, VA
Chapter 20 (page 1053): Central Park, Manhattan, NYC

For the text integrative cases photos, credits are as follows:

PhotoEdit, page 374
Unicorn Stock Photos, page 375
PhotoEdit, page 379
Unicorn Stock Photos, page 622
Tony Stone Images, page 627
Unicorn Stock Photos, page 630
SuperStock, page 838
PhotoEdit, page 1086
SuperStock, page 1097

(*Continued from inside front cover*)

No. 52. Foreign Currency Translation 1981
No. 53. Financial Reporting by Producers and Distributors of Motion Picture Films 1981
No. 54. Financial Reporting and Changing Prices: Investment Companies 1982
No. 55. Determining Whether a Convertible Security Is a Common Stock Equivalent 1982
No. 56. Designation of AICPA Guide and Statement of position (SOP) 81-1 on Contractor Accounting and SOP 81-2 Concerning Hospital-Related Organizations as Preferable for Purposes of Applying *APB Opinion 20* 1982
No. 57. Related Party Disclosures 1982
No. 58. Capitalization of Interest Cost in Financial Statements That Include Investments Accounted for by the Equity Method 1982
No. 59. Deferral of the Effective Date of Certain Accounting Requirements for Pension Plans of State and Local Governmental Units 1982
No. 60. Accounting and Reporting by Insurance Companies 1982
No. 61. Accounting for Title Plant 1982
No. 62. Capitalization of Interest Cost in Situations Involving Certain Tax-Exempt Borrowings and Certain Gifts and Grants 1982
No. 63. Financial Reporting by Broadcasters 1982
No. 64. Extinguishment of Debt Made to Satisfy Sinking-Fund Requirements 1982
No. 65. Accounting for Certain Mortgage Banking Activities 1982
No. 66. Accounting for Sales of Real Estate 1982
No. 67. Accounting for Costs and Initial Rental Operations of Real Estate Projects 1982
No. 68. Research and Development Arrangements 1982
No. 69. Disclosures about Oil and Gas Producing Activities 1982
No. 70. Financial Reporting and Changing Prices: Foreign Currency Translation 1982
No. 71. Accounting for the Effects of Certain Types of Regulation 1982
No. 72. Accounting for Certain Acquisitions of Banking or Thrift Institutions 1983
No. 73. Reporting a Change in Accounting for Railroad Track Structures 1983
No. 74. Accounting for Special Termination Benefits Paid to Employees 1983
No. 75. Deferral of the Effective Date of Certain Accounting Requirements for Pension Plans of State and Local Government Units (an amendment of *FASB Statement No. 35*) 1983
No. 76. Extinguishment of Debt (an amendment of *APB Opinion No. 26*) 1983
No. 77. Reporting by Transferors for Transfers of Receivables with Recourse 1983
No. 78. Classification of Obligations That Are Callable by the Creditor (an amendment of *ARB No. 43,* Chapter 3A) 1983
No. 79. Elimination of Certain Disclosures for Business Combinations by Nonpublic Enterprises (an amendment of *APB Opinion No. 16*) 1984
No. 80. Accounting for Futures Contracts 1984
No. 81. Disclosure of Postretirement Health Care and Life Insurance Benefits 1984
No. 82. Financial Reporting and Changing Prices: Elimination of Certain Disclosures (an amendment of *FASB Statement No. 33*) 1984
No. 83. Designation of AICPA Guides and Statement of Position on Accounting by Brokers and Dealers in Securities, by Employee Benefit Plans, and by Banks as Preferable for Purposes of Applying *APB Opinion 20* (an amendment of *FASB Statement No. 32* and *APB Opinion No. 30* and a rescission of *FASB Interpretation No. 10*) 1985
No. 84. Induced Conversions of Convertible Debt (an amendment of *APB Opinion No. 26*) 1985
No. 85. Yield Test for Determining whether a Convertible Security Is a Common Stock Equivalent (an amendment of *APB Opinion No. 15*) 1985
No. 86. Accounting for the Costs of Computer Software to Be Sold, Leased, or Otherwise Marketed 1985
No. 87. Employers' Accounting for Pensions 1985
No. 88. Employers' Accounting for Settlements and Curtailments of Defined Benefit Pension Plans and for Termination Benefits 1985
No. 89. Financial Reporting and Changing Prices 1986
No. 90. Regulated Enterprises—Accounting for Abandonments and Disallowances of Plant Costs (an amendment of *FASB Statement No. 71*) 1986
No. 91. Accounting for Nonrefundable Fees and Costs Associated with Originating or Acquiring Loans and Initial Direct Costs of Leases (an amendment of *FASB Statements No. 13, 60,* and *65* and a rescission of *FASB Statement No. 17*) 1986
No. 92. Regulated Enterprises—Accounting for Phase-in Plans (an amendment of *FASB Statement No. 71*) 1987
No. 93. Recognition of Depreciation by Not-for-Profit Organizations 1987
No. 94. Consolidation of All Majority-Owned Subsidiaries (an amendment of *ARB No. 51,* with related amendments of *APB Opinion No. 18* and *ARB No. 43,* Chapter 12) 1987